T0300396

Energy Economics

Three-quarters of our current electricity usage and transport methods are derived from fossil fuels, and yet within two centuries these resources will dry up. *Energy Economics* covers the role of each fossil and renewable energy source in today's world, providing the information and tools that will enable students to understand the finite nature of fossil fuels and the alternative solutions that are available.

This textbook provides detailed examinations of key energy sources—both fossil fuels and renewables including oil, coal, solar, and wind power—and summarizes how the current economics of energy evolved. Subsequent chapters explore issues around policy, technology, and the possible future for each type of energy. In addition to this, readers are introduced to controversial topics including fracking and global warming in dedicated chapters on climate change and sustainability.

Each chapter concludes with a series of tasks, providing example problems and projects in order to further explore the proposed issues. An accompanying Companion Website contains extensive additional material on the history of the major types of fuel as well as technical material relating to oil exploration, the development of solar power, and historical environmental legislation.

This textbook is an essential text for those who study energy economics, resource economics, or energy policy.

Roy L. Nersesian is Professor at the Department of Management and Decision Sciences, Monmouth University, USA.

Energy Economics

Markets, History and Policy

Roy L. Nersesian

Routledge
Taylor & Francis Group

LONDON AND NEW YORK

First published 2016
by Routledge
2 Park Square, Milton Park, Abingdon, Oxon OX14 4RN

and by Routledge
711 Third Avenue, New York, NY 10017

Routledge is an imprint of the Taylor & Francis Group, an informa business

British Library Cataloguing in Publication Data
A catalogue record for this book is available from the British Library

Library of Congress Cataloging in Publication Data
Catalog record for this book has been requested

ISBN: 978-1-138-85837-4 (hbk)
ISBN: 978-1-315-71806-4 (ebk)

Typeset in Bembo
by Book Now Ltd, London

To Friends of the Family
Taffy, Daisy, Rue, Heather, Ginger, Quincy, Marco, Maya, and Copper

Contents

Figures

Tables

Online Material

Please visit the Companion Website at www.routledge.com/cw/nersesian for the following additional sections.

Chapter 6
Earth as an Oil Manufacturer
Formation of Oil
 Biotic Theory of Origin
 Abiotic Theory of Origin
Oil Exploration and Production
 Drilling Rights
 Drilling Operations
 Offshore Exploration Rigs
 Offshore Production Rigs
 Decision to Drill a Production Well
 Getting Oil to a Refinery
 Refining

Chapter 7
History of Coal Gas
History of Natural Gas
 Battle over Lighting
 Long Distance Transmission
Federal Regulation
 War Years
 Last Stop before Total Regulation

Chapter 8
Nuclear Incidents and Accidents
 Three Mile Island Incident
 Chernobyl Nuclear Accident
 Fukushima Daiichi Accident
 Disposal of Spent Fuel
Birth of the Environmental Movement
 Saga of the Hoover and Glen Canyon Dams
 Saga of Aswan High Dam

Chapter 9
Solar Power
 Historical Development of Thermal Solar Power
 Thermal Solar Energy for Heating Water
 Thermal Solar Energy for Generating Electricity
Wind Power
 Historical Development
 Government Involvement in Developing Wind Turbines

Preface

Many of life's greater expectations remain unfulfilled, but on a more mundane level our lives are ones of fulfilled expectations. We expect the radio alarm will awaken us in the morning, there will be light when we turn on the light switch, water will flow when we turn on a faucet, food in the refrigerator will still be cold, and burner on the stove will fry an egg. We expect a newspaper at our front doorstep and something to look at if we turn on the television. If we commute, we expect the bus or train will be running, or the car will run and the gas station will be open for fueling. In our office, we expect the mail will be delivered, the computer boots up when we turn it on, our e-mail has received all messages that had been sent to us, and there is a dial tone when we pick up the telephone (or iPhone). There is an endless list of fulfilled expectations necessary for our modern way of life to continue for another day.

All this depends on energy: electricity for the lights, refrigerator, computer, and communications; natural gas or electricity for the stove; gasoline or diesel fuel for the car, bus, and train; jet fuel for the airplane; heating oil or natural gas to heat a home or a building. Electricity itself is derived for the most part from burning coal and natural gas and, to a lesser extent, from nuclear and hydropower. A rather small but rapidly growing contribution is made from alternative sources such as wind, solar, and biofuels, with a smaller contribution from geothermal and other forms of renewables. Of these, biofuels and wind have made the most progress in becoming a meaningful alternative supply of energy followed by rapidly expanding solar. Yet while progress in certain nations is 20 percent renewables or more, overall renewables (solar, wind, biofuels) only satisfy 2.5 percent of global energy consumption. Pretty small contribution when one considers how many pages of this book are dedicated to renewables. The bulk of energy demand for electricity generation is and will continue to be fulfilled by conventional means (fossil fuels, hydro, nuclear). The problem is that fossil fuels are finite with perhaps a century or so at best left—then the lights go out. The main thrust of this book is concerned with the transition from fossil fuels to renewables (nuclear, hydro, wind, solar, geothermal, wave, and tides). We have time to make this transition, but we are also running out of time. When one thinks about it, the ultimate solution to climate change is to exhaust our fossil fuel resources!

This book examines the role of the principal sources of energy both in the aggregate and by specific types (biomass, coal, oil, natural gas, nuclear and hydro, wind and solar, and other sustainable sources) for a balanced view on energy. Nations exhibit enormous variance in energy consumption both in amount and the degree of reliance on different types of energy. Moreover, their energy plans to satisfy future needs vary markedly. Energy diversity on a national level is too great for the global community of nations to adopt a common policy approach to energy. The only international convention that bears on energy is the Kyoto Protocol. However, one can argue that the Protocol is more environmental in orientation in that its primary concern is reducing greenhouse gas emissions. However, in complying with the Protocol, nations favor natural gas, nuclear and hydro, and wind and solar over coal and oil.

Having divergent and perhaps mutually exclusive energy policies prevents integration into a single, coherent, and consistent policy toward energy. The world will have to live with a portfolio of energy policies that fit each nation, not one that applies globally. While it may be possible to develop regional energy policies, such as the European Union or North America, even here there is a great deal of diversity among individual nations within Europe or provinces within Canada or states within the US on their dependence to various types of energy and their aims in establishing energy policies.

This book is the third edition with the incorporation of economics. I felt that the subject of energy economics was present in the second edition in verbal form, but in this edition, problems and projects have been added that will be handy for this book to be a classroom textbook. In addition to problems on energy economics, there are also spreadsheet formulations. Some are adapted from my book *Energy Risk Modeling* written for a course I taught at SIPA at Columbia University. Others provide the basis for particular charts or assertions made in the text. For instructors' access to problem and spreadsheet solutions, please contact Customer Service.

The book, however, can be read by anyone interested in energy without having to get involved with the problems at the end of each chapter. The book is written for those who are in a particular facet of energy and desire to broaden their knowledge, or for those just plainly interested in energy. I tried to present a balanced view without succumbing to the temptation to tell one side of the story, though I show partiality from time to time. In preparing to write the book, I discovered to my amazement divergence of opinion rather than consensus on simple matters such as where oil comes from, relationship between global warming and rising concentration of carbon dioxide in the atmosphere, and even whether we are running out of oil and natural gas. There is a wide range of opinions on energy issues. Some are far from settled and others are more like questions begging for answers.

My initial thought on writing essentially the third edition of a book working off the second edition was that while it would not be a "piece of cake," it would be far less effort than starting from scratch. I was stunned by the degree of effort which reflected how much has changed in 6 years between the writing of the second edition and the submission of the third. I suppose that I should be grateful that the historical background did not change, but little good that did. Energy is evolving, and evolving fast; the status quo changes from day to day. The effort reflected these changes. In this regard, I would like to thank Rob Howard, Chris Maier, and Mogens Petersen for their assistance.

Lastly I plan to make good a promise I made to my wife Maria that I will spend more time with her and less on the computer, so she can no longer dub herself an "author's widow." I have been cutting back on my activities as hints of aging make themselves known in a subtle fashion such as looking in a mirror. Although I failed to keep my promise to Maria in the past, I have no major project in mind to take the place of this book. To pass my time, I intend to continue teaching at Monmouth University for as long as I am physically (and mentally) able, much to the distress of my students. In contemplating the possibility of an unintended consequence, Maria may not be terribly happy over my wandering aimlessly about the house poking my nose into areas I have ignored for a half-century of marriage. Maybe I had better think of another project!

1   Energy Economics and Policy

What Is Energy?

Believe it or not, there is no clear definition of energy. What we understand are the various forms of energy. The most common is heat—we turn on a stove and a kettle of water soon begins to boil. Then we pour the hot water into a cup with a tea bag and we are enjoying a cup of hot tea. If asked "what is energy?" we would respond with "energy made the water hot," which is not a definition, but an observation. We watch a workman with a jack hammer breaking up cement. We associate the result as an output of energy, but broken cement is still not a definition.

There is potential energy such as a rock perched precariously on top of a cliff or a rocket on a launch pad, where nothing happens until the rock is somehow nudged or the launch key is pressed. Thus energy can be associated with nothing happening. When the rock falls off the cliff, we witness gravitational energy; when the rocket is launched, it is chemical energy. Electrical energy is at work whenever a switch is thrown to turn on an electric appliance. Magnetic energy surrounding the earth diverts harmful solar radiation from striking the planet. Radiant heat is felt by standing in front of a burning fireplace in winter, which is transmitted mainly by conduction via heated air molecules colliding with one another. The sun's radiant heat is electromagnetic energy, but so too is a portion of a burning fireplace as infrared radiation. Sun's rays warm the earth, but can also be transformed directly into electrical energy by solar panels. The unequal warming of the earth by the sun creates weather patterns from which we extract wind, current, and wave energy to generate electricity. Gravitational attraction between the moon and earth provides tidal energy. The hydrologic cycle begins with the sun evaporating water that condenses in clouds and eventually falls, nourishing the earth only to evaporate again to complete the cycle. Some rainfall ends up in a reservoir as potential energy until transformed to kinetic energy on its way to the generator turbines to be transformed again to electromagnetic energy and then again to mechanical energy in a food grinder or heat energy in a toaster. Energy associated with sound waves allows us to hear and that associated with light waves allows us to see. The nucleus of an atom contains energy which we have unlocked via nuclear fission—for bombs to destroy mankind and reactors to serve mankind (Chernobyl and Fukushima excepted). Freeing up energy in the atom originated with Einstein's revelation through $E = mc^2$ that mass and energy are equivalent. So what is energy? Perhaps this question should be best left in the hands of the physicists, who, by the way, do not have a clear definition.

Let us just leave the definition in limbo and simply note that energy can take many forms and can be transformed from one form to another. A good example is a roller coaster ride where energy alternates between potential and kinetic energy. Mechanical energy is first expended to move the roller coaster cars to the highest point of the ride that is then potential energy when the cars are almost still. The cars whizzing down the first leg of the ride transforms potential energy into kinetic energy, the energy in the movement (momentum) of the speeding cars. Then kinetic energy is mostly transformed back to potential energy as the cars slow as they approach the next peak, which is lower in height and in potential energy than the first to compensate for energy losses, or increasing entropy. Energy is repeatedly transformed between potential and kinetic energy on a lose-lose basis until the end of the ride. This marks the point where the mechanical energy to move the roller coaster cars to the highest peak has been dissipated in pushing air away from the moving cars and in frictional heating of the wheels and track and in the final stopping of the cars. Entropy is the downhill flow of energy from usefulness to uselessness. The slight warming of the environment and movement of air surrounding the roller coaster is the same as the mechanical energy expended in bringing the roller coaster cars to the highest point of the track. While energy cannot be created or destroyed, the final state of that energy expended to move the roller coaster cars to the initial peak has been reduced to where it is no longer useful. The entropy of the system has increased. These observations are contained in the three laws of thermodynamics:

1   The first law states conservation of energy; energy cannot be created or destroyed.
2   The second law states that the entropy of any isolated system not in thermal equilibrium increases until it is in thermal equilibrium (a cup of hot tea will cool to the ambient temperature of a room).
3   The third law states that the entropy of a system approaches a constant value when the temperature of a system approaches absolute zero.

The transformation of energy to move a roller coaster to the highest point is eventually dissipated into a slight warming of the environment. This dissipated energy cannot be collected and used again, but it has not been destroyed. The second law outlaws perpetual motion machines. The second law can be applied when order disintegrates into disorder. Suppose that a box is filled with layers of differently colored marbles. Entropy increases when the box is picked up and shook, destroying the ordered nature of the layers.

One day the entire universe will reach a state of constant entropy where energy is evenly spread everywhere and can no longer be transferred from a higher to a lower state. It will be a universe whose temperature everywhere will be close to absolute zero. Modern theory of dark matter and dark energy and an accelerating universe suggests that the very atoms in the universe and their sub-atomic components and space itself will be eventually shredded into nothingness. On a brighter note, life can be considered reverse entropy because life consumes a lower level of energy as food and transforms it to a higher level of energy in the form of physical and mental activity. Ultimately though, life is mortal and it's back to increasing entropy!

Energy and Economics

Human societies before the Industrial Revolution were primarily agrarian, employing 80–90 percent of the people. Life for the common folk was oftentimes brutish, dirty, hard, and, perhaps as a side benefit, mercifully short. For the ruling, merchant, landowning, and priestly classes, life was a bit different. Despite the plight of common folk, great empires flourished. During their heydays, magnificent buildings and monuments, now in ruins, were erected. These empires made remarkable progress in organizing society for internal control and external expansion, establishing a legal foundation to guide human conduct and in fostering arts and sciences. Empires rose and fell in Mesopotamia, Egypt, Persia, Greece, Rome, and Mesoamerica. China is the only extant empire with a beginning before the Common Era. These empires harnessed wind power for sailing vessels to move cargos in domestic and international trade and, along with water power, ground grain. But wind and water power contributed little in the grand scheme of things. From the building of the pyramids to the Colossus of Rhodes, economic activity was constrained by the limits of manual labor with a major assist from animals.

The precursor to the Industrial Revolution was development of the metal and glass industries whose fuel demand leveled the forests of England. Moreover, trees were needed to support a major expansion of the English fleet by Queen Elizabeth to combat the Spanish Armada. The shortage of lumber, particularly fully mature trees for ship masts, spurred the exploitation of newly discovered forested lands in North America. The energy crisis for fueling the metal and glass making was eventually solved not by importing wood from North America or Scandinavia but by the discovery of coal lying on the surface near Newcastle—actually a rediscovery as coal was burned during Roman times. Coal lying on the ground was gathered up, and when depleted, holes were dug into the exposed coal seams; then tunneling, which when extended far enough became mines. The downward tilt of the coal seams eventually put the miners below sea level, and flooding threatened to terminate the birth of fossil fuels. The intellectual capital of England was dedicated to solving this one problem since a return to wood was out of the question. The invention of the Newcomen steam engine, which burned coal to produce steam to operate a water pump, marks the beginning of the Industrial Revolution.

What differentiates our civilization compared to previous civilizations is our dependence on energy and the marked improvement of the standard of living of not just the rich but the common folk. The standard of living of various peoples on this planet can be directly related to their per capita energy consumption. It is no surprise that the higher standard of living in the US compared to a subsistence existence endured by about one-third of the world's population can be seen by the difference in per capita energy consumption. Indeed the war on poverty led by the United Nations Development Programme has an objective, among others, to make electricity accessible to 1.4 billion people not connected to an electricity grid and another billion with limited access to unreliable electricity supplies. About three billion people rely on biomass to meet their basic needs, a condition that can be improved by upgrading to fossil and renewable energy sources. Universal access to electricity is considered transformational in the quality of life for billions of people by lighting schools and health clinics and homes, pumping water for irrigation and sanitation, and powering communications and light manufacturing.

Energy and the Environment

Pollution takes many forms—from the air we breathe to the water we drink, to the food we eat, to the garbage dump down the street or dumped in the street. The more we consume material goods, our judge of economic success, the greater the degree of pollution plaguing the planet. Huge landfills or open, infested garbage dumps surround metropolitan centers. In some parts of the world, people are dying from eating fish and vegetables and drinking water contaminated with dangerous levels of toxicity. According to the Environmental Protection Agency, the average American produces 4.3 pounds of waste per day, of which 54 percent ends up in landfills, 34 percent recycled or composted, and 12 percent burned at combustion facilities.[1] Waste is big business; so is reducing waste, particularly in manufacturing goods, because waste detracts from profitability. Recycling and converting waste to something useful over throwing it away is not only socially responsible but a money maker by transforming a cost to a revenue stream. One of the focuses of green manufacturing is the reduction of emissions. Cutting emissions can be easily done by increasing fuel efficiency. General Electric's advertising of green locomotives and green jet engines is based on reduced emissions from greater fuel economy. But greater fuel economy also cuts operating costs for railroads and airlines, increasing their profitability. "Green" in General Electric's products translates to "green" in the corporate bottom line.

Air Pollution

The common air pollutants are ozone, particulate matter, carbon monoxide, nitrogen and sulfur oxides, and lead. Other airborne pollutants include ground level ozone, aerosols and propellants, asbestos, chlorofluorocarbons and hydrochlorofluorocarbons, mercury, radiation and radon, and volatile organic compounds. Sources of air pollution are from burning fossil fuels (coal, natural gas, and oil) and biomass for cooking and heating; burning crop residues and garbage including used tires and batteries; emissions from motor vehicles, steel mills and metal smelters, pulp and paper mills, and chemical and cement plants; insecticides, herbicides, dust from fertilizers, and other agricultural activities; and mining operations. Much, but not all, pollution is associated with energy consumption.[2]

Greenhouse Gas Emissions

Greenhouse gas (GHG) emissions have been legally classified as pollutants. Some may object, citing that the principal component of GHG emissions, carbon dioxide, is vital for life. Without carbon dioxide, plants die and the planet becomes frigid because of the role of carbon dioxide in retaining heat in the atmosphere. Both would decimate life as we know it—thus carbon dioxide is not a pollutant in the same sense as sulfur and nitrous oxides. Nevertheless, the concentration of carbon dioxide in the atmosphere is increasing. It is estimated that one-third of anthropogenic (mankind-related) carbon dioxide added to the atmosphere is not being absorbed by plants, earth, and oceans. That one-third cumulative buildup in the earth's atmosphere can account for the incremental growth in the concentration of atmospheric carbon dioxide. Hence carbon dioxide is deemed by governments, but not entirely by everybody, as being responsible for global warming—now called climate change from growing awareness of the significant divergence between earth's temperature and the predicted output of global warming models. Anthropogenic carbon dioxide emissions are 57 percent from burning fossil fuels, 17 percent from burning biomass and deforestation, and 3 percent from other activities for a total of three-quarters of GHG emissions. Another 14 percent of GHG emissions is methane, which is about 25 times more effective than carbon dioxide as a heat retention gas. Anthropogenic methane sources are natural gas leaks from oil and gas operations and methane generated by agricultural and waste disposal activities (natural gas also seeps "naturally" from the earth into the atmosphere). The remaining 9 percent of GHG emissions is mainly nitrous oxides from agricultural activities.[3] It is clear that energy consumption should include not just the economic benefit of our well-being but also the environmental consequences on air we breathe, water we drink, and food we eat.

Energy and Policy

Public policy guides governments in determining an objective in pursuit of the common good of society. It is not for the common good of society to exhaust a principal energy source in a very short period of time. The consequences threaten civilization itself. Public policy provides the framework upon which laws and regulations are drafted to allocate resources and guide behavior in pursuit of a social objective. The statement of purpose of the Center of Global Energy Policy at the School of International and Public Affairs at Columbia University is an example of defining the role of public policy with regard to energy.[4]

> In just a few years, the global hydrocarbon outlook has rapidly shifted from scarcity to abundance as a result of new technologies… These changes have significant economic, geopolitical, security, and environmental implications that demand independent, balanced, data-driven analysis.
>
> At the same time, the cost of clean energy technologies continues to fall, and there are increasingly urgent calls…to take meaningful action to address climate change. Energy policy makers must balance the economic, security, and geopolitical benefits of increased oil and gas resources with the need to drive the development, cost reduction, and deployment of emerging clean energy technologies and improve the energy productivity of the economy.
>
> The policy choices made in the coming years, both domestically and globally, will be of profound importance in balancing these multiple objectives. Smart policies will be key to meeting the defining challenge of the next generation—how to provide billions more people with reliable, affordable, secure access to energy supplies that enable more rapid rates of economic growth while sustaining the planet.

Any energy policy has an economic consequence. It is fortuitous when policy considerations and economics line up together. US energy policy on coal fired power plants is not to build new ones and phase out the oldest. The economics of electricity generation is that it is cheapest to build and fuel natural gas fired power plants. This assertion assumes that there is an economic benefit from replacing old, energy inefficient, fully amortized coal fired power plants with some years of remaining useful lives with new energy efficient plants with higher capital costs but lower fuel costs. If this analysis shows that there is an economic benefit in replacing old coal plants with new natural gas plants, then economic and policy goals are mutually reinforcing. This, of course, is not always the case. For instance, the fall in the price of coal from retiring US coal fired plants and much more costly natural gas in Europe induced utilities in Germany and the UK to switch from natural gas to coal. The added emissions by burning coal conflicts with the

European energy policy to reduce carbon emissions. This is known as an unintended consequence.

One problem with policy is that it may not be backed with economic analysis. And the problem with economic analysis is that it may not include all cost factors. For instance, the cost of environmental degradation from sulfur and nitrous oxide emissions along with toxic metals such as mercury was at one time not included in the economics of building a coal fired plant. These factors, referred to as externalities, were not taken into account because a utility did not have to write a check on the environmental consequences of its pollution emissions; that is, pollution did not affect profitability. Back then, environmental externalities may not have been associated or even known for a coal plant—and if known, difficult to quantify.

To address local pollution, coal fired plants in Ohio were built with high smokestacks that removed the environmental consequences of particulate and sulfur oxide (SOx) and nitrous oxide pollution on the local population. It took a while to realize that coal emissions were being channeled by prevailing wind patterns to the Adirondack Mountains in upper New York State and to New England, acidifying lakes and despoiling forests. This externality was not included in the economic analysis for Ohio coal plants because it was not even known. Even if known, it would be difficult to quantify the damage. However, there was no point in analyzing a cost for which the utility did not have to write a check. And what would be the amount of the check? What is the cost of an isolated Adirondack lake becoming acidified, resulting in a fish kill when no one relies on fishing for a livelihood? What is the cost of an isolated fisherman not catching as many fish as would have been caught before acidification?

Public energy policy response to this situation was incorporated into the Clean Air Acts where an economic incentive was provided by internalizing an externality; that is, putting a value on SOx pollution. Coal utility operators had to reduce SOx pollution either by reducing emissions or buying what essentially were rights to pollute, thus establishing a quasi-cost that affected profitability. By reducing this quasi-cost, which was a real cost determined by regulations sanctioned by law, profitability could be improved. This could be done by installing scrubbers to remove SOx from smokestacks or buying low sulfur coal, switching energy sources to wind or natural gas, and other means. While the energy policy embodied in regulations to cut SOx stipulated the amount of reduction and timing, it left the choice of a proper course of action to the individual utility. Another way for energy policy to induce burning less coal in favor of natural gas or renewables would be the institution of a carbon tax that would make it economical to consider alternative fuel sources over coal. A pseudo-cost based on a legal requirement affects the bottom line just as any real cost such as the purchase of coal. Internalizing an externality is a strong and effective means of swaying the behavior of those who make decisions primarily by economic considerations.

An energy policy with regard to carbon emissions can be garnered from an analysis of carbon emissions embodied in the 2013 International Energy Agency's (IEA) special report entitled *Redrawing the Energy-Climate Map*. In this report, a quantitative analysis was performed to evaluate every nation's contribution of anthropogenic GHGs to the global atmosphere. The conclusion of this analysis was that China and the US were responsible for two-thirds of carbon emissions on an unequal basis; that is, China outranked the US as a GHG emitter. This gives a meaningful insight for a global energy policy to reduce the rate of growth of carbon emissions by focusing on two nations. This is not to imply that the rest of the world can get away with doing nothing, but does guide actions to be taken in drafting an appropriate global energy policy. Hence policy should be based on quantitative analysis in order to be able to evaluate the most effective way to deal with a problem. Staying with qualitative feel-good, knee-jerk reactions mouthed by demagogues should not be the basis of an energy policy. Interestingly, the next major contributor to carbon emissions after China and the US was not India, but deforestation in Indonesia and Malaysia. Here burning jungles and heavy undergrowth to clear land for agriculture adds carbon dioxide because plant mass associated with agricultural crops is less than the original jungle. Deforestation even if replaced by agricultural crops reduces Earth's capacity to absorb carbon dioxide from the atmosphere. Hence a public policy focused on four nations, not two hundred, can go a long way to achieving a climate change objective.

Granted that renewables generate more costly electricity, what energy policy with regard to tax incentives, subsidies, and renewable portfolio standards (obligatory minimum generation of electricity from renewables) should be pursued to best act as an incentive to switch from fossil to renewable energy sources? Should fossil fuels continue to receive government subsidies, which they do at this time? Granted that solar and wind are less reliable than fossil fuels, what energy policy would best straddle the dichotomy between a greater share of renewable sources with less electricity grid reliability? It is a known fact that Americans react by buying smaller automobiles with greater fuel efficiency when gas prices are high and switch almost immediately to heavy, low mileage SUVs when gas prices fall. Should public policy on cutting gasoline consumption be based on a high gasoline tax to keep gasoline prices high regardless of the price of crude oil, or should higher fuel efficiency standards be imposed on automobile manufacturers by government fiat? Which energy policy can best pursue the goal of energy efficiency? If fracking is a game changer in the production of natural gas and oil, what should be the proper energy policy in response to instances of ground water pollution by natural gas or oil leakage through well casings or disposal of contaminated water from fracking hard shale and tight sands? These are examples of policy issues to deal with energy challenges. The final decision should be based on a fair minded approach backed by quantitative analysis to ensure that intended consequences both in terms of economics and environment are identified and thoroughly understood. The challenge is that unintended consequences are unknown when a decision is made and can have profound ramifications once they emerge.

Measuring Energy

Striking a match initiates a chemical reaction that rearranges organic molecules of mainly hydrogen, carbon, and oxygen in the matchstick and oxygen in the atmosphere to form carbon dioxide, water, and heat, plus a little ash residue and other minor products of combustion. Heat generated from burning a match can warm water, which is measured in British thermal units (Btu). A Btu is defined as the amount of heat required to raise the temperature of one pound of liquid water from 60°F to 61°F at atmospheric pressure. There are minor variations on the definition of a Btu with different water temperature references, but still separated by 1°F. Burning a wooden match releases about 1 Btu of energy.

A Btu is a woefully minuscule unit for measuring energy when dealing with world energy consumption. A quad improves the understanding of the energy picture by introducing a unit that is scaled to a more comprehensive measure for the human mind. To get to a definition of a quad, it is best to start with a therm, a measure of the energy content associated with natural gas for billing households. A therm is 100,000 or 10^5 Btu, and a home natural gas utility bill of 420 therms is more easily understood than 42,000,000 Btu of energy and is better for doing a comparative analysis with other homes or for different months. A million Btu (mmBtu) is 10^6 Btu, a billion 10^9 Btu, a trillion 10^{12} Btu, and a quadrillion, or quad, 10^{15} Btu. These are large numbers; a trillion dollar bills stacked with no air spaces between the bills is 70,000 miles high, about one-quarter of the way to the moon. A stack of a quadrillion dollar bills would reach from the sun nearly to Venus. Measuring distance in quadrillions of stacked dollar bills makes no sense, but in consuming energy, quads do make sense. The world consumes about 500 quads and the US 100 quads, easier units for the mind to grasp.

One more transformation is necessary. The primary source of energy data in this book is the *BP Statistical Review of World Energy*.[5] It should be no surprise that an oil company would define energy in terms of barrels per day or tons per year of equivalent oil consumption. This is fortunate as it places energy in all its forms on the same scale. From the *BP Statistical Review*, one million tons of oil equivalent (mmtoe) have the energy content of 39.7 trillion Btu. Hence a thousand million or billion tons of oil equivalent are the same as 39.7 quads (a thousand trillion), or 1 quad is equivalent to 25.2 mmtoe.

The Problem Is the Size of the Problem

The central problem of reducing the role of fossil fuels in the energy diet is the size or magnitude of the problem. The 2015 issue of the *BP Statistical Review* contains data on energy consumption from 1965 to 2014. In 2014, total energy consumption was 12,477 mmtoe, which is equivalent to 495 quads. US energy consumption was 2,209 mmtoe or 87 quads or 17.7 percent. While US consumption is relatively flat, the rest of the world, particularly China, India, and other Asian nations, is consuming a lot more. Renewables are made up of biofuels (not biomass), solar, wind, and geothermal output and contributed an aggregate of 237.4 mmtoe or 9.4 quads or 1.9 percent of total energy consumption. As an aside, biomass, which is not included in the *BP Statistical Review*, is estimated to be about 10 percent of total energy consumption. Between 2011 and 2012, world energy consumption, excluding biomass but not biofuels, grew by 2.05 percent and renewables by 15.5 percent. Between 2013 and 2014, world energy consumption grew by only 0.9 percent, whereas renewables maintained a rather brisk pace of 14 percent. A growth rate of 15 percent doubles output of renewables every 5 years. A 15 percent growth rate of doubling capacity every 5 years is ultimately nonsustainable in terms of physical, managerial, and capital constraints. The renewable energy curve in Figure 1.1 assumes that overall energy growth is 1 percent, down from previous levels of around 2 percent and a sustained average growth rate for renewables of 12 percent, a doubling every 6 years, which could also be constrained by physical factors.

If total energy demand can be kept at 1 percent per year, the time span for renewables to reach about one-half of total energy demand is about 30 years. The remaining half would be supplied by traditional fossil fuels plus nuclear and hydropower. Thus, coal will be part of the energy picture even with natural gas playing an increasingly important role accompanied by rapid growth in renewables. However, after this point, renewables can conceivably supply most energy requirements in half a century, which means that

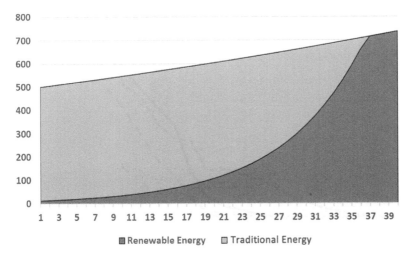

Figure 1.1 Replacing Traditional Energy Sources with Renewables

coal will be significantly phased out of electricity generation and oil will be phased out as a motor vehicle fuel in favor of electricity. For higher overall energy growth rates, the longer it will take for renewables to displace fossil fuels. This is not going to be an easy transition. But it can be helped if capital and physical resources dedicated to no-win wars to secure oil supplies can be diverted to improving the energy infrastructure—a tall order given our proclivity for war.

Another illustration of the time to make a major transition in the pattern of energy consumption is shown in Table 1.1, which shows the time spans for Japan to switch from wood to coal and from coal to other forms of energy.

Phasing out wood as a major source of energy and substituting it with coal required 60 years. Oil became a dominant source of energy for motor vehicles plus a portion of electricity generation over a 30-year period. Developing a natural gas distribution system for LNG imports took 40 years, as did developing nuclear power, both of which being substitutes for coal and oil for electricity generation. This generational time span is again reflected in Figure 1.2, which shows the time required for oil, coal, natural gas, and nuclear power to make the ascent from a small to major contributors to satisfy energy needs.[6]

Table 1.1 Distribution of Energy Sources for Japan

	Wood	*Coal*	*Oil*	*Natural Gas*	*Hydro*	*Nuclear*
1880	85%	14%	1%			
1900	39%	57%	4%			
1940	10%	66%	8%		16%	
1970		22%	71%	1%	6%	0%
1990		18%	57%	10%	5%	10%
2010		23%	43%	17%	4%	13%

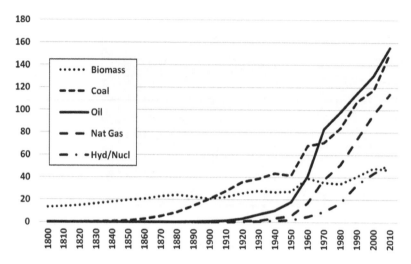

Figure 1.2 Growth of Major Sources of Energy (quads)

Figure 1.3 shows the cumulative contribution of each energy source. Biomass has been increasing in absolute terms, but if expressed as a percentage of overall energy consumption, it would show a Niagara-type drop because other energy sources, primarily fossil fuels, have been satisfying the unprecedented increase in energy demand.

Figures 1.2 and 1.3 illustrate that there is no such thing as status quo in energy since the start of the Industrial Revolution. Up to then, biomass (wood) was the principal source of energy, augmented by diverting some agricultural output for animal power. The animal feed included in biomass played an important role in agriculture and transportation to sustain millions of horses, mules, and oxen that pulled plows and wagons and

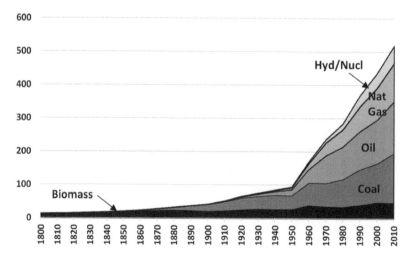

Figure 1.3 Cumulative Distribution of Major Sources of Energy

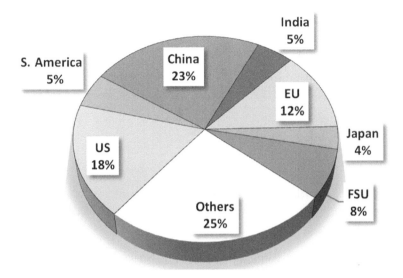

Figure 1.4 Percentage Distribution of Global Energy Consumption

carriages. At the start of the twentieth century, coal became much more significant, fueling factories, steel mills, and railroads, which displaced horses in transportation. Coal as a percentage of energy consumed peaked around 1915 to make room for the growth of oil to fuel motor vehicles (transforming horse power to horsepower), ships, and airplanes. It took a while for a pipeline infrastructure to be built to allow natural gas to make a major contribution. All this points to the expectation that it will take three to four decades for renewables to make a meaningful contribution in satisfying total energy needs, which also implies overcoming current technological hurdles such as increasing the efficiency of solar panels and developing high capacity, low cost storage batteries.

Figure 1.4 shows the distribution of percentage energy consumption among principal consuming nations and regions for a total of 513 quads in 2014. In 2009, China's aggregate energy consumption was 95 percent compared to that of the US; in 2010, 103 percent; in 2011, 112 percent; in 2012, 124 percent; in 2013, 126 percent; and in 2014, 129 percent. The US is no longer the energy hog of the world—that mantle has been taken over by China, and the disparity between the two nations will continue to grow.

Figure 1.5 shows the comparative percentage reliance on principal sources of energy for China and the US. China is clearly a coal driven economy, but is taking significant remedial actions to increase dependence on other forms of energy. The US is an oil driven economy with a better balance in its usage of coal and natural gas. Nuclear and hydro in the US are not increasing, but renewables will become increasingly more important over time. Figure 1.6 shows the detailed usage of energy in the US in 2014.[7]

In 2014, US electricity generation required the entire output of solar, nuclear, hydro, wind, and geothermal, 82 percent of coal, and 30 percent of natural gas. The remaining 18 percent of coal energy is for industrial use, primarily in steelmaking. In addition to the 30 percent of natural gas consumed in generating electricity, 19 percent is consumed

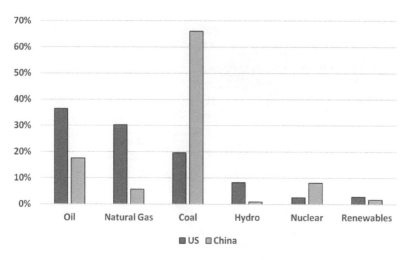

Figure 1.5 Comparative Percentage Reliance on Energy for China and the US

by residential users, 13 percent by commercial users, 35 percent by industrial users, and 3 percent by transportation. Energy consumed by residential users is to heat water, cook food, and power household appliances and space heating and cooling systems. Commercial users including hospitals, schools, office buildings, and business establishments consume natural gas in a similar manner as residential users, but with additional thermal needs to fulfill intended commercial functions such as heating ovens in a bakery. Industrial users burn natural gas for a wide range of processes associated with chemicals, food and paper products, cement, aluminum, glass, and metals. Natural gas is a raw material for ammonia and ammonia based products, fertilizers, and power pipelines, and is consumed in transformational processes such as corn to bioethanol conversion. Petroleum is 71 percent consumed in transportation (motor vehicles, trucks, busses, railroads, airlines, ships). The remainder of oil is primarily consumed by the industrial sector as a feedstock for pesticides, fertilizers, and petrochemicals for the making of plastics. Nearly half (48 percent) of biomass made up of waste wood, dried sewage, and organic residue from food processing and papermaking plants is burned as fuel in industrial plants. Another 27 percent is in the form of biofuels for motor vehicles. Remaining biomass is chiefly firewood and reconstituted wood chips for heating.

Figure 1.6 is full of useful information. In 2014, petroleum made up 35 percent of energy sources to power the US, natural gas 28 percent, coal 18 percent, nuclear 8 percent, biomass 5 percent, and hydropower and wind 2 percent each, with quite small contributions from solar and geothermal. Electricity generation absorbed 35 percent of energy supply, residential users 11 percent, commercial users 8 percent, industrial users 22 percent, and transportation 24 percent. Much of the 98.3 quads of energy to fuel the economy is simply passed to the environment as waste heat (increased entropy). Useful energy listed as Energy Services is 40 percent of total energy input, whereas Rejected Energy, that which is lost to the environment as low level heat, is 60 percent of input energy for an overall energy efficiency of 40 percent. Of the 38.4 quads of energy input to generate electricity, 25.8 is passed to the environment as waste heat to warm the atmosphere,

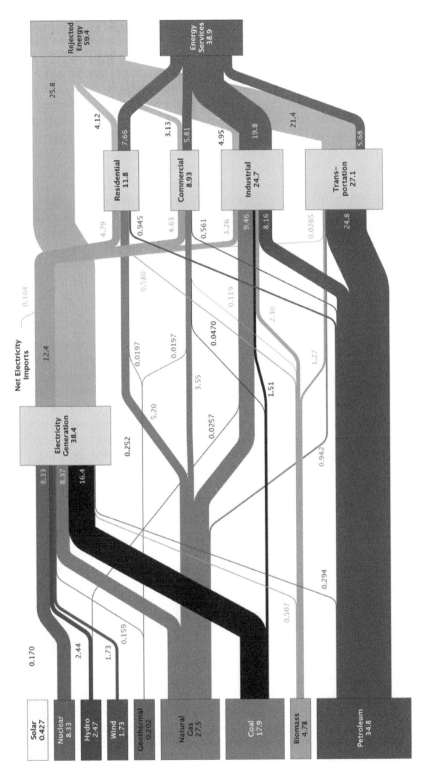

Figure 1.6 Estimated US Energy Use in 2014: ~98.3 quads

ocean, bay, or river for an overall efficiency of 33 percent. Thus, an electric stove requires three times the heat to boil a cup of water than a natural gas stove, assuming the distribution for electricity and natural gas require about the same energy. This low efficiency has nothing to do with the technology of generating electricity, but the nature of thermodynamics. Turbine exhaust steam must be converted back to water to be fed into the boiler. The heat of vaporization consumed to convert water to steam is given up to the environment. In the boiler, the heat of vaporization is again required to convert water to steam. This cycle essentially passes the heat of vaporization (energy required to make water boil) to the environment. Residential, commercial, and industrial consumptions of energy have much higher efficiencies than generating electricity, but the most inefficient use of energy is transportation. Transportation absorbs 27.1 quads, while 21.4 quads, or 79 percent of energy input, passes to the environment as heat from the engine block, radiator, and exhaust system, plus pushing air away to accommodate the forward motion of the motor vehicle along with the friction between wheels and pavement, and in warming brake pads. An efficiency of only 21 percent is an economic driver for an energy policy to improve automobile and truck mileage in order to cut oil consumption without curbing driving.

Forecasting Energy Demand

Figure 1.6 can serve as an outline for forecasting energy demand. Starting with electricity, future demand can be projected by examining past consumption patterns among residential, commercial, and industrial users. Taking residential as an example, new home and apartment buildings fitted with new, efficient appliances and better insulation, less retirement of older homes with inefficient appliances and poor insulation, are taken into account in determining their respective energy needs. One has to assess whether home appliances, air conditioning, and heating systems in new homes will be fueled by natural gas or electricity and compared to natural gas or electricity consumption of homes being retired. Another factor is the age profile of household appliances, air conditioning units, and water and space heating units—the older portion being phased out in time and most likely replaced by energy saving units. Phasing out of incandescent light bulbs in favor of fluorescent light bulbs meant a significant reduction in electricity demand for lighting. On the other hand, modern, wall-mounted, high definition televisions draw far more electrical current than their mundane, standard definition, table-mounted predecessors.

The general format of this process has to be repeated for commercial and industrial users except that their demand is strongly affected by economic activity as is electricity demand. Thus, a forecast of economic activity lies at the core of an energy demand forecast. Projections of commercial and industrial users should cover new energy efficient equipment replacing old energy inefficient equipment plus incremental demand for new equipment. A project on electricity demand can be based on past demand projected forward reflecting population growth, economic activity, adoption of energy efficient appliances and equipment, and weakening of the link between economic activity and electricity demand. Once a projection of electricity demand is obtained, supply of electricity has to be addressed. Like any asset, electricity generating plants do not last forever. The oldest segment of the age profile of generating plants has to be assessed as to which units will be retired. The oldest units are probably coal fired, but we are approaching a point where nuclear power plants may start to retire—the first smaller units have already been removed from service and certain other larger units are expected to retire in the near future. Mothballed nuclear power plants in Germany and Japan have to be assessed as to their likelihood of returning to service. Then one has to have an assessment as to which type of electricity generating plants will replace retired units plus new units necessary to accommodate incremental demand. Part of this question is addressed by power generation projects already underway or likely to be approved. Beyond this time horizon, energy policies that affect renewable energy and fossil fuel powered plants have to be brought into the picture. Then by assessing utilization and thermal efficiency rates, one can obtain a projection of the number and size of generating plants fueled by renewables, nuclear and hydro, coal, and natural gas to satisfy future electricity demand.

Seventy percent of natural gas is consumed generating electricity and the remaining 30 percent serves primarily the thermal needs of residential, commercial, and industrial consumers. A close look at what changes are in store that affect energy consumption patterns for residential, commercial, and industrial users, which are far more complex than that covered for electricity generation, has to be performed. This includes an analysis of retiring older natural gas fueled equipment, which covers a plethora of uses, and introduction of new and more efficient units to meet both replacement and incremental demand. The interplay between electricity and natural gas powered appliances and equipment has to be considered along with the respective roles of oil and natural gas for space heating in areas that both serve residences and commercial establishments. For areas not served by natural gas, there is an interplay between biofuels (wood pellets) and oil. These interplays are a function of price differentials between electricity, natural gas, and oil, which means that a price forecast of each is necessary to perform the analysis.

Oil consumption is dedicated to transportation. The automobile fleet has to be examined for retirements and the size of the future fleet as it relates to demographics (population growth) and number of vehicles per thousand people, an example of double exponential growth. For instance, the number of automobiles in the US is getting close to one per person and thus automobile population would be a single exponential growth function linked to population. However, in China and India, double exponential growth is applicable where future automobile population is linked to both growth in population and the rising portion of automobiles per thousand people. Consequently, US automobile growth will be much lower than that of India and China. Incremental demand for automobiles plus replacements determines new car production. Gasoline demand is a function of existing cars and those retired plus new cars. Those being retired generally have poorer fuel mileage than new cars. This affects gasoline demand along with changes in annual miles driven. Another factor of future oil demand is the total annual miles driven for automobiles, which is no longer in an upward trend in the US, but is in China with the building of superhighways, which have resulted in 250-mile-long traffic jams!

US car buyers have gone through several cycles of wanting fuel efficient cars versus gas guzzlers in the form of pickup trucks, vans, and SUVs depending on the price of gasoline. This changing preference for new cars complicates the assessment of future demand along with the emergence of electric and hybrid vehicles. In addition to a forecast on economic activity, a forecast is needed on oil prices as it affects car buying preferences and miles driven per year. While forecasts are needed for oil prices and economic activity, the task is complicated that each influences the other. High oil prices depress economic activity because money diverted to oil producers by high priced motor vehicle fuels reduces the amount of consumer spending, which accounts for 70 percent of gross domestic product (GDP).

Oil demand is also affected by the injection of ethanol into the gasoline stream and the introduction of natural gas as a motor vehicle fuel. A similar exercise has to be repeated for trucks and airplanes. Fuel demand for trucks is a function of ton-miles, the combination of how many tons are carried for various distances. Piggy-back inter-modal transportation combining the fuel efficiency of railroads with the flexibility of trucks affects transportation energy demand. Truck and rail traffic are also influenced by economic activity. Airplanes have larger passenger carrying capacity and are more fuel efficient, reducing fuel consumption on a passenger-mile basis, but this is countered by a greater number of passengers taking long distance flights that affect the demand driver of passenger-miles. Ton-miles is the economic driver for ships carrying bulk commodities such as oil and iron ore, coal, and grain. Container vessels, due to their higher speed, are heavy consumers of fuel, which is affected by the cost of crude oil. When oil prices are high and international trading subdued, container vessels slow up to achieve significant savings in fuel consumption. Other forms of shipping demand such as cruise ships and a host of specialized shipping assets are part of the calculus of projecting fuel demand. Shipping is unique as larger vessels consume bunkers, a residue of the oil refining process. Smaller vessels depend on diesel fuel, a refined product. In all of this, the consequences of various environmental regulations and policies with regard to encouraging one form of energy at the expense of another and an analysis of pollution emissions for the various fossil fuels have to be undertaken.

This overall description of what has to be considered in assessing the future demand for various sources of energy does not do full justice to the actual depth of effort needed to develop a vital planning tool to guide energy policy makers and regulators in governments and planners and decision makers in corporations. But not every organization has to perform this task as there are a number of consulting companies and government agencies that do. *The Annual Energy Outlook with Projections to 2035*, published by the US Energy Information Administration (EIA), 240 pages in length, covers only the US. But world oil prices, production, and demand are included as international oil prices affect domestic economic activity and driving habits.[8] Projections are made for different scenarios on oil prices and economic activity. The totality of the effort to provide an energy outlook can be seen by the list of over 20 specialists as primary contacts for specific areas of the report. The international or global energy picture is provided by the IEA located in Paris and operated under the auspices of the OECD. Its flagship publication, *World Energy Outlook*, also includes analysis of particular nations and special focus issues.[9] A complex mathematical model has been developed to assist in arriving at a forecast as described in the *World Energy Outlook* (2010).

> Since 1993, the IEA has provided medium to long-term energy projections using a World Energy Model. The model is a large-scale mathematically construct (about 16,000 equations) designed to replicate how energy markets function and is the principal tool used to generate detailed sector-by-sector and region-by-region (24 regions) projections for various scenarios including the Reference Scenario (now called Current Policies). Developed over many years, the model consists of six main modules: final energy demand (with sub-models covering residential,

services, agriculture, industry, transport and non-energy use); power generation and heat; refinery/petrochemicals and other transformation; fossil-fuel supply; carbon dioxide emissions and investment.

The *World Energy Outlook* lists over 20 team leaders responsible for specific aspects of the outlook, over 20 internal experts, about 50 representatives of external energy and industrial organizations who provide input, and a small army of 200 peer reviewers for various facets of the outlook. In the 2012 issue, three scenarios were analyzed. The Current Policies scenario assumes no policies are implemented other than those in effect. The New Policies scenario assumes that existing energy policy commitments plus recently announced policies will be implemented. The 450 Scenario establishes an energy pathway to limit global carbon dioxide concentration in the atmosphere to 450 ppm by 2020 (current level is 400 ppm), which is assumed to have a 50 percent probability of containing global warming within 2°C. The 2012 *World Energy Outlook* was 385 pages long with another 285 pages on special topics regarding energy in Iraq, the role of water in energy, and progress being made to make energy accessible for all. As with the EIA's *Annual Energy Outlook with Projections to 2035*, this first brush description of both publications barely does justice to the full extent of the effort to project global energy demand.

Short Cut for Projecting Energy Demand

Rather than forecasting energy demand accounting for every detail and nuance, a more simplistic approach is to project energy demand utilizing a mathematical model that works off a few macroeconomic drivers. It is clear from simple observation that there are four principal causal variables influencing energy demand: per capita energy consumption, per capita economic activity, population, and oil prices. In essence, a projection of each is necessary to obtain a projection of energy consumption. One might ask why one would substitute four projections for one. This is a fair question. The primary reason is that it might be easier to forecast population and economic activity growth on a long-term basis than energy consumption. For this reason, oil prices will be left out of the proposed energy consumption forecast because oil prices, being extremely volatile, cannot be projected with any degree of confidence. Thus the proposed model for projecting energy demand will use per capita energy and per capita economic activity and population as dependent variables.

The problem with this approach is that economic activity is affected by oil prices, which should be part of the projection. But projecting oil prices by a simple extrapolation using trend analysis is impossible, or meaningless if done. However, some consulting firms do a detailed analysis of supply and demand factors for making oil price forecasts. If such a forecast is available, then that could be incorporated into the proposed model. But most forecasts of oil prices are a likely range of values and that inhibits their use in this model that requires discrete values.[10] However, if discrete values are available, or if one is content using mid-range values, then oil prices could be a dependent variable. An alternative would be to do high-price, medium-price, and low-price scenarios to evaluate the role of oil prices in projecting energy demand. One possible outcome is that oil prices may not have a significant impact, but this can only be known by incorporating oil prices into the model and viewing the results (t-stats are useful in judging the strength of a variable's contribution to the final model).

Population

Energy usage and pollution can both be linked directly to population. Indeed, there are those who advocate population reduction as the primary countermeasure to cut land, air, and water pollution. Having identified the true culprit of energy exhaustion and environmental pollution, their suggested means of correcting the problem is by a small step-down of 90 percent in the global population. It is interesting to note that audiences listening to this proposal applaud vigorously to show their approval—they must have already made their reservations to be on Noah's Ark. Figure 1.7 shows world population since the beginning of the Common Era and its phenomenal growth since the start of the Industrial Revolution.[11]

The world's population was remarkably stable up to 1000 CE. War and disease worked wonders in keeping the population in check. High death rate of infants and children and short, dirty, brutish lives of those who survived childhood, coupled with periodic disintegrations of society and outbreaks of contagious diseases, prevented runaway population growth. The Dark Age of political disorder and economic collapse following the fall of the Roman Empire around 400 CE further suppressed population. Interestingly, the advent of the Dark Age was a time of global cooling, with some making a connection between climate change and the collapse of civilization. After the Dark Age was over, population began to grow accompanied by a period of global warming, another instance of pre-Industrial Age climate change affecting civilization. This continued until the Black Death starting around 1350, which occurred in the early decades of what would be nearly a 500-year period of global cooling, which affected civilization with falling crop yields and social stress. Infected fleas on rats seeking warmth in human habitats played a key role in the spread of this dread disease. After several recursions over the next hundred years, the Black Death wiped out massive numbers of people in Asia and Europe. More than one-third of Europe's population fell victim with as much as two-thirds in certain areas. It took over a century for the population of Europe to recover to pre-plague levels. The first billion in the world's population was reached around 1840. The second billion

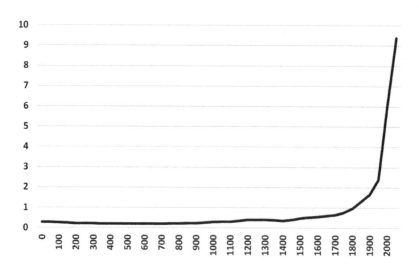

Figure 1.7 World Population (in billions)

was reached around 1930, only 90 years later, despite the horrendous human losses during the First World War, the Russian Revolution and Civil War, and the Spanish Flu, a pandemic that wiped out 30–40 million lives. This pandemic cost more in human life than the combined efforts of those involved with perpetrating war and revolution and numerically, but not percentage-wise, exceeded lives lost in the Black Death. Yet it only took 30 years for the world population to reach its third billion in 1960 despite Stalin's execution of millions of his own people by starvation and firing squad, Hitler's extermination of 12 million Jews and Slavs, plus the deaths of untold tens of millions of military personnel and civilians during the Second World War. The fourth billion was reached 14 years later in 1974 despite Mao Zedong's failed Great Leap Forward that caused the deaths of tens of millions from starvation plus genocide perpetuated by the Khmer Rouge in Cambodia, who thought social progress was worth executing a quarter of their own people. Mounds made of skulls of these victims are today tourist attractions. The fifth billion occurred 13 years later in 1987, the sixth billion 12 years later in 1999, and the seventh billion also 12 years later in 2011.

We should be justifiably proud of the medical advances that have drastically reduced infant mortality rate and childhood diseases. No one espouses going back to the days of Queen Anne (1665–1714), ruler of England from 1702 until her death. Anne had the best medical care that royalty could buy. Yet she had the misfortune of having around six stillbirths plus another 12 who survived birth. She died at 49 without an heir to the throne, spurring a war over her succession. As much as we are grateful for advances in treating disease, there are mathematical consequences. The quickening pace of adding increments of a billion to the population is not an increase in the growth rate, but a property of the mathematics of growth. Going from 1 to 2 billion is a 100 percent gain in population, 2 to 3 billion 50 percent, 3 to 4 billion 33 percent, 4 to 5 billion 25 percent, 5 to 6 billion 20 percent, and 6 to 7 billion 17 percent. Eventually only a 10 percent growth in population would be necessary to go from 10 to 11 billion. Thus, each billion increment of the world's population occurs more quickly for a constant population growth rate.

The earth is rapidly getting more crowded, yet there are some who say that we can sustain a much larger population. If every human being were to stand next to one another, how much of the earth would be covered with people? If we place every individual in a 3′ × 3′ square, enough space to stand, but not lie down, we can get just about 3.1 million people into a square mile. The area to accommodate 7.3 billion people in 2015 is about 2,360 square miles, or a square a 48.5 miles on a side. Thus, the world's population could fit, standing room only, in Delaware, the nation's second smallest state at just under 2,500 square miles, with a little room to spare. With a population density of Manhattan including Central Park, the world's population could fit into half of Texas.

Demographics affect energy consumption since more people consume more energy. One way to judge the future population is to calculate the portion of a nation below 15 years of age. A disproportionately high youthful population portends higher than average population growth as this segment reaches its childbearing years. On this basis, future population growth will be centered in the Middle East, Asia (excluding Japan), and South America. On the other hand, Europe, the US (net of migration from Latin America), Russia, and Japan have to deal with a growing geriatric generation that has ramifications on future population size and energy consumption and the viability of old age social programs. As Europe and Japan exhibit essentially stagnant to negative population growth, other nations would like to curb theirs. Some years ago, China took draconian efforts to contain its population growth at one billion people by restricting families to one child through forced abortions, financial fines, and even corporal punishment for having more than the authorized number of children. Families restricted to one child preferred boys, which resulted in abortions or abandonment of baby girls, of whom quite a number were adopted by American families.[12] Having a society where males outnumber females may create a serious social problem as large numbers of males, unable to find mates, bond to form roving gangs of disaffected bachelors, disrupting social cohesion. Despite Herculean efforts to the contrary, the social experiment to contain the nation's population at one billion has obviously failed; China's current population is 1.4 billion and slowly climbing. Perhaps too slowly, as there is now fear that China too may become a geriatric state about two decades behind Japan.

The rate of world population growth expanded between 1950 and 1965, peaked at 2.1 percent per year, and then went into a long-term decline of 1.8 percent in the 1970s, 1.7 percent in the 1980s, 1.4 percent in the 1990s, and 1.2 percent in the 2000s. The current population growth rate is 1.04 percent and is projected to be 0.45 percent by 2050.[13] On a global scale, the average number of children per family has to decline to reduce the population growth rate to this level. But other forces are at work that may effectively cut the increase in population growth, if not population itself. The fall of communism in 1991, and the subsequent political and economic turmoil, brought about a decade of a declining birthrate and a shortening of the average life span, resulting in a negative population growth in Russia. Diseases such as HIV/AIDS ravage the population in Sub-Saharan Africa along with social disintegration, civil upheaval, tribal warfare, and, on occasion, tribal holocausts. In 2014–2015, the fear that Ebola would spread globally was countered by successful efforts to contain the disease within three nations in West Africa. Some rapidly growing nations such as flood-prone Bangladesh, with 156 million people in an area of 57,000 square miles (a bit smaller than Georgia), must be close to reaching, or have already exceeded, their capacity to adequately feed, clothe, and shelter their populations. Further population growth will only foster extreme poverty. Aswan dam, when built in the 1950s, made Egypt self-sufficient in food. Today Egypt is one of the world's largest food importers because of its rapid population growth. Whoever governs Egypt must face the problems associated with severe shortages in domestic production of food and energy. Under these conditions, can Egyptians continue to propagate as in the past? And if so, how are they going to feed themselves and have energy to fuel their society?

Despite success in containing Ebola, there are other forms of flu on the verge of jumping from animals to humans, which could bring on a new Spanish Flu-type pandemic. Modern means of travel make it nearly impossible to isolate or quarantine an outbreak of contagious diseases as feared with Ebola. Swift actions taken by airlines and governments were successful in containing Ebola. Weapons of mass destruction and terrorism are other threats to human survival. Considering all these factors, the projected population of over 9.3 billion people by 2050, a 27 percent increase from current levels, is not a foregone conclusion. Exponential growth of humans, like bacteria overflowing the confines of a Petri dish, has its limits. Figure 1.8 shows the actual and projected annual growth rates for population and the annual increment being added to the population.

Population growth rates are projected to continue to decline as they have been since 1965. Annual increments to population have been relatively flat, adding about another

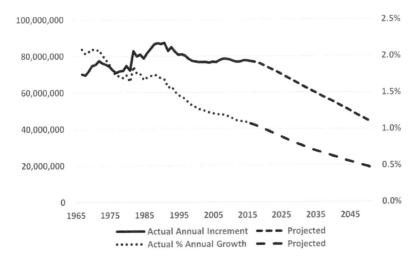

1965	1975	1985	1995	2005	2015	2025	2035	2045	

—— Actual Annual Increment ▬ ▬ ▬ Projected
•••••• Actual % Annual Growth ▬ ▬ Projected

Figure 1.8 Actual and Projected Annual Growth Rates and Increments to Population

equivalent US in population every 4 years. Annual increments are projected to decline after 2015 more in line with birth rates. Unfortunately these positive increments will continue to boost population to 9.3 billion in 2050, but at a slower pace.[14] But not all agree with 9.3 billion by 2050. Some see 11 billion by 2100 from higher than anticipated birth rates particularly in Africa.[15] Others see a peaking at 8.5 billion with a decline thereafter as a consequence of a continuing decline in population birth rates. The replacement rate for developing nations is 2.3 children per family and 2.1 children per family in developed nations. Nations already below the replacement rate are Azerbaijan, Bahrain, Brazil, Georgia, Iran, Japan, Lebanon, North Korea, Qatar, Tunisia, and Uzbekistan. Nations whose birth rate is nearing the replacement rate are Argentina, India, Indonesia, Mexico, Saudi Arabia, Turkey, and UAE.[16] Several nations in Europe and Russia have stagnant population growth.

Per Capita Energy Consumption

Figure 1.9 is per capita consumption of energy in tons of oil equivalent per year. Thus, every man, woman, and child consume, on average, energy equivalent to 1.8 tons of oil per year. With 7 barrels of oil in a ton and 42 gallons of oil in a barrel, each person consumes 529 gallons of oil equivalent per year, or 1.45 gallons per day. This is not oil, but the oil equivalent of all energy consumed. Of course, this is an average—a large portion of the human population (one to two billion) consumes mainly biomass and virtually no fossil fuels. Not surprisingly, the best fitting trend line is fairly close to linear. Per capita energy consumption has been in an upward trend for over a century except during the Great Depression. Nowadays its upward trend includes higher per capita energy consumption in Asia, the Middle East, and South America that will probably continue for another two or three decades before leveling off. Then perhaps it will be the turn of the one to two billion of the world's poorest people who may see some upward adjustment in their living standards.

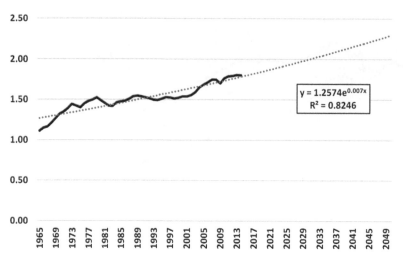

2.50

2.00

1.50

1.00

0.50

0.00

$y = 1.2574e^{0.007x}$
$R^2 = 0.8246$

1965 1969 1973 1977 1981 1985 1989 1993 1997 2001 2005 2009 2013 2017 2021 2025 2029 2033 2037 2041 2045 2049

Figure 1.9 Per Capita Energy Consumption (toe)

Economic Activity

A common measure of economic activity is GDP, which is defined as the monetary value of all finished goods and services produced annually within a nation, net of trade imbalances. It is also treated as total spending of all the principal activities of a society (personal, corporate, government, and capital investment, net of savings). GDP is not above criticism. For instance, there is no contribution to GDP if two individuals mow each other's lawns for free; but if they each charge the other $20, then $40 becomes part of GDP. Yet the lawns are mowed in both cases. Of greater concern, there is no link between GDP and productivity. If a society educates one million specialized tax lawyers and accountants to create and wade through 100,000 pages of complex tax regulations replete with innumerable loopholes in order for the rich and famous as individuals and corporations to minimize their tax payments at the expense of the plebeians who must shoulder the full brunt of the tax bill, all this effort is incorporated into GDP, but it is hardly productive. The same is true in the acquisition and distribution of cocaine and other harmful drugs and the concomitant cost to society of the spread of crime and disease by drug addicts; all this is part of GDP (police and public services and healthcare costs). How about building entire cities in China, known as ghost cities, where the only inhabitants are those responsible for security and maintenance of empty or "see-through" buildings built in the unpopulated hinterlands? Spending associated with their construction becomes part of a nation's GDP, but it is not (as of yet) productive spending.

Let us take a look at two families with the same income. The first family lives within its means and has a certain demand for goods and services incorporated into the GDP. The second family has the same income, but lives far beyond its means by collecting credit cards like postage stamps and continually refinancing their home in a rising housing market, spending twice as much as the first family. The contribution of the second family will be twice that of the first family to the GDP. In fact, if you have much of the population spending more than they earn, the GDP will grow, as President George Bush knew full well when he recommended to the American people at least twice during his administration to continue to borrow based on refinancing their homes and spend the proceeds "to keep the economy going."

But what happens when house prices no longer rise, cutting off a chief means of funds from refinancing mortgages? Banks then become wary of customers whose income would have to be largely dedicated to servicing debt if they were not offered more debt to tap. This then becomes the excuse to cut off offering more credit card debt. This point has to occur because, mathematically, it is possible for a person to acquire enough debt whose service charges would be equal to gross income if no more debt were available. When new sources of debt are no longer available to service existing debt, the second family's disposable income collapses as a large chunk of gross income is consumed in actually paying off existing debt. Consumer spending is 70 percent of US GDP. Cut consumer spending and GDP takes a hit. Its growth is not as robust—in fact it may even shrink. The housing and the credit card bubbles artificially inflated GDP, which ended in 2007–2009 with the bursting of these bubbles.

In recent years, towns and counties have gone bankrupt from growing budget deficits exhausting market willingness to continue buying new issues to be added to their bloated debt. What do these government agencies do? They fire government workers, try to renege on overly generous pension and medical care obligations, cut services, and raise taxes. This means that some government people will have less income either in reduced direct pay or retirement benefits and residents in the town will be contributing more to paying taxes rather than spending on goods and services. The added tax revenues do not support higher levels of government spending that would add to the GDP, but are dedicated to retiring debt that can no longer be refinanced by acquiring new debt. Under these circumstances, the contribution of the town or county to GDP declines.

Look at Greece—the poster child of Europe. It can only borrow from the European Central Bank to make good on current debt servicing charges, which only transfers risk from one bank to another. To obtain such funds, the Greek government must raise taxes and cut costs by firing employees or reducing wages and pension benefits. Unemployment climbs and these people are no longer in the spending stream, which negatively affects GDP. Those with more heavily taxed incomes will have less to spend. As GDP sinks, loan covenants are triggered where aggregate debt is not allowed to exceed a certain level of GDP, forcing yet another round of firing/cutting benefits to government employees and, for those still left with a job, another round of tax hikes, which cuts their spending. Again, GDP contracts, prompting another round in cutting government expenditures and raising taxes. This is an excellent example of a positive feedback system where the consequences of pursuing a course of action only makes the problem worse. It is clear that this situation is going to continue until the economy of Greece is reduced to dust and ashes or until the patience of the people to endure being sent to a poor house is utterly exhausted. Youth facing a bleak future for the remainder of their lives with little or no hope of ever securing a job have nothing to lose by taking to the streets with pitch forks and shovels. Cyprus has introduced the world to "bail-ins" where collapsing banks seize depositors' savings. What happens to GDP when retirees no longer have the funds to spend on their necessities and businesses have to close because the government has seized their working capital?

While Zimbabwe and post-World War One Germany come to mind when one thinks of hyperinflation, the fact is that the number of nations in the history of paper currencies that have managed to destroy the value of their currencies is legion.[17] Why should today's paper currencies being stuffed to fill gigantic cracks in the economic foundation be exempt from this historical process? Be that as it may, GDP artificially inflated through unwarranted or uncontrollable credit creation is not a proper measure of actual economic activity. Neither is it a proper way to run a government, as history has amply shown. Massive credit expansion with little or no growth in the underlying economy to support such debt is ultimately self-destructive. These unwelcomed macroeconomic factors have to be integrated into any forecast of GDP as indeed they have when one views the barely positive forecasts in recent times. GDP forecasts are also adjusted for inflation, which has plainly been understated for a number of years in order to minimize adjustments to inflation-protected government benefits (e.g., US social security payments). Expressing GDP with inflation rates that more accurately reflect reality would swing GDP calculations from positive to negative. This in itself is another major reason why governments underestimate inflation. Nevertheless, relying on the conventional definition of GDP as a measure of economic activity, Figure 1.10 shows per capita economic activity for the first 1,800 years of the Common Era.[18]

Basically nothing happened until 1400, the start of the pre-Industrial Age, marked by the beginning of metallurgy and glass making in the West. These activities were known during the time of the Roman Empire, but were lost in the chaos of the Dark Age. These lost technologies were rediscovered and brought back to Europe by knights returning from the Crusades. The UK was the first nation to experience per capita GDP growth, followed very closely by Germany, but the UK maintained a substantial lead on per capita GDP. The US lagged the UK by about 200 years before industrialization started (as a British colony where the economic theory of mercantilism ruled, manufacturing was prohibited to force the colonists to buy manufactured goods from Britain). However, by 1800, US per capita economic activity was equal to

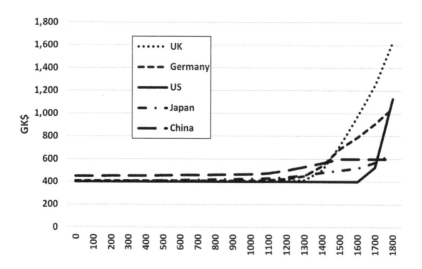

Figure 1.10 Per Capita Economic Activity Before 1800

that of Germany. The Meiji Restoration in 1868 marked Japan's entry as an industrial power, and China, under the emperors, was disinterested in Western technology and did not become an industrial state until the early twentieth century.

Growth in per capita economic activity between 1800 and 2000 in Figure 1.11 shows that the UK and US were essentially tied in terms of per capita economic activity, with Germany lagging from 1800 to 1940. In the aftermath of the war, US per capita economic activity surged as the victor that had suffered no domestic war damage. The UK and Germany were tied for second and third place by 1960 and were joined by Japan in 1970 as a consequence of its post-war economic awakening. The three nations remained about equal in per capita economic activity to 2000. China's economic awakening was stunted by Mao Zedong's Great Leap Forward (1958–1961). Economic and political recovery took over 10 years before China embarked on what was a state sponsored free market. China now has the world's largest GDP, slightly ahead of the US. With four times the population, its per capita economic activity would be about one-quarter that of the US, a highly significant advance since 2000.

Figure 1.12 is per capita economic activity on a global basis. It is constructed in GK$ for global economic activity, which is in current dollars, and is converted to constant 2014 dollars by adjusting for inflation.[19] Dividing two exponential growth curves for economic activity and population did not yield a best fitting exponential curve.[20]

The downward slope shows that energy intensity of economic activity decreased sharply from 1971 to the early 1980s when oil prices were very high. The nations of the world worked wonders to introduce greater efficiency in transportation, machinery, and equipment and in installing insulation and encouraging conservation. As a result, the world economy could operate with less energy intensity. Oil prices weakening from 1981 to 1989 removed the incentive to be overly efficient. Energy intensity significantly slowed and has pretty much leveled out since 1990. The selected projection calls for a continuing slight decline of energy intensity per unit of economic activity.

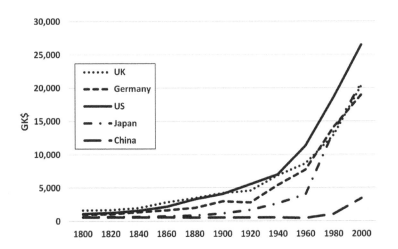

Figure 1.11 Per Capita Economic Activity Post-1800

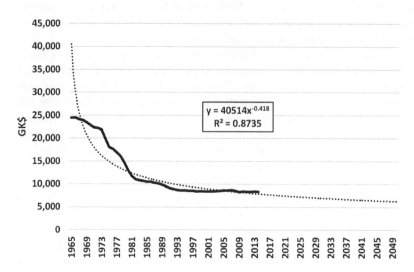

Figure 1.12 Per Capita Economic Activity in Constant GK$

A Model to Project Total Energy Demand

The proposed model incorporates the following equation.

Global energy consumption = a + b1*GDP per capita + b2*Energy per capita + b3*Population (millions)

The values for a, the y-intercept, and b1, b2, and b3, the coefficients for the variables, can be obtained from a multiple regression output for the actual values for GDP per capita, energy per capita, and population in millions from 1965 to 2014 contained in Figures 1.12, 1.9, and 1.7, respectively. The resulting three variable model has an R^2 value of 99.8 percent, indicating an excellent fit between the model and actual data. Having obtained the values for a, b1, b2, and b3 from the regression output, the projected values for Global Energy Demand were calculated using the formulas shown for trend lines depicting per capita energy consumption in Figure 1.9 and per capita economic activity in Figure 1.12 and projected population derived from information in Figure 1.7.[21] Figure 1.13 is the resulting forecast of global energy demand.

One may well ask whether this was worth the trouble as a child can draw a continuation of an existing line. A response to that valid observation is that the projection encompasses one's assessments on per capita economic activity and per capita energy consumption and population growth. While the economy becomes slightly less energy intensive with time, growth in per capita consumption and in population keeps the past trend intact. This should instill some degree of comfort and confidence over a projection done by a child arbitrarily extending an existing curve even though both turn out to be the same! The exercise showed that any hope for energy consumption leveling out given greater per capita energy consumption and population growth is wishful thinking. The trend line will remain intact as long as the underlying trends that generated the trend line remain essentially unchanged. Energy demand would level out only if a calamity struck

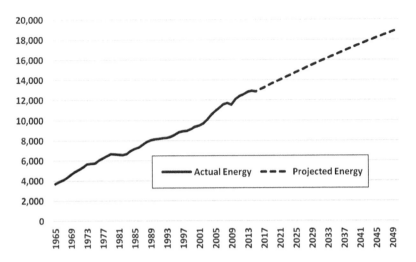

Figure 1.13 Global Energy Demand Projection (mmtoe)

such as a sharp contraction in economic activity from a financial collapse, or outbreak of a major war, which would cause energy demand to climb or could lead to a constriction on energy supplies that would cut energy consumption, or any number of potential disaster scenarios, which with time seem to be getting greater in number and less remote in possibility. But given a relatively stable society, energy consumption will be growing at a modest annual rate of 1.1 percent, yet by 2050, total energy demand will increase by 47 percent, the power of exponential growth!

Problems and Projects

Problem 1.1

Take a major nation from the *BP Statistical Review* and plot either a cumulative line or an area chart of the principal sources of energy in quads (1 quad = 25.2 million tons of oil equivalent) from 1965 to the latest year. If quads turn out to be too small in value for charting purposes, then use million tons of oil equivalent. Obtain the growth rate for overall energy consumption and its principal components for 10-year segments. Goal Seek under What-If Analysis (Data ribbon) can be used. The general formula is cell 1*(1+cell 2)^10. Cell 1 is the beginning value; cell 2 is the growth rate determined. "By changing cell" and "To value" is the ending value after 10 years. For each decal year (1965, 1975, etc.), construct a pie chart showing the percentage distribution of each of the major sources. Write a short paper on how energy consumption and its components changed over this period of time.

Problem 1.2

We consume food for energy—a proper diet is somewhere between 2,500 and 3,000 calories per day. Using the approximate conversion that 1 calorie is equivalent to 0.004 Btu and consuming 3,000 calories per day, what is the equivalent consumption in Btu per hour?

This is hardly the beginning of how much energy is necessary to keep us alive. The response to the above question is the last step in the conversion of food to keep us alive. There are agricultural activities associated with growing crops and raising animals that consume energy. Energy is consumed in producing pesticides and fertilizers and manufacturing tractors and farm implements. Crops and animals have to be converted to food and shipped to market and to the consumer before being prepared for meals, all of which requires energy. It is difficult to establish where this process should start when figuring out daily energy requirements to keep us alive. But there may be sources available that quantify these elements. Do an internet or a library search to assess the actual energy required to keep us alive for one day!

Problem 1.3

The 100 watt (W) bulb was quite common in US homes. A watt is a unit of power. Energy is power over time. A 100 W bulb shining for 1 hour is 100 watt-hours (Wh) of energy. A Btu is a unit of energy. There are 3.412 Btu in a watt-hour or 341.2 Btu per 100 Wh. A typical home requires about 400 kWh, where kW is a thousand watts per month. What is the equivalent amount of energy in Btu? How much fossil fuel in terms of Btu has to be burned to supply a home with 400 kWh per month of energy, given that electricity generation along with transmission losses has a net efficiency of 33 percent?

Problem 1.4

Given that there are 20 million Btu in a short ton of coal (2,000 pounds), how many pounds of coal have to be burned to supply a home with electricity for 1 month? This, too, underestimates the energy required as in Problem 1.3 because energy is required to mine and transport coal to the electricity generating station. Taking a wider spectrum, energy is consumed on a one time basis to develop a mine, manufacture transport and mining equipment, and build a utility plant. Calculating energy requirements is not an easy exercise, depending on how encompassing is the energy envelope.

Problem 1.5

Create a bar graph of per capita energy consumption for 10 nations including the US, China, India, and World Average using the latest year in the *BP Statistical Review* and population from the US Census Bureau Website. Sort the nations and their respective per capita energy consumption from highest to lowest. This can be done by putting the cursor on the first per capita energy consumption figure and then selecting both columns of data. On the Data ribbon, select the icon Z A to sort the data in descending order and then select a bar chart on the Insert ribbon. This is the Pareto diagram. Describe the disparity in per capita energy consumption—are you surprised at the degree of disparity?

Problem 1.6

If India and China were to increase their per capita energy consumption to 50 percent that of the US, what would be the incremental annual demand for each nation? How much does this increase compare to global energy demand? Do you think that this can be accommodated?

Problem 1.7

A statement was made that if the world's population density was that of Manhattan Island, then the world's population would fit into half of the state of Texas. Is this statement true?

Project 1.1

Take any OECD or BRIC nation of your liking and construct a projection of total energy consumption to 2050 incorporating trend formulas and the results of the regression analysis. Past and future population data can be obtained from the US Census Bureau Website (www. census.gov/population/international/data/idb/informationGateway.php). GDP data can be obtained from www.ggdc.net/maddison/maddison-project/home.htm up to 2008. Obtain percentage growth rate for selected nation from http://data.worldbank.org/indicator/ NY.GDP.MKTP.CD and apply these to the Maddison 2008 data to obtain GDP values beyond 2008. This is probably not strictly comparable. Alternatively, you can use the World Bank GDP data, which is in current US dollars, and adapt the analysis to its start date of 1980. Whatever the source of data, convert to constant dollars if in current dollars using www.usinflationcalculator.com.

Project 1.2

Do a projection for oil using the same methodology for any nation of your choosing where you can obtain the necessary underlying data. If you select China or India, annual oil consumption figures reflect both population growth and a rapidly growing population of automobiles. A future reduction in automobile sales from, say, congested roads or market saturation would affect future growth rates. Future growth in oil should be tempered with saturation of automobiles when people are less inclined to purchase a motor vehicle just to be trapped in a 250-mile traffic jam. In other words, a significantly growing trend line in per capita oil consumption may have to be tempered to reflect this phenomenon at some point in the future. Blindly following trend lines should be avoided!

Project 1.3

Modify both projects 1.1 and 1.2 by including a fourth variable for oil prices. Oil prices in constant dollars are in *BP Energy Statistics*. Obtain if possible high, medium, and low priced assessments of future oil prices. Alternatively, think about what would be your assessments. Run the multiple regression model for each of these oil prices and examine the projection of energy and oil demand. Are oil prices important drivers in projecting future energy and oil demand? If they are, what oil price scenario would you select and why?

Notes

1 Katharine Gammon, "Pollution Facts," Website www.livescience.com/22728-pollution-facts.html.
2 "Air Pollutants," Environmental Protection Administration, Websites www.epa.gov/airquality/urba nair; www.epa.gov/air/airpollutants.html.
3 "Greenhouse Gas Emissions," Environmental Protection Administration, Website www.epa.gov/ climatechange/ghgemissions/global.html.

4 Extracted from "Launch of the Center on Global Energy Policy," SIPA, Columbia University, Website www.sipa.columbia.edu/cgep/opportunity.html.

5 *BP Statistical Review of World Energy* can be downloaded from British Petroleum Website, www. bp.com.

6 Data source for Figures 1.2 and 1.3 is https://nextbigfuture.com/2010/11/world-energy-in-exa joules-by-energy.html. A bar graph version of Figure 1.3 can be found at www3.weforum. org/docs/WEF_EN_IndustryVision.pdf, extracted from Vaclav Smil, *Energy Transitions: History, Requirements, Prospects* (Santa Barbara, CA: ABC-CLIO, 2010).

7 "Estimated U.S. Energy Use in 2014," Lawrence Livermore National Laboratory (2012), Website https://flowcharts.llnl.gov. Image used with permission of Lawrence Livermore National Laboratory.

8 *The Annual Energy Outlook with Projections to 2035*, US Energy Information Administration, Website www.eia.gov.

9 *World Energy Outlook*, International Energy Agency (IEA), Website www.iea.org. In addition, IEA offers other publications that bear on various aspects of energy.

10 R. Nersesian, *Energy Risk Modeling* (Ithaca, NY: Palisade, 2013). Sections 12–14 deal with uncertainty on assessing variables in projecting demand and oil prices.

11 "Historical Estimates of World Population," US Census Bureau, Website www.census.gov/popu lation/international/data/worldpop/table_history.php. Post-1950 world population from www.cen sus.gov/population/international/data/worldpop/table_population.php.

12 There are about 30 adopted Chinese girls and no adopted Chinese boys in my home town who, as throw-away babies, would not be alive today.

13 World Population Clock, Website www.worldometers.info/world-population/#growthrate.

14 "World Population Prospects: The 2012 Revision," United Nations Department of Economics and Social Affairs, Website http://esa.un.org/wpp.

15 Brad Plummer, "New Forecast: The Earth Could Have 11 Billion People by 2100," *Vox Topics* (September 18, 2014), Website www.vox.com/2014/9/18/6412059/population-11-billion-UN-forecast.

16 David Merkel (Aleph Blog), "Analyst: World Population Will Peak at 8.5 Billion in 2030," *Business Insider* (November 30, 2012), Website www.businessinsider.com/analyst-world-population-will-peak-at-85-billion-in-2030-2012-11.

17 I was in a Czech restaurant that displaced four currencies that were once of value in Czechoslovakia— notes from the Austrian-Hungarian empire, notes after World War One as an independent nation, notes after Hitler seized control, and notes after the Soviet Union seized control. All are worthless other than as collectibles.

18 Data for Figures 1.10 and 1.11 from the Maddison Project, Website www.ggdc.net/maddison/mad dison-project/home.htm. GK$ are defined as international Geary Khamis (not US) dollars, with the intent of placing economic activity for each nation on an equal footing based on purchasing power parity. Many more nations are represented than those included in Figures 1.10 and 1.11. What is important is the relative standing of the individual nations. The Maddison Project Website offers references for more material on GK$. Further information may be available from Ed Jones at Ed.Jones@efpublishing.com.

19 US Inflation Calculator, Website www.usinflationcalculator.com. Enter $1 as cost in indicated year for 2014 base year and the factor to be applied to GDP is given as "same item would cost." The resulting inflation factor has to be multiplied by the indicated year's GDP in current dollars to obtain GDP in constant 2014 dollars. See following footnote for source of global GDP and corrections made to update last 2008 figure to 2014.

20 Regional economic activity drawn from the Maddison Project was totaled to obtain a global eco nomic output. It was noted that its 2008 value of $50 trillion GK dollars was less than the nominal US dollar estimate of close to $63 trillion dollars. The reason for this is GK dollars are not US dollars. The Maddison Project database allows extraction of economic data for many nations extending back to 1965 to match the start time for *BP Energy Statistics*. The Maddison Project data was projected to

2012 by utilizing World Bank data that the global economy shrank by 2.1 percent in 2009 versus 2008, with growth rates of 3.9 percent in 2010, 3.7 percent in 2011, 3.8 percent in 2012, 2.7 percent in 2013, and 2.4 percent in 2014. Expressing economic activity in GK dollars is not a problem as long as consistency is maintained and that these growth rates for global GDP in US$ would apply to GDP in GK$.

21 The X values in the trend line formulas do not refer to the specific year, for example 2015, but to its ordinal number 51, where 1965 has an ordinal number of 1. A population of six billion people is entered as 6,000 million.

2 Electricity and Utility Industry

The primary fuels are coal, oil, natural gas, nuclear, hydro, biomass, and renewables, but these are not the forms of energy we encounter most often. Other than driving a car and heating a home, the most common form of energy we encounter is turning on an electrical switch. We use electricity for lighting and running all sorts of electrical appliances and equipment. Electricity is a secondary form of energy derived from primary fuels and is absolutely essential to running a modern economy. Its essentiality was demonstrated during Hurricane Sandy in 2013 when loss of electricity to homes, businesses, banks (including ATMs and credit card processors), and food stores, plus inability to pump gas at filling stations, brought life to a standstill.

From this experience, it is no wonder that the ultimate weapon envisioned is an atmospheric explosion of a nuclear device that can generate an electromagnetic pulse sufficient to knock out a nation's communication system and electricity grid, which would also render inoperative home computers, automobiles, and iPhones. Sad to say, this would totally immobilize modern society. It is possible, by the way, for the sun to do the job. In 1859, an electromagnetic pulse from an intense solar storm facing the Earth, which was observed and described by astronomer Richard Carrington, knocked out the nation's telegraphic system, including electrically shocking operators and sparking fires.[1] Other Carrington events occurred in 1972, affecting interstate telephone lines in the Midwest, and in 1989, causing a major blackout in eastern Canada when electrical currents induced by a solar flare burned out transmission lines and melted transformers. In 2000 a Carrington event short-circuited radio satellites; in 2003 destroyed spacecraft solar flare measuring devices; and in 2006 disrupted satellite-to-ground communications and Global Positioning System navigation. In July 2013, a potentially devastating Carrington event from a coronal mass ejection crossed Earth's orbit at a point where the Earth would have been two weeks later. Those who walked on the moon risked their lives if they were directly exposed to the radiation of a solar flare. The crew in the international space station moves into a protected area when the space station is exposed to a solar flare. It goes without saying that modern technology has increased our vulnerability to the unexpected and the unanticipated. This chapter deals with electricity, its origin, the organizational structure and system operation of utilities, energy sources, and electricity consumption.

See the Companion Website for sections on the Early History of Electricity and Generating Electricity Commercially: www.routledge.com/cw/nersesian.

Electricity Is Derived Energy

Electricity and oil, while both forms of energy, are far different from each other. Crude oil, sometimes considered a common indistinguishable commodity, which it is not as different grades of crude oil have different properties, is made into a myriad of different petroleum products and petrochemicals, which can be stored. Various forms of energy generate electricity where one electron is identical with others, which cannot be stored, at least not yet in commercial quantities. Electricity is a form of just-in-time production with no delay between generation and consumption. Oil product flows are directed by pipelines, tankers, and tank trucks from one location to another and stored for future use, a process that can be described by flow and stock diagrams in systems analysis. Electricity, on the other hand, follows the path of least resistance unless phase-angle regulators are installed that can control power flow through interconnected power systems. Ultimately there is no way to identify one electron from another or to direct electricity from a generating plant to a particular customer unless, of course, a single generator is serving a single customer. A customer has no idea of the origin of electricity regardless of the identity of the payee on an electric bill in systems where electricity from different generating plants is fed into a common transmission and distribution system.

Electricity is a charge measured in coulombs; electrical energy is measured in joules and is the flow of electrical power over time. Electrical power is measured in watts (W; one joule per second) to honor James Watt for his pioneering work in developing the steam engine. James Watt needed some measure of the output of a steam engine for marketing purposes. He decided that a horse, a primary source of power at that time known by all, could pull with the force of 180 pounds to turn a mill wheel 2.4 times per minute. With a radius of the mill wheel of 12 feet, one horsepower was initially defined as 32,572 foot-pounds per minute, which was subsequently standardized as the power necessary to lift 550 pounds 1 foot in 1 second (550 foot-pounds per second or 33,000 foot-pounds per minute). For short spurts in time, we can operate at 1.2 horsepower, while a trained athlete can get up to 2.5 horsepower. One horsepower turned out to be equivalent to 745.7 W. But a watt is not defined in terms of horsepower but as the power of 1 joule per second, and a joule is in turn defined as energy required to accelerate a 1 kilogram mass with 1 newton of force for 1 meter. A newton of force is defined as the force necessary to accelerate a mass of 1 kilogram at 1 meter per second. A joule is also defined as the power in an electric circuit where the potential difference is 1 volt with 1 ampere of current. Perhaps it is better to think of a watt as one-hundredth of the power needed to light a 100 W bulb.

The terms electricity and electrical energy are used interchangeably even though they are technically quite different. Generators cannot make electricity (technically electrical energy) because electricity similar to temperature is a property of matter. An electricity generator "pumps" an electrical charge back and forth inside a wire 60 times per second, and electromagnetic fields created around the wire are what is known as electrical power. Electrical power flowing through a motor, heater, or light bulb over time becomes electrical energy that turns the rotor and warms or lights a room. Electrical energy is electrical power performing some function over time. One hundred watts can light a 100 W bulb—that is power. Keeping the bulb lit for 1 hour is 100 Wh—that is energy. A watt is a measure of "capacity" to deliver power, whereas watt-hour is the amount of energy or power delivered over time. Power is what can be delivered at a moment in time, and energy is the integral of power over time. Kilowatt-hours (kWh) charged in an electricity bill from the local utility represent the electrical energy consumed by the customer.

To produce electricity, a turbine is rotated to drive an electricity generator. Steam is the most common motive force of rotating a turbine and is produced by burning coal, oil, natural gas, and biomass, or from a geothermal or nuclear source. Falling water, tidal currents, river flow, wave action, and wind are other motive forces to rotate a turbine. The only manmade source of electricity not created by rotating a turbine is a solar photoelectric cell that converts sunlight directly into electricity. Our capacity to generate electricity pales to insignificance when compared to nature. Enormous circulating electrical currents surrounding the Earth's core create the magnetic field that deflects charged particles from the sun that would otherwise strip away the protective ozone layer, allowing harmful ultraviolet and cosmic radiation to destroy life on Earth. Lightning occurs when the buildup of static electricity at different cloud levels, or between a cloud and Earth, creates a voltage differential large enough to overcome the resistance of air to conduct electricity. If lightning could be harnessed, it would easily fulfill humanity's dream of unlimited and free electrical power.

System Operation

Electricity is generated at about 35,000 volts and then stepped up by transformers in voltage to anywhere from 250,000 volts for older generating plants to 800,000 volts for modern. Power transported by an electric line is equal to current multiplied by voltage. Energy lost in the power line (mostly as heat) is the square of current multiplied by the resistance of the line. Thus, the same amount of power can be transmitted with less line losses if the voltage is increased to lower the current. Since line losses are lower for higher voltages, transmission systems transmit electricity with as high a voltage as possible to a point close to consumers. A distribution system starts when the high voltage electricity is stepped down to lower voltages. The initial step-down at a transformer station may be to 70,000 or 130,000 volts to distribute electricity to major industrial users. Another step-down may be to 15,000 or 25,000 volts at a transformer substation to distribute electricity to large commercial enterprises. Voltage step-downs vary considerably from one utility to another. For residences and small commercial establishments, the final step-down to 120 or 240 volts is done by transformers mounted on the nearest telephone/electric pole. Step-downs for those connected to underground electric cables are done as close as possible to end users to minimize line losses. Care has to be exercised in locating transformers to ensure safety from potential sparking.

Unlike fossil fuels, there are few ways to store electricity. Conventional batteries are incapable of storing the amount of electricity required to support the operations of a utility. Development of a cheap means to store enormous quantities of electrons would be a game changer in the world of electricity. Until this occurs, the electricity business is the only one that operates without an inventory. Some maintain that water in the back of a dam can be considered stored electricity. Using this logic, a pile of coal sitting outside a generating facility is also stored electricity. But water and coal are not electricity until they provide the motive force to rotate a turbine to drive a generator. Once generated, electrical energy flows close to the speed of light between the generator and the consumer when the switch is turned on and stops just as abruptly when the switch is turned off.

Unlike oil or natural gas in a pipeline, throttling a valve does not control or direct the flow of electricity. Unless directed by phase–angle regulators, electricity follows the path of least resistance. If that path leads to overloading a transmission line and melting the wires, so be it. Although breakers protect transmission lines from overloading, the usual way to decrease flow of electrical energy through transmission lines from region A to B is to raise output of electricity at B and cut output at A, assuming power providers at both locations. Changing outputs at A and B can have unpredictable effects on the flow of electricity between A and B and other nodes in an electricity distribution system.

During times of low demand, when transmission systems are not limited by capacity constraints, electricity rates are fairly uniform throughout a region. During times of heavy demand, transmission capacity constraints create local rate disparities if a system is established that involves an auction-like process to determine local rates at principal node or connecting points. For instance, reducing output at A, to prevent overloading the transmission system may involve a low-cost electricity generator, and increasing output at B, as a substitute source, may involve a high-cost electricity generator. This creates a price disparity between points A and B. Another cause of a price disparity between two points is line losses; that is, what goes into a transmission system is not what comes out.

Handling Peak Demand

Other than pumped storage plants and proposed systems to utilize compressed air and spinning fly wheels and until the technological development of a super battery, there is no way to store large quantities of electricity. The system of generating and transmitting electricity must adjust to variation in demand instantaneously. Variation in demand is significant over the course of a day when peak day time demand may be double that of night time, over the course of a week when more electricity is consumed on weekdays than weekends, and over the course of a year when electricity demand peaks from air conditioning during summer hot spells. In cold climates in areas where electricity heats homes such as in eastern Canada, peak demand occurs during the winter. Some areas have a morning peak and an afternoon peak, while others have one during the afternoon and an even higher peak during the early evening hours, but more typically a single mid-afternoon peak. To meet peak demand, peaking generators have to be purchased, but there are exceptions, such as where there is ample hydropower capacity available to satisfy peak loads. Peaking generators are usually combustion turbines (modified jet engines) fueled by natural gas that have a fast startup time to react to surges in power demand. They may run for only a few hours on weekdays during summer hot spells to meet air conditioning demand in homes and offices. Amortizing the annual cost of peaking generators over such a short period of operating time makes for extremely expensive electricity. Yet, if peaking generators were not available, blackouts would ensue unless other arrangements have been made to curb demand.

There are a number of ways to handle peak demand by either supply or demand management. One example of supply management is to pay operators of office buildings and factories to disconnect from the grid during times of peak seasonal demand and supply themselves with power by operating their emergency backup generators. Another arrangement is for heavy users of electricity to slow operations during times of peak demand and shift some of their load to times of reduced demand. Some plants (e.g., aluminum smelting) have their own electricity generating capacity. During times of peak demand, it may be more profitable for these plants to curtail production and sell excess electricity to utilities. Other companies pay a lower rate for an interruptible supply of electricity and are willing to be disconnected for a few hours a day during peak seasonal demand to benefit from lower electricity cost for the rest of the year. They may, of course, have backup generators to support their operations when this occurs. Companies desiring uninterrupted service pay a higher rate to ensure that there is always enough generating capacity available to sustain their operations.

One way to handle peak demand is installing timers on appliances, such as hot water heaters, so that they operate only during nighttime lulls in electricity demand. The more common form of demand management is time-of-day metering, with electricity rates varying by the hour in response to demand. More costly electricity during times of peak demand creates an incentive for individuals and businesses to reduce their electricity load by cutting back on their air conditioning for an hour or two when rates (and temperatures) peak. With flat rates that now prevail for most consumers, the cost of running an air-conditioning unit is the same regardless of the time of day. Consumers are not sensitive to fluctuations in market priced electricity during times of peak demand. Demand management makes them sensitive to time of day and day of the week. Running washers and dryers at night and on weekends can significantly reduce electricity bills. The last resort for accommodating peak demand without sufficient generating capacity is controlled by rolling blackouts that cover different areas for relatively short periods of time, announced or otherwise, to reduce demand below generating capacity. Failure to take effective action when demand exceeds supply will result in a loss of system control and an unplanned blackout.

Ancillary Services

System operation is a critical function that controls the output of generators to satisfy demand in real time, where electrical energy flows at the speed of light over the path of least resistance, without the benefit of being able to draw down on inventory. The system operator must deal with imbalances between supply and demand, congestion (overloading transmission lines), and ancillary services. Ancillary services include scheduling and dispatch, a commitment and coordination in generation and transmission to maintain the reliability of the power grid. Other aspects of ancillary services are reactive power to compensate for voltage drops, frequency control to maintain frequency (cycles per second) within intended bounds, and operating reserves to ensure that capacity can be quickly dispatched for sufficient energy generation to meet unexpected load fluctuations. Spinning reserves are generators already online that are able to rapidly increase their output to meet sudden changes in demand. Backup power is needed to meet unexpected demand, generator failure, low water in a hydro dam reservoir, calm winds for wind turbines, and cloudy days for solar arrays. The system operator is responsible for scheduling (planning future starting and stopping of generators) and dispatching (real-time starting and stopping). Scheduling and dispatching have to be carefully coordinated to prevent overloading transmission lines while maintaining system stability with continually fluctuating demand. Overloading transmission lines and/or losing system stability are the root causes for blackouts that can spread over large areas of a nation through utility interconnections and last for extended periods of time.

Clearly a cost effective, high capacity storage battery would provide an inventory of electricity that could be drawn down during periods of peak demand, which would reduce the need for peaking generators. High capacity storage batteries would stabilize the system by providing electricity during times of operational difficulties or load imbalances or transmission constraints. Storage batteries would be recharged at night with cheap electricity generated from excess capacity. Generally speaking, wind energy is useless at night and storage batteries would allow night-time generation to be sold when needed during the day. An inventory accumulated when electricity is cheap and sold when electricity is dear reduces the average cost of electricity. Enhancing utilization of electricity generating capacity at night whose output can be stored for day-time consumption flattens the demand curve, requiring fewer generating units that can be operated nearly continually over the course of day and night. This reduces capital charges, another source of savings for the consumer. However, one of the benefits of a non-flat demand curve is that there is time when a generator is not needed and maintenance can be conducted while it is idle. For a flat demand curve, extra capacity would be needed to stand in while units are taken out of service for maintenance and repair.

Methods of Rate Regulation

The roots of regulation go back to the days of manufactured gas that preceded natural gas. Electricity faced the same problem as manufactured gas where customers must deal with a natural monopoly. A natural monopoly occurs when there is a single electrical wire or single manufactured gas pipeline entering a house, originating from a single provider. Multiple transmission and distribution lines from a number of competitive generators for electricity or a number of competitive pipelines from different manufactured gas plants connected to individual households and businesses would give consumers a choice of provider. But the electricity rate or manufactured gas price would be inordinately high because of what amounts to a gross redundancy of productive and distributive capacity. The investment would be far smaller having a single wire entering a household or business from a single generator or a single pipe from a manufactured gas plant. This would result in lower electricity or manufactured gas rates to amortize a smaller investment in highly utilized assets.

Focusing on electricity, a natural monopoly comes into being once a decision is made to have only one wire from a generator connected to each consumer from a single provider. Once a monopoly is established, a company might be tempted to take advantage of the situation and raise the price of electricity to the point where it would become cheaper to have competitive suppliers with multiple generators and transmission and distribution lines. In a monopoly, there is no inherent impediment from charging high rates other than the monopolist's conscience, usually seared in the process of becoming a monopolist, plus the threat of consumers throwing the switch and doing without. To prevent a natural monopoly from behaving like a true monopoly, government bodies granting franchises to create natural monopolies also established regulatory agencies to govern rates and oversee business and operating practices. Rates set by regulators cover operating costs and provide a fair rate of return on the monopolist's investment. A fair rate of return takes into consideration the return that can be earned by investing in other businesses of similar risk in order for a natural monopoly to attract sufficient capital to support its operations. A regulated utility serving a franchise area, with rates set to cover costs and provide a return on investment, has little risk compared to a manufacturing company. A manufacturer must compete against others for the consumer's dollar with little in the way of consumer allegiance if a competitor brings out a better product at a lower price. A fair return reflecting the inherent risks ensures that a regulated utility can attract sufficient capital to build its asset base to satisfy customer demand. Normally the rate of return for a regulated utility is less than that of a manufacturer because risks associated with a utility, where rates are legally obligated to cover costs, are far less than a manufacturer having to sell its wares in a competitive and fickle marketplace. The rate of return on the equity of a public utility is often some premium over interest rates of its bonds to cover the additional risk faced by equity holders in case of a liquidation, which, in theory, should never occur.

From the perspective of regulators, the simplest way to organize a utility is as an integrated utility company that provides the complete package of generation, transmission, and distribution for a designated area covered by a single rate. Integrated utility companies can obtain high credit ratings if the regulators ensure that electricity rates provide ample cash coverage over interest expense. Whether cash coverage is one time interest expense or three times interest expense makes a great deal of difference in investors' willingness in buying a utility's bonds and in the credit rating awarded by third-party institutions such as Standard & Poor, Moody, and Fitch. A high credit rating results in lower interest rates on debt issued for capital expenditures, which in turn reduces interest expense and, thus, electricity rates. Too high a regulated rate on electricity would be reflected in a higher return on investment than warranted for the business risks faced by a regulated utility. If, on the other hand, regulators are too eager to squeeze electricity rates for the benefit of consumers, they are also reducing cash flow coverage of interest expenses that can lead to a cut in a utility's credit rating. This results in higher interest rates as investors compensate for the greater perceived risk of default by demanding a higher return. Rates then have to be increased to compensate for the increased interest expense. If the regulators squeeze rates too far for the benefit of consumers, then a utility may not be able to raise the necessary capital to sustain its asset base, making it unable to meet its obligation to provide a reliable and ample supply of electricity to a growing population with higher living standard expectations. Too little pressure by regulators results in high electricity rates and a return on the utility's investments above that, reflecting its inherent risks (a phenomenon for which there appears to be no historic precedent!). Too much pressure on rates (the prevalent phenomenon) can threaten a utility's operational as well as its financial viability. Regulators must walk a fine line in approving rates, balancing the opposing needs of providing low-cost electricity to the public and ensuring that a utility has the financial wherewithal to carry out its obligation to the public. Rate-setting guidelines for regulatory commissions were established by the Supreme Court Hope Natural Gas case of 1944 when it was decided that rates should be determined not on a formula basis or some overarching methodology but on a pragmatic basis. Rates should be set at a level sufficient to ensure reliable operation and to attract capital to maintain the company as a viable entity with a return on investment commensurate with risks assumed by investors.[2]

The general approach to rate setting is for the utility to initiate action by filing a rate case to its public service commission (PSC). The PSC staff reviews the application and intervenors submit their opinions to PSC, which takes 2–3 months. Intervenors can be larger consumers of electricity who are not willing to pay more than necessary or could be public advocates representing the collective interests of homeowners and small businesses. Upon submission, the utility submits its rebuttal to PSC and public hearings are held. This step of the process, which takes 6–8 months to complete, ends with a recommendation by an appellate law judge based on expressed opinions. The next step is PSC issuing the final rate order whose findings are confined to the record of the rate case itself. A PSC decision can be appealed by intervenors to the PSC or judicial courts. While these avenues of intervention are available, as a practical matter few PSC decisions have been reversed once promulgated. Obviously a rate case can be a multi-year event.[3]

Rate base is the value of property on which a public utility is permitted to earn a specified rate of return in accordance with rules set by a regulatory agency. In general, the rate base consists of the value of property used by a utility in providing its service. Allowed profit is the rate base multiplied by the allowed return on equity and the equity ratio. To obtain required revenue, allowed profit is grossed up to compensate for taxes along with adding costs in the form of interest, and operating and maintenance (O&M). While fuel costs are generally treated as a pass-through expense, an estimate of their future cost is built into the electricity rate to be charged. An electricity rate is required revenue, including fuel, divided by expected electricity sales for a stipulated period of time. This rate is often divided into two parts, a fixed monthly charge and the rest dependent on actual demand.

On the surface, regulation of rates based on costs, including a reasonable return on investment, appears to be a sound approach for ensuring that a natural monopoly is properly funded to provide its intended service at a reasonable cost, including an adequate capacity to meet future needs. However, two problems are associated with regulation of cost-based rates. The first is absence of any incentive to be efficient because all operating costs are rolled into the regulated rate charged to customers. In fact, there is an incentive to be a little inefficient when rates are being negotiated to obtain a higher rate, then improving efficiency after the rate has been set to enhance profitability. The second is the incentive to overinvest in plant capacity as the return is not only competitive but also more or less guaranteed by the rate-setting mechanism. To combat these drawbacks of cost-based rates, regulators review a utility's operations and have the power to replace management if operations are not up to a reasonable set of standards. With regard to overinvestment, regulators normally insist that a utility clearly demonstrate that new electricity generating capacity, or any significant capital investment, is needed before approving the expenditure of funds. Despite the best attempts by regulators, who are themselves subject to influence by those being regulated, a lingering suspicion existed that cost-based rates were higher than necessary.

This turned out to be the case when rates fell after privatization of the British electricity industry, a process that started in 1988. At that time, the British government under Margaret Thatcher became concerned over what was perceived to be overpriced electricity from cost-based rates and announced its intention to privatize the government owned and operated electric utility industry. The transformation of a socialized industry to several competing commercial enterprises as part of a national energy policy began in earnest in 1990 and was essentially completed by 1999. During this period, retail rates for individual consumers and households fell by 20 percent, 34 percent for small industrial customers, and 7–8 percent for medium and large industrial consumers. The overall decline in wholesale electricity rates averaged 2.1 percent per year, demonstrating the ability of market pricing to lower electricity costs to consumers over regulatory cost-based pricing.[4]

In the US, the roots of deregulation—some prefer to call it liberalization because the utility industry is still highly regulated under deregulation—go back to the 1973 oil crisis. President Nixon's Project Independence was aimed at reducing the nation's dependence on oil and natural gas by switching to other fuels and encouraging energy efficiency and conservation to cut overall energy demand. At that time, oil and natural gas each contributed 20 percent of the fuel consumed in electricity generation. Project Independence sought to cut oil consumption in electricity generation to reduce imports. Though natural gas was indigenous, there was a belief that a natural gas shortage might develop if there were a significant switch from oil to natural gas for generating electricity. Project Independence focused on the development of nuclear power, coal, and renewables for generating electricity.

The electricity generating industry operated under the Public Utility Holding Act of 1935, a law that had dismantled the pyramid utility holding companies of the 1920s that collapsed during the Great Depression of the 1930s. The Act restored the utility business to its original state in which a single corporate entity provided electricity (and natural gas) to a franchise or specified area protected from competition. Within their franchises, utilities were lords and masters of generation, transmission, and distribution, subject, of course, to regulatory oversight. A cozy arrangement existed between electricity providers and regulators because of continual falling of electricity rates due to economies of scale and improved technology. As these advantages were fully exploited and it became more difficult to maintain falling rates, friction developed between regulators and utilities. The cozy relationship ended with the 1973 oil crisis. Congress, fearing that utilities would resist adopting new technologies that would further reduce rates, passed the Public Utility Regulatory Policies Act (PURPA) of 1978 under President Jimmy Carter. PURPA required state regulatory commissions to establish procedures for qualifying facilities (QFs) that were not utilities to sell electricity to utilities generated from renewable energy sources, waste, and natural gas fueled cogeneration plants. Cogeneration plants were favored for their high thermal efficiency, double that of a conventional plant, because of their utilization of waste heat from generating electricity as a source of hot water for apartment complexes and industrial processing plants. PURPA could be viewed as a form of government coercion in support of cogeneration plants and renewable energy sources, but that turned out to be only part of the story. PURPA made it obligatory for utilities to buy electricity from QFs paying the "avoided" cost, the amount that a utility would have to pay for replacement electricity if it did not buy electricity from the QF. If the avoided cost made it profitable for independent power producers (IPPs) to invest in qualifying electricity generating facilities whose output had to be purchased by utilities, so be it. Some states, most notably California, required utilities to buy electricity at a rate above avoided cost in order to jump-start new electricity generating technologies involving solar, wind, and biomass.

The overall effect of PURPA was to raise electricity rates, and by this narrow definition, it could be considered a failure. But PURPA was the first intrusion of independent third parties into the monopoly of electricity generation and also challenged the concept of having a few large nuclear and coal fired plants supplying a wide area through long distance transmission lines. These centralized plants were burdened with billions of dollars of cost overruns and years of construction delays, resulting in a cost of electricity far higher than originally envisioned. As these plants established avoided cost, PURPA opened the door to having a more distributive system in which renewables and natural gas cogeneration plants serve smaller areas.

Fear that utilities would exercise their monopoly control over transmission lines to make it difficult for QFs to develop a competitive market for major utility customers was dealt with in the Energy Policy Act of 1992 and the Federal Energy Regulatory Commission (FERC) Order 888 of 1996, which began the transformation of electricity transmission under the strict control of a utility or a group of utilities into a common carrier. As a common carrier, the transmission company was open to all generating plants charging the same rate exactly like a railroad charging the same rate for all shipments regardless of the shipper. These three legislative acts (PURPA, Energy Policy Act of 1992, and FERC Order 888) established the opportunity for the emergence of wholesale competition in electricity within the regulatory framework governing natural monopolies. In addition to federal support, there was state support. California was a particularly strong supporter of deregulating the electricity industry (again deregulation does not mean doing away with regulation, but introducing competition). California had among the highest electricity rates in the nation, caused in part by its enthusiastic support and endorsement of PURPA legislation to support renewable energy sources, particularly wind.[5]

Deregulation/liberalization entails the unbundling of generation, transmission, distribution, and system operation. As an integrated utility, one rate covered all operating and capital costs associated with generating and delivering electricity. In order for IPPs to compete for the business of the utility's customers, it was necessary to break a single cost for integrated service into three separate cost components for generation, transmission, and distribution—an accountant's delight to say the least. An immediate problem arose for integrated utilities when shifting from cost-based to market-priced electricity. Under the old regulatory regime, cost overruns such as those associated with building nuclear powered plants were simply rolled into the rate base where higher electricity rates generated the revenue to amortize the cost overrun plus interest (Long Island Lighting not being reimbursed by its customers for costs associated with the closure of Shoreham nuclear plant was an exception). With third-party access to generation permissible and with IPPs relying on more energy efficient, lower capital cost generators run on natural gas (whose price had fallen when the natural gas "bubble" appeared and hung around for two decades after the first energy crisis), market-priced rates for electricity fell below cost-based rates. The market rate of electricity applied to nuclear power and other large plants plagued with huge cost overruns, which when discounted into the future did not create a book value for these generating assets that was even close to covering their capital costs. This would have necessitated writing down the book value of the assets to their market value, resulting in a diminution and, in some cases, an elimination of shareholders' equity. This difference in asset value between cost-based and market-priced electricity rates was given a name: stranded costs. To save utilities from having their creditworthiness impaired—resulting in lower bond ratings and higher interest rates—an incremental charge was added to electricity rates to cover stranded costs. This increment, charged to all sources of electricity including IPPs, was paid to the affected utilities until their stranded costs were liquidated. The existence of stranded costs was proof positive that rates based on costs were not the most economical way to generate electricity.

Operating Models in an Era of Deregulation/Liberalization

Where once there had been one model for the electricity business, now there are four. The first model is the traditional, vertically integrated monopoly, still operating in many parts of the world, where rates are regulated to cover costs and provide an acceptable rate of return on capital assets. This model still exists in the US where population density is not large enough to support competition afforded by deregulation. The second model resulted from PURPA legislation in 1978 that gave IPPs third-party access to utilities. This initial step in liberalizing the industry took the form of a utility entering into a long-term, life-of-asset contract to buy the entire output of the IPP's generating plant. An IPP was forced to enter into a life-of-asset contract with the utility; otherwise, its investment was at risk because an IPP did not have access to transmission lines, and without such access, an IPP could not compete with the utility to supply the electricity needs of the utility's customers. This made an IPP entirely dependent on the utility for its return on and of the investment. This model has been adopted fairly widely in Asia and South America as a means to attract private capital for increasing the generating capacity of state-owned utilities. Creditworthiness for financing building of a generating plant relies primarily on the nature of the contract between an IPP and a state-owned enterprise, not on an IPP's creditworthiness. Of course, potential investors scrutinize an IPP to ensure that it can carry out its operational responsibilities, but security for repayment of debt is based almost exclusively on the sales contract. By issuing what essentially is a self-funding life-of-asset contract to buy the entire output of an IPP's generating plant, a state-owned enterprise does not have to tap external sources of funds or borrow from the government to increase its generating capacity.

The third model gives IPPs access to the transmission system and the ability to enter into contracts with major consumers such as large industrial enterprises and even a utility's distribution company that serve the general population and businesses. This model opens up direct competition by IPPs for the utility's major customers and was first put into effect in Chile, followed by Argentina, the United Kingdom, and New Zealand. The US does not have a national policy on how the utility industry is to operate, but the third model was instituted in parts of the US through utility pools. In the third model, each generator, whether owned by a utility or an IPP, pays a fee for the use of the transmission system. The fee covers the operating and capital costs of the transmission system, in effect converting the transmission system into a common carrier in operation, if not in actuality. The rate can be a "postage stamp" rate, which is the same regardless of the distance of transmission, or be based on distance. While the latter may be preferable because distance plays a role in determining the cost of a transmission system, most transmission projects have rates set on costs, not distance, partly because there is no way to track electricity.

Each generator becomes an independent supplier regardless of its ownership, selling electricity under a variety of contractual arrangements with buyers. Term contracts run for a period of time and cover the generation of electricity for specific times during the day. They could be for 24 hours a day, 365 days per year for life-of-asset to cover base demand or, more commonly, contracts focus on day-time demand and may cover a number of months or years. Negotiated in a market environment, term contracts fix the cost of electricity for consumers and revenue for providers. Term contracts account for the bulk of generated electricity and are arranged directly between a utility and IPPs as suppliers and a utility distribution company and large industrial enterprises as consumers, or indirectly through intermediate market makers. Care has to be taken on the part of the utility either owning or not owning generating units (e.g., Con Edison) not to enter into too many term contracts to avoid the take-or-pay provisions whereby the utility must pay for all the electricity covered by the term contract regardless of whether it can be used. If this provision were not in term contracts, then the term contracts would not have the financial wherewithal to serve as collateral for building new electricity generating capacity.

Thus, there is some margin between the amount of electricity covered by term contracts and ownership and perceived demand. This margin is handled by the spot market. On the spot market, consumers (utilities) indicate the amount of estimated electricity that they need to cover specified time frames in the current and day-ahead market. Providers, usually IPPs, submit bids for what they are willing to sell the output of particular generating units in that time frame, net of term contract commitments. As an example, a provider may fix 75 percent of the output of a generating unit with term contracts and let the remaining 25 percent be available for spot market sales. Term contracts usually provide minimum revenue to allow a project to be financed largely by debt, with the ultimate profitability of the project determined by the state of the spot market. Bids may apply to hourly intervals in the day-ahead market or to the current spot market or some other time interval such as 5 minutes. A computer program determines the clearing price or rate where supply meets demand for a specific time interval of the day-ahead and current spot market. The clearing price is the bid of the last generator needed to meet demand and this bid becomes the clearing price of all selected generators regardless of what they actually bid.

Day-ahead spot market is a contractual arrangement that meets anticipated needs not covered by ownership or term contracts with other utilities and independent power providers. Current spot market handles differences between planned and actual consumption of electricity. Part of this difference is intentional to ensure that a utility is not paying for electricity that it cannot use. The rest is random in nature from buyers not needing all, or needing more, electricity than anticipated, unexpected generator and transmission problems that reduce availability of contractual electricity, and actions necessary to keep the system stable. Day-ahead and current spot rates are not determined for an entire region, but at node points (usually sites of generating capacity) or defined zones. Rate disparities between nodes or zones are primarily determined by system transmission capacity constraints, line losses, and differences in generating costs. Rate disparities provide vital economic signals for determining the size and location of additional transmission and generating capacity, something entirely missed under cost-based rates of a vertically integrated utility.

Obviously generators have different fixed and variable costs depending on their capital investment, efficiency for converting energy to electricity, type and price of fuel, operating and maintenance costs, and nature of ownership. Generating plants owned by the US government and by state and municipal authorities operate in a tax-free environment and have access to more favorable financing alternatives than investor-owned utilities and privately owned generators. Capital costs and fixed costs of operation and marginal (variable) cost of operation determine the electricity rate under a term contract. Having a lower capital cost such as operating in a tax-free environment gives the operator an advantage over those who do not. Marginal costs play an important role in the spot rate-setting mechanism. Marginal costs reflect the variable costs of operation, mostly fuel with other relatively minor costs that vary with output, but do not cover fixed operating and capital costs, which are considered sunk costs in setting marginal rates. Continual operation at marginal costs will eventually drive an IPP out of business. It is like a taxi fare that only covers variable costs for fuel, but not fixed costs of a driver, maintenance, insurance, and financing charges, with no allowance to accumulate funds to buy a replacement cab. Obviously operating at marginal costs cannot last forever.

Coal, nuclear, and hydro powered plants have the lowest marginal costs because of their relatively low fuel costs (hydro plants have no fuel costs). Nuclear power and coal fired plants do not respond well to fluctuating demand as they require considerable time to ramp output up and down, measured in days for startups and shutdowns. These plants normally supply base load electricity and enter into term contracts for their entire output or are owned by the utilities. Generators whose output is more easily adjusted (natural gas and hydro) tend to serve fluctuating day-time demand. Coal and nuclear plants bid on a 24-hour/7-day-a-week rate for the life-of-asset for base load employment, locking out higher marginal cost generators fed by natural gas. However, the lowering of natural gas prices from fracking along with lower capital costs for natural gas generators, coupled with higher energy efficiency, are challenging the economic viability of new coal and nuclear plants to serve the base load market, and for that matter the economic viability of unsubsidized solar and wind power.

Higher load demand during the day calls for a different type of term contract where generators may supply electricity for 12 hours a day or less for a period of time that may cover years. Much of the variable load demand is satisfied by term contracts at a rate that supports the economic viability of the generator. Obviously, this will have to be a higher rate than that paid for base load plants to take into account extended periods of idleness. Ownership and life-of-asset term contracts of base load plants and a variety of term contracts for variable demand fix the electricity rate for the utility up to a point of comfort that demand will fully utilize the electricity purchased from take-or-pay term contracts. The spot market handles the difference between actual demand and electricity supplied by owned plants and term contracts. Degree of reliance on the spot market is to minimize the obligation to pay for unneeded electricity from term contract holders. While the spot market represents a relatively small portion of overall demand, the economic signals it provides for the expansion of electricity generating capacity are absolutely vital. This is the element missing in a natural monopoly—costs are merely totaled and presented to the customers as an electric bill. There was little guidance as to where and when and how much to expand capacity, but the existence of a spot market covering distinct node points commonly centered at generating plants does provide that guidance. This can then be used to decide to increase transmission capacity from a generator not being fully utilized or to build new generating capacity at the site with a high spot market rate.

As demand increases in the spot market, natural gas and other types of generators submit bids for different quantities of electricity at higher rates reflecting both higher marginal costs and fewer available generators to submit a bid. Bids are tallied until demand is satisfied. Then the entire spot market rate for an hour's worth of time, or other time interval, is set by the last rate to clear the market, that is, the rate submitted by the last generating plant whose output, when added to all the others, is sufficient to satisfy demand. This rate becomes the clearing rate or single rate paid to all providers regardless of their actual bids. This introduces game theory into the picture. In the submission of bids for the day-ahead or current spot market, those who entered a low bid near marginal costs not only place themselves on the list to be selected but will receive a higher rate depending on the bid of the last generating unit to clear the market to meet demand. This higher wholesale rate provides the additional revenue to pay sunk costs such as fixed costs of operation, servicing debt to bondholders, and dividend payments to equity investors. As attractive as this may sound, there is a real risk in this strategy. If too many electricity plants are bidding low in the spot market to get on the list, the electricity rate for the last bidder will reflect some improvement over the lowest bidding plants, but not enough for these plants to operate profitably. If an IPP lacks sufficient term contracts to cover financing charges, and if there is excess IPP capacity resulting in a weak spot market, then an IPP risks insolvency. IPPs risk their capital when operating in the third model, which has led to bankruptcies that would have rarely occurred in a fully regulated environment. On the other hand, if too few generating plants are competing in the spot market, bidders will become more aggressive, resulting in a higher clearing rate and profitability in owning a generating plant with spare capacity. An IPP with fewer term contracts and a greater exposure to the spot market can "clean up" by submitting a low bid to make sure that some units are on the list and then withholding bidding on other units to force the market up before submitting a much higher bid, that if accepted affects all the units on the acceptance list. Even if not accepted by submitting too high a bid, the provider will still benefit by another generator on the acceptance list receiving the highest rate that cleared the system. Moreover, the provider may withhold bidding at all and not mind being a loser on one generating unit if others on the acceptance list are enjoying a bonanza of high rates. The shifting aggressiveness in bidding on the part of IPPs for employment of their units in the spot market when there are too many or too few generating units available has a markedly strong impact on spot rates. Hence the spot market is a powerful indicator of the financial health of third-party providers along with being a signal to expand transmission or generating capacity. As attractive as the spot market may be, most IPPs prefer to enter into fixed term contracts to ensure their solvency, which would be required by those providing the funds, and look to that portion of their output not fixed by a contractual arrangement as the determinant of their ultimate profitability.

The fourth model gives IPP access not just to principal utility customers but also to individual households and small businesses, which are handled by distribution companies under the third model. In the third model, the transmission company becomes a de facto common carrier to serve a buyer, which includes large-scale buyers such as distribution companies, which supply thousands or millions of individual consumers. In the fourth model, the distribution company also becomes a de facto common carrier and is paid a tariff that covers its operating and capital costs. Individual consumers select a provider (be it the utility or an IPP) to supply their needs. An electricity bill then has three components: the contractual arrangement with the electricity provider, a common-carrier charge for the transmission company, and another for the distribution company. The transmission common-carrier charge may be incorporated into the cost of electricity.

The great advantage of the fourth model is the introduction of a choice of competitive suppliers along with a means to control costs through demand management, also available in the third model for large industrial users and distribution companies. Demand management can only occur if time-of-day automated reading meters or smart meters are installed in order for rates to reflect what is being paid to wholesale providers in terms of term contracts and spot market purchases. This gives individuals and businesses an incentive to reduce electricity usage during hours of peak demand when rates are high by shifting a portion of electricity demand to periods of base demand, when rates are low. By individuals and businesses managing their load, electricity bills are lowered and utilities experience less peaking of demand and thus less dependence on high-cost peaking generators.

The third and fourth models of direct access to large and small consumers require separate control over transmission independent of generation. In England, it was relatively easy to separate transmission from generation, and transmission from distribution, during privatization of a government-owned industry. The government simply organized new corporate entities to serve these three functions as they wished, without much ado other than from those directly involved in managing and operating the proposed companies. Restructuring the electricity utility business is much more complicated in the US where generating plants are owned by private and public institutions. Regulation of investor-owned utilities is by individual states and, by definition, not regional or national in scope. Municipal-owned utilities are regulated by municipalities, and the US government-owned utilities are under the control of the federal government. FERC regulates electricity transmission lines, natural gas pipelines, wholesale rate of electricity between utilities, and wholesale power trading.[6] But FERC is not really in a position to impose a national policy on electricity. This confused and complex regulatory environment makes it difficult for the US to develop a national policy on electricity generation and distribution, which may seem strange considering the importance of electricity in the national economy. On the other hand, the system seems to work effectively without strong leadership or guidance on a national level.

Municipal utilities own generating plants along with investor-owned utilities and also the US government, which owns hydro and nuclear powered plants under the Tennessee Valley Authority in the east and under the Bonneville Power Administration in the west for hydro plants on the Columbia River. The dichotomy of ownership also exists for transmission lines in the US. Transmission systems within an integrated utility's franchise area are owned by the utility. Interconnecting transmission systems may be owned piecemeal for those portions of the system passing through a utility's franchise area or by a separate corporate entity or the US government. The US government owns transmission lines associated with its generating plants and has also played an active role in providing loans and grants for utilities to build transmission lines to rural America under the Rural Utilities Service (formerly the New Deal Rural Electrification Administration).

In a deregulated system, utilities continue to own, operate, and maintain transmission lines, but they cannot have any real or perceived influence or control over their usage. If utilities could influence or exercise control over transmission, then the transmission system could be employed to their advantage and to the detriment of IPPs. This would hinder the formation of a competitive market for electricity where rates are determined by supply and demand, not by those who have control over access to the transmission system. In addition to open access to the transmission system, the rate-setting mechanism for wholesale providers of electricity utilities and IPPs cannot allow any single provider to dominate the market. Studies have indicated that market domination might occur if any single participant has more than a 20 percent share of the business. This implies that a market free of manipulation that responds only to underlying shifts in supply and demand must consist of at least a half dozen independent and somewhat equally sized participants. Of course, the more participants, the better the market in terms of depth (volume of transactions and number of parties buying and selling) and freedom from potential manipulation. The mechanism for determining rates should be efficient (similar to a stock exchange), liquid (easily transferable obligations to buy or sell electricity), and transparent (transactions displayed and known to all participants). Besides equal access to transmission and the right to compete in order to get the business of distribution companies and major consumers, no cross-subsidies (regulated activities underwriting unregulated activities) can be allowed, and a mechanism for dealing with environmental issues must be instituted that does not interfere with the workings of the marketplace.

Deregulation requires a restructuring of integrated utility companies, separating generation from transmission, if not in ownership, certainly in operation. Historically the system operator was responsible for the operations of a single integrated utility that owned the generating units, transmission, and distribution systems within its franchise area. The allegiance of a system operator cannot be dedicated to a utility when IPPs are trying to cut deals with the utility's customers. An Independent Systems Operator (ISO) must be established that acts impartially and is not beholden to any provider. ISO is responsible for scheduling and dispatching (turning generators on and off) and for accommodating demand—taking into consideration bilateral sales agreements between buyers (consumers) and sellers (owners of generating units), transmission constraints, and system stability. ISOs in the US and Canada are responsible for operation of groups or pools of utilities that cover a number of states and provinces. ISOs also control the system operation of large areas of Australia and China and entire nations such as Argentina, England, France, Mexico, and New Zealand.

Ideally transmission and distribution companies would become separate corporate entities that own assets rather than assets being owned by investor and government owned utilities. However, they would be considered quasi-utility stocks since the rate they charge is regulated to cover their operating and financial costs. Ownership of transmission companies in the US is split among integrated utilities, transmission utilities, and the US government, with each owning various sections of the national transmission grid. This arrangement makes decision making on expanding capacity cumbersome. Decision gridlock has not been the cause of limited building of new transmission lines in the US; rather, the cause is local opposition or BANANAS (building absolutely nothing anywhere near anybody syndrome), which affects many industries. One problem with a proposal to build new transmission lines is that they affect people over a very wide area, whereas new power plants affect a local area. Opposition against transmission lines is more difficult to handle as it involves people along its entire length. Without building new transmission lines, the US is consuming the spare capacity of an aging system that spells future trouble.

Europe is making much more progress than the US in instituting a universal transmission grid system. The European Network of Transmission System Operators for Electricity also serves as a model for natural gas. Originally founded in 1999 to deal with emergence of an internal EU electricity market, it was greatly expanded in 2008 as a combination of 36 different European electricity transmission system operators (TSOs), since expanded to 42 TSOs covering most of Europe. Its purpose is to enhance transparency and promote integration of the individual TSOs. The organization establishes common network codes, ensures coordination of network operation with common operational tools, develops a 10-year development plan, and publishes reports to promote understanding of the organization's mission. It measures success in terms of ensuring generation and transmission adequacy for its members and establishing a European-wide energy policy at least in regard to transmission.[7]

Distribution companies can be treated as a utility and indeed some are. The best example is Con Edison, whose only business is distribution after having shed all its electricity generating plants to third parties. Normally distribution is part of an integrated utility as in the first model, with no change of function as the electricity system evolved into the second and third and fourth models. Distribution also becomes a separate operation in the third and fourth models. In the third model, the utility cannot influence the distribution company's electricity purchases. But there is nothing that precludes a distribution company from entering into a term contract with its owning utility as long as other IPPs have been given equal access to bid for the business. The distribution company charges a regulated tariff that covers its operating and capital costs plus its electricity purchases. Under the first two models, regulated rates for distribution companies cover all costs, including the cost of electricity. This is also true for the third model. Under the third model, distribution companies can make separate deals with IPPs, but there really is no incentive for distribution companies to buy from the lowest cost source because the cost of purchasing electricity, no matter what it is, is a pass-through direct to the customer. There has been some movement by regulators to set up an incentive system that rewards distribution companies if they can demonstrate that they have been more successful in seeking the best deal for their customers than other distribution companies. This reward could be in the form of incremental profits based on a portion of the difference between actual purchases and average purchases by other distribution companies.

Under the fourth model, the customers must select a provider, thereby reducing the role of the distribution company to that of a conduit or common carrier for direct sales between generator owners (utilities and IPPs) and individuals and businesses. This places the responsibility for purchasing electricity squarely on the shoulders of consumers, not distribution companies. If an IPP offers a better deal than that offered by the distribution company, then the distribution company loses what a customer pays for electricity, which is essentially a pass-through to the provider, but still receives payment for distributing electricity, which is the bulk of its expenses. For the fourth model to work most effectively, consumers need time-of-day smart meters that continually communicate electricity usage to the utility. This way the utility/IPP can charge for electricity by time increments that reflect rates charged by electricity providers, which, in turn, are influenced by supply and demand, plus allowing consumers to benefit by shifting loads to times of lower cost electricity.

Europe is paving the way in the development of demand management, starting in England and Wales, Scandinavia, and Spain. Demand management is now much more widespread, with the number of smart meters expected to be 100 million in 2016.[8] The US lags with 50 million smart meters installed in 2014.[9] These meters read electricity consumption frequently, perhaps as small as 5-minute increments, and send the data via wireless satellite to providers. Smart meters save money by not having to employ an army of meter readers. Signals from smart meters keep providers informed of customer usage and whether or not they are receiving service. This allows providers to quickly identify power disruptions and initiate action to restore service. Smart meters also benefit providers beyond billing, collections, and customer service. The wealth of information gathered by smart meters can be integrated into asset management, energy procurement, operational control, risk management, and field operations. While first-generation smart meters collect information as automatic readers, ultimately smart meters will be capable of controlling usage of appliances that place a heavy load on the system, putting utilities firmly in the driver's seat for managing demand. However, some are opposed to smart meters if use of appliances is no longer under consumer control. Control in the hands of the provider can force consumers to wash and dry clothes at night or on weekends and reduce output of air-conditioning units during times of peak demand. Those opposed feel that there is enough intrusion in their lives without a provider having instantaneous information on electricity usage and the ability to control energy consuming appliances.

Nevertheless, demand management benefits consumers by shifting electricity loads from high- to low-cost periods. Only a portion of the peak day load can be shifted to night, but whatever that portion is, it represents significant savings to the consumer. Demand management also benefits providers. With the shifting of a portion of demand from peak to low demand periods, the base load of the utility is increased, with a commensurate reduction in peak demand and the need to invest in peaking generators. Demand management under the fourth model also encourages aggregators to represent groups of consumers. An example of the power of aggregators to lower costs can be seen in some office buildings that aggregate telephone service for all their tenants into one account. The office building enters into a single contract with a communications company. The communications company bills only the office building, which then breaks down the billing to the individual tenants within the building, and receives a fee for this service that represents a portion of the savings. This gives office buildings, as aggregators of phone service, a powerful negotiating presence when dealing with competing communications companies lacking when each tenant must arrange for their communication needs. In the same way, aggregators of electricity representing a group of industrial and commercial users can increase the group's bargaining power with providers in contracting for electricity services. Aggregators could someday represent hundreds or thousands of individual households and small businesses as a single bargaining group.

Smart Meters/Smart Grids

Smart meters and smart grids are being introduced into the utility business. As mentioned, a smart meter can tell the occupant of a house or manager of a factory what the cost of electricity is on a real-time basis. Knowing the cost of electricity, an occupant of a house may decide to run a washing machine or dryer at night, or a manager may be able to shift some energy intensive operations to times when electricity rates are lower. Alternatively, a smart meter can make these decisions without the occupant's consent, but not on a routine basis if it involves a commercial or industrial enterprise. A smart grid adds an entirely new dimension to demand management. A smart grid will be able to integrate a centralized electricity generating system feeding a transmission system with small combined heat and electricity generation plants, along with solar panels and wind turbines feeding local distribution systems. Depending on further developments in storage battery technology, smart grids will control the charging of storage batteries when demand is low and draw down electricity when demand is high. Smart grids combined with smart meters will manage electrical loads during peak times by reducing electricity demand from refrigeration and air-conditioning units in homes and buildings. Commercial electricity storage batteries, when available, and demand planning for load reduction will have a powerful influence on electricity demand by reducing daily peaks in electricity demand, sharply reducing the need to invest in peaking generators, with a greater investment in generators that operate nearly continually. Total generator capacity will be much closer to average demand than it is today. A nationwide system of plug-in hybrid electric automobiles can be realized by the smart grid controlling timing and electrical load when recharging vehicles. Reliability of transmission and distribution systems can be enhanced by smoothing out peaks and valleys of electricity demand and by the smart grid being able to take corrective action as problems in load, generation, and distribution begin to emerge. Rather than responding to load changes, a smart grid can actively control loads to prevent blackouts and other service disruptions. A smart grid allows an electricity system to run more efficiently without the need for spinning or backup generators to handle unanticipated fluctuations in demand. It transforms a "dumb" grid passively reacting to changing loads to a "smart" grid proactively managing loads for increased efficiency, stability, and reliability.[10] In summary, the economic benefits of a smart grid would be in more efficient transmission of electricity, more rapid restoration of electricity after power disruptions, reduced peaking demand, better integration of renewable energy systems and customer-owned power, and reduced capital investments that should ultimately lead to lower electricity rates for consumers net of investments in smart grid technology.

EU legislation is far ahead that of the US in smart meters. Besides integrating the European transmission system for pursuing a common cause such as the smart grid, Europe is also making progress in encouraging and implementing a legal framework for installing smart meters. Smart meters are becoming more prevalent throughout Europe and are on the energy policy agenda of most nations. *Landscape Report 2012* (updated 2013) depicts smart meter development in each country using a common methodology and displays progress being made in smart meter adoption. "Dynamic movers" such as Estonia, Finland, France, Ireland, Italy, Malta, the Netherlands, Norway, Portugal, Spain, Sweden, and the UK have instituted a mandatory rollout for adopting smart meters with a specified timetable and a clear legal foundation to support the mandatory rollout. "Market drivers" such as Germany, the Czech Republic, and Denmark have not established legal requirements for a full rollout, but have made smart meters mandatory for newly built and renovated houses. Other nations in Europe lag behind and are considered "waverers" or "laggards."[11] Regulatory authorities in certain states in the US have given strong support for the installation of smart meters. Benefits of smart meters are operational savings, customer choice energy management, better grid reliability, greater energy efficiency and conservation options, increased use of renewable energy sources, and support for intelligent home appliances, which turn themselves off when not in use. Smart meters also require a smart transmission system incorporating an information and communication infrastructure. The "brain" of a smart transmission system can be coordinated with the "brawn" of delivering power to charge plug-in electric motor vehicles while maintaining a stable power load.

Technological progress is being made in developing superconductivity transmission materials where temperatures below a critical temperature present zero resistance to direct current and only minimal resistance to alternating current, virtually eliminating line losses for long-distance transmission. An example of a low-temperature superconductivity material is niobium-titanium alloy that becomes a superconductor at −441°F in a liquid helium medium. A "higher" temperature superconductivity material is bismuth-based copper oxide ceramic with a critical temperature of −265°F in a liquid nitrogen medium. Besides no line losses, another advantage of superconductivity is that a conductor can carry up to 150 times the amount of power over ambient temperatures. This enhanced flow of power through a superconductivity transmission system allows the widespread adoption of plug-in electric vehicles. Superconductivity coupled with a smart grid can relieve grid congestion, enhance grid utilization, efficiency, and resilience against attack and natural disaster, and anticipate and respond to power surges.[12]

Telecommunications, computer, and Internet industries have adapted well to sophisticated technology with an average lifespan of 3 years. This may not be possible for an electrical distribution network with an average lifespan of half a century. Utilities are in uncharted waters in determining which devices should be installed on their networks today that will be able to interact with the technology of tomorrow. One way to address this is collaboration among utilities throughout the world to share their challenges, insights, and knowledge base. This way they can begin the process of assisting one another in developing approaches to innovative technology processes and concepts, human resource demands, and regulation.

Utility Pools

Utility pools predate deregulation and had a vital role to play at the start of the electricity industry. Pools were set up not to challenge the concept of an integrated regulated utility but as a means of increasing system reliability among independent integrated utilities. In this way, surplus capacity for one utility would be available to meet demand for another utility short on capacity. A tight pool is a pooling of utilities with membership restricted to a specific region. Two tight pools, one for New England and one for New York, were formed to share generating capacity among pool members for greater system reliability. New transmission lines were built to interconnect the pool members to allow one utility with surplus electricity generating capacity to support another facing a shortage. This ability to share capacity enhanced reliability, reducing the risk of blackouts. It also increased the productivity of generating capacity and reduced the need for peaking generators. But the exchange of electricity between utilities required an agreement on a rate for settling accounts, thereby creating a wholesale market between utilities in addition to the retail market between utilities and their customers. In addition to New England and New York pools, three other pools were organized. PNJ was originally an open pool organized by utilities in Pennsylvania and New Jersey, but soon morphed into the PJM pool when utilities in Maryland joined the pool. The Texas pool is a closed one, limited to utilities in Texas. The California pool is an open one, including utilities in the western part of the US and Canada. Having pooled their generation and transmission resources and created a wholesale market, it was relatively easy for the pools to admit IPPs when required by PURPA legislation.

Pools had a major impact on the involvement of FERC in electricity markets. As independent utilities serving their franchise areas, utilities are exclusively under state or municipal regulation. FERC originally had jurisdiction over wholesale buying and selling of electricity and transmission of electricity between utilities in different states. But court rulings determined that wholesale buying and selling between utilities within states provides no assurance that such electricity might end up being transmitted to other states. Thus, all wholesale sales of electricity fall under the purview of FERC—even the Texas pool, which operates solely within the state of Texas and does not transmit electricity to other states. The spread of pools increased FERC involvement in electricity markets via wholesale deals and interstate transmission to a degree not envisioned when FERC was first established.

FERC's limited jurisdictional authority to act was improved by the Energy Policy Act of 2005, which better reflected the reality that electricity generation and transmission were no longer best handled by local regulatory authorities. Electricity generation and transmission had become a regional matter and a growing national matter as a result of the increased tying together of transmission grids and generating stations through pools and utility-to-utility marketing arrangements. The US has three regions where transmission systems are tied together: Eastern Interconnection, Western Interconnection, and ERCOT (Electric Reliability Council of Texas). The only way to tie these different interconnections into one national system is with a high voltage direct current (HVDC) tie because the frequencies of the systems are not in sync. In addition, a large-capacity cross-Rocky Mountain transmission system would have to be built to fully integrate the electricity grid of the nation. This would allow electricity to flow from where it is least needed to where it is most needed. Moreover, there is an increasing flow of electricity both ways across the borders with Mexico and Canada, which could result in a continental electricity grid.

Two pools deserve mention. One is the highly successful PJM pool, the poster child for how to organize and run a pool, and the other is the California pool as operated in 2000, the poster child of what not to do. The PJM pool was the world's first electricity power pool, formed by three utilities in 1927 to share their resources. Other utilities joined in 1956, 1965, and 1981, which led to the PJM pool covering most of Pennsylvania, New Jersey, and Maryland. Throughout this period, system operation was handled by one of the member utilities. In 1962 PJM installed an online computer to control generation in real time and in 1968 set up the Energy Management System to monitor transmission grid operations in real time. The transition to an independent neutral organization began in 1993 and was completed in 1997 with the formation of the PJM Interconnection Association, the nation's first fully functioning ISO approved by FERC. PJM also became the nation's first fully functioning Regional Transmission Organization (RTO) in 2001 in response to FERC Order 2000. RTOs operate transmission systems on a multistate or regional basis to encourage the development of competitive wholesale power markets. PJM Interconnection coordinates the continual buying, selling, and delivery of wholesale electricity throughout its region, balancing the needs of providers and wholesale consumers as well as monitoring market activities to ensure open, fair, and equitable access for all participants. PJM Energy Market operates much like a stock exchange, with market participants establishing a rate for electricity through a bidding process that matches supply with demand.

PJM Energy Market uses location marginal pricing that reflects the value of the electricity at specific locations and times. During times of low demand and no transmission congestion, rates are about the same across the entire grid because providers with the lowest priced electricity can serve the entire region. During times of transmission congestion that inhibit the free flow of electricity, location marginal price (LMP) differences arise that can be used for planning expansion of transmission and generation capacity. PJM Energy Market consists of day-ahead and real-time markets. The day-ahead market is a forward market for hourly LMPs based on generation offers, demand bids, and scheduled bilateral transactions. The real-time market is a spot market where real-time LMPs are calculated at 5-minute intervals, based on grid operating conditions. The spot market complements that portion of total market not covered by term contracts between buyers and sellers and unforeseen adjustments that have to be made for buying and selling transactions originally made on the day-ahead market.

PJM has expanded from its original base in Pennsylvania, New Jersey, and Maryland to include Virginia, West Virginia, the District of Columbia, a large portion of Ohio, and smaller portions of Indiana, Illinois, Michigan, Kentucky, and Tennessee. It is the world's largest competitive wholesale market operating in 13 states plus the District of Columbia, serving a population of 61 million, with nearly 1,400 generating plants with a total capacity of 183 GWs (for comparison purposes, a large nuclear or coal fired generating plant is between 1 and 1.5 GW for the most part) and 62,500 miles of transmission lines, with about 850 members and growing.[13] In addition to creating and serving this market, PJM is also in charge of system reliability including planning for expansion of transmission and generator capacity. System reliability was sorely tested during the polar vortex in January 2014, but PJM Interconnection successfully kept its system online during trying times.[14] PJM has become a model emulated both in the US and elsewhere in the world.

Another pool under the auspices of the Gulf Cooperation Council connects Kuwait, Saudi Arabia, Bahrain, Qatar, the United Arab Emirates, and Oman.[15] Electricity is purchased on term deals for base load with spare capacity available, whose rate is determined by an auction process. System rates were low enough to close higher cost facilities with greater dependence on lower cost facilities. The grid is capable of shifting electricity to prevent blackouts that had previously plagued local areas, particularly in the peak summer months from air-conditioning demand. The grid utilizes HVDC and high voltage alternating current (HVAC) transmission with back-to-back converters. Technological improvements in recent years to direct current transmission have made HVDC transmission cost competitive with less line losses than traditional HVAC transmission.[16] HVDC is particularly useful in connecting asynchronous systems such as Saudi Arabia's 60-cycle frequency, with the remaining countries operating on 50-cycle frequency. Underwater transmission with HVDC has far less line losses than transmitting HVAC underwater.

The Central American Electrical Interconnection System (SIEPAC) grid creates an integrated regional electricity market for six Central American countries: Guatemala, El Salvador, Honduras, Costa Rica, Nicaragua, and Panama.[17] The system is also based on HVDC transmission because the various local utilities making up the system are not synchronized. SIEPAC allows for the retirement of older and more costly sources of electricity and for tapping lower cost hydro and geothermal sources. System reliability is enhanced by connecting small utilities to a far larger integrated system where one generating plant can serve as backup for another. Electricity rates are expected to continue falling from economies of scale in new, efficient generating facilities and retiring, outmoded, and costly running units. The grid may open up trading opportunities in electricity with neighboring Mexico and possibly with the proposed Andean Electrical Interconnection System that would connect Colombia, Ecuador, Peru, Bolivia, and Chile into a single electricity market.[18]

The newest HVDC transmission lines operate from 800,000 to 1.1 million volts to transmit electricity over long distances with less line losses.[19] State Grid Corporation of China, China's largest utility, operates a vast network of power distribution lines across 26 of China's 32 provinces and regions.[20] The company is building an ultra-high 1–1.1-million-volt transmission system that will connect Beijing and Shanghai and other eastern cities to dams in southwest China and coal powered plants in northwest China. Coal powered plants will have electricity generating plants at mouths of mines, eliminating the need to transport coal to utilities located near or within population centers. Thus, pollution abatement in populated areas is accomplished by substituting transmission of electricity for movement of coal.

See the Companion Website for sections on When Demand Exceeds Supply and the Real Lesson of California: www.routledge.com/cw/nersesian.

It Takes Energy to Make Energy

On a global scale, the entire output of renewable, geothermal, hydro, and nuclear power, plus about 80 percent of coal production and about 40 percent of natural gas production, is dedicated to generating electricity. Figure 2.1 shows the percentage distribution of world energy consumption in 2012, including the shares of coal and natural gas dedicated to electricity generation.[21] Electricity consumes 44 percent of global energy, of which half is supplied by coal.

The *BP Statistical Review* lists electricity generation in terms of terawatt-hours (tWh), where a terawatt is a trillion watts.[22] To gain an appreciation of what tWh mean, energy is power over time. A 100 W bulb lit day and night for 1 year or 8,760 hours is 876,000 Wh. A kilowatt is a thousand watts, a megawatt is a million watts, and a giga-watt is a billion watts. While a gigawatt might be beyond comprehension, actually it can be easily understood. A thousand megawatts or a gigawatt is the size of a typical large-sized coal or nuclear powered generating plant, which is about 1,000–1,500 megawatts (mW) or 1–1.5 gigawatts (gW). A terawatt is equivalent to 1,000 gW or 1,000 large-sized electricity generating plants. In terms of energy, providing 1 tW of power for an entire year would require 8,760 tWh of energy. A 1 gW plant can power the electrical energy requirements for about 700,000 people in the US, one million people in Europe, or two million people in Asia where per capita electricity consumption is less. To get a more overall figure on how many people can be served by a gigawatt plant, the *World Energy Outlook* listed 5.429 tW of installed electricity generating capacity in 2011. At that time there were 7,000 million people, of which about 5,700 million people were

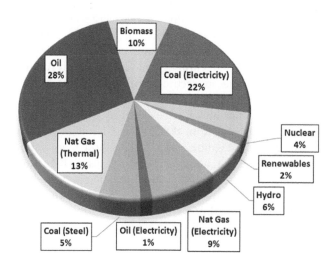

Figure 2.1 2012 World Energy Consumption (percentage)

attached to the electrical grid. Thus, on a global basis, a million people required almost 1 gW or 1,000 mW of electrical generating capacity. This, of course, is capacity. Actual usage would be less.

From the *BP Statistical Review*, 22,050 tWh of electrical energy were generated in 2011. Dividing this by 8,760 hours yields the world's average power demand of 2.52 tW if generating units were 100 percent utilized. But 100 percent utilization cannot be, as there are significant differences between peak and base load demand plus the need for reserve capacity to ensure reliability. The 5.429 tW of actual installed electricity capacity is necessary to handle peak demand with still some spare capacity to provide coverage for outages of operating units. The ratio of 2.15, obtained by dividing actual installed capacity of 5.429 tW by average demand of 2.52 tW, means that over twice as much capacity is installed than what is needed on an average basis. This excess capacity accommodates peak demand, taking into consideration that capacity really has to exceed peak demand to have enough reserve capacity to ensure reliability and to compensate for generating capacity taken out of active service for repairs and maintenance. Moreover, the inventory of generating capacity includes units not normally used either from economic or physical obsolescence. They sit in inventory until a decision is made to dispose of these units, an ongoing activity for utility managers. Thus, a portion of newly built generating capacity to meet growing demand has to first substitute for phased-out units before installed capacity can expand. If demand management were successful in flattening the demand curve, which would involve large-scale storage batteries along with smart meters and smart grids, the investment in generating capacity could be substantially reduced.

Figure 2.2 shows the growth in electricity generation in tWh. Electricity demand has grown in South America, the Middle East, and Africa, but when combined with Europe and North America, aggregate demand has been growing more slowly since 2010. It is normally assumed that electricity is forever in an upward track requiring the building of more generating units. This is no longer true. The US, 19 nations in Europe and FSU (actually all of Europe and FSU), South Africa, Australia, Japan, New Zealand, and

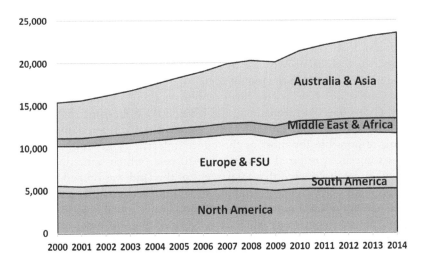

Figure 2.2 Growth in World Electricity Demand (tWh)

Pakistan consumed less electricity in 2014 than in 2010. Much of this fall in demand is from less energy intensity of the economy (energy content of a unit of GDP has decreased) from greater efficiency and conservation. Social disintegration in the developing world also cuts electricity consumption.

Nearly all of global growth is concentrated in Asia, particularly China, which generated 4.2 times in 2014 than what it did in 2000. Other Asian nations showing high gains in electricity generation since 2000 are Vietnam (5.5×), Bangladesh (3.7×), Indonesia (2.5×), Malaysia (2.2×), and India (2.2×). China generated 56 percent of Asian electricity demand, India 12 percent, and Japan 11 percent; together these three nations accounted for nearly 80 percent of Asian generation. Between 2000 and 2014, global electricity growth averaged 3.1 percent per year and 2.4 percent per year between 2010 and 2014. The *World Energy Outlook* projects 2.2 percent annual growth between 2010 and 2035 for overall growth of 70 percent. The respective shares of natural gas, hydro, and nuclear are expected to remain the same, with the share for coal falling from 41 percent to 33 percent, with further diminution of oil (already a small percentage) by another 1 percent. Renewable fuels will substitute for the decline of 9 percent for the shares in coal and oil by the share of renewables expanding by 9 percent from its present 3 percent. Thus by 2035, renewables will have a 12 percent share of electricity generation at that time. While there will be new generating units powered by natural gas, nuclear, and hydro built to keep the respective shares of these energy sources constant, the *World Energy Outlook* assumes that renewables will supply all new electricity generating capacity additions necessary to meet projected 2035 demand. This is the only way that the share of renewables can grow from 3 to 12 percent. There will have to be strong growth in renewables to achieve this goal of quadrupling the share of renewables despite overall growth in electricity demand.

This cut in the percentage share of coal does not translate directly to a drop in coal consumption because electricity generation is expected to climb by 70 percent. With 2010 coal production at 7.25 billion tons and reducing 2010 production by 20 percent to compensate for coal consumed in steel production, about 5.8 billion tons were consumed in 2010 to generate electricity. If coal's share of electricity generation of 41 percent is maintained, then the expected coal production in 2035 would be 70 percent higher or 9.9 billion tons. Correcting this for a loss of share from 41 percent to 33 percent would indicate that coal production in 2035 would be 7.9 billion tons plus that needed for steel production. The notion that coal is dead is absurd. Coal is not dead—at most its global growth rate will lag overall global growth rate in electricity consumption despite herculean efforts in some nations to reduce the role of coal.

Figure 2.3 shows the share of electricity generation for nations consuming the most electricity in 2014. China literally zoomed past the US in 2011 to become the world's largest electricity generating nation. This is a classic Pareto chart where relatively few causes (nations) are responsible for most of the effects (electricity generation). The Pareto principle is sometimes referred to as the 80–20 rule, which Vilfredo Pareto observed in 1906 when he discovered that 80 percent of the land was owned by only 20 percent of the population. A common thumb rule of business is that 80 percent of sales come from 20 percent of customers. Figure 2.3 shows only a vital few nations are responsible for most of global electricity generation. Most of the remaining nations in the world can be numbered among the trivial many. With nearly 200 nations in this world, only two, China and the US, generate 42 percent of the world's electricity, and the top five nations generate 56 percent. Sixteen nations in Figure 2.3 generate

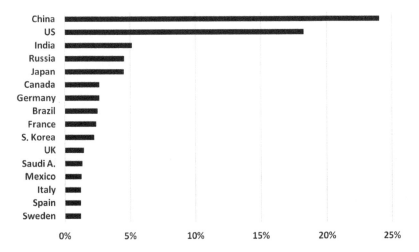

Figure 2.3 Leading Nations' Share of Electricity Generation (2014)

76 percent of the world's electricity. The top 20 nations, which is 10 percent of all nations, generate close to 80 percent of the world's electricity. Clearly the 80–20 rule does not hold; it is more like 90–10! Any policy to reduce carbon emissions from electricity generation should focus its attention on the top five nations, not completely neglecting, of course, the remaining nations. Thus, energy policies with regard to electricity generation in China and the US are critical for advocates of reducing carbon emissions.

Projects and Problems

Project 2.1

The purpose of this assignment is to acquaint you with PJM. As described in the text, PJM is a forward-looking pooling arrangement of utility companies that encompasses much of eastern US. This company is a source of information and inspiration on how to pool utilities for those desiring to establish pools both in the US and elsewhere in the world. For this assignment, pretend that you are a *New York Times* journalist writing a special interest article on PJM for its Sunday edition. Visit the company Website at www.pjm.com. Write the article including a general description of the activities of this pooling arrangement, its size, members, service area, and in general how it works, expanding on the information contained in the text. This can include, but not limited to, PJM EnvironTrade, Sage Auction system (what it does and how it does it), the purpose of ISO and RTO as it pertains to PJM, and the ISO/RTO Council, of which PJM is a member. Other aspects of this pooling arrangement described on the Website can be included in the article.

Project 2.2a

Levelized cost of electricity is a cost in dollars per kilowatt-hour that takes into account the capital cost of the generating unit, fixed operating and maintenance costs, and variable costs that are primarily fuel. Levelized cost is a flat cost that applies for every year of operation of the unit. Normally the levelized cost is done on the basis of the life of the plant. The levelized cost of energy (LCOE) is defined as total life cycle cost divided by total lifetime energy production at a prescribed discount rate. Total life cycle cost is the investment, less the depreciation tax shield, plus the total cost of operation in terms of operating and maintenance and fuel costs, less the salvage value, divided by total energy produced. Here, levelized cost will be calculated for the first year, with the presumption that it remains constant every year at the same utilization rate.

There are pitfalls in the LCOE methodology in that data may be preselected on the basis of supporting a modeler's goal such as assuming low costs for capital investment or operating costs or too high a utilization rate. Another area where managing results can be done is by adjusting model inputs. Suppose that it is desired to compare a natural gas with a coal plant. The levelized cost over the life of the plant would be affected, to say the least, by future assessments on coal and natural gas prices. Both of these are unknown at the start of the analysis, and an analyst with the freedom to assume future prices can affect the decision as to whether to build a coal or a natural gas plant. One way to handle the imponderables of assessing future energy costs is the use of simulation whereby thousands of energy cost scenarios are run to obtain the mean cost of electricity and an associated probability distribution of costs about the mean. The mean between two plants can be compared along with the risk (probability) of electricity costs exceeding a certain level. This methodology can be applied to a group of different types of plants to obtain an overall electricity cost probability curve, and then by changing the type of plants within the group, one can take a more systems approach to planning for the future.[23]

In this chapter, only the first step of this process, determining the appropriate capital recovery factor (CRF), will be covered. The remainder of obtaining the levelized cost of electricity for a coal burning plant will be completed in the problems section in Chapter 4. The following provides guidance on how to convert capital cost of a new generating capacity for a utility to an annual capital charge to assure return of and on an investment known as the CRF. The first step is to obtain the appropriate discount factor that will ultimately determine the CRF. The traditional methodology to obtain the appropriate discount factor is to rely on the total capitalization of a company as the sum of long-term debt and shareholders' equity found in the lower right side of a balance statement. What is the percentage share of each?

The next step is to obtain the hurdle rate, which is the minimum return an investment must earn to satisfy the weighted cost of capital. In Project Table 2.2b, the interest rate that a company must pay on its long-term debt can be obtained from the financial manager and let us suppose that it is 6 percent. However, a company is not really paying 6 percent because interest expense is tax deductible. The effective interest rate is one adjusted for the tax benefit and is calculated by: Interest rate × (1 − Tax rate). If the interest rate is

Project Table 2.2a

Amount Listed in Balance Sheet		Percentage Share
Long-term debt	$800 million	
Shareholders' equity	$1,200 million	
Total capitalization		

Project Table 2.2b

	Percent Return	*Percent Share*	*Weighted Return*
After-tax long-term debt			
Equity			
Hurdle rate			
Risk increment			
Discount rate			

6 percent and the tax rate is 33 percent, the effective interest rate is 4 percent. The company pays 6 percent to the bank as interest on the loan, but taxes paid to the government are reduced by the equivalent of one-third of the interest payments for a tax rate of 33 percent. Our tax system actually subsidizes debt financing by making interest payments tax deductible, but not dividends. Dividends are taxed twice—once by the company as funds earned, as profits are taxed at the corporate rate before they can be paid out as dividends. Then once paid, shareholders are taxed on their dividend income. This is why companies, when they can, prefer to issue debt over equity. Assume an interest rate on long-term debt and a tax rate to obtain the after-tax cost of debt. The percent share is the same as derived in the previous table. The weighted return for debt is the multiplicand of the percent return with the percent share.

Now it is time to determine the appropriate return on equity. In the traditional approach, the return on equity is a management decision. As a first stab, it must be higher than the interest rate on debt because bondholders have first claim on a company's asset in a liquidation or bankruptcy. In a liquidation, voluntary or otherwise, the company's assets are sold and all funds garnered are dedicated to paying off the bondholders. If there are insufficient funds to pay off the bondholders, the equity holders receive nothing. The equity holders only receive what is left after the bondholders are made whole. Thus, equity holders need a higher return to compensate for the additional risk of being left with nothing in case a company fails. Other than that, the return on equity is a management decision. For a utility, it could be some increment over the cost of debt, say 8 percent, considering the assurance of being able to make debt payments via rate adjustments. Companies may select 10, 12, or 15 percent or more depending on their perception of risk. Companies have markedly different returns on equity because determining a return is a management prerogative. Returns on equity for companies even in the same business or industry can vary widely. Obviously the return on equity plays a part in management investment decisions as it affects the discount rate, which in turn affects the required CRF.

In the above table, assume a return on equity and obtain its weighted average. The sum of the weighted averages for debt and equity is the hurdle rate, the minimum rate that reflects the weighted cost of capital. Any investment that does not meet the hurdle rate can be likened to borrowing money at 10 percent and lending it out to someone for 5 percent. It does not make sense. To compensate for this possibility, some companies add a risk increment of 0.5 or 1 percent just in case a new investment does not generate funds that reflect the hurdle rate. The risk increment should reflect the inherent risk of an investment. If a company is investing in a machine to improve its operations, the risk increment can be zero as there is or should be no risk doing what the company normally does. If a company is investing in a new business that it does not fully understand, the risk increment should reflect the inherent degree of risk. Adding the hurdle rate and the risk increment is a company's discount rate.

Project 2.2b

A more up-to-date approach is the weighted average cost of capital (WACC) derived from the Capital Asset Pricing Model (CAPM). There are different approaches and degrees of sophistication—what is represented here should be considered the garden-variety WACC. To begin with, there are some major departures from the traditional methodology. Calculating percentage shares of equity and debt to arrive at a discount rate is not at all related to a company's balance sheet. Equity is calculated by the number of outstanding shares multiplied by the stock price, and debt is the market value, not the book value, of a company's long-term debt. If a company issued debt publicly, then the market value is the price of the bond easily obtainable from the financial press. For private debt entirely held by pensions and other financial institutions with no public trading, a market value can be assessed by examining the market value of debt issued by companies with a similar credit rating for the remaining tenure of the debt at the same interest rate. It is possible, in this manner, to estimate a company's debt as if all were being traded on the public market. Suppose that the market value of a company's debt has been estimated to be $450 million and there are 40 million shares outstanding selling for $60 per share. The sum of these is considered the company's capitalization, regardless of what is on its balance sheet. What is the percentage share of the company's debt and equity in its capital structure?

The first difference with WACC over the traditional approach is that a company's capitalization is no longer a constant derived from the balance sheet, but varies with changes in the markets for stocks and bonds. Another difference with the traditional approach is that return on equity is no longer management's prerogative. Return on equity is determined by the relative performance of the company's stock price to the stock market average as a whole, which can change along with the stock market. The relative performance is measured by a stock's beta, which compares changes in the company's stock price with changes in an overall market average such as S&P500. Beta measures what is called systemic risk—it is the movement of the price of a stock determined by stock market conditions. Systemic risk is a risk outside management control. In this case, if the stock price declines because of a fall in the market, it is not the fault of the company's management. Management has no influence over the stock market, but management does affect a stock's price by its decisions.

If percentage changes in stock and market prices are about the same, then beta has a value of 1. If the market goes up or down by 10 percent, so does the company's stock. A beta of 1.2 means that swings in the company's stock are more volatile than the market where a 10 percent change in the market price becomes a 12 percent change in the stock price whether the market rises or falls. A beta of 0.8 means that the stock price is less volatile than the market, and a 10 percent change results in an 8 percent change for stock price. High betas are associated with technology stocks and low betas with utility stocks. The beta for every stock is in the public domain such as S&P and Moody's individual stock listings.

Assuming that the long-term return on the S&P500 including dividends is 10 percent, then the return on equity for a company is 10 percent multiplied by the company's beta.

With a utility's beta of 0.9, what would be its return on equity? Redo the calculation for the WACC as before to obtain a revised discount rate. Suppose there is a market downturn and the company's stock value falls in half. What is the new WACC? Some corporate executives are bothered by corporate investment decisions being influenced by the stock market.

Project 2.3

The next step is to derive the CRF that can be applied to any investment in order to arrive at the annual capital charge. Instructions are provided to allow you to set up a spreadsheet to calculate the CRF. As you progress, you should be obtaining the values in the worksheet included in this project.

On an Excel spreadsheet in cell A5, put in "Year" followed by 1 and 2. Select both cells, obtain the black cross in the lower right corner of the cell, hold down the left mouse button, and drag down to 30 for a 30-year horizon. Column B is revenue. In cell B3 put in "Revenue," $1,000 in cell B4, and =$B$4 in cell B6 using the F4 key. Get the black cross in the lower right hand corner of cell B6, double click, and the formula will be replicated down to the last value in column A. There are no operating costs and fuel charges in this model as the CRF only applies for obtaining the annual capital charges. Column C is the write-off of the investment over the life of the project. In cell C1 put in "Investment," $10,000 in cell C2, "Depreciation" in cell C3, =C2/30 in cell C4, and =$C$4 in cell C6 and replicate down. Column D is the amortization of debt, assumed to be 20 years. In cell D1 put in "% Debt," 70% in cell D2, "Amount" in cell D3, =C2*D2 in cell D4, and =$D$4/20 in cell D6 and replicate down to year 20 and not beyond. This model is not being set up to accommodate changes, and care has to be exercised in formulation if the tenure or term or repayment period of the loan is changed. The same is true for the depreciation period. Column E is the amount of outstanding debt that will be used to calculate interest in column F. In cell E3 put in "Amount," "Outstanding" in cell E4, =D4 in cell E5, and =E5-D6 in cell E6 and replicate down to year 20 when the outstanding debt has been fully amortized. Column F calculates interest based on the amount of debt outstanding in column E. In cell F3 put in "Interest," "Rate" in cell F4, and 6% in cell F5. In cell F6, enter the formula =AVERAGE(E5:E6)*$F$5 and replicate down. This methodology of averaging the start and end-of-year balances of the loan, which is then multiplied by the interest rate, agrees closely with a 6-month schedule of interest and amortization payments frequently specified for large bank loans and corporate debt issues. Column G calculates tax payables. In cell G3 put in "Tax," "Rate" in cell G4, and 35% in cell G5. In cell G6 enter the formula =$G$5*(B6-C6-F6), which states that taxes payable is Revenue less Depreciation less Interest Payments (again, no operating costs are in this model), and replicate down to year 30. Column H shows the projected cash flow; in cell H3 put in "Cash" and in cell H4 "Flow." Year 0 equity investment is negative as it represents a cash outflow and the amount of equity is the portion of the investment not funded by debt or (1 − Percent debt) multiplied by the investment, or in cell H6: =-(1-D2)*C2. The cash flow for year 1 and succeeding years is Revenue less Debt amortization less Interest payments less Tax payables, or in cell H7: =B6-D6-F6-G6, and replicate down to year 30. Depreciation is not included as it is a noncash expense that affects tax payables.

In cell I1 put in "Discount" and in cell I2 "Rate"; in cell I3 put in the WACC that you had calculated (8.5 percent is assumed here), in cell I5 "NPV:" and in cell I7 "IRR:".

Project Table 2.3

	A	B	C	D	E	F	G	H	I	J	K
1									Discount		
2			Investment	% Debt					Factor		
3		Revenue	$10,000	70%					8.5%		
4		$1,000	Depreciation	Amount	Amount	Interest	Tax	Cash			
5	Year		$333	$7,000	Outstanding	Rate	Rate	Flow			
					$7,000	6%	35%	($3,000)	NPV:	$276	
6	1	$1,000	$333	$350	$6,650	$410	$90	$150	IRR:	9.2%	
7	2	$1,000	$333	$350	$6,300	$389	$97	$164			
8	3	$1,000	$333	$350	$5,950	$368	$105	$178			
9	4	$1,000	$333	$350	$5,600	$347	$112	$191			
10	5	$1,000	$333	$350	$5,250	$326	$119	$205			
11	6	$1,000	$333	$350	$4,900	$305	$127	$219			
12	7	$1,000	$333	$350	$4,550	$284	$134	$232			
13	8	$1,000	$333	$350	$4,200	$263	$141	$246			
14	9	$1,000	$333	$350	$3,850	$242	$149	$260			
15	10	$1,000	$333	$350	$3,500	$221	$156	$273			
16	11	$1,000	$333	$350	$3,150	$200	$164	$287			

Goal Seek [? X]

Set cell: $J$5
To value: 0
By changing cell: B4$

OK   Cancel

Net present value (NPV) is the sum of the discounted cash flows, and internal rate of return (IRR) is the discount rate that reduces the NPV to zero. In cell J5 enter the formula =NPV(I3,H5:H35), and in cell J7: =IRR(H5:H35). As it now stands for a discount rate of 8.5 percent, NPV has a positive value of $276 with an internal rate of return of 9.2 percent. If we entered this transaction as is, and the projected cash flow actually materialized, shareholders' equity would be $276 higher at the end of the project life than it was at the start. The reason for this is that the internal rate of return of 9.2 percent exceeds the required WACC of 8.5 percent. This is similar to borrowing money at 8.5 percent and lending it out at 9.2 percent.

To find the CRF, enter What If Analysis/Goal Seek on the Data ribbon and set the NPV value in cell J5 to 0 by changing revenue in cell B4. The CRF is revenue in cell B4 of $957 divided by the investment of $10,000 or 9.57 percent. Of course, this CRF only works for the terms of debt that have been built into the model. A "universal" CRF can be obtained by changing the percent debt in cell D2 to zero and rerunning Goal Seek. Now the required revenue is $1,252 for a CRF of 12.52 percent. For both of these alternatives, NPV equals zero and the IRR equals the discount rate of 8.5 percent. Depending on which one is deemed applicable, this investment proposal would not add to shareholders' equity as long as the NPV is equal to zero—it is like borrowing money at 10 percent and lending it out at 10 percent. This is why investment proposals are selected on the basis of a positive NPV and an IRR higher than the discount rate. There is possibly an argument for adding an increment to the discount rate to ensure that shareholders' equity will grow if the investment is approved, but this is not necessary as long as one realizes the implication of approving a project whose NPV is zero.

Two alternatives have been presented here where the investment is leveraged with debt and is treated as pure equity. Academics in financial management favor the non-leveraged alternative as the proper way to analyze project investments partly because the same CRF applies to all projects. They argue that the investment is already leveraged by virtue of the derivation of the discount factor that includes the share of debt in the company's financial structure. Presumably, if a company approves a major project and has to raise funds to finance it, both debt and equity (new shares) will be issued. However, financial practitioners in corporations may favor the leveraged alternative because corporate funds are only supplying the equity while the remainder of the project is being financed by external "cheap" debt provided by a financial institution. The problem with this approach is that the CRF depends on the underlying assumptions of the debt financing in terms of amount, tenure (debt duration), and interest rate. Frankly, CRF is subject to financial engineering (or finagling) on the part of an analyst in the sense that increasing the amount of debt and extending its amortization period reduces the required CRF. Freedom to alter the terms of the assumed debt means a different CRF for each project proposal depending on its capacity to attract debt. This is an inconsistent way to analyze projects. One way to address this issue is to assume a debt structure for calculating the CRF that does not vary with each project under analysis.

The purists who say that a project should be analyzed in terms of being nonleveraged are not entirely free of inconsistencies. Cutting the stock price in half during a stock market break reduces the equity component and expands the debt component in determining the discount rate. This cuts the discount rate, reducing the CRF, which affects whether a project is approved. Thus, the WACC becomes a variable that affects investment decisions depending on the vagaries of the stock and bond markets. The ultimate answer as to whether one should calculate the CRF on a nonleveraged or leveraged basis is a decision that has to be made by the corporate officer in charge of financial analysis.

One might also ask why the CRF is higher than the discount rate. Why not make the WACC of, say, 8 percent the CRF and judge new projects on that basis? Let us say you invest 10-year $1,000 in a bond with an 8 percent coupon. You are making 8 percent on your money for 10 years and you receive $1,000 back when the bond matures. So what do you have? You have both a return on investment and a return of investment. When this cash flow is discounted at 8 percent, the NPV is zero and the IRR is 8 percent (you should do this). Now suppose that you invest $1,000 in a project that is reduced to a salvage value of zero at the end of 10 years. Each year you receive 8 percent for 10 years and then the return ceases and you do not get your investment back. You are clearly not earning 8 percent. In fact, the NPV is −$429 and the IRR is −3.9 percent when the payment in the tenth year is changed from $1,080 to $80. An IRR of zero means a return of investment, but with no return on investment; that is, cash inflow is just equal to the investment (cash outflow). A negative IRR means that the cash inflow is not capable of recouping the investment. Thus, investing using the discount rate as a measure for approving projects is a guarantee for losing money even though the discount rate reflects the cost of funds to a company.

A project must have a return both on and of the investment. A higher CRF generates the funds necessary to repay the investment with the stipulated return. This means it must operate at a profit to accumulate funds to repay the investment and provide a return. But in operating profitably, the company must now pay taxes because depreciation only shields the investment from taxation, not the return on investment. If you treat the equity as a loan with an interest charge equal to the discount rate and each year charge the previous year's "balance" of the loan by the discount rate and reduce the loan amount by the cash flow, the ending balance of the loan will be zero. When you do this, and this is a good spreadsheet exercise, it becomes clear that discounting cash flows treats equity as a form of subordinated debt without a set amortization schedule. The "loan" is amortized by the annual cash flows. You can see that the discount rate is the "interest" charge on the outstanding amount of the loan and the loan is fully repaid in the last year of the project. Thus, the CRF generates the cash required both to provide a return on investment at the discount rate and to return or repay the investment. The equity investment in the leveraged case is 30 percent of the project cost and 100 percent for the nonleveraged case. This explains why the CRF is so much higher for the nonleveraged case. For both cases, the CRF treats the investment as though it were a special form of subordinated debt. Applying the CRF to a generating plant to obtain the levelized cost of electricity will be considered in the problem set in Chapter 4.

Problem 2.1

Complete Problem Table 2.1 for converting one unit of fuel to the equivalent kilowatt-hour given that 3,413 Btu is the energy content of 1 kWh.[24] How would you summarize the findings?

Problem 2.2

The efficiency of a power plant is described as the heat rate of the plant, which measures the amount of heat energy (Btu) needed to produce one unit of electrical energy (kWh).

Problem Table 2.1

Fuel	Unit	Btu/Unit	kWh
Dry wood	Pound	5,800	
Natural gas	Cubic foot	1,000	
#2 Diesel	Gallon	138,500	
#6 Bunker	Gallon	148,000	
Lignite coal	Pound	8,300	
Western coal	Pound	9,000	
Interior coal	Pound	11,000	
Appalachian coal	Pound	12,000	

Problem Table 2.2

Technology	Btu/kWh	Efficiency
Early plants	30,000	
Peaking generator	12,000	
Coal	10,000	
Integrated gasification combined cycle	8,700	
Combined cycle gas turbine	7,000	

If a power plant were 100 percent efficient, it would have a heat rate of 3,413 Btu/kWh, the number of Btus in 1 kWh. The lower the plant heat rate, the more efficient the plant. Efficiency is 3,413 Btu/kWh divided by the heat rate. Complete Problem Table 2.2.

Problem 2.3

Problem Table 2.3 shows the average growth rates for the indicated decades. The ratio of electricity to GDP growth rates is a measure of the electricity intensity of the US economy. Obtain the growth rates for GDP and electricity for the 2000s via a search. Why do you think there was a spurt in electricity growth rates in the 1940s which essentially continued to the 1960s? What is the trend of the intensity of electricity in the economy? What factors may explain the trend?

Problem Table 2.3

	Real GDP	Electricity Growth	Ratio GDP Growth to Electricity Growth
1930s	1.86%	3.51%	
1940s	4.69%	7.68%	
1950s	3.24%	8.37%	
1960s	4.16%	6.70%	
1970s	3.22%	4.10%	
1980s	3.01%	2.11%	
1990s	2.82%	1.89%	
2000s			

Problem 2.4

The spark spread is the profitability of converting natural gas into electricity and is the best indicator of a gas fired plant's profitability. It consists of the market price of electricity ($/mWh) minus the conversion price of gas to power, which is the market price in terms of $/mmBtu × Heat rate divided by 1,000. If a utility is selling electricity at 7 cents/kWh, this is equivalent to $70/mWh. So if the purchase price of gas is $4 per mmBtu and there is a $70 per megawatt-hour market price for electricity, with a 7,000 heat rate, the spark spread in $/mWh would be equal to $70 − $4*(7,000/1,000) or $70 − $28 or $42 per megawatt-hour. The spark spread measures profitability based on variable costs, which is largely fuel costs. A zero spark spread means that the plant is operating at break-even with respect to variable costs without recouping anything to satisfy fixed costs. A negative spread would indicate that the utility would be better off selling natural gas than electricity. A positive spread does not mean that the plant is operating profitably net of fixed costs. Obtain the purchase price of gas and the electricity rate for two cities of your choice for a heat rate of 9,000 and calculate the spark spread and the relative profitability of having an electricity generating plant in both cities.

Problem 2.5

The US electric utilities transmission and distribution systems operate under a cost of service formula as generation has been deregulated where the rules guiding deregulation vary with each state. But the general approach would be as follows.

Permitted or authorized earnings are equal to the Rate base × Equity ratio × Return on equity. Rate base is the value of property allowed to earn an authorized return. Regulators determine which property can be added to the rate base that is both prudent and needed for the service of rate payers. Retired and depreciated property are removed from the rate base to obtain what the utility is spending on construction in excess of depreciation. Equity ratio is the ratio of equity to total capitalization of a company that includes equity, preferred stock, and long-term debt. Normal equity levels are about 45–50 percent of capitalization. The return on equity (ROE) is calculated in a fashion approved by the regulators such as the utility's WACC based on the risk-adjusted return calculated from the CAPM. Other methods such as the discounted cash flow or other recognized methodologies can be used with approval from regulators. The national average ROE for utilities is a bit under 10 percent, reflecting both a weak electricity market and falling interest rates.[25]

Suppose that a utility has a rate base of $12 billion, an equity ratio of 40 percent, and an authorized ROE of 10 percent. The authorized earnings is $12 billion × 40% × 10% or $480 million. With this permitted profit, grossed up by taxes and adding in all expenses, the utility can calculate the level of revenue that would allow them to earn this profit. The grossed-up authorized earnings to have $480 million as after-tax profit is $480 million divided by (1 minus the tax rate) or $738 million. If this were earned, then net of a 35 percent tax rate, the authorized earnings of $480 million would be achieved. Further suppose an interest expense of $500 million, depreciation of $400 million, O&M expense of $1.2 billion, and a fuel expense of $700 million. Thus, the revenue requirement is $480/(1 − 35%) + $500 + $400 + $1,200 + $700 or $3.54 billion. If expected sales are 50 billion kWh, then the rate will be $3.54 billion/50 billion kWh or $0.071 per kilowatt-hour. Since this is an anticipated rate, the utility will charge $0.071

per kilowatt-hour, but will earn something more or less than its authorized earnings. Actual earnings will reflect selling less electricity than expected because of abnormal weather, poor business conditions or more electricity from robust business conditions, O&M expenses being over or underestimated, or, perhaps the toughest item to predict, fuel costs may be off the mark. Sometimes there are quasi-automatic rate adjustments to take care of variances from budgeted figures or from variances in fuel costs, or these adjustments become another rate case.

Suppose that a utility has a rate base of $20 billion, an equity ratio of 45 percent, and a return on equity of 9.5 percent. Furthermore, it has a tax rate of 40 percent, interest expense of $800 million, depreciation of $900 million, O&M expense of $1.5 billion, and a fuel expense of $1.1 billion. It anticipates selling 60 billion kWh. What is its electricity rate for customers when 70 percent of output is for residences, 20 percent for commercial customers, and 10 percent for industry where commercial customers pay 90 percent and industry pays 85 percent of the rate paid by residential customers?

Problem 2.6

The *World Energy Outlook* indicates that the share of renewables was about 3 percent in 2010 and is projected to be 12 percent in 2035 to compensate for the decline in the percentage share for coal and oil. This, of course, assumes that the percentage shares of natural gas, hydro, and nuclear remain the same by these sources, growing at 2.2 percent per year along with total energy. Lay out a spreadsheet with years 2010 to 2035. All you need to enter is 2010 and 2011 and select both cells and get the black cross, depress the left button, and drag down until you reach 2035. In the next column, total energy is depicted as 100 for 2010 growing at 2.2 percent per year. Year 1 is 100, year 2 is year 1 × (1.022), and year 3 is year 2 × (1.022). Put in a third column for renewables with an initial value of 3 depicting its 3 percent share and a formula referring to a growth rate contained in a separate cell. What is the total projected energy in 2035 based on an initial value of 100 and what is 12 percent of that value? With What If/Goal Seek on the Data ribbon, what growth rate is necessary for a value of 3 to grow to 12 percent of the projected 2035 energy starting out with a value of 100 in 2010? Does this growth assessment seem feasible?

Problem 2.7

The purpose of this problem is to demonstrate the degree of savings that can accrue by shifting loads from day to night time when rates are lower. Problem Table 2.7 shows the incremental cost in cents per kilowatt-hour versus the load factor where the load factor of 100 represents the base load. There is a significant increase in cost from 3.5 cents per kilowatt-hour at base load of 100–45 cents per kilowatt-hour at peak demand of 250 (250 percent of base load).

Problem Table 2.7 calculates the cost of electricity as demand goes from 100 to 250. Columns A and B show the incremental cost of electricity for load varying from base to peak demand using the derived formula from trend analysis. The formula in cell B4 is =0.0017*A4^2-0.3172*A4+18.229. Columns D and E are the actual demand over a 24-hour day, column F is the cumulative demand of 3,500, and column G is the incremental cost derived similarly to column B. Column H is the cost figured on the basis

Problem Table 2.7 Cents per Kilowatt-Hour versus Load Factor

	A	B	C	D	E	F	G	H	I	J	K	L	M
1													
2		Incremental			Before	Cumulative	Electricity	Rate		After	Cumulative	Electricity	Rate
3	Load	Cents per kW-Hr			Hourly Demand	Demand	Rate Cents/kW-Hr	X Demand		Hourly Demand	Demand	Rate Cents/kW-Hr	X Demand
4	100	3.51		1	100	100	3.51	$3.51		105	105	3.67	$3.69
5	105	3.67		2	100	200	3.51	$3.51		105	210	3.67	$3.69
6	110	3.91		3	100	300	3.51	$3.51		105	315	3.67	$3.69
7	115	4.23		4	100	400	3.51	$3.51		105	420	3.67	$3.69
8	120	4.65		5	105	505	3.67	$3.69		105	525	3.67	$3.69
9	125	5.14		6	110	615	3.91	$3.90		110	635	3.91	$3.90
10	130	5.72		7	115	730	4.23	$4.14		115	750	4.23	$4.14
11	135	6.39		8	135	865	6.39	$5.75		135	885	6.39	$5.75
12	140	7.14		9	160	1025	11.00	$10.11		160	1045	11.00	$10.11
13	145	7.98		10	190	1215	19.33	$20.91		190	1235	19.33	$20.91
14	150	8.90		11	200	1415	22.79	$26.30		200	1435	22.79	$26.30
15	155	9.91		12	220	1635	30.73	$40.38		220	1655	30.73	$40.38
16	160	11.00		13	235	1870	37.57	$54.23		220	1875	30.73	$40.38
17	165	12.17		14	250	2120	45.18	$71.28		220	2095	30.73	$40.38
18	170	13.44		15	230	2350	35.20	$49.27		220	2315	30.73	$40.38
19	175	14.78		16	215	2565	28.61	$36.41		215	2530	28.61	$36.41
20	180	16.21		17	180	2745	16.21	$16.48		180	2710	16.21	$16.48
21	185	17.73		18	140	2885	7.14	$6.37		140	2850	7.14	$6.37
22	190	19.33		19	110	2995	3.91	$3.90		110	2960	3.91	$3.90
23	195	21.02		20	105	3100	3.67	$3.69		110	3070	3.91	$3.90
24	200	22.79		21	100	3200	3.51	$3.51		110	3180	3.91	$3.90
25	205	24.65		22	100	3300	3.51	$3.51		110	3290	3.91	$3.90
26	210	26.59		23	100	3400	3.51	$3.51		105	3395	3.67	$3.69
27	215	28.61		24	100	3500	3.51	$3.51		105	3500	3.67	$3.69
28	220	30.73						$384.87					$333.32
29	225	32.92											
30	230	35.20											
31	235	37.57											
32	240	40.02											
33	245	42.56											
34	250	45.18											

that base demand is a fixed cost, whereas demand above base demand is priced at the incremental cost. In reality, of course, term contracts with fixed costs would have to be entered, but to demonstrate a point, all demand above base demand is priced at the incremental cost, although the curve could reflect term contracts. The formula in cell H4 is =IF(E4=100,100*$B$4,100*$B$4+(E4-100)*G4)/100, which prices base demand as 100*$B$4 and any portion of demand above that at the incremental cost. The total cost of $385 is in terms of percent demand per hour over a 24-hour period.

Columns J–M is a copy of columns E–F with demand management, where it is possible to maintain a maximum demand of 220 by shifting load to the night-time hours by various means described in this chapter. Care has to be taken to ensure that the total of 3,500 demand-hours is maintained. By so doing, the cost to consumers falls from $385 to $333, a saving of $52.

Set up the spreadsheet and assume that demand management can hold demand peak at 210 by changing 220 to 210 and adding hours during the night time to preserve a total of 3,500. What are the savings? Reduce peak demand to 200 and calculate the savings. From this exercise, one can begin to appreciate the cost savings possible through demand management. However, keep in mind the assumption that demand over base demand is priced at the incremental cost—this simply is not true in reality where a goodly portion of demand over base is covered by term contracts.

Problem 2.8

The cost of electricity is $0.031 per kilowatt-hour for base load demand. What is the cost per megawatt-hour given that there are 1,000 kWh in 1 mWh? Suppose that we are dealing with a city of a few hundred thousand people and the base load is 500 mW. What is the cost of electricity per hour to serve the base load needs of a city this size for 1 hour, 1 day, and 1 year? What do you think of the magnitude of the annual cost to supply the city?

Suppose the local utility has entered into a number of term contracts. Up to the base load of 500 mW, the cost is $31 per megawatt-hour. From 500 to 700 mW, the cost of electricity is $50 per megawatt-hour; from 700 to 1,000 mW, the cost is $80 per megawatt-hour; and above 1,000 mW, it has been estimated that the average cost of electricity purchased on the spot market will be $120 per megawatt-hour. Copy column E of Problem Table 2.7 to column A in a new worksheet with consumption in column B being five times column A. A single embedded IF statement can do the calculations. The first part of the IF statement covers demand in B4 being less than or equal to 500 (it is important that each demarcation point is covered by an equal sign, otherwise a "<" condition followed by a ">" condition will leave out, in this case, consumption being exactly 500 mWh). If the first part of the embedded IF statement is true, then the cost is $31 per megawatt-hour up to 500 mW. If this statement is not true, then a second embedded IF statement checks to see if consumption is less than or equal to 700 mWh. If this condition is true, then consumption is between 500 and 700 because the first IF statement covered consumption at or below 500 mWh. Thus, cost will be $31*500 for the first 500 mWh plus consumption less 500 multiplied by $50, which takes care of consumption between 500 and 700 mWh. If this condition is not true, then a third embedded IF statement checks to see if consumption is less than 1,000. If this is true, then consumption has to be between 700 and 1,000 because the previous two IF statements covered consumption of less than 700 mWh. Thus, cost is \$31*500 for the first 500 mWh plus \$50*200 for the next 200 mWh plus anything over 700 mWh being charged \$80. If none of these IF statements apply, then consumption has to be over 1,000 mWh. Now the cost is \$31*500 plus \$50*200 plus \$80*300 plus the excess over 1,000 being charged \$120. Try to formulate this IF statement on your own without referring below.

$$= IF\left(B4 <= 500, 31*B4, IF\left(\begin{matrix} B4 <= 700, 31*500 + (B4 - 500)*50, IF \\ \left(\begin{matrix} B4 <= 1,000, 31*500 + 50*200 + B4 - 700 \\ *80, 31*500 + 200*50 + 300 \\ *80 + (B4 - 1,000)*120 \end{matrix} \right) \end{matrix} \right) \right)$$

Notes

1 "A Super Solar Flare," National Aeronautics and Space Administration Science News (2008), Website http://science.nasa.gov/science-news/science-at-nasa/2008/06may_carringtonflare.

2 "The Hope Natural Gas Case and its Impact on State Utility Regulation," *Maryland Law Review*, University of Maryland, Website http://digitalcommons.law.umaryland.edu/cgi/viewcontent.cgi?article=1288&context=mlr.

3 Jefferies' Utility Primer, Jefferies & Partners, Website www.jefferies.com.

4 Sally Hunt, *Making Competition Work in Electricity* (New York, NY: John Wiley & Sons, 2002), is well worth reading for a more comprehensive view of deregulation. Many of the concepts described herein are drawn from this book without individual citations.

5 *1994 Electricity Report*, California Energy Commission, Website www.energy.ca.gov/reports/ER94.html.

6 "An Overview of the Federal Energy Regulatory Commission," FERC (December, 2010), Website www.ferc.gov/about/ferc-does/ferc101.pdf.

7 European Network of Transmission System Operators for Electricity, Website www.entsoe.eu/Pages/default.aspx.

8 Geert-Jan van der Zanden, "100 Million Smart Meters to Be Installed in Europe by 2016, but Are End-Users Engaged?" greentechgrid (August 25, 2011), Website www.greentechmedia.com/articles/read/100-million-smart-meters-to-be-installed-in-europe-by-2016-but-are-end-user.

9 "Utility-Scale Smart Meter Deployments: Building Block of the Evolving Power Grid," Institute for Electric Innovation (The Edison Foundation) (September, 2014), Website www.edisonfoundation.net/iei/Documents/IEI_SmartMeterUpdate_0914.pdf.

10 "The Smart Grid, an Introduction," Office of Electricity Delivery & Energy Reliability of the US Department of Energy, Website www.doe.energy.gov.

11 *Smart Regions Landscape Report 2012* (updated 2013), Website www.smartregions.net/default.asp?sivuID=26927.

12 American Superconductor, Website www.amsc.com.

13 PJM, Website www.pjm.com.

14 "Analysis of Operational Events and Market Impacts during the January 2014 Cold Weather Events," *PJM Interconnection* (May 8, 2014), Website www.pjm.com/documents/reports.aspx.

15 Cooperation Council for the Arab States of the Gulf, Website www.gcc-sg.org/eng/index.html.

16 Clean Line Energy Partners, Website www.cleanlineenergy.com/technology/hvdc.

17 "Central American Electric Interconnection System (SIEPAC) Transmission and Trading," Economic Consulting Associates (March, 2010), Website www.esmap.org/sites/esmap.org/files/BN004-10_REISP-CD_Central%20American%20Electric%20Interconnection%20System-Transmisison%20&%20Trading.pdf. Study commissioned by the Energy Sector Management Assistance Program, a global knowledge and technical assistance program administered by World Bank, Website www.esmap.org.

18 Justin Miller, "How Soon Could We See a Single Andean Power Market?" Nexant (May 9, 2014), Website www.nexant.com/resources/how-soon-could-we-see-single-andean-power-market.

19 "HVDC Status in China," EPRI Conference (August, 2013), Website http://dsius.com/cet/HVD CinChina_EPRI2013_HVDC.pdf.

20 State Grid of China, Website www.sgcc.com.cn/ywlm/projects/index.shtml.

21 World steel production was 1.5 billion tons (www.worldsteel.org/statistics/statistics-archive/2012-steel-production.html) and world coal production was 7.86 million tons (*BP Statistical Review*). Using an approximation that a ton of steel requires 2 tons of iron ore plus 1 ton of coal, the estimated percentage of coal consumed in steel production is 20 percent rounded. The *World Energy Outlook* (2012) shows that of the 3.3 billion cubic meters of natural gas consumption in 2010, 1.35 billion cubic meters was for power generation or 40 percent rounded and that 5 percent of oil is consumed in power generation. Source of energy consumption is the *BP Statistical Review* except for biomass, which is not included. Biomass is difficult to estimate because its use is so diffuse in Africa, Asia, and South America, but is estimated to be 10 percent of total traditional energy consumption.

22 Among the many sources for energy measurements and conversions, one handy guide can be obtained from www.extension.iastate.edu/agdm/wholefarm/pdf/c6-86.pdf, which also contains links to other Websites that perform conversions.

23 R. Nersesian, *Energy Risk Modeling* (Ithaca, NY: Palisade, 2013). Sections 5–7 deal with combining solar arrays and wind turbines to obtain an output simulation that can be used to select the optimal number of each.

24 Problems have been adapted from Jefferies' Utility Primer, Jefferies & Partners.

25 "Rate Case Summary," Edison Electric Institute, Website www.eei.org/resourcesandmedia/industry dataanalysis/industryfinancialanalysis/QtrlyFinancialUpdates/Documents/QFU_Rate_Case/2013_Q2_Rate_Case.pdf.

3 Biomass

Energy is not as it always was. Yesterday's world was entirely dependent on biomass, particularly wood for heating and cooking. Today biomass is generally viewed with disfavor as something associated with abject poverty. Yet there is a resurgence going on for biomass. As fossil fuel prices increase, biomass promises to play a more active role as a utility fuel (biofuel), a motor vehicle fuel (bioethanol and biodiesel), and a supplement to natural gas (biogas). Biomass is displacing heating oil and propane as homes heated with split wood or processed wood pellets burned in highly efficient burners gain in popularity. Biomass will never replace fossil fuels, other than on the margin, nor is there any hope that we can return to a world where biomass played a significant role in satisfying society's energy needs. But that does not mean that biomass is dead or that we can ignore its contribution to satisfying energy demand. This chapter examines the past and present roles of biomass and its potential as tomorrow's energy fuel.

Yesterday's Fuel

Until about 300 years ago, the world depended nearly exclusively on biomass as a source of energy. The population was low in relation to the number of trees. Nature simply replaced those chopped down for heating and cooking. The environmental impact was minimal because carbon dioxide released by burning wood was absorbed by plant growth that replaced the burnt wood. With no net loss of tree resources, carbon dioxide was recycled, which is described by contemporary proponents of biomass as a closed carbon sustainable system. Fossil fuels, on the other hand, release carbon dioxide locked away eons ago as partially decayed plants, animals, and marine organisms.

Despite environmental benefits of recycling carbon dioxide and emitting less nitrous and sulfur oxides than coal and oil, pollution—in the form of smoke from burning wood—would have filled a cave, tent, hut, or dwelling before someone invented the chimney. While the first chimney can be traced back to the twelfth century, they did not become common until the sixteenth and seventeenth centuries in Europe and North America. Yet the common chimney is not so common in Africa and Asia. According to the World Health Organization, cooking and heating homes by burning biomass and coal by three billion people primarily in Africa and Asia without the benefit of chimneys results in two million people dying prematurely annually from illnesses attributable to indoor air pollution along with another million people contracting chronic obstructive pulmonary disease, plus the death of nearly 50 percent of children who contract pneumonia from inhaling particulate matter.[1]

Early explorers observed smoke from American Indian fires filling the Los Angeles basin with smog long before the automobile age and in the Smokey Mountains from caves for smoking meat.[2] In the modern era, smoke from burning biomass joined by emissions from automobiles and coal burning utilities operating with virtually no safeguards against pollution has created a highly publicized brown cloud overhanging much of southern Asia. The brown cloud, visible from space, has resulted in serious health problems. Naturally, of course, the brown cloud is not confined to Asia, subject as it is to global wind patterns.

Biomass maintained its dominance as a fuel source up to the Industrial Revolution. Coal entered the picture first in Britain, followed by Germany, the US, and later Japan. Its progress to becoming a major source of energy was slow—in 1850, coal made up only 10 percent of the energy mix and biomass satisfied nearly all the remainder. By the mid-1870s, biomass still contributed twice that of coal in fulfilling energy needs even with coal replacing charcoal for producing steel and split logs for fueling railroad locomotives and heating homes. Gas piped into homes and businesses to supply lighting and heating at that time was actually manufactured from coal. What little energy demand remained after biomass and coal was filled by hydropower (water mills turning shafts that, via gears or belts, powered grinding wheels and machinery). Even as late as 1900, biomass still played an important role in satisfying energy, although coal was rapidly gaining ascendency as the dominant source of energy.[3] By then, natural gas had joined manufactured gas from coal to light buildings and streets in city centers. Hydropower for generating electricity was in its infancy. Oil was still a fuel for lighting (kerosene), as the birth of the automobile age had just begun. Hardly a decade after Ford began to mass-produce automobiles and the Wright brothers flew the first airplane, oil had become a strategic fuel for waging war. Natural gas began its ascent as a fuel of choice during the 1920s and 1930s with the development of long-distance transmission pipelines. Nuclear power made its debut after the Second World War, and renewables (solar and wind) not till the latter part of the twentieth century.

Today's Fuel

Biomass is still a major source of energy, though often, but not entirely, excluded from energy statistics because of its inherent difficulty of gathering reliable data from remote areas of the world far beyond the reach of record keepers. As noted in Chapter 1, biomass and organic waste are estimated to make up 10 percent of total energy consumption—still an impressive amount of energy considering the growth in overall energy consumption in the last hundred years. The *World Energy Outlook* assessed bioenergy as 1,277 million tons of oil equivalent (Mtoe) in 2010, which contributed 9.7 percent to world energy consumption. The *World Energy Outlook* projects bioenergy consumption at 1,881 Mtoe in 2035, an annual growth of 1.6 percent. While looking a bit anemic, nearly all this growth will be in power generation, whose share of the bioenergy pie will grow from 9 to 22 percent, and also motor vehicle fuels from 5 to 11 percent. Thus, the implied annual growth rates for bioenergy in power generation of 5.3 percent and 4.8 percent for motor vehicle fuels are, in the world of energy, impressive.

Biomass takes many forms. Women carrying biomass on their heads in semi-arid regions of Africa and Asia may trudge as much as 10 to 20 miles a day to find dead tree limbs and camel dung. Once dried in the open sun, camel dung becomes the preferred fuel for mud ovens because of its slow burning, evenly releasing a great deal of heat. Unfortunately, burning dung for fuel robs the ground of a valuable fertilizer. Moreover, demand for dung from a growing human population is beginning to exceed the supply of camel droppings. Introducing an energy efficient oven with a means of control over the heating rate would reduce demand for biomass fuels. But a woman who depends on dung and dead tree branches for cooking most likely would not have the financial wherewithal to acquire the latest in biomass ovens. Besides, if something is gathered freely from the environment by those who work for nothing and apparently have the time, what is the economic justification for buying a fuel efficient oven? Though treks into the hinterland for wood and dung make for interesting TV documentaries and fascinating photographs in *National Geographic,* the reality is not so attractive. How many of these women would gladly give up the romance of walking 10–20 miles per day gathering wood and animal droppings for small kerosene or propane stoves to heat their huts and cook their food?

See the Companion Website for sections on the Role of Charcoal and Wood Pellets: www.routledge.com/cw/nersesian.

Around the World with Biomass

Wood residue is an important source of biomass. As much as 75 percent of a tree becomes residue, beginning with the leaves, tree top, branches, and stump left in the forest, to the bark, edgings, and sawdust produced when a log is transformed into lumber, and to the shavings, edgings, and sawdust of transforming lumber into furniture and other products. Bark and wood residue can be used for residential heating, as an industrial fuel to supply power either as steam or electricity for lumber mills and other activities in the developing world and in the developed nations such as Finland and Germany, and for being transformed to pellets for heating homes in North America and Scandinavia.

Some African nations such as Burundi and Rwanda are over 90 percent reliant on biomass energy, while others are 70–80 percent reliant for their total energy needs, which includes commercial as well as residential demand. In terms of residential demand, nearly all rural households in Kenya, Tanzania, Mozambique, and Zambia rely on wood, and 90 percent of urban households rely on charcoal for cooking. Heavy biomass users in Asia are Indonesia, the Philippines, Thailand, Myanmar (formerly Burma), Vietnam, Bhutan, Laos, and Cambodia; and in the Western Hemisphere, Guatemala, Honduras, Nicaragua, and Haiti. Many of these nations are sustainable in that replacement growth is greater than consumption. A major exception is Haiti, where most of the land has been stripped bare of forests. This is clearly visible from spacecraft, where the brown of Haiti stands out in vivid contrast to the green of the neighboring Dominican Republic, except in border regions where Haitians have been poaching on the Dominican Republic's forests. Arid regions of Africa with the highest per capita dependency on biomass are also consuming biomass faster than it can be replaced, as evidenced by the ever longer daily treks. However, technology may slow the nonsustainable consumption of biomass. Envirofit offers fuel efficient and environmentally beneficial wood and charcoal burning stoves for about $100. The stoves are specially designed to reduce harmful emissions by 80 percent and demand for fuel by 60 percent compared to open-air burning of wood and charcoal. More than 700,000 have been sold in 40 different nations and have saved users over six million working weeks from collecting firewood.[4] West Africa is a significant market—perhaps some of the oil money is trickling down to the people. Sub-Saharan Africa would need outside financial support for these or other similar types of stoves to counter the harmful environmental effects of open-air burning; likewise for the indigent poor of India, China, and Southeast Asia.

Of the world population of seven billion people, an estimated 1.5 billion have no, and another one billion have limited, access to electricity. Almost by definition, those without electricity depend almost entirely on biomass. Even with limited access to electricity, many cannot afford to buy electricity to serve all their needs and restrict their use to lighting, a small refrigerator, and perhaps an appliance or two. Heavy energy consuming activities such as cooking, heating water, and space heating are fueled by biomass. Not only does burning biomass pose health problems, but it also contributes to ecological problems such as loss of dung as a fertilizer and deforestation occurring in parts of Africa, India, Indonesia, Brazil, and elsewhere. As one may surmise, there is a direct link between poverty and dependence on biomass.

As a counterpoint to deforestation, India initiated an afforestation program in an area stripped of its indigenous evergreen forests. The aim of the program is to transform what had become wasteland from deforestation back to forestland. If successful, new forests will reduce soil erosion and increase groundwater. Improved fertility and productivity of soil will benefit agriculture in the surrounding area, while the forest itself will provide employment opportunities and fuel. The goal of the National Forestry Action Program is afforestation of a significant portion of the nation that has been stripped of trees, with the local population supplying labor and government supplying material.[5]

Many remote and isolated islands making up nations in Southeast Asia are not well served by commercial forms of energy. Over 70 percent of the population of Indonesia and Malaysia depend on biomass for heating and cooking. Biomass is burned in developing nations for smoking fish, curing tobacco, processing food, drying bricks and lumber, and making furniture and ceramics. Biomass would be an ideal fuel for micro-electricity generating plants that could bring the advantages of electricity to the isolated islands of Southeast Asia. While the most likely fuel is wood, it could also be bagasse, a residue from processing sugarcane, and rice husks. But such plans oftentimes face insurmountable hurdles of few local individuals having the requisite technical knowledge to generate and distribute electricity and a community having the means to garner external sources of financial support.

Special Case of Biomass in Brazil

Biomass plays an important role in Brazil. Similar to other nations, biomass as wood and charcoal are consumed for cooking and heating in rural areas; but what is different about Brazil is that over half of biomass is consumed as commercial and industrial fuel. Companies in mining, cement, paper and ceramic making, and food processing rely on biomass (mostly charcoal) as a fuel more than any other nation in the world. Most nations use coal to make steel, but Brazil has little in the way of coal reserves suitable for steel production. While Brazil imports metallurgical coal, it is unique in partially depending on charcoal to produce steel. Brazil stands out for its greater reliance on biomass not only as commercial and industrial fuel but also as biofuel for motor vehicles. Brazil's energy pie consists of 18 percent ethanol, 14 percent hydro, 10 percent wood and other biomass such as burning bagasse for power, and 4 percent other renewables. Thus, the total slice of renewables is 46 percent of energy demand, something few nations have achieved.[6] For nations 90 percent reliant on biomass, nearly all is wood or charcoal for cooking and heating, quite unlike Brazil where biofuel and hydro make important contributions.

Biomass for Electricity Generation

Land dedicated for growing biomass for electricity generation is unused or marginal land unfit for agricultural use, but suitable for fast-growing trees (poplars, willows) and grasses (switchgrass). *Miscanthus x giganteus*, a hybrid (indicated by the "x" in its name) of an Asian grass-like plant related to sugarcane, sprouts annually, requires little water and fertilizer, thrives in untilled fields and cool weather, and grows rapidly to 13 feet tall. After its leaves drop in the fall, a tall bamboo-like stem can be harvested and burned to generate electricity. It is estimated that about half of the electricity needs of Illinois would be satisfied if marginal land, making up 10 percent of the state, were dedicated to growing miscanthus.[7] Another plant gaining recognition are shrub willows that grow 10–15 times faster than trees. It is particularly suited for poorly drained marginal soils. While new to North America, Sweden has 34,000 acres of shrub willows supplying fuel for heat and power generation.[8]

The benefits of biomass as a fuel for electricity generation are that biomass:

- is plentiful, with large regions of the earth covered by forests and jungles;
- can be increased by planting marginal lands with fast-growing trees and grasses;
- stabilizes soil and reduces erosion;
- is renewable and recyclable and does not add to carbon dioxide emissions;
- stores solar energy until needed, then is converted to electricity, whereas solar panels and wind turbines generate electricity, whether needed or not, and then only when the sun is shining and the wind is blowing;
- does not create an ash waste disposal problem since ash can be spread in forests or fields to recycle nutrients and not to landfills as is coal ash;
- creates jobs in rural areas.

Some environmentalists are critical of biomass plantations because they deplete nutrients from the soil, promote aesthetic degradation, and cause loss of biological diversity. While growing biomass as a fuel depletes the soil of nutrients, spreading ash from combustion replenishes the soil with what was removed with the exception of nitrogen. Interspersing nitrogen-fixing plants among the biomass plants can replenish nitrogen rather than relying on nitrogen-based fertilizers made from fossil fuels. On the plus side, biomass plantations can reduce soil erosion and be managed in a way to minimize their impact on the landscape and on biological life. In fact, there is no reason why biomass plantations cannot make a barren landscape more attractive and encourage biological life such as India's afforestation program. However, birds and mammals seem to prefer natural environments of diverse trees and plants over monocultures if given a choice.

The province of Ontario in Canada has decreed the elimination of coal-fired electricity generation which was supposed to have been completed by 2007 and which has proven to be more costly than expected.[9] Nevertheless, in compliance with this decree, Ontario Power Generation converted the Atikokan Generation Station from coal to biomass. The station was opened in 1985 as a coal burning plant and the conversion was completed in 2014, which entailed removal of coal handling systems with internal modifications to boilers and other components of the plant to burn biomass. Biomass fuel is wood pellets produced in two plants on a sustainable basis where forest growth exceeds removal of wood mass for conversion to wood pellets. A 200 mW plant consumes 10 truckloads of pellets per day at 35 tons per truck five days a week, stored in two 5,000 ton storage silos, for an annual throughput of 90,000 tons of biomass. Pellets are pulverized prior to combustion to achieve a thermal efficiency of about 35 percent in line when the plant was coal-fired. Planning and designing has been aimed at constructing a plant that can be replicated to serve other areas of Ontario.[10]

Ash waste from this plant is only 1–3 percent of the volume of pellets compared to 25 percent for coal. Ash from burning biomass and captured particulate matter from smoke emissions are spread on land as a low-grade fertilizer versus coal ash that must be disposed in a landfill. Spreading ash on the forest land is actually necessary to replenish nutrients removed in harvesting trees. If not done, continued harvesting will deplete the ground of needed nutrients to support growing biomass unless fertilizer is applied to replace the nutrients. Thus, sustainability of forest land has to take into consideration how nutrients contained in harvested trees are replaced. Besides eliminating coal by substituting biomass, Ontario Power will satisfy some electricity demand with solar and wind power.

Not All Favor Biomass for Electricity

Biomass for fuel has generally been well received by the public as environmentally desirable, particularly recycling of carbon emissions. However, not everyone is in favor of biofuels. An example of the growing opposition is contained in a study, *False Claims of Carbon Neutrality Conceal Climate Impacts*, published by Greenpeace Canada in their November 2011 magazine, with a tell-tale cover title of "Fuelling a BioMess."[11] Two of the principal arguments are that decades separate burning a tree and growing its replacement before carbon neutrality can be achieved and that biomass-fired electricity generating plants emit far more carbon dioxide and carbon monoxide and particulate matter to produce the same amount of electricity as a coal-fired plant. The former criticism does not hold for biomass that replaces itself annually such as grasses and corn and sugar for biofuels, but a replacement tree sprouting out of the ground does not absorb the carbon released by burning a mature tree. Carbon recycling is postponed until such time when the tree reaches maturity, although it absorbs carbon dioxide from the moment it sprouts. One has to compare the total carbon dioxide absorbed by a plant seedling growing into a mature tree to that released by burning the tree. As a thought experiment, if a seedling absorbs, say, 1 percent of a mature tree on average for the first 3 years, 5 and 8 percent for the next 2 years, then 10, 20, 40, 70, and 100 percent each year thereafter, then the replacement tree has absorbed about 2.5 times the carbon dioxide released by burning the original tree. The counterargument is that leaving the tree alive would have absorbed 10 times the amount of carbon dioxide over the same time period. Thus, the debate over environmental consequences continues unabatedly without even a tenuous resolution.

The point that there are more particulate emissions can be handled by precipitators. The contention of greater carbon emissions reflects the fact that biomass has less energy content per unit volume than coal: 125 pounds of oven-dried wood has the same energy content (one million Btu) as 90 pounds of coal and therefore more biomass has to be burned for the same release of energy. The ratio is much higher for green wood that can have moisture content as high as 50 percent. Moisture evaporated during combustion reduces heat available for generating steam to drive turbines. But to present a fair and impartial view, coal also has some moisture content. Thus, it is incumbent for any analysis on energy released by burning wood versus coal to take into account the respective water moisture of both fuels. Even this analysis may be flawed if there are major energy differences between gathering and shipping biomass versus mining and shipping coal. Anyway, according to Greenpeace Canada, burning coal emits significantly less carbon emissions and actually is a comparatively "clean" energy source compared to biomass. Would anyone believe Greenpeace even back-handedly praising the virtues of coal?

As a counterpoint, a paper entitled "A Look at the Details of CO2 Emissions from Burning Wood vs. Coal" argues that emissions by burning wood and coal are about the same, but that the advantage of wood is replacement plants absorbing most of the carbon emissions.[12] Therefore, the end result is that burning wood has less carbon emissions than burning coal. So who is correct—Greenpeace Canada or FutureMetrics? Analysis of biofuels (and energy in general) is full of such contradictory outcomes—for instance, some maintain that corn-based ethanol reduces carbon emissions, although its contribution is ranked from significant to marginal. Others maintain that it actually increases carbon emissions on an energy equivalent basis with gasoline. Someone has to be wrong, but one also has to be aware that there is always a question as to the extent of the envelope in an analysis of energy and its impact on the environment. In other words, are all key factors being considered? And if so, are estimates of key factors realistic and reliable? Another consideration is that the analysis of those associated with organizations with a particular view, either pro or con to some environmental or energy position, always seem to pick those models or methodologies and select those values for key variables that support their parochial view. Energy policy administrators cannot make decisions on such constructs— they need an impartial and fair view of an environmental or energy issue done by analysts who have no axe to grind.

Biomass Fuels for Electricity Generation

Biomass for electricity generation can be forest residues including imperfect commercial trees, noncommercial trees thinned from crowded forests, unhealthy trees, deadwood from fire-prone forests, and debris from logging operations. Though "free," there is the cost of collecting and shipping a thinly dispersed energy source from remote locations to an electricity generating plant. More promising from a logistics point of view is collecting bark, edging, and sawdust residues at lumber mills. Lumber mills are generally located closer to population centers and collect logs over a wide area, concentrating wood residues at a few sites, making transport to an electricity generating plant easier and less costly. Some of this waste is already being utilized for supplying power to a lumber mill or being available to those living nearby for home heating.[13] In northern Europe, logging and lumber mill wastes are burned to generate electricity. Furniture manufacturing facilities are also concentrated sources of wood waste. Pulp waste from producing paper from wood biomass is burned to fuel the plant.

A second source of biomass is residue from harvesting agricultural crops. These include wheat straw, corn stover (leaves, stalks, and cobs), orchard trimmings, rice straw and husks, and bagasse. Sugarcane harvested and shipped to a sugar processing plant concentrates bagasse at a single location, which can then be burned to supply power to a sugar processing plant. Agricultural wastes are generally left in the field and decay to become part of the soil. The high cost for collecting and shipping would make agricultural wastes as commercially unattractive as forest residue. Furthermore, agricultural wastes are seasonal, although they could be combined with wood residues to feed a biomass electricity generating plant over the course of a year. Total removal of agricultural waste would have adverse consequences on soil fertility. However, agricultural wastes left in the field are beginning to be collected as feedstock for cellulosic ethanol plants.

A third source is so-called energy crops grown specifically for fuel on marginal land. These crops are preferably fast-growing, drought- and pest-resistant, and readily harvestable by mechanical means. Depending on growing conditions, hybrid poplars and willows can be harvested every 6–10 years. Trees can be cut and shipped to the utility plant as wood chips, shipped whole as round wood (logs cut to an appropriate length for ease of transport), and converted to chips at the plant prior to burning them whole in specially designed boilers. Switchgrass does not require replanting for up to 10 years; after cutting, it is dried a few days in the sun if desired, baled, and shipped to a utility plant and ground up prior to burning. However, none of these sources is strictly carbon-neutral in that fuel consumed by tractors and trucks in growing, harvesting, and shipping biomass adds to carbon emissions. Overall carbon emissions should still be lower than burning fossil fuels because of the carbon dioxide absorbed by replacement plant growth.

For biomass fuel for electricity generating plants to be feasible, land area dedicated to replacement plant growth should be sufficient to support sustainable operations. This is not a minor consideration because a great deal of land has to be set aside to ensure sustainability. The reason for this is that photosynthesis is actually inefficient from a human viewpoint: only about 3 percent of the sun's energy is converted to biomass. Rate of growth in energy content depends on type of plant and length of growing season. One should not be surprised if the area necessary to support biomass electricity generating plants increases with latitude. As an example, it is estimated that 6,600 square kilometers in the UK are necessary for sustainable growth to support a 2,000 mW electricity generating plant.[14] This is a lot of land by any measure, particularly in a highly developed and densely populated nation as the UK. The area of land would be considerably less in a tropical region where the growing season extends for most, if not all, of the year. This makes biomass electricity more feasible in South America and Southeast Asia where there is considerable undeveloped land (jungles or savannahs) not far from major population centers. This land could be converted to tree farms to support a sustainable biomass generating plant. Burning biomass for electricity generation that leads to deforestation is self-defeating from an environmental viewpoint since carbon emissions from burning biomass cannot be absorbed by replacement plant growth. It is also self-defeating from an economic viewpoint since costs will escalate, as more distant biomass sources have to be tapped to continue generating electricity.

Another option is to use biomass as a co-fuel in existing coal burning plants instead of burning it in specialized electricity generating plants. These facilities would have dedicated storage and material-handling systems for biomass in addition to their existing facilities for handling coal. Biomass would be mixed with coal for burning, but while this sounds attractive, it turns out that technical problems begin to emerge when more than 10 percent biomass is mixed with coal in a conventional coal burning plant. These problems have to be dealt with before higher portions of biomass can be mixed with coal. There are a few specially designed facilities that can burn either 100 percent coal or 100 percent biomass. At high-load factors, coal is favored for its higher heat content. Despite the apparent desirability of biomass-fed electricity generating plants, the fact is that coal can generate electricity at 6 cents per kilowatt-hour versus biomass at 9 cents per kilowatt-hour, a 50 percent cost premium.[15] This higher cost of electricity paid in the form of biomass subsidies to the electricity providers is facing growing opposition from taxpayers in the UK and elsewhere.[16]

Research is being conducted on "torrefied" biomass, which is similar to wood pellets, but designed for mixing with coal to fuel electricity generating plants. Torrefaction gives wood pellets coal-like properties with energy content similar to coal. Pellets require no special attention when mixed with coal. They can be pulverized along with coal and used at any desired concentration. While technology for producing torrefied wood has been developed, it has not yet reached a commercial stage where large volumes can be produced at prices competitive with coal. If this could be achieved, or if a carbon tax were put into effect, a massive market for biomass would open up for electricity generation.[17]

Vegetable oils and paper trash have also been suggested as biomass fuels for electricity generating plants. Used vegetable oils are not available in quantities necessary to run electricity generating plants and the cost and effort of collecting used vegetable oils from a million-and-one burger joints would be prohibitive. However, a few imaginative and entrepreneurial owners of diesel trucks have discovered that they can stop at a friendly fast food restaurant for a bite of food and then do a favor for the proprietor by disposing of used vegetable oil free of charge. A concoction of vegetable oil and diesel fuel, if suitable adjustments are made to the engine, burns just as efficiently as pure diesel fuel, generating savings for the driver while odorizing a stretch of highway with a piquant aroma of French fries or fried hamburger, chicken, or fish, or some combination thereof. The disposal problem associated with used vegetable oil would dissipate if an entrepreneur built a permanent business around recycling used vegetable oil as biodiesel fuel. Paper trash has a higher value if not burned as fuel for electricity generation, but reprocessed and sold as recycled paper and cardboard products. Over half of US paper waste is exported to China for recycling since China does not have forest reserves necessary to support a large-scale paper making industry.[18]

Biomass Electricity Generating Plants

Biomass energy accounts for less than 1 percent of the US electricity generation and 2 percent in Europe, where much of the available biomass is waste from lumbering operations in Sweden, Finland, and Germany. Most biomass electricity generating facilities are small, dedicated to meeting the needs of a local industry or community. Their most important contribution is that they demonstrate the potential for biomass to generate electricity and serve as platforms for improving technology. One such plant in Vermont burns waste wood from nearby logging operations, lumber mill waste, and discarded wood pallets. In addition, there is a low-pressure wood gasifier capable of converting 200 tons per day of wood chips to fuel gas, which is fed directly into the same boiler for burning wood waste. Hot water from generating electricity is pipelined to nearby buildings for heating.[19] Net carbon dioxide emissions, taking into consideration the sustainable growth of biomass, is less than burning fossil fuels, although this assertion has been challenged by Greenpeace Canada.

For special circumstances, biomass can generate electricity, but the economic viability of large-scale use of biomass to generate electricity remains questionable. Growing, harvesting or collecting, and shipping biomass by truck are costly compared to the alternative of mining and shipping coal, which can be looked upon as concentrated biomass, by rail. Biomass electricity generating facilities built in the US in response to the 1973 oil crisis were economically sound when oil and natural gas prices were at historic highs, but became financial albatrosses either for utilities if operated under long-term contracts or for their investors if operated under short-term contracts when energy prices subsequently fell.

Biomass for large-scale electricity generating facilities does not appear to be on the cards simply because biomass cannot compete with fossil fuels. To underscore this point, the UK Tilbury biomass burning plant was the largest of its kind in the world with a capacity of 750 mW, enough to supply 1.5 million households. This seems to contradict the estimate that a 1 gW plant can support a city of 1 million people in Chapter 2, so how can 0.75 gW support 1.5 million households? Easy—this is an example of elasticity of choice associated with energy statistics: 1.5 million households mean 1.5 million homes and, to make matters a bit worse, a household is usually 2–4 people. These homes may not use electricity for space heating or for hot water. A city of one million people, considerably less in terms of households, includes not just homes and apartment buildings but commercial and industrial enterprises, office buildings, schools and hospitals, hotels and restaurants, stores and warehouses, public street lighting, traffic signals, commercial signs, and so on. The two measures are not comparable.

The Tilbury plant was originally coal-fired when built in 1969 and was converted to biomass (wood pellets) in 2011. Plant closure occurred in 2013 in the wake of a government report on continued support for renewable energy (could the report have cast doubt on the continuance of government subsidies for this plant?). But this should not be interpreted as the end of biomass for electricity generation. Drax Power operates six coal-fired power plants that supply 4 gW of power, enough to supply electricity to six million homes. The company is in the process of converting three of these plants to biomass. The first source of biomass was tapping the local market for baled straw and contracting with farmers to grow miscanthus on marginal lands, which once planted grows every year without need to fertilize. But these sources could not satisfy the demand for biomass. The company set up a subsidiary in the US to manufacture wood pellets from sustainable forest lands, which will be shipped by bulk carrier to the UK. If these plants prove successful, the company intends to convert all its units to biomass.[20]

As an additional counterpoint to the closure of the Tilbury plant, construction has begun on an electricity generating plant that will be fueled with waste and rubbish supplied by the citizens of Copenhagen. The Amager Bakke plant is expected to be finished in 2017 and will supply electricity and heating to over 150,000 homes. The plant is actually a replacement for an existing plant and will increase energy output by over 25 percent and reduce nitrous oxide emissions by 85 percent and sulfur emissions by 99.5 percent.

To demonstrate the plant's environmental friendliness, a recreational area is going to be built on its roof top complete with a ski run to the ground.[21] Underscoring the nation's commitment to renewable fuels, Denmark imports trash from nearby nations as fuel for generating electricity. Denmark's Dong Energy is switching half of its coal generators to biomass by 2020 as part of Denmark's plan to be coal-free by 2025.

Stockholm's oldest power plant has burned coal, oil, and natural gas since its construction in 1903. The plant is now being converted to the world's largest combined heat and power generator that will burn only wood chips and timber scraps.[22] The people of Scandinavia are strong advocates of renewable energy and are willing to pay more in taxes and utility bills to reduce their nations' reliance on fossil fuels. This is not to say other European nations are not environmentally conscious, but to say that the Scandinavians are particularly so and their efforts in renewable energy serve as an example for others. Germany, for instance, produces 30 million tons of straw. Thought is being given to consider straw as a renewable energy source. Netting out the uses of straw as livestock feed and bedding and a source of humus for soil, between 8 and 13 million tons are estimated to be available as a renewable energy source. This amount of straw, when burned, could provide two to three million households with electricity and three to five million households with hot water and heating.[23]

Since biomass is not competitive with coal, government subsidies are necessary for biomass plants to be built and operated and survive in a competitive market. This exposes the vulnerability of all subsidy-dependent renewable energy projects to the vagaries of the government budgeting process. Frequently, subsidies provide temporary support for just a few years and their renewal is subject to government review and approval while project life is decades long. This is a particular problem in nations such as the US where most renewable energy subsidies generally have short lives whereas renewable energy projects have long lives. Without subsidies, projected profits disappear. Thus, their continuance depends on Congress passing new legislation to renew subsidies. If Congress does nothing, subsidies automatically expire, a real risk that strongly affects investors' appetite for financing renewable energy projects. Even feed-in-tariff rates where consumers directly bear the extra costs of renewable energy are not immune to risk. Feed-in-tariffs means that consumers pay the full cost of renewables in the form of higher electricity rates without government subsidies. If electricity from fossil fuels costs 10 cents per kilowatt-hour and 25 cents per kilowatt-hour for renewables and renewables make up 5 percent of electricity generation, the weighted average price to consumers of 10.75 cents per kilowatt-hour would not be that noticeable. But if renewables make up 30 percent of electricity, then the weighted average price of 14.5 cents per kilowatt-hour, approaching a 50 percent premium, would be noticeable. Renewables are at risk if a government is under public pressure, as in Spain, to do something about spiraling electricity rates from a greater reliance on renewable energy. In the case of Spain, the government cancelled subsidies outright, leaving investors in renewable energy high and dry, killing the prospects for investing in new sources of renewable energy.

Advocates of renewable energy point out that permanent subsidies such as favorable tax treatments and other means of hidden support enjoyed by fossil fuel companies ought to be eliminated to put renewable fuels on a level playing field with fossil fuels. It is amazing that fossil fuels, in business for over two centuries for coal and over a century for oil and natural gas, are subsidized, particularly when one considers their history of profitable operations. These subsidies are not subject to an expiration date: once on the legislative books, always on the books. They are not only hard to get rid of, but also, in some industrialized nations, exceed subsidies to renewable energy.

The business of biomass electricity generation can change if current research and development efforts result in a technological breakthrough that significantly lowers biomass energy costs or if prices of fossil fuels (coal and natural gas) rise to levels that make biomass for electricity generation economically attractive. The latter is not likely in the US where there is no reason for a radical rise in prices for coal and natural gas since both are bountiful resources. But in Europe, coal is very expensive to mine, and some European governments (the UK, Germany) phased out massive subsidies which led to mine closures (subsidies can be phased out if there is political will to do so). Moreover, natural gas from Russia is not only expensive but also heavily taxed by European governments, making it costly for consumers. Russian gas is also vulnerable to geopolitical risk of intentional interruptions in service (always during the coldest part of winter, of course) to encourage utility buyers to concede to an arbitrary price hike and revision of payment terms. (These interruptions have generally been associated with Ukraine not paying its gas bill to Russia.) To combat both high-priced coal and natural gas, biomass projects fueled by forests in Scandinavia are certainly feasible to consider as long as they operate on a sustainable basis where forest growth outpaces demand for wood products and biofuel.

Lithuania was entirely dependent on Russian natural gas. Its third largest city, Klaipeda, completed a combined heat and power plant of 60 mW fueled by biomass and waste that displaced 40 percent of Russian gas consumed in electricity generation.[24] This, along with building similar units in other cities and a LNG receiving terminal for an alternative supply of natural gas, plus interconnecting the nation's electricity grid with Sweden and Poland, may back out most of Russian natural gas imports. Other nations are looking at Lithuania as a blueprint for reducing dependence on Russian natural gas partially by substituting biomass for electricity generation.

If we take the position that carbon emissions contribute to climate change, which of itself represents a cost for those who link the two, then one can justify a tax on carbon emissions. A carbon emissions tax placed on burning fossil fuel to generate electricity would make sustainable biomass energy economically attractive because of its associated reduction in carbon emissions by replacement plant growth. If something on its own merits cannot be economically justified, then it can be made economically justifiable by discriminatory taxation. At the end of the 1970s, during the oil crisis, heating oil made up 90 percent of fuel for Swedish district heating plants utilizing combined heat and power plants that generate both electricity and hot water for apartment heating and commercial use. Sweden placed a carbon tax on fossil fuels to make renewables economically competitive. The effect of the carbon tax on district heating was that, by 2010, fossil fuel supplied 2 percent and 70 percent was supplied by forest products' waste and other sources of biomass, with the remainder natural gas.[25] Nevertheless, it would be preferable if technology could make something environmentally desirable also economically attractive without subsidy gimmicks of one sort or other. A principal argument against a carbon tax is that it raises the price of electricity to the point where it can have a negative impact on economic activity.

Even without technological breakthroughs, biomass energy is ideal for electricity generation in isolated areas in temperate and tropical regions, such as the island nations of Southeast Asia, sparely populated areas of South America, and non-arid areas of Africa not connected to an electric power grid. Micro-electricity generating plants could serve the local needs of such communities. Unfortunately, areas already facing deforestation would be worse off if biomass were to become a source of energy for generating electricity unless an associated tree or energy plant farm large enough to supply fuel to the plant on a sustainable basis was an integral part of the project. Micro-electricity generating plants dependent on sustainable sources of biomass fuel would provide basic services such as lighting and communications to a village and encourage cottage enterprises to provide jobs and amenities. This, of course, presumes that the people consider it a desirable outcome. Some indigenous people would rather continue living the way they have for countless generations than adopt the ways of modern society. And who is to say that they are wrong?

Biogas

In the presence of dissolved oxygen, aerobic microorganisms decompose biodegradable organic matter releasing carbon dioxide, water, and heat. In the absence of dissolved oxygen, an anaerobic digestion process takes place that releases carbon dioxide and methane, which can be collected as a fuel. Aerobic digestion normally occurs in compost heaps. Anaerobic digestion occurs wherever concentrations of organic matter accumulate in the absence of dissolved oxygen such as bottom sediments of lakes and ponds, swamps, peat bogs, and landfills.

A number of steps involving different microorganisms are necessary to produce biogas. It starts with a hydrolytic process that breaks down complex organic wastes into simpler components. Then fermentation transforms these organic components into short chains of fatty acids plus carbon dioxide and hydrogen. Next a syntrophic process converts the short chains of fatty acids to acetic acid, thereby releasing heat and more carbon dioxide and hydrogen. One type of bacterium converts the acetic acid to methane and carbon dioxide, while another type combines hydrogen with carbon dioxide to produce more methane. Still another bacterium reduces any sulfur compounds to hydrogen sulfide, which in turn reacts with any heavy metals that may be present to form insoluble salts. Thus, the simple process of decay turns out to be biologically and chemically complex: imagine the complexity of processes involved with new bio-based energy technologies!

Biogas from anaerobic decay is approximately two-thirds methane and one-third carbon dioxide and can be made from sewage, animal manure, and other organic matter such as wood chips, household refuse, and industrial organic waste. Biogas generation is very slow at ambient temperatures, but can be sped up by raising the temperature of the organic matter up to a point. Energy for heating is generated from organic decomposition, and, if necessary, a portion of the biogas production can be siphoned off and burned to further increase temperature. Gasification of raw sewage involves an initial screening to remove inorganic objects before being pumped into sedimentation tanks, where solid organic matter settles as sludge. Sludge is pumped into large anaerobic digester tanks where decomposition takes place at a heightened temperature. In about 2 months, half the sludge will be converted into gas. What is left can be dried and used as a fertilizer, burned as a fuel, or dumped into a landfill.[26] The public does not accept sludge from human waste as a desirable fertilizer for the backyard tomato patch and relatively little is burned as a fuel.

Most sludge from human sewage is buried in a landfill or dumped at sea mainly because the investment in anaerobic digester tanks is huge considering the 2-month stay time to reduce volume by half. But this has not stopped a waste treatment plant in Johannesburg, South Africa, from producing biogas from sludge to generate electricity. The plan is to expand capacity by four-fold to 4.5 mW to eliminate outside purchases of electricity.[27] The world's largest technologically advanced digestion plant generates enough electricity to supply 25,000 homes from the sewage of 1.2 million people in Manchester, England, that had formerly been dumped into the Irish Sea. The plant uses a thermal hydrolysis technology where waste input is heated to 165°C at high pressure. When pressure is suddenly released, organic substances are "smashed," releasing 50–60 percent more biogas than by conventional techniques. Gas is stored in large inflatable bags, then cleaned and fed as fuel to generate electricity. Remaining sludge is safe for use as free fertilizer or can be incinerated.[28] Another example is the UK retailer Sainsbury intending to power one of its supermarkets with 100 percent renewable electricity produced by methane from an anaerobic digester fed by biodegradable materials from its entire UK supermarket chain.[29]

Biogas generating systems are being set up where animal and poultry manure present a disposal problem. In the past, poultry, beef, and pig farms had sufficient land, fertilized by animal waste, to grow crops to be sustainable. Now spreading manure may be prohibited because runoff may be considered a contaminant of local streams. More importantly, modern poultry, beef, and pig farms are run like factories and buy their feed. This industrial approach to agriculture does not require much land. Animal waste normally kept in a void space eventually becomes a waste disposal problem, which can at least be partially offset by a biogas generator. For biogas to be an effective fuel, carbon dioxide has to be separated from methane, taking advantage of carbon dioxide being heavier than methane. Biogas is burned locally in a turbine or fed as a gaseous fuel into a specially adapted internal combustion engine to power a generator for local consumption of electricity. Biogas is not only a source of power for running the farm, but also reduces the volume of organic waste by half. What is left can be spread on fields, if permissible, dried and used as fertilizer, burned as a fuel, or disposed in a landfill.

Severn Trent, a British publicly traded water company, completed a treatment plant in 2014 that produces "green gas" from the human sewage of about 2.5 million people. Part of the methane gas from 16 anaerobic digesters is consumed within the company for fuel and the remainder (after treatment for smell) is fed into natural gas lines for public consumption. The company has significantly reduced its natural gas bill, and buyers of its methane gas are expected to see savings of about 5 percent in their billings. Severn Trent is not the first; Thames Water Utilities built a plant in 2010 that turns sludge into biogas. Severn Trent is building a plant that will turn food waste into energy, with plans to build others.[30]

Carbon dioxide emissions from generating and burning biogas are a closed carbon cycle. Human sewage comes from eating plants either as grain, vegetables, or fruits, or meat from plant-eating animals. Animal waste comes from plant food fed to animals. Biogas from human and animal waste is not a completely closed carbon cycle because growing and harvesting crops, processing and distributing food, and manufacturing fertilizer and pesticides require a great deal of fossil fuels in the form of gasoline, diesel fuel, natural gas, and also electricity, about three-quarters of which is generated by burning coal and natural gas. Nevertheless, biogas reduces carbon dioxide emissions by reducing fossil fuel demand.

Europe has taken the lead in producing biogas from organic matter, but biogas contributes less than 1 percent to electricity generation.[31] Finland is working on a number of renewable energy projects including biogas from anaerobic digestion of waste from sludge and biowaste from households and restaurants. Synthetic gas (syngas) made from wood biomass will supply fuel for city and airport busses and service trucks plus supplement natural gas.[32] These projects are economically feasible as they displace costly Russian gas, but probably still require some form of government assistance to bring them to fruition. Even if government assistance does not make these projects wholly competitive with Russian gas, the geopolitical risk associated with Russian gas is a consideration for paying a premium for biomass energy. The premium can be viewed as insurance against an interruption in Russian gas supplies. It then becomes a matter of judging whether the insurance is an economically attractive means of risk mitigation.

As organic matter decays in a landfill, biogas normally finds its way to the surface and disperses to the atmosphere. If landfill is covered with an impermeable layer of clay or plastic liner to prevent escape to the atmosphere, biogas can be extracted by sinking tubes into the landfill. Biogas can fuel an internal combustion engine or turbine to generate electricity for local use. The problem here is that a covered landfill is probably full and the investment must be justified by the amount of biogas generated from a finite and nonreplenishable source.

Disposal of Biowaste

In addition to disposing of sludge, disposing of garbage as biowaste is a major problem for the principal population centers of the world. Ocean dumping and landfills are not desirable ways to dispose of garbage. Ocean dumping off New York City has created a marine dead zone, and fish that live nearby have a high incidence of cancer and/or suffer from grotesque mutations, with their flesh containing a nice concoction of toxins. Landfills near metropolitan areas are usually undesirable, although they have a role to play in urban development. LaGuardia Airport in New York City is built on top of a landfill as are other airports, but a residential development built on top of a landfill might be a hard sell, although some exist. Time has a way of erasing memory of prior use for subsequent buyers of attractive tract homes carefully tendered and conveniently located near city centers that were originally constructed on top of landfills or cemeteries. Marshes buried under enormous mounds of garbage capped with a layer of soil are becoming less available near populated areas and are negatively perceived by the public. Now landfill sites may be hundreds of miles away from metropolitan areas, and trucking garbage that distance cannot be cheap.

There is an alternative to transforming picturesque countryside into landfills. Modern garbage disposal starts with separating recyclables such as paper, cardboard, and items made from plastic, glass, aluminum, tin, and other metals. Recycling reduces energy intensity because glass and aluminum require 90 percent less energy when made from glass and aluminum scrap than from sand and bauxite. Paper and cardboard made from paper trash and steel made from scrap also require a lot less energy than making paper from trees and steel from iron ore and coal. After removing recyclable waste, what remains can be burned to produce steam, which can be superheated by also burning natural gas to enhance turbine efficiency for generating electricity. Garbage is ultimately reduced to ash, a small fraction of its former volume, which can be buried in a landfill.

Though this may be considered an attractive means of disposing of garbage, it is also costly to build an electricity generating plant that runs on garbage. However, fuel is not only free, but a charge for disposing of garbage becomes another source of revenue in addition to selling electricity. Even so, revenue from selling electricity and disposing of garbage may not be sufficient to justify the investment. Burning garbage does not generate nearly the same amount of electricity as burning coal or natural gas. Communities may still find it cheaper to dump garbage in the ocean or ship it to a distant landfill rather than pay for it to be burned under controlled conditions for generating electricity.

As long as there is no cost associated with dumping garbage into the ocean or in transforming the countryside into landfills, other than shipping and dumping fees, there is an economic incentive for municipalities to continue doing business as usual. An environmental degradation tax would internalize the cost of external damage to the environment by dumping garbage in the ocean or in landfills and make these alternatives more costly. If this were done, then sharp-eyed pencil pushers determining whether to pay shipping and dumping or landfill fees along with an associated environmental degradation tax, versus using a garbage burning electricity generating plant without an environmental degradation tax, might have a change of heart. As long as pencil pushers are weighing the relative merits of alternatives strictly in terms of dollars and cents, then internalizing an externality (putting a cost on environment degradation) is a way to sway these single-focused individuals to select an environmentally sound way to dispose of garbage. Persuasive arguments and appeals to their better nature mean little when there is a cheaper, though less desirable, alternative.

In one way it is unfortunate that pencil pushers make decisions by scribbling figures on a pad of paper without thought to social or environmental consequences; but in another way, it is fortunate. You can depend on their making a decision based on selecting the least cost alternative, and this makes it relatively easy to shape their decisions. All one has to do to make a desirable outcome attractive is to ensure that it is the least cost alternative, which an environmental degradation tax would do. Moreover, the proceeds of the tax can be dedicated to funding the building of environmentally sound garbage disposal plants whose output of electricity would reduce the need to burn fossil fuels. Such a simple solution to a complex problem seems to escape human attention. Unfortunately, in the case of local garbage burning electricity generating plants, the not-in-my-backyard syndrome makes it difficult to site plants within city limits where they belong from a logistics standpoint. Another drawback has been the discovery that these plants emit mercury and other noxious metal fumes from burning discarded batteries and electronic gear found in household trash. However, a modern waste-to-energy plant can incorporate features that remove most of the nitrogen oxide, mercury and dioxins, acid gas, and particulates.[33]

The US Air Force has been underwriting the development of a garbage-in, energy-out plasma gasification system that transforms 10 tons of garbage daily to 350 kW sufficient to run the test plant. A mechanical shredder reduces garbage to 2-inch lengths that are transferred by an air-tight auger to an oxygen-poor gasification chamber where two graphite electrodes generate an arc of electricity at 9,000°F. The resulting plasma, or cloud of ionized particles, reduces wood, plastic, medical waste, polychlorinated biphenyls, asbestos, hazardous hydrocarbons, and any other organic material to a syngas of hydrogen and carbon monoxide. Metals and glass are liquefied into a molten pool at the bottom of the chamber. The bottommost layer is liquid metals, which are drawn off and recycled. The layer of silica above the liquid metal is also drawn off, cooled, and used as construction aggregate. Manufactured syngas exits the furnace and in this test plant generates enough electricity for sustainable operations. In commercial applications, syngas would be transformed not just to electricity but also various fuels via the Fischer-Tropsch process. Another advantage is that conventional incinerators emit dioxin and furan, mercury, and other harmful emissions, which the plasma gasification system can cut by 99 percent. This system is being scaled up by Fulcrum BioEnergy to handle 200,000 tons of garbage annually, whose syngas will produce 10 million gallons of transportation fuels (jet fuel, diesel) at a cost equivalent to $50 per barrel crude oil. The plant is expected to be in operation in 2016.[34] If the technology and economics prove successful, there would be no need for further landfills for municipal waste.

Tapping Biomass for Electricity Generation

Brazil has been a model nation in having a national energy policy aimed at reducing the consumption of fossil fuels in electricity generation by developing low-cost hydropower resources. Its original goal was to have hydropower supply all the nation's electricity needs until a drought in 2002 caused severe power outages throughout the nation. Faced with the need to find alternative backup ways to generate electricity, Brazil turned to natural gas. Brazil decided to build pipelines to tap natural gas fields in Bolivia, Argentina, and remote regions of the Amazon, and to import natural gas in a liquefied state. Rather than pursue electricity generating plants fueled by largely imported natural gas, why not plant sustainable tree farms to supply biomass fueled electricity generating plants? Biomass seems to be a neglected fuel for large-scale generation of electricity in Brazil. Bolivia's nationalization of its natural gas reserves in 2006, which caused Petrobras, the national oil company of Brazil, to lose a significant amount of money, should have induced Brazil to view biomass in terms of energy security much as we view coal, but apparently not.

The UN Development Programme (UNDP) is responsible for implementing UN conventions on biological diversity and climate change. Global Environment Facility, the financing arm of the UNDP, has funded, along with private corporate support, the developmental stage of a biomass integrated gasification/gas turbine (BIG/GT) in Brazil fueled by wood chips from tree plantations. Brazil already leads the world in having huge pine and eucalyptus tree plantations for paper pulp. BIG/GT transforms wood chips into a clean burning gas and steam, both of which can be used to generate electricity. BIG/GT plants would create many more jobs in planting and harvesting trees than hydropower and natural gas plants over their project lives. If proven commercially and technologically feasible, BIG/GT installations can be sized to serve local communities and built wherever there is land fit for growing trees on a sustainable basis to avoid deforestation.

A centralized electricity generating system requires high-density population centers to financially support the construction of large conventional plants with long-distance transmission lines. Such systems cannot economically serve remote areas of the Philippines, Indonesia, Malaysia, and Africa, but a distributive electricity generating system, such as BIG/GT, can be sized for the local population and be fueled by sustainable tree farms to neutralize carbon dioxide emissions. Yet micro-electricity, biomass-fueled plants, capable of serving the needs of about one to two billion people dispersed in low-density population areas outside the main power grids, have made little progress. Even those villages with biomass-fueled plants for local industrial activities such as lumber mills and food processing plants are, for the most part, without electricity for light and comfort. One would think that generating electricity for a lumber mill or a food processing plant would be scaled up to supply power to a local community. This should be a no-brainer, but is not being done. It could be recognition that few in the village can pay for the electricity no matter how low its price. The absence of electricity prevents the development of cottage enterprises that provide basic amenities and goods along with paying jobs to buy these amenities and goods and pay for the electricity that they require. No electricity keeps people hopelessly locked in poverty. But supplying electricity would induce development of cottage enterprises that would provide income and jobs to pay for electricity after the fact. This is a clear case of chicken and egg: free or heavily subsidized electricity must come first before there is sufficient economic development that would provide a means to pay for it.

One would think that building a micro-electricity generating plant fueled by freely available biomass in a remote village would be a high-priority item for governments in pursuit of social and economic development, but this is apparently not the case. All one sees is a fairly uniform lack of progress. However, if BIG/GT technology proves technologically and commercially feasible, distributive BIG/GT installations serving local needs along with solar and wind could contribute to the economic development of large areas of the world that cannot be served by conventional electricity generating grids. But this depends on external financing, which, other than a few showcase projects, is apparently not readily available.

A proposal has been made for opuntia or nopal, a prickly pear cactus, to be a biomass crop for biogas production. Prickly pear cactus pads degrade five to ten times faster than manure, and only 4 hectares of the opuntia can produce an estimated 800 cubic meters of biogas per day. It is estimated that as much as 2.5 kWh of methane can be obtained from 1 kg of dry opuntia. Opuntia grows to maturity in 1–3 years and then harvested, chopped, and consumed by methanogenic bacteria in anaerobic digesters releasing a 50–50 mixture of methane and carbon dioxide.[35]

Biofuels

Biofuels are bioethanol and biodiesel; bioethanol will be handled first. Ethanol can be made in an oil refinery by the catalytic hydration of ethylene with sulfuric acid as a catalyst and also from coal gas, but fossil fuel derived ethanol is used almost exclusively for industrial purposes and only accounts for 5 percent of world ethanol production. "Ethanol" herein refers to hydrous bioethanol (around 5 percent water) and anhydrous bioethanol (no more than 1 percent water). Anhydrous bioethanol is the same as 200-proof White Lightning whisky (100 percent ethyl alcohol) except being denatured with 2–5 percent gasoline or natural gas liquids to make it unfit for human consumption (if one considers White Lightning fit for human consumption!). Hydrous ethanol can be used as a 100 percent substitute for gasoline, or E100 (technically E95 taking denaturing into consideration). Brazilian automobiles that run on E100 consume hydrous ethanol, which is cheaper than anhydrous ethanol, as the final drying process of removing residual water is not necessary. Gasohol, a mixture of gasoline and ethanol, requires anhydrous ethanol. Ethanol figures exclude alcoholic beverages and ethanol found in consumer products such as cosmetics, paints, and ink, and consumed in commercial and industrial processes.[36]

As seen in Figure 3.1, Brazil and the US account for 83 percent of world ethanol production and the US has overtaken Brazil as the world's largest producer.[37] US and

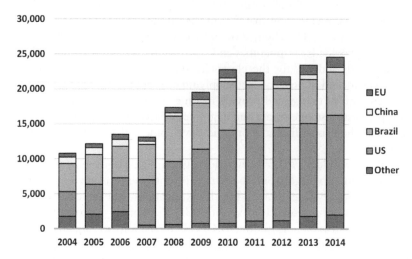

Figure 3.1 Global Ethanol Production (million gallons)

Brazilian production were even in 2005, but since then, Brazilian production increased about 45 percent, whereas US production has grown 235 percent. Global ethanol production increased 7.8 percent between 2010 and 2014, reflecting 2 years of declines and 2 years of advances. Other contributors are Canada, India, Thailand, and Argentina.

The US relies on corn (maize) to produce ethanol, whereas Brazil relies on sugar. Although the US is in first place, Brazil has much greater potential to expand sugarcane production than the US has in further converting corn to ethanol. Comparing ethanol production in Figure 3.1 with oil consumption in *BP Energy Statistics* for 2014, ethanol is estimated to be about 9.8 percent of gasoline in the US, 31.3 percent in Brazil, and 4.4 percent of global gasoline. In 2013 the US was pushing against the 10 percent limit of ethanol in gasoline imposed by warranties issued by automobile engine manufacturers, the so-called blend wall. While the Energy Independence and Security Act of 2007 required increasing amounts of alternative fuels for transportation fuel, the US Environmental Protection Agency (EPA) proposed a lower volume of renewable fuels, which is mainly ethanol, of 13.4 billion gallons in 2015 and 14 billion gallons in 2016 versus actual production of 14.3 billion gallons in 2014. This had to be done because mandated consumption of ethanol was up against the blend wall; that is, there was no room left to absorb ethanol in the gasoline stream. With Brazil showing modest growth in the last few years, it will be up to the EU, Canada, India, and other nations to pick up the slack to meet the *World Energy Outlook* forecast for the role of biofuels in 2035. However, a fall in the international price of sugar and a rise in crude oil prices would significantly increase Brazilian ethanol production. Moreover, the *World Energy Outlook* forecast includes biodiesel, whose growth could contribute to achieving the forecast.

The process for making ethanol was well established in ancient Egypt when beer was the common beverage for working people, just as it is today throughout the world where alcohol consumption is allowed. Distillation of wine to raise the alcohol content was discovered by the Chinese around 3000 BCE, reaching its zenith as 200-proof first recorded in the eighth and ninth centuries in eastern Europe, today known as vodka.

Interestingly, the distillation process for making whisky was adapted in the earliest days of the oil industry to refine kerosene from crude oil, and the same barrel for aging, storing, and shipping whisky became the proverbial 42-gallon barrel of oil.

Ethanol is a renewable transportation fuel that adds carbon dioxide to the earth's atmosphere to the extent that fossil fuels are consumed in its production and transportation. If ethanol could be produced without fossil fuels, then its contribution to carbon emissions would be hypothetically zero as the carbon dioxide released during combustion would be absorbed by replacement plant growth. But this is not the case. In the US, other than ethanol proponents, many observers believe that ethanol made from corn represents only a marginal reduction in carbon emissions, while others believe that ethanol actually increases carbon emissions when fossil fuels associated with its production are fully taken into account. If it can be shown that ethanol increases carbon emissions, then there is no longer any justification from an environmental point of view. From an energy point of view, ethanol can be justified to the extent that it reduces reliance on oil imports. Producing ethanol in Brazil from sugar is effective both in cutting carbon emissions and in reducing reliance on oil imports.

Photosynthesis absorbs energy from sunlight to convert carbon dioxide and water to glucose (sugar), the simplest form of carbohydrate, and oxygen:

$$6CO_2 + 6H_2O + \text{Light (photosynthesis)} \rightarrow C_6H_{12}O_6 + 6O_2$$

The fermentation process decomposes glucose into ethanol and carbon dioxide:

$$C_6H_{12}O_6 \rightarrow 2C_2H_6O + 2CO_2$$

The chemical formula for ethanol is sometimes written as C_2H_5OH; either way, ethanol reacts with oxygen during combustion to produce energy that can power an engine along with the waste products of carbon dioxide and water:

$$2C_2H_6O + 6O_2 \rightarrow \text{Energy} + 4CO_2 + 6H_2O$$

One difference between ethanol and gasoline is that the ethanol molecule contains oxygen, whereas gasoline is a blend of hydrocarbons ranging from C_5H_{12} to $C_{12}H_{26}$. Ethanol is an oxygenate that improves fuel combustion, reducing carbon monoxide, unburned hydrocarbons, and particulate emissions in comparison to gasoline. However, some oxygen in ethanol reacts with atmospheric nitrogen during combustion, producing ozone-forming nitrous oxides, the precursor to smog. Ethanol has no sulfur emissions and is a cleaner-burning fuel than gasoline with 13 percent less emissions even with its higher nitrous oxide emissions. Moreover, ethanol, along with biodiesel, is biodegradable if spilled on the ground. Biofuels are eligible for carbon credits where a cap and trade program has been instituted for reducing carbon emissions.

Though theoretically carbon-neutral, ethanol is not carbon-neutral when netted of fossil fuels consumed during planting and harvesting. In the US, fossil fuels are also consumed in pesticide and fertilizer production and distribution and in converting corn to ethanol and distributing the end product. Both natural gas and electricity are needed to run ethanol producing plants where electricity is 75 percent derived from burning coal and natural gas. At best, US ethanol production is a means to convert fossil fuels (coal, natural gas, and oil) to a gasoline substitute. The major difference between the US and Brazil is that sugar requires less energy than starch to be converted to ethanol and that bagasse is burned to generate electricity for the ethanol conversion process.

But fossil fuel (petrodiesel) is still consumed for agricultural activities and transportation of sugarcane and ethanol. While Brazilian ethanol is more effective as a substitute for gasoline consumption and in reducing carbon emissions than US ethanol, it will become more so when biodiesel is substituted for petrodiesel for agricultural activities and transportation.

The energy content of 87 octane gasoline is around 115,000 Btu per gallon versus 76,000 Btu per gallon for ethanol (E100).[38] On an energy equivalent basis, ethanol requires about 1.5 gallons to be burned to obtain the same energy output as 1 gallon of gasoline. But ethanol has a higher octane rating of 98–100 compared to 86–94 for gasoline. The higher octane improves engine performance by reducing engine knocks, which occur from premature fuel combustion during acceleration or pulling a heavy load. The higher octane of ethanol is cleaner burning and better performing and improves engine power by about 5 percent. Taking both factors into consideration, an automobile burning E100 ethanol will get 70 percent of the mileage of one burning gasoline. In other words, a car getting 30 miles per gallon on gasoline would be expected to get 21 miles per gallon on pure ethanol. The reduction in mileage from burning gasohol is directly related to its ethanol content. Besides lower mileage, another drawback of a high percentage of ethanol in gasoline is difficulty in cold weather starts.

Ethanol requires special conditions for shipping and storage. The existing pipeline and storage infrastructure system for oil products is unsuitable for ethanol, which has an affinity for water. If gasohol is carried in petroleum pipelines and absorbs residual moisture, a phase separation occurs making it virtually impossible to reblend ethanol with gasoline. Ethanol is also a solvent that absorbs rust, gums, and other contaminants in piping and storage tanks, making it unfit to be a motor vehicle fuel. Depending on the metallurgy of the pipeline, it is possible for ethanol's electrical conductivity to increase corrosion rates. Ethanol in gasohol can also strip off certain corrosion inhibitor coatings on the interior surface of pipelines and promote stress corrosion cracking. Another problem with moving ethanol in petroleum pipelines is that it is much more difficult to segregate batches of ethanol–gasoline blends. Petroleum pipelines operate on the principle of fungible products where what is shipped by a seller may not be what is received by a buyer. However, the buyer is assured that what is received has the same specifications of what was purchased. Batches of various blends of gasohol are not fungible because they cannot be easily identified and separated for final delivery to the buyer.

Ethanol and gasohol can be carried in dedicated pipelines built to withstand the technical challenges posed by ethanol. In the US, the logical ethanol pipeline would run from the Midwest to the Northeast, with entry points at various centers of corn growing regions for delivery of ethanol to markets in Chicago, Philadelphia, and New York City. The associated pipeline toll for building an ethanol pipeline must reflect the cost and time hurdles of obtaining government environmental approvals and permits, a high capital cost to reflect the special nature of handling ethanol, and the most likely throughput volume. Of vital concern is the question of whether the resulting pipeline toll provides a clear economic advantage over the present logistics system; if not, the pipeline cannot be economically justified.

The present logistics system does not involve pipelines, but tank trucks, rail tank cars, barges, and tankers. Ethanol is shipped in tank trucks for short-distance movements within the Midwest from ethanol plants, not to refineries but to distribution points, where ethanol is "splashed" into gasoline being pumped into tank trucks for final delivery to retail filling stations. Rail tank cars ship ethanol to distribution points beyond the Midwest. Ethanol is also moved on inland waterway barges down the Mississippi River to terminals for transfer to tankers for export and to coastal barges to serve US east and west coast port terminals for final delivery by tank trucks to gasoline distribution points. Ethanol shipments in tankers do not require double hulls as do petroleum products. Double hulls reduce the chance of a spill because petroleum spills are highly polluting, whereas ethanol spills are biodegradable. The cost to move ethanol or any liquid is lowest by vessel, if possible, then in ascending order, pipeline, barge, and rail, with truck being a factor of up to 10 times more expensive than rail for long hauls.

History of Ethanol as a Motor Vehicle Fuel

The history of the nonalcoholic use of ethanol started as a fuel for lighting in the nineteenth century. In the 1850s, nearly 90 million gallons of pure ethanol were consumed annually as a fuel for lamps. In 1862 an excise tax on alcoholic beverages of $2 per gallon knocked ethanol out of the lighting market for the benefit of other sources such as kerosene, whale oil, and methanol. The reason why the tax applied to all ethanol was that tax authorities were unable to monitor whether ethanol was being drunk or burned in a lamp.

Early automobile engines ran on a variety of fuels including ethanol, such as Nicholas Otto's first spark-ignition engine and Henry Ford's first automobiles in 1896. With repeal of the liquor tax in 1906, Ford wanted ethanol to be the fuel of choice for his Model Ts to counter a farming depression.[39] Converting grain to alcohol would create incremental demand, raising its price to improve the living standards of farmers plus boosting rural job opportunities, the same benefits espoused by biofuel aficionados today. The problem facing Ford was the oil industry built on kerosene for lighting. At the turn of the century, kerosene faced a dim future with the invention of Edison's electric light bulb. Naphtha, the light end of the refining process, was considered a waste product often dumped into the nearest stream. The advent of the automobile meant salvation to the oil industry. A new market in gasoline made from the waste product naphtha would be a substitute for a declining market in kerosene.

Cheap gasoline forced Ford to modify the Model T in 1908 to have two fuel tanks—one for ethanol and the other for gasoline. The carburetor was adjustable for either fuel or a mix of the two, the precursor of today's flex fuel vehicles. Ford and Standard Oil entered into a partnership to distribute corn-based ethanol blended with gasoline. In the 1920s, gasohol represented about 25 percent of Standard Oil's sales in the corn growing region under the brand Alcogas. But as time went on, gasoline became the motor fuel of choice with ethanol primarily an additive for better engine performance. Prohibition, which lasted from 1919 to 1933, made it illegal for farmers to produce ethanol from the family still for any purpose including being a fuel. Tetraethyl lead took over ethanol's role as an antiknock agent. After the repeal of prohibition, bioethanol again became part of the gasoline stream. With falling corn prices during the 1930s depression, Midwest states sought alternative uses for farm products. Alcolene and Agrol were gasoline blends ranging between 5 and 17.5 percent ethanol sold in 2,000 retail outlets from Indiana to South Dakota. Nonetheless, the oil industry lobbied against blending of alcohol in gasoline, as the Depression worsened the financial prospects for oil. Interest in ethanol waned after the Second World War as it could not compete against gasoline. But interest revived in the wake of the 1970s oil crisis beginning with Brazil's National Alcohol Program (ProAlcool).

Why Sugar?

The agricultural feedstock of choice for ethanol is sugar, also known as glucose, the simplest form of carbohydrates. The human body can easily convert sugar to energy. White refined sugar has virtually no nutritional value, while brown sugar, a less refined state of white sugar, retains some vitamins and minerals. Molasses is the residue of the sugar refining process and is mixed with cattle feed or fermented under controlled conditions to produce rum or mixed with water for another run through the ethanol making process. Sugar causes tooth decay by metabolizing into an acid that eats away at tooth enamel and contributes to obesity, diabetes, and perhaps hyperactivity when consumed in excess. Sugar may not be a good food, but is sure a good biofuel!

The history of sugar by the evaporation of sugarcane juice can be traced back to 500 BCE in India. From there it spread to the Middle East and China. Arabs and Berbers introduced Europeans to sugar during their conquest of the Iberian Peninsula in the eighth century. Crusaders brought sugarcane plants back with them on their return to Europe where, in the fourteenth century, advances in sugar presses made it economical to grow sugar in southern Spain and Portugal, and from there to the Canary Islands and Azores. Spanish and Portuguese explorers and early settlers introduced sugarcane to the Caribbean and Brazil, both perfect environments for growing sugarcane whose low cost undercut supplies from Asia and Europe. Market demand for sugar and molasses in Europe and North America provided rich rewards for growers, but there was a shortage of labor. Native Americans could not survive the rigors of working in the sugar plantations, but Africans could—the economic impetus for the slave trade. Sugarcane rapidly exhausts soil of its nutrients, which was addressed by abandoning nutrient-depleted land and bringing new land into cultivation. Before Castro, Cuba was a major producer of sugar not only from its favorable growing conditions but also from the technological leadership displayed by Cuban sugar growers on how to optimally apply fertilizers to prevent soil exhaustion and how to improve the sugar-making process to reduce costs—knowledge that spread throughout the world of sugar. Today much of these capital investments in sugar processing plants lie in ruins or operate with equipment more than a half century old. Technological leadership displayed by Cuban sugar growers may be an historical footnote in Cuba, but not necessarily a footnote in other Caribbean nations. A similar story can be told about cigar making.

Discovery of sucrose in sugar beets and the process for making sugar from sugar beets occurred in Europe in the 1700s, but its cost was not competitive with imported sugar from sugarcane. Napoleon, when cut off from sugar imports by the British blockade, banned sugar imports (interesting timing), which provided the economic impetus for advancing the technology to convert sugar beets to sugar. Sugarcane is grown in tropical and subtropical regions, whereas sugar beets are grown in temperate regions of the Northern Hemisphere. Sugar from sugarcane is cheaper than from sugar beets, even though sugar beets have a higher sucrose yield, because the process of separating sugar from sugar beets is more complicated. Sugar production is estimated to be 173.4 million metric tons for 2015/2016, down from a peak of 177 million metric tons in 2012/2013. Over 100 nations grow sugar, of which about 80 percent come from sugarcane and the remainder sugar beets. Figure 3.2 shows the world's top 11 producers, accounting for 78 percent of world sugar production.

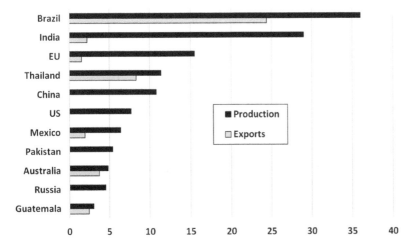

Figure 3.2 2015/2016 Estimated Sugar Production and Exports (million tons)

Total exports are 55.8 million tons, or 32 percent of production. Figure 3.2 shows the relationship between production and exports for the major sugar producers.[40] Brazil is by far the world's largest producer (20 percent of world production) and exporter of sugar (43 percent of world exports). Brazil as a nation exports 71 percent of its production as sugar or ethanol. Thailand exports 72 percent of its production, Australia 77 percent, and Guatemala 80 percent. Larger producers such as India and the EU export little of their production. The cost of production for sugar from sugar cane and sugar beets in Euros per metric ton is in Figure 3.3.[41]

The lowest cost sugar producer is Brazil by far, with other low-cost producers being Australia, Thailand, and South Africa. India is a medium-cost producer. The cost of sugar from sugar beets is significantly higher than that of sugar from sugar cane, with Poland the lowest and Germany the highest cost sugar producer. The US is a high-cost producer of sugar from sugarcane and sugar beets. The EU, the US, and Japan protect their domestic sugar growers by imposing high tariffs on imports.

Brazil—The Great Leap Forward for Biofuels

The development of the ethanol industry in Brazil was not entrepreneurial in nature, but was nurtured by decades of an active pro-ethanol energy policy pursued and financially supported by the government. In 1975 Brazil imported much of its oil needs, aggravating its negative balance of trade. Brazil also had a social challenge of doing something about the enormous numbers of unemployed workers in the rural Center-South and North-Northeast regions of Brazil. The solution for both problems was bioethanol. The Brazilian government implemented a program to stimulate ethanol production to reduce reliance on imported oil, provide job opportunities for large numbers of unemployed workers, and convert fallow land to agricultural use. The government provided billions of dollars in low-interest loans for entrepreneurs and landowners to finance the construction

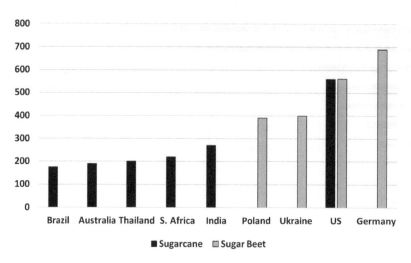

Figure 3.3 Cost of Sugar Production (Euros per metric ton)

of ethanol production plants and convert mostly fallow and underutilized grazing land to sugarcane plantations.

The government also required Petroleo Brasileiro SA (Petrobras), the state oil company, to purchase ethanol to blend a vehicle fuel with a minimum of 22 percent ethanol (E22). Petrobras had to refit its gasoline stations to sell gasoline, gasohol, and pure ethanol. A differential tax was placed on motor vehicle fuels to ensure that hydrous ethanol sold initially at a 65 percent discount from the price of gasoline. This, along with tax incentives to purchase automobiles fueled by hydrous ethanol, provided a clear incentive for Brazilians to buy automobiles that ran on E100. Ethanol consumption grew rapidly from 1983 to 1988, with 90 percent of new car sales being pure ethanol vehicles. By 1990, over five million pure ethanol vehicles made up about half of the population of the motor vehicle fleet. The subsidy on ethanol was eventually reduced to 35 percent, making the ethanol price competitive with gasoline on an energy content basis.

The Brazilian automobile industry had to modify engines to burn high concentrations of ethanol in gasoline or pure ethanol by eliminating materials such as aluminum, zinc, brass, and lead whose metal deposits from ethanol would eventually damage an engine. Nonmetallic materials that cannot come in contact with ethanol include natural rubber, polyurethane, cork gasket material, leather, polyvinyl chloride polyamides, methyl-methacrylate, and certain thermal plastics. Fiberglass reinforced with nonmetallic thermoset was found suitable for the storage and piping of ethanol in automobiles. Conventional automobiles can burn gasohol of 10 percent ethanol (E10) with no modifications. For automobiles to burn between E10 and E25, modifications may have to be made to the fuel injection, pump, pressure device, filter, tank, and catalytic converter, along with the ignition and evaporative systems, depending on the automobile design. Between E25 and E85, further modifications may have to be made to the basic engine design and the intake manifold and exhaust systems. A cold-start system may have to be installed for automobiles to burn E100.

A metric ton of sugarcane (2,205 pounds) can produce either 305 pounds of refined sugar or 21 gallons of ethanol. Although Brazilian sugarcane growers are free to sell to either the sugar or ethanol market, whichever is more profitable, Petrobras is required to buy ethanol to ensure that the regulatory minimum content of ethanol in gasoline is satisfied. This creates the market for ethanol. However, during the latter part of the 1980s and 1990s, Petrobras discovered offshore oilfields which promised to eventually make Brazil self-sufficient in oil, reducing the negative trade balance associated with oil imports. Moreover, the price of oil fell significantly in the mid-1980s from the crisis levels of the late 1970s and early 1980s. The decline in oil imports and oil prices weakened the government's resolve to support biofuels. In 1988 the government permitted the free export of sugar to reduce the amount of subsidies being paid to ethanol producers. As sugarcane growers diverted sugar to the international export market to take advantage of higher prices, ethanol producers were squeezed between a high cost for their raw material input and a low price for their output. The fall in ethanol production in the 1990s was so great that Brazil became the world's largest ethanol importer. But imports were not enough to avert shortages, which resulted in a loss of consumer confidence in pure ethanol burning automobiles. Brazilians switching from pure ethanol to gasohol burning automobiles ended the era of pure ethanol automobiles.

In 2000 Brazil deregulated the ethanol market and removed all subsidies, but depending on market conditions, motor vehicle fuels were required to be blended with a minimum of 20–25 percent ethanol. Brazil stopped importing ethanol and became an exporter. Flex fuel vehicles were introduced in 2003 that could run on straight ethanol, straight gasoline, or a blend of the two—the same as Henry Ford's early Model Ts. This protected Brazilian drivers from the vicissitudes that had previously plagued pure ethanol burning vehicles. New cars built in Brazil are flex fuel, with 12 automobile manufacturers offering Brazilians a choice of 90 models. The 2012 fleet of automobiles, which includes all previously built automobiles, is 51 percent flex fuel, 47 percent gasoline, and 2 percent pure ethanol. The 2020 projected fleet is 81 percent flex fuel, 18 percent gasoline, and 1 percent pure ethanol, reflecting the preponderance of flex fuel automobiles being built in Brazil.[42]

Filling stations have pumps for gasoline, ethanol, or ethanol-blend (gasohol). Motorists can choose what makes best sense for them, which means that the competitive price of pure ethanol must be at a 30 percent discount from gasoline to reflect its lower energy content. Automobile drivers can play the arbitrage game as the price of gasoline changes with respect to the price of crude oil and ethanol with respect to the price of sugar. Most ethanol distilleries are part of sugar mill complexes, and their owners can also play the arbitrage game between shifting prices for ethanol and sugar by the portion of sugar sold as sugar or ethanol. Advocates of bioethanol in the US point out that it would be necessary to copy the Brazilian model of having most gasoline stations offering both ethanol (E85) and gasoline and for auto manufacturers to produce mostly flex fuel cars before bioethanol can play a significant role as a substitute for gasoline.

Figure 3.4 shows oil consumption in Brazil in millions of barrels per day (Bpd) from 1965 to 2014. The conclusion one may reach is that the impact of bioethanol has been to interrupt growth in oil demand between 2000 and 2007, but that the historic growth rate has been restored and in fact appears to be accelerating as Brazil, a member of the BRIC nations, is undergoing rapid economic development.

About 40 percent of oil consumption goes into gasoline that is then mixed with ethanol. Ethanol does not affect the consumption of diesel and jet fuel, lubes, petrochemical feedstocks, and fuel oil. However, ethanol can be substituted for high-octane aviation gasoline to power prop-driven airplanes. Eleven hundred Brazilian crop dusters, about

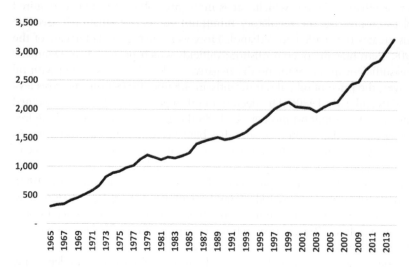

Figure 3.4 Oil Consumption in Brazil (million Bpd)

75 percent manufactured by Ipanema, have logged about one million hours of flight time on pure ethanol.[43] The energy density of ethanol is too low for commercial jet engines, but a blend of biodiesel and jet fuel has been successfully tested by several major airlines.

At the beginning of 2012, two important changes were made with respect to US ethanol subsidies that affected Brazil. One was a $0.45 per gallon Volumetric Ethanol Excise Tax Credit that basically meant that ethanol did not have to pay the gasoline excise tax. This was a major price support for US ethanol producers. The other subsidy was a discriminatory tariff on imported ethanol only from Brazil of $0.54 cents per gallon. This was to protect US ethanol producers from Brazilian competition. Both subsidies had expiration dates that required Congress to pass new legislation for the subsidies to remain in place. Since Congress chose not to act, they simply expired. The expiration of both subsidies placed the price of ethanol in the US and Brazil on the same footing, which meant that Brazilian ethanol was worth a dollar a gallon more in 2012 than in 2011.[44] On the surface, this could be a major impetus for Brazilian exports to the US.

Before 2012, in response to a distinct economic disincentive for exporting to the US, Petrobras embarked on an aggressive plan to seek ethanol outlets in Japan and China and other nations that viewed bioethanol as a means to reduce reliance on imported oil. Europe was looked upon as a potential export market to fulfill the EU objective of having renewables supplying 20 percent of energy needs by 2020. In 2012 almost half (49 percent) of Brazilian sugar production was converted to ethanol, amounting to 20 billion liters. Of this, three billion liters (15 percent of production) were exported where the largest market was, not Asia or Europe but the US, receiving two billion liters.[45] The reason for this was that sugar-based ethanol could most economically fulfill EPA's advanced biofuels mandate, which designated sugar-based ethanol not made in the US as an advanced biofuel.

In 2013, US ethanol producers were facing a blend wall that placed pressure on US ethanol imports until this problem was resolved. Moreover, there was growing opposition to biofuels in Europe in reaction to the perceived impact of biofuels on food production and doubt over the effectiveness of biofuels to cut greenhouse gas emissions.[46] This has a major ramification on the projected *World Energy Outlook* growth of biofuel consumption. Clearly a significant global ethanol export market has not yet developed, nor is apt to develop, taking a lot of the air out of the slogan "Brazil, the Saudi Arabia of Ethanol."

Though sugar production in Brazil is free of subsidies, there is still a subsidy by Brazilian government to support research programs to improve sugarcane varieties and fertilizer applications. New varieties have been developed to make sugarcane more resistant to drought and pests while yielding higher sugar content. There are now over 500 commercial varieties of sugarcane, but only 20 are used for 80 percent of sugarcane production. Diversification of varieties is essential for pest and disease control. Rapid replacement of varieties has stemmed highly damaging disease epidemics. While pesticides are used to control damaging insects, Brazil's first line of defense is biological countermeasures such as parasitoids to control sugarcane beetles and certain fungi to control spittlebugs. In 30 years, the yield of sugar from sugarcane increased from 55 tons per acre in 1975 to over 90 tons per acre in 2003 with a 14.6 percent sugar content, which of itself has increased by 8 percent between 1975 and 2000. As a result of this government investment in research, ethanol yields increased from 242 gallons per acre in the 1970s to 593 gallons per acre in the late 1990s. The success of this research program has more than paid for itself. Oh, that other government programs could make such positive contributions!

Waste products of making sugar from sugarcane are bagasse and vinasse. Bagasse is the residue of sugarcane stalks after the sugar is extracted. Electricity produced by burning bagasse is estimated to be 1,350 mW as compared to Brazil's Angra I nuclear power plant of 657 mW (a typical large coal or nuclear electricity generating plant is about twice this size). Most of the electricity is consumed internally (1,200 mW) for converting sugar to ethanol and the remaining 150 mW is sold to electric utilities. This electricity is generated during the dry season when hydropower, the principal source of electricity in Brazil, operates at reduced capacity. Electricity output could be enhanced by replacing low-pressure steam boilers with more efficient high-pressure boilers. Mechanization in harvesting sugarcane has increased the volume of biomass that can be burned for electricity generation by eliminating burning of sugarcane fields. Burning bagasse for electricity generation produces little ash and no sulfur, and its nitrous oxide emissions are low as bagasse is burned at relatively low temperatures. Bagasse is also sold to other processing industries as a substitute for burning heavy fuel oil.

Vinasse is a liquid residue from alcohol distillation. Every liter of ethanol produces 10 to 15 liters of vinasse, which contains high levels of organic matter, potassium, and calcium, and moderate amounts of nitrogen and phosphorus absorbed by sugarcane. The volume of vinasse is about the same as the entire sewage waste of Brazil and was initially dumped into streams and rivers, resulting in algae blooms and fish kills. With a similar chemical composition to fertilizer, it is now spread on the ground along with another waste product, filtercake, and other waste water from making ethanol. Application of vinasse is optimized for the soil and environmental conditions in order to reduce the amount of fertilizer required for sugarcane cultivation—an example of fertilizer recycling. Spraying vinasse on soil can also be for irrigation, but Brazil is fortunate in having sufficient rainfall to support this water-intensive crop. As a counterpoint, irrigation in the sugar growing region in India is depleting the water table—clearly a nonsustainable agricultural practice.

Sucrose from sugarcane is normally converted into 83 percent sugar and 17 percent molasses. Molasses is sold at 10–35 percent of the price of sugar, either for direct human consumption or mixed with livestock feed or for making rum. A sugarcane producer can obtain a near-equivalent price of sugar for a portion of molasses by diluting with water and adding it back into the sugarcane juice stream to produce more ethanol. Sugar and ethanol mills operate for 5–6 months during the sugar season in Brazil versus 3–4 months for corn ethanol plants in the US. The longer duration of unused capacity in the US adds to capital costs per unit of ethanol produced.

Unlike the US where most arable land is under cultivation, there is plenty of room to expand agricultural output in Brazil. Brazil's land mass is about two-thirds of South America. Pastures and grazing land make up 23 percent of Brazil's land mass and crop lands 8 percent, of which sugar growing is 1 percent of the total land mass and, of this, sugar for making ethanol 0.5 percent. Considering the area of pastures and grazing lands, enormous tracts are available for expanding agricultural output not just for sugarcane, but also other food crops like soybeans. Sugarcane production climbed from 300 million tons in 2000 to 550 million tons in 2012. The question of why ethanol production has leveled out while sugarcane production is growing at slightly over 5 percent per year is that sugar growers are free to sell sugar and ethanol in the domestic or international markets, whichever is more profitable. Clearly, with level ethanol production and rising sugar production, the international sugar market is where the action is. However, if Brazilian authorities desire to increase the minimum ethanol content in gasohol to dampen oil imports, then ethanol prices would increase, creating a financial inducement for sugar growers to produce more ethanol and export less sugar; or alternatively, expand sugar production by increasing the number of sugar-ethanol plantations. However, with relatively low oil prices in 2014–2015, increased ethanol consumption would require more government funding of subsidies to make ethanol price-competitive with gasoline on an energy content basis.

There are 70,000 sugarcane growers utilizing 400 sugar mills, with 85 percent in the Center-South region and the remainder in the North-Northeast region. In the past, sugarcane growers employed many day laborers for cutting sugarcane during the harvest season that extends from November to March. Criticism was directed at plantation towns having less than desirable living conditions; yet for these workers, working for the sugar industry, even on a seasonal basis, was an attractive alternative to stark poverty. Cane workers actually received premium pay compared to other Brazilian workers, but were expected to harvest 12 tons of sugarcane per ten-hour day. This led to numerous personal injuries and ailments. Sugarcane was burned prior to harvesting to reduce the weight of its foliage to ease harvesting by hand, but its smoke became a leading cause of air pollution in Brazil. Moreover ash clinging in the air resulted in lung fibrosis among cane workers, a leading cause of occupational death.

Environmental and human problems of burning sugarcane fields are rapidly becoming something of the past as mechanization of harvesting sugarcane replaces labor. Not burning sugarcane, made possible by mechanical harvesting, increases the amount of biomass waste that can be burned for electricity generation under controlled conditions. While mechanization takes the place of labor in harvesting sugarcane, many of the displaced day laborers have been rehired on a more permanent basis to man new sugar plantations and other agricultural enterprises springing up on the vast tract lands of Brazil. About 1.2 million workers are employed on sugar plantations.

There is no need to deforest the Amazon jungle to increase sugarcane production as there is plenty of grazing and pasture and fallow land that can be upgraded to grow agricultural crops. Deforestation of the Amazon is largely cut and burn farming where a swath of jungle is burned and growing crops for food and grass for grazing cattle are supported by the residual nutrients found in the ash. But this lasts only a few years before another swath of forest has to be burned. Cut and burn is the only way for increasing numbers of Brazilians living in the jungle to sustain their food supply. What Brazil needs is the rediscovery of the method of making terra preta, which allowed a large population of Indians to live in permanent communities without having to slash and burn. To the degree that deforestation is being caused by lumbering activities, Brazil leads the world in tree farms for making charcoal and paper pulp. Lumbering in forests, while admittedly difficult to control, should be suppressed in favor of tree farms suitable for lumber for the Brazilian people and for export. If lumber from organized tree farms with access to low cost transportation can undercut the price of haphazard deforestation, or if lumber mills are only allowed to buy trees from certified sources, then the incentive to slash and burn for lumber would be diminished.

Notwithstanding the above, Brazil has succeeded in reducing deforestation from 30,000 square kilometers per year (the area of Belgium) in the 1990s to 7,500 square kilometers in 2005 to 5,800 square kilometers in 2013, almost an 80 percent reduction. A series of bans and restrictions between the 1990s and 2004 were largely unsuccessful both from compliance and enforcement points of view. In 2005 the Brazilian government made cessation of deforestation a high priority national objective and beefed up enforcement in terms of police and prosecutors. Agricultural improvements were made such that cattle could be raised on less land. A public boycott of beef induced farmers to slow down their destruction of forests. Beginning in 2009, farmers not in compliance with rules controlling deforestation were denied cheap credit needed for agriculture. Farmers also had to register their land holdings with the government for monitoring by environmental regulators. Monitoring and enforcement were placed in the hands of local governments. No incentives were provided to stop deforestation, only prohibitions and fines, which are to be kept in place until deforestation has essentially ceased.[47]

As in the US, thought has been given to improving the transport infrastructure by building ethanol carrying pipelines from the sugar producing regions to ports with substantial terminal storage capacity for the use of larger sized tankers to promote ethanol exports. However, exports would have to exhibit considerable growth from current levels to justify large-scale investments in ethanol pipelines and associated facilities. Brazil's dream of becoming the "Saudi Arabia of Ethanol" was based on its low-cost ethanol being able to compete against high-priced gasoline in the world market in order for nations to diversify motor vehicle fuels for energy security and to cut carbon emissions. Though the dream may have lost some of its luster, it has not daunted Brazil's confidence in the future of ethanol. Brazilian authorities have expressed their willingness to share their technological achievements with other sugar producers in the Caribbean and Latin America. Brazilian confidence is anchored to their being the low-cost producer of ethanol. It is felt that oil could drop as low as $50 per barrel and the equivalent ethanol price would still cover costs. Of course, this excludes the sugar market—a high price for sugar even if crude oil prices fell would still bring smiles to the faces of plantation owners. Their nightmare would be a low price for both crude oil and sugar.

The ratios of energy output to fossil fuel input for producing ethanol from different crops are shown in Figure 3.5.[48]

Figure 3.5 Energy Output/Fossil Fuel Input

Output is the energy contained in ethanol, while input is energy contained in fossil fuels consumed in the production of ethanol. Sugarcane produces eight times the energy output compared to fossil fuel input. The major reason for this is that biomass (bagasse) is burned to supply electricity for conversion of sugar to ethanol, not fossil fuels (coal and natural gas) as in the US. Vinasse greatly reduces the need for fertilizer, which is a major user of fossil fuel energy in its manufacture and transportation. Whereas pesticides, some of which are petroleum-based, are widespread in growing corn in the US, Brazil depends more on biopesticides and choice of sugar variety types to control infestations. Moreover making ethanol from sugar is far less energy intensive than ethanol from starch. The energy output/fossil fuel input for Brazil would be even greater if tractors and trucks employed by the sugar plantations were powered by biodiesel rather than petrodiesel. Corn ethanol in the US has a ratio of only 1.3, meaning that 1.3 units of energy in the form of ethanol are obtained from consuming 1 unit of fossil fuel. Some may take the position that corn ethanol can be looked upon as a conversion of fossil fuels (coal, natural gas, oil) to a gasoline substitute that reduces reliance on oil imports and environmental emissions at least on a marginal basis. Others would say that the statistical evidence of a reduction in US oil imports is scant in that a lot of diesel fuel is consumed growing and harvesting corn and distributing ethanol. Moreover there are those who remain unconvinced of the environmental benefit of corn ethanol in the form of reduced emissions. At best, corn ethanol acts as a price support for corn; at worst, ethanol has been a very expensive political payoff by the Republicans to secure the Midwest vote. Incidentally, the energy output/input for gasoline is 5, less than 8 for making ethanol from sugar in Brazil, but far better than making ethanol from corn in the US.

The US—The Great Leap Forward for Corn Growers

One of the chief advantages of ethanol from corn is that the nutritional value, other than starch, is preserved. Ethanol only consumes the starch content in corn, and its residues along with the added nutrition of the waste products of fermentation are highly valued as a livestock feed.

See the Companion Website for a section on Two Processes for Making Ethanol: www.routledge.com/cw/nersesian

Biobutanol

Over a dozen companies are pursuing the development of biobutanol as the next significant change in renewable biofuels. Biobutanol has a molecular structure more similar to gasoline than ethanol and is compatible with existing vehicle technology. Its energy content is 110,000 Btu per gallon versus 115,000 for gasoline and 76,000 for ethanol. Biobutanol can be easily added to conventional gasoline because of its low vapor pressure and similar energy content. It can be blended at much higher concentrations than bioethanol in standard vehicle engines and is well suited to current vehicle and engine technologies. It can also be blended up to 40 percent in diesel fuel. Biobutanol is less susceptible to separation in the presence of water than gasohol and, most importantly, can be used in the oil industry's existing distribution infrastructure without modifications in blending facilities, storage tanks, pipelines, or retail station pumps. Moreover biobutanol significantly cuts hydrocarbons, carbon monoxide, and nitrous oxide emissions.

Biobutanol is produced from the same agricultural feedstocks as ethanol (i.e., corn, wheat, sugar beet, sorghum, cassava, and sugarcane), and existing ethanol capacity can be cost-effectively, or nearly so, retrofitted to biobutanol production with relatively minor changes in fermentation and distillation. Biobutanol will fit into future developments in cellulosic ethanol from energy crops such as grasses and fast-growing trees and agricultural waste. Emission reduction for biobutanol is on a par with ethanol. Biobutanol has the potential to expand the market for biofuels because of its greater compatibility with gasoline and relative ease of distribution (there is no blend wall). Several ethanol plants have been purchased by biobutanol, producers for conversion to biobutanol. DuPont in partnership with British Petroleum has developed a process (Butamax) that transforms ethanol to biobutanol and a demonstration plant is being built in the UK. Other technologies are in the latter part of their development stage and anticipated to be fully developed in less than 2 years. It is felt that biobutanol can compete with crude oil priced at greater than $80 per barrel.[49]

The Great Sugar–Corn Debate

Although sugarcane is grown in Florida, Louisiana, Texas, and Hawaii, the climate in the US is generally too cold for large-scale sugar production, leaving corn as the principal source for ethanol. However, there are definite benefits of utilizing sugar over corn to produce ethanol. Corn is an annual crop requiring plowing, harrowing, and planting, whereas sugarcane is replanted every 6 years. Corn requires heavy applications of fertilizers and pesticides, which require fossil fuels to produce and distribute. Sugarcane takes less in the way of fertilizers, which are recycled via vinasse, and less in the way of pesticides, which are partly controlled by biological means and by switching sugarcane varieties. Producing ethanol from corn is four times greater in energy consumption to first convert starch to sugar before it can be converted to ethanol. Although both processes consume electricity, electricity is generated from burning bagasse in Brazil, whereas electricity generated in the US is largely from fossil fuels. Brazilian ethanol makes a much greater contribution to reducing oil demand and greenhouse gas emissions than US ethanol. Brazil's sugar crops can expand without affecting food production, whereas diversion of corn to ethanol in the US may affect food production unless there are countervailing influences such as higher yield. All in all, there is not one advantage of using corn over sugar other than ethanol from corn being an effective price support mechanism.

Well-to-wheels is a measure of energy that was originally applied to oil where the energy envelope was expanded to encompass as many factors as possible that influence producing and consuming energy. Its purpose was to better assess energy output/input ratios and associated environmental effects. For oil, the energy envelope was extended to include every step from pumping oil from a well to combusting oil products. But even here there is disagreement on the reach of the envelope; for instance, should an analysis include energy consumed not only in pumping oil, but also in drilling the well and perhaps constructing the drilling rig? Should the energy envelope include making steel that goes into the rig, perhaps reaching back to iron ore and coal mines to include the manufacture and operation of mining equipment and transport of raw materials to steel mills? Somewhere a boundary has to be drawn, and this boundary varies with analysts and affects their findings.

Applying well-to-wheels analysis to biofuels, the system boundary encompasses energy inputs for agricultural activity for growing biofuel feedstocks, for producing fertilizer, and for converting feedstock to a biofuel. Energy output would be biofuel combustion in motor vehicles. Pollution for biofuels is centered on greenhouse gas emissions, primarily CO_2 emissions from agricultural activities to fermentation to combustion net of absorption through photosynthesis. Other factors in well-to-wheels analysis may include change in soil carbon content and the impact of growing corn or sugar on alternative crops or land uses and coproducts (distillers' grains for corn ethanol and electricity generation by burning bagasse for sugar ethanol). There are considerable variations within studies and among studies. Variation within studies normally results from assuming a likely range of values that better reflect growing conditions and agricultural practices over a region rather than a discrete set of values that would apply to a specific location. Variation among studies reflects differing assessments on energy consumption for agricultural activities and the nature, type, and degree of application for fertilizers, including perhaps natural gas consumption in ammonia-based fertilizers and oil content in pesticides. Some studies take into account the environmental impact of growing biofuel crops on soil condition including erosion, plus impact of rainfall and irrigation on crop growing and ground water resources. For corn ethanol, variation encompasses yield per acre, moisture content, and type of ethanol plant with regard to energy usage and efficiency, possibly including the energy/environmental impact of distillers' grains plus enzymes and yeast. For sugarcane ethanol, variation encompasses yield per acre, type of sugarcane plant, fertilizer usage net of recycling vinasse, and energy consumption net of burning bagasse. Variation is also caused by applying different analytical techniques along with the choice of computer software model utilized in a study. Computer models have differing inputs and outputs and algorithms to calculate energy ratios and environmental impacts. A sampling of software acronyms (CARB, CCLUB, CENTURY, COLE, GREET, GTAP, STELLA) indicates not only their availability, but also the potential for differing results leading to an array of conclusions and recommended policies.

In an arbitrarily selected study, greenhouse gas (GHG) emission reduction was 34 percent for corn ethanol, 51 percent for sugar ethanol, 96 percent for corn stover (higher reduction in that stover is waste picked up off the ground or harvested with corn—corn is not planted to harvest stover!), 88 percent for switchgrass, and 108 percent for miscanthus. Corn stover, switchgrass, and miscanthus imply commercialization of cellulosic ethanol where the whole plant is converted to biofuels. For miscanthus to have GHG emission reduction of over 100 percent, the implication is that CO_2 absorbed by photosynthesis is greater than emissions released with planting, harvesting, converting miscanthus to biofuels, and combusting biofuels. The ratio of energy output to energy input in this study is 1.61 for corn ethanol, 4.32 for sugar ethanol, 4.77 for corn stover, 5.44 for switchgrass, and 6.01 for miscanthus.[50] The calculated energy ratio for corn ethanol is higher than the previously mentioned value of 1.3, with an energy ratio of sugar ethanol lower than the previously mentioned value of 8.

In another study for one hectare (2.47 acres), energy input for corn ethanol was 65.02 gigajoules versus an energy output of 71.44 gigajoules for a ratio of 1.098, less than 1.3. The corresponding figures for sugar ethanol was energy input of 42.43 gigajoules versus energy output of 155.27 gigajoules for a much improved ratio of 3.67, but still less than 8. A ratio of only about 1.1 between energy output and energy input is a poor use of resources and not a hearty endorsement of corn ethanol as a source of energy. CO_2 released in this study was 3,122 kilograms per hectare for sugar ethanol and 5,030 kilograms per hectare for corn ethanol. The major differences in higher CO_2 emissions for corn ethanol were energy required for conversion of starch to sugar and its associated release of CO_2, plus greater energy input for fertilizers and agricultural activities. GHG emission reduction was not explicitly stated as these values would have to be netted of CO_2 absorption during photosynthesis, plus differences in bioethanol output per hectare.[51]

The findings of energy ratios of 1.3 for corn ethanol and 8 for sugar ethanol quoted herein are in relation to fossil fuel input, not total energy input. In order for corn ethanol to be on a comparable basis, the energy input of electricity would have to be netted of non-fossil hydro and nuclear power to obtain a fossil fuel input. For sugar ethanol to be on a comparable basis, energy input would have to be netted of the benefit of burning bagasse and recycling vinasse. The ratio of 8 for sugar ethanol will improve when the major fossil fuel input of petrodiesel for agricultural activities and transportation is substituted by biodiesel in the coming years.

There are other studies concerning corn ethanol that support a marginal greenhouse gas emission reduction and a relationship of energy output to energy input of close to one based on energy input, not limited to fossil fuel input. This signifies little advantage to corn ethanol either in terms of energy ratio or GHG emission reduction. One has to be careful in dealing with energy ratios because the conversion of one form of energy to another has an associated loss of energy in the conversion process, which means a gain in entropy. For instance, biofuel energy ratios do not include sunlight in growing plants as part of energy input. If it were, the energy ratio would be far less than one. This is true for other energy sources. Energy release of coal does not include sunlight absorbed by plants millions of years ago. Sunlight is certainly consumed in plant growing, but is left out of the calculation of energy ratios for good reason as it is freely available. Energy input is restricted to energy consumed in terms of fossil fuels and electricity, which should also be netted of its renewable energy content.

In dealing with studies on energy ratios and environmental effects, one has to be cognizant that these are not experiments affirming the ratio of oxygen and hydrogen in water, which is immutable and verifiable. Energy and environmental studies have a large qualitative component associated with model structure, degree of reach of the energy envelope, mode of analysis, and value assignments. Thus findings can vary considerably among researchers. If the research is being conducted by an organization that has a parochial leaning for a predetermined viewpoint, then models/modes/variables and their assigned values may be preselected to support that viewpoint. This is one of the major criticisms leveled against climate models—the conclusion has been predetermined. Now it is just a matter of finding the necessary support. This is not to say that findings are necessarily prejudiced; but if they are, this can have a profound effect on establishing a public policy on energy and the environment already agreed to by the powers-that-be.

Corn has one other nonfood use. Polylactide (PLA) is a polymer made from corn for manufacturing a wide variety of everyday items such as clothing, packaging, carpeting, recreational equipment, and food utensils. Products made from PLA offer the environmental benefits of being biodegradable and made from a renewable resource. The potential market for PLA is enormous considering pollution of the world's oceans by non-biodegradable petroleum-based plastics where biodegradation is measured in decades or centuries depending on the type of plastic. But widespread application of food for plastics would not fare any better in the public's mind than food for fuel.

A major argument against corn for ethanol is its impact on the price of food. Corn is generally thought of as corn on the cob for a summer lobster fest. Sweet corn is consumed fresh, frozen, or canned and, as the name suggests, has higher sugar content than commercial or field corn, but its yield in bushels per acre is less. About 260 acres of field corn are planted for every acre of sweet corn. Only about 10 percent of field corn is for human consumption in the form of corn oil, high-fructose corn syrup, corn chips, and flakes. Corn is chiefly a food for livestock first and foremost, with humans a far distant second.[52] In the US, field corn provides 95.3 percent of livestock feed, with 2.7 percent from sorghum, 1.5 percent from barley, and 0.5 percent from oats. Since the 1980s, about 80–85 million acres of corn have been planted annually, with about 95 million acres in recent years.[53] Corn yield has climbed from about 100 to 170 bushels per acre during that time period. Corn availability for domestic consumption has remained about flat and exports have been about 20 percent of rising production. This means that ethanol production consuming 40 percent of the corn crop in 2012 has not cut into corn as a source of livestock feed, taking into consideration distillers' grains, and has seemingly not affected rising corn exports. The price of corn was roughly stable averaging a little over $2 per bushel from 2000 to 2006, then escalating to $3.39 in 2007 and $4.78 in 2008, before declining to $3.75 in 2009 and $3.83 in 2010. The average price then jumped to $6.01 in 2011, $6.67 in 2012, and $6.15 in 2013, and then declined to $4.11 in 2014. In mid-2015, the price of corn was $3.75.[54] The actual rate of inflation is not the government published rate because fuel and food are conveniently left out of the calculations, and fuel is a major cost component in agriculture. But if the true or actual rate of inflation were applied to the $2 per bushel that prevailed in the early 2000s, the 2015 price of $3.75 per bushel barely compensates for inflation.

Although corn farmers were better off in 2011 and 2013 than in the early 2000s, they are essentially back to where they were in the early 2000s. Furthermore, subsidies for corn growers have fallen from $10 billion in 2000 to $1.8 billion in 2012.

Bearing in mind that only the starch portion of a corn kernel is lost for making ethanol, and considering the price of corn, it is hard to argue that food for fuel has caused food prices to rise. Gains in acreage planted in corn and higher levels of productivity have made up for corn "lost" in producing ethanol. Nevertheless the price of corn is an important determinant of food prices. Rising corn prices affect the price of soybeans through the corn–soybean complex where corn and soybean oil and meal can be, to some extent, substituted for one another depending on their relative prices and the nature of consumption. Any rise in corn and soybean oil prices in North America affects the price of other forms of vegetable oil such as canola, more common in Europe, but would have little impact on palm oil prices in Asia because of limited substitutability.

Some organizations such as the World Bank have been critical of biofuels being responsible for higher food prices.[55] But agricultural advocates blame most of the rise in food prices on inflation. Inflation has been rampant, affecting cost factors of all enterprises, including every element of the food supply chain. Consumers tell endless tales about price increases for goods and services, food being but one. As to higher corn prices, one pundit remarked that a box of corn flakes has about a nickel's worth of corn with corn at $4.40 a bushel. Doubling corn prices raises the price of a box of corn flakes to about a dime for its corn content (one may begin to wonder what is being purchased when one buys a box of corn flakes!).

Ethanol spokespeople maintain that food prices, including corn, are more affected by oil and other energy costs than by the diversion of corn to ethanol since agriculture is a heavy consumer of energy at every stage of production. Moreover the conversion of agricultural products to food items in a store is also energy-intensive. There is a possibility of farmers switching from wheat to corn production, but it is marginal as most wheat is grown in areas of the nation where corn does not grow well such as Kansas and Nebraska. The center of corn growing is Iowa, Illinois, and Indiana. Some 10 million extra acres now in corn production did not come from farmers switching crops, but by expanding the corn belt into traditional grasslands in the Dakotas and southern Iowa, which are not particularly well suited for growing corn.

Some new acreage dedicated to corn growing could be from declining acreage enrolled in the Conservation Reserve Program (CRP).[56] CRP provides an annual rental income to farmers who agree to remove environmentally sensitive land from agricultural production to reduce erosion, improve water quality, and promote the natural growth of grasslands and trees. Still another source of land for corn growing is soybean growers switching to corn. But this has to be balanced against the enormous expansion of soybean production in Brazil and Argentina that would amply substitute for any diversion of crops for food to crops for fuel in the US. Anti-biofuel advocates have to take into consideration higher grain yields, substitution of one crop for another, rise of South American soybean and other grain exports, and reversion of grasslands to crop lands before a definitive position can be supported on the impact of biofuel on food—few take the trouble.

US corn exports in 2014 were 45.7 million metric tons, up from 31.8 million tons in 2013, followed by Brazil at 20.5 million tons, Ukraine at 16.5 million, and Argentina at 15 million tons, then a large step down to 3 million tons for the next exporter.[57] In addition to corn, the US is by far the world's largest wheat exporter. An agricultural failure in

North America would have ripple effects throughout the world, as many nations depend on US agricultural output to feed their people, such as Egypt, Haiti, and a host of others in Asia and Africa. An agricultural disaster would no doubt divert food away from being made into fuel. In examining the agricultural situation, one has to conclude that "No Food for Fuel," a mantra gaining strength in the public realm, has a bit of a hollow ring at least in the US. Nevertheless the shibboleth is a tough one to overcome.

Whatever criticism is leveled against ethanol made from corn, most Americans are in favor of biofuels to reduce the nation's oil imports, particularly from the Middle East. America's pro-biofuels stance was reflected in the Indianapolis 500 declaration that its official fuel would be 100 percent (E100) ethanol, not mentioning that E100 has several distinct advantages over gasoline as a racing fuel.[58] President Bush enunciated the US commitment to biofuels at the Renewable Fuels Association Summit meeting in Washington, DC, in April 2006:

> Ethanol is good for the whole country . . . We owe it to the American people to be promoting alternative ways to drive their cars so as to make us less dependent on foreign sources of oil. We owe it to the American people to be aggressive in the use of technology so we can diversify away from the hydrocarbon society. That is exactly what we are doing.

How close we have come to achieving these goals is not a matter of conjecture; we have made significant progress in becoming less dependent on foreign sources of oil, but not through biofuels. Biofuels are a mute witness to reduced oil imports by technological advances in fracking to tap the nation's enormous domestic oil resources locked in hard shale. It is misleading to show a chart originated by ethanol proponents of rising ethanol production and declining gasoline imports and let the observer conclude that there is a causative relationship between the two. Gasoline imports have virtually ceased because oil from shale is light with a high content of gasoline. Since oil cannot be exported as crude oil, it is refined in the US, creating a glut of gasoline. Thus rising gasoline exports and falling imports are caused by what is happening in the oil patch, not the ethanol patch.

The US Is Following Brazil's Footsteps in a More Complex Way

Biofuel programs require government intervention and support. The US biofuel support program was more gradual than Brazil's, starting with the US Energy Tax Act of 1978 that officially defined gasohol as a blend of gasoline of at least 10 percent nonfossil fuel ethanol by volume (excluding oil-refinery ethanol). The Act exempted ethanol from the gasoline excise tax; in effect, providing a direct subsidy for ethanol blended in gasoline. The US EPA became interested in ethanol as an octane booster and volume extender in the 1980s, but this role was ultimately filled by methyl tertiary butyl ether (MTBE), a petroleum-based oxygenate preferred by the oil industry with the banning of tetraethyl lead. Despite the general disinterest in ethanol other than the E10 gasohol sold in the corn-producing regions of the nation, Congress approved several tax benefit packages along with loan and price guarantees to support ethanol producers and blenders. Nothing came of these incentives when oil prices collapsed in the mid-1980s. The Alternative Motor Fuels Act of 1988 provided credits to automobile manufacturers for building vehicles capable of burning E85, a blend of 85 percent ethanol and 15 percent gasoline. These credits could be applied to meet the requirements of the Corporate Average Fuel Economy (CAFE) standards. This Act had little impact as there were very few fuel retailers offering E85. The Energy Policy Act of 1992 required primarily government-owned automobile fleets to begin purchasing alternative fuel and flex fuel vehicles capable of burning E85 fuel.

During the 1990s, motorists in the Midwest voluntarily paid a premium for gasohol (E10) as a means of supporting the local corn growers. Growth in US ethanol production started after 2002, with increasing restrictions being imposed on the use of the oxygenate MTBE. This movement to ban MTBE as a carcinogen finding its way into drinking water supplies was led by California. MTBE lost 42 percent of its market when New York and Connecticut joined California in banning the product. This forced the EPA to drop the requirement for MTBE (an example where state initiatives forced the Federal government's hand). This provided the opportunity for ethanol to be a substitute for MTBE, but quickly ended with the repeal of the oxygenate requirement for reformulated gas by the Energy Policy Act of 2005. While seemingly negative for ethanol, the Energy Policy Act of 2005 also contained the Renewable Fuel Standard (RFS). RFS guaranteed a market for ethanol by mandating that 4 billion gallons of ethanol be incorporated into gasoline in 2006, an amount nearly met in 2005, to be expanded to 7.5 billion gallons by 2012. The mandate left it to the oil companies on how to infuse this amount of ethanol into the gasoline pool, which would result in gasoline containing about 7 percent ethanol by 2012 depending on future gasoline consumption. This is still a far cry from Brazil's success in achieving 20–30 percent ethanol in gasoline, but Brazil consumes a far smaller volume of motor vehicle fuel.

Though ethanol was to be derived from corn, another feature of the Act was providing an incentive for the development of cellulosic ethanol. A crediting procedure was set up whereby cellulosic ethanol has a 2.5 advantage over corn ethanol in terms of meeting minimum ethanol requirements. That is, 1,000 gallons of cellulosic ethanol would be treated the same as 2,500 gallons of corn ethanol in fulfilling minimum usage requirements. There was also a mandate for 250 million gallons of cellulosic ethanol to be produced and incorporated into gasoline by 2013, but technology for making cellulosic ethanol was not fully developed despite a guaranteed market.

The Energy Independence and Security Act of 2007 contained provisions bearing on a number of energy issues. Titles I and II are most pertinent to motor vehicle fuels. Title I—Energy Security Through Improved Vehicle Fuel Economy—is to reduce energy demand through greater efficiency. Title II—Energy Security through Increased Production of Biofuels—defines RFS-2, replacing the aforementioned RFS, renamed RFS-1, and calls for a massive growth in mandated fuels, as shown in Figure 3.6, such as slightly more of a doubling of the 2012 ethanol requirement from 7.5 to 15.2 billion gallons.

Advanced cellulosic and non-cellulosic biofuels include ethanol derived from cellulose, hemicellulose, or lignin, sugar or starch other than corn starch, waste material and crop residues, ethanol produced from biogas including landfill and sewage waste treatment gas, butanol and other alcohols produced from organic matter, and any other fuel derived from biomass including algae, recycled cooking oil, and grease. In other words, these two categories cover everything but corn ethanol. By 2022, conventional corn ethanol is to be stabilized at 15 billion gallons, consuming about half of the corn crop, biodiesel 1 billion gallons, advanced non-cellulosic biofuels 4 billion gallons, and advanced cellulosic biofuels 16 billion gallons.

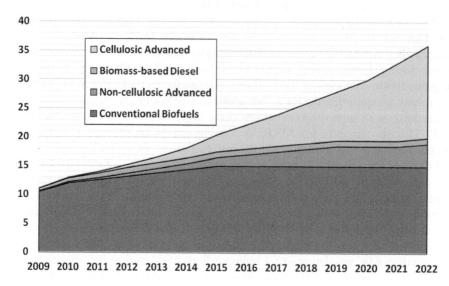

Figure 3.6 The US Renewable Fuels Standard (RFS-2) in Billion Gallons

Conventional gasoline-fueled vehicles can burn E10 with no alterations. The fleet of E85 flex fuel vehicles is quite small. Automobiles built since 2001 can burn E15 and now make up a significant part (62 percent) of the total gasoline powered fleet of 230 million vehicles.[59] However, vehicles built before 2001, still a large portion of the fleet, are limited to E10. But a number of studies has shown that automobiles, regardless of their age, burning E15, have suffered no engine damage.[60] In 2009, the ethanol industry made a proposal, endorsed by the EPA, to raise the ethanol content in gasoline to a maximum of E15 to meet the volumetric requirements of the Act. The proposal raised concerns from automobile manufacturers that their engine warranties on vehicles built before 2001 would not apply for engines burning more than E10. Objections came from gasoline distributors whose storage and pumping facilities are designed for E10, and to also accommodate E15 would require a large investment in new storage and pumping facilities to serve what was then perceived as a small fraction of automobiles new enough to be able to burn E15. In 2014, 60 percent of new cars sold are warranted to burn E15, but they can only buy E15 at 60 service stations in 12 states. However, this number will grow. Small engine manufacturers of outboard motors and lawnmowers have expressed concerns over poor engine performance if fueled by E15.[61] The ultimate solution is for all new automobiles built in the US to be flex fuel in order to accommodate higher levels of ethanol. In 2012 Ford Motor Company switched entirely to flex fuel vehicles, a nice tribute to Henry. In 2014 about one quarter of sales by the US automobile manufacturers are flex fuel.

But accommodating E85 would require a massive investment in gasoline service stations. Even if most gasoline stations made the investment in E85 facilities and all new automobiles could burn E85 (flex fuel), there would be a resulting shortage of E85. Considering that 40 percent of the corn crop is dedicated to meeting E10, then approximately 60 percent of the corn crop would be required to meet E15, and E25 would require the entire conversion of the corn crop to ethanol, an intolerable situation.

Even if this were tolerable, it would be necessary that E85 be available at many of the 150,000 service stations counting truck stops, convenience stores, and marinas, down from 200,000 in 1994 mostly from low profitability. This in itself shows that massive investments in gasoline service stations are quite unlikely. Most of the 2,638 gas stations in 2015 that served E85 were located in the Midwest and represented only 1.8 percent of the total.[62]

The Blend Wall

Renewable Identification Numbers (RINs) are serial numbers assigned to batches of renewable fuel as they leave ethanol plants by EPA as part of the Renewable Fuel Standard (RFS) to track progress in reaching energy independence goals established by Congress. Under the Energy Policy Act of 2005, EPA was authorized to set annual quotas in terms of volume even though reality limited the percentage of ethanol in gasoline to 10 percent because higher levels would void engine manufacturers' warranties. Companies that refine, import, or blend fossil fuels are obliged to meet individual RFS quotas based on the volume of fuel they provide to the market. This volume is expressed as a range with a minimum and maximum that seems reasonable given the level of ethanol production. Compliance is assured by obligated parties having met their RFS quota when they submit the requisite number of RINs to EPA. This permits EPA to assure the government that the energy industry collectively satisfied the overall national volume quota.

All motor vehicle fuel produced for US consumption must contain either adequate renewable fuel in the blend or the equivalent in RIN credits if they do not. RINs are tracked throughout every link in the supply chain, as title is transferred from one party to the next, until the point in time where the biofuel is blended with petroleum products. Once renewable fuel is in the petroleum product, RINs are separated from the renewable fuel. With each refiner, blender, and importer having a volume requirement with a minimum and maximum, it is possible that the volume of renewable fuel exceeds the minimum. If companies blended more than their required minimums, they are rewarded with RIN credits that can be sold to those who fail to meet their minimum requirements. RIN credits are tradable, but have a finite life of about 1 year unless extended another year for special reasons.[63] This becomes the supply of RINs for refiners who do not have enough ethanol available to meet the stipulated minimum. When this occurs, the refiner is obliged to buy RINs to cover the shortfall. The presence of RIN buyers and sellers establishes a market and, hence, a price. RIN credits are used by obligated parties to certify compliance with meeting mandated renewable fuel volumes. RINs had a very low value before 2012/2013 because refiners, blenders, and importers who exceeded minimum volumes established by EPA sold excess RINs into a market of few buyers because there was more than sufficient ethanol to meet minimum volumes. All this changed in 2012/2013 when the price for RINs spiked to $1.50 per gallon as refiners ran up against the blend wall.

The first reason for the existence of a blend wall was that the ethanol requirement was in terms of volume, not percentage of gasoline consumption. As volume of mandated ethanol production grew under RFS-2 on the presumption that volume of gasoline would also grow consistent with its past trend, the volume of actual oil consumption declined. US motor gasoline consumption peaked at 142 billion gallons in 2007 and has declined since then to 137 billion gallons in 2014, off 4.5 percent from the peak, contrary to its history of perpetual growth. The principal causes were an overall reduction in driving linked to a soft US economy (for those without a job, less commuting and fewer cross-country family vacations) and improved fuel efficiency. A smaller pool of gasoline reduced demand for ethanol for E10 below that mandated by RFS-2.

To compensate for this, EPA raised the minimum amount of ethanol to E15, which would have covered the RFS-2 mandate. However, there were virtually no gasoline service stations offering E15. EPA then urged the industry to take a more aggressive stand selling E85, but the buying public did not respond. Thus refiners were caught in a vise of ethanol being presented to them for blending at minimum volumes above E10, dictated by EPA regulations, but could not be sold as dictated by commercial reality. Thus blenders and refiners could not meet their EPA imposed minimum requirements, which made it mandatory for them to buy RINs for ethanol that, if placed in the gasoline stream, could not be sold. As demand for RINs grew, supply collapsed, because there was little opportunity left to blend ethanol in excess of a minimum requirement of 10 percent of gasoline volume. So before 2012 there was a plethora of RINs with no demand because no one was up against the blend wall, which reduced the commercial value of RINs to nil. Then in 2012/2013, there was demand for RINs, but no supply, as there was very limited opportunity to exceed EPA imposed minimums. This had all the earmarks of a failed market mechanism for clearing RINs between buyers and sellers. The equilibrium price was either nil or a level so high that it adversely affected the price of gasoline.

See the Companion Website for a section on Proposed Solutions: www.routledge.com/cw/nersesian

In 2015 the RIN crisis was over. The cure was commercial. It paid to buy ethanol not for blending 10 percent into gasoline, but to sell as E85 and separate their associated RINs that could be sold very profitably to those who needed RINs. The sale of RINs covered the "loss" of selling E85 at $1 per gallon less than gasoline. This incentivized owners of flex fuel vehicles to switch to E85, gas stations to offer E85, and car buyers to purchase flex fuel vehicles. Greater consumption of discounted priced E85 saved the day. Meanwhile exports of ethanol increased from 600 million gallons to 800 million gallons between 2013 and 2014, with 43 percent of exports to Canada, 13 percent to Brazil, 10 percent to the UAE, 8 percent to the Philippines, and 6 percent to the EU. Imports fell from 400 million gallons to 50 million gallons, with the cut in sugar ethanol fulfilling the advanced biofuels requirement. But in a market of over 14 billion gallons, this rise in exports and cut in imports did not play a significant part of the solution. The permanent solution to demolishing the blend wall was EPA reducing the mandate for renewable fuels to 13.4 billion gallons in 2015 and 14 billion gallons in 2016, much more in line with market realities.

Other Developments in the World of Ethanol

Peru is rapidly developing sugar plantations and ethanol plants for both domestic consumption and export potential. A sugar plantation in the Peruvian desert features drip irrigation fed by water flowing from the Andes Mountains to the Pacific Ocean. Drip irrigation is the most efficient way to irrigate crops. While sugarcane cannot be harvested during the rainy season, which lasts for seven to eight months in the Caribbean and Central America, the benefit of an irrigated sugar plantation in a desert is higher yields from year-round harvesting. Since the US and EU ethanol markets are under pressure not to import and with exports from this Peruvian project managed by a Japanese trading company, Japan would probably end up being the ultimate buyer (Peru being closer to Japan than Brazil).[64]

Another bioethanol crop is sugar beets, which have the highest yield of ethanol per acre. In France, sugar beets produce 7,000 liters per hectare (750 gallons per acre); in Brazil, sugarcane 5,500 liters per hectare (590 gallons per acre); and in the US, corn 3,000 liters per hectare (320 gallons per acre). Sugar beets grow in temperate regions of the Northern Hemisphere and are harvested solely for their sugar content. The root is about one foot long, weighing 3–5 pounds and containing 15–20 percent sugar. Sugar beets, while yielding more sugar than sugarcane on a per acre basis, consume more fertilizers and pesticides and are more difficult to harvest as a root than sugarcane as a stalk. Pest infestations prevent sugar beets being cultivated more than once every 3 years on the same ground. Moreover the process of obtaining sugar from sugar beets is more energy intensive and costly than sugarcane. Sugar beet molasses and pulp, byproducts of sugar beet ethanol plants, are sold as wet or dry livestock feed. Worldwide sugar beet production peaked at just over 300 million metric tons in 1990 and has been in a slow decline to 250 million tons in 2013.[65] Sugar beets' future role as an ethanol producer is not promising.

Some are advocating agave as a bioethanol crop. Agave is a desert plant from which tequila is made. It has high sugar content and grows quickly in dry and poor quality soils unfit for food crops and thus does not affect food production. Agave is said to produce three times more ethanol than sugarcane, six times more ethanol than corn, and three times more cellulosic ethanol than switchgrass or poplar trees on a per acre basis. Harvesting is year-round with little or no water and fertilizer requirements to encourage growth and, consequently, a very low cost of production independent of food prices. If these contentions on ethanol yield are true, then agave would be an ideal biofuel crop in Mexico or any dry and infertile locale where the plant can grow.[66]

Making ethanol from the residue of a plant after the food portion has been removed is a way to increase its value. Cassava is an edible starchy tuberous root. Tapioca is the starch removed from the cassava root and is a major source of carbohydrates. Cassava, known by a variety of names, is the second most popular crop in Africa, fourth in Southeast Asia, fifth in Latin America and the Caribbean, and seventh in Asia. Its highest yields are achieved in Thailand because of less exposure to disease and pests and intensive crop management including irrigation and fertilizers. Cassava has a high tolerance for marginal soils and drought, which explains its popularity throughout the developing world. A demonstration plant is being built in Thailand by a Japanese company to produce ethanol from residue after extracting tapioca.[67]

Germany and France depend mostly on wheat as feedstock for ethanol production. Rye and barley are two relatives of wheat that grow better in drier and cooler weather and acidic soils in Sweden and other parts of northern Europe. The problem with biofuels in Europe is a relative scarcity of cropland and lower ethanol yields from wheat, rye, and barley compared to corn (maize) and sugarcane. Incremental ethanol production in Europe is under pressure from public opposition to food for fuel. A bill before the European Parliament will, if passed, cap the volume of first generation biofuels derived from food crops. The bill proposes that 10 percent of transport fuel be from renewable sources by 2020, but no more than 6 percent from first generation biofuels. The difference will be from second generation biofuel technologies such as cellulosic or other non-food ethanol.[68] This bill reflects growing opposition of food for fuel in Europe, but its impact will be nil. Europe produces 235,000 Bpd of biofuels (ethanol and biodiesel) and consumes 10.2 million Bpd of light and middle distillates, which is largely, but not entirely, gasoline and diesel fuel. Six percent of 10 million Bpd is 600,000 Bpd, about 250 percent over current consumption. If it becomes law, it may dampen interest for EU imports of ethanol. Looking forward, major importers will most likely be China, Japan, Korea, and Singapore and major exporters will be Brazil and Thailand, with smaller contributions from the Philippines, southern Africa, and Peru.

Cellulosic Ethanol

First generation biofuels are bioethanol and biodiesel, both of which impinge on food production. It is felt that successful development of second generation biofuels such as cellulosic ethanol will consign the first generation biofuel producers to the dustbin of history; hopefully after their investments have been recouped with a positive return. This statement is more applicable to the US than to Brazil since an argument can be made that Brazil's sugarcane production does not impinge on food crops because of the extent of fallow land available for conversion to sugar and other food crops.

Nevertheless, in the first generation, only the kernels of the corn are transformed to bioethanol. In the second generation, the whole plant, kernels, cob, stalk, leaves, tassels, and silk, will be turned into cellulosic ethanol; same with the stalk and leaves of sugarcane. Ethanol production is significantly increased when using the whole plant rather than just its sugar or starch content. The cellulosic content of agricultural crops can be increased without affecting crop yield. The best example is short and tall varieties of soybeans. If a tall variety of soybean is substituted for a short variety, the soybean crop remains the same, but the amount of cellulosic biomass doubles. With the technological development of cellulosic ethanol, the first feedstocks are most apt to be agricultural wastes such as corn stover, bagasse, and wheat straw followed by municipal sewage waste (MSW) and waste wood. Conversion of corn stover and bagasse to cellulosic ethanol will have a significant impact on the total ethanol yield from corn and sugarcane.

The US has an estimated capacity to produce one billion dry tons of biomass feedstock per year. Sources of cellulosic feedstocks are forest-derived biomass (dead trees removed to reduce fire hazards and residue from logging), thinning trees as part of a robust forest management program, wastes from urban construction and furniture manufacturing and other wood processing activities, agricultural waste (crop residues, particularly corn stover and wheat straw and food processing residues), and special fuel crops grown for their cellulosic content.

Cultivating perennial biomass crops on marginal and idle land has its detractors, who maintain that biomass crops will place constraints on equipment, labor, and transport availability for food crops. Removal of large quantities of plant residues such as corn stover and straw from cropland could reduce soil quality, promote erosion, and lead to a loss of soil nutrition that might lower crop productivity. Biomass crops may consume some pesticides and fertilizers, although the degree of application is much less than food crops, which may, nevertheless, affect the cost of pesticides and fertilizers for producing food crops. In addition there is also the question of water availability for perennial biomass croplands that may need irrigation. On the plus side, perennial plants grown for biomass fuel would provide a habitat for birds and animals and increase availability for animal feed if protein can be separated from cellulosic biomass in the ethanol-production process. Wildfires would be less menacing if removal of excess plant growth and dead trees were permitted in public forests along with removal of logging wastes in forests where lumbering is permitted. Cellulosic crops can be grown on land that does not require irrigation or fertilizers. The advantage of the extensive use of MSW for biofuels would be reduced pollution of surface and ground water and cost of disposing of municipal waste.

Farmers in Nebraska and the Dakotas participated in the 5-year study sponsored by the US Department of Agriculture and the University of Nebraska of planting switchgrass, carefully recording all costs for fuel, fertilizer, and other energy-related costs. The study concluded that cellulosic ethanol production would be 300 gallons per acre, almost the yield of ethanol from corn starch, and have a 5.4 energy output/fossil fuel input. This compares favorably with the 1.3 energy output/input for corn ethanol and 5 for gasoline from crude oil, and is beaten only by the energy output/input of 8 for sugar ethanol in Brazil.[69]

The estimated one billion tons of cellulosic biomass and forest residues that can be harvested each year in the US can produce 340 billion liters of ethanol. With gasoline demand at 760 billion ethanol-equivalent liters, cellulosic biomass has the possibility of supplying 45 percent of gasoline demand in terms of ethanol-equivalents. Given the upper limit of ethanol concentration in gasoline, the potentially vast quantities of cellulosic ethanol would have to be converted to biobutanol in order to be fed directly into the gasoline stream as a biofuel substitute or flex fuel automobiles would have to become the norm. This would make North American oil independent; that is, oil imports from Mexico and Canada to the US would be sufficient to eliminate imports from elsewhere.

Cellulosic ethanol technology based on acids converting (hydrolyzing) cellulose and hemicellulose into simple sugars has a 100-year history. Germans and Russians employed this technology during wartime to produce alcohol fuels and chemicals from wood. During peacetime, interest in this process waned when poor yields, high wastage, and unmarketable byproducts made the process noncompetitive with low-cost petroleum products. Interest was rekindled by the oil crisis in the mid-1970s and also by a DuPont article published in *Science* magazine at that time citing 250 chemical products made from petroleum that had previously been made from sugar or sugar ethanol. This spurred government and university laboratories, led by the Tennessee Valley Authority and Mississippi State University, to study the hydrolysis of cellulose using acids or enzymes.

Three primary components in cellulosic biomass are cellulose, hemicellulose, and lignin. As an approximation, the biomass composition of plants is about 45 percent cellulose, 25 percent hemicellulose, 25 percent lignin, and 5 percent others, such as sulfur, potassium, and calcium carbonate or oxide, a major constituent of ash. Cellulose is made up of long chains of glucose molecules with six atoms of carbon per molecule (six-carbon sugar). Hemicellulose consists of a mixture of six- and five-carbon sugars and is easier to break down to sugar than cellulose. Lignin is the "glue" in cell walls that provides the overall rigidity and strength to plant structure. Trees have more lignin in their cell structure to grow taller than other plants. The challenge of cellulosic ethanol is penetrating the lignin surrounding the cellulose and hemicellulose within a cell without adversely affecting their integrity. Lignin is very difficult to break down into simpler forms of glucose. Some approaches to cellulosic ethanol call for burning the separated lignin to fuel the process with the potential of selling excess electricity capacity to the grid.

See the Companion Website for a section on Traditional Means of Making Cellulosic Ethanol: www.routledge.com/cw/nersesian

Biodiesel

The first diesel engines invented by Rudolf Diesel ran on a heavy grade of kerosene, but at the Paris Exposition in 1900, the demonstration diesel engine ran on peanut oil. The smell of peanut scented engine exhaust drew visitors to the demonstration, much to Diesel's delight. A number of explanations have been put forth for why Diesel chose to burn peanut oil, including no other available fuel, Diesel wanting to demonstrate that the diesel engine could run on a wide variety of fuels, or the French government wanting to promote a potential market for peanuts grown in its African colonies. Regardless of the reason why Diesel used peanut oil at the Paris Exposition, as the years passed, Diesel became a strong advocate for the use of vegetable oils as a fuel, as in this 1912 quote:

> The use of vegetable oils for engine fuels may seem insignificant today, but such oil may become, in the course of time, as important as petroleum and coal-tar products of the present time. . . . Motive power can still be produced from the heat of the sun, always available, even when the natural stores of solid and liquid fuels are completely exhausted.[70]

Like 200 proof White Lightning, biodiesel can also be home brewed. "Anyone can make biodiesel in a blender. The recipe calls for some dangerous ingredients such as methanol and lye." After duly providing safety precautions, "put 200 milliliters of methanol in the blender. Dump in 3.5 grams of lye. Blend." Again some precautionary words over not ingesting methanol and the resultant methoxide. "Once you have a successful methoxide reaction, add a liter of vegetable oil and blend for about fifteen minutes. This is the bio-diesel reaction, and if the mixing is done correctly you get two nicely defined layers. One is glycerin, the byproduct of the reaction, and the other biodiesel. Glycerin is nontoxic and composted for disposal and the biodiesel can go right into the fuel tank."[71]

Vegetable oil does not have to be "virgin oil," but can be anything such as sausage fat from a pizza restaurant or waste vegetable oil from fast food restaurants—the difference is the amount of lye that has to be added and the smell of the exhaust (some devotees of home brew avoid waste cooking oil from fast food fish restaurants). Methanol and potassium in the lye are entrapped in the glycerin. Heating the glycerin vaporizes the methanol, which can be recovered for recycling by condensing the vapors. Reclaiming potassium is too complicated for the blender operation. The glycerin is not commercial grade, and purifying blender glycerin is much more difficult than making biodiesel. Even if purified, glycerin cannot be considered commercial grade for making soaps, pharmaceuticals, cosmetics, toothpaste, and other consumer products because glycerin used in these products, since they could be ingested, must be certified as kosher. It would be difficult to guarantee no pork fat ending up in the blender. Moreover, certification for being kosher prohibits the mixing of feedstocks such as different seed oils. With no commercial value, home brewed glycerin can be disposed by mixing it with hay, wood chips, horse manure, and other ingredients for compost or mixed with alfalfa and fed to goats.

Biodiesel fuels are oxygenated organic compounds—methyl or ethyl esters—derived from vegetable oil, animal fat, and cooking oil. Oxygen in biodiesel requires stabilization to avoid storage problems. Methyl ester diesel made from vegetable oil and fats mixed with methanol is by far the most common form of biodiesel. In Europe, rapeseed (canola) oil is the most common form of vegetable oil in biodiesel, in the US and Brazil soybean oil, and in Asia palm oil. Brazil is providing incentives for family farms to grow castor seeds as biodiesel feedstock. Collectively these fuels are referred to as fatty acid methyl esters (FAME).

Commercial biodiesel is produced by first crushing seeds to extract oils followed by a catalytic process called transesterification in which oils (triglycerides) are reacted with an alcohol such as methanol or ethanol into alkyl esters. Fossil fuel-derived methanol is normally used, but Brazil is experimenting with sugarcane-derived ethanol. If successful, this would make biodiesel entirely renewable. Because biodiesel marketed today is made with methanol, emissions and health standards as well as fuel specifications are based on methyl, not ethyl, esters. Glycerin (also called glycerol and sometimes spelled glycerine) and water are byproducts of the reaction and have to be removed along with traces of alcohol, unreacted triglycerides, and catalyst before biodiesel can be sold to the public. Non-kosher glycerin can be used in paints and other commercial products. But some biodiesel producers are finding glycerin an unwanted byproduct and are quietly disposing of it in the nearest stream. Glycerin is gelatinous flotsam that absorbs oxygen, killing fish and marine life. Like an oil spill, it can be traced to its source by downstream residents.

There is a significant purity problem associated with the glycerin byproduct of biodiesel production for kosher products. Glycerin produced by transesterification is only about 50 percent pure, containing a significant amount of contaminants such as methanol, soap, and catalyst. The first step of purification is relatively easy by adding hydrochloric acid to acidify glycerin to split soap into fatty acids and salt. Fatty acids are separated as they rise to the top of the glycerin and methanol is removed by evaporation. These relatively simple steps can make the glycerin 80–90 percent pure, but it needs to be 99.7 percent pure to be commercially acceptable as kosher. This takes a much more sophisticated process of vacuum distillation or ion exchange refining. Vacuum distillation is capital intensive, and ion exchange columns, while less capital intensive, generate large volumes of waste water during regeneration that has to be treated. Even if commercially pure glycerin were produced, there is the matter of supply and demand. The total demand for glycerin is about one million tons per year. Large-scale incremental supplies of commercial grade glycerin from biodiesel processing plants would flood the market and depress prices, making investments in glycerin purification equipment unprofitable. Research is underway to transform glycerin byproduct into something of greater value such as isoprene, the main ingredient in synthetic rubber.

The majority of alkyl esters produced today rely on the catalyst-reaction process because its operating temperature (150°F) and pressure (20 psi) are relatively low, has a high conversion rate (98 percent) with no intermediate steps, minimal side reactions, and short reaction time. No exotic materials are needed for plant construction. It is a cost-effective way to produce biodiesel with inputs of 87 percent vegetable oil, 12 percent methanol, and 1 percent catalyst, generating outputs of 86 percent methyl ethyl (biodiesel), 9 percent glycerin, 4 percent methanol recapture, and 1 percent fertilizer, with no waste![72]

Cetane number is an empirical measure of a diesel fuel's ignition delay measured by time required for ignition after injection into a compression chamber. Biodiesel has a favorably high cetane number and contains essentially no sulfur and aromatics (benzene, toluene, and xylene), and burns with less particulate (soot), unburned hydrocarbons, and carbon monoxide emissions. Soot may become a major environmental issue. There is scientific speculation that the increased concentration of soot in glacial ice in the Northern Hemisphere leads to more rapid melting. Soot decreases reflection of sunlight, increasing albedo or energy absorption that accelerates glacial meltdown. The primary contributors of soot in the atmosphere are smokestack emissions from burning coal for electricity generation and as an industrial fuel and exhaust of diesel-fueled motor vehicles and machinery. In other words, it may not be just global warming that is melting glaciers, but also soot accumulation. Average tailpipe emissions from burning 100 percent biodiesel (B100) is a reduction of 43 percent in carbon monoxide emissions, 56 percent in hydrocarbon emissions, 55 percent in particulates (soot), and 100 percent in sulfur emissions, but a 6 percent increase in nitrous oxide emissions.

Care must be exercised in mixing biodiesel with petrodiesel since its specific gravity of 0.88 is higher than the 0.85 for petroleum diesel. Thus biodiesel should be splashed on top of petrodiesel to assure proper mixing. B20 is considered a "safe" blend that would not have any meaningful impact over the use of petrodiesel similar to E10 gasohol in automobiles. B20 minimizes the impact of higher cost biodiesel and keeps nitrous oxide increases within 1–4 percent that satisfy legal emission standards for diesel engines. B20 also reduces the engine emissions of soot, particulates, hydrocarbons, carbon monoxide, and carbon dioxide by more than 10 percent. B20 keeps the increase in cloud and pour points to manageable levels, which can be controlled through normal cold flow additives. There are also few material compatibility problems with B20, whereas higher-level blends can create problems with rubber seals, gaskets, and hoses unless replaced with biodiesel resistant materials. In short, B20 is a good starting point for new users of biodiesel.

B100 is biodegradable if spilled, making it especially suitable for marine or farm applications. Tourist boats and yachts on Lake Constance, Europe's second largest drinking water source, are required to use B100 to keep the lake free of toxic fuel spills. Biodiesel is safer to transport and store because of its higher flashpoint (over 260°F compared to 125°F for petrodiesel). Biodiesel lubricity is better than petrodiesel and is particularly desirable for blending with low and ultralow sulfur petrodiesels to improve their lubricity. The higher viscosity range of biodiesel helps to reduce barrel-plunger leakage and increases injector efficiency in engines. Its exhaust smell is slightly reminiscent of French fries even without recycled cooking oil. Biodiesel has a heat content of about 121,000 Btu per gallon compared to 135,000 Btu for diesel fuel. Its oxygen content of around 10 percent is higher than petrodiesel, which lowers emissions and enhances combustion efficiency by about 7 percent. Taking the lower energy and higher oxygen content into consideration, B100 has a net 5 percent loss in torque, power, and fuel efficiency compared to petrodiesel—a much better relative performance than E100 is to gasoline.

Biodiesel has less oxidative stability, a tendency of fuels to react with oxygen at ambient temperatures, than petrodiesel. This adversely affects combustion, resulting in varnish deposits, and sediments, and becomes a serious problem if storage of biodiesel exceeds six months. Another problem associated with long term storage is microbial growth, but this can be treated with antioxidants and biocides. Petrodiesel can form sediments, sludge, and slime on the bottom and sides of storage tanks that have not been adequately maintained. Biodiesel, a mild solvent, will dissolve these sediments and carry dissolved solids to the fuel filters. Fuel filters will catch much of the sediments, but can become plugged, stopping the flow of fuel and possibly leading to fuel injector failure unless frequently changed. Thus it is best to start out with B20 until sediments and sludge are removed before using higher grades of biodiesel.

Petrodiesel begins to "cloud" at 20°F with the formation of paraffin crystals, which can clog fuel filters, preventing the engine from starting or causing it to stall. At lower temperatures, diesel fuel reaches its pour point, a temperature where it will not pour or flow through fuel lines, causing the engine to stop running. Normally, cloud and pour points are about 15–20°F apart. At even lower temperatures, diesel fuel gels with a consistency of petroleum jelly. Biodiesel suffers from all these problems, but at higher temperatures. The rule of thumb is that B100 should be stored at temperatures at least 15°F higher than petrodiesel. Biodiesel made from palm oil has worse cold-weather performance than biodiesel made from other vegetable oils. The same winterizing and antigel agents used in petrodiesel can be applied to biodiesel. Shipping biodiesel in winter requires tank cars equipped with heaters such as steam coils. Adding kerosene in winter decreases the cloud and pour point temperatures of petro and biodiesel. It might be advisable to burn B20 during the winter and a higher concentration of up to B100 in summer. Having said this, B100 has been successfully employed in extremely cold climates such as Yellowstone National Park as long as the vehicles are equipped with suitable diesel fuel winterizing packages.[73]

Both petro and biodiesel fuels oxidize and create sediments in the presence of brass, bronze, copper, lead, tin, and zinc. Suitable metals for both are stainless steel and aluminum. Acceptable storage tank materials include aluminum and steel coated with fluorinated polyethylene or polypropylene or Teflon. Certain types of seals, gaskets, and adhesives including natural and nitrile rubber should be avoided. Most engines built after 1994 have been constructed with gaskets and seals that are biodiesel resistant. Diesel engine warranties are affected by using biodiesel; the impact of biodiesel usage on engine warranties varies among engine manufacturers.

Biodiesel can substitute for home heating oil with no special precautions. However, for older systems where there may be sludge in the tank, biodiesel should initially be B20 until biodiesel has removed sediments to avoid clogging filters. It is best for heating oil tanks to be inside a house as outdoor temperatures may fall below the pour point. With these precautions, B100 has been successfully substituted for home heating oil. Biodiesel as a fuel or for heating oil is susceptible to microbial growth, which is accelerated by the presence of water. Hence care has to be taken to remove water from fuel tanks, and biocides may be necessary for biodiesel stored for extended periods of time.

Palm Oil as a Biodiesel Feedstock

There are hundreds of oil-producing plants such as the avocado, almond, sesame, and tobacco seed and a host of nonplant sources including fish oil and animal fats that can be made into biodiesel. Figure 3.7 shows crops with the highest yield of oil, including tallow (animal fat) for a comparative measure.

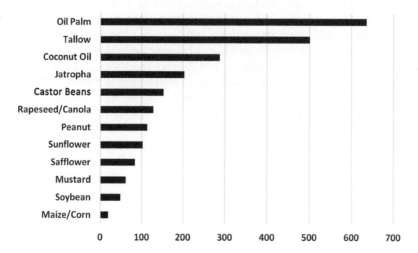

Figure 3.7 Biodiesel Output by Plant Type in Gallons per Acre

Two other sources of biodiesel that are even more highly productive than those listed in Figure 3.7 are the tropical rainforest tree *Copaifera langsdorffii* and algae. Copaifera, also known as the diesel or kerosene tree, produces large quantities of terpene hydrocarbons in capillaries honeycombed in its porous structure, which can be collected by tapping. A plantation of copaifera trees can yield 1,280 gallons per acre of biodiesel, double that of palm oil. Even more productive are algae, with the potential of up to 10,000 gallons of biofuels (biodiesel and ethanol) per acre.[74]

African oil palm is the highest yielding commercial oil-yielding plant producing biodiesel comparable to Brazilian ethanol from sugar. It grows in Africa and Southeast Asia with a stout tree trunk topped with a spray of fronds. Palm tree plantations have increased from 1 million hectares in 1994 to 10.8 million hectares (2.47 acres in a hectare) in 2013, or 41,700 square miles, close to the size of Ohio. Uncontrolled burning is the primary means to convert tropical forests to palm tree plantations. Smoke from burning tropical forests in Indonesia can be seen from space and affects air quality as far away as Singapore. Environmental opposition to the destruction of tropical forests and pollution of air has resulted in a 2 year moratorium on new plantation development, but the moratorium is seen as having limited effect.[75]

The palm is a highly efficient producer of vegetable oil, which is squeezed from the thick bunches of plum-size bright red fruit. An acre of oil palms yields as much oil as 13 acres of soybeans or five acres of rapeseed/canola. Palm oil is a major source of cooking oil and an important source of calories for Asians, rivaled only by sugarcane in terms of calories per acre. Two types of oil are extracted from this plant. The fleshy part of the fruit contains 45–55 percent oil used mainly in cooking oil, soaps, candles, and margarine. The kernel is about 50 percent oil and used mainly in ice cream, mayonnaise, baked goods, soaps, and detergents. The pressed pulp after extraction of the oil is an animal feed. Biodiesel from palm oil has a high cloud point, the temperature when wax crystals begin to form, making biodiesel from palm oil less desirable in colder temperatures unless treated.

Palm oil is intended to be the principal biodiesel feedstock in Asia. In 2014, total palm oil production was 61.6 million metric tons, of which Indonesia produced 33 million tons and Malaysia 19.8 million tons, or 86 percent of world production. Third and fourth leading nations are truly significant step-downs, with Thailand at 2 million tons and Colombia at 1 million tons.[76] Large palm tree plantations have been organized in Papua New Guinea and Borneo where environmentalists have expressed concern over their threatening the habitat for orangutans. Vast expansion of oil palm plantations for bio-diesel production will dramatically increase palm oil production, as palms reach maturity 8 years after planting. Their output can be sold for human or motor vehicle consumption as circumstances dictate.

Environmentalists are becoming increasingly concerned over growing evidence that the act of clearing (burning) tropical forests not only adds to carbon dioxide emissions, but also the replacement biofuel crop is less effective in removing carbon dioxide than the original habitat. This is clearly evident when viewing a photograph showing both a palm tree plantation and surrounding tropical forest; the decrease in carbon-absorbing foliage is self-evident. The concept of sustainable biofuels is rooted in looking at the whole picture of what was replaced before biofuel crops are cultivated in addition to the capacity of biofuel to reduce carbon emissions. Palm oil from plantations replacing tropical rainforests is not considered effective in reducing carbon emissions when carbon absorption of palm plantations is compared to that of tropical forests in addition to carbon dioxide released when the tropical forest was razed. For these reasons, carbon emission reduction of biodiesel from palm oil is considered negligible, if not negative. This is a parallel argument against corn ethanol in not being effective in reducing greenhouse gases when the total picture of fossil fuel consumed for growing and harvesting and processing is taken into account.

The United Nations Food and Agricultural Organization estimates that 104,000 square kilometers, the area of Iceland, is deforested each year globally. Deforestation is caused by lumbering, conversion to agricultural croplands, and forest fires, natural or otherwise. Deforestation does not include conversion of tropical forests to fruit tree or oil palm plantations or agroforestry operations where trees are replanted after harvesting such as for lumber or wood pulp for making paper. Thus the conversion of tropical forests to oil palm plantations is not considered deforestation regardless of their impact on carbon dioxide absorption. Reforestation counters deforestation. Reforestation can be organized such as in India to restore previously forested lands or grow biomass crops (trees) on marginal land in North America, Europe, and China. Reforestation can also be natural, such as the reversion of crop lands to forests.[77] Despite reforestation, the world is suffering from net deforestation, where nearly half of the world's loss of forest cover is in Brazil (27 percent) and Indonesia (17 percent) for either animal grazing, crop cultivation, or lumbering. Slash and burn is the primary means of deforestation preceded by logging of valuable native trees. However, Brazil has been active in recent years in sharply reducing its rate of deforestation.

Biorefinery Spread

Cooking oil is a critical foodstuff among the poor in Asia. Even those who raise or grow much of their food must purchase cooking oil. The price of palm oil is particularly critical to those who live on the edge of economic survival barely sustaining themselves for food, shelter, and clothing. Palm oil prices over the years have fluctuated widely from small changes, mere nuances in the relationship between supply and demand. The creation of vast palm plantations will sharply increase the supply of palm oil, conceivably reducing its cost as a food. However, these plantations were organized with the idea of selling biodiesel, not palm oil. From the point of view of a biorefinery dedicated to producing biodiesel, it is not high petroleum oil prices that economically support a biorefinery, but the spread or difference in price of a biofuel less the cost of feedstock. The price of biofuels is determined by petrofuels, and the cost of palm oil is determined by a host of factors affecting the supply and demand of a food commodity. Biorefinery spreads shown in Figure 3.8 are snapshots for August of the indicated year, calculated as the difference between the price of diesel oil and palm oil in dollars per metric ton.[78]

Diesel prices exceeded palm oil prices in 2008, resulting in a positive spread that ben-efited Malaysian and Indonesian biodiesel processing plants built to consume palm oil. But biorefineries stood idle in 2009–2011 when a negative spread made palm oil more valuable as food than as biodiesel feedstock. Idle biodiesel production plants do not earn revenue to support debt servicing charges, which for some meant bankruptcy. The spread in 2012 turned positive, but not necessarily enough to generate profits after the conver-sion cost of palm oil to biodiesel is taken into account. However, the spread in 2013 and 2014 of high diesel prices in relation to low palm oil prices provided the necessary incen-tive to start existing plants, if possible.

The positive spread did, however, support the operations of two of the world's larg-est biodiesel refineries, both owned by Neste Oil. The Singapore plant has an annual capacity of 800,000 tons of diesel fuel, similar to the company's plant in Rotterdam. Neste Oil also operates two smaller plants in Finland. The Singapore plant was intended to run exclusively on palm oil, but with strong criticism from those opposed to food for fuel, the Singapore plant ran mostly on tallow and other animal and fish wastes, the principal feedstocks for the company's European plants. Opposition to biodiesel from palm oil detractors against Neste Oil will be faced by other biodiesel producing plants in Southeast Asia.

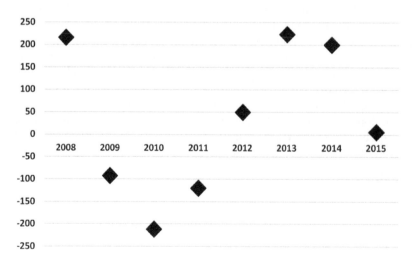

Figure 3.8 Biorefinery Spread of Diesel Oil Less Palm Oil (dollars per metric ton)

Managing Biodiesel Waste

In addition to "no food for fuel," environmentalists object to discarded husks, shell kernels, and fibers from the clusters holding the palm fruit rotting on the sides of roads and fields and discarded liquid wastes from extracting the oil palm seeds being dumped into open air lagoons to bio-degenerate. Discarded plant and liquid wastes make up 90 percent of the weight of the harvested cluster. Yet it is possible to utilize every part of the palm cluster. A plant in Honduras sells crushed meal after the oil is removed as chicken and livestock feed. All remaining plant waste is burned to produce hot water, steam, and electricity consumed by the plant, with excess electricity sold into the local power grid. Liquid waste is mixed with char from the furnace burning waste for generating electricity, some of which can be sold as a means to remove unwanted chemicals such as hydrogen sulfide. The remainder is placed in four cement biogas converters to produce carbon dioxide and methane. Carbon dioxide is separated and methane is burned to generate electricity. Perhaps someday carbon dioxide in concert with liquid waste may be a source of nutrients for an algal pond to produce biofuels and livestock feed. Recycling of waste contributes to the profitability of the plant by being self-sufficient in energy, with sales of excess electricity augmenting revenue.[79]

Another potential means of cleaning waste waters from biodiesel and other bioenergy plants is duckweed, one of the smallest (just a few millimeters in width) and simplest of freshwater plants. Duckweed floats on the surface and is more easily removed from water than algae and more easily dried and stored. Duckweed thrives on pollution-laden water and can be utilized for cleaning municipal waste and sewage water and waste from animal and poultry farms. Under proper circumstances, harvesting can occur every three days with the removal of half, leaving the other half to double in volume in the interim. Duckweed may prove to be a much cheaper form of tertiary wastewater treatment than conventional chemical plants. It is felt that duckweed may lend itself to bio-engineering to improve its content of either sugar, starch, or protein to produce different portions of bioethanol, biodiesel, or livestock feed. One researcher concluded that duckweed can produce four times the amount of starch as the same area of corn.[80] Another proposal is to feed duckweed into a process that employs a heated coil to produce hydrogen and methane, raw materials for motor vehicle hydrocarbons. Carbon residue can be burned to heat the coils for the next batch of feedstock. Carbon dioxide released during the process can be channeled back into greenhouses to further encourage growth of duckweed.[81]

Existing biodiesel refineries in Asia, fed mainly by fats and used cooking oil collected from restaurants, institutions, street vendors, and private citizens, will continue to expand their output. Excluding virgin palm oil will have a definite impact on the future growth of biodiesel in Asia, but a potential problem looms as recently planted palm plantations reach maturity and flood the market with new supplies. If palm oil prices plunge, pressure to divert excess supplies to biorefineries may be overwhelming to save the palm growers. As with corn in the US and sugar in Brazil, biodiesel may become a price support mechanism for palm oil. However, taking the growing opposition of food for fuel into consideration, it is problematic whether the future supply of biodiesel will be able to sustain its historical growth rate.

Other Biodiesel Feedstocks

Coconut is the world's third most-produced vegetable oil after peanuts and soybeans. Its output of biodiesel is comparable to the ethanol output of corn. Oil is pressed from the meat of the coconut after it has been husked and dried and the residue is fed to domesticated animals. Coconut oil is found in soaps, lubricants, hydraulic fluids, paints, synthetic rubber, margarine, and ice cream. The coconut tree is also a raw material for making twine or rope, mattress padding, matting, mats, rugs, and other products. Coconut trees grow along coastlines of tropical regions. Plans to build biodiesel processing plants using coconut oil as a feedstock in the Philippines and Papua New Guinea have been stymied by the same factors that have adversely affected biodiesel plants elsewhere in Southeast Asia.

Rapeseed in Europe (canola in the US) is cultivated half in Germany and most of the rest in France, the Czech Republic, and Poland, and also in Canada and Russia. Rapeseed is the principal feedstock for biodiesel in Europe, and the seed cake after the oil is removed is a high-protein animal feed. Rapeseed is the largest source for making biodiesel since global biodiesel production is currently centered in Europe. Rapeseed needs to be crop-rotated to avoid the spread of plant disease. This, along with soil quality considerations and growing European opposition of food for fuel, dampens expansion opportunities for rapeseed as a biofuel. While China and Japan are looking into rapeseed and used cooking oils and Australia and New Zealand are eying their plentiful supplies of animal fats as biodiesel feedstock, progress in these nations to develop biodiesel as a fuel has been slow.

Soybean is a major supplier of protein and is the largest source of vegetable oil by far, dwarfing the production of all other oilseed plants. Soybean oil is found in salad oil, margarine, and shortening and is used industrially in paints, printing inks, soap, insecticides, disinfectants, and other products. Though most biodiesel made in the US and Brazil is based on soybean oil, its consumption for making biodiesel is much less than Europe's consumption of rapeseed oil. On the surface, soybeans should not be considered for biodiesel production as its output of oil only exceeds corn, yet soy-diesel is heavily promoted in the US. Its support stems from the enormous acreage of land in the US dedicated to soybean production and the political clout of various soybean associations. While the relatively low vegetable oil yield of soybeans may be a problem, this is not the determining factor. The determining factor is the cost of soybean oil versus canola and castor oil and other vegetable oils. If soybeans can make a lower cost soy-diesel than biodiesel made from any other biofuel crop then this, in the last analysis, will make soybeans the desired feedstock.

Other potential vegetable oils for biodiesel are derived from peanuts, sunflowers, safflowers, and mustard. Peanut oil is used for cooking and in margarine, salad dressing, and shortenings, as well as in pharmaceuticals, soaps, and lubricants. Peanuts, native to South America, are now widely cultivated in warm climates and sandy soils particularly in West Africa. Sunflower, native to the western US, is cultivated primarily in Europe and Russia for biodiesel feedstock. It grows in both temperate and tropical regions and its oil is for basically the same purposes as peanut oil, with its seed cake, after the seed hulls are removed, also being a high-protein animal feed. Safflower is a thistle type of herb and is grown mainly for edible oil from its seeds. Safflower oil is high in unsaturated fatty acids and is found in salad dressings, cooking oil, margarine, candles, and as drying oil in paints and varnishes. Safflower is grown in Europe and in North and South America in areas favorable for wheat and barley cultivation. Mustard or carinata (*Brassica carinata*), a relative of rapeseed, is grown for its vegetable greens and is valued for its seeds, whose oil can be found in lubricants and hair oil. Its seed residue is an animal feed, fertilizer, and an organic pesticide. Research is being conducted on its suitability as a biodiesel feedstock, including genetic engineering to boost its oil content. Based on yield per acre and make-up of its carbon chains, mustard may be able to produce more fuel per acre than other oilseeds and, as another benefit, can be grown on semi-arid land not suitable for most oilseeds.[82]

Modern agricultural research and development efforts have been responsible for dramatic improvements in crop yields by such means as optimal fertilizer and pesticide applications, plant hybridization, genetic engineering, and greater productivity through mechanization. Corn yields in the US are up 65 percent since the mid-1970s and oil palm by 200 percent since the 1960s, with soybeans in Brazil up by over 300 percent since 1940. Despite gains in crop yields, there are limits on agricultural output of oilseeds in meeting biofuel demand. Considering both ethanol and biodiesel, for the EU to obtain a 10 percent share of biofuels for transport fuels, a large portion of its agricultural land for growing food crops would have to be dedicated to producing biofuel crops. This fact alone may be the reason behind the growing opposition to food for fuel in Europe. To meet this same objective of a 10 percent share of biofuels in transport fuels (gasoline and diesel fuel), about one-third of US and Canadian agricultural land would have to be converted to biofuel crops. But on a world basis, only 8 percent, and for Brazil only 2 percent, of its agricultural land would have to be converted to biofuel crops for every 10 percent incremental share of biofuels in transport fuels. The world has an enormous capacity to increase biofuel production, such as expanding jatropha and castor plant cultivation on marginal nonagricultural lands throughout Africa, Asia, and South America.

Biodiesel from Jatropha

Jatropha (*Jatropha curcas*) is a weed that grows in the tropical regions of Africa, South America, India, China, and Southeast Asia. It is thought to have originated in Central America and was introduced into other parts of the world by early explorers. The plant can grow on virtually barren land with little water, needs little fertilizer if cultivated, and produces inedible seeds rich in oil whose biofuel yield per acre beats many biofuel crops. Jatropha needs no fertilizer if residue after extracting oil, inedible seed cake, is placed around the plant (another example of fertilizer recycling). In Mali, jatropha is grown in long rows as a living fence to keep grazing cattle, repelled by its smell, off crop fields. It can be grown in rows interspersed with agricultural crops, fruit groves, and tree plantations. Jatropha prevents soil erosion and can be grown alongside rail and road right-of-way and on land not suited for agricultural crops—a perfect cash crop for the rural poor, generating both income and employment opportunities.

Jatropha begins to bear seeds 2 years after planting and its yield increases fourfold in 10 years, maintaining this yield throughout the remainder of its 50-year life. It is conceivable that African and Asian oil importing nations could become biodiesel exporters earning foreign exchange rather than spending their meager hard-currency reserves on petroleum imports. Myanmar (Burma) planned to cultivate 700,000 acres in jatropha to completely replace 40,000 Bpd of oil imports. While the plan failed in 2005/2006 partly from reliance on forced labor and a lack of commitment on the part of growers, it does point to the concept of jatropha or other oil seeds replacing oil imports. Myanmar is looking at less draconian approaches to biofuels at this time. Perhaps the Brazilian model for private farmers growing oil seeds on their land as a cash crop would be better, but this would require an entire remake of Myanmar's political system.

For jatropha or other oil seeds to replace oil imports, biodiesel conversion plants would have to be built. Conversion plants require both capital and operating funds and a source of feedstock. To assist growers, India has devised a system of microcredit to ease poverty among women by financing their growing jatropha to be sold to processing plants. Jatropha is planted along the railroad tracks between Mumbai (Bombay) and New Delhi supplying about 15–20 percent of locomotive fuel.

Biodiesel from Castor Beans

Castor bean or castor oil plant (*Ricinus communis*) is a labor-intensive crop that can provide jobs for the unemployed. India is the largest producer and exporter of castor oil followed by China and Brazil. Castor bean contains a poisonous toxin called ricin, is a food preservative and a medicinal laxative, and can be found in industrial adhesive, brake and hydraulic fluids, and paints and lacquers. Brazil considers castor oil a promising feedstock for biodiesel because, unlike food crops, castor bean has little value and can be grown on nonagricultural lands. Its cost is established by planting, harvesting, and shipping, which are primarily fixed, and its production has no impact on food crops. A fixed cost feedstock removes much of the risk of biorefineries whose spread is linked to a food crop.

Petrobras, through its Research Center (Cenpes), has been studying biodiesel production from castor oilseed and other oleaginous plants for which the company has patented technology. Despite the role of soybean oil in making biodiesel in Brazil, Petrobras is in favor of producing biodiesel from castor oilseed for the following reasons:

- Castor plant is robust and can be planted in several regions of the country (particularly the semi-arid Northeast) with relatively little demand on soil nutrients and water.
- Castor crop provides jobs for rural workers in areas too dry for normal agriculture.
- Plant residue after removing the seeds can be left for soil recovery or be a source of cellulosic ethanol or be converted to livestock feed or fertilizer.
- Castor seeds have high oil content (45–55 percent) and are not edible.
- After oil is removed, the seed cake can be used as a fertilizer or animal feed, but the latter requires detoxification.
- Castor seed plant leaves can be used to grow silkworms; the flower draws bees for honey production; the stalk can be used for firewood; and the seed's shell is rich in organic fertilizer.

Yet Brazil uses soybeans for 85 percent of its feedstock for biodiesel, with most of the remainder being tallow. The reason for soybeans as biodiesel feedstock is not its yield, which is the lowest except for corn, as shown in Figure 3.7, but its availability. Castor beans would require a capital investment and time for developing large-scale production, whereas soybeans are already grown on millions of acres. However, progress is being made to have castor beans be a cash crop for indigenous farmers to supplement their income. One idea is to incorporate castor oil plants with soybeans. In northeast Brazil, soybean farms lie idle during the dry season before soybeans can be replanted. Evofuel, an advocate of castor seed as a competitive biodiesel feedstock, is developing a high yield castor seed that thrives during the dry season in northeast Brazil. Evogene, its wholly owned subsidiary, and SLC Agricole are conducting a test program to develop castor plants for crop rotation with soybeans with castor seed sowed after soybeans are harvested and harvested before soybeans are sowed. Thus castor oil production would not compete with the food crops, providing farmers with an additional revenue source.[83] Petrobras has also initiated a program for family farms to grow oleaginous plants for conversion to biofuels. The company has begun production of a biodiesel fuel based on a blend of 30 percent castor bean oil and 70 percent sunflower seed oil produced by family farms. This program is active in semi-arid regions of Brazil and presently has 55,000 enrolled farms with the objective of 80,000 farms.[84]

Biodiesel from Algae

Biodiesel can be made from algae, which grow everywhere—oceans, ponds, swimming pools, goldfish bowls. Although these single-celled organisms have the same photosynthetic capacity to convert sunshine into chemical energy as plants, they lack roots, stems, leaves, and the reproductive organs of flowers, seeds, and fruits characteristic of plants. Algae's single-celled structure is extremely efficient in absorbing light and nutrients to reproduce by cell division. Certain types of algae produce oils similar to vegetable oils at 30 to 100 times per acre of pond water greater than the per acre yield of soybeans or corn. Moreover, algae require 99 percent less water than what biofuel crops absorb in their life cycle, neglecting evaporation of pond water (a major omitted factor in making this assertion). Oil produced by algae can be converted to biodiesel, and the residue containing carbohydrates can then be converted to ethanol and the remaining proteins and fermentation products a nutritious livestock feed with no waste.

Productivity depends on photosynthesis. The critical aspect of algal ponds is not depth, but surface area and amount of sunshine. This makes deserts an ideal location as long as there is a ready supply of water to replace that lost by evaporation. Water need not be fresh but can be drawn from saline aquifers, which otherwise have no use. Not only do algae grow vigorously in saline water, but their productivity can be enhanced by building the pond near a coal-burning electricity generating plant. Stack emissions percolating through the pond water allows algae to consume most of the carbon dioxide and nitrous oxides. Carbon dioxide enhances photosynthesis, and nitrous oxides act as fertilizer. Other fertilizers can be animal and human waste. Carbon dioxide present in stack emissions from a utility plant is recycled by being absorbed by algae and released when algae-made biodiesel and bioethanol are burned. Burning of algae-made biodiesel and bioethanol adds little carbon dioxide to the atmosphere as its fossil fuel energy input is quite low. Algal cultivation is a perfect conversion of waste (smokestack emissions, sewage water) into useful products. Algal ponds built around the Salton Sea in the Sonora desert in California can feed off polluted waters heavily laden with nitrogen and phosphate fertilizers.[85]

Groundwork for producing biodiesel from algae was laid in a nearly 20-year program (1978–1996) conducted by the US Department of Energy's Office of Fuels Development. The peak funding year for the Aquatic Species Program (ASP) was only $2.75 million, yet from this program came the entire framework of identifying the right type of algae and right conditions for maximum productivity. The conclusion of the program was that the process was not economic. But that was 1996. With current prices of crude oil and with the possibility of selling carbon credits, the economic equation has changed considerably. Moreover, technological progress has been made since the cessation of ASP to further reduce capital and operating costs and enhance productivity.

Algal ponds are shaped like racetracks where algae, water, and nutrients circulate, powered by paddlewheels to keep the algae suspended. Water and nutrients are continually fed to the ponds, and a portion of pond water is continually drawn off to harvest algae. Ponds are shallow to keep algae exposed to the maximum degree of sunlight for photosynthesis, and individual raceways can be connected into a single algal factory. Displacement of croplands dedicated to food crops for the production of biofuels is a major concern. In the US about 450 million acres of land are used for growing crops, much of that for animal feed. Another 580 million acres are grassland pasture and range. Croplands and grazing account for nearly half of the 2.3 billion acres within the US, with only 3 percent, or 66 million acres, considered urban land. It has been estimated that a pond system covering nearly 15,000 square miles or 9.5 million acres would produce enough biofuel to replace petroleum-derived motor vehicle fuels. This is a huge area of ponds that have to be constructed, yet it represents only 2 percent of the 580 million acres of grazing and rangeland. If these ponds were built in deserts, there would be no impact on agriculture or grazing land. The cost would be high, but so is acquiring oil from overseas and maintaining a continual military presence in the Middle East.

Photobioreactors contain algae within a closed system that drastically reduces land necessary to grow algae and water lost to evaporation, but adds considerably to capital costs. There is a great deal of biological science involved with photobioreactors to select the right type of algae from thousands of varieties, the correct temperature and pH of water, and the right mix of carbon dioxide and nutrients. Technological challenges include the design of an effective photobioreactor for high productivity, ease of removing algae, and low capital costs. As with algal ponds, a portion of algal water in a photobioreactor is removed and run through a centrifuge to remove algae, which must be dried before being pressed to remove the oil. The residual press cake can be used for a variety of purposes including bioethanol production, with the remaining residue being a nutritious animal feed. Drying and pressing oil out of algae is a fairly expensive process and more economical processes are being explored.

But developmental cost can be prohibitively high. The Arizona Public Service Company and its partner GreenFuel Technologies experienced initial success in a pilot plant to create biofuels from algae. Algae were grown in specially designed containers (bioreactors) fed with power plant emissions. Carbon dioxide absorbed by algae and nitrous oxides as fertilizer promoted growth. However, the widely publicized project was liquidated in 2009 when the next stage of commercial development could not be economically justified. The torch for algae grown at utility plants has been passed to Duke Energy. Its East Bend Station has a photobioreactor to convert carbon dioxide in flue gas to algal biomass under the auspices of the University of Kentucky Center for Applied Energy Research.[86]

Sapphire Energy is converting algae grown in racetrack shaped ponds straight to jet fuel, gasoline, and diesel fuel, bypassing the usual route of bioethanol, biodiesel, and livestock feed. Like all algae projects, it is heavily subsidized by the government. Sapphire's Green Crude Farm, started in 2010 in New Mexico, received funding from the American Reinvestment and Recovery Act plus a federal grant from the US Department of Energy and a loan guarantee from the US Department of Agriculture Bio-refinery Assistance Program. Green Crude Farm began operating in a commercial test phase in 2012. Green crude oil is extracted from algae and concentrated and refined as an oil to produce gasoline and jet and diesel fuel. Sapphire Energy's process requires only sunlight and carbon dioxide. Algae grow in nonpotable salt water ponds on nonarable desert land, not impacting fresh water resources or croplands. It takes advantage that algae are the most efficient photosynthetic plants as no energy goes into making roots, stems, seeds, or flowers. The annual energy capture of algae is 6–50 times more per acre than other biofuel feedstocks.

Every gallon of algae crude oil absorbs 13–14 kilograms of carbon dioxide from the atmosphere. Sapphire estimates that Green Crude has a well to wheels life cycle carbon impact that is about 70 percent less than fossil-based fuels and less than other biofuels. The refined products of Green Crude are totally compatible with petroleum transportation fuels for automobiles, trucks, and airplanes, with equivalent or better energy density. They can be used in the existing infrastructure of refineries, pipelines, and distribution centers, quite unlike bioethanol and, to a lesser extent, biodiesel. Sapphire believes that its production facilities are scalable, requiring only sunlight, a source of saline water, and desert land.[87]

Solazyme harnesses the prolific oil-producing capacity of microalgae acting on sugar with proprietary strains of algae that convert sugar to oil. Microalgae are heterotropic, which means that they can grow in the dark in fermenters consuming sugar that has already harnessed the sun's energy. Microalgae's natural oil production time is just a few days and it is possible to scale up the technology to make commercial quantities of oil.[88] Algenol Biofuels has a special technology that can produce ethanol for around $1.20 per gallon at a production rate of 10,000 gallons per acre in photobioreactors. The company plans to scale up to 20 million gallons per year and then to 1 billion gallons per year by 2020. Not all companies in algae are focused on energy products. Heliae is exploring algae in nutrition, therapeutics, health and beauty, and agrosciences. Aurora Algae, Cellana, and Earthwise are developing or providing algae-based omega-3 fatty acids, protein, and animal feeds along with biofuels. Phycal has a plant that makes sugar from cassava, which is then transformed by algae into ethanol.[89]

Research is being conducted on tunicates, a common marine species best described as a yellowish, slimy growth that consumes microorganisms and can be converted to a combustible biofuel. Kelp is a macroalgae that can grow over 100 feet in length from the bottom of the ocean where it is rooted to the surface. It can grow over one foot a day and can provide prodigious amounts of feedstock for potential conversion to ethanol and biomethane gas. The challenge is in harvesting seaweed and kelp mechanically and dewatering macroalgae, which is 60–70 percent water and laden with salt, in an energy-efficient way. Another avenue of algal research is dealing with a pond crash where algae suddenly die from fungi, rotifers (microscopic zooplankton that feed on microalgae), viruses, and competitive and undesirable forms of algae. Pond crashes can lead to tremendous costs in cleaning and removing dead algae along with the cause of their demise and reestablishing growth of desired algae.

Niche markets for high value algae products are already commercially successful or are well-along in becoming technically and commercially feasible. These include nutraceutical products such as heart-healthy omega 3–6 oils, DHA fish oils, and cosmetic products such as facial creams, environmentally friendly green chemicals, detergents, and solvents, biodegradable polymers for plastics, and protein and carbohydrate supplements for animal feed. These products may be able to fund the development of algae production facilities able to produce higher volumes than necessary for niche products. Excess production could be dedicated to biofuels. In other words, development of low volume, high value algal products may clear the way for production of high volume, low (relatively speaking) value biofuels.[90]

At the present time, biofuels from algae are not commercially competitive, but the US military has been a reliable customer for some companies, paying substantial premiums to ensure that these companies are kept in operation in its quest to find and develop alternatives to petrofuels in case of an interruption of oil supplies.

Biodiesel from Other Feedstocks

China is looking at guang-pi, an oil-bearing tree that can be grown on marginal land in addition to other oil seeds, animal fats, and used cooking oils. Biodiesel from rapeseed has reportedly been increasing, but China's demand for agricultural products stands in the way of massive areas of cultivated croplands being dedicated biofuels (China's prohibiting corn from being converted to ethanol in 2008 is a case in point). On the other hand, China possesses large areas of marginal land not particularly well suited for agricultural crops that could be brought into cultivation for biofuel crops. Japan is looking into biodiesel and has a growing number of entrepreneurial businesses being set up to convert used cooking oil from local restaurants and households into biodiesel. Some biodiesel is made from rapeseed grown on idle plots of land or rotated with rice crops. Like China, Japan has enormous demand placed on its land for food crops, but marginal land could be dedicated to biofuel crops. Other nations in Asia are mandating low levels of biodiesel such as B3. All in all, Asia is just starting to get its feet wet in the biofuel revolution.

Indigenous peoples of Africa and Asia should take to heart the fact that large inputs of outside capital are not necessary for them to bootstrap themselves into the biofuels age. In the 1930s, the British Institute of Standards in Calcutta examined inedible oils as potential diesel fuels. In 1940, a textile mill in the state of Andhra Pradesh was powered, as well as supplying power to the surrounding community, with inedible oils as fuel. This lesson was lost until 1999 when the people of Kagganahalli in the state of Karnataka told Dr. Udupi Srinivasa, a mechanical engineering professor at the Indian Institute of Science, about inedible oil from seeds of the honge tree that had been previously used for lamp oil. Dr. Shrinivasa initiated a project that resulted in a local company converting its diesel electric generators to run on honge oil, sharply reducing energy costs. Now the villagers of Kagganahalli possess electric generators fueled by biodiesel that pump water to irrigate their crops, and the previously dry and desolate village has been transformed into a thriving oasis of agricultural enterprise. Dr. Shrinivasa repeated this again with the villagers of Kammeguda in Andhra Pradesh, who now take seeds from karanji trees to produce biodiesel to power a diesel electric generator for lights and running water. He is also advocating oil from the mahua seed, which when mixed with ethanol produces a superior diesel fuel than petrodiesel.[91] A few other Indian villages have done the same. Thus, relatively small capital investments in diesel electricity generators fueled by biodiesel made from local seeds can become the first step in raising living standards and transforming the lives of impoverished people. This lesson in "micro-bootstrapping" should be taken to heart—there is no reason why this process has to stop at a handful of villages.

As much of the vegetable oil supply is used for cooking, there is a sizable market emerging from recycling waste vegetable or cooking oil for biodiesel feedstock. Waste vegetable oil must be filtered to remove residues and treated for acids produced by high-temperature cooking. Apart from this, used or waste vegetable oils can be easily converted to biodiesel as in China and Japan and other nations. Animal fats or tallow from cattle, pig, fish, and chicken processing plants are gathered for conversion to biodiesel in the US, Australia, New Zealand, and elsewhere. Some biodiesel facilities are located near meat processing plants to take advantage of their waste.

There are now a few companies converting animal fats and greases along with vegetable oils to biodiesel in commercial quantities. Renewable Energy Group has nearly 20 years of experience producing biodiesel from ten operating plants, with four in the pipeline. The company in 2014 produced 287 million gallons of biodiesel made from natural fats, oils, and grease.[92] DAR PRO Solutions has developed a biodiesel plant fed by recycled fats and used cooking oils. Its Diamond Green Diesel refining center, a 50–50 venture with Valero Energy, began operation in 2013 and now has a capacity to annually convert 1.1 billion pounds of animal fat and used cooking oil (11 percent of the nation's annual output of animal fat and used cooking oil) into 147 million gallons (10,000 Bpd) of green diesel. The plant is located at Valero's St. Charles, Louisiana refinery and is tied into Valero's oil product distribution system.[93]

Organic waste can produce biopetroleum by utilizing a thermal conversion process that mimics the geological and geothermal processes of nature to produce oil. In what was the world's first operating organic waste biorefinery, turkey and pig slaughterhouse wastes, called offal (and is awful!), were converted to fertilizer and fuel oil at a thermal conversion processing plant in Carthage, Missouri.[94] The process starts with grinding offal, followed by heat and pressure in a first-stage reactor to start a chemical breakdown. A sudden drop in pressure flashes off excess water and minerals, and the residue, when dried, produces a high-calcium powdered fertilizer. The remaining concentrated organic soup is heated to 500°F (260°C) and pressurized to 600 pounds per square inch in a second reaction tank. In 20 minutes, the process replicates what happens over millions of years to dead plants and marine organisms buried deep in the earth's sedimentary rock layers. Complex molecular chains of hydrogen and carbon are chopped into shorter chain molecules of fuel oil. A centrifuge removes water laden with nitrogen compounds and amino acids to be sold as a potent liquid fertilizer. What is left is fuel oil superior in quality to crude oil. It can be sold to an industrial plant as fuel or to a refinery for upgrading to high-end petroleum products. At peak production, 500 barrels of high quality fuel oil were made daily from 270 tons of turkey offal and 20 tons of pig fat. The process is energy-efficient, consuming only 15 percent of the plant's energy output to power its operations.[95] Despite these attributes, neighbors around the plant complained about the smell, forcing the plant to be closed while the litigants battled it out in court. The company failed to solve its olfactory problem and, in 2013, was acquired by Ridgeline Energy Services.[96]

Biodiesel Development

World biodiesel production increased from 61,000 Bpd in 2005 to 226,000 Bpd in 2008 and to 369,000 Bpd in 2011, an annual growth rate of 35 percent. Between 2009 and 2011, growth fell by half to 16 percent. In 2011, the chief producing areas were Europe at 165,000 Bpd, mostly in Germany and France; South America 94,000 Bpd, chiefly in Argentina, Brazil, and Colombia; North America 66,000 Bpd, and another 28,000 Bpd in Asia, mostly in Thailand and China. The chief consuming nations were the US at 58,000 Bpd, Germany 47,000 Bpd, Brazil 45,000 Bpd, Spain 32,000 Bpd, and Italy 31,000 Bpd.[97]

Europe

Biodiesel played a major role in Europe's quest for a 10 percent allotment of biofuels for transportation, which may be cut back to 6 percent. Development of a biodiesel market in the EU was set in motion by several public policy programs. One was the Common Agricultural Policy, a supranational farm policy for EU member nations that had established a "set-aside" program to reduce farm surpluses. The program allowed producers of grains, oilseeds, and protein crops to receive direct payments if they removed a specified percentage (up to 10 percent) of their farmland from production as a price support mechanism. However, nonfood crops were permitted on set-aside land. It turned out that farmers were better off growing crops for biofuels than receiving payments for idle land, which they did. The European Community Scrivener Directive laid the groundwork for tax relief for biofuel production plant investments. The EU also established incentives to make it attractive for Europeans to buy diesel-powered automobiles by partial subsidization of their purchase price and to make diesel fuel attractive over gasoline by reducing diesel taxes about 50 percent (at times 90 percent) in relation to petrodiesel taxes. These collective actions were necessary to compensate for the cost of biofuels being 2–3 times greater than petrofuels. This program was very successful, as a great preponderance of motor vehicles in Europe are now diesel-powered, giving preference for biodiesel over bioethanol as a biofuel. The objective of this government public policy to encourage switching from gasoline to diesel was to take advantage of the better mileage of diesel-powered automobiles to reduce oil imports.

Europe's production of biodiesel was 8.9 million metric tons in 2013, which grew by 16.3 percent to 10.4 million tons in 2014, and then more than doubled to 23.1 million tons in 2015. Germany produces 20 percent, followed by the Netherlands and France at 11 percent each.[98] In Germany, biodiesel is available at 1,900 filling stations, with the average distance between filling stations selling biodiesel being about 30 kilometers, although there are substantial regional variations.[99] Assuming biodiesel is 7.3 barrels per metric ton and with 42 gallons in a barrel, 23.1 million tons is equivalent to 7.1 billion gallons. Europe's largest biodiesel producer is Neste Oil, a Finnish oil company, with four biodiesel production facilities, two at its Finnish refinery and one each at its Rotterdam and Singapore refineries. Total output is 2 million tons per year of biodiesel using a variety of feedstocks, including waste animal and fish fats, and oils from rapeseed, camelina, jatropha, soybean, corn, and palm trees. Greenhouse gas emission reductions for vegetable and palm oils are around 47 percent, whereas waste animal and fish processing fats are around 90 percent.[100]

United States

Military vehicles and fleets owned by federal and state agencies and the US Department of Energy made up much of the initial biodiesel market required by the Environmental Protection Act of 1992. A part of incentivizing consumption of biodiesel in Germany was attributable to establishing and enforcing a universal set of biodiesel quality standards to allow engine manufacturers to have a design that burns either biodiesel or petrodiesel. In like fashion, the American Society of Testing and Materials (ASTM) issued detailed specifications for bio and petrodiesel fuels to ensure usage of both fuels in any engine design. The National Biodiesel Board established the National Biodiesel Accreditation Commission to develop and implement a voluntary program for accrediting producers and marketers of biodiesel under "BQ-9000, Quality Management System Requirements for the Biodiesel Industry."

In 2015, the number of biodiesel filling stations serving over B20 numbered about 670, concentrated in the Carolinas, Tennessee, and California.[101] Many other stations serve B2, B5, B10, and other percentage mixes less than 20 percent. In 2008, 700 million gallons of biodiesel were sold in the US and subsequently declined to 315 million gallons in 2010. But in 2011, biodiesel production surged to 1.1 billion gallons, satisfying the EPA biofuel mandate on biodiesel, which guaranteed a market for 1 billion gallons of biodiesel. Biodiesel production further improved to 1.1 billion gallons over the next 2 years and, in 2013, surged to 1.8 billion gallons, exceeding the biodiesel requirement under the Federal Renewable Fuel Standard, plus satisfying the majority of the Advanced Biofuel requirement as a substitute for imported sugar ethanol from Brazil.[102] While 1.8 billion gallons of biodiesel seems impressive, it is not quite so impressive when compared to Europe's 7.1 billion gallons.

Brazil

In addition to being the second largest ethanol producer in the world and being at the forefront of incorporating biofuels into automobiles, Brazil may be playing an additional role in developing biodiesel as well. Nearly all of the world's biodiesel production relies on methanol, but ethanol can be used. While biodiesel made from methanol contains an oil product, biodiesel made by substituting bioethanol for methanol would contain none. Researchers at the University of Sao Paulo have succeeded in developing a biodiesel formula that uses ethanol instead of methanol, making biodiesel entirely renewable. Biodiesel substituted for petrodiesel in sugar production would make ethanol entirely renewable.

Beginning in 2008, Brazil mandated 2 percent biodiesel (B2) in diesel fuel. This mandate is currently being filled by soybean oil. Soybeans have a relatively low yield of seed oil compared to castor seed, but soybeans are plentiful and available. In addition to Brazil, Argentina and Colombia are important producers of biodiesel, with other nations in South and Central America looking into biodiesel as an alternative for petrofuels. The future of castor bean as a feedstock for biodiesel remains problematic at this time.

Asia

Thailand is planning to revise upwards its biodiesel production target to 7.3 million liters per day (46,000 Bpd) by 2021 compared with an earlier target of 5.9 million liters per day under its Alternative Energy Development Plan (2012–2021). The current biodiesel production of 3 million liters per day is produced by 11 biodiesel refineries with a combined capacity of 5 million liters per day. Hence these biorefineries operate at 60 percent of capacity, but utilization will increase by expanding the mandated volume from the present B7 to B10 by 2019 with palm oil as the primary feedstock. The mandate for advanced biodiesel from jatropha, seaweed, wood, used vegetable oils, and other biomass has been severely cut back from cost considerations. The Thai biodiesel program is justified in savings from reduced oil imports.[103] Maturing of the palm plantations throughout Southeast Asia will have a strong impact on the growth of the biodiesel market in Asia unless detractors have their way.

Biodiesel Prospects

Rudolf Diesel ran his diesel at the Paris Exposition on peanut oil, not biodiesel. Straight vegetable oil (SVO) does not need to be converted to biodiesel, but diesel engines have to be adapted to burn SVO. SVO is cheaper than biodiesel with no conversion costs and does away with the glycerin disposal problem. However, SVO requires a heated auxiliary tank in order not to clog the fuel system in cold weather. Diesel conversion kits are available to adapt diesel engines to SVO. The kits consist of modified fuel injector nozzles, stronger glow plugs, dual fuel heaters, temperature controls, and parallel fuel filters. The converted diesel can run on SVO, biodiesel, or petrodiesel, or any combination of the three stored in separate tanks. However, free used cooking oil, which may include animal fats and fish oils, may not be acceptable fuels for the conversion kits. Some maintain that untreated SVO does not cause engine problems; it can go straight from the oil seed crusher to the fuel tank. Others maintain that SVO must be treated (de-gummed, deacidified, and usually winterized), and factories in Europe process fuel-grade vegetable oils as others process food-grade vegetable oils. In the respective arguments over whether biodiesel or SVO is better, one should not lose the point that both replace petrodiesel.[104]

There is a great deal of entrepreneurial activity that may shape the prospects for biodiesel. Steeper Energy Aps of Copenhagen has proprietary hydrofaction technology to convert low value organic feedstocks such as coppice (periodic cutting of scrub and young trees to ground level to stimulate growth), peat, and lignite coal to liquid fuels. Success of its pilot plant has led to a contract with the port of Frederikhavn to produce marine fuel that can easily meet stringent environmental standards. Annual production of 50,000–100,000 tons of marine fuel is only a small part of the 900,000 ton market that serves 100,000 vessels passing through the Skagen strait. Wood requirement is 2–3 times the output of marine fuel and is anticipated to be sourced from Russia, the Baltic nations, Sweden, Finland, and possibly Canada.[105] This same thermal conversion technology can also be adapted to process sewage, old tires, and mixed plastics. Perhaps someday, towns and cities will build biorefineries at their sewage and waste collection facilities to sell motor vehicle fuels to the public in competition with oil companies!

Amyris produces renewable diesel in Brazil and fuels 300 public transit busses in Sao Paulo and Rio de Janeiro. Its diesel fuel is made from sugar, with an 80 percent reduction in greenhouse gas emissions, no sulfur emissions, and significant lowering of nitrous oxides and particulate matter emissions. It is superior to petrodiesel, with a high cetane number, very low cloud point, and ideal lubricity, and is made from Biofene, which, in turn, is a product of microbial reactions with sugar. Biofene has also been used in cosmetics, perfumes, detergents, industrial lubricants, and even medical applications. Amyris has also developed an approved renewable aviation fuel in a joint venture with the French oil company Total. Renewable jet fuel is made from a bio-derived chemical farnesane that is mixed with regular jet fuel to fuel aircraft flights in Brazil.[106]

Research is underway to genetically-engineer a hydrocarbon-rich tobacco plant that will yield 1,000 gallons of biofuel per acre of land, three times that of corn ethanol. It is envisioned that biofuel tobacco would supplant growing tobacco for smoking. Other research is being conducted on the molecular level to improve the efficiency and effectiveness of biofuel processes. As an example, scientists are performing research on how to model molecules on supercomputers to simulate production of cellulosic ethanol. Use of microbes in producing biofuels is considered third generation, with ethanol and biodiesel as first and cellulosic ethanol and algae as second generation.

An apartment complex in Hamburg, Germany, features algae growing between the glass panels to create biofuel, produce heat, shade the building, and abate street noise. The cost of electricity, however, is considerably more expensive than solar panels. If this could be further developed, vertical algae farms built into apartment complexes and office buildings may become a future architectural rage.[107] Algae.Tec in Australia has succeeded in growing and harvesting microalgae in enclosed, used shipping containers. Algal farms within the shipping containers are not exposed to light, but light is fed into the containers through optical fibers from solar collecting disks. Containers are also fed carbon dioxide from fumes from a coal-fired power plant along with phosphorous and nitrogen fertilizers. It is anticipated that each container will produce 250 tons per year of triacylglycerol oils, which can be chemically converted to biodiesel and pelletized animal feed. Part of the profitability is the coal plant having to pay less in carbon taxes.[108] The US Navy is experimenting with using electricity to extract carbon dioxide and produce hydrogen from seawater. In the presence of an iron-based catalyst, carbon dioxide and hydrogen are converted to an olefin, a precursor to jet fuel. This is part of an ambitious Navy program to half petroleum fuel demand by substituting various sorts of synthetic fuels.[109]

The International Renewable Energy Agency (IRENA) in its 2014 report concluded that consumption of biomass in terms of cooking and heating for the indigent will decline in favor of more desirable fuels, but that other biomass consumption segments will increase. It is anticipated that there will be a 2.6 percent growth of demand for heating modern buildings, nearly 5 percent growth as a fuel for industry, and a 10 percent growth both as a motor vehicle fuel and in district heat generation, supplanting, to some degree, natural gas. Incremental sources will be biogas from human and animal waste, agricultural, forest, and wood residues, plus greater consumption of wood pellets for generating electricity and home heating and biomass in co-firing coal burning plants. These will also be accompanied by greater growth of motor vehicle and aircraft biofuels (cellulosic ethanol and biodiesel from non-edible vegetable oils and conversion of wood waste). From the perspective of 2030, nations with the greatest growth potential for biomass demand are the US, China, India, Brazil, Indonesia, and Russia. Nations with the highest share of biomass as a fuel are anticipated to be Brazil, Nigeria, Indonesia, Denmark, France, Germany, and Ecuador. This will be achieved by a more organized approach to gasify human and animal and food wastes, forest and wood residues, and more intense growing of biomass fuel crops on currently nonproductive land. Since the weighted overall growth rate for biomass consumption of 3.7 percent is higher than overall energy growth, biomass will be playing a greater role in satisfying aggregate energy demand in 2030 than in the past.[110]

Biofuel Risks

Production of biofuels (mainly ethanol, but also biodiesel) in 2014 was 1.4 million Bpd and is expected to grow to 2.5 million Bpd by 2020.[111] For this to be achieved, revenue must pay all capital, operating, and feedstock costs. No business is without its risks, and biofuels are no exception. Biofuels have historically been more costly than petroleum products, requiring various forms of government intervention in the form of subsidies and mandates to keep biofuel companies afloat. One risk is the fickleness of governments to arbitrarily and abruptly change established policies. In the 1980s, the government of Brazil faced increased subsidy payments to support ethanol producers stemming from falling oil prices. Rather than pay more in subsidies, the government, after nurturing and fostering the biofuels revolution, walked away from its energy child. All subsidies to the ethanol producers were abruptly ended and sugar growers were permitted to sell into the international market, which had a higher price than the domestic market. Cutting government expenditures and increasing the nation's export earnings benefited the government at the expense of the ethanol producers. Unable to operate profitably, many producers were forced into financial restructuring. Despite ethanol imports, the resulting shortages of E100 led to a loss of consumer confidence in the availability of pure ethanol. Sales of pure ethanol automobiles plummeted and, in response, automobile companies concentrated on producing gasohol vehicles. Government policies that brought about the pure ethanol automobile ultimately led to its demise. The advent of the flex fuel vehicle gives drivers complete flexibility on the degree of ethanol and gasoline in fueling the vehicle, mitigating the risk of another shift in government policy.

Another example of the fickleness of government mandates is the political reaction to the no food for fuel movement, which is growing in Europe. As discussed, the proposed cutback of 10 percent biofuels to 6 percent first generation biofuels in Europe will not have any impact; but if actual consumption were near or above 6 percent, this would have a negative impact on capital investments. However, the no food for fuel movement may have a real negative impact on the enormous investment in palm plantations in Southeast Asia.

In addition to abrupt changes in government policies toward biofuels, another major risk faced by biofuel providers is the biorefinery spread, the price differential between petroleum products and the cost of the biofuel feedstock. In Brazil, the fall in the price of oil accompanied by a hike in the international price of sugar when sugar growers were given the right to sell in the higher-priced international market financially squeezed the ethanol producers. The price for ethanol declined to remain competitive with gasoline on an energy-content basis and the cost for sugar rose to the international price. It is not the price of oil that is critical for a biorefinery operator, but the spread between the price of oil and the cost of feedstock. This is similar to the classic refinery margin or spread between the price of refined products (gasoline and diesel) and the cost of crude oil, with one major difference. The classic oil refinery margin deals with one commodity in two forms, with crude oil on one side and refined products on the other, where there is a strong price linkage between the two. Even so, oil refiners can be trapped in a spread where the difference between the price of oil products and the cost of crude oil is too narrow for profitable operations. The biorefinery margin is the price difference between two disparate commodities of crude oil on one hand and foodstuffs (sugar, corn, vegetable oils) on the other. There is no statistical linkage between the two, which means both behave as independent variables.

Figure 3.8 tells the whole story. Biodiesel producers in Indonesia and Malaysia suffered from a negative biorefinery margin between the prices of crude oil and palm oil in 2009. As crude oil prices set record highs, one would expect prosperity for the biodiesel producers; but not when palm oil is selling at an even higher price. Caught in this financial vise, with the government unwilling to pay a promised subsidy to keep biodiesel producers financially whole, Indonesian biodiesel production fell by 85 percent. While oil palm plantation owners were making a financial killing, oil palm biodiesel producers were taking a financial beating. Further investments in biodiesel plants ceased. The general retreat from biodiesel plants was not confined to Indonesia and Malaysia. In 2008 and 2009, ethanol plants in the US came under financial pressure during times of record high gasoline and corn prices that drastically reduced the biorefinery spread. This caused some plants to shut down and a few firms to declare bankruptcy. Then in late 2008 and 2009 both gasoline and corn prices fell, but the biorefinery spread did not improve sufficiently to prevent the bankruptcy of a leading ethanol producer.

As seen in Figure 3.8, 2012 was a year of transition where the spread was positive, but not sufficient to cover the costs of operation of a biodiesel plant. But 2013 and 2014 were good years for the biodiesel producers, followed in 2015 by a narrowing of the spread to the point of closing plants unless some government aid package or subsidy was activated. Closure means zero revenue. Costs have to be drastically cut, which means disbandment of nearly all of the workforce. If none are left, then the plant will rapidly decay from hot humid weather, lack of maintenance, and no security against vandalism. Moreover, resumption of operations means hiring previously fired personnel with attendant morale problems. If key people are kept on the payroll, how are they paid? How are debt financing costs paid? The history of profitable operations depicted in Figure 3.8 should give investors pause, since risk inherent in the biorefinery spread is far greater than the oil refinery spread.

Of course, there are means of risk mitigation. Oil refiners have the ability of taking opposite derivative positions in futures, forwards, and swaps in crude oil and in gasoline and diesel fuel to lock in a spread. This also exists for biofuel producers except that, rather than locking in a spread of two forms of the same commodity, biofuel producers must lock in a spread between two disparate commodities: agricultural crops and petroleum. This, of course, makes it more difficult to mitigate risk in that biofuel producers have to be knowledgeable of market outlooks for both petroleum and agricultural crops. Moreover there is a basis risk because taking a position in petrodiesel to lock in revenue may not fully protect biodiesel, as prices for petrodiesel and biodiesel, while presumably close, are not guaranteed to be close.

There are other ways to mitigate risk of a negative biorefinery spread. One is to use feedstocks not grown for food such as jatropha and castor beans. Prices for these feedstocks are closely related to their production costs and are relatively fixed, quite unlike the volatile market value for foodstuffs like sugar, corn, rapeseed oil, palm oil, and other vegetable oils. Similarly cellulosic ethanol is made from biomass wastes or cellulosic crops like fast-growing trees and grasses, whose costs are collecting or planting and harvesting, and shipping. These costs are not affected by the price of food. With the cost of cellulosic ethanol feedstock more or less fixed, there is no point in taking a derivatives position to protect against an adverse price change of raw material feedstock. This simplifies risk mitigation as cellulosic ethanol producers need only worry about the market outlook for oil. If it is possible to separate the protein content from the biomass sources of cellulosic ethanol, then food prices become a source of incremental revenue, not a source of incremental cost or a risk to be considered. The same can be said about the possibility of using algae as a feedstock for biodiesel and bioethanol where the residue is a source of protein for animal feed.

A mandatory requirement for a certain percentage of bioethanol in gasoline or biodiesel in petrodiesel is not a guarantee that biofuel producers can cover their costs. Mandatory requirements only work when the biorefinery spread between oil prices and feedstock costs cover the operating and financial costs of a biofuels plant. A volume mandate does not cover the biorefinery spread. However, if biofuel producers cannot fulfill a mandate, then petrofuel providers must bid up the price of biofuels to secure supplies. But the equation changes when the biofuel providers produce more than what is required under the mandate. Now competition to have one's output volume included in the mandate lowers the price. If the price no longer covers costs, then biofuel firms will find themselves in financial distress even with a mandate to purchase a large portion of their output.

Biofuels and petrofuels are both technologically challenging. In some respects, biofuels are less challenging in that oil exploration and development give way to agricultural pursuits or waste collection. But biofuels can be more challenging in that the refining process, particularly for cellulosic ethanol and algae, has a long way to go before becoming commercially viable. Cellulosic ethanol and algae are the future as second generation biofuels versus the first generation biofuels whose feedstocks are food crops. If cellulosic technology can become commercially viable, there is enough cellulosic feedstock in our backyard to make North America independent of oil imports, but the ethanol would have to be transformed to biobutanol for national distribution. Cellulosic ethanol has the potential to make corn and grain ethanol transitional biofuels. What would be the point of extracting just the starch from corn and grains to make ethanol when the whole plant can be utilized?

For biodiesel, jatropha and castor beans can fix the cost of raw material to production and shipping and not by their value as a foodstuff. Algae have a great potential for biodiesel and bioethanol production and as livestock feed. Algae can also make green crude oil that can be transformed to petrofuel products without having to extract oils, starch, and sugars. As demonstrated in India, local communities can bootstrap themselves into energy independence, relying on low-cost inedible oleaginous seeds from weeds and trees for feedstocks to generate power. Impoverished oil importing nations in Africa and Asia have the potential of becoming biodiesel exporting nations, improving the living standards of their people.

The greatest risk faced by biofuel producers is low oil prices as experienced in late 2008 and early 2009 and again in 2014 and 2015. Dealing in ranges that include variation in price of feedstocks, ethanol producers in Brazil require a minimum oil price between $35 and $45 per barrel in order to price ethanol to cover costs. The minimum oil price to support ethanol producers in the US is between $50 and $60 per barrel. Ethanol from grain in the EU requires a minimum crude oil price between $75 and $100, for biodiesel made from vegetable oils the minimum crude price is between $90 and $110, and for cellulosic ethanol a minimum crude price between $100 and $130 is necessary for existing technology to be commercially feasible. Thus the thrust to lower the capital and operating costs of biofuel plants to improve profitability also mitigates the risk of low oil prices.

Projects and Problems

Project 3.1a

What are the comparative carbon emissions in burning wood versus burning coal? This is a critical question if biomass is to displace fossil fuels. As the text indicates, this is a controversial issue. The assignment is to search the available information and write a short paper addressing this issue replete with supporting statistics and your belief about which of these contentions is true.

Project 3.1b

As an alternative to Project 3.1a, what are the carbon emissions for burning ethanol made from corn in the US as compared to gasoline? Some feel that carbon emission reduction is at least marginal, whereas others feel that carbon emissions have increased in substituting ethanol for gasoline. Ethanol proponents indicate the carbon emissions are down by about 40 percent. This, too, is a contentious issue because if it is found that ethanol increases carbon emissions, then dedicating 40 percent of US corn production to motor fuels simply does not make sense from an environmental viewpoint. Research this subject and write a report with your findings.

Project 3.1c

The other major argument for corn ethanol is that it displaces crude imports, making the US less vulnerable to an interruption in world oil flows. What evidence is there that ethanol does reduce foreign dependence on oil imports—can you quantify the impact of ethanol on US oil imports? How has fracking oil from hard shale affected gasoline imports? How about gasoline consumption—has that affected gasoline imports?

Project 3.2

Whereas biomass was once welcomed as a source of electricity, there has been growing opposition. What is the nature of this opposition? Suppose you are a manager of a project to build a biomass electricity generating plant. What would be your reaction to these assertions? Remember no plant, no job.

Problem 3.1

As per the text, the *World Energy Outlook* projects bioenergy consumption at 1,881 million tons of oil equivalent (mmtoe) in 2035, which represents annual growth of 1.6 percent from the 2010 bioenergy consumption of 1,277 mmtoe. Verify the growth rate for power generation of 5.2 percent if the power generation share of the bioenergy pie will grow from 9 to 22 percent, and the growth rate for motor vehicle fuels of 4.8 percent if its share of the bioenergy pie increases from 5 percent to 11 percent.

Problem 3.2

Calculate what percent of US, Brazil, and world ethanol production is represented in gasoline production. For 2014, obtain the figures for US, Brazil, and world oil consumption in thousands of barrels per day from *BP Energy Statistics*. Multiply US oil consumption by 0.5 to estimate gasoline production and 0.4 for the others. (US refineries have been designed to have the higher gasoline yield on refining crude oil.) Take these figures and multiply by 42 gallons per barrel and 365 days per year and divide by 1,000 to obtain millions of gallons of gasoline consumption. The 2014 production of ethanol in the US is 14,300 million gallons; for Brazil 6,190 million gallons; and for the world 24,570 million gallons. What percentage does ethanol production represent with respect to gasoline production in terms of volume (gallons) for the US, Brazil, and the world? Should you reduce ethanol by 30 percent to place ethanol on the same energy equivalent basis as gasoline? If so, what is your share of ethanol on an energy equivalent basis? Which should be used when the share of ethanol is being represented to the public and why?

Problem 3.3a

Suppose that gasoline costs $3.50 per gallon and an automobile gets 25 miles to the gallon on gasoline. Suppose that a 70 percent plus ethanol mix (E70+) gets 20 miles to the gallon. What should be the price of the ethanol mix to be price equivalent to gasoline? If the price of the ethanol mix sold above this price, what would be your reaction?

Problem 3.3b

Suppose that premium gasoline sells for $4 per gallon and regular gasoline for $3.50 per gallon. If E85 is priced the same as premium gasoline, what is its equivalent price compared to regular, taking into consideration its energy content being 30 percent lower than regular gasoline and that premium gasoline can increase your mileage by 7 percent over regular?

Problem 3.4

Suppose that an acre of corn can produce 300 gallons of ethanol. A 250,000 Bpd oil US refinery can produce 112,500 Bpd of gasoline (50 percent gasoline at 90 percent utilization). Further suppose that a 250,000 Bpd refinery including some allotment for the producing wells, tanks, pipelines, etcetera takes up 1 square mile of land, more than a generous allotment of land. Taking into consideration that ethanol has 70 percent of the energy content of gasoline and that land requirements for growing corn should be expanded by 25 percent to take into consideration the roads, towns, ethanol plants, and all the other things that make up a community, how many square miles of land (640 acres in a square mile) are necessary to replicate the oil refinery? The District of Columbia is 68.3 square miles—what is the equivalent area in DC units?

Problem 3.5

Redo the calculations for a sugar plantation in Brazil where the output is 600 gallons of ethanol per acre. What is your conclusion regarding the comparative land requirements for corn and sugarcane in making ethanol?

Problem 3.6

Obtain the cost estimate of building a 250,000 Bpd refinery. This is the capital cost to produce 112,500 Bpd gasoline. Obtain the cost estimate for a standard sized ethanol production plant. What is its output in ethanol production and how many of these plants do you need to substitute for a 250,000 Bpd refinery, taking into consideration the lesser energy content of ethanol? Remember that an ethanol plant may be in production around 3–4 months per year, starting with the harvest plus whatever is put into inventory. It is possible for an ethanol plant to run 12 months a year if the inventory is high enough, but this is not normal practice. Whatever you assume, how do the capital costs for a 250,000 Bpd oil refinery compare with the total capital costs for the number of ethanol plants needed to produce the same amount of ethanol on an energy equivalent basis as the refinery?

Problem 3.7

A 2,000 mW biomass fueled electricity plant requires 6,600 square kilometers for sustainable biomass growth to support the plant in the UK. How many square miles of woodland is this? This assessment probably incorporates the idea that not all land area can be used for biomass production, as roads and villages and ponds and streams will affect biomass production. Assuming this is true, how many equivalent Washington DCs (68.3 square miles) is this? What would be your assessment for an equivalent plant in Brazil?

Problem 3.8a

DuPont is building a cellulosic plant in Iowa as described on their Website, which has some interesting facts (http://biofuels.dupont.com/cellulosic-ethanol/nevada-sitEcEfacility). One is that there are 815,000 acres of corn grown within a 30 mile radius of the plant. This provides a measure of the percentage of land that can be cultivated, as Iowa is an intensely agriculturally devoted state. Calculate the square miles of a circle with a radius of 30 miles (remember Pi R^2?). Translate this to acres (640 acres per square mile) and compare the acres under cultivation with what is available. What do you think of the result?

Problem 3.8b

The harvest rate is 2 tons of stover per acre. How many tons are available if all 815,000 acres were available for making ethanol? What is the total output of ethanol if cellulosic ethanol is 150 gallons per acre and ethanol from corn kernels is 300 gallons per acre?

Problem 3.8c

This figure is gallons per year—what would be the equivalent barrels per day? Reducing this by 0.7 to make cellulosic ethanol energy-equivalent to gasoline, how does this compare with the output of a 250,000 Bpd oil refinery (50 percent gasoline with an effective utilization of 90 percent)? What would be the land requirement for stover to be equal to one 250,000 Bpd oil refinery? How many equivalent Washington DCs (68.3 square miles) is this?

Problem 3.8d

The above ethanol applies for corn stover plus corn kernels for an output of 450 gallons per acre. How many Washington DCs are necessary if miscanthus is substituted for corn with an ethanol yield of 780 gallons per acre to be equivalent to the gasoline output of a 250,000 Bpd refinery? Switchgrass has a wide range of ethanol yield per acre of 400 to 640 gallons per acre per year. What would be your assessment if switchgrass is substituted for corn (obviously switchgrass would be grown on land conducive to higher yields)? Generally speaking biomass such as fast growing trees have yields varying from 400 to 800 gallons per acre per year. Construct a curve that would answer the above where the number of DCs is the dependent variable and gallons per acre per year for various feedstocks is the independent variable to have the same output as a 250,000 Bpd refinery.

Problem 3.8e

Giant King Grass (GKG) can be grown on marginal land, but requires water and fertilizer. In comparison to corn stover, its energy content per dry pound is higher at 7,900 Btu versus 7,560 Btu per dry pound of stover. However, its maximum yield is up to ten times greater than corn stover.[112] For argument's sake, suppose that its yield can be maintained in a sustainable manner at eight times that of stover, taking into consideration the difference in heat content. If the cellulosic output of corn stover is 150 gallons per acre, then GKG can produce 1,200 gallons of ethanol per acre. What would be the number of DCs to equate to a 250,000 Bpd oil refinery using the same approach as Problem 3.8b? What would be some of the considerations that should be included in evaluating the relative cost of cellulosic ethanol from GKG to corn ethanol? What would be the impact if GKG were grown in tropical regions where two crops can be harvested annually?

Problem 3.8f

Corn, sugar, miscanthus, and switchgrass are annual crops—poplar trees are harvested about every 10 years. How does this affect your approach to Problem 3.8c?

Problem 3.8g

Myanmar (Burma) had a grand plan to convert 700,000 acres of land for jatropha plantations to produce 40,000 Bpd of diesel fuel that would displace the nation's oil imports. This land allotment probably included non–jatropha growing activities such as villages, roads, waterways, and water bodies. Be that as it may, suppose that 30 percent of this allotment will not be dedicated to growing jatropha. How does this land requirement fit in with your assessments of land use per unit oil output in the previous problems?

Problem 3.9a

The yield of biodiesel from soybeans is 48 gallons per acre and 151 gallons per acre for castor beans. The average annual price for soybeans 2003–2015 varied from $6 per bushel to $14 per bushel. Assuming that the cost for transforming soybean and castor oil to biodiesel is the same, how much can you afford to pay for a bushel of castor beans to be competitive with soybeans during this period of time? Draw a chart using XY Scatter showing the relationship.

Problem 3.9b

The national average yield of soybeans in the US is 40 bushels per acre and castor 30 bushels per acre in Brazil. Both are planted annually; how does this difference in yield affect the relative cost of growing castor beans versus soybeans?

Problem 3.9c

A ton of castor oil is estimated to cost $400 per ton in Brazil and soybean oil $160 per ton. The cost of castor oil does not change as it is inedible. But while soybean oil can be produced at $160 per ton, it is also sold for food. The relevant cost comparison is $400 per ton for castor oil versus the price of soybean oil in dollars per ton. A bushel of soybeans weighs 60 pounds and a bushel of castor beans 46 pounds. What price can be obtained from soybeans in dollars per ton when its price varied from $6 per bushel to $14 per bushel? What is the breakeven soybean oil price in dollars per ton with the fixed price of $400 per ton for castor beans in Brazil? This assessment presumes that the outputs of biodiesel from a ton of soybean oil and a ton of castor oil are the same, which should be checked.

Problem 3.10

Indonesia produces about 31 million tons and Malaysia 19 million tons of palm oil, and all, or nearly all, are being consumed as vegetable oil. Let us suppose that another 50 million tons of palm oil is in the form of planted, but not yet mature, oil palm plantations throughout all of Southeast Asia and that this will be converted to biodiesel. Assuming 7 pounds weight for a gallon of palm oil, what would be the gallons per year and then the barrels per day output of 50 million tons of palm oil? If all 50 million tons were converted to biodiesel, which may not be possible from environmental objections, how many standard sized 250,000 Bpd refineries is this equivalent to if a refinery's product slate is 25 percent petrodiesel? Assuming an output of 600 gallons of palm oil per acre, how many acres does 50 million tons of palm oil represent? Put in a 25 percent factor for nonagricultural activities; how many DC equivalents does this represent?

Problem 3.11

The best biofuel output is algae, which is estimated to be able to produce up to 10,000 gallons of oil per acre of open pond. This could be converted to biodiesel with the starch residue converted to bioethanol. Assuming this is true and working off 10,000 gallons per acre, assuming that 80 percent of the output of a 250,000 Bpd refinery is petrofuels, plus a 25 percent factor for nonproductive activities associated with an algae plantation, how many DC equivalents of ponds would be needed to substitute for the refinery?

Thought Question

It was mentioned at the beginning of this chapter that "Biomass will never replace fossil fuels, other than on the margin, nor is there any hope that we can return to a world where biomass played a significant role in satisfying society's energy needs." Do you agree with this statement, and if so, why?

Notes

1 World Health Organization, Website www.who.int/mediacentre/factsheets/fs292/en.

2 The "smoke" in the Smokey or Smoky Mountains has been attributed to vegetation exhaling volatile organic compounds that have a high vapor pressure and easily form a mist at normal atmospheric conditions. It has also been attributed to warm humid air from the Gulf of Mexico cooling rapidly as it rises to higher elevations. This is an example of confusion over causes of natural events: a human phenomenon repeated time and again.

3 My father, a boy at that time, told me that each family on Long Island (New York) would chop down one large tree near their home to satisfy their annual energy needs for cooking and heating. Naturally there came a time when all the large trees were gone and fossil fuels had to fill the gap. He also reminisced about wading into Long Island Sound to gather all the oysters he wanted by feeling them with his feet and picking them up with his hands!

4 Envirofit, Website www.envirofit.org.

5 United Nations, Website www.un.org/esa/forests/pdf/national_reports/unff5/india.pdf.

6 Sources are Balanço Energético Nacional (BEN) (2011) and International Energy Agency World Statistics (2010).

7 For further information about *miscanthus x giganteus*, contact Professor Stephen Long, University of Illinois at Urbana-Champaign, 1401 West Green Street, Urbana, Illinois 61801.

8 Bruce Dorminey, "Is Shrub Willow a Viable Biomass Feedstock for the US?" *Renewable Energy World* (November 14, 2013), Website www.renewableenergyworld.com/rea/news/article/2013/11is-shrub-willow-a-viable-biomass-feedstock-in-the-us.

9 Parker Gallant, "Ontario Power Trip," *Financial Press* (January 17, 2013), Website http://opinion.financialpost.com/2013/01/17/ontarios-power-trip-mcguintys-legacy.

10 Ontario Power Generation, Website www.opg.com/generating-power/thermal/Pages/thermal.aspx. See also "Sneak Peek: Inside the Atikokan Biomass Plant Conversion," Power Engineering (September 12, 2013), Website www.power-eng.com/articles/2013/09/sneak-peek-inside-the-atikokan-biomass-plant-conversion.html.

11 Greenpeace, Website www.greenpeace.org/canada/Global/canada/report/2011/10/ForestBiomess_Eng.pdf. This concern is also cited in N. Armaroli, V. Balzani, and N. Serpone, *Powering Planet Earth* (Weinheim, Germany: Wiley VCH, 2013).

12 William Strauss and Laurenz Schmidt, "A Look at the Details of CO2 Emissions from Burning Wood vs. Coal," FutureMetrics (January, 2012), Website www.bcbioenergy.ca/wp-content/uploads/2012/02/c02_whitepaper.pdf.

13 When my brother lived in Maryland, he would take his pick-up truck to a nearby lumber mill for a load of bark and other tree and lumber waste conveniently cut in foot long lengths, as did others, to load a furnace that heated his home.

14 "Bonfire of the Subsidies," *The Economist* (April 6, 2013).

15 B. Mendell and A. Lang, *Wood for Bioenergy* (Durham, NC: Forest History Society, 2012).

16 Lisa Gibson, "Facing the Vocal Opposition," *Biomass Magazine*, Website http://biomassmagazine.com/articles/3741/facing-the-vocal-opposition. See also Craig Rucker, "U.K. Biomass Plants Fuel Local Opposition," CFACT (2013), Website www.cfact.org/2013/05/28/u-k-biomass-plants-fuel-local-opposition.

17 New Biomass Energy, Website http://newbiomass.com. See also "Torrefied Pellet Pursuit," *Biomass Magazine* (April 4, 2013), Website http://biomassmagazine.com/articles/8836/torrefied-pellet-pursuit.

18 It is a sad commentary on today's economic situation that used paper is the chief US export item to China considering all that is imported from China.

19 McNeil Generating Station, Website www.ieabcc.nl/database/info/cofiring/115.html.

20 Drax Power, Website www.drax.com, and also their presentation on biomass at Website http://draxbiomass.com/about-us/our-story.

21 "Waste-to-energy CHP Amager Bakke Copenhagen," State of Green, Website www.stateofgreen. com/en/Profiles/Ramboll/Solutions/Waste-to-energy-CHP-Amager-BakkECopenhagen.

22 Jesper Starn, "Stockholm Power Goes Green as Wood Ousts Coal: Carbon & Climate," *Bloomberg* (February 6, 2015), Website www.bloomberg.com/news/articles/2015-02-09/stockholm-power-goes-green-as-wood-ousts-coal-carbon-climate.

23 Tilo Arnhold (Helmholtz Centre for Environmental Research), "Is Straw Germany's Next Big Energy Resource?" *Renewable Energy World* (October 21, 2013), Website www.renewableenergyworld. com/articles/2013/10/is-straw-germanys-next-big-energy-resource.html.

24 "Klaipeda Combined Heat and Power Plant, Lithuania," Website www.power-technology.com/ projects/klaipeda-combined-power-plant.

25 Kjell Andersson, "Bioenergy: The Swedish Experience—How Bioenergy Became the Largest Energy Source in Sweden," Svebio (Swedish bioenergy industry association), Website www.svebio. se/english/publikationer/bioenergy-swedish-experience.

26 US Environmental Protection Agency's Website www.epa.gov/epaoswer/non-hw/compost/bio solid.pdf. See also Zia Haq, "Biomass for Electricity Generation," US Department of Energy, Website www.eia.doe.gov/oiaf/analysispaper/biomass.

27 Tshepiso Mokhema (Bloomberg), "South Africa Utility to Expand Biogas Plant for Power," *Renewable Energy World* (October 28, 2013), Website www.renewableenergyworld.com/news/2013/10/south-africa-utility-to-expand-biogas-plant-for-power.html.

28 Randall Hackley, "Sludge Treatment at U.K. Facility Turns Waste into 'Black Gold,'" *Bloomberg News* (September 1, 2014), Website www.renewableenergyworld.com/rea/news/article/2014/09/sludge-treatment-at-u-k-facility-turns-waste-into-black-gold. See also "Thermal Hydrolysis: The Missing Ingredient for Better Biosolids?" Water World (October 26–29, 2014), Website www.waterworld. com/articles/wwi/print/volume-27/issue-4/editorial-focus/slidge-processing-biosolids/thermal-hydrolysis-the-missing-ingredient.html.

29 "UK Supermarket to be Powered Exclusively by Waste-to-Energy Plant," *Renewable Energy World* (August 20, 2014), Website www.renewableenergyworld.com/rea/news/article/2014/08/uk-supermarket-to-be-powered-exclusively-by-waste-to-energy-plant.

30 Louise Downing, "Severn Trent 'Poo Power' Helps Fuel Homes, Save on Costs," *Bloomberg* (October 1, 2014), Website www.bloomberg.com/news/2014-10-01/severn-trent-poo-power-helps-fuel-homes-save-on-costs.html.

31 "Biomass Heat and Power and Bioelectricity for Transport," European Biofuels Technology Platform (2012), Website http://biofuelstp.eu/bioelectricity.html, contains a listing of biomass and biogas projects in Europe.

32 Tildy Bahar, "Finland Looks to the Future of Bioenergy," *Renewable Energy World* (July 22, 2013), Website www.renewableenergyworld.com/rea/news/article/2013/07/finland-looks-to-the-future-of-bioenergy.

33 Thomas Stringfellow and Robert Witherell (CH2M HILL Engineers), "An Independent Engineering Evaluation of Waste-to-Energy Technologies," *Renewable Energy World* (January 15, 2014), Website www.renewableenergyworld.com/rea/news/article/2014/01/an-independent-engineering-evalu ation-of-waste-to-energy-technologies?cmpid=WNL-Wednesday-January15–2014.

34 Randy Leonard, "Plasma Gasification Raises Hopes of Clean Energy from Garbage," *The New York Times* (September 11, 2012). See also Fulcrum BioEnergy, Website http://fulcrum-bioenergy.com/ facilities.

35 Bruce Dorminey, "Prickly Pear Cactus: Nuisance or Bioenergy Opportunity?" *Renewable Energy World* (January 15, 2013), Website www.renewableenergyworld.com/rea/news/article/2014/ 01/prickly-pear-cactus-nuisance-or-bioenergy-opportunity?cmpid=WNL-Wednesday-January15–2014. See also Elqui Global Energy, Website www.elquiglobalenergy.com/english.

36 Roy Nersesian, *Biofuels: Fuels of the Future* (New York, NY: Energy Intelligence Research, 2008). This study includes a complete listing of citations and is a source of information for this chapter.

37 Renewable Fuels Association (RFA), Website www.ethanolrfa.org.

38 "Fuel Properties Comparison," Alternative Fuels Data Center, Website www.afdc.energy.gov/fuels/fuel_comparison_chart.pdf.

39 The history of alcohol in motor vehicle fuel is described on the Website http://66.147.244.135/~enviror4/people/henry-ford-charles-kettering-and-the-fuel-of-the-future. Hemp enthusiasts maintain that Ford was thought to have hemp in mind as a source for ethanol and in 1941 made a car out of biomass (thought to be soybeans) that was lighter and tougher than steel. Hemp's fibers can be made into rope, cloth, and paper. Hemp grew profusely in the Midwest, and today, variants of the hemp plant is a source of cannabis. Website www.hemp.com/2011/01/henrys-hemp-car-not-so-much-hemp.

40 "Sugar: World Markets and Trade," US Department of Agriculture: Foreign Agricultural Service (May, 2015), Website http://apps.fas.usda.gov/psdonline/circulars/Sugar.pdf.

41 Martin Thelen (AgroConcept, Bonn), "Sugar Beet vs. Sugar Cane: What are the Main Forces Operating on the World Market?" Bayer Crop Science (2004), Website http://origin-www.bayercropscience.com/bayer/cropscience/cscms.nsf/id/Sugarbeet_Agro/$file/sugarbeet.pdf.

42 "Overview & Outlook: Brazilian Sugarcane Industry," EIA presentation, Website www.eia.gov/biofuels/workshop/presentations/2012/pdf/leticia_phillips.pdf. See also USDA Global International Agricultural Information Network (GAIN) Report, Website http://gain.fas.usda.gov/Recent%20GAIN%20Publications/Biofuels%20Annual_Sao%20Paulo%20ATO_Brazil_7-25-2014.pdf, for a wealth of statistical information on biofuels in Brazil.

43 Fabio Carretto (Embraer Aircraft Ipanema), "Ipanema: Efficiency and Sustainability in the Field," AgAir Update, Website http://agairupdate.com/article_detail.php?_kp_serial=00000903.

44 "With Tariff Gone, US and Brazil Can Trade Ethanol without Restrictions," Biofuels, Website www.greentechmedia.com/articles/read/With-Tariff-Gone-US-and-Brazil-Can-Freely-Trade-Ethanol (site no longer available).

45 David Brough, "Brazil Sugar, Ethanol Exports at Peaks," Reuters (January 8, 2013), Website www.reuters.com/article/2013/01/08/brazil-sugar-ethanol-idUSL5E9C8A9S20130108.

46 Ewa Krukowska, "EU Should Phase Out Support for Land-Based Biofuels, Lobbies Say," *Bloomberg News* (February 21, 2013).

47 "Cutting Down on Cutting Down (the Amazon Rainforest)," *The Economist* (June 7, 2014).

48 Dr. Christoph Berg, "World Fuel Ethanol Analysis and Outlook," Website www.distill.com/World-Fuel-Ethanol-A&O-2004.html.

49 Websites www.biobutanol.com and www.butamax.com.

50 Michael Wang, Jeongwoo Han, Jennifer B. Dunn, Hao Cai, and Amgad Elgowainy, "Well-to-Wheels Energy Use and Greenhouse Gas Emissions of Ethanol from Corn, Sugarcane, and Cellulosic Biomass for US Use," Environmental Research Letters (2012), Website http://iopscience.iop.org; doi:10.1088/1748-9326/7/4/045905.

51 M.E. Dias de Oliveira, B.E. Vaughan, and E.J. Rykiel, "Ethanol as Fuel: Energy, Carbon Dioxide Balances, and Ecological Footprint," *American Institute of Biological Science*, Vol. 55, No. 7, Pages 593–602 (July, 2005).

52 To exemplify the magnitude of difference between sweet and field corn, my father grew about 30 acres of field corn for silage for the cows and 4–6 rows of sweet corn in the family garden. He planted each row about a week apart so that we would have fresh corn for much of the summer. I remember going out to the garden to pick a half dozen ears of corn that were immediately steamed—by far the sweetest and best tasting corn I've ever had.

53 "Crop Production Historical Track Record," US Department of Agriculture (2014), Website www.nass.usda.gov/Publications/Todays_Reports/reports/croptr14.pdf.

54 US Department of Agriculture Economic Research Service, Website www.ers.usda.gov/topics/crops/corn.aspx#.UhExcpK1E1I. Price quotes from University of Illinois, Website http://farmdoc.illinois.edu/manage/uspricehistory/USPrice.asp.

55 "Rising Food Prices: Policy Options and World Bank Response," World Bank, Website http://siteresources.worldbank.org/NEWS/Resources/risingfoodprices_backgroundnote_apr08.pdf.

56 Interview with Christopher Wright, "The Disappearing Act," Federal Reserve Bank of Minneapolis Fedgazette (July, 2013).

57 Index mundi, Website www.indexmundi.com/agriculture/?commodity=corn&graph=exports.

58 Website www.ethanolproducer.com refers queries on Indy's Super Fuel article to author Craig Johnson's email cjohnson@bbibiofuels.com.

59 "Population Update Overview," EPA, Website www.epa.gov/oms/models/moves/documents/faca-meeting-jul2013/02-population-2013-07-09.pdf.

60 "Falling Walls and Rising Tides: 2014 Ethanol Industry Outlook," Renewable Fuels Association, Website www.ethanolrfa.org/pages/rfa-publications.

61 "Ethanol Industry's 15% Solution Raises Concerns," *The New York Times* (May 8, 2009).

62 Alternative Fuels Data Center, Website www.afdc.energy.gov/fuels/ethanol_locations.html. I'm a New Jersey resident with a flex fuel automobile and I have a choice of all of the three gas filling stations that sell E85 in the entire state. One is near Newark Airport, which makes sense for flex fuel taxis and other vehicles serving the airport, the other is in the southern part of the state, and the third only four miles from my home. Several round trips of eight miles to fuel with E70+ never provided a price discount sufficient to induce me to permanently switch.

63 Dennis K. Burke Inc., Website www.burkeoil.com/renewablEenergy/rins.

64 Maple Energy, Website www.mapleenergy.com/index.aspx.

65 "Sugar Beet Production Worldwide from 1965 to 2013," statista, Website www.statista.com/statistics/249609/sugar-beet-production-worldwide.

66 Arturo Velez presentation on agave, Website www.slideshare.net/agaveproject.

67 Erin Voegele, "Cassova Residue Ethanol Demo Planned for Thailand," *Ethanol Producer* (December 26, 2012).

68 Biofuels' Digest article "European Parliament Votes to Cap First Generation Biofuels at 6%," Biofuels' Digest, Website www.biofuelsdigest.com/bdigest/2013/09/11/european-parliament-votes-to-cap-first-generation-biofuels-at-6.

69 Crop Watch, University of Nebraska-Lincoln, Website http://cropwatch.unl.edu/bioenergy/switchgrass.

70 Greg Pahl, *Biodiesel* (White River Junction, VT: Chelsea Green Publishing, 2005).

71 Lyle Estill, *Biodiesel Power* (Gabriola Island, BC: New Society Publishers, 2005).

72 Biodiesel, Website www.biodiesel.org, contains a wealth of data and material on biodiesel.

73 "Biodiesel Handling and Use Guide," National Renewable Energy Laboratory (2009), Website http://biodiesel.org/docs/using-hotline/nrel-handling-and-use.pdf?sfvrsn=4.

74 Wikipedia, The Free Encyclopedia, Websites http://en.wikipedia.org/wiki/Table_of_biofuel_crop_yields and http://en.wikipedia.org/wiki/Copaifera_langsdorffii.

75 US Department of Agriculture, Website www.pecad.fas.usda.gov/highlights/2013/06/indonesia.

76 Index mundi, Website www.indexmundi.com/agriculture/?commodity=palm-oil&graph=production.

77 On a personal note, my father's farm in upstate New York prevented surrounding woodlands from encroaching on farm land because tree seedlings sprouting in fields were either harvested with crops or eaten by cows or plowed under. With the farm subdivided into private residences, fields and pastures not converted to lawns are now covered with mature woodlands—a common phenomenon with the decline of dairy farming in the Northeast.

78 Palm oil prices in dollars per metric ton and diesel in dollars per gallon at index mundi, Website www.indexmundi.com/commodities/?commodity=palm-oil&months=60&commodity=diesel; diesel prices were converted to dollars per metric ton using 42 gallons per barrel and 7.34 barrels per metric ton.

79 Brian Thomas blog, Website http://lifeobservationsfromorangehouse.blogspot.com/2011/08/african-palm-trees-real-power-plant.html.

80 Bruce Dorminey, "The Ugly Duckling: Can Duckweed Find Its Way to Bioenergy Commercialization?" *Renewable Energy World* (2014), Website www.renewableenergyworld.com/rea/news/article/2014/06/the-ugly-duckling-can-duckweek-find-its-way-to-bioenergy-commercialization.

81 Andy Polhamus, "East Greenwich Man to Start Bioenergy Farm," *South Jersey Times* (April 20, 2013), Website www.nj.com/gloucester-county/index.ssf/2013/04/east_greenwich_man_to_start_bi.html.

82 Don Konantz (Falyx BioVentures), "Pass the Mustard: Why Carinata is Taking Root as Biofuel," *Renewable Energy World* (2011), Website www.renewableenergyworld.com/rea/news/article/2011/06/pass-the-mustard-why-carinata-is-taking-root-as-biofuel.

83 Shiri Habid-Valdhorn, "Evogene Reports Castor Oil Biofuel Success," *Globes* (September 16, 2013), Website www.globes.co.il/en/article-1000879801.

84 Petrobras, Website www.petrobras.com.br/en/news/biodiesel-with-castor-bean-oil-is-already-a-reality (site no longer available).

85 Michael Briggs, "Widescale Biodiesel Production from Algae," University of New Hampshire (2004), Website www.resilience.org/stories/2004-10-03/widescale-biodiesel-production-algae.

86 "CAER Scientists, Duke Power Demonstrate Algae-Based Carbon-Capture System," University of Kentucky, Website http://uknow.uky.edu/content/caer-scientists-duke-energy-demonstrate-algae-based-carbon-capture-system.

87 Sapphire Energy, Website www.sapphireenergy.com/sapphire-renewable-energy.

88 For current biofuel developments see the Amyris Website at www.amyris.com, the Solazyme Website at www.solazyme.com, and the Advanced Biofuels Association blog at http://advancedbiofuelsassociation.com/blog.

89 Algae Biomass Organization, Website www.algaebiomass.org/wp-content/uploads/2010/06/ABO_project_book_lo-res_July2013.pdf.

90 Jim Lane, "Are We There Yet? The Positioning and Repositioning of the Algae Industry," *Renewable Energy World* (July 2, 2014), Website www.renewableenergyworld.com/rea/news/article/2014/07/are-we-there-yet-the-positioning-and-repositioning-of-the-algae-industry.

91 Laiqh Khan, "Engineering College Staff Run Engine on Bio-Fuel," *The Hindu* (January 6, 2006), Website www.hindu.com/2006/01/06/stories/2006010603570200.htm.

92 Renewable Energy Group, Website www.regfuel.com.

93 DAR PRO Solutions, Website www.darpro.com/diamond-green-diesel.

94 Changing World Technologies, which started the plant in 2004, went bankrupt in 2009 and reopened in 2012 under its subsidiary Renewable Environmental Solutions. Despite reducing smells, a class action has been stayed by a judge. Turkey offal is no longer a raw material. See Website http://en.wikipedia.org/wiki/Changing_World_Technologies.

95 Brad Lemley and Tony Law, "Anything into Oil," *Discovery Magazine* (May, 2003), Website http://discovermagazine.com/2003/may/featoil.

96 "Ridgeline Completes Acquisition of Missouri Facility," PR Newswire (April 15, 2013), Website www.prnewswire.com/news-releases/ridgeline-completes-acquisition-of-missouri-facility-202957471.html.

97 Index mundi, Website www.indexmundi.com/energy.aspx?region=xx&product=biodiesel&graph=production. See also index mundi, Website www.indexmundi.com/energy.aspx?product=biodiesel&graph=consumption&display=map.

98 European Biodiesel Board, Website www.ebb-eu.org/stats.php.

99 A partial view for the situation for biodiesel by country can be obtained from the Wikipedia Website at http://en.wikipedia.org/wiki/Biodiesel_by_region.

100 Neste Oil, Website www.nesteoil.com.

101 Biodiesel, Website http://biodiesel.org/using-biodiesel/finding-biodiesel/retail-locations/retail-map.

102 Biodiesel, Website http://biodiesel.org/production/production-statistics.

103 Platts Commodity Week, Website www.platts.com/latest-news/oil/singapore/thailand-plans-to-raise-biodiesel-output-target-27287876. See also Apiradee Thammanomai, "Thailand Biofuel Policies," Department of Alternative Energy Development and Efficiency, International Energy Agency, Website www.iea.org/media/technologyplatform/workshops/southeastasiabioenergy2014/Thailand.pdf.

104 "Straight Vegetable Oil as Diesel Fuel," Journey to Forever, Website http://journeytoforever.org/biodiesel_svo.html.

105 Steeper Energy, Website http://steeperenergy.com, and Maritime Executive, Website www.maritime-executive.com/article/BioRefinery-For-Sustainable-Marine-Fule-to-Be-Built-in-Denmark-2013-09-11.

106 Amy Yee, "Airlines Fly the Skies on a Sugar High," *New York Times Energy Section* (October 8, 2014). See also Amyris, Website www.amyris.com.

107 David Wallace, "When Algae on the Exterior Is a Good Thing," *The New York Times* (April 25, 2013).

108 Algae.Tec, Website http://algaetec.com.au.

109 Roxanne Palmer, "How the Navy Might Spin Seawater into Jet Fuel," *International Business Times* (December 17, 2013), Website www.ibtimes.com/how-navy-might-spin-seawater-jet-fuel-1512712.

110 "Global Bioenergy: A Working Paper for Remap 2030," International Renewable Energy Agency (September, 2014). The report can be downloaded from Website www.irena.org.

111 Shankar Rampalli, "Don't Count It Out: Biofuels Industry Holds Much Promise," Mordor Intelligence (June 16, 2014), as reported on Website www.renewableenergyworld.com/rea/news/article/2014/06/dont-count-it-out-biofuels-industry-holds-much-promise.

112 "Giant King Grass to Fuel Bioenergy Plants in California," *Renewable Energy World* (March 25, 2014), Website www.renewableenergyworld.com/rea/news/print/article/2014/03/biomass-and-biofuel-plants-under-development-in-california-using-giant-king-grass.

4 Coal

See the Companion Website for sections on First Energy Crisis and the Origin and History of Coal: www.routledge.com/cw/nersesian.

Coal suffers from an incredibly bad image. It has few advocates other than the hundreds of thousands whose livelihoods depend on mining and burning coal by the trainload for generating electricity. No one strikes it rich in coal; that metaphor is reserved for oil. For some, coal brings back an image of a young man with healthy lungs who goes in hock to buy a set of tools and quits decades later with an aged body and black lung still in hock to the company store. That might be one of the better images. Another would be the mangled bodies caught in mine mishaps or trapped by cave-ins awaiting their fate in pitch blackness. Still another would be youngsters harnessed to sleds dragging coal up narrow underground passageways on their hands and knees like pack animals, or straddling precariously above fast-moving conveyor belts of coal picking out rocks. For still others, the image of coal is as a pollutant of the first order that has to be eliminated under any or all circumstances. Nothing short of unconditional surrender can appease these environmental militants.

Yet at the same time, this biomass fuel from ages past is irreplaceable and absolutely essential to ensure that the lights go on when we flick the switch. Figure 4.1 shows the consumption of coal in million tons of oil equivalent (mmtoe) since 1965 and its percentage share of satisfying global energy demand.

In the last half century, consumption of coal has increased 280 percent, but its share of the energy pie declined from 37 percent in 1965 to 25–27 percent from 1990 to 2004. Since then its share has increased to 30 percent. Annual growth in coal consumption was 1.6 percent from 1965 to 2002 and then increased to 4.7 percent until 2011 when it slowed to 0.9 percent. Its relatively rapid growth from 2002 to 2011 and its increasing share of the energy pie is primarily caused by the economic development and industrialization of China and to a lesser degree India. Global consumption of 3,880 mmtoe of coal is equivalent to 8,165 million short tons of mined coal, with 2.1 short tons of coal having the same energy equivalence as a metric ton of oil.[1] While the world is consuming more coal, there has been a 14 percent decline in US consumption since 2010 as a result of the Obama administration's war on coal. Some of the decline was pure economics where substitution of low-cost natural gas from fracking generated lower cost electricity.

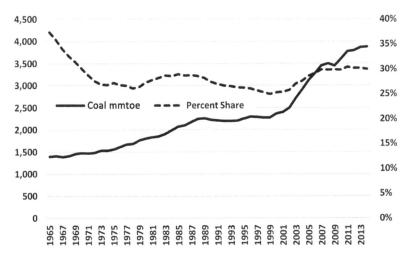

Figure 4.1 Global Coal Consumption (mmtoe) and Percentage Share

Part of the switch to natural gas and renewables was to avoid costly regulatory burdens being placed on coal-fired utilities by the EPA. Coal may be on the defensive in the US and elsewhere, but it is not enough to curb its growth on a global scale. Figure 4.2 shows the largest consumers of coal.

China consumes half of global coal despite herculean efforts to diversify energy sources to natural gas, nuclear, hydro, solar, and wind. The US and Europe, including the Former Soviet Union, each consumes 12 percent of global coal, with India, Japan, and S. Korea being significant coal consumers. Individual

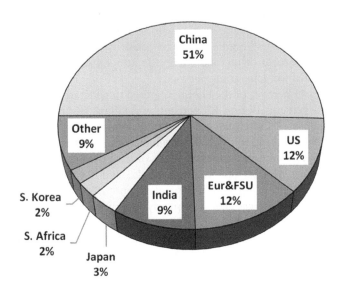

Figure 4.2 Percent Share of World Coal Consumption by Nation (2014)

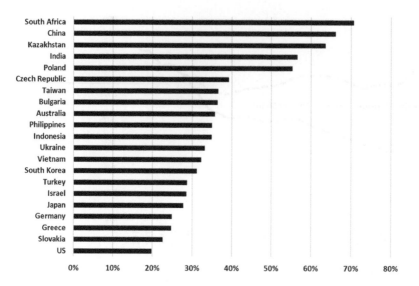

Figure 4.3 Nations Most Dependent on Coal to Satisfy Energy Needs (2014)

nations having a high dependence on coal to satisfy their total energy needs are shown in Figure 4.3.

Coal satisfies 30 percent of global energy demand. South Africa depends on coal for 71 percent of its energy needs and China for 66 percent. Other coal dominated nations are Kazakhstan, India, and Poland. China is making some progress in reducing the role of coal when, in 2000, coal made up 70 percent of total energy demand. However, total energy demand in China has grown so rapidly that coal consumption nearly tripled in the interim. Sixty-five percent of coal production is consumed in generating electricity, 15 percent in steel production, most of the remainder in powering industries, and the rest in heating buildings, feedstock for coal-to-liquid plants, and other uses.[2] Interestingly, Israel is dependent on coal for 28 percent of its total energy. Figure 4.4 shows nations with the highest dependence on coal for generating electricity.[3]

On a global basis, coal supplies 41 percent of the energy required to generate electricity. But South Africa obtains 93 percent, Poland 87 percent, and China 79 percent of their electricity from coal. Australia and Kazakhstan as coal producing nations are heavily dependent on coal to generate electricity. Israel obtains 58 percent of its electricity from coal. Israel, a small nation to be sure, is much more dependent on coal than many other nations including the US, yet it has no coal reserves! Figures 4.3 and 4.4 show that, despite rhetoric to the contrary, the US is not overly dependent on coal for electricity generation nor as a source of energy. Whereas coal is primarily consumed in electricity generation and steel production in the West, Asia also relies on coal as an industrial fuel, plus burning coal in homes, along with biomass, for heating and cooking. Thus, coal plays a more pervasive role in the economic life in the East than in the West.

During 2002–2011 when coal was growing 4.7 percent annually, global energy growth net of coal was 2.0 percent. Since 2011, growth in coal consumption has been much closer to growth in overall energy consumption. Between 2013 and 2014, world coal

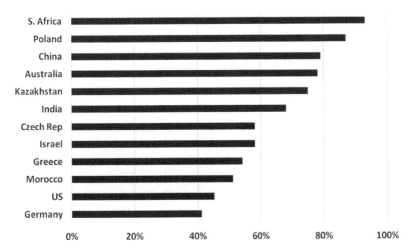

Figure 4.4 Percent Share of Electricity Generation Supplied by Coal

consumption grew by only 14 mmtoe compared to 166 mmtoe between 2011 and 2012, of which nearly all was additional consumption in China. Between 2013 and 2014, China's coal consumption flatlined, with India consuming 36 mmtoe more than in 2013, exceeding aggregate world growth of only 15 mmtoe. Declines in coal consumption were registered in a number of nations such as the US, Brazil, Chile, and Peru in the Western Hemisphere, and Europe had double-digit declines in Denmark, France, the UK, Ukraine, and Kazakhstan. Even so, on a historical basis, coal consumption over the last 50 years has grown 2.8 times, with a stunning expansion of 17 times for China and S. Korea, 13 times for Taiwan, and 10 times for India. Another view on the future potential for coal is that there are 2,300 coal-fired generating plants in the world with 620 located in China. However, there may be several coal-fired generating units within a single plant; counting these, there are about 7,000 coal-fired generating units in the world.[4] In 2012, there were 1,200 proposed coal plants in the global pipeline (mostly China and India) that, if built, will supply 1,400 gW of electricity capacity. As a point of comparison, the entire US power grid in 2011 was 1,050 gW for all sources of energy.[5] Another indication of the future role of coal is anticipated growth by 60 percent in coal-fired generating capacity between 2010 and 2035.[6] Nearly all this expansion will take place in China and India. These figures virtually guarantee long-term demand for coal for decades to come.

For the EU, coal's role is anticipated to remain unchanged in absolute terms, but decline in relative terms to aggregate energy demand. For the US, the prognosis for coal's decline is considered temporary before steadying out at a level determined by the number of surviving coal-fired plants. However, a great deal of uncertainty is associated with the nature of "temporary." In August 2013, EPA issued a proposed ruling that new coal plants will be required to emit less than 1,100 pounds of carbon dioxide per megawatt-hour and, after some time to allow for suitable adjustments, average between 1,000 and 1,050 pounds over an 84-month operating period. As a point of reference, the average US coal plant emits 1,768 pounds of carbon dioxide per megawatt-hour versus natural gas plants at 800–850 pounds per megawatt-hour.[7]

Clearly a line has been drawn in the sand. On one side are the coal detractors led by EPA that want to minimize, if not eliminate, the role of coal in electricity generation. On the other are coal supporters that consider coal the backbone of the nation's energy infrastructure. Spokespeople for the coal industry reacted strongly, pointing out that the most efficient and environmentally advanced technologies proven to be workable cannot comply with the proposed ruling. Thus, the proposed ruling would essentially eliminate new coal-fired power plants unless a utility wants to gamble on an unproven technology. Since utilities would be averse to spending billions to develop a new technology that may miss the EPA mark, the proposed ruling would inhibit further corporate-sponsored development of clean coal technology.[8] A yet-to-be-published EPA ruling will provide guidance on carbon dioxide emissions for existing plants. Critics were quick to predict the potential closure of between 200 and 300 plants in the US plant inventory of 500 equivalent sized 500 mW coal-fired plants, whose average age, by the way, is 35 years.[9] Retiring upwards of half coal-fired electricity capacity has the potential of severely disrupting the economy. Many older and more polluting plants have already been culled, most victims of low-cost natural gas and potential cost of meeting government regulations. As of mid-2015, final rulings for both new and existing plants have not yet been issued.[10] Thus, there is a real question as to where US coal consumption will level out depending on how many coal plants survive the final version of EPA guidelines. Substitute and incremental growth in electricity demand will be primarily satisfied by natural gas and renewables, with little contribution from nuclear and hydro.

Even with a partial phase out of coal-fired electricity generation in the US, on a global scale coal is expected to continue increasing in absolute, but not in relative, terms. Nothing can be done to avert this inevitability unless China and, to a lesser extent, India and other Southeast Asian nations curb their voracious appetites for energy and invest heavily in non-coal energy sources. To be fair, China is investing heavily in non-coal energy sources, but this may be a case of too little too late. China had been building an equivalent of two 500 mW coal-fired plants per week for a number of years, adding more coal-fired plant capacity in 1 year than electricity generating capacity in the UK. However, leveling off of coal consumption in 2014 indicates that this feverish building of coal plants has subsided. Reflecting this, growth in volume of carbon emissions ceased in 2014 in relation to emissions in 2013 as a result of stabilization in fossil fuel consumption and growth in renewables.[11] Unfortunately, most coal-fired plants built in China and India and elsewhere in Southeast Asia lack all but the most elemental pollution control equipment. Retrofitting existing plants with pollution controls is far more expensive than incorporating these features when the plants were initially designed and built. But air pollution in China has long reached such hazardous levels that an active program to retrofit existing plants with pollution control equipment has belatedly begun. China is embarking on several broad fronts to cut air pollution.[12] Whether fitted with pollution controls or not, the existence of so many coal-fired plants assures a market for coal for decades.

Types of Coal

Aside from peat, a precursor to coal, there are four types of coal. The lowest quality coal is lignite, a geologically young, soft, brownish-black coal, some of which retains the texture of the original wood. Of all coals, it has the lowest carbon content, 25–35 percent, and the lowest heat content, 4,000–8,300 Btu per pound. Lignite is burned to generate electricity even though it has a low heat content and emits more pollution than other coals. Lignite is strip-mined in Germany, Poland, and the Czech Republic.

Lignite coal is plentiful and cheap in Germany, although more polluting than other forms of coal. Lignite was brought into the energy picture as a consequence of Germany retiring its nuclear reactor plants in the wake of the Fukushima tragedy. In 2015 Germany announced its intention to phase out half of its lignite-fired generating plants (13 percent of its electricity generating plant capacity). The worst polluting lignite-fired generating plants will be placed into reserve status in 2017 for operation only when absolutely needed, with the intention of phasing out these units by 2021. In 2014 lignite provided 25.4 percent of power, hard coal 18 percent, and renewables 26.2 percent.[13] Lignite provides low-cost electricity, as seen in Figure 4.5, and counters high-cost sources of electricity that drive away value creating investments and jobs.[14]

Clearly lignite provides the lowest cost of electricity. The cost premium associated with green energy is still high in comparison to fossil fuels, although marked progress has been made in lowering costs for electricity generated from solar and wind. Onshore wind is now cost-competitive with coal, and utility sized photovoltaic (solar) energy is cost-competitive with natural gas. Lignite also enhances energy independence by reducing the need for Russian natural gas imports. Obviously Germany is striving for a balance between low-cost electricity from lignite to support its economy and high-cost green electricity to protect its environment while reducing the geopolitical risk associated with Russian gas imports.

The next step up is sub-bituminous coal, a dull black coal with a carbon content of 35–45 percent and heat content 8,300–13,000 Btu per pound. Both lignite and sub-bituminous coals, known as soft coals, are thermal coals for generating electricity. Some sub-bituminous coals have lower sulfur content than bituminous coal, an environmental advantage. Next are the hard coals: bituminous and anthracite. Bituminous is superior to soft coal in terms of carbon content, 45–86 percent, and energy content, 10,500–15,500 Btu per pound. Bituminous coal is the most plentiful form of coal in the US and is mostly

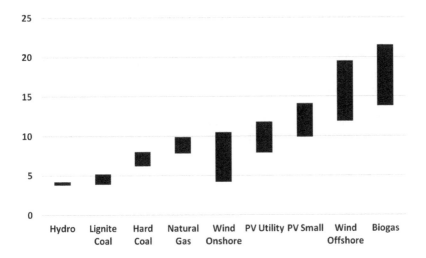

Figure 4.5 Levelized Cost of Electricity in Germany in Euros per kWh

burned as thermal coal to generate electricity. However, if the coal has the right physical properties, it is used as coking or metallurgical coal for steel production. Thermal and metallurgical coals are two distinct markets. It is possible for a large bulk carrier to move thermal coal from Australia to Europe with the vessel returning with a cargo of metallurgical coal from the US or South Africa to Japan. Anthracite coal has the highest carbon content, 86–98 percent, and a heat content of nearly 15,000 Btu per pound. Anthracite coal was closely associated with home heating because it burned nearly smokeless. As desirable as anthracite is, anthracite coal is scarce. In the US, anthracite coal is found in only 11 counties in northeastern Pennsylvania and its reserves are largely exhausted.

Coal Mining

Coal mines have historically been subterranean where accidents and black lung have taken their toll. Mining coal in the twenty-first century is an activity carried out differently than in the past. In developed nations, no gangs of men swing pickaxes to remove the over- and underburden of rock to gain access to the coal, then again to chip out the coal. No gangs of men shovel rock or coal into small wagons or carts for the trip to the surface. Now the most popular way of removing coal is continuous mining machines with large, rotating, drum-shaped cutting heads studded with carbide-tipped teeth that rip into a seam of coal. Large gathering arms scoop the coal directly into a built-in conveyor for loading into shuttle cars or a conveyor for the trip to the surface. Continuous cutters ripping and grinding their way through coal seams can do in minutes what gangs of miners with pickaxes and shovels took days to accomplish.

Another popular method for removing coal is a machine resembling an oversized chain saw that cuts out a section of coal to allow for expansion in preparation for blasting. Holes are then drilled for explosives that blast large chunks of coal loose from the seam. Loaders scoop coal into conveyors that fill shuttle cars to haul coal out of the shaft. For both methods of mining, long rods or roof bolts are driven into the roof of a mine to bind layers of weak strata into a single layer strong enough to support its own weight. If necessary, braces are used for additional support. Wood is favored because it makes a sharp cracking sound if the roof begins to weaken.

An increasingly popular and efficient means of mining introduced into the US from Europe in the 1950s is longwall mining, where a rotating shear moves back and forth in a continuous, smooth motion for several hundred feet across the face or wall of a coal seam. The cut coal drops into a conveyor and is removed from the mine. Some of the rock on top of the coal also collapses, which is removed either in the mine and piled where coal has been removed or is removed at the surface. Main supports for rooms created by longwall mining are pillars of solid coal, which are last to be mined before a mine is abandoned. An associated environmental problem in abandoning underground mines of all types is that they may eventually fill with water that can range from being nearly fit for drinking to containing dangerously high concentrations of acids and metallic compounds. Abandoned mine water may end up contaminating ground and drinking water. No big surprise that it is difficult to identify the responsible party once an abandoned mine poses a public health risk.

Regardless of type of mining technology, mine shafts for transporting miners and coal either slope down to coal seams that are not too deeply located in the earth or are vertical to reach coal seams more than 2,000 feet beneath the surface. Huge ventilation fans on the surface pump air through the mineshafts to reduce coal dust in the air, prevent accumulation of dangerous gases, and ensure a fresh supply of air for miners. In recent decades, surface mining has gained prominence over subterranean mining. In the western part of the US, 75 percent of coal is obtained from surface mines with coal deposits up to 100 feet thick. Surface mining also occurs in Appalachia. Surface mines produce 60 percent of the coal mined in the US, while the remaining 40 percent comes from underground coal mines primarily in Appalachia. Although there are large open-pit mines in other parts of the world, such as Australia, Indonesia, and Colombia, globally speaking, about two-thirds of coal comes from underground mines.

After mining, coal is processed to ensure a uniform size and washed to reduce its ash and sulfur content. Washing consists of floating coal across a tank of water containing magnetite for the correct specific gravity. Heavier rock and other impurities sink to the bottom and are removed as waste. Washing reduces ash and pyretic sulfur-iron compounds clinging to the surface of coal, but not sulfur chemically bonded within the coal. Washing can reduce carbon dioxide emissions by up to 5 percent. Magnetite clinging to the coal after washing is separated with a spray of water and recycled. In some cases, chemicals such as 4-methylcyclohexane methanol are added to create a frothy, heavy consistency that enhances the washing process. This chemical escaped from a storage tank in West Virginia in January 2014, affecting water supplies to 300,000 people in nine counties and sending hundreds to hospitals.[15]

After treatment at the mine, coal is then shipped by rail or barge to power plants, although a few utility plants are located at the mouths of mines. Most coal is loaded on barges and railroad cars for transport to electricity generating plants or export ports. Some power plants run off a single source of coal, while others buy various grades of coal that are mixed together before burning in order to obtain optimal results in heat generation, pollution emissions, and cost control. In the US, about 60 percent of the coal mined is moved by railroad to consuming utilities, often in unit trains of a hundred coal cars, each holding 100 tons of coal, or 10,000 tons of coal in a single trainload. Coal is unloaded by opening hoppers in the bottom of coal cars to drop the coal onto a conveyor belt below the rails. At some export terminals, a rotating mechanism empties 100 tons of coal by turning coal cars upside down as though they were toys. Coal is still a major revenue generator for railroads around the world. Steam locomotives have not been entirely relegated to the dustbin of history; they can be found hauling coal in China, India, and South Africa. Coal in the US not moved by rail is primarily moved by barge on 25,000 miles of inland waterways. One unconventional way to move coal is to pipeline pulverized coal mixed with water as a slurry from a coal mine to a power station, where water is then decanted.

Coal mining operations are highly regulated in the developed world. In the US, a company must comply with hundreds of laws and thousands of regulations, many of which have to do with the health and safety of the miners and impact of coal mining on the environment. Legal hurdles may require 10 years before a new mine can be developed. A mining company must provide detailed information about how coal will be mined, precautions taken to protect the health and safety of the miners, and the mine's impact on the environment. For surface mining, the original condition of the land must be carefully documented to ensure that reclamation requirements have been successfully fulfilled. Other legal requirements cover archeological and historical preservation, protection and conservation of endangered species, and special provisions to protect fish and wildlife, forest and rangeland, wild and scenic river views, water purity, and noise abatement.

In surface or strip mining, specially designed draglines, wheel excavators, and large shovels strip the overburden to expose the coal seam, which can cover the entire top of an Appalachian mountain. Overburden is normally dumped into the adjacent valley, appropriately dubbed "valley fill." Draglines extract coal from seams, and huge mechanical shovels, or draglines themselves, load coal into specially designed trucks capable of carrying from one hundred to several hundred tons of coal. The trucks carry coal either for pretreatment or directly to awaiting railroad cars or barges. Sometimes conveyor belts run from the surface mine to load river barges. Large truckloads fit for road traffic are used if shipping is to a nearby coal burning utility.[16] Surface mining has lower operating and capital costs and provides a safer and healthier environment for the workers than underground mining.[17] After coal is removed, overburden is replaced and replanted with plant life to restore land as closely as possible to its original state. Reclaimed land can be transformed into farmland, recreational areas, or residential or commercial development, as permitted by regulators.

Critics of surface mining point out the damage done to the landscape when overburden removed from the top of a mountain is dumped into an adjacent valley. In addition to the destruction of the landscape and vegetation, valley fills form dams, creating contaminated ponds of acid runoff from sulfur-bearing rocks and heavy metals such as copper, lead, mercury, and arsenic exposed by stripping off the mountain top. They also object to the dust and noise of strip mining operations and "fly-rocks" raining down on those unfortunately residing nearby. The scars of surface mining are clearly seen from the air. Residents in West Virginia are split between those who support the economic benefits of surface coal mining and those who want to transform West Virginia into a recreational destination for tourists.[18]

Critics point to examples of land reclamation after the coal has been removed that hardly qualifies for that term. Much of this lies with fly-by-night companies that fold without meeting their light-of-day responsibilities. Of course the record also shows that there are large established companies mindful of their legal obligations to restore the landscape and protect the environment. There are instances of reclamation carried out so effectively that, with the passage of time, there is no apparent evidence that strip mining had ever taken place.[19] Aside from corporate ethics, there are sound business reasons for being a responsible corporate citizen such as the desire to remain in business for decades to come. For these companies, extra costs in protecting the health and safety of miners and safeguarding the environment generate huge payoffs by allowing them to remain in business over the long haul. Private ownership is a right granted by governments on the basis that conduct of business is better handled by businesspeople than government bureaucrats. If in reality, or if in the perception of the electorate, the supposed benefits of private ownership are not forthcoming, then private ownership itself is in jeopardy.

While critics of coal extraction in developed nations abound, developing nations, most notably China, seem to exist on another planet. Few critics in the West acknowledge the situation in China where coal mining, particularly in tens of thousands of small mines, violates elemental concerns over the health and safety of workers and the environment. Whereas employment of coal miners in much of the world has changed drastically as machines replaced labor, most of the world's coal miners today are in China, where picks and shovels are the dominant coal mining technique. No one seems to care about the thousands of killed or maimed workers or the spontaneous combustion of coal mining residues that burn on forever, or about drinking water and agricultural lands permanently contaminated with poisonous metal compounds. Not only is China's coal mining productivity lowest in the world from lack of mechanization, but China also has the highest death and injury rates with 7.29 deaths per million tons of coal mined. As a counterpoint, in the US, there are 0.04 deaths per million tons mined, 0.47 deaths in India, and 0.23 deaths in Poland.[20] Interestingly, the death rate in India, though ten times that of the US, is only a small fraction of that in China despite pick and shovel being the prevailing mode of coal mining. There are nearly as many daily fatalities in Chinese mines as annually in US mines.

Most casualties in China are associated with small mines employing women and children, not large state-owned mines. Methane explosions from lack of proper ventilation and gas monitoring are responsible for half the deaths. These figures reflect mine mishaps, not deaths from health impairment from mining. A nonfatal occupational risk for miners and for many industrial workers throughout the world is loss of hearing. Loss of hearing from noisy machinery in close quarters to workers occurs slowly and often without their awareness. With regard to fatal occupational risks, the most common is a miners' disease, pneumoconiosis, commonly known as black lung, from long-term exposure to coal dust. Black lung has dropped precipitously for mines with ample ventilation, but still remains a problem in China and other nations where relatively little is invested in protecting workers' health. China's terrible record in protecting miners extends to end users. Drying chilies with coal contaminated with arsenic was responsible for thousands of cases of arsenic poisoning.[21] Drying corn with coal contaminated with fluorine caused millions to suffer from dental and skeletal fluorosis.[22] The workers' paradise that communism espouses is far from standards on worker health and safety established in capitalist societies.

Coal in the Twenty-First Century

Coal's retreat in relative standing among other energy sources ended in 2000. Coal is here to stay and is gaining ground in absolute and relative terms. Despite criticisms leveled against coal, it does have virtues that cannot be ignored, such as being:

- abundant—frequently reserves are measured in hundreds of years;
- secure—in that coal is available in sufficient quantities without the need for large-scale imports for most coal consuming nations;
- safe (does not explode like natural gas, but of course mine safety is an issue);
- nonpolluting of water resources as oil spills (although there are other adverse environmental consequences of mining and burning coal);
- cost-effective—by far the lowest cost source of energy (other than in the US where natural gas in recent years is lower in cost).

Figure 4.6 shows the world's largest consumers and producers of coal in 2014 in terms of mmtoe. China is the world's largest consumer and producer of coal and both exports and imports coal. China suffers from a poorly developed internal logistics system. Movement from inland distributions to coastline population centers relies on China's river systems and railroads. Movement of goods and commodities along China's long coastline, where

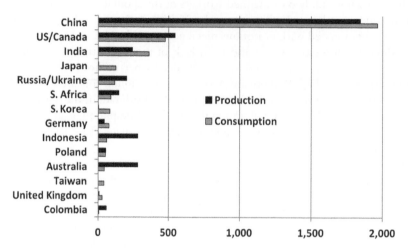

Figure 4.6 World's Leading Producers and Consumers of Coal (mmtoe)

many of its principal population centers are located, is mainly by water rather than by land, although China is in the midst of major expansion of its logistics infrastructure. As a substitute for moving commodities along its coastline, China selectively exports and imports. Thermal coal to utilities located on its southern and central coastal region is imported from Australia and Indonesia and thermal coal is exported from its northern region to neighboring North and South Korea and Japan. This reduces the need to transport coal inland and along coastal waterways from north to south China. While China is a major producer of coal, it is now an important importer of coking and metallurgical coal to support its steel production. The difference between production and consumption in Figure 4.6 for China is its net imports of both coking and thermal coals. In terms of coking coals, China was the largest importer at 77 million tons in 2013 followed by Japan at 54 million tons and India at 38 million tons. The world's largest exporters of coking coal in 2013 were Australia at 154 million tons, the US at 60 million tons, and Canada at 33 million tons.

The relative importance of China in relation to the US along with Canada as consumers and producers of coal can be seen by the huge step down. China is by far the largest player in the coal market. As seen by the difference between production and consumption, the US and Canada are large exporters, whereas India is a significant importer on the scale of China for both coking and thermal coals. Coal exports from Russia and Ukraine satisfy nearby import demand for Germany and other European nations. Clearly Indonesia and Australia stand out as major world exporters of coal followed distantly by South Africa and Colombia. Japan, South Korea, and Taiwan are entirely dependent on coal imports. The largest steam and coking coal importers in 2013 were China (327 million tons), Japan (196 million tons), India (180 million tons), South Korea (126 million tons), Taiwan (68 million tons), Germany (51 million tons), and the UK (50 million tons). The largest steam and coking coal exporters in 2013 were Indonesia (426 million tons), Australia (336 million tons), Russia (147 million tons), the United States (107 million tons), Colombia (74 million tons), South Africa (72 million tons), and Canada (37 million tons). Japan, South

Korea, and Taiwan view coal as a means of reducing their reliance on Middle East oil. The UK, once the world's largest exporter of coal, now imports a large share of its coal needs. Both the UK and Germany have phased out large subsidies paid to keep their costly domestic coal mines economically alive in favor of far cheaper imports.

South Africa has abundant coal resources and limited oil resources. In the past, oil exporting nations were reluctant to trade with South Africa because of its apartheid policies. As a consequence, South Africa became a world leader in producing petroleum products (synthetic fuels) and chemicals from coal. The Fischer-Tropsch process, dating back to the 1920s, transforms low quality coal to high grade petroleum fuels plus other products.[23] The Nazis relied on this technology to make gasoline from their plenteous supplies of coal during the Second World War to compensate for not having indigenous oil resources to run its war machine. These plants were the highest priority targets during the Allied bombing of Nazi Germany. South African synthetic fuel plants have been producing 160,000 barrels per day of a mix of about 20–30 percent naphtha and 70–80 percent diesel, kerosene, and fuel oil since 1955. About 0.4 tons of coal are consumed for every barrel of oil produced with an overall energy efficiency of 40 percent (60 percent of the energy content of coal is consumed either in transforming coal to liquids or as waste heat). Coal is first gasified to yield a mixture of hydrogen and carbon monoxide, which, when passed through iron or cobalt catalysts, is transformed into methane, synthetic naphtha, gasoline or diesel fuel, waxes, and alcohols, with water and carbon dioxide as byproducts. Synthetic fuels from coal are higher in quality than those made from oil. For instance, diesel fuel made by the Fischer-Tropsch process has reduced nitrous oxides, hydrocarbons, and carbon monoxide emissions with little or no particulate emissions compared to petrodiesel.[24] However, the Fischer-Tropsch process is a large emitter of carbon dioxide as a waste product.

China has built coal-to-liquid plants in Inner Mongolia to take advantage of newly discovered coal deposits. One major plant, Shenhua Group, can annually convert 4.1 million metric tons of coal into 1.1 million metric tons (6.9 million barrels) of diesel fuel for China's growing fleet of heavy duty vehicles. More of these plants were intended to be built, but coal-to-liquid plants are also heavy consumers of water. It takes 10 to 12 cubic meters (2,641–3,170 gallons) of water to produce a metric ton (6.3 barrels) of fuel at the Shenhua plant. Water of this volume is in short supply in Inner Mongolia. The future of coal-to-liquid plants was placed on hold until the coal-to-liquid process was reengineered to cut water consumption at least by half.[25]

But in 2015, China's coal conversion projects are proceeding ahead with at least 16 coal-to-liquid plants already built or under construction or in an advanced planning stage. Their cumulative production capacity is over 22 million tons of oil products, equivalent to about 450,000 barrels per day. While water is still a consideration and every effort is being made to recycle water to cut usage, a major drag in 2015 on coal-to-liquid plants is that $70 per barrel oil is not sufficient to economically justify investments in these plants.[26]

Coal Reserves

Unlike oil, where the world's total proven reserves divided by current consumption is 53 years, over a century (110 years) would be required for current coal consumption to eat away at proven reserves. The reserve to production (R/P) ratio has to be handled gingerly as reserves are made up of known reserves plus estimates of probable reserves.

We have a knack for discovering new reserves not included in past R/P ratios (Theodore Roosevelt estimated that oil reserves would be exhausted in 20 years, given consumption and known reserves in the 1910s). Thus there is a tendency to underestimate reserves. R/P ratios are also based on current, not future, consumption and to that extent over-estimate the life of reserves. Unlike oil, there is no active ongoing search for new coal reserves other than Mongolia, which means that coal reserves could be substantially upgraded if searching for new reserves became more of an economic imperative.

The US has the world's largest reserves of coal of 237 billion tons with an R/P ratio of 262 years, meaning that it would take 262 years of present consumption to exhaust reserves. The R/P ratio will grow accordingly if coal consumption continues to drop. Russia has 157 billion tons with an R/P ratio of 441 years. Other nations with enor-mous longevity of coal reserves as measured by R/P ratios are Kazakhstan at 309 years, Germany 218 years, Australia 155 years, and India 94 years. A few nations have compa-rable R/P ratios but their reserves are small and essentially untapped. Clearly, enormous coal reserves enhance a nation's view of its energy self-sufficiency.

The nation that started the Industrial Revolution with the world's largest supply of known coal reserves, the UK, has surprisingly low reserves and an R/P ratio of 20 years. The UK has essentially exhausted its coal reserves. This, along with scant anthracite reserves in the US, shows that natural resources can be exhausted. The world's largest consumer of coal, China, has reserves of 115 billion tons with an R/P ratio of only 30 years. The R/P ratio for China is dropping as its annual consumption is increasing at a faster pace than growth in its coal reserves. In this light, one can see why new coal discoveries in Mongolia are going to figure large as a potential supplier to China. Figure 4.7 illustrates the size of coal reserves and how long they can last at the present rate of consumption.

Reserves are listed as either hard coals (anthracite and bituminous) or soft coals (sub-bituminous and lignite). Premium bituminous coals for making coking coal for steel production are found in Australia, the US, Canada, and South Africa. Significant

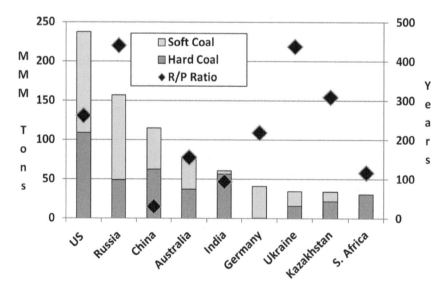

Figure 4.7 Known Coal Reserves (billion tons) and R/P Ratio (years)

portions of reserves in Russia, Ukraine, and China are soft coals, generally perceived to be greater pollutants than hard coals. But there are exceptions. India has only hard coal, but of poor quality in terms of heat, ash, and sulfur content.

Coal Prices

Coal has another very important virtue: low cost with a stable price in comparison to oil and natural gas, shown in Figure 4.8.[27]

A picture is worth a thousand words. Since the oil crisis of 1973, coal prices have been much lower than oil on an equivalent energy basis and, generally speaking with some exceptions, lower than natural gas and more stable. Since 2008, however, natural gas prices have been lower than coal. But a picture does not include everything. What cannot be seen is that coal is a reliable domestic source of energy not subject to the whims of oil potentates. Whereas coal has been close to or below the price of natural gas throughout much of the time since 1960, a major change has occurred in the price of natural gas in recent years. Success in fracking has sharply lowered the price of natural gas by increasing its availability, playing havoc with the economics for building large coal plants as well as undermining the economics for nuclear and renewable power. Low natural gas prices have been an inducement, along with tougher regulations, for utilities to switch from coal to natural gas. Less demand lowered coal's domestic price, which, in 2013, resulted in an increase in US coal exports. While one might guess that China would be a likely buyer, the actual buyers were the UK and Germany, where low-priced US coal was too attractive to ignore when faced with high-priced Russian natural gas.

However, the fall-off in coal consumption in the UK and Germany in 2014 may have taken their toll on US coal exports, but the fall-off may have merely switched the destinations of coal exports from Europe to elsewhere. International trade is very complex and quickly responds to changes in underlying conditions. While the US is a traditional

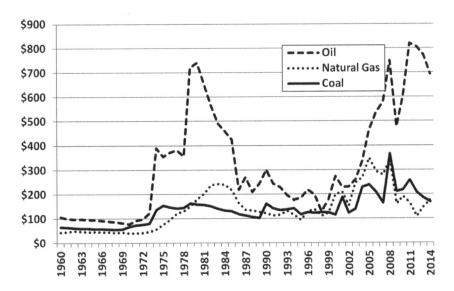

Figure 4.8 US Dollars Per Ton Oil, Natural Gas, and Coal Prices (constant 2014 dollars)

coal exporter, in 2014 it imported coal from Russia. This is not a "coal to Newcastle" phenomenon, as low-level US imports compared to exports have a longstanding history. Colombia and Indonesia are traditional providers of imported coal. What is different is the expectation of increasing volume from Russia. Coal receiving terminals for Russian coal were Tampa (Florida) and Boston, which served nearby utilities. The rationale for importing coal rather than depending on domestic sources was increasing demand for generating electricity coupled with declining coal stockpiles. Bottlenecking problems with US railroads moving large quantities of shale oil and ethanol became an obstacle for replenishing coal stockpiles in a timely fashion. There was also an economic incentive to purchase Russian coal with its higher heat and lower sulfur content, and lower price, than US coal. Russia became a more aggressive coal exporter partly in response to lower natural gas shipments to Europe.[28]

The price of coal in China and India is low, reflecting low mining costs from lack of investment in mechanization, near-slave wages for miners with little regard for personal safeguards for their health and safety, and little in the way of environmental safeguards to protect the population from pollution. This heavy reliance on low cost coal affects their competitive position in world trade since cost of energy is an element in the price of exported goods. On the surface, India is in a better position than China because it is less dependent on coal. From another perspective, India is in a worse position than China. China has an enormous trade surplus supporting the development of alternative sources of energy to coal (natural gas, hydro and nuclear, and renewables). India suffers from a negative trade balance and is less able to finance the development of alternative energy sources or import cleaner burning but more expensive natural gas. It is possible to import clean energy if energy providers are willing to accept rupees rather than dollars (one liquefied natural gas import scheme calls for rupee payments). But this is a rare occurrence, as the rupee has a long history of losing value faster than other currencies. Thus greater coal consumption may be the primary solution to India's growing energy needs. Until there is a slowing of their economic locomotives as has occurred in China, coal consumption in India and other parts of Asia will continue to expand both in volume and possibly in share of the energy pie.

Case against Coal

The case against coal can be put simply in one word—pollution. Pollution from lower grade coals, whether soft or hard, is greater than higher grade coals in terms of the quantities of ash and nitrous and sulfur oxides released during combustion. A greater quantity of lower grade coals has to be burned for the same release of energy. Plant thermal efficiency also plays a major role in determining the quantity of coal that must be burned; the lower the efficiency, the more coal has to be burned for the same generated output. Nitrous oxides once in the atmosphere contribute to smog, and sulfur oxide droplets collect on the upper surfaces of clouds, enhancing their reflectivity. This reduces the amount of sunshine reaching the Earth and, paradoxically, is a counter-pollution measure to carbon dioxide that reduces the amount of heat escaping from the atmosphere. Eventually sulfur and nitrous oxides return to Earth as acid rain, which harms plant and marine life and erodes stone buildings and statues. Mercury, arsenic, cadmium, selenium, and other heavy metals are also released when coal is burned. Surface mining destroys the landscape and, along with abandoned underground mines, affects water supplies.

Abandoned coal mines can catch fire and burn underground. Once on fire, there is little that can be done to stop coal mine fires other than entering the mine with earth-moving equipment and removing the coal feeding the fire, a hazardous undertaking by any measure. In 1962, burning trash near the mouth of an abandoned mine near Centralia, Pennsylvania, started an underground fire that has been spreading ever since despite several attempts to extinguish it. Fire is burning 300 feet beneath the surface, giving off enough heat to threaten the cremation of bodies buried in the local cemetery. There is also venting of poisonous gases and the opening up of holes large enough to swallow automobiles. It is thought that the fire will continue for another 250 years encompassing 3,700 acres before it runs out of fuel. Centralia has been largely abandoned except for a few diehards.[29]

Coal fires are not all the fault of men. Lightning igniting brush fires can cause the spontaneous combustion of coal exposed to the atmosphere. Burning Mountain in Australia has been on fire for an estimated 6,000 years. Most of the thousands of coal mine fires that threaten towns and roads, poison air and soil, and worsen carbon emissions are, however, inadvertently started by man. The estimate of coal burned each year in mine fires in China varies between 20 and 200 million tons per year; the high-end estimate being an appreciable fraction of China's total coal consumption. India has 68 underground coal fires burning beneath a 58 square mile region of Jhairia coalfield near Dhanbad spewing toxins into the atmosphere. Underground coal fires have raised surface temperatures and injected toxic byproducts into groundwater and soil, turning formerly populated areas into uninhabitable wastelands.[30]

Clean Coal Technologies

If the position is taken that coal is indispensable for generating electricity, then it becomes worthwhile for corporate and government sponsored research to be dedicated to producing a clean coal, termed an oxymoron by critics. Modern coal burning utility plants remove 99 percent of ash produced as a residue falling to the bottom of the combustion chamber and by electrostatic precipitators removing ash from flue gas. A flue gas desulfurization unit can reduce sulfur oxide emissions by 90–97 percent. A spray mixture of limestone and water is injected into flue gas where sulfur oxides chemically combine with limestone to form calcium sulfate, or gypsum.[31] In past years of rising coal consumption, sulfur emissions have fallen 2–3 percent per year in the US through greater use of scrubbers to remove sulfur and greater reliance on low sulfur coal. The role of the EPA cap and trade program in reducing sulfur emissions is covered in Chapter 11.

After mining and washing, coal is transported by train, barge, or truck and piled outside the electricity generating plant until needed. A conveyor then moves coal into a plant where it is first crushed and pulverized into a fine powder before being blown by powerful fans into the combustion chamber of a boiler in a conventional plant. In a conventional coal-fired plant, coal is burned at 1,300°C–1,400°C to transform water in tubes lining the boiler to high pressure steam fed to a turbine. A fluidized bed combustion chamber can burn pulverized coal of any quality including coal with a high ash and sulfur content. Pulverized coal is burned suspended in a gas flow with heated particles of limestone at half the temperature (1,500°F) of a conventional coal-fired boiler. At this lower temperature, about 90 percent of the sulfur dioxide can be removed by limestone absorbing sulfur dioxide to form calcium sulfate or gypsum without an expensive scrubber. In a conventional plant, water tubes in the combustion chamber generate steam to drive a steam turbine while, in a fluidized bed combustion plant, both steam and hot combustion gases drive two types of turbines. Steam from the boiler tubes is fed into a conventional steam turbine, and hot combustion gas, after ash and gypsum have been removed, is fed into a gas turbine. Both steam and gas turbines power electricity generators. If configured with high and low pressure gas turbines, spent combustion gases from the high pressure gas turbine can be passed through a low pressure gas turbine to produce more electricity. Spent gases from gas turbines pass through a heat exchanger to further warm condensed water from the steam condenser returning to the combustion chamber. Two advantages of fluidized bed combustion are an enhanced energy efficiency of 45 percent compared to 35 percent for a conventional plant and a reduction of about 40–75 percent in nitrous oxide emissions from a lower temperature of combustion. Fluidized bed combustion chambers normally operate at atmospheric pressure, but one currently being developed would operate at a considerably higher pressure.[32]

The first thermal steam turbine plants built in the early twentieth century to drive electricity generators were only about 20–25 percent energy efficient, consuming about half the energy required by a steam engine for the same electrical output. In 1975, the efficiency of US coal-fueled electricity generation plants was about 35 percent, the same as in 2006. European nations as a group increased their efficiency from 30 percent to 35 percent; China improved from 25 percent to a little over 30 percent, whereas India declined from 30 percent to 25 percent over the same time period.[33] Increasing energy efficiency is a major action item for reducing carbon dioxide emissions because less coal is burned to generate the same output of electricity.

Coal Gasification

Coal-to-liquids, already covered, is a way to convert coal to clean oil products that are less polluting than refined oil products. Likewise coal gasification is a way to create products from coal, avoiding the pollution generally associated with coal. Coal gasification is a thermochemical reaction of coal, steam, and oxygen to produce synthetic gases or syngas largely made up of carbon monoxide and hydrogen. The integrated coal gasification combined cycle (IGCC) process is more complicated than fluidized bed combustion, but in some ways is a step back in history. Manufactured gas, the predecessor of natural gas, reduced coal to a mixture of hydrogen, carbon dioxide, carbon monoxide, and methane that was distributed by pipeline to consumers. Similarly, coal is not burned in coal gasification, but processed to produce gas products essentially free of ash, sulfur, nitrous oxides, and other pollutants.

The process begins with an air-separation plant that separates oxygen from nitrogen. Coal is milled and dried in preparation for being mixed with oxygen and hot water for gasification. Synthetic gases (syngas), mainly carbon monoxide and hydrogen, are then treated to remove solids (ash) and sulfur. Some of the nitrogen separated out by the air separation plant is added to clean syngas prior to burning to control nitrous oxide generation. Syngas is then burned in a combustion chamber to drive a gas turbine and, in turn, an electricity generator. In addition to burning syngas to drive a gas turbine, a steam turbine runs off steam produced in the gasifier and in cooling synthetic gas from the gasifier. Spent steam is partly reheated by exhaust from the gas turbine and fed back into the steam turbine and partly condensed to water to feed the gasifier (the combined cycle part of IGCC).

Byproducts of an IGCC plant can be hydrogen for the hydrogen economy or a range of motor vehicle fuels. The advantages of IGCC are increased energy efficiency of over 50 percent, less generation of solid waste, lower emissions of nitrous oxides and carbon dioxide, and recovery of chemically pure sulfur. In a conventional coal plant, carbon dioxide emissions are mixed with intake air and cannot be separated from flue gas. Carbon dioxide emissions from an IGCC plant are pure carbon dioxide that can be sold or captured. The government-subsidized Wabash River coal gasification plant, in operation since 1971, removes 97 percent of sulfur, 82 percent of nitrous oxides, and 50 percent of mercury from plant emissions. Higher thermal efficiency of an IGCC plant reduces carbon dioxide emissions for the same amount of power output produced by conventional coal-fired plants that operate at a lesser degree of thermal efficiency. A newer IGCC plant, Duke Energy's Edwardsport Generating Station in Knox County, Indiana, began commercial operations in 2013 and is one of the world's cleanest coal-fired power generating stations. It is the first to use IGCC technology on such a large scale (618 mW). The plant has substantially reduced the environmental impact of burning coal to generate electricity.[34] IGCC plants cost considerably more than conventional plants and represent a higher level of technological sophistication both in construction and operations.

Advanced hybrid systems combining the best of both gasification and combustion technologies are under development. Here the coal is not fully gasified, but partially gasified to run a gas turbine with the residue of gasification burned to run a steam turbine. Again, higher energy efficiencies with even lower emissions are possible. Ultra-low emissions technology is being funded by the 10 year, multi-billion dollar FuturGen project to build the world's first integrated sequestration and hydrogen-producing research power plant. FuturGen employs coal gasification technology integrated with combined cycle electricity generation. FuturGen will be the world's first zero-emissions fossil fuel plant capable of transforming coal to electricity, hydrogen, and carbon dioxide. Hydrogen can fuel pollution-free vehicles using low cost and abundant coal as the raw material. Electricity can be sold as well as the carbon dioxide byproduct. While FuturGen was killed by the Bush Administration in 2007 for cost overruns, it has been reinstated in 2009 by the Obama Administration.[35]

Gasification plants operate with a wide variety of feedstocks and outputs. In the US, small capacity gasification plants consume biomass and wastes to produce steam, electricity, fuel gas, syngas, hydrogen chloride, or hydrochloric acid. Larger plants can be fed by petroleum, petroleum coke, natural gas, and coal, with outputs of oxochemicals (a family of alcohol based chemicals made by adding carbon monoxide and hydrogen to olefins), acetic acid, methanol, ammonia, and others. Favorite feedstocks for worldwide gasification plants are low grades of coal (lignite and sub-bituminous) and oil refinery waste products (asphalt and petroleum coke). Products in order of volumes are gaseous fuels, chemicals, liquid fuels, and power. Whereas gasification plants were once more or less spread evenly around the world, now they are concentrated in China and other Asian nations, dwarfing output in other parts of the world.[36]

Synthetic Natural Gas (SNG) from Coal

Producing natural gas (methane) from coal has the advantage of transforming a dirty fossil fuel to a clean fossil fuel. The preferred commercial method is the steam oxygen process where coal is gasified with steam and oxygen separated from air. Coal is reduced to ash and a mixture of gases consisting of carbon monoxide, hydrogen, and methane, along with higher order hydrocarbons such as ethane and propane, depending on temperature and pressure. After particulates and tars are removed, the gas mixture enters a water-gas shift reactor, where in the presence of steam and a catalyst gases are reduced to carbon monoxide, carbon dioxide, and hydrogen. Carbon dioxide is removed and carbon monoxide and hydrogen enter a methanation reactor, where in the presence of a catalyst the two gases react to form methane (SNG) and water. Water is removed in the condensation unit and SNG enters a natural gas pipeline for distribution.[37]

China seized on this technology as a means to tap coal reserves in Xinjiang province in western China and Inner Mongolia for transformation to SNG to meet energy demands in population centers in eastern China. Substituting SNG for coal burning would reduce air pollution from burning coal in eastern China. Fifty plants were originally planned for construction, but in 2014 with two pilot plants built, three under construction, and 16 more in the advanced stages of planning. Opposition from environmental groups emerged when it was realized that much more carbon dioxide would be emitted to the atmosphere via coal gasification projects than in burning coal directly. Twelve million tons of coal will be consumed to produce SNG that displaces 9 million tons of coal burned directly for power generation increasing the volume of emitted carbon dioxide. An estimated 1.1 billion tons of additional carbon dioxide emissions will enter the atmosphere annually if the 50 plants were built.[38] This is a measurable increase to 35 billion tons of carbon dioxide already being emitted annually from burning fossil fuels.

Carbon Capture

As with everything else that has to do with this planet, nothing is constant. Concentration of carbon dioxide over the ages from ice core samples shows that carbon dioxide generally cycled between 200 parts per million (ppm) and 250–280 ppm for the last 700,000 years. Unfortunately the start of the Industrial Revolution coincided with a cyclical peak of 280 ppm. Since then humanity has added another 120 ppm from burning fossil fuels to bring the total up to 400 ppm in 2014 and slightly above 400 ppm in 2015.[39] This level of carbon dioxide concentration has never occurred before in the 700,000 year climatic record based on ice core samples, although there were previous geological epochs when carbon dioxide was far higher. This places us clearly in unchartered waters with no precedent for judging the impact of such high levels of carbon dioxide in the atmosphere, at least in terms of the last 700,000 years. However, this period was dominated with glaciation infrequently interspersed with short periods of interglacial warming. We are presently in one of those warming periods.[40]

No practical way exists to capture 3 tons of carbon dioxide emitted by driving a 30 mile per gallon automobile 10,000 miles.[41] However, a stationary coal-fired power plant does lend itself to capturing and storing carbon dioxide emissions. A typical large coal burning power plant of 1,000 mW produces about 6 million tons per year of carbon dioxide, equivalent to the emissions of 2 million automobiles. There are about 1,000 of these plants in the world. Flue gas is roughly 15 percent carbon dioxide and the remainder mainly nitrogen and water vapor, plus of course nitrous and sulfur oxides (NOx and SOx), depending on type of coal and plant design. A technology for removing carbon dioxide from flue gas is to pass flue gas through an absorption tower containing amines that absorb carbon dioxide. An associated stripper tower heats the amines, releasing carbon dioxide and regenerating amines for another cycle through the absorption tower.[42] The question centers on what to do with carbon dioxide from the stripper tower assuming it has no commercial value.

If the power plant sits on top of impermeable caprock below which is a horizontal porous sand formation filled with brine, carbon dioxide can be pumped down a vertical pipeline that reaches the porous formation and then is dispersed via horizontal pipelines running through the formation. The brine formation should be more than 800 meters beneath the surface, where pressure is sufficient for injected carbon dioxide to enter into a "super-critical" phase where its density is near that of the brine that it displaces. In addition to carbon dioxide displacing brine, brine also absorbs some of the carbon dioxide. When carbon dioxide saturates an area of the formation, more horizontal pipelines are necessary to open up new areas. Huge volumes of carbon dioxide can be safely stored in this manner, but the geologic formation has to be about six times larger than a giant oil field to contain the 60 year lifetime plant output of about 100,000 barrels per day of carbon dioxide condensed to a super-critical phase.[43]

Carbon sequestering also means that about one-third more coal has to be burned for a given level of power generation to dispose of carbon dioxide, but it may be possible to also get rid of sulfur dioxide along with carbon dioxide as a side benefit. The cost of carbon dioxide sequestering would be a substantial surcharge to cover higher capital and operating costs plus additional coal that has to be burned. But any process to remove the relatively low percentage (15 percent) of carbon dioxide in flue gas in conventional plants is costly. One idea being explored is burning coal with pure oxygen and then recycling flue gas back through the combustion chamber to significantly raise the concentration of carbon dioxide in flue gases for potential separation.

An economic payback can be generated if carbon dioxide sequestering enhances fossil fuel production. Carbon dioxide pumped into methane-rich fractured coal beds displaces methane, which can then be gathered and sold. Carbon dioxide can also be pumped into older oil reservoirs, where its interaction with residual crude oil eases its migration through porous reservoir rock to production wells, known as tertiary oil recovery. One coal burning plant pipelines its flue gas emissions over 200 miles for tertiary oil recovery. Another idea is carbon capture utilization storage (CCUS) where carbon dioxide is stored as a substitute for water for carbon dioxide plume geothermal energy. Here much higher flow rates of carbon dioxide compared to water can remove far larger quantities of heat energy from geothermal sources.[44]

Carbon sequestration is not without its risks. Lake Nyos in Cameroon sits in a volcanic crater where carbon dioxide seeps into the bottom of the lake and is contained in place by the weight of the overlying water. One night in 1986, the lake overturned and released between 100,000 and 300,000 tons of carbon dioxide. Carbon dioxide, heavier than air, poured down two valleys, asphyxiating 1,700 individuals and thousands of livestock while they slept.[45] Any geologic formation including depleted oil and natural gas fields holding carbon dioxide must act as an effective lock against escape.

There is some experience with sequestration. Carbon dioxide associated with natural gas production in certain fields in the North Sea and Algeria is separated and sequestered in nearby porous geological formations. Not all research is space age for reducing carbon emissions. One project is exploring the possibility of adding 10 percent biomass to existing coal burning plants, which may reduce greenhouse gas emissions by up to 10 percent.

One Japanese utility adds 1 percent biomass in the form of solid municipal sludge to its coal intake, which has improved utility performance.

Ash Disposal

Two types of ash are fly ash removed by electrostatic or mechanical precipitation of dust-like particles in flue gas and coal ash found in the bottom of a combustion chamber. Ash differs in concentration and composition for each type of coal. For instance, bituminous coal from Appalachia is 10–14 percent ash, whereas lignite from Texas is 25 percent ash. The chemical composition of ash varies greatly, but primarily consists of oxides of silicon (silica), aluminum, calcium, iron, and sulfur trioxide, a solid form of sulfur oxide found in ash (not all sulfur found in coal leaves as sulfur oxides in smoke-stack fumes).[46] Ash represents a disposal problem; most ends up in landfills. Alternatively ash from burning coal, gypsum from flue gas desulfurization units, and boiler slag can be made into "cinder" construction blocks, which consume less energy and release less pollution than cement construction blocks. Fly ash added to concrete makes it stronger, more durable, less permeable to water, and more resistant to chemical attack. Gypsum can be used as a low grade fertilizer. These waste products can also be used as aggregate or binder in road construction. The Japan Fly Ash Association, Asian Coal Ash Association, and American Coal Ash Association are dedicated to conducting research for recycling fly and coal ash and boiler slag into useful products or disposal in an environmentally sound way.[47] Disposal of ash became an active environmental issue when a storm drain broke underneath a 27 acre ash pond close to Dan River in North Carolina. This allowed over 50,000 tons of coal ash to flow through the storm drain into the river. The coal-fired plant, owned by Duke Energy, had been previously decommissioned. The environmental impact on drinking water and recreation was significant from both the muck-like nature of coal ash and its arsenic and possibly other harmful metals content.[48] Obviously a better utilization of ash as recycled products would reduce the need for storing vast quantities of coal ash under such circumstances.

Eliminating Coal Not So Easy

Carbon dioxide is the result of a chemical reaction that occurs during combustion. Switching from coal to oil or natural gas reduces, but does not eliminate, carbon dioxide emissions. For the US, much greater reliance on natural gas would put upward pressure on prices, reducing the economic benefit of switching to natural gas. Switching from coal to oil for electricity generation is out of the question as oil is far more expensive on an energy equivalent basis and would result in increased oil imports and dependence on Middle East oil. Switching to nuclear and hydropower, renewables (wind, solar), and the hydrogen fuel economy would eliminate carbon dioxide emissions altogether, but major impediments have to be overcome to entirely replace coal. Switching from coal to nuclear power cannot occur unless public opposition to nuclear power is lessened, which is highly unlikely in the wake of the Fukushima tragedy. Switching from coal to hydro is hampered by a lack of suitable sites for damming. Switching from coal to wind and solar, while certainly beneficial as incremental sources of power, cannot replace coal because the generating capacity of wind and solar would have to be expanded by several orders of magnitude before an effective substitution can be achieved. Moreover, wind and solar are dependent on the wind blowing and sun shining and require some sort of backup to enhance reliability. Switching from coal to hydrogen, while environmentally desirable, is stymied by a less than fully developed and commercially feasible technology.

Much can be done to reduce coal burning emissions without resorting to clean coal technologies. Physical washing removes sulfur-iron compounds (pyretic sulfur) on the surface of raw coal, but not sulfur embedded in coal's molecular structure. While coal washing is prevalent in the US, Europe, Japan, and other developed nations, it is not in China and India, whose high ash and sulfur content coal would benefit most from washing. Although China and India are making headway in washing coal, there are capital constraints in establishing washing facilities, and possibly a shortage of available water in certain areas. A shortage of capital might apply for India, but China, with a huge balance of payment surplus, does not lack capital. In the past, China lacked the national will to deal with pollution because capital invested in pollution controls could not be dedicated to its economic development. China is beginning to rethink its position and is becoming more concerned over the environmental consequences of its economic policies. From one perspective, having Beijing submerged in the Asian brown cloud should be enough of an incentive for Communist government officials to take action against pollution, but apparently not to the degree necessary to take truly effective remedial action. While China is starting to take preliminary steps with regard to pollution emissions, the cost of retrofitting utility plants and motor vehicles is probably insurmountable at this point. New plants and new motor vehicles fitted with pollution devices would be the first logical step in addressing this problem.[49]

Closing small and inefficient coal mines can improve the environment and better protect the miners. Fewer and larger mines ease inspection efforts by government authorities and larger coal volumes more easily justify investments to protect the health and safety of workers and minimize harm to the environment. Using coal and biomass in home cooking and heating is a major source of uncontrolled pollution in Asia; electricity and propane are likely substitutes. On the surface, greater amounts of coal would have to be burned in order to switch home cooking from coal to electricity, but burning coal in a few locations rather than dispersed in millions of households provides the best means of monitoring and controlling pollution emissions; and, in fact, may be more efficient.

The future of coal is certain: it plays too significant a role in generating electricity to be dismissed out of hand. What is uncertain is what is going to be done to reduce its adverse environmental impact. Two projects may point to the industry's future. Prairie State Energy Campus (PSEC) is a $4 billion joint venture comprising eight public electric utilities and Peabody Coal, the world's largest coal company.[50] The venture is unique in that the participants own both the electricity generating plant and coal reserves set aside to service the plant. Coal is from a mine located adjacent to the plant that supplies 6.4 million tons per year on a continuous basis using the room and pillar technique. The plant, completed in 2012, is the largest of its kind at 1,600 mW compared to more typical large-sized plants of 1,000 mW capable of serving around 2 million households. The plant burns pulverized coal ground at the consistency of talcum powder, which in conjunction with supercritical steam generating technology has an efficiency advantage that cuts the carbon footprint by 15 percent compared to existing plant technology.

The plant is among the cleanest coal-fueled plants in the nation. The special design of the boiler and burner tips, along with burning coal at a lower temperature, reduces nitrogen oxide (NOx) emissions, which is cut further by 80–90 percent employing selective catalytic reduction technology. Here exhaust gas passes through anhydrous ammonia in the presence of a catalyst to transform NOx to nitrogen and water. Dry and wet electrostatic precipitators remove 99.9 percent of particulates in emissions and an advanced sulfur dioxide scrubber using limestone and water removes 98 percent of sulfur oxides (SOx). Mercury emissions are significantly reduced by the collective action of the selective catalyst reduction unit and dry and wet electrostatic precipitators. Total emissions are expected to be cut in half compared to existing plants.[51]

American Electric Power's John W. Turk, Jr. Power Plant, built in 2012, sets a new standard for clean, energy efficient coal-fueled generation. It relies on ultra-supercritical generation technology that consumes less low sulfur coal and produces fewer emissions including carbon dioxide with state of the art emission control technologies than traditional pulverized coal plants. Turk Plant can meet emission limits that are among the most stringent ever required for a pulverized coal unit. Chrome and nickel-based alloys are incorporated into the plant's steam generator, turbine, and piping systems to allow higher temperature (1,100°F) and pressure steam (3,200 psia) to achieve greater efficiency and hence a reduced environmental impact.[52]

Other projects under contemplation are chilled ammonia isolating carbon dioxide from flue gas plus oxy-coal combustion (burning coal in pure oxygen) as another means of isolating a pure stream of carbon dioxide for sequestration or tertiary oil recovery or carbon capture utilization storage. Some companies are taking a safer route in building coal plants by pushing the technology envelope without having to originate a new technology. All these initiatives being undertaken by the US coal burning utilities are in danger of being placed in abeyance in reaction to what many consider will be draconian EPA environmental restrictions placed on new and existing coal burning plants when their final rulings are issued.

This is one side of the ledger. Critics of the US coal industry utterly fail to recognize hundreds of coal burning utility plants in China and India operating without regard for pollution. Pollution controls are viewed as an unnecessary expense that adds to the cost of electricity. Cheap electricity is considered a competitive advantage to produce low cost consumer goods for the world export market. Socialist and communist leaders in these societies act more like nineteenth century capitalist robber barons and are not criticized by the Western media, although mention is made of the degree of pollution. It is true that China and to a lesser degree India are adopting clean technologies for generating electricity such as hydro, nuclear, and renewables, but the magnitude of their growing demand for electricity is such that they are forced to rely heavily on coal despite efforts to the contrary. Both nations appear wary of adding to their energy costs as long as economic performance outweighs environmental concerns, again a supposedly capitalist trait. Considering the number of coal plants that have been built in recent decades, any effort to clean up these plants is a bit too late with an effort a bit too small to make much of a difference for ameliorating the environmental consequences of their economic policies.

Problems and Project

Problems 4.1a–c below show the power of "runaway" exponential growth and its ultimate nonsustainability. The time it takes a quantity to double remains the same for a given growth rate regardless of its absolute value. If population doubles from 1 thousand to 2 thousand in 30 years, it also takes 30 years to double from 1 trillion to 2 trillion.

These problems pave the way for Problem 4.2, which covers what appears to be an eventual energy crisis for China to meet its future demand from its relatively low level of coal reserves. In solving Problem 4.2, you will sense how long China can sustain its growth in energy consumption without hitting the brick wall of reality that resources are finite.

Problem 4.1a

Manhattan Island was purchased from the Indians for an estimated $24 worth of glass beads, cloth bolts, and other paraphernalia by Peter Minuit in 1626. Suppose that the Indians deposited $24 in a savings bank at 5 percent interest compounded each year since 1626. What value would that be at this time? What would be the equivalent value of an acre of land (not including buildings) given that the land area of Manhattan is 23 square miles with 640 acres in a square mile? How would this differ if the interest rate were 3 percent? How do you think these values compare with average land values in Manhattan?

Problem 4.1b

Suppose that Mary and Joseph deposited one penny at the first Christmas at a local savings and loan bank that gave 3 percent interest on the outstanding balance. No withdrawals were ever made. At 3 percent compound growth, what is the current value of the deposit? Taking the current value of gold per troy ounce, what would be the value of the deposit in terms of troy ounces? There are 10.17886 troy ounces in a cubic inch. A cubic foot is 12" × 12" × 12" or 1,728 cubic inches or 17,589 troy ounces. How many cubic feet of gold does the balance represent? What is the radius in feet of a solid sphere of gold that could be purchased today given that volume is equal to 4/3 Pi R^3? Redo for 5 percent growth: the compounding factor makes a big difference!

Problem 4.1c

Refer to the tab Primary Energy Consumption in the *BP Statistical Review of World Energy* and check out how many years it has taken to double world primary energy consumption. On this basis, what will be the year it doubles again and again? Or if you wish, obtain the growth rate for the last two, five, or ten years. In what year will it double yet again? Take a look at the magnitude of energy consumption. Do you think this will happen, and if so, why?

Problem 4.2

Referring to China in the *BP Statistical Review of World Energy* and ignoring oil, which is a fuel for transportation, what's left is primarily energy consumed for electricity generation and as an industrial fuel.

a   Using historical growth rates, what would be the overall energy consumption (ex-oil) in 30 years when China may be exhausting its coal supplies (recent discoveries of coal in Mongolia notwithstanding)?
b   Suppose that China's coal production and imports are at present levels of consumption at that time (current R/P ratio is 30 years). Further suppose that hydro and

nuclear power continue to grow at historical rates out to 2040. What would be the deficit in energy that has to be satisfied by natural gas and renewables?

c   Suppose that natural gas can continue its historic growth rate based on Russian pipe- line imports and larger numbers of LNG import terminals. What would have to be the growth rate in renewables (solar and wind) to fill the gap?

d   How many doublings will solar and wind experience to fill the gap? Suppose that $10 billion were spent this year in renewables—how much would have to be spent in 2040 to fill the gap?

e   What is your overall assessment of the approach taken to assess future energy needs in China? Is it feasible or realistic? What would you do to make the approach more realistic?

f   What is your overall assessment of the energy situation in China in 2040? This ques- tion is more of a discussion on the nature of the solution rather than on obtaining a solution.

Problem 4.3

How many Btus are required to run a 1 gW base load plant demand for one hour operat- ing at 95 percent utilization for three different plant types? Plant 1 is an outdated plant with an operating efficiency of 25 percent, Plant 2 is a modern conventional plant with an operating efficiency of 35 percent, and Plant 3 is a modern plant with a fluidized bed combustion chamber with an operating efficiency of 45 percent. One watt-hour is equal to 3.412141633 Btu.

Problem 4.4

How much coal must be burned for two types of coal on an hourly basis? Type A is a high grade bituminous coal with a heat content of 14,000 Btu per pound and Type B is low grade lignite coal with a heat content of 9,500 Btu per pound. Figures are for dry coal where the moisture content has been removed. A typical coal train is 100 hopper cars each with 100 tons of coal or 10,000 tons of coal per trainload. How many trainloads are necessary to keep the plant running each day?

Problem 4.5

How much carbon and carbon dioxide will be emitted in tons per day for both types of coal for the three plants? Type A coal is 75 percent carbon and Type B is 35 percent car- bon. Assume complete combustion where the entirety of the carbon content is converted to carbon dioxide (no carbon monoxide). First calculate daily tons of carbon. Convert carbon to carbon dioxide-equivalent by utilizing the atomic mass of carbon of 12 and 16 for oxygen. Tons of carbon dioxide is tons of carbon × the ratio of the weight of a mole of carbon dioxide to a mole of carbon or $(12 + 16 + 16)/12$.

Problem 4.6a

How many tons of sulfur are emitted daily if Type A coal is 1.5 percent sulfur and Type B is 2.5 percent sulfur for the three plants?

Problem 4.6b

Assume that half of the sulfur is emitted in the flue or smokestack gas as SO_2 and the other half is contained as solid sulfur compounds in the boiler ash. Calculate the tons of sulfur as a percentage of the coal burned and reduce by half to account for particulate emissions. Multiply the remaining tons of sulfur by the ratio of $(32 + 16 + 16)/32$ where the atomic mass of sulfur is 32 to obtain tons of SO_2. What would be SO_2 emissions in tons per day if a scrubber is installed that can remove 98 percent of SO_2 airborne emissions?

Problem 4.7

Suppose that the ash content for Type A coal is 5 percent and Type B is 25 percent. Further suppose that the ash is evenly divided between boiler ash and flue ash. How many tons per day of flue ash enter the atmosphere as soot for both types of coal for each of the three plants? What would be the flue ash emissions if precipitators are installed that can remove 95 percent of particulate matter in the flue gas?

Problem 4.8

Suppose that a 1 gW advanced pulverized coal plant has an all-inclusive capital cost of $3,000 per kilowatt capacity.[53] What is its capital cost? Suppose that the capital recovery factor (CRF) covered in Projects 2.2–2.3 in Chapter 2 is 10 percent. The CRF includes both debt repayment obligations and satisfies a desired rate of return on the equity investment. What is its annual capital cost?

a   Suppose that the plant's fixed operating and maintenance (O&M) costs are $32 per kilowatt-year—what are the fixed annual costs?
b   The plant's variable (O&M) costs are $4.50 per megawatt-hour—what are its variable costs at 95 percent utilization?
c   The fuel cost is the cost of coal consumed to run the plant. Assume coal prices of $70 and $90 per ton and an average operating efficiency of 35 percent and an average utilization of 95 percent. What is the cost of fuel for the two coal prices?
d   What is the cost of electricity in dollars per kilowatt-hour for the two prices of coal?

Problem 4.9

How would the price of electricity be affected by a carbon tax of $20 per ton?

Problem 4.10

Redo the calculations for a 1 gW IGCC plant operating at 95 percent utilization with carbon sequestration. The cost is $3,800 per kilowatt-year, a fixed cost of $51 per kilowatt-year, and a variable cost of $7.20 per megawatt-hour. Plant efficiency is 50 percent. Suppose that hydrogen produced by the plant is burned as a fuel and is incorporated into plant efficiency. Moreover the operation of the IGCC plant with carbon sequestration increases coal consumption by one third. What is the cost of electricity in dollars per kilowatt-hour for the two prices of coal?

Problem 4.11

What carbon tax would have to be applied to the advanced pulverized coal plant in order for its electricity cost to be equivalent with the IGCC plant with carbon sequestration?

Project

Using the values derived in Problems 4.3–4.11, write a briefing paper for guiding a utility on its considering another 1 gW plant incorporating the two plant types, efficiency, and coal types on cost and pollution emissions.

Notes

1 *BP Statistical Review of World Energy*, British Petroleum (2015), unless indicated otherwise, is the primary source of data in this chapter.
2 *World Energy Outlook*, International Energy Agency (2012), and World Coal Association, Website www.worldcoal.org/resources/coal-statistics/coal-steel-statistics.
3 "Coal and Electricity," World Coal Association, Website www.worldcoal.org/coal/uses-of-coal/coal-electricity. Data originally from International Energy Agency (2012).
4 World Coal Association, Website www.worldcoal.org/resources/frequently-asked-questions.
5 *MIT Technology Review*, Vol. 116/No. 3 (2013), Website www.techologyreview.com.
6 *World Energy Outlook*, International Energy Agency (2012).
7 Jeff Postelwait (Electric Light & Power), "US EPA Issues Revised Rules for New Power Plants," *Renewable Energy World* (August 9, 2013), Website www.renewableenergyworld.com/rea/news/article/2013/09/gina-mccarthy-introduces-epas-revised-rules-for-new-power-plants.
8 "Reaction to EPA Revised Carbon Emission Rules," World Coal, Website www.worldcoal.com/news/coal/articles/Reaction_to_EPA_revised_carbon_emission_rules_68.aspx#.UsXGBrTWOkI. See also "The Future of Coal," Massachusetts Institute of Technology (2007), Website http://web.mit.edu/coal/The_Future_of_Coal.pdf.
9 William F. Jasper, "Obama EPA War on Coal to Shut 200+ Coal-Fired Plants, Devastate Economy," *New American* (August 9, 2013), Website www.thenewamerican.com/tech/energy/item/16250-obama-epa-war-on-coal-to-shut-200-coal-fired-plants-devastate-economy.
10 "FACT SHEET: Clean Power Plan & Carbon Pollution Standards Key Dates," EPA, Website www2.epa.gov/carbon-pollution-standards/fact-sheet-clean-power-plan-carbon-pollution-standards-key-dates.
11 Vince Font, "Renewable Energy Responsible for First Ever Carbon Emissions Stabilization," *Renewable Energy World* (June 17, 2015), Website www.renewableenergyworld.com/articles/2015/06/renewable-energy-responsible-for-first-ever-carbon-emissions-stabilization.html.
12 Jack Perkowski, "China: Getting Serious about Air Pollution?" *Forbes* (September 29, 2013), Website www.forbes.com/sites/jackperkowski/2013/07/29/china-getting-serious-about-air-pollution.
13 Stefan Nicola and Tino Andresen, "Germany Gives Dirtiest Plants Six Years for Phase Out," *Bloomberg* (July 2, 2015), Website www.bloomberg.com/news/articles/2015-07-02/germany-to-close-coal-plants-in-effort-to-curb-pollution.
14 Andrew Topf, "Why King Coal Will Keep Its Crown," OilPrice.com, Website http://oilprice.com/Energy/Coal/Why-King-Coal-Will-Keep-Its-Crown.htm, from data drawn from Fraunhofer ISE, Germany (November, 2013).
15 "Chemical Spill Shuts off Water to 300K in West Virginia," CBS News (January 10, 2014), Website www.cbsnews.com/news/some-people-treated-for-water-related-issues-in-w-va.
16 Interesting information on coal mining can be found at Website www.coalwoodwestvirginia.com/coal_mining.htm. Photos of coal mining equipment of various types are available by doing a search on "types of coal mining equipment" and selecting Images. One Website with images is

http://images.search.yahoo.com/yhs/search;_ylt=A0oG7o4OY8BSQw8AjfAPxQt.?p=coal+mining+equipment+pictures&fr=&fr2=piv-web&hspart=avg&hsimp=yhs-fh_lsonsw&type=ff.26.w7.hp.17-01.us.dis_ts.test8._.

17 "Description of Coal Mining," World Coal Institute, Website www.worldcoal.org/coal/coal-mining.

18 John McQuaid, "Mining the Mountains," *Smithsonian Magazine* (January, 2009).

19 Images of reclaimed land can be seen by doing a search on "reclaimed surface mining land" and selecting Images. One Website with images is http://images.search.yahoo.com/yhs/search;_ylt=A0oG7qSKZMBSGmIABv0PxQt.?p=reclaimed+surface+mining+land&fr=&fr2=piv-web&hspart=avg&hsimp=yhs-fh_lsonsw&type=ff.26.w7.hp.17-01.us.dis_ts.test8._.

20 "Coal Mine Safety, Deaths and Injuries in China," Facts and Details, Website http://factsanddetails.com/china/cat13/sub85/item321.html.

21 Dong An, Dasheng Li, Yin Liang, and Zhengjin Jing, "Unventilated Indoor Coal-Fired Stoves in Guizhou Province, China: Reduction of Arsenic Exposure through Behavior Changes Resulting from Mitigation and Health Education in Populations with Arsenicosis," *Environmental Health Perspectives* (April, 2007), Website www.ncbi.nlm.nih.gov/pmc/articles/PMC1852693.

22 Robert B. Finkelman, Harvey E. Belkin, and Baoshan Zheng, "Health Impacts of Domestic Coal Use in China," *Proceedings of the National Academy of Sciences of the US* (March, 1999), Website www.pnas.org/content/96/7/3427.full.

23 Sasol Corporation, Website www.sasol.com.

24 "Clean Alternative Fuels: Fischer-Tropsch Fact Sheet," US Environmental Protection Agency, Website http://slate.wvu.edu/r/download/37739.

25 Keith Schnieder, "Water Needs Curtail China's Coal Gasification for Fuel, Yet Conversion to Chemicals Pushes Ahead," Circle of Blue (2011), Website www.circleofblue.org/waternews/2011/world/water-needs-curtail-chinas-coal-gasification-for-fuel-yet-conversion-to-chemicals-pushes-ahead.

26 Coco Liu, "Chinese Companies Plunge into Coal-to-Liquids Business, Despite Water and CO_2 Problems," ClimateWire (February 23, 2015), Website www.eenews.net/stories/1060013819.

27 The source in Figure 4.8 for the price of coal at FOB (free on board, used to specify that a product is delivered and placed on board a carrier at a specified point free of charge at the mine mouth) is the US Department of Energy, Website www.eia.gov/totalenergy/data/annual/pdf/sec7_21.pdf, for bituminous coal in short tons. The source for the price of oil is *BP Energy Statistics* for $/bbl (dollar cost per barrel), FOB West Texas Intermediate; the $/bbl price was multiplied by 7 in order to obtain $/metric ton (cost in dollars per metric ton). Natural gas prices in $/1,000 cf were obtained from tonto.eia.doe.gov and translated to bbls at 5,610 cf/bbl. The price of coal was multiplied by 1.1 to convert from short tons to metric tons and then by 2 to convert physical tons to tons of oil equivalent to approximate the relationship between oil and coal in terms of equivalent energy released; these figures do not include shipping costs. Adjustments were made to price all three energy sources in 2014 dollars.

28 Mario Parker, "Hungry U.S. Power Plant Turns to Russia for Coal Shipment," *Bloomberg*, Website www.bloomberg.com/news/print/2014-07-15/hungry-u-s-power-plant-turns-to-russia-for-coal-shipment.html.

29 Kevin Krajick, "Fire in the Hole," *Smithsonian Magazine* (May, 2005).

30 Sapient-Horizons, Website http://sapient-horizons.com/Sapient/Underground_Fires.html, contains a global map of clusters of underground coal fires.

31 World Coal Institute, Website www.worldcoal.org, for clean coal technology.

32 Further information on coal-fired power plants can be obtained from National Energy Technology Laboratory (NETL), part of DOE's national laboratory system, Website www.netl.doe.gov/technologies/coalpower/cfpp/technologies/fluidizedbedcombustion.html.

33 "Power Generation from Coal," Coal Industry Advisory Board (CIAB), International Energy Agency (2010), Website www.iea.org/ciab/papers/power_generation_from_coal.pdf.

34 Duke Power, Website www.duke-energy.com/about-us/edwardsport-overview.asp.

35 FuturGen is described by the US Department of Fossil Energy, Website www.fe.doe.gov.

36 Gasification Technologies Council, Website www.gasification.org/what-is-gasification/the-gasifica tion-industry.

37 Munish Chandel and Eric Williams, "Synthetic Natural Gas (SNG): Technology, Environmental Implications, and Economics," Climate Change Policy Partnership of Duke University (January, 2009), Website www.canadiancleanpowercoalition.com/pdf/SNG3%20-%20synthetic.gas.pdf.

38 Edward Wong, "China's Energy Plans Will Worsen Climate Change, Greenpeace Says," *The New York Times* (July 24, 2014).

39 "Atmospheric Concentrations of Greenhouse Gases," EPA, Website www.epa.gov/climatechange/science/indicators/ghg/ghg-concentrations.html. See also Earth System Research Center, Website www.esrl.noaa.gov/gmd/ccgg/trends.

40 Considering the climatic record for the last 700,000 years, higher levels of carbon dioxide may not be harmful if it helps to delay the next onslaught of glaciation!

41 Robert H. Socolow, "Can We Bury Global Warming?" *Scientific American* (July, 2005), p. 33ff.

42 Dan Chapel, Carl Mariz, and John Ernest, "Recovery of CO_2 from Flue Gases: Commercial Trends," National Energy Technology Laboratory (NETL), Website www.netl.doe.gov/publications/proceed ings/01/carbon_seq/2b3.pdf.

43 *Carbon Capture Journal*, associated with the *Digital Energy Journal*, covers developments in industrial scale carbon capture and geological storage technology including major projects and development with government policy. A free subscription to *Carbon Capture Journal* is available at Website www.carboncapturejournal.com/allnews.aspx.

44 Sonal Patel, "Using Carbon Dioxide to Produce Geothermal Power," *Power* (February 1, 2014), Website www.powermag.com/using-carbon-dioxide-to-produce-geothermal-power.

45 University of Arizona Geosciences Department, Website www.geo.arizona.edu/geo5xx/geos577/projects/kayzar/html/lake_nyos_disaster.html.

46 "Quality Guidelines for Energy System Studies—Detailed Coal Specifications," National Energy Technology Laboratory Office of Program Planning and Analysis, Website www.netl.doe.gov/energy-analyses/pubs/QGESS_DetailCoalSpecs_Rev4_20130510.pdf.

47 "An American Recycling Success Story," American Coal Ash Association, Website www.acaa-usa.org/Portals/9/Files/PDFs/ACAA-Brochure-Web.pdf.

48 Associated Press, Website http://finance.yahoo.com/news/broken-pipe-spills-coal-ash-145423646.html.

49 It is quite amazing that huge misallocations of capital would be made in building what are now called "empty cities" while pollution abatement is studiously ignored.

50 Prairie State Energy Campus, Website www.prairiestateenergycampus.com.

51 Duke Energy, Website www.duke-energy.com/environment/air-quality/control-technologies.asp, discusses control technologies to reduce coal plant emissions.

52 American Electric Power, Website www.aep.com/about/MajorBusinesses/PowerGeneration/New Generation.aspx.

53 Cost estimates on electricity generating plants throughout this book are approximate values contained in *Updated Capital Cost Estimates for Utility Scale Electricity Generating Plants* published by the US Energy Information Administration (April, 2013).

5 The Story of Big Oil

When we think of oil, we think of gasoline and diesel fuel for motor vehicles, but the beginning of the oil industry was kerosene for illumination. Kerosene was the foundation of the Rockefeller fortune and marked the birth of Big Oil. Oil provided an alternative fuel for lighting; if oil ran out, it would be back to whale oil, tallow, and vegetable oils. Thus oil was not indispensable or vital to the running of the economy; now, no oil, no economy. The transmogrification from a preferred fuel for lighting to something without which modern society could not survive started with Henry Ford putting America on wheels in the early 1900s and was completed by the First World War when military vehicles, tanks, and fighter aircraft fueled by oil played a pivotal role in securing victory for the Allies. Oil had become as important as armaments and ammunition in the conduct of war. During the Second World War, one of the principal targets of the Allies' bombing was coal-to-liquid plants that produced gasoline to fuel the Wehrmacht. Sinking oil tankers was a prime submarine activity in the theaters of war in the Atlantic by German U–Boats and in the Pacific by US submarines. To achieve dominance over much of world oil supplies, Hitler intended that one army would sweep across the Soviet Union and then south from Stalingrad to meet up in Baku with Rommel's army that would sweep across North Africa and up through the Middle East. This grand plan was thwarted at Stalingrad and El Alamein, not far from Cairo.

But things have changed. As a depleting resource, oil has moved beyond being a fuel for war to being a cause of war. Never-ending and never-winning Middle East wars evolve around oil; yet, in the aftermath of all these wars, is the Middle East more secure as a source of oil for the global economy? Is the Middle East more socially and politically stable for its people? Is terrorism on the run? The irony is that the US is not actually dependent on Middle East crude oil. US imports of Middle East crude can be easily replaced by western hemisphere oil exports to Asia. Our need for imported oil will continue to diminish by increasing supply via fracking, improving internal pipeline distribution, and reducing demand via better motor vehicle mileage. Another irony is that those who benefit most from Middle East oil (China, India, Japan, Korea, and other Asian nations) do not participate in "stabilizing" the Middle East nor compensate the US for over two trillion dollars spent for accrued benefits, real or imagined. In contemplating the situation, one can only ask "Why?"

This chapter looks at the historical development of two of the world's largest oil companies and the role that Big Oil will play in supplying the world with energy products as we proceed towards "Beyond Petroleum."

See the Companion Website for sections on the History of Lighting and the History of Oil through to Opening Up the Middle East: www.routledge.com/ cw/nersesian.

History of Oil

Early Attempts at Oil Price Controls

Rockefeller, of course, was the first to attempt to control prices, and he pretty much succeeded when he achieved 90 percent control over the US refinery industry. His idea of an acceptable price for kerosene was the price that would not encourage outsiders to build refineries. Too high a price would only create more problems for Rockefeller to maintain his monopoly by providing an incentive for others to get into the refining business.

The first to attempt to bring order to the oil industry on a global scale was the oil power brokers of the day, Teagle of Exxon (a distant relative of Maurice Clark, Rockefeller's first partner) and Deterding of Shell. In 1922 they stood together, along with others, to present a united front in dealing with oil sales by the Soviet Union, which they viewed as buying back stolen property. While the two power brokers were shaking hands and expressing mutual dismay over Soviet duplicity in expropriating their oil properties without compensation, Deterding secretly purchased a large quantity of Soviet oil at less than the agreed price with Exxon, which he promptly dumped in the Far East. Subsequent attempts by Teagle and Deterding to restore some semblance of order sometimes worked and sometimes didn't. In 1927 their bitter cross-accusations ended with Deterding abandoning any further pretext of cooperating with Exxon over the matter of Soviet oil, starting what turned out to be a disastrous price war. The Soviets thought that they had succeeded in creating chaos in the world oil patch by successfully playing one oil company off another, perhaps bringing back memories of Nobels and Rothschilds. Soviet satisfaction over spreading confusion in the capitalistic world stemmed not so much from their conspiratorial intentions, or Deterding's ill-fated venture into a price war, but from a world flooded with crude from the Soviet Union, Mexico, and Venezuela.

The 1920s started with a feeling that oil would be in short supply, which is why the US government forced Exxon and Mobil to get involved with Middle East oil through its interest in the Turkish Petroleum Company. By the late 1920s, and continuing on through the global depression of the 1930s, the world was awash in oil. Something had to be done. Oil companies had made massive investments on the basis of a certain projected price of crude oil; as crude prices sank, so did return on these investments. To thwart further weakening of oil prices, Deterding (known as the Napoleon of Oil) held a social and sporting affair at Achnacarry Castle in Scotland in 1928 that included, among others, Teagle of Exxon and Sir John Cadman, director of the Anglo-Persian Oil Company, half owned by BP (BP acquired the other half of Anglo-Persian Oil in 1954). Intimate business conversations during this social and sporting affair led to a pooling arrangement to control price through cooperation in production and in sharing incremental demand among the cartel of supposedly competing oil companies called the Achnacarry Agreement. The reference price would be American oil in the US Gulf, with adjustments to take into account freight from the US Gulf.

Once this system was initially proposed, four other major oil companies joined, forming what became known as the Seven Sisters. If a participating oil company purchased oil in the Middle East and sold it in France, the selling price would not be the FOB price in the Middle East plus freight from the Middle East to France, but the price of oil in the US Gulf plus freight from the US Gulf to France. This system stabilized the price regardless of the actual source at a healthy level for the oil companies, as long as others joined, which they did. With a mechanism in place for allocating incremental production to meet growing demand among the participating oil companies, the global oil business, with the exception of Soviet oil, was under the control of a cartel of oil companies. Rockefeller's dream of world control over oil, for the most part, had finally come true, but not with domination vested in the hands of an individual, but a small group of executives who, in the aggregate, controlled most of the world oil. The success of this agreement hinged on all the individuals continuing to cooperate, something rarely seen in the world of oil. Of course US oil companies involved in this arrangement to fix price and control volume were acting in direct violation of the Sherman Antitrust Act.

In 1930, only 2 years after the system was set up, price stability was threatened by yet another mammoth oil discovery. Like Drake, Higgens, and Reynolds, an old wildcatter, Dad Joiner, persisted where others had given up. Joiner did not drill on land that had promising geologic characteristics, but on land owned by promising widows who might invest in Joiner's ventures. Joiner was an avid reader of obituaries in search of prospective clients. Joiner must have had a way with widows for they were all financially disappointed with Joiner's ventures; except for one, on whose east Texas farm in Kilgore Joiner brought in a gusher. Joiner had proved oil geologists wrong and Kilgore became another Pit Hole and Spindletop all rolled into one with oil derricks almost on top of one another pumping with all their might. Unfortunately Joiner was in financial straits from his past ventures and could not hold onto his holdings. Forced to sell out to H.L. Hunt, who made billions on Joiner's and other east Texas properties, Joiner was to die as poor as Drake and Higgens. One would have thought that Hunt out of gratitude would have given Joiner a pittance to make life a bit more comfortable considering his role in making Hunt a billionaire, but that was not to be!

The east Texas oil boom was fed by discovery of other oil fields in east Texas much larger than anyone imagined, all of which were crowded with producing wells. These fields ran north and south. Once one was discovered, success was virtually assured by drilling north and south of a producing well and failure east and west. Wildcatters spudded wells east and west and endured the risk of failure for the promise of discovering other north–south oriented fields, which they eventually found. Enough fields were discovered to create a glut during the Great Depression sufficient for local oil prices to collapse to 10 cents a barrel, where, as in Pit Hole, a barrel was worth more than the oil contained therein. Teagle and Deterding were powerless because they had no means of control over east Texas oil fields. Faced with financial ruin, Texas "independents" demanded federal and state intervention. Texas and Oklahoma obliged and declared martial law on the basis that independents were squandering a valuable natural resource, particularly at 10 cents a barrel. Using conservation to justify states' intervention and with local militia to enforce their will, oil production was stopped. Then the Texas Railroad Commission was authorized to set up a rationing system to control production for every well in the two states. Although individual producers initially cheated whenever they could, the Texas Railroad Commission eventually got the upper hand over producers and was able to ration production of individual wells and prices rose. Government action to protect and conserve a natural resource would be viewed today as environmentally desirable. Paradoxically it also served the interests of the global oil cartel as well, since stabilizing the price of east Texas oil also stabilized the US Gulf price and, consequently, the world price of crude oil. Thus capitalism and conservation joined hands with a common objective, but different goals. Deterding's pooling arrangement and the Texas Railroad Commission's rationing of production were valuable lessons for OPEC when it gained control over oil prices and production in the 1970s.

Enter Saudi Arabia and Kuwait

With the price of oil reestablished by controlling east Texas production, the last thing oil companies wanted was another east Texas discovery. Another oil rogue, New Zealander Frank Holmes, believed that oil was waiting to be discovered in Arabia. Gulbenkian's Red Line Agreement prohibited exploration in Arabia without the joint cooperation of the signatories. Socal (Standard Oil of California), progenitor to Chevron, was not a signatory of the Red Line Agreement, and for $50,000 bought Holmes's concession in Bahrain, an island nation off Arabia, and in 1931 struck oil. While Bahrain would never become a major oil producer, it indicated that Holmes might also be right about nearby Arabia.

In 1927 the desert king Ibn Saud subdued his rivals along the Red Sea coastline and named his new kingdom after his clan. In 1930, desperate for money, King Saud inveigled Socal to buy a concession in Saudi Arabia. The major oil companies, bound by the Red Line Agreement and in no mood to discover more oil, passed up the opportunity to make a deal with King Saud. Socal did some exploration, which turned out to be promising, but was short on capital if oil were discovered. Socal teamed up with Texaco, another nonsignatory to the Red Line Agreement, and Texaco bought a half share of Socal's interests in Bahrain and Saudi Arabia. Eventually oil was discovered in Saudi Arabia, and in 1939 King Saud opened a valve and oil began to flow into an awaiting tanker. The king was so pleased that he increased Socal's and Texaco's concession to an area as large as Texas, Louisiana, Oklahoma, and New Mexico combined.

Frank Holmes was involved with opening up Kuwait, also outside the Red Line Agreement. Eventually BP and Gulf set up a joint venture after a fair degree of behind-the-scenes maneuvering by the British and US governments and, in 1938, oil was discovered. Although Frank Holmes was instrumental in opening up oil exploration in Bahrain, Saudi Arabia, and Kuwait, all successful finds, he made no fortune from the enormous wealth that he was instrumental in creating for oil companies and producers, although he had a comfortable retirement. Originating and transforming a good idea to reality does not necessarily translate into personal wealth. This is the lesson of Drake, Higgens, Joiner, and Holmes; something else is needed.

Exit the Key Players

Hitler inadvertently took down three leading oil company executives. The first to fall was Deterding, who was showing signs of mental imbalance (megalomania) as his management style became increasingly dictatorial. In his memoirs, composed in 1934 in the midst of the Great Depression, with tens of millions of unemployed workers desperately seeking work, he wrote that all idlers should be shot on sight. Upset over the loss of

Shell properties in Russia after the revolution, Deterding's position against communism hardened with his second marriage to a White Russian. With his third marriage to a German, Deterding became a Nazi sympathizer because of their determination to rip communism out root and branch. Deterding would not be the only industrialist, states-man, monarchist, or church leader to support the Nazis for this reason. Alarmed over Deterding's managerial style and his extremist views, the board of directors removed Deterding from his position in 1936 by forcing him to retire and he died 6 months before the war started. Shell's penchant for collegiality and corroboration in the decision-making process might be partly in reaction to Deterding's last years of dictatorial rule.

The second to fall was Rieber, the head of Texaco. In 1937 Rieber diverted Texaco tankers taking oil to Belgium to support Franco in Spain, and in 1940 got around a British oil embargo against Germany by shipping oil to Germany from neutral ports. Unable to take money out of Germany, Rieber worked out a barter agreement whereby he accepted German-built tankers in exchange for oil. Rieber was forced to resign in 1940 in the wake of a British intelligence revelation that a Texaco employee was sending information to Germany about American war preparations.

The third to fall was Teagle, who had entered into an agreement before the rise of Hitler with I.G. Farben, a German chemical company. Farben was to research and develop synthetic rubber for Exxon in exchange for Exxon's patents for tetraethyl lead, a vital ingredient in aviation fuel. Teagle was unable to see the military implications of this arrangement after Hitler's rise to power and Japan's seizing of rubber plantations in Southeast Asia. Teagle refused to break what he considered first and foremost a busi-ness deal, which remained in force until revelations of its existence by the US Justice Department led to his resignation in 1942.

All three were counterpoints to Marcus Samuel, who put civic duties and patriotism above business. Deterding, Rieber, and Teagle put business above all else. Buy for a little less here, sell for a little more there—this was their key to success. Business plans are to fit the immutable laws of supply and demand. The name of the game is making money. Politicians come and go and have little use other than passing laws and establishing regu-lations that protect business interests or guarantee their success. Governments rise and fall, but business remains forever; it is the Great Constant.

Shareholders and Stakeholders

The modern corporation is based on the premise that its mission is maximizing share-holder wealth. One way to do this is to spawn new products and expand market reach to millions of individuals as Rockefeller did. Another way to maximize shareholder wealth is to widen the spread between the price received for a product and its cost of production, also a Rockefeller practice, although Rockefeller focused more on reducing the cost of production than raising the price of kerosene.

While maximizing wealth for a corporation's shareholders is what the game is all about, there are other constituencies, or stakeholders, affected by the operation of a pri-vate corporation. For instance, an oil company has some degree of latitude concerning where profits are assigned. Profits can be shifted between upstream activities (crude oil production) or downstream activities (refining and marketing) through internal transfer prices. If an oil company has its oil fields, refineries, and distribution system, and mar-kets its products within the border of a single nation, such as the US, it does not matter how profit is assigned internally when a company consolidates its financial statements and tax returns. The federal government collects the same in income taxes regardless of how internal transfer prices are set, although internal transfer prices can affect state income taxes. When an oil company is buying crude oil from one nation, processing in a second, and selling in a third, the internal assignment of profits through transfer pricing can heavily influence the taxes and royalties paid by oil companies to host governments. This in turn affects the well-being of the people of oil exporting nations, who are, in every sense of the word, stakeholders in a company that is exploiting their nation's natural resources.

Deterding noted the importance of the triangle linking the mutual interests of an oil company with the people and with the host government where all three should benefit from developing a nation's oil resources.[1] Shell operated in Mexico, and despite assertions by Deterding to the contrary, the Mexican government and people felt they were getting a raw deal from the oil companies and, in 1938, nationalized the industry. Oil companies struck back by refusing to buy Mexican oil until they received restitution. Pemex, the newly formed national oil company of Mexico, could not ship oil to a foreign port without having it legally attached by oil companies. Ultimately Pemex was forced to pay restitution in order to gain access to foreign markets. Now two nations, the Soviet Union and Mexico, directly controlled their oil resources. Yet oil companies had not learned the essential lesson of Mexico—a one-sided relationship in which an oil company exploited the oil resources of a nation with limited benefit to the people or the government, either real or perceived, was not in the best long-term interests of the oil company. No one viewed Mexico as a harbinger of more to come when new oil discoveries in Venezuela diverted oil company attention away from Mexico.

Development of Saudi Arabia's Oil Fields

Saudi Arabia was the answer to Washington's worry, one that had first vexed Theodore Roosevelt and would come back now and then to haunt government energy policy-makers—the world was going to run out of oil. Socal and Texaco operated in Saudi Arabia under the corporate umbrella of Aramco, the Arabian-American Oil Company. Socal and Texaco advanced the idea during the early years of the Second World War of the US government setting up a Petroleum Reserve Corporation to buy a controlling interest in Aramco and construct a refinery in the Persian Gulf. The idea was well received by Franklin D. Roosevelt, who, like Churchill, was attracted by the idea of government ownership of a foreign oil field. However, oil companies abruptly broke off negotiations in 1943. Only in hindsight can one see the timing between the success of Rommel in North Africa and the proposal for the Petroleum Reserve Corporation and Rommel's defeat in 1943 with the proposal's demise. Obviously oil company investments in the Middle East would be in danger if Rommel succeeded in his master plan to link his army in North Africa with Hitler's in Baku. Oil companies generally oppose government intervention in their operations unless, of course, such intervention promotes their agenda.

The US government then proposed constructing a thousand-mile pipeline to carry Saudi crude to the Mediterranean with the oil companies' guarantee of a 20 percent interest in the oil fields as a naval reserve. The Trans-Arabian Pipeline (Tapline) was completed, without US government involvement, in 1950 when Saudi crude was loaded on a tanker in Sidon, Lebanon. The pipeline, passing through Saudi Arabia, Syria, and Lebanon, was shut down in 1975 during a time of turmoil in Lebanon. Its carrying oil cheaply to Europe while in operation meant a great deal to Socal and Texaco.

Having achieved such success in Saudi Arabia, Socal and Texaco passed up an opportunity to become dominant players in the oil business by not wanting to challenge other major oil companies. They felt that involvement of the majors was necessary for access to oil markets, capital to develop Saudi oil resources, and garnering diplomatic support if there were an unfriendly successor to King Saud. Admitting Exxon and Mobil and excluding other signatory oil companies violated the Red Line Agreement. Using American antitrust legislation as a lame excuse, Exxon and Mobil walked away from the Red Line Agreement and joined Aramco, thereby locking BP, Shell, and CFP out of Saudi Arabia.

Aramco proved to be a model for a company operating in a host nation. Its employees had their own town and concentrated on the business of finding, developing, and operating oil fields, and building and running refineries, pipelines, and terminals. By any measure, Aramco was considered a "good corporate citizen." Aramco permitted the US to have two allies diametrically opposed to one another. The state department dealt directly with Israel and, when necessary, relied on Aramco as a go-between in its dealings with Saudi Arabia. In the aftermath of the 1973 oil crisis, Aramco transmogrified into Saudi Aramco with 54,000 employees, of whom 86 percent are Saudis. The company prides itself on its ability to manage Saudi energy resources and contribute to the nation's development. It is a model national oil company for others to emulate.[2]

Shoes Begin to Fall

It is one matter when foreign producers supply 10 percent of the world's oil, which can easily be replaced by other sources. This keeps producers in a weak bargaining position, as they learned in Mexico. Their bargaining position is not quite so weak when their share grows to 30–40 percent and is more difficult to replace. Oil companies failed to realize the growing bargaining strength of oil producers that accompanied growing world dependence on foreign oil. The next shoe to fall after the Mexican nationalization of its oil industry came in 1948 when Venezuela passed a law for a 50:50 sharing of profits. This was an idea of Juan Pablo Perez Alfonso, Venezuelan oil minister and who would one day be the chief architect of OPEC. The idea was not total anathema to the oil companies if sharing profits meant forestalling nationalization, as had occurred in Mexico (better to have half than none). Moreover oil companies had the power to define profitability via transfer pricing.

King Saud, whose huge family's lifestyle had become incredibly expensive, joined the fray and demanded a share of profits. Aramco turned to the US government for support, and the government, fearing a communist takeover in the Middle East, agreed to have Aramco partners treat additional payments to Saudi Arabia as a foreign income tax. This was a great boon to the Aramco partners because this meant, under rules on double taxation, that taxes paid to the US government would decrease one dollar for every dollar paid in taxes to Saudi Arabia. In other words, the US government, and hence US taxpayers, were subsidizing the extra cost of oil. Such a ruling could not be restricted to some oil companies and some nations; equal treatment demanded that this apply for all oil companies and all nations. Oil companies could reduce their US taxes by what they were paying in taxes to foreign suppliers, something that would not apply to an oil company with only US producing properties. The upshot of this ruling was that it became more profitable for oil companies to develop oil properties overseas than domestically. Another tax bonanza for the oil companies was applying the oil depletion allowance to foreign as well as domestic sources of oil. These two tax rulings placed oil companies in a quasi tax-free environment at that time, which is not true today. Thus oil companies could acknowledge the principle of sharing profits with producers because it did not represent an actual cost by virtue of fanciful accounting with transfer pricing and a fortuitous change in tax laws.

BP, still half-owned by the British government, had expanded into activities far beyond those envisioned by Churchill. While its principal source of oil was still Iran, BP had a major position in Iraq and Kuwait and had developed a worldwide marketing network served by its fleet of tankers. In 1951, a new Iranian leader appeared on the scene, Mohammad Mossadegh, who called for the nationalization of Iranian oil fields after BP's refusal to adopt a deal similar to that between Aramco and Saudi Arabia. The Iranian prime minister, who opposed Mossadegh, publicly stated that he would not allow Iran to repudiate its concession with BP. That remark sparked his assassination by those who thought otherwise, paving the way for Mossadegh to become prime minister and nationalize BP's oil fields. The Labour Party, then in power in Britain, was hardly in a position to enforce this legacy of colonialism. With no help from the British government, BP took legal action, not in Iran, but in every nation where a cargo of Iranian oil landed, mimicking what was done to Pemex cargoes after Mexico had nationalized its oil industry. This lasted 2 years. By then civil unrest from loss of oil revenue led to a coup, encouraged by the CIA, which placed a son of a previous shah on the throne. In 1954, an agreement was hammered out whereby the National Iranian Oil Company (NIOC), formed by Mossadegh, would remain owner of the oil fields along with the Abadan refinery. However, oil would be sold through a consortium in which BP had a 40 percent share and Shell 14 percent, with most of the remainder divided among CFP and the seven sisters. In other words, oil companies had total market control over Iranian oil production. The agreement taught oil companies a valuable lesson in that ownership of an oil field is not nearly as critical as access to its oil.

Later on five small US oil companies inveigled a 5 percent share. Among these were Getty Oil and Tidewater, both owned by Jean Paul Getty. Getty was the son of a lawyer who struck it rich in oil in Oklahoma. The son was just as talented, if not more so, as his father. Getty became a billionaire, partly as a result of his flying with an oil geologist serving as a consultant over the Neutral Zone between Saudi Arabia and Kuwait. The Kuwait side of the Neutral Zone was already producing oil. The geologist noted from the air that a certain sector of the Neutral Zone in Saudi Arabia had geologic features very similar to that of the oil producing sector in Kuwait. Based on this visual observation, Getty immediately started negotiating with Ibn Saud for a concession. Drilling revealed a huge oil field, big enough to make Getty a billionaire and for the geologist to be reimbursed for his travel expenses.

Besides Getty, there was Hunt, another billionaire not given to sharing with those responsible for his wealth (Dad Joiner comes to mind), and Armand Hammer. Hammer received a medical degree but did not practice medicine, as had his father, who, in the course of events, had befriended Lenin. Hammer took advantage of his father's relationship with Lenin to consummate commercial deals in the Soviet Union including setting up a pencil factory and purchasing Russian art treasures for pennies on the dollar. Hammer, at an age when many contemplate retiring, got interested in oil and eventually took over a small oil company called Occidental Petroleum. By dint of his determination and driving force, Hammer transformed Occidental Petroleum into an international oil company with the discovery of three major oil fields in Libya. Hammer would play a pivotal role in the oil crisis of 1973.

Another thorn in the side of the seven sisters was Enrico Mattei, head of the Italian State Oil Company, who was able to prick the seven sisters by negotiating an independent concession with NIOC in 1957 and making a private deal with Khrushchev for cheap Soviet oil, much as Deterding had done. On top of this, the seven sisters had to contend with CFP's discovery of oil in Algeria. New discoveries of supply remained ahead of rapidly growing demand. Despite the best efforts of the seven sisters to put a lid on production, a glut of oil kept prices low. Unbeknownst to the Iranian government, oil companies in the consortium that purchased NIOC's production made a secret side agreement to reduce Iranian volume in order to avoid a global glut of oil. Neither the Shah nor NIOC knew about this agreement, which effectively made Iran a swing producer to maintain world oil prices.

Despite falling shoes, which could be looked upon as a premonition of what was to come, this period also marked the zenith of oil company power. Oil companies had reinstated their position in Iran even though their properties had been nationalized by preventing access to the world market, the same stratagem used in Mexico. Mossadegh's political demise served as a warning to other interlopers. Notwithstanding the success of Hunt, Getty, Hammer, and Mattei, there were limited opportunities for third parties to reach the market unless they went through one or more of the seven sisters. The seven sisters exerted the power of Rockefeller's horizontal monopoly on a global scale. Table 5.1 lists the shareholders of the various Middle East oil concessions on the eve of the 1973 oil crisis.

Nasser's 1956 takeover of the Suez Canal did not affect oil companies as much as it created fortunes for tanker owners. Because it took longer to get the oil around South Africa, Humble Oil, the Texas subsidiary of Exxon, took advantage of the temporary shortage of oil in Europe and hiked crude prices by 35 cents per barrel. This incurred the wrath of Congress, which from a contemporary perspective appears ludicrous when price changes of 35 cents per barrel are hardly noticeable. Of course, 35 cents per barrel of oil at around $2 per barrel was a noticeably large percentage change. What this showed was a major consuming government's keen interest in keeping a lid on oil prices; in fact, one might conclude that consuming governments depended on oil companies to keep a lid on oil prices. Keeping communists out of the oil producing nations and keeping oil prices low for consumers were the reasons why the US government never seriously pursued antitrust actions against American oil majors, who clearly violated the Sherman Antitrust Act when they cooperated with competitors to fix prices and control production. The British government took a far more pragmatic view of the situation and did not share the US government's vexation with oil companies' attempts to stabilize the price of something as critical to the world economy as oil.

Birth of OPEC

By the late 1950s cheap Soviet crude was cutting into the seven sisters' markets in Italy, India, and Japan. The seven sisters had to lower their prices in these nations to maintain

Table 5.1 Shareholders' Ownership Percentage

	Iran Consortium	Iraq IPC	Saudi Arabia Aramco	Kuwait KOC	Abu Dhabi Petroleum
BP	40	23.750	–	50	23.750
Shell	14	23.750	–	–	23.750
Exxon	7	11.875	30	–	11.875
Mobil	7	11.875	10	–	11.875
Gulf	7	–	–	50	–
Texaco	7	–	30	–	–
Socal	7	–	30	–	–
CFP	6	23.750	–	–	23.750
Others*	5	5	–	–	5

*Getty, Hunt, and Hammer for Iran Consortium and Mr. Five Percent (Gulbenkian) for IPC and Abu Dhabi Petroleum.

their market presence, which, of course, meant lower profit margins. In 1959 Exxon resolved that it must cut posted prices to oil producers to preserve its profit margin. When other oil companies followed suit, Arab oil producers organized the first meeting of the Arab Petroleum Congress, the fruit of private talks between the oil ministers of Venezuela and Saudi Arabia. A second round of Exxon-inspired cuts provoked a stronger surge of unity among the oil producers. Another meeting in 1960 of the oil ministers of Saudi Arabia, Iran, Iraq, Kuwait, and Venezuela gave birth to the Organization of Petroleum Exporting Countries (OPEC).[3] The purpose of OPEC was not to raise oil prices, but to prevent further erosion of posted prices. The original unity of purpose was gone by the second OPEC meeting in 1961, when a rough and tumble battle broke out among OPEC members as each sought to garner a larger export volume at the expense of others. OPEC was behaving no differently than the earliest oil drillers in Pit Hole; it was every man for himself as each strove to maximize revenue by maximizing production.

By no measure could OPEC be considered a success during the 1960s. There was little coordination among members and politics kept getting in the way of negotiations. Meanwhile new sources were coming on stream, such as Nigeria, putting more pressure on OPEC. In 1965 OPEC failed at an attempt to gain control over future increases in production just as it failed to gain control over current production. The seven sisters meanwhile were trying to restrain production to prevent further declines in oil prices. The irony is that, in only 10 years, OPEC would take over the oil companies' role of restraining production to control prices. Role reversal would not be a mirror image, as OPEC's idea of price in the 1970s would be radically different than that of the oil companies in the 1960s.

The 1967 Six-Day War between Israel and Egypt sparked the first Arab boycott. The war was over before the boycott had any effect, which was doomed anyway when Venezuela and Iran refused to join. Formation of the Organization of Arab Petroleum Exporting Countries (OAPEC) within OPEC in 1970 did not succeed in strengthening the resolve of OPEC to bring order to the oil market. Order, of course, meant maximizing each member's respective production volume to maximize revenue, which, all the while, neglected price as a determinant of revenue. Oil company attempts to rein in production to maintain prices, which varied for each member of OPEC, irritated oil producers who now had to contend with new production from Qatar, Dubai, Oman, and Abu Dhabi.

In 1970, the Alyeska Pipeline Company was formed to handle the 1968 oil discovery by Arco (then Atlantic Richfield) in Prudhoe Bay on the north slope of Alaska. Compared to the Middle East exporters, this was expensive oil. Arco, short on crude, viewed the development of the North Slope field as vital to its survival. Two other major participants were Exxon and BP, the latter having acquired Sohio to gain greater access to the US market. These two companies, with more cheap Middle East oil than they wanted, did not need expensive North Slope oil. At first the environmentalists were successful in blocking the building of an 800-mile pipeline to Valdez. Congress set an interesting precedent by overriding environmental concerns in the wake of the 1973 oil crisis and authorized the construction of the pipeline. Alaskan oil began flowing in 1977.

Another source of high-cost oil was the 1969 discovery of the Ekofisk oil field in the Norwegian sector of the North Sea by Phillips Petroleum. This was followed a year later by the BP discovery of the Forties field north of Aberdeen and the following year by the Shell and Exxon discoveries of the Brent field off the Shetland Islands. The involvement of Exxon, BP, and Shell in oil fields far more costly to develop than buying Middle East crude, intentionally or unintentionally, could be interpreted as manifesting their concern over the rising dependence on Middle East oil.

The 1973 oil crisis was not caused by a shortage of oil. Indeed, the greatest worry right up to the eve of the crisis was how to keep new production from flooding the market, further eroding oil prices. Producers fretted over anything that would shrink their export volumes. The Shah of Iran wanted to increase export volumes in order to expand Iran's military power and develop its economy, and saw his role as guarantor of stability in the Middle East, for which he had received President Nixon's blessing. Other oil producers had their agendas on why their export volumes should be increased.

1973 Oil Crisis

Figure 5.1 shows the growth of world oil consumption from the beginning of the oil age and OPEC production since 1960 in millions of tons per year (mmtpy).[4]

From the birth of the automobile age around 1900, oil consumption began to double about every decade. Even the Great Depression did not dampen growth in oil consumption, but the age of oil did not begin in earnest until after the Second World War, when successive doublings really started to kick in (one penny doubled is two pennies, two pennies doubled is four, doubled again eight, doubled again 16, doubled again 32). The slopes of the curves for both world oil consumption and OPEC production appear about the same from 1960 to 1973, which implies that nearly all incremental oil demand was coming from OPEC nations. This can only happen if OPEC had an increasing share of world oil production, which it did. In 1960 OPEC's production was equivalent to 41 percent of world oil consumption, 45 percent in 1965, and 52 percent in 1973. Much of the rapid growth in incremental consumption was in Europe and Japan, both in their mature stages of recovery from the Second World War. While oil consumption growth in the US was more subdued, nevertheless the US was heavily responsible for growth in OPEC demand as it made the transition from being the world's largest oil exporter in the days of Rockefeller to the world's largest oil importer after World War II

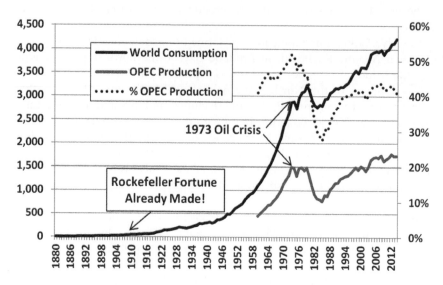

Figure 5.1 Growth in World Oil Consumption and OPEC Production (mmtpy)

from declining domestic production. Figure 5.2 records the consequences of supply lagging demand in thousands of barrels per day (000 Bpd).

The early 1970s was a period of rapidly rising US oil imports, of which a greater portion was Middle East exports because incremental production from South America and North and West Africa could not keep up with growing US demand. The 1973 oil crisis halted growth in US consumption, and over 20 years were to pass before US consumption would surpass its 1978 peak. Middle East production peaked in 1977 and did not exceed that peak until 2003. Though the US is criticized as the energy hog of the world, its share of the oil pie was far larger in the past. The US portion of world oil consumption of 42 percent in 1960 declined by little over half to 20 percent in 2014, nearly the same as Europe including the Former Soviet Union. Obviously, incremental growth in oil consumption has been concentrated elsewhere—elsewhere being primarily Asia. Asia, including Australia and New Zealand, consumes one-third of world oil. The largest consuming nations in Asia are China at 12.4 percent followed by Japan at 4.7 percent and India at 4.3 percent of world oil, collectively accounting for two-thirds of Asian consumption. The US still remains by far the world's largest consuming nation, but as seen in Figure 5.2, US imports of 7.4 million Bpd are declining rapidly from success in fracking oil. If North America is considered a single entity for oil production and consumption, North America's net imports of 4.6 million Bpd are less than China's imports of 6.8 million Bpd.

The high point of oil company ascendancy over national powers was the BP-inspired embargo against Mossadegh that led to his downfall from power in 1953 and brought Iran to heel. Between then and the 1973 oil crisis, there was a shift from a buyers' to a sellers' market that occurred without public fanfare. The question raised by Figure 5.1 is, why did it take so long? Another way of putting it, from the consumers' perspective, would be that oil companies should be congratulated for keeping the lid on oil prices for as long as they did. Yet there had to be an underlying unease with respect to the state of the oil

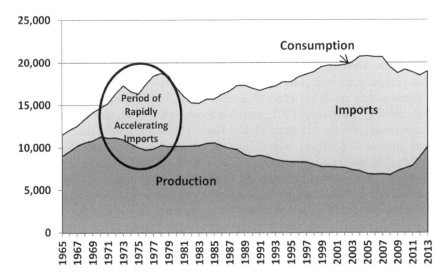

Figure 5.2 US Oil Consumption, Production, and Imports (000 Bpd)

market. Why else would major oil companies start searching for oil in such high-cost areas as the North Slope and the North Sea?

The underlying shift from a buyers' to a sellers' market needed a precipitating event to make it manifest. Actually, there were a series of events, starting with Colonel Gadhafi's successful military coup in Libya in 1969. At that time, Libya was supplying about one-quarter of Europe's needs with high-quality and low sulfur crude. Moreover Libya is located on the advantageous side of the Suez Canal from the point of view of European buyers. The Canal was closed in 1956 and reopened in 1957 when Nasser nationalized it, then closed again in 1967 during the Israeli–Arab War, and was not reopened until 1975. Libya received no premium for its oil reflecting its quality and nearness to market. Gadhafi was not to be cowed by the major oil companies' resistance to a price change. In 1970 Gadhafi struck at the weakest link in the supply chain, the independents, particularly those highly dependent on Libyan crude. Of these, the most dependent was Occidental Petroleum. Gadhafi chose his target wisely.

Hammer pleaded with the majors to sell him replacement oil at the same price he was paying for Libyan oil before Gadhafi raised his price. In their shortsightedness, they offered Hammer higher priced oil. Facing a disastrous interruption to supply, Occidental caved in to Gadhafi's new price and tax demands, which were relatively modest from today's perspective. Flushed with victory, Gadhafi went after the majors. To everyone's surprise, the majors did not embargo Libyan crude and replace it from other sources as they had with Mexico and Iran. Instead they capitulated to Gadhafi's demands, a stiff price to pay for not coming to Hammer's aid. The difference in reaction by the oil companies to a price hike was a hint to producers that a fundamental change had taken place in the market. The world was psychologically shifting from a buyers' to a sellers' market long after the physical shift had occurred.

As a consequence of Gadhafi's success, a hastily convened OPEC meeting in Caracas in late 1970 agreed to higher minimum taxes and higher posted prices that, when announced, only made Gadhafi leapfrog with even greater demands, followed by Venezuela. This infuriated the Shah, who viewed Gadhafi as a challenge to his leadership. To shore up the resistance of independents to further OPEC demands, the majors agreed that appropriately priced replacement oil would be provided to prevent more independents from caving in to producer demands. It was too late.

With US government support, oil companies attempted to get oil producers to agree to common terms and to moderate their demands, that is, to get control over Gadhafi. A meeting was held in Tehran in 1971 attended by delegates from the oil producing nations, oil companies, and the US State Department. The Shah insisted that Libya and Venezuela not attend. The majors hoped that the presence of the State Department would aid in their negotiations, but it proved to be a weak straw. The State Department wanted to avoid a confrontation between oil companies and producers because of its policy for Iran and Saudi Arabia to act as regional police to suppress Communist-inspired radicals. The State Department and oil majors were not on the same page. Similarly government representatives of several European nations and Japan proved equally inept at influencing the outcome. Without strong government backing, and considering the importance of OPEC oil in the general scheme of things, oil companies made no new demands and shifted their approach from confrontation to a call for moderation. It was now a matter of damage control.

The capitulation of oil companies to oil producers was the final piece of evidence that convinced oil producers that the market had indeed shifted in their favor. One top oil executive publicly quipped that the buyers' market was over, not the wisest remark to make under the circumstances. The agreed price increase in February of 1971 was an extra 30 cents per barrel on top of the posted price, escalating to 50 cents per barrel in 1975. This price adjustment held for the Gulf producers; now a meeting was necessary with Libya. A separate Tripoli agreement, signed six weeks after the Tehran agreement, called for a higher price for Libyan oil without Libya providing a similar guarantee on future price hikes as contained in the Tehran agreement. The Shah was infuriated by Gadhafi's leapfrogging once again over what he had already agreed with the major oil companies.

Whereas the 1960s were years of worry over looming oil gluts, the early 1970s were years of growing concern over a potential shortage, a reversal of the change in perception that had occurred between the early and late 1920s. This change in sentiment spurred oil producers to increase their demands for part ownership of their natural resources in the 2-year hiatus between the Tehran agreement and the oil crisis of 1973. Oil producers felt that the original concessions granted to oil companies belonged to a bygone age of colonialism and imperialism. They wanted to move into the modern era and control their national resources through joint ownership rather than merely collecting taxes and royalties on their exports. Oil producers initially favored joint ownership with oil companies over nationalization because nationalization removed oil companies' incentive for making money in the upstream, or production, side of the business. By limiting their profits to the downstream side of refining and marketing, oil companies would only be interested in buying crude at the cheapest price and oil producers would be back to undercutting one another as the only way to attract oil companies' attention.

Joint ownership turned out to be an idle thought. British withdrawal of their military presence from the Middle East in 1971 created a power vacuum that allowed Iran to seize some small islands near the Strait of Hormuz. As the world focused on Iranian aggressions, Gadhafi took the opportunity to nationalize BP's holdings in Libya along with

Bunker Hunt's concession, and then 51 percent of the remaining concessions, including Hammer's. Algeria and Iraq joined in the frenzy of nationalizing oil assets. In early 1973 the Shah announced his intention not to have NIOC renew its operating agreement with the oil companies when it expired in 1979 and to transform NIOC from a domestic oil producer into a major global oil company.

By making separate deals with oil companies, oil producers were fast learning how to play one of the seven sisters off another just as effectively as the seven sisters used to play one producer off another. Oil companies were beside themselves as their oil fields and physical assets were transferred from their books into the books of oil producers. They were at loggerheads over a common approach that would minimize their loss of power and enable them to obtain restitution. Their appeals to the US government for help were interpreted as a sign of weakness by the oil producers. Then independent oil companies broke ranks with the seven sisters and began a bidding war to assure their oil supplies, another sign of weakness. The imposing facade of oil company power was being exposed for what it was: an imposing facade.

With governments standing helplessly aside, oil companies prepared to meet with OPEC producers in Vienna in October 1973. The meeting took place just as Syria and Egypt invaded Israel, hardly an auspicious omen. The meeting broke down when oil producers demanded a price hike to $5 per barrel. Oil companies played a weak hand and tried to refer the matter to their respective governments before making a formal reply. Oil companies had never appealed to their governments for permission before, so why now unless they were in desperate straits? Shortly after, in mid–October, King Faisal delivered an ultimatum to Nixon for immediate cessation of US military aid to Israel or face an embargo. The ultimatum arrived just as the US Senate had overwhelmingly voted to send reinforcements to Israel.

Events were now entirely out of the hands of oil companies and consuming nations. In quick response to the continued US military support of Israel, members of OPEC meeting in Kuwait unilaterally raised the price of a barrel of oil from $3 to $5, accompanied by a 5 percent cutback in production. The oil weapon, mentioned in the past, was now taken out of its sheath for the first time. The production cut was intended to sway the US not to continue supporting Israel. Then, three days later Saudi Arabia announced a 10 percent cutback in production plus an embargo of oil to the US and the Netherlands, the oil gateway to Europe. This embargo had to be carried out by the oil companies themselves, even though a majority of them were US companies. Of course, Saudi Arabia could not stop oil companies from supplying oil to the Netherlands and the US from other sources. Nevertheless the embargo created a hiatus in oil moving into the US, resulting in long lines at gasoline stations in November only a month later. The irony was that on October 21, when the embargo went into effect, Israel agreed to a ceasefire. But Humpty Dumpty of the old world could not be put back together again. Oil companies made fruitless attempts to regain control over market prices. The first oil shock reached its apogee in December, when Iran conducted an auction, which of itself manifested oil company loss of control. During the auction, independents panicked over oil supplies, bidding the price up to a high of $17 per barrel.

One argument advanced for raising oil prices by producers was the fact that European governments collected more in taxes on a barrel of crude than what they received for selling a finite and depleting resource (this relationship still holds). Another was that oil displacing coal proved that oil was underpriced with respect to coal. Hence it was in the long-term interests of energy consumers to reinstate coal as a source of energy. According to the Shah, this could be accomplished if crude were priced at $11.65 per barrel, the price necessary to make oil products from coal and shale oil at that time. The benefit to consumers was that a higher price of oil would cut oil consumption and postpone the time when the world would run out of oil.

The Shah was absolutely right. If the oil crisis had not happened and oil consumption kept doubling every decade, there would have been four more doublings between 1973 and 2013. World oil consumption averaged 2,750 million tons in 1973/1974, which, if doubling every decade held, would be 5,500 million tons in 1983, 11,000 million tons in 1993, 22,000 million tons in 2003, and 44,000 million tons in 2013 compared to 4,127 million tons actually consumed in 2013, less than 10 percent of projected exponential growth! An oil crisis was inevitable at some point because there was no way for production to continue doubling every decade to keep up with demand—a perfect illustration of the nonsustainable nature of exponential growth. Any system that doubles every decade is doomed to break down or explode or implode—take a choice. It is interesting that there has not been even a single doubling in consumption in the 40 years since the oil crisis; in fact, current consumption is "only" up by 50 percent from 1973.[5]

As the Shah was justifying why oil prices had to be increased, an oil auction held in Nigeria fetched a whopping $23 per barrel, although the winner did not show up to take delivery. At the end of 1973, with an OPEC meeting to determine the appropriate price for a barrel of oil, the Shah unilaterally announced a price of $11.65 per barrel, much to the chagrin of the other producers.[6] Even though the Shah would be accused of moderation in a sea of immoderation by other producers, his price still represented a doubling of the then-posted price and a quadrupling of the posted price only a few months earlier. He accompanied his announcement of the new price with the warning that Western living styles would have to change and everyone would have to learn to work harder. The world no longer had to face a cartel of oil companies, but a cartel of oil producing states. The greatest transfer of wealth in history was about to occur.

First Occasion for High Oil Prices

Figure 5.3 shows the history of oil prices in constant dollars and dollars of the day. Dollars of the day are actual prices of oil paid at points in time. Constant dollars reflect the purchasing power of 2014 dollars. Crude prices expressed in constant 2014 dollars are higher than in current dollars or dollars of the day, reflecting loss of purchasing power from inflation. In 1979/1980, crude prices were about $37 per barrel in dollars of the day or current dollars, whereas in constant 2014 dollars, prices were $106 per barrel, reflecting a two-thirds loss of purchasing power of the US dollar in the interim.

Although the peak price in 2008 was $147 per barrel in current dollars that occurred in a single moment of time, the average annual price shown in Figure 5.3, reflecting prices throughout the year, was $97 per barrel in current dollars and $107 per barrel in constant 2014 dollars. In constant 2014 dollars, the highest annual average price occurred in 1864, when prices averaged $122 per barrel. This explains a lot about the frenzy in Pit Hole. With Rockefeller in control by 1880, oil prices in terms of 2014 dollars averaged $22 per barrel, ranging $15–$39 per barrel until 1930. Thus, oil prices were fairly stable for a half century. The period 1930–1960 saw another 30 years of essentially constant prices,

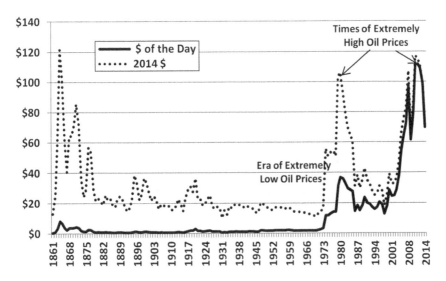

Figure 5.3 History of Crude Oil Prices ($/bbl)

although lower, averaging $17 per barrel, ranging $10–$20 per barrel, again in 2014 dollars. From 1960 up to 1972 was the absolutely worst period for oil producers, with an average price of $13 per barrel, ranging $11–$15 per barrel. It is ironic that the oil producers were facing the lowest prices in history in real terms while export volumes were virtually exploding. As long as exploding export volumes stayed ahead of exploding import volumes, oil companies could maintain the upper hand. As soon as exploding export volumes fell below exploding import volumes, which happened when Saudi Arabia imposed its embargo, all hell broke loose. The free market works on the principle that when supply exceeds demand, prices fall to the marginal producer—how fast they fall depends on the degree of oversupply; when demand exceeds supply, chaos prevails. Pricing in the free market economy is somewhat predictable when supply exceeds demand in that prices will eventually decline to the marginal producer, but pricing is entirely unpredictable when demand exceeds supply. The free market is not a place for the faint of heart.

After the 1973 price hikes, the Shah now had the means to make Iran the military powerhouse of the Middle East and NIOC a global oil powerhouse while pursuing the economic development of the nation including important social advances such as making education and professions accessible to women. Rather than giving him the means to fulfill his grandiose dreams, all he got for the financial bonanza was exile (he went on a vacation from which he never returned in early 1979). The Iranian Revolution, which broke out in 1978 as national strikes, ended in 1979 with the ascendancy of Khomeini, a cleric with a decidedly anti-Western bent. The Iranian Revolution marked the second oil shock when cessation of Iranian crude exports of over 5 million barrels per day (Bpd) caused oil prices to climb precipitously to $37 ($106 in current dollars) per barrel on an average annual basis, prices that would not be seen again until 2004, in terms of dollars of the day, but not until 2008 in constant dollars.

Cessation of Iranian production and accompanying panic buying and hoarding brought about a reoccurrence of long lines of automobiles at gasoline filling stations. As Khomeini was finding his way around Tehran, Saddam Hussein staged a coup making himself dictator of Iraq. Two years later, in 1981, Saddam cast his eye on Khomeini's army, whose weapons were no longer being supplied by the US, and whose officers, commissioned by the Shah, had been purged and replaced by loyal, but untrained, revolutionaries. Saddam decided that Khomeini's army, unlike the Shah's, was no match for Iraq's army, newly equipped by the Soviet Union, and so he invaded Iran.[7]

While Iranians and Iraqis were waging war and Saudi Arabians were having problems digesting their newfound wealth, changes in the world of energy were at work that would come back to haunt the oil producers. Among these was a worldwide economic decline that reduced overall energy demand. High oil prices instigated a desperate search for alternative sources to oil, leading to a resurgence of coal, an accelerated pace in building nuclear power plants, and a greater reliance on natural gas and anything else not called oil, including woodburning electricity generating plants. There were great gains in energy efficiency where cooling a refrigerator, heating a home, and running an automobile, truck, locomotive, marine, or jet engine could be achieved with significantly less energy. Conservation of energy took the form of keeping indoor temperatures higher in summer and lower in winter made more tolerable by wearing warmer clothing, driving the family car fewer miles, and recycling energy intensive products such as glass, aluminum, and paper. Companies set up energy managers to scrutinize every aspect of energy use in order to identify ways to reduce consumption.

In addition to slashing demand, high-priced oil caused an explosion in non-OPEC crude supplies, best exemplified in the North Slope of Alaska and in the North Sea. The North Slope of Alaska is an inhospitable place to develop and operate an oil field and necessitated the construction of an 800-mile pipeline to the port of Valdez over mountain ranges and tundra. North Slope production peaked at 2 million Bpd a few years after the pipeline started operating in 1977 and went into a slow, but inexorable, decline as government permission was not forthcoming in drilling more wells to sustain production. The North Sea was an even greater challenge with its hundred-knot gales and hundred-foot seas. Floating oil drilling platforms explored for oil in waters a thousand feet deep. "Oceanscrapers," structures higher than the Empire State Building, were built on land and floated out to sea on their sides. The location of the site was selected by analyzing exploratory well results for the optimal tapping of an oil reservoir. When on site, platoons were flooded (carefully) for an oceanscraper to first upright itself and then sink under controlled conditions. More water was added to the platoons as it sank to increase its sinking rate. A prescribed momentum was necessary for the oceanscraper to bury itself in the bottom at a designed depth to ensure that it remained upright in an ocean environment. Then production wells would be drilled from the oceanscraper to become a production platform. North Sea oil started with 45,000 Bpd of output in 1974 and grew to over 500,000 Bpd in 1975, to 1 million Bpd in 1977, to 2 million Bpd in 1979, to 3 million Bpd in 1983, and eventually peaking at 6 million Bpd in the mid-1990s. Every barrel from the North Slope and the North Sea was one barrel less from the Middle East.

Pricing After the Oil Crisis

Oil exporters attempted to dictate prices after the 1973 oil crisis, but continually changing prices implied that OPEC could not control price as well as the oil companies had. With oil prices fluctuating widely, no one knew, including oil producers, what would be tomorrow's price. This provided speculative opportunities for traders who tried to outwit or outguess oil producers. All they needed was a place where they could place their bets. Once the traders started placing bets, the buyers and sellers of oil had an opportunity to hedge their investments against adverse price changes.

Future and forward contracts of commodities with wide price swings were already traded, providing buyers with a means to hedge against the risk of a rising price and sellers a means to hedge against the risk of a falling price. The first futures were traded in grain in the nineteenth century. Before the advent of futures, farmers would ship their grain to Chicago and prices would collapse from supply overwhelming demand. Grain prices fell so low that unsold grain was left to rot. Farmers were not getting a fair price for their hard work. Then months later, grain prices would soar from supply falling short of demand. People were not paying a fair price for their bread. Once a futures market was established and sufficient grain storage facilities built, grain growers could short the futures market and lock in their revenue, whereas bakers could buy futures and lock in their costs. Futures and storage capacity stabilized prices in the cash market, serving both the interests of buyers and sellers. Futures then spread to other agricultural products and industrial metals to stabilize prices, provide a means of hedging against price swings, and function as chips in a gambling casino for speculators, whose buying and selling add depth to the market. Up until the 1970s there was no reason to have futures in gold and in interest and currency exchange rates, as these were essentially fixed by government fiat. As governments lost control over gold prices and interest and currency exchange rates during the 1970s, future contracts were developed to help buyers and sellers deal with the risk of price and rate volatility.

When oil companies controlled oil prices within a narrow range, there was no point in having futures. When they lost control over pricing, and with oil prices gyrating widely from a combination of oil producer greed, political instability, and Middle East conflicts, it was only a matter of time before someone would create a futures contract in oil. The New York Mercantile Exchange (NYMEX), with a long history in butter, cheese, eggs, and potatoes, needed a new trading commodity to keep its doors open. In the early 1980s NYMEX started trading futures in heating oil, then gasoline, and finally crude oil. First attracting primarily speculators, soon oil companies as buyers and oil producers as sellers started trading. The development of a cash and futures market spawned contracts that could be settled in monetary or physical terms. New contracts in market crudes expanding from West Texas Intermediate to a variety of specific crudes in the Middle East, West Africa, and the North Sea offered traders a much wider spectrum of opportunities. Cash and futures markets started to erode oil producers' direct control over price. Since the mid-1980s the primary determinant of oil prices has been the relationship between supply and demand, with supply as the control lever firmly in OPEC's hands. OPEC attempts to influence price by cutting back or expanding production, and in this indirect way affect oil prices, a practice put into place in the 1920s by oil oligarchs and the Texas Railroad Commission in the 1930s. The circle was complete with the reversion to the age-old practice of manipulating supply to affect price.[8] But the single control lever of production quotas was not quite as responsive because of the shrinking share of OPEC exports in relation to world production.

End of High Oil Prices

With consumers doing everything they could to reduce oil consumption and with economies crumbling under the weight of high oil prices, Middle East exports fell precipitously,
as seen in Figure 5.4.

The 12 current OPEC members are Algeria, Angola, Ecuador, Iran, Iraq, Kuwait, Libya,
Nigeria, Qatar, Saudi Arabia, the United Arab Emirates, and Venezuela, with Middle East
production currently making up 78 percent of OPEC production. Figure 5.4 shows production and domestic consumption of Middle East oil, with the difference representing
Middle East exports. Middle East exports satisfied 28 percent of world oil consumption
in 1970 and peaked at 37 percent in 1974. It remained between 31 and 37 percent from
1971 to 1979, then precipitously declined to 13 percent in 1985. From there it recovered
to 22 percent in 1998 and remained between 21 and 24 percent since then, with the
2014 share being 22 percent. These figures differ from previous figures of OPEC production compared to global consumption because OPEC includes non-Middle East members.
Furthermore Middle East oil exports have been netted of domestic consumption.

Every OPEC and non-OPEC producer operated full out (shades of Pit Hole and
Spindletop), taking advantage of the price bonanza to maximize revenue after the 1973
crisis. As time went on and demand began to drop from nations reacting to high oil
prices, it was becoming increasingly difficult to maintain price. There had to be a swing
producer to maintain a balance between supply and demand to keep prices high and, as
Figure 5.5 clearly shows, that swing producer was Saudi Arabia.

Saudi Arabia's production was initially boosted as replacement crude during the
Iranian Revolution in 1978 and 1979 and during the early years of the Iran–Iraq War.
After production in Iran and Iraq was restored, Saudi Arabia had to cut back sharply to
maintain price. Those holding huge inventories in anticipation of further price increases
had a change of heart when some semblance of order was restored and prices began to
decline. Liquidating excess inventories caused OPEC oil demand to slump just as panic

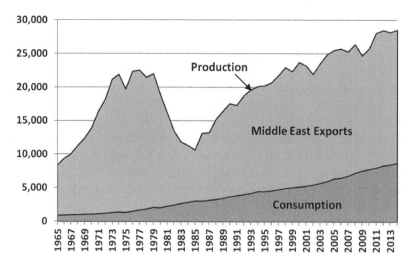

Figure 5.4 Middle East Production versus Consumption (000 Bpd)

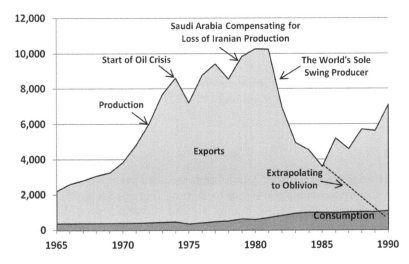

Figure 5.5 Saudi Arabia Oil Production, Exports, and Consumption (000 Bpd) 1965–1990

buying and hoarding caused it to jump, illustrating how changes in inventory sentiment can affect supply and, hence, price. With OPEC members producing full out, Saudi Arabia had to cut production again and again to keep prices from eroding further. Saudi Arabia was now playing the same historical role played by the US when the Texas Railroad Commission had the authority to control production to maintain oil prices. The US ceased being a swing producer in March 1971 when the Commission authorized full production for all wells under its jurisdiction—another noteworthy sign of the transformation from a buyers' to a sellers' market.[9]

From the perspective of 1985, cessation of Saudi Arabian exports was just over the horizon that could be pinpointed by simply extending the trend line. The days of being the world's swing producer were about to end. Something had to be done to prevent Saudi exports from collapsing. In 1985 Saudi Arabia unsheathed the oil weapon, not against the consuming nations, but against its fellow OPEC members. Rather than raise prices by cutting production as in 1973, Saudi Arabia opened the oil spigot and flooded the market with oil, forcing oil prices to collapse below $10 per barrel, threatening to financially wipe out OPEC. Saudi Arabia then invited its fellow producers to sit around a table to reach agreement on production quotas and a mechanism for sharing production cutbacks whereby Saudi Arabia would cease being the sole swing producer. The cartel would now act as a cartel. These episodes in 1973 and 1985 clearly showed that while price may be determined by the relationship between supply and demand as taught by traditional economics, in oil, supply is a control lever to establish its relationship to demand, and hence influence price. Saudi Arabia has demonstrated its willingness on several occasions since 1986 to unsheathe the oil weapon to lower or raise prices in a less draconian fashion to discipline erring OPEC members or to maintain price stability as circumstances dictated.

A cartel is a small group of suppliers with a share large enough to control the market and having an organizational will to divide the market among themselves. A mechanism has to be in place for determining the size of the quota for each member, with a means to identify violations and punish violators. Enforcement of cartel decisions is under the control of the cartel, not an individual member. A cartel has the power to prevent prices from becoming too high that would erode its market and encourage substitution or too low to be financially painful for cartel members. On nearly all these markers for a cartel, OPEC is not a cartel comparable to other cartels such as exist for diamonds, coffee, bauxite, tin, and rubber. But this is not to discount OPEC's influence over prices, even if not all-encompassing.[10]

Era of Moderate Oil Prices

The era of moderate oil prices began after Saudi Arabia sheathed its oil weapon in 1987. Immediately world and US consumption began to increase (Figures 5.1 and 5.2) along with OPEC (Figure 5.1) and Saudi Arabia (Figures 5.4 and 5.5) production. What happened to energy conservation and efficiency? By the mid-1980s most of the means to achieve energy conservation and efficiency were in place. Energy conservation and efficiency are noble undertakings; wasting a nonreplenishable resource cannot be justified. But the dark side of energy conservation is that it only works when prices are high. If energy conservation and efficiency succeed in decreasing demand to the point where prices fall, then it becomes a different ball game. Suppose an individual buys a fuel-efficient car when the price of gasoline is high. The individual is using less gasoline. If repeated over millions of individuals, reduced consumption may be sufficient for the price of gasoline to fall. Once gasoline is cheaper, there is a temptation to take an additional vacation trip, perhaps as a reward for having a fuel-efficient automobile, which, when repeated millions of times over, increases gasoline consumption.

A house has been insulated, and the temperature is lowered to consume less heating oil in winter. If repeated in millions of homes, the cut in consumption may be sufficient to cause the price of heating oil to decline. When this occurs, the temptation is to increase the indoor temperature for greater comfort, causing heating oil consumption to rise. Fuel-efficient jet engines cut jet fuel consumption. If the airline industry converts to fuel-efficient jet aircraft in response to high fuel costs, reduced consumption eventually cuts the price of jet fuel. Savings in jet fuel justify the purchase of fuel-efficient aircraft. Suppose that fuel-efficient jet aircraft are underemployed from airlines buying too many aircraft. With low jet fuel prices, the temptation is to take advantage of savings in jet fuel to underwrite a discount in airline fares to attract more business. Cheaper fares encourage more passenger traffic and thus more flights, increasing jet fuel consumption. Likewise as jet fuel prices fall, fresh fruits and vegetables can be flown from far-distant New Zealand and Chile, and flowers from Colombia to Europe and the US, at a cost that the market can bear. Lower priced tickets and increased food and flower shipments cause jet fuel demand to rise, negating the benefit of conservation and efficiency in reducing consumption.

If conservation and efficiency succeed in cutting demand to the point where energy prices decline, then lower cost energy will reinvigorate consumption, closing the gap between usage and what was consumed before conservation and efficiency measures were put in place.[11] This phenomenon is clearly seen in Figures 5.1, 5.2, and 5.5—a quintessential example of a negative feedback system. Ultimately conservation and efficiency are self-defeating, which does not mean that energy conservation and efficiency should be discarded. What it means is that high prices have to be sustained in order to maintain the benefits of conservation and efficiency, and provide incentives for people to continue practicing conservation and improving efficiency.

Second Occasion for High Oil Prices

The second time for high oil prices was from 2007 to late 2008 with the all-time record price of $147 per barrel (average price would of course be lower), the highest since 1865 in constant dollars. Pseudo-economic growth fueled by enormous debt acquisition by US consumers resulted in greater crude oil consumption. Asian oil growth was fueled by China transforming itself from depression-level economic egalitarianism under communism to Manufacturer of the World under capitalism. This growth in economic activity occurred throughout Asia to varying degrees. While there is an enormous difference in the degree of permanence between economic activity spurred by acquiring debt or by producing goods and services, the outcome of both is higher energy consumption. Spare capacity for the OPEC producers fell to about 1–2 million barrels per day at this time, a far cry from the late 1970s/early 1980s when Saudi Arabia could make up for the cessation of exports from Iran of nearly 6 million barrels per day and still have capacity to spare. A low level of spare capacity is just another way of saying that demand is getting too close to supply, which introduces price instability. Price instability was described in Chapter 2 with regard to electricity rates in California when Enron intentionally cut electricity supply to California and again in this chapter when Saudi Arabia intentionally cut oil supply to the US and the Netherlands.

Inventory Accumulation and Liquidation Affects Price

During the upswing in prices in the latter part of the 1970s, oil companies and traders anticipating further price increases scrambled to build up inventories. Removing oil from available supply to store in tanks rather than satisfying demand affects price. In fact, if inventory accumulation continues over a long enough period of time of shunting supply to storage at a significant pace, a rising price may become a self-fulfilling prophecy. As long as the feeling that price will continue to rise, market participants are tempted to expand inventories far beyond what's needed to handle normal variation in demand. When price begins to weaken, as it did in the early 1980s, holding on to inventories for a higher price is no longer wise, but foolish in the eyes of investors and speculators. Wholesale liquidation of bloated inventories adds to supply weakening price, which if carried out with enough conviction becomes another self-fulfilling prophecy. This behavior on the part of investors and speculators is not unique to the crude market, but all commodity markets. However, the same phenomenon of inventory accumulation and liquidation occurs if OPEC is too slow in adjusting production to changing demand. If demand for oil begins to fall, and OPEC keeps supply unchanged, extra production will accumulate as inventory; if demand for oil begins to rise, and OPEC does not respond, then production failing to meet demand will drain inventory. This makes it difficult to pin the primary responsibility for price changes on those accumulating or liquidating inventories or on those with their hands on the supply control lever reacting too slowly. OPEC's capacity to adjust supply does not operate like a light switch. A great deal of time-consuming communication is necessary to develop consensus among oil ministers. Moreover it is necessary for oil ministers to ensure concurrence from OPEC's respective heads of state before production can be curtailed or expanded as a group activity. Further complicating the negotiations is that OPEC is not entirely a cohesive group, as seen by members who routinely cheat by exporting more than their allowed quota.

Futures as a Substitute for Investing in Commodities

Futures are supposed to be a risk mitigation tool—this is the historical reason for creating them. Futures reduce a loss from a price decline for producers and a price hike for consumers. If a producer of any commodity with a futures market shorts (sells) futures, and if the commodity price declines, loss of revenue in selling the physical commodity is mitigated by gains in the paper commodity. For consumers of a commodity, buying futures is a way of mitigating a loss from rising prices. Losses incurred in paying a higher price for the physical commodity are mitigated to the extent of profiting in the paper commodity. The cost of hedging wrongly (shorting futures when price then rises or buying futures when price then falls) can be considerable in the sense of either foregoing profits or foregoing cost savings, but not in going out of business. Buying and selling futures by speculators provide sufficient market depth for commodity suppliers and consumers to carry out their risk mitigation plans or to offset hedged positions on the wrong side of the market. Speculators can go bankrupt if they find themselves on the wrong side of a market.

Buying and selling futures with a cash settlement rather than a physical settlement can be viewed as side bets on what happens in the cash market. As side bets, futures should in theory have minimal impact on cash prices for a commodity. Settling a futures position in cash when it expires is simply a transaction between the buyer and the seller of a futures contract—a settlement of a side bet or wager with no relation to the physical market. It is the same as two individuals betting whether the market will go up or down on a daily basis. Their settling accounts at the end of the day does not affect the market. But what if there is a change of attitude and buying futures becomes an investment vehicle in addition to a risk mitigation tool? This is what happened during a prolonged upward trend in oil prices from 1998 to 2008, which drew Wall Street attention of buying either the commodity itself or rolling over futures in the commodity to profit from what appeared to be a continuing and perhaps never-ending escalation of price. Pension plans rarely invest in commodities, preferring bonds as a means of providing future benefits to plan participants. This time pension funds joined hedge funds and followed Wall Street advice to take a position in a commodity. While buying physical oil is an investment choice, most preferred paper oil. Physical oil required 100 percent cash to purchase oil, which then had to be stored, generating both interest and storage fees. Paper oil required only 5–10 percent margin with no obligation to take delivery. A 5–10 percent price increase doubled the investment with paper oil while generating only a 5–10 percent gain on physical oil less interest and storage costs. Of course a decline of 5–10 percent would wipe out the paper holder while the physical holder would suffer a manageable loss. People investing in futures must keep their trigger fingers ready in case the market moves against their position. But as long as there is a general price escalation, futures can be rolled over when they expire with the cash proceeds reinvested in new futures. Hence futures are transformed from risk mitigation to a substitute investment in physicals. At this point, cash settlement of futures has no impact on the cash market for the physical.

Supply and demand in Economics 101 held sway as growing demand for futures as a quasi-long-term investment pushed up the prices of paper oil in relation to physical oil, known as a market in "contango." The spread between the paper and physical market, the price of futures with respect to the cash price of oil, became wide enough for investment bankers and fund managers to invest in profitable and riskless arbitrages. Arbitragers bought oil for cash, usually on borrowed funds, and placed purchased oil in shore side storage tanks; or if none were available, in more expensive floating storage by chartering tankers. At the same time, they would short (sell) 90-day (or other duration) futures contracts to investors who intended to roll over the futures when they expired. There was no risk for the arbitragers because, in effect, buying and selling a position was accomplished in one fell swoop. Whatever might be the actual cash price when the futures contract expired was immaterial from the point of view of the arbitragers as the futures contract fixed the selling price. But this would not be true for those who purchased futures as a substitute for investing in the physical who bore the financial risk, and opportunity, of the cash price differing from the futures price on expiry of the futures contract. However, for an arbitrager to profit from a fully hedged position, the spread between cash and futures markets had to be wide enough to cover the cost of capital invested in oil plus storage costs. Once this breakeven spread was exceeded, arbitragers would make money with no risk of loss, and if oil is purchased with borrowed funds, no cash investment other than interest.

Now there is a relationship between the futures contract and the cash market for the physical. What is the impact on the physical price of oil when a portion of its available supply is withdrawn from the market and stored in shore side and floating tanks until their associated futures expire? This is no different than hedging against a price increase by inventory accumulation. Shouldn't a portion of supply immobilized by physical oil covering paper oil affect prices just as inventory accumulation affects prices? Economics 101 states that removing supply should increase price with no change in demand. If done to excess, continual removal of oil from the market either by inventory accumulation or taking riskless arbitrage positions could become a self-fulfilling prophecy of ever-rising prices. This would encourage more buying of futures as a substitute for the physical opening up of more opportunities for arbitragers. How much of the upward sweep of prices reflected oil producers and consumers making deals in a public marketplace in an environment of growing consumption? And how much was price simply responding to diminishing supply by withdrawing oil from the physical market to either expand inventories in the physical market or cover arbitrage positions in the paper market?

The answer to this question requires a knowledgeable person with the authority and access to underlying data to measure the relationship between physical oil available for sale to that tied up in inventory to cover arbitrages in paper oil. One major investment house made such an assessment and opined that every million barrels tied up in storage increased the cash price by 10 cents per barrel. In February 2012 when crude oil futures contracts covered 233.9 million barrels of oil, the estimated price escalation was a whopping $23.39 per barrel, which, if true, the then current price of $108 per barrel would have been about $85 per barrel in the absence of speculative futures trading.[12] A Saudi Arabian oil minister about the same time noted, perhaps self-servingly, that conventional supply and demand analysis could not support high oil prices and therefore the cause of high prices can be blamed on speculative pressures, not oil producer greed.[13] During times of large volume arbitrages, tanker rates rose as a consequence of reduced tanker supply for carrying cargoes. While oil futures may or may not have influenced cash prices for oil, they certainly influenced cash prices for tankers.[14]

Oil Prices Vulnerable to Manipulation

Any commodity is subject to manipulation under the right conditions. A great amount of oversight is exercised by regulatory bodies to ensure that prices reflect supply and demand, not the whims of a manipulator. In the US, regulators overseeing the spot natural gas and electricity markets become nervous when a single participant represents 25 percent or more of transactions. The fear is that a large-scale market participant may throw his or her weight around to influence price one way or the other; that is, manipulate the market. Even with regulatory authorities standing guard over an exchange in a single nation, trading commodities from some presumably unregulated offshore location with sales channeled through one exchange and purchases through another may escape regulatory scrutiny. A trader hiding his or her actual intent may be entirely legitimate in that the trader is trying to accumulate or liquidate a large position without alerting market participants. Or it could be a trader attempting to carry out some nefarious plan to hoodwink others without alerting regulatory authorities.

Rumors abound of price manipulation by playing paper against physicals. The following unsubstantiated rumors were reported, though not confirmed. They're offered simply to provide examples on how it would be feasible to manipulate price for gain as long as the manipulator had the desire, motive, power, position, and means to do so. Saddam Hussein was rumored to have purchased oil futures for his personal account, then ordered a reduction in Iraqi production to cause world oil prices to rise, manipulating the market for his personal gain at the expense of his people. Another rumor of price manipulation was a group of ship owners who purchased freight rate futures and then refused to charter their vessels. By cutting supply, freight rates rose and the owners made more money on their paper or virtual fleets than losses from idling their physical fleets. Still another rumor was a pool of Wall Street speculators who, as call writers, sold a large volume of naked call options on a relatively thinly traded stock. Then they dumped physical stock before the exercise day to lower its price below the strike price. Call writers were able to profit by the inability of call buyers to exercise their options, which, had they been able, would have forced the call writers to buy stock to cover their naked calls. They avoided this potential loss by manipulating price to prevent exercise of the options. Since the options were not exercised, the call writers kept the proceeds from selling calls. Needless to say, price rapidly rose after the expiration date as call writers purchased back stock they had previously dumped. Any losses taken on the stock (the physical transaction) were more than made up by keeping the premiums on writing naked calls (the paper transaction).

When an individual buys a futures contract, someone has to short the futures contract to bring it into existence. It may not be in the interest of the individual, often an investment banking firm, who created a futures contract for it to be exercised. Paper exceeding the physical by a factor of hundred or more encourages manipulation by dumping the physical to depress the value of the futures, which for highly leveraged investors on the long side forces liquidations, allowing futures writers to profitably close out their positions. While the normal presumption is that manipulation is to artificially inflate prices, manipulation may be to artificially depress prices.

Oil Prices and Delusional Madness

Delusional madness is where investors blindly make one-sided bets that can strongly affect prices. In 1841 Charles Mackay wrote *Memoirs of Extraordinary Popular Delusions and Madness of Crowds* with the purpose "to collect the most remarkable instances of those moral epidemics which have been excited, sometimes by one cause and sometimes by another, and to show how easily the masses have been led astray, and how imitative and gregarious men are, even in their infatuations and crimes." Delusion and mania can be epidemic in scale, spreading through the investing public at an astonishing pace.

In 1593 a botanist brought some tulip bulbs from Constantinople to Holland to investigate their medical properties. Some of the bulbs were stolen, which when planted gave birth to a new industry. For decades, demand for tulip bulbs exceeded their capacity to reproduce and prices rose as one would expect. The continuing rise in prices induced people to believe that the upward trend would last forever. Once this delusion set in, it was impossible to shake. Rather than planting bulbs to produce more bulbs, bags of bulbs became the media for frenzied trading that overtook the nation. The Dutch government was aware of the situation, but chose to do nothing, much like President Calvin Coolidge's failure to address the 1920s stock market bubble and the failure of Alan Greenspan, head of the Federal Reserve, to address the 1990s–2000s housing bubble. They feared the consequences of bursting a bubble when it was small, and by their failure to act, let it grow to a humongous size. When the bubble finally burst, as all bubbles surely do, the floodtide of adverse consequences was enormously direr.

People abandoned worthwhile occupations to speculate in tulips. Buy, hold, and sell; then buy some more became a mantra for untold wealth. Supply being short of demand morphed into delusional mania, making price increases a self-fulfilling prophecy, which reached a level of over $1,000 in current dollars for a single bulb, with exotic bulbs fetching several multiples more. Fortunes were made (and some presumably lost) trading bags of bulbs in a volatile market. One of the first option markets in history occurred when one could buy tulip bulbs for 10 percent of their value with the remaining 90 percent due 90 or so days in the future. These call options were traded as paper tulips or tulip derivatives alongside the cash market for physical tulips. Would having to pay only 10 percent of the purchase price for paper tulips affect the value of physical tulips in the cash market? The answer would be affirmative if enough bags of tulips were withdrawn from the physical market to back up transactions in the paper market. On the other hand, there may have been no bags of tulips set aside to cover writing calls. In writing naked calls, the underwriter takes the risk of a price rise. The transaction is simply a side bet on what's going to happen in the cash market. As long as derivative buying and selling are treated as side bets to changes in market prices, there will be little or no impact on the cash price for the physical. But if paper trading results in bags of tulips being withheld from the physical market as collateral for the paper market, then reduced availability will impact prices. This is a key challenge, or imbroglio, for those who want to link prices of paper derivatives to physical commodities.[15]

A tulip bulb trader died leaving his orphaned children with nothing but a bag of tulip bulbs found among his personal effects. Fortunately for them, they sold the bulbs and the money was sufficient to support them for the rest of their lives. Had they waited until after the tulip bubble burst, they would have died paupers. Bubbles don't last forever. This one burst during the winter of 1636/1637 when a single consignment of tulip bulbs at an auction drew no bidders. Another version was that a buyer failed to show up to pay for his bag of bulbs. Either way, a single act was enough to awaken speculators from their stupor as to the true value of a tulip bulb. Prices crashed by a factor of a hundred in a few days, with financial panic and ruin in its wake.

A market implies rational investment decisions, while manipulation or mania or bubbles are the earmark of irrational investment decisions (buy not for any rational reason, but as a simple act of faith that price, which was up from yesterday, will be up further tomorrow). Some people wonder about those who rely blindly on computer algorithms for trading stocks or commodities. Algorithms make irrationality appear rational. Suppose that computer algorithms contain a rule that says sell dollars when oil prices go up. The rule is based on a statistical analysis of the past relationship between dollars and oil prices. A statistical relationship is not a scientific law such as the law of gravity. The law of gravity is unchanging; statistical relationships are like relationships between individuals—they're subject to change and may even become irrelevant with time. When incorporated into computer algorithms, a statistical relationship becomes a hard and fast dictum as unchanging and unyielding as any irrational thought that overtakes a mob of gullible and hysterical speculators. If the preponderance of transactions is fixed by computer algorithms, it is going to be hard to break the rule to sell dollars when oil prices go up without being wrong. At some point, however, the algorithm for one computer system may be changed in recognition that the rule is not working quite as well as it had in the past. This could potentially trigger changes to other computerized algorithms, leading to a rapid unwinding of positions, which in the old days was called a market panic.

The degree of trading controlled by computer algorithms can be judged by the portion of trading that appears to be the continual buying and selling of small positions that are closed out at the end of a trading day, called flash or high-frequency trading. Conservative estimates are that flash trading makes up half or more of trading activity; some say it is the preponderance of trades. Flash trading establishes price by pitting one set of computer algorithms against another. The winner is the firm with the superior set of computer algorithms and whose computers are located at the shortest possible distance from processors handling orders. This allows a firm to gain an electronic edge, measured in microseconds, for front running (taking advantage of knowing the flow of orders to buy and sell before others). This has little to do with the economic basis for determining price by buyers and sellers continually negotiating with each other for the best deal in an open and transparent market.

Oil Prices Reflect Declining Value of Dollar

One of the principal concerns of oil exporters is the loss of value of the US dollar as the world's petrocurrency for buying and selling oil and as a world's reserve currency. The loss of purchasing power from 1913 to 2015 can be seen in that it takes $23.55 of 2015 dollars to buy $1 worth of goods in 1913 when the Federal Reserve gained control over the management of the nation's currency. Under the guidance of the Federal Reserve, the dollar has depreciated nearly continually since its formation except for a few years during the Great Depression.[16] Loss of over 95 percent of purchasing power means that an average workman who made $2 a day in 1913 must make at least 20 times more or $40 a day to stay even (on an after tax basis). This is not an enviable record of achievement for the private banks (US and foreign) who own and manage the Federal Reserve.

Currency depreciation is measured by the Consumer Price Index (CPI) compiled by the US Bureau of Labor Statistics (BLS). Some feel that the calculation of the CPI may involve a statistical sleight of hand since 1990 by deemphasizing or omitting food and fuel in the calculation process to reduce the impact of their volatility on the published CPI. Unfortunately there is an enormous incentive for the government to underestimate inflation since cost of living adjustments (COLA) are built into social security and government retirement programs. Shadow Government Statistics compiles a revised CPI based on the BLS methodology employed in 1990. Their conclusion is that the reported CPI has been understated by about 2.5–3.5 percent in absolute terms *per year* from 2000 to 2014 and to a lesser extent between 1990 and 2000.[17] According to Shadow Government Statistics, the BLS-reported CPI of 1.5 percent in 2013 should have been 5 percent using the 1990 BLS methodology for calculating CPI. The cumulative impact of this understatement of the actual inflation rate, if true, for over two decades would have doubled social security and retirement benefits by 2014. If Shadow Government Statistics is anywhere near being true, then actual currency depreciation may be of the order of 98 percent or more, meaning that an average workman who made $2 a day in 1913 would have to make $100 or more per day on an after-tax basis to be even in purchasing power. After-tax basis is no small adjustment given that taxes on wages since 1913 rose from none to a significant portion of pre-tax income in the form of Federal and state income taxes and compulsory contributions to entitlement programs. Sleight of hand statistics do not fool anybody holding on to vast quantities of US debt securities. They are well aware of the rising value of oil reserves below ground versus the falling value of petrodollar reserves above ground. Higher priced oil of around $100 per barrel both restores the purchasing power of an ever-depreciating currency and reimburses purchasing power losses of petrocurrency primarily held in low-yielding US government debt.

Oil Prices Reflect the Cost of Social Stability in Oil Producing Nations

People of oil exporting nations feel that a benefit of being born in an oil exporting nation is their being provided basic amenities free of charge. This is not endemic to Middle East nations, but to any nation where there is an escape from drudgery. The domestic economy of Spain collapsed in the wake of an influx of gold from the New World during the reign of Philip II and his successors. Gold sparked inflationary pressures that ran up prices of domestically made goods. People chose to rely on lower priced imports for their supply of goods, leading to the withering away of the domestic economy. With cessation of gold from the New World, Spain was bereft of domestic industry to support its economy. Its fall from power and decline in living standards was quick and unstoppable. The same phenomenon occurred when the Groningen gas field was found offshore the Netherlands in 1959, becoming the largest natural gas field in Europe and the tenth largest in the world at that time. The Groningen gas field spawned the so-called "Dutch Disease" where the run up in the value of the domestic currency from selling natural gas to Europeans resulted in inflation, which adversely affected the price competitiveness of Dutch-made goods. This induced consumers to purchase lower priced imported goods in preference to domestic goods. Consequently, the domestic economy of the Netherlands withered in the wake of the natural gas bonanza just as it had in Spain centuries earlier from the New World gold bonanza. The Dutch Disease occurs anywhere when there is an easy way to avoid work. In the US, higher paying positions in gambling on price changes on Wall Street drew talented people away from manufacturing on Main Street that harmed the domestic economy. Worse yet, easy credit policies made it possible to borrow money on continually rising home values and seemingly endless creation of lines of credit. Purchase of goods from "made in America" to "made in China" eroded the domestic economy. Ballooning debt removed the necessity of working harder to achieve a higher standard of living. When the debt bubble finally burst, Americans could no longer refinance their debt and what jobs were left disappeared. Many packed what they could in the family SUV and rode off into the sunset, leaving furniture, personal belongings such as wedding pictures and computers, and pets behind in their newly purchased homes. The pathology of Dutch Disease can be blamed on the US becoming a consuming society built on a house of credit cards rather than a producing society built on a solid foundation.

With oil revenues pouring into the national coffers of oil exporters, many people do not see why they have to work or at least work hard to support their families. While this sounds attractive to the ears of many, what have been the lasting benefits of oil producers finally receiving just compensation for their oil resources? Are the people of Iraq, Iran, Nigeria, Venezuela, and Sudan better off? Wars and corruption have taken their toll. Moreover the Dutch Disease has affected the domestic economies of oil exporting nations, even though they didn't have much of an economy before oil prices boomed in 1973. Figure 5.6 is the per capita gross domestic product (GDP) of Saudi Arabia and Venezuela, founding members of OPEC, and Japan, a leading oil importer, indexed at 100 in 1972. Admittedly, this is not the best way to determine whether the population has benefited from higher oil prices, but it's at least an indication of the nation's capacity to produce goods and services. While Saudi Arabians are better off today than they were in 1973, it is more a result of government programs to provide medical, educational, and social services and fund mammoth imports than Saudi factories producing goods for the people.

Figure 5.6 shows that per capita GDP contracted in Japan immediately following the price hikes in 1973, then resumed its upward course despite the high price of oil. Ironically the Japanese benefited from the oil crisis even though they import all their energy needs. In the early 1970s Japan was producing higher quality, more fuel-efficient automobiles than the mediocre quality gas guzzlers produced in the US. In the wake of the oil crisis, the Japanese succeeded in capturing a significant share of the US automobile market, which they managed to keep long after Detroit began producing higher quality automobiles with better gas mileage. Per capita GDP for other nations in Asia, particularly the Industrial Tigers (South Korea, Taiwan, Singapore, and Hong Kong), shows an even more dramatic rise than Japan.

For the oil exporters, Saudi Arabia and Venezuela, per capita GDP expanded in the years immediately following the 1973 oil crisis, particularly for the former. However, these gains began to evaporate during the era of high oil prices and continued to erode during the era of moderate oil prices. What is surprising is that the decline in per capita GDP has fallen below 100. This implies that these nations are producing fewer goods and services now on a per capita basis with oil around $100 a barrel in 2014 than when oil was around $2–$3 a barrel in current dollars. This does not necessarily mean a lower standard of living because per capita GDP may not fully reflect the portion of petroleum revenue distributed to the people in the form of social, educational, and medical services, and the role of imports in sustaining living standards. Maybe the Shah's advice

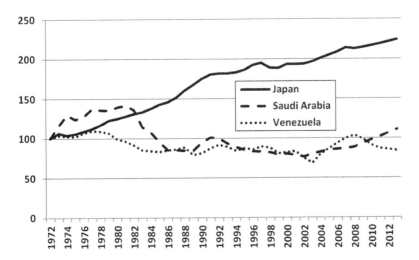

Figure 5.6 Per Capita GDP for Japan, Saudi Arabia, and Venezuela from 1972 to 2013 (Index 1972=100)

for Westerners to learn to work harder should be heeded by oil exporters suffering from the Dutch Disease.

Another contributing factor for the declining per capita GDP in Venezuela and Saudi Arabia is their booming populations. The population of Venezuela has almost tripled from 11 million in 1972 to nearly 31 million in 2015, while the population of Saudi Arabia has quadrupled from 6.6 million in 1972 to 30 million in 2015. There is a large immigrant population in Saudi Arabia performing menial tasks avoided by the Saudis. Domestic production of goods and services, as measured by GDP, would have to multiply several times over for Venezuela and Saudi Arabia to restore per capita GDP to the same level of 1972 when oil prices were low.

Part of Venezuela's decline in per capita GDP in the early 2000s was a consequence of civil unrest. Unrest still prevails for a people whose expectations on government largesse from oil revenues are not fulfilled; nor will they be fulfilled from declining oil production, a result of "politicizing" the oil industry workforce; nor will the return of lower oil prices help. Perez Alfonso, principal architect of OPEC and Venezuelan oil minister in the 1970s, called oil the "devil's excrement" that would eventually ruin Venezuela. Maybe he was right. Venezuela, Iran, Nigeria, Mexico, Russia, and other oil exporters need high-priced oil to fulfill social promises that they've made to their people. Political instability and civil unrest in these nations would follow a prolonged period of low oil prices, although political instability shows signs of existence even with high oil prices. Saudi Arabia may be able to extract crude oil including a return on investment for $5 per barrel or less, but they cannot afford to sell at that price for the government to fulfill its promises. For instance, in 2012, King Abdullah bin Abdulaziz announced by royal decree that all civil servants and military personnel would be given two months of salary, university students would receive a two-month stipend, job seekers would receive an equivalent of $533 per month while job hunting, minimum wages would be increased, 60,000 law enforcement jobs would be created, and 500,000 new houses would be built for nearly $70 billion as part of a $130 billion spending program. Estimates are that with this announced program, Saudi Arabia would need about $100 per barrel to sustain its oil infrastructure and social programs. The United Arab Emirates needs $85 per barrel, $119 for Bahrain, $120 for Russia, and similar amounts for other oil exporting nations.[18]

Oil Prices Reflect the Marginal Cost of New Productive Capacity

Unfortunately for OPEC, oil price to ensure domestic tranquility and preserve value of their petrodollar reserves is high enough to develop not only high-cost non-OPEC conventional oil fields, but nonconventional sources of oil such as oil sands in Canada, fracking of oil in tight sand and shale formations in the US and elsewhere, and deep water oil fields in an ocean depth of two miles where wells must be drilled five miles into the ocean bottom to reach oil. As an example of the cost of marginal oil, while the UK sector of the North Sea produces a little over half of UK energy needs, production is off by 70 percent from its peak in 1999 and still falling. It is five times more expensive to extract a barrel of North Sea oil in 2014 than in 2002 (part of the problem have been three major tax increases in 2002, 2006, and 2011 on oil firms).[19] Figure 5.7 is illustrative of the price of oil necessary to support incremental additions to capacity.

As long as the relationship of world oil supply/demand is such that new sources have to be brought on stream, the necessary investment in these sources will not be forth-coming unless the price of oil justifies the investment. The price of oil is set by the most costly marginal producer needed for supply to keep ahead of demand. World oil consumption has been more or less increasing since the start of the oil age. Since 1965 annual oil consumption increased every year except for 1979–1983 during the Iranian Revolution and 2008–2009, both periods of high oil prices. Regardless of the cause, high oil prices depress demand. Disposable spending for goods and services is income net of taxes and nondiscretionary spending such as food, fuel, and housing. Disposable spending is a major driver of GDP via the manufacturing of goods and providing services. High-energy prices reduce disposable spending by shunting purchases from goods and services to fuel. Fewer goods being sold depresses manufacturing demand, which reduces GDP and, consequently, energy demand. On the other hand, falling energy prices means more disposable income, and more goods being purchased encourages manufacturing, which in turn enhances GDP, leading to a greater demand for energy, including oil.

This is a negative, self-correcting feedback system. As oil consumption rises, more expensive sources of oil must be brought into production to increase supply. Thus oil prices must rise to meet the marginal cost of incremental supply; otherwise, such invest-ments will not be made. Without new investments, supply of oil does not stagnate, but falls, since production from existing oil fields declines as reserves are consumed. New sources of oil must be put in place just to maintain production. If this does not occur, supply diminishes and there comes a time when the supply curve gets too close to the demand curve, forcing prices to rise to cover the cost of increasing production. If draco-nian measures are taken to control price, scarcity may result, accompanied by rationing. The story of controlled natural gas prices in the US in Chapter 7 shows the inevitable outcome of market distortions caused by the government punishing suppliers by legisla-tively keeping prices too low in relation to demand to garner voter favor.

If demand falls in relation to supply or if supply rises above demand, price will decline as the need to invest in costly incremental sources of oil diminishes. This does not mean that already existing costly oil projects will lose money, but they will operate with lower

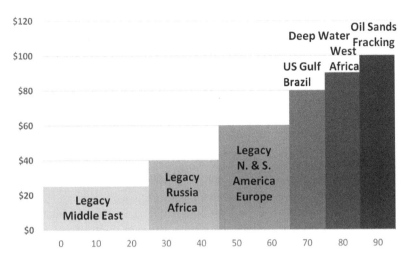

Figure 5.7 Incremental Cost ($/bbl) versus Cumulative Oil Production (mmBpd)

profit margins. As price continues to decline, projects will continue to operate as long as they can throw off enough funds to pay operating (OPEX) and debt financing costs (CAPEX) regardless of the degree of profitability. If price falls further and a shortage of cash to support CAPEX occurs, then debt holders (bankers) usually redefine the terms of the loan in order to keep the company solvent and recoup their investment over a longer period of time, possibly at a lower interest rate. Further price declines make bankruptcy a realistic option. Bankruptcy essentially removes the claim of the equity investors on a project's assets, bolstering the security position of the debt holders. However, if cash flow is so diminished that there is now a shortage to cover OPEX, the project may be shut-tered until the financial storm clouds pass or be permanently abandoned. Thus existing production capacity will be kept in operation as long as cash generation exceeds OPEX and provides a modicum of support for CAPEX.

In 2014 oil prices fell by more than half at their low point. The reason for this was that the success of oil fracking in the US was threatening to reduce the market for OPEC oil. Saudi Arabia, the only nation in OPEC willing to play the role of swing producer, decided that maintaining its market share overruled its traditional role. Continued pro-duction pushed down oil prices below the point of supporting drilling new wells for fracked oil. Boom times in North Dakota and other states evaporated almost overnight. Wells partly completed were completed, but no new ones were drilled. The number of idle oil rigs spiraled upward, drilling crews were laid off, and prospects for companies in fracked oil considerably dimmed. Continued low oil prices cannot support proper well maintenance and production volume declines over time. Thus times of low oil prices are self-correcting as oil development ceases and production in legacy oil fields continues their unrelenting decline, eventually closing the gap between supply and demand. This decline can be quite precipitous for tight oil shale where well production is effectively over in 3 years. Once a balance is restored between supply and demand, the first price escalations support remedial work on wells to recoup their output. If this is not sufficient to meet demand, then price must continue to rise to financially support more expensive forms of remediation to extract oil from existing fields. Still not sufficient, then price has to rise to cover OPEX and CAPEX for drilling new wells and developing new sources.

Thus the real threat to the financial health of the oil industry is not declining demand, which is self-correcting by declining supply, but discovery of huge reserves of low-cost oil. Iraq may turn the tables on the oil industry if, for instance, it begins exporting huge volumes of oil from discovery of vast deposits of low-cost oil in largely unexplored areas of the nation. Another potential for large volumes of low-cost oil yet to be discovered is in the relatively shallow waters of the largely unexplored South China Sea. If sizable sources of low-cost oil are brought into production, then the right hand side of Figure 5.7, representing the highest cost sources of incremental supply, would be shoved off the chart leaving them perched high and dry. Marginal prices would decline to financially support high-cost producers still needed to meet demand. Financial backers of the most costly and no longer needed projects will be saddled with enormous losses.

But discovery of large oil fields in Iraq and the South China Sea is problematic to say the least considering the geopolitical risk in both areas. Barring discovery of a giant low-cost oil field, the oil industry is burdened with spending more for getting less. An energy advisory service scrutinized the annual reports of publicly traded oil companies on their capital expenditures.[20] Aggregate capital expenditures in 2000 were about $50 billion, with aggregate production around 14 million Bpd. Initially oil production grew along with capital expenditures. Oil production peaked at about 15 million Bpd in 2010 and then declined, but capital expenditures continued to grow. By 2012, capital expenditures had ballooned to about $250 billion and oil production was back to 14 million Bpd. Essentially flat production with increasing capital expenditures places pressure on oil company profits with oil prices contained within a narrow range. During this time, in order to maintain their dividends, some oil companies were resorting to disposal of assets, a form of liquidation—not a good long-term survival strategy.[21] Another indication of the oil companies digging themselves into a financial hole while trying to maintain their position is that, in 2013–2014, 127 oil companies generated $568 billion in cash from their operations and spent $677 billion in capital expenditures. This deficit of $110 billion has to be funded by increasing their debt load or selling assets. The corresponding deficit in 2010 was only $10 billion. The only way to cover the higher cost of spending more for standing still is a boost in the price of oil.[22] While higher prices to support "spending more for standing still" has a negative feedback effect on demand, that was not a problem for oil companies. The real problem was oil prices dropping, which has forced oil companies to abandon plans to enhance production from new and costly oil fields.

Oil Price Feedback Loop

Most energy modeling starts with a projection of economic growth. Since there is a strong statistical relationship between economic and energy or oil demand growth, one can obtain a projection for energy or oil demand based on a projection of economic activity. Staying with oil, the general presumption is that supply of oil will increase to fill any gap and to maintain some degree of spare capacity. The effect on price of increasing demand can be minimal if the increase in demand is largely satisfied by Saudi Arabia drawing down on its spare capacity. There have been fairly numerous occasions of this happening. Some industry observers maintain that the Saudis have been good world citizens by using their productive capacity to maintain some semblance of order in the oil markets. However, if the Saudis are getting close to exhausting their spare capacity or are unwilling to draw down on their spare capacity, then price will begin to rise until it reaches a level sufficient to finance new and costly sources of supply. The freedom of choice possessed by the Saudis makes it very difficult to project oil prices based on a projection of demand.

Frequently a projection of oil prices is not included in a projection of oil demand because price is to a certain extent a controllable variable depending on how Saudi Arabia reacts to changing demand with its spare capacity as a control variable. But Saudi Arabia doesn't have total control over prices, as seen by episodes of very high prices that have adversely affected world economies. A high oil price depresses economic activity, reducing oil demand, which, in turn, frees up oil to counteract high prices. A low oil price enhances economic activity, increasing oil consumption that can result in rising oil prices. This negative, self-correcting feedback loop has to be incorporated into a projection of oil demand for it to have any validity. Obviously this last step of the process of projecting oil demand, while admittedly very difficult, cannot be ignored. As difficult as the question on the future price of oil may be, the follow-on question on how the future price will affect economic activity also has to be dealt with. And lastly one has to deal with the question of how the change in economic activity will affect oil consumption. This is a reiterative process until all the pieces of the puzzle, supply and demand and price, fit nicely together in a coherent fashion. The oil price feedback loop is normally left out of an oil supply–demand projection because of the inherent difficulty in predicting oil prices; nevertheless leaving it out is not doing anyone a favor. The oil price feedback loop is real and cannot be ignored, although it often is when projecting oil demand, for understandable reasons.

Challenge in Predicting Price

It is well and good to discuss the necessity of incorporating a projection of price into a forecast of oil demand to assess its impact on economic activity, which, in turn, affects demand. Then adjusted demand, whether up or down, when compared to supply, yields a revised price, which, in turn, affects demand. This reiterative process is a challenging exercise to say the least. But this process depends ultimately on the reliability of price forecasts and on how well energy experts are in projecting future prices.

The short answer is terrible. A history of price forecasts from 1977 through 2001 showed the almost futility of assessing future prices. During the peak in oil prices, on the very eve of a major price collapse, all but one forecaster predicted a continuing upward trend, differing only by the slope of the projecting curve; that is, the rate of future price growth. The single forecaster who correctly predicted a downturn in prices also predicted a leveling off of prices that turned out to be substantially higher than what occurred. In 1985–1986, about midway in the collapse of oil prices, projections were for either an immediate turnaround or a turnaround about 2–3 years hence with a stabilization of prices in the interim. Rather than steady out, oil prices continued their retreat. When oil prices stabilized after 1987, nearly every projection for the next 14 years called for an increase in oil prices, differing only in the rate of increase. All were proven wrong when oil prices remained essentially stagnant.

Except for one, projections were consistently optimistic. What can explain an overly optimistic view of the future of escalating oil prices? Well, one factor is, who is paying the bill? If an oil company is paying for a projection on oil prices, it is difficult to tell your client that doom is right around the corner. In Chapter 2, the discussion on the "check-shaped" forecast is pertinent. Things are bad now, they'll be bad for the next year or two, but after that, for innumerable reasons, things will get better. These check forecasts can run for years long after the client has succumbed to reality.[23] But in any case, who knows, maybe things will get better! And, in fact, they eventually do; it is in estimating the "when" that is critical. Sometimes the blame lies with miscalculating supply availability or the magnitude of demand, but part of the problem is the psychological aspects of the forecasting process.[24]

Geopolitical Risks

There is no geopolitical risk associated with US domestic production and with oil imports from Canada and Mexico. It is highly unlikely that the US would impose sanctions against Canadian and Mexican imports, and it is also highly unlikely that Canada and Mexico would impose an embargo against exports to the US. The prohibition against building the Keystone pipeline is neither a sanction nor an embargo in that Canadian crude oil from its vast oil sand deposits passes over the border in other pipelines and by rail. Failure to build the Keystone pipeline may restrict the volume of flow over the Canadian border. But this is not a crippling blow to Canada, as it is free to build a pipeline to a west coast terminal to export Canadian crude to Asia or to US west coast refineries by tanker or to build or reverse the direction of existing pipelines to export Canadian crude from east coast Canadian terminals. These options may not be economically optimal, but not preventative of Canada exporting its crude if it so desires. More crippling to Canadian oil sands is not the Keystone pipeline, but low oil prices in 2014/2015 which has stunted expansion of oil sand capacity.

However, there is a geopolitical risk associated with Venezuela, which has a policy of at least minimizing exports to the US because of differing political persuasions. If Venezuela could find enough buyers for its crude exports, it would be in a position to embargo oil exports to the US. This is tempered by Venezuela being a participant in the US oil industry through its wholly owned CITGO Petroleum subsidiary with its nearly 750,000 Bpd of refining capacity. A Venezuelan embargo against the US, or any embargo, is regarded by some as a farce because oil is fungible; that is, US refiners can easily buy crude from other sources. Venezuela selling oil to China in preference to the US, as an example, frees up oil that China was buying from other sources. The freed-up oil then becomes available for sale to the US. An embargo as a means of punishing the US accomplishes nothing other than altering world oil trades, adding to the profitability of owning tankers.

Sanctions mean that exports from a particular nation are to be avoided—this reduces supply and can have a price impact on the oil market. The most well-known sanction is the US-led coalition not purchasing Iranian oil as a means to persuade Iran to abandon its nuclear weapon program. If a full sanction could be imposed on Iran, the world supply of oil would be reduced and the Iranian economy would most probably collapse. But the US cannot impose a full sanction on Iranian crude exports because the coalition mainly involves the US, which has imported very little Iranian oil for nearly four decades, and Europe. India, China, and other Asian nations are major nonparticipants and continue to import large volumes of Iranian oil. US government efforts to make it difficult for Iran to purchase needed imports by prohibiting US dollar banking transactions has been sidestepped by Iran's willingness to pay for its imports in gold and non-dollar currencies and by an exchange of goods for oil.

Geopolitical risk is associated with the unsettled political and civil and social conditions in oil exporting nations such as Nigeria and Sudan and others, which threaten to boil over at any moment affecting oil production and exports. Oil producers employing offshore rigs felt that they were immune to political instability that affected onshore rigs. But Nigerian dissidents have taken over offshore rig installations, demonstrating that offshore facilities scores of miles out to sea are not safe from civil disturbances.[25] Geopolitical risk is associated with military adventures or misadventures such as the British pulling out of the Middle East in 1971, leaving a power vacuum that was filled by Iran, and which contributed to the unfolding of events leading to the 1973 oil crisis. Before the 1973 oil crisis, the US military presence was limited to providing military weapons and advice to Saudi Arabia and Iran either for cash or as part of a military aid package. After the oil crisis, the US military presence and involvement ballooned, starting under President Carter in 1979 when forces loyal to Khomeini held US embassy personnel hostage for 444 days, a situation worsened by a failed rescue mission. The US Navy was charged with keeping the Arabian Gulf sea lanes open during the long Iran–Iraq War from 1981 to 1989. Failing to vanquish Iran, and desperate for money to repay loans for military equipment from the Soviet Union, Saddam Hussein cast his eye south to its neighboring state, Kuwait. Furious over Kuwait's refusal to cancel Iraq's debts as he had requested and short on funds, the temptation to take over Kuwait's enormous oil fields proved too much for Saddam to resist.

The US led the coalition forces in the first Gulf war of 1990–1991. The retreating Iraqi forces set fire to Kuwait's oil fields, creating an environmental disaster in their wake. The US military presence in the Middle East remained strong between the first and second Gulf wars. In 2003 it was Iraq's turn to be devastated. The Iraq War was finally over with the withdrawal of most US forces from Iraq under President Obama in 2009–2011, marking the end of President George Bush's unsuccessful policy of transforming Iraq to an island of democracy in a sea of autocracy. The hope that Iraq would be led by a stable government capable of keeping terrorist elements at bay was not to be. The geopolitical risk of reduced or curtailed Iraqi oil production and exports is higher today than under Saddam Hussein as the nation is threatened with dissolution into three regions: one nationalistic (Kurds) and two religious (Sunni and Shi'a Muslims). The same can be said of allied involvement is disposing Gadhafi in Libya. As bad as he was, the political dissolution of the Libyan government and the resulting anarchy since his overthrow cannot be viewed as a positive outcome for the people of Libya. In addition the Libyan economy has suffered with a sharp curtailment of oil exports. The dream of an Arab Spring is now a nightmare. The same can be said of our involvement with the overthrow of Mubarak, although Egypt is not an oil exporter. The long Afghan war, while not directly associated with oil, hampers US capacity to act militarily in other regions. Fighting in Afghanistan has a long history of disasters for invading nations. Only Alexander the Great successfully invaded Afghanistan and maintained control by nurturing a positive working relationship with ruling tribal leaders. Britain lost an entire army in the 1840s, the collapse of the Soviet Union is partially linked to its failed invasion during the 1980s, and it's problematic whether the US may fare much better after years of grueling war.

Choke points are another form of geopolitical risk where tankers crowd in narrow channels on global sea routes that can be easily interdicted by pirates, terrorists, and unfriendly naval forces. Blockage of a choke point can lead to a substantial rise in oil and possibly liquefied natural gas prices.[26] The world's most critical and most vulnerable choke point is the Strait of Hormuz, a narrow waterway between Qatar and Iran that separates the Arabian (Persian) Gulf from the Gulf of Oman and the Indian Ocean beyond. Although 20 miles wide, each sea lane for inbound and outbound tankers is restricted by water depth to two miles wide for each of two lanes separated by two miles. Thus seizure of a six-mile stretch of water can interrupt about 20 percent of the world oil and liquefied natural gas supply. It is a relatively simple matter for Iran to close the Strait from military installations and naval forces stationed nearby on the mainland and on islands in and around the Strait made available to Iran by the British withdrawal in 1971. In case of closure of the Strait, some oil can be diverted to fill any unused capacity of pipelines that carry oil overland from Iraq to a Mediterranean port in Turkey and from eastern Saudi Arabia to a Red Sea port. The Trans-Arabian pipeline from Saudi Arabia to Lebanon has been out of service since 1976 except for that portion serving Jordan, which has been out of service since 1990. The pipeline would require a complete renovation before being capable of diverting oil from the Strait. A pipeline from oil fields in Abu Dhabi in the Arabian Gulf to Fujairah in the Gulf of Oman bypasses the Strait of Hormuz. Still, a cutoff of the Strait would interrupt supply, amounting to about 15 percent of world oil consumption. Since an interruption of this magnitude cannot be made up from other sources, high oil prices would not be the worse of the consequences—not having enough oil to sustain a global economy would be the true consequence of a prolonged closure of the Strait.

Not all countries would be equally affected. The strategic oil reserves in the US and China would certainly dampen the impact for a period of time, much longer for the US that is far less reliant on Middle East crude than China. Most nations have limited oil storage capacity to handle a major interruption in oil supply. They would feel the price impact immediately and the impact on availability within a month or two depending on shore side inventory and the number of tankers on the high seas loaded with cargoes before the crisis erupted.

The volume of oil and liquefied natural gas cargoes passing through the Strait of Malacca between Indonesia, Malaysia, and Singapore is close to that passing through the Strait of Hormuz. Its narrowest point is 1.7 miles wide for ships passing in both directions at the Phillips Channel in the Singapore Strait. The Malacca Strait has been a center for piracy, but increased surveillance and interdiction by naval forces of the littoral states have significantly reduced this threat. Unlike the Strait of Hormuz that has the potential to cut off all cargo flow to and from the Arabian Gulf nations, closure of the Malacca Strait would simply reroute traffic through the Lombok and Sunda Straits in Indonesia. These longer voyages would add to voyage time and costs, but would not affect the availability of oil and liquefied natural gas. Oil and gas pipelines from Myanmar (Burma) to China reduce traffic flow through the Malacca Strait and thus lessen the impact of its closure.

The Bab el-Mandad Strait is the entry point between the Indian Ocean and Red Sea and has been the center of piracy in recent years. Much of the oil passing through the Suez Canal and the parallel Sumed pipeline, representing about 5 percent of world oil consumption, passes through the Bab el-Mandad Strait. Its narrowest point is 18 miles, with two 2-mile-wide channels for inbound and outbound shipments. Closure of the Strait or the closure of the Suez Canal and/or the Sumed pipeline would divert tanker traffic to a much longer voyage around the Cape of Good Hope (South Africa). This would cause voyage costs to increase considerably, but oil supply would not be affected. Another choke point is the Turkish Strait, which consists of the Bosporus and Dardanelles Straits, separating Europe from Asia and connecting the Mediterranean and Black Seas. All oil flowing from the Black Sea to the Mediterranean Sea would cease if the Turkish Strait were closed as there are no bypass pipelines. But some Black Sea oil can be diverted to Russian pipelines for shipment to Russian and Baltic ports and inland European destinations. The Panama Canal has relatively few transiting tankers compared to container vessels and the highly remote chance of closure would simply reroute oil on either side of the Canal, although some oil can be moved from the Caribbean to the Pacific side of Panama via the Trans-Panama pipeline.

From the perspective of 2014, exports from Syria of 400,000 Bpd have ceased and, with the fall of Mubarak in Egypt, natural gas exports to Israel were curtailed. The 1.5 million Bpd exports from Libya have swiveled considerably with the overthrow of Gadhafi. Moreover there are serious reservations about whether Libya will be able to restore production to its former levels given the fractured nature of the nation now under tribal rule, with terrorists threatening whatever semblance of order exists. Takeover of western Syria and the Sunni-dominated portion of western Iraq by the Islamic State of Iraq al-Sham (ISIS) occurred rapidly in mid-2014. Al-Sham, sometimes referred to as Levant (ISIL) or the Islamic State, has made territorial claims that includes Cyprus, Palestine, Jordan, Iraq, Syria, Lebanon, Israel, and southern Turkey. That is merely its first objective, as ISIS has instituted a Caliphate, whose ambitions cover the entire Islamic world. The Islamic State's takeover not only threatens Iraq's production of 2.5 million Bpd, but also cripples its prospects of expanding to 4.4 million Bpd in 2015 and to 6 million Bpd by 2020.

Thus the geopolitical risk of a major Middle East disruption of oil production is real. Cessation of just Iraqi crude cannot be made up by spare capacity and would most likely be accompanied by a price spike. It was originally thought that Kurdish production might improve as the Kurds consolidated their control over the oil center at Kirkuk, which is connected by pipeline to the eastern Mediterranean. Kurdish (not Iraqi) output could be sold to international buyers at the pipeline terminal at Ceylon, Turkey, and by pipeline and truck to buyers in Turkey.[27] But loadings of tankers of what is considered Kurdish oil by the Kurds and Iraqi oil by Iraq cannot be sold with a clean bill of sale. Moreover the initial thought that Kurds could defend themselves was dashed in August 2014 by the Islamic State taking over oil fields, hydroelectric dams, and villages previously in Kurdish hands. Oil stopped flowing through the Iraq–Turkey pipeline. A massacre of Kurds and Christians forced Obama's hand to recommit the US forces to Iraq for both humanitarian and military reasons. In other words, since we "broke" Iraq, we're going to have to "fix" it. The US cannot extricate itself from the Middle East regardless of who holds political power.

Oil and Diplomacy

Oilmen, most of whom have engineering backgrounds, often end up playing a diplomatic role to negotiate making investments in foreign nations and protecting them once made. One such example before the 1973 oil crisis was Great Britain's imposition of a trade embargo against the then existing nation of Rhodesia (now Zimbabwe). South Africa deemed such an embargo illegal for oil companies operating in South Africa. No matter what BP and Shell did, as British companies operating in South Africa, they were breaking someone's law. If they continued to trade with Rhodesia, they violated

British law. If they stopped trading, they violated South African law. During this time of apartheid, Shell was sharply criticized by the general public for dealing with South Africa and, perversely, reprimanded by the South African government for its practice of hiring, training, and giving blacks positions of responsibility and authority in violation of apartheid. As a result, Shell found itself breaking the law in both Britain and South Africa and, simultaneously, being criticized by outsiders for having investments in South Africa, and by insiders (the South African government) for not upholding the spirit of apartheid.

Another time when oil companies found themselves on the proverbial horns of a political dilemma was during the Yom Kippur War in 1973 when US oil companies had to enforce an embargo of Saudi crude to America, although they did everything possible to secure supplies from other sources. Helping Russia to reopen its oil resources in the wake of the collapse of communism put oil companies at loggerheads with the Russian government over its predilection to unilaterally change tax laws and contractual terms with no means of judicial appeal. Oil company executives and Russian government officials had to work together to hammer out some sort of compromise that affected Russian regulations on taxation, contractual law, judicial appeal, and the rights of minority shareholders before major investments could be made. The laying of pipelines in the Caspian Sea region brought oil companies in contact with governments hostile to one another through which the pipelines must pass. Tariff structures, security measures, and ways for resolving disputes had to be just as carefully planned as selecting the pipeline route and engineering its construction.

Another instance of the coupling of oil with diplomacy is in East Africa. Oil fields are in South Sudan and a pipeline must run through Sudan for an outlet to the Red Sea to export oil. South Sudan and Sudan have been at loggerheads with one another since oil was discovered and developed by China. Oil fields are in the south, the African populated portion of Sudan, and a pipeline had to be laid through the Arab populated portion of Sudan to reach a Red Sea port. The "reward" for discovering oil in an impoverished nation was not the amelioration of the plight of the people, but a civil war and genocide, leaving Sudan divided into two nations. South Sudan would benefit from building connecting pipelines to Ethiopia, Kenya, and Tanzania, which would both provide alternative port access to the Red Sea and new customers. A pipeline connection to landlocked Uganda would also diversify South Sudan's market. These nations cannot agree on which of several pipeline alternatives should be pursued, whether refining should be part of the picture, and all have promising exploratory efforts underway, which if successful would undermine the need for a South Sudan distribution pipeline project. It is problematic whether this imbroglio can be resolved.[28] Resolving conflicting interests of different peoples and governments to determine a fair share of the benefits of oil exports for the people and their governments, along with participating oil companies, has and still poses daunting challenges.

Oil and Environmentalists

In more recent times, oil executives have had to learn to deal with environmental groups that pursue their agendas not only through public media and demonstrations, but also through direct pressure on governmental institutions. Environmentalists have learned how to influence lawmakers and bureaucrats, who in turn affect laws, rules, and regulations. In 1995 Shell's plans to dispose of an abandoned North Sea oil platform by essentially sinking the rig were challenged by environmental groups.[29] They successfully lobbied for a UK government ruling that resulted in a far more costly means of disposal of towing the rig to shore for dismantling. In addition to being active in sponsoring environmental laws, environmental groups have achieved their objectives through loan covenants, conditions that have to be satisfied before funds can be advanced. In response to environmental group lobbying efforts, the World Bank imposed environmental conditions as loan covenants that affected construction of two pipeline projects. One was for moving oil from an oil field in Chad to a port in Cameroon and the other for moving oil in Ecuador from an oil field in the Amazon over the Andes to an exporting port.[30] These loan covenants ensured that a portion of the oil revenues would be paid directly to indigenous peoples along with changes in pipeline routing to deal with environmental concerns. Both national and independent oil companies responsible for building and operating the pipelines had to agree to comply with these loan covenants to obtain World Bank financing.

An earlier gas project in Peru was assessed by road. The same road was then used by illegal loggers who were also responsible for the spread of a fatal disease among the native Indian population. A later project in 2014 has no access road, with helicopters carrying in men, materials, and drilling equipment. Drilling sites are quite small in area, employing horizontal drilling to minimize land requirements. Dense forests and rules prohibiting contact with the native Indians control spread of disease. Native Indians are employed as environmentalist monitors to detect leaks. Gas transmission pipelines are buried in the jungle and are visible only at river crossings. The Indian tribe receives payments from gas revenues. All this was prearranged with the government in order to obtain permission to develop the project. The success of this project may act as a model for another similar project in Ecuador.[31]

Environmentalists point to oil as being a major source of pollution primarily through motor vehicle exhaust. Reduction of pollution emissions, a concept that no one can really oppose, can pose significant operational challenges for oil companies. Yet these seemingly insurmountable barriers to their continued existence are surmountable. The oil companies have learned to cope, if not thrive, in this changing business environment. "Beyond Petroleum" of BP—once a company shibboleth, which must have sounded sacrilegious to the ears of oilmen of yore—is now incorporated into "better people, better products, big picture, beyond petroleum." Oil companies have learned to operate in an environmentally friendly, socially desirable way considering issues beyond their focus on oil. Oil companies have learned to cooperate with engine manufacturers by redesigning gasoline specifications to better support engine modifications to cut emissions. Their success in this endeavor gives them an edge over their competition and promotes a more positive image of what they do.

Of course, this world of environmental concern exists mostly in North America, Europe, Japan, Australia, and New Zealand. Much, but not all, of the rest of the world is more interested in making economic progress without being overly sensitive to adverse environmental consequences. This attitude is epitomized by the nonreaction of most Asian nations to a brown cloud of pollution that overhangs a large portion of the continent, recognized as a severe respiratory health hazard. Nevertheless oil companies have been responding in a positive fashion to environmental challenges in the quality of their product and in the nature of their operations. If they don't, they face a monumental mountain of lawsuits and fines and a daunting public relations challenge. This is epitomized by the *Exxon Valdez* 1989 oil spill in Alaskan waters that cost Exxon billions of dollars in cleanup, rehabilitation, and lawsuits over damages, real or imagined. BP's 2010 natural gas release and subsequent explosion and sinking of the Deepwater Horizon oil rig drilling the Macondo well resulted in a massive crude oil leak in the Gulf of Mexico and billions of dollars in cleanup costs, lawsuits, and fines.[32] These costs can justify a much larger budget in doing everything possible to avoid environmental accidents. If oil companies operate in an environmentally sound manner, they can ensure their profitability and survival as long as oil remains a major source of energy in the modern world.

Role of Oil Companies after the Oil Crisis

Although oil companies were literally thrown out of producing nations after the 1973 oil crisis, there has been a return of sorts to the situation that existed prior to the oil crisis. Oil companies are, to widely varying degrees, involved with oil production with nearly all producers that had previously nationalized their oil fields and facilities. The major difference is that any accounting entries for oil reserves in OPEC nations have been obliterated from oil companies' books. These were always fictional because oil fields were located outside the nations of domicile of the oil companies. Oil companies never had any legal recourse to protect their property rights against actions taken by host governments, although in the case of expropriation by Mexico and Iran oil companies were able to place liens on cargoes once outside their national jurisdictions. But the oil companies were not able to restore ownership of their property however that is defined. This makes ownership a spurious claim, to say the least.

National oil companies operate under encumbrances that Big Oil does not have. National oil companies are limited in their activities to exploiting a nation's wealth of oil and natural gas and, by government fiat, do not and cannot look outside the box. Most national companies are not run as government bodies even though they are wholly owned by their respective governments. Normally they operate as quasi-independent oil companies. While some have managed their nations' energy resources and infrastructures quite well, others have less than a stellar record. Some oil exporting nations are looking at privatization, at least in part, as an alternative to a nationalized oil company or to introduce a taste of competition to reinvigorate a moribund state run organization. Lest we forget, *privatization* would not be a word had it not been for the failure of government owned and operated companies to deliver goods and services that they were set up to provide.

While national oil companies do not worry about making a profit or surviving in an extremely competitive world, their financial life is not one of idle comfort. National oil companies are the chief revenue generators for many oil producing nations and have to fight over every dollar with their exclusive shareholders, their national governments. National oil companies sometimes come up short in the struggle over whether a dollar of revenue should be spent on a social program or be plowed back into the oil infrastructure.

Another problem that affects the financial viability of national oil companies are subsidies in the form of low fuel prices for the people. Oil sold to nationals for sale in the domestic market may receive a mere pittance of what is received for exported oil. Low-priced fuel induces profligacy in domestic oil consumption that reduces export potential. Energy subsidies have a negative impact on the economy by putting pressure on government budgets that affect funding of other government services. Although local citizens benefit and feel entitled to cheap energy, the true beneficiaries are the rich who own and operate companies that consume a great deal of energy. Many nations are trying to phase out subsidies. Iran limits the amount of subsidized gasoline that can be purchased and has been raising the price in steps that minimizes public outcry. Chinese state oil companies have been saddled with billions of dollars removed from their coffers by buying crude at market prices to be refined and selling gasoline and diesel at low prices without any form of restitution by the state. Publicly traded Petrobras is forced to sell gasoline and diesel within Brazil at a loss of $21 billion over a 3-year period that adversely affects the company's activities in developing new sources of oil and, of course, its earnings and dividends and stock price.[33] Another example of a national government robbing an oil company's piggy bank to the detriment of its performance as an oil company is Argentina re-nationalizing YPF 6 years after it was privatized.[34] Nigeria as an oil exporter subsidizes local consumption of gasoline and diesel. Despite the financial distortion, one can argue that Nigerians shouldn't have to pay the world market price for gasoline and diesel because clearly they can't afford it. But cheap prices enforce wasteful practices that ultimately cost the national government revenue in the form of reduced exports. Even if that position can be justified for oil exporters, how can oil subsidies be paid to the people of India and Egypt, nations that do not export oil and have large negative trade deficits? Egypt also subsidizes food prices as a major world grain importer. These subsidies grossly imbalance the government budget, leaving little for education, health, and economic development.[35]

Some national oil companies of oil exporting nations are short on funds needed to maintain their oil infrastructures. Drained of funds by their respective governments, they have maintained their oil infrastructure by borrowing huge sums of money whose repayment is now crippling their operations. Others lack technical expertise to expand or maintain their oil infrastructure or have limited access to markets. Having chased the oil companies out with a broom, oil companies are back under a variety of contractual arrangements to assist national oil companies with capital infusions, technical expertise, and market access. Since these are the same functions oil companies provided before their oil reserves and properties were nationalized, the circle has been closed.

Oil companies have learned that what counts is not who owns the oil fields but who has access to oil. Access is provided under a variety of joint venture and production sharing agreements with producers. These agreements would not be necessary if national oil companies could fully replicate the oil companies' contributions in capital, technology, and market access. Having tapped publically owned oil companies for various reasons, some national oil companies have become more like integrated publicly owned oil companies by acquiring refineries and service stations in consuming nations and tankers to ship their oil. Kuwait purchased Gulf Oil's refinery and distribution system in northern Europe. Venezuela purchased refineries offshore and in the US along with a chain of gas stations. Kuwait, Venezuela, Saudi Arabia, and Iran have tanker fleets to transport a portion of their oil exports. These investments assure oil exporters of market outlets for their oil and secure transportation. A few national oil companies have morphed into so-called hybrid oil companies that behave as independent oil companies, but have large government shareholdings. Chief among these are Petrobras (Brazil) and Statoil (Norway) whose behavior, as a government policy, is much more as independent oil companies than national oil companies. These moves by producing nations to become more like integrated oil companies have not diminished the role for the major oil companies and hundreds of independents in the global oil business. Just as Marcus Samuel remarked that there was room for both Shell and Royal Dutch to succeed in an expanding Asian oil market (although he may have lived to regret that remark), so too is there room for government-owned national oil companies and publicly owned independent oil companies to succeed in an expanding world oil market.

A Changing World

The world of the twenty-first century is different for the oil companies, but in one respect it is easier. They need not worry about pricing. That is no longer in their hands and not nearly as much in the hands of the oil producers as they would like. Pricing is a combination of factors where the relationship of supply and demand is simply another lever running the oil machine. Moreover they're no longer concerned about ownership of oil in foreign lands as long as they have access to that oil. Before the oil crisis, the goal of the oil companies was to reduce costs, a principal cost being the price of crude oil. The irony is that profits are not based on costs but on the spread between the price of oil products and the cost of crude oil. It does not matter what the cost of oil is as long as a sufficient spread can be maintained between crude oil they buy and oil products they sell. In addition an oil company can enter into a variety of contracts and financial derivatives such as swaps, futures, and forwards to hedge against the risk of an adverse price change. The record of oil company profits since the 1973 oil crisis shows that they have survived the crisis quite well.

One can expand this concept to the environmental cost of doing business. It does not matter what incremental costs are placed on an oil company's operations to safeguard the environment as long as every oil company bears the same cost. Then it becomes just another cost of doing business, such as the cost of crude oil or the obligation to pay taxes, all of which are simply passed on to consumers in the form of higher prices. Ultimately it is the consumer who pays for higher priced crude, increased environmental costs, and additional tax burdens. As long as these costs are approximately equally borne by all oil companies and can be passed on to consumers, why should they care? However, oil companies do care when a particular project is singled out for costly environmental requirements, higher taxation, and other costs added on by government fiat that affect its profitability. If these extra costs are too much of a burden, the oil company always has the freedom to walk away. For costs that affect oil companies in general, all they have to focus on is maintaining their margins, which in the last analysis means covering their costs. Furthermore they really do not have to be overly concerned about security of supply. Before the 1973 oil crisis, it was not a significant concern and, since the crisis, responsibility has been assumed by taxpayers who foot the bill for an American and Allied military presence in the Middle East.

Are Oil Companies' Margins All That Great?

Some politicians accuse oil companies of making unconscionable profits. In all fairness, any politician who does so is at a minimum misleading the public, at worst a demagogue. Oil companies do make a lot of money in tens of billions of dollars for the same reason that Henry Ford made a lot of money on the Model T: volume. In Figure 5.8, oil company profit is estimated to be about 12 cents per gallon.[36]

The estimate on refinery costs may include a profit element for the refiner, but 12 cents per gallon profit estimate does not include corporate income taxes paid on this

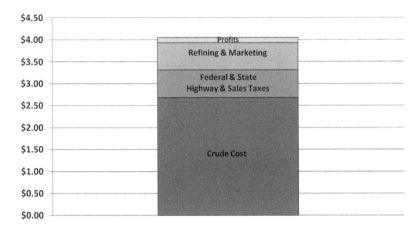

Figure 5.8 Cost Factors for Average $4.05 per Gallon of Regular Gasoline in 2012 in California

profit. Let's assume that combining these two factors would yield an effective profit of 10 cents per gallon, which is the normally accepted estimate for after tax profits on a per gallon basis.[37] This is a bit more than the 9 cents per gallon that California makes on every gallon of gasoline as a sales tax. The California Highway Tax is over three times greater and the Federal Highway Tax is nearly twice that of oil company profit. The largest component of the price of gasoline is money paid to the oil producers, which include independent oil companies along with national oil companies.

Figure 5.9 shows the comparison between European and American prices where Europeans pay between two and three times what Americans pay for gasoline. Motor vehicle fuel taxes are an important source of revenue for European governments and the primary reason why Europeans prefer fuel-efficient, smaller sized automobiles and are more sensitive about their driving habits than Americans.[38]

European oil consumption slowly expanded from 1990 to 2006 and then began a slow retreat such that 2014 oil consumption is less than that in 1970. This is a result of high taxes on motor vehicle fuels, a weakening of overall economic activity, and a determination in Europe to subdue growth in oil consumption. European governments still make far more in tax revenue from selling a gallon of gasoline or diesel fuel than oil producers get for selling a gallon of a depleting natural resource—one of the justifications of the price hikes in 1973. Assuming that the US price is what is needed to maintain and build highways, just taking the difference in gasoline prices between Europe and the US as a pure revenue contribution to European coffers, the difference of $186 per barrel is far in excess of the average crude oil price of $100 per barrel received by oil producers in 2014.

The value of a gallon of gasoline, which can drive an automobile 20 or 30 miles, can be better appreciated by comparing it to the value of a gallon of mineral water that can sell at a substantial premium to gasoline. Bottled water costs between $10 and $20 per gallon, as do many soft drinks. When one compares the effort to explore, develop, refine, distribute, and market one gallon of gasoline with the cost of bottling one gallon of mineral water, plus taking into consideration the amount paid to governments in the form of sales and

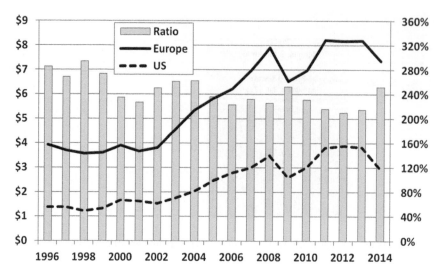

Figure 5.9 Average Annual Price of Gasoline, Europe versus the US, $/Gallon

highway taxes and paid to the producing nations for crude, the oil industry has got to be one of the most efficiently run operations on Earth. We get far more on the 10 cents per gallon we pay the oil companies than the $1 we pay to fill government tax coffers or the $2–$3 we pay the oil producers.

Future Role of Oil Companies

Most oil companies specialize in some facet of the oil business. They have neither the capital nor the technical expertise nor the desire to explore energy alternatives outside the oil box. Big Oil is a relatively small group of publicly traded corporations that play a paramount role in finding and developing large oil fields and in refining and marketing oil. Unlike smaller oil companies, they have an eye on the future of energy with or without oil. Big Oil is aware that the energy business goes beyond getting crude out of the ground and gasoline into a tank. They realize that the era of oil may draw to a close much as the era of biomass in the nineteenth century and the era of coal in the twentieth. This is not to say that oil will disappear any more than biomass and coal have disappeared. If not enthusiastic endorsers of developing alternative energy technologies, oil companies are certainly cognizant of their own well-being. Oil is but one facet of the energy industry, and if the role of oil changes, Big Oil wants to be part of that change as the only way to ensure their survival as major players in the energy game.

Big Oil's ability to adjust to a changing business environment has been amply demon-strated. They've survived the greatest assault imaginable on their privileged position by losing control over vast oil resources once considered their own. They have also lost the ability to determine the price of oil. Such losses could have led to their demise, yet they are prospering now more than ever before. Once unceremoniously thrown out of oil pro-ducing nations, they have long since been invited back by the national oil companies that had taken over their oil fields and distribution and refining assets. Mexico incorporated into its Constitution that oil companies would have no part in the nation's oil industry. While oil companies have been involved with service contracts, there has been nothing on a major scale. The primary reason for this is that oil companies want to participate in the output of an oil field and bear the risk of not being successful in their endeavors. By having a share of the output, the oil companies have the incentive to do the best job they can to enhance production. If Mexico needs the technical expertise that only oil companies can provide, then its declining oil production may force the nation to rethink a fundamental decision made three-quarters of a century ago. As of 2014, the thinking of the Mexican government is to prohibit the privatization of any Pemex activities, but to possibly permit a variety of contractual activities, including production sharing, in areas where Pemex lacks technical expertise such as hard oil and gas shale development and offshore drilling in deep waters. However, much has to be accomplished in the legal and regulatory framework before foreign oil companies can enter into contractual arrangements to develop Mexican oil resources.[39]

There are some who say that oil (or any basic business) is too important to be left in the hands of businesspeople bent on making a buck. Oil should be in the hands of a benign government body that knows best how to serve the wide interests of people rather than the narrow interests of shareholders. As alluring as this sounds, privatization of the ex-Soviet oil industry revealed outmoded technology, managerial ineptness, and a total disregard for the environment of a government-owned and operated oil company. YPF, an Argentinian oil company nationalized under Peron, eventually became an enormous cash drain on the government to fund its losses, and its management, as government employees, did little to upgrade the company's operations or maintain its oil reserves. After a half-century of draining the public coffers, the company was privatized and its umbilical cord to the public treasury cut. Faced with declaring bankruptcy if life went on as usual, public servants running YPF decided to make the transformation to corporate managers. In about 5 years' time, the company was contributing to the government coffers by paying taxes on its profits and Argentina went from an oil importing to an oil exporting nation. YPF became a poster child on how wrong the London School of Economics was in promoting nationalization of basis industries. It also vindicated Adam Smith's dictum that the best way of organizing commerce is to put business in the hands of business people and hold their feet to a profit and loss statement and they can only make a profit by pleasing the market. YPF has been back in the news again as the Argentinian government seized a major portion of its ownership (renationalize), presumably to garner the "excess" profits being earned by the company (those who forget history are condemned to repeat it).

Unfortunately profit has a bad name. For many, all profit means is the right of unscrupulous individuals or companies to gouge the public when the opportunity arises, as was exercised by certain energy companies who supplied electricity to California during the 2000 energy crisis. Allegations have been proven that supplying companies, most notably Enron, held back on generating electricity to create an artificial shortage that hiked electricity rates. In fairness, the California state regulatory body that established a flawed energy policy and provided poor oversight must bear some of the blame. Nevertheless this crisis—along with the exposure of executive compensation for certain companies aggregating in the hundreds of millions at the expense of corporate liquidity and stakeholder value—reinforced the public's generally negative image of corporate executives as profit-gouging, irresponsible, selfish, self-serving gluttons. These accusations rose again when executives of top financial houses paid themselves aggregate bonuses of untold tens of millions of dollars for creating what turned out to be pseudo-profits, which required government bailouts totaling in the hundreds of billions. Ironically, despite the survival of top financial houses depending on government handouts, they continued to pay their top executives huge bonuses. One justified his bonus on the basis of the amount of tax-payer money that had to be poured into the bank to ensure its solvency. In other words he should be rewarded for his incompetence in putting the bank in such financial peril that untold billions of taxpayer funds were needed to prop up the bank. Not one of these bankers were brought up on charges of corporate impropriety as were Enron executives.

Profit means revenue covers costs. No one can seriously argue against the concept of a public or private undertaking covering its costs; that is, having enough money in the bank to pay its bills. The only objection that can be raised against profits is the degree of coverage. As has been shown, profits made by oil companies expressed in cents per gallon are quite modest in comparison to what consuming governments receive in the form of taxes and what producing governments receive in the form of revenue. The key question is whether we are getting value for what the oil companies charge for their services. By focusing on making money, oil companies have been able to bridge the gap between consumers and suppliers (primarily oil exporters), acting as a neutral third party serving the widely divergent interests of both.

Oil companies' possession of engineering technology, capital resources, and market access cannot be duplicated. Major oil companies view themselves as energy companies with a particular focus on oil, with that focus subject to change as conditions warrant. If tar deposits in Canada and Venezuela, and oil shale deposits around the world, become technologically and economically feasible, which they were when oil was $100 a barrel, oil companies will be there. If another fuel replaces gasoline as the fuel of choice, the oil companies have to be part of the transition. Their survival as major global companies hinges on their ability to adapt to changing times. This adaptation would be relatively easy if there were a major shift from gasoline to natural gas, but would be relatively difficult if the shift involved electricity. Barring this, as this chapter readily shows, oil companies have proven their adaptability in the past and there is every reason to expect that they will do so in the future.

Projects and Problems

Project 5.1

An Excel spreadsheet template is to be constructed to perform a gasoline consumption projection based on the number of automobiles in various age segments. The problem is pro forma and its intent is to set up a template that can be modified as appropriate to fit an actual situation. Year 0 is the present time and goes out to year 10. The gasoline consuming motor vehicle population at year 0 is 270 million and is expected to grow at 0.5 percent per year. If cell D9 has the population of 270 and the percentage growth is in cell D7, then the applicable formula in cell D10 is =D9*(1+$D$7) replicated down the column. Obviously, the choice of cells is up to you, but this shows the general structure.

There are four subgroups of motor vehicles. At time 0, Group A has a population of 50 million motor vehicles and represents the oldest segment. The decay rate for year 1 is 7 percent in cell F10 that increases by 0.5 percent per year thereafter. Cell G9 is the time 0 population of 50 and cell G10 is the year 1 population given by the formula =G9*(1-F10) replicated down the column. Cell H5 is the distance factor associated with miles driven per year of −2%, which assumes that older cars are being driven less as they age. Cell H9 is the miles driven per year at time 0 of 11,000. Cell H10 reflects miles driven in subsequent years with the formula =(1+H$5)*H9, replicated down the column. Cell I3 contains the average miles per gallon for Group A motor vehicles of 16, but this has to be corrected because the automobiles actually run on gasohol that is 10 percent ethanol. The corrected mileage in gasohol is a weighted average of 90 percent × 16 mpg plus 10 percent × 16 mpg × 0.667, reflecting that ethanol has only two thirds of the energy of gasoline. Cell I9 calculates the annual amount of gasohol consumed in millions of gallons with the formula =G9*H9/I$4.

Columns F through I can be copied to columns K through N for Group B. Some editing and data changes will have to be made to the formulation. Group B has 100 million motor vehicles with an initial population decay rate of 3 percent that escalates by 0.5 percent per year thereafter. Time 0 miles driven are 12,000 miles and the associated distance factor is −1% per year. Group B motor vehicles get 18 miles per gallon gasoline, which has to be corrected for its 10 percent ethanol content. Copying columns K through N to columns P through S establishes Group C, the newest of the existing motor vehicle fleet. Its decay rate is 0.25 percent for time 1, escalating 0.25 percent per year thereafter. Its time 0 population is 120 million motor vehicles that are driven 13,000 miles per year with a 0 percent distance factor and consume an average of 20 miles per gallon before correcting for its ethanol content.

The last group is the New Vehicle population that does not exist at time 0. For time 1 and beyond, its population is total number of vehicles less the populations in Groups A, B, and C. At year 1, the number of non-gasoline-fueled motor vehicles (electric and natural gas) is 0.1 million or 100,000, escalating at 50,000 vehicles per year. Adjusted New Vehicles is New Vehicles less non-gasoline-fueled vehicles. The average mileage of this group is 25 miles per gallon gasoline, escalating at 0.5 miles per gallon and reflecting further progress in improving mileage plus growth in the number of hybrid motor vehicles that get significantly better mileage. Each individual year will have to include the ethanol correction. Gasohol consumption is based on 14,000 miles driven per year that increases with a distance factor of 1 percent, depicting that families with multiple cars tend to take longer trips in a new vehicle over an old vehicle. Dividing annual miles driven by annual miles per gallon and multiplying by the population (all these figures differ by year) yields gasohol consumption for the New Vehicle group.

Total gasohol consumption is the sum of the four groups. The non-oil portion is ethanol, which makes up 10 percent by volume—thus gasoline consumption is 90 percent of gasohol consumption (the lower energy content of ethanol has already been taken into account). Biobutanol is a straight gasoline substitute made from ethanol. Suppose that success in development will be 25,000 Bpd (0.025 million Bpd) year 1, escalating by 25,000 Bpd thereafter, multiplied by 365 to obtain annual production. Adjusting for biobutanol consumption yields net gasoline consumption. This can be indexed at a value of 100 by dividing year 1 gasoline consumption values by itself with an absolute address and multiplying by 100 before replicating down. This provides a convenient visual measure of how gasoline consumption is projected to grow or decline with respect to time 0. Using Goal Seek, what growth rate for the overall population is necessary for the gasoline consumption index in year 10 to be equal to the initial value of 100?

Project 5.2

The purpose of this project is to introduce the concept of lag and regression analysis as a means of projecting oil prices. Casting past data forward in time often involves exponential smoothing and other akin methodologies. An example is the TimeSeries function offered by @RISK, a Microsoft Excel add-in simulation software provided by Palisade Corp. A set of past oil prices or any data of interest is selected and the TimeSeries function develops envelopes for high and medium probabilities of occurrence for projected price paths. Watching an interactive display of individual paths randomly generated by the TimeSeries function should alert the observer to the wide variety of potential paths that can be generated from a given set of historical data. @RISK simulation can generate future price patterns for evaluating the nature of risk and the efficacy of various risk mitigation means to reduce risk.[40]

Another approach to projecting oil prices is regression analysis. Suppose that you believe that a causal relationship exists between US gasoline inventories and gasoline prices. A causal relationship in this instance would be a rise in inventories accompanied by a fall in prices as traders and market participants move to reduce inventories by selling larger quantities of gasoline from inventory, which reduces their purchases of refinery output, putting pressure on prices. Falling inventories may be accompanied by increased buying of refinery output to rebuild inventories to a desired level, which should prop up prices. Since changes in inventories affect the volume of purchases of refinery output, one might suspect that a causal relationship exists between stock or inventory changes and price.

To illustrate this methodology, copy about six months of weekly gasoline inventories (stock levels) and gasoline prices to a spreadsheet from the US Department of Energy Website.[41] For purposes of discussion, suppose that column A contains dates, column B gasoline prices in cents per gallon, and column C stock levels in thousands of barrels and that the data on price and stock levels are in cells B6 to C43. Run a regression on y values B6:B43 and x values C6:C43. You now have a regression equation for projecting next week's price by substituting next week's stock levels as the independent variable. The problem, of course, is that you are no better off in assessing next week's stock level than in assessing price. Thus, you may as well project next week's price using the @RISK TimeSeries function or some other means.

However, there may be a causal relationship between this week's announced stock levels and next week's gasoline price. In other words, there may be a lag between announced changes in inventory stock levels and prices to take into account reaction time by oil traders. To explore this possibility, rerun the regression analysis with y values B7:B43 and x values C6:C42. The regression equation now contains a one week lag where next week's oil price is keyed to this week's stock levels. This is a great boon because one does not have to assess next week's stock level to project next week's oil price. The advantage of this week's independent variable not being utilized to derive the regression equation is that it can be substituted in the regression equation to obtain a projected price. Uncertainty associated with price is the projected price plus or minus two times the Standard Error in the regression output, which is the 95 percent confidence range about the projected price. The higher the R Squared value, the narrower the confidence range and the more comfortable, statistically speaking, one is about the output.

Now explore introducing a two week lag by obtaining the regression equation for y values B8:B43 and x values C6:C41 to project oil prices for the next two weeks using

stock levels for the preceding and present week in the regression equation. This procedure allows price projections for different lag times. By comparing projected values with
actual data, one can evaluate whether a causal relationship exists between gasoline prices
and stock levels. Moreover, this model can be expanded to include multiple independent
variables such as refinery throughput and gasoline consumption and crude oil prices and
others that may affect price. If the independent variables are in columns C, D, E, and F,
then the regression equation for a three week lag would have y values of B9:B43 and x
values of C6:F40.

   Model performance for different lags using past data is one facet of assessing the usefulness of the model. Another is the extent of the historical data. Adding data may decrease
the R Square, illustrating that this model is not deterministic like the law of gravity.
Rather it is a statistical model where the coefficients for the various independent variables
in the regression equation change with time. The more dramatic the change in coefficient
values for additional data, the shorter should be the database. Thus, the final selected
model includes not just the degree of lag, but also the period of past data to derive the
regression equation. The final judge of a model is how well it projects oil prices for different lags and time periods of historical data. While R Square is certainly part of the
evaluation, a better evaluator is the absolute or relative valuation of how well projected
prices compare with actual prices.

   What is your evaluation of lag with one independent variable? Construct a lag model
using a multiple regression model similar to the one described. Do an evaluation of which
model seems better.

Problems 5.1a and 5.1b

These problems develop spreadsheet templates to measure the comparable economics
of buying a hybrid over a conventional gasoline powered automobile. Problem 5.1a
generates the capital recovery factor to be used for each automobile type and Problem
5.1b does the comparable economic analysis to identify the highest price to be paid
for the hybrid that equates to the cost of transportation for both types of automobiles.
Thus there would be an economic benefit to buy the hybrid if its cost is lower than
that calculated.

Problem 5.1a

Suppose that the life of the hybrid is 7 years before the battery has to be replaced and its
residual value at that time is estimated to be 7 percent of the purchase price if one does
not desire to buy the second battery. Life of the gasoline powered automobile is 12 years
with a residual value of 5 percent, and the desired return on the equity investment is
8 percent. This represents the opportunity cost in not investing the equity in the stock
market whose long-term gain is 8 percent. For both cars, financing is 90 percent of the
cost with mortgage-type debt of monthly payments at 4 percent annual interest. For
the hybrid, time goes from 0, when the equity investment is made, to 7 years. To ease
formulation, put Time in cell D5. Column E is the annual finance charge that will be
determined in order to cover the financial aspects of the investment. The financial charge
that meets all criteria will become the annual financing charge or capital recovery factor
that will be applied against the acquisition cost.

Suppose that cell E5 contains an arbitrarily selected value of $3,000 for the financial charge. The financial charge in cell E7 is =$E$5 replicated down. Column F is the mortgage-type payment given by the formula =12*PMT (monthly interest rate, # payments, principal amount). The monthly interest is the annual interest divided by 12, the number of payments is 12 × number of years, 7, for 84 payments, and the principal amount is 90 percent of the nominal cost of the automobile of $10,000. The residual value in selling the car in year 7 is 7 percent of the nominal cost and the equity payment is 10 percent of the nominal cost. Obtain the cash flow and enter the formula for IRR such as =IRR(I6:I13). Employ Goal Seek to set the cell containing the IRR formula to have a value of 0.08 by changing cell E5. Try to set up the spreadsheet with an input section so that different financial structures can be explored. For this case, the annual financing charge or capital recovery factor (CRF) is 15.9 percent.

For the conventional gasoline fueled automobile, modifications involved extending the life out to 12 years when the car is sold for 5 percent of its original value. With suitable formulation changes including changing the IRR formula to reflect the longer period of time, the appropriate CRF for this type of car is a significantly lower 11.26 percent.

Problem 5.1b

Suppose that the hybrid gets 50 miles per gallon and the conventional automobile 25 miles per gallon and gasoline costs $4 per gallon. The hybrid has a higher charge of $250 per year for maintenance and insurance and both cars are driven 15,000 miles per year. Further suppose that the conventional automobile costs $35,000—what would be the breakeven price for the hybrid based on full costing of $/mile?

Using $40,000 as an estimate for the breakeven price as a starting point, the hybrid cost would be the price × CRF for hybrids, plus the charge of $250 for higher maintenance and insurance costs, plus the total gasoline bill for 15,000 miles at 50 miles per gallon and $4 per gallon. Do the same for the gasoline fueled automobile with a CRF of 11.26 percent. Do the calculation on the basis of a single year, which would apply for the first seven years, and use Goal Seek to obtain the breakeven price for the hybrid.

Problem 5.1c

Because of the higher CRF being applied against the shorter life of the hybrid without battery replacement, what price of gasoline would be necessary to justify a $40,000 price for the hybrid? Enter $40,000 for the price of the hybrid, formulate a cell for the difference between total costs, and use Goal Seek to set the difference to zero by varying the price of gasoline. What gasoline price is necessary to justify the purchase of the hybrid at this price?

Problem 5.1d

So far, the economics are clearly against the hybrid. How would you handle the situation that a battery estimated to cost 20 percent of the hybrid price can be made in the eighth year that would extend the life of the hybrid to 14 years? Redo the CRF for 14 years for both car types. For the hybrid, enter a new column for the same type of payment schedule as for the car for years 8–14 reflecting the value of the new battery, which is 20 percent of the nominal cost of $10,000. This significantly narrows the two CRFs. Both cars are sold for 5 percent of the nominal value at the end of the 14 years. This significantly narrows the difference between the two CRFs. With these new CRFs, what is now the hybrid breakeven price at $4 per gallon?

Problem 5.2

In the *BP Energy Statistics* tab Regional Consumption for oil, light distillates can be used as a proxy for gasoline consumption. Starting in 2005, perform a trend analysis for light distillates for North America, the US, Europe, the Middle East, Asia-Pacific, China, Japan, and total world. The selection of the appropriate trend line involves an implicit analysis of one's perception of the future for gasoline consumption. As such, trend line analysis really reflects what one thinks about the future rather than being a mathematically precise methodology where the world abides by the trend line with the highest R Square value. Write a short paper on what you feel is the future demand for gasoline for each of these regions/nations and for the world, including your thinking of factors affecting future consumption.

Problem 5.3

CO_2 emissions from burning a gallon of gasoline is 8,887 grams.[42] If you drove an automobile 12,000 miles per year at 22 miles per gallon, how many metric tons of carbon dioxide do you add to the atmosphere? There are 1,000 grams in a kilogram and 1,000 kilograms in a metric ton. With around 260 million gasoline fueled automobiles, pickup trucks, and light vans in the US, this is no small number!

Problem 5.4

a   Suppose that a gasoline fueled automobile is driven 12,000 miles and gets an average of 22 miles per gallon and gasoline costs $3.50 per gallon. What is the total fuel bill for a year and what is the average cost per mile?
b   Suppose that an electric vehicle with the same driving pattern gets an average of 2.90 miles per kWh. How many kWh does this vehicle consume in a year?
c   If the efficiency of charging to consumption is 85 percent, how much electricity must be charged into the electric vehicle?
d   If the cost of electricity is 11 cents per kWh, what is the annual cost and cost per mile? Suppose that time-of-day electricity rates are available and the night-time rate is 6 cents per kWh—what is the new cost per mile?

Problem 5.5

a   Suppose that the battery pack has a capacity of 24 kWh. What would be the maximum number of miles between charges assuming that recharging occurs when 90 percent of the battery capacity has been consumed? Do you think this is a convenient or an inconvenient distance between charges? This depends on how you charge the car—if it is in your garage at night, maybe it wouldn't be inconvenient. What if your commute is 100 miles per day?

b   What if the battery pack is $500 per kWh—what is the cost of the battery pack? Suppose that the battery is good for 3,000 cycles at maximum drawdown (90 percent of battery capacity). What is the battery depreciation cost per cycle given a 15 percent residual value for the battery?

c   How many full charge cycles would a car need to do if driven 12,000 miles per year? What is the annual cost for battery depreciation? Add this in with the annual electricity usage charge and calculate the per mile cost of electricity plus battery depreciation. How does this compare with gasoline fuel?

Problem 5.6

Suppose that oil has a current cash value of $100 per barrel and the futures market is in contango (futures are priced higher than the cash market). Oil can be purchased using funding costing 2 percent interest per year. Low-cost land storage is not available. But a very large crude carrier is available at $33,000 per day for 90 days which can be used for floating storage. This figure includes all costs for chartering a vessel plus an allowance for the ship's fuel consumed for electrical loads and discharging cargo and any other associated expense. What is the breakeven value for a 90-day futures contract for an individual to buy oil in the cash market, store it on board the vessel, and convert the futures contract to a cash settlement to repay the initial loan? What is the profit potential on this non-cash transaction (all funding is borrowed) for every penny increment over the breakeven rate?

Notes

1 Stephen Howarth, *A Century in Oil: The "Shell" Transport and Trading Company, 1897–1997* (London, UK: Weidenfeld & Nicolson, 1997).
2 Saudi Aramco, Website www.saudiaramco.com.
3 Charles Mason and Stephen Polasky, "What Motivates Membership in Non-renewable Resource Cartels? The Case of OPEC," *Resource and Energy Economics*, Vol. 27 (2005).
4 *BP Energy Statistics* (London, UK: British Petroleum, 2013) is the principal data source of the figures.
5 At that time I was working for a shipping company on a forecasting model for tanker demand. I was using growth rates in oil demand that applied in the early 1970s without ever giving a thought to the idea that such rapid growth in consumption might be nonsustainable. Looking back, I had all the data necessary to conclude that the world could not continue indefinitely on its track of plentiful cheap oil. Nor did anyone who worked for oil companies; at least, they did not make it public. As humans, we are incredibly poor at sensing when the world reaches a tilting point, the edge of a cusp of significant change. So few seem capable of announcing it; fewer yet acting on it.
6 A detailed chronology of events prepared by National Public Radio (NPR), "Gas & Oil Prices: A Chronology," Website www.npr.org/news/specials/oil/gasprices.chronology.html.
7 Daniel Yergin, *The Prize: The Epic Quest for Oil, Money, and Power* (New York, NY: Simon & Schuster, 1991), is the primary source for the post-1975 history.
8 A.F. Alhajji and David Huettner, "OPEC and Other Commodity Cartels: A Comparison," *Elsevier Science Energy Policy*, Vol. 28 (2000). See also "The Target Revenue Model and the World Oil Market: Empirical Evidence from 1971 to 1994," *The Energy Journal*, Vol. 21, No. 2, IAEE (2000).
9 Energy Is Constant, Website www.energyisconstant.com/index.php?page=production.
10 A.F. Alhajji and David Huettner, "OPEC and Other Commodity Cartels: A Comparison," *Energy Policy*, Vol. 28 (2000).
11 Herbert Inhaber, *Why Energy Conservation Fails* (Westport, CT: Quorum Books, 2002).

12 Robert Lenzner, "Speculation in Crude Oil Adds $23.39 to the Price per Barrel," *Forbes* (February 27, 2012), Website www.forbes.com/sites/robertlenzner/2012/02/27/speculation-in-crude-oil-adds-23-39-to-the-price-per-barrel. See also Douwe Miedema, "Funds, Speculators Pushing up Energy Prices—U.S. Regulator," *Reuters* (February 13, 2013), Website www.reuters.com/article/2013/02/13/energy-speculators-idUSL1N0BCHJS20130213, and L. Randall Wray, "The Commodities Market Bubble (Money Manager Capitalism and the Financialization of Commodities)," *The Levy Economics Institute* (No. 96, 2008), Website www.levyinstitute.org/pubs/ppb_96.pdf.

13 Michael Greenberger, "The Relationship of Unregulated Excessive Speculation to Oil Market Price Volatility," University of Maryland School of Law report prepared for the International Energy Forum (March, 2010), Website www.michaelgreenberger.com/files/IEF-Greenberger-AppendixVII.pdf.

14 Storing oil affected tanker rates during the First Gulf War when Saddam Hussein invaded Kuwait to make it a province of Iraq in August 1990. During the conflict, both Saudi Arabia and Iran chartered about 100 very large crude carriers as strategic oil storage outside the Middle East in case their production was affected by the war. Ship tonnage removed from active service to hold crude oil in storage amounted to about 25 percent of the world fleet of 400 very large crude carriers. This removal of such a large portion of the fleet from active or trading service to inactive storage caused a rate spike. The spike disappeared when war was over in March 1991 and crude carriers unloaded their stored cargoes and resumed trading. In times of active speculation in oil futures, this same phenomenon was noted when a significant portion of the very large crude carrier fleet was committed to storing oil for covering positions in oil futures. It may be difficult to prove that removing oil from current supply availability to cover future positions was responsible for actually causing the cash market for oil to rise, but it can be shown that it was sufficient to cause the cash market for tankers to rise.

15 My opinion is that paper transactions are primarily side bets that do not affect the cash value of a commodity. Only if paper transactions are affecting the physical availability of the commodity as with the arbitrage transactions in oil is there a potential of a financial link depending on how much of available supply is being stuffed into storage. There is no doubt that massive inventory accumulation and liquidation affect prices.

16 See Website www.usinflationcalculator.com based on Bureau of Labor Statistics.

17 John Williams' Shadow Government Statistics, Website www.shadowstats.com/alternate_data/inflation-charts.

18 Jeff D. Opdyke, Editor of *Profit Seeker*, "The Hidden Cost of Oil" (December 18, 2012), as reprinted in *The Sovereign Investor* (July 8, 2014), Website http://info@thesovereigninvestor.com.

19 "The North Sea: Running on Fumes," *Economist* (March 1, 2014).

20 Douglas-Westwood, Website http://douglas-westwood.com. See following footnote.

21 "Beginning of the End? Oil Companies Cut Back on Spending," *Our Finite World* (February 2, 2014), Website http://ourfiniteworld.com/2014/02/25/beginning-of-the-end-oil-companies-cut-back-on-spending. The article, prepared by Douglas-Westwood, includes an in-depth philosophical treatise on whether oil extraction depends on supply growth or demand growth.

22 Andrew Nikiforuk, "A Big Summer Story You Missed: Soaring Oil Debt," *The Tyee* (August 29, 2014), Website http://thetyee.ca/opinion/2014/08/29/Soaring-Oil-Debt-Summer.

23 I'm ashamed to admit that I authored check forecasts where things are bad now, they'll be worse in the next year or two, but after that things will get better for any number of plausible and positive happenings. The reason for this cop-out was simple—even if I knew the truth, there was no way to tell the company's clientele that they faced certain liquidation. Besides, I may be wrong!

24 An excellent paper on the subject of the difficulty of forecasting is Michael C. Lynch, "Forecasting Oil Supply: Theory and Practice," *The Quarterly Review of Economics and Finance*, Vol. 42 (2002), Website www.aspo-australia.org.au/References/Lynch-july-02.pdf?origin=publication_detail.

25 Dr. Mikhail Kashubsky, "Protecting Offshore Oil and Gas Installations: Security Threats and Countervailing Measures," *Journal of Energy Security* (August, 2013), Website www.ensec.org/index.php?option=com_content&id=453:protecting-offshore-oil-and-gas-installations-security-threats-and-countervailing-measures&catid=137:issue-content&Itemid=422.

26 World Oil Transit Chokepoints from US Energy Information Administration (EIA), Website www. eia.gov/countries/regions-topics.cfm?fips=wotc&trk=p3.

27 "Oil and Iraq: Burning at Both Ends," *Economist* (June 21, 2014).

28 "Pipeline Poker: East Africa is in Danger of Throwing Away Part of Its New-Found Oil Wealth," *Economist* (May 25, 2012).

29 Shell Oil Co. and Rig Dumping (SHELLRIG), Website www1.american.edu/TED/SHELLRIG.HTM.

30 Paul Brown, "Chad Oil Pipeline under Attack for Harming the Poor," *Guardian* (September, 2002), Website www.theguardian.com/environment/2002/sep/27/internationalnews. See also "West LB Finances OCP Oil Pipeline through the Mindo Important Bird Area, Ecuador," Website www. worldtwitch.com/ecuador_pipeline.htm.

31 "Drilling in the Wilderness: Energy Extraction Can Coexist with Native Peoples and Forests," *Economist* (April 26, 2014).

32 Exxon-Mobil policy with regard to spill prevention and response at Website www.corporate.exx onmobil.com/en/environment/emergency-preparedness/spill-prevention-and-response. See also British Petroleum, Website www.bp.com/en/global/corporate/gulf-of-mexico-restoration/deep water-horizon-accident-and-response.html.

33 "Petrobras: Two Heads are Worse than One," *Economist* (April 5, 2014).

34 "Fill'er Up: Cristina Fernandez Sacrifices Her Country's Relationship with Its Biggest Foreign Investor to Satisfy Her Hunger for Cash and Nationalist Symbolism," *Economist* (April 21, 2012). In 2014, Argentina lost in a decision made by the International Centre for Settlement of Investment Disputes and had to compensate the Spanish company Repsol for the expropriation of its shares in YPF. See "A Good Week for Some Investors," *Economist* (June 21, 2014).

35 "Price Squeeze: Popular and Harmful, Energy Subsidies are Hard—But Not Impossible—to Kill," *Economist* (June 14, 2014).

36 California Energy Commission, Website http://energyalmanac.ca.gov/gasoline/margins/index.php.

37 The average oil profit per gallon for 2007 was reported as 10 cents per gallon by Oxford Club Investment, Website www.investmentu.com/IUEL/2007/20070323.html, and the Associated Business Press quoted Exxon's earnings in the first quarter of 2008 as 4 cents per gallon of gasoline and diesel, down from 8 cents per gallon from the previous year's first quarter, as listed on Website www.wmi.org/bassfish/bassboard/other_topics/message.html?message_id=298879. In the first edi- tion of this book, I estimated that the Shell Group made 8.5 cents per gallon and Amerada Hess made 6.6 cents per gallon on its oil sales in 2003. The following article estimated that Exxon made 7 cents per gallon in 2011: Drew Johnson, "Who Really Gets Rich off High Gas Prices," *Wall Street Journal Opinion* (August 2, 2012), Website http://online.wsj.com/news/articles/SB1000087239639044368 750457756338398241853 6?mg=reno64-wsj&url=http%3A%2F%2Fonline.wsj.com%2Farticle%2 FSB10000872396390443687504577563383982418536.html. In my opinion, 10 cents per gallon is a fair estimate during good years for the oil companies, while 5–10 cents per gallon is a fair estimate of overall profitability for more typical years.

38 US Energy Information Agency, Website www.eia.gov/countries/prices/gasolinewithtax.cfm, for data up to 2013. 2014 data from *Bloomberg*, Website www.bloomberg.com/visual-data/gas- prices/20144.

39 Adrian Lajous, "Mexican Energy Reform," Center on Global Energy Policy, Columbia University (June, 2014).

40 Roy Nersesian, *Energy Risk Modeling* (Ithaca, NY: Palisade, 2013). Chapters 12, 13, and 14 provide guid- ance on simulating future oil prices using @RISK simulation. Chapter 12 illustrates the TimeSeries function in @RISK. Chapter 15 examines swaps, and Chapter 16 simulates a swap manager charged with reducing risk of adverse price movements. Chapter 17 looks at trailing stops and Chapter 18 puts and calls as risk mitigation tools. Website http://blog.palisade.com/blog/decision-making-under- uncertainty-2/palisade-publishes-new-book-energy-risk-modeling-by-professor-roy-nersesian.

41 Department of Energy, Website http://tonto.eia.doe.gov/dnav/pet/pet_pri_gnd_dcus_nus_w.htm.

42 "EPA Greenhouse Gas Emissions from a Typical Passenger Vehicle," US Environmental Protection Administration, Website www.epa.gov/otaq/climate/documents/420f11041.pdf.

6   Oil

This chapter describes the journey oil takes from deep in the Earth until it reaches consumers in a wide range of products from motor vehicle fuels to plastics to fertilizers to pesticides. The sojourn starts with the exploration and development of oil wells onshore and offshore, refining and transportation of oil products, and enhanced recovery methods to get the most out of oil fields. Adequacy of oil reserves to continue to fuel our economy, and potential of nonconventional oil sources including the game-changer, fracking, and synthetic crude, will be covered. The impact of improved energy efficiency and progress in developing alternative fuels on gasoline consumption will be discussed along with geopolitical aspects of oil, with a belated call to internalize an externality called oil security. Despite rising US oil production and surplus production in Mexico and Canada, North America is far from being energy (oil) independent. Greater support for the development of oil resources and alternative fuels is necessary to reduce our vulnerability to global oil shocks.

See the Companion Website for sections on the Earth as an Oil Manufacturer, the Formation of Oil, and Oil Exploration and Production: www.routledge.com/cw/nersesian.

Oil Reserves

Oil resources are the totality of oil in the ground, known and unknown. Half of this is irretrievable, even with the most costly recovery methods. Oil resources that are both known and retrievable are called reserves. Reserves of an oil and gas field are not known with certainty until the last well is dry. Reserves are an estimate of the amount of oil and gas that can be removed from a reservoir under current oil prices employing current extraction technology, not the amount of oil resources actually in the ground. Thus an improvement in the price of oil that can support more costly recovery methods, or an advance in oil extraction technology, can change the amount of proven reserves. Oil resources are fixed by what is in the ground, whereas reserves are a variable dependent on oil prices and extraction technologies. Proven oil reserves can be considered working inventory, but not an inventory that appears on the balance sheets of oil companies. Proven oil reserves are reported as a footnote in an annual report. The reported book value of a share of oil company stock based on its balance sheet does not include the value of the company's proven reserves. However, a company's proven reserves affect its stock price and are accepted as collateral for bank loans.

Proven reserves are reserves that can be calculated with reasonable accuracy based on field production and the results of appraisal or development wells that measure the potential size of an oil field. Calculation of proven reserves is based on volume of a pay zone, porosity and permeability of a reservoir, degree of oil saturation, and recovery factor. Porosity is obtained from well logs or cores and oil saturation from a resistivity well log. Recovery factor is estimated by reservoir drive, nature of oil, and permeability of reservoir rock. Another method of estimating proven reserves is based on the decline curve, falloff in production over time. The materials balance method is another mathematical approach that correlates volume of oil, water, and gas produced with a change in reservoir pressure.

Proven reserves are either developed (within reach of existing wells) or undeveloped (new wells would have to be drilled to access the oil). Probable and possible reserves are calculated in a fashion similar to proven reserves, but their lower classification reflects a greater degree of uncertainty associated with underlying data. Rule 4.10(a) of Regulation S-X under the US Securities Act of 1933 was promulgated to protect investors from being fleeced by unscrupulous speculators selling east Texas oil properties. The required methodology for calculating proven reserves is based on actual production. In 2004 the US Securities and Exchange Commission (SEC) ordered Shell Oil to remove over 4 billion barrels of oil, equivalent to 20 percent of its reserves, from proven reserves because Shell had not followed the prescribed methodology. Shell had categorized certain deep water reserves as proven based on the results of exploratory wells and a 3D seismic analysis of their reservoir structures. Shell retorted that SEC was using a dated methodology applicable to onshore reservoirs, not deep water offshore reservoirs. The SEC response was that its rules are clear—an assessment of proven reserves must be based on actual production from existing wells using an analytical approach that can substantiate at least a 90 percent chance of recoverability. Without following the SEC script for determining reserves, a portion of Shell's reserves could not be considered proven, but could be considered probable if a 50 percent chance of recoverability could be demonstrated or, lacking that, reserves could be considered possible. Thus, while Shell's total proven, probable, and possible reserves remained unchanged, the portion considered proven took a significant hit. Shell Oil abided by the decision, but members of the investment community were free to interpret Shell's reserves as they desired.

In 2012, a study indicated the 1,750 square mile Monterey Shale formation in central California contained 13.7 billion barrels of recoverable oil. This then became the basis for estimating as many as 2.8 million new jobs to California, boosting tax revenue by $24.6 billion annually, with an eventual substantial cut in US oil imports. In June 2014, the US Energy Information Administration (EIA) reduced reserves of recoverable oil by 96 percent to 600 million barrels. The firm conducting the original study assumed that oil would be as easily recoverable as the flat shale formations in North Dakota and Texas. But Monterey Shale turned out to be folded and shattered by earthquakes and tectonic plate movements, ruling out conventional fracking techniques, which resulted in a sharp mark down of reported reserves. However, EIA pointed out that the potential for recovering oil could rise if new technology were developed and the price of oil were high enough to economically support developing this resource. This incident demonstrates that oil in the ground as a resource is fixed, while oil in the ground as a reserve is a variable, depending on technological and economic and other circumstances.[1]

What does this write-down mean in terms of US oil reserves? Based on conventional oil, total world reserves are 1.7 trillion barrels or 1,700 billion barrels and US reserves are 49 billion barrels.[2] As of the start of 2013, worldwide Technically Recoverable Resources (TRRs) for oil found in hard shale were 345 billion barrels.[3] Of this, 58 billion barrels are in the US. However, the net reduction of 13.1 billion barrels in TRRs in the Monterey Shale formation reduces US TRRs to 45 billion barrels, still a significant increase of a bit under 100 percent compared to 49 billion barrels of conventional oil. In 2009 SEC made it easier for companies to claim untapped proved reserves for wells that wouldn't be drilled up to a maximum of 5 years.[4] As a consequence, hard shale producers added 9.7 billion barrels of untapped proved oil and gas reserves to garner $230 billion in bonds, loans, and stock sales to support fracking operations. This was accomplished when oil was $95 a barrel and confidence high that these reserves would be tapped within 5 years. However, in 2015, with prices at $60 per barrel and low confidence that oil would return to $95 a barrel within 5 years, it was felt that over half, 5.4 billion barrels out of 9.7 billion barrels, would have to be removed from the books of 44 US hard shale frackers, of which 10 companies have over 60 percent of their proved reserves at risk. This will impact their ability to refinance billions of dollars of debt placed on the books when oil was at $95 a barrel, which if not accomplished may affect their corporate liquidity if not survival. All this changes, of course, if oil prices surge upward within the next few years.[5] Again, reserves are a variable depending on the circumstances.

Reserves are not necessarily revised downward. Table 6.1 shows reserve increases made by OPEC nations during the 1980s when OPEC was setting production quotas based on proven reserves. A warranted or unwarranted write-up of proven reserves would have resulted in a higher oil production quota and higher revenue. These write-ups have been generally considered suspect as they were not accompanied by new discoveries. But it could have been that reserves at that time were intentionally underestimated by oil companies as a way to subdue the exuberance of oil exporting nations for higher royalties. Regardless of one's position, the write-up of 270.5 billion barrels during this time added almost 35 percent to the 1984 reserves of 774 billion barrels.

Another write-up occurred in 1999 when Canada added 130 billion barrels to its reserves in recognition of its potential to produce synthetic crude oil with the same properties of conventional crude oil from its vast resource in oil sands. In like manner Venezuela decided to count its Orinoco bitumen, another nonconventional source of

Table 6.1 Write-Up of OPEC Reserves

Nation	Year	Billion Barrels
Kuwait	1983	25.7
Venezuela	1985	26.5
Iran	1986	33.9
Iraq	1986–1987	35.0
United Arab Emirates	1986	64.2
Saudi Arabia	1988	85.4

oil capable of producing synthetic crude similar to conventional crude oil, as part of its oil reserves in 2006. Venezuela included 8 billion barrels of Orinoco bitumen in 2006, 20 billion barrels in 2007, 94 billion barrels in 2008, 133 billion barrels in 2009, and 220 billion barrels thereafter. Canada also lists the portion of Canadian oil sands "under active development," which amounted to 21 billion barrels in 2006 and increasing to 25 billion barrels in 2014. Are these write-ups in what is normally considered conventional oil reserves justifiable? The response by Venezuela and Canada would probably be that though bitumen and oil sands are not the same as conventional crude found in an oil field, technology exists to convert these unconventional sources to synthetic crude similar to certain types of conventional crude. Since syncrude can be profitably produced at oil prices around $100 per barrel, it would have been misleading not to include these unconventional sources as conventional. But at $60 per barrel, the economics cannot support further development of these unconventional sources of crude oil. Should they still be counted as reserves? If they are, then fracking oil from tight rock formations may one day be counted as conventional sources if oil prices were to rise to $100 per barrel, which would further expand the global reserves to production ratio (R/P Ratio).

Is Hubbert's Peak Oil Dead?

Comparing oil reserves with oil production assesses how long the age of oil will last. Since the beginning of the oil age, predictions of the world running out of oil have been made, and all have been proven wrong. In 1879 the US Geological Survey was formed in response to a fear of an oil shortage. In 1882 the Institute of Mining Engineers estimated that there were 95 million barrels left, an amount that would be exhausted in 5 years at the then present consumption rate of 25 million barrels per year. In the early 1900s Theodore Roosevelt opined that there were about 20 years of reserves left and hearings were held in Washington on the adequacy of supply. In 1919 *Scientific American* warned that there were only 20 years of oil left in the ground and made a plea for automobile engines to be designed for greater energy efficiency (*déjà vu?*). In 1920 the US Geological Survey estimated that US reserves were only 6.7 billion barrels, including what was known and remaining to be discovered (current US reserves are 49 billion barrels after 80-odd years of production).[6] In the 1920s the US government, worried over the adequacy of oil supplies, secured an interest in the Turkish Petroleum Company and had to almost coerce reluctant US oil companies to get involved with Middle East oil.

In 1956 M. King Hubbert, a geophysicist with a background in exploration for Shell Oil, postulated that US oil production would peak in the early 1970s based on an assessment of discoverable oil (known oil reserves plus that yet to be discovered). Scorned by his contemporaries, he turned out to be basically right. Hubbert was off a bit on the actual timing of the peak in production because, since he had made his original prediction, more oil was discovered in Alaska and in the Gulf of Mexico than he anticipated. But he was not off by much.

Indonesia and the UK have three things in common—they were once oil exporters, their production has already peaked, and they are now importers. While Indonesia is the first OPEC nation to become a net oil importer and is no longer a member, it is still a net energy exporter when natural gas and coal exports are taken into consideration. Nations whose oil production is less in 2014 than in 2000 in the Western Hemisphere include Argentina, Mexico, Trinidad & Tobago, and Venezuela; in Europe Denmark,

Norway, Romania, and the UK; in the Former Soviet Union (FSU) Turkmenistan and Uzbekistan; in Africa Algeria, Congo, Gabon, Libya, Sudan, and Tunisia; in the Middle East Iran, Oman, Syria, and Yemen; and in Asia Brunei, Indonesia, and Malaysia, plus Australia. In some cases, the fault is not finding sufficient replacement oil and in others mismanagement of oil resources, and in still others political and social upheaval. The actual reason is immaterial—this rather large grouping of nations is producing less today than 14 years ago while world demand is expanding.

Another indication of peaking of oil is the dearth of discoveries of new supergiant oil fields. Table 6.2 lists the world's largest oil fields. The cumulative percentage is based on adjusted proven reserves of a little over 900 billion barrels for 1986, net of the write-ups in Table 6.1. The Ghawar field represents 7 percent of the world's proven resources in 1986. Both the Ghawar and Greater Burgan fields represent 10 percent of the world's proven reserves, and so forth.[7] The ultimate recovery oil for these supergiant fields has, for the most part, not been updated after decades of production.[8]

These 18 supergiant fields account for one-third of the world's known proven reserves in 40,000 oil fields. Two-thirds of these were discovered in and prior to 1960, over half a century ago. All but three are in the Middle East. Figure 6.1 shows the historical record for discovering giant oil fields of greater than 500 million barrels.

Clearly the peak of discovery for supergiant fields has passed. Prior to 1968, the problem faced by oil executives was how to control production to maintain price in the face of mounting discoveries. Since 1968, with the exception of 2 or 3 years, discoveries have not kept up with consumption by a significant margin. The US Geological Survey evaluated growth of petroleum reserves between 1996 and 2003.[9] During this 8-year period (including 2003), oil reserves increased 240 billion barrels, of which 69 billion barrels were new discoveries and 171 billion barrels were write-ups of existing

Table 6.2 World's Largest Oil Fields

Ultimate Recovery Oil, Millions Bbls	Country	Field Name	Discovery Year	Cumulative Percentage
66,058	Saudi Arabia	Ghawar	1948	7
31,795	Kuwait	Greater Burgan	1938	10
22,000	Iraq	Rumaila North & South	1953	13
21,145	Saudi Arabia	Safaniya	1951	15
17,223	Abu Dhabi	Zakum	1964	17
17,000	Iraq	Kirkuk	1927	19
16,820	Saudi Arabia	Manifa	1957	20
13,390	Venezuela	Tia Juana	1928	22
13,350	Iran	Ahwaz	1958	23
13,010	USA (Alaska)	Prudhoe Bay	1967	25
13,000	Kazakhstan	Kashagan	2000	26
12,631	Iran	Marun	1964	27
12,237	Saudi Arabia	Zuluf	1965	29
12,000	Iraq	Majnoon	1977	30
11,800	Iran	Gachsaran	1928	31
10,276	Abu Dhabi	Murban Bab	1954	32
10,265	Saudi Arabia	Abqaiq	1940	33
10,000	Iran	Fereidoon	1960	34

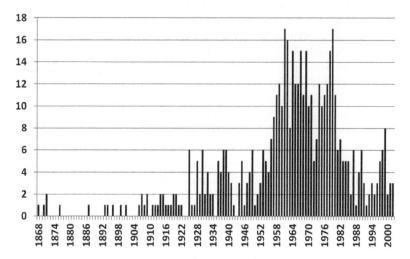

Figure 6.1 Number of Giant Oil Field Discoveries

oil reserves. Discoveries compensating for only one-third of consumption appear to be a sure-fire prescription for running out of oil. However, this contention implies that write-ups have been purely fictional. Write-ups are valid and should be made if production or further development work indicate that reserves are higher than previous estimates. On the other hand, proven reserves of major OPEC exporting nations with no discoveries of note remain the same year after year despite significant production. This cannot be, but any write-down would reduce their production quotas. Reserves should take into consideration both new discoveries and depletion and write-ups of existing reserves. A particular geographic area may be a very strong candidate for harboring enormous oil reserves, but exploration may be intentionally postponed on the theory that what may be in the ground will be worth more if discovered tomorrow rather than being discovered today. Reserves are underestimated by the degree of oil resources that may be found in areas where exploration is either postponed or cannot be conducted because of civil instability or conflicting territorial claims. Upgrading probable and possible reserves by improved technology and higher oil prices and including unconventional sources of oil that are technologically and economically feasible would also increase reserves. The problem facing oil reserves is a general lack of third-party verification of reserves in many oil fields where political and economic ramifications prevent telling the truth. This obfuscation over the extent of reserves has been a part of the oil business since the earliest days of estimating reserves. Oil reserve statistics are subject to manipulation upward or downward for political or commercial reasons. An OPEC nation may exaggerate its reserves to get a higher production quota. Private companies may not want the world to know the true extent of their reserves to discourage corporate takeovers or renegotiation of royalties and taxes.

Figure 6.2 shows the percentage distribution of the world's proven oil reserves by nation. The Pareto effect is clear; the top three nations hold 44 percent of the world's oil reserves, which include two OPEC nations. The top eight nations out of nearly 200 nations hold 79 percent of the world's oil resources, of which six are OPEC members and

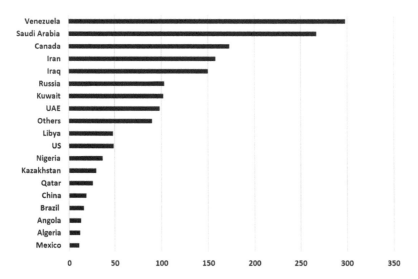

Figure 6.2 Distribution of the World's Proven Oil Reserves

four are in the Middle East. In the aggregate, OPEC holds 72 percent of the world's oil reserves. Oil reserves are highly concentrated among relatively few nations.

Dividing reserves in billions of barrels by global daily production in millions of barrels per day over 365 days, the reserves to production (R/P Ratio) was 36 years in 1983. That is, current production in 1983 could be maintained for 36 years before reserves are exhausted with no new discoveries and no increase in the rate of production. Hypothetically this means exhaustion of oil reserves in 2019, clearly not in the cards. Nevertheless this simplistic approach for measuring the comfort level for reserves with no allowance for new discoveries or changes in production is still useful as long as one understands its limitations. In 1993, the R/P Ratio was 43 years, meaning that new discoveries of smaller than supergiant fields outpaced growth in production. In 2003, the ratio was 47 years, and it was 53 years in 2014. While no discoveries of supergiant fields for decades support peaking, an increasing R/P Ratio with increasing annual production supports the contention that peaking is moving further into the future. But if write-ups by Venezuela and Canada totaling 350 billion barrels of unconventional crude are removed and R/P Ratios recalculated based on what was traditionally considered conventional oil, the 2014 R/P Ratio would be cut from 53 to 42 years. On this basis, the R/P Ratio has remained essentially constant for the last two decades even with higher production levels, still an argument that peaking is retreating into the future.

Modern-day followers of Hubbert assess the quantity of ultimately discoverable oil and compare that to cumulative production on a global scale. Oil production peaks when cumulative production has consumed half of the ultimately discoverable reserves. This assumes the impossible that one knows when a resource has been half-consumed without knowing the true extent of a resource. Ultimately discoverable reserves consist of known reserves, including enhanced production from played-out fields through secondary and tertiary recovery methods, and an assessment of what has not yet been discovered.

When on the downhill slope of a bell-shaped curve, exploration and extraction become more expensive as fewer and smaller oil fields are discovered in more remote areas and more costly methods have to be employed to maintain production in aging oil fields. Furthermore, oil becomes more viscous as a field ages, increasing refining costs.

The fact that the R/P Ratio for conventional oil continues to increase by incorporating Canadian oil sands and Venezuelan bitumen, or remains about the same without these additions, shows that the world is still on the left hand side of Hubbert's curve—we have not peaked when prognostications of just a few years ago were that it either had already occurred, or was about to occur, or will occur in just a few more years. From this perspective, Hubbert's peak is dead, at least for now.[10] But from the point of view of cheap oil, we have peaked. Unless supergiant fields of low-cost oil are discovered in largely unexplored areas in Iraq and the South China Sea, both problematic at this time, extraction costs will keep rising as exploration and development of oil fields take place in more inhospitable and remote and challenging locations.[11] The higher degree of offshore drilling rig sophistication to drill in ever deeper waters vividly attests to the increasing technological challenge of finding new oil fields. Deepwater oil, Canadian syncrude, and oil from fracking are costly. Wells drilled in two miles of sea water and several miles into the sea floor are expensive, as is the process for making syncrude. A well for fracked oil has only a 3-year useful life compared to 20–30 years for wells associated with conventional oil and gas fields. Cessation of drilling wells for fracked oil would cause an incipient fall in output over a 3-year horizon when these wells will be down to residual output. Oil prices would have to rise to cover the cost of fracking new wells. A strong dependence on fracked oil outlaws a return to cheap oil for any extended period of time.

While new oil being added to conventional oil reserves from deep water oil fields, oil shale, and bitumen deposits is more expensive, so is the increased cost of coaxing conventional oil out of the ground relying on tertiary recovery methods. Oil production from legacy oil fields declines over time necessitating drilling of new wells to sustain production. Most legacy oil fields suffer from declining production despite new wells as production inexorably exhausts a resource. Costs add up quickly if tertiary recovery methods are employed to maintain production. When this is coupled with growing demand, and with incremental oil from more costly sources gaining a larger share of the conventional oil pie, higher priced oil is in the cards. But more costly oil slows or depresses economic activity in industrialized nations as individuals pay more for gasoline at the expense of spending less in discretionary spending, a large component of a nation's GDP (70 percent for the US). High-cost oil financially stresses developing nations with little indigenous supplies of oil, which contributes to perennial negative trade balances. Oil may not have peaked, but the impact of higher prices to extract oil affects global economic activity as though oil had peaked. From that point of view, the concept of Hubbert's peak oil if applied to low-cost legacy oil has already occurred. But with the addition of costly sources of oil, physical peaking has been deferred into the indefinite future.[12]

There is another factor that has to be considered in asserting that Hubbert's peak applies to low-cost oil. In large measure, low-cost oil no longer exists. Yes it's true that oil coming out of the ground in the Middle East may cost $20 per barrel or less selling into a world market when oil was $100 per barrel, but that is grossly misleading. OPEC producers have entered into a social contract with their citizens to provide medical, educational, pension, and whatever other benefits that are necessary for a population that is largely unemployed by volition. Many people, certainly not all, feel that it is their prerogative to live off the riches of oil rather than toil for a living. Otherwise what is the point of being a citizen of an OPEC nation? Oil producers have piled on sufficient social obligations to maintain social stability to raise the breakeven price of oil to levels generally in excess of $100 per barrel, as illustrated in Figure 6.3.[13]

The fall in oil prices to about $80 per barrel in November 2014 and to $55 per barrel in December, which continued into 2015, was blamed on a host of plausible explanations, which may or may not have played a role in the fall in oil prices. One was economic doldrums, with supply overwhelming anemic growth in demand. Another was that the decline in oil prices was not so much a change in the relationship between supply and demand, but an intentional act by Saudi Arabia at the instigation of the US to put financial pressure on Putin with regard to the Ukrainian situation. For Saudi Arabia, the real reason for placing financial pressure on Putin was to discourage his support of Assad in Syria. The Russian budget was constructed at $100 per barrel oil, and $60 per barrel oil is enough to create large budget deficits, which has already affected the Russian economy. Interestingly Saudi Arabia's breakeven price is also about $100 per barrel, but their large cash reserves are more than ample to tie them over to better days. Another plausible reason, or rumor, put forth for the price drop was to put financial pressure on Iran, whose breakeven price is $140 per barrel, to cease its nuclear weapons development program. Here both the US and Saudi Arabia had the same objective, but Saudi Arabia is not happy about the US brokering a deal in July 2015 allowing sanctions against Iran to be lifted on what some feel are weak inspection protocols and basically permission for Iran to develop nuclear weapons after a 10-year hiatus. An unintentional consequence for the US encouraging lower oil prices as an oil weapon to achieve geopolitical goals is that the breakeven for US shale oil projects varies from $40 to $150 per barrel, averaging about $80 per barrel.[14] But an $80 per barrel breakeven is misleading as oil frackers do not receive the published price of oil. In North Dakota and other remote areas, frackers may have to pay as much as $10 per barrel for oil to reach the market by rail and pipeline

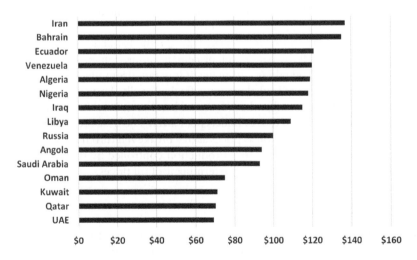

Figure 6.3 Estimated Breakeven of Brent Crude $/Bbl for 2014 Government Budgets

where published oil prices prevail. Their lower netback value effectively prohibits drilling of new wells. By December 2014, companies were already scaling back their plans. When wells being drilled were completed, rig owners were left with inactive rigs and drilling crews laid off, and the economies of towns where oil fracking was active suffered accordingly. This state of affairs will continue until oil prices are restored to former levels, which could happen quickly if a geopolitical event takes place that affects Middle East oil production. Fracking both gas and oil wells is a significant portion of US Capex (capital spending), and cessation of oil fracking for any length of time adversely affects the nation's economic activity. Cessation of drilling new wells will, within 3 years, reduce the entire output of fracked oil to residual levels. If low prices persist this long, and they might if OPEC does not cut back on its production to maintain market share, this will have major financial ramifications on billions of dollars of debt that has been issued in recent years to support fracking and will restore American dependence on imported oil. Both events would please the Saudis. Other ramifications of a prolonged period of low oil prices is increasing the pace of economic distress in Venezuela that could lead to a regime change and quicken the pace of social disintegration in Nigeria. Again, this whole episode demonstrates that the price of oil is not a matter driven by supply and demand, but by the power plays of major producers and behind-the-scene maneuverings of political forces to achieve geopolitical objectives. Saudi Arabia and other OPEC members could have maintained high prices by cutting production, but they chose not to do so. They had to have a reason besides not losing market share since maintaining market share at sharply lower prices hurts their revenue generating capacity. This will worsen with the lifting of sanctions against Iran that will allow Iran to export much more crude, assuming it's capable of doing so. If OPEC does not cut back to accommodate increased Iranian exports, soft oil prices may persist a bit longer than originally contemplated.

One does not have to be too prescient to realize that the days of cheap oil are indeed over and that we've passed Hubbert's peak if the peak is confined to low-cost oil. Even $100 per barrel oil is placing financial pressure on oil regimes to provide all that they had promised to a population that may become restless if promises are broken. In a way OPEC governments are held hostage by their own people to provide an expected level of goods and services or be replaced by other than a comfortable retirement. In this regard, OPEC may have sown the seeds of its own destruction.

American frackers, facing liquidation, have been taking remedial actions to cut the cost of drilling new fracked oil wells by better well placement, improvements to fracking fluid to enhance its effectiveness, and taking advantage of low rates from idle drilling rigs. Moreover they have greatly improved oil flow from fracked wells. Lower capital and operating costs plus greater lifetime oil flow have lowered breakeven costs for fracked oil not in dollars per barrels but possibly in tens of dollars per barrel. The new breakeven cost may determine the world price for crude oil as prices above breakeven turn fracking "on" and prices below breakeven turn fracking "off." Production controlled by throwing the fracking switch could conceivably be the future determinant of oil prices.

Oil Consumption and Production

Figure 6.4 shows that the growth rate in global oil consumption has been in a long-term decline, although it is still positive. US oil demand has been essentially flat since the mid-1990s from lower annual miles driven and better fuel efficiency despite a growing

Figure 6.4 Annual Growth Rate in Oil Consumption

population of motor vehicles. The same is true for Europe including the FSU. Excluding the FSU, European oil consumption has been declining partly as a consequence of Europe's switching from gasoline to diesel as a motor vehicle fuel. Diesel fuel, because of its higher energy content, gets better mileage than gasoline and thus less diesel oil has to be consumed for the same motor vehicle performance. The other reason is economic malaise from stagnating economic growth for a number of years. The world may be nearing an end of a debt cycle where accumulated debts are not spurring, but hampering, economic activity, of which Greece is the poster child. Just as higher energy costs shrink consumer spending, so does debt repayment that can no longer be financed by accumulating even more debt. Japan has also been in a long-term decline with regards to oil consumption, reflecting partly a rapidly growing retired population that may be driving less for economic reasons, an economy also in the doldrums since bubbles in real estate and stock market burst in the late 1980s, and an overburden of debt weighing down on society. On the positive side of the ledger, there has been noteworthy growth in oil consumption in Brazil and in smaller nations in the Middle East and Africa. Without China and India, whose oil consumption growth of 3 percent in 2014 has been much more subdued than in previous years, the rest of Asia's consumption was flat between 2013 and 2014.

The logarithmic trend line best fits the consistent decline in oil consumption since 1965. The average oil consumption growth rate since 2005 is only 1 percent per year. There is no reason why this should change materially in the coming years.

Figure 6.5 shows those nations consuming more than 2 million Bpd. As a group, they are responsible for 60 percent of world consumption. While the US is still the top consumer, China is catching up, but still has a long way to go to challenge the US position. Japan is consuming less oil, and India is consuming more and may overtake Japan as the third largest oil consuming nation, but it has a ways to go. Germany and South Korea have steady consumption, but others have an increasing appetite for oil.

Two major oil exporters, Saudi Arabia and Iran, are now among the top consumers. Increased domestic consumption affects export capacity. This reflects a problem common

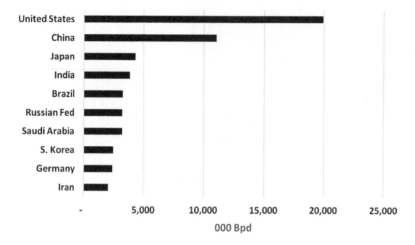

Figure 6.5 Major Oil Consuming Nations over 2 MmBpd

to all oil exporters in that their populations believe that they have the right to pay a low price for motor vehicle fuels. While perfectly understandable, particularly when most of the population is poor, the consequence has been rapid growth in domestic consumption at the expense of a nation's export capacity. Measures have been undertaken to increase the domestic prices of motor vehicle fuels in a number of oil exporting nations, but popular opposition and resentment have prevented any meaningful success.

Figure 6.6 shows the top 13 oil producing nations, who in the aggregate are responsible for 72 percent of global production. The top three nations, the US, Saudi Arabia, and Russia, dominate the producers and are responsible for 38 percent of global production. Canada and Mexico direct their exports to the US. While the OPEC share of global production is 41 percent, in the aggregate, OPEC production has exhibited little growth since 2005.

Figure 6.7 shows the "race" for the top contender as global crude oil producer. Saudi Arabia reached its low point as a producer in 1985 as the world's sole swing producer, but has managed to recoup its standing as one of the world's most important oil producers. Russia shows the debilitating impact on its economy with the breakup of the Soviet Union, but has also recouped its role as being a major world producer. The US was in a long-term decline from matured conventional oil fields. Figure 6.7 clearly shows the emergence of "Saudi America"! A previous forecast of US production reaching 10 million Bpd by 2015 and then leveling off was broached in 2013 with no hint of leveling off until the oil price collapse stopped further fracking of new wells in late 2014.[15]

In 2014, the US took first place by a smidgeon and it is problematic how long it can hold first place. With the cessation of fracking new oil wells, production did not decline immediately as partly completed wells were brought on line and improvements were made to increase flow from existing wells. However, it is felt that production peaked in April 2015, but an EIA forecast calls for declines of a relatively modest 200,000 Bpd per year for the next 2 years. Still this is enough for the US to lose its tenuous hold on first place.[16]

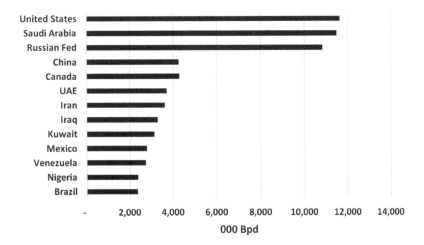

Figure 6.6 Major Oil Producing Nations

Oil Trade Patterns

Table 6.3 shows the net export/import status of major regions of the world.[17] North America is made up of the US, an importer, and Canada and Mexico, exporters primarily to the US. While the US, Canada, and Mexico export to other nations, on balance, North America is a net importing region that has grown less dependent on imported oil with the advent of oil fracking. Europe including the FSU is a small net oil importing region, meaning, presumably, that FSU oil and North Sea oil remain within the FSU and Europe. This is not true, as Russia exports oil to many nations including pipeline and rail shipments to China plus Black and Caspian Sea oil by tankers via the Turkish Straits.

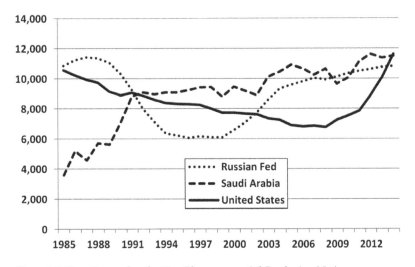

Figure 6.7 Top Contenders for First Place among Oil Producing Nations

Table 6.3 Net Export/Import Status of World's Major Regions in 2014 (mmBpd)

Region	Production	Consumption	Net Exporter	Net Importer
North America	18,721	22,481		3,760
Europe + FSU	17,198	17,576		378
South America	7,613	6,861	752	
Asia Pacific	8,324	29,713		21,389
Middle East	28,555	8,383	20,172	
Africa	8,263	3,659	4,604	

North Sea oil is also exported to non-European nations. But these exports have to be matched by imports; so on balance, there is a small volume of net imports. The Asia Pacific is by far the largest oil importing region strongly dependent on the Middle East and Africa. Africa is an important source of oil for importers, whereas South America is actually a minor participant in international trade because much of its production is consumed domestically.

Future trading patterns will be affected by changes in where oil is produced and consumed. Total world oil production is expected to rise from 87.2 million Bpd (mmBpd) in 2010 to 97.6 mmBpd in 2020 or about a gain of 1 mmBpd per year or 1.1 percent per year.[18] Of this 10.4 mmBpd gain in production, the largest incremental contributor was originally assessed to be North America at 6.6 mmBpd, with the Middle East incrementally contributing only 2.8 mmBpd, which is quite low on a historical basis, and West Africa, Russia, China, and Brazil each contributing between 0.5 and 0.7 mmBpd. Of course, this study assumed that fracking would continue to grow; that is, oil prices would remain around $100 per barrel. Soon after this study was released, oil prices plummeted and North America oil production will at best level off, and more realistically decline. This will place the Middle East back in the driver's seat. This forecast was decimated by events soon after it was published. This is by no means a criticism of the forecast, but an illustration of the difficulty faced by forecasters in contemplating the future. The lesson here is that the best laid plans of forecasters often go awry by exogenous and unanticipated "wild cards," here the halving of oil prices.

From a consumption point of view, the greatest gains between 2010 and 2020 will be non-OECD Asia at 6.7 mmBpd, led by China at 3.8 mmBpd, the Middle East at 1.7 mmBpd, which affects export availability, South and Central America at 0.9 mmBpd, led by Brazil at 0.5 mmBpd, and North America at 0.8 mmBpd, with declining consumption in Europe and Japan. Assuming that these consumption figures hold for a lower price of oil, in examining Table 6.3, changes in the export/import matrix by 2020 would be increasing imports by the North America, self-sufficiency for South America, and increasing imports by the Asia Pacific, most of which will be coming from the Middle East with some from Africa.

Logistics of Oil

Although one may think otherwise, world oil trade patterns are not exclusively based on shortest distance to minimize shipping costs. A good example of this is Venezuela that once shipped all its oil to the US Gulf for processing, its most logical market not only in terms of distance, but also in the presence of refineries built to handle heavy sour

Venezuelan crude. In recent years, Venezuela has elected to sell as much of its crude to Asia as possible, halfway around the world, for political reasons, tempered by the fact that Venezuela owns refinery capacity in the US that has to be supplied with crude oil. Thus, the US must find another source, which, by definition, is going to be further afield than Venezuela. Tanker owners profit when Venezuela shifts its market from 2,000 miles away to 12,000 miles and when the US loses a source 2,000 miles away and must find another such as Brazil or Africa more than double the distance away.

In addition to the loss of Venezuelan crude as refinery feedstock, another problem has emerged that complicates the operations of the US Gulf refineries and has a direct bearing on logistics. Unlike other nations, the US prohibits export of crude oil, but permits export of refined products. US Gulf refineries are forced to process light sweet Bakken crude because this is the only way to dispose of excess Bakken crude since it can't be exported, although its refined oil products can. The logical solution would be for the US to export Bakken light crude and import heavy Middle East crude for its Gulf coast refineries. Another logical solution would be to build the Keystone XL pipeline to increase the flow of heavy Canadian oil sands crude to Houston for processing rather than importing heavy crude coupled with exporting Bakken crude. Of course, these logical solutions cannot be accomplished with a policy of prohibiting crude oil exports and opposing the Keystone XL pipeline. Still another logical solution would be to permit export of Canadian crude from Houston, but this is not possible because the ban on oil exports from the US does not distinguish between US and Canadian crude. Canadian crude was not available as export crude when the regulations were put in place. The Energy Department is mulling a policy change that would permit export of Canadian crude from Houston if it can be demonstrated that Canadian crude has been kept segregated from US crude at every stage of transport and storage, which would not be easy to do.

But logical solutions cannot be carried out when opposed by a regulatory authority set up to administer a law written four decades ago. Yet the economic imperative cannot always be ignored by a regulatory authority. In the latter 1990s and mid-2000s, individual cargoes of Alaska crude were permitted to be exported to Japan and South Korea in response to a glut of crude on the US west coast that depressed prices. Exports stopped when declining Alaska crude production could be absorbed by west coast refineries at an improved level of profitability.[19] This certainly set a precedent for permitting exports of Bakken crude. In 2014 the Energy Department granted permission for the export of a few cargoes of condensate. Fracking for oil and gas produces more natural gas liquids (NGLs) and condensate than needed and exports were necessary to address accumulating surpluses. Separating condensates from crude was deemed "refining" in order to classify condensates as a refined product that could be exported. Some oil industry observers believe that permission being granted in 2014 for the export of a few condensate cargoes may be a harbinger to a fundamental change in policy, which would require Congressional action, to permit crude oil exports. Or the law can remain intact with the Energy Department easing administrative requirements to get permission or licenses to export crude oil cargoes such as occurred for the export of Alaska crude. Or perhaps this isn't even necessary, as a tanker left Galveston, Texas, with a 400,000 barrel cargo of crude oil bound for South Korea, the first unrestricted export of crude oil in four decades.[20] A study published by the General Accountability Office opined that the impact of crude oil exports would initially increase the price of US crude oil from a greater interaction between domestic and higher priced international crude oils. The resulting increase in supply from enhanced US oil production would ultimately put pressure on crude oil prices with a concomitant decline in the prices of oil products. The study also concluded that the Strategic Petroleum Reserve, originally established when crude oil imports were at a higher level, should be reviewed. One outcome could be that strategic reserves can be safely reduced and still provide adequate protection to the nation in case of an oil supply interruption given reduced dependence on oil imports.[21] Of course, the halving of crude oil prices would probably affect the conclusions of this study; again, the best laid plans of forecasters and planners often go awry.

Prohibiting oil exports was established four decades ago under President Carter in the 1975 Energy Policy and Conservation Act (EPCA) during a time of declining production and a global oil crisis. This law was partially reversed by President Reagan in the 1980s to permit the export of refined oil exports. A policy adopted four decades ago to prevent oil exports at a time of declining domestic production ill-fits a time of rising production forcing suboptimal performance on both Canadian and American oil producers. Regulations once placed on the books are hard to exorcise even when they become outdated and irrelevant, and distort the smooth functioning of the oil or any market.

Another reason for oil not always being shipped to the closest market is oil security. Importing nations in Asia feel more comfortable not relying solely on relatively nearby Middle East crude to reduce geopolitical risk. For greater security of supply in case of an interruption in Middle East exports, China and India have purchased more distant crude from Nigeria, Angola, and Venezuela. Any differentials in delivered costs between Atlantic basin crude and Middle East crude are treated as an insurance premium for risk mitigation in case of an interruption of Middle East supply. However, China and India buying Atlantic basin crude oil backs out Middle East crude from the Asia market. Displaced Middle East crude must now be shipped from the Pacific to Atlantic basins to compensate for the Atlantic to Pacific basin oil movement. Tanker owners profit by moving crude cargoes from the Pacific to Atlantic basins coupled with crude cargoes from the Atlantic to Pacific basins.

Another reason for not shipping to the closest market is that exporting nations do not want to rely on a single market and few customers simply because they're close-by. Most oil exporting nations attempt to diversify customers in order to prevent any single customer from having enough clout to demand special price concessions or protect against the repercussions of a major customer bolting to another supplier. Having a greater number of customers or buyers, not necessarily close, mitigates risk of overreliance on one or just a few customers. Again tanker owners profit when oil exporters cast their eyes further afield to diversify buyers.

Netback Analysis

While the nearest source of oil may offer logistics savings, it may not optimize a refinery's financial performance. Logistics is just one element of netback analysis where refiners attempt to maximize profit. Netback values start with the FOB (free on board) price of crude at the oil exporter's terminal. The crude market is diverse, with different crude oil markers having unique pricing structures. For instance, the FOB price of Arab heavy is less than North Sea light because of its inferior product yield and greater refining challenge and more remote location at least for Atlantic basin refiners. The next step in arriving at netback values is to calculate the CIF (cost, insurance, and freight) of crude at the refinery terminal. The cost of logistics (shipping) is not as straightforward as one might expect because the nearest source may not have the lowest shipping cost. A nearby source that relies on smaller sized tankers because of water depth and terminal capacity restrictions at the loading port may not offer the lowest shipping cost compared to a crude exporter further afield who can utilize much larger sized tankers that offer significant economies of scale that lower shipping costs.

CIF netback value is still insufficient to select the optimal source of crude oil. Each refinery has a different yield and output depending on the crude oil grade and type where grades are generally variations within a particular crude oil type or mix of crude types.[22] Strictly speaking, crude oil is not truly fungible because refinery yield varies with crude oil types. Hence the value of each crude type depends on the processing capabilities of refineries. Heavy sour crude usually sells at a discount from light sweet crude because of its lower yield of high-end products and added refining complexity. Changes in the spread between the price of light sweet crude and heavy sour crude reflect their relative desirability by global refiners. Moreover, spreads between various refined products also play a role in selecting the appropriate crude. A higher refinery spread for gasoline over diesel would work in favor of a greater demand for light crudes at the expense of heavy crudes. Hence the optimal choice of crude type determined by netback analysis depends on market prices for various refined products, refinery yield for each crude type, shipping cost from the oil exporter, and the oil exporter's FOB crude oil price. This calculation would hold for a simpler designed refinery. Merchant refineries are more sophisticated with various modes of operation that affect yield even for the same crude type. Variable costs associated with different modes of refining should also be part of the netback calculation. For instance, the choice of whether to operate a coker affects refinery yield, and a coker's associated variable cost should also be incorporated into netback analysis.

Changing Nature of US Oil Imports and Middle East Exports

Figure 6.8 shows crude oil sources satisfying US demand. In 2013, domestic production made up 51 percent of total supply (up from 46 percent the previous year), with nearly 59 percent of imports from the Western Hemisphere. In 2014, domestic production made up 56 percent of total supply, with 63 percent of imports from the Western Hemisphere. Further increases in US and Canadian oil production will come at the expense of imports from Europe (North Sea), South America, Africa, and the Middle East. As mentioned earlier, outflow of oil from the Atlantic basin (primarily West Africa and Venezuela) exceeds US imports from the Middle East by a 2:1 margin. Diversion of the outflow can easily substitute for Middle East imports when this is vital to the continued functioning of the US. (An adaptation of the Monroe Doctrine to forbid Atlantic basin exports enforced by a couple of destroyers stationed off the Cape of Good Hope in South Africa would do the trick!)

Figure 6.9 shows Middle East exports in 2014. Eighty percent of Middle East exports of 19 million Bpd were to Asian destinations ("Other Asia" includes Taiwan, Thailand, Malaysia, and the Philippines) and 10 percent each to North America and Europe (in the 1970s, 70 percent of Middle East exports were destined to the Atlantic basin and the remainder to the Pacific basin). Reducing exports to North America in the coming years, if oil prices rise to a level to support fracking of new wells, along with slowly declining

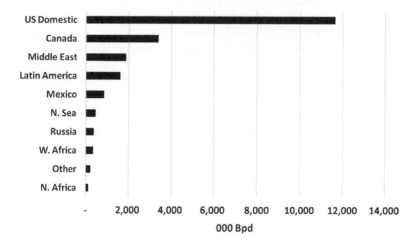

Figure 6.8 Sources to Satisfy US Oil Demand

oil consumption in Europe possibly accompanied with greater oil imports from Russia, will make the Middle East even more dependent on Asian buyers.

The $2.2 trillion spent on ultimately unsuccessful US military adventures to "stabilize" the Middle East cannot be justified by our dwindling dependence on Middle East oil, which, in any event, can be replaced from Atlantic basin crude oil sources if necessary. Nor can it explain why the true beneficiaries of Middle East crude exports contributed just about nothing for the US to essentially guarantee their oil supply. Rising Middle East turmoil possibly as a consequence of the US withdrawing its forces from the Middle East will affect Asia's energy security much more than the US. This being the case, why didn't China, Japan, India, Korea, and other nations shoulder a part of the responsibility to maintain political stability in the Middle East? Will they step up to the plate if the US withdraws possibly unilaterally from the Middle East? Maybe noninvolvement is a better

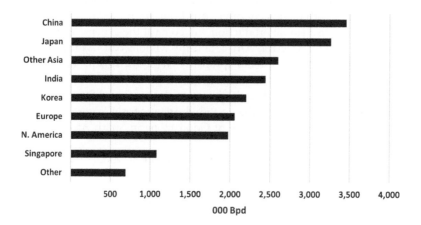

Figure 6.9 Middle East Oil Exports (mmBpd)

approach considering the outcome of military intervention, but doing nothing isn't much of a government policy for major oil consumers whose economies would collapse if not fed by a steady flow of Mideast oil.

Oil Shale—Game Changer

An issue on nomenclature concerning two different sources of hydrocarbons in shale has to be resolved. The first hydrocarbon in shale to be covered is oil in hard shale or oil shale whose reserves shall be called oil shale reserves. The second is kerogen, a primitive form of crude, also found in hard shale, which will be referred to as shale oil and shale oil reserves. In practice, these terms are used interchangeably, which can be confusing. Here, oil shale and oil shale reserves or resources refer to crude oil in hard shale, whereas shale oil and shale oil reserves refer to kerogen in hard shale. Oil shale can be refined directly, whereas shale oil (kerogen) must be further processed before being fit as a synthetic crude for refinery operation.

Fracking is a game changer. It was developed in the US as a means to increase natural gas production; and for this reason, the development and discussion of fracking will be covered in the next chapter on natural gas. As soon as fracking showed signs of success to coax natural gas out of nonpermeable hard shale and hard sand and any hard non-permeable rock, the same technique was applied to oil. The US is far ahead of the rest of the world in fracking. In 2014 fracking for oil began in Argentina, but other nations are making progress in forming partnerships with oil companies to exploit their oil shale resources. US production of gas in billions of cubic feet and oil in millions of barrels per day since 1990 is shown in Figure 6.10. The age of fracking, defined as when fracking turned the corner to reverse declining domestic production, occurred in 2005 for natural gas and 2008 for oil.

One major advantage of fracking is that it avoids the necessity of drilling explora-tion wells to identify an oil reservoir, which may be no more than a dot on the map, or in any case a very small percentage of the land area of a nation. "Exploration" in fracking requires only the demarcation of an oil bearing geologic formation in terms of

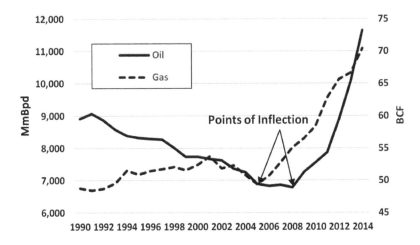

Figure 6.10 Turning Points in US Oil (mmBpd) and Natural Gas Production (BCF)

depth, thickness, and area, which cover thousands or tens of thousands of square miles encompassing large portions of entire states. Some regions within a geologic formation of oil shale may be more prolific than others in hydrocarbon yield and this knowledge is highly valuable for those in the fracking business. Fracking for oil in the US is concentrated in three geologic formations. The largest is the Bakken formation, with oil shale resources estimated to be 14.7 billion barrels located mainly in North Dakota, extending into South Dakota and Montana, and in Saskatchewan province extending into Manitoba.[23] The second largest is the Eagle Ford formation, with 13.6 billion barrels of estimated oil shale resources located in southern Texas extending into Mexico. The third largest is the Permian formation, with 9.7 billion barrels of oil shale resources located primarily in western Texas extending into eastern New Mexico. These three formations total 38 billion barrels or nearly 80 percent of total US oil shale resources of 47.7 billion barrels.[24]

Figure 6.7 shows the impact that fracking has had on US oil production compared to two world oil producers Russia and Saudi Arabia. The trend line is unmistakable—the US was projected to become the world's largest oil producer, but it occurred sooner than expected. A past estimate of US oil production reaching 9.6 million Bpd by 2019 was shattered in 2013 when oil production exceeded 10 million Bpd for the first time since 1987. As domestic production increases, the US becomes more resilient to international oil supply disruptions and oil price shocks.[25] However, cessation of new oil fracking wells will slow or end the upward sweep of the trend line and the US may well lose being in first place. If oil prices ever surge upward again, then the trend line will be restored.

Fracking oil shale is going to have a major impact on many nations.[26] In the US, oil shale reserves increased conventional oil reserves by 130 percent, no small contribution. In oil exporting nations such as Russia and Libya, reserves climbed by 85 and 55 percent respectively. Russia and Ukraine have formed partnerships with oil companies to look into the possibility of fracking, although current hostilities between these two nations have made these projects moot. Moreover, sanctions imposed on Russia by the US because of the political situation in eastern Ukraine have caused two major oil companies, Exxon and Shell, to pull out of high technology oil projects. This left Russian oil companies in the lurch as they were dependent on the technological input from these companies to develop oil in the Arctic and from fracking. In 2014, it was expected that development of these sources would eventually be responsible for as much as 23 percent of Russian domestic production.[27] Argentina, short on conventional oil reserves, has seen its reserves grow by a factor of ten and is already exploiting its tight oil resources. Pakistan, without oil reserves, now has the possibility of producing some oil rather than importing all its oil needs. Figure 6.11 compares oil shale with conventional crude oil reserves for various nations.

China, the second largest world oil importer, may be able to reduce future imports and Indonesia may one day regain its position as an OPEC member by developing their tight shale oil resources. Mexico can maintain its position as a major oil supplier to the US in addition to meeting its own needs by tapping the Eagle Ford formation that does not stop at the US–Mexico border. Mexico has to first clear the way on permitting outside oil companies to participate in fracking activities. In 2014, President Enrique Pena Nieto proposed a Constitutional change that would partially end the state energy monopoly of Pemex by permitting foreign firms to drill in deep water oil fields and frack oil shale to allow

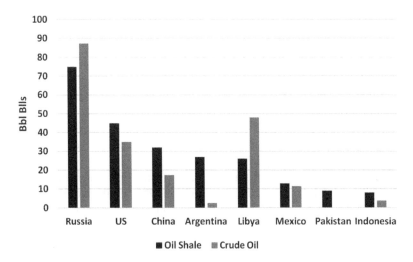

Figure 6.11 Oil Shale versus Conventional Crude Oil Reserves

Pemex to acquire their technical expertise.[28] In August, both houses of Mexico's Congress approved legislation to break the 76-year-old monopoly of Pemex on the oil industry by allowing foreign oil companies to form joint ventures under terms that would involve the sharing of profits with Pemex, with Pemex retaining exclusive rights to 83 percent of proven and probable reserves.[29] In 2015, the first ever auction of shallow water exploration blocks in the Gulf of Mexico had disappointing results when only 2 of 14 exploration blocks were awarded. Part of the problem for the poor results was lower oil prices and Mexico's wariness about ceding control to oil companies in developing these leases. This problem of trust will have to be dealt with before a next round of bidding on deep water leases is scheduled.[30] Like Mexico, nations with large geologic formations containing oil shale require technical expertise that now resides fairly exclusively with US oil companies. Deals will have to be structured to the satisfaction of both host governments and independent oil companies possessing the requisite technical expertise. If these deals can be consummated, oil shale will indeed be a game changer once again if and when oil prices improve above breakeven rates.

Fracking in the US and elsewhere takes on added importance when it is realized that Mexico is not the only oil exporter with declining production. Venezuela's oil industry was crippled when Hugo Chavez fired 18,000 employees in 2003, half the workforce of the state oil company PDVSA, for supporting a strike protesting government interference in internal operations. Many of those fired were managers and key technicians. As a consequence, Venezuelan oil production went into a gradual decline from 3.3 million Bpd in 2003 to 2.7 million Bpd in 2011, which has stabilized since then. Many of the displaced personnel migrated and contributed to production gains in Colombia and Canada.[31] Algeria is another nation suffering from an inexorably slow decline in oil production since 2007 from a fall in exploration activity and lack of investment. Similar to other oil exporters, much of the nation's oil revenues are shunted to support various government social and other type of programs rather than maintaining its oil infrastructure. From past actions, foreign investors are wary of legal enforceability of Algeria's contractual arrangements and lack confidence in the nation's capacity to provide physical security at energy installations. Facing this problem of declining production head-on, Algeria decided to make a major investment in Sonatrach, the state oil company, to augment production and take actions that would make foreign investment more attractive.[32] On the other hand, massive investments in investor-friendly environments such as the UK, Norway, and the US (before fracking) were not able to stem long-term declines in oil output.

Relying on fracking to produce a significant share of world oil production may be problematic. Unlike conventional oil fields that require several dozen new wells per year to sustain production, oil shale may require hundreds of new wells per year or more to accomplish the same. The International Energy Agency estimated that maintaining production in the Bakken geologic formation at 1 million Bpd would require 2,500 new wells each year, while a million Bpd field in Iraq would require 60 new wells per year.[33] At $8 million per well, annual investment to maintain the 1 million Bpd output is $20 billion, possibly more since this degree of activity will probably be reflected in higher costs. Moreover, such high levels of activity may reach constraints in the form of availability of drilling pipe, equipment, and crews. Most projections prior to 2014 showed a leveling-off of fracked oil production after 2020, which may have reflected physical limits to drilling activity. Leveling-off may occur in 2015 as a result of lower oil prices. But if oil fracking does return, fracked oil and gas will continue the trend of oil and gas companies spending more and more money just to stand still.

The reason why such intense effort is needed to maintain production is the short life of a fracked well. About two-thirds of the total lifetime output of a fracked well occurs during the first year and most of the remainder over the succeeding 2 years. Other estimates are less skewed to over half of total production occurring during the first year, but are consistent in that the effective life of the well is over in 3 years with some residual output. Moreover, total output of a fracked well over its effective 3-year life will be far below the average conventional well over its 20–30-year life. Thus oil shale will require a much greater continual investment in new wells with concomitant demand on drilling rigs, drill pipes, and drilling crews than conventional oil. Any leveling-off of fracking activity does not mean that incremental production from fracking will level off, but production will decline after new wells are completed and existing fracked wells rapidly come to the end of their short lives, coupled with continuing decline from oil wells from conventional mature fields. To maintain oil production where fracked wells are the main contributors, the number of fracked wells must increase in time as fracked oil must also substitute for declining conventional oil. Fracked wells beget fracked wells! It may be that the ultimate constraint is the availability of fresh water required to frack new wells. Present activity has been estimated to be consuming 2 or more percent of US fresh water supply. Moreover a nation with a strong dependence on oil shale will eventually have its countryside littered with abandoned fracked well sites unless multiple wells are drilled from the same site over succeeding years. The cost of plugging abandoned wells along with the cost of rebuilding roads and bridges worn out by untold thousands of trucks filled with water and equipment is another unfunded cost along with damage to water tables and possibly even the ultimate disposal of used fracked water.

Another factor to be taken into consideration is that there have already been enormous reductions as high as 90 percent of oil shale reserves once wells were drilled and the geologic nature of the tight shale was better understood, as had occurred in Poland, Romania, China, and the US (Monterey). If we assume that the best sites are exploited first, then there may be a case of diminishing returns in terms of oil output as the industry is forced to move into less promising formations (of course, this does not rule out the discovery of "sweet" finds where the shale has a higher concentration of hydrocarbons that can be more easily removed). Moreover there have been improvements in oil technology to extract more fracked oil per well from a given geologic formation.

As previously mentioned, another consequence of depending on fracked oil for a meaningful portion of crude oil needs is that any fall in the price of crude oil sufficient to stop fracking activities will see oil production plummet in the subsequent 3-year period. Fracked wells will actually transform oil production to a variable much as a nozzle on a water hose. Today's oil production from conventional oil fields can be likened to a water hose without a nozzle since most wells operate close to capacity most of the time. A rapid falloff in fracked well production assures that low crude prices cannot last for long. Fracked oil production is quite literally a nozzle that is rapidly throttled down if crude prices cannot sustain drilling new fracked wells. A strong dependence on fracked wells means the end of low oil prices for an extended amount of time. In fact, strong and growing dependence on fracked wells may mean even higher oil prices to financially sustain wells being drilled in less promising tight rock formations.

Despite the glow over the prospects of fracking, there are those who are warning that fracking may not be the full solution to avert a future oil supply crunch. While US production climbed at an average of 1.3 million Bpd per year between 2012 and 2014, world consumption expanded by an average of 1.6 million barrels per day over the same time period. Saudi Arabia, the home of world spare capacity, is operating at nearly full capacity along with the United Arab Emirates and Kuwait to make up for shortfalls from other OPEC members such as Libya, Nigeria, and Iran, non-OPEC Syria and Sudan, plus declining production in a number of other nations. Growing geopolitical risk that threatens to disrupt Middle East exports may require more spare production capacity than is available for risk mitigation purposes.[34] The possibility of Iran returning to the oil market would help to mitigate the risk of a production shortfall. If supply cannot keep up with demand, chaos will break out in the oil patch and the public will experience skyrocketing oil prices that can easily set off an economic downturn.

Synthetic Crude

Oil shale is considered nonconventional in the sense that it does not come from a traditional or conventional oil field, but from a geologic formation covering thousands of square miles. Oil from oil shale can be fed directly into a refinery. Shale oil is another nonconventional source of oil in that its source is not a conventional oil field, but a geologic formation of hard shale or other hard (impermeable) rock containing kerogen, a precursor to the formation of crude oil. Kerogen must be processed to produce an acceptable grade of crude oil before it can be fed into conventional refineries. This makes shale oil a synthetic crude oil, or syncrude. At this time the only major source of commercially available synthetic crude is bitumen; shale oil will have to wait for further technological development before being economically feasible. However, both bitumen and shale oil possess the potential of becoming major sources of crude oil in the future.

Bitumen

Major bitumen deposits are in Canada, Venezuela, and Russia. Bitumen is a thick, sticky form of crude oil, sometimes called extra heavy oil, with the consistency of molasses; too viscous to flow in a pipeline unless mixed with a light petroleum liquid diluent such as condensate, naphtha, or propane, which can be recycled. Bitumen is the end result of the burial of partially decayed marine organisms several miles into the Earth, which when transformed to light hydrocarbons began their migration back to the Earth's surface. If impeded by an impermeable layer of cap rock, hydrocarbons would become conventional oil and gas fields. If not impeded, hydrocarbons continue to lose their light ends through evaporation and emerge on the Earth's surface as seep oil. Bitumen is seep oil, viscous and impregnated with a high sulfur and metals content picked up during migration. Bitumen must be upgraded to syncrude before being fit for processing by a conventional refinery.

These undesirable traits are offset by enormous deposits of bitumen, currently estimated to be 1.2 trillion barrels in Venezuela alone compared to known world reserves of conventional oil of about 1.4 trillion barrels net of Venezuelan and Canadian inclusion of bitumen in their oil reserves. Venezuelan bitumen nearly doubles global conventional oil reserves if it were entirely recoverable. The mind boggles over the quantity of hydrocarbons that had to start their migration to become trillion barrel deposits of bitumen on the Earth's surface considering the loss of light end hydrocarbons through evaporation.

Bitumen deposits in Venezuela are located in the Orinoco region, lie on the surface, and unlike Canada are relatively free of contamination other than sulfur and metals. To commercially tap this resource, Venezuela originated a product called Orimulsion, a mix of 30 percent water and 70 percent bitumen, sold to utilities as a coal substitute. Orimulsion turned out to be easy and safe to produce, transport, handle, and store as a liquid. It had good ignition and combustion characteristics, and coal burning utilities could easily convert from solid coal to liquid Orimulsion carried in oil tankers. However, there were no environmental benefits in burning Orimulsion over coal in terms of sulfur and metals emissions. Many felt that Orimulsion had a bright future, but it turned out that mixing bitumen with a particular Venezuelan light crude formed a blend that could be processed by refineries designed for heavy sour crude, entirely voiding the necessity of syncrude treatment plants. Thus the value of bitumen improved in 2004 from being related to coal at $4–$5 per barrel to being related to heavy sour crude at $30 per barrel.[35] This erased the economic incentive to continue producing Orimulsion other than honoring existing contracts.[36]

Transforming bitumen to a heavy grade crude oil by simply mixing with a light crude also eradicated the economic basis of syncrude plants in Venezuela. These had the advantage over Canadian syncrude plants in that Venezuelan bitumen could be mixed with naphtha or another light hydrocarbon to reduce its viscosity for pipelining to a syncrude plant. There the light hydrocarbon was recovered and pipelined back to the bitumen deposit for recycling. The costs of getting bitumen to a syncrude plant and preparing it for processing were far less in Venezuela than in Canada where bitumen is mixed with sand (only 12 percent of Canadian oil sands is actually bitumen).

Venezuela had entered into four grassroots joint ventures with foreign oil companies, but eventually these plants were taken over by Venezuela without due compensation to investors. Having scared off further foreign investment by oil companies, Venezuela began courting China and Iran as potential investors in new syncrude production facilities, but neither nation seemed anxious to consummate a deal. Then Venezuela discovered that mixing bitumen with a light grade of crude produced a heavy sour crude, called Merey 16, which could be refined in traditional refineries built for heavy sour crude oil.[37] Refineries that handle heavy sour crude in politically safe locations can take advantage of Venezuela's enormous reserves of bitumen and avoid the risk of investing in Venezuela. The impact of Merey 16 on Venezuela's syncrude plants regardless of ownership amply demonstrates both the geopolitical and technological risks of investing in oil projects. Availability of light sweet crude in Venezuela should cap the amount of bitumen counted as reserves.

In Canada, huge volumes of oil migrated horizontally and vertically through more than 70 miles of rock without entrapment by anticlines or faults, preventing the formation of oil reservoirs. Seep oil emerging on the surface mixed with sand and some clay became a feast for microorganisms that transformed it into bitumen. It is estimated that bacteria consumed between two and three times the present volume of bitumen, an incredible amount of seep oil when one considers that what was originally called tar sands, now oil sands, hold about 1.8 trillion barrels of bitumen, significantly more than the bitumen deposits in Venezuela. This implies that the original source rock generated 3–5 trillion barrels of oil, enormous when compared to the volume of about 1 trillion barrels of oil consumed since Drake's discovery in 1859. That amount of hydrocarbons required a whole lot of ocean plankton, algae, and other forms of simple marine life to die and settle to the bottom in oxygen-starved waters and be buried by miles of sediment in a single province of Canada before it could start its migration back to the surface: a phenomenon that must surely tax one's imagination about the biotic origin of oil.

As a recoverable resource using present technology, Canadian oil sand is equivalent to 168 billion barrels of crude oil reserves, somewhat less than the 266 billion barrels of proven oil reserves in Saudi Arabia. More recent estimates are greater—between 178 and 315 billion barrels, higher than Saudi Arabia's reserves.[38] These estimates are based on a price of crude oil high enough to financially justify the capital investment and operating costs of current technology. With improved technologies and higher prices for crude oil, reserves can be significantly expanded, hypothetically, even up to total reserves of 1.8 trillion barrels. And higher prices are necessary to keep developing oil sands. In 2009, syncrude plants required about $30 per barrel to construct and sustain operations, more recent and more costly plants $60 per barrel, whereas new grassroots oil sands projects require $80–$90 per barrel to justify their investments. Much of this increase has to do with rising labor and equipment costs, reflecting a dollar of ever diminishing value compensated by improvements in technology that increases efficiency and reduces operating costs. Further technological advances could considerably raise the estimated amount of recoverable oil. Improvements in technology coupled with higher oil prices are responsible for the growing volume of syncrude production of 0.8 million Bpd in 2003, 1.2 million Bpd in 2008, and 2.1 million Bpd in 2013 (up 8 percent from 2012), and projected to be 4.1 million Bpd by 2023.[39] Higher estimates of production outputs are 4.9 million Bpd in 2020 and 6.7 million Bpd in 2030.[40] But these estimates will not be achieved as long as oil prices remain below the $80–$90 per barrel breakeven rate.

Athabasca deposit in Alberta is the world's largest oil sand deposit, containing about two-thirds of Canadian bitumen resources. Oil sand containing about 12 percent bitumen by weight is mined similar to the surface mining of coal. Overburden is first removed and stockpiled for future reclamation after cessation of strip mining operations. Superficially reclamation sounds desirable, but environmentalists point out that not only does mining operations scar the land surface as in strip mining coal, but also destroys the aboriginal peat bogs, a carbon dioxide absorption medium, that cannot be restored to its original condition by land reclamation.

At the present time, Canadian oil sands production depends largely on giant mining shovels working 24–7 filling huge trucks with 360–380 tons of oil sand for transport to an upgrading plant.[41] But strip mining has its limits as a means to mine oil sands. To gain access to deeper deposits of oil sands beyond the reach of strip mining, which comprise 80 percent of oil sand resources, two *in situ* (Latin for "in place") methods are currently in use. One is called cyclic steam stimulation (CSS) where directional wells are drilled and injected with high pressure steam to melt surrounding bitumen. A well switches to a production mode of operation when melted bitumen enters a well and is pumped to the surface. Environmental safeguards prevent hydrogen sulfide emissions, a poisonous gas, from escaping to the atmosphere. When production slows, a repeat cycle of "huff and puff" or CSS melts another batch of bitumen. The second method is called steam assisted gravity drainage (SAGD), which involves two parallel horizontal wells drilled from the same well pad with one well above the other. Steam injected in the top well melts bitumen that flows to the lower well by gravity and is pumped to the surface. Both CSS and SAGD are replacing strip mining and will be utilized to a much greater extent as oil sands are removed from the surface.[42] This will reduce some of the negative environmental impact of strip mining.

After mining and transporting to an extraction plant, oil sand is crushed and mixed with hot water and then sent to a large separation vessel where sand falls to the bottom and bitumen, entrapped in tiny air bubbles, rises to the top as froth. The froth is then skimmed off, mixed with a solvent, and spun in a centrifuge to remove residual water and sand. Water and sand residue, called tailings, are placed in a settling pond where the remaining bitumen is skimmed off the surface. Sand mixed with fresh water is returned to the mine site by pipeline to fill in mined-out areas. Water residue from separating bitumen from oil sand is pumped to a settling pond for recycling. Recycling minimizes the undesirable consequences of releasing water to the environment, recovers over 90 percent of bitumen in sand, and reduces the amount of water needed to support oil sand operations.

Extracted bitumen is ready for upgrading to synthetic, or processed, crude with a density and viscosity similar to conventional heavy crude oils. Upgrading involves removing carbon and sulfur and adding hydrogen. Coking removes carbon atoms from the large, carbon-rich hydrocarbon chains, breaking them up into shorter and more valuable chains. Hydrotreating removes sulfur from the hydrocarbon chains, which is sold to fertilizer manufacturers. Hydrocracking adds hydrogen to hydrocarbon chains to increase the yield of light end products when syncrude is refined in a conventional refinery. Processed syncrude is mixed with condensate as a diluent for pipelining to a refinery where condensate is refined along with crude oil to further enhance the yield of light end products.

Syncrude production from oil sands requires a lot of natural gas, as a source of condensate diluent, to heat up bitumen and water mixture for separation, and to supply hydrogen for hydrocracking and hydrotreating, and energy to generate steam for CSS and SAGD extraction of bitumen. A great deal of water is used for separating bitumen from sand and in pumping spent sand back to the mine site. While water can be recycled up to 17 times, its residue is a black foul liquid collected in tailing ponds. Care has to be exercised that this contaminated liquid does not escape to the environment. Thus enormous reserves of bitumen are ultimately dependent on the availability of water, a naturally replenishable resource up to a point, and natural gas, a wasting resource. Syncrude production creates value for stranded gas without access to a commercial market. With a pipeline that can move natural gas to markets in Canada and the US, the issue then becomes whether to consume natural gas locally for syncrude production or sell as commercial pipeline natural gas to the Lower 48. A natural gas provider can play one buyer off another to get a better price, whereas a provider of stranded gas is in the unenviable position of negotiating with a single buyer. The price paid for natural gas, whether stranded or with an alternative market, affects the cost of syncrude. In terms of the environment, natural gas consumed in producing syncrude and treating oil sand, plus the energy consumed in mining and transporting bitumen to the syncrude treatment plant, significantly increases the carbon emissions of gasoline made from Canadian oil sands over traditional crude oil when these activities are included in the carbon footprint. The Obama administration is not a proponent of gasoline from syncrude because of this marked increase in its carbon footprint compared to gasoline made from conventional oil. This is why permission to build the Keystone XL pipeline has not been forthcoming.

Alberta's 166 billion or more barrels of proven reserves are surface oil sands that can be strip mined or tapped by "huff and puff" steam methods of removal. This still represents only a small fraction of bitumen deposits. To improve the effectiveness of recovery of deep oil sands deposits, various proposals have been made such as drilling a deep well and igniting oil sand at its bottom controlled by air injection. Burning oil sands deep underground heats up surrounding bitumen to allow flow to the surface via producing wells. Another idea is pumping a solvent into the oil sands such as propane that absorbs bitumen. The mixture of solvent and bitumen is separated at the surface for recycling of the solvent. Still another idea is to force hot, high pressure air into oil sands to heat crude so that it can flow to the surface. Another extraction possibility is a series of wells filled with electrodes for melting the surrounding bitumen that is then collected in a nearby production well. Still another envisions insertion of a hot vaporized solvent that dissolves the bitumen, which not only flows more easily to a production well, but also enhances the efficiency of extracting bitumen from sand. It is possible that this method may partially refine bitumen by the time it emerges at the surface, reducing the effort involved in synthetic crude treatment. The development of *in situ* refining would be a great boon to this industry if bitumen comes to the surface as a relatively sulfur-free fuel oil. Fuel oil can be burned directly for electricity generation or industrial enterprises or be fed into refineries to make light end products. Other research projects are underway with the intent to reduce fresh water usage, improve recovery factors in separating bitumen from sand, enhance energy efficiency, and cut greenhouse gas (GHG) emissions. These research efforts point to the day when Canadian oil sands may play a significant role in satisfying global oil demand with a reduced impact on the environment.

Logistics of Canadian Syncrude

An existing Keystone pipeline operating at full capacity moves Canadian syncrude to Nebraska for connections with other pipelines that can ship crude to Houston. Another pipeline is needed to move the larger quantities of Canadian syncrude being produced. The proposed Keystone XL pipeline will run between the same terminal points, but to the west of the existing pipeline, in order to also transport Bakken oil from North Dakota and Montana to the Nebraska terminal. This will reduce the Bakken producers' dependence on more costly rail transport. The proposed 36-inch pipeline will be nearly 1,200 miles long, capable of pumping 830,000 barrels per day.[43]

Even in the absence of the proposed pipeline, the Canadian National and Canadian Western Railways transported 200,000 Bpd of Canadian crude to US and Canadian refineries in 2013. Unlike Canadian syncrude that requires a diluent (condensate) for pipeline transport, rail tank cars do not contain a diluent as crude is shipped heated in insulated tank cars to assure flow when the train arrives at a refinery. Moreover there are enough insulated rail tank cars under construction to transport 800,000 Bpd of Canadian crude, effectively negating the need for the Keystone XL pipeline.

It is interesting that Canadian crude can be carried into the US on rail tank cars and in existing pipelines, but not in a new pipeline. The proposed Keystone XL pipeline requires US State Department approval since it crosses an international border. This permission has not been forthcoming because of strenuous environmental objections over the carbon footprint of Canadian syncrude oil.[44] Some feel that the environmental case against Canadian syncrude is overstated. One study by the Congressional Research Service concluded that GHG emissions of gasoline made with Canadian syncrude will be 14–20 percent higher than the weighted average of transportation fuels now sold in the US. Based on selected imports, Canadian syncrude would have a carbon footprint that ranges about 9–19 percent greater than Middle East sour crude, 5–13 percent more than Mexican Maya crude, and 2–18 percent higher than Venezuelan crude, depending on the grade and type of crude oil. In addition, steps can be taken to reduce carbon dioxide emissions while processing Canadian syncrude such as collecting and feeding treatment plant carbon dioxide emissions to conventional oil fields for tertiary recovery and potential use of solar and wind as power sources for processing Canadian oil sands.[45] Another report disputed the findings of the State Department on carbon emissions associated with the Keystone XL pipeline because the $3 per barrel projected reduction in crude oil prices from lower logistics costs would induce Americans to consume more oil, resulting in 121 million tons of more carbon dioxide being pumped into the atmosphere, an admittedly small fraction of global carbon dioxide emissions of 36 billion tons. This report again illustrates the fluid boundaries of energy and environmental studies plus the implicit assumption that lower oil prices may be good for the economy but bad for the environment, which really complicates the decision-making process.[46]

The Keystone XL pipeline allows more Canadian syncrude to be processed in the US Gulf region where refineries are adapted to heavy sour crude and allows Bakken oil to be shipped from North Dakota and Montana for processing in the US or possibly for export from the Gulf if permission to export crude oil were granted by the government. Without State Department approval, Canadian syncrude will still flow into the US via existing pipelines, relying on more costly and less environmentally sound railroads. There have been several headline catching train derailments resulting in loss of property and life from exploding and burning tank cars within populated areas. The worst was a runaway train carrying Bakken crude derailing in the Quebec town of Lac-Megantic in July 2013 with the loss of 47 lives from exploding and burning tank cars.[47] Both Canadian and American railroad regulatory authorities are seeking new measures for the quicker phase-out of older tank cars, building of stronger and more crash-resistant tank cars, lowering speeds of tank car trains in populated areas, advanced notification of tank car train transits, and inauguration of comprehensive emergency oil response spill plans.[48] Despite these efforts, in February 2015, a train of 109 upgraded tank cars of Bakken crude derailed in West Virginia. Dozens of tank cars left the tracks and 19 caught on fire filled with light volatile Bakken crude. Explosions and intense fires caused the evacuation of hundreds of families living in the vicinity and the shutdown of two water treatment plants. Luckily no crude spilled into waterways serving the treatment plants.[49] In March 2015, 8 tank cars from a 105 tank car train derailed in Galena, Illinois, where 2 tank cars burst into flames in a non-populated area. Tank cars on this train had been modified to increase rail safety.[50] There were four tank train derailments in the province of Ontario during the first ten weeks of 2015.[51] In May 2015, an oil tank train derailed in Heimdal, North Dakota, where six tank cars burst into flames causing an evacuation of the town.[52] It is quite curious that environmental advocates remain strangely silent on railroad spills and yet remain highly critical of an environmentally safer means of transporting crude by pipeline.

While economics and safety considerations favor pipelines, a drawback is that a pipeline is fixed in location serving only those refineries connected to the pipeline. Railroads serve refineries not connected by pipeline to Canadian syncrude and Bakken crude and can deliver in terms of quantity and timing advantageous to the refiner. Railroads expand the market for oil producers beyond limitations imposed by pipelines. Nevertheless the preferred mode of transporting oil is by pipeline for as far a distance as possible before switching to rail. Alternatives to the Keystone XL pipeline are two Canadian pipeline proposals to move crude from Alberta to Canada's west coast for export of oil sand syncrude to refineries in China.[53] One is a new pipeline (Northern Gateway) to Kitimat, a port in British Columbia. The residents of Kitimat and native First Nations through whose lands the pipeline must pass oppose the project for environmental reasons. Native Americans are taking a more aggressive stand against pipeline and energy projects. The Rosebud Sioux Indian tribe in South Dakota contends that the House vote to approve the Keystone XL pipeline in 2014 violates the 1851 and 1868 Fort Laramie Indian treaties that gave the Black Hills, through which the pipeline would pass, to the Sioux Nation.[54] Some feel that giving Native Americans an economic stake in an energy or pipeline project would be beneficial in gaining their support. The other proposal is the expansion of the capacity of an already existing Trans Mountain pipeline from Alberta to Vancouver, but again environmentalists are out in force over the potential consequences of increased tanker traffic in Vancouver Bay. Shipping Canadian crude to China may not be optimal from the viewpoint of US energy security, but it is not in Canada's economic interests to shut in its oil production by being unable to obtain a pipeline permit from the State Department.

Another pipeline alternative that has a relatively high probability of materializing is to convert an existing natural gas pipeline (Energy East) to move Canadian oil sand crude from Alberta to eastern Canada. A pipeline extension will be built to serve refineries in Montreal, Quebec City, and Saint John (New Brunswick). This alternative would substitute Canadian crude for foreign imports at eastern Canada refineries with any excess crude exported to Europe or even the US.[55] The choice of whether to pipeline crude oil west to reach the market in China or east to reach the market in the Atlantic basin is partly a matter of netback calculations involving crude price delivered to refineries in China or to refineries in eastern Canada, Europe, or the Gulf coast. It is also a matter of dealing with environmental resistance, particularly in western Canada, to pipelines and oil terminals.

Another way around the problem is that prohibition of the US exporting crude oil does not apply to Mexico and Canada. US crude oil exports to Canada are normally associated with refinery balancing when it is more convenient for certain refineries in Canada to import US crude rather than consume Canadian crude. Historically this has been a small volume of about 20,000 Bpd. But in 2014, it was estimated that 200,000 Bpd of US crude would be exported to Canada with a potential of growing to 1 million Bpd over the next few years, including permitted exports of condensate cargoes.[56] Clearly this larger volume of exported US crude to Canada is displacing Canadian crude in its domestic market, which can then be exported. Exporting US crude to Canada for consumption to allow the export of Canadian crude, or exporting US crude to Mexico for consumption to allow the export of Mexican crude, is just another demonstration that oil will reach its market despite obstacles from government bureaucrats. Sidestepping regulatory obstacles increases logistics costs and lowers netback values to Canadian producers, but all have the same environmental effect. The redirection of Canadian oil sand crude from the US to Asia or eastern Canada or anywhere else makes the carbon footprint objection by environmentalists moot: whether extra carbon dioxide is released in Asia or Canada or the US or elsewhere has the same impact on global GHG emissions.

Some years ago, the US prohibited the burning of high sulfur petroleum coke for environmental reasons, reducing its economic value to nil. Cement manufacturers in Korea discovered this cheap source of energy, and purchased, shipped, and burned it in Korea. Sulfur emissions still entered the atmosphere. While the location of combustion had changed, wind patterns assured that the environmental impact would remain unchanged. The same is true for the Keystone XL pipeline—if not built, Canadian oil sand crude will find an alternative market and its environmental impact will remain unchanged. The same cannot be said for energy security if Canadian syncrude is redirected from the US to Asia.

Carbon Footprints

For Canadian syncrude, the larger carbon footprint is directly related to the energy associated with the large volume of natural gas consumed to transform oil sand to synthetic crude oil. But there is a greater carbon footprint for all alternative means of producing petroleum products. Using 1.0 for the carbon footprint of petroleum products made from conventional crude oil, the carbon footprint for petroleum products made from natural gas is 1.1 or 10 percent more carbon emissions; for petroleum products using crude oil requiring enhanced (tertiary) oil recovery 1.2; for petroleum products made from oil sands and heavy oil 1.4; and for petroleum products made from coal 1.9. Thus on the surface, petroleum products from oil sands are 40 percent more polluting in terms of GHG emissions than conventional oil.

However, these values are maximum assessments; petroleum products from oil sands may be only 5–15 percent higher than conventional crude. As discussed earlier, the extent of the energy/carbon envelope in analyzing an alternative is critical. For instance, the carbon footprint of oil sands can be significantly higher if the desolation of peat bogs associated with oil sand strip mining is taken into consideration in terms of future loss of carbon dioxide sequestration.[57] Thus the extent of an energy/carbon envelope in analyzing an energy alternative gives analysts a great deal of leeway to produce desired results. All that can be asked is that the extent of energy/carbon envelopes be as consistent as possible for each alternative. But this may be well-nigh impossible given the diverse nature of approaches and circumstances surrounding energy alternatives, further confounded by any preconceived notions analysts may have with regard to a particular energy source. It is best if analyses of energy/carbon footprints are carried out by neutral parties having no vested interest in outcomes.

Shale Oil

Oil found in hard shale and other rock, called oil shale, is not considered syncrude as no additional processing is necessary to make oil shale acceptable for refinery intake. In fact, oil shale is a light sweet crude ideal for refining. Oil shale should not be confused with shale oil! Oil shale is produced by fracking nonpermeable hard shale and other rocks for its oil content. (Some commentators prefer tight oil as a less confusing descriptive term.) Shale oil is found in shale rock and other hard rocks in the form of kerogen, a primitive form of oil that has not gone through Earth's pressure cooker to become conventional crude oil. Kerogen impregnated rock, found in various parts of the world, must be processed to produce a synthetic crude oil called shale oil before it can be refined into oil products.

Similar to bitumen, the potential supply of shale oil is huge. Five trillion barrels of shale oil exist, of which 4.3 trillion barrels lie mostly in a 16,000 square mile Green River formation in Wyoming, Utah, and Colorado. About three-quarters of this hard impermeable rock, called mari, may be too lean for commercial development given the current state of technology, but this still leaves 800 billion to 1 trillion barrels that could be developed.[58] If this source were developed, this would be another factor responsible for the fading horizon of peak oil. According to the US Geological Survey, there are 24 billion barrels of recoverable oil from oil shale, 19 billion barrels of recoverable oil from tar sands in Utah, 86 billion barrels of recoverable oil in the Outer Continental Shelf, and 800 billion barrels of recoverable oil in the Green River formation. Including other sources of nonconventional oil, the US may have as much as 1.44 trillion barrels of recoverable oil as compared to 44 billion (0.044 trillion) barrels of proven conventional reserves.

If all this can be developed, the fading horizon for oil peaking becomes inconsequential. But this does not make oil peaking a dead subject. Oil peaking of low-cost legacy oil is very much alive and has probably already occurred unless mega-oil fields are discovered in Iraq or the South China Sea, both with unexplored areas large enough to contain undiscovered oil fields of this magnitude. Without such discoveries, legacy oil will become more expensive as greater efforts will be necessary to tease oil out of nearly depleted oil fields. Peaking of high-cost oil, demanding a much greater input of technology and capital, is a long way off.

Other nations with shale oil resources in order of importance are China, Brazil, Morocco, Jordan, Australia, Thailand, Israel, Ukraine, and Estonia. Shale containing kerogen is burned directly for power generation in Estonia. A recent discovery of shale oil near Coober Pedy, a town in southern Australia, may have as much as 200 billion barrels of recoverable oil. However, this shale oil is unusual in that it is not kerogen entrapped in rock, but droplets of crude oil. While still considered shale oil, far less costly fracking techniques could be employed. This find, when developed, would be sufficient to transform Australia from an oil importing to an oil exporting nation.[59]

The traditional approach to shale containing kerogen is mining shale, which is then transported, crushed, and heated to a high temperature (450°C) in the presence of hydrogen to produce a low quality crude oil. The process requires a great deal of water, a commodity in short supply in the western US, plus natural gas as a source of energy to heat shale and be a source of hydrogen. Crushed rock residue takes up more volume than the original rock, presenting a significant disposal problem in the scenic Rockies. The US invested a great deal of money during the oil crisis in the 1970s to commercially develop shale containing kerogen, but to no avail. As promising as shale oil may appear, in a practical sense, the mining of shale does not offer a viable solution to a shortfall in conventional oil production.

For over 30 years, it was thought that this negative outlook would change with Shell Oil's Mahogany Project in northwest Colorado. This project took a different approach to shale oil. Rather than mining shale and then extracting kerogen, electric heating elements were embedded between 1,000 and 2,000 feet below the surface to heat shale rock to 650 to 750°F. Over time, *in situ* refining of kerogen would produce a hydrocarbon mix of about one-third natural gas and two-thirds light high grade oil. A surrounding ice barrier contained hydrocarbons for retrieval by traditional drilling. High grade oil can easily be refined to gasoline, jet fuel, and diesel oil. The process has an EROEI of greater than one; that is, the energy consumed in heating shale rock and maintaining a surrounding ice barrier is less than energy supplied by the resulting hydrocarbons; but, of course, not as energy-efficient as simply drilling for oil. Started by Shell in 1981, the project was abandoned in 2013 primarily because of a sharp reduction of allowable land available for shale oil leasing.[60]

Just when a source of oil that could contain as much as nine times conventional oil is consigned to commercial oblivion, another twist in the road of energy progress restores hope in shale oil. The government of Jordan has entered into an agreement with an Estonian company to build a 540 mW shale-fueled electricity generating plant. Shale is heated in an oxygen-free environment to separate oil and natural gas. Residual kerogen in crushed rock is burned to generate steam to run an electricity generator. Natural gas can also be burned as a power source if necessary or be pipelined to commercial consumers. Synthetic crude can be transformed into diesel and jet fuels. Other companies are taking a serious look at shale oil.[61]

Challenge of Oil: The Automobile

Oil is the fuel of choice for automobiles, trucks, busses, locomotives, aircraft, and ships. Ships' bunkers are the waste or residue of the refining process. While one might be tempted to dismiss ships' bunkers from further consideration in the general scheme of things, bunkers have become a major headache for shipowners. Ships' fuel, or bunkers, is sold at a discount from crude oil since the valuable refined products have been removed. With crude oil at $100 per barrel, and considering the amount of fuel necessary to move a ship in water, bunkers have become the most expensive component in operating a ship. In times of low rates, it is not unusual for much of the freight revenue to be paid directly to bunker suppliers leaving little to support a ship's operational and financial expenses. Suppose that bunkers cost $70 per barrel with crude oil at $100 per barrel. A very large crude carrier can burn, say, 90 tons per day or nearly 600 barrels at 6.5 barrels per ton or $42,000 per day. For comparison purposes, operating costs (crew, insurance, maintenance, supplies, etc.) are about $9,000–$12,000 per day with another $20,000–$40,000 per day for debt financing charges neglecting a return on equity. Thus bunkers, once a small portion of total costs (600 barrels at \$2 per barrel for bunkers or \$1,200 per day pre-1973 oil crisis), made up about half of required daily revenue when sailing with a cargo with oil at \$100 per barrel. Life gets really tough for tanker owners of large crude carriers or other vessel types when freight rates are not sufficient to pay cash costs. In response to this, the latest generation of ships being built by shipyards are more fuel efficient than their predecessors. Motivation for buying these vessels is that fuel savings are so pronounced that they can operate in a weak market, knocking out competition from less efficient vessels.

Bunkers are the "gunk" of the refining process and burning bunkers is a way to get rid of a waste product. Burning bunkers has now been recognized as a major source of pollution, particularly sulfur emissions. Environmental regulations are forcing shipowners to burn low sulfur bunkers in waters surrounding certain regions (the Baltic and North Sea and within 200 miles of US and Caribbean coasts), exacerbating ship operation by markedly increasing bunker costs. In response has been the development of low sulfur and ultralow sulfur bunkers to meet demand.[62] An alternative is to install a scrubber to remove sulfur from engine exhaust, but this increases capital costs. To illustrate the complexity of dealing with environmental issues, calcium sulfates, a chemical product of a scrubber, if dumped into the ocean, contributes to the acidification of the world's oceans. Now the problem is how to deal with calcium sulfates now that exhaust fumes are nearly free of sulfur! As will be discussed in the next chapter, a potential substitute fuel for ships is liquefied natural gas (LNG), which not only opens a new market for natural gas, but also places a burden on refinery operators on how to dispose of a waste product.

Trucks, busses, and railroads consume diesel fuel (distillates) and airlines jet fuel (kerosene). For the most part, automobiles run on gasoline, although Europe has succeeded in inducing a switch from gasoline to diesel fueled automobiles through tax incentives. This is reflected in US refinery output that is 42 percent gasoline and 27 percent diesel oil, whereas OECD Europe is almost the opposite at 19 percent gasoline and 41 percent diesel oil. Seventy percent of US oil production is consumed by transportation. The rest is feedstock for the petrochemical, fertilizer, and pesticide industries, industrial fuel to power machinery and water and pipeline pumps, fuel for agricultural, off-road, lawn and landscaping activities, lubricating oils, kerosene for lighting, power for emergency and backup power supplies, and other miscellaneous needs.

Of the 70 percent of oil dedicated to serving transportation needs in the US, 30 percent is consumed by automobiles and 28 percent by light trucks, which include pickup trucks, minivans, and sports utility vehicles (SUVs), which are nearly all gasoline fueled. Another 22 percent is diesel fuel consumed by medium and heavy trucks, 2 percent for rail, and 1 percent by busses. Jet aircraft consumed 9 percent as kerosene. Remaining transportation fuel is primarily diesel consumed by marine vessels in US waters including tug-barge units on inland waterways, and in operating pipelines (along with natural gas and electricity), a primary form of transport for oil and natural gas.[63]

In the US, petroleum makes up 93 percent of transportation fuel, with alternative fuels making up the remaining 7 percent. An overwhelming percentage of alternative fuels is ethanol, accounting for 6 percent, with compressed natural gas, liquefied petroleum and natural gas, and electricity for the remaining 1 percent. Only Brazil has a higher percentage of alternative fuels in the form of ethanol in its transportation fuels. Europe has some alternative fuels primarily as biodiesel. For the rest of the world, petroleum reigns supreme.

Automobile Population

Henry Ford pioneered the motor vehicle industry in the US in the early 1900s. Even as late as 1950, 76 percent of the world's automobiles of 53 million were registered in the US. Figure 6.12 shows the growth in the world automobile registrations and the decline in the percentage registered in the US.

Figures for the US include automobiles only. The US is unique in that minivans and pickup trucks, used almost exclusively for commercial purposes in other countries and therefore classified as trucks, are commonly for passenger use in the US. Moreover SUVs are classified as trucks and serve almost exclusively as passenger cars. This distorts Figure 6.12 in that the number of automobiles of 121.4 million in 2011 is only about half of the number of motor vehicles in the US of 248.9 million including automobiles, minivans, pickup trucks, and SUVs. Hence about half of US motor vehicles are automobiles and half are minivans, pickup trucks, and SUVs.

Rapid growth of the US automobile population was over before the Second World War. Rapid growth in motor vehicle population after the Second World War first began in Europe (1960–1985), then Japan (1970–1985), afterward in the emerging economies of the Industrial Tigers (Korea, Taiwan, Singapore, and Hong Kong), from there to South America and eastern Europe, and now India and China. Figure 6.13 shows the dramatic shift in the production of automobiles between 2000 and 2011.

Growth in automobile production in China between 2000 and 2011 has been an astounding 1,565 percent followed by 310 percent in India and 85 percent in Brazil. US production has declined by 46 percent along with a relatively minor decline of 14 percent in Japan. Truck production figures over the same period follow the same general trends, with China up 470 percent, India 415 percent, and South Korea 240 percent. Japan is down 30 percent, and the US down 22 percent. Figure 6.14 shows the number of vehicles owned per 1,000 people. US figures include automobiles, SUVs, pickups, and minivans, whereas vehicles for other nations are automobiles only. This assumes pickups and minivans are being used exclusively for passengers, which is not strictly true as pickups and minivans are also used for commercial purposes.

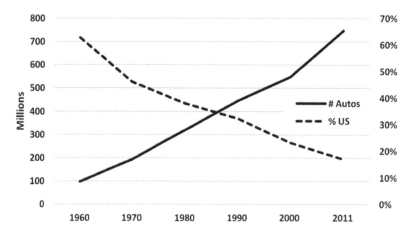

Figure 6.12 World Automobile Population and Percent of US Registered

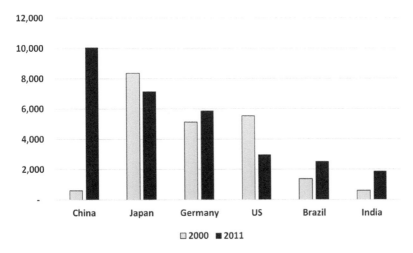

Figure 6.13 Production of Automobiles between 2000 and 2011 (in millions)

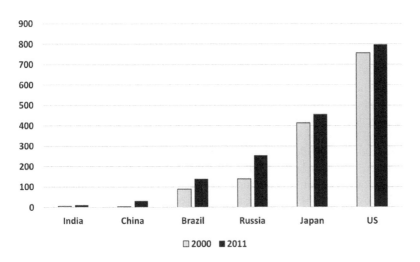

Figure 6.14 Motor Vehicles per 1,000 People between 2000 and 2011

Greatest potential growth in automobile ownership is in China and India. Even though China has tripled the number of motor vehicles per 1,000 people, and India has doubled, the figures are absolutely dwarfed by the number of motor vehicles per 1,000 Americans. Robust growth in per capita motor vehicle growth also occurred in Brazil and Russia, whereas there was modest growth in Japan and the US.

Automobile Miles Driven Per Year

From the point of view of motor vehicle fuels, consumption is keyed to the number of vehicles, miles driven per year, and mileage (miles per gallon). While population of motor

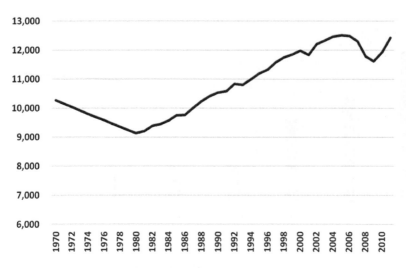

Figure 6.15 Annual Miles Driven Per US Vehicle

vehicles is growing year by year, in the case of the US, annual miles driven per vehicle as shown in Figure 6.15 declined twice before resuming its traditional growth. Miles driven declined during the energy crisis in the 1970s and the economic crisis between 2006 and 2009. Annual miles per vehicle increased up to the time of the 1973 oil crisis, then retreated as a consequence of the economic decline from high oil prices. The extra cost to fill up a tankful of gasoline comes mostly from disposable income, a primary driver of economic activity. Declining annual miles per vehicle continued to 1980 when high oil prices fell precipitously. Economic activity began to pick up as dollars no longer having to be spent filling up the automobile were diverted to consumable goods.

Annual miles driven per vehicle continued to expand until 2007 when the curve turned downward from the economic repercussions of a series of bursting financial bubbles. Individuals who lost their jobs no longer needed to commute to work nor did they have the financial wherewithal to pack up their families for the traditional cross-country summer vacation.

Automobile Fuel Efficiency

The average age of the US automobile fleet was 8.5 years in the mid-1990s, growing to 9 years in 2000, and continuing to increase to 11 years by 2010. This means that automobiles may be built to last longer, but it could also mean that individuals cannot afford to trade automobiles in as frequently as in the past. The same phenomenon can be seen for the light truck fleet (SUVs, pickup trucks, and minivans) except they lag automobiles by about 1 year (average age was 10 years in 2010). This is important because it takes time for a new generation of fuel-efficient automobiles to influence the fuel economy of the entire fleet. Figure 6.16 shows the steady progress that has been made in improving fuel economy since 1975.

There has been substantial private and governmental support to enhance engine efficiency. Increased efficiency has two benefits: better mileage with less pollution. Doubling

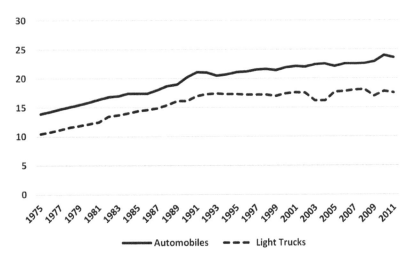

Figure 6.16 Average Miles Per Gallon of US Motor Vehicles

mileage cuts both fuel consumption and pollution emissions in half. Part of the improve-ment has to do with the price of gasoline—when it costs $50 or more to fill up a tank of gas, drivers become concerned over gas mileage. SUVs are extremely popular among Americans, and SUV sales increase as gasoline prices fall, but decrease as gasoline prices rise. There is a direct correlation between sales of gas guzzlers and the price of gasoline. Automobile companies are sensitive to those nuances affecting sales and have been tech-nologically creative in both increasing mileage and cutting pollution emissions.

The other major thrust to greater fuel efficiency are CAFE (Corporate Average Fuel Economy) standards, government imposed mileage standards that automobile manufac-turers must satisfy or face fines. Standards are proposed and administered by the National Highway Traffic Safety Administration (NHTSA), which acts under the authority granted by the Energy Policy and Conservation Act (EPCA), as amended by the Energy Independence and Security Act (EISA).[64] CAFE standards were an overall 18 miles per gallon in 1978, and expanded to 27.5 miles per gallon in 1990 and remained at that level to 2010. These standards are fleet wide, but separate standards exist for various categories of motor vehicles. Thus the number of automobiles for different makes and models is averaged to ensure that the overall standards are met in addition to their specific standards. Allowances are made for foreign built automobiles and automobiles fueled by alterna-tive fuels. The averaging process coupled with special allowances provides automobile manufacturers with an opportunity to sell some gas guzzlers to satisfy this segment of the market by ensuring that sales of fuel efficient automobiles are sufficient for the overall average to comply with CAFE standards. While CAFE standards restrict the number of gas guzzlers that can be built to maintain an overall mileage standard, the point is that they are built. Buyers must pay a gas guzzler tax when purchasing these models that starts at $1,000 for automobiles with a gas mileage between 22 and 22.5 miles per gallon and escalates to $7,700 for automobiles whose mileage is under 12.5 miles per gallon. There are over 80 models of high performance or luxury automobiles that have an associated gas guzzler tax. Despite efforts by CAFE standards to place a lid on allowable mileage, an egregious example of regulatory gamesmanship was reclassifying SUVs from automobiles to light trucks. This allowed automobile companies faced with compliance issues with CAFE standards to satisfy surging demand for SUVs and avoid fines for noncompliance and gas guzzler taxes for buyers.

In 2012 NHTSA and EPA issued joint final rules to further improve fuel economy and reduce GHG emissions for passenger cars and light trucks for model years 2016 through 2025. EPA established national GHG emissions standards under the Clean Air Act where automobiles must achieve a carbon dioxide emission standard of not exceeding 163 grams per mile by 2025. CAFE standards will start at about 38.5 miles per gallon in 2017, growing at about 4 percent annually to about 55.5 miles per gallon (there is a little leeway in the actual CAFE standards depending on which NHTSA forecast of automobile growth turns out to be more applicable).[65] These are overall standards— standards also apply to specific vehicle types. For instance, compact cars with a model footprint of 40 square feet have a 2025 target of 61.1 miles per gallon and carbon dioxide emissions of 131 grams per mile, whereas full size cars of 53 square feet have a target of 48 miles per gallon and carbon dioxide emissions of 170 grams per mile. Standards apply to other automobile size categories and to light duty trucks that include SUVs, minivans, and pickup trucks.

How Can Higher CAFE Standards Be Met?

Over the years improvements have been made to engine and materials technology that provide greater power with less engine mass. Substituting aluminum and plastic for steel has substantially reduced vehicle weight that augments vehicle fuel efficiency. Computer controls also enhance fuel efficiency while reducing emissions. Improvements to automobile efficiency will continue to be made. One recently introduced to the market is Ford's EcoBoost engines, which offer a unique combination of torque, horsepower, performance, utility, durability, and reliability that generates a saving of 20 percent in fuel consumption. Other automobile manufacturers are sure to offer their versions of these more efficient engines to maintain their competitiveness. Added fuel economy makes conventional engines more competitive with hybrids.[66] Another threat to hybrids is the development of advanced diesel engines that can obtain 30 percent better mileage than comparable gasoline engines. Modern diesel engine designs have traded off some power output for improved combustion to reduce soot particles and smog-forming nitrogen oxides. Diesel engines are very common in European automobiles and are one reason why hybrids have not caught on as much as in the US.[67]

Better mileage is an example of diminishing returns. Suppose that a fleet of automobiles has an average mileage of 10 miles per gallon and an improvement is introduced that increases fleet mileage to 12 miles per gallon. Keeping all else constant (the same population of motor vehicles and the same annual miles driven), gasoline consumption will drop by 20 percent. Now suppose that the fleet of automobiles averages 20 miles per gallon and improvements are made to increase the average to 22 miles per gallon. Gasoline consumption now drops by 10 percent, half of what it was before. With the fleet average increasing from 40 to 42 miles per gallon, gasoline consumption would fall by 5 percent. Thus improvements to gasoline mileage, as laudable as they are, will not produce the same impact on gasoline consumption as motor vehicles become more fuel-efficient.

Higher CAFE Standards can be achieved through some combination of improved gasoline and diesel engine design and greater public acceptance of hybrid electric vehicles (HEVs). Since the 1973 oil crisis, the US Department of Energy, through the National Renewable Energy Laboratory, has funded development costs for HEVs to enhance fuel economy and reduce emissions. Honda and Toyota were early entries in offering HEVs to the buying public. HEV sales began in 2000 with 9,400 sold and subsequently climbed to a little over 200,000 by 2005. Annual sales varied between 250,000 and 350,000 from 2005 to 2011. In 2012 sales jumped to 435,000 from positive word-of-mouth advertising by owners who were pleased with their HEVs' performance. This provides confidence for other buyers to purchase hybrids. This upward trend is expected to continue as hybrids become more generally accepted among the buying public, a trend noticed by automobile manufacturers. Thirty-three hybrid models were offered by Acura, Audi, Cadillac, Ford, Honda, Hyundai, Lexus, Lincoln, Mercedes Benz, Porsche, Toyota, and Volkswagen in 2013. In 2014, the number of hybrid models increased to 50.

Hybrids cost more because a large capacity battery is necessary to store electricity for propulsion. Fuel savings of 30–60 or more miles per gallon can justify a higher acquisition cost. These savings vary with each hybrid model and with the underlying assumptions on price of gasoline and annual miles driven to calculate fuel costs. This is then compared to a gasoline powered automobile with similar performance characteristics to obtain fuel savings. The extra financing cost for a hybrid, net of any government tax subsidies, has to be calculated using a consistent return on money invested and expected life of the automobile. Battery replacement is another cost factor, but recent improvements in battery technology have extended battery life to 12 or more years, the effective life of an automobile. Premium differentials for an HEV and a conventional gasoline fueled automobile should be calculated between models of the same manufacturer with the most similar characteristics. One such study concluded that the annual net cost (not savings) of a hybrid averaged nearly $1,400 over a conventional gasoline powered automobile. That is, on average, the fuel savings of a hybrid cannot justify the premium on price. But there was a very large spread in outcomes of cost–benefit analyses for individual hybrids. The best amounted to an annual saving of $6,400 and the worst an additional annual cost of $9,200. Thus an individual considering a hybrid should do a comparative analysis for a hybrid under consideration and not be content with an overall assessment that applies to some subset of hybrids.[68]

An HEV obtains higher mileage by converting energy normally lost during deceleration to electrical energy that can be stored in a battery. HEVs can be designed in a series or parallel configuration. In a series configuration, the primary gasoline engine drives a generator that powers an electric motor that, in turn, provides power to the front wheels of the vehicle and charges the battery. The vehicle is driven solely by the electric motor and electrical power is either generated by the gasoline motor or drawn down from a battery. HEVs now on the market have a parallel configuration in which the car is driven directly from a single axis or drive train that is, in turn, powered either by a gasoline fueled engine or by an electric motor. There are different designs as to how the engine and electric motor interact with the drive chain such as individually or in tandem. The electric motor is run by electricity stored in a battery that supplements power from the gasoline engine and can cut in when the car needs extra power. A nickel metal hydride or a lithium ion battery is not only recharged during deceleration, when regenerative braking captures energy normally passed to the environment as waste heat, but also during normal motor operation if a charge is necessary. The design criteria of an HEV in terms of engine size and battery capacity are to provide better fuel economy and lower emissions with the same performance of a conventional automobile.

A plug-in electric hybrid (PHEV) can also be charged by plugging into a conventional electricity outlet. PHEVs can be more reliant on the battery and can be driven in pure electrical mode at low or high (unchanging) speeds. Being able to charge at home or at public charging stations allows greater reliance on the battery over the gasoline engine as a means of propulsion. This increases fuel savings by purchasing less gasoline and cuts emissions accordingly. A PHEV is generally viewed as the precursor to an all-electric car.[69]

Supplemental acceleration using an electric motor means that automobiles can be built with gasoline or diesel engines of lower horsepower, which consume less fuel. Fuel efficiency is further enhanced by "cutting out" firing of a cylinder at cruising speed on level ground. In addition, an HEV has less weight because its engine components are made from lighter weight aluminum and magnesium despite the additional weight of a battery. The vehicle's body, also made of lightweight aluminum and plastic, is aerodynamically designed to reduce wind resistance. Depending on the make of HEV, mileage can range from 30 to more than 60 miles per gallon. An HEV's mileage performance, compared to that of a conventional automobile, is more impressive in stop-and-go traffic than in steady highway driving, although some models essentially have the same mileage regardless of driving conditions. HEVs' engine emissions meet California's stringent ultra-low vehicle emission standards. HEV sales jumped when gasoline prices spiked during the summer of 2008, sending SUV sales into a slump. But the opposite occurred when oil prices fell and HEV sales slumped while SUV sales jumped. This lesson is vital for automobile manufacturers in planning future production: a projection of future oil prices must be part of the planning process!

Role of Alternative Fuels

One way to attack oil demand for motor vehicles is to find an alternative fuel to gasoline. The US Department of Energy defines alternative fuels as substantially nonpetroleum that enhance energy security and the environment. The list includes methanol and ethanol fuels of at least 70 percent alcohol, compressed natural gas (CNG), liquefied natural gas (LNG), liquefied petroleum gas (LPG), hydrogen, coal-derived liquid fuels, biofuels, and electricity. On a total cost basis, all are currently more costly than gasoline and diesel oil fueled automobiles. However, there are significant fuel cost savings for natural gas and electricity, which can justify at least a portion of the higher cost for the automobile adapted to run on these fuels. Table 6.4 shows that the energy content of alternative fuels is lower than gasoline and diesel oil, which means that motor vehicles that use alternative fuels will get lower mileage (miles per gallon) than those running on gasoline and diesel fuel.

Anti-gasoline public sentiment is "fueled" by the desire to improve air quality and concern over oil security. Since the 1970s when California suffered from the worst polluted air in the nation, state energy authorities became acutely aware of the impact on oil security of declining California and Alaska oil production. The state has led and continues to lead the nation in initiating legislation to promote the demise of the conventional gasoline engine and has made marked progress in cleaning up the air in the Los Angeles basin. Many states look to California as a model for motor vehicle pollution legislation.

Table 6.4 Energy Content of Motor Vehicle Fuels

Fuel	Btu/Gallon
Diesel	129,000
Gasoline	111,400
E85(3)	105,545
Propane	84,000
Ethanol (E100)	75,000
Methanol (M100)	65,350
Liquid hydrogen	34,000
CNG at 3,000psi	29,000
Hydrogen at 3,000psi	9,667

California in common with all the states must deal with the one critical factor holding back the development of alternative fuels: lack of an infrastructure for serving customers. Table 6.5 shows the number of motor vehicles and the number of service stations for each type of alternative fuel.[70]

The population of gasoline fueled vehicles includes automobiles, SUVs, minivans, and pickup trucks. The number of alternative fueled vehicles of 1,191,000 is less than ½ percent of the total gasoline fueled motor vehicle fleet. Moreover, 72 percent of alternative fueled vehicles use E85. Stations that sell E85 are concentrated in the corn growing regions of Illinois, Indiana, Iowa, Michigan, Minnesota, Missouri, and Ohio. While there are relatively few gas stations that sell E85 elsewhere in the nation, more recently built vehicles are actually flex fuel, meaning that they can burn any combination of gasoline and ethanol. Given the relative scarcity of E85 service stations, most flex fuel automobiles burn gasoline more often than E85. From this perspective, the number of alternative fueled vehicles is overstated.

There are no specially built biodiesel fueled trucks. Diesel trucks can burn up to B20 without engine modifications. A small but growing number of biodiesel stations sell B100, and diesel trucks that burn more than B20 require modifications to their engines depending on the percentage of biodiesel in petrodiesel. Fueling stations that sell B20 or greater are concentrated in North and South Carolina, Tennessee, and along the west coast. However, there are considerably more stations that sell B1, B2, B5, and B10 biodiesel.

Table 6.5 Alternative Fuel Vehicle Population and Number of Service Stations

Fuel	US Vehicle Population	Number of Service Stations
Gasoline	248,932,000	121,446
E85	862,837	2,394
LPG	139,477	2,723
CNG	118,214	713
Electric	67,294	8,291
LNG	3,436	53
Biodiesel (B20+)	Many	300
Hydrogen	Few	12

Natural gas fueled vehicles will be discussed in Chapter 7. Hydrogen as a motor vehicle fuel is another possibility. Its chief advantage is that its only combustion product is water and is the preferred fuel for a fuel cell. Hydrogen fueled vehicles and fuel cells are discussed under Hydrogen Economy in Chapter 10; but for now the prognosis for large numbers of automobiles, powered by either direct combustion of hydrogen in a conventional engine or hydrogen feedstock for a fuel cell, is quite dim.

Electric vehicles are at their beginning stages of public acceptance primarily through the Nissan Leaf, Chevy Volt, and Tesla. The Chevy Volt is a hybrid that can only travel 38 miles (effectively 30 miles) on a full charge and then reverts to a gasoline engine. The Nissan Leaf is a pure electric vehicle that can get about 80 miles per charge and Tesla, also a pure electric vehicle, can get around 350 miles between charges. With a safety factor so as not to "run out of electricity," the effective mileage on a Nissan Leaf may be closer to 60 miles per charge and 300 miles for Tesla, the same as a full tank of gas for a gasoline fueled vehicle. Electric vehicles have far fewer moving parts, brake fluid is the only fluid that needs to be changed, regenerative braking reduces brake wear (the same is true for hybrids), and their electrical systems do not require regular maintenance.[71]

However, electric vehicles require considerable time to fully charge the battery at charging stations and there is a question on availability of charging stations when driving electric vehicles "off the beaten track." Of course, every home is a recharging station and every place an electric automobile is parked that has access to an electric outlet can also be considered a recharging station. Recharging an electric vehicle either at home or at work when the car is not being used sidesteps the issue of the large amount of time required for charging at public charging stations. Careful planning has to be made on trips off the beaten track to ensure that the vehicle can be recharged. There are over 8,000 recharging stations with 20,000 charging outlets to ensure that more than one car can be charged at a time. However, charging stations are concentrated along the eastern and western and Gulf coasts and extend inland in the Carolinas and upper Midwest and around Denver. Cross-country trips in an electric vehicle could pose a challenge; yet, in an emergency and if a motel operator is willing, an extension cord can provide an overnight battery charge.

Battery life has been improved and is now expected to last the life of the vehicle. Most battery warranties run for 7 years or 100,000 miles, whichever occurs first. Tesla has an unlimited mileage warranty on its battery. A disincentive for buying an electric vehicle is the extra cost of the battery over a conventional engine, but its cost is coming down from technological developments and economies of scale in having to produce larger numbers of batteries. The cost of a battery in 2009 was $1,200 per kilowatt-hour of capacity and in 2014 around $500–$600 per kilowatt-hour. Its projected cost is around $200 per kilowatt-hour in 2020 and $160 per kilowatt-hour in 2025. The cost of fuel (electricity rates versus gasoline prices in 2014 dollars) works out to be equivalent to 95 miles per gallon on gasoline. The fuel efficiency of an electric vehicle is 85 percent versus 15 percent with a gasoline fueled engine. Of course this neglects the inefficiency of generating electricity from fossil fuels plus transmission and distribution losses. While electric vehicles have zero emissions and lower operating costs by being entirely divorced from gasoline, electric vehicles are not entirely green depending on the type of fuel consumed for generating electricity. But to the extent that electricity is generated from hydro, nuclear, solar, wind, and other renewables, electric vehicles reduce GHG emissions.[72]

Another factor working in favor of electric vehicles is their gaining market traction. The 2014 sales of electric vehicles including plug-in hybrid vehicles were about 125,000, of which 30,200 were the Nissan Leaf, 18,800 the Chevy Volt, and 18,500 the Tesla Model S.[73] With total automobile sales of 16.5 million, electric vehicles were short of 1 percent of automobile sales; they may reach 1 percent of automotive sales in the not too distant future. While this still sounds low, it is also promising. Suppose that reaching 1 percent represented seven doublings from some very low initial population level. Then the mathematics of exponential growth is that the next six doublings will raise sales of electric vehicles to 64 percent of automotive sales. Of course, this probably won't happen, but significant growth can occur once a product reaches 1 percent of aggregate market sales—it's all in the mathematics of exponential growth. Moreover each doubling of sales is expected to drive down the overall cost of the vehicle by 20 percent, the same which had occurred with solar panels and computer chips. Electric stations fitted with recharging outlets will surely grow if electric vehicle sales continue to escalate in a significant manner. But millions of electric vehicles simultaneously being charged would severely challenge the electricity industry. Off-peak charging would be a necessity, and low-cost electricity during these periods would provide a necessary incentive for electric car owners to recharge their vehicles at night. A growing number of utilities offer sharply reduced rates during the night time lull in electricity demand from about midnight to the start of the daytime load around 6 am. Charging electric vehicles at night helps to even out the grid load over a 24-hour period, which can generate significant savings in electricity rates by reducing the number of generators that operate only a few hours per day. Ultimately a smart grid would have to be set up to handle the charging of millions of electric vehicles particularly when a large portion of electricity is from unreliable sources such as solar and wind. Some electric vehicle owners are installing solar panels at home to charge their vehicles during the day, selling any excess electricity generation to the grid. While still in its infancy, electric vehicles with a 300 mile range such as Tesla that are winning increasing public acceptance may well be the harbinger to a major change in motor vehicle propulsion and investments in the electricity generation, transmission, and distribution infrastructure.

Europe lags the US in electric vehicle sales. Pure battery and plug-in hybrid sales were only 38,600 in 2013, up from 24,200 in 2012. Similarly market share increased from 0.21 percent in 2012 to 0.34 percent in 2013. Lagging sales is primarily cost-related where the price for electric vehicles is double that of an equivalent gasoline or diesel car even after government subsidies of up to $8,000 in some countries. There is also the question of availability of charging stations. Only Norway and the Netherlands offer tax subsidies and use-incentives to make the purchase of electric vehicles a rational choice. In Norway, high taxes on buying vehicles and a 23 percent sales tax are avoided when buying an electric vehicle. Moreover owners have free access to toll roads, free parking, and, in Oslo, access to bus lanes. Consequently Norway's electric vehicle sales of 7,900 in 2013 were second only to France's 8,800 vehicle sales. On the other extreme, Germany does not offer subsidies for electric and plug-in hybrids.[74] China is looking at electric vehicles as a means to cut pollution from automobile emissions and is currently building an industrial infrastructure sufficient to produce one million electric vehicles per year by 2020. To jump start electric vehicle production, China requires that 30 percent of government purchases of motor vehicles be electrically driven.[75]

Nevertheless, in reviewing the number of alternative fueled vehicles in Table 6.5, and despite intense government and private efforts to support the technological development of vehicles run by alternative fuels, including fuel cells, over the past 40 years (all of this started in the aftermath of the 1973 oil crisis), the overwhelming share of the world's fleet of automobiles and trucks is still powered by gasoline and diesel fuel. Progress made since the 1973 oil crisis, when the necessity of divorcing the automobile from reliance on oil was first widely recognized, has been pitiful to say the least. But things may change, and change relatively rapidly. It is possible that long-term oil consumption could be affected by technological breakthroughs that bring the capital and operating costs of alternative fueled vehicles closer to that of gasoline and diesel fueled vehicles. With growing instability in the Middle East, the price of gasoline may escalate to a level that can rationalize a switch to alternative fuels. Alternative fuels that would benefit the most would probably be natural gas, for which the US has a plentiful supply at low prices, and electricity.

One thing is certain: lack of significant progress for motor vehicles fueled by alternative fuels is not being hampered by the automobile industry. Automobile manufacturers share the general public sentiment that the conventional gasoline engine is becoming archaic and needs to be replaced. Carmakers are not wedded to the oil industry, but they are wedded to a technology that works and a fuel that is readily available. Until there is an alternative fuel that works and is readily available, oil will remain the preferred fuel. There will be no easy divorce from oil. But the future of oil has to be tempered by improvements in fuel efficiency and development of hybrids and electric vehicles. While oil consumption is still increasing, its rate of growth is slowing. Rapid automobile population growth in China, India, and elsewhere in Asia compensates for stagnant or declining oil consumption in OECD nations. The prospects for major oil companies will be adversely affected if oil consumption, not supply, is approaching a peak. Total capitalization of major oil company stocks has lost position relative to Walmart and Apple.[76] Major oil company investments in natural gas may be influenced by the comparative long-term prospects of oil and natural gas as a motor vehicle fuel.

Fuel Savings with Piggybacking

The advantage of trucks over railroads is their flexibility—they can go anywhere there is a road. The advantage of railroads is their inherent efficiency—a train crew of only three members can haul several hundred containers or truck trailers on flatbed railcars, a number that would require an equal number of truck drivers. Aside from significant labor savings, a railroad with steel wheels on steel tracks is far more energy-efficient than a truck with rubber wheels on concrete or asphalt. CSX Railroad advertises that it's capable of moving one ton of freight about 450 miles on one gallon of diesel oil and this presumably includes moving the train itself. An optimal blend of both modes of transport is intermodal transport (piggyback) of combining trucks for short-distance delivery with rail for long-distance hauling. A large percentage of containers arriving at west coast ports are hauled by dedicated unit trains handling containers only across the nation to central depots for transfer to trucks to take containers to their ultimate destinations. Piggybacking reduces oil consumption and highway congestion including investments in expanding highway capacity for the benefit of truckers. Ferries play a similar role in Europe in getting trucks off the highways and the US has been toying with the idea of a roll-on roll-off (Ro-Ro) vessel service for transporting trucks and containers up and down both coasts, relieving highway congestion and saving fuel.

Internalizing an Externality

The government supports the oil industry by ensuring security of supply. This is not a subsidy to oil companies because they are not in the business of military interventions to secure supplies of oil. Government participation in the civilian economy is common. The automobile industry would have been truncated (to say the least) if town, county, state, and federal governments did not step up to the plate and build roads. It would be just as unfair for automobile companies to be responsible for building roads as it would be for oil companies to ensure oil security. The big difference is in the method of payment. The cost of building and maintaining roads falls on the user as highway taxes placed on every gallon of gasoline and diesel sold. The more one drives or, to be more exact, the more one consumes gasoline and diesel fuel, the greater his or her contribution to highway trust funds. However, the cost of oil security falls on the taxpayer as a government expenditure regardless of whether the taxpayer even owns a vehicle. It is high time that those who benefit from oil bear the full cost of oil through an oil security tax. The US has consumed about 18 million Bpd on average since 1980. Let's say two-thirds of this represents gasoline and diesel fuel for automobiles and trucks. Twelve million Bpd of motor vehicle fuels is about 500 million gallons per day (42 gallons in a barrel) or 180 billion gallons per year. A $1 tax on each gallon of gasoline will support $180 billion in annual defense expenditures. How long would this tax have to be in effect to pay for the estimated $2.2 trillion spent in military misadventures in the Middle East? Twelve years would be necessary. Thus if a $1 per gallon oil security tax had been added to gasoline and diesel fuel just after or perhaps during the Gulf War in 1990, the first major direct military intervention into the Middle East, it would have funded military activities until now. Support given to Iraq during the Iraq–Iran War in the 1980s was a low-cost prelude to what happened thereafter. An oil security tax imposed at that time would have been sufficient to internalize an external cost actually borne by the US taxpayer.

Adding a dollar to the price on gasoline would affect both miles driven and type of automobile purchased. Higher priced gasoline and diesel fuel would also support the development of alternative fuels. It would not have been lethal to automobile owners. When gasoline prices rise, people are not deprived of the driving experience, they just think more carefully about how they drive their cars. Carpooling, taking the bus or train to work, not visiting the shopping mall every day, letting the kids take the bus to and from school rather than running a personal escort service, and shortening the distance traveled for family vacations have a significant impact on the number of miles driven in a year. In addition to driving less, people are incentivized to buy fuel-efficient automobiles and hybrids over gas-guzzlers epitomized by SUVs. Today's higher priced gasoline is opening the pathway to ultra-efficient automobiles like the Mini Cooper that gets 30 or more miles per gallon for combined highway and city driving.[77] CityCars, a Massachusetts Institute of Technology project at this time, are foldable electric vehicles sized for two people. When folded, 3.5 vehicles can fit in a space for one conventional car. CityCars will be starting its test phase for intra-city use in the near future.[78] A price of gasoline of the order of $5 per gallon would probably be sufficient to cut oil consumption to the point of eliminating Middle East imports. If North America could become nearly self-sufficient with some imports from South America (Venezuela or Brazil) or Africa, then Americans would be somewhat isolated by what's happening in the Middle East, relaxing the necessity of having a large military presence in a part of the world that does not want our presence.

Is This Politically Acceptable?

Internalizing an externality by incorporating Middle East military expenditures as a security tax on gasoline and diesel fuel would not be politically acceptable, but what relevance is that? The money is being spent anyway, it is the manner of payment that is up for discussion. Even with US oil production rising rapidly, the world remains dangerously close to supply not being able to satisfy demand. Surplus capacity is concentrated in the Middle East, and that region of the world is fraught with danger to say the least. The problem with being on the razor's edge of oil supply is that one can easily fall off. In the world of oil, an extended supply disruption in Nigeria or Venezuela, or any number of other possibilities, can reduce oil supply below demand. Once this occurs, there is no upper limit on oil prices.

What we should learn from high oil prices in 2008 was that a gasoline price of $3–$4 per gallon at that time appeared sufficient to persuade US drivers to drive less and buy fuel-efficient automobiles. Today gasoline prices would probably have to be $4–$5 per gallon to have the same impact and $5 per gallon to more or less ensure a permanent cut in consumption. This in turn will allow us to extricate ourselves from the Middle East, saving billions, if not trillions, of dollars and many lives on military efforts that do not seem to accomplish anything and surely do not enhance political stability. Our partially excising the import market from increased domestic production enhances oil availability elsewhere, easing the strain on global oil supplies.

Stated in the most simplistic way, we have a choice of paying $4–$5 per gallon or paying $4–$5 per gallon. The choice is only differentiated by when and where the money flows, either to the US government to ease budget deficits or to the coffers of oil exporters. Either way, there will be an economic incentive for the development of alternative fuels, but it may be too late to save the economy if we continue to procrastinate. Despite fracking, the US still remains a major oil importer. Total North American consumption in 2014 was 23.3 million Bpd with production of 18.7 million Bpd. The resulting difference of 4.6 million Bpd was significantly down from 6.5 million Bpd in 2013. A major disruption in Middle East exports would affect the US regardless of success in fracking oil shale. The time to wean our dependence on oil imports in favor of alternative fuels was yesterday, but nothing can be done about that. The time is now before the next crisis strikes.

We had our first warning in the 1973 oil crisis that life will not be the same, and we managed to do nothing in the subsequent four decades to deal with a highly explosive situation. Matters are not getting better, and each subsequent oil crisis will bring even higher prices that will last longer. It is about time that we do something to at least curb our dependence on imported oil. This can be done by becoming serious about developing alternative motor vehicle fuels along with continuing to enhance North American oil production. This can be done with fracking and syncrude along with expanding conventional oil production by allowing drilling in offshore waters and in Alaska. If pandemonium breaks out in the Middle East, nations including the US will run out of oil. The old saw that alternative fuels cannot be developed because of our enormous vested interest in the infrastructure of oil production facilities, refineries, and associated processing plants, pipelines, ships, storage tanks, and distribution facilities is not going to be a persuasive argument if this infrastructure goes dry.

Problems and Project

Problem 6.1a

Suppose that you're operating a refinery whose year 1 output is 115,000 Bpd gasoline and 65,000 Bpd diesel. Gasoline demand is expected to drop 1,000 Bpd annually, whereas diesel demand is expected to increase 3,000 Bpd annually. What are the gasoline, diesel, and total outputs of the refinery in year 15? What are the annual growth rates for all three?

Problem 6.1b

Focusing on year 1, there are three types of crude with the indicated cost in $/bbl and percentage yields for gasoline and diesel. The marketing assessments on the minimum and maximum volumes that can be sold are as indicated. The solution spreadsheet is shown in Problem Table 6.1b.

For setting up the problem for a Solver solution, the gray cells are variables; the actual production volume of both gasoline and diesel in cell F8 is the sum of cells F6 to F7. The cost is the SumProduct of the volume of the three crudes and their respective costs, which is to be minimized. Constraints are that solution variables in column F should be greater than column G and less than column H. Set up the problem with 0 values for the variables. Problem Table 6.1b is the solution.

Problem 6.1c

Suppose that gasoline can be sold for $110 per barrel and diesel for $107 per barrel. Change the objective to be profit to be maximized. Revenue is the SumProduct of column I and column F and profit is the difference between revenue and costs. Since only 30 percent of the barrel is being consumed to make gasoline and diesel, the applicable cost should be 30 percent of the total purchase of crude. The remaining 70 percent of crude purchased is assumed to be made into products that generate revenue just to cover the cost of crude.

Problem Table 6.1c is the solution spreadsheet. Minimizing costs generally leads to minimum use of crude oil and maximizing profits generally leads to maximum use of crude oil. It is interesting here that the actual volume of gasoline and diesel is not at its maximum allowable value. Comparing the two spreadsheets shows that the solution hinges on whether costs are being minimized or profits being maximized. Some

Problem Table 6.1b

	B	C	D	E	F	G	H
4					Actual	Min	Max
5		Crude1	Crude2	Crude3	Volume	Volume	Volume
6	Gasoline	10%	15%	20%	110,000	110,000	120,000
7	Diesel	20%	15%	10%	65,000	60,000	70,000
8	Volume	66,667	0	516,667	175,000	175,000	185,000
9							
10	Cost	$95	$100	$105	$60,583,333		

Problem Table 6.1c

	B	C	D	E	F	G	H	I
4					Actual	Min	Max	
5		Crude1	Crude2	Crude3	Volume	Volume	Volume	Price
6	Gasoline	10%	15%	20%	110,000	110,000	120,000	$110
7	Diesel	20%	15%	10%	70,000	60,000	70,000	$107
8	Volume	100,000	0	500,000	180,000	175,000	185,000	
9								
10	Cost	$95	$100	$105	$62,000,000			
11								
12	Profit				$990,000			

problems are cost minimization by nature, but when there is an opportunity to set up a problem between minimizing costs and maximizing profits, the general recommendation is to go with the latter.

Problem 6.2

Suppose that a company has two refineries and a choice of two different crude oils. Based on netback values, you have to decide which crude should be selected for each refinery and, in the case of Refinery A, which mode of operation.

Yield of gasoline, diesel, and jet fuel totals 60 percent in all cases. Suppose that products from the remaining 40 percent of the barrel are sold for $42. The wholesale price of gasoline is $2.90 per gallon, for diesel $2.85 per gallon, and for jet fuel $2.80 per gallon (42 gallons in a barrel). Price for Crude1 is $110 per barrel plus a shipping cost of $1 per barrel to Refinery A and $1.25 per barrel to Refinery B. Price for Crude2 is $105 per barrel plus a shipping cost of $3 per barrel to Refinery A and $2 per barrel to Refinery B. Extra cost for Mode 2 operation for Refinery A is $0.50 per barrel. For each refinery, what is your selection of crude oil and, for Refinery A, which mode of operation based on netback analysis of profitability and costs?

Problem 6.3

Suppose that an oil shale well costs $8 million. The desired revenue of $12 million recoups the investment, provides a return on the investment, and pays for operating costs. The well produces 60 percent of its output in year 1, 25 percent in year 2, and 15 percent in year 3. What would be the minimum output of the well in Bpd to generate $12 million if oil is sold for $100 per barrel? (Problem Tables 6.2a and 6.2b provide guidance.)

Problem Table 6.2a

	B	C	D	E	F	G	H	I	J	K	L	M	N
4					Crude1						Crude2		
5													
6			Refinery A		Refinery A		Refinery B		Refinery A		Refinery A		Refinery B
7	Yield		Mode 1		Mode 2				Mode 1		Mode 2		
8	Gasoline		30%		40%		20%		20%		25%		15%
9	Diesel		20%		15%		30%		25%		20%		35%
10	Jet Fuel		10%		5%		10%		15%		15%		10%

Problem Table 6.2b

	A	B	C	D	E	F	G	H	I	J	K	L	M	N
13		Price/gal	Price/bbl											
14	Gasoline	$2.90	$121.80	$71.40		$72.03		$70.98		$70.77		$70.98		$70.77
15	Diesel	$2.80	$117.60											
16	Jet Fuel	$2.70	$113.40											
17														
18	Revenue remaining 40% of barrel			$42.00		$42.00		$42.00		$42.00		$42.00		$42.00
19														
20	Total Revenue			$113.40		$114.03		$112.98		$112.77		$112.98		$112.77
21														
22	Extra op cost/bbl					$0.50						$0.50		
23														
24														
25	Net Revenue			$113.40		$113.53		$112.98		$112.77		$112.48		$112.77
26														
27	Cost of Shipping $/bbl			$1.00		$1.00		$1.25		$3.00		$3.00		$2.00
28														
29	Cost of Crude $/bbl			$110.00		$110.00		$110.00		$105.00		$105.00		$105.00
30														
31	Netback Value			$2.40		$2.53		$1.73		$4.77		$4.48		$5.77

Problem 6.4a

Suppose you're in charge of drilling activities for a company with a combined output of 100,000 Bpd from 20 conventional oil wells. The production manager has estimated that production will decrease by 5,000 Bpd per year until production from existing wells is exhausted. The decision has been made to exploit the company's leases of hard shale. Each well will require fracking and the average output is estimated to be 400 Bpd the first year, 200 Bpd the second year, and 100 Bpd the third year. What will be your shale drilling program for the next 25 years?

Production rate for each shale well is in column B. Both column D and row 2 run for 30 years. Column D is the production of the existing oil fields dropping off by 5,000 Bpd. Starting in column F, row 3 is the number of fracked wells to be completed in any given year. Put in an initial value of 1 as this is the solution spreadsheet. In year 1, one completed fracked well will produce 400 Bpd in the first year of its operation, 200 in the second year, and 100 in the third and final year of operation. Hence 12.5 wells (fractional wells result from the Solver solution) produce 5,000 Bpd, which when added to the conventional field production of 95,000 Bpd maintains production at 100,000 Bpd. In the second year, shale wells must make up for a 10,000 Bpd decline in the conventional field production. This is accomplished by drilling 18.75 wells (in reality, only whole number wells can be drilled). These produce 7,500 Bpd, which when added to the 2,500 Bpd from the wells drilled in the first year maintains production at 100,000 Bpd. The formulation for year 1 is =$B$6*F$3 in cell F4, year 2 =$B$7*F$3, and year 3 =$B$8*F$3. These three cells are simply copied and pasted accordingly for 30 years.

Problem Table 6.4a

	A	B	C	D	E	F	G	H
2					Year:	1	2	3
3				Year	100,000	12.5	18.75	25
4		Annual		1	95,000	5,000		
5	Year	Output		2	90,000	2,500	7,500	
6	1	400		3	85,000	1,250	3,750	10,000
7	2	200		4	80,000		1,875	5,000
8	3	100		5	75,000			2,500

Problem Table 6.4b

	AG	AH	AI	AJ
2	28	29	30	Total
3	142.9	142.9	0.0	2,867.35
4				100,000
5				100,000
6				100,000
7				100,000
8				100,000

Cell AJ3 is = SUM(F3:AI3) and cell AH4 is = SUM(F4:AI4) replicated down. The Solver menu is set up to minimize the total number of wells needed (cell AJ3), with variables being the number of wells drilled in cells F3 to AI3 with the constraint that the total for the first 28 years in column AJ will equal 100,000. Other production levels of fracked wells can be explored by changing the values in cells B6 to B8.

The purpose of this problem is to demonstrate the enormous number of wells that have to be drilled to maintain production—here 143 wells per year must be drilled once the conventional field is exhausted. Total wells that have to be drilled over 28 years total nearly 2,900 wells. Fracking oil is going to provide plenty of jobs for drillers and builders of pipe and associated equipment to maintain production. Any letup in the relentless pace to maintain production will almost immediately be felt in terms of declining production.

Problem 6.4b

Once the conventional oil fields are exhausted and all production is from fracked wells, 143 wells have to be drilled each year. Consider that a well has a 3-year life and suppose that each well requires $4 million annually during its 3-year life to cover CAPEX and OPEX. The wells as a group will produce 100,000 Bpd. What will have to be the minimum price of oil to sustain this operation profitably? Given the number of wells that have to be drilled over this 28-year period, will abandoned fracked wells become an environmental problem? What would you suggest as a means of reducing abandoned sites?

Problem 6.5a

China's automobile registrations were, in thousands of automobiles, 351 in 1980, 1,897 in 1990, 3,750 in 2000, 8,900 in 2005, 18,270 in 2008, 34,430 in 2010, and 43,220 in 2011. Using these figures as the independent variable or Y-values and oil consumption from *BP Energy Statistics* for these years as the dependent or X-values, run a linear regression to obtain the statistical relationship between automobile population and oil consumption. Plot the independent and dependent variables along with the regression equation. What is your interpretation of this as a projection tool? What is your projection if automobile registrations grew to 80 million, 120 million, and 160 million? Saudi Arabia has a production of about 10 million Bpd, which could be considered a unit of production. How many Saudi Arabian production units have to be added to world production to accommodate your forecasts?

Problem 6.5b

In examining the chart of the regression curve versus the data points, it is clear that eliminating the first three data points would result in a regression equation with a higher R Squared reflecting a better fit between the data points and the regression line. Rerun the regression analysis with only the last four points and obtain a revised linear regression equation. Compare the standard errors between the two equations; what does that mean to you? What is your projection now if automobile registrations grew to 80 million, 120 million, and 160 million and you have the revised number of Saudi Arabian production units? The 95 percent confidence interval is the projection $+/- 2*$Standard Error. What is your 95 percent confidence interval? Which of these two projections would you select and why? Click on all the data again and select from the trend analysis menu different types of regression lines like exponential, polynomial, and others. You can scrutinize these visually and view the R Square to discriminate one from the other. Select the trend equation that you prefer and perform a projection with that and compare with the linear projection.

Problem 6.5c

Redo this problem with India, where the automobile registrations were 2,300 in 1990, 5,150 in 2000, 7,654 in 2005, 9,400 in 2008, 13,300 in 2010, and 14,165 in 2011.

Problem 6.6

According to the EPA, burning a gallon of gasoline releases 8,887 grams of CO_2 and burning a gallon of diesel releases 10,180 grams.[79] It is felt that both are essentially equivalent when adjusted for the better mileage of diesel fuel. Suppose that a gasoline motor vehicle averages 20 miles per gallon and drives 9,000 miles per year. What are the CO_2 emissions in metric tons? What would it be for US registered motor vehicles (250 million) and for all registered motor vehicles (900 million)? How does this compare to the annual 35.5 billion metric tons of carbon dioxide emissions from all fossil fuel sources? See *BP Energy Statistics* for a breakdown of carbon dioxide emissions by nations. How are these calculated?

Problem 6.7 (Futures)

You are in charge of risk management for an airline. Risk is a high price on jet fuel, which can threaten the financial viability of the company if it rises above a certain level. Suppose that the price of jet fuel is $100 per barrel and the forecast for the future is that there is a 50–50 chance that the price in three months will be above or below $100 per barrel, which is a pretty innocuous forecast. The agreed probability distribution for prices in 90 days is 10 percent chance of the price being $92 and $108 per barrel, 30 percent chance of $97 and $103 per barrel, and 20 percent chance of $100 per barrel.

The company consumes 5,000 barrels of jet fuel per day. Suppose that a 90-day futures contract is available for 1,000 barrels of jet fuel, which is an obligation to buy 1,000 barrels at the futures price. Five contracts would be necessary to fully hedge the company's exposure for just a single day in 90 days in the future. Risk mitigation can be accomplished by buying a futures contract because losses generated by a rising price of jet fuel are mitigated by profits in the derivative. Suppose also that there is fear of an outbreak of hostilities that affects jet fuel prices from massive military purchases and the market is in contango anticipating rising prices. The price of the futures is $101 per barrel. Margin is 5 percent of the futures price. Futures contracts can be sold at any time; they do not have to be held to maturity. For the sake of simplicity, suppose that the decision is to hold the futures contract to maturity and to fulfill the obligation of the futures by purchasing 1,000 barrels at $101 using the 5 percent margin that has already been paid in addition to a cash infusion for the remaining 95 percent. How does the purchase of a single futures contract affect the risk profile if it is held to the day of maturity using the aforementioned probability distribution (ignore any cost associated with funding margin three months before purchase)? Construct the following spreadsheet where the variables are the number and price of futures and measure performance accordingly across the probability distribution.

Problem Table 6.7a Non-hedged Position

	B	C	D	E	F	G	H	I	J
2			# Futures		Futures				
3			Contracts		Price				
4			0		$101				
5									
6	Price	Volume	Futures	Market	Futures	Market	Total		Expected
7	in 90 Dys	Required	Volume	Volume	Purchase	Purchase	Cost	Probability	Cost
8	$92	5000	0	5000	$0	$460,000	$460,000	10%	$46,000
9	$97	5000	0	5000	$0	$485,000	$485,000	30%	$145,500
10	$100	5000	0	5000	$0	$500,000	$500,000	20%	$100,000
11	$103	5000	0	5000	$0	$515,000	$515,000	30%	$154,500
12	$108	5000	0	5000	$0	$540,000	$540,000	10%	$54,000
13									
14								Total	$500,000

Problem Table 6.7b Hedged Position

	B	C	D	E	F	G	H	I	J
2			# Futures		Futures				
3			Contracts		Price				
4			1		$101				
5									
6	Price	Volume	Futures	Market	Futures	Market	Total		Expected
7	in 90 Dys	Required	Volume	Volume	Purchase	Purchase	Cost	Probability	Cost
8	$92	5000	1000	4000	$101,000	$368,000	$469,000	10%	$46,900
9	$97	5000	1000	4000	$101,000	$388,000	$489,000	30%	$146,700
10	$100	5000	1000	4000	$101,000	$400,000	$501,000	20%	$100,200
11	$103	5000	1000	4000	$101,000	$412,000	$513,000	30%	$153,900
12	$108	5000	1000	4000	$101,000	$432,000	$533,000	10%	$53,300
13									
14								Total	$501,000

Notice that the purchase price when jet prices are high is reduced by the presence of futures contracts—this is the benefit of risk mitigation. But also notice that the average price has increased—this is the cost of risk mitigation. Plot the benefit versus cost of risk mitigation from 0 to 5 futures contracts. What is your advice as to how many contracts should be purchased? Suppose that the market is in backwardation with a futures price of $99 per barrel. What is your recommendation now?

Problem 6.8 (Calls)

Unlike a futures contract where there is an obligatory purchase or sale, a call is an option with no concomitant obligation. Suppose that a call is available for the purchase of 1,000 barrels of jet fuel 90 days in the future at $100 per barrel with a 5 percent premium or $5,000 (5 percent of $100 per barrel for 1,000 barrels). American call and put options can be exercised at any time during the option period up to the expiry date and European options can only be exercised on the expiry date. The Bermudan options can only be exercised during specified narrow periods of time. For purposes of analysis, the exercise of the call option is limited to the expiration day (European option). The call is exercised if the price is above $100 per barrel with only a portion of the call price recouped until the price reaches $105 per barrel. Beyond that, the price of jet fuel is $100 per barrel up to the call volume. The call is said to "be in the money." The problem is set up as a modification of Problem 6.7.

Problem Table 6.8a Non-hedged Position

	B	C	D	E	F	G	H	I	J
2			# Futures		Futures				
3			Contracts		Price				
4			0		$101				
5									
6	Price	Volume	Futures	Market	Futures	Market	Total		Expected
7	in 90 Dys	Required	Volume	Volume	Purchase	Purchase	Cost	Probability	Cost
8	$92	5000	0	5000	$0	$460,000	$460,000	10%	$46,000
9	$97	5000	0	5000	$0	$485,000	$485,000	30%	$145,500
10	$100	5000	0	5000	$0	$500,000	$500,000	20%	$100,000
11	$103	5000	0	5000	$0	$515,000	$515,000	30%	$154,500
12	$108	5000	0	5000	$0	$540,000	$540,000	10%	$54,000
13									
14								Total	$500,000

The call exercise volume column has an IF statement that the call is not exercised if the price is $100 and below. This is denoted by zero volume. If exercised, the call exercise volume is the number of calls times the call volume of 1,000 barrels. The market volume is 5,000 barrels less the call volume. The market cost reflects market prices, whereas the call volume is the exercise price. Set up the spreadsheet in order to be able to analyze the benefit and cost of various numbers of calls. What is your recommendation?

Problem Table 6.8b Hedged Position

	B	C	D	E	F	G	H	I	J
1			# Call		Call				
2			Contracts		Exercise				
3			1		$100				
4									
5			Call						
6	Price	Volume	Exercise	Market	Call	Market	Total		Expected
7	in 90 Dys	Required	Volume	Volume	Purchase	Purchase	Cost	Probability	Cost
8	$92	5000	0	5000	$0	$460,000	$460,000	10%	$46,000
9	$97	5000	0	5000	$0	$485,000	$485,000	30%	$145,500
10	$100	5000	0	5000	$0	$500,000	$500,000	20%	$100,000
11	$103	5000	1000	4000	$100,000	$412,000	$512,000	30%	$153,600
12	$108	5000	1000	4000	$100,000	$432,000	$532,000	10%	$53,200
13									
14								Total	$498,300
15									
16								Option Cost	$5,000
17									
18								Total	$503,300

The option cost is the number of options multiplied by the option premium of $5,000. Again notice that the high-end price is reduced, the benefit of risk mitigation, but the total cost including the call premium has increased, the cost of risk mitigation. The American call option depends on the daily price of jet fuel. An interesting variation used in the oil business is the Asian option, which is keyed not to daily prices, but to a monthly average. Thus settlement is based on a less volatile price and the option premium is reduced, reflecting the lesser volatility associated with monthly over daily prices.[80]

Problem 6.9

Futures are obligations to buy or sell a commodity at some point in the future. They can be settled in cash or by an exchange of physicals. Calls and puts are options that are only exercised if the option is in the money and have no relationship to physicals. Swaps are also simply a business arrangement with a swap counterparty where one counterparty pays another if the market price is above the swap price, or the cash exchange is reversed if the market price is below the swap price, for the volume covered by the swap or the swap volume. For instance, suppose that a swap is entered into with a swap counterparty to cover 1,000 Bpd of jet fuel at $100 per day for a 30-day period where the exchange of funds is based on the average monthly price. Funds actually exchanged are the difference between the market price and the swap price multiplied by the volume. Suppose that the current market price is $100 per barrel and a swap is available with a swap price of $100 for 30,000 barrels settled on the average price for a month with the swap covering 6 months. As risk manager for an airline, you want money to flow in when jet fuel prices are above $100. If average monthly prices for the next 6 months are $100, $102, $98, $99, $101, and $105 per barrel, what would be the associated swap payments and direction of payments? Notice that up to the swap volume, the airline is protected totally for jet fuel price increases above $100. This benefit has to be weighed against the cost of risk mitigation of passing savings from jet fuel prices being below the swap price to the swap counterparty.

Problem Table 6.9

	C	D	E	F	G
1			Swap Volume		
2			30,000		
3					
4				From	From
5			Difference	Swap	Airline to
6		Average	from	Counterparty	Swap
7		Monthly	Swap Price	to Airline	Counterparty
8	Month	Price	$100		
9	1	$100	$0	$0	$0
10	2	$102	$2	$60,000	$0
11	3	$98	($2)	$0	$60,000
12	4	$99	($1)	$0	$30,000
13	5	$101	$1	$30,000	$0
14	6	$105	$5	$150,000	$0

Futures and options are normally conducted through established markets where institutional brokers stand behind buyers and sellers; that is, there is no counterparty risk of a buyer or seller defaulting on performance. This is not true for the swap market, which is over the counter, where swaps are arranged by brokers with no third-party guarantee of performance. Thus swap counterparty risk is real and, for this reason, swaps are normally done between major corporate and banking institutions.

Project

The purpose of this project is to optimize a refinery operation in Excel using Solver to determine the choice of crude oils and their respective amounts to be purchased for refinery input and the slate of products to be sold as refinery output to maximize profits.[81] The refinery produces three blending stocks that are subsequently mixed to produce Ultra, Premium, and Regular brands of gasoline, each with their respective octane rating and vapor pressure specifications. The refinery also produces jet fuel and distillates (diesel fuel and heating oil), and sells blending stocks to third parties. Blending stocks, either mixed to produce gasoline or sold separately, along with jet fuel and distillates, are the high end of the barrel called clean or white products where refinery profits are made. What is not evaporated in the distillation or fractionation column to make high-end products is called low-end dirty or black products. The bottom of the distillation column is called straight-run resids, which can be sold separately or fed into a catalytic cracker (catcracker), where under special conditions of temperature and pressure and in the presence of a catalyst, long hydrocarbon chains are broken up into shorter hydrocarbon chains of high-end products. Residue left in the catcracker can be sold as heavy fuel oil or ships' bunkers or be fed into a coker. The coker smashes long hydrocarbon chains using a "hammer" of intense temperature and pressure to produce more high-end products. Residue from a coker is asphalt for road paving or petroleum coke, which has the appearance of oily charcoal briquettes and is burned as fuel. The waste products of the refining process, be it in the form of straight run, fuel oil, or petroleum coke/asphalt, are sold at a substantial and progressively greater discount from the price of crude oil with the increased removal of clean product content.

Refiner's margin is the difference between price of refined products and cost of crude oil per barrel (bbl). There are various ways of measuring refiner's margin for judging the overall financial health of the refinery industry. One is the wholesale price of two barrels of gasoline plus one barrel of distillates less cost of three barrels of crude oil. Another is the wholesale price of three barrels of gasoline, two barrels of distillates, and one barrel of jet fuel less cost of six barrels of crude. The choice of which to use depends on the general type of refinery one has in mind to assess potential profitability. Refiner's margin multiplied by the refinery run (crude oil intake) is an estimate of the gross profit of a refining company. Alternatively refiner's margin can be calculated for a particular refinery by dividing its gross profit by crude oil input in barrels, as will be done here.

Rather than absolute values for crude oil and product prices, the spreadsheet is built on price spreads to maximize refiner's gross profit because it is not the price of refined products or the cost of crude that determines profitability *per se*, but the spread or difference between the two. Refiner's gross profit is not net profit, as fixed operating, overhead, depreciation, and financial costs have not been taken into account. As these do not change with refinery throughput, maximizing gross profit also maximizes net profit. For the purposes of dealing in price spreads, the cheapest crude oil (crude1) is deemed the benchmark or marker crude where better grade crude oils are priced at a $/bbl premium. Refined products will also be priced at a $/bbl premium above the benchmark or marker crude except for resids, which are sold at a substantial discount. An overview of the spreadsheet will help to gain an appreciation of what's involved with this project accompanied with detailed instructions.

General Overview of the Refinery Model

The refinery can handle eight different types of crude oil with varying yields of high-end products. Crude1, the marker crude, has the poorest yield of high-end products, and crude8 the best. The numerical values in Project Figure 1 are a result of a Solver optimization run.

Overall View of Spreadsheet Formulation 1

In rows 4–7, columns B and E contain the spread in price for the various grades of crude oil in relation to crude1. Columns C and F are the quantity to be purchased of each grade of crude. These are not variables, but reference variables in row 40, to be shown shortly, whose values have been determined by Solver. Cost in cell H4 is the respective spread and volume for the eight crude oils plus the variable cost of operation of the catcracker and coker, also to be described shortly. Rows 11–17 show two refinery outputs—ultra and regular brand gasolines. Each section for a particular brand contains the price spread for the product referenced to crude1, minimum and maximum quantities as guided by marketing, and actual amount produced. Also shown are specifications for minimum octane and maximum vapor pressure plus actual specifications of produced gasoline. Rows 20–26 perform the same function for regular gasoline plus price for third-party sales of the three blends, minimum and maximum quantities provided by marketing, and amount actually produced for sale. Rows 29–32 show spreads for jet fuel and distillates

Project Figure 1 Spreadsheet Formulation 1

	A	B	C	D	E	F	G	H	I
1	Refinery Control Board								
2								($000)	
3		$/Bbl	Quantity		$/Bbl	Quantity	Revenue	$9,816	
4	Crude1	$0.00	171,607	Crude5	$3.50	180,235	Costs	$5,064	
5	Crude2	$1.00	174,294	Crude6	$4.00	184,308	Profit	$4,752	
6	Crude3	$2.00	178,910	Crude7	$4.50	192,242			
7	Crude4	$3.00	178,893	Crude8	$5.00	239,512	Ref. Margin	$3.17	
8									
9	Marketing Information Next Cycle								
10									
11	Ultra Brand Gasoline					Premium Brand Gasoline			
12		Min	Max	Prod			Min	Max	Prod
13	$/Bbl	Qty	Qty	Qty		$/Bbl	Qty	Qty	Qty
14	$10.00	100,000	250,000	127,842		$9.00	125,000	300,000	125,000
15	Octane		Vapor Pressure			Octane		Vapor Pressure	
16	Mininum: 105		Maximum: 5.0			Mininum: 100		Maximum: 6.0	
17	Actual: 105		Actual: 5.0			Actual: 100.380162		Actual: 5.8	
18									
19					3rd Party		Min	Max	Prod
20	Regular Brand Gasoline				Sales	$/Bbl	Qty	Qty	Qty
21		Min	Max	Prod	Blend1	$9.00	5,000	30,000	5,000
22	$/Bbl	Qty	Qty	Qty	Blend2	$8.00	5,000	15,000	5,000
23	$8.00	150,000	600,000	518,720	Blend3	$7.00	5,000	10,000	10,000
24	Octane		Vapor Pressure						
25	Mininum: 80		Maximum: 6.0						
26	Actual: 80.0		Actual: 5.1						
27									
28									
29	Jet Fuel					Distillates			
30		Min	Max	Prod			Min	Max	Prod
31	$/Bbl	Qty	Qty	Qty		$/Bbl	Qty	Qty	Qty
32	$6.00	100,000	300,000	214,079		$5.00	-	500,000	382,638
33									
34					Straight Run	Fuel Oil	Petroleum		
35					$/Bbl	$/Bbl	Coke/Asphalt		
36					($10.00)	($15.00)	($20.00)		
37				Amt Produced	-	-	6,722		

(diesel fuel and home heating oil) along with their minimums and maximums. Rows 34–37 show the quantities of three residual products of the refining process. Straight run can be sold all or in part with the remainder as input to a catcracker. The catcracker enhances production of the white products, with fuel oil, sometimes referred to as heavy fuel oil, as a residual product. Fuel oil can be sold all or in part with the remainder as input to a coker for producing more white products with the residual product being asphalt or petroleum coke. Residual products are sold at a discount from crude1, a loss akin to a disposal cost. Revenue in cell H3 is price multiplied by production volume of three brands of gasoline plus jet fuel and distillates and, using the SumProduct function, price times production volume of third-party sales of three blends and three types of residual products. The difference between revenue and cost is gross profit which, when divided by refinery throughput in thousands of barrels, yields actual refinery margin. Over time, the delivered $/bbl spread for each crude oil type changes, reflecting its competitive market dynamics with respect to the marker crude plus changes in shipping costs. Refinery spreads for oil products also change with time along with volume, responding to shifting demand patterns such as seasonal variations, where demand for heating oil is less and gasoline greater in summer and vice versa in winter.

Overall View of Spreadsheet Formulation 2

In Project Figure 2, cells B40:I40 are the quantity in barrels to be purchased for each type of crude oil, which will be designated in the Solver menu as variables. These are totaled

Project Figure 2 Spreadsheet Formulation 2

	A	B	C	D	E	F	G	H	I	J
39		Crude1	Crude2	Crude3	Crude4	Crude5	Crude6	Crude7	Crude8	Qty to Buy
40		171,607	174,294	178,910	178,893	180,235	184,308	192,242	239,512	1,500,000
41										
42										
43										
44										Cost:
45										
46										
47										
48										Refinery
49										Production
50	Blend1	5%	6%	6%	9%	10%	12%	16%	18%	159,884
51	Blend2	7%	8%	10%	11%	12%	15%	18%	20%	195,305
52	Blend3	11%	13%	15%	17%	19%	20%	21%	22%	262,953
53	Jet Fuel	11%	11%	12%	12%	13%	13%	13%	13%	184,504
54	Distillates	29%	27%	23%	25%	25%	22%	15%	11%	323,487
55	Resid	30%	28%	27%	19%	14%	11%	10%	9%	268,867
56	Total %	93%	93%	93%	93%	93%	93%	93%	93%	

in cell J40 and will be constrained to equal the desired weekly refinery run of 1.5 million barrels in cell K40 (not shown). This constraint ties crude input with desired output.

Percentage distributions of high-end products for each crude oil are in rows 50–54 along with the percentage of straight-run resid in row 55. Yield from each crude type totals 93 percent, as 7 percent of crude is consumed internally to run the refinery. In addition to total crude consumption, Column J also contains production quantities of three blending stocks, jet fuel, distillates, and residual products in cells J50–J55, which are the SumProduct of the volume of each crude type multiplied by the products' respective yields. Considering that residual products are sold at a loss and money is made on gasoline, and to a lesser degree jet fuel and distillates, it is obvious that Crude7 and Crude8 are the best choices to maximize the refinery output of high-end products. But as one may suspect, they are also the most costly with the highest spreads with respect to the marker crude.

Overall View of Spreadsheet Formulation 3

The model incorporates a catcracker and a coker. In Project Figure 3, volume of straight-run resids is 268,867 barrels (cell J55), of which 100 percent (cell K47) becomes feedstock for the catcracker. If the value were not 100 percent, the volume not directed to the cat-cracker would be sold separately (cell J59), which is referenced in cell E37 in Project Figure 1. The catcracker produces more high-end products (15 percent blend1, 20 percent blend2, 25 percent blend3, 10 percent jet fuel, and 20 percent distillates), with the remainder heavy fuel oil. The percentage of heavy fuel oil to be fed into the coker is in cell L47 and amount

Project Figure 3 Spreadsheet Formulation 3

	J	K	L	M	N	O	P	Q	R	S	T	U	V
43		$2.00	$1.00										
44	Cost:	CatCracker	Coker										
45		Production	Production										
46		Input	Input										
47		100%	100%										
48	Refinery	268,867	26,887	Total									
49	Production			Production									
50	159,884	40,330	2,689	202,903	202,903 Blend1 produced must equal Blend1 consumed in Ultra, Premium, and Regular gasolines and sold separately								
51	195,305	53,773	4,033	253,112	253,112 Blend2 produced must equal Blend2 consumed in Ultra, Premium, and Regular gasolines and sold separately								
52	262,953	67,217	5,377	335,547	335,547 Blend3 produced must equal Blend3 consumed in Ultra, Premium, and Regular gasolines and sold separately								
53	184,504	26,887	2,689	214,079									
54	323,487	53,773	5,377	382,638									
55	268,867	26,887	6,722										
56													
57													
58													
59	-	-	6,722										

Project Table 1 Designation of X Variables

Variable	Meaning
X1	Blend1 in Ultra
X2	Blend2 in Ultra
X3	Blend3 in Ultra
X4	Blend1 in Premium
X5	Blend2 in Premium
X6	Blend3 in Premium
X7	Blend1 in Regular
X8	Blend2 in Regular
X9	Blend3 in Regular
X10	Blend1 Third-Party Sales
X11	Blend2 Third-Party Sales
X12	Blend3 Third-Party Sales

sold as heavy fuel is in cell K59 and referenced in cell F37. The coker makes more high-end products (10 percent blend1, 15 percent blend2, 20 percent blend3, 10 percent jet fuel, and 20 percent distillates), with the remainder in cell L59 sold as petroleum coke or asphalt and referenced in cell G37 in Project Figure 1. The percentage shares of resids as feedstock to the catcracker and the coker in cells K47 and L47 will also be designated variables or adjustable cells in the Solver menu along with the quantities of each crude type. Total production of high-end products in column M is the sum of refinery and catcracker and coker output. Constraints will be constructed linking production to desired sales volumes of three brands of gasoline, jet fuel, and distillates, to be described shortly in column N.

In addition to the volumes of the eight types of crude oil and percentage utilization of the catcracker and coker, cells X1–X12 are also designated variables in the Solver menu, with the meanings described in Project Table 1.

Vapor Pressure and Octane Specifications

The refinery produces three blending stocks, but sells three brands of gasoline. Gasoline brands are made by mixing blending stocks, Blend1, Blend2, and Blend3, which have the characteristics shown in Project Table 2.

As already shown in Project Figures 1 and 2, three brands of gasoline must satisfy the specifications with regard to minimum octane rating and maximum vapor pressure (psi) in Project Table 3.

Project Table 2 Blending Stock Characteristics

Blending Stock	Octane	Vapor Pressure (PSI)
Blend1	108	5
Blend2	90	7
Blend3	73	4

Project Table 3 Gasoline Specifications

Gasoline Brand	Minimum Octane	Maximum Vapor Pressure (PSI)
Ultra	105	5
Premium	100	6
Regular	80	6

Mixing Constraints

When three blending stocks are mixed together, the amount of Ultra gasoline produced is X1+X2+X3, Premium X4+X5+X6, and Regular X7+X8+X9. Blend1 production is equal to X1+X4+X7+X10, the amount of Blend1 in each of the three brands of gasoline plus the amount sold separately. Similarly Blend2 production is X2+X5+X8+X11 and Blend3 is X3+X6+X9+X12, where X11 and X12 are third-party sales of Blend2 and Blend3.

Focusing on Ultra brand gasoline, octane rating and vapor pressure are the weighted averages of the constituent parts of the three blending stocks. For instance, if gasoline is produced by mixing 50 percent Blend1 and 50 percent Blend2, its vapor pressure would be 50 percent * 5 psi + 50 percent * 7 psi, or 6 psi, and its octane rating would be 50 percent * 108 + 50 percent * 90, or 99. The following formula is the weighted average of the vapor pressure for the mix of Blend1, Blend2, and Blend3 making up the Ultra brand, which must be less than, or equal to, 5:

$$\frac{5*X1+7*X2+4*X3}{X1+X2+X3}\ \frac{}{X1+X2+X3}\ \frac{}{X1+X2+X3} <= 5$$

or in terms of a common denominator:

$$(5*X1+7*X2+4*X3)/(X1+X2+X3) <= 5$$

This nonlinear expression can be transformed to a linear equation by cross-multiplying and combining terms:

$$5*X1+7*X2+4*X3 <= 5*(X1+X2+X3)$$
$$5*X1+7*X2+4*X3 <= 5*X1+5*X2+5*X3$$

2*X2–X3<=0, which will be designated a constraint associated with the vapor pressure for Ultra gasoline.

Alternatively vapor pressure could be left as a nonlinear expression. Cell D17, the actual vapor pressure of Ultra brand gasoline, could have the formula (5*X1+7*X2+4*X3)/ (X1+X2+X3), with cell D16 containing the maximum vapor pressure, with a constraint for cell D17 being less than cell D16. Generally speaking, in Solver applications, it pays to convert nonlinear to linear constraints to shorten run time. If complete linearity can be achieved, the Solver solution is global. A global solution means that no matter what the starting point (the assignment of initial values to the variables), the same solution will always result. A local optimal solution occurs when nonlinear relationships exist. A local optimal solution means that a change in the assignment of initial values to the variables may affect the solution. Thus it is important to rerun Solver when in the nonlinear mode with different initial values for the variables to see whether better solutions exist.

Following the procedure already demonstrated for vapor pressure, the nonlinear expression for the octane rating can be reduced to a linear constraint. In cell B16, the minimum octane rating for Ultra is 105. Cell B17 contains the nonlinear expression for the actual octane rating:

$$= (108 * X1 + 90 * X2 + 73 * X3)/(X1 + X2 + X3)$$

The associated linear constraint is:

$$(108 * X1 + 90 * X2 + 73 * X3)/(X1 + X2 + X3) > 105$$
$$108 * X1 + 90 * X2 + 73 * X3 > 105 * X1 + 105 * X2 + 105 * X3$$
$$3 * X1 - 15 * X2 - 32 * X3 > 0$$

This then becomes the constraint associated with Ultra gasoline with regard to octane. Other vapor pressure and octane constraints are similarly constructed as those for the Ultra brand, but reflecting different adjustable cells: X4, X5, and X6 for the Premium brand, and X7, X8, and X9 for the Regular brand, plus different maximum vapor pressure and minimum octane ratings. The constraints shown in Project Figure 4 have been placed in a single location to ease incorporation into the Solver menu.

The first set of constraints handles minimum and maximum production of the various indicated products. The formulation in Project Figure 4 does not contain any variables, but references particular cell locations in the spreadsheet. For instance, cell L4, the production volume of Ultra gasoline, references D14 (contains the formula =D14). Cell M4 references cell B14 for the minimum, and cell N4 references cell C14 for the maximum; the remainder are similarly constructed. Octane constraints must satisfy a minimum, and

Project Figure 4 Solver Constraints

	K	L	M	N	O	P	Q	R	S
2			Min	Max	Equal		Notes		
3	Production						Production between Min and Max		
4	Ultra	127,842	100,000	250,000			Ultra gasoline		
5	Premium	125,000	125,000	300,000			Premium gasoline		
6	Regular	518,720	150,000	600,000			Regular gasoline		
7	Jet Fuel	214,079	100,000	300,000			Jet fuel		
8	Distillate	382,638	-	500,000			Distillates		
9	Blend1	5,000	5,000	30,000			Blend1 - 3rd party sales		
10	Blend2	5,000	5,000	15,000			Blend2 - 3rd party sales		
11	Blend3	10,000	5,000	10,000			Blend3 - 3rd party sales		
12									
13	Ultra Octane	0	0				Octane values are > Min constraints		
14	Premium Octane	47520.3023	0						
15	Regular Octane	0	0						
16									
17	Ultra Vapor	-		-			Vapor pressures are < Max constraints		
18	Premium Vapor	(19,504)		-					
19	Regular Vapor	(453,539)		-					
20	Max catcracker	100%		1			% limit of straight run to catcracker		
21	Max coker	100%		1			% limit of catcracker resid to coker		
22									
23	= Constraints								
24	Refinery Run	1,500,000			1,500,000		This ties actual refinery output to crude input		
25	Bl1 Sup=Demand	202,903			202,903		These 3 constraints tie production of Blend1,		
26	Bl2 Sup=Demand	253,112			253,112		Blend2, and Blend3 to the volume of Blend1,		
27	Bl3 Sup=Demand	335,547			335,547		Blend2, and Blend3 consumed in the production		
28							of ultra, premium, and regular gasolines plus		
29							the third party sale of Blend1,2,3		

Project Figure 5 Solver Menu

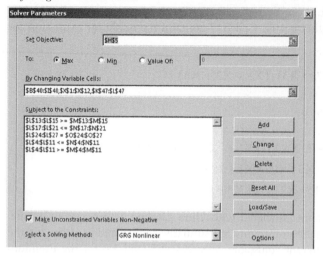

vapor pressure constraints must satisfy a maximum, value. The percentages of feedstock to the catcracker and coker cannot exceed 100 percent. The equal constraints equate crude purchased to the desired refinery throughput and ties the production of blending feedstocks to what is required to produce the indicated refinery output of gasolines and third-party sales. For instance, for Blend1, what is produced is the sum of refinery, catcracker, and coking output and what is required is X1+X4+X7+X10, the amount of Blend1 in the three gasoline brands plus what is sold to third parties. The others are similarly constructed following the variable definitions in Project Figure 4. Project Figure 5 is the Solver menu.

Selection of "Make Unconstrained Variables Non-Negative" ensures that all variables have positive values. The GRG Nonlinear Solving Method was necessary, as a solution could not be achieved using the Simplex LP Solving Method despite the effort made in reducing nonlinearity associated with octane and vapor pressure constraints. The problem with the nonlinear Solver solution is that it is not global. The initial conditions were established by setting all variables equal to zero prior to running Solver. Unfortunately this is a local optimal solution, which may or may not be the global optimal solution. Only by changing the initial conditions by setting different values to the variables can one feel confident that the local optimal solution may also be the optimal solution. Even doing so is not a guarantee that the global optimal solution has been identified. It is possible that another set of starting values for the variables could result in a better solution.

Evaluation of a catcracker investment can be done by setting the limits on the variables associated with the catcracker and coker to a minimum and maximum of zero and rerun Solver to obtain the optimal solution without the catcracker and coker. Then to make the maximum of the variable for catcracker use 1, leaving the coker with a maximum of zero, and rerun Solver. The two runs will furnish all the information necessary for analysis on not only the difference in profitability, but also the change in product output and possibly crude input. The analysis can be repeated to evaluate an investment decision of adding a coker.

Notes

1 Louis Sahagun, "U.S. Officials Cut Estimate of Recoverable Monterey Shale Oil by 96%," *Los Angeles Times* (May 20, 2014), Website www.latimes.com/business/la-fi-oil-20140521-story.html.

2 Unless indicated otherwise, oil reserves are from *BP Energy Statistics* (London, UK: British Petroleum, 2013).

3 EIA/ARI World Shale Gas and Shale Oil Resource Assessment, Table 5, Page 10, US Energy Information Administration (EIA) (May, 2013), Website www.eia.gov/analysis/studies/worldshale gas/pdf/overview.pdf.

4 "SEC Final Rule: Modernization of Oil and Gas Reporting," Securities and Exchange Commission (2009), Website www.sec.gov/rules/final/2008/33-8995.pdf.

5 Asjylyn Loder, "Millions of Barrels of Oil are about to Vanish," Bloomberg (May 21, 2015), Website www.bloomberg.com/news/articles/2015-05-21/oil-s-whodunit-moment-coming-with-millions-of-barrels-to-vanish.

6 Bill Kovarik, "The Oil Reserve Fallacy: Proven Reserves are Not a Measure of Future Supply," Website www.radford.edu/~wkovarik/oil/oilreservehistory.html.

7 Michel T. Halbouty, *Giant Oil and Gas Fields of the Decade (1990–1999)* (Tulsa, OK: American Association of Petroleum Geologists, 2003).

8 Matthew R. Simmons, *Twilight in the Desert: The Coming Saudi Oil Shock and the World Economy* (New York, NY: Wiley, 2005). This is a contentious book that argues that the world should not take too great a degree of comfort on depending on Saudi Arabia to remain the oil producer of last resort.

9 An Evaluation of USGS World Petroleum Assessment 2000—Supporting Data (Open-File Report 2007–1021), US Geological Survey (2007).

10 In the second edition to this book, which was published in 2010, meaning that I last reviewed it in 2009, I concluded that peaking would occur in 15–20 years (Page 210). Without fracking, we are adding more conventional oil reserves than what is being consumed. Fracking makes the problem worse for advocates of oil peaking unless oil peaking is restricted to low-cost oil fields. Those have definitely peaked. References used in the second edition concerning peaking included: "Deepwater Oil Discovery Rate May Have Peaked, Production Peak May Follow in Ten Years," *Oil & Gas Journal* (July 26, 2004), one of a six-part series on Hubbert Revisited, Tulsa, OK. See also Association for the Study of Peak Oil and Gas, Websites www.asponews.org and www.peakoil.net; C.J. Campbell, "Peak Oil," Website www.geologie.tu-clausthal.de/Campbell/lecture.html; "The Wolf at the Door: Beginner's Guide to Oil Depletion," Website www.wolfatthedoor.org.uk; "Future World Oil Supplies," Website www.dieoff.org; and "Hubbert Peak of Oil Production," Website www.hubbertpeak.com.

11 Bryan Walsh, "The Future of Oil: Extreme Oil … Is Replacing Dwindling Supplies at a Heavy Economic and Environmental Cost," *Time Magazine* (April 9, 2012). See also Mark Scott, "Out of Africa (and Elsewhere): More Fossil Fuels," *The New York Times* (April 11, 2012).

12 Sig Silber, "Peak Oil Deferred" (July 21, 2013), Cached at Global Economic Intersection—Econintersect, Website http://econintersect.com/wordpress.

13 "Cheaper Oil: Winners and Losers," *The Economist* (October 25, 2014).

14 Tom Randall, "Break-Even Points for U.S. Shale Oil," Bloomberg New Energy Finance (October 17, 2014), Website www.bloomberg.com/news/2014-10-17/oil-is-cheap-but-not-so-cheap-that-ameri cans-won-t-profit-from-it.html.

15 "Saudi America: The Benefits of Shale Oil are Bigger than Many Americans Realise. Policy Has Yet to Catch Up," *The Economist* (February 15, 2014).

16 Nick Cunningham, "EIA Confirms Oil Production Peaked," OilPrice.com (July 12, 2015), Website http://oiprice.com/Energy/Energy-General/EIA-Confirms-Oil-Production-Peaked.html.

17 *BP Energy Statistics* (London, UK: British Petroleum, 2013). There are differences between world consumption and production statistics as the former includes stock changes and consumption of nonpetroleum additives and refinery gains. Consumption figures were reduced to keep total consumption equal to total production.

18 International Energy Outlook 2014, US Energy Information Administration, Tables A2 and A4 (September, 2014).

19 Larry Kumins, "CRS Report for Congress: West Coast and Alaska Oil Exports" (May 25, 2006), Website www.cnie.org/NLE/CRSreports/06jun/RS22142.pdf.

20 Clifford Krauss, "Reversing the Flow of Oil," *The New York Times Energy Section* (October 8, 2014).

21 "Changing Crude Oil Markets: Allowing Exports Could Reduce Consumer Fuel Prices, and the Size of the Strategic Reserves should be Reexamined," US Government Accountability Office (GAO-14-807) (September, 2014), Website www.gao.gov/assets/670/666274.pdf.

22 A partial listing of crude oil grades and types can be found on Intertek's Website www.intertek.com/petroleum/crude-oil-types.

23 Shale oil reserves from Technically Recoverable Shale Oil and Shale Gas Resources, US Energy Information Administration, Attachment C, Table A-1 U.S. Remaining Shale Gas and Oil Reserves and Undeveloped Resources (June, 2013), Website www.eia.gov/analysis/studies/worldshalegas/pdf/overview.pdf.

24 Interestingly Table A-1 above did not include Monterey Shale Oil in its estimated shale oil resources of 47.7 billion barrels.

25 Philip K. Verleger, Jr., "The Amazing Tale of U.S. Energy Independence," *International Economy* (Spring 2012).

26 Shale oil reserves from Technically Recoverable Shale Oil and Shale Gas Resources, US Energy Information Administration, Table 5, Top 10 Countries with Technically Recoverable Shale Oil Resources (June, 2013), Website www.eia.gov/analysis/studies/worldshalegas/pdf/overview.pdf. Crude oil reserves from *BP Energy Statistics* (London, UK: British Petroleum, 2013). US shale oil reserves reflect the recent reduction (essentially elimination) of Monterey Shale Oil as described in the text. Venezuela has 13 billion tons of shale oil and Canada 9 billion tons. When compared to their reserves of 298 billion barrels and 174 billion barrels respectively, shale oil is a mere drop in the bottle and both nations have been omitted from Figure 6.11.

27 Alexei Lossan, "Foreign Oil Majors Pull Out of Russia," from a special advertising feature, "Russia Beyond the Headlines," provided by Rossiyskaya Gazeta, *The New York Times* (October 15, 2014).

28 Morelos and Queretaro, "Mexico's Reforms: The Power and the Glory," *The Economist* (July 5, 2014).

29 Laurent Thomet, "Mexico Congress Gives Final Nod to Landmark Oil Reform," AFT (August 7, 2014), Website http://news.yahoo.com/mexico-set-implement-historic-oil-reform-000510599.html.

30 "Oil in Latin America: The Good Oil Boys Club," *The Economist* (July 18, 2015).

31 "Venezuela Oil Diaspora: Brain Hemorrhage," *The Economist* (July 19, 2014).

32 "Algeria's Sonatrach to Spend $100 bln Over 5 Years to Boost Oil, Gas," Reuters (July 21, 2014), Website http://af.reuters.com/article/investingNews/idAFKBN0FP0KH20140720.

33 "The Benefits of Shale Oil are Bigger than Many Americans Realise. Policy has Yet to Catch Up," *The Economist* (February 15, 2014), Website www.economist.com/news/US/21596553. The estimate of 2,500 annual new wells for the Bakken field and the estimate for 60 new conventional wells for a field in southern Iraq are drawn from the International Energy Agency. See also Asjylan Loder, "Dream of U.S. Oil Independence Slams Against Shale Costs," Bloomberg (February 26, 2014), Website www.bloomberg.com/news/2014-02-27/dream-of-u-s-oil-independence-slams-against-shale-costs.html.

34 Ajay Makan and Neil Hume, "IEA Warns of Future Oil Supply Crunch," IEA (November 12, 2013).

35 Humbert Marquez, "Oil-Venezuela: Orimulsion R.I.P.," Inter Press Service News Agency (June 3, 2004), Website www.ipsnews.net/2004/06/oil-venezuela-orimulsion-rip.

36 "PDVSA Plans to Scrap the Expansion of Orimulsion Fuel," Alexander's Oil and Gas Connections (March 18, 2004), Website www.gasandoil.com/news/ms_america/7ab7f7e4a6f661bd4edfe1a05b36aa02.

37 The characteristics of Merey 16 crude compared to other Venezuelan crude can be found at Website www.genesisny.net/Commodity/Oil/OSpecs.html.

38 Alan Harvie, Partner at Norton Rose Fulbright, "Canadian Legislative Update," AIPN Spring Conference (April, 2014).

39 "Alberta Oil Sands Output to Nearly Double by 2023—Regulator," Reuters (May 29, 2013), Website www.reuters.com/article/2014/05/29/canada-crude-alberta-idUSL1N0OF1ZZ20140529. "Alberta's Energy Reserves 2012 and Supply Demand Outlook 2013–2022," Energy Resources Conservation Board publication ST98-2013, calls for production of 3.8 million Bpd by 2022.

40 Clifford Krauss, "'Saudi America': Mirage?" *The New York Times* (April 22, 2014). The source of production figures in this article was the Canadian Association of Petroleum Producers.

41 "Canada's Oil Sands and Heavy Oil," Petroleum Communication Foundation (2000), Website www.centreforenergy.com.

42 "Alberta Sands Quarterly Update," Alberta Government (Summer 2013), Website https://alberta canada.com/files/albertacanada/AOSID_Quarterly_Update_Summer2013.pdf.

43 TransCanada Keystone XL, Website http://keystone-xl.com/about/the-keystone-xl-oil-pipeline-project.

44 Three opposition sites to Canadian oil sands are: Tar Sands Network, Website www.no-tar-sands.org; Visual Carbon, Website www.saxifrages.org/eco; and "Climate Impacts of the Keystone XL Tar Sands Pipeline," National Resources Defense Council (NRDC) Issue Brief (October, 2013), Website www.nrdc.org/energy/dirtyfuels.asp.

45 The US government position is laid out in Richard K. Lattanzio, "Canadian Oil Sands: Life-Cycle Assessments of Greenhouse Gas Emissions," Congressional Research Service 7–5700 R42537 (March 15, 2013), Website www.fas.org/sgp/crs/misc/R42537.pdf. A more constructive approach to approving the Keystone pipeline is in Michael B. McElroy, "Should the President Approve Construction?" *Harvard Magazine* (December, 2013).

46 Peter Erickson and Michael Lazarus (Stockholm Environment Institute) in an article published by the journal *Nature Climate Change* (August 10, 2014), Website http://finance.yahoo.com/news/study-keystone-carbon-pollution-more-figured-171016712--finance.html.

47 PBS News Hour Special on train derailments, Website www.pbs.org/newshour/bb/explosive-train-derailments-prompt-u-s-advocate-safety-improvements-oil-transport.

48 Jad Mouawad, "U.S. Proposes Faster Changes in Oil Trains," *The New York Times* (July 24, 2014). See also "Crude Errors," *The Economist* (August 23, 2014).

49 Dan Heyman and Richard Perez-Pena, "Spilled Oil Keeps Flames Burning After a Train Derailment in West Virginia," *The New York Times* (February 18, 2015).

50 "BNSF: Oil Train Derailment Near Galena Involved Safer Tank Cars," *Chicago Tribune* (March 6, 2015), Website www.chicagotribune.com/news/local/breaking/chi-galena-train-derailment-20150305-story.html.

51 "Huge Fire: Train Carrying Crude Oil Derails in Ontario," *RT News* (March 7, 2015), Website http://rt.com/news/238693-canada-train-derailment-gogama.

52 "North Dakota Town Evacuated after Oil Cars Derail and Catch Fire," *Bismarck Tribune* (May 6, 2015), Website http://bismarcktribune.com/bakken/north-dakota-town-evacuated-after-oil-cars-derail-and-catch/article_992b4c53-24f4-54fd-a657-9943d69fca0c.html.

53 Finbarr Bermingham, "Canada Pushes Ahead with Pacific Oil Pipeline Amid Environmental Protests," *International Business Times (IBT)* (June 18, 2014), Website http://uk.news.yahoo.com/canada-pushes-ahead-pacific-oil-pipeline-amid-environmental-093901384.html#zHr8oAr. See also "Canada's Northern Gateway Project: A Go or a No?" *The Economist* (June 21, 2014).

54 Andrew Hart, "Rosebud Sioux Tribe: House Vote on Keystone XL Pipeline an 'Act of War,'" *The Huffington Post* (November 16, 2014), Website www.huffingtonpost.com/2014/11/16/rosebud-sioux-keystone-war_n_6168584.html.

55 "The Great Pipeline Battle: The Energy Industry and Stephen Harper's Government Try to Ensure Tar-sands Oil Gets to Market," *The Economist* (May 26, 2012).

56 Remarks by Dr. Edward Morse (Global Head of Commodities Research at Citigroup), "Instability in Iraq and Implications for Global Energy Markets," Panel discussion held by the Columbia University/SIPA Center of Global Energy Policy (June 19, 2014).

57 Bill Chameides, "The Carbon Footprint of Oil Sands Oil," Duke University Nicholas School of the Environment (March 26, 2012), Website http://blogs.nicholas.duke.edu/thegreengrok/carbonfoot print-tarsands.

58 "Oil Shale vs. Shale Oil," Colorado Oil & Gas Association (June 18, 2013), Website www.coga.org/pdf_Basics/Basics_OilShale.pdf.

59 "$20 Trillion Shale Oil Find Surrounding Coober Pedy 'Can Fuel Australia,'" *The Advertiser* (January 24, 2013), Website www.adelaidenow.com.au/news/south-australia/trillion-shale-oil-find-surrounding-coober-pedy-can-fuel-australia/story-e6frea83-1226560401043.

60 Kerry Sloan, "What's Next for Oil Shale?" *The Business Times* (October 8, 2013), Website http://thebusinesstimes.com/whats-next-for-oil-shale. See also Shell Oil, Website www.shell.us/about shell/projects-locations/mahogany.html. (Site no longer available, but may be cached in Shell Oil's archives.)

61 "Flaming Rocks: A Second Shale Revolution May Be Coming, Squeezing Out Yet More Oil," *The Economist* (June 28, 2014).

62 Larry Axelrod, "ULSFO Prognosis," Presentation at Platts Bunker and Residual Fuel Conference (June 25, 2015), Website www.axelrodenergyprojects.com.

63 Unless indicated otherwise, the principal source of information is the *Transportation Energy Data Book* (Washington, DC: US Department of Energy, 2013). Most data applies for 2011.

64 CAFE standards are described on the National Highway Traffic Safety Administration Website at www.nhtsa.gov/fuel-economy.

65 Select the "Read the Final Rule" link to obtain the 2017–2025 Final Rule pdf file at NHTSA, Website www.nhtsa.gov/About+NHTSA/Press+Releases/2012/Obama+Administration+Finalize s+Historic+54.5+mpg+Fuel+Efficiency+Standards.

66 Full-Race Motorsports, Website www.full-race.com/articles/what-is-ecoboost.html.

67 "The Rebirth of the Diesel Engine," *The Economist Technology Quarterly* (September 7, 2013).

68 A private company, Vincentric, provides data, knowledge, and insight to measure and analyze the cost of owning and operating vehicles: Website http://vincentric.com/Home/IndustryReports/HybridAnalysis.aspx.

69 A good explanation of the workings of the hybrid power drive train is in the Free Encyclopedia, Website http://en.wikipedia.org/wiki/Hybrid_vehicle_drivetrain.

70 The source of number of fueling stations for each alternative fuel is National Alternative Fuels Data Center (US Department of Energy), Website www.afdc.energy.gov (2014); the source of gasoline fueling stations is Statistical Brain, Website www.statisticbrain.com/gas-station-statistics (2014); and the source of number of vehicles for each fuel is the *Transportation Energy Data Book* (Washington, DC: US Department of Energy, 2013). Data applies for 2011. Motor vehicles for gasoline include SUVs, minivans, and pickup trucks.

71 "Vehicle Technologies Program," US Department of Energy/Energy Efficiency & Renewable Energy (May, 2011), Website www.cleancities.energy.gov.

72 Tam Hunt, "Are Electric Vehicles Already Halfway to Market Dominance?" (December 18, 2013), Website www.renewableenergyworld.com/articles/2013/12/are-electric-vehicles-already-halfway-to-market-dominance.html.

73 EVObsession, Website http://evobsession.com/tesla-sales-updates-estimates.

74 Neil Winton, "Electric Car Sales in Western Europe Spurt, But from Miniscule Base," Forbes (February 6, 2014), Website www.forbes.com/sites/neilwinton/2014/02/06/electric-car-sales-in-western-europe-spurt-but-from-miniscule-base.

75 Alexandra Ho, "China Requires Electric Vehicles to Make Up 30 Percent of State Purchases," *Bloomberg News* (July 14, 2014).

76 "Today's Fuel: The World's Thirst for Oil Could Be Nearing a Peak," and "Supermajordammerung: The Day of the Huge Integrated International Oil Company is Drawing to a Close," *The Economist* (August 3, 2013).

77 Mini Cooper, Website www.miniusa.com/content/miniusa/en.html.

78 MIT, Website http://video.mit.edu/watch/the-city-car-10146.

79 US EPA, Website www.epa.gov/cleanenergy/energy-resources/calculator.html#results. This is a handy reference for calculating GHG emissions in terms of carbon dioxide emissions and in terms of various sources of carbon dioxide emissions.

80 Excellent coverage on the subject of forward oil markets in futures, swaps and options, and managing oil price risk is in Chapters 17–20 of Morgan Downey, *Oil 101* (New York, NY: Wooden Table Press, 2009). The application of incorporating simulation into risk analysis of oil is contained in select sections of Roy Nersesian, *Energy Risk Modeling* (Ithaca, NY: Palisade, 2013).

81 This project is an adaptation from Roy Nersesian, *Energy Risk Modeling*, Section 3: From Solver to Evolver (Ithaca, NY: Palisade, 2013).

7   Natural Gas

This chapter covers the history of natural gas from its beginning as a manufactured gas made from coal. It is the most regulated of fossil fuels because only one natural gas pipeline can be connected to a house, just as a house can only be connected to one cable for electricity. Like electricity, deregulation/liberalization has changed the nature of regulation considerably in North America and Europe to allow market forces to influence price, but the mechanism by which market forces affect price is still well regulated. How natural gas travels from a resource in the earth to a point of consumption will be described along with growth in the international trade in natural gas and the development of nonconventional sources of methane, including fracking and coal bed methane. The future of natural gas as a replacement for coal and as a motor vehicle fuel will also be covered.

Background

Natural gas is made up of primarily methane, a carbon atom surrounded by four hydrogen atoms. It is the cleanest burning fossil fuel with only water and carbon dioxide as products of combustion. Carbon monoxide emissions are caused by insufficient oxygen to support combustion. Natural gas, with no nitrogen within its chemical structure, releases far less nitrous oxides than oil and coal. Formation of nitrous oxides by oxidization of nitrogen in air during combustion is a function of boiler and burner tip design, not a property of the fuel. Burning natural gas produces virtually no sulfur oxides, and no particulate and metallic emissions. Table 7.1 shows the comparative emissions of the three types of fossil fuels in terms of pounds per billion Btu of energy generated.[1]

Its greater ratio of hydrogen to carbon atoms releases less carbon dioxide per unit of energy than coal and oil. Moreover, cogeneration plants fueled by natural gas have a higher thermal efficiency than coal and oil, further lowering carbon dioxide emissions for the same output of electricity.

Reservoir recovery of natural gas fields is about double (70–80 percent) that of oil (30–40 percent), which lessens the need to continually find new gas fields. Unlike oil, natural gas requires relatively little processing to become "pipeline-quality." On the minus side, natural gas has always been a logistics challenge. In the beginning decades of the oil age, much of the natural gas found with crude oil (associated natural gas) was flared (burned) or vented to the atmosphere. Discovery of a natural gas reservoir was treated in the same light as drilling a dry hole! The primitive state of pipeline technology and reliance on reservoir pressure as a motive force to move natural gas through a pipeline restricted natural gas to local markets. Large volumes of natural gas associated

Table 7.1 Emissions in Pounds of per Billion Btu of Energy Generated

	Natural Gas	*Oil*	*Coal*
Carbon dioxide	117,000	164,000	208,000
Carbon monoxide	40	33	208
Nitrogen oxides	92	448	457
Sulfur dioxide	1	1,122	2,591
Particulates	7	84	2,744
Mercury	0	0.007	0.016

with oil production were available with developing oil discoveries in the US Southwest. With natural gas stranded with no nearby markets and no means to get it to distant markets, vast quantities of associated natural gas from oil production were vented to the atmosphere. This waste of a "free" energy source in the Southwest and the waning of natural gas fields in Appalachia provided an economic impetus to improve pipeline technology to connect suppliers with consumers over long distances in a safe, reliable, and cost-effective manner.

Another drawback is that natural gas is odorless and leaks can asphyxiate occupants of a building or trigger a fire or an explosion that can level not only a building, but also, on occasion, an entire city block. Eventually an odorant was added to give natural gas a distinctive smell. Fires fueled by broken gas mains in the aftermath of earthquakes, such as occurred in San Francisco in 1906 and Kobe, Japan, in 1995, exacerbated damage, suffering, and loss of life. In particular, the San Francisco earthquake also broke the city's water mains. With no way to extinguish fires fueled by escaping gas from a piping system short on cut-off valves, people trapped in buildings awaited a dreadful fate. Unlike liquid petroleum products, consumers have no way of storing natural gas. Natural gas delivery systems must be designed to handle extreme variations in demand.

A long-standing and complex relationship exists between natural gas and electricity, as the proliferation of "electric and gas" utilities suggests. Natural gas both supplies fuel to generate electricity and competes with electricity to supply consumers with a means to cook, heat water and living spaces, and run appliances. Manufactured gas from coal was first regulated by municipalities in the mid-1800s followed by natural gas and electricity being regulated by states in the late 1800s and early 1900s. Both became federally regulated in 1930s as a consequence of growth in interstate transmission, which posed a challenge to state regulation. Later on, natural gas interstate pipeline regulation was expanded to include natural gas suppliers. This experiment in total regulation of an industry turned into a bureaucratic quagmire of internal contradictions and unintended and undesired consequences plaguing regulators, suppliers, and consumers. This drama is covered in some detail to show that regulation by fiat simply cannot respond to the complexities and nuances of a market economy without introducing major distortions. The final solution to the regulatory question was deregulation of natural gas production, transmission, and distribution beginning in the late 1970s.

The link between electricity and natural gas can be seen in the parallel deregulation of electricity generation, transmission, and distribution. The breakdown of natural monopolies for natural gas and electricity has been completed in the US and UK, although regulatory oversight is ubiquitous and always in need of fine-tuning. Europe has just recently put the finishing touches on deregulation (called liberalization in the UK and Europe) whereby consumers have the right to switch suppliers and negotiate prices in a quasi-free market environment. Some form of deregulation (liberalization) is being considered or pursued elsewhere in the world. But deregulation (liberalization) is not at all a return to the rough and tumble-free market of Rockefeller and Carnegie. Regulatory watchdogs are in place to ensure that the system is not co-opted by special interest groups pursuing objectives not in the public interest. Yet within this framework the principles of a market economy hold where suppliers seek the highest price from buyers while buyers are free to seek suppliers with the lowest cost. The resulting price, established in an open and transparent setting, balances supply and demand, providing an economic signal about whether suppliers should expand or idle operating capacity. Price coupled with volume determines profitability, which, in turn, incentivizes energy companies to improve their efficiency and productivity. Profitability plays a paramount role in adjusting utilization of capital assets for optimal long-term performance along with influencing decisions on capacity expansion. Through competition among energy companies for market share, some of the enhanced profitability is diverted to customers in the form of lower prices for electricity and natural gas. Deregulation (liberalization) is a complete negation of rates and capacity expansions determined by regulators sitting around a table.

See the Companion Website for sections on the History of Coal Gas, the History of Natural Gas, and Federal Regulations: www.routledge.com/cw/nersesian.

Road to Deregulation

The 1976 Carter campaign for presidency pledged "moral equivalent of war" on the ongoing energy crisis. Following through on his campaign pledge, Carter created the Department of Energy (DOE) as part of the National Energy Act of 1978, which was preceded by Congress reorganizing the Federal Power Commission as the Federal Energy Regulatory Commission (FERC). The Natural Gas Policy Act of 1978 permitted FERC to price natural gas that came into production in and after 1978 into nine categories, with subcategories depending on well depth, source, and other factors, until 1985 when all post-1978 gas would be deregulated. Old gas in production prior to 1978 would be indefinitely regulated with three price tiers. The significantly higher priced new gas flowing into the system had "unexpected" Economics 101 consequences—it provided an incentive for consumers to reduce demand by switching to other sources of energy and taking steps to conserve energy, at the same time providing an incentive for producers to expand supply. New gas prices dropped when controls were lifted in 1985 because gas shortage of too little supply chasing too much demand had become a gas "bubble" of too much supply chasing too little demand. The word "bubble" was intentionally used to describe what FERC thought would be a transient state of oversupply, but "transient" lasted for nearly two decades. Natural gas prices fell to the point where synthetic gas, Alaskan gas, and liquefied natural gas (LNG) were far from being economically viable. A fall in natural gas prices as a result of letting the market work its magic (higher prices spurring exploration to expand supply and conservation and energy-switching to dampen demand) made it easy for Congress to pass the Natural Gas Wellhead Decontrol Act of 1989 abrogating price controls on all wellhead gas.

Unfortunately pipeline companies had arranged for 20-year, back-to-back, take-or-pay, fixed price contracts between electric utilities and natural gas suppliers at prevailing high natural gas prices of the late 1970s. The growing presence of lower priced gas during the first half of the 1980s placed a great deal of pressure on utilities to break their high-priced gas contracts. FERC bent to their demands and, through various rulings, allowed utilities to walk away from these contracts and buy natural gas directly from producers at lower prices and pay a fee to the pipeline companies for transmission services. This started the transformation of natural gas transmission companies from merchants to transporters, the first step in breaking a monopoly in which a consumer had no choice but to buy from the transmission company.

Once utilities were allowed to break their contracts with pipeline companies, pipeline companies were stuck with the other side of take-or-pay contracts to buy natural gas at high prices. Faced with multi-billion dollar liabilities, in 1987 FERC issued Order 500, the first step toward breaking take-or-pay contracts with natural gas producers, allowing pipeline companies to set up a system of pipeline transmission credits against producers' take-or-pay claims. While not an entirely satisfactory resolution of the matter, Order 500 turned out to be the precursor to a series of orders that ended up with Order 636 in 1992, which mandated the final solution to the national gas regulatory problem: deregulation.

To its credit, regulation either fostered or, at least, did not prevent the building of hundreds of thousands of miles of interstate gas pipelines linking natural gas producers to consumers throughout the nation. Under sanction of the FPC, natural gas pipeline merchants acquired natural gas, transmitted it through their pipelines, and sold gas in their respective franchised territories. Pipeline merchants generally made more money buying and selling gas than transmitting it. This system ended with Order 636. The whole natural gas system was unbundled into three distinct activities: natural gas producers, pipeline transmitters, and end-use buyers—either local distribution companies (LDCs) or major consumers such as utilities and industrial plants.

Order 636 restricted the service offered by interstate pipeline companies to the transmission of natural gas at a regulated rate that provided a fair and reasonable return on their investments. LDCs and major consumers would be responsible for arranging their own supplies by contracting with natural gas producers to cover their needs. This created a marketing opportunity for companies to acquire natural gas production or represent the interest of natural gas producers and sell to end users. Pipeline transmission carriers were reduced to contract carriers and were obligated to set up Electronic Bulletin Boards in order for buyers and sellers to keep track of gas flows and pipeline allocations.

In 1983, 95 percent of all interstate commerce gas was purchased by pipeline companies from natural gas producers and sold to LDCs and major consumers. By 1987, pipeline companies arranged for the buying and selling of less than half of the gas going through their pipelines, and by 1994, they were fully converted to common carriers. Thus ended the world of the pipeline companies where they dealt with producers for a supply of gas and then marketed gas to LDCs and large end users. Now the pipeline company was no longer a gas merchant but a common contract carrier like a railroad. Marketing firms were the intermediaries between natural gas producers and LDCs and large end users. However, pipeline carriers were free to set up marketing organizations to compete with independent marketers in arranging and brokering deals between natural gas buyers and sellers. The marketing arms of pipeline companies gained a significant share of the market, but they had to operate independently of their associated pipeline transmission organizations; any collusion between the two, or less than arms-length transactions, were subject to heavy fines.

   This process of unbundling of services is essentially completed. LDCs buy natural gas from producers, pay a toll to an interstate natural gas pipeline as a common carrier at a rate determined to provide a reasonable return, and supply gas to their customers through their distribution system for a fee that provides a reasonable return for the LDC. This principle of deregulation can be expanded to include customers of LDCs, in theory down to individual households, who can arrange for their natural gas needs directly with producers, pay the interstate pipeline company one toll for use of its transmission system, and then pay another toll to the LDC for use of its distribution system at a rate that represents a fair return.[2]

Life under Deregulation

The simple days when gas producers sold to interstate pipeline companies which then sold to LDCs, who in turn sold to residential and commercial markets, plus direct pipeline sales to large industrial and electric utilities at regulated prices based on costs, are gone. Natural gas suppliers are no longer regulated. Pipeline transmission companies have lost their status as natural monopolies. No longer merchants, they have become common carriers with regulated long-term transmission rates. Life is now more complex for customers because they must examine many options such as buying direct from gas producers via independent marketing firms, the marketing arms of transmission companies, storage providers, or other gas transmission pipelines and their natural gas suppliers via hubs. This process is made easy in that natural gas is fungible (identical in specifications) so that a purchaser has no idea who the actual supplier is because all suppliers are providing an identical product. All that is required of a purchaser is a connection into the system and the same is true for the supplier to fulfill its obligation to supply the system with a sufficient volume of natural gas to match sales. Transmission and distribution systems must also purchase natural gas to meet their operational requirements to transmit and distribute gas, but this cost is covered in their tolls.

   While natural gas consumers are doing their best to buy at the lowest cost, natural gas producers are doing their best to sell at the highest price. Producers look at the basis price at every hub that they have access to and net the basis price of transmission costs to obtain the netback value for their gas and then sell to the hub with the highest netback value. The enormous number of individual transactions among buyers seeking the lowest delivered cost and sellers seeking the highest netback price creates a market. Regulators, as watchdogs, ensure that no individual company dominates the market place by attempting to manipulate price or reduce the transparency of transactions or in any way to game the system. Regulators also ensure that buy and sell transactions are simplified, transferable, and transparent. The resulting natural gas price reflects the relationship between supply and demand, not a regulated price based on cost plus a guaranteed profit.

   In a commodity market, where providers are all selling at the same approximate price, differentiation among natural gas providers becomes one of value-added services. A buyer selects a provider based not only on price, but also on reliability, dependability, and behind-the-meter services. Behind-the-meter services can include maintenance and repair of natural gas equipment owned by the buyer or advice on how to utilize natural gas more efficiently. In the future, it is possible, but perhaps not probable, that companies may provide a bundled service in which gas is combined with other utility services such as electricity and water, or even communication, to woo customers away from competitors.

HEDGING RISK

Deregulation has not made life easy for transmission companies because increasing revenue means attracting more customers by, perhaps, cutting rates on spare capacity, reducing operating expenses and capital commitments, and providing value-added services behind-the-meter. Nor is life easier for the consumer. With natural gas prices fluctuating widely and long-term contracts becoming less available, there is a greater exposure to adverse price fluctuations in the spot and short-term markets. Independent gas marketers can also be at risk if their buy and sell commitments do not match up in either volume or time duration, exposing them to potentially large financial losses from an adverse change in natural gas prices.

The risk of adverse price changes generates a need for risk mitigation among natural gas suppliers, consumers, and marketers. Swaps protect suppliers from low prices and consumers from high prices that may threaten their financial well-being. Banks and other financial institutions provide an active over-the-counter market for swaps tailored to meet the particular needs of suppliers and consumers. NYMEX is the nation's leading center for buying and selling natural gas futures contracts. In addition to traditional hedging, the public trading of natural gas futures contracts opens up the opportunity for individuals (including hedgers turned gamblers) to speculate on the future price of natural gas, which is why futures volume far exceeds physical volume. Speculators add depth to the market by accepting risk that hedgers are trying to shed. However, not all risks can be mitigated by financial instruments such as volume risk (a customer uses more or less than the nominated amount), counterparty risk (one of the parties to a swap transaction does not honor its commitment), execution risk (a transaction is not properly concluded), regulatory risk (possibility of a change in rules after a transaction has been signed), operational risk (system failure), and basis risk (possibility of the price at a hub such as Boston moving differently than expected from the Henry Hub price used to hedge a risk).

LOCAL DISTRIBUTION COMPANIES (LDCs)

The demarcation point between transmission and distribution is the city gate where gas regulators reduce the pressure; scrubbers and filters remove any remaining traces of contaminants and water vapor, and mercaptan is added as an odorant to detect gas leaks. The nation's million-mile distribution system is made up of 2- to 24-inch pipe with pressures from 60 psi down to one-quarter psi (above atmospheric) for natural gas entering a home or business, and higher for industrial and utility customers. A distribution pipe was traditionally made of steel, but nowadays plastic or PVC is used for its flexibility, resistance to corrosion, and lower cost.

To ensure an adequate supply of natural gas, LDCs contract with transmission companies for pipeline volume capacity that meets peak demand. The rate charged to LDCs is the regulated rate that ensures a fair and reasonable return on the interstate pipeline investment. However, during times of less than peak demand, LDCs are free to sell their spare transmission capacity to third parties. While these rates are generally less than what LDCs are paying, revenue so earned reduces LDC transmission costs. This creates a market for interstate pipeline capacity that generally disappears during times of peak demand. But if an LDC finds itself in a position with spare capacity during times of peak demand, it can sell this spare capacity at either the market or a maximum rate imposed by government regulations.

In addition to the marketing of spare transmission capacity, another opportunity has opened up to address nomination imbalances. The major customers of transmission pipelines (LDCs, industrial plants, utilities, etc.) must address an imbalance between their nominated and actual usage of more than 10 percent either way or face a monetary penalty. Rather than face a monetary penalty, customers can contact a marketing outfit that specializes in finding other users with the opposite imbalance.

The unbundling of services has created a plethora of marketing opportunities and commercial dealings that have commoditized not only natural gas, but also natural gas transmission and storage capacity, nomination imbalances, and risk mitigation. The buying and selling of natural gas has become just like any other commodity such as grain or metals or petroleum products. Yet there is still a great deal of regulation in the natural gas industry. FERC establishes services to be provided by interstate pipelines, determines pipeline rates based on a fair and reasonable return, and approves the construction of new interstate pipelines. LDCs are regulated by states and, in some cases, municipalities, which determine rate structures, approve the construction of new facilities, and address consumer complaints.

Rates charged by LDCs are based on covering operating and capital costs including the purchase of natural gas. Consistent with interstate transmission companies, a fair and reasonable return for LDCs is based on determining the appropriate rate of return that induces shareholders to invest in plant and equipment consistent with the inherent risk of the business and opportunity to invest elsewhere. A balancing account keeps track of the difference between required and actual revenue, which eventually leads to upward or downward rate adjustments. Rates also reflect customer categories (residential, commercial, industrial, utilities, etc.) to take into account peculiarities associated with each. The capital and service requirements for hundreds of thousands of residential and commercial customers in a local distribution system are quite different than those for a comparative few industrial and utility customers.

Various states are experimenting with unbundling LDC services, but progress is slow. It is possible that regulation may not be deregulated but transformed to incentive regulation, which gives a regulated LDC an opportunity to profit from exceptional performance. One form of incentive is performance-based regulation in which an LDC's cost of procuring gas for residential customers is compared to an index value for other LDCs. If its cost is lower than the index value, then LDC shareholders and ratepayers benefit by splitting the savings. If higher, the incremental cost is again split and shareholders suffer along with ratepayers. Incentive regulation can take the form of benchmarking with adjustments for both inflation and productivity gains. If productivity gains exceed the impact of inflation, then both shareholders and ratepayers share the benefit; if not, both suffer. Another alternative is rate caps, a method whereby shareholders either suffer or benefit from actual rates being above or below the cap. Incentive regulation provides an opportunity for LDCs to enhance their profitability by becoming more astute in gas purchases and more eager to pursue productivity gains. Of course none of this applies if a consumer has a right to contract for his or her supply of natural gas directly with providers and merely pays an LDC for distribution costs.

European Road to Liberalization

Europe never had a regulatory regime similar to that of the US. Excluding the UK, European nations carried out their respective energy policies through "championed" energy companies. Championed energy companies had the support of their respective governments to dominate a phase of a nation's electricity or natural gas business almost as quasi-monopolies. European governments exercised semi-control over these companies by having seats on boards of directors and approving the appointment of top executives. This comfortable relationship between private and public realms resulted in European governments being assured of a secure supply of energy delivered in a dependable and reliable manner; of championed companies operating profitably in a low-risk, almost competitive-free business environment; and consumers paying a high price for energy.

The UK did not have this arrangement, having previously nationalized their energy providers. In common with nationalized industries the world over, efficiency, cost controls, and performance were of little concern for wards of the state with direct access to the public till. The result was high energy costs both in terms of what consumers paid in rates and what the government paid in subsidies. The first European leader to react against high-priced energy was Prime Minister Thatcher, who cut subsidies to coal companies, privatized national energy companies, and started the process of major consumers having direct access to energy providers. Direct access gave major consumers the opportunity to negotiate on price and terms and choose from various electricity and natural gas suppliers, introducing competition in what had previously been a grouping of government monopolies. Thus the two paths taken by the US and UK arrived at the same destination, but from markedly different starting points. For the US, the path was deregulation of a regulated industry; for the UK, the path was cutting the umbilical cord to subsidized energy companies and privatizing previously nationalized companies. The common destination for both nations was a competitive marketplace where major consumers had third-party access to natural gas and electricity suppliers. The upshot of this effort was declining costs for electricity and natural gas. Figure 7.1 shows the price of US electricity in dollars per kilowatt-hour from 1979 to 2014 in terms of dollars of the day and constant 2014 dollars.[3]

Figure 7.1, corrected for monetary inflation by expressing rates in constant 2014 dollars, clearly shows a downward trend. However, non-inflationary induced changes in the cost of fuel affect the trend. Primary fuel sources are coal, natural gas, nuclear, and hydro. The latter two costs, accounting for 25 percent of electricity generating energy, have been relatively flat. Historically coal fueled half of electricity generation and coal prices showed little volatility. Natural gas supplying 25 percent of energy requirements for electricity generation was usually higher in price than coal and much more volatile. The switch from coal to natural gas from 2005 to 2009 for environmental reasons substituted more expensive energy for less costly energy and contributed to the rise in electricity rates in terms of 2014 dollars. Another contributing factor was the greater role of solar

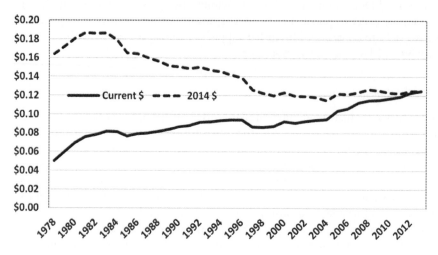

Figure 7.1 US Average Annual Consumer Electricity Rate ($/kWh)

and wind, both more expensive than natural gas. The decline in electricity rates since 2009 was caused by the fall in natural gas prices from fracking and in coal prices from coal companies reacting to a significant loss of business (coal now supplies about one-third of the energy for electricity generation). Moreover, solar and wind have made marked technological progress in reducing their respective costs to generate electricity. Thus, Figure 7.1 shows that deregulation in the US has lowered electricity rates if changes in fuel costs and energy technology are taken into consideration, and this observation holds for all consumers be they individual residences, commercial establishments, industrial complexes, and electricity generating utilities. Deregulation was responsible for a drop in natural gas prices as a consequence of additional supplies (the 20-year "bubble"). After the 20-year "bubble" waned, natural gas prices rose with the realization that US supply was lagging demand. Prices peaked when it was concluded that there would have to be relatively costly large-scale LNG imports to meet demand. But this spike in natural gas prices was cut short by the advent of fracking.

UK electricity rates and natural gas prices similarly declined after liberalization was enacted about the same time as deregulation in the US, but not as dramatically. One reason is that natural gas for electricity generation and natural gas sold to consumers was formula-priced, based primarily on the price of oil. Thus deregulation was not accompanied by a fall in natural gas prices as in the US, but there was a decline in electricity rates. UK electricity and natural gas buyers did benefit from competition among suppliers. Previously nationalized electricity and natural gas providers were incentivized to improve performance through efficiency and productivity gains with some of the enhanced profitability flowing to consumers in the form of lower prices.

The unbundling of UK natural gas and electricity markets stands apart from Europe. European nations were reluctant to break up the comfortable relationship between governments and selected championed companies who provided a secure and reliable delivery system of natural gas and electricity for a price that also assured the companies of a comfortable profit. Governments and championed companies did not want to liberalize their energy markets that would give buyers the right to negotiate with suppliers. While high-cost energy was widely recognized as a deterrent to European economic growth in the mid-1980s, the first EU directives for liberalizing electricity and natural gas did not appear until the latter half of the 1990s. These directives established a time frame for specified percentages of natural gas and electricity that had to be satisfied in a competitive marketplace. In 2003 a second EU directive was issued to accelerate the process of liberalization. Independent transmission and distribution system operators were to be created to separate services formerly provided by integrated transmission and distribution companies with a target year of 2007 for the unbundling of gas and electricity markets. In 2009 the third EU legislative package was issued consisting of two directives and three regulations to establish common rules for internal markets for electricity and natural gas, cross-border exchanges of electricity and gas, and open access to the electricity and gas transmission networks to be overseen by the Agency for the Cooperation of Energy Regulators (ACER). In addition energy production was to be unbundled, eliminating conflicts of interests, preventing network operators from favoring any particular producing and supplying companies, increasing the transparency of retail markets, and strengthening consumer protection rules and regulatory oversight.

The European Network of Transmission System Operators for Electricity representing 41 transmission system operators in 34 nations, along with Gas Infrastructure Europe (GIE) with 68 member companies in 25 European countries representing the interests of transmission, storage, and LNG terminal operators, were active in bringing together EU electricity and gas grid operators to develop common commercial and technical codes and security standards.[4] Rules were established to prevent companies involved in the transmission, production, and supply of energy from using their privileged position to prevent or obstruct access of their competitors to the network. Electricity and natural gas providers would be given nondiscriminatory third-party access to the transmission network while customers would be given the right to choose providers as they deemed fit. ACER oversaw the activities of these and other public and private organizations, guiding their progress while ensuring the cooperation of national regulatory authorities. The objective to form a single, sustainable, and competitive electricity and natural gas market with a stable and predictable regulatory framework conducive to sound investments was achieved when the third package became law in March 2011.[5]

From Source to Consumer

Natural gas comes from a well as a mixture of hydrocarbons. For instance, Southwest natural gas has average proportions of 88 percent methane, 5 percent ethane, 2 percent propane, and 1 percent butane, plus heavier hydrocarbons and impurities. A methane molecule is 1 carbon atom and 4 hydrogen atoms; ethane 2 carbon atoms and 6 hydrogen atoms; propane 3 carbon atoms and 8 hydrogen atoms; and butane 4 carbon atoms and 10 hydrogen atoms. Heavier hydrocarbons of pentane (5 carbon atoms and 12 hydrogen atoms), hexane (6 carbon atoms and 14 hydrogen atoms), and heptane (7 carbon atoms and 16 hydrogen atoms) are in a gaseous state when in a natural gas (and oil) reservoir, but "fall out," or condense, to a liquid called condensate when brought to the surface. Condensate is separated from natural gas (and oil) and sold separately, as described in Chapter 6. Ethane is fairly expensive to separate with its low liquefying temperature and normally remains in the natural gas stream. Propane and butane are easily separated by fractionation, or cooling of natural gas, and are sold separately as liquefied petroleum gases (LPGs). Impurities such as hydrogen sulfide, carbon dioxide, nitrogen, and water have to be removed. "Pipeline-quality" natural gas is primarily methane with some ethane, cleansed of impurities and stripped of condensates and petroleum gas liquids, with a heat content of 1,000–1,050 Btu per cubic foot at standard atmospheric conditions.[6] A close relationship exists between volumetric and energy measures of natural gas. With an average heat content of natural gas of 1,025 Btu per cubic foot, there are 1,025,000 Btu in 1,000 cubic feet (Mcf) or 1 Mcf is equivalent to 1.025 million Btu (mmBtu). One therm, the unit of usage for natural gas bills for residences, is 100,000 Btu or 0.1 mmBtu.[7]

Cleaning and stripping functions are performed in a million-mile pipeline gathering system connecting a half million producing wells with transmission pipelines.[8] The last step is raising the pressure of natural gas to transmission system pressure. Transmission pipelines are typically 24 or 36 inches in diameter and operate between 600 and 1,200 psi pressure, although there are wider diameter pipelines operating at higher pressures. Compressor stations are located about every 70 miles, and speed of gas varies between 15 and 30 miles per hour depending on gas pressure, compressor capacity, and pipeline diameter.

Monitoring devices and shutoff valves are strategically placed about every 5–20 miles to deal with potential pipeline ruptures and routine pipe maintenance. Both inner and outer pipe surfaces are coated to protect against corrosion. The inner surface is kept clean by running a "pig" through the pipeline for routine maintenance; a "smart pig" transmits data on the internal condition of a pipeline. Routine maintenance inspections of the external condition of pipelines detect leaks, measure corrosion, and look for potential problems. One major potential problem is construction crews inadvertently affecting the integrity of a natural gas pipeline by the careless handling of earthmoving equipment, which have, on occasion, set off explosions.[9]

Storage facilities are available along a pipeline, but not in above-ground tanks, as those are constructed for manufactured gas. A manufactured gas tank or holder in the nineteenth and early twentieth centuries had an internal set of rollers and guide rails that allowed the tank to telescope; that is, change its internal volume by rising and falling in height above the ground. Height depended on holdings of manufactured gas, while weight helped maintain internal pressure to transmit manufactured gas to customers. In the Gulf region, natural gas is stored under pressure in salt caverns where salt has been leached out. In Appalachia, abandoned or played-out natural gas reservoirs are used for storage. Natural gas reinjected into these reservoirs under pressure during times of weak demand and low prices is withdrawn during times of strong demand and high prices. The placement of these storage "facilities" is much closer to the peak winter market in the Northeast than natural gas wells in the Southwest, which evens out demand placed on transmission and gas production systems over the course of a year.

Before deregulation, natural gas was stored during the summer in played-out Appalachian gas fields and drawn down during the winter. Since deregulation, natural gas in storage is recycled several times a year in response to changing prices, not necessarily related to times of peak demand. Underground storage in played-out natural gas fields dot the nation.[10] Storage may not be necessary if natural gas wells and their connecting pipelines and compressors are sufficient to deliver natural gas during times of peak demand.

The 300,000 miles of transmission pipelines in the US have an inherent storage capacity that can be enhanced by increasing their internal gas pressure. Metering is a vital operation as gas enters and leaves gas transmission systems and associated storage facilities for the accurate paying of suppliers, charging of customers, and system control.

Gas planning for a transmission company depends on long- and short-term forecasting models. Long-term forecasts determine investments in order for the pipeline system to meet future demand. Short-term forecasts ensure that volume of gas can accommodate current demand. Nominations are made one to two days in advance to ensure that enough gas enters the upstream system to match downstream demand without exceeding pipeline capacity. Scheduling acceptances of gas from thousands of suppliers and deliveries of gas to thousands of consumers, each with their specific needs and different contractual arrangements, is both complex and crucial for the smooth operation of a system. A system of allocation cuts based on a previously arranged and agreed-on priority ranking is activated when nominations exceed pipeline capacity limits.

In today's deregulated climate, natural gas can be drawn from storage or obtained directly from natural gas producers or from other interstate transmission companies via hubs. About 30 major hubs in the US connect various interstate pipelines into essentially a common system whereby natural gas consumers connected into one interstate pipeline can obtain supplies from natural gas suppliers connected into others. The most important one is Henry Hub in Louisiana, where a multitude of interconnected pipelines provide the base price for the nation.[11] Other hubs are generally priced at the Henry Hub price plus transmission costs with local market-related variations.

As an example, three interstate pipelines serve New York City. Through local interconnections, major gas purchasers can bargain for natural gas from suppliers in three different natural gas regions. Continual negotiations for the best price create a pricing center in New York City, where price does not vary much regardless of which transmission pipeline is actually supplying the gas. If a price gap does appear among transmission companies, then consumers' continual quest for the cheapest source of natural gas tends to close the gap. Thus the New York price is closely related to the Henry Hub price plus transmission costs. Another pricing center is in Boston, where gas from two interstate pipelines from the Southwest and two pipelines from the western and eastern provinces of Canada are interconnected, providing major customers with an opportunity to buy gas for the best price from suppliers in four different natural gas producing regions. The search by large consumers for the best price ends up with a more or less common price in Boston, regardless of the source. Natural gas prices in New York and Boston are not the same. Whereas the New York basis price reflects the price in Henry Hub plus transmission costs, the presence of Canadian producers in the Boston market affects its basis price along with Southwest gas. It is possible that Canadian gas may lower the price of gas in Boston in relation to New York. If this were true, Canadian gas could penetrate the New York market by reversing the Algonquin pipeline between New Jersey and Boston. If this pipeline were made truly reversible, that is, capable of moving gas in either direction, then there would be a stronger relationship between Boston and New York basis prices separated only by the Algonquin pipeline toll. This, in turn, would link both New York and Boston basis prices to the Henry Hub basis price. Thus making the Algonquin pipeline reversible and perhaps increasing its accessibility to the New York pipeline distribution system would tie together five natural gas producing regions, three in the US and two in Canada, in terms of price and availability with two major population centers in the Northeast. However, this benefit of making the Algonquin pipeline reversible will have to wait until natural gas supplies are increased in the Boston area by building more pipeline capacity.[12] Nevertheless, deregulation has introduced a dynamic in the natural gas business that was lacking under regulation and has lowered overall natural gas prices by allowing major natural gas producing regions to compete for business in major consuming centers.

Natural Gas as a Fuel

On a global basis, OECD nations consumed 55 trillion cubic feet (Tcf) and non–OECD nations 58 Tcf in 2010. By 2040 the projected consumption for OECD nations is 75 Tcf and 100 Tcf for non–OECD nations, representing 1.2 percent and 2.5 percent annual growth respectively, for an overall global annual growth of 2.1 percent. The non–OECD nation showing the greatest growth in natural gas consumption is China by far, although other nations will be increasing consumption to a lesser extent. In terms of natural gas consumption, global electricity generation is expected to grow from 20 trillion kilowatt-hours to 39 trillion kilowatt-hours in 2040 for an average annual growth rate of 2.25 percent. The natural gas contribution is expected to increase from 22 percent to 24 percent, which would imply a global growth in natural gas of 2.55 percent over this time span to supply primarily new electricity generation. Interestingly, while coal is slated to lose share as an energy source for global electricity generation from 40 percent to 36 percent, more coal will be burned in 2040 to produce electricity than in 2010.[13]

Natural gas provides nearly 24 percent of world energy demand in 2014, remaining virtually unchanged for the last decade, somewhat surprising given the well-publicized virtues of natural gas over coal. In the aggregate, the increased consumption of natural gas has been the same as average growth in world energy demand. Limiting attention to total volume of oil and natural gas, natural gas made up 36 percent of the two fossil fuels in 2005, climbing to nearly 39 percent in 2014. This signifies that oil is in a slow retreat with respect to natural gas. With oil falling behind natural gas and natural gas just keeping up with aggregate energy consumption, renewables and coal are taking up the slack despite the negative publicity given to coal. But this negativity is concentrated in the US, whereas Asia still depends heavily on coal to fuel new electricity generating capacity. Figure 7.2 shows the distribution of natural gas consumption by region.

North America and Europe, including the Former Soviet Union (FSU), account for nearly 60 percent of global consumption. China, the largest consumer of natural gas in Asia, grew by 13 percent between 2012 and 2013, and retreated to 9 percent growth between 2013 and 2014, both below 14 percent compound growth since 2010. The second largest major consumer in Asia is Japan, whose natural gas consumption exhibited no growth between 2012 and 2013 and a 1 percent decline between 2013 and 2014. The Fukushima Daiichi nuclear disaster occurred in March 2011 with the subsequent shutdown of essentially all nuclear plants in Japan. LNG was the substitute fuel for generating electricity and grew by 20 percent between 2010 and 2012. Restarting nuclear plants in Japan, while problematic, would back out natural gas imports as a source of energy for Japan. Figure 7.3 shows the respective natural gas growth for various regions of the world between 2009 and 2014.

While South America, Africa, the Middle East, and, most particularly, Asia show dramatic annual growth in natural gas consumption over a 5-year period, overall growth of

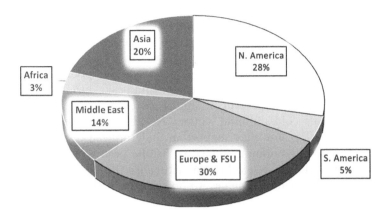

Figure 7.2 Percent Distribution of Natural Gas Consumption by Region

only 2.7 percent reflects the situation in North America and Europe, which make up nearly 60 percent of the market. While North America's growth is slightly above aggregate growth, Europe's growth is negative, reflecting long-term economic doldrums that have plagued all but the northern part of the continent and dampening effect on demand of expensive natural gas. Natural gas in Europe is priced much higher than the US and, in addition, is highly taxed as an energy source. Out of 31 nations making up Europe and the FSU, a remarkable 25 are consuming less natural gas in 2014 than they did in 2010. Declining energy demand in general plus growth in renewables (primarily solar and wind) have taken their toll on EU natural gas and coal consumption. Over time the share of consumption of natural gas in Europe and the FSU will decrease with respect to other regions and, to a lesser degree, so will North America.

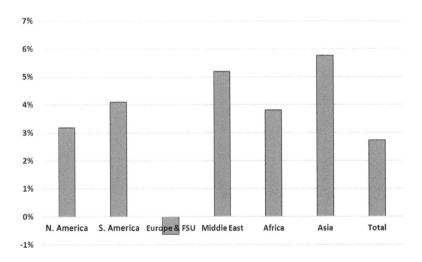

Figure 7.3 Average 5-Year Natural Gas Growth by Region

Natural Gas in the US

Figure 7.4 shows the distribution of natural gas consumption in the US by end users based on 2020 projections.[14] Fifteen percent of natural gas consumption is residential, which as individual customers number 67 million. The primary uses of natural gas in residences are space and water heating, cooking, clothes drying, pool heating, central air conditioning, and gas fireplaces. Residential demand peaks during winter months, accounting for as much as 70 percent of annual gas consumption, which of itself can vary greatly between cold and mild winters. Residential customers pay the highest rates for natural gas because they support an underutilized distribution system connected to each individual home designed to handle peak winter needs. Residential customers consume the greatest volume of natural gas during winter, and this seasonal peak in residential demand coincides, to no surprise, with the seasonal peak in prices.

Close to 5.4 million commercial customers consume 12 percent of natural gas, paying the second highest price. The commercial sector consists of restaurants, motels and hotels, retail establishments, hospitals and healthcare facilities, schools, and office and government buildings. Though commercial customers have similar usages for natural gas as residential customers, there is less of a seasonal swing in demand between summer and winter. Space cooling for commercial establishments is usually powered by natural gas, whereas space cooling for residences is usually powered by electricity (window mounted air conditioning units) except for homes fitted with natural gas fed central air systems that provide both warm and cool air. Moreover, commercial customers have higher base load demand that reduces the prominence of peak usage for space heating and cooling. In addition to weather, general business activity also influences consumption among commercial customers.

The industrial sector with 192,000 customers is the second largest consumer at 30 percent of total demand. Natural gas supplies the energy needs of a host of manufacturing

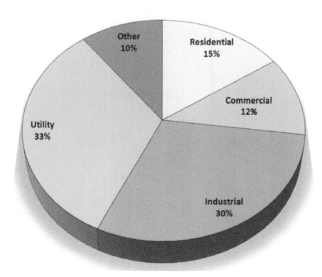

Figure 7.4 US Projected 2020 Consumption of Natural Gas (Tcf per year)

processes such as metal, glass, pulp and paper, and food processing industries. Natural gas is an energy source for waste treatment, incineration, drying and dehumidification processes, and a feedstock for fertilizer, chemical, and petrochemical industries. Natural gas prices directly affect food prices as it is a raw material for making ammonia-based nitrogen fertilizers and a source of energy for drying crops, pumping irrigation water, and processing food. While seasonal variations are less than those of residential and commercial users, the industrial sector experiences significant fluctuations in demand from changes in economic activity. Moreover, one-third of industrial users can switch to propane and fuel oil if natural gas prices get out of line with these alternative fuels. In 2014 fuel oil was much higher priced than natural gas, and therefore not consumed by industrial users as long as natural gas was available. But fracking is responsible for creating surpluses of propane that can be competitive with natural gas for some industrial applications. The industrial sector ranks third in what is paid for natural gas, while plants that generate electricity pay the lowest price. The electricity sector consists of about 1,000 electricity generating utilities that consume 33 percent of total natural gas demand. While seasonal demand is less pronounced, daily fluctuations are much greater as natural gas plays a prominent role in satisfying variable electricity demand above base load.

"Other" in Figure 7.4 amounts to 10 percent of consumption and represents natural gas consumed in operating wells, separating liquid gas components, cleaning and removing impurities, pressurizing natural gas for pipeline transmission, and powering natural gas compressors to move gas through the transmission and distribution systems. A very small part of this category is transportation fuel, only 0.04 Tcf in 2012, but this doubles by 2020 and grows seven-fold to 0.28 Tcf in 2030. Although volume is small, the implication is that there will be a 14-fold increase in natural gas as a transportation fuel between 2012 and 2030, or roughly a 14-fold increase in the population of motor vehicles fueled by either liquefied or compressed natural gas.

During the 20-year gas bubble, electricity generation was the fastest growing market segment, numbering about 5,500 natural gas electricity generating plants, not counting cogeneration units run by commercial and industrial customers. Nearly all incremental electricity generating capacity was fueled by natural gas. After bursting of the gas bubble in 2000, coal fired plants were in the ascendancy, but some natural gas plants were still being built. With the collapse of natural gas prices from fracking and political pressure via new environmental regulations imposed on coal burning plants by the Obama administration, natural gas plants are again being built at the expense of coal plants.

Figure 7.5 shows the projected US consumption of natural gas in 2020 and 2030. Very little growth is exhibited by the residential and commercial sectors. The industrial sector exhibits more pronounced growth as a power source substituting for diesel fuel in powering machinery and equipment. However, natural gas as a utility fuel is not capturing market share given up by coal as renewables, solar and wind, are expanding rapidly. This can be seen in Figure 7.5 where consumption for natural gas for electricity generation actually declines by 2020, but grows thereafter.

Overall projected growth in US natural gas consumption from 2012 to 2040 is only 0.7 percent for electricity generation, while projected growth for total electricity demand is 0.6 percent. Low growth in electricity reflects sluggishness in economic activity and continued efficiency gains that suppress electricity consumption in relation to economic activity. Growth in coal demand for electricity generation of 0.3 percent indicates that the current cutback in coal has a short time to run its course before some growth in coal

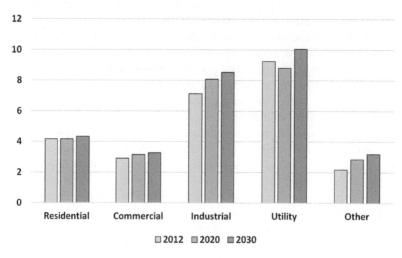

Figure 7.5 US Projected Consumption of Natural Gas (Tcf per year)

is necessary to satisfy overall electricity demand. It is possible that this could be translated into more natural gas plants, resulting in less growth for coal. Growth in nuclear power of only 0.2 percent represents the completion of units under construction before the Fukushima disaster. No other orders for nuclear plants are expected at this time. To meet overall growth of 0.6 percent, part will come from natural gas, but the primary contribution will be renewables that will have to grow by 1.7 percent per year to fill the gap.[15] If electricity generated by renewables exceeds 1.7 percent, the most likely result would be backing out coal generated electricity.

Natural gas usage in electricity generation is affected by seasonal factors, changes in economic activity, and the relative cost of electricity generated from natural gas compared to coal, oil, nuclear, hydropower, and renewables, taking availability into consideration. Some dual-fueled electricity generating plants can easily switch between natural gas and fuel oil depending on their relative costs. When oil prices are $100 per barrel, these plants are running on natural gas. With oil prices cut in half, the economics become more favorable for fuel oil.

Natural Gas in Europe

OECD Europe's 20 Tcf of natural gas consumption in 2014 is 30 percent electric power, 33 percent commercial, and 37 percent residential, including other uses, of which 10 percent is probably related to system performance as in the US. Growth is expected to reach 24.7 Tcf by 2040, representing an average annual growth rate of 0.8 percent. Fifty-seven percent of the overall increase in natural gas consumption will be for electric power, possibly signaling greater reliance on LNG imports in the future.

The pricing of natural gas is a real problem in Europe. Unlike the US where regulated gas prices were kept artificially low to the detriment of providers leading to shortfalls and supply disruptions, Europe is plagued by high natural gas prices that have had a negative impact on economic activity. The problem is historical, beginning with the

1958 discovery of the huge Groningen natural gas field offshore the Netherlands. This introduction of natural gas into Europe brought forth the matter of price for resolution. Esso and Shell, developers of the field, suggested to the Netherlands government that its revenue would be higher if the price of natural gas were indexed to oil rather than being based on its low production costs. (Of course the oil companies did not have a hidden agenda in making this suggestion!) The rationale was that by linking price of natural gas to oil, an already established market, buyers and traders would be able to use oil derivatives to hedge risks in natural gas. The original Groningen formula was 40 percent heavy fuel oil and 60 percent light fuel oil (gas oil or diesel fuel oil), reflecting that natural gas would substitute for heavy fuel oil in generating electricity and light fuel oil in powering industrial enterprises. The formula changed over the years, but was always strongly linked to oil. The 2005/2006 pricing formula for natural gas was 29.5 percent heavy fuel oil, 44.8 percent light fuel oil (thus 75 percent linked to oil), 9.8 percent gas, 4.4 percent fixed, 4.1 percent inflation adjusted, and the remainder coal, electricity, and other minor factors. The Groningen pricing formula is adjusted for gas sources (Russia, the North Sea, Algeria, and Libya) and gas consumers (Eastern and Western Europe and the UK).[16]

High prices persevered for decades by this oligarchy of suppliers who were not tempted to compete on price and tied their customers to long-term contracts. However, in recent years, liquefied natural gas (LNG) import terminals have been constructed to take advantage of what was conceived to be excess LNG production from the proliferation of LNG production facilities around the world. Pricing of this incremental production is divorced from the Groningen formula and other pricing formulas associated with long-term LNG projects serving Europe and Asia. With European consumers having third-party access to LNG terminals and with a potential for a surfeit of LNG cargoes, eventually from the US, it was thought that potentially excess LNG production would exert sufficient commercial pressure on traditional suppliers to break their common front and create a truly competitive market. Up to 2014, this had been an idle thought from lack of available LNG cargoes as a consequence of Japan substituting LNG for nuclear power. Moreover, high-priced LNG did not offer much economic benefit over natural gas priced under the Groningen formula. However, in 2014, the mere threat of US LNG exports in 2015 impacted the market for natural gas suppliers. The need to secure new contracts for European natural gas suppliers in an environment where there may be a new entrant to the market has put pressure on natural gas prices for the benefit of buyers. As US LNG cargoes become available along with increases in the output of global liquefaction capacity, the potential of consumers switching to LNG suppliers and affecting natural gas pricing in Europe will become real. Europe has the capacity to import over 200 million cubic meters of LNG annually and only about 20 percent of LNG capacity was utilized in 2014.[17] Pricing hubs in the UK, the Netherlands, Belgium, Germany, France, Austria, Spain, and Italy will play the same role as in the US for consumers to contract with pipeline transmission operators to secure their natural gas supplies from different sources including LNG import terminals.

Facing the Geopolitical Risk of Natural Gas

Unlike Americans, Europeans face geopolitical risk for their natural gas supplies. The North Sea and the Netherlands are, of course, secure sources of supply. Algeria is a citadel of stability compared to Libya, which, in the aftermath of the "Arab Spring" that brought down Gaddafi, has become a chaotic jungle of warring tribal fiefdoms. Of particular concern is the geopolitical risk associated with Russia.

While Russia imposed high-priced natural gas on Western Europe in accordance with the Groningen formula, under communism, natural gas in the Soviet Union was free, obviating the need for meters and thermostats. Torridly hot rooms were cooled by a blast of frigid Arctic air from partially opened windows. Since the fall of communism, meters and thermostats were installed and charging for natural gas usage stemmed wasteful practices, freeing up supplies for hard currency exports. However, gas sold within the Russian Federation was still far less than that paid by Western European importers. The conflict between Russia and Ukraine in 2006 and 2009 on natural gas pricing focused on this point. Russia would choose the timing of these negotiations during the peak cold period in winter and would reduce pipeline flow to Ukraine to enhance its bargaining position. This put pressure on Ukrainians from a negotiating point of view, but it also created a shortage of natural gas in Europe during the coldest part of the year. The Russians thought that this would induce Europeans to put pressure on Ukraine to concede to Russian demands. The actual European reaction was quite different: Europeans realized the geopolitical risk in relying too heavily on Russian gas. They began thinking about ways to minimize Russian natural gas to counter its unreliability. The Ukraine–Russia confrontation in 2014 whereby Crimea has been ceded by Ukraine to Russia and Russian sympathizers in eastern Ukraine are seeking Russian hegemony has sharpened European concern over the security aspects of Russian gas imports. Russia considers the potential for cutting pipeline supplies to Ukraine, which is tantamount to cutting pipeline supplies to Western Europe, as a strategic weapon in its arsenal of dealing with Ukraine and also dealing with sanctions that the EU has imposed on Russia in reaction to the political and military situation in eastern Ukraine. These sanctions take the form of US and EU finance and technological restrictions along with US export controls over oil equipment sold to major Russian oil and gas companies. Technological restrictions are bans on supporting drilling for oil in deep Arctic waters over 500 feet deep and in developing oil shale resources. Access to capital markets is limited to short-term (30 and 90 days) debt, which will interfere with refinancing large amounts of external debt for Russian oil and gas companies. Sanctions are anticipated to slow the development of oil resources in Russia, increasing the importance of natural gas as a foreign exchange earner.[18]

Europe is 24 percent dependent on Russian gas on an aggregate basis, which varies considerably for individual nations, as shown in Figure 7.6.[19] Nations not indicated receive less than 1 percent of their gas from Russia.

Clearly Europe is not entirely dependent on Russian gas. Natural gas fields in the Netherlands, the North Sea, Algeria, and Libya are connected into the European gas grid, with the latter pipelines among the first major undersea pipelines. One pipeline from Algeria crosses Morocco, then under the Mediterranean to Spain near Gibraltar, while the other crosses Tunisia, then under the Mediterranean to Sicily, and again under the Strait of Messina to mainland Italy. Libya's undersea Mediterranean pipeline connects Libya with Sicily and then to mainland Italy. Undersea pipelines are a growing phenomenon. A major 750-mile-long undersea pipeline in operation since 2003 is Blue Stream passing north–south under the Black Sea, transmitting 16 billion cubic meters (bcm) of gas per year from Russia to Turkey.[20] Another major undersea pipeline is Nord

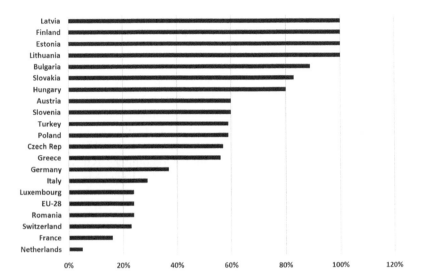

Figure 7.6 Europe's Dependency on Russian Gas by Nation

Stream, also 750 miles long, connecting Russia (near St. Petersburg) to Germany under the Baltic Sea. Its twin pipelines can move 55 bcm per year and has been in operation since 2012.[21] These pipelines have no undersea pumping stations. A powerful gas compressor located onshore provides the necessary pressure and power to move the requisite volume of gas through the entire length of the undersea portion of the pipeline.

Dealing with the Geopolitical Risk of Russian Gas

Russian gas enters Europe through a number of major pipelines. The principal pipelines with the highest throughput volume are Nord Stream, Yamal, Soyuz, and Bratstvo. The two major pipelines that do not pass through Ukraine are Nord Stream, with a capacity of 55 bcm that runs directly from Russia to Germany under the Baltic Sea, and Yamal, with a capacity of 33 bcm that runs through Belarus and Poland. Northern Lights parallels the Yamal pipeline to western Belarus and then turns south into Ukraine, joining up with the Brotherhood and Soyuz pipelines. This cluster of pipelines transits Ukraine and then into Slovakia and the Czech Republic before entering Germany, where they connect to various other European gas pipelines for access to the European gas market.[22] Eastern European nations most affected by the cessation of the natural gas pipeline flow through Ukraine that occurred in January 2015 and affects 60 percent of Russian exports, besides Ukraine, are Bulgaria, Greece, Macedonia, Romania, Croatia, and Turkey.[23] Other nations such as Slovakia and the Czech Republic are also affected.

Short-term alternatives Europeans have for dealing with the 2015 cessation of Russian gas exports for pipelines passing through Ukraine are somewhat limited. One is to increase imports from Russian pipelines that do not cross Ukraine and from non-Russian traditional suppliers such as Libya, Algeria, the North Sea, and the Netherlands. Libyan gas exports are down from civil commotion, and Algerian gas exports are also down from booming domestic demand cutting into export availability. Both are unlikely to make significant additions to European gas supplies. North Sea natural gas production is dwindling away from exhaustion of its fields, while the Groningen gas field is holding its own. Neither can be a source of meaningful additions to natural gas supplies. The only real option is switching to LNG imports as an alternative source of natural gas. Europe has more than adequate LNG receiving terminals to import relatively large volumes of LNG if cargoes can be found. But world liquefaction capacity is busy supplying Japan with LNG as a substitute for nuclear power and available spot cargoes may be in short supply compared to incremental demand. US LNG imports are certainly part of a solution, but the first US LNG export terminal will not be in service until late 2015. Aside from importing LNG cargoes, Europe actually has limited means to counter a Russian cut-off of natural gas exports via Ukraine unless it abandons sanctions that have been imposed in support of US pressure on Russia to resolve the Ukrainian crisis.

Europe has a number of long-term alternatives to consider to mitigate the geopolitical risk associated with Russian gas. One alternative to reduce dependence on Russian gas is exemplified by the South Caucasus Pipeline, which has been in operation since 2006. The pipeline moves 18 bcm per year of Azerbaijan natural gas via Georgia and Turkey with pipeline connections to Greece, Albania, and Italy. From Italy, Azerbaijan gas can reach much of Europe.[24] As this non-Russian gas does not transit Russia, Azerbaijan is free to negotiate the best deal among buyers keen on diversifying their gas sources. Another pipeline that would have been a source of non-Russian gas is the now defunct Nabucco pipeline proposal to transport 31 bcm per year of Caspian natural gas in a 2,050-mile, 56-inch pipeline stretching from the Caspian region across Turkey, Bulgaria, Romania, Hungary, and Austria where it would have connected into the European pipeline distribution system. The pipeline was cancelled in 2013 after a series of setbacks partly by being too large for the market and too ambitious, and perhaps political repercussions of avoiding both Russian gas and a Russian transit.[25] The South Stream pipeline was under construction that would have transmitted Russian gas east–west under the Black Sea avoiding transiting both Ukraine and Turkey, coming onshore in Bulgaria. There the pipeline was to split with one segment traversing the Balkans and then under the Adriatic Sea to connect to Italy. The other segment would go to Austria and Hungary with both segments serving intervening nations along the way. The complexity of this $45 billion project can be seen in that the pipeline transits seven nations and organizers must deal with and resolve the differences of opinion of six regulatory systems and over a dozen investing companies and gas buyers involved in the endeavor. In 2014 Bulgaria was forced to stop pipeline construction from EU and US pressure over presumably Bulgaria's violating EU law in its administration of public tenders.[26] In late 2014, Russia abandoned the South Stream project in favor of increasing exports to Turkey as a conduit into Europe. Turkey has indicated its willingness if price discounts of the nature offered to Germany were applicable to Turkey.[27]

A little-publicized project known as White Stream, initiated by Ukraine, was supposed to bring gas from the Caucasus (Azerbaijan) under the Black Sea to Romania for pipeline connections to other Central European destinations. A branch of the undersea pipeline would have come ashore in Crimea (now part of Russia) to serve Ukrainian gas needs. The project is defunct given the political animosity between Ukraine and Russia and, of course, Russian objection to a Ukrainian sponsored project that would have reduced their dependence on Russian gas.

However, the dream of Nabucco of Caspian gas substituting for Russian gas is not dead. The proposed Trans-Caspian pipeline would transmit gas from Turkmenistan to Azerbaijan including a link under the Caspian Sea to bolster natural gas supplies in Azerbaijan to service planned pipelines to Europe.[28] The Interconnector Turkey–Greece– Italy (ITGI), to be operational in 2015, increases the volume of gas in Turkey that can be exported to Greece and Italy. Trans-Caspian and ITGI are to be incorporated into a larger system including the Trans-Adriatic Pipeline (TAP) that connects Italy with the Trans-Anatolian Pipeline (TANAP) at the border of Turkey and Greece.[29] TANAP, in turn, extends through Turkey and Georgia to Azerbaijan. Its first stage of completion is planned for 2018 to transmit 16 bcm with plans to ultimately reach 60 bcm by 2026.[30] The four pipeline projects, taken together, would fulfill the Nabucco dream. A less likely project is the proposed Azerbaijan–Georgia–Romania Interconnector (AGRI) to transport Azerbaijani gas by pipeline to a Black Sea port in Georgia for liquefaction for transport in an LNG carrier across the Black Sea to Romania for gasification and pipeline transmission through existing pipelines to Hungary and on to the rest of Europe. The AGRI project appears unlikely to materialize unless European demand exceeds that supplied by TANAP and its associated pipelines.[31] Russia might reduce the risk of being an unreliable supplier by becoming a reliable supplier via pipelines that do not transit Ukraine. In 2015 Putin inked a deal with Greece for a pipeline with an annual throughput of 47 bcm that would be an extension of the Turkish Stream pipeline into Greece for transit into Europe.[32]

Middle East natural gas pipeline proposals can have significant geopolitical implications for the EU gas market. Both Iran and Qatar have enormous natural gas reserves and both nations are proposing natural gas pipeline projects to serve Europe. The proposed Iranian pipeline would transit Iraq and Syria, where it would terminate at a liquefaction plant for shipment by LNG carriers to various LNG receiving terminals in Europe. The proposed Qatari pipeline would transit Saudi Arabia, Syria, and Turkey for pipeline connections into Europe. Both projects are stymied by the civil war in Syria. But are they even necessary? The Middle East has plenty of liquefaction plants (now dedicated to serving Japan) that could be expanded to serve Europe with LNG. Of course, the economics of the situation may favor pipeline transmission over LNG shipments, but there is no physical impediment other than LNG production capacity preventing the Middle East from selling natural gas to Europe.

Shale gas resources have been found in France, Poland, and Ukraine. The initial attempt to bring Polish shale gas into production was abandoned because of the nature of the rock structure, which made American-style fracking techniques difficult to apply plus lack of popular support for fracking. Whether France and Ukraine can develop a sufficient volume of shale gas to make a difference is problematic, particularly in Ukraine. In either case, it'll take years to bring shale gas into production at meaningful levels as will the aforementioned pipelines.

Europe is busy expanding its 145 underground gas storage facilities by nearly a third in capacity. Lacking played-out natural gas fields and salt domes, European storage facilities are tanks built both under and above ground that hold natural gas under pressure. As in the US and elsewhere, European storage satisfies fluctuations in seasonal demand while keeping production on a more even keel. By expanding storage capacity, natural gas storage can serve as a strategic reserve to compensate for a stoppage in Russian gas. However, storage volume under construction would only be effective for an interruption, not a stoppage, of Russian gas.

Another means of addressing the issue on a more long-term basis is to enact the EU Commission plan to lower primary energy consumption by 30 percent primarily by enhancing energy efficiency.[33] Using tons oil equivalent per million dollars of GDP in terms of purchasing power parity as a metric of energy input to generate economic activity, the EU average is 103. Ukraine stands at 349, a grossly energy inefficient economy that makes its dependence on Russian gas all the more intense. Ukraine's objection to Russia raising the price of natural gas could be addressed by enacting an energy efficiency program to significantly cut its consumption. Russia itself is also energy inefficient at 300, which means its domestic consumption of energy is quite wasteful, detracting from its hard currency export potential. Generally speaking, Eastern Europe is energy inefficient, although far less than Ukraine and Russia, measuring between 110 and 200. These nations could also take positive actions to enhance their energy efficiency, and in so doing, reduce their energy consumption and, in turn, their dependence on Russian gas.[34]

While natural gas options available to the EU for reducing the geopolitical risk associated with Russian gas appear limited, at least in the short term, Europe has been active in developing substitute sources of electricity from solar and wind and, to a much lesser extent, biofuels at the expense of natural gas. Moreover, some utilities in the UK switched to US imported coal whose price has softened with the closure of coal-fired plants. Germany is burning low-cost domestic lignite to generate electricity. Time, money, and sustained political effort can reduce Europe's dependence on Russian gas, but it'll not be an easy task.[35]

Natural Gas in Asia

China is 67 percent reliant on coal and only 5 percent on natural gas. China's natural gas reserves are insufficient to meet the nation's demand for a clean fuel to counter pollution associated with burning low-grade coal with little in the way of environmental protection. China's aggressive stand in offshore exploring in the China Sea can be understood in this context. A major development in expanding the availability of natural gas in China is Russia and China signing a deal in 2014 for 38 bcm of Russian natural gas per year. This natural gas is to be moved via the Power of Siberia pipeline eastward from the Irkutsk region in central Siberia so it reaches a north–south gas pipeline from gas fields on Sakhalin Island in eastern Russia to Vladivostok. There the Power of Siberia will run south parallel to the Sakhalin gas pipeline with both pipelines entering China near Vladivostok. The pipeline is scheduled for completion in late 2017 and its throughput of 38 bcm will represent 23 percent of China's 2013 natural gas consumption of 162 bcm.[36] Of course this percentage will be reduced when measured against a higher consumption of natural gas in 2017. At the Asia Pacific Economic Conference held on November 9–11, 2014, Putin announced that Russia and China were near to an agreement for export of another 30 bcm from Russian gas fields in Siberia via the Altai pipeline that runs almost due south into western China. This will almost double exports from the Power of Siberia pipeline when the pipeline is operational in 2018.[37]

Power of Siberia and Sakhalin natural gas exports to China complement Russian crude oil exports of 1 million barrels per day via the Eastern Siberia–Pacific Ocean (ESPO) pipeline that runs from oil fields in eastern Siberia to Vladivostok for seaborne export to Japan and Korea and other Asian nations. The ESPO pipeline has a major spur to the Daqing oil field, the principal oil field in China.[38] The Daqing oil field is in decline and field production is maintained by Siberian oil pipeline imports. The mix of two crudes feeds an already existing distribution pipeline system to supply crude oil to refineries in China. Coupling the Power of Siberia and ESPO pipelines with the well-established oil and gas pipeline distribution system from Russia to Europe makes Russia the lynchpin in Eurasian oil and natural gas markets. Adding to the importance of Russia as an oil and gas supplier to China is the discovery of a billion barrel field in the Kara Sea in the Arctic. This discovery, the result of teamwork between Exxon and Rosneft, indicates that geologic structures in the general vicinity of the discovery may translate into more oil than in the Gulf of Mexico. It will take a number of years to evaluate the true reserves in the region including further exploratory wells to confirm the size of the field followed by building production platforms that can operate in the Arctic environment.[39] This discovery extends the volume of reserves that can be corralled to meet China's and Europe's future energy needs; but unfortunately, the project was curtailed by US sanctions against Russia.

China is actively seeking oil and gas elsewhere to mitigate overreliance on a single source. China and Myanmar have entered into an agreement for two parallel pipelines from Myanmar's west coast to Yunnan province in southwest China. One pipeline to be completed in 2015 is to transmit 440,000 Bpd of oil from a port in Myanmar, which reduces the amount of oil that has to pass through the Malacca Strait between Indonesia and Thailand, mitigating the geopolitical risk of the strait being closed by hostile powers. The second pipeline already in operation is to transmit 12 bcm of natural gas from gas fields in Myanmar into China.[40] China and Tajikistan are discussing the possibility of constructing a 25–30 bcm per year pipeline between the two nations.[41] Another source of natural gas supplies is the building of LNG receiving terminals in China. The combination of pipeline and LNG imports could have a significant impact on natural gas pricing in Asia.

Natural Gas in the Rest of the World

Important discoveries of natural gas in different parts of the world will affect the global market for natural gas. One, while not a major find, is the first major indigenous source of energy for Israel. The offshore Leviathan, Tamar, and Dalit fields represent only 1 percent of Middle East gas reserves, but are of paramount importance for Israel. These gas fields lie within the Exclusive Economic Zone (EEZ) of Israel, which extends 200 nautical miles from its shoreline. Within the EEZ, a sovereign nation has the right to explore, exploit, and manage natural resources, living and nonliving, of the seabed and subsoil and in the waters, including producing energy from currents, tides, and wind. There are two problems associated with EEZs. EEZ borders are drawn perpendicular at the point where the shoreline of two nations meet. As anyone who has visited a shoreline knows, shorelines are not straight lines. Thus it is possible for two nations to refer to a same point along the shoreline for drawing a perpendicular line and end up with two different "perpendicular" lines depending on the curvature of the shore at that point. This results in overlapping claims and counterclaims for mineral rights. Another problem is that overlapping claims occur when two nations are less than 400 miles apart. The gas fields, located directly offshore Israel, are also claimed by Cyprus, Lebanon, and Egypt as being all or partly within their EEZs. Gaza, while not an independent nation, views the small Mari-B offshore gas field located just off its border with Israel as its own. While offshore fields are producing natural gas for Israeli consumption and with announced plans to export natural gas to Egypt, full development will not take place until conflicting demands by nation states have been satisfactorily resolved. This dilatory action on the part of Israel may prove costly in the wake of a 2015 discovery of a supersized offshore gas field within the territorial waters of Egypt. The Nohr field has the potential for 850 bcm of lean gas in an area of 100 square kilometers at a depth of 1,450 meters. The discovery has major implications on the energy policies for both Egypt and Israel.[42]

African oil reserves have grown by 40 percent in the last 20 years, with much of this growth in East Africa. Recent discoveries of natural gas in Mozambique have raised its reserves to that of Indonesia, which ranks thirteenth in the world. Negotiations are underway for the building of an LNG export plant to monetize a portion of these largely stranded reserves.[43] While a major offshore gas discovery was made in Kenya in 2013, work is continuing on an LNG import terminal as part of a much larger project to increase Kenya's electricity generation capacity by 5 gW. Kenya plans to build an electricity transmission system connecting electricity generating plants in Kenya to the neighboring region as part of a larger integrated system. It is not known how the discovery of offshore gas will affect the LNG import project whose construction was to start in 2014. Another LNG export plant is under negotiation to monetize a portion of stranded gas discovered offshore Tanzania.[44] A gas transmission system is being proposed where a main pipeline would run from northern Ethiopia through Kenya, Tanzania, Malawi, and Mozambique to Swaziland in South Africa, with a branch pipeline from Kenya to serve Uganda, Rwanda, and Burundi. This would essentially tie all East Africa into a common gas transmission system.[45] Coupling this with a regional electricity transmission system would be vital for the economic development of East Africa.

South America has only 4 percent of the world's reserves of conventional natural gas, and nearly three-quarters of this is in Venezuela. Very little is occurring to commercialize Venezuelan gas reserves under the current government, which because of its domestic policies has little funds to develop or maintain its hydrocarbon resources. GasBol is the largest pipeline in South America, which feeds natural gas from Bolivia into Brazil and Argentina. The pipeline is nearly 2,000 miles long and has a capacity of 11 bcm per year. Natural gas is needed in Brazil as backup to hydropower during times of droughts. Discovery of large hard shale oil and gas reserves in Argentina, Colombia, and Chile will determine the future direction of natural gas activity in South America. Hard shale reserves are being developed in Argentina, but there are no projects to develop shale gas in Colombia and Chile.[46] A few LNG import terminals are planned or have been built, but many related issues must first be resolved.[47]

Transforming Natural Gas to Electricity

Natural gas in electricity generation employs a variety of technologies including conventional steam generators, combustion turbines, and combined cycle plants. Natural gas burned in a steam generator is similar in context to burning coal or oil to produce steam that passes through a turbine that drives an electricity generator. Efficiency is about 35–40 percent for new plants and about 25–35 percent for older plants, regardless of the fuel. Most of the remaining energy passes to the environment as the latent heat of vaporization (the heat absorbed by water to change to steam). Combustion turbines are basically modified jet engines attached to turbines to generate electricity for peak shaving during relatively short periods of time of seasonal peak demand such as satisfying air conditioning demand during a heat wave. For most of the year, peak shaving combustion turbines are idle and the electricity they generate is extraordinarily expensive, not from their thermal inefficiency, but from the need to amortize an investment in a very short period of operation. If a generator runs all year long such as coal and nuclear, the investment can be written off over 8,640 hours of operation (360 days × 24 hours per day with five days set aside for maintenance and repair). For a natural gas generator running during daylight hours, the investment must be written off at a maximum of 4,320 hours, and probably less. For a peak shaving combustion turbine operating 6 hours a day for 60 days, 360 hours of operation must bear the entire burden of an annual write-off of the investment. Hence low capital cost combustion turbines are best for peak shaving. However, they are also energy-inefficient. About two-thirds of energy consumed in a combustion turbine is for compressing incoming air prior to burning natural gas and the remaining one-third turns the generator. In other words, a combustion turbine of 300,000 horsepower output will expend 200,000 horsepower compressing air in readiness for injecting natural gas for burning, leaving 100,000 horsepower to turn an electricity generator. One hundred thousand horsepower is equivalent to 73 mW (1 horsepower is equivalent to 0.735 kW) or about 70 mW taking into account the efficiency of the electric generator. This implies an overall efficiency of 25–30 percent taking into account heat loss from combustion. But the real cost in dollars per kilowatt-hour ($/kWh) is amortizing the investment in a very short period of time.[48]

A combined cycle plant directs the escaping exhaust gases from a combustion turbine through a steam generator to drive an electricity generating turbine. A combined cycle plant can increase thermal efficiency up to 50 percent, higher than that of an oil or coal fired steam generating plant, by inclusion of a combustion turbine in addition to a steam generator. Besides higher thermal efficiency, a combined cycle plant has lower capital costs than coal or nuclear plants, shorter construction times, and greater operational flexibility, and is the preferred choice for medium capacity plants. Combined cycle plants of various generating capacities are built to meet the variable needs of electricity generating utilities, leaving base load generation to large coal and nuclear plants. Hydro plants would be ideal for base load generation since their fuel cost (water) is free. However, it is difficult to ramp the power output of coal and nuclear plants up and down rapidly in response to changing electricity demand. Coal and nuclear plants are best employed at nearly full capacity operation at all times as suppliers of base load electricity. Hydro plants in the US are normally employed to meet variable demand as they can be easily ramped up or down by changing the flow of water through the turbines. In nations where hydro is a principal source of power as in Norway, Canada, Brazil, and many small nations, hydro satisfies both base and variable needs. As a general rule, natural gas plants satisfy variable needs because of their relative ease to respond to changing electricity demand. They are also used as backup for hydro plants during times when water levels in reservoirs are low and as backup for solar plants when skies are cloudy and for wind turbines when air is calm. The cost of inclusion of natural gas fired electricity generating plants as backup to hydro, solar, and wind is generally neglected in calculating the cost of electricity for these renewable sources.

Many companies require large quantities of hot water in their operations and have historically purchased electricity for both powering a plant and for heating water. These companies are increasingly installing cogeneration plants that do not necessarily have to be fueled by natural gas. When fueled by natural gas, a cogeneration plant is a combined cycle plant with both a combustion turbine and a steam turbine to produce electricity with none of the line losses associated with offsite electricity generation. Moreover, water containing the latent heat of vaporization from the steam turbine condenser can be substituted for hot water that has previously been heated with electricity. Being able to utilize "free" hot water raises the overall efficiency of cogenerating plants to 65 percent or higher. The latest version of a combined cycle plant utilizing a Brayton cycle gas turbine with a Rankine cycle steam generator can achieve 60 percent efficiency without having to utilize the hot water from the turbine condenser. Presumably this may mean that also being able to utilize hot water from the condenser would result in an even higher efficiency.[49]

Combined cycle plants is combined heat and power (CHP) plants, commonly associated with district heating in Scandinavia. These can be fueled partly by biomass or natural gas or fuel oil. Fuel selection is optimized, generally minimizing, if not eliminating, the need for fuel oil. Electricity is consumed by commercial and/or residential users residing in the local area and waste water is for space heating, personal use, clothes and dishwashers, and any other commercial or industrial equipment requiring hot water. A commercial and/or residential area served by a CHP is optimized in order to achieve a high utilization for the generation of both electricity and waste hot water to maximize overall performance. CHPs are popular as a means to conserve energy. District heating is a residential area served by a common source of hot water, but not electricity.

Carbon Emissions of Natural Gas

A joule is a unit of energy, as is Btu, where one Btu is equal to 1,055.0559 J. A Btu can heat one pound of water in 1°F, making a joule a rather small unit of energy. Table 7.2 shows the amount of carbon dioxide given off per terajoule (trillion joules) and tons of oil equivalent for the three fossil fuels, taken from *BP Energy Statistics* (Toe is ton oil equivalent).

Clearly natural gas emits much less carbon dioxide per unit of energy released than oil and coal. Natural gas as primarily methane (CH_4) when combined with oxygen (O_2) yields carbon dioxide and water as combustion products.

$$CH_4 + 2O_2 = CO_2 + 2H_2O$$

Coal and oil are more complex hydrocarbon molecules where carbon atoms outnumber hydrogen atoms to a far greater extent than in natural gas, producing more carbon dioxide for an equivalent release of energy plus other undesirable contaminants such as nitrous and sulfur oxides, particulates, and metals. At 100 percent conversion between heat energy and electricity, 1 kWh is equal to 3,412 Btu. However, for 30 percent thermal efficiency, 11,373 Btu would have to be expended to generate 1 kWh and 6,824 Btu for 50 percent thermal efficiency.[50] Using this relationship, carbon dioxide emissions can be determined for a 1 gW plant (1,000 mW), sufficient to meet the needs of 1 million

Table 7.2 Carbon Dioxide Emissions

	Kg CO₂ per TJ	*Tons CO₂ per Toe*
Natural gas	56,100	2.35
Oil	73,300	3.07
Coal	94,600	3.96

Table 7.3 Annual Carbon Dioxide Emissions from a 1 Gigawatt Generating Plant

	Kg CO_2 per TJ	Thermal Efficiency	Metric Tons CO_2 Emissions
Natural gas	56,100	50%	3,538,000
Natural gas	56,100	30%	5,897,000
Oil	73,300	30%	7,705,000
Coal	94,600	30%	9,944,000

people, in terms of residential, commercial, and industrial demand, over the course of a year. Table 7.3 shows the carbon dioxide emissions generated by fossil fuel plants of 30 percent thermal efficiency and a natural gas plant of 50 percent thermal efficiency.

A more efficient natural gas plant has about one-third the carbon emissions of a coal plant with the same power output, better yet with cogeneration (CHP) plants, which explains why there is a great interest in phasing out coal plants in favor of natural gas (and renewables) plants. CHP plants cannot be universally adopted because there has to be a need for hot water to achieve their higher efficiency. Without this need for hot water, a cogeneration plant becomes a conventional combined cycle natural gas generating plant.

Selection Procedure for Electricity Generating Plants

As mentioned, the three principal types of natural gas generating plants are the combustion turbine, combined cycle (combustion turbine plus conventional steam turbine), and cogeneration (combined cycle plus the ability to use waste heat for heating and industrial purposes). Each has its place in generating electricity. Moreover a utility operator has to consider the possibility of coal fired plants, nuclear and hydro plants, and renewables usually in the form of solar and wind, but also geothermal and marine tides and waves.

The normal approach for examining the economics of each of these options utilizes the levelized cost methodology. The basic elements of a levelized cost model are the capital, fixed, and variable costs of operating an electricity generating plant. There are various approaches to obtaining the levelized cost.[51] One levelized cost model calculates total cost of operating a plant for 20 years and total amount of generated electricity to obtain cost in dollars per kilowatt or megawatt-hour. Another calculates the annual cost over the life of the project, which is then discounted to obtain the levelized cost. Variable costs are predominantly fuel costs, but could include other costs that are a function of the utilization rate of a generating plant. Other than fuel costs, most operational costs are fixed. Utility workers are not hired and fired as utilization rates rise and fall. Property taxes, insurance, salaried personnel, and nearly every other cost remain the same (fixed) regardless of the power output of a generating plant. Capital costs take into account the equity investment and its associated return on equity, the amount of the asset financed by debt and its associated interest rate and amortization schedule, and taxes on profits.

If the capital cost factor changes with time, or inflation is taken into account, or noninflationary changes in energy costs occur, then the 20- or 30-year (life of asset) approach has to be taken, including discounting future costs. However, the annual capital cost factor calculated with the net present value (NPV) methodology is usually constant throughout the economic life of the asset. For a constant capital factor, and for fixed and variable costs expressed in constant dollars, the levelized cost model can be constructed for a single year as long as the remaining years have identical assessments of values. Inflation can be built into the model, but this then brings into question the appropriate inflation and discount rate. The same observation is true if fuel costs vary in terms of constant dollars. Doing the calculation in constant dollars obviates this higher level of complexity by not having to estimate future inflationary rates and fuel costs and the appropriate discount factor. But, of course, this more complex approach can be taken if desired by management to perform a greater in-depth analysis for making a more informed and intelligent decision regarding a major long-term capital investment.

Suppose that the annual capital cost factor is 10 percent and the investment is $10 million; the annual capital cost would then be $1 million. This would be sufficient to pay off the underlying debt with its applicable interest rate, provide a desired return on the equity investment along with the recoupment of invested equity funds, and payment of taxes on profits over the investment horizon. By adding in the fixed and variable costs of operation, one can obtain the corresponding minimum electricity rate that covers capital, fixed, and variable costs. There is no impact on income taxes as long as the stipulated electricity rate just covers fixed and variable costs. If the actual electricity rate departs from this minimum rate, then there would be repercussions on taxable profits. Normally electricity rate calculations are done on the basis of satisfying the charge on capital along with covering fixed and variable costs.

Cash flow analysis incorporating NPV treats equity as a form of subordinated debt where cash flow provides first for the return on equity in the manner of applying interest to any outstanding debt. Any funds left over are applied to the return of equity similar to amortization of debt; if there is a shortfall, then the amount of outstanding subordinated debt increases accordingly. At the end of the investment horizon, equity as a form of sub-ordinated debt, like any loan, is completely paid off (return of investment). In addition to receiving a return of the equity investment, an investor also earns "interest" in the form of a return on equity equal to the internal rate of return (IRR) embodied within an NPV analysis. Equity as subordinated debt differs from true debt in that its amortization is not set, but varies with the cash flow. With actual debt, amortization is fixed, and a company that can-not pay debt amortization or interest on a loan can be forced into bankruptcy. Equity can be viewed as a form of subordinated debt, with amortization being a variable depending on cash flow, with the proviso of being entirely paid off at the end of the investment horizon. A shortfall in cash flow to pay for the return on equity increases the amount of subordinate debt. This continues until cash flow is sufficient to cover return on equity, with any excess dedicated to reducing the principal (amount of equity). Despite these caveats, equity has properties consistent with subordinate debt in that cash flow must provide a return on equity (interest) and a return of equity (repayment of subordinated debt). This can be dem-onstrated by taking a project cash flow and breaking it down into two components: one for a return on the outstanding amount of equity equal to the project's IRR, and the other a return of the equity investment. The balance of the equity investment is zero at the end of project life just as the balance of debt is zero when a loan is fully amortized.

Screening Curves

Screening curves are used to obtain the cost per kilowatt-hour or megawatt-hour for different utilization rates. From examination of the screening curve for a desired level of output, one can choose which type of plant would best fit the needs of a utility. To construct a screening curve, capital and fixed costs are constant, but fuel costs are variable depending on the utilization rate of the plant. The effective rate for electricity covers capital, fixed, and variable costs for various utilization rates. If a generating plant operates at a utilization of 10 percent, or 10 percent of 8,640 hours, or 864 hours, then the entire year's capital and fixed costs are applied to that time duration. Adding in variable costs in the form of fuel for that period of time, one should not be surprised that the cost of electricity is rather high at low utilization rates. A screening curve provides the minimum charge in dollars per megawatt-hour to satisfy all costs (capital, fixed, and variable). Screening curves can be constructed in incremental steps of utilization from 5 percent to 95 percent and multiplied by the power output of the three types of natural gas plants under consideration. Table 7.4 lists the principal plant characteristics and costs, which are *pro forma* for illustrating the general method for constructing screening curves.

The procedure for obtaining the screening curve is to calculate output at 5 percent of design output and then in incremental steps of 5 percent up to 95 percent (nothing operates at 100 percent output over the course of the year—there's always some planned downtime for maintenance and repairs). The variable energy cost is calculated for each output increment and actual hours of operation are calculated for each utilization rate. The entire annual capital and fixed costs are applied to the actual hours of operation to obtain the capital and fixed costs for each 5 percent increment of utilization (capital and fixed costs are treated as *de facto* variable costs in being applied to actual hours of operation). The variable fuel cost is added to the capital and fixed costs for each increment to obtain the dollars per megawatt output. The screening curve can then be plotted as in Figure 7.7.

While the screening curves for the remaining two natural gas electricity generating plants can also be plotted, the problem is a lack of consistency in comparing the three. For instance, 10 percent utilization represents 7 mWh of output for the combustion turbine, 50 mWh for the conventional plant, and 70 mWh of output for the cogeneration plant. A direct comparison can be made if the x-axis is in terms of megawatt-hour output, not utilization rates, as in Figure 7.8.

Clearly the combustion turbine should be used during short periods of time when electrical demand peaks such as extraordinary hot summer weather. Installing a larger, but more efficient, plant that would only be used 10 percent of the time over the course of a year is clearly uneconomic. Low capital and operating costs of combustion turbines coupled with thermal inefficiency provide a much better economic solution for peak shaving than grossly underutilizing larger types of plants. For the assumptions in Table 7.4, the cost of electricity is lower for the cogeneration plant than for the conventional combined plant, although the differential is narrow, as can be seen in Figure 7.8. At 500 mW, the conventional combined cycle plant delivers electricity at $54 per megawatt-hour, whereas the cogeneration combined cycle is $51 per megawatt-hour. For power levels above 500 mW,

Table 7.4 Principal Plant Characteristics and Costs

	Combustion Turbine	Conventional Combined Cycle	Cogeneration Combined Cycle
Design Output, mW	70	500	700
Thermal Efficiency	20%	50%	65%
Capital Cost	$1,000,000	$10,000,000	$11,000,000
Fixed Cost	$300,000	$3,500,000	$3,600,000

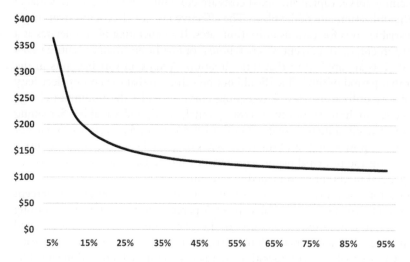

Figure 7.7 Screening Curve for the 70 mW Combustion Turbine

the 700 mW cogeneration plant has a clear advantage with a cost of $42 per megawatt-hour at full power. However, if the hot water waste from the cogeneration plant cannot be put to good use, then its efficiency falls to that of the conventional plant and, with its higher capital and operating cost, would generate more costly electricity.

Since the relationship between Mcf (thousand cubic feet) and mmBtu is so close (1 Mcf is 1.025 mmBtu), practitioners in the utility business use a shortcut to obtain what is called the heat rate of a plant. The advantage is that the fuel cost of generating power can be easily obtained by multiplying the current gas price by the heat rate. The heat rate is the energy content for 1 kWh of electricity divided by efficiency (3,142

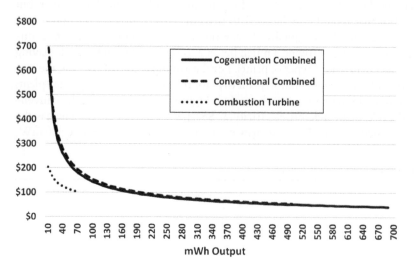

Figure 7.8 $/mWh Output

Btu for 1 kWh divided by efficiency, say 50 percent), or a heat rate of 6,284 Btu per kilowatt-hour. The heat rate when multiplied by natural gas selling for $4/Mcf gas yields a fuel cost of $0.025/kWh or $25/mWh.

Fracking

Just a few years ago, the outlook for US natural gas, like oil, was a depleting resource. Forecasts by knowledgeable individuals and energy consulting companies and government think-tanks called for imminent large-scale natural gas imports by the US just as had occurred with crude oil. This opened up the floodgates to build LNG import terminals spurred on in part by remarks made by Alan Greenspan: "a major expansion of US import capability appears to be under way. These movements bode well for widespread natural gas availability in North America in the years ahead."[52]

Luckily for most of these promoters, the government took so long to grant approvals that they could quietly shelf their plans without financial loss when it was realized that the US would not become a natural gas importer. Just a few LNG import terminals were built, and while opening their doors for receiving LNG cargoes, the projection for US natural gas imports was transformed to a projection for US natural gas exports. For the swift in foot, brand new LNG import terminals were converted to LNG export terminals. This is an unbelievable rapid and dramatic change in outlook for any commodity and why fracking is truly considered a game changer. This had to be a bitter pill for the most astute industry specialists and observers to totally miss one of the biggest changes in the outlook of any commodity—the best laid plans of planners and forecasters *aft gang* astray.

Fracking is fracturing rock to ease the flow of oil and gas to a well bore. Fracturing rock has a long history, but not the word "fracking." It is felt that the first use of "fracking" was in the late 1970s as a substitute curse word in the science fiction series *Battlestar Galactica*.[53] Fracking is normally associated with hard shale, an impermeable rock which essentially locks in hydrocarbons, preventing their flow to a well bore. But fracking can be done on any impermeable rock such as tight sand formations where the particles making up sand stone form a barrier to lock in natural gas or oil hydrocarbons. Fracking of hard shale is now a generic term that applies to hydrocarbons found in any impermeable rock, but which most often is shale.

The concept of fracturing rock dates back to the Civil War when a Union officer noticed that a column of water would shoot straight up when an artillery shell exploded in a narrow canal. After the war, he developed a torpedo mechanism that lowered nitroglycerine capsules into an oil well, which directed the explosion sideways to fracture rock around a well, increasing the flow of oil into the well bore. The concept of fracturing rock was essentially born, along with the oil industry. In the 1930s, guns and bullets became the way to pierce the well casing and fracture nearby rock, followed in the 1950s with bazookas, culminating with experiments with nuclear weapons by the US and USSR.

Fracking as now practiced is the brainchild of George Mitchell. George's father, a penniless Greek immigrant, worked on railroad gangs (the paymaster could not write his Greek name and renamed him after his own). Eventually he opened up a shoe-shine parlor in Houston. Although life was a financial struggle, one of his sons, George, eventually earned a degree in petroleum engineering in 1940 and served in the US Army Corps of Engineers during World War Two learning how to manage projects that employed hundreds of men. After the war he developed a knack for picking productive wells by scrutinizing their logs. He teamed up with his brother who developed a knack for raising funds. George's success in picking winners (not all his picks were winners, but enough were) allowed the brothers to open shop to what would eventually become Mitchell Energy.

By the late 1970s George faced a serious problem. Mitchell Energy's conventional natural gas fields were declining in volume to the point where meeting long-term contractual arrangements on supplying gas was in doubt. The company's mineral rights to conventional natural gas fields also contained hard shale formations, but natural gas entrapped in the hard shale could not be tapped by conventional means. Exploring for new sources of conventional gas proved unsuccessful and George took a new look at the Barnett shale formation lying a mile or so below land whose mineral rights were held by Mitchell Energy. In 1981 George made a strategic decision to stem declining production by concentrating the company's effort on developing fracking to tap natural gas in the Barnett geologic formation. The US government was also looking into fracking with a series of demonstration projects.[54] The Gas Research Institute received funding for investigating hydraulic fracturing from FERC. Regardless of any assistance from these sources, it would take Mitchell and his team a decade and $35 million of company funds to successfully find the right combination of water, sand, chemicals, and pressure to successfully frack Barnett shale.

Although George was a major (but not a majority) shareholder in Mitchell Energy, and held a top-level position, he faced vociferous objections by top senior management and the board of directors representing shareholders on the years of time and millions of dollars expended with little to show in progress of perfecting a successful technique for fracking. There was dissension within George Mitchell's own ranks on what should be the next step considering that all previous steps had failed. He became the butt of jokes by industry experts for pursuing the impossible dream and his efforts were deemed, like Colonel Drake's, pure folly. Major oil companies held him in disdain if not derision as they abandoned the US to pursue conventional oil and gas development in foreign lands.

George Mitchell's breakthrough in technological development in fracking wells did not reach its full potential until it was joined with horizontal drilling. Hard shale formations were relatively shallow in depth but extended horizontally over wide areas. Vertical wells only tapped a tiny portion of a formation, whereas horizontal wells could penetrate miles of pay zone. Once the technology of fracking and horizontal well drilling were perfected, the race was on to develop this new source of hydrocarbons and huge fortunes were made (and lost), perhaps best personified by the principal founder of Chesapeake Energy, Aubrey McClendon, an extremely aggressive champion of commercializing fracking.[55] Underpinning the rapid development of the gas shale industry was a widespread reliance on natural gas futures and swaps to assure future cash flows to appease bankers' yearning to sleep comfortably at night. Increased lending to gas shale producers whose risk was mitigated by offsetting positions in futures and swaps was vital for the rapid expansion of fracking as a new source of energy. A shale gas producer taking the short side of a futures or swap is protected by a fall in natural gas prices; but there is a cost in the form of passing profits to the futures or swap counterparty in case of a rise in natural gas prices. Thus protection against bankruptcy came at a price of reduced profitability; nevertheless, derivatives permitted huge amounts of investment dollars to flow into companies, leading the way in developing a new source of oil and gas.[56] But, of course, this did not prevent the founders of these companies including McClendon, as individuals, to take the opposite position their companies were forced to take by the bankers to person-ally profit if natural gas prices rose. To some, this opened the door to a conflict of interest of an individual making a private investment on one side of a derivative transaction and then as an executive making a corporate investment on the opposite side.

Horizontal Drilling

Horizontal drilling starts with a conventional drilling of a vertical drill hole until safely beyond the fresh water table. The drill is removed and a casing installed and filled with cement forced up through the bottom of the well to surround the casing by high pres-sure water in the drill pipe. All that is left in the casing from cementing is a bottom cement plug. This isolates the fresh water aquifer from contamination by hydrocarbons that will be flowing up the drill pipe and also forms the foundation for the blowout pre-venter. Then the drill pipe and bit are reinserted and they drill through the cement plug and continue to drill vertically to about 500 feet above the horizontal zone called the kickoff point. The drill pipe and bit are again withdrawn and a downhill drilling motor and an associated "measurement while drilling" instrument are lowered to begin the angle building process. A vertical well is drilled by rotating the drill pipe with a tricone drilling bit at its end. Mud forced down the center of the drill pipe clears away the debris from drilling, which passes up the annulus between the drill pipe and the inner wall of the casing. Beyond the kickoff point, the drill pipe does not rotate, but mud passing down the center of the pipe powers the drilling motor. The "measurement while drill-ing" equipment informs the drilling team of the exact location of the drilling motor and the nature of any surrounding hydrocarbons. The distance from the kickoff point of a vertical well to the well becoming horizontal is about one-quarter of a mile. Once the well is horizontal, drilling proceeds in what is called the lateral. The pipe used to drill a horizontal well is 30 feet in length and just short of 500 pounds. It takes 350 pipe lengths to drill 10,500 feet of horizontal well (about 2 miles). Depending on the circumstances, the lateral distance can be as much as 7 miles.[57] The drill pipe, now referred to as the drill string because of its apparent flexibility to follow and drill a curved path, has to be removed from time to time, tripped out, to renew the drill bit.

When the horizontal well is drilled to its full extent, the drill pipe and bit are removed, the casing installed, and cement pumped down the middle and out the end to fill the annulus outside the casing and the inner surface of the well bore. Cement is forced out of the inside of the casing by high pressure water, leaving only a cement plug at the end. This completes the drilling phase. The next phase is to frack the well, starting with the removal of the drilling equipment and installing a temporary wellhead. From this a per-forating gun (pipe with holes to direct the explosive force) is lowered by line wire to a targeted segment of the horizontal leg, starting at its furthest end. The targeted segment is generally between 350 and 1,000 feet. An electrical current through the line wire sets off explosives that penetrate the casing, creating small cracks in the hard shale rock. The per-forating gun is then withdrawn and water with sand and chemicals is pumped down the well. About 98–99 percent of the mixture is water and a sand called proppant, which can be a man-made ceramic material with better properties than sand in keeping cracks open for easier passage of hydrocarbons to the well bore. The remaining 2 or less percent is an industry secret, but involves chemicals similar in nature to those found under a kitchen sink.[58] Gels, foams, compressed gases, and polymer friction reducers change turbulent flow to laminar flow and act as suspension agents to ensure that proppant does not fall out of the liquid. Chemical additives including certain types of gels increase the viscosity of the fracturing fluid to hold proppant in the fluid, whereas chemical breakers (enzymes and oxidizers) reduce the viscosity of fracturing fluid, exiting a crack to leave proppant behind to keep cracks open. Other chemicals include isopropyl alcohol, antifreeze (ethylene glycol), alkalis, biocides, scale inhibitors, surfactants, and acids to normalize pH levels. This cocktail mix of so many varied chemicals illustrates the challenge that Mitchell faced, the proportions of which had to be determined through endless experimental changes to the fracking fluid menu along with different fracking pressures.

Once fracking fluid is in place, its pressure is suddenly raised to 3,500 psi, possibly as high as 15,000 psi, to greatly expand the small cracks made by the perforating gun by several hundred feet up to as much as nearly 2,000 feet. Sand particles in the fracking fluid become entrapped in the cracks, preventing them from closing when the pressure is released. This keeps the cracks in the fractured rock open to allow the escape of hydrocarbons to the well bore. It is necessary that fracked rock has the right properties because hard shale with too much clay or which is pliable for other reasons will fill in around the proppant, preventing release of gas or oil. Upon release of pressure, much of the water and chemicals are flushed out. The well bore is prepared for the next fracking operation, which begins with a plug inserted at the terminal end of the previous perforated segment to prevent refracking a completed section. The perforating gun is inserted and the process is repeated for the next segment, which is repeated again until the entire horizontal well bore has been fractured. Up to 40 percent of fractures are duds in that little or no oil or gas escape into the well bore.[59] Once fracking is completed, the well plugs for each segment are removed and a permanent wellhead Christmas tree is installed with connections made to a nearby oil or gas gathering system.[60]

Hard Shale Natural Gas Resources

US natural gas reserves were 9.3 trillion cubic meters (tcm) in 2013, up from 5.8 tcm in 2005 when hard shale gas was still in its infancy stage. With conventional gas reserves declining about 0.1 tcm per year prior to 2005, the difference in reserves between 2005 and 2013 of 3.8 tcm plus including conventional gas reserve declines of 0.1 tcm per year infers that US gas reserves have increased about 4.6 tcm or 162 Tcf from fracking hard shale. On top of this, it is estimated that shale gas resources (not proven reserves) are estimated to be 1,161 Tcf. Figure 7.9 compares known gas reserves with estimated shale gas resources to illustrate the dramatic impact shale gas has on US gas reserves/resources.[61]

Figure 7.9 shows that natural gas reserves/resources have nearly quadrupled with the advent of gas fracking. The figure also includes the major individual shale gas geologic formations in the US. Marcellus and Utica are west of the Appalachian mountains primarily in Pennsylvania and with extensions into New York and Ohio. Haynesville is smaller area-wise, straddling the Texas–Louisiana border, and Eagle Ford straddles the Texas–Mexico border. Global conventional natural gas reserves adjusted for the shale gas component in US reserves are 6,550 Tcf, and global shale gas resources are estimated at 6,634 Tcf, a doubling of known reserves. Figure 7.10 shows the nations with the largest shale gas resources.

Other nations with exploitable resources of shale gas are Brazil, Venezuela, France, Poland, Ukraine, Libya, Egypt, India, and Pakistan. Poland was considered an early bright

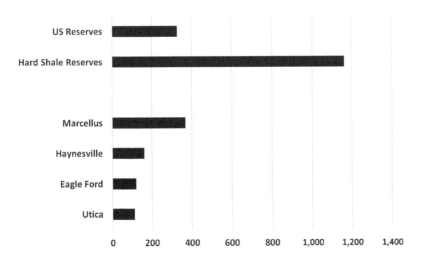

Figure 7.9 Conventional Gas Reserves and Shale Gas Resources (Tcf)

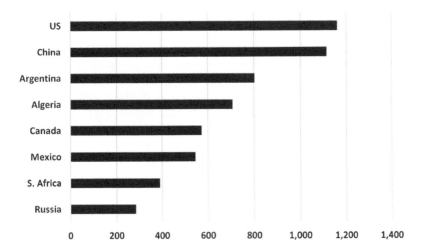

Figure 7.10 Global Shale Gas Resources (Tcf)

light for fracking in Europe, but major oil companies have retreated from fracking in Poland because of doubts over estimated shale gas resources and difficulties in fracking the shale rock.[62] Civil commotion in Ukraine has put fracking on hold. Argentina has started a successful fracking project, which may be further expanded as results become better known. One small aspect of this doubt was the write-down of the Chaco-Parana basin's gas shale reserves from 162 to 3 Tcf by EIA. While this casts serious doubt on Argentina's ultimate gas shale reserves, a much greater uncertainty exists in the financial risk of investing in Argentina. While a "partial" default on an international loan in 2014 raised the eyebrows of foreign investors, more ominously, the passage of a bill in the Argentine Senate that would allow the government to "establish, at any stage of the economic process, profit margins, reference prices, maximum and minimum prices, or all or any of these measures," would greatly discourage companies from investing in Argentina.

The risk of developing hydrocarbon resources can be seen in China's original announced intention to develop shale gas with an objective of producing 6.5 bcm per year in 2015 rising to 60–100 bcm per year by 2020. In 2014 the objective was scaled back to 30 bcm per year, barely able to satisfy 1 percent of China's current energy needs. This scaling-back is a result of shale being much deeper and containing more clay than anticipated, making it difficult to utilize US fracking techniques. Moreover the drilling region turned out to be seismically active, inhospitable to drilling, and short on water.[63]

Fracking Water Disposal

Disposal of huge quantities of fracking water varying between 2 and 8 million gallons per well has become a major environmental problem. Fracking water cannot be reused because it is contaminated by salts and minerals absorbed during fracking. The preferred method to dispose of water from fracking (including any salt water from hydrocarbon extraction) is Class II salt water disposal wells espoused by the Environmental Protection Agency (EPA). Disposal wells are monitored, inspected, and maintained in accordance with EPA regulatory standards going back to the 1970s. Any oily residue in the salt water waste is removed prior to injection. A typical disposal well is an oil or gas well no longer producing hydrocarbons. Casing and piping should form a multi-layered protection to ensure the integrity of the disposal well. Casing of a disposal well should extend some hundreds of feet below the fresh water table to prevent any contamination of fresh water aquifers by contaminated salt or fracking water. Salt or fracking water is normally injected into a permeable water zone whose water content has a similar chemical makeup to water being disposed. Perforations at the bottom of the well provide a gateway for the disposal of water, if necessary, and packing prevents any upward flow of water through the annulus. Nonpermeable rock layers above the salt water zone keep fracking water trapped within its disposal zone. Superficially, if fracking water is being disposed into salt waters of similar chemical makeup in permeable rock zones, it seems unlikely that disposal water would be a cause of minor earthquakes as has been claimed. However, if disposal is not in a salt water zone between impermeable rock layers, but within a rock layer itself, then water could act as a lubricant, resulting in minor earthquakes. Some state and local authorities are seeking bans on fracking and/or on disposal of waste waters until this issue is resolved.

Case against Fracking

For some, fracking is costly by being energy and materials and water intensive. High decline rates in production create a drilling treadmill of fracked wells begetting more fracked wells along with expansion of gas gathering systems to maintain production. Fracking is facing local opposition from its impact on lifestyles, landscape, and environmental degradation. Although there have been isolated instances of natural gas contaminating drinking water, which would not occur if the casing were properly installed, EPA has found that fracking for oil and gas has not adversely affected drinking water supplies.[64]

The recovery rate of shale gas varies between 15 and 25 percent, averaging 20 percent. This means about 80 percent of the gas in a fracked well is still contained within the rock as only natural gas at or very close to a cracked surface can migrate to the well bore compared to a conventional gas well that can remove about 75 percent of reservoir gas. Whether higher recovery rates can be achieved by refracking a well or drilling and fracking an entire new well does not seem to be entirely resolved. As poor as the recovery rate is for shale gas, it is much better than oil shale, whose recovery rate varies between 3 and 5 percent, meaning that 95–97 percent of the oil resource is still locked in shale rock when a fracked well stops producing. A conventional oil well can tap about a third of the oil in a reservoir without resorting to a variety of recovery enhancing methods. Poor recovery rates are reflected in the 3-year effective life of fracked wells, whereas conventional wells can last 20–30 or more years. Having to replace a fracked well every 3 years or so is going to place a great deal of strain on available trained and competent crews, drilling equipment and pipe, and on financial resources for companies that own and operate fracked wells. It has been noted that the debt load on companies that frack wells balloon within a rather short period of time. If revenue from fracked wells cannot pay down this debt over the short life of the well, then it is entirely possible that a company reporting profits on its operation of fracked wells can go bankrupt from its inability to pay down its burgeoning debt load. Think of it this way: if 10 year debt is placed on a well that only produces for 3 years, how are the remaining 7 years of debt to be serviced? One way is to keep on fracking as many new wells as possible and dedicating the new influx of short-term funds to pay off past and new debt. Under these conditions, a company can't stop drilling new wells because this may place remaining debt in jeopardy. This is precisely the problem being faced by oil companies actively involved with fracking: low oil prices have stopped drilling new wells. It is feared that falling production that terminates in 3 years will cause a financial crisis for many of these companies.

This is a problem for companies in oil fracking, not natural gas fracking. But there are some who believe that natural gas prices have to rise to $6–$7 per Mcf to justify a continuing investment in fracked wells and gathering systems to maintain production. Others feel that a substantial rise in natural gas prices is not necessary because of gains in fracked well productivity. Productivity per fracked well is increasing as a consequence of the learning experience from drilling multiple wells under varying conditions. In 2010 a new Marcellus shale well was estimated to produce nearly 1.5 million cubic feet per day and this has increased to an amazing 8 million cubic feet per day in 2014. This, of course, translates to far fewer fracked wells for the same output.[65] Thus advances in technology and an increased understanding of the fracking process have caused the breakeven price of fracked gas to fall from $5–$6 to $4–$5, with some maintaining that the breakeven price in 2014 was below $3 per million Btu or 1,000 cubic feet for those who have best mastered the fracking process.

Given the short lifetime of a fracked well, the countryside may eventually be littered with abandoned fracked wells. It might be possible that the vertical well bore of a fracked well can be reused by drilling a horizontal well in a different direction and at a different depth, creating what might look like spokes on a wheel. This would considerably enlarge the area that can be served by a single well. It may even be possible to have more wells drilled from the horizontal portion of a fracked well, forming what one could consider roots on an underground tree. While this sounds attractive, it may not be feasible. But one step in this direction is Continental Resources' ECO-Pad that is a drilling platform that "walks" on hydraulic "feet" to four close-by locations drilling four horizontal wells in different directions (and different pay zones), where the operation for all the wells is accomplished at a single site.[66] This concept is akin to so-called Octopus technology where many wells are being drilled from one pad site. Given that a fracked well requires about 50–80 acres for its operation, multiplying the number of wells from one site makes good sense, particularly when one considers the impact on land use of tens of thousands of fracking wells.

Some point out that the 3-year effective life lowers the energy output/energy input ratio for fracked wells. The energy input for fracked wells is primarily diesel fuel to drill wells, power associated equipment including transporting water to the site and fracked water from the site, and running the facility. But, of course, this is not a concern as long as revenue from output covers costs, which includes energy input. Of greater concern is that fracking is water intensive, consuming 2–2.5 million gallons, perhaps as high as 8 million gallons, per well. This volume far exceeds the internal volume of a well bore because of repeated fracking for each segment of the lateral plus water expended creating cracks in formation rock. While recycling fracking water is an attractive sounding idea, the chemistry of fracked water is affected by absorbing salts and metals during fracking, which prevents recycling. Thus fracking water is used once and then disposed. There is a safe method of disposal, but fracking may not be near an authorized disposal site. Hundreds of tank loads of water for fracking and disposal of waste fracking water put an enormous strain on rural roads that were not built for this level of activity. (A typical tank truck holds 9,000 gallons; how many truck loads are necessary to move, say, 3 million gallons of fluid to a site before and during fracking and from the site to a disposal facility after fracking?)

Efforts are underway to identify a fracking fluid that does not present a disposal problem. Ideas being floated around include use of carbon dioxide, gels, and propane as fracking fluids. Memsys Clearwater, located in Germany and Singapore, has developed a vacuum multi-effect membrane distillation used for distilling sea water that could be used for purifying fracking fluids. The end result of this process is pure water that can be reused for fracking and a highly concentrated brine containing all the chemicals, which can be safely disposed.[67] GasFrac in Canada has originated a process for substituting a gel made from LPG. The gel does not dissolve salts or clay in the shale and doesn't sweep natural contaminants back out of the well. Since the fracking fluid is a hydrocarbon, for gas wells it can be recaptured for recycling, or for oil wells it can be sold to refineries as part of the well's output. A hydrocarbon fracking medium eliminates water and its associated disposal problem.[68]

There are other environmental objections to fracking. Some people object to the aesthetic quality of pristine pastures transformed to a production well with pipelines and sounds of diesels competing with the birds.[69] Prometheus Energy, a joint venture of Shell and Cargill, is offering a service to supply natural gas either as compressed or liquefied to run diesels used in fracking. The benefits are less nitrous oxide and particulate emissions and elimination of diesel oil contaminating soil.[70] Occurrences of fracking water and natural gas getting into drinking water are usually traced to faulty casing, which can be regulated by authorities to ensure compliance with suitable standards. The purpose of casing is not only to safeguard the environment, but also to safeguard revenue by not allowing natural oil or gas to escape from the well. There is a financial benefit of companies following environmental and construction standards that prevent hydrocarbons escaping into the water table. A DOE study of six wells at one site found no drinking water pollution from fracking fluids. One interesting aspect of this study was the discovery that fracking cracks can extend up to 1,900 feet from the well bore, much further than the usual estimates of a few hundred feet.[71] Despite this, there is a growing body of evidence that fracking, in common with any industrial activity, has a negative effect on human health.[72] Europe has instituted a thorough regulatory program for shale gas with directives that involve the environmental impact assessment of chemicals, industrial emissions, mining waste, biocides, and extraction activities on human health. Directives have also been issued on hydrocarbon licensing, safeguarding groundwater, and protecting birds.[73]

There is a question between fracking activity and the occurrence of minor earthquakes that has yet to be resolved. There appears to be a greater number of small earthquakes, or swarm of earthquakes, occurring near fracking sites, and public attention is more focused on reinjection sites of fracking waste than in fracking itself. In Oklahoma, the incidence of earthquakes has grown at an alarming pace. For all detectable earthquakes with a magnitude greater than zero, there were less than 100 annually before 2010 and since then between 900 and nearly 3,000 annually. For earthquakes above magnitude three, there were about 10 annually before 2010 and between 20 and nearly 200 since then.[74] To be fair, earthquakes are occurring in the center of the state and fracking in other areas of the state. The earthquake pattern does not seem to be "following" fracking activity. Nevertheless there is a growing interpretation of statistical data by the scientific community supporting causality between reinjection of fracking water and earthquake swarms.[75] The question of whether shattering formation rock contributes to earthquakes is still open, particularly if fracking is occurring near existing, but unknown, faults. Interestingly small earthquakes are occurring in areas where the water table is dropping, as in California. It is thought that draining the water table via irrigation reduces the weight on the crust, which springs upward, inducing small earthquakes.[76]

One important point in looking to the future is that fracking will become an ever larger component in the production of oil and gas. With fracked wells being short-lived and with the number of wells increasing to support higher levels of production, it is entirely possible, indeed inevitable, that production from oil and gas fracked wells will level off when constraints stand in the way of fracking a greater number of wells. It is possible to run out of permissible sites or trained crews, but probably not drill pipe and other equipment. Once a constraint is hit, the number of new fracked wells will remain constant and production will stabilize unless further technological progress can be made in increasing the productivity of each well.

LPG: Prelude to LNG

Liquefied petroleum gas (LPG) is propane and butane produced either as an oil refining byproduct or stripped out of natural gas and oil at the wellhead by a fractionating unit. In the 1910s light-end gases from a barrel of crude were kept in a liquid state under pressure and fueled early automobiles, then blowtorches for metal cutting, and, in 1927, gas stoves. Butane was one of the propulsion fuels for dirigibles until the market for dirigibles crashed in 1937 with the *Hindenburg*. An entrepreneur began selling unwanted bottles of butane as fuel for gas stoves in Brazil. All went well until he ran out of dirigible fuel. To replace butane, he began to import cylinders of pressurized butane on cargo liners, thus marking the humble beginning of the international trade of LPG.[77]

A single company possessed the legal right of proprietorship to the LPG fractionating process until a 1927 court decision made it available to industry, thus opening the door to development of the LPG business. With an increased availability of supply came the opportunity to develop a new market. The industry grew slowly with bobtail trucks delivering pressurized propane in a liquid state to refill cylinders that fueled stoves, water heaters, clothes dryers, and space heaters in rural areas and towns not served by natural gas pipelines. LPG was also used for crop drying. Propane was a preferred fuel for bakeries, glassmaking, and other commercial and industrial enterprises that required a greater degree of control over temperature and flame characteristics. Cleaner burning propane became a motor fuel of choice over gasoline for forklift trucks and other vehicles that operated in semi-enclosed environments such as terminals and warehouses. Butane eventually found a home as a fuel for cigarette lighters and taxicabs. LPG became a gasoline blending stock and a feedstock for steam crackers to make ethylene, the precursor to plastics and petrochemicals. Railroad tank cars were the primary means of moving LPG over long distances until they were replaced by pipelines in the late 1960s.

Wells drilled into a salt dome at Mont Belvieu in Texas leached out salt to form a cavern to store LPG. This would eventually become the nation's principal storage hub and central marketplace for LPG, with extensive gas liquid pipeline connections to major suppliers and buyers in the Gulf Coast, Midwest, and Northeast. Another storage hub in Kansas played the same role satisfying LPG demand in the upper Midwest via pipelines. LPG-carrying rail tank cars served areas beyond the reach of pipelines. LPG was carried in pressurized tanks mounted on vessels and barges along the eastern seaboard and the Mississippi River. In 1971 President Nixon put price controls on oil, which happened to include LPG. Not surprisingly, this encouraged the consumption of LPG because of its lower cost compared to other fuels.

In the US, refinery produced LPG was generally consumed internally for gasoline blending or pipelined as feedstock to an associated petrochemical plant. The commercial market for LPG was primarily supplied by stripping gas liquids from natural gas and oil at the wellhead. In contrast, LPG development in Europe was based on refinery operations and railcar imports from the Soviet Union because of no indigenous supplies of natural gas until the late 1970s when North Sea natural gas fields came onstream. LPG consumption in Europe was primarily propane in the north and butane in the south because propane vaporized more easily in warm climates. Italy promoted the use of butane as a motor vehicle fuel. Small shipments in pressurized tanks installed on vessels carried LPG from refineries in Rotterdam to destinations in northern Europe and from refineries in Italy, Libya, and Algeria to southern Europe and the eastern Mediterranean.

In Japan, the LPG market grew out of the desires of Japanese housewives and restaurant owners to cook with propane rather than kerosene. Switching from kerosene to propane was a sign of a rising standard of living. Unlike the US and Europe, Japan had to import much of its LPG aside from that produced as a byproduct in domestic refineries. Shipping LPG at sea was costly because LPG was carried in cargo tanks built to withstand the pressure necessary to keep LPG liquid at ambient temperatures. The weight of the steel in the cargo tanks to contain a pressurized cargo was about the same as the weight of the cargo, restricting the cargo-carrying capacity of the vessel.

To counter high shipping costs, Japanese shipyards designed and began building fully refrigerated LPG carriers in the 1960s. Cargo temperature was reduced to keep LPG liquid at atmospheric pressure (−43°C for propane and −1°C for butane). Cargo tanks had to withstand a lower temperature cargo and were insulated to minimize heat transfer from the outside environment. An onboard cargo refrigeration unit kept the cargo at the requisite temperature to prevent pressure buildup in the cargo tanks. Fully refrigerated cargoes made it possible to use a simpler design for the cargo tanks, which could be built to conform to the shape of the hull with no structural requirements of a pressurized cargo. This allowed an order of magnitude increase in the carrying capacity from several thousand cubic meters to 30,000–50,000 cubic meters. Parenthetically, with a specific gravity of about 0.6, a cubic meter of LPG weighs about 0.6 metric tons, compared to close to 1 metric ton for a cubic meter of crude oil. A fully loaded LPG carrier transports less cargo weight-wise than a crude carrier of the same cargo volume because of density differences. The first large-sized LPG carriers were employed shipping LPG between Kuwait and Japan. By 1970 the Japanese LPG carrier fleet numbered a dozen vessels, with the largest being 72,000 cubic meters, or about 43,000 metric tons of cargo.

The US was primed for large-scale imports with adequate storage at Mont Belvieu, inland pipeline connections (the Little Inch was converted from natural gas to gas liquids), and LPG import terminals in the Northeast and terminals in the US Gulf originally built for export, which had failed to materialize. All that was missing was an LPG shortage, appearance of a major new export source, and a means of transport. All missing elements fell into place following the oil crisis of 1973. Shortages in natural gas stemming from the consequences of government price regulations of natural gas in interstate commerce reduced the domestic supply of LPG. Fractionating plants built in the Middle East and Europe to strip out gas liquids from natural gas destined for LNG liquefaction plants greatly increased overseas supply. Transport was available as more shipyards began building large-sized, fully refrigerated LPG carriers.

While all the elements fell in place for the US to become a major LPG importer, large-scale imports never quite got off the ground. The appearance of new supplies of natural gas from deregulation increased the domestic availability of LPG. LPG demand slackened when oil (and LPG) price controls were partially lifted, and finally dismantled, by President Reagan in 1981. Increased availability, coupled with a decline in demand from higher prices, reduced the need for large-scale imports. Without the US import market developing to any significant degree, the enormous capacity of new LPG export plants in Saudi Arabia and elsewhere in the Middle East and Europe created a glut. There is nothing like a glut to present an opportunity for entrepreneurs to develop a market, as had happened with the glut created by discoveries of huge natural gas reserves in the US Southwest.

Western Way of Conducting Business

The international price for LPG swung between a premium and a discount from the price of crude oil on an energy-equivalent basis and thus was far more volatile than oil. These price swings determined the success or failure of suppliers and entrepreneurs in finding a home for new supplies of LPG. Those who bought a cargo of Middle East LPG and loaded it on a ship without a firm commitment from someone to buy the cargo when delivered a month later in the US or Europe were at the mercy of a fickle market while the vessel was at sea. Millions of dollars could be made or lost during a single voyage depending on whether the buyer was on the right or wrong side of a price swing. When playing dice in a volatile market over a long enough time horizon, the chance of survival becomes zero![78] To support this contention, many of the founding firms instrumental in developing the international LPG market were merged or liquidated when they eventually found themselves on the wrong side of the market. The same thing happened to independent LPG carrier owners when more vessels were delivered from shipyards than there were cargoes to fill the vessels. Lining up long-term deals between suppliers and buyers, along with the ships to carry the cargoes, would drastically reduce the degree of commercial risk, but long-term deals were not always available and, when available, were not always to the liking of either the buyer or seller.

Japanese Way of Organizing Business

While Western firms were enjoying either a financial bonanza or going bust, Japanese LPG players just kept rolling along in a secure business environment, the result of how different business is conducted in Japan. Having concluded that propane was preferable over kerosene, the Japanese began by ensuring a substantial market for propane as a substitute for kerosene by making bottles of liquid propane available to the public and by mandating conversion of Tokyo taxi cabs to butane fuel. If these two markets proved inadequate to absorb imported LPG, then LPG would be substituted for naphtha for steam crackers to produce petrochemicals. With the beginnings of a substantial market for imported LPG, the Japanese then proceeded to establish a fully integrated logistics supply chain by arranging long-term contracts with Middle East exporters for volumes that could be absorbed in Japan. Building a sufficient number of vessels to move the cargoes was timed to the start of long-term contracts whose volume was timed to anticipated growth in demand. Terminals with adequate storage were constructed to unload vessels, along with setting up a nationwide distribution system for bottles of LPG.

Development of an integrated supply chain was under the guidance of the Ministry of International Trade and Industry (MITI), now the Ministry of Economy, Trade and Industry (METI). MITI coordinated activities with keiretsu, massive agglomerations of Japanese companies representing major industrial sectors of the nation, who agreed to a national energy plan, sitting around the table with MITI. Whatever each keiretsu agreed to do was tantamount to a legal obligation (such a meeting in the US would be in violation of the Sherman Anti-Trust Act). Peace among the keiretsu was maintained by a "moral code" to respect each other's "corporate turf" to avoid disruptive competition. MITI was in a position to dictate the volume of LPG consumed by the petrochemical industry to smooth out any bumps and wrinkles in establishing a smoothly running supply chain.

LPG carriers received a "regulated" rate to cover costs and ensure a modest return on vested funds over the life of the vessel, reflecting little risk of unemployment for vessels tied into a well-run logistics supply chain. This investment philosophy was shared by other elements in the supply chain. Thus the price of LPG sold in Japan was essentially regulated, taking into consideration the cost of acquiring LPG and the capital and operating costs of transportation, storage, and distribution. The regulated price reflecting a low profit margin tied to long-term financing for each element of the supply chain was as favorable as possible for the Japanese people while ensuring the financial viability of all participants in the supply chain. Since the Japanese people did not object to this arrangement, there was no political advantage for the Japanese government to curry the favor of the electorate by underpricing a fuel. Japanese government guidance of energy policy proved to be superior to the regulatory experience in the US where energy policies seem to be a series of "fits and starts" that eventually have to be scrapped. Experience gained in managing LPG imports on a system or supply chain basis would become the prelude to LNG imports.

Evolution of the International LPG Business

The history of LPG consumption is a series of developing markets that started at a point in time and reached maturity at another. The US market began in earnest in 1950 and reached maturity around 1975; for Europe the growth stage spanned 1960 to around 1980, for Japan from 1965 to 1985, and for Korea from 1980 to the late 1990s. In the 2000s, China entered the growth phase of a new LPG market, and India will join in the future. Although the rate of growth in aggregate LPG consumption is somewhat constant, its center of activity travels around the world as one market begins to develop and another matures. Thus what appears to be a stable business growing at a modest rate to outsiders is, in reality, a continual opening up of new opportunities for entrepreneurs, marketers, traders, and suppliers. The LPG business, like so much of the energy business, is a challenge for those who like to be on the cusp of change where money can be made by correctly assessing its twists and turns.

The US is the world's leading LPG consumer and was essentially self-sufficient, importing and exporting only about one million tons per year (mmtpy) annually until the 1990s when imports began to increase, reaching 4.5 mmtpy by 2005. By 2012 imports had been transformed to exports of 3.7 million tons and grew to 9 mmtpy in 2013 as a result of fracking, a profuse producer of light-end hydrocarbons.[79] Export LPG terminals and pipelines are being built or expanded in capacity to deal in response to this new market. The emergence of the US as an LPG exporter caused LPG carrier rates to spiral upward from demand to transport relatively large quantities of LPG to far-off Atlantic and Pacific basin destinations.

After the US, the second largest consumer is Europe and the Mediterranean that both imports LPG to meet its domestic needs and exports LPG from the North Sea and North Africa. The Europe and Mediterranean region exports 18 mmtpy and imports 21 mmtpy and so is a net importer. While simultaneously importing and exporting large quantities of LPG may not make immediate sense, LPG is made of two distinct products, propane and butane, each of which can be long or short on a regional basis. Furthermore it may pay to export from one location and import into another, rather than ship directly between the two, to take advantage of price disparities.

The world's largest exporter is the Arabian Gulf at 33 mmtpy, of which Saudi Arabia is the largest exporter by far. The world's largest importer, on a regional basis, is Asia at 38 mmtpy, of which Japan imports 13 mmtpy and South Korea 6 mmtpy. As Asia imports more than what the Arabian Gulf exports, the deficit is covered by stripping LPG from natural gas inputs to LNG liquefaction units in Indonesia, Malaysia, Australia, and elsewhere, plus, if needed, from more distant sources such as the US and the North Sea.[80]

China is a fast growing importer of LPG, with India beginning to move into the growth stage. In a way, Korea and China mimicked Japan. Burning propane for cooking is a status symbol and indicates a rising standard of living. In Japan, propane displaced kerosene, while in Korea propane displaced charcoal briquettes, and in China propane is displacing coal and biofuels (charcoal, wood, and agricultural waste such as straw and animal dung). The next market to be developed is India, where coal and biofuels dominate home cooking. Substituting propane for coal and biofuels is a big step toward a cleaner environment because propane does not emit air particulates (smoke), carbon monoxide, nitrous oxides, and, in the case of coal, sulfur oxides and metals (cadmium, arsenic, and mercury). However, a high price for oil becomes a high price for propane. For millions of the world's poor, high-priced propane means continued cooking with coal and biofuels, ingesting pollution along with food.

In shipping, the longer the voyage, the larger the size of the optimal vessel as long as there are sufficient cargoes to fully employ a vessel. As seen in Table 7.5, the very large gas carrier fleet is undergoing a rapid expansion from growth in long haul trades such as the Arabian Gulf to Asia and the newly emerging US to Asia. Most of this fleet segment has a capacity between 70,000 and 80,000 cubic meters.

Semi-refrigerated means that the tanks are built to withstand some pressure above ambient pressure from cargoes whose temperatures are maintained above that of a fully refrigerated cargo. Semi-refrigerated vessels cost more because of the need for the tanks to withstand some degree of cargo pressure, but operate for less because of less refrigeration required to maintain cargo temperatures. The decision of which to build is partly owner-preference and partly the relative economics of transporting LPG cargoes in a fully or semi-liquefied state, which might be affected by whether the vessel is employed in mostly cold or hot climates.

Fully refrigerated medium-sized gas carriers and semi-refrigerated large gas carriers have approximately the same range of cargo capacity and trade, for example, between the North Sea and South America and between Southeast Asia and Japan and China. These fleet segments are experiencing growth from a greater volume of US exports to Atlantic basin destinations. Pressurized LPG carriers have tanks that can withstand the pressure of an LPG cargo in a liquefied state without refrigerating the cargoes. The greater cost of building tanks to hold a pressurized cargo and the impact of their weight on cargo-carrying capacity are compensated by not having the capital and operating costs of refrigeration plants. Small semi-refrigerated and large pressurized LPG carriers are in the same general cargo size range and are involved in short haul trades such as between the US Gulf and Caribbean islands or between Singapore and Southeast Asia. Small pressurized LPG carriers are employed on short haul trades supplying LPG to lightly populated remote islands in the Caribbean or Southeast Asia or within or near a port area or to isolated river ports.

In addition LPG carriers can also carry liquid cargoes of ammonia, butadiene, iso-propane, propylene, and vinyl chloride monomer (VCM). The ammonia trade is large enough to employ large-sized LPG carriers on long haul routes, but short haul routes employ smaller sized LPG carriers. Other types of liquefied cargoes generally employ small- and medium-sized LPG carriers because voyages are generally short and cargo volume limited, along with storage space at load and discharge terminals. Another subgroup of liquefied gas carriers is ethylene carriers whose cargo temperature of $-104°C$ is much

Table 7.5 World LPG Carrier Fleet

Vessel Type	Capacity (Cubic Meters)	Number Existing	Number Building
Fully Refrigerated Very Large Gas Carrier	>60,000	158	78
Fully Refrigerated Large Gas Carrier	40,000–60,000	19	3
Fully Refrigerated Medium Gas Carrier	18,000–39,999	94	20
Semi-Refrigerated Large Gas Carrier	12,000–35,000	74	44
Semi-Refrigerated Small Gas Carrier	3,000–11,999	239	5
Pressurized Large Gas Carrier	5,000–11,600	47	19
Pressurized Small Gas Carrier	<5,000	640	22

lower than LPG, but higher than LNG. This fleet segment is growing from excess ethane production from fracking. Ethane is then converted to ethylene in new and expanded ethylene production plants whose output exceeds domestic needs.[81] Ethylene carriers can carry LPG cargoes, but not LNG cargoes. While LPG cargoes are a substitute for ethylene cargoes, the real money is in ethylene cargoes that cannot be carried on LPG carriers.

International Natural Gas Pipeline Trade

Natural gas is constrained by logistics. The development of long-distance pipeline transmission was crucial to natural gas becoming a commercial energy resource. Pipelines as fixed installations are an inflexible mode of transmission connecting specific suppliers with specific consumers not unlike a railroad. Most pipelines are physically located and regulated within a single nation. Pipelines crossing national boundaries bring international political considerations into the picture, where the Keystone XL pipeline is a case in point.

A proposed pipeline from Iran to India that would cross Pakistan was, for many years, considered impossible because of the rivalry and bitter feelings between Pakistan and India. However, the parties are at least talking because Pakistan needs natural gas for energy and transit fees for revenue. Although progress has been stymied by US opposition to Iran's building of export pipelines, talks have actually been expanded to include China as part of the project.[82] A pipeline connection between Turkey and Greece, long-time bitter foes, is moving gas between the two nations and may well be expanded under Putin's initiative to help Greece. Another example of long-time foes cementing better relationships through energy was a pipeline supplying Egyptian gas to Israel. None is currently moving after the pipeline was sabotaged by the Muslim Brotherhood when in control of Egypt during 2011–2012. Egyptian gas exported as LNG is declining, squeezed between rising domestic consumption and falling production. Talks are proceeding between Israel and Egypt to reverse the pipeline and have excess Israeli offshore gas pipelined to Egypt for both domestic consumption and international sale as LNG.[83] Pipelines can be lifelines for peace—"when goods don't cross borders, armies will."[84]

Bearing in mind that 30 or more billion cubic meters per year is equivalent to a major pipeline on its own merits, the 2014 international pipeline trade between North American nations, involving a number of individual pipelines, was 75 bcm from Canada to the US, 22 bcm from the US to Canada, and 21 bcm from the US to Mexico. The only major pipeline gas exporter in South America was Bolivia that sent 5 bcm to Argentina and 11 bcm to Brazil. The world's largest pipeline exporter by far is Russia, including Central Asian Republics, that sent 153 bcm to Europe and another 18 bcm to Belarus and 13 bcm to Ukraine (about half that of 2013). Turkmenistan sent 7 bcm to Iran, 9 bcm to Europe, and 26 bcm to China; Iran sent 6 bcm to Russia and 2 bcm to China; Algeria 11 bcm (2013 figures) and Libya 18 bcm (surprising that this pipeline is still operating considering the political and social collapse of this nation) to both Spain and Italy; and Qatar 18 bcm to the UAE via an underwater pipeline. In Asia, Myanmar sent 10 bcm mostly to Singapore and the remainder to Malaysia via an underwater pipeline.[85]

Natural Gas Reserves

Total world natural gas reserves are 187 tcm in 2014, virtually unchanged from 2011, but up from 157 tcm in 2004, 133 tcm in 1999, 119 tcm in 1994, and 109 tcm in 1989.

In 2014 with world consumption at 3.39 tcm, the reserve-to-production ratio was 54 years. Dealing only in conventional proven reserves of natural gas (neglecting nearly all hard shale gas), 43 percent is in the Middle East, of which 18 percent of the world's reserves are in Iran and 13 percent in Qatar. Russia possesses 17 percent of world reserves. These three nations account for 48 percent of the world's reserves; all other nations pale in comparison (for instance, fourth place is Turkmenistan at 9 percent, fifth place the US at 5 percent (as discussed there is some inclusion of hard shale reserves), and sixth place Saudi Arabia with only 4 percent of the world's reserves). Reserves can be misleading. For instance, proven reserves in Alaska exclude potentially vast gas fields in the North Slope that have not been sufficiently assessed to classify them as proven. More importantly, nearly all hard shale gas resources, except a relatively small amount associated with the US, are not listed as reserves for good reason. Resources have to be proven to exist, with a high degree of certainty before they can be included in reserves.

International Trade of Liquefied Natural Gas

Compressed natural gas (2,000–4,000 psi) can be transported in specially built tanks. The problem is the cost of building large-capacity cargo tanks that can withstand this magnitude of pressure with a cargo still four times greater in volume than in a liquefied state.[86] However, there are special circumstances where compressed natural gas carriers are feasible such as small natural gas fields in remote areas of the Amazon River where reserves are not sufficient to justify building a long-distance pipeline or a liquefaction plant. Compressed natural gas carriers are useful for natural gas delivery to lightly populated Caribbean or Southeast Asian islands whose consumption is far too small to sustain an LNG import terminal, but where less costly natural gas can be substituted for diesel fuel for electricity generation. Compressed natural gas is not conducive to high volume, long-distance transport of natural gas.

With the exception of Russia and the US, much of the world's natural gas reserves would be stranded if pipelines were the only means of transmission. The construction of long-distance undersea pipelines to connect remote fields in Iran, Qatar, Nigeria, Venezuela, Indonesia, and Malaysia with industrially developed nations thousands of miles away in waters that may be 2–3 miles deep with undersea mountains replete with deep chasms would be either impossible to construct or prohibitively expensive. The natural gas reserves for these nations remained stranded with no commercial value until a new means of transmission was devised. Just as liquefied gas liquids (propane and butane) are refrigerated for transport as a liquid at ambient pressure, so too can natural gas. As a liquid, natural gas takes up 610 times less volume than at ambient conditions with a specific gravity a little less than LPG. The problem is that natural gas is a liquid at atmospheric pressure at a much colder temperature of −161°C (−258°F), which imposes severe constraints on tank design and insulation to prevent LNG from coming in contact with the hull. Conventional steel in ship hulls, if exposed to the cold temperature of LNG, is subject to instantaneous cracking, known as brittle fracture. A few mass-produced Liberty freighters during the Second World War sunk after their hulls split open from brittle fracture when the vessels sailed into cold north Atlantic waters. A steel belt welded around the hull of Liberty vessels resulted in no further losses from this cause. Better quality steel prevents brittle fracture at freezing ocean temperatures, but not from the cold of liquefied natural gas.

Historical Development of LNG

A much greater technological challenge in tank design and insulation than LPG carriers had to be faced before natural gas could be transported as a liquid. The success of independent research efforts in the 1950s led to the first LNG delivery in 1964 from a liquefaction plant in Algeria to a regasification terminal on an island in the Thames River. From this time forward, Algeria would remain a major force in the LNG business, expanding its export capacity in 1973, 1978, 1980, and 1981. Small-scale LNG plants were built to export LNG from Alaska (Cook Inlet) to Japan in 1969 and from Libya to Europe in 1970. Brunei was the first large-scale LNG export project to serve Japan, starting operations in 1972 and relying on 75,000 cubic meter LNG vessels. This project was followed by other large-scale LNG export projects in Indonesia and Abu Dhabi in 1977, Malaysia in 1983 (a second in 1994), Australia in 1989, Qatar in 1997 (a second in 1999), Trinidad and Nigeria in 1999, Oman in 2000, and Egypt in 2005, employing 125,000 cubic meter LNG carriers. Many of these nations have subsequently expanded their LNG production capacity.[87]

In the wake of the energy crisis in the 1970s, Japan adopted an energy policy of diversifying its energy sources to reduce dependence on Middle East crude oil. The first-generation large-scale LNG projects were long-term contractual arrangements of 20 or more years for the entire output of a liquefaction plant dedicated to a small group of Japanese utilities. LNG carriers of 125,000 cubic meters were assigned to a project for their entire serviceable lives. As such, the first LNG export projects were as inflexible as long-distance pipelines and were organized similarly to LPG projects serving Japan as totally integrated supply chains.

The price of LNG built into long-term supply contracts arranged between Japan and oil exporters was based on the delivered cost of crude oil. Low crude oil prices during the latter part of the 1980s and much of the 1990s kept a lid on LNG prices and, consequently, on the value of stranded gas. New LNG projects could not be economically justified until the passing of the natural gas bubble in the US. This was the dawn of a new day for LNG projects because it was perceived that the US might become a major LNG importer, spurring new LNG projects in Egypt, Qatar, Nigeria, Oman, and Trinidad. More importantly, crude prices rose, which raised the price of LNG in Asia to a point where new projects could be entertained. But this time, building new or expanding existing LNG export plants was not based entirely in response to a policy to diversify energy sources on a long-term basis as in Japan and later Korea and Taiwan. Something happened to open the eyes of the industry that LNG need not be entirely dedicated to a single quasi-pipeline project.

During the late 1990s Korea's demand for LNG declined in the wake of the Southeast Asia economic meltdown. Korea was stuck with take-or-pay contracts where an LNG cargo that could not be consumed must still be paid (a provision in contracts to ensure repayment of debt). This put Korea in a position of desiring to sell some cargoes. Moreover, liquefaction trains had removed bottlenecking impediments within LNG trains over the years and found that they could produce 25 percent in excess of their nameplate capacity. Idle LNG carriers from failed LNG projects in the US (El Paso and Trunkline) and Nigeria plus a few unemployed vessels built on speculation were available. Finally there was demand for more LNG in the US and Europe. All that was left was for an entrepreneur to put all the elements for the first spot purchases of LNG together and a new idea swept the industry.

From this point forward, although a large portion of the financing of new or expanded LNG liquefaction capacity depended on having 20-year contracts to ensure adequate debt coverage, these contracts did not cover the entire plant output. This allowed an LNG plant owner to participate in commercial opportunities from single cargoes (spot deals) to short- and medium-term (1–5 years) contracts. The leader in the transformation of looking at commercial opportunities in addition to securing long-term contracts for project financing was the Trinidad Atlantic LNG project.[88] Ironically, as with LPG, the US did not become a large-scale LNG importer as anticipated; and as with LPG, the US is rapidly turning into a major LNG exporter.

LNG Projects

LNG business is unique in several aspects. One is the sheer size of the investment. Unlike oil, coal, and other commodity businesses that start small and become large through accretion, LNG starts out as a multi-billion dollar large-scale project. LNG projects are rivaled in size, complexity, and capital requirements only by nuclear power plants. But unlike a nuclear power plant connected to a local electricity grid, an LNG project involves two sovereign powers—a nation with stranded gas reserves and a nation in need of natural gas. Though an LNG project is like a long-distance pipeline, which requires that suppliers and consumers be lined up before the pipeline can be built, an LNG Sales and Purchase Agreement (SPA) is more akin to a commercial agreement between two sovereign powers. One is the nation with the gas supply, whose interests are pursued by its national energy company, and the other is the nation with an energy policy that calls for greater consumption of natural gas, whose interests are pursued by its receiving utilities. In both cases, a sovereign power has made a policy decision to either export or import LNG and has delegated oversight to a national energy company or receiving utilities. The respective governments take a keen interest in negotiations leading up to the SPA.

The SPA establishes the commercial link between buyer (receiving utilities) and seller (national energy company), laying the foundation for the financial structure of the project. Laying the foundation for the physical structure is the engineering, procurement, and construction (EPC) contract. The EPC contract selects a consortium of companies with the requisite skill set in project management and technical expertise to design the plant, procure the necessary equipment, build a liquefaction plant in a rather remote part of the world, and put it in operation. Shipping contracts have to be arranged with the delivery of ships timed to start up and subsequent step-ups in liquefaction plant output. It can take as long as 4 years for a multi-train liquefaction plant to reach its full capacity.

For Japan, and later Korea and Taiwan, it was not a simple matter of building a receiving terminal with sufficient storage capacity and berths to off-load the LNG carriers, along with a regasification plant to convert LNG back to a gas. These nations had to create a market for natural gas. The first customers were electricity generating plants located adjacent or near to receiving facilities. Eventually an entire nationwide natural gas pipeline distribution infrastructure, replete with customers, had to be designed, planned, organized, and built for natural gas to become an important contributor to a nation's energy supply. Getting approvals for the requisite permits to build a natural gas pipeline grid would have been impossible if the government had not endorsed the LNG project. As with LPG, government support, particularly in Japan and Korea, was instrumental in establishing an integrated LNG supply chain. Both governments relied on corporations within the keiretsu or the Korean-equivalent chaebol to play their respective roles in fulfilling the objectives of a national policy to significantly expand the role of natural gas in satisfying energy demand.

LNG Supply Chain

An LNG supply chain consists of three major segments. The first segment is the upstream end of natural gas fields with producing wells and a gathering system. A gas treatment facility removes undesirable elements (nitrogen, carbon dioxide, hydrogen sulfide, sulfur, and water) and separates gas liquids and condensate from the natural gas stream. These, along with any sulfur, are sold to third parties to provide additional revenue. A pipeline delivers treated natural gas from gas fields to the second segment, the downstream end, which consists of a liquefaction plant and LNG carriers. After the last remaining contaminants are removed, a mixed refrigeration process cools methane, along with any ethane in the natural gas, to its liquefaction temperature using various refrigerants, starting with propane and switching to butane, pentane, ethane, methane, and finally nitrogen. Terminal storage capacity at the liquefaction plant is between 1.5 and 2 shiploads of cargo plus berthing facilities and a sufficiently sized fleet of LNG carriers to transport the desired throughput from loading to receiving terminals. The third segment is the market end of the supply chain, which is made up of the receiving and storage facilities and regasification plant at the importing nation to warm LNG (mainly by cooling sea water) to a gaseous state before entering a natural gas pipeline distribution system. Vessel arrivals are on a fairly regular schedule, whereas demand can be heavily skewed for winter heating. Receiving facilities must have sufficient storage for not only unloading a vessel, but also satisfying transient and seasonal fluctuations in demand plus accommodating potential delays in vessel arrivals. Early regasification plants were connected to utilities to generate electricity. Now regasification plants are connected to a natural gas pipeline distribution grid with sufficient customers to consume large volumes of imported LNG.

Organizing the LNG Supply Chain

Three segments of the LNG supply chain can have different organizational structures. The simplest is to have the same participants throughout the supply chain. This "seamless" structure avoids the need for negotiating transfer price and sales conditions as natural gas or LNG passes through each segment of the chain. But this form of organization can lead to management by committee in which representatives of each segment of the supply chain vote on critical matters that apply to a single segment. This can have undesirable repercussions if the representatives of other segments are not well versed in the technical aspects of a particular segment. Moreover, funding of the project may be in jeopardy if a participant in one segment does not desire or does not have sufficiently deep pockets to fund its share of the entire project.

The second alternative with regard to ownership is the upstream and downstream segments of the project (natural gas fields and the liquefaction plant) being a separate profit center that sells LNG either free on board (FOB) at the loading terminal or delivered at the receiving terminal, where the price of LNG includes cargo, insurance, and freight (CIF). Profit for the upstream and downstream portions of an LNG supply chain is revenue from selling LNG less all operating and capital costs, the acquisition cost of natural gas, taxes, and royalties. A floor price for LNG may be incorporated into the SPA to ensure a positive cash flow. The third alternative is the liquefaction plant being a cost center that simply receives a toll for services rendered that covers its operating and capital costs. Profit or loss is concentrated in the downstream portion of the project. These last two alternatives can have different participants with different shares within each segment of the LNG supply chain. Segmented ownership arrangements among the participants can create interface problems in transfer pricing and risk sharing. A conflict resolution mechanism has to be established to resolve potentially contentious issues as, or preferably before, they arise. Splitting the ownership of various supply chain segments has the advantage of having participants who are interested in dedicating their financial and technical resources to a single segment of a project.

Financing the LNG Supply Chain

An LNG project can be entirely funded by equity. The return on equity is determined by the cash flow (revenue less operating costs, taxes, royalties, and acquisition costs for natural gas). The advantage of equity funding is that participants are not beholden to outside financial institutions. The disadvantage is that participants must have deep pockets. Dedication of funds to a single multi-billion dollar project may preclude becoming involved in other LNG projects. On the other extreme, an LNG project can be financed entirely by debt. Debt may be supplied by the sovereign nation that borrows on the basis of its creditworthiness or provides a sovereign guarantee. Revenue is funneled into a special account from which debt service charges are drawn off first and what remains pays for operating costs, royalties, and taxes; whatever is left determines the value of natural gas consumed by the project.

The proceeds of an LNG project from a government's perspective are its receipts of royalties and taxes and what the national hydrocarbon company earns on its natural gas sales to the LNG project plus return on its investment in the project, if any. The split in government payments in the form of royalties and taxes on profits is critical for LNG project participants in the event of a drop in LNG prices. Royalty payments remain fixed and independent of the price of LNG. Taxes on profits, on the other hand, decline as the price of LNG falls. Risk of a negative cash flow can be better dealt with by favoring taxes over royalties. A higher tax rate over royalties mitigates the risk of low LNG prices by paying less to the government, but more money will be paid in taxes when LNG prices are high (this is the cost of mitigating risk via taxes).

Project Financing

A popular form of raising capital is project financing. Here the LNG supply chain is set up to be self-financing, with debt holders looking only to the financial wherewithal of the project itself, not the project sponsors, for interest and debt repayment. Debt issued by an LNG supply chain project is initially limited recourse debt—sponsors assume full liability for funds advanced only during construction. Once the plant operates at its defined specifications, debt becomes nonrecourse and project sponsors assume no liability for debt service obligations; debt repayment relies exclusively on the financial performance of the project.

Project financing is usually equity and debt, whose mix is determined by a cash flow analysis that takes into account the price for LNG, the operating costs of the liquefaction plant and upstream natural gas field, the acquisition cost of the natural gas, the LNG carriers (if part of the project), royalties and taxes, and debt servicing requirements. In early LNG projects, the price of LNG was tied to the value of fuel oil, crude oil, or coal on a formula basis. In later LNG projects, other determinants may be affecting price or price may simply be set by the contractual arrangement between seller and buyer. Degree of debt in financing a project depends on the nature of the cash flow—buyers of debt like to see a comfortable cash cushion in case price projections or operational performance don't materialize. Project financing exposes an LNG supply chain to the scrutiny of third parties when they exercise due diligence prior to making a commitment. Sponsors and host governments are more likely to agree to an organizational and legal structure imposed by a third party because of the benefit of garnering external sourcing of capital. In this sense, project financing has been a healthy influence by discouraging one party to an LNG project from insisting on conditions that not only would be detrimental to others, but also would jeopardize the external funding of the project.

Project financing removes the necessity for sponsors to have sufficient internal funds to finance the entire project by equity alone. By reducing funding requirements, sponsors are free to participate in other LNG projects, spreading their risk and expanding their presence in the LNG business. Project financing also allows the importing nation to participate directly in an LNG supply chain by purchasing a meaningful portion of the debt. These benefits of project financing have to be balanced by the costs of satisfying third-party due diligence requirements, managing lender–project relationships, and arranging creditor agreements with various financial institutions.

Underwriters for project financing face the challenge of making an internationally oriented LNG project attractive to prospective buyers of the underlying debt. In packaging securities, underwriters must deal with the sovereign risk of the host country (e.g., a Middle East nation), a variety of contractual arrangements with several receiving utilities from one or more nations (e.g., Europe), vessel chartering agreements involving a number of legal jurisdictions (e.g., Korea as shipbuilder, London as center of operations, Bermuda as legal owner, and Liberia as ship registrar), and multiple equity participants incorporated into different nations with unequal shares in various segments of an LNG project. Financial institutions funding LNG projects include pension funds seeking long-term maturities, and commercial banks and private investors focused on short- and medium-term maturities. Another source of debt funding is low-interest credits issued by governments to finance the exports of liquefaction plant components manufactured by domestic companies.

Depending on the distance between liquefaction plant and receiving facility, LNG carriers may account for 25–40 percent of the total investment in an LNG project, the same general magnitude of investment as the liquefaction plant. The remaining investment is primarily the development of natural gas fields. The regasification system is usually the responsibility of the receiving utility, but for Japan, Korea, and Taiwan, a natural gas pipeline distribution system also had to be built, which is now progressing in China and India. The development of natural gas fields, the construction of the liquefaction plant, and the building of ships and the receiving terminal, including the regasification plant and a natural gas distribution system with a sufficient number of consumers to absorb LNG imports, have to be coordinated on a fairly tight schedule for all elements of an LNG project to fall in place in a synchronous fashion. As large and as complex as LNG projects are, few have failed. Most have been successfully completed and LNG trade has blossomed.

LNG Suppliers and Consumers

In 2014 the total volume of LNG in international trade was 333 bcm (gaseous equivalent) versus a total volume of 664 bcm of natural gas moved in international pipelines. The world's largest suppliers of LNG were Qatar (31 percent), Malaysia (10 percent), Australia (10 percent), Nigeria (8 percent), Indonesia (7 percent), Trinidad (6 percent), Peru (6 percent), and Algeria (5 percent), with smaller shares from Russia, Oman, Yemen, the UAE, Brunei, Equatorial Guinea, Papua New Guinea, and Norway.

Asia was the major recipient of LNG cargoes, absorbing 73 percent, followed by Europe at 16 percent, South America 6 percent, North America 4 percent, and the Middle East 1 percent. Within Asia, Japan consumed 36 percent of world production of LNG, South Korea 15 percent, China 8 percent, India 6 percent, and Taiwan 5 percent. Asia absorbed nearly the entire output of LNG export plants in Australia, Brunei, Equatorial Guinea, Papua New Guinea, Indonesia, Malaysia, Russia, Oman, the UAE, and Yemen. Europe received 16 percent of world LNG, with Spain consuming 5 percent of world production, followed by the UK at 3 percent and France and Turkey at 2 percent each. Principal suppliers to Europe are Qatar, Algeria, and Nigeria. South America receives 6 percent of world production principally to Argentina, Brazil, and Chile, supplied primarily by Trinidad and much of the remainder from Nigeria and Norway. North America received 4 percent of world LNG production principally from Peru, Trinidad, and Nigeria. Qatar, Trinidad, Nigeria, and Algeria sell cargoes worldwide with a greater emphasis on short- and medium-term deals. Other LNG exporters have more restrictive markets, signaling a greater reliance on long-term contracts.[89]

LNG Liquefaction Plants

The characteristics of LNG vary with its source and is generally made up of 88–99 percent methane, with ethane being the second most important gas, followed by relatively small portions of propane and butane.[90] Propane and butane may be removed before liquefaction and sold separately or retained in LNG. Ethane is normally left in LNG, but can be separated if desired. Figure 7.11 shows the principal LNG exporting nations along with the number of operational liquefaction facilities and total capacity in millions of tons of LNG per year. Liquefaction units in Libya did not operate for much of 2013 and 2014, as the plant was damaged during the "Arab Spring" and also suffers from unresolved technical issues. The US plant in Cook Inlet in Alaska was among the first built (1969) and exports LNG to Japan when in operation.

The global number of liquefaction facilities in 2015 was 34 (up from 23 in 2009), with another 16 under construction.[91] LNG liquefaction plants under construction in Australia, including the world's first floating liquefaction plant of gargantuan size built by Shell, will make a significant contribution in expanding LNG availability.[92] Four equivalent sized floating liquefaction plants are to be built.[93] There are plans to increase export capacity to 85 million tons per year, possibly to 100 million tons per year by 2020, rivaling or exceeding Qatar. Canada may become a major world producer of LNG if National Energy Board approved plans to liquefy unconventional gas production materialize. Five proposed LNG projects located on the west coast of Canada would total 100 million tons of output per year. These plants will be fed by unconventional natural gas (hard shale gas) that has yet to be developed. Moreover, these projects must obtain permission from Indian tribes for transit pipelines over their lands and from citizens where LNG

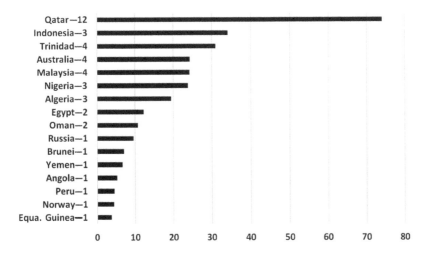

Figure 7.11 Number of Liquefaction Facilities and Combined Capacity (mmtpy)

liquefaction plants are to be built. These are the same people who have already rejected proposed pipelines and export terminals for oil from Canadian oil sands. A new Canadian approach to Native Americans is to have them share in the project for their long-term economic benefit rather than pay them for right-of-way. Nevertheless Canada becoming a major LNG exporter seems problematic indeed. To worsen the situation, LNG prices in Asia are linked to crude oil, which with the collapse of crude oil prices must have compromised the economics of these projects. LNG liquefaction plants are planned or under construction in Colombia and Russia (Yamal). LNG plants are being considered in several locations such as Mozambique and Tanzania, where large quantities of stranded natural gas have recently been discovered.

LNG Regasification Terminals

In 2015, there were 110 regasification receiving terminals (up from 82 in 2009), with another 18 under construction, including 15 floating facilities. Regasification storage may be considerable if there is highly seasonal consumption of natural gas where LNG arriving during the summer has to be stored to meet peak winter demand. Most LNG regasification plants are built on land. The first floating regasification plants were early-built LNG vessels that were converted to floating receiving terminals by installing a regasification plant on the vessel. Aside from the cost of the regasification plant, these floating terminals offered a low-cost alternative to building storage facilities on land as the storage tanks were already in the vessel. Moreover, floating storage provides mobility if it is desired to move the terminal from one location to another. Floating terminals today are purpose-built, with both storage tanks and a regasification plant as integral parts of the vessel. Floating storage removes LNG storage from within populated areas. For traditional onshore terminals, about two dozen receiving terminals are in Europe providing many marketing options/opportunities for imported LNG when LNG availability improves. There are a dozen terminals in South America serving Brazil, Argentina, Chile, and Peru. The largest concentration of regasification terminals are in Japan, followed by Korea, China, and Taiwan. China and India are rapidly building more regasification terminals and Israel, Malaysia, and Singapore installed their first regasification terminal in 2013.

LNG cargo in insulated storage tanks at the receiving terminal has to be warmed to a gaseous state and pressurized before entering a natural gas pipeline system for distribution to consumers. The most common way to heat LNG is to pass through a seawater heat exchanger where seawater is cooled and LNG warmed to about 5°C (41°F). A gas-fired vaporizer may be employed. A few Japanese import terminals tap the "waste cold" of LNG to cool brine or Freon for freezing food and for chemical and industrial processes that require large volumes of cooled water.

Commodization of LNG

LNG plants to be built in the US will advance the commodization of LNG on a global basis where LNG prices would be influenced by LNG carriers moving cargoes from low-cost suppliers in North America, Africa, the Middle East, and Southeast Asia to willing buyers in Europe, South America, and South Asia. The greater the traded volume, the closer natural gas becomes a commodity where LNG cargo volumes move on the basis of netback values between producers and consumers. This commodization of natural gas would reduce regional price disparities similar to what has occurred in the oil market. The disparity in natural gas prices in 2014 was pronounced. In August 2014 the landed prices of LNG in $/mmBtu were $12 in South America, $11 in Asia, $7–$10 in Europe, and $4 in the US as a source of LNG.[94] This rosy projection of landed prices of LNG changed radically four months later at the end of 2014 when oil prices collapsed unexpectedly (as usual) to $50 per barrel. Superficially this should have no bearing on LNG, yet it does because the contracted price for LNG in Japan is keyed to crude oil prices. A lower oil price lowers LNG costs to Japan and this affects the price of what Japan may be willing to spend for commercially arranged spot cargoes and term contracts beyond the volumes covered by long-term contracts.

The US could play a key role of making natural gas a global commodity. The first US plant is Cheniere's Sabine Pass plant, expected to be on stream in 2015 with a capacity of 16 mmtpy, followed by Freeport (13.2 mmtpy), Lake Charles (15 mmtpy), Cove Point (5.25 mmtpy), and Cameron (12 mmtpy), all to be in operation in the 2017–2019 time frame. Total capacity of the US LNG export project is about 60 mmtpy, not far from Qatar's output of 74 mmtpy. This large quantity of LNG entering the market should have a strong impact on global natural gas prices and will eventually have a profound effect on European gas suppliers hiding behind the Groningen oil-based pricing formula. But to keep 60 mmtpy in perspective, it represents 9.6 percent of 2013 US natural gas production, a bit less than 2 percent of global production, and a 17 percent increase in global LNG availability. However, by 2019 when all the already approved US export plants are in operation, gains in US shale gas production will most aptly compensate for the incremental demand represented by LNG exports, leaving more than adequate supplies of natural gas for the domestic market. In other words, natural gas prices may not escalate in the face of large-scale LNG exports. Excluding applications to expand the volume output of approved projects, there are nearly two dozen applications for additional US export plants under consideration by the DOE.[95] A project must be financially self-sustaining when presented to the DOE. This can take the form of a variety of contracts normally running 20 years, with volumes that may change over the term of the contract, coupled to a variety of pricing packages involving minimum prices, floating prices with Henry Hub, and perhaps a tolling fee to cover the cost of liquefaction. These purchasing contracts are conditional in a project winning approval, and their terms and conditions determine the degree that lenders will support the financing of a project. Obviously not all, if any, of these will be approved, but the potential for the US to expand its LNG exports is pronounced.

Regulatory Hurdles for LNG Facilities in the US

In addition to lining up buyers and financial support, each of the approved projects had to pass the regulatory process for both the DOE and FERC. The DOE authorizes the license to import and export natural gas. The authority of the DOE lies in the 1938 Natural Gas Act where the presumption is in favor of approving export applications unless opponents can demonstrate that the project is not in the public interest. The DOE's review considers the economic, energy security, and environmental impacts as well as public comments for and against the application, which can number as many as 200,000 for a single application. Federal law requires approval of LNG exports to Free Trade Agreement (FTA) nations, which may not include nations buying LNG. For this case, the DOE has the power to grant export authorizations to non-FTA nations as long as these authorizations are in the public interest. The National Environmental Policy Act (NEPA) designates FERC as the lead federal agency to prepare an Environmental Impact Statement that involves various state and federal agencies. Under the Natural Gas Act, FERC is responsible for authorizing the siting and construction of LNG import or export facilities and to issue certificates of public convenience and necessity for LNG facilities engaged in interstate natural gas transportation by pipeline.[96]

A sampling of organizations involved with LNG facilities being built in the US shows the regulatory complexity that does not have to be faced in its entirety in building facilities in other nations. Licenses are required from the Department of Transportation, Coast Guard, and Maritime Administration along with permissions from the Research and Special Programs Administration, which enforces deepwater-port pipeline regulations (if applicable), and the Department of the Interior for pipeline right-of-way. The Fish and Wildlife Service is concerned with the ramifications of LNG facilities on endangered species; the Minerals Management Service with potential hazards and underwater artifacts of archeological interest; and the Environmental Protection Agency with carrying out the provisions of the Clean Air Act. Other federal agencies involved are the Department of Defense, Department of State, the Department of Commerce, the National Oceanic and Atmospheric Administration, the Bureau of Oceans, the Army Corps of Engineers, and the Advisory Council on Historic Preservation. Besides these, various state bodies involved with coastal zone management, pollution control, wildlife and fisheries, and historical preservation present their own hurdles for building a facility. And a final hurdle: an LNG facility cannot be built without a permit from the municipality within which it would be located, and for this to occur, the local population must be in support of the project.

LNG Contracts

In the past, most LNG plants' production was largely fixed by long-term contractual arrangements of 20 years or more. This is still true for new LNG export plants where prospective creditors demand long-term commitments to safeguard their investments in the long-term debt portion of the plant's financing structure. In 2013, 20-year contracts were arranged for new LNG plants in the US, Australia, Russia (Yamal), Israel, and others. Established LNG exporters can profit from the flexibility afforded by five or less year contracts such as those entered into by LNG exporters in Qatar, Brunei, and Malaysia. There were also short-term contracts entered into by LNG merchants who buy a portion of the output of an LNG plant and then sell smaller quantities to buyers with short-term needs. Spot sales are becoming more important, as sellers with extra cargoes, oftentimes from liquefaction plants operating safely and reliably above their original nameplate capacity, satisfy buyers with an immediate or short-term need. A great advantage of spot and short-term deals is that the receiver is not locked into a term contract where there is a risk of not being able to utilize the cargo throughout the contractual period. This was exemplified by European importers under medium- and long-term contracts who were not able to dispose of all their imported cargoes within Europe. They re-exported some cargoes to other destinations where buyers either purchased spot cargoes or entered into short-term deals.

LNG Carriers

LNG carriers can be owned by the project for delivered sales where price at the receiving terminal includes insurance and freight or they can be owned by the buyer for purchase at the loading terminal for free on board sales. Alternatively vessels do not have to be owned by either buyer or seller, but can be chartered from third parties (independent shipowners, energy companies, or financial institutions) under a variety of arrangements. Charters shift the responsibility for raising capital to finance vessels from the LNG project to vessel owners.

LNG Carrier Containment Systems

LNG carriers are classified by their containment systems: spherical or membrane. In the spherical containment system, a thick aluminum spherical shell covered by insulation and an outer steel shell is supported by a freestanding skirt that accommodates the expansion or contraction of the cargo tank. Propagation of a crack, should any occur, is very slow, with little chance of leakage. While there is no need for a full secondary barrier, a partial barrier prevents any LNG leakage from coming in contact with the hull. Spherical tanks are entirely filled with cargo to limit the sloshing of cargo when at sea for improved ship stability. However, their protrusion above the main deck affects visibility from the bridge, also a problem for modern container vessels. The principal disadvantage of spherical tanks is inefficient utilization of space within a ship's hull. Spherical tanks are also used for storage at loading and receiving terminals.

An alternative containment system is a membrane design in which cargo tanks conform to the shape of the ship's hull, increasing a vessel's cargo-carrying capacity. Rather than thick aluminum, the membrane is a thin primary barrier covering insulation installed on the inner hull surface of the ship. This considerably reduces the weight of metal in an LNG tank. Membrane tanks are not self-supporting, but an integral part of the ship's hull that directly bears the weight of cargo. The structure holding the insulation material must be strong enough to transfer cargo weight to the inner hull, be an effective insulator, and prevent any liquid gas from coming in contact with the ship's hull.

The membrane for the Gaz Transport system is made of a special stainless steel alloy called invar of 36 percent nickel with a very low coefficient of thermal expansion, eliminating the need for expansion joints. Both primary and secondary insulation consists of a layer of thin (0.7 mm) invar membrane covering plywood boxes filled with perlite, a naturally occurring insulating material made of volcanic glass. Primary and secondary insulation provides 100 percent redundancy. The membrane for the Technigaz system is thin (1.2 mm), low-carbon corrugated stainless steel with a relatively high coefficient of thermal expansion. Corrugation is designed to accommodate the expansion and contraction of the metal from temperature changes. Earlier LNG carriers of this design used balsa wood as insulation material. Now two layers of reinforced polyurethane panels, separated by a secondary membrane made of a thin sheet of aluminum between two layers of glass cloth, form the primary and secondary insulation. The latest membrane system (CS1) combines the Gaz Transport and Technigaz technologies with a membrane of invar and insulation of reinforced polyurethane panels. The membrane design requires less material, but construction is more labor-intensive. Spherical tanks require more material, but their construction is more automated, reducing labor requirements. Thus the comparative cost of LNG carriers of spherical or membrane design depends on shipyard labor costs. The spherical tank design is favored in Japan because labor costs are higher, while the membrane design is favored in Korea and China where labor costs are lower.

Whereas the early LNG fleet was dominated by the Moss design, the membrane design became more popular as shipbuilding activity shifted from Japan to Korea. The share for each design became about equal in the early 2000s as Korea rose to dominate LNG carrier construction. Of 458 LNG carriers in existence and on order, Korea has built and will be building 61 percent of the LNG carrier fleet, with Japan at 22 percent and the remainder in China, France, and other nations. Of 134 LNG carriers built since 2009, 100 were in Korea, 20 in China, and 13 in Japan.[97] Of 15 large LNG carriers with a carrying capacity between 155,000 and 177,000 bcm delivered from shipyards in 2013, all but one were of the membrane design. Of 45 new LNG carriers ordered in 2013, 37 were the membrane design and 8 the spherical design. In the future, more LNG carriers featuring the membrane design are expected to be built in China.

LNG Carrier Fleet Segments

The first generation of LNG carriers built in the 1970s was 75,000 cubic meters, but relatively few of these were built after the Brunei project. They were quickly followed by what turned out to be the early work horses of the LNG carrier fleet: standard sized vessels of 125,000 cubic meters. The 1980s was not an active time for new LNG projects with little demand for new LNG carriers, but vessels built in the 1990s were typically 135,000 cubic meters, becoming even larger in carrying capacity in time. In 2015, there are six LNG carriers less than 50,000 cubic meters, with one below 25,000 cubic meters for local distribution of LNG and possibly for carrying ethylene cargoes when LNG cargoes are not available. Eleven mainly 75,000 cubic meter vessels are associated with the Brunei–Japan LNG project. The middle portion of the size spectrum between 125,000 and 170,000 cubic meters is made up of 327 vessels, with many of the more recently built vessels above 138,000 cubic meters. Another 35 vessels are under construction. The newest portion of the fleet above 170,000 cubic meters consists of 68 vessels, with another 45 vessels, under construction.[98] Within this group are Qatar Gas Transport's 31 Q-Flex vessels of 210,000–220,000 cubic meters and 14 Q-Max vessels of 260,000–270,000 cubic meters. Q-Flex vessels can be dedicated to Qatar's LNG projects or trade commercial cargoes to existing terminals, many, but not all, of which are large enough to accommodate these vessels. Q-Max vessels are too large for existing terminals and will trade on dedicated trades where regasification terminals are built with enough capacity to accommodate these vessels.

Prior to completion of improvements to the Panama Canal, only 9 percent of LNG carriers could transit the Panama Canal because their physical dimensions exceeded the limitation imposed by the locks. After completion in 2016, 88 percent of LNG carriers will be able to transit the canal.[99] Q-vessels are among the few LNG carriers unable to transit the improved Panama Canal, introducing a degree of trading inflexibility. While Q-vessels will not be able to carry cargoes from the US to Asia via the Panama Canal, the longer Suez Canal route may still be economically feasible. However, Q-Max vessels were built to service long-term contracts (Qatar to Asia or Europe), which do not involve passage through the Panama Canal. Q-Flex and Q-Max vessels generate significant shipping cost savings of the order of 20–30 percent from economies of scale of their larger cargo-carrying capacity coupled with better fuel economy. Figure 7.12 shows the employment of the LNG fleet in terms of discharging cargoes. Obviously Japan receiving 38 percent of all discharges attests to its importance in determining the financial health of the LNG business. The Pareto effect can be seen by the total share of Europe, South Korea, and Japan making up 70 percent of vessel discharges.

In 2015, the order book of 81 vessels included 10 FSRUs (floating storage regasification units). FSRUs are purpose-built LNG tankers with onboard equipment to vaporize LNG and deliver high pressure natural gas to an offshore pipeline. Thus these vessels do not have to enter port and no port facilities are necessary. The ship itself acts as a regasification plant with storage tanks, but vessel discharge time is measured in days rather than hours. FSRU vessels load the same as standard LNG tankers at liquefaction terminals and have the flexibility to discharge cargoes as a liquid at a conventional LNG receiving

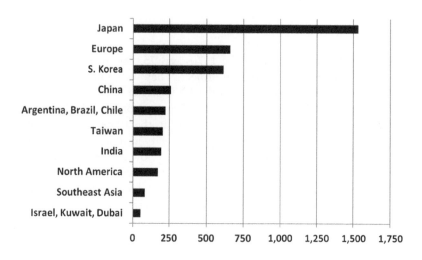

Figure 7.12 Completed Loaded LNG Voyages (2013)

terminal, as a high pressure gas through a connection in the ship's hull to a subsea pipe-line, or as high pressure gas from the vessel's LNG loading arms at a terminal without a regasification unit.[100]

LNG Carrier Cargo Boil-off

Heat passing through the insulation can warm the cargo and increase its pressure within the cargo tank. Unlike LPG cargoes where a refrigeration plant keeps the cargo cool enough to remain liquid at atmospheric pressure, an LNG cargo is kept liquefied by boil-off, which removes heat transmitted through the insulation into the cargo. The better the insulation, the less the boil-off; typical boil-off for older vessels was about 0.15 percent of the cargo volume per day, but now is 0.01–0.1 percent per day for newer vessels from improved cargo tank insulation.[101] While nearly all merchant vessels have diesel engine propulsion plants that burn heavy fuel oil, older LNG carriers have dual fuel steam tur-bine propulsion systems that burn either heavy fuel oil or LNG boil-off, which typically provides 60 percent of the fuel requirements. This avoids wasting boil-off by flaring or venting to the atmosphere. Not all LNG cargo is discharged at a receiving terminal; a heel or small amount of LNG is left in cargo tanks to keep tanks cold via boil-off on the ballast voyage to the loading port. This eliminates the necessity of cooling cargo tanks before loading the next cargo and minimizes stress from repeated thermal cycling. The ship is charged for the boil-off burned for ship propulsion on an energy-equivalent basis with heavy fuel oil.

LNG Carrier Propulsion Systems

The 1970s built LNG carriers' steam turbines for propulsion were more fuel inefficient than diesel engines, but this was compensated by lower fuel costs prior to the oil crisis in 1973 and sufficient boil-off to supply about 60 percent of a ship's fuel. The steam turbine with its 30 percent efficiency became economically obsolete with the advent of high-priced oil. The only commercial steam turbine vessels left in the world fleet are older LNG carriers; the rest have been scrapped. As oil prices increased and engineering crews aged with no young graduates from merchant marine schools having training or experi-ence in steam turbine plants, the economics and human resource constraints swung in favor of diesel propulsion for LNG carriers.

Higher priced oil increased the value of LNG, and some LNG carriers were built with reliquefaction units to keep boil-off as part of the cargo. The choice of vessel with or without a reliquefaction unit was the result of an economic cost–benefit analysis. The benefit of diesel engines with a reliquefaction unit was discharging a larger cargo of LNG, but the cost was the capital and operating costs wrapped up in an onboard reliquefaction unit and loss of boil-off as a propulsion fuel. Early experience with reliquefaction units proved to be operationally unreliable and the idea was abandoned.

Today owners have a choice of engines. One is the modern dual fuel slow speed diesel having 50 percent thermal efficiency. The engine can burn heavy fuel oil or diesel oil. Heavy fuel oil as a residual fuel, fit for only an industrial or ship's fuel (bunkers), is far cheaper than diesel fuel, a refined product widely used in land transportation, machinery, and equipment applications. The economics favor burning low sulfur heavy fuel oil over diesel oil, but new environmental rules on allowable sulfur emissions are having an effect on the type of fuel that can be burned. Another choice is dual fuel diesel–electric propulsion plants where the diesel runs a generator and electricity drives the propulsion shaft, similar in principle to a railroad locomotive. The dual fuels are boil-off (natural gas) or diesel fuel to avoid flaring boil-off. This type of propulsion plant is gaining in popularity. A third choice is a dual fuel gas turbine plant where the propulsion shaft is driven by a turbine fueled by natural gas from boil-off and a dedicated tank holding LNG for a ship's fuel.[102]

The engine of choice for recent orders is the tri-fuel diesel electric engines that run on either heavy viscosity fuel oil, diesel oil, or LNG including boil-off. Unlike conventional diesel engines that are located near the propeller for direct drive, diesel engines generating electricity are connected by electric cables to electric motors that turn the propellers. This introduces greater flexibility of design by allowing diesel engines to be in a location that increases cargo volume and enhances vessel stability.[103] A great preponderance of recently built LNG carriers along with those on order have dual or tri-fueled diesel electric propulsion plants. While the role of boil-off as a ship's fuel has been vastly diminished by improvements in the cargo insulation of modern vessels, a few LNG carriers are being built to run exclusively on natural gas carried in special LNG fuel tanks to fuel electricity generation. The advantages of relying on natural gas as a fuel are simpler engine design and greater fuel economy.[104]

LNG Pricing

Pricing LNG in Japan is formula-based on the blended cost of crude oil imports (Japan Customs Cleared Crude) on an energy-equivalent basis, later adopted by South Korea and Taiwan. Thus the exporting nation received a natural gas price that reflected the blended cost of crude delivered in Japan. Its profit would be revenue net of operating and capital costs associated with the natural gas gathering system, liquefaction plant, and LNG carriers (regasification facilities are owned by the receiving nation's gas utility). A floor on LNG price, if incorporated into the SAP contract, assured the exporting nation of a minimum price for its gas exports and debt providers of a positive cash flow. The price relationship between LNG and crude oil is tempered by essentially taking a running average to partially protect LNG importers from oil price shocks. The pricing of LNG imported into Europe under long-term contracts is based on a formula containing the cost of Brent crude oil, high and low sulfur fuel oil, European pipeline gas, and coal. The pricing of LNG by formula in Asia and Europe does not apply to the spot or short- or medium-term markets where deals are done on their commercial merits. The pricing of LNG imports into the US is based on natural gas at Henry Hub as indicated by cash or near-term futures trading of natural gas contracts on the New York Mercantile Exchange (NYMEX). LNG exports will be based on Henry Hub prices. Unlike Asia and Europe, US LNG import and export pricing was and will continue to be based on market, not formula, prices.

There are several factors that until recently have lowered LNG prices. One is a continual decline in the shipbuilding cost of LNG carriers. In 1995 the cost of building a large LNG carrier was three times that of a large crude oil carrier ($280 million). Since an LNG carrier can only transport about one-third as much energy as a large crude carrier of the same cargo volume, LNG shipping costs were nine times higher than crude oil on a Btu basis. By the 2000s shipbuilding cost had fallen to $150–$160 million, or a 50–60 percent premium over large crude carriers, knocking down the premium on an energy basis to about five times. The discernible downward trend in shipbuilding costs when measured in constant dollars came about by shipyards specializing in building LNG carriers incorporating automation such as robotic welding of steel plate and in labor-saving manufacturing processes to construct LNG tanks. Building a near-identical series of LNG carriers allows shipyards to move down the learning or experience curve where repetition irons out or eliminates problems that had been previously encountered including debottlenecking the production cycle. Whereas only a few shipyards were capable of building LNG carriers in the 1970s, in the 2000s there were a dozen, with their number increasing with new LNG carrier building yards in China. The improved system design of liquefaction trains coupled with greater output resulted in a one-third reduction in capital and operating costs for liquefying natural gas for units built in the 2000s versus those built in the 1970s.

This trend abruptly changed in the early 2010s. Up until then newbuilding and liquefaction plant prices tended to follow declining costs as profit margins for shipbuilders and liquefaction train manufacturers remained relatively stable. However, costs to build should not be confused with price to buy. Price is strongly affected by the relationship between supply and demand. The role of cost is in establishing a minimum price to avoid liquidation of a builder or manufacturer. Outside of this, price is a product of market forces. LNG carrier prices rose considerably in the early 2010s to about $250 million by the mid-2010s when shipyard deliveries could not satisfy incremental demand to transport LNG to Japan and serve the emergence of new LNG projects. Prices to build new liquefaction plants jumped considerably from the same demand factors bidding up the price for LNG carriers. Enormous cost overruns and construction delays at this time seem counterintuitive when one realizes that there were more firms participating in EPC consortia and more energy companies with the requisite project management skill set, technical expertise, and financial wherewithal to organize LNG supply chain projects. Cost overruns and project delays indicated that demand for new LNG projects outstripped available engineering and managerial resources. As a counterweight, there have been offsetting savings in financing cost. More investment bankers well versed on structuring LNG projects design a more attractive capital structure to attract potential investors. Greater reliance on low interest debt in a capital structure reduces the role of more expensive equity, the amount of money that LNG project participants have to raise, lowering the required capital recovery factor. The annual financing cost of LNG projects benefited from central banks pushing short-term rates close to zero percent interest.

A slowdown in the feverish pitch to inaugurate new LNG projects should have a calming effect on price volatility for all components making up an LNG project. Then previous cost reductions through productivity gains would be able to re-exert themselves and be better reflected in price, which is another way of saying that profit margins would regress back to their historical mean.

Outlook for LNG Projects

Despite economic obstacles facing LNG projects, LNG will play a greater role in satisfying future energy needs. Natural gas as the cleanest fossil fuel is already a hefty substitute for coal in the US and Europe. China represents an enormous market for natural gas pipeline and LNG imports to clean up its horrific atmosphere. India will be next in line.

The availability of natural gas for LNG has increased substantially from discoveries of conventional natural gas fields and the development of unconventional sources, namely fracking. By 2018 new LNG projects will have to be built to handle projected growth in LNG demand to one-third above 2014 levels and double 2014 levels by 2025.[105] Continued robustness in LNG will lead to the further internationalization and commodization of natural gas, with long-term contractual pricing of LNG tied to coal and oil prices giving way to pricing LNG on its commercial merits. This rosy view may have to be tempered by impact of low oil prices on long-term contractual volumes into Japan and on what Japan and other Asian nations may be willing to pay for excess cargoes above their contractual volumes.

Natural Gas as a Transportation Fuel

Natural gas has certain advantages over oil as a transportation fuel. First, it's environmentally desirable, eliminating gasoline fumes and spillage that escape from gasoline powered motor vehicles, and virtually eliminating particulate matter (soot) and sulfur oxides in engine exhaust along with a significant reduction in carbon monoxide (90–97 percent), nitrous oxides (35–60 percent), and toxic and carcinogenic volatile organic compounds (50–75 percent).[106] From the point of view of greenhouse gas emissions, natural gas offers a significant reduction in carbon dioxide emissions of 25 percent, but this has to be tempered with increased methane emissions from leakages in pipe fittings and hose connections. Limiting methane emissions is an important design consideration in natural gas vehicles (NGVs) since methane is over 20 times more powerful as a greenhouse gas than carbon dioxide. Second, natural gas availability is increasing dramatically from new discoveries of conventional gas fields and from fracking. Third, natural gas is generally viewed as relatively secure with less geopolitical risks that plague oil. This observation is not as true as it once was. Europeans face increased geopolitical risk with Russian gas since the outbreak of hostilities between Russia and Ukraine. While oil importers fret over a threatened cut-off of Middle East oil by Iran seizing the Strait of Hormuz, such a seizure would also cut off exports from Qatar, the world's largest LNG exporter. Fourth, the price of natural gas with its increased availability is less than petroleum fuels on an energy equivalent basis with less price volatility. Fifth, natural gas allows crude exporters to increase their exports and crude importers to decrease their imports if their domestic motor vehicle fleets are converted to natural gas. Sixth, natural gas can substitute for oil as a transportation fuel for all modes of transport (ships, railroads, trucks, and automobiles) except airplanes. However, the NASA space shuttle carried an external tank of LNG.[107]

LNG as a Ship's Fuel

One of the problems facing the world's shipowners is that bunkers, a ship's fuel, have become the single most important cost factor in operating a ship. Furthermore sulfur emissions in port and along restricted waterways from burning heavy fuel oil laden with sulfur has become a major environmental problem plaguing shipowners. The International Maritime Organization has set up Emission Control Areas (ECAs) in the Baltic and North Seas, which have been subsequently expanded to North America and the Caribbean.[108] The North American ECA extends 200 miles off the east and west coasts and 200 miles surrounding the Hawaiian Islands and essentially the entire Caribbean.[109] Within ECAs, the sulfur content of fuel oil must be less than 1 percent by weight, falling to 0.1 percent after January 1, 2015. Outside an ECA, the limit is 3.5 percent (typical sulfur content of heavy fuel oil is 2–3 percent), falling to 0.5 percent after January 1, 2020. This date could be deferred to January 1, 2025 depending on a review of the availability of low sulfur fuel oil. The price premium for 1 percent low sulfur heavy fuel oil has been substantial at times, and lowering sulfur content to 0.1 per cent simply rules out heavy fuel oil. However, a scrubber can be installed on a ship's exhaust funnel at a cost of $5 million plus associated operating costs including reduced energy efficiency to transform sulfur in a ship's exhaust to sulfur sulfate. The most popular type of scrubber, the open loop, flushes sulfur sulfate overboard and, in 2014, this emerged as a disposal problem in Europe's ECA waters. The only other choice for shipowners is using low sulfur medium diesel oil (MDO) in the ship's diesel engines. MDO, a refined product, is extremely expensive compared to low sulfur heavy fuel oil, which in any case can't be burned in an ECA after January 2015.

The obvious solution is adapting diesel engines to burn heavy fuel oil at sea and low sulfur diesel fuel in ECAs. Shifting from heavy fuel oil to diesel oil poses operational problems, something to be avoided particularly in congested waters. For new construction, the solution could be to build ships with dual fuel diesel electric propulsion systems as described for LNG carriers. Ships will burn LNG when available, or otherwise low sulfur diesel fuel. Ships operating in the Baltic and North Seas whose operations are restricted to a single port such as harbor work boats and tug boats or a scheduled service between or among designated ports such as ferries have been converted to either dual fuel (LNG and low sulfur diesel fuel) propulsion units or LNG fueled vessels. In 2014 there were 47 LNG fueled vessels other than LNG carriers in operation—not even a drop in the bucket compared to nearly 60,000 cargo-carrying vessels and about 90,000 vessels of all types above 100 gross tons (small vessels to be sure).[110] Nevertheless it is a beginning, just as the first oil burning vessels was a beginning in a world of coal burning vessels. LNG fueled vessels operate mostly in Norwegian waters where citizens living along the shoreline are acutely aware of ship exhaust pollution. The idea of abandoning diesel for LNG fueled ships operating in local waters is spreading. Poland expects as many as 500 LNG fueled vessels to be plying the Baltic Sea within 5 years.

An obvious candidate for conversion to heavy fuel oil and LNG is container vessels operating between Asia and Europe where LNG terminals already exist at both ends of their trade that could be used for bunkering (fueling) purposes. Container vessels when operating at their normal speed are heavy consumers of heavy fuel oil, and the owners of these vessels may find it economically attractive to convert to dual fuel slow-speed diesels relying heavily on LNG, with heavy fuel oil serving as backup. Alternatively they may depend entirely on LNG, as are ten LNG container vessels on order as of January 31, 2015, part of a total of 78 LNG fueled vessels on order.[111]

A new alternative for shipowners to consider is the introduction of low sulfur heavy distillate marine ECA (HDME), a fuel specifically made for compliance with environmental restrictions in ECAs. HDME burns efficiently and performs well in diesels that burn heavy fuel oil. Ships can easily switch from burning HDME to heavy fuel oil as they enter or leave an ECA without the operational risk of losing propulsion.[112] However, the cost of HDME, a refined oil product, could still make dual fuel (heavy fuel oil/diesel fuel and LNG) diesel electric propulsion desirable for ships yet to be built.

LNG/CNG as a Railroad Locomotive Fuel

Railroads run primarily on diesel oil worldwide except for coal fired locomotives hauling coal in South Africa, India, and China. Conversion of diesel fueled locomotives to either LNG or CNG is open for debate as no conversions have yet occurred. While railroads are fuel-efficient compared to trucks, they still burn a considerable amount of diesel fuel; for instance, US railroads consume 3.5 billion gallons of diesel fuel per year or 230,000 barrels per day.

Small locomotives work as switchers in rail yards and large locomotives pull freight trains between rail yards. The heavier gauge steel and larger volume tanks for holding CNG over LNG are not an impediment for railroads as they are for trucks. The nation's largest switch railroad carrier, the Indiana Harbor Belt Railroad, has received a $34.5 million grant to facilitate the conversion of 31 of the railroad's 46 diesel powered locomotives to CNG over 4 years and to build a centralized CNG refueling station. Estimated fuel savings of $2.7 million per year would have to be applied to the project investment to determine the economic feasibility for further conversions.[113]

There is some thought that large locomotives moving freight trains over long distances would be better served by LNG. For LNG to be a fuel, an entire infrastructure has to be built to distribute LNG from liquefaction plants or import terminals to refueling stations employing LNG-carrying tank cars. Another cost would be modifying locomotives to burn LNG as a fuel in diesel electric engines. LNG has less energy density than diesel fuel and would require larger sized tanks, but not nearly as large as CNG tanks. LNG tanks would be about 1.6 times larger than diesel fuel tanks of an equivalent energy basis and would consist of two concentric cylinder tanks where the inner tank holds LNG with a vacuum between the two being the primary insulation (conductive heat cannot be transmitted in a vacuum). The inner tank would be built of lighter material than a CNG tank as the design pressure of 140 psi is far less than the design pressure of a CNG tank measured in thousands of psi. Of course, there will be some heat transfer through the internal structure that holds the inner cylinder in place within the outer cylinder, causing boil-off. The material for this internal structure should have both favorable insulating and mechanical strength properties to hold the inner tank in place while minimizing heat transfer. Boil-off has to be dealt with to prevent over-pressurizing the tanks. The best way is by consuming boil-off as a fuel on a more or less continuous basis. While an idling locomotive can consume boil-off, stopping a locomotive engine for any length of time would require venting to prevent a dangerous pressure build-up in the inner tank in a way that does not present a health or fire hazard. Locomotive design will probably be initially dual fueled to take care of the contingency of not enough LNG refueling stations. But railroads, as point-to-point transportation, are amenable to full conversion to LNG. Certain point-to-point railway tracks where locomotives routinely shuttle back and forth would be best for initial conversion. BNSF, CSX, and Canadian National Railway are currently running pilot-programs to evaluate LNG as a locomotive fuel. Once the feasibility of LNG as a locomotive fuel has been demonstrated, then an LNG distribution system would have to be established and locomotive engines modified before full conversion of railroads to LNG can be accomplished. Again, fuel savings in switching to LNG would have to support the required investment in modifying engines and setting up a distribution system.

LNG/CNG as a Truck Fuel

Trucks already run on LNG and CNG. LNG fueled trucks are generally associated with local distribution of LNG from LNG terminals to customers not connected to the terminal by a natural gas pipeline.[114] If railroads were converted to LNG, then LNG fueled trucks can operate from railroad refueling depots. Tanks for holding LNG as a fuel are larger than tanks holding diesel fuel on an equivalent energy basis, but are far smaller in size and lighter in weight than CNG fuel tanks. A major drawback to CNG as a fuel for large trucks is the 3,000 pound weight of a tank that safely holds a sufficient volume of pressurized natural gas for a comparable refueling frequency as diesel trucks. This directly detracts from both the volume and weight-carrying capacity of a truck and thus its revenue generating potential. The prime advantage of LNG as a fuel is its smaller and lighter weight tank with a much smaller impact on revenue generation.

But LNG lacks a distribution infrastructure except in the vicinity of LNG terminals. CNG is more popular as a truck fuel than LNG because a distribution system to serve CNG refueling stations already exists in areas served by natural gas pipelines. Trucks including busses and taxis operating out of a central service facility with access to a natural gas pipeline are prime candidates for conversion to CNG. The service facility has to be fitted with equipment to pressurize and store CNG, and truck, bus, and taxi engines have to be converted to burn CNG. Cummins Engine and Westport Innovations have formed a joint venture (Cummins Westport) to provide conversion kits for existing heavy duty trucks and CNG equipment for truck manufacturers. Another 10 or so companies provide conversion kits for light and medium-sized trucks, and others for passenger cars. Not only does CNG provide a less costly fuel alternative, but ultra-low sulfur standards in diesel fuel are causing engine problems partly from the fuel's poor lubricant properties (lubricity).[115] More stringent regulations on particulate emissions are behind a greater frequency of expensive filter replacements. These unintended and costly consequences from stricter environmental regulations regarding diesel fuel add to the economic incentive of switching to CNG.

Refuse trucks operating out of a single station averaging over 150,000 miles per year and consuming 25,000 gallons of diesel fuel are prime candidates for conversion to CNG. In 2014, 5,000 refuse trucks ran on natural gas, of which two-thirds were operated by Waste Management. It is expected that 3,000 FedEx, 3,000 Ryder, and 1,000 UPS trucks will be running on CNG in the near future. While these are dwarfed by nearly 16 million diesel fueled trucks, the success of these trucks converting over to CNG may act as a magnet for others to emulate if CNG lives up to its promises.

The relative scarcity of CNG refueling stations limits CNG conversions to trucks, busses, and taxis operating from a single station that can be sufficiently fueled to be able to return to the station at night. Refueling time can be 5–20 minutes (fast-fill) or several hours (time-fill). Time-fill is cheaper in that a compressor pressurizes incoming natural gas from a pipeline direct to the truck's tank. Fast-fill is refueling motor vehicles from tanks that already contain pressurized natural gas at 5,000 psi, which adds significantly to the investment in CNG filling stations. There are 1,100 CNG filling stations in the US, half serving the public and half for onsite fueling of captive fleets.[116]

Like railroads, thought is being given to establishing an LNG distribution system and installing LNG refueling stations along the interstate highway system. As a start, truck traffic on certain heavily trafficked point-to-point interstate highways where rigs shuttle back and forth would be initially amenable to LNG conversion. Once a toehold is established, then it becomes easier to expand LNG availability throughout much of the interstate highway system. Trucks would not be able to leave the interstate highway system, at least for long distances, without the risk of running out of fuel unless they are dual fueled to run on diesel fuel and LNG. For trucks fueled exclusively by LNG, it would be possible to drop truck trailers at staging depots for switching to diesel driven rigs for off-interstate highway distribution. It may be possible to switch drivers to keep LNG fueled rigs running day and night to amortize their larger investment and to keep from having to vent natural gas when the rig is not operating. As such, LNG trucks would be acting like mini-trains using the interstate highway system as "truck-track." This is reminiscent of the Pony Express where a new horse was waiting at each staging depot for the rider. Staging depots were more or less 10 miles apart depending on the terrain and its effect on the practical limit for a galloping horse. Riders were changed between 170 and 200 miles. Unlike LNG trucks, the means of locomotion (horses) were rested whereas riders, as drivers, had little rest.[117]

CNG as an Automobile Fuel

Entrepreneurial grassroots efforts in Iran and Colombia as in Pakistan and Bangladesh convert gasoline powered automobiles and light trucks to natural gas. Private individuals have mastered the technique of installing tanks to hold compressed natural gas and in adapting the engine fueling systems to substitute natural gas for gasoline. Conversion kits are available in the US and other nations for the mechanical-minded.[118] By converting gasoline powered motor vehicles to natural gas, Iran and Colombia, as oil exporters, can augment their export earnings. Pakistan and Bangladesh, as oil importers, can reduce their hard currency trade deficits. Governments in oil exporting and importing nations with spare or stranded natural gas resources encourage their citizens to convert to natural gas and provide financial assistance for private interests to build pressurized natural gas dispensing stations. Relatively minor involvement by a sponsoring government is required if there is popular support for converting gasoline powered motor vehicles to natural gas other than in ensuring that natural gas is priced with respect to gasoline to provide an economic incentive.

An average gallon of gasoline contains 114,500 Btu or 1.145 therms (100,000 Btu in a therm). The figure most often quoted is 1.25 therms as equivalent to a gallon of gasoline to compensate for the energy expended to pressurize natural gas to 3,600 psi. At $6 per million Btu for natural gas, this works out to about $0.75 per equivalent gallon of gasoline. However, there is the extra cost of buying a CNG vehicle and the impact on mileage of carrying a 200 or 300 pound tank strong enough to safely contain pressurized natural gas. Natural gas can be purchased from public dispensing units or, in the US, in any of 67 million private residences, excluding apartment complexes, hooked up to natural gas. If automobiles are refueled in the family garage, there is an added cost of installing an in-house compressor plus paying for electricity for an overnight charge. The cost of equipment and use of electricity appear reasonable.[119] It is estimated that the all-inclusive charge for natural gas taking these added expenses into consideration is an equivalent cost of $2 per gallon of gasoline. As with electric cars, trips beyond normal commuting and around town chores have to take locations of CNG refilling stations into consideration. However, it may be possible to have a bi-fuel CNG and gasoline engine that eliminates the risk of being in a region with no CNG refueling facilities. Brazil builds a tri-fuel automobile that can run on CNG, gasoline, and ethanol either alone or any mix with gasoline (flex fuel), giving drivers a full range of fuel choices.

CNG tanks made of steel can weigh up to 300 pounds when filled with fuel. This extra weight affects the mileage performance of a CNG car. CNG tanks are sized for an equivalent energy content of a 12–15 gallon conventional gasoline tank. However, lighter weight, more costly CNG tanks are available made of aluminum liner overwrapped with carbon fiber. The dimensions of such a tank pressurized at 3,600 psi with a capacity equivalent to 12.6 gallons of gasoline are 15.9 "in diameter (width) and 60" long, weighing 118 pounds when empty and 185 pounds when full.[120] A CNG tank can easily take up much of an automobile's luggage space.

CNG tank weight and pressure can be reduced if the tank is filled with a technologically advanced, yet-to-be-developed porous material with a high surface area that increases the energy density of compressed natural gas. A relatively low pressure tank would then be able to hold the same amount of natural gas as a conventional CNG tank, but with less weight. A search is underway for such a material by government and corporate research centers; if successful, lighter weight tanks would increase the appeal of CNG vehicles.[121]

On a global basis, NGVs of all types from motorcycles to heavy lift trucks are growing at an annual rate of 20 percent. Annual growth in Asia is 36 percent, followed by Africa at 16 percent, Latin America 15 percent, Europe 14 percent, and North America (somewhat surprisingly) nil. World population of NGVs is 16.7 million, of which 19 percent are in Iran and in Pakistan, 13 percent in Argentina, 11 percent in Brazil, and 7 percent each in India and China. In terms of saturation, the percentage of NGVs to all motor vehicles is 77 percent in Armenia, 65 percent Pakistan, 37 percent Bolivia, 21 percent Iran, 18 percent Bangladesh, 17 percent Argentina, and 15 percent Uzbekistan. Clearly some nations with relatively low automobile populations have made significant progress in converting from gasoline to compressed natural gas. As impressive as these figures appear to be, NGVs make up only 1.28 percent of the world's motor vehicle population. Out of 84 nations, the US stands 80th with 128,000 NGVs out of a total population of over 250 million motor vehicles, with NGVs representing a 0.05 percent share. The number of public and private filling stations in the US grew from 1,100 in 2008 to 1,120 in 2012, a clear testament to the lack of popular interest in NGVs. Quite obviously, with the exceptions of Waste Management and a few other trucking firms, the US is a real laggard in adopting NGVs for transportation.[122]

It is quite unlikely that liquefied or compressed natural gas emerging as a motor vehicle fuel would affect the price of natural gas or petroleum fuels because of the enormous disparity of the number of natural gas versus petroleum fueled vehicles. That said, there is a great deal of interest in pursuing the opportunity afforded by NGVs and they will certainly expand in number with time; if not in the US, then elsewhere. The question of how many depends on the relationship between oil and natural gas prices, the degree of geopolitical risk associated with oil, the availability of domestic natural gas, government support in encouraging and permitting CNG dispensing stations, and popular perception on the benefits of owning an NGV.

Transformational Technologies

Technology for converting natural gas to liquid motor vehicle fuels exists and gives natural gas access to the same delivery system that serves petroleum. The volume of natural gas consumed in producing gas-based petroleum liquids would be far from the point of affecting the price of natural gas or motor vehicle fuels. Other transformation technologies turn sour gas to sweet, tap coal bed methane, and "mine" methane hydrates.

Gas to Liquids (GTL) Technology

Reservoirs of stranded gas too remote for access by pipeline, and lacking sufficient reserves to support an LNG export project, or being wasted by flaring, can be made accessible to the market by gas to liquids (GTL) technology. While LNG is a physical process of changing natural gas from a gaseous to a liquid state, GTL is a chemical process of transforming natural gas into oil products. GTL technology combines methane with oxygen at high temperatures to produce a stream of synthetic gas (syngas) of carbon monoxide and hydrogen. The Fischer-Tropsch process, developed during the 1920s by the two German scientists Franz Fischer and Hans Tropsch, utilizes iron or cobalt catalysts to transform syngas into hydrocarbon chains of LPG, naphtha, kerosene, diesel fuel, lubricating oil, and wax. The process can also create hydrocarbon fuels from coal and biomass. Oil-starved Nazi Germany depended on the Fischer-Tropsch process to produce gasoline from coal to fuel its war machine. Sasol, a world leader in GTL technology, operates the world's largest 150,000 Bpd GTL plant that runs on coal to make motor vehicle fuels. The plant was built to reduce South Africa's vulnerability to the threat of a Middle East oil embargo when apartheid reigned as a national policy.

The first step of the GTL process is to clean natural gas of water, hydrogen sulfide, and carbon dioxide. After that, LPG, condensates, and ethane content in the natural gas are separated to obtain a stream of pure methane, which is then combined with a stream of pure oxygen separated from air to produce a syngas of carbon monoxide and hydrogen. The Fischer-Tropsch process transforms syngas into a variety of hydrocarbon fuels by controlling the nature of the catalyst, process temperature and pressure, and mode of operation. The output of oil products from the GTL process is markedly different than from an oil refinery. An oil refinery may have an output of 3 percent LPG, 10 percent naphtha, 27 percent gasoline, 40 percent middle distillates (jet fuel/kerosene and gas oil/diesel), and 20 percent fuel oil. A GTL plant's output may range from zero to a few percent LPG, 15–25 percent naphtha, 65–85 percent middle distillates, and up to 30 percent lubes/wax.[123] This wide range of output for various motor vehicle fuels allows a design of a GTL plant to be tailored to fit expected demand.

Shell Oil has a long history of involvement with GTL technology and has been producing over 14,000 Bpd of liquid petroleum products from its Bintula plant in Malaysia since 1993. Qatar has been actively seeking joint venture partners to build GTL plants to take advantage of its enormous gas reserves.[124] The oryx GTL plant, a joint venture between Qatar and Sasol of South Africa, began operations in 2006 consuming 330 million cubic feet of natural gas per day and producing 34,000 Bpd of petroleum products (24,000 Bpd of diesel fuel, 9,000 Bpd of naphtha, and 1,000 Bpd of LPG). Shell, utilizing its experience from the Bintula plant, built the Pearl GTL plant in a joint venture with Qatar. The plant was completed in 2012 and produces 140,000 Bpd of naphtha, kerosene, diesel fuel, lubricating oils, and paraffin plus 120,000 Bpd of natural gas liquids and ethane stripped from 1.6 million cubic feet per day of natural gas feedstock.[125] Chevron, utilizing its experience in a GTL project with Sasol, built a 33,000 Bpd GTL plant in Escravos, Nigeria, in partnership with the Nigerian National Oil Company. The plant began initial operations in 2014, 9 years late and over five times its original cost estimate, partly reflecting the difficulty of constructing a highly sophisticated plant in a rather remote location. Plans are to expand its output to 100,000 Bpd within 10 years of completion.[126] About a dozen GTL projects with an output between 50,000 and 100,000 barrels per day of petroleum products are in various stages of feasibility studies.[127]

Selling GTL petroleum products is a virtually unlimited market from the perspective of natural gas producers. One drawback to GTL production is the cost of the plant, which is far higher than a comparable oil refinery with a similar output. The cost has been reduced from technological advances and economies of scale in building larger sized plants, but these plants have also been plagued by cost overruns and missed deadlines not unlike certain LNG projects. Another drawback is that the GTL process is about twice as thermally inefficient as an LNG liquefaction plant. This means that a lot more of the original energy content of natural gas is lost when natural gas is converted to petroleum products than to LNG. In addition the Fischer-Tropsch process produces a large volume of carbon dioxide as a waste product (the process has been dubbed a carbon dioxide production plant by critics). While petroleum products made by the Fischer-Tropsch process are cleaner-burning than those made from crude oil, the carbon footprint is larger when emissions from the production process are taken into account. The carbon footprint would be smaller if the GTL plant consumed natural gas that would otherwise be flared (another example of the possibilities of managing outcomes). Earlier projections of the contribution of GTL as a source of motor vehicle fuels have not materialized from a combination of higher capital costs for building a GTL plant, the thermal inefficiency of the process, and a larger growth in LNG markets in Europe and Asia than anticipated. Moreover the price of LNG improved considerably after Japan shut down its nuclear plants. Since LNG liquefaction and GTL plants monetize stranded natural gas, no conclusion can be made for nations with stranded natural gas resources as to which course to follow until a netback analysis is completed. The analysis will determine whether they're better off exporting natural gas in a liquefied state or as liquid oil products.

Technological progress is being made to convert natural gas to gasoline in a much less costly fashion. A proposed technology envisions breaking down a molecule of methane into its constituent elements of carbon and hydrogen and then reassembling them into gasoline in the presence of a catalyst. Although this Midas touch to creating gasoline from natural gas has not yet succeeded, progress has been made by Siluria, a start-up company that has developed new tools for making and screening potential catalysts hundreds at a time. The company has also developed viruses that can assemble atoms of inorganic materials into precise shapes utilizing nanotechnology and has improved the technology of transforming methane into ethylene in the presence of catalysts. Ethylene is but one short chemical step away from gasoline. Siluria is building two pilot plants, one in San Francisco to make gasoline and the other in Houston to make ethylene.[128]

Sweetening Sour Gas

Sour gas is natural gas with a significant content of either hydrogen sulfide or carbon dioxide or both. While not considered a transformational technology, sour gas does require technology to make it commercially acceptable. Sour gas reserves are plentiful, amounting to 40 percent of global and 60 percent of Middle East gas reserves.[129] Hydrogen sulfide is normally converted to sulfur and sold to industrial enterprises.[130] Sour gas with hydrogen sulfide requires special alloys of steel pipe to prevent corrosion.

Another gas constituent of sour gas is carbon dioxide, which at high concentrations can create a disposal problem that affects natural gas production. The Natuna gas field, the largest offshore gas field in Southeast Asia, has a carbon dioxide concentration ranging from just a few percent to over 70 percent. Natural gas production from the Natuna field has been in areas where carbon dioxide concentration is low. Safe disposal must be addressed before natural gas with a high concentration of carbon dioxide can be tapped. There are a few examples of successful sequestration of carbon dioxide from gas fields. One gas field in Norway and another in Algeria have successfully separated carbon dioxide from natural gas, which is disposed by injection into nearby depleted gas fields, providing useful data and experience on carbon sequestration. Depleted oil fields and salt water aquifers are other means of disposal. But there is a cost of separating carbon dioxide from natural gas and in sequestering (compressing, transporting, and injecting carbon dioxide into underground formations) that has to be taken into account when conducting an economic feasibility study.

Methane from Coal Beds

Methane found with coal has been responsible for the death of many miners. Coal bed methane (CBM) is "mining" coal beds not for coal, but for methane. CBM works best for mines too deep for mining (below 3,000 feet) with fractured methane-rich coal submerged in water. The water surrounding coal absorbs and retains methane as long as the water is under pressure. Methane has a low solubility in water and readily comes out of solution when water pressure is dropped.

A well is drilled to the coal seam to allow the water to rise to the surface, where it is capped and kept under pressure by a pump. From time to time, pumping is stopped and water released to drop the well's pressure, allowing methane to come out of solution. The released methane is collected and diverted to a gathering system that connects a number of wells to a natural gas pipeline. After the release of methane, the well is capped and water pumped in to increase its internal pressure. The process is repeated after a sufficient wait for water to reabsorb methane from the coal bed.

The principal region for CBM wells in the US is the San Juan basin encompassing Four Corners regions (northwestern New Mexico, northeastern Arizona, southwestern Colorado, and southeastern Utah), the Powder River basin (southeastern Montana and northeastern Wyoming), and other basins and regions such as Appalachia. CBM production in the US was 1.6 Tcf in 2003, rising to 2 Tcf in 2008 and falling back to 1.5 Tcf in 2013, representing 1.6 percent of natural gas production.[131] While the US is the most advanced nation in developing CBM, its potential resources (not reserves) of 4–11 tcm are small compared to Australia (8–14 tcm), China (30–35 tcm), Russia (17–80 tcm), and Canada (17–92 tcm).[132] Canada, Australia, China, and India are likely candidates for the development of coal bed methane. China has taken a more aggressive stand on CBM in its quest to reduce its reliance on coal. Coal bed methane output was 13.8 bcm in 2013 and 15.5 bcm in 2014. One of the problems facing the developers of CBM in China is that gas output does not pay off the investment. However, tight gas deposits have been found at different layers than coal bed methane. The plan is to tap both sources simultaneously to enhance output and increase return on investment.[133] While the US still dominates, production is expected to continue falling from resource maturity and depletion. Australia may displace the US as the top-ranked producer by 2020.

CBM production in China and India suffers from more challenging geological conditions and low well productivity.[134]

Environmentalists object to the pristine Western wilderness being crisscrossed with gathering pipelines and its quiet disturbed by the noise of equipment pumping water into wells and compressors moving gas in pipelines. The water from CBM wells is saline and can damage agricultural and natural plant life if it penetrates fresh water aquifers. Saline water is kept in ponds, but some seeps into surface groundwater. Reinjecting saline water into the CBM well avoids the risk of surface water contamination, but at the present time not all is reinjected.[135] These environmental objections are similar to those associated with fracking.

Enhanced coal bed methane involves injecting carbon dioxide into the coal bed. Fractures in a coal bed can absorb twice as much carbon dioxide as methane. Carbon dioxide remains trapped in the coal bed, displacing methane. This has the double benefit of sequestering carbon dioxide while enhancing methane production. Between 0.1 and 0.2 tons of methane can be recovered for every ton of injected carbon dioxide. Experimentation of enhanced CBM is being undertaken in the US, China, Japan, and Poland. Sequestering carbon dioxide in coal beds would require separating carbon dioxide from flue gases and pipelining carbon dioxide from an electricity generating plant to a CBM site, which, as one might expect, would be quite costly at this time.

A new methodology is being explored for stranded coal mines located too deep for conventional mining. Underground coal gasification (UCG) has been around since the nineteenth century, but has never been commercially viable. Advances in UCG technology have reached a point to support pilot projects in Uzbekistan, Australia, and South Africa with other nations looking into UCG. Interest in UCG technology has been kindled by the development of horizontal drilling. Two vertical wells are drilled from the surface to each end of a horizontal well bore through the coal seam. Oxygen and steam are forced down the injection well to feed the combustion process at one end of the horizontal well bore, reducing coal to char and releasing a mixture of hydrogen, methane, carbon monoxide, and carbon dioxide gases (same as manufactured gas). These gases move through the horizontal well bore and come to the surface via the production well. Carbon dioxide can be separated and sequestered in the coal seam. Methane can be directed to a natural gas distribution system. Hydrogen can be sold separately or combined with carbon monoxide to form a syngas to produce more methane or other hydrocarbon fuels. A start-up company called Five-Quarter Energy is exploring substituting solid state chemical engineering for the combustion process in UCG.[136]

Methane Hydrates

Clathrate compounds are water molecules that under certain conditions bond to form an ice-like cage that encapsulates a gas molecule, which if methane is called methane hydrate.[137] Methane hydrates are essentially natural gas molecules trapped in a lattice of ice whose structure is maintained in a low-temperature and moderate-to-high pressure environment. Methane hydrates can be shaped into an ice ball like those carefully sculpted by Calvin in the "Calvin and Hobbs" comic strip to throw at Suzie. The only difference is that a methane hydrate ice ball can be ignited. One cubic meter of methane hydrates contains enough embedded natural gas that, when released, expands to an incredible 160 cubic meters at atmospheric pressure.

Methane hydrates are found beneath large portions of the world's permafrost as well as in offshore sediments. They are thought to have been formed by migrating natural gas or seep gas that came in contact with cold seawater at sufficient depths to form hydrates or by the decay of marine life in bottom sediments. Cold and pressure keep the methane entrapped in the ice lattice, which can be released by increasing the temperature or reducing the pressure.[138] Some climatologists fear that global warming of the tundra regions could release methane now entrapped as methane hydrates in the permafrost, leading to runaway global warming as methane is 20 times more effective than carbon dioxide in reflecting infrared radiation back to earth. Some speculate that one of the largest landslides that ever occurred may have been set off by the disintegration of methane hydrates. The Storegga Submarine Landslide occurred off the coast of Norway during the Holocene epoch about 8,000 years ago. It is thought that the rapid decomposition of hydrates from temperature changes near the end of the last ice age may have destabilized sediments, setting off the landslide that traveled 500 miles down the continental slope. This, in turn, triggered a mega-tsunami possibly as high as 82 feet that struck Scotland and Norway. There has also been speculation that a massive amount of methane released from entrapped hydrates might have been a "global warming" event that hastened the end of the last ice age.

Methane hydrates are not limited to the arctic regions. Large deposits of methane hydrates have been found in coastal regions around Japan, both coasts of the US, Central and South America, and elsewhere. While known world reserves of conventional natural gas are over 6,600 Tcf, the worldwide estimate of methane trapped in methane hydrates is over 100 times greater at 700,000 Tcf, but only a small portion of this would likely be mined. For the US, the estimate is 200,000 Tcf versus natural gas reserves of 330 Tcf, almost 700 times larger, but, again, relatively little would be available for exploitation. It is estimated that of the 11,000–34,000 Tcf in the northern Gulf of Mexico with a mean of 21,400 Tcf, only about 6,700 Tcf would likely to be mined. Nevertheless there is an awful lot of methane locked up in methane hydrates, and such a potential cannot be ignored. The challenge is how to mine methane hydrates considering their inherent instability.

Japan has taken a keen interest in methane hydrates because of large deposits offshore that could substitute for imported LNG to fuel the nation in the aftermath of the Fukushima Daiichi disaster. Japan is the first nation to succeed in extracting natural gas from a methane hydrate deposit 900 feet below the seabed in the Nankai Trough, offshore central Japan. Japan Oil, Gas, & Metal National Corporation drilled a pipe into the deposit and then lowered the pressure that caused methane to disassociate from ice at the bottom of the pipe. Gas flowed up the pipe to the surface. It is thought that sending warmed water down the pipe would accomplish the same effect, but it is feared that warming might consume nearly all the released energy.

In another joint venture project between the US and Japan in 2012, a successful test in releasing methane was by injecting carbon dioxide into a methane hydrate deposit. Carbon dioxide molecules changed places with methane molecules within the ice lattice freeing methane while sequestering carbon dioxide. Substituting carbon dioxide for methane also avoids the instabilities associated with methane hydrates by raising temperature or reducing pressure.[139] Commercialization of methane hydrates is decades away, but Japan, the US, Canada, Norway, and China have collaborative research projects in progress to develop methane hydrates as a commercial source of energy.[140]

The current cost estimate to develop methane hydrates is $30–$50 per million Btu as compared to $6 per million Btu or less from fracking natural gas in the US.[141] The first methane hydrates to be exploited would be the thousands of Tcf trapped in highly porous and permeable sandstone in the Arctic. This would be followed by tens of thousands of Tcf in marine sands, which represent a higher degree of technological effort. Hundreds of thousands of Tcf in marine muds would be much more technologically difficult to extract. The challenge of methane hydrates is maintaining their integrity to keep methane locked within an ice lattice through the mining or extraction process until methane can enter a natural gas gathering system.[142]

It has been speculated that ships lost in the Bermuda Triangle may have actually been caught in a gigantic bubble of methane released from methane hydrates and floundered from a loss of buoyancy. Similarly, aircraft passing through a cloud of methane-enriched air might suffer from loss of power by methane displacing oxygen or from an explosion or fire from a methane cloud coming in contact with the hot engine exhaust. However, there is nothing speculative about brine pools with an extreme concentration of salt containing high levels of methane found at the bottom of certain areas of the ocean. These pools are surrounded by colonies of mussels, which have formed a symbiotic relationship with methane-metabolizing bacteria that live on their gills. Methane-metabolizing bacteria have also been found living symbiotically with worms in methane hydrate deposits at the bottom of the Gulf of Mexico. These pools have their own surface characteristics that are as distinct from sea water above as pools on land are distinct from air. Methane in brine pools flourishing with life and a methane atmosphere of Saturn's moon, Titan, with rain, rivers, and lakes of LNG show that we live in an amazing world in an amazing universe.

Problems

Problem 7.1

This problem is to calculate the volume of carbon dioxide emissions of coal and natural gas and oil to generate 1 gW for 1 year to obtain metric tons of carbon dioxide emissions listed in Table 7.3. Thermal efficiency is 30 percent to translate energy to electricity with plants fueled by natural gas, oil, and coal, and also, for comparison purposes, a natural gas plant with a higher thermal efficiency of 50 percent. The approach is one of translating energy terms consistent with their definitions in a logical fashion for the four plants. Btu data expended to produce 1 kWh of electricity, which takes into account applicable thermal efficiencies, have been derived in the text following Table 7.2. From this information, calculate Btu per kilowatt-day and kilowatt-year, then Btu per megawatt-year and gigawatt-year. With one Btu equal to 1,055.0559 J, calculate joules per gigawatt-year, then trillion joules per gigawatt-year, and then translate to kilograms of carbon dioxide from the relationship shown in Table 7.1.

Problem 7.2

The purpose is to calculate return on equity for an annual capital charge of 10 percent assumed in the chapter and to show that this charge is sufficient to satisfy debt requirements, associated taxes on profits, and provide an attractive return on equity. The investment is $10,000 and a 10 percent capital charge is an annual revenue of $1,000. The capital charge is dependent on the underlying financial structure and will most apt not be 10 percent for other applications.

Problem Figure 7.2

	D	E	F	G	H	I	J	K	L
1		Investment	$10,000						
2		Depreciation	20 Years						
3					Loan				
4			Loan	$7,000	Amount	Interest	Before	Tax	Net
5			Years	15	Outstanding	4%	Tax	Payable	Cash
6	Year	Revenue	Depreciation	Amortization			Income	30%	Flow
7	0				$7,000				-$3,000
8	1	$1,000	$500	$467	$6,533	$271	$229	$69	$194
9	2	$1,000	$500	$467	$6,067	$252	$248	$74	$207
10	3	$1,000	$500	$467	$5,600	$233	$267	$80	$220

Revenue in year 1 in cell E8 is a capital charge of 10 percent or $1,000. The remaining cells reference cell E8 (=$E$8). Depreciation is the write-off of the investment over 20 years (=$F$1/$F$2). The amount of the loan is $7,000 to be paid over 15 years. Annual amortization in cell G8 is =IF(D8<=$G$5,1,0)*$G$4/$G$5 where the first part of the formula stops amortization payments after the loan has been paid off. The loan amount is placed in cell H7, and the outstanding amount of the loan at the end of the previous year/start of present year in cell H8 is =IF(D9<=$G$5,1,0)*(H8-G9) where the first part of the formula prevents negative values from occurring after the amortization period is over.

Interest payments in column I in year 1 is =$I$5*(H7+H8)/2 where interest is based on the average amount of debt outstanding between the start and the end of the year (this is very close to semi-annual or 6-month debt repayment often used in financing capital investments). Before tax income is revenue less depreciation less interest. Tax payable is before tax income times the applicable tax rate. Annual cash flow starts with the outflow for equity and is thereafter revenue less amortization less interest less taxes. The IRR in cell L29 (not shown above) is =IRR(L7:L27). In a more general approach where the capital charge is not known, but the return on equity is, then the capital charge can be obtained by Goal Seek by changing revenue in cell E8 to reflect the desired return on equity in cell L29. Then revenue, divided by $10,000, is the desired capital charge. But here with the revenue set at 10 percent capital charge, the return on equity is 9.1 percent. Thus a 10 percent capital charge is applicable to an investment 70 percent financed with 15-year debt with an interest rate of 4 percent, an effective tax rate of 30 percent, and a desired return on equity of 9.1 percent. For a utility, a 9.1 percent return is attractive considering it is paying 4 percent on its debt. Thus a 10 percent capital charge can be used in a general sense to assess electricity rates, which would also include fixed and variable costs at full utilization. Suppose that the desired rate of return for a utility is 8 percent; using Goal Seek, what would be the required capital charge as a percent of an investment? Suppose that 10-year debt is available at 3 percent interest; what would be the required capital charge for a 9 percent desired return on investment?

Problem 7.3

Referring to the cash flow in column L of Problem 7.2, demonstrate that treating equity as a form of subordinate debt where "interest" is the return on equity and where "debt," equal to the equity investment, is fully repaid at the end of the project horizon is a valid assertion. This can be done by placing the equity investment in cell N7 as a positive value and cell N8 containing the formula =N7*(1+$L$29)-L8 replicated to the end of the project. The first term applies the "interest" charge as the return on equity in cell L29, the IRR of the cash flow stream. This is then netted of the first year's cash flow. In this case, since cash flow is less than the "interest" charge on subordinated debt, the outstanding amount of the "loan" grows to year 10 before cash flow finally exceeds return on equity. After year 10 the enhanced "loan" amount is steadily, but slowly, being repaid until year 15, when the "loan" is quickly paid off with the cessation of amortization payments on actual debt. Its balance at the end of the project horizon is zero, meaning that the equity "loan" has been paid off, plus providing the stipulated return on equity.

Problem 7.4

To create a screening curve, list utilization rate from 5% to 95% and calculate the output for the three natural gas plants described in Table 7.3. With 3.412 million Btu in 1 mWh at 100 percent thermal efficiency for converting thermal energy to electrical output, calculate the Btu to produce 1 mWh for each plant. Using the relationship that 1,000 cubic feet (Mcf) is equal to 1.025 million Btu, calculate the Mcf to produce 1 mWh of electricity and charge this $6 per Mcf. This is the cost to produce 1 mWh; multiplying this for the three plants and for the various utilization factors generates the variable cost for energy. Each of the utilization factors represents so many hours of operation given 8,640 hours at full utilization. Apply the annual capital charge at 10 percent of capital cost and fixed cost to each of the 5 percent increments. The cost per megawatt-hour for each utilization rate can be obtained by adding in the variable energy costs to the capital and fixed costs and dividing by the applicable megawatt-hour output. From this, screening curves can be obtained for the three electricity generating plants. Figure 7.7 shows the screening curve for the 70 mW combustion turbine.

Problem 7.5

Screening curves are not comparable because each utilization rate presents a different megawatt-hour output for the generators. To obtain a chart that is comparable for each plant, it is necessary to obtain the $/mWh for the same output of three plants whose maximum output is different. Rather than plotting $/mWh versus utilization in percentage terms, the object of this problem is to plot $/mWh for the megawatt output of the three plants.

A number of steps are needed to adjust the screening curve from utilization to power output. For each plant, do the screening curves for output 5 to 95 percent in increments of 5 percent. Then calculate the thermal input for 1 mWh of output in mmBtu; adjust for Mcf with the factor of 1.025 mmBtu in 1 Mcf and multiply by $6 per Mcf to obtain the cost for 1 mWh of output. Then multiply this by the screen curve figures to obtain the variable fuel cost for each of the 5 percent increments for each plant. For each plant, obtain the capital costs by multiplying the capital investment by 10 percent and add in the fixed costs as per Table 7.4. Translate the 5 percent increments to hours per year with 8,640 hours for 100 percent utilization and divide these hours into the total capital and fixed costs plus variable fuel costs already calculated. At this point, you have $/mWh for each plant for each 5 percent increment of utilization.

For each plant copy the megawatt-hour output from the screen curves that correspond for each 5 percent increment in one column and associated $/mWh output next to it and do an X-Y scatter chart (not line chart). Right click on the curve for trend lines and obtain the best fitting trend line along with the equation and R square value (these are selected at the bottom of the trend line menu). For simplicity, you may select the Power curve for each. The reason for selecting the X-Y scatter diagram is that x-values in the regression equation are actual x-axis values, whereas for a line chart, ordinal values would have to be entered into the Excel generated trend line formulas. Now equipped with the best fitting trend lines, the final step is to incorporate them into a table for x-values from 10 mWh output to 700 in increments of 10. The equation for the combustion turbine will go from x-axis values up to 70, for the conventional plant up to 500, and for the cogeneration plant up to 700. These were plotted to obtain Figure 7.8.

Problem 7.6

Suppose that a new Marcellus well has an initial output averaging 9,000 cubic feet (mcf) per day the first year, 3,000 mcf the second year, and 1,000 mcf the third year. What is the total output over the lifetime of the well in billion cubic feet (bcf)? What is the total revenue of the life of the well if natural gas is priced at $4 per thousand cubic feet?

Suppose that a sampling of fracked gas wells had the following distribution of total output in billion cubic feet: 3% for an output of 0.5 bcf, 8% for 1 bcf, 10% for 1.5 bcf, 12% for 2 bcf, 10% for 2.5, 3, and 4 bcf, 6% for 4.5, 5, and 5.5 bcf, 3% for 6 bcf, and 1% for 6.5 and 7 bcf all the way to 14 bcf in steps of 0.5 bcf. What is the average output? If the total cost of drilling and operating a well for 3 years, the life of the well, is $8 million, and the price of natural gas is $4 per mcf, what is the risk of earning less than $8 million (this is the cumulative probability of lifetime revenue being less than or equal to $8 million)? Suppose that the lifetime drilling and operating cost is $12 million; what is the risk of the well not making $12 million?

Problem 7.7

Although a tank truck can haul up to 11,600 gallons, a typical tank truck found on the road hauls 9,000 gallons. Suppose that a fracked well is 12 inches in diameter (see Website http://science.howstuffworks.com/environmental/energy/hydraulic-fracking1. htm) and extends down 7,000 feet before going horizontal for 10,000 feet (nowadays the maximum assessment for horizontal wells is 2–3 miles). How many gallons of water (7.48 gallons per cubic foot) are required to fill the well prior to the initial fracking (well bore is 7,000 feet plus 9,000 feet)? Once the furthest 500 feet is fracked, pressure is released and much of the water gushes out on the surface. Assuming that all the water is removed to ensure the chemical integrity of new fracking water entering the well, how much water is necessary to fill the well less the initial 500 foot segment which is isolated to prevent further fracking (say 9,500 feet has to be filled with water, sand, and chemicals, then 9,000 feet all the way back to the start of the horizontal well bore at 7,000 feet in 500 foot segments)? What is the total number of tank truck loads necessary to supply the water at 9,000 gallons per truck load?

Problem 7.8

The Cheniere LNG export plant has the capacity to export 16 million tons per year (mmtpy) of LNG when it comes on stream in 2015. Using nominal 155,000 cubic meter LNG carriers, how many vessels are required to handle this volume given 0.58 metric ton per cubic meter of LNG and an average of eight round trip voyages per year for some mix of destinations to Europe and the Far East? How many would be required in 2020 if all the currently approved export plants are on line exporting 60 mmtpy?

Problem 7.9

A very large crude carrier moving around 250,000 tons consumes 90 tons per day of heavy fuel oil costing about $60 per barrel. What would be the daily fuel cost when at sea? Compare this with $10,000–$12,000 per day for operating cost including crew, insurance, maintenance and repairs, supplies, and a contribution to meeting office over-head. What if total operating and capital costs were $40,000 per day? What would the comparable fuel bill be if the vessel was fueled by LNG costing $8, $10, or $12 per mmBtu given that a ton of crude oil is energy-equivalent to 40 mmBtu assuming energy equivalence between crude oil and residual fuel oil?

Problem 7.10

Suppose that you are considering converting a gasoline motor vehicle to an NGV where 1.25 therm (100,000 Btu) is equivalent to one gallon of gasoline. If 1 mmBtu of natural gas delivered to your home is $6, what is the equivalent cost of gasoline? Suppose your automobile gets 25 miles to the gallon and you drive 10,000 miles per year; what is your annual savings on gasoline if gasoline costs $3.00 per gallon? Further suppose that variable costs to pressurize and pump natural gas into your automobile is $200 per year in extra electricity; how much can you pay for the conversion kit on the basis of 5 years of net savings?

Problem 7.11

A gallon of diesel contains 139,000 Btu. Suppose that a truck has a tank size of 100 gallons of diesel and the truck is to be converted to burn natural gas. While an actual tank would be a cylindrical tank with hemispherical end heads, for ease of calculation, assume that the tank is rectangular in shape. The tank holding natural gas will be built to withstand a pressure of 3,500 psi and the inner base of the rectangular tank must be no larger than 4" by 4". How high does the inner height of the tank have to be to carry the equivalent of 100 gallons of diesel fuel?

First figure out the amount of Btu required in a tankful of natural gas and the equivalent cubic feet where 1,000 cubic feet have a heat content of one million Btu. Boyle's law states that, at the same temperature, P1V1 = P2V2 where the atmospheric pressure, 14.7 pounds per square inch, multiplied by the indicated volume, is equal to 3,500 pounds per square inch times a compressed volume. Applying Boyle's law at this elevated pressure does not take into account the non-ideal behavior of natural gas, but for the purposes of this exercise it is assumed that Boyle's law is applicable.[143] The height of the tank can be calculated knowing the base area of the rectangular tank.

Notes

1 Fang-Yu Liang, Marta Ryvak, Sara Sayeed, and Nick Zhao, "The Role of Natural Gas as a Primary Fuel in the Near Future, Including Comparisons of Acquisition, Transmission and Waste Handling Costs of as with Competitive Alternatives," *Chemistry Central Journal* (6[Supp 1]:54, 2012), Website http://journal.chemistrycentral.com/content/6/S1/S4.

2 As a customer of Public Service of New Jersey, I was given an opportunity to buy natural gas and electricity from third-party providers. I accepted the opportunity in part for writing this book and teaching a course in energy. The utility bill contained two PSE&G distribution charges to serve my house with natural gas and electricity and two charges for the amount of natural gas and electricity used. The charges for energy usage were forwarded directly by PSE&G to the third-party providers. There was no separate transmission bill, which must have been incorporated into the rates offered by the providers. I was also supplied with information on what PSE&G would have charged for natural gas and electricity had PSE&G been my provider to make it easy for me to judge the effectiveness of third-party providers to lower my utility costs. Moreover I had the right to switch from third-party providers back to PSE&G at my volition. Today I purchase natural gas and electricity directly from PSE&G as sole provider—a personal testament of the effectiveness of third-party providers to lower my utility bill!

3 Source of data before 2005: US Bureau of Labor Statistics, Website http://data.bls.gov/pdq/SurveyOutputServlet (site no longer available). Post 2005: Electric Power Monthly, Website www.eia.gov/electricity/monthly/epm_table_grapher.cfm?t=epmt_5_03.

4 ENTSO-E (European Network of Transmission System Operators for Electricity), Website www.entsoe.eu/Pages/default.aspx. See also Gas Infrastructure Europe, Website www.gie.eu.com.

5 "Single Market for Gas and Electricity," European Commission, Website http://ec.europa.eu/energy/gas_electricity/legislation/legislation_en.htm.

6 Bob Shively and John Ferrare, *Understanding Today's Natural Gas Business* (San Francisco, CA: Enerdynamics, 2004).

7 "Natural Gas Frequently Asked Questions," US Energy Information Agency, Website www.eia.gov/tools/faqs/faq.cfm?id=45&t=8.

8 "U.S. Natural Gas Number of Gas and Gas Condensate Wells," US Energy Information Agency, Website www.eia.gov/dnav/ng/hist/na1170_nus_8a.htm.

9 Brigham A. McCown, "New Jersey Explosion Serves as Reminder for Safety Vigilance," *Huffington Post* (originally written in 1994 shortly after time of explosion, but updated May 6, 2014), Website www.huffingtonpost.com/brigham-a-mccown/new-jersey-explosion-serv_b_4907186.html.

10 *Annual Energy Outlook 2011* (Washington, DC: Energy Information Administration, US Department of Energy, 2011), Table 14 and Figure 16, Website www.eia.gov/naturalgas/annual/pdf/nga11.pdf.

11 "Natural Gas: Natural Gas Market Centers and Hubs in Relation to Major Natural Gas Transportation Corridors," US Energy Information Agency (2009), Website www.eia.gov/pub/oil_gas/natural_gas/analysis_publications/ngpipeline/MarketCenterHubsMap.html.

12 Housley Carr (RBN Energy), "Polar Vortex Spurs Catch-22 Workaround—Getting New England Gas Pipeline Capacity Built" (February 10, 2014), Website https://rbnenergy.com/polar-vortex-spurs-catch-22-workaround-getting-new-england-gas-pipeline-capacity-built.

13 *Annual Energy Outlook 2014* (Washington, DC: Energy Information Administration, US Department of Energy, 2014). The figures for 2010 and 2015 were essentially identical and were assumed to apply for 2014. See also "Natural Gas," International Energy Outlook, Website www.eia.gov/forecasts/ieo/nat_gas.cfm, for source of data on electricity from Electricity section.

14 *Annual Energy Outlook 2014* (Washington, DC: Energy Information Administration, US Department of Energy, 2014), Table A13: Natural gas supply, disposition, and prices, Website www.eia.gov/forecasts/aeo/pdf/0383%282014%29.pdf. Number of customers was obtained from EIA, Website www.eia.gov/dnav/ng/ng_cons_num_dcu_nus_a.htm.

15 *Annual Energy Outlook 2014* (Washington, DC: Energy Information Administration, US Department of Energy, 2014), Table A2: Energy consumption by sector and source, Website www.eia.gov/forecasts/aeo/pdf/0383%282014%29.pdf.

16 Andrey A. Konoplyanik, "European Gas Market under Third Energy Package," Slides 17–19 of presentation given at European Gas Conference 2011 (January 25–28, 2011), Website http://core. theenergyexchange.co.uk/agile_assets/1279/09.40_Andrey_Konoplyanik.pdf.

17 "Energy in Europe: The Gas Man Cutteth," *The Economist* (September 20, 2014).

18 James Henderson, The Oxford Institute for Energy Studies, Oxford University, "Sanctions and the Future of Russian Oil and Gas," presentation at Center on Global Energy Policy, Columbia University (December 4, 2014).

19 "Briefing European Energy Security: Conscious Uncoupling," *The Economist* (April 5, 2014).

20 Blue Stream, Website www.gazprom.com/about/production/projects/pipelines/blue-stream.

21 Nord Stream, Website www.nord-stream.com; the video on how the pipeline was built is of interest.

22 Jonathan Stern (Director of Gas Research), "Natural Gas in Europe—The Importance of Russia," Oxford Institute for Energy Studies, Map 6 (2003), Website www.centrex.at/en/files/study_stern_e. pdf.

23 Robert Lea, "Europe Plunged into Energy Crisis as Russia Cuts off Gas Supply via Ukraine," *The Daily Mail* (January 19, 2015), Website www.dailymail.co.uk/news/article-1106382/Europe-plunged-energy-crisis-Russia-cuts-gas-supply-Ukraine.html.

24 South Caucasus pipeline project, Websites http://az-scpc.com; www.bp.com/en_az/caspian/opera tionsprojects/pipelines/SCP.html.

25 Charles Recknagel, "Nabucco Pipeline Suffers Setback as Rival Expected to Get Azeri Gas," Radio Free Europe (June 27, 2013), Website www.rferl.org/content/nabucco-gas-pipeline-rivals-future-in-doubt/25030223.html. See also John Daly, "Romania Pulls Plug on Nabucco Pipeline," oilprice. com: Oil and Energy Insider (August 25, 2013), Website http://oilprice.com/Geopolitics/Europe/Romania-pulls-plug-on-Nabucco-pipeline.html.

26 "Russia's South Stream Pipeline in Deep Freeze as EU Tightens Sanctions Noose," *The Telegraph* (September 13, 2014), Website www.telegraph.co.uk/finance/newsbysector/energy/oiland gas/10750840/Russias-South-Stream-pipeline-in-deep-freeze-as-EU-tightens-sanctions-noose. html. See also "Screams and Streams," *The Economist* (June 21, 2014), for a detailed description of pressure placed on the Bulgarian government which led to South Stream's downfall.

27 Darya Korsunskaya, "Putin Drops South Stream Project to EU, Courts Turkey," Reuters (December 1, 2014), Website www.reuters.com/article/2014/12/01/us-russia-gas-gazprom-pipeline-idUSKC N0JF30A20141201. See also "Gazprom Announces Final Nail in the South Stream Coffin," RT (January 14, 2015), Website http://rt.com/business/222619-bulgaria-south-stream-gazprom.

28 "Trans-Caspian Gas Pipeline Vital to Nabucco," Petroleum Economist (October 17, 2011), Website www.petroleum-economist.com/Article/2918721/Trans-Caspian-gas-pipeline-vital-to-Nabucco. html.

29 See TAP, Website www.tap-ag.com, and TANAP, Website www.tanap.com/en.

30 "PM Davutoglu Calls TANAP Project 'Dream Come True,'" World Bulletin (September 19, 2014), Website www.worldbulletin.net/turkey/144684/pm-davutoglu-calls-tanap-project-dream-come-true.

31 "AGRI LNG: Potential for Project High If European Demand Remains Firm," Natural Gas Europe (April 22, 2013), Website www.naturalgaseurope.com/agri-pipeline-lng-potential.

32 Germain Moyon and Marina Koreneva, "Greece Seals Russia Pipeline Plan as Putin Pledges to Work with West," Yahoo News (June 19, 2015), Website http://news.yahoo.com/russia-greece-agree-build-gas-pipeline-104935019.html.

33 Ewa Krukowska and Jonathan Stearns, "EU Regulators Propose 30% Energy-Savings Target for 2030," Bloomberg News (July 23, 2014), Website www.bloomberg.com/news/2014-07-23/eu-regu lators-propose-30-energy-savings-target-for-2030.html.

34 Jason Bordoff and Trevor Houser, "American Gas to the Rescue?" Columbia/SIPA Center on Global Energy Policy (September, 2014).

35 "Conscious Uncoupling: Reducing Europe's Dependence on Russian Gas is Possible—But It Will Take Time, Money and Sustained Political Will," *The Economist* (April 5, 2014).

36 "Power of Siberia," Gazprom, Website www.gazprom.com/about/production/projects/pipe
lines/ykv.

37 "Putin: Russia, China Close to Reaching 2nd Major Gas Deal," RT Business (November 7, 2014),
Website http://rt.com/business/203087-putin-china-gas-deal.

38 Vadim Kravets, "ESPO Holding Back Production," Russian Oil and Gas Technologies (September
10, 2014), Website www.rogtecmagazine.com/blog/tag/espo-pipeline.

39 Ilya Arkhipov, Stephen Bierman, and Ryan Chilcote, "Rosneft Says Exxon Arctic Well Strikes Oil,"
Bloomberg News (September 27, 2014), Website www.bloomberg.com/news/2014-09-27/ros
neft-says-exxon-arctic-well-strikes-oil.html#disqus_thread.

40 Christina Larson, "China's Oil Pipeline through Myanmar Brings Both Energy and Resentment,"
Business Week (February 4, 2014), Website www.businessweek.com/articles/2014-02-04/chinas-oil-
pipeline-through-myanmar-brings-both-energy-and-resentment.

41 "Tajikistan, China to Build Natural Gas Pipeline," *Asia Energy Journal* (September, 2013),
Website http://asiaenergyjournal.com/tajikistan-china-to-build-natural-gas-pipeline-2684. See also
"Turkmenistan, Tajikistan to Discuss Construction of Gas Pipeline Branch to China," Trend
(September 12, 2014), Website http://en.trend.az/business/energy/2311032.html.

42 "'Supergiant' Gas Field Discovered off the Coast of Egypt," Aljazeera News (August 30, 2015), Website
www.aljazeera.com/news/2015/08/gas-field-discovered-coast-egypt-150830172919161.html.

43 "Mozambique—The Emergence of a Giant in Natural Gas," SPTEC Advisory (January, 2013),
Website www.sptec-advisory.com/SPTEC_Advisory-Mozambique-The_Emergence_of_a_giant_
in_Natural_Gas.pdf. See also Devon Maylie and Daniel Gilbert, "Anadarko's Controversial
Mozambique Project Shows Appetite for Natural Gas," *The Wall Street Journal* (August 11, 2014),
Website http://online.wsj.com/articles/anadarkos-controversial-mozambique-project-shows-
appetite-for-natural-gas-1407810602.

44 "On the Brink of a Boom: Africa Oil and Gas Review," PwC (PricewaterhouseCoopers) (September,
2014), Website www.pwc.co.za/en_ZA/za/assets/pdf/oil-and-gas-review-2014.pdf. See also
Mikael Holter, "Statoil, BG to Build Tanzania LNG Plant in Lindi, Minister Says" (February 14,
2014), Website www.bloomberg.com/news/2014-02-14/statoil-bg-to-build-tanzania-lng-plant-
in-lindi-minister-says.html.

45 "Potential for Regional Use of East Africa's Natural Gas," Briefing Paper by the Sustainable
Engineering Lab of Earth Institute, Columbia University (May, 2014).

46 Alexis Arthur, "Shale Oil and Gas Latest Frontier for South America," oilprice.com (June 5, 2014), Website
http://oilprice.com/Energy/Energy-General/Shale-oil-and-gas-the-latest-energy-frontier-
for-South-America.html.

47 L. Barroso, H. Rudnick, S. Mocarquer, R. Kelman, and B. Bezerra, "LNG in South America: The
Markets, the Prices, and Security of Supply," IEEE (2007), Website ieee.org. The article can also be
obtained by a Google search of title.

48 "How Do Combustion Turbines Work?" Duke Energy, Website www.duke-energy.com/about-
energy/generating-electricity/oil-gas-fired-how.asp.

49 David L. Chase, "Combined-Cycle Development Evolution and Future," GE Power Systems,
Website http://site.ge-energy.com/prod_serv/products/tech_docs/en/downloads/ger4206.pdf.

50 The new Siemens H-class combined-cycle power plant has an efficiency of over 60 percent versus
the US average of 42 percent, *Popular Science*, Page 59 (June, 2013).

51 Black and Veatch, "Levelized Cost of Energy Calculation," Website http://csep.efchina.org/rep
ort/20112844913435.70772110666485.pdf/Levelized%20Cost%20of%20Energy%20Calculation_
BV_EN.pdf. See also "Levelized Cost of Electricity: Renewable Energy Technologies Study,"
Fraunhofer Institut for Solar Energy Systems (ISE) (November, 2013), Website www.ise.fraunhofer.
de/en/publications/veroeffentlichungen-pdf-dateien-en/studien-und-konzeptpapiere/study-leve
lized-cost-of-electricity-renewable-energies.pdf.

52 Chairman of the Federal Reserve Board Alan Greenspan's testimony before the House of
Representatives Energy and Commerce Committee (June 10, 2003), Website www.federalreserve.
gov/boarddocs/testimony/2003/20030610/default.htm.

53 The main source on the background of fracking is Gregory Zuckerman, *The Frackers* (London, UK: Penguin Group, 2013). See also Russell Gold, *The Boom* (New York, NY: Simon & Schuster, 2014).

54 The Eastern Gas Shales Project results are contained in Pennsylvania Department of Conservation and Natural Resources, Website www.dcnr.state.pa.us/topogeo/econresource/oilandgas/marcellus/marcellus_egsp/index.htm.

55 Gregory Zuckerman, *The Frackers* (London, UK: Penguin Group, 2013). The book covers the principal leaders in developing the shale gas industry including Aubrey McClendon of Chesapeake Energy.

56 Philip K. Verleger, Jr., "The Amazing Tale of U.S.: Energy Independence," International Economy (Washington, DC: Spring, 2012). The conflict with hedging as an executive of a company to mitigate risk at the behest of the lenders by shorting futures and of gambling (seeking out risk) by simultaneously buying futures is also covered in *The Frackers*.

57 "The Unsung Masters of the Oil Industry," *The Economist* (July 21, 2012).

58 In 2005, Dick Cheney as Vice President under President G.W. Bush and as former CEO of Halliburton, supplier of fracking fluids, obtained an exemption in 2005 of fracking fluids from the provisions of the Safe Drinking Water Act (SDWA), part of the Energy Policy Act of 2005 and the Clean Drinking Water Act. This permits fracking fluids suppliers from revealing their ingredients to state and federal EPAs to protect their intellectual property rights.

59 Dajahi Wiley, "The Questionable Staying Power of the U.S. Shale Boom," Wall St. Cheat Sheet (June 7, 2014), Website http://wallstcheatsheet.com/business/the-questionable-staying-power-of-the-u-s-shale-boom.html/?ref=YF.

60 The American Petroleum Institute has a video that describes the fracking process at Website www.api.org/oil-and-natural-gas-overview/exploration-and-production/hydraulic-fracturing/hydraulic-fracturing-safe-oil-natural-gas-extraction. Answers to common questions concerning the disposal of waste water from oil and gas operations including fracking are provided by the Independent Petroleum Association of America, Website http://energyindepth.org/wp-content/uploads/2015/02/Wastewater-Disposal-Q-and-A1.pdf.

61 "Technically Recoverable Shale Oil and Shale Gas Resources," US Energy Information Administration, Attachment C, Table A-1: U.S. Remaining Shale Gas and Oil Reserves and Undeveloped Resources (June, 2013), Website www.eia.gov/analysis/studies/worldshalegas/pdf/overview.pdf. Natural gas resources are estimated by Advance Resources International, Website www.adv-res.com. Global assessments are from Tables 4 and 5.

62 Sarah Miller Llana, "As Poland's Fracking Future Turns Cloudy, So Does Europe's," *The Christian Science Monitor* (July 24, 2013), Website www.csmonitor.com/World/Europe/2013/0724/As-Poland-s-fracking-future-turns-cloudy-so-does-Europe-s.

63 Summary of Shale Gas Workshop at Peking University sponsored by Peking University, Columbia University Center on Global Energy Policy, and Columbia University Law School (January 8, 2014).

64 "Assessment of the Potential Impacts of Hydraulic Fracturing for Oil and Gas on Drinking Water Resources (External Review Draft)," Environmental Protection Agency (June 4, 2015), Website http://cfpub.epa.gov/ncea/hfstudy/recordisplay.cfm?deid=244651.

65 "EIA Marcellus Region Drilling Productivity Report," EIA (August, 2014), Website www.eia.gov/petroleum/drilling/pdf/marcellus.pdf.

66 A description of ECO-Pad can be found on the Continental Resources Website www.contres.com/operations/technologies/eco-pad.

67 Memsys Clearwater has a clear explanation of how the system works on Website www.memsys.eu.

68 GasFrac explains its process on Website www.gasfrac.com.

69 Suzanne Goldenberg, "Fracking Hell: What It's Really Like to Live Next to a Shale Gas Well," *The Guardian* (December 14, 2013), Website www.theguardian.com/environment/2013/dec/14/fracking-hell-live-next-shale-gas-well-texas-us. See also Alex Halperin, "Texas: When Fracking Comes to Town," Aljazeera America (April 28, 2014), Website http://america.aljazeera.com/features/2014/4/texas-when-frackingcomestotown.html.

70 "Profitable Green Drilling," Prometheus Energy (September, 2014), Website www.prometheusenergy.com.

71 Kevin Begos, "Landmark Fracking Study Finds No Water Pollution," Associated Press (September 16, 2014), Website http://finance.yahoo.com/news/landmark-fracking-study-finds-no-160237470. html.

72 Roxana Witter, Lisa McKenzie, Kaylan Stinson, Kenneth Scott, Lee Newman, and John Adgate, "Use of Health Impact Assessment for a Community Undergoing Natural Gas Development," *American Journal of Public Health*, Vol. 103, No. 6, Page 2002 (June, 2013).

73 Mary Begg-Saffar, Co-Chair, International Association of Oil and Gas Producers Legal Committee presentation "Recent developments from the European Union affecting the E&P (Exploration and Production) Industry," made at AIPN (Association of International Petroleum Negotiators), Spring Conference, New York (2014).

74 Leonard Geophysical Observatory of the Oklahoma Geological Survey, Website www.okgeosurvey1. gov/pages/earthquakes/faq.php.

75 "Scholarly Articles for Fracking and Earthquakes," Website www.google.com/search?q=fracking +and+earthquakes&ie=utf-8&oe=utf-8&aq=t&rls=org.mozilla:en-US:official&client=firefox-a&channel=np&source=hp. A more definitive link between fracking and earthquakes is A. McGarr, B. Bekins, et al., "Coping with Earthquakes Induced by Fluid Injection," *Science Magazine*, Vol. 347, No. 6224 (February 20, 2015), Website www.sciencemag.org/content/347/6224/830.

76 Rong-Gong Lin II, "Depletion of Central Valley's Groundwater May be Causing Earthquakes," *Los Angeles Times* (May 14, 2014), Website www.latimes.com/local/la-me-quake-water-20140515-story. html.

77 Colin Shelley, *The Story of LPG* (New York, NY: Poten & Partners, 2003).

78 This is no different than playing dice in a gambling casino—in the long run, the casino wins! This was verified in a television interview with Steven Wynn, a Las Vegas gambling palace tycoon; when asked whether he knew anyone who was a net winner in gambling over the long haul, his response was an unequivocal "no!"

79 "US Shale Gas Realigns LPG Carrier Fleet," Shipping Herald (April 4, 2013), Website www. shippingherald.com.

80 All LPG statistics, including fleet numbers, from *LPG in World Markets* (New York, NY: Poten & Partners). Fleet data as of April 2014.

81 "Quarterly Natural Gas Liquids Report," Energy Ventures Analysis, Website http://evainc.com/ publications/quarterly-ngl-report.

82 "Iran–Pakistan Gas Pipeline could be Extended to China," *The Times of India* (August 24, 2013), Website http://timesofindia.indiatimes.com/business/international-business/Iran-Pakistan-gas-pipeline-could-be-extended-to-China/articleshow/22030498.cms.

83 Shoshanna Solomon, "Israel Nears Gas Sales to Egypt as Mideast Unrest Flares," Bloomberg (August 21, 2014). See also "Confirmed: Israel to Supply Gas to Egypt in $4 Billion Deal," Israel National News (October 20, 2014), Website www.israelnationalnews.com/News/News.aspx/186340#. VEUn_CfD-Ma.

84 Attributed to Frederic Bastiat, Website http://mises.org/page/1447/Biography-of-Frederic-Bastiat-18011850. But others disagree; see Website http://econlog.econlib.org/archives/2013/08/ when_goods_dont.html.

85 *BP Energy Statistics* (London, UK: British Petroleum, 2014).

86 Altair provide a PDF file on CNG (compressed natural gas) vessels that can be downloaded from its Website at www.altairproductdesign.com. See also EnerSea Transport, Website http://enersea.com/ understanding-cng.

87 Michael Tusiani and Gordon Shearer, *LNG: A Nontechnical Guide* (Tulsa, OK: PennWell Books, 2007).

88 The story of the Trinidad LNG project is chronicled in a series of articles on the Atlantic LNG project in *Energy Day* (June, 1999) and also Alexei Barrionuevo, "How Trinidad Became a Major U.S. Supplier of Liquefied Natural Gas," *The Wall Street Journal* (March 13, 2001). See also Atlantic LNG, Website www.atlanticlng.com.

89 *BP Energy Statistics* (London, UK: British Petroleum, 2014).

90 The International Group of Liquefied Natural Gas Importers (GIIGNL) consists of 74 member companies in 24 countries whose purpose is to exchange information among its members to improve the safety, reliability, and efficiency of LNG imports. Much of the information that follows is from its publication "The LNG Industry for 2013," Website www.giignl.org/sites/default/files/PUBLIC_AREA/Publications/giignl_the_lng_industry_fv.pdf.

91 "World's LNG Liquefaction Plants and Regasification Terminals," Global LNG Info, Website www.globallnginfo.com/world%20lng%20plants%20&%20terminals.pdf.

92 David Shukman, "The Largest Vessel the World has ever Seen," BBC News (December 16, 2014), Website www.bbc.com/news/science-environment-30394137.

93 "World LNG Report," International Gas Union, Website www.igu.org/sites/default/files/node-page-field_file/IGU%20-%20World%20LNG%20Report%20-%202014%20Edition.pdf, provides a thorough analysis of the status of world LNG. Figures are primarily in LNG throughput capacity rather than units.

94 "World Estimated LNG Landed Prices," Website www.ferc.gov/market-oversight/mkt-gas/overview/ngas-ovr-lng-wld-pr-est.pdf.

95 "Applications Received by DOE/FE to Export Domestically Produced LNG," Department of Energy (January, 2014), Website http://energy.gov/sites/prod/files/2014/02/f7/Summary%20of%20LNG%20Export%20Applications.pdf.

96 "A Guide to LNG: What All Citizens Should Know," FERC, Website www.ferc.gov/industries/lng.asp. See also Cheniere presentation by Charif Souki delivered to the Howard Weil Energy Conference (2012) and Christopher Smith, "Oregon LNG Granted Approval to Export to Non-FTA Countries," *Oil and Gas Journal* (July 31, 2014), Website www.ogj.com/articles/2014/07/oregon-lng-granted-doe-approval-to-export-to-non-fta-countries.html.

97 "Asian LNG Tanker Builders Vie for Market Share," *Wall Street Journal* (December 20, 2013), Website http://online.wsj.com/articles/SB10001424052702304866904579269290895618508.

98 Shipbuilding History, Website www.shipbuildinghistory.com/history/highvalueships/lngactivefleet.htm.

99 PFC Energy Shipping Database, Website http://pfcenergy.com.

100 Excelerate Energy, Website http://excelerateenergy.com.

101 "Problem of Boil-Off in LNG Supply Chain" (2013), Website http://hrcak.srce.hr/file/161548.

102 "Guide for Propulsion Systems for LNG Carriers," American Bureau of Shipping (ABS) (February, 2014), Website https://www.eagle.org/eagleExternalPortalWEB/ShowProperty/BEA%2520Repository/Rules%26Guides/Current/112_PropulsionSystemsforLNGCarriers/Pub112_LNG_Propulsion_GuideDec05. See also "LNG: Mathematical Solution for Selection of LNG Carrier Propulsion Systems," MAN B&W Diesel.

103 "Advantages of Dual Fuel Diesel Electric Propulsion of LNG Carriers," Liquefied Gas Carrier (Safety and Operational Matters), Website www.liquefiedgascarrier.com/advantages-electrical-propulsion-LNG-carrier.html. See also Sriram Balasubramanian, "Operational Advantages of Tri-Fuel Diesel Electric Propulsion (TFDE) Over Diesel Propulsion," Marine Insight (August 23, 2011), Website www.marineinsight.com/tech/main-engine/operational-advantages-of-tri-fuel-diesel-electric-propulsion-tfde-over-diesel-engine-propulsion.

104 "Total's LNG Newbuilding Duo Flipped to Gas Fueling," Tradewinds (2014), Website www.tradewindsnews.com/weekly/343244/Totals-LNG-newbuilding-duo-flipped-to-gas-fuelling.

105 "Bubbling Up: An International Gas Market Is Developing. Buyers Will Gain More than Sellers," *The Economist* (May 31, 2014).

106 "About Natural Gas Vehicles," Questar Gas, Website www.questargas.com/FuelingSystems/NGVInfoSheet.pdf.

107 Lockheed Martin, Website www.lockheedmartin.com/us/news/features/2013/lng-michoud.html.

108 "Special Areas under Marpol," International Maritime Organization (IMO), Website www.imo.org/en/OurWork/Environment/SpecialAreasUnderMARPOL/Pages/Default.aspx.

109 "Information on North American Emission Control Area (ECA) Under MARPOL Annex VI" (May 13, 2010), Website www.epa.gov/otaq/regs/nonroad/marine/ci/mepc1-circ-re-na-eca.pdf.

110 Shipping Research and Finance, Website http://shippingresearch.wordpress.com/2012/07/31/how-many-ships-are-there-in-the-world.

111 "Shipping Industry's Response to ECA 2015," *International Shipping News* (February 9, 2015).

112 "ExxonMobil Launches ExxonMobil Premium HDME 50 Marine Fuel," ExxonMobil Marine Fuels and Lubricants (July 9, 2014), Website www.exxonmobil.com/MarineLubes-En/Files/exxonmobil-premium-hdme-50.pdf.

113 "Fuelcast Special Report: Gas Demand in the Transportation Sector," Energy Ventures Analysis (March, 2014).

114 Elengy operates LNG terminals in France including trucking of LNG to customers. Website www.elengy.com/en/commercial-section/lng-truck-loading.html.

115 Jerome Sava, "Taking the Mystery out of Lubricity," *Fuel Oil News* (March, 2010), Website http://fueloilnews.com/2010/03/04/taking-the-mystery-out-of-lubricity.

116 "CNG Station Design: What You Need to Know," NGV Advantage, New Jersey Natural Gas, Website www.njng.com.

117 As a footnote to history, the iconic Pony Express only lasted about 18 months until Western Union completed the first transcontinental telegraphic line. Message delivery time dropped from 10 days to seconds and was far cheaper, stopping the Pony Express dead in its tracks!

118 Information on converting automobiles and other information on CNG vehicles can be obtained from CNG Now, Website www.cngnow.com/Pages/information.aspx.

119 "Refueling at Home," CNG Now, Website www.cngnow.com/vehicles/refueling/Pages/refueling-at-home.aspx. 800 W for an assumed 10 hour charge is 8,000 Wh or 8 kWh; at 10–12 cents per kWh, this is a very low cost, as is the cost of acquiring the compressor. However, these costs may not be representative, but even so, owning and operating a home compressor may not be as costly as one would expect. One industry has opined that the all-inclusive cost of natural gas is equivalent to $2 per gallon for gasoline.

120 Critical measurements of various sized CNG tanks are available at Luxfer Gas Cylinders at Website www.luxfercylinders.com/products/alternative-fuel-cylinders/443-type-3-alternative-fuel-cylinder-specifications.

121 Advanced Research Projects Agency-Energy (ARPA-E), Website http://arpa-e.energy.gov/?q=slick-sheet-project/efficient-conversion-natural-gas. See also Gas Technology Institute (GTI), Website www.gastechnology.org/news/Pages/New-NGV-Storage-Material-Technologies-to-Lower-Cost-of-Light-Duty-Vehicles.aspx.

122 "Natural Gas Vehicle Knowledge Base," NGV Global, Website www.iangv.org.

123 Egheosa Onaiwu, "How Much of a Future Is There for Gas-to-Liquids (GTL) as a Gas Monetisation Option?" Centre for Energy Petroleum, University of Dundee (circa 2010), Website www.dundee.ac.uk/cepmlp/gateway/index.php?view_all&pg=162 and select article.

124 A listing of Qatar Petroleum's GTL projects can be found on the Website http://extranet.qp.com.qa/qp.nsf/web/bc_new_projects_gtl.

125 "Pearl GTL—An Overview, Shell Global," Shell Oil, Website www.shell.com/global/aboutshell/major-projects-2/pearl/overview.html.

126 "Chevron's Escravos GTL Project Finally Gets off Ground," *BusinessDay* (September 3, 2014), Website http://businessdayonline.com/2014/09/chevrons-escravos-gtl-project-finally-gets-off-ground/#.VGetfsmDD-s.

127 "GTL Projects Blossoming Around the World," J.E. Sinor Consultants, Website http://edj.net/sinor/sfr1-01art9.html.

128 Kevin Bullis, "Chasing the Dream of Half-Priced Gasoline from Natural Gas," MIT Technological Review (January 15, 2014), Website www.technologyreview.com/news/523146/chasing-the-dream-of-half-price-gasoline-from-natural-gas.

129 "The Global Sour Gas Problem," Stanford Energy Club (November 26, 2012), Website http://energyclub.stanford.edu/journalitem/the-global-sour-gas-problem.

130 "Sour Gas: A History of Expertise," Total, Website www.total.com/sites/default/files/atoms/file/total-sour-gas-history-expertise.

131 "U.S. Coal Bed Methane Production," Energy Information Agency, Website www.eia.gov/dnav/ng/hist/rngr52nus_1a.htm.

132 "Coal Bed Methane," World Coal Institute, Website www.worldcoal.org/coal/coal-seam-methane/coal-bed-methane. Data extracted from IEA Clean Coal Centre 2005.

133 Yuhan Zhang, "China's Unconventional Gas Potential," Economist Intelligence Unit (March 4, 2015), Website http://country.eiu.com/article.aspx?articleid=1032927687&Country=China&topic=Economy&subtopic=Regional+developments#.

134 "BCM Around the World," BCM Asia Development, Website www.mudomaha.com/sites/default/files/lng.pdf.

135 "Integrated Process of Coalbed Brine and Methane Disposal," National Energy Technology Laboratory, Website www.netl.doe.gov. See also "Coal Mine Methane Use in Brine Water Treatment," Environmental Protection Agency, Website www.epa.gov.

136 Richard Anderson, "Coal Gasification: The Clean Energy of the Future?" BBC News Business (April 13, 2014), Website www.bbc.com/news/business/26921145. See also UCG Association, Website www.ucgassociation.org, and Five-Quarter Energy Company, Website www.five-quarter.com/#!five-quarter-and-the-big-picture/cf65, for a description of its process.

137 "Methane Hydrates," Oak Ridge National Laboratory, Website http://web.ornl.gov/info/reporter/no16/methane.htm.

138 William Harris, "How Frozen Fuel Works," How Stuff Works, Website http://science.howstuffworks.com/environmental/green-tech/energy-production/frozen-fuel4.htm.

139 "Methane Hydrate: The Next Energy 'Game Changer,'" Geoscience News and Information, Website http://geology.com/articles/methane-hydrates.

140 Sarah Battaglia, "Japan's Methane Hydrates and the Future of Global Energy," The Oil Boom Investor (March 19, 2013), Website http://theenergycollective.com/sbattaglia/200361/methane-hydrate-future-of-energy.

141 Darren Spalding and Laura Fox, "Challenges of Methane Hydrates," *Oil & Gas Financial Journal* (May 7, 2014), Website www.ogfj.com/articles/print/volume-11/issue-5/features/challenges-of-methane-hydrates.html.

142 "Energy Resource Potential of Methane Hydrate," National Energy Technology Laboratory, Website www.netl.doe.gov/File%20Library/Research/Oil-Gas/methane%20hydrates/MH-Primer2011.pdf.

143 "Volume of a Compressed Gas in a Cylinder," Air Liquide, Website www.alspecialtygases.com/volume_of_gas_in_a_cylinder.aspx.

8 Nuclear and Hydropower

Nuclear power supplies 4.4 percent of global energy demand in 2014 and hydro 6.8 percent. Nuclear power generates 10.8 percent of global electricity, supplying 22 percent of electricity in Europe and the Former Soviet Union (FSU), 18 percent in North America, and 4 percent in Asia. Hydropower supplies 16.5 percent of global electricity, supplying 17 percent of electricity in Europe and the FSU, 13 percent in North America, 54 percent in South America, and 15 percent in Asia. The public generally views nuclear power as dangerous, while hydro is considered benign. This is not quite true for either. There have been over 16,000 reactor-years of safe commercial plant operation in 33 nations over 60 years, and one can add about the same equivalent span of safe operation for nuclear powered warships.[1] The two worst accidents by far were Chernobyl, a case of an unsafe reactor design unsafely operated, and Fukushima Daiichi, a case of ignoring tsunami warnings etched on prehistoric monoliths. Hydropower has its environmental opponents and dam failures have drowned tens of thousands. This chapter covers the principal aspects of nuclear and hydropower as energy sources and their future contribution in meeting mankind's seemingly insatiable demand for energy.

Promise of Nuclear Power

Nuclear power is the outgrowth of the nuclear weapons program to transform the world's most destructive weapon to peaceful uses. The 1953 launching of the Atoms for Peace program foretold a world where commercial nuclear energy would be safe, clean, abundant, and too cheap to even meter! Three Mile Island buried the myth that nuclear power was inherently safe. Nuclear power is clean as it does not generate greenhouse gas emissions and air pollutants such as sulfur and nitrous oxides, particulates, toxic and carcinogenic hydrocarbons, and heavy metals. But Chernobyl showed that nuclear power is not clean if the integrity of the reactor is violated. Fukushima Daiichi is an ongoing disaster continuing to spew forth huge quantities of radioactivity into the Pacific Ocean, affecting background radiation level over vast areas of the Pacific as far away as 5,500 miles on the US west coast. Fukushima is an ongoing disaster as no way has yet been devised to contain radioactive leakage. Fukushima has cast a pall over the entire industry that may never go away.

Nuclear power is abundant in terms of uranium resources to power the world, but there are physical constraints on how many nuclear reactor plants can be built in terms of industrial capacity to manufacture reactors and containment systems, means to dispose of spent fuel assemblies, and availability of suitable sites. Another constraint, which is most critical, is public acceptance. And nuclear power is not cheap, with construction cost overruns in the billions of dollars and project delays lasting a decade or more. Furthermore, nuclear generated electricity rates do not cover the ultimate disposal of spent fuel assemblies, a hidden government subsidy for the industry, along with providing insurance to cover the contingency of a plant accident. More importantly, they do not cover the incalculable costs on human health and suffering from Chernobyl and Fukushima. Yet there may be a new day for nuclear power emerging from the rubble of Chernobyl and Fukushima: fail-safe reactors—reactors that cannot suffer a core meltdown because there is no core!

Contribution of Nuclear Power to Satisfying Energy

Figure 8.1 shows the growth in nuclear consumption in terms of the amount of oil that would have been burned to generate an equivalent amount of electricity.[2]

The upward sweep in nuclear power output for North America during the 1980s did not result from building more nuclear plants. Reorganization of the electricity industry from a regulated cost-plus regime to a more liberalized competitive business environment was chiefly responsible for the higher nuclear power output. Under a cost-plus regulatory regime, there was no incentive to get more out of a nuclear power plant than what was convenient. In a liberalized competitive environment, the profit motive residing within deregulation (or liberalization) improved capacity utilization from 65 percent in 1980 to 90 percent in 1990 by better scheduling of maintenance and refueling to reduce downtime and greater reliance on nuclear power to take advantage of its low variable cost.

Nuclear power's contribution to meeting global energy demand leveled off in the early 2010s. Decline in Europe's nuclear output was from retiring the older segment of German nuclear power plants in the wake of Chernobyl. The halving of Asian output was the shutting down of Japanese nuclear power plants in the wake of Fukushima. Aggregate

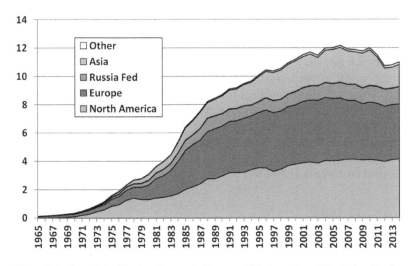

Figure 8.1 Growth in Nuclear Power in Terms of Displaced Fossil Fuels (mmBpd)

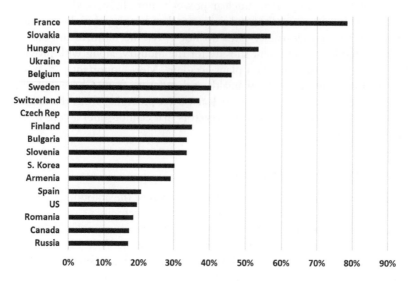

Figure 8.2 Percentage of Electricity Generated by Nuclear Power

nuclear power output enjoyed an uptick in consumption in 2014, but it is possible that more plants will be shut down, particularly in the US. But the long-term trend for nuclear output is up as China, India, and Russia roll out their nuclear plant construction program. The role of nuclear power in satisfying electricity generation shows a dramatic difference in attitudes toward nuclear power among various nations (Figure 8.2).[3]

France leads with 78 percent of its electricity generated by nuclear power. France is a leader in standardizing nuclear plant design and in generating relatively low-cost electricity, which is exported to other European nations. Japan was a major world nuclear producer of electricity before Fukushima. The center of operating nuclear power plants in Asia is now S. Korea. While in relative terms over half of electricity generated in Slovakia and Hungary is from nuclear power, and the US and Russia are near the bottom of Figure 8.2 in terms of share of electricity from nuclear power, this does not accurately portray these nations in absolute terms. Figure 8.3 shows the nations that generate the most electricity by nuclear power.

The US leads the world in nuclear energy output. With global output of nuclear energy at 2,537 tWh, the US alone accounts for 33 percent and, in conjunction with France and Russia, 57 percent of output, the top five nations account for 69 percent, and all 11 nations account for 87 percent (Figure 8.3). Japan accounted for 11 percent of world nuclear power in 2010 before shutting down its nuclear power plants. While S. Korea was included but not China in Figure 8.2, in Figure 8.3 China is on stage to become a major contributor to nuclear power.

Future Contribution of Nuclear Power

Despite predictions of a phase-out of nuclear power plants and general pessimism over prospects for nuclear power since Fukushima, there are 66 nuclear power plants under construction in 2015 (24 in China, 9 in Russia, 6 in India, 5 in the US, and 4 in S. Korea)

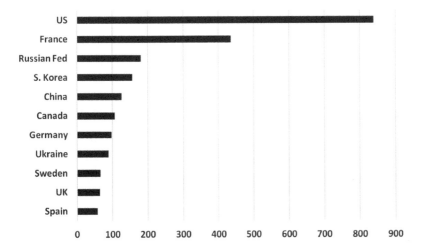

Figure 8.3 Nuclear Generated Electricity by Nations (tWh)

on top of a world fleet of 437.[4] The future of nuclear power is hinted at in Figure 8.4 where some nations are contemplating massive numbers of reactor construction projects.

The world inventory of nuclear reactors numbers 437, but over 50 of these have been taken out of service. Nearly all 43 reactors in Japan were shut down in reaction to the Fukushima tragedy, but a few may be reactivated if the government can obtain public support. Eight older German reactors are permanently retired, with the remaining nine scheduled for shut down by 2022 in reaction to the Chernobyl tragedy. Five US nuclear reactors may be retired. This loss of operating capacity will be more than made up by the 66 reactors under construction. Moreover, there are 168 reactors in the planning stage

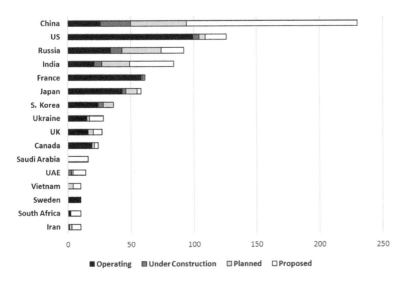

Figure 8.4 Reactors Operating, Under Construction, Planned, and Proposed (2015)

and 322 reactors in the proposal stage, the sum of which exceeds the present population of nuclear plants. While planned and proposed reactors do not mean that they will actually materialize, they do reflect the perceived role of nuclear power on the minds of energy policymakers. With regard to planned reactors totaling 168 reactors, China leads by far with 136, 35 in India, 18 in Russia, 17 in the US, 16 in Saudi Arabia, 11 in Ukraine, and 10 in the UAE. Nuclear plants in the Middle East will back out natural gas in generating electricity, which can then be exported as LNG. China is taking a very aggressive view toward nuclear power as a source of clean energy with no airborne pollution and greenhouse gas emissions. Although one may surmise that nuclear power in China and India is a means of attaining a cleaner environment by reducing the role of coal in generating electricity, the fact remains that future energy demand for these nations will maintain coal consumption close to current levels. Nuclear power is to satisfy incremental growth in energy demand. On the other hand, Poland has six reactors in the planning stage as part of a policy to curb carbon emissions and air-borne pollution by reducing coal generated electricity.[5]

A large portion of the population of US nuclear plants have been in service for four decades as the US was a very early entrant into nuclear power. Some reactors are already being phased out from age, repair costs, and the changing electricity market. Phase-outs will accelerate in 2025 for a phase-out age of 55 years, or 2030 for a phase-out age of 60 years. Over the subsequent 20 years, essentially all existing US reactors will be retired. Given that nuclear plants generate nearly 20 percent of the nation's electricity (and account for 63 percent of its carbon-free electricity), even a modest increase in electricity demand would require 13.2 gW of new nuclear capacity by 2025, or about 13 new plants of 1 gW average output (1 gW is sufficient to supply the needs of a city of one million). With five nuclear plants currently under construction, another eight would have to be built for nuclear power to maintain its 20 percent share of electricity generation if the nuclear plant phase-out age is 55 years. While 22 plants are in the planning or proposal stage, intense opposition by environmental groups and those who may find themselves living near a nuclear power plant would make building of new nuclear reactor facilities in the US problematic. If nuclear plants retire after 60 years of operation, 22 gW of new nuclear capacity would be needed by 2030, and 55 gW by 2035, to maintain a 20 percent nuclear share.[6] At a cost of replacement of $8,000 per kilowatt for plant construction, a 1 gW plant would cost $8 billion, or $176 billion to replace 22 gW of nuclear plant capacity by 2030. In this light, all 22 reactors in the planning or proposal stage would essentially be replacements for retiring plants, not expansion of nuclear capacity. Conceivably there could be some expansion of nuclear capacity as new plants have a higher electricity output and greater utilization rate than those being retired, but siting for these new plants and getting approval to proceed with construction are going to be extremely challenging.

Retirement may occur sooner rather than later in the US. Eleven risk factors have been identified for nuclear plants such as competition from lower cost energy sources, falling electricity demand, safety retrofit expenses, costly repairs, and rising operating costs. Thirty-eight US reactors out of a total fleet of 100 exhibit four or more of these risk factors and are vulnerable to an earlier-than-expected retirement.[7] In addition to five nuclear power plants currently closed or scheduled to be closed, six others seem likely to be closed.[8] Reasons for the Vermont Yankee nuclear plant closing in 2014 were intense environmental objections to its continued operation, high regulatory costs, competition from natural gas power plants that provide lower cost electricity, and "disadvantageous market structures." The cost of decommissioning this plant is not cheap: $1.24 billion of decommissioning costs include terminating the Nuclear Regulatory Commission operating license ($817 million), spent fuel management ($368 million), and site restoration ($57 million).[9] It should not be surprising if natural gas and renewable solar and wind substitute for nuclear power at least in the early years of needed replacement. To the extent that this occurs, nuclear power will not be able to maintain its 20 percent share of the electricity market. And this appears to be happening. Of the applications for 24 new reactors received by the Nuclear Regulatory Commission, only two are being built, nine applications have been withdrawn, and serious doubt exists about the prospects for the remainder.

The primary culprit is not opposition from environmentalists and townspeople, but natural gas, whose price has fallen so dramatically as a result of fracking that nuclear power is no longer competitive. Estimates of $40 per megawatt-hour of capacity for natural gas places $100 per megawatt-hour for nuclear power in a disadvantageous position.[10] Even though a natural gas plant must buy fuel, fixed costs for a nuclear power plant are higher compared to a natural gas plant's fixed and variable costs at this time. One benefit of a nuclear power plant is that once built the cost of electricity in constant dollars shows little variation over time. Much of the cost of electricity is associated with financing the plant established at the time of completion. Remaining costs are primarily fixed such as personnel, repair, and maintenance expenses. Variable costs are minor, quite unlike electricity from fossil fuel plants whose fuel costs are significantly affected by fluctuations in coal and natural gas prices. Though fuel assemblies have to be continually replaced over the life of a nuclear plant, an annualized fixed cost element covers the manufacture and installation of new fuel assemblies. Thus, the only variable cost is in acquiring uranium for the manufacture of fuel assemblies, which is not a major cost driver in the grand scheme of things. From the perspective that nuclear generated electricity is relatively insensitive to fluctuations in uranium costs, the electricity rates for nuclear power are similar in structure to fuel-free hydro, solar, and wind power, but not quite the same. Hydro, solar, and wind have lower fixed operating costs than nuclear, which makes nuclear power more vulnerable to inflation.

Subsidizing Nuclear Power Plants

Nuclear power in the US has been criticized for being heavily subsidized. Figure 8.5 shows the sharing of $14.9 billion of subsidies to specific energy sources for electricity generation in 2013.[11] This is not an inclusive listing of energy subsidies—only those subsidies directly attributable to electricity generation excluding subsidies paid to biofuels (ethanol) and loan guarantees. Subsidies paid to the natural gas and oil industry are substantially higher than those indicated in Figure 8.5, as little oil is dedicated to electricity generation. The $14.9 billion in subsidies excludes $1.2 billion in subsidies to smart grid and transmission facilities, which are more or less shared by all electricity sources. However, subsidies for transmission might favor solar and wind farms to the extent that these facilities are located in remote areas. Renewables in Figure 8.5 are aggregated subsidies for biomass, geothermal, hydropower, and others. Out of a total of $14.9 billion, 50 percent is for direct subsidy payments and grants, 39 percent in tax benefits, 9 percent for research and development, plus 2 percent for others.

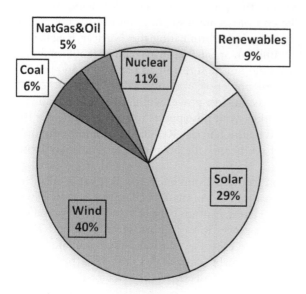

Figure 8.5 Sharing of Electricity Subsidies among Energy Sources (2013)

The largest share of subsidies, 40 percent, is paid to wind, followed by 29 percent for solar. Counting biomass, geothermal, hydropower, and others, the renewable energy slice of the electricity subsidy pie is 78 percent. Nuclear power is only 11 percent, followed by fossil fuels, also at 11 percent. However, there are hidden subsidies for nuclear power such as the government obligation to dispose of spent fuel in permanent storage, which is currently in abeyance, plus a contingent liability in the form of catastrophic insurance in case of a nuclear accident. Nevertheless, the subsidy argument against nuclear power does not have much in the way of substance.

A different view occurs when the annual subsidy is divided by megawatt-hours of electricity output in Figure 8.6.[12] Bearing in mind that the average retail price of electricity being in the vicinity of $0.12 per kilowatt-hour, most subsidies represent a very small portion of the retail price—that is, eliminating subsidies paid by the government and substituting a surcharge on retail electricity rates pertinent to the source of electricity would not be that noticeable except for solar and, to a lesser extent, wind.

The subsidy for solar in terms of cents/kWh is huge and perhaps should be excluded. Unlike other forms of energy, solar power receives heavy state (California and others) support for installing private solar systems, which, understandably, is not accounted for in federal figures. Superficially the high cents/kWh for solar power is caused by the amount of electricity generated by solar being far smaller than wind with somewhat comparable sized federal subsidies. Of concern is that the statistics for solar electricity output may be understated. Data on electricity are provided by utilities, independent power providers, and commercial and industrial sources, which would account for essentially all electricity generated by renewables and traditional fuels except solar. Solar output data appears to exclude installations generating electricity for internal consumption by individuals and businesses. Furthermore, it is not clear whether federal subsidies to electricity sources cover subsidies

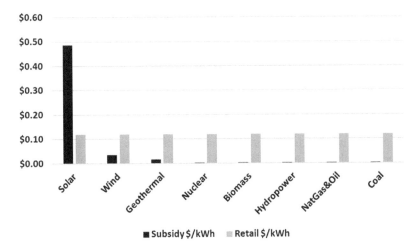

Figure 8.6 Annual Subsidy Cost Expressed as Cents/kWh of Output (2013)

paid for private installations. It is possible that the calculation for solar power subsidies expressed as cents/kWh is greatly distorted. The point of this diversion is not so much to question the validity of the cents/kWh assessment in Figure 8.6, but to question published figures for solar power output. They may be significantly understated if private solar power installations for internal consumption are excluded from official oversight.[13]

The high cost of nuclear plants in the US is that each one is uniquely designed. Capital costs can be significantly reduced in building nuclear plants by standardizing "cookie-cutter" plants, built principally in the way Ford manufactured Model Ts. Series production of just a few types of plants in terms of output would eliminate enormous cost overruns and construction delays associated with the one-of-a-kind nuclear plants that dominated the American landscape. Advancements in nuclear power technology, coupled with series production of a standard plant design built as modules in a central manufacturing facility and shipped to a plant site, would make the cost of electricity from nuclear plants more attractive compared to fossil fuel plants. This is how France addresses nuclear power plant construction, totally different than having a unique design for every plant as practiced in the US. An economic analysis would further favor nuclear power plants if a cap and trade program for carbon credits or a tax on carbon had been enacted. At this point in time, what has to be accomplished before any renaissance of nuclear power becomes possible is assuring the public that human errors and circumstances responsible for the Three Mile Island incident and the Chernobyl and Fukushima accidents cannot happen again. This was not an easy sell after Chernobyl, but after Fukushima, it is a hard sell.

Comparing Nuclear with Coal

Base load needs are most commonly handled by large nuclear and coal-fired plants. In 2013, the US generated 1,586,000 gWh of electricity from coal, consuming 858.35 million short tons.[14] This implies that a gigawatt-hour requires 540 tons of coal. A 1 gigawatt coal-fired power plant operating one full year, or 8,640 hours, at 100 percent utilization consumes 4.67 million tons of coal, releasing 8.73 million tons of carbon dioxide each year.[15] In addition, a potentially large quantity of sulfur dioxides can be released into the environment, depending on the sulfur content of coal and the effectiveness of the plant's scrubbers. Moreover, there are emissions in the form of particulate matter (soot) unless removed by precipitators; nitrous oxides; plus health-affecting emissions of mercury, cadmium, and arsenic. A nuclear plant of the same size releases none of these emissions and consumes about 25 tons of enriched uranium (3.5–5 percent of the isotope U235) per year, which requires over 200 tons of uranium oxide concentrate produced by mining 25,000–100,000 tons of ore depending on the uranium concentration. The annual waste from a nuclear power plant is less than 30 tons of spent fuel, albeit a highly radioactive and toxic waste. If reprocessed (chopped up and dissolved in acid to recover fissionable material for recycling), the volume of spent fuel can be reduced significantly, easing the burden of providing permanent storage facilities.

Uranium

Uranium is as common as tin and is mined both on the surface and underground. Of the world's reserves of 5.4 million tons of uranium (not uranium ore), 31 percent is located in Australia, 12 percent in Kazakhstan, 9 percent each in Canada and Russia, and 5 percent each in South Africa, Namibia, Brazil, Niger, and the US.[16] Figure 8.7 shows the share of 56,217 tons of uranium production (not uranium ore) by nations in 2014.

Kazakhstan is the world's largest uranium producer, accounting for 42 percent. The top three nations, including Canada and Australia, account for two-thirds of world production. In terms of individual mines, the largest is McArthur River (Canada) supplying 13 percent of world production, Tortkuduk and Myunkum (Kazakhstan) each 8 percent, Olympic Dam (Australia) 6 percent, and Somair (Niger) 5 percent. These mines are responsible for one-third of output. The top nine mines produce 50 percent and the top 15 nearly two-thirds of world uranium. Nearly half of uranium ore is mined on the surface or underground and nearly half by uranium extraction by in situ leaching (ISL) and a small amount as a byproduct

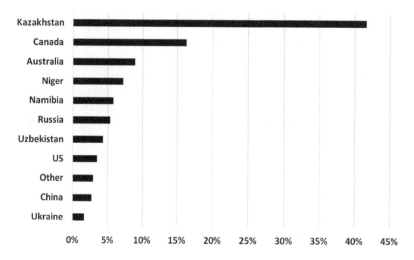

Figure 8.7 Share of Uranium Produced by Nations (2014)

of other mining activities. ISL or in situ recovery is the fastest growing method of mining and accounts for nearly all production in the US, Kazakhstan, and Uzbekistan and is being introduced into Australia, China, and Russia. A local supply of water is needed and ore must be permeable to allow liquid passage. An impermeable layer of rock should separate the ore body from fresh groundwater to prevent contamination. However, in many uranium ore bodies, no prevention has to be taken because groundwater is not potable with high concentrations of salt, uranium, radon, arsenic, sulfides, and other minerals. Groundwater is pumped to the surface and an oxidant is added, the most common oxidants being sulfuric acid and hydrogen peroxide depending on type of ore. Water with oxidant passing through the ore body chemically unites with uranium (this method can also be used for gold and copper), and "pregnant" water is pumped to the surface into evaporation ponds. After water is evaporated, uranium residue is processed the same as in mining. With sufficient recycling of water and oxidants, up to 70–90 percent of the uranium can be removed from the ore body. Besides high recovery rates, the other advantages of ISL are no disturbance to the geology by moving earth and ore, no tailings, and no unsightly landscape common in surface mining.[17]

Uranium ore is first finely ground, then leached with sulfuric acid to remove uranium, called yellow cake, which is about 80 percent uranium oxide concentrate (U_3O_8). In the next stage of production, yellow cake is transformed to uranium fluoride gas. Both gaseous diffusion and high-speed centrifuge processes take advantage of U235 being slightly lighter than U238. These processes create two streams of uranium fluoride gas: one enriched and the other depleted of U235. Starting with a concentration of 0.7 percent U235, the enriched stream ends up with a concentration of about 3.5–5 percent U235, depending on the type of reactor, and a depleted stream of nearly pure U238. Pure U238 is 1.7 times as dense as lead and can be used for reactor shielding and armor piercing shells. Although most is stockpiled, some U238 has been drawn down to mix with highly enriched uranium released from Russian and US weapons programs for transformation to reactor fuel. Enriched uranium fluoride is converted to uranium dioxide (UO_2), pressed into small cylindrical ceramic pellets, and inserted into thin tubes of zirconium alloy or stainless steel to form fuel rods. These are then sealed and assembled into reactor fuel assemblies and placed in the core of a nuclear reactor. The core of a 1,000 mW or 1 gW reactor contains about 75 tons of enriched uranium. The presence of a moderator such as water or graphite slows down neutrons sufficiently for the U235 isotope to fission (or split) in a chain reaction that produces heat to transform water to steam. From that point on, generation of electricity is the same as in a fossil fuel plant.

Uranium reserves for conventional reactors can last over a century. Reserves can be extended by a factor of 100 or more by reprocessing spent fuel to capture plutonium generated by the fission process and any residual U235 left in the fuel, by breeder reactors designed to create their own fuel, and by utilizing thorium, which becomes fissionable when transformed to U233 in a nuclear reactor. Taking into consideration uranium life extension through reprocessing, breeding, and transforming thorium to fissionable material, some view nuclear energy as a virtually inexhaustible source of energy that can last thousands of years.

Physics of a Nuclear Reactor

U235 fissions or splits into fission byproducts such as barium and krypton, releasing about 2.5 prompt or fast neutrons and other products. Fission byproducts also decay, releasing delayed (or slow) neutrons. Both prompt and delayed neutrons are necessary to maintain criticality (a constant rate of fission). Slowing down fast neutrons in a moderator such as graphite or water is necessary for the neutrons to be absorbed by fissionable material in a conventional reactor. The exception is fast breeder reactors that depend only on prompt or fast neutrons to maintain criticality. The total mass of fission byproducts is less than the original U235 atom, and heat released is equivalent to the loss of mass multiplied by the square of the speed of light (Einstein's famous $E = mc^2$). This equation implies that mass can be viewed as a highly concentrated form of energy.

From the perspective of converting matter to energy, a nuclear bomb and a nuclear reactor are similar. But a nuclear bomb is designed to have a runaway reaction, whereas a nuclear reactor is designed to prevent a runaway reaction. A nuclear bomb concentrates over 90 percent fissionable material for a single explosive event. A nuclear reactor disperses a low concentration (3.5–5 percent) of fissionable material within a fuel assembly, along with channels for the coolant to pass through and to insert neutron-absorbing control rods. It is impossible for a nuclear reactor to sustain a nuclear explosion, but it is possible for the core to melt down from heat generated by radioactive decay during a loss of coolant accident. Core meltdown would result in a release of radioactivity, possibly creating conditions within a compromised core for a chemical explosion. If the primary and secondary containment systems are breached, radioactivity can escape to the environment.

A reactor is shut down when control rods are fully inserted. Control rods are made of a neutron-absorbing material such as cadmium that removes slow neutrons from sustaining a chain reaction. To operate a reactor, control rods are pulled out until a critical mass is formed where a self-sustaining chain reaction can occur (a constant number of fissions over time). The power output of a reactor is increased by pulling control rods further out to increase the fission rate. A reactor control system scrams (shuts down) the reactor by rapid insertion of control rods if system performance does not fit a tight set of conditions. Heat is generated within a reactor by the transfer of kinetic energy from fission byproducts to molecules in the fuel rod and then to molecules in the coolant and by the slowing down of neutrons in the moderator. With exceptions, the coolant is normally water flowing through channels within assemblies of fuel rods and control rods. Nearly all fission products are locked in the fuel rod to ensure that the coolant has a low degree of radioactivity. Water not only serves as a moderator to slow down neutrons but also transfers heat from reactor to steam generators to drive the electricity turbine generators.[18]

See the Companion Website for a section on Nuclear Incidents and Accidents: www.routledge.com/cw/nersesian.

Weapons Proliferation

The chain reaction within a reactor core transforms some of the U238 to various plutonium isotopes. What is of particular concern is fissionable plutonium 239 (Pu239) that remains in the spent fuel when about 75 percent of the U235 has been consumed. A typical light water reactor breeds about 8 kg of Pu239 per month of operation, although one-third undergoes fission, supplying more power to the reactor. The possibility of nuclear weapons made from Pu239 extracted from spent fuel has been of concern to the world community for many years. With regard to weapons proliferation, only 15 kg of Pu239 can make a crude nuclear weapon, and more sophisticated varieties require less, which represents about 2 or 3 months of reactor operation. Pu239 can be separated chemically from spent fuel after it is ground up and dissolved in acid. The International Atomic Energy Agency (IAEA) was set up by the United Nations in 1957 to ensure that nuclear materials at reactor sites and at enrichment and reprocessing facilities are not diverted to nuclear weapons manufacture. The IAEA undertakes regular inspections of civilian nuclear facilities to verify the accuracy of submitted documentation, checks inventories, and undertakes the sampling and analysis of materials. Safeguards are designed to deter diversion of nuclear material by early detection and export controls on sensitive technology from the UK and the US and other nations.

Safeguards are backed up by the threat of international sanctions encompassed in the Nuclear Nonproliferation Treaty to curb the diversion of uranium from civilian to military use. Nearly every nation with a nuclear capability is a signatory of the treaty, except Israel, Pakistan, and India.[19] The potential, real or otherwise, for diversion of Pu239 from spent fuel from a reactor in Iran for nuclear weapons is unsettling the world community. Particularly, Iran has publicly announced its intention to use these weapons against Israel, even noting that it will only take two nuclear bombs to destroy the nation. Sanctions placed against Iran to stop any diversion of Pu239 to weapons use may have caused personal hardship for the people and perhaps even slowed the development of nuclear weapons, but they have not stopped Iran in its quest to become a Middle East nuclear power. Iranian mullahs assert that if Pakistan, India, and North Korea have developed nuclear weapons without world sanctions, why cannot Iran? The US–Iran nuclear deal signed in 2015 will allow Iran to effectively have a nuclear bomb in 10 years in return for an immediate lifting of sanctions after the treaty is approved. This will change the nuclear dynamic in the Middle East. Considering the one-sided terms of the treaty, one wonders how the US benefited—certainly Israel and the Arab states wonder. There is also some doubt about whether the treaty will be approved by a two-thirds vote of the senate or whether their vote would have any meaning.

A new weapon of mass destruction has arisen for the terrorists' arsenal. It consists of a metal container filled with highly radioactive spent fuel ground to fine particles, surrounded by conventional explosives. When detonated, the explosion vaporizes and disperses particles as an aerosol, spreading lethal amounts of radioactivity over a wide area. It takes only a few micrograms of ingested or inhaled Pu239 to prove fatal. It is known that terrorists have considered flying an airliner into a nuclear power plant. While containment systems, with walls typically 4 feet thick of steel-reinforced concrete, are designed to sustain an unintentional crash of a jet liner, they may not be able to sustain the intentional head-on ramming of an airliner at full speed.

Disposal of Spent Fuel

About one-third of fuel assemblies are removed from nuclear reactors each year as spent fuel and replaced with fresh fuel. Spent fuel still contains about 96 percent of its original uranium with its fissionable U235 content reduced to less than 1 percent. Highly radioactive spent fuel gives off heat and is normally stored in a spent fuel pool at the reactor site; water prevents radiation into the environment and absorbs radioactive decay heat. After 3 years, the heat rate has been reduced enough for dry storage where air ventilation is sufficient to keep the fuel assemblies cool, but this has to be considered temporary storage because radioactivity will persist for tens of thousands of years, far beyond the life of the plant.

Spent fuel can either be sent to permanent storage or reprocessed. Reprocessing plants, located in Europe, Russia, and Japan, separate uranium and plutonium. Recovered uranium is converted back to uranium fluoride and reenriched with U235. Plutonium can be blended with enriched uranium to produce a mixed oxide fuel called MOX. MOX has been used commercially since the 1980s with about 2,000 tons fabricated and loaded in power reactors. Europe has about 40 reactors in Belgium, Switzerland, Germany, and France licensed to use MOX, with 30 reactors loaded with MOX. Japan has about ten reactors licensed, with several loaded with MOX. MOX fuel assemblies generally make up about one-third of a core, but some may have as much as half. France and Japan (before Fukushima) planned to expand the role of MOX and some new advanced light water reactors are able to accept complete fuel loadings of MOX if desired. The US has done some development work in the past with MOX, but does not favor reprocessing of spent fuel assemblies as a result of a decision made early on. Considering the build-up of the number of spent fuel assemblies with no permanent facility for storing them, perhaps it is time to reconsider this decision.

Fifty percent MOX does not change the operating characteristics of a reactor, but a reactor has to be designed to accept MOX, including having more control rods. An advantage of MOX is that the fissile concentration of fuel can be increased easily by adding plutonium, whereas enriching uranium to higher levels of U235 is relatively expensive. Higher levels of U235 or MOX fuel extends the time between refueling. Higher uranium prices act as an economic incentive to reprocess spent fuel. The separated fissionable plutonium in MOX reduces the need for uranium. MOX also reduces the volume of spent fuel. Seven spent fuel assemblies give rise to one MOX assembly plus high-level radioactive waste, reducing the volume, mass, and cost of disposal by about a third.[20] The reduced but more radioactive waste is disposed by vitrification where it is mixed in liquefied Pyrex glass, which contains neutron-absorbing boron, and poured into steel canisters. One ton of reprocessed waste is embedded in five tons of glass.[21]

The problem now is where to store the canisters. Final disposition sites for these canisters have not been built, but geological formations made of granite, volcanic tuff, salt, or shale are being examined. One proposal is to drop glass canisters into ocean trenches for "natural" disposal. Glass does not corrode or crack, preventing the escape of radioactive material into the environment. Canisters are adequately shielded with 5 to 7 miles of ocean water. If the ocean trench is also a subduction zone, over millions of years, canisters will be dragged into the earth's mantle, melted, and dispersed. It is possible that waste could return to the earth's surface in volcanic lava in some tens of millions of years; but by then its radioactivity will have been long gone.

Public objections to dumping nuclear toxic waste in ocean trenches have ruled out what may be a very practical solution to nuclear waste. Yet, there is a precedent. About two billion years ago, at a place called Oklo in Gabon, West Africa, six "nuclear reactors" operated naturally within a rich vein of uranium ore that went critical when saturated with water. The water acted as a moderator and the "reactors" remained critical, producing heat that evaporated the water, stopping the nuclear reaction. New water entering the uranium vein restarted the nuclear reaction. It is felt that the nuclear reaction lasted for about 30 minutes and switched off for about 2.5 hours.[22] The pulsing reactor, similar to what happened in the 1999 nuclear incident at Tokaimura, continued to operate for several hundred thousand years, generating radioactive fission byproducts until running out of fuel. Radioactive residue, which once totaled over 5 tons of fission products and 1.5 tons of plutonium, has all decayed into harmless nonradioactive stable elements. This is the natural disposal of spent fuel waste. It has been theorized that another natural reactor or reactors exists in the earth's core, maintaining its high temperature and keeping its outer layer liquid and rotating to induce enormous flows of electricity responsible for the protective magnetic field. Evidence for this is radioactive fission products found in the mantle and unexplained changes in geomagnetic strength that may be linked to variability (pulsations) in natural reactor output.[23]

The problem with land storage is that radioactivity will persist for many tens of thousands of years, far exceeding recorded history. Any water seepage into the storage area could become contaminated and affect the surrounding water table. There are a number of proposals that are being advanced for developing permanent storage facilities, but none making much headway. The most publicized proposed permanent storage site was Yucca Mountain in Nevada. Congress approved this site in 2002 after $4 billion and 20 years of study (another subsidy for the nuclear power industry). It was to be licensed by the Nuclear Regulatory Commission after it had examined the suitability of Yucca Mountain's geology, hydrology, biology, and climate. Factors favoring Yucca Mountain were its remote location with regard to population centers, its dry climate, and large depth of an underlying water table. An unexpected source of opposition was the state of Nevada, which had second thoughts about becoming the nation's sole nuclear waste depository (dumpsite). Nevada filed a lawsuit against the US Department of Energy for using public rail transport to ship spent fuel to the site. This suit became moot when in 2009 the Obama administration cut off further funding for studying the feasibility of Yucca Mountain as a national depository for nuclear waste. Consequently, several utilities have filed suit since the federal government agreed to provide a permanent storage facility as a precondition for building nuclear reactor plants.

Sweden advanced the idea of burying highly toxic radioactive waste in 25 ton copper capsules 500 meters deep in granite that was essentially free of cracks and fissures.[24] This project was placed in abeyance soon after the Fukushima accident. Without any permanent storage on line or scheduled to be constructed, spent fuel will continue to be kept in cooled water at nuclear plant sites, accumulating in volume with the passage of time.

Commercial Reactors

Enrico Fermi, "father of the atomic bomb," built the first nuclear reactor in a squash court at the University of Chicago as part of the Manhattan Project in 1942. The nuclear "pile" consisted of slotting pellets of uranium into a pile of graphite bricks in a carefully arranged geometry with embedded cadmium control rods to absorb neutrons. The pile eventually grew sufficiently in size to allow a nuclear reaction to start when the control rods were withdrawn from the center of the pile. An axe man was stationed on top of the pile to chop a rope that would send the main control rod crashing back into the core to stop the reaction if it were starting to get out of control. "Scram"—or shut down a reactor—is the acronym for "safety control rod axe man."

The start of the peaceful use of nuclear power was a small boiling water reactor (BWR) built for a nuclear submarine, a project spearheaded by Admiral Hyman Rickover in 1954. The first commercial reactor was a pressurized water reactor (PWR) built in 1957 at Shippingport, PA—since decommissioned. Others were to follow, but these early reactors were really prototypes built to gain expertise before building larger units. A BWR feeds steam directly from the reactor to the turbines that drive the generators. This introduces a low level of radioactivity to the steam turbines, condensers, and associated piping, but is simpler in design, though with less thermal efficiency than a PWR. A PWR operates under higher pressure and contains a heat exchanger between the reactor coolant and water to feed a steam generator. This precludes any reactor coolant from entering the steam generator, turbine, and associated equipment, and higher temperatures possible with a PWR design improve thermal efficiency. PWRs, operating at higher pressures than a BWR, present a more dangerous situation in case of a reactor vessel rupture. Most reactors in the US are either BWRs built by General Electric or PWRs built by Westinghouse, and both use light or normal water as a moderator. Nuclear reactors are found in 30 nations, with half in the US, Japan, and France. The world fleet of 437 reactors, including those not in operation in Germany and Japan, are capable of producing 372 gW of electrical power for an average of 0.86 gW per reactor. Of these, 277 are PWRs and 80 are BWRs used worldwide. Pressurized heavy water reactors use natural uranium, but the coolant/moderator is not light water but heavy water with deuterium (a proton and neutron) in place of hydrogen (a proton) in water molecules. While light water absorbs neutrons, deuterium does not and is a more efficient moderator than light water. While heavy water reactors generate cost savings in not having to enrich uranium, there is a cost in producing heavy water and these costs have to be analyzed to decide which type of reactor to build. Forty-nine heavy water reactors (CANDU and an improved CANDU 6) are located mainly in Canada (22 reactors), India (10 and building more), S. Korea (7), Pakistan (3), Romania (3), China (2), and Argentina (2).[25] There are also 15 gas-cooled reactors in the UK, with carbon dioxide as the coolant and graphite as the moderator. Carbon dioxide circulates through the core where it is heated before passing through steam generator tubes contained within a concrete and steel pressure vessel. Steam from the generator passes through the pressure vessel to steam turbines that drive electricity generators. Russia has 15 light water-cooled graphite moderated reactors and two fast neutron reactors.[26]

Fast Neutron and Fast Breeder Reactor

Fast neutron and fast breeder reactors depend only on prompt or fast neutrons, not delayed or slow neutrons, to maintain a chain reaction, requiring a greater degree of technological sophistication. A fast breeder reactor is designed to create more plutonium 239 from irradiating uranium 238 than fissionable material consumed. Thus, fast breeder reactors can extend uranium reserves forever, at least from the perspective of human existence. A fast neutron reactor does not create more plutonium 239 than fissionable material consumed and thus has an extended core life compared to conventional reactors. Over 400 hours of operating history are associated with 22 fast neutron reactors, most built for experiment or as prototypes. Those still in operation include one experimental fast reactor in China, an experimental and a demonstration (400 mW) fast reactor in India, an experimental and a demonstration (714 mW) fast reactor in Japan, and two experimental fast reactors, a demonstration (1,470 mW) and a commercial (2,100 mW), in Russia.[27]

European Pressurized (Evolutionary Power) Reactor

France has been a leader in nuclear power and is still a leader in the post-Chernobyl world. The major differences between nuclear power in the US and in France are public attitudes toward nuclear power and the organization of nuclear power activities.[28] After the oil crisis of 1973, France did not have the requisite coal and natural gas reserves of the US to rely on for electricity generation. French people accepted a government decision to pursue nuclear power because of their respect for and trust in their civil servants and government officials, many of whom by training were scientists and engineers. Moreover, the nuclear power industry organization was placed under government oversight for every facet of its activities. The government was responsible for selecting a reactor design, which comes in three sizes (1,450, 1,300, and 900 mW of electricity). The "cookie-cutter" approach by limiting reactors to three varieties of a single design reduced the manufacturing and construction costs of nuclear components and facilities and simplified the process of licensing and permitting.[29] Efficiencies gained from progressing down the learning or experience curve of permitting, building, and licensing multiple units of essentially identical plants reduced scheduling delays, cost overruns, and capital costs.

The chosen design is simple and rugged, has a long life, is easy to operate, and is less vulnerable to operator errors and circumstances that could lead to a nuclear accident. Nuclear reactor plants are manufactured by the publicly traded corporation Areva (85 percent owned by the French government) and the German company Siemens. But nuclear electricity generating facilities and reprocessing plants are in government-owned companies with the government responsible for dealing with nuclear wastes. Government ownership reduces the risk premium that would have to be paid if financing were in private hands. Government involvement ensures a simpler regulatory regime and positive guidance over the future role of nuclear power in satisfying the nation's electricity needs. In the US, nuclear power plants satisfy base load needs, which means that they operate close to full capacity at all times. In France, nuclear power plants supply power for both base and variable needs. Some contend that continual cycling of power output when serving both base and variable needs affects safety from potential power surges and stressing of internal components, but apparently this does not seem to be a problem.[30]

The second-generation European pressurized reactor has been upgraded to the third-generation evolutionary power reactor (EPR) manufactured by a joint venture between Areva and Siemens. EPR has an output of 1,650 mW (1.65 gW) using a 5 percent enriched uranium oxide fuel or a 50 percent uranium plutonium mixed oxide fuel. A heavy neutron reflector surrounding the reactor core improves fuel utilization and protects the reactor pressure vessel against aging (metal fatigue). An axial economizer in each steam generator enhances steam pressure and plant efficiency. In addition to its enhanced and more efficient output, a major improvement incorporated into the EPR is safety built around a quadruple redundant safeguard of four independent emergency cooling systems. Its foundation is built to withstand the largest potential earthquake. A leak-tight containment system surrounding the reactor is augmented by an extra or secondary containment and cooling area built under the reactor base. This acts as a core catcher to handle the potential accident of a molten core penetrating the bottom of the primary reactor containment. The outer containment has a two-layer concrete wall, each 2.6 meters thick, designed to withstand an impact by aircraft and internal pressures from a reactor accident.[31]

These safety enhancements increase the cost of EPR, but economy of scale associated with its greater output can reduce the cost of electricity by 10 percent from existing plants. Unfortunately, in common with building the first of anything, the first EPR being built in Finland is suffering from huge cost overruns (three times over original budget) and scheduling delays (nearly 10 years behind schedule). But the learning or experience curve associated with series production should reduce cost overruns and scheduling delays for follow-on orders such as the two ordered by China's Guangdong Nuclear Power Company and one by Électricité de France. Another contract has been signed for two EPRs for nuclear steam generation by the UK firm EDF Energy (a consortium led by Électricité de France) for construction later in the decade. Unfortunately, these expected economies may not materialize as Areva itself, from a lack of sales and difficulties associated with the construction of EPRs, may have its reactor division purchased by Électricité de France, also 85 percent owned by the French government. To make matters worse for Areva, a new law coming into force in 2015 calls for the reduction of French dependence on nuclear power from 75 to 50 percent by 2025.[32]

Other Commercial Reactors

Westinghouse (once a leading US corporation, now owned by Toshiba, Shaw Group, and Ishikawajima-Harima Heavy Industries) has a third-generation AP1000 PWR with an output of 1,100 mW. AP1000 has a simple design incorporating standardization and modularity to reduce costs. The plant has both passive and active safety means to shut down the reactor. Passive safety depends on natural driving forces such as gravity flow, natural circulation, and pressurized gas to react to a hazardous condition without operator intervention and no electrical power for the first 72 hours. After that, operator interaction is necessary, but the reactor can remain in a safe mode indefinitely. This reactor would presumably have survived the Fukushima tsunami without violating its integrity.[33] Four units are being built in the US and four in China. General Electric with its partner Hitachi of Japan has introduced a third-generation advanced BWR (ABWR) of 1,350–1,460 mW of electricity generation with improved efficiency, safety, and reliability, as well as lower cost. The reactor has more protection against core damage, its design has been standardized and modularized to optimize construction, and has a demonstrated capital and operating cost structure from existing units. Four ABWRs have been built in Japan, with two plants under construction in Japan and another two in Taiwan.[34]

Pebble Bed Reactor

The concept of the pebble bed reactor is not new. It was proposed at the dawn of the nuclear age in 1943 when the Manhattan Project team led by Enrico Fermi sustained the first nuclear chain reaction in a pile of uranium-impregnated blocks of graphite at the University of Chicago. Farrington Daniels, a chemist, who joined the effort a short time later, proposed the harnessing of nuclear power for cheap, clean electricity using a reactor containing enriched uranium "pebbles" (a term borrowed from chemistry) cooled by helium transferring energy to a turbine driving an electricity generator. Under President Eisenhower's "atoms for peace" program, the newly created General Atomics division of General Dynamics assembled 40 top nuclear scientists in 1956 to brainstorm reactor designs. Edward Teller, "godfather of the H-bomb," argued that reactors must be inherently safe and advocated that the only acceptable design being one where every control rod could be pulled out without causing a meltdown. But Admiral Hyman Rickover's competing idea of building a water-cooled and moderated pressurized reactor with control rods to power submarines prevailed over a gaseous pebble bed reactor that satisfied Teller's criterion. Rickover's proposed design was adopted not only for nuclear powered submarines but by the utility industry to generate electricity.[35]

The pebble bed reactor idea did not entirely die with Rickover's decision. Rudolf Schulten, a German physicist, picked up on the pebble bed idea and spearheaded the building of a 15 mW demonstration reactor known as the AVR (Arbeitsgemeinschaft Versuchsreaktor) at the Julich Research Center in West Germany. The reactor was online in 1966 and ran over 20 years before being decommissioned in 1988 because of Chernobyl plus certain operational problems that occurred at that time. AVR was originally intended to breed uranium 233 from the much more abundant thorium 232, but pebbles of the AVR contained the fuel so well that transmuted fuels could not be economically extracted. Background radiation given off by the AVR was only one-fifth of that which would have been given off by a conventional reactor. Following this, a 300 mW thorium fueled pebble bed reactor was built in 1985 and operated for 3 years with over 16,000 hours of operations. It too was decommissioned as a result of Chernobyl along with the consequences of a jammed pebble in a feeder tube that released radiation.

Although there were research activities in the US and the Netherlands on pebble bed reactors, the baton for the next step of development passed to South Africa. In the mid-1990s, the national utility company, Eskom, petitioned to build a pebble bed reactor both for domestic use and for export. Opposition from the environmental group Earthlife Africa along with a lack of investor interest and commercial orders killed the ultimate objective of the program to build 20–30 165 mW pebble plants, each holding 450,000 pebbles to produce an aggregate output between 4 and 5 gW of electricity. In 2010 South Africa ceased funding the development program.[36] The baton of technological leadership has been handed over to China.

A pebble is a tennis ball sized micro-reactor made primarily of graphite with a diameter of 60 mm. The outer coating cannot be graphite. Graphite is slippery when cool but, when heavily radiated at high temperatures, becomes sticky, affecting the movement of pebbles within a reactor. Another problem is the need to protect heated graphite coming in contact with air and water, which would generate a hazardous chemical reaction as occurred at Chernobyl. Both problems are countered by coating the outer surface of a pebble with silicon carbide or a similar substance. Below this surface coating is a 5-mm graphite shell surrounding a graphite matrix containing 10,000–15,000 microspheres of coated particles within which is uranium fuel. The coated microspheres consist of an outer shell of pyrolytic carbon, then a barrier shell of silicon carbide, and then the inner shells of pyrolytic carbon and porous carbon buffer. In the center of a microsphere is enriched U235 or some combination of thorium and plutonium with unenriched uranium or MOX (a mixture of uranium and plutonium) from reprocessing conventional nuclear fuel assemblies or decommissioned nuclear weapons. Any release of radioactivity from a coated particle would be extremely small.

The primary safety feature of a pebble bed reactor is its low fuel density with a power density only one-thirtieth that of a PWR. The reactor is inherently safe for a total loss of coolant—no core meltdown occurs in a PWR as there is no core. A loss of coolant heats the pebbles up to a maximum temperature of 1,600°C, well below the 2,000°C needed to melt the ceramic coating surrounding each bit of fissionable fuel. As pebbles heat up, the frequency of fissions drops, which lowers the power output of a pebble reactor to a level where more heat escapes through the reactor wall than is produced by nuclear reactions. The reactor cannot crack, explode, melt, or spew hazardous materials: it simply remains at an idle temperature with pebbles intact and undamaged. Known as passive nuclear safety, the reactor's low fuel density allows more heat to escape than is generated in the absence of coolant rather than having to depend on an active nuclear safety feature such as inserting control rods and maintaining coolant. A pebble bed reactor is inherently safer than traditional reactors. It is impossible to have a runaway reaction as occurred at Chernobyl by a sudden withdrawal of control rods that caused the reactor to go supercritical or to have a partial core meltdown as at Three Mile Island or a total core meltdown as at Fukushima by a loss of coolant.

In order to ensure this inherent safety, the output capacity of pebble reactors is kept relatively small between 100 and 250 mW versus 1,650 mW for the EPR. Over a half dozen pebble reactors would have to be built at a single site for the same power output of an EPR. These increments in reactor capacity can be added at a central facility in response to growing demand, obviating the building of a large facility that must operate at partial power until demand grows to utilize its full capacity. Alternatively, pebble reactors can be built at diverse locations for a more distributive form of electricity generating system, reducing transmission costs. The modular design of pebble reactors allows for mass production at a central location for shipment by truck or rail to a facility site. The modular construction of a single design at a central site can significantly lower construction and safety certification costs.

Criticality is achieved by loading several hundred thousand pebbles in a reactor. Helium, an inert gas, is heated by passing through the spherical pebbles to a temperature of 500°C (932°F) at a pressure of 1,323 pounds per square inch (psi). Helium can be directly fed into turbines that drive generators to produce electricity, but this exposes turbines to low levels of radioactivity. An indirect system eliminates this problem by exchanging heat from reactor helium with helium fed to turbine generators, but this adds to costs. Helium, being less dense than steam, requires larger sized turbines. The energy output of the reactor is controlled by the flow of helium coolant passing through the pebbles. The higher temperature and lower pressure of a pebble reactor results in greater thermal efficiency (nearly 50 percent) than conventional reactors. As with conventional turbines, energy exchange is a function of pressure drop across the turbine, which can be maximized by cooling the exhaust helium with air. It is possible that hot helium exhaust from the turbines, rather than being cooled by air, can be used as a source of energy to heat water via a heat exchanger and generate more electricity via steam or be a source of hot water for industrial purposes. Cooled exhaust helium is then pressurized by compressors for recycling through the reactor. Lower operational pressure reduces the cost of protecting against pressure breaks and hydrogen embrittlement of the reactor vessel and components. Redundant safety systems found in conventional nuclear reactors are not required in a pebble reactor and its pebbles are far less radioactive. Containment building must be capable of resisting aircraft crashes and earthquakes and the internal pressure from a release of hot pressurized helium if the reactor vessel failed. This pressure would be far less than that experienced by the release of coolant in a PWR.

Inside the containment building is a thick-walled room containing the pebble reactor. Fuel replacement is a continuous process where pebbles are recycled from the bottom of the reactor to its top. Center pebbles of pure graphite act as moderators to slow down and reflect neutrons into pebbles containing fuel. The inner wall of the reactor container also has a graphite lining to reflect neutrons back into the reactor. A fuel-loaded pebble will recycle through the reactor 10 times over its normal 3-year life and is examined and tested for integrity when removed from the bottom of the reactor. If expended of fuel or damaged, a pebble is transferred to a nuclear waste area and replaced by a new one. Unlike spent fuel rods, it is exceedingly difficult to extract plutonium from a pebble. A 165 mW plant will produce about 32 tons of spent fuel pebbles per year, of which 1 ton is spent uranium. Storage for spent pebbles does not require the safety cooling system necessary to prevent the release of radioactive material from spent fuel assemblies. A pebble reactor plant facility will have sufficient storage for spent pebbles to cover its 40-year operational life.

China started with a prototype pebble bed reactor HTR-10 fueled by 27,000 pebbles, which achieved initial criticality at Tsinghua University in 2003 under the leadership of scientist Qian Jihui. Based on the continuing successful operation of this prototype, two fourth-generatoin high-temperature pebble bed modular nuclear reactor plants of 100 mW each have begun to be constructed at the Shidaowan plant (Huaneng Power International) in Shandong Province for completion in 2017.[37] These plants will produce electricity for the national grid, but could be used for cracking steam to produce hydrogen for fuel cell powered motor vehicles. Eighteen similar plants are in the planning stage. While China's massive expansion of nuclear energy will be primarily traditional PWRs, a small portion of the nuclear energy will be satisfied by pebble bed reactors. If successful in a commercial environment, pebble bed reactors are intended to fulfill a larger share of nuclear energy production.

Other Advanced Reactor Designs

Advances in nuclear technology have not been curtailed by Chernobyl. Active members of the Generation IV International Forum (GIF), organized in 2001, include Canada, China, Euratom, France, Japan, Russia, South Africa, South Korea, Switzerland, and the US. GIF works closely with the IAEA's International Project on Innovative Nuclear Reactors and Fuel Cycles (INPRO). Its recent efforts have been centered on the safety considerations of a sodium cooled fast reactor, which is felt to be the first fourth-generation nuclear reactor type under the GIF umbrella to be brought to a demonstration phase. (The pebble reactor being built in China is a fourth-generation nuclear reactor type not under the GIF umbrella.) In addition to the sodium cooled fast reactor (SFR), five other reactor designs under consideration are the lead cooled fast reactor (LFR), supercritical water cooled reactor (SCWR), very high temperature reactor (VHTR), and molten salt reactor (MSR). GIF pursues research and development activities to advance the technology and safety of these reactor types.[38]

The sodium cooled fast reactor (SFR) is a fast neutron, sodium cooled reactor with a closed fuel cycle for the efficient management of actinides, a group of 15 metallic radioactive elements found in spent fuel waste, plus plutonium. Important safety features of the system include a long thermal response time, a large margin to coolant boiling, it operates near atmospheric pressure, and it has an intermediate sodium system between the radioactive sodium in the primary system and the steam generator for the power plant. The problem with sodium as a coolant is that it reacts violently if in contact with water and is potentially highly corrosive outside the reactor. The lead cooled fast reactor (LFR) had its beginnings in Soviet submarines as a fast neutron reactor operating at high temperature and low pressure. The coolant is molten lead or a mixture of molten lead and bismuth (the mixture is eutectic, meaning that the boiling point of the mixture is less than the components that make it up). Lead and bismuth are chemically inert with good thermodynamic properties, which enhances the safety of the reactor and simplifies the design. Molten lead coolant passing through a steam generator powers a turbine driven electricity generator. The supercritical water cooled reactor (SCWR) is a combination of two known technologies: BWR and a supercritical water system that is in operation in hundreds of fossil fueled power plants. Supercritical water is at a temperature and pressure above a critical point where distinct liquid and gas phases do not exist; that is, it is not possible to distinguish supercritical water as either liquid or gas. Water is heated to supercritical conditions in the BWR (374°C and 3,205 pounds per square inch) and, as in a BWR, passes directly to a turbine to drive a generator. Advantages of SCWR are higher thermal efficiencies of 44 percent versus 35 percent for existing reactors and no reactor coolant pumps. The only pumps are feed water and condensate extraction pumps. The very high temperature reactor (VHTR) was originally developed in the 1970s–1980s and consists of fully ceramic coated particle fuel, graphite as the neutron moderator, and helium as the coolant. Leadership in developing VHTR is not GIF, but China constructing a variant of VHTR, the pebble reactor, for commercial operation.

Molten Salt Reactor (MSR)

MSR technology is only partly developed, with current research efforts taking place in Russia. One type of MSR that has great interest is the thorium reactor. Thorium is four times more plentiful than uranium. Of the estimated 6.4 million tons of thorium resources, 13 percent is in India, 10 percent in Brazil, and 9 percent each in Australia and the US. India has very little uranium. With six times more thorium than uranium, India is independently advancing nuclear technology to take advantage of its ample thorium supplies. India has inaugurated a three-stage reactor program of building a pressurized heavy water reactor to produce plutonium. In the second stage, plutonium will be fissionable fuel for a fast breeder reactor to breed uranium 233 from thorium. In the third stage, uranium 233 will be the fissionable fuel for an advanced heavy water reactor.[39] A simpler, but less developed, technology could be the thorium reactor.

The problem is that thorium (Th232) is not directly usable (fissionable) in a thermal neutron reactor. However, it is fertile when transmuted to uranium 233 (U233), an excellent fissile fuel. Thorium is similar to uranium 238, which transmutes to fissionable plutonium 239 by absorbing a neutron. Thorium reactors require that Th232 first be irradiated in a reactor to provide the necessary neutron dosing. Once created, U233 can either be chemically separated from the parent thorium and recycled as a new fuel or consumed in situ in molten salt reactors.

An example of a molten salt reactor is a liquid fluoride thorium reactor (LFTR) where thorium is in a molten salt of beryllium and lithium fluorides whose melt temperature can be reduced from 1,110°C to 360°C by adjusting the mix, another example of a eutectic mixture.[40] A core of U235 is initially needed to supply neutrons to transmute thorium to U233. At some point there is sufficient U233 for a self-sustaining production of neutrons and the initial loading of U235 is no longer needed. U233 fissions produce heat and sufficient neutrons to transform thorium, suspended in the liquid salt, to U233. The process remains self-sustaining as long as thorium is added and fission byproducts removed from the liquid salt. Heated fluoride salt liquid is pumped through a heat exchanger to another stream of nonradioactive liquid salt, which in turns heats helium or carbon dioxide or air to run a turbine generator. Safety is inherent in a reactor operating at atmospheric pressure with no danger of blowing itself apart. If the temperature rises too much, liquid salt is allowed to expand into empty tubes, which slows down the fission rate. If this turns out to be insufficient and temperature rises too high, power is cut to a cooling coil to maintain a plug of solid frozen salt. By cutting power, the plug melts and fluoride salt liquid within the reactor is diverted to an empty container that shuts down the nuclear reactions. Some of the advantages of LFTR are:

- thorium being four times more plentiful than uranium and almost free as a byproduct of rare earth mining;
- only 1 percent of the radioactive waste of a light water reactor with virtually no fissile materials;
- radioactive decay to safe levels is accomplished in hundreds of years, not tens or hundreds of thousand years, for conventional reactors;
- inherently safe by thermal expansion shutting down fissions with increasing temperatures;
- core is already in a molten state—no risk of coolant flashing to steam and no need for control rods;
- no periodic shutdowns for refueling;
- higher thermal efficiency of 44–50 percent compared to 33 percent for PWRs and BWRs;
- highly compact plants and scalable from small to large size capacity;
- operates at atmospheric pressure;
- simpler containment structure without having to contain potential escape of high pressure steam and hydrogen.[41]

Ideas Being Considered

An idea being considered is the addition of beryllium oxide to uranium dioxide in fuel pellets. Uranium dioxide has very poor heat conductivity properties, which means the center of a pellet has a much higher temperature than its edge. This temperature gradient shortens its useful life. By adding beryllium oxide, heat conductivity improves, resulting in a more uniform distribution of temperature within a pellet, extending its life, which, in turn, lowers nuclear fuel cycle and disposal costs. Beryllium, while expensive, can be retrieved from spent fuel and recycled.[42]

Another idea is small reactors. There have been a few in service to serve extremely remote communities in Antarctica and northern Russia with an output of 25–35 mW. Other small reactors serving local needs are in Argentina, Pakistan, India, and China. Pebble reactors being built in China are considered small reactors as their output is less than 300 mW. Another eight different types of small reactors are being offered as power sources for locations far removed from the main power grids.[43] Some thought has been given in burying small unmanned reactors deep in the ground where they would supply power to local communities. One market for small reactors are communities being served by diesel generators where the logistics cost of fuel is very high. These communities are focusing more on renewable sources (wind and solar) complemented by diesel than small reactors. A more likely market is military installations. Babcock & Wilcox is proposing a 180 mW reactor 13 feet in diameter and 83 feet tall. It is a modular reactor, meaning that it can be delivered to the construction site by truck.[44] NuScale Power has a proposed ultra-safe small modular reactor of 45 mW that can be scaled up to over half a million megawatts.[45]

Thought is being given to floating large sized nuclear power stations that would take advantage of two known technologies: nuclear power plants and offshore structures. The plants would be built at shipyards experienced in offshore drilling rigs, then installed with a nuclear power plant and towed to an offshore sight for mooring. Underwater power cables would connect the plant to shore. Offshore reactors would overcome the increasing difficulty of finding suitable sites, the ocean would be in effect an infinite heat sink, and the reactor can be cooled passively without electricity driven pumps if the core is below the sea surface. If moored in waters more than 100 meters deep, the height of a potential tsusami wave would not be sufficient to do any damage. At the end of the reactor's life, the nuclear power station would be towed away for dismantling at a suitable site. Russia is building two floating 35 mW nuclear power plants scheduled for completion in 2016. The power stations were intended to support Russia's energy requirements in developing Arctic Ocean oil and gas resources.[46]

Fusion Power

Whereas fission is the splitting of heavy atoms, fusion is uniting light atoms. The sun and stars produce heat when hydrogen atoms fuse to form helium, transforming matter into energy. Thus for fusion to work on Earth, an environment equivalent to being at the center of the sun has to be created, requiring temperatures over 15 million degrees Celsius and pressures over 340 billion times greater than atmospheric pressure. Hydrogen fusion on Earth is obviously quite a technological challenge, but fusion of deuterium and tritium, isotopes of hydrogen, is less demanding than hydrogen. Deuterium can be extracted from seawater and tritium is a byproduct of fission. The challenge is to design a magnetic field strong enough to contain plasma, a heated mix of electrons and ions, under conditions conducive to fusion (100 million degrees Celsius, much hotter than the center of the sun, to compensate for the sun's much higher pressure).

Neutrons are produced when fusion takes place and become a source of heat when trapped in a stainless steel containment vessel wall surrounding the fusion chamber. Heat is transferred to a water blanket outside the vessel to produce steam to run an electricity generator. Once fusion is triggered, it has to be controlled and kept self-sustaining by adding more fuel from a surrounding blanket of lithium in which neutrons react with lithium to produce tritium and helium. Leakage of plasma from the magnetic field is a major problem as it stops the fusion process. Until recently, more energy (electricity) was consumed to maintain the plasma than extracted from fusions. A positive energy balance has been achieved with fusion. With improved technology, it is estimated that half the electricity produced by fusion would be consumed to contain plasma within a magnetic field.

Fusion is inherently safe. A hydrogen bomb environment cannot be created because any "runaway" condition stops the fusion process by removing plasma. The trick is knowing how to keep plasma together long enough for fusion to occur. Alternative approaches to magnetic confinement as a means of trapping the hot plasma are lasers or particle beams. If fusion could be perfected, energy would be virtually inexhaustible. Radioactivity is limited to high-energy neutron bombardment of the containment vessel. This radioactivity is short-lived (100 years) compared to the radioactivity of a fission reactor (many thousands of years). An additional health hazard is the possibility of tritium leaking into the environment. Tritium is a radioactive proton with two neutrons and has a half-life of 12.4 years. Tritium can be bound with an oxygen atom and form an isotope of water. The body does not discriminate with water made of hydrogen and oxygen or tritium and oxygen. Once ingested, tritium is easily absorbed by the human body and becomes a constituent part of cells and remains in a human body for a long time, posing a serious threat to human health as it decays. The advantage of the deuterium–deuterium fusion process is that no tritium is involved.

Research in nuclear fusion is being conducted in the US, Russia, various European nations, Japan, Korea, China, Brazil, and Canada. In 2005, France was selected as the host nation for a multi-billion dollar experimental nuclear fusion reactor, the ITER (International Thermonuclear Experimental Reactor), to be funded by the European Union, the US, Japan, S. Korea, Russia, and China. Its goal is to produce 500 mW of power for hundreds or thousands of seconds at a time. Construction began in 2006 for completion in 2019.[47] It may take as long as 25 years before an acceptable design for a commercial fusion plant can be developed.

Another serious approach to achieving fusion is being taken by the National Ignition Facility (NIF). The NIF is a consortium of government and private organizations dedicated to creating conditions found in the cores of stars for fusion to occur. Housed in a ten-story building covering an area of three football fields, a spherical plastic capsule the size of a small pea filled with 150 micrograms of two heavy isotopes of hydrogen, deuterium and tritium, are exposed to the combined output of 192 giant lasers of 500 trillion watts, lasting a 20 billionth of a second. For a 10 billionth of a second, the capsule will be compressed to a density 100 times greater than lead and heated to 100 million degrees Celsius, hotter than the center of the sun. It is hoped that fusion will result producing ten to one hundred times the energy consumed.[48] When the NIF was completed in 2009, experiments were conducted to see if energy generated through fusion reactions exceeded the energy input to create the laser beam. The first experiments had an energy deficit where the energy consumed by lasers was greater than the energy generated by fusion. However, in 2014, after a number of changes, an energy surplus resulted where the energy generated by fusion reactions exceeded the energy consumed by lasers.[49] If this project can be scaled up successfully, the world energy problem would be potentially solved, but the solution will take time. The project would have to prove that fusion can safely generate enough energy for commercial electricity generation and fusion plants would have to go through the long drawn-out process of receiving permission to be built.

In 1989 there was great excitement over the possibility of cold fusion, creating energy in a test tube (so to speak), which turned out to be either a case of vain hope or scientific sleight of hand. In 2009 the idea of cold fusion got back in the limelight when researchers at a US Navy laboratory announced that there was significant evidence of cold fusion (low-energy nuclear reaction) producing neutrons and other subatomic particles at room temperatures. Although nothing more was heard from this, the idea of cold fusion is still alive.[50]

Hydropower

History

Dams have a long history of supplying water to meet human needs. Ancient dams in Jordan, Egypt, Yemen, Greece, and Turkey were built to supply water for human and animal consumption, irrigate crops on land too dry to sustain agriculture, and control flood waters; the same purposes for building dams now. A few of these ancient dams have been in more or less continual operation for two or more millennia. The ruins of the Jawa Dam built around 3000 BCE still stand in Jordan. The Ma'rid Dam in Yemen in operation today was originally constructed over 2,700 years ago. Beginning in the first century, the Romans built a number of dams to impound river waters around the Mediterranean such as the Cornalvo and Proserpina dams in Spain still in service after 1,700 years.[51]

Hydropower has been around a long time in the form of waterwheels. Waterwheels turned by running water that lifted water for irrigation and grinding grain have been in existence since Roman times—a definite improvement over tread wheels operated by humans or animals. The first waterwheels were horizontal and drove a vertical shaft to rotate millstones that ground grain on a floor above the waterwheel. Vertical waterwheels were vastly superior to horizontal waterwheels because they could more efficiently capture the momentum of moving or falling water. Gearing was now necessary to change the direction of a rotating shaft from horizontal to vertical in order to operate millstones, something that different societies found not always technically feasible. Over the centuries waterwheels were applied to a variety of tasks such as sawing wood, crushing ore, stamping, cutting, grinding, polishing, and powering bellows to force air into a furnace to refine metals. Ruins have been found in France of a center for grinding grain consisting of two series of eight waterwheels built at different heights on a cascade of water. Although built during the fourth century by Romans, it has all the earmarks of a water-powered factory, a very early precursor to industrialization.[52] In the 1680s a large installation of waterwheels pumped water to supply fountains at the Versailles palace. Factories in England and New England, the first centers of industrialization, continued to be powered by waterwheels long after the advent of the steam engine. Waterpower had the virtue of being free, but steam from burning coal eventually overtook waterpower in the nineteenth century as steam could deliver a lot more power with greater reliability.[53]

What is new is using hydropower to generate electricity. There are 45,000 dams in the world with a vertical distance of 50 feet or more. These dams catch 14 percent of precipitation runoff, providing 40 percent of water for irrigated land and more than half of electricity for 65 nations.[54] Many of these are in developing nations in Central and South America, Africa, and Asia. Africa is home to two dams with the world's largest reservoirs. One is Owen Falls Dam in Uganda whose reservoir is Lake Victoria. Lake Victoria existed long before the dam was built three miles downstream on the White Nile, but is now considered a reservoir since its depth is controlled by the dam. The other is Kariba Dam on the border of Zimbabwe and Zambia whose reservoir is Lake Kariba. Owen Falls supplies hydropower to Uganda and Kariba to Zambia and Zimbabwe, each for over a half-century.[55] Kariba Dam is considered unsafe by some from a weakening foundation (a contention denied by the dam's operators).[56]

One hundred and fifty dams are considered major in terms of generating electric power, reservoir capacity, and height. As a group they generate 40 percent of energy produced by hydropower, but not all dams generate electricity. Some are built to provide water for some combination of human consumption and recreation, irrigation, and flood control. Flood control dams contain heavy rains and snowmelt to reduce the flooding of low-lying areas such as those built by the Tennessee Valley Authority (TVA) in Appalachia. Smaller dams span rivers to allow the navigation of deeper draft, larger sized vessels. Ships sailing on major rivers, such as the Mississippi and its tributaries and the Danube, bypass these dams via locks that raise and lower a vessel to the height of the water on either side of a dam. Large vessels could not navigate these rivers were it not for these dams eliminating rapids and increasing depth of water.

Hydroelectric dams raise the level of water to create a hydraulic head to power turbines that drive electricity generators. Reservoirs compensate for fluctuations in the inflow and outflow of water. Inflow is determined by the amount of rainfall in a dam's watershed. Spillways and gates control the discharge of excess water from a reservoir, while intake valves control the flow of water through a tunnel (penstock) to hydraulic turbines that drive electricity generators. Long distance transmission lines are necessary as many dams are located far from population centers. A few hydroelectric dams have locks that allow ships to pass around them and others have steps, called ladders, to allow fish to get to and from their spawning grounds. Some low powered, outmoded, century-old hydroelectric dams are being or have been dismantled as the economic benefit of restoring fisheries and recreational areas destroyed by a dam now outweigh the value of its generated electricity (if even in operation).[57]

The principal advantage of hydropower is that it utilizes a cost and pollution free renewable source of energy. However, some environmentalists maintain that hydroelectric dams built in tropical regions contribute to carbon dioxide emissions since preexistent forests now covered by their reservoirs no longer absorb carbon dioxide. This is somewhat misleading in that a mature forest is carbon neutral and that carbon dioxide absorbed by living plants is balanced by carbon dioxide released by decaying plants. Plants absorb carbon dioxide on balance during reforestation when unproductive land is planted with trees, but not after the trees reach maturity. But reservoirs in the tropics more than elsewhere emit carbon dioxide and methane from the decay of a flooded forest. These emissions do not stop because decaying plant debris continually flow into reservoirs. This latter point is also misleading as rotting plant debris is going to emit carbon dioxide and methane no matter where it comes to rest; it is just that the tropics generate more plant debris than temperate climates.[58]

Though hydropower has no fuel cost and a low operating cost, it has a high capital cost and is site-specific. Unlike fossil fueled plants, hydropower dams are not built where they're needed. Prospective dam sites require ample supplies of water plus favorable geological conditions suitable for building a dam whose reservoir is sufficiently large with a type of bottom that limits water absorption. The capital cost of a dam includes preparation of a site, construction of the dam, and installation of an electricity generating plant and long distance transmission lines. From a fuel standpoint, hydropower is environmentally friendly, but other environmental concerns still have to be addressed such as the impact of dams on fish and wildlife both upstream and downstream of a dam, resettlement of people living upstream of a dam, and potential of catastrophic structural failure for those living downstream.

With tens of thousands of dams, some fail each year, mostly without catastrophic results other than local flooding. The 2013 failure of a dam on the Elbe River forced the evacuation of 50,000 people with no loss of life and minimal property damage.[59] Not all dam failures are so benign. The 1889 Johnstown flood from the failed South Fork Dam caused a loss of over 2,200 lives and devastated Johnstown. The rich folk, steel magnates of the day, used a dammed lake purely for recreation and spent a lot of money in building classy vacation homes, but not in fixing a clearly deteriorating dam that formed the lake. Nor were they held financially liable for the consequences of their neglect.[60] In 1928 the 2-year-old St. Francis Dam in California failed, leaving more than 450 dead. This occurred 12 hours after the builder declared the dam safe (a builder is always a good source for an unbiased opinion), even though water was leaking right through the middle of the dam. Cause of the dam failure was the unsuitable geology of the site.[61] In 1975 unprecedented rainfall caused the Shimantan Dam in China to fail and its floodwaters destroyed the downstream Banqiao Dam. The combined deluge of water and dam debris carried away other downstream dams and dikes, drowning 140,000 people (other sources state 85,000 people).[62] In 1976, after seven months of filling the newly constructed Teton Dam in Idaho, with the reservoir only three feet below the spillway, three leaks were found: one at the bottom of the gravel filled cement dam, another alongside one of its abutments, and still another about 100 feet below the top of the dam. Less than two hours later, the dam was breached and water poured through the dam. In a matter of hours the breach widened, carrying away a large portion of the dam and emptying a 17-mile-long reservoir over a wide area of Idaho with a loss of 14 lives.[63]

Heavy rainfall can cause dams to fail, but dams are also affected by a lack of rainfall or a drought that fails to replenish the waters they hold. The California energy crisis in 2001 was sparked by a drought in Oregon and Washington that curtailed the export of hydroelectricity to California. That same year Brazil suffered power disruptions from a drought in the rain basins serving its principal dams that significantly cut hydroelectricity generation, the primary source of electricity. This spurred Brazil to seek energy diversification once hydropower was deemed unreliable in times of severe drought.

Hydropower in Brazil and other nations with a high dependence on hydropower fulfills both base and variable load. Hydropower is amenable to satisfying variable power because its output can be easily controlled by varying the flow of water through the turbines. In the US, base load electricity demand is satisfied primarily with coal and nuclear power. A large coal fired plant takes days to reach full power and days to shut down. Since coal and nuclear power cannot handle quick changes to power demand easily, these plants generally run at full power to satisfy base load demand while hydropower (despite its free energy) and natural gas primarily satisfy variable demand. The design of nuclear power plants in France is more amenable to changing loads.

The first commercial site for generating electricity was New York City's Pearl Street station built by Thomas Edison in 1882. The plant produced direct current electricity from generators driven by coal burning steam engines and was the progenitor of other plants to electrify the city. The second commercial site for generating electricity was Niagara Falls, where a hydropower plant built by George Westinghouse produced alternating current electricity. No dam was involved; the construction of a tunnel to divert water upstream of the falls to a downstream power plant began in 1890. Commercial sales started in 1895, and the plant's generating capacity was continually expanded until 1927. With increasing availability of cheap electricity generated from hydropower, industry rapidly developed along the Niagara River. Today the US side of Niagara Falls produces 2.7 gW and the Canadian side 2.3 gW.[64] In 2013, on the Canadian side, a 10 kilometer tunnel, 12.7 meters wide, was completed to replace a tunnel that had served for 100 years with another that will last for another 100 years to supply water to a 2 gW hydroelectric power plant.[65]

Birth of the Environmental Movement

The first recorded public outcry over the environmental consequences of energy was the ban on burning coal in London during the thirteenth century. At the turn of the twentieth century, New Yorkers demonstrated against black smoke emissions from early electricity generating plants. While the environmental movement can be traced back in time to a number of such instances of public outcries over polluted air and water, the major thrust that propelled environmentalism to the forefront of public limelight, that initiated the entire environmental movement as seen today, was a dam powered by one of the cleanest sources of energy.

See the Companion Website for a section on the Birth of the Environmental Movement: www.routledge.com/cw/nersesian.

Hydropower: Today and Tomorrow

Hydropower once provided a significant portion of electricity generation capacity in the US (40 percent in 1920, increasing to over half during the 1930s). Since the Second World War, fossil fuel and nuclear generating plants were built in large numbers, pushing hydropower to the background. North American hydropower development is now centered in eastern and western Canada. Hydropower plants in eastern Canada are built and operated by Hydro-Québec, a publicly owned company, with 59 hydropower generating stations encompassing 560 dams and 25 large reservoirs with an installed capacity of 35.3 gW, with another 1.5 gW under construction. The company has access to another 5.4 gW of output at Churchill Falls plus 2.4 gW through purchase agreements with independent wind power producers. Churchill Falls, a joint project between Newfoundland and Labrador, is being expanded in what is called the Lower Churchill project, with an output of 3 gW to be added in several phases.[66] Churchill Falls projects involve no dams, but water tunnels bypass the falls similar to Niagara Falls. Hydro-Québec owns and operates a 33,900 kilometer transmission system with interconnections to other transmission systems in Ontario and Québec Provinces, the Midwest, Middle Atlantic, and New England states.[67] It has applied to FERC for permission to run new transmission lines into New England. Selling electricity both in Canada and the US helps to even out the base load for Hydro-Québec where a winter peak to heat homes and office buildings in Canada is balanced by a summer peak to cool homes and office buildings in the US. The company has spearheaded technological advances in long distance transmission to reduce transmission losses (an imperative considering the remote location of its hydropower plants), and shares its expertise by getting involved with hydropower projects in other lands.

On the other side of Canada in British Columbia, BC Hydro, a government owned company, produces 11 gW of electricity, of which over 90 percent is hydroelectric, at

31 integrated generating stations.[68] Like Hydro-Québec, a significant portion of its electricity output is consumed in the US. BC Hydro expects to invest heavily in the future in response to rapid population growth, beginning with a 1.1 gW hydropower dam on Peace River to start construction in 2015.[69] A 22 mW hydropower project in Ontario, Canada, has demonstrated a new business model where the ownership of the project is split between three First Nation communities, a local municipality, and a private developer. Rather than a top-down imposition of a hydropower project on the people by government authorities, here the project was organized from bottom-up by people both owning and reaping the benefit of the project.[70] Perhaps this type of organization, modified to reflect a much larger capital investment, would have prevented the failure of the 2.75 gW HidroAysen Hydroelectric project in Chile from popular opposition.[71] The counterpart to Hydro-Québec in the US is the Tennessee Valley Authority in Appalachia and, to BC Hydro, the Bonneville Power Administration in the Pacific Northwest. But the days of building large dams in the US ended with the Glen Canyon dam.

The leading hydroelectric regional producer is Asia with a 39 percent share of hydropower production, with China alone having a 27 percent global share. Europe including the FSU accounts for 22 percent of hydropower, with major producers being Russia and Norway, but with France, Sweden, Turkey, and Italy having noteworthy shares. South America has an 18 percent share, dominated by Brazil and augmented by Venezuela, Colombia, and Argentina. North America has an 18 percent share, with Canada producing more hydropower than the US. The remaining 3 percent is mainly Africa, with a small contribution from the Middle East. The historical growth of hydropower in Figure 8.8 is in terms of millions of barrels per day of energy equivalent that would have been consumed to generate the equivalent electricity with a 38 percent thermal efficiency.[72]

The overall growth rate in hydropower production was 3.7 percent from 1965 to 2003. Since then, as is plain in Figure 8.8, the growth rate escalated to 8.8 percent primarily from massive additions to hydropower capacity in China.[73] Figure 8.9 shows those nations with the greatest dependence on hydropower for electricity generation. The listing does

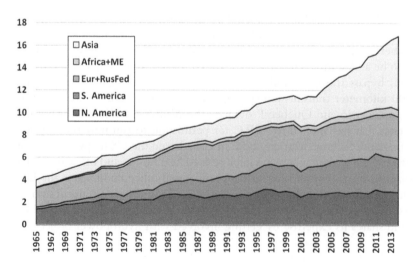

Figure 8.8 Historic Growth in Hydropower (mmBpd)

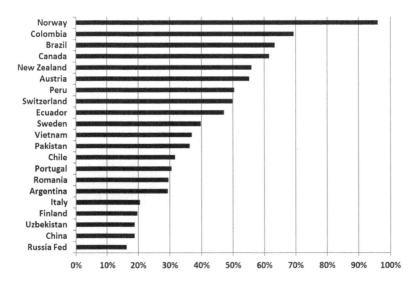

Figure 8.9 World's Largest Hydropower Producers (percent of total electricity output)

not include smaller nations in Central and South America, Africa, plus Iceland that generate a large share of their electricity from hydropower.

Norway is almost entirely dependent on hydropower for electricity generation. Colombia is nestled in the Andes and along the Pacific and Atlantic coasts with plentiful rainfall in the mountains. Its wide variation in elevation between mountains and coastline is a perfect setting for building dams. While Colombia is highly dependent on hydropower, droughts and dry seasons affect its reliability. Colombia has entered into contracts with independent natural gas electricity producers for standby power in case a lack of rainfall cuts hydropower output. Natural gas producers are paid to have plants on standby and, of course, paid when electricity is generated. These plants are the fossil fuel backup for a renewable energy source, something in common with solar and wind power.

Brazil was once over 82 percent dependent on hydropower and had a national energy policy to become entirely dependent much like Norway. In pursuit of this objective, the Itaipu hydroelectric power project was built between 1975 and 1991 with 18 generating units for a total output of 14 gW of electricity. This single dam complex has an output equivalent to about 14 nuclear or large coal power plants of 1,000 mW (1 gW) each. Itaipu is a binational development project on the Paraná River between Brazil and Paraguay, not far from the border with Argentina, and provides 25 percent of electricity supply in Brazil and 80 percent in Paraguay. The height of the dam is 643 feet (196 meters) with a length of nearly five miles (7.8 kilometers) and a reservoir 106 miles (170 kilometers) long. The dam has become a major tourist attraction as a construction marvel, much like the Hoover and Glen Canyon dams.[74] While under construction, wet cement was refrigerated before pouring to decrease the setting time rather than installing refrigerated water pipes as at the Hoover and Glen Canyon dams. Whereas it took 17 years to fill Glen Canyon reservoir, Itaipu reservoir was filled in a matter of weeks—water rising so fast that an intensive effort had to be launched to save animals from drowning.

Brazil's dream of achieving full reliance on hydropower for generating electricity was shattered in 2001 when a severe drought lowered reservoir levels throughout the nation to the point of cutting electricity generation by 20 percent, causing widespread power disruptions and economic dislocations. Brazil is now pursuing a policy of energy diversification for electricity generation rather than total reliance on hydropower and has significantly increased the contribution of natural gas to satisfy national energy needs from LNG imports and by pipeline from Bolivia. Natural gas resources are known to exist in remote areas of the Amazon, but these are not being tapped at this time. Economics was probably behind Brazil's decision not to resort to its massive biomass resources for generating electricity. In 2014, Brazil was 48 percent dependent on oil, 28 percent on hydro, 12 percent natural gas, 5 percent each for coal and renewables, and 1 percent nuclear. For comparison purposes, global dependence on energy sources was 33 percent oil, 7 percent hydro, 24 percent natural gas, 30 percent coal, 2 percent renewables, and 4 percent nuclear.

Dam building is not over in Brazil. The 11.2 gW Belo Monte dam on Xingu River is still expected to be completed in 2016 despite cost overruns and indigenous groups' protests and occupation of construction sites. The dam can only produce its rated output during four months of the rainy season, otherwise its expected output will be 40 percent of capacity.[75] In 2014 another drought hit the region around Sao Paulo state, causing serious water shortages to 20 million people. This fast growing region, home to a fifth of Brazilians and producing a third of the nation's GDP, has outgrown its water reservoirs. Moreover the drought became so severe that six reservoir lakes that also produce hydropower have been shut down from extremely low levels of water (3 percent of capacity). Substitute electricity is being generated at fossil fuel plants. In the future dams will have to be built not just to generate hydropower, but to provide drinking water.[76] Of course, agricultural output in Sao Paulo state is vulnerable to drought along with other regions of Brazil if the drought persists and expands in area.

Major Dams

Dams are ranked all sorts of ways such as by height, type, reservoir size, spillway capacity, irrigated areas, volume for flood protection, and other measures. In terms of electricity generating capacity, Three Gorges Dam in China is by far the world's largest dam at 22.5 gW, as shown in Table 8.1.[77]

The Myitsone dam project in Myanmar is sponsored by China. The dam was started in 2007 and stopped in 2011 as a result of intense environmental opposition that also included some degree of xenophobia because of the China connection plus internal strife between the government and rebel forces fighting for autonomy in the region where the dam is being built. China is trying to get the project reactivated, but resumption of construction is problematic.[78] Another project facing strong local opposition is building two large dams across the Mekong River. Riparian nations Cambodia, Laos, Thailand, and Vietnam signed the Mekong Agreement in 1995 to coordinate river management. The dams in question are Xayaburi Dam (partially completed) in Laos and the proposed Don Sahong Dam between Cambodia and Vietnam. Fifty million people depend on fish in the Mekong region for protein in their diet and many fear that dams threaten fish spawning grounds, food supply, and a way of life.[79] China and Myanmar are also riparian nations, and China is planning to build a dam across the Mekong—one among 11 proposals to dam the Mekong.[80]

Table 8.1 World's Largest Dams in Electricity Generating Capacity (gW)

Name of Dam	Rated Capacity (gW)	Year Completed	Nation
Three Gorges (Sanxia)	22.5	1991	China
Itaipu	14	1991	Brazil/Paraguay
Baihetan	14	2020 (est)	China
Xiluodu	13.8	2013	China
Belo Monte	11.2	2011	Brazil
Guri	10	1986	Venezuela
Tucurui	8.4	1984	Brazil
Grand Coulee	6.8	1942	US
Sayano-Shushenskaya	6.4	1980	Russia
Xiangjiaba	6.4	2013	China
Longtan	6.4	2009	China
Krasnoyarsk	6	1967	Russia
Myitsone	6	?	Myanmar

The potential for hydropower is enormous for both India and China because their major rivers start 15,000 feet above sea level on the Tibetan plateau. The Indian government is a strong advocate of hydroelectricity as an alternative to coal burning plants to reduce air pollution by utilizing a free source of clean energy. However, the government faces strong environmental opposition to its plans for hydropower.[81] Environmental opposition has succeeded in stymying dam construction in India, although not entirely. Of the top ten dams being built in India, two are 1.9 gW, one 1.0, one 0.3, two 0.2, and the remainder less than 0.1 gW respectively. The aggregate of these ten dams might just make the listing of single dams in Table 8.1. India may have found a way around the opposition posed by environmentalists by pursuing hydropower development in Nepal. These are not dams, but tunnels built along swiftly flowing water on steep inclines. One such project is an 11.2 kilometer tunnel, 6 meters wide, where water will flow down a 627 meter incline to turbines capable of generating 600 mW. Electricity from this and similar projects will not only supply Nepal with electricity, but also can generate foreign exchange earnings by exporting electricity to satisfy shortfalls in northern India. Using pipelines to shunt water from upriver to downriver, similar to that at Niagara and Churchill Falls, has a potential for generating 40 gW of power in Nepal, 24 gW in neighboring Bhutan, and 59 gW in Pakistan, in addition to its present capacity of 6.6 gW of hydropower.[82] A proposal has been made of constructing low dams in parallel rows across fast moving streams and rivers. These dams will not create reservoirs, but water piling up behind the dams will be forced to pass through turbines to generate electricity.[83] This is akin to building low run-of-river dams, again without reservoirs, and capturing river flow to generate electricity. Locks can be built around the dams to allow passage of vessels.

Unlike India, China has embraced hydropower along with nuclear power as a solution to its energy problems. This is epitomized by Three Gorges Dam on the Yangtze River, the world's third longest river. Completed in 2009, the dam stretches 1.3 miles (2 kilometers) across and towers 610 feet above the river bed. Its reservoir covers land reaching 360 miles upstream of the dam and forced the resettlement of 1.5 million people.[84]

Its installed capacity of 22.5 gW is the largest in the world, equivalent to 23 nuclear power plants, and supplied about 18 percent of China's electricity needs in 2014. As huge as the output of Three Gorges Dam is, it only covered about 50 percent of the increase in electricity consumption in China between 2012 and 2013, but 90 percent of the increase between 2013 and 2014 when growth in electricity consumption slowed (by China's standards). If the rate of growth keeps up at this slower pace, China would have to build one equivalent Three Gorges Dam every year to meet incremental demand. This type of growth in electricity consumption probably explains why the 12th Five-Year Plan proposes to build 120 gW of new hydropower plants on the Nu/Salween, Lancang/Upper Mekong, Jinsha/Upper Yangtze rivers plus Yarlung Tsangpo, the world's highest river that flows through the "Grand Canyon of Tibet" before becoming the Siang River in India and then the Brahmaputra River in Bangladesh. In theory, the Five-Year Plan averages 24 gW every year for 5 years or about one new Three Gorges Dam every year, more than any nation has ever built.[85] Of course this is just a plan, but from this, one can sense the imperative for completing massive energy projects. In the past, it meant completing 2 gW of coal burning utility capacity per week. With the recent slowdown in economic growth, such a furious pace of building coal fired utility plants may no longer be necessary.

Three Gorges Dam increased the freight capacity of the Yangtze River six-fold while dropping shipping costs by 25 percent by allowing deeper draft vessels of up to 10,000 tons to navigate the Yangtze. Ship locks lift and lower ships over 300 feet between water levels on each side of the dam. Five locks are needed for gates to withstand the water pressure. There are two sets of these staircase locks, one for moving ships downstream and the other upstream, with a transit time of two to three hours.[86] There is also a ship lift for smaller vessels of less than 3,000 tons, which lifts vessels directly between the two levels of water like a water elevator.

Three Gorges Dam is also a flood control measure for a river notorious for disastrous floods throughout China's history. Recent major floods occurred in 1870, 1931, 1954, and 1998. The 1931 flood killed over 300,000 people and left 40 million people homeless.[87] The benefit of flood control, along with the substitution of clean hydropower for dirty burning coal in electricity generation, has made little impact on those opposed to the dam. Human rights organizations criticized resettlement plans, archaeologists were concerned about submergence of over 1,000 historical sites, and others mourned the loss of some of the world's finest scenery. Moreover, tens of millions of Chinese downstream of the dam are at risk if there were a catastrophic structural failure (memories of the Shimantan dam disaster still persist).

As large as Three Gorges Dam is, it may be overtaken by the Grand Inga dam complex in the Democratic Republic of Congo. Construction has begun on the first of six phases of development, Inga 3, a 4.8 gW hydropower dam being built on the Congo River. After serving the needs of the Democratic Republic of Congo (over 90 percent of the people are currently without electricity) and its mining industry, much of the electricity will be sold to South Africa via Zambia and Zimbabwe.[88] These nations along with Angola and Namibia will be served by this project. Raising $80 billion for all six phases to achieve 40 gW of output is problematic. Prospective sites for large hydropower projects are nearly exhausted in the US and Europe. South America still has a great deal of potential that can be tapped, as does Asia, the present world center of dam building. Africa is emerging as a center of hydropower plant activity.

While the focus is on large dams, small hydro plants are being vigorously pursued for the same purposes as large dams, but on a much smaller scale, serving isolated communities, farms, and ranches. Small hydro plants are considered nonthreatening nor disruptive to people or environment. They range in size categories of pico dams (up to 5 kW), micro (5 to 100 kW), mini (100 kW to 1 mW), small (1 to 10 mW), and medium (10 to 100 mW).[89] The 1,800 kilometer interconnector integrates the electricity systems of Guatemala, El Salvador, Honduras, Costa Rica, Nicaragua, and Panama. Its 283 mW of additional power in 2012 was provided by seven small and medium sized (run-of-river) hydro plants whose individual capacities were 5, 13, 26, 34, 57, 59, and 88 mW respectively.[90] These individual additions were sized and located to handle the nature of incremental demand along the length of the interconnector. They can take advantage of limited hydropower potential and their capital costs are within the bounds of capital availability. A number of small hydropower projects can be built to better accommodate annual growth in demand rather than one large dam whose output capacity may not be fully utilized for a long period of time, thereby negating the advantage of a large dam's inherent economies of scale.

Dams Affect International Relations

There are more conflicts over access to water as growing populations further tax nations' agricultural resources, such as the one that erupted between Lebanon and Israel in 1978. Israel felt that a plan to divert the headwaters of Litani River in Lebanon, needed for irrigation and drinking water in Israel, was tantamount to an act of war.[91] Conflicts over water rights are becoming larger in scope, more frequent in time, and more serious in nature.

Turkey versus Iraq

The headwaters of the Euphrates and Tigris rivers are in Turkey. The Tigris flows from Turkey, forms a border with Syria for a short distance, and then enters Iraq. The Euphrates flows from Turkey, down through the middle of Syria, before entering Iraq. Both rivers join together before flowing into the Persian Gulf (Shatt al-Arab). Turkey has inaugurated a massive dam-building scheme called the Güneydoğu Anadolu Projesi (GAP) that will encompass, when completed, 22 dams and 19 hydropower plants across the Tigris–Euphrates basin. Dams will store water for irrigation that will be distributed by hundreds of kilometers of canals to irrigate 75,000 square kilometers—almost 10 percent of the land area of Turkey. GAP is about 70 percent complete and is expected to be finished in 2017. Building of dams throughout Turkey may add as much as 70 gW of capacity, a huge contribution by any measure, to a starting point of 15 gW.[92] Turkey's use of water has already cut the flow of water downstream in the Tigris and Euphrates rivers. It is projected that, when completed, GAP will reduce the flow of water into Iraq by 70–80 percent for the Euphrates River and about 40 percent for the Tigris River.[93] This will definitely place irrigation-dependent agricultural output in Iraq in a precarious position. The problem will worsen when Syria begins to construct new dams on the Euphrates River.

The potential for international conflict already has precedence. Completion of Syria's Tabqa Dam in 1975 brought Syria and Iraq to the brink of war, which coincided with a drought in Iraq that created serious water shortages. In 1990 Turkey mobilized its forces when it cut the Euphrates' flow to fill the Atatürk Dam, temporarily reducing water flow into Syria and Iraq by 75 percent. Iraq threatened to blow up the dam, which led Turkey to threaten to completely cut off water flow to Syria and Iraq. An Iraqi dam made front page news during the summer of 2014 when Islamic State seized the Mosul dam, the largest dam in Iraq and a vital source of water for irrigation and hydropower. This seizure brought forth allegations that Islamic State might blow up the dam, subjecting those living downstream to a horrific flood. Fortunately Islamic State lost control shortly after its capture of the dam.[94] However, its seizure made known to the public that the dam is considered one of the most dangerous dams in the world. Its foundation is deteriorating because the dam was built on top of gypsum that dissolves when in contact with water. This necessitates a continuing maintenance program of injecting materials to maintain its foundational strength, a maintenance program that Islamic State might neglect if it retook control.

In mid-2009, what was feared most happened. Flow in the Euphrates River fell from 950 cubic meters per second to 230 cubic meters. Part of the decreased flow was blamed on dams in Turkey and Syria plus the repercussions of a 2-year drought, which also affected flow in the Tigris River. The UN Food and Agriculture Organization (FAO) maintained that Iraq had its worst cereal harvest in a decade and its wheat harvest was set to fall to one million tons from an annual average of 3.5 million tons over the previous decade. Domestic rice production also fell from an average 500,000 tons a year to an estimated 250,000 tons.[95] Moreover, water management practices in Iraq are generally poor, resulting in wasteful consumption. Lack of water crippled a large swath of Iraqi agriculture along the Euphrates and forced Iraq to import once homegrown fruits, vegetables, and grain. Low flow rates in the two rivers allowed salt water to penetrate 160 kilometers from the mouth of Shatt el-Arab. Poisonous snakes, losing their natural habitat in the reed marshes, attacked cattle and humans. Although an appeal to Turkey to release more water was successful, Turkey is under no obligation to maintain an increased flow.[96] At this time, reed marshes are being restored by rediverting water flows previously diverted by Saddam Hussein in his war against the reed people.[97] Recent remarks by the Iraqi agricultural minister promises a blossoming of Iraqi agricultural output by increased rainfall and better management of water and soil resources, which had been previously lacking.[98] Nevertheless, significant reductions in water flow of the Euphrates and Tigris rivers do not augur well for Iraq's agricultural output.

Egypt versus Nile River Riparian Nations

Another international water problem is the Nile River. Egypt's legal claim to Nile's water is a 1929 document between Egypt, then a colony, and Britain to allocate 48 billion cubic meters of the Nile's water to Egypt and two billion to Sudan, with Egypt holding veto power over any significant diversion of the Nile's waters to other nations. A 1959 treaty between Egypt and Sudan apportioned 55.5 billion cubic meters to Egypt and 18.5 billion cubic meters to Sudan with no mention of the other riparian nations. The Nile River Basin Initiative (NBI) was launched in 1999 by the riparian nations to develop Nile Basin water resources in a sustainable and equitable way to ensure prosperity, security, and peace for all peoples.[99] The Nile River is made up of the Blue Nile starting in Ethiopia, source of 85 percent of its waters, and the White Nile whose headwaters is Lake Victoria, making the Nile the longest river in the world. The riparian nations are Egypt, Sudan, Burundi, Democratic Republic of Congo, Ethiopia, Eritrea, Kenya, Rwanda,

Tanzania, and Uganda. NBI developed the Cooperative Framework Agreement among the riparian nations as all want at least the right to share Nile waters. Egypt will not sign the agreement unless there is a provision requiring that future upstream users of Nile waters do not interfere with the current downstream users' (Egypt and Sudan's) consumption of Nile waters—a provision that the other riparian states reject.[100]

Ethiopia is the first nation to upset the apple cart with its active dam building program. Its first major dam does not affect the Nile River. The Gibe III hydroelectric dam being built in Ethiopia will rise 243 meters above the Omo River (a river self-contained within Ethiopian borders) and have an upstream reservoir 150 kilometers long to accommodate the river's annual flooding. The dam will control the river's flow below the dam and will generate 1.87 gW of electricity, doubling the nation's generating capacity. Anticipated to be completed in 2015, the dam will solve Ethiopia's energy (electricity) problems and allow Ethiopia to become an energy exporter to Sudan and Kenya. Food production in the vicinity of the reservoir will rise from irrigation. The dam faced environmental criticism over its potential environmental impact on Lake Turkana, the world's largest desert lake that depends on the river for 80 percent of its water inflow, and on the people who depend on the river for their livelihoods.[101] The Omo and Okavango (from the wet region of Angola to Botswana) Rivers are unique in that their mouths are not the sea, but deserts.

While Gibe III does not affect Egypt, its building whet the appetite of Ethiopia to build another dam: the Grand Ethiopian Renaissance Dam (formerly the Grand Millennium Dam) that'll span the Blue Nile. Grand Ethiopian Renaissance is larger than Gibe III and its two hydropower plants will have the capacity to generate 3.5 and 1.75 gW respectively.[102] Taking into account irrigation, the government of Egypt believes this project, only 30 percent complete in 2014, will reduce Egypt's share of Nile River flow by 20–30 percent and cut electricity generation at the Aswan dam by a third. Egypt has threatened military intervention or sabotage if Ethiopia does not stop construction.[103] Ethiopia is adamant about completing these projects as a means to emerge from grinding poverty through greater food production by irrigating currently unproductive dry land, having plentiful electricity to support economic development, and adding to foreign exchange earnings by selling electricity to its neighbors. Meetings between the two nations have taken place to find some compromise solution. But there can be no compromise solution: a dam across the Blue Nile either will or will not be built; it cannot be half-built!

Indus River

Since their formation in 1947, India and Pakistan have fought three major wars and countless skirmishes. It is not a territorial dispute over Kashmir, but a water dispute, that may initiate the next conflict between two nations each armed with over 100 nuclear warheads. The Indus River is the lifeblood of Pakistan, but its source waters rise in India. Both nations have soaring populations, taxing their water resources. India wants to build dams across the Indus River and rivers feeding into the Indus River within its domain to generate power to satisfy its electricity shortfalls. Generating electricity may interrupt the flow of the Indus River, but ultimately water passes through the dams and into Pakistan. But India also wants to irrigate crops and supply water for its rapidly growing population, which directly affects Pakistan.

Pakistan is one of the most "water-stressed" countries in the world, not far from being classified as "water-scarce." In 1947 annual water availability on a per capita basis was 5,000 cubic meters and is now down to 1,000 cubic meters, an 80 percent decline in nearly 70 years. Pakistan has drawn so much water from its reservoirs that its emergency water supplies are down to 30 days, a small fraction of what is considered prudent. At the current rate of population growth, Pakistan will be 33 percent short of its needed water supplies by 2025. Thus Pakistan feels that its very existence is threatened by India's construction of dams on rivers feeding into the Indus River, a potential *causa belli* between the two nations.[104]

Hydropower for Peace

One potential hydropower project under consideration that should not be a source of conflict, but hopefully may ameliorate tensions in the Middle East, is the Red Sea to Dead Sea project. The Dead Sea, 1,370 feet below sea level, is the lowest spot on Earth. It is bordered by Israel and Jordan and the West Bank under the control of the Palestinian Authority. For thousands of years, the flow of the Jordan River was sufficient to replenish water lost to evaporation. Being "at the end of the road," the Dead Sea accumulates salts carried by the Jordan River. Whereas the world's oceans have a salinity content (salts of sodium, magnesium, calcium, potassium, and others) of 3.5 percent and Great Salt Lake in Utah has a salinity of 27 percent, the Dead Sea's 33 percent is almost ten times that of ocean waters. Dead Sea waters are thought to have therapeutic properties and have an oily sensation. A person floating in the Dead Sea finds it hard to stand up and leaves the water caked with salt.

The problem is that the Dead Sea is no longer being replenished with water. The Jordan River and its tributaries have been thoroughly tapped by Israel, the Palestinian-controlled West Bank, Jordan, and Syria for the region's scarcest resource, which has cut the flow of the Jordan River by nearly 90 percent. What now flows into the Dead Sea is mainly sewage and other waste waters dumped into the Jordan River after its clean waters have been drawn off. Depending on where it is done, baptism by submergence in the Jordan River can be hazardous to one's health.[105] The idea to build sewage treatment plants to remove wastes being dumped into the Jordan actually worsens the problem. Once treated, the water would probably be diverted for irrigation, reducing the flow in the Jordan from a trickle to nothing.

With this massive diversion of water for irrigation, the Dead Sea is falling about 1 meter per year and its shoreline has retreated 500 meters over the last few decades, resulting in the loss of one-third of its area.[106] To counter this, the possibility of building a 108 mile (174 kilometer) system of canals and pipelines to bring seawater via gravity flow from the Gulf of Aqaba on the Red Sea to the Dead Sea has long been considered. The original design incorporated no pumping stations. Pipelines would siphon water over intervening highlands. Siphoning occurs when water leaves the pipeline at a lower elevation than where it enters the pipeline, eliminating the need for pumping. The end point of the Red-to-Dead project would be a hydropower plant with a hydraulic head of 500 or more meters, higher than most dams. The potential output of electricity, presently envisioned at 0.55 gW, could be far larger, depending on the flow of water from the Red Sea. Electricity generation can be partly dedicated to desalinizing water for human and agricultural use. The project requires the cooperation of Israel, Jordan, and the Palestinian Authority to arrive at a way to fairly share electricity and desalinized water and its estimated $5 billion cost. The project has to deal with environmental objections on the possible biological and chemical consequences of pouring vast quantities of Red Sea water into the Dead Sea basin. On the other hand, doing nothing means another environmental calamity when, in about 150 years, continued evaporation transforms the Dead Sea into a supersaturated solution of salt incapable of further evaporation.

In December 2013, Israel, Jordan, and Palestine signed a general agreement to pursue what is now called the Red-Dead Conduit or Two Seas Canal proposal.[107] In February 2015, a final agreement was signed. As part of this agreement, Israel would release a further 50 million cubic meters annually from Lake Kinneret (Sea of Galilee) to serve water-starved northern Jordan. An annual 65–80 million cubic meter desalinization plant will be built in the Gulf of Aqaba, of which 35 million cubic meters will be purchased by Israel and the rest by Jordan. The saline output of the desalinization plant will be pumped through a 200 kilometer pipeline to the Dead Sea. Unlike the original proposal where siphoning would substitute for pumps, pumping will occur for the first third of pipeline length to its high point and then gravity fed for the remaining length of the pipeline. This first stage $800 million project will be completed and evaluated before advancing to the next stage.[108]

Problems and Project

Problem 8.1

How much electricity can be generated by converting one gram of mass into energy over a period of 1 year assuming a net thermal efficiency of 38 percent in transforming energy to electricity?

Treating mass as frozen energy (E), the equation $E = MC^2$ needs to be evaluated in units where mass (M) is in kilograms and the speed of light (C) is expressed in meters/second or almost 300 million (3×10^8) meters/second. Speed of light squared is 9×10^{16} meter^2/second^2. Without providing a derivation or explanation, the indicated source (www.1728.org/einstein.htm) states that a mass of one kilogram contains the equivalent of energy of 9×10^{16} joules. A gram is 1/1000 of a kilogram and a watt-second equals 1 joule. There are 3,600 seconds in an hour for a watt-hour and 8,640 hours in a year for a watt-year. Assuming one gram is converted to energy and this energy is then converted to electricity at a net efficiency of 38 percent over a 1 year period, what is the equivalent electrical power for the entire year? For perspective, the conversion table at the bottom of the referenced Website shows that 1 gram of mass is equivalent to the energy released by the Hiroshima atomic bomb.

Problem 8.2

High scale radiation readings near Fukushima station were 10 Sv/hour. Referring to Table CW8.2, what does that mean to you? The Website www.world-nuclear.org/info/Safety-and-Security/Safety-of-Plants/Appendices/Fukushima--Radiation-Exposure/ contains the recommended maximum allowable radiation dose for adults; how does this affect your initial response?

Problem 8.3

Avogadro's number 6.02×10^{23} is the number of atoms in a mole of an element where a mole is the atomic weight of an element in grams. For cesium 137 isotope, the atomic weight is 132.9 grams (Website www.webqc.org/molecular-weight-of-Cs137.html). How many atoms is in one gram of cesium 137? Cesium 137 has a half-life of 30.2 years. What would the weight of cesium 137 be after 30.2 years? What would the radiation be in becquerel (one becquerel is defined as one atomic decay per second) over this period? This is average radiation; actual radiation would be higher at the start of the half-life than at the end when there are fewer atoms to decay. Starting with x being the initial radiation and x/2 being end radiation with the derived radiation as the average, what was radiation in becquerel at the start and end of the half-life? From this exercise, one can also see that the shorter the half-life, the higher the radiation. Damage in Sieverts is dependent on both radiation strength in becquerel and the type of radiation.

Problem 8.4

A 1.5 gW nuclear plant net of operating factors can be built for $8,000 per kW capacity. Suppose that the plant has a capital recovery factor of 10 percent on its investment and can be operated at a fixed cost of $1 billion annually, which includes the fabrication and installation of fuel assemblies. What is the cost of electricity? Is this low cost electricity?

Problem 8.5

Take the difference in terawatt-hours between 2013 and 2014, or any two recent consecutive years, from *BP Energy Statistics* on China's electricity demand. How many 22.5 gW Three Gorges Dams is this demand change equivalent to? There are 1,000 gW in a terawatt, and terawatt power output can be transformed to energy in the form of terawatt-hours by multiplying by 8,640 hours per year.

Problem 8.6

You're standing on the edge of a stream whose water speed appears to be 2 miles per hour. The stream is 100 feet wide and 3 feet deep. The water drops 40 feet over a waterfall. Suppose that you can capture this energy by building a dam with a penstock that can direct all this water through a hydraulic turbine to power a generator. At a system efficiency of 90 percent and with line losses at 7 percent, how many 100 W bulbs can you light continuously, assuming a static situation? Before you start the problem, write down your best estimate.

The problem can be solved by ensuring the dimensions are laid out correctly. First translate miles per hour to feet to second (round if you wish). An area of water 100' × 3' is multiplied by feet/second to get cubic feet per second as the velocity going over the edge of the waterfall. Power is derived by taking into account the density of water of 62 pounds/cubic foot to obtain pounds/second. There are 550 foot pounds/second in one horsepower and 1.34 horsepower per kilowatt. With 90 percent efficiency and 7 percent line losses through transmission and distribution, calculate the number of 100 W lightbulbs that can be kept lit as long as flow and conditions remain unchanged (i.e., static situation).[109]

Project

This is an Excel spreadsheet exercise to set up a model for measuring the performance of a hydropower dam during the wet and dry seasons and seasonal periods of high and low demand for electricity.[110] Hydropower has a number of variables that affect performance to satisfy desired power output such as rainfall in the reservoir basin, reservoir capacity, water consumption for different power outputs that depends on water height above the intake, and losses from evaporation and bottom leakage.

When water is at the intake level, the hydropower dam can produce 30 percent of rated power. Thus when X, the distance above the intake, is zero, power output, Y, is 30 percent of maximum capacity. This defines the y-intercept. When X is 100 signifying that the water level is at its maximum height of 100' above the intake, power output, Y, is 100 percent of maximum capacity. Calculating delta Y and delta X defines the slope of the line, which along with the y-intercept establishes the indicated linear relationship between water depth and power output. Derive the linear relationship linking power output to reservoir depth between 0' and 100' above the intake.

Let's suppose that the dam is 300' high and the intake is 200' above the bottom of the dam. If the water level is below 200', output of the dam is zero as the water level is below the intake. If the water level is at 200', water can flow down the penstock producing 30 percent of the dam's rated power output. Let's assume that this consumes 10' of the reservoir's depth on a monthly basis, assuming that rainfall during the month is sufficient to keep the water level above the intake. If the water level is 300', or 100' above the intake, then 10' of reservoir depth generates 100 percent of the dam's rated power output for a month. For a desired monthly power output of 50 percent of the dam's rated power output with the water level 200' above the bottom of the reservoir, the maximum output is 30 percent, consuming 10' of reservoir depth; if the dam is full, 50 percent of the dam's output can be achieved with a water depth reduction of 5'.

Quantifying these observations: if water depth of the dam is below 200', output is zero. For a given water level above 200', maximum output is provided by a straight line relationship just derived. If desired output is less than maximum, then the reservoir level will fall by a direct proportion of desired output divided by maximum output multiplied by 10'. If desired output is greater than maximum, the hydropower plant will operate at maximum capacity with a decrease in water level of 10'; output is lesser of maximum or desired.

These conditions are contained in Project Table 1 below.

Cell C26 contains reservoir depth. In cell D26, if this depth is below 200', power output is zero; otherwise maximum output is the previously derived relationship between power output and height of water above the intake. Cell E26 contains desired power. Delivered output power in cell F26 is maximum output or desired output, whichever is less. The decreased reservoir depth over the course of the month from operation at

Project Table 1

	C	D	E	F	G
23					Decrease
24	Reservoir	Maximum	Desired	Delivered	in Water
25	Depth	Power	Power	Power	Depth
26	200	=IF((C26-200)<0,0,0.3+0.007*(C26-200))	0.15	=IF(E26<D26,E26,D26)	=10*F26/D26

Project Table 2

Reservoir Depth	Maximum Power	Desired Power	Delivered Power	Decrease in Water Depth
200	30%	15%	15%	5

Reservoir Depth	Maximum Power	Desired Power	Delivered Power	Decrease in Water Depth
200	30%	50%	30%	10

Reservoir Depth	Maximum Power	Desired Power	Delivered Power	Decrease in Water Depth
250	65%	50%	50%	7.69

delivered power is the proportion of delivered power to maximum power multiplied by 10'. Project Table 2 above is a sample of outputs.

At a reservoir depth of 200', water level is at the intake and 10' of reservoir depth can generate a maximum of 30 percent output (it is assumed that rainfall is enough to keep the level at the top of the intake or that the top of the intake value is at a depth of 200' and that the vertical width of the intake is 10', but once depth is below 200', it is assumed that no electricity can be generated). For a desired output of 15 percent, water depth will fall 5'. If the desired output is 50 percent, the dam can only generate 30 percent output with a fall of 10' in water depth. However, for a water depth of 250', maximum output is 65 percent. Thus the desired output of 50 percent can be achieved with a loss of water depth of 7.7' (10 times 50/65). Project Table 3 determines monthly allowable ranges on desired output, rainfall, and evaporation.

The formula in D6 is =B6+RAND()*(C6-B6) and replicated down. Formulas in columns H and L are similarly constructed. The working part of the spreadsheet is in Project Table 4.

Formulas in columns D, E, F, and H have already been described. Cell C26 is 250 and cell C27 refers to the previous end of month's depth: C27=L26. Cells G40 and K40 are not shown. Cell G40 is the percentage of months that the hydropower plant cannot deliver desired power and cell K40 is the percentage of months that water passes over the spillway. The formulations of the applicable cells are in Project Tables 5 and 6.

By pressing the F9 function key, an iteration of a simulation is performed. By recording cells G40 and K40 with each iteration, a data base can be generated to measure risk:

Project Table 3

2	A	B	C	D	E	F	G	H	I	J	K	L
3		Minimum	Maximum	Actual		Minimum	Maximum	Actual		Minimum	Maximum	
4		Desired	Desired	Desired		Rainfall	Rainfall	Rainfall		Evaporation	Evaporation	Actual
5	Month	Output	Output	Output		in Feet	in Feet	in Feet		in Feet	in Feet	Evaporation
6	1	20%	30%	20%		10	20	18.0		0.1	0.3	0.19
7	2	15%	30%	19%		10	17	16.1		0.1	0.3	0.29
8	3	20%	35%	30%		7	12	8.0		0.1	0.4	0.37
9	4	25%	40%	39%		5	10	7.5		0.2	0.6	0.31
10	5	50%	70%	55%		3	7	3.2		0.4	1.0	0.97
11	6	70%	100%	84%		0	5	0.7		0.6	1.0	0.61
12	7	80%	100%	89%		0	5	0.5		0.8	1.0	0.86
13	8	90%	100%	92%		0	5	0.9		0.6	1.0	0.88
14	9	80%	100%	100%		3	7	6.0		0.3	0.6	0.51
15	10	60%	80%	75%		5	10	5.8		0.2	0.4	0.34
16	11	30%	50%	41%		7	15	13.8		0.1	0.3	0.16
17	12	25%	35%	27%		10	17	10.2		0.1	0.3	0.14

Project Table 4

A	B	C	D	E	F	G	H	I	J	K	L
22		Start of					Decrease				End of
23		Month				Occurrence	in Water				Month
24		Reservoir	Maximum	Desired	Delivered	of Power	Depth	Rainfall	Evaporation	Spillage	Reservoir
25	Month	Depth	Power	Power	Power	Shortage	in Feet	in Feet	in Feet	(1-Yes 0-No)	Depth
26	1	250	65%	27%	27%	0	4.2	12.9	0.30	0	258.4

Project Table 5

Cell G6	Cell I6	Cell J6	Cell K6
=IF(E26>F26,1,0)	=H6	=L6	=IF(C26–H26+I26–J27>300,1,0)

Project Table 6

Cell L6	Cell G40	Cell K40
=IF(C26–H26+I26–J26>300,300,C26–H26+I26–J26)	=SUM(G26:G37)/12	=SUM(K26:K37)/12

percentage of time that the hydropower plant fails to meet demand in cell G40. A minimum of 25 iterations should be recorded and the Excel/Data Analysis/Histogram can be used to create a probability distribution. All this is done automatically in the @Risk simulation software package provided by Palisade Corporation.

Notes

1 "Safety of Nuclear Reactors," World Nuclear Association, Website www.world-nuclear.org/info/Safety-and-Security/Safety-of-Plants/Safety-of-Nuclear-Power-Reactors.
2 *BP Energy Statistics* (London, UK: British Petroleum, 2014). A thermal efficiency of 38 percent is assumed in translating electricity output to energy equivalent input.
3 Data in Figures 8.2 and 8.3 from *BP Energy Statistics*.
4 Data on the population of nuclear reactors in operation, under construction, planned, and proposed as of June 2015 from World Nuclear Association, Website www.world-nuclear.org/info/reactors.html. US nuclear plants under construction are listed on the US Nuclear Regulatory Commission Website www.nrc.gov/reactors/new-reactors/col-holder.html.
5 "Polish Energy Policy: A Different Energiewende," *The Economist* (February 8, 2014).
6 World Nuclear Association, Website www.world-nuclear.org/info/country-profiles/countries-T-Z/USA--Nuclear-Power.
7 "Report: Over Three Dozen U.S. Nuclear Reactors at Risk of Early Retirement, 12 Face Greatest Shutdown Pressure," PRNewswire (July 17, 2013), Website www.prnewswire.com/news-releases/report--over-three-dozen-us-nuclear-reactors-at-risk-of-early-retirement-12-face-greatest-shutdown-pressure-215857411.html. See also M. Ragheb, "Restarting the USA Stalled Nuclear Renaissance," Website http://mragheb.com/NPRE%20402%20ME%20405%20Nuclear%20Power%20Engineering/Restarting%20the%20USA%20Stalled%20Nuclear%20Renaissance.pdf. The article has insight on all reactors at risk plus a wealth of information on the US nuclear situation.
8 Jeff McMahon, "6 Nuclear Plants That Could Be Next to Shut Down," *Forbes* (November 7, 2013), Website www.forbes.com/sites/jeffmcmahon/2013/11/07/6-nuclear-plants-that-may-be-next-to-shut-down.

9 Mary Serreze, "Vermont Yankee Nuclear Power Plant Unplugs from the Grid This Week," Mass Live (December 29, 2014), Website www.masslive.com/news/index.ssf/2014/12/vermont_yan kee_nuclear_plant_u.html.

10 "Nuclear Power: Fracked Off," *The Economist* (June 1, 2013).

11 "Direct Federal Financial Interventions and Subsidies in Energy in Fiscal Year 2010," US Energy Information Administration (EIA), Table ES4, Fiscal year 2013, Electricity production subsidies and support, Website www.eia.gov/analysis/requests/subsidy/pdf/subsidy.pdf. Table ES4 differs from other tables that show higher subsidies to natural gas and oil plus subsidies in the form of loan guarantees and biofuels. Table ES4 was selected because its title seemed more focused on subsidies directed to electricity generation than Table ES2. Missing loan guarantees are not material, and not listing subsidies paid to biofuels is pertinent in that biofuels are not used to generate electricity. Subsidies paid to the natural gas and oil industry are substantially reduced from the values in Table ES2 as only those subsidies directly attributable to electricity generation are included.

12 "Net Generation by Energy Source for 2013," US Energy Information Administration (EIA), *Electric Power Monthly* (May, 2015), Table 1.1, Website www.eia.gov/electricity/monthly/pdf/epm.pdf. Subsidies in Figure 8.4 are for the year 2013 and their source is cited in the previous note.

13 It seems clear to me that private solar installation output is not part of the *Electric Power Monthly* statistics, as their source is utilities, IPPs, and commercial and industrial suppliers. Solar output in *BP Energy Statistics* is the same as in *Electric Power Monthly*, hence if my interpretation of solar output is true, the reported figures on solar output may be significantly understated in nations where there is significant installation of private solar panels.

14 US Energy Information Administration (EIA), *Electric Power Monthly* (November, 2014), Table 6.2, Coal Consumption per Sector for 2013, Website www.eia.gov/totalenergy/data/monthly/pdf/mer.pdf.

15 Carbon dioxide emissions weigh more than the original fuel because, during complete combustion, each carbon atom in the fuel combines with two oxygen atoms in the air to make carbon dioxide (CO_2). The addition of two oxygen atoms with a combined atomic weight of 32 combined with one carbon atom with an atomic weight of 12 has a total atomic weight of 44, 3.6667 times the atomic weight of carbon 12. Sub-bituminous coal of an average of 51 percent carbon will have 1,020 pounds of carbon in a short ton (2,000 pounds). Carbon dioxide emissions from burning a short ton of sub-bituminous coal are 3.67 times the weight of the carbon in a short ton of coal or 3,740 pounds, or 1.87 times the weight of a short ton of coal. Website www.eia.gov/tools/faqs/faq.cfm?id=82&t=11.

16 "Uranium Mining Overview," World Nuclear Association (May, 2015), Website www.world-nuclear.org/info/Nuclear-Fuel-Cycle/Mining-of-Uranium/World-Uranium-Mining-Production.

17 "World Uranium Mining Production," World Nuclear Association, Website www.world-nuclear.org/info/Nuclear-Fuel-Cycle/Mining-of-Uranium/World-Uranium-Mining-Production.   See also "In Situ Leach Mining of Uranium," World Nuclear Association, Website www.world-nuclear.org/info/Nuclear-Fuel-Cycle/Mining-of-Uranium/In-Situ-Leach-Mining-of-Uranium.

18 Edward S. Cassedy and Peter Z. Grossman, *Introduction to Energy* (Cambridge, UK: Cambridge University Press, 1998).

19 "Safeguards to Prevent Nuclear Proliferation," World Nuclear Association (September, 2014), Website www.world-nuclear.org/info/Safety-and-Security/Non-Proliferation/Safeguards-to-Prevent-Nuclear-Proliferation.

20 "Mixed Oxide Fuel," World Nuclear Association (September, 2014), Website www.world-nuclear.org/info/Nuclear-Fuel-Cycle/Fuel-Recycling/Mixed-Oxide-Fuel-MOX.

21 "The Disposal of High-Level Radioactive Waste," Nuclear Energy Agency (January, 1989), Website www.oecd-nea.org/brief/brief-03.html.

22 Alex Meshik, "The Workings of an Ancient Nuclear Reactor," *Scientific American* (January 26, 2009), Website www.scientificamerican.com/article/ancient-nuclear-reactor. See also Evelyn Mervine, "Nature's Nuclear Reactors: The 2 Billion Year Old Natural Fission Reactors in Gabon,

Western Africa," *Scientific American* (July 13, 2011), Website http://blogs.scientificamerican.com/guest-blog/2011/07/13/natures-nuclear-reactors-the-2-billion-year-old-natural-fission-reactors-in-gabon-western-africa.

23 D.F. Hollenbach and J.M. Herndon, "Deep-Earth Reactor: Nuclear Fission, Helium, and the Geomagnetic Field," *Proceedings of the Natural Academy of Sciences of the United States of America* (2001), Website www.pnas.org/content/98/20/11085.full. See also Richard Ball, "Are There Nuclear Reactors at Earth's Core?" *Nature News* (May, 2008), Website www.nature.com/news/2008/080515/full/news.2008.822.html.

24 "Sweden Plans First Ultimate Storage Site for Nuclear Waste," DW Media Center (March 22, 2011), Website www.dw.de/sweden-plans-first-ultimate-storage-site-for-nuclear-waste/a-14935527.

25 Various sources were examined, but some were contradictory; data may not be entirely correct.

26 "Nuclear Power Reactors," World Nuclear Association, Website www.world-nuclear.org/info/Nuclear-Fuel-Cycle/Power-Reactors/Nuclear-Power-Reactors. These total 438 versus 437 total reactors also mentioned on this Website.

27 "Fast Neutron Reactors," World Nuclear Association, Website www.world-nuclear.org/info/Current-and-Future-Generation/Fast-Neutron-Reactors.

28 Jon Palfreman, "Why the French Like Nuclear Energy," PBS, Website www.pbs.org/wgbh/pages/frontline/shows/reaction/readings/french.html.

29 As a former engineering officer onboard a nuclear submarine, I could easily be transferred from one submarine to another because reactor and steam propulsion systems were essentially identical. There was only one plant layout and one set of manuals to learn for operating instructions and emergency procedures. Frankly I always felt comfortable and secure with power produced from a nuclear plant. It was safe, reliable, and gave me and other crewmembers confidence of a safe return. Submarine casualties were all non-nuclear related just as Fukushima.

30 My personal experience with a naval nuclear reactor, which is far more compact than a civilian reactor, was that the reactor was designed to accommodate rapid cycling between different power outputs.

31 "Evolutionary Design Meets Cutting Edge Technology," Areva, Website www.areva.com/EN/operations-1723/epr-reactor-evolutionary-design-meets-cutting-edge-technology.html.

32 "France's Nuclear Industry: Arevaderci," *The Economist* (May 23, 2015).

33 Passive safety features of the Westinghouse AP1000 reactor described in greater detail on Website http://westinghousenuclear.com/New-Plants/AP1000-PWR/Safety.

34 "ABWR Nuclear Power Plant," GE Hitachi, Website https://nuclear.gepower.com/build-a-plant/products/nuclear-power-plants-overview/abwr.html.

35 Andrew Kadak, "MIT Pebble Bed Project," Massachusetts Institute of Technology (March 11, 2007), Website http://web.mit.edu/pebble-bed/papers1_files/MIT_PBR.pdf. See also "Pebble Bed Reactor," Princeton University, Website www.princeton.edu/~achaney/tmve/wiki100k/docs/Pebble_bed_reactor.html.

36 Linda Nordling, "Pebble-bed Reactor Gets Pulled," *Nature News* (February 23, 2010), Website www.nature.com/news/2010/100223/full/4631008b.html. See also "SA Mothballs Pebble Bed Reactor," South Africa.info (September 17, 2010), Website www.southafrica.info/news/pbmr-mothballed.htm#.VJhioP8ADM.

37 "Construction Progresses on China's High Temperature Pebble Bed Nuclear Reactors," *World Nuclear News* (April 9, 2014), Website www.world-nuclear-news.org/NN-First-CAP1400-reactor-under-construction-0404144.html. See also Christina Larson, "China Wants Nuclear Reactors, and Lots of Them," *Bloomberg Businessweek* (February 21, 2013), Website www.businessweek.com/printer/articles/98266-china-wants-nuclear-reactors-and-lots-of-them.

38 Generation IV International Forum, Website www.gen-4. Annual Report, provides a detailed description of the status of the six reactor types.

39 "Thorium," World Nuclear Association (September, 2014), Website www.world-nuclear.org/info/current-and-future-generation/thorium.

40 "Thorium Reactors: Asgard's Fire," *The Economist* (April 12, 2014).

41 Robert Hargraves, *Thorium: Energy Cheaper than Coal* (Hanover, NH: 2012).

42 Mehran Nezir, "BeO-UO$_2$ Fuel," Course Work Paper, Stanford University (March 18, 2012), Website http://large.stanford.edu/courses/2011/ph241/nazir2. For more detailed information, see references at bottom of paper.

43 "Small Nuclear Power Reactors," World Nuclear Association, Website www.world-nuclear.org/info/nuclear-fuel-cycle/power-reactors/small-nuclear-power-reactors.

44 "Small Modular Reactors," Babcock & Wilcox, Website www.babcock.com/nuclear-energy/pag. See also Matthew Wald, "The Next Nuclear Reactor May Arrive Hauled by a Truck," *The New York Times* (April 24, 2013).

45 NuScale Power, Website www.nuscalepower.com.

46 "Nuclear Power: All at Sea," *The Economist* (April 26, 2014).

47 The 2nd Edition of this book listed 2013! Status of construction of ITER on Website www.iter.org/construction.

48 National Ignition Facility and Photon Science, Website https://lasers.llnl.gov.

49 Steven Rose, "Viewpoint: Encouraging Signs on the Path to Fusion," Physics (February 5, 2014), Website http://physics.aps.org/articles/v7/13. See also "Physics World Names National Ignition Facility Fuel Gain Top Ten Breakthroughs of the Year," *Physics World* (December 15, 2014), Website www.llnl.gov/news/physics-world-names-national-ignition-facility-fuel-gain-top-10-break-through-year, and Ian Sample, "Scientists have Moved a Step Closer to Achieving Sustainable Nuclear Fusion and Almost Limitless Clean Energy," *The Guardian* (February 12, 2014), Website www.theguardian.com/science/2014/nuclear-fusion-breakthrough-green-energy-source.

50 Sebastian Anthony, "Cold Fusion Reactor Verified by Third-Party Researchers, Seems to Have 1 Million Times the Energy Density of Gasoline," ExtremeTech (October 9, 2014), Website www.extremetech.com/extreme/191754-cold-fusion-reactor-verified-by-third-party-researchers-seems-to-have-1-million-times-the-energy-density-of-gasoline.

51 A listing of the world's oldest dams not including those cited in the text built during the Common Era are at the International Commission of Large Dams Website www.icold-cigb.org/GB/World_register/general_synthesis.asp?IDA=212. See also Miguel Arenillas and Juan Castillo, "Dams from the Roman Era in Spain" (January, 2003), Website www.traianvs.net/textos/presas_in.htm, for information on the Cornalvo and Proserpina dams and other Roman era built dams in Spain.

52 Roger Hansen, "The Roman Flour Mill at Barbegal," WaterHistory.org, Website www.waterhistory.org/histories/barbegal.

53 Vaclav Smil, *Energy in World History* (Boulder, CO: Westview Press, 1994).

54 Fen Montaigne, "Water Pressure," *National Geographic* (September, 2002).

55 "Golden Jubilee Uganda," New Vision (February 3, 2012), Website www.newvision.co.ug/news/628782-owen-falls-dam--powering-uganda-for-five-decades.html.

56 "Kariba Dam: About to Collapse?" *Zambia Daily Mail* (March, 2014), as reported on the Infrastructurenews Website www.infrastructurene.ws/2014/03/25/kariba-dam-about-to-collapse.

57 Michelle Nijhuis, "World's Largest Dam Removal Unleashes U.S. River After Century of Electric Production," *National Geographic* (August 26, 2014), Website http://news.nationalgeographic.com/news/2014/08/140826-elwha-river-dam-removal-salmon-science-olympic.

58 "Reservoir Emissions," International Rivers, Website www.internationalrivers.org/campaigns/reservoir-emissions.

59 Martin Schlicht and Oliver Kirk, "Thousands of Germans Evacuate as Dam on Elbe River Breaks," Reuters (June 10, 2013), Website http://in.reuters.com/article/2013/06/09/us-europe-floods-idINBRE9580EF20130609.

60 "History of the Johnstown Flood," Johnstown Area Heritage Association, Website www.jaha.org/FloodMuseum/history.html.

61 Doyce Nunes (Editor), "The St. Francis Dam Disaster Revisited," based on an original report by J. David Rogers, Historical Society of Southern California (1995), Website www.owensvalleyhistory.com/ov_aqueduct1/st_francis_disaster.html.

62 "Engineering Failures: The Banqiao Reservoir Dam Failure," Engineering Failures (June 19, 2012), Website http://engineeringfailures.org/?p=723.

63 Arthur Sylvester, "Teton Dam Failure," Earth Science, University of California, Santa Barbara, Website www.geol.ucsb.edu/faculty/sylvester/Teton_Dam/welcome_dam.html.

64 "Niagara Falls: History of Power," Niagara Frontier, Website www.niagarafrontier.com/power.html.

65 Michael Harris, "Niagara Tunnel Completion Important Piece for Ontario's Hydroelectric Power Supply," HydroWorld (April 9, 2013), Website www.hydroworld.com/articles/2013/04/niagara-tunnel-completion-imporant-piece-for-ontario-s-hydroelec.html. See also "Niagara Tunnel Project," Ontario Power Generation, Website www.opg.com/generating-power/hydro/projects/niagara-tunnel-project/Pages/niagara-tunnel-project.aspx.

66 Michael Harris, "Northern Exposure: Canadian Hydro in the Spotlight," HydroWorld (December 9, 2013), Website www.hydroworld.com/articles/hr/print/volume-32/issue-10/cover-story/northern-exposure-canadian-hydro-in-the-spotlight.html.

67 Hydro-Québec Annual Report for 2013, Website www.hydro.qc.ca.

68 BC Hydro, Website www.bchydro.com.

69 "Site C Clean Energy Project," BC Hydro (December, 2014), Website www.bchydro.com/energy-in-bc/projects/site_c.html.

70 Stephanie Landers, "Hydropower Project on the Kapuskasing River Is a First for Many Reasons," Ontario Waterpower Association (July 18, 2014), Website www.hydroworld.com/articles/hr/print/volume-33/issue-2/articles/aboriginal-project-ownership-on-the-kapuskasing-river.html.

71 Michael Harris, "Chile Rejects Proposal for 2,750-MW HidroAysen Hydroelectric Project," HydroWorld (June 11, 2014), Website www.hydroworld.com/articles/2014/06/chile-rejects-proposal-for-2-750-mw-hidroaysen-hydroelectric-project.html.

72 Hydropower data from *BP Energy Statistics*.

73 "IHA Hydropower Report," International Hydropower Association, Website www.hydropower.org, provides a global view of what's happening in hydropower.

74 A description and photos of Itaipu dam can be found at Website www.solar.coppe.ufrj.br/itaipu.html.

75 Kenneth Rapoza, "Was Brazil's Belo Monte a Bad Idea?" *Forbes* (March 7, 2014). See also "Dams in the Amazon: The Rights and Wrongs of Belo Monte," *The Economist* (May 4, 2013).

76 "Sao Paulo's Water Crisis: Reservoir Hogs," *The Economist* (December 20, 2014). See also Gregory Poindexter, "Brazil's Drought Brings Water Supply to Near Zero Capacity at Hydroelectric Facilities," HydroWorld (January 28, 2015), Website www.hydroworld.com/articles/2015/01/brazil-s-drought-brings-water-supply-to-near-zero-capacity-at-hydroelectric-facilities.html.

77 International Commission on Large Dams, Website www.icold-cigb.org/GB/World_register/general_synthesis.asp?IDA=213.

78 Yun Sun, "China, Myanmar Face Myitsone Dam Truths," *Asia Times* (February 19, 2014), Website www.atimes.com/atimes/Southeast_Asia/SEA-01-190214.html.

79 Michelle Nijhuis, "Dam Projects Ignite a Legal Battle Over Mekong River's Future," *National Geographic* (July 11, 2014), Website http://news.nationalgeographic.com/news/special-features/2014/07/140711-mekong-river-laos-thailand-dams-environment.

80 Liyuan Lu, "China Mekong Dam Project Generates Growing Controversy," Voice of America (February 26, 2014), Website www.voanews.com/content/china-mekong-dam-project-generates-growing-controversy/1859964.html.

81 An example of the opposition to hydropower projects is Friends of the River Narmada, Website www.narmada.org.

82 Jagat Village, "Bad Politics Should No Longer Prevent Nepal and Its Neighbors Making the Most of Some Amazing Geology," *The Economist* (November 29, 2014).

83 "Hydro Power Invention," Alternative Energy (April 11, 2007), Website www.alternative-energy-news.info/hydro-power-invention.

84 "Great Wall Across the Yangtze," Public Broadcasting System (PBS), Website www.pbs.org/itvs/greatwall/dam1.html.

85 Li Hong, "China's Government Proposes New Dam Building Spree," International Rivers (February 28, 2011), Website www.internationalrivers.org/resources/china%E2%80%99s-government-proposes-new-dam-building-spree-3419.

86 "Three Gorges Dam Five-Step Ship Lock," Yangtze River Attractions, Website www.viator.com/Yangtze-River-attractions/Three-Gorges-Dam-Five-Step-Ship-Lock/d4440-a6664.

87 "Yangtze River Floods," Encyclopedia Britannica, Website www.britannica.com/EBchecked/topic/1503369/Yangtze-River-floods.

88 "Grand Inga Dam, DR Congo," International Rivers, Website www.internationalrivers.org/campaigns/grand-inga-dam-dr-congo.

89 "What is the Difference between Micro, Mini and Small Hydro?" Renewables First, Website www.renewablesfirst.co.uk/hydro-learning-centre/what-is-the-difference-between-micro-mini-small-hydro. See also "World Small Hydropower Development Report," available at Website www.smallhydroworld.org.

90 David Appleyard, "Hydropower Outlook," Hydro Review Worldwide (June 28, 2014), Website www.hydroworld.com/articles/print/volume-22/issue-3/article/market-guide/hydropower-outlook.html.

91 "ICE Cases: Litani River Dispute," American University (Washington, DC), Website www1.american.edu/ted/ice/litani.htm.

92 David Appleyard and Bethany Duarte, "Reaching for Turkey's Hydropower Summit," Hydro Review Worldwide (October 8, 2014), Website www.hydroworld.com/articles/print/volume-22/issue-5/features/reaching-for-turkey-s-hydropower-summit.html.

93 "Water-Shortage Crisis Escalating in the Euphrates–Tigris Basin," Future Directions International (August 28, 2012), Website www.futuredirections.org.au/publications/food-and-water-crises/678-water-shortage-crisis-escalating-in-the-tigris-euphrates-basin.html.

94 Alex Milner, "Mosul Dam: Why the Battle for Water Matters in Iraq," BBC News (August 18, 2014), Website www.bbc.com/news/world-middle-east-28772478.

95 "IRAQ: Food Insecurity on the Rise, Says Official," IRIN (UN Office for the Coordination of Humanitarian Affairs) (November 8, 2009), Website www.irinnews.org/report/86926/iraq-food-insecurity-on-the-rise-says-official.

96 *The Independent*, Website www.independent.co.uk/environment/nature/as-iraq-runs-dry-a-plague-of-snakes-is-unleashed-1705315.html. See also Campbell Robertson, "Iraq, a Land Between 2 Rivers, Suffers as One of Them Dwindles," *New York Times* (July 14, 2009), and "Fertile Crescent will Disappear this Century," *New Scientist*, Website www.newscientist.com/article/dn17517-fertile-crescent-will-disappear-this-century.html?DCMP=OTC-rss&nsref=climate-change.

97 Richard Porter, "Marsh Flooding Brings New Life to Iraq's 'Garden of Eden,'" BBC News (June 1, 2013), Website www.bbc.com/news/magazine-22706024.

98 "Iraq to Export Agricultural Products in Five Years," Alsumaria TV News (July 25, 2012), Website www.alsumaria.tv/news/60367/iraq-to-export-agricultural-products-in-five-years/en.

99 Nile Basin Initiative, Website www.nilebasin.org.

100 Ashenafi Abedji, "Nile River Countries Consider Cooperative Framework Agreement," Voice of America (March 17, 2011), Website www.voanews.com/content/nile-series-overview-11march11-118252974/157711.html.

101 Desalegn Sisay and Will Ghartey-Mould, "Ethiopia: Ministers Condemn Gibe III Dam Critics as Bank Finalizes Evaluation," Afrik-News (April 6, 2009), Website www.en.afrik.com/article15536.html.

102 Grand Millennium Dam, Website http://grandmillenniumdam.net.

103 Cam McGrath, "Nile River Dam Threatens War between Egypt and Ethiopia," Common Dreams (December 30, 2014), Website www.commondreams.org/news/2014/03/22/nile-river-dam-threatens-war-between-egypt-and-ethiopia.

104 Palash Ghosh, "What Are India and Pakistan Really Fighting About?" *International Business Times* (December 27, 2013), Website www.ibtimes.com/what-are-india-pakistan-really-fighting-about-1520856.

105 It is rumored that an Austrian Archduke insisted on being baptized in the Jordan River and subsequently died from typhoid fever.

106 Joshua Hammer, "The Dying of the Dead Sea," *Smithsonian Magazine* (October, 2005).

107 "Dead Sea Neighbors Agree to Pipeline to Pump Water from Red Sea," *The Guardian* (December 9, 2013), Website www.theguardian.com/world/2013/dec/09/dead-sea-pipeline-water-red-sea.

108 Sharon Udasin, "Israel, Jordan Sign Historic Plan to Save Dead Sea," *Jerusalem Post* (February 27, 2015), Website www.jpost.com/Israel-News/New-Tech/Israel-Jordan-sign-historic-plan-to-save-Dead-Sea-392390.

109 Robert Herendeen, *Ecological Numeracy: Quantitative Analysis of Environmental Issues* (New York, NY: Wiley, 1998).

110 Roy Nersesian, *Energy Risk Modeling* (Ithaca, NY: Palisade, 2013).

9 Solar and Wind Power and Their Storage

Sustainable energy sources are solar, wind, geothermal, and ocean (tidal, wave, and thermal). This chapter covers solar and wind power, the principal sustainable sources, including their contribution to meeting world energy needs, prospects, and reliability compared to fossil fuels. Two sources of sustainable energy have already been dealt with: biomass in Chapter 3, and hydropower in Chapter 8. Some feel that nuclear power also qualifies as a sustainable energy source if reprocessing of spent fuel and breeding fuel can extend the life of uranium reserves for thousands of years, further augmented with developing the thorium reactor. Solar and wind are the focus of renewable energy source development, but are inherently unreliable as cloud cover or wind speed are not predictable. Unlike a fossil fuel plant, electricity dispatchers cannot issue an order to increase output up to full capacity unless the sky is cloudless or wind speed falls within an optimal range. Moreover, full capacity output for a solar plant is time dependent. The chapter ends with storage of electricity, the *sine qua non* that has to be solved for solar and wind to make the transition from being an unreliable energy source on the periphery of energy supply to a mainstream contributor of reliable energy.

Solar Power

Sol means sun in Latin. Like other free sources of energy, solar energy is not free as major capital investments have to be made and the price of electricity from renewable sources, even with no fuel cost, must reflect fixed costs of operation plus a return of and on the capital investment. Moreover, particular conditions apply for renewable energy sources. For solar power, it is a function of the sun's position in the sky. Solar power can only be generated during daylight hours, with peak output on clear days when the sun is directly overhead. Fortunately, solar power peaks when electricity demand is highest, reducing the need for peaking generators. Unfortunately, solar power does not help the surge in electricity demand late in the day and in the early evening. The effectiveness of solar power is affected by cloud cover, times of day when the sun is near the horizon (early morning and late afternoon), seasons during which the sun does not rise high in the sky (winter at high latitudes), and even humidity and temperature. Solar (and wind) power cannot be relied upon without a backup. And like wind power, the best location for solar power may be in remote areas, necessitating the building of long-distance transmission lines. In full costing of solar and wind power, attention should be paid to necessary investments in backup support and/or electricity storage and transmission.

There are two types of solar energy: thermal and photovoltaic (PV). Thermal solar is a source of hot water that can be used for heating or for making steam to generate electricity. PV solar is the direct conversion of solar energy to electricity.

See the Companion Website for a section on Solar Power: www.routledge.com/cw/nersesian.

PV Solar Energy

PV solar energy is the direct conversion of the sun's radiation to electricity, obviating the need to convert thermal energy to steam in order to generate electricity by conventional means. PV solar energy represents the most significant growth in renewable energy at this time, beating out thermal solar and overwhelming other renewable sources. While wind power generates more electricity than solar, the growth in PV solar power is significantly higher than that of wind in recent years.

Development of the PV Solar Cell

Capturing solar energy in the form of electricity began with Edmund Becquerel, a French physicist, who studied the PV (electricity from light) effect. In 1839, he noticed that an electrical current through two metal electrodes submerged in a conducting medium increased when exposed to light, but did not pursue the matter further. In 1873, Willoughby Smith, an Englishman, experimented with the photoconductivity of selenium. The first solar cell is credited to an American, Charles Fritts, who coated the semiconductor selenium with a thin layer of gold in 1883 to produce the first working PV solar cell. It was constructed with two layers of semiconductor material. One layer has an abundance of electrons and the other a shortage. Sandwiching these together forms an electrical field at the interface, which acts as a battery when exposed to sunlight, forming a device that can convert sunlight to direct current (DC) electricity. However, high cost and low efficiency of 1 percent for converting solar energy to electricity left Fritts' idea dormant until 1941 when another American, Russell Ohl, used silicon to improve the conversion rate to 5 percent at far less cost. Russell Ohl received a patent for what is recognized as the first modern solar cell. In 1954, three scientists at Bell Laboratories were able to design a silicon solar cell with a conversion rate of solar energy to electricity of 6 percent along with another reduction in cost, opening the door to the commercialization of solar cells. The first commercial solar cells made their debut in 1956 to power radios and toys, but were very expensive at $300 per watt. AT&T built the first solar arrays to power the Earth satellite Vanguard I launched in 1956. Hoffman Electronics improved the conversion rate of silicon cells to 10 percent in 1960. In 1963 Japan built the largest ground based PV array installation of 242 W with a storage battery to supply electricity for a lighthouse. The energy crisis in 1973 provided an incentive to increase funding on solar technology with the result that the price of solar cells dropped dramatically to about $20 per watt (today it is $2–4 per watt). In 1973, the University of Delaware built "Solar One," a roof-installed integrated PV/thermal hybrid system that supplied heated water as well as provided electricity to a home. Since PV solar cells produce DC, output had to be converted to alternating current (AC) by means of an inverter for home-use. Excess output during the day was sold to a utility that supplied the home with electricity at night and during times of cloud cover.

One hour's worth of solar energy striking the Earth is greater than all the energy consumed by the world's population in 1 year. Desert land 100 miles on a side (10,000 square miles, which is equivalent to 9 percent of the area of the state of Nevada) could generate enough electricity to supply the US if laid end-to-end with solar panels, weather permitting, making the southwest the Saudi Arabia of solar power! However, the intent is not to concentrate the nation's solar power in one location, but to install solar power plants on rooftops and over parking lots and landfills dispersed throughout the nation to reduce reliance on electricity from conventional sources.[1]

Many nations are pursuing the solar option, and research is being conducted under a wide assortment of public and private programs sponsored by governments, universities, and private enterprises. The objective is to make electricity from solar power competitive with conventional sources by reducing front-end costs such as material costs for semiconductors, manufacturing and installation costs of solar arrays, and enhancing efficiency. The greater the efficiency in converting sunlight to electricity, the smaller the solar array has to be to deliver a given amount of electricity. In 2013 the leading nations for solar energy research and development were Germany ($251 million), the US ($194 million), Australia ($170 million), Korea ($118 million), and Japan ($90 million).[2] Success in these programs coupled with private industry efforts has led to a significant reduction in the cost of solar PV electricity. An example of private industry making an advance in technology in pursuit of its commercial interests is one that applies an etching 100 nanometers deep on both sides of the outer solar panel glass. Etching reduces reflectance and increases transmittance of light through the glass, enhancing the efficiency of transforming solar energy to electricity by 3 percentage points and annual energy output by 8–10 percent.[3] Another company has "etched" the surface of the silicon in a solar cell to increase the conversion efficiency by trapping sunlight inside PV microstructures where photons remain for a longer time, enhancing electrical output. The solar cell also has a special wide-angle feature on its surface to capture more light when the sun is low in the sky, also enhancing its efficiency.[4] Other companies are researching the possibility of solar cells using a wider spectrum of light, including infrared.[5]

Manufacturing Solar Installations

Most commercial PV solar cells are made of crystalline silicon cut in wafers as thin as 200 microns, usually 12.5 to 15 square centimeters and up to 20 square centimeters in area (about 1.5–1.75 square inches). Single-crystal PV cells account for 80 percent of all PV cells and are "grown" from melted silicon and can convert solar energy to electricity at an efficiency of 16–24 percent (up from 15–18 percent as reported in the previous edition of this book). In a laboratory setting, the highest efficiency from a solar cell was 46 percent.[6] The remaining 20 percent is largely multicrystalline PV cells produced using a less expensive melting and solidification process, but have a marginally lower efficiency of 14–21 percent. An even lower cost alternative is a solar film of extremely thin layers of PV semiconductor materials such as amorphous silicon deposited on a backing of glass, stainless steel, or plastic. While cheaper to make, thin-film PV arrays have a lower efficiency of 7 percent if made from amorphous silicon, but this could be increased to almost 22 percent by using more expensive copper-indium-gallium-diselenide.[7] Lower efficiency of commercially available thin films requires more area to produce the same output than conventional solar panels. The advantage of thin films is avoiding the glass coverings and mechanical frames of conventional solar panels. Thin films covering long strips of metal roofing panels are an economical way of generating electricity from the sun.[8] There are research efforts searching for a way to spray paint solar film on any surface to generate electricity.

In 2013, 230,000 tons of polysilicon, the raw material for making silicon wafers, was produced, with four companies accounting for half of production: Wacker Chemie (Germany), GCL-Poly Energy (China), OCI (Korea), and Hemlock Semiconductor (the US). China produces 58 percent of PV cells, with a large step down to Taiwan in second place with 18 percent, followed by Japan with 8 percent and Malaysia with 7 percent. In terms of PV modules, 65 percent are manufactured in China, 9 percent in Japan, and 6 percent in Malaysia. The top ten companies in PV module manufacturing are Trina Solar (China), Yingli (China), Canadian Solar (Canada), Jinko Solar (China), JA Solar (China), Sharp Solar (Japan), Renesola (China), First Solar (the US), Hanwha SolarOne (Korea), SunPower (the US), and Kyocera (Japan).[9] Qatar is mulling over entering into PV module manufacturing to take advantage of the opportunities presented by solar PV projects in the Middle East.[10] The Sahara Forest Project pilot plant in Qatar takes advantage of what is available (salt water and sunlight) to make what is needed (fresh water and fresh vegetables). Sea water enters the plant and cools greenhouse air via filters and then is desalinized using solar power. Desalinized water is potable and plants thrive on drip irrigation. Some thought is being given to capture carbon dioxide from nearby industrial plants for growing algae for fuel and food. Successful performance of the pilot plant could lead to a more commercially sized project.[11] Saudi Arabia is considering adding 41 gW of PV solar capacity by 2020. This would certainly be business for building a PV module manufacturing facility in Qatar or Saudi Arabia. The purpose of this amount of solar energy is to reduce 523,000 Bpd of oil being consumed in power stations.[12] In addition to conventional oil reserves, Saudi Arabia has enormous heavy oil reserves that have to be heated by steam before heavy crude can flow into a well. Normally the energy source is natural gas, but natural gas has more valuable uses as a feedstock for the petrochemical industry or exported as LNG. A massive planned expansion of solar power would be used for generating electricity and steam for enhanced oil recovery projects while enhancing oil and LNG exports.[13]

India suffers from electricity brownouts and blackouts from its poor electricity infrastructure. A significant load on the system is rural water pumps for irrigation. These are powered either by electricity if near to a grid or by diesels, consuming expensive diesel fuel. An idea is to substitute solar water pumps. Solar arrays would be built near the water pumps to minimize distribution costs. Since solar arrays have no fuel cost, it is feared that the solar pump would be used too extensively, contributing to a falling level of groundwater. To deal with this outcome, Indian farmers will have to switch to water-saving drip irrigation in exchange for subsidies to buy solar water pumps. Savings in diesel fuel purchases and in less subsidy payments to electricity consumers justifies the investment.[14] One mitigating factor against solar power in India is the long monsoon season when there is extended cloud cover, but this is the season when water pumps are not needed.

A massive investment in PV module manufacturing is vulnerable to disruptive technology. One such company, 1366 Technologies (named after solar radiation in the upper atmosphere of 1,366 W per square meter), has opened a demonstration factory for a more efficient way of manufacturing solar wafers. Wafers are conventionally made by first forming large blocks of crystalline silicon and then cutting them with diamond-coated wire saws, wasting as much as half of the original silicon as dust. 1366 Technologies makes wafers in a single step directly from molten silicon with equipment that costs a third as much as conventional equipment. If the demonstration plant succeeds, the company plans to take the next step toward manufacturing the product on a commercial scale.[15] MIT is conducting research on recycling discarded car batteries into solar panels. Recycled lead would be transformed to organolead halide perovskite that may one day be competitive with silicon based solar cells. Perovskite PV film is only a micrometer thick. Lead from a single car battery can make sufficient solar cells to power 30 households.[16] Zep Solar has a unique mounting design where the solar panels "snap together," reducing installation time for residences from 2–3 days to 4–5 hours.[17] On a global scale, there are 23,000 companies (including 15,000 installers) involved in providing and installing equipment, components, materials, and panels, plus others specializing in marketing, solar applications, and conferences.[18] This large number of corporate entities, like 1366 Technologies and Zep Solar, spur entrepreneurial effort to establish a competitive niche in this rapidly emerging industry.

Solar cells have a higher efficiency if surrounded by cool rather than warm air. Solar arrays in Antarctica operate at a higher efficiency than those in the Sahara. The efficiency of solar arrays can be enhanced by incorporating a tracking system to keep the array facing the sun; a single-axis tracking system increases irradiation by 25–35 percent and a double axis by 35–45 percent. The space program normally uses more expensive PV cells made of gallium arsenide and other semiconducting materials such as cadmium telluride or copper-indium-gallium-diselenide, whose efficiency in transforming solar energy to electricity can exceed 40 percent. There is also research on employing nanotechnology to produce organic solar cells of molecular polymers, which, if successful both technically and commercially, would be a game-changer in manufacturing solar cells.[19] Sandia National Labs is pursuing an inexpensive way to synthesize titanium dioxide nanoparticles that would allow a solar cell to capture more light, enhancing its efficiency.[20] Swiss Federal Laboratories for Materials Science and Technology are working on photo-electrochemical cells that utilize sunlight to split water into hydrogen and oxygen. Light capturing is enhanced by iron oxide that absorbs visible light and tungsten oxide that absorbs ultraviolet light. The combination can absorb as much as 35 percent of sunlight in spheres measured in nanometers. The hydrogen produced can be used as fuel or converted to electricity in a fuel cell at night or when needed.[21]

Solar Arrays

A PV or solar cell is the basic building block, small in size, and capable of producing 1 or 2 W of power. These are combined into larger units, called modules or panels, which produce 50–300 W of power, which are then joined together to form solar arrays sized to meet the desired power output. Historically solar arrays were primarily for off-grid applications providing power to isolated buildings in sunny climates such as lodges in national parks, lighthouses, telecommunications stations, navigational aids, and any facility far from an electricity grid. Smaller solar modules provide power for light signs, streets, gardens, pools, and remote telephones or automatic teller machines, or any need with similar power requirements. Off-grid applications normally have an associated battery that is charged by day in order to supply power at night or during inclement weather. A recent development in Africa is a low-cost solar powered electric light that can effectively compete with a kerosene lamp for internal lighting. An integrated battery and PV cell (8–10 hours for a daily charge) provides 4–5 hours of clear light from highly efficient white LEDs. The battery is an improved version that requires less replacing. The cost of $10 per solar lamp plus battery replacement compares favorably with a kerosene lamp plus fuel. The solar lamp is safer, with environmental benefits.[22]

Off-grid solar arrays have been instrumental for governments to launch economic development in areas too remote and/or sparsely populated to justify building an electricity grid. An independent solar (or wind) power system in isolated locations obviates the need for building a generation, transmission, and distribution system. A good example of this is a 950 kW solar power project on the island of Mindanao in the Philippines. Its purpose was to augment hydropower that had become inadequate to serve the needs of a community. Hydropower output is curtailed when solar power is available to conserve water for times when solar power is not available. Another company plans to build a 6.25 mW solar power plant also in Mindanao to replace aging diesel engine electricity generators. Both these projects are part of a Philippine government plan to increase solar power from 50 to 500 mW.[23]

Ground mounted solar arrays in non-desert environments can have vegetation growing under the array that may affect its performance. Popular means to control vegetation include mowing, spraying herbicides, relying on grazing animals such as sheep and goats, and covering the area with weed control sheets. Repeated spraying with herbicides and covering land with weed control sheets do not fit the picture of solar energy being an environmental poster child. There is a growing movement in favor of grazing animals and emus.[24] An associated issue is alternative land use of solar farms. Solar farms built in the desert or on top of landfills or on land unfit for agriculture do not affect food production. The image of solar farms does not seem compatible with loss of agricultural lands, but one can argue that placing solar farms on agricultural lands is no different than real estate developers transforming a farm into a housing development. But in Japan, finding available land for solar farms is difficult. Japan has resorted to the construction of solar farms built on high-density polyethylene floats. These floating solar farms are placed in protected waters. Solar arrays have also been placed on the face of dams and, of course, could be floated in dam reservoirs. Maintenance is higher for solar arrays floating on water and access is more difficult.[25]

Solar and wind power, when displacing diesel generators, eliminates the purchase of normally imported fuel in developing nations. But diesel generators are still needed for backup, running infrequently rather than continually. Cycling diesel or natural gas powered backup electricity generators create more carbon dioxide than running at a constant speed. The greenhouse gas emissions of the intermittent use of backup sources of power should be included in the greenhouse gas footprint of clean energy. Solar and wind power, either singly or together, with diesel backup, are viable means of supplying electricity on a local or distributive basis to one to two billion people who live in isolated communities far from electricity grids or in areas of low population density. The chief benefits of introducing renewable electricity to remote locations is improving health and providing light and power for education, communication, and commerce.

Capital investment in off-grid solar power includes solar panels, mounting structure, installation, inverter to change DC output to AC, and a storage battery, along with a charge controller for battery operation. Off-grid installations are still important, but they are losing relative importance to grid-connected installations. In 1992 about 75 percent of installations were off-grid and 25 percent were grid-connected. In 2000 the off-grid share dropped to 47 percent, and to 19 percent in 2004, 6 percent in 2008, and 1 percent in 2011. This is not to say that off-grid solar installations are declining in volume or importance; in fact they are expanding at 3 percent since 2007, but are simply overwhelmed by the enormous growth in grid-connected solar installations.[26]

Explosive Growth in Solar Power

Figure 9.1 shows that the growth in solar power is far beyond the take-off phase at 177 gW at the end of 2014 (versus 8 gW in 2007 from the previous edition of this book!).[27]

Compound growth in solar power is 45 percent between 2000 and 2014, starting, of course, from a minuscule base. Growth between 2013 and 2014 was 26 percent, probably reflecting that it is impossible to sustain at the pace of 45 percent compound growth over a long period of time as constraints on various aspects of manufacturing and installation would take their toll; nevertheless, growth is expected to remain robust.[28] While 177 gW is a large contributor to electricity, it is not the same as 177 gW from a fossil fuel or a nuclear plant. Fossil fuel and nuclear plants can operate at or near full capacity 24 hours a day. The output of a solar array is at full capacity in the hours around high noon—other than that, it operates at partial capacity while the sun is still visible. In terms of comparison with a fossil fuel plant, a solar plant capacity has only one-third of its energy output. However, if one takes the view that solar electricity is available during times of high or peak demand, then perhaps it does not matter. Solar power can be viewed as a substitute for peaking generators, and their economic analyses should reflect the need for fewer peaking generators. Solar power is not a threat to base load demand served by coal and nuclear power; its threat is directed at power

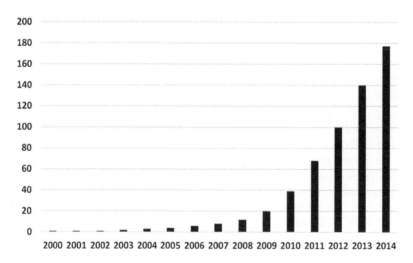

Figure 9.1 Historical Development of Solar Power (gW)

sources that satisfy heightened daytime demand. However, there have been occurrences in Germany of having to cut back base load generation in the face of simultaneous high outputs of solar and wind power. However, the energy output for solar power in terms of megawatt-hours is going to be only one-third of a comparable fossil fuel or nuclear plant, which, of course, affects the cost of solar electricity. Figure 9.2 is the installed capacity of solar PV power by nation.

Germany has over 35 gW of installed PV capacity as a result of an aggressive Feed-in Tariffs (FiTs) program to incentivize the building of solar capacity. FiTs were set at rates that made it profitable to install solar arrays, and the higher cost of solar power was then borne by all utility rate payers. It is a bit ironic that Germany, known for its overcast skies, would become a world leader in solar installations, but that happens with high FiTs. In 2013 Germany cut the tariff incentive as it felt that solar supplying 5.3 percent of its electricity met its national goals.[29] Of the 40 gW of additional solar power capacity added in 2013, 13 gW (32 percent) was in China, 7 gW (17 percent) in Japan, 5 gW (13 percent) in the US, and 3 gW (8 percent) in Germany. Again China dominates in its headlong drive to expand its energy portfolio with more environmentally friendly forms of energy. Many Japanese households invested in solar installations along with a battery to counter the risk of unreliable service following Fukushima. Tokyo Electric Power Company established attractive Time-of-Use rates, making it financially attractive to sell PV-generated electricity to the grid at a FiT premium and also purchase and store electricity from the grid during off-peak hours. A PV installation with battery storage allowed PV solar owners to receive the lowest rate when buying electricity and the highest rate when selling.[30] It is apparent in examining PV capacity added in 2014 that Germany's lead as the nation with the largest solar PV capacity will soon be challenged by China and later by the US and Japan. The US output of 12.6 gW includes private or residential installations of solar panels, as it is higher than the 9.1 gW quoted in the previous chapter.[31]

There are nearly 80 solar PV power plants above 50 mW in the world, with the largest two being 550 mW, both located in the US. For solar PV power plants above 200 mW, nine are in the US, three in China, and one in India. For the 54 solar PV plants under

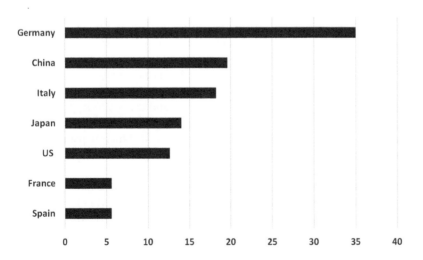

Figure 9.2 Installed Solar PV Power (gW)

construction or in the planning stage, 26 are above 200 mW, showing the shift to larger sized plants. Of these, the largest is in Greece of 10,000 mW (10 gW), being planned in 2,000 mW segments, which have yet to be sited. The next largest is 2.7 gW to be built in the US, followed by 2.0 gW to be built in China. One-gigawatt plants are to be built in the UAE and Pakistan. Half of the large plants above 200 mW are to be built in the US, with only two in China. It is clear from this that China is building many smaller sized PV plants which, in the aggregate, will make a very large contribution to global PV capacity. Some of this capacity is in remote areas of China, a portion of which had not been previously served by electricity. Other nations building large-sized PV plants are Australia, Chile, Japan, and Spain.[32]

Government Incentives to Promote Growth in Solar Power

The development of solar power, as with wind, started in the US (California, to be precise) as a result of the Public Utility Regulatory Policies Act (PURPA) of 1978 to spur the development of solar and wind and other alternative forms of power. This Act required state regulatory commissions to establish procedures for nonutility companies to sell electricity to utilities generated from renewable energy sources, waste, and cogenerating plants run on natural gas. California took an aggressive view of PURPA legislation that played a key role in the development of wind and solar power. Significant government monies were invested in the development of solar power by other nations. Japan, Germany, Spain, the US, and other nations offered incentives for individuals and businesses to install solar and wind and other alternative power sources. These come in various forms such as a direct grant or rebate paid to the individual or business for installing solar and other renewable power units, and various tax benefits both in terms of a tax deduction or a direct dollar-for-dollar reduction in taxes such as investment and production tax credits. An investment tax credit is a specified percentage of the total capital cost, say 7.5 percent, that can be written off immediately against tax payables when an installation is completed. Production tax credits also reduce tax liabilities and apply to solar as well as wind, geothermal, micro-hydroelectric, open-loop biomass, refined coal, livestock and municipal solid waste, and landfill gas as defined by the legislation. Production tax credits have resulted in negative electricity rates.[33] Wind power is generally not needed at night, but it can take business away from base load nuclear and coal plants by selling for less than base load rates. In fact, electricity from wind can be sold at a negative rate, paying the utility to buy the electricity. Suppose that a production tax credit is worth $20 per megawatt-hour and a wind farm sells electricity for a negative $5 per megawatt-hour. The wind farm spends $5 to get a utility to buy the output and earns $20 in production tax credits with which to reduce its taxes to the federal government. This, of course, only works when wind turbine owners have taxable income to shield. Nuclear plant owners have objected to this practice as they have to cut back in generating electricity to accommodate intrusion of wind electricity.[34]

Other forms of subsidies include soft loans at below-market interest rates and long payout periods, the right to sell production to a utility at an agreed rate (FiT), which are direct cash payments for power generated. FiTs can be at the average cost of electricity generation for the utility. Utilities object to FiTs based on cost of generation because it does not include the transmission and distribution costs that a utility must face. FiTs are often higher than normal utility rates, as in Germany, and the extra cost of renewable energy is passed on to utility customers. For home installations, a system of debits and credits can be set up where credits are earned by the homeowner when the solar installation is generating excess electricity that can be transmitted to the grid. Debits result when electricity from the grid is being supplied to the home. On some scheduled basis, the account is liquidated with a payment being made or received by the homeowner depending on the net balance. Net metering is similar in that the meter spinning backward from solar panel electricity generation being fed into the grid is simply subtracted or netted from actual consumption. Government mandating sustainable building standards requiring PV panels is another way to boost solar power. In the US, most states have some sort of program to encourage the development of solar energy, ranging from personal, corporate, sales, and property tax exemptions plus loan and grant programs as a means of inducement. Significant rebates of the order of 50 and 60 percent were offered by various states. Direct grants in the 2009 American Recovery and Reinvestment Act encourage installing alternative energy systems.

Supports for Solar Power

Solar power works better if electricity rates are based on time-of-day metering when rates track actual demand. This improves the economics of solar power immensely since the day rate for electricity is higher than the night rate. Night rates reflect low rates charged by base load electricity providers of nuclear and coal powered plants, while day rates are set by the marginal supplier. If incentives to install solar power are profitable, then one can consider oversizing an array and selling excess power back to the utility. Regardless of the outcome of an economic analysis, one may still choose solar power just for the satisfaction of having a home that does not require burning a fossil fuel or relying on nuclear power.

Installing a 454 kW solar array for Monmouth University in New Jersey in 2005 had a capital cost, including installation, of $2,860,000. A substantial rebate was available from the state of New Jersey in the amount of $1,715,000 (60 percent of capital cost). This reduced the capital investment to $1,145,000. Table 9.1 summarizes the economic analysis of the installation assuming a cost of purchase of 10 cents per kilowatt-hour, which applied at the time of the installation. The cost of solar power remains fixed over its 20–30-year life regardless of subsequent hikes in utility rates. Since a portion of the output can be sold to the utility at commercial rates, the greater the escalation of utility rates, the higher the return on investment.

Table 9.1 Economic Analysis of Actual Solar System

	Aggregate Savings (Costs) over 25-Year Life of Project
Avoided electricity purchases	$2,415,000
Avoided transformer losses	$50,000
Estimated sales of electricity back to utility (first 4 years only)	$315,000
Maintenance of solar system and roof	($110,000)
Aggregate savings	$2,670,000
Cost of system net of rebate	$1,145,000
Internal rate of return over 25-year period	8.3%

The net capital investment of $1.1 million earns a healthy return, primarily in the form of avoided electricity purchases from the utility. Any hike in electricity rates above 10 cents per kilowatt-hour, which occurred as a consequence of higher natural gas prices for the utility, increases the rate of return on the investment. However, as the analysis plainly shows, the internal rate of return is positive only because of a significant commitment on the part of the state government to support the development of solar power. A review of the project in 2014 showed that its profitability was greater than originally anticipated because of the magnitude of subsequent hikes in electricity rates that were effectively hedged by that portion of demand satisfied by solar. Its fixed electricity rate lowered the overall cost of electricity.

In 2012 other buildings on campus were fitted with solar panels on the basis of no cost to the university—only an obligation to buy the output at a fixed price, reflecting electricity rates when the rooftop solar panels were installed with no escalation in price thereafter. These solar panels are not fixed, but are free-standing, with a heavy bottom to prevent movement by wind or rain. From the point of view of the university, a fixed price for 20 or 30 years for another portion of its electricity needs with no upfront investment was a good deal along with any revenue that could be earned by selling excess electricity back to the utility at higher rates. Obviously, from the point of view of the installing company, the net cost of the installation after government rebates and benefits in the form of tax deductions and tax credits for a tax paying company was sufficient, when combined with lease revenue to be earned from the university, for this to be a sound financial investment.

Sizing Home Installations

The controlling variable is the electric bill, which determines the number of panels. Oversizing an installation that results in a negative electric bill should be based on a careful economic analysis. Sometimes electric utilities pay the wholesale rate for electricity, which is of the order of one-half the retail rate, which may not economically justify an oversized installation. If the price paid by a utility is the retail price, then this may change the decision. However, 75 percent of installations are constrained by the roof area suitable for installing solar panels, which removes oversizing from the table. The north side of a roof should not be used as the sun normally does not rise high enough in the sky to provide sufficient radiation. The best location is the south side of a house, followed by east and west sides, in areas with a minimum of shading by trees or house structure or chimney.[35]

A typical solar panel measures 65" × 40" and costs about $1,000 per panel (dimensions and cost vary, of course, by contractor and type of installation). Besides the retail price of electricity, an economic analysis should be net of any available subsidies offered by state or federal governments for installing solar arrays. Typical electricity consumption is 1,000 kWh per month or 12,000 kWh per year. Electricity usage peaks in summer in warm climates for air conditioning and in winter in cool climates for electric heating or electric forced air blowers. In San Jose, California, with 5.6 peak hours of sunlight and an average roof tilt of 18°, a typical home requires 32 solar panels with a 260 W output. A home in northern New Jersey, with 4.2 peak hours of sunlight with an average roof tilt of 30° to avoid snow accumulation, requires 42 solar panels. The number of panels is affected by location, suitable roof area, degree of shade, and tendency to become soiled. Dirty solar panels degrade output between 5 and 10 percent, but can be up to 20 percent in dry areas with more airborne dust or sand particles. A good rainfall cleans dirty panels and restores their efficiency. Installers do not have to climb a roof to plan a panel layout as this can be done on special solar panel software using satellite pictures and computer graphics to plan placement of panels. Higher output panels of 300 W are available for roofs short on space, but of course their cost is higher. Some thought should be given to the possibility of eventually owning an electric vehicle when making a decision on installing solar panels. New solar installations are generally amenable to adding panels at a later time if desired. Reputation of installer and preferably being a local businessman are other factors that have to be integrated into the decision.

Renewable Portfolio Standards

Governments or regulators have established renewable portfolio standards (RPS) where utilities must have a certain percentage of their electricity generation from renewable energy, typically about 20 percent of their output, to be accomplished over a reasonable period of time. The US and Canada do not have a uniform RPS for the entire nation. However, individual states and provinces have imposed RPS, such as Arizona (15 percent by 2015); California (20 percent by end of 2013, 25 percent by end of 2016, and 33 percent by 2030); and New York (29 percent by 2015).[36] The extra costs for renewable energy sources are borne by rate payers or by tax payers depending on the nature of government support for the development of renewables.

The Arizona Power Service (APS) operates in the US Southwest where the company can take advantage of 300 days of sun and plentiful desert land. The logical choice to meet its required renewable energy standard is solar. APS buys the entire output of 800 mW of solar installations in its region including the 280 mW Solana Generating Station that serves 70,000 customers. The parabolic trough plant generates electricity and also heats up tanks of molten salt to 700°F during the day that can be tapped for up to 6 hours of electricity generation after dark. The solar plant is 1,700 football fields large, or 3 square miles, of parabolic troughs plus a steam and electricity generating plant and molten salt tanks.[37] A new program starting in 2015 is a residential rooftop solar program. About 1,500 customers across Arizona (not a large number, but a start) will be able to install APS-owned rooftop solar panels on their homes free of charge and receive a $30 credit each month on their electricity bill for the next 20 years. There are no upfront or maintenance fees for participants. APS owns the solar array and is responsible for arranging installation. The benefit of excess electricity production would accrue to APS. This is a start of a distributive type of electricity generating system within a utility system that normally depends on a few centralized generating stations; perhaps this program is a harbinger of the future. A customer considering this program also has the right to buy and install solar panels on his or her roof; the relative economics of both alternatives should be checked out first. The chief benefit of the APS program is that it requires no investment.

The approach of the EU is to set a goal to be attained, not by utilities, but by member nations. The 2009 Directive of the European Parliament, which supersedes previous directives on renewable energy standards, establishes an overall policy for renewable sources to fulfill at least 20 percent of its total energy needs and at least 10 percent of transport fuels from renewable sources by 2020. Each member state is to adopt a national renewable energy action plan with national targets for the share of energy from renewable sources consumed in transport, electricity, and heating and cooling in 2020.[38] For instance, France has a renewable energy standard of 23 percent, Spain 22.7 percent, Germany 18 percent, and Italy 17 percent by 2020. The most common method for achieving renewable energy source goals is FiTs, where the tariff is set at a level to make renewable energy sources profitable for investors. Russia's goal is to have 4.5 percent of electricity generated from renewable sources; China 11.4 percent for nonfossil fuels by 2015 including hydro; India 9 percent renewable electricity generation excluding hydro; Japan 10 percent renewables by 2020; and Australia 20 percent electricity generation by 2020.[39]

Solar Co-ops

Co-ops are common in the US, numbering 30,000 with 100 million members, and can be made up or owned by workers, residents, consumers, farmers, and communities, or any combination thereof. Co-ops for the most part are not about making profits but in sharing benefits as, for instance, a purchasing co-op where members reap the benefit of savings by aggregating small purchases that would have to pay retail prices to large group purchases at wholesale prices. Installing solar installations on its customer rooftops in a collaborative effort between a utility and their customers can be expanded to a cooperative of individuals acting together to meet a common need or aspiration. Co-ops can be formed to share knowledge. Amicus is a solar cooperative jointly owned by 33 independently owned and operated solar PV installers, who share best practices among themselves and also pool their buying power for installation materials.[40] Community residential owners are forming solar co-ops where the discovery process on deciding to install rooftop panels is shared among the members, including contracting for their installation. Rather than install solar panels on their roofs, people are forming solar gardens where they share the cost and maintenance of a single solar array in a good location and proceeds of the sale of electricity to a utility are credited to their electricity bills.[41] NRG Energy is building five community co-op projects totaling 8.2 mW that allow homes and buildings unfit for installing solar panels to buy solar electricity from a nearby project—another example of a beginning of a utility's shift from centralized to distributive power generation.[42]

California: Major Supporter of Alternative Fuels

An example of government support for solar power occurred at the end of 2005 when California Public Utilities Commission unveiled a plan to install 3 gW (3,000 mW) of capacity over the next 11 years. This plan would double then-existing global solar power capacity and would supply 6 percent of California's peak electricity demand. The California Solar Initiative (CSI) would provide $3.2 billion in rebates over the subsequent 11 years with an objective of installing solar panels on one million homes and public buildings. Funding would also be eligible for solar water heating along with other solar power technologies. CSI was actually an expansion of an existing program that added a surcharge to consumer utility bills with the proceeds dedicated as rebates for solar power installations. The plan was to add about 80 mW of power by 2013, making California the largest state in the union in solar power generation.

The success of CSI can now be judged. In 2014 California has over 2,000 solar companies employing over 47,000 people, and in the previous year, California installed 2.7 gW (2,700 mW) of solar capacity at a cost of $7 billion to the state budget, bringing the total installed capacity to 8.5 gW, the highest in the nation. PV solar prices have fallen 39 percent since 2010. Clearly California has exceeded CSI's original objectives by a wide margin.[43] California intends to maintain this growth and has an ambitious renewable energy standard of being 33 percent reliant on renewable energy by 2020.

US Bureau of Land Management: Major Supporter of Solar Sites

Solar radiation levels in the Southwest rank among the best in the world and the US Bureau of Land Management (BLM) has control over more than 19 million acres of public lands in California, Nevada, Arizona, New Mexico, Colorado, and Utah. Since 2010, BLM has approved 29 utility-scale solar energy projects including transmission construction authorizations for 8.5 gW of solar power and has 70 pending solar energy applications. The Western Solar Plan established an initial set of 17 Solar Energy Zones, totaling 285,000 acres of public lands, which were given priority for commercial-scale solar development. Two additional Solar Energy Zones were designated in 2013 in Arizona and California. If fully built out, projects in the designated areas could produce as much as 27 gW of solar power.[44]

Companies: Major Supporters of Solar Growth

Envision Solar's EV ARC (Electric Vehicle Autonomous Renewable Charge) provides solar powered recharging of electric driven plug-in motor vehicles parked under a canopy. Units are completely self-containing without the need for building foundations, getting building permits, or being connected to the grid. The solar canopy has an automatic solar tracking system to maximize power production and delivers 16 kWh per day, which at 3.5 miles per kilowatt-hour is only about enough to power an electric vehicle 60 miles. An associated battery is charged when no car is under its canopy, which can hasten the recharging of an automobile's battery.[45] Of course an individual can place solar panels on top of the roof of a home or car port and use the output for home use, recharging an electric vehicle's battery, or feeding excess generation back into the grid. Expanding on this concept, shopping centers and hotels are installing car ports covered with solar panels in their parking lots. A car port provides shade for parked automobiles for a cooling effect when people leave their automobiles. Solar panels on the car port provide electricity that can substantially decrease the electricity bill for a shopping center or hotel.[46] Walmart enters into third party contracts with solar developers who install, own, and operate solar arrays on Walmart rooftops. Walmart locks in low cost, long term rates to buy electricity and benefits from any green credit from generated electricity. Walmart's solar power output is greater than the solar power of 38 states![47] Other Big Box retailers such as Costco and Ikea are installing solar panels on their roofs and in their parking lots to generate power and provide shade for customers parking their cars.[48] Amazon, Google, Microsoft, and Apple have and are making noteworthy investments in solar power to meet their electricity needs. Most of these projects are between 100 and 400 mW, and Google's capacity will reach 1 gW of solar power.[49]

Economics of Solar Power

In terms of 2013 dollars, the median installed cost of a 10 kW residential sized solar array was $7 per watt in 2010 and $4.40 in 2013 for an annual decline of 14.4 percent per annum over this 3 year period. The median installed cost of a 100 kW commercial sized solar array was $6 per watt in 2010 and $4 in 2013 for an annual decline of 12.6 percent. The median installed cost of a utility sized solar array of 5 mW was $3.90 per watt in 2010 and $3 in 2013 for an annual decline of 8.4 percent. There is no reason to believe that these decline rates will not continue into the foreseeable future.[50] Solar power is getting cheaper, but still can be relatively expensive compared to fossil fuel generated electricity if not supported by government incentives.

To translate $/W to $/kWh, the capital cost for a plant with a capacity of C kilowatts is the multiplicand of one thousand times C and the indicated $/W for the plant. With an assumed capital recovery factor of 10 percent, the annual cost is 10 percent of the capital cost assuming nil maintenance expenses (alternatively it may be possible to approximate maintenance expenses as a percent of capital and incorporate it into the capital recovery factor). Suppose that a solar array can deliver an equivalent full power of C kilowatts for 6 hours a day for 365 days per year. Six hours a day takes into consideration daylight hours where the few hours after sunrise and before sunset are just a fraction of the power delivered at high noon with further adjustments for average cloud cover and latitude (the sun does not rise high above the horizon in winter at high latitudes). Cost in the numerator is divided by watt-hours in the denominator and both contain the variable C, which cancel one another. Thus the resulting cost in dollars per kWh is independent of the size of the solar installation. What discriminates different sized solar installations is that the cost per watt of larger sized installations is less than smaller sized installations. Figure 9.3 is the required dollars per kWh to support different sized installations whose dollars per watt differ with size.

The $/watt installed cost does not take into consideration any rebates or any other form of subsidized taxes and other gimmickry. Whether the installer is paid partly by the government and partly by the owner is immaterial to the installer. Whatever tax benefits accrue to the owner are of no interest to the installer. Thus Figure 9.3 can be considered the actual cost of solar power in terms of $/kWh without subsidies, which can be compared to the average residential cost of $0.12/kWh. For the median cost of

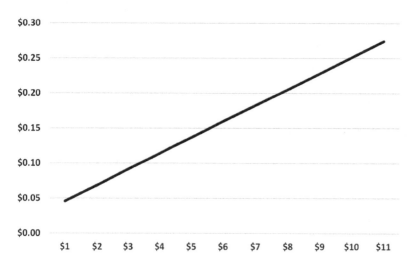

Figure 9.3 Required $/kWh versus $/W Installed Cost

$4.40/watt for a residential solar array in 2013, the resulting electricity charge is $0.20/kWh and, for commercial at $4/watt, $0.18/kWh. This can still be considered expensive electricity even in light of substantial improvements in the cost and efficiency of solar installations. However, if the installation cost were financed by a 50 percent rebate by the government, then the $/kWh cost would be cut in half, providing cheap electricity for the consumer and demonstrating the influence of government subsidies on decisions to proceed with a solar installation. A utility sized solar array at $3.90/watt would be $0.137 per kWh, but this would have to be compared to the average wholesale rate, which, of course, is less than $0.12 per kWh. Again various forms of government assistance can make the utility solar array economically attractive for an owning utility or independent power provider.

Subsidizing solar power has been successful in providing financial incentives that have given birth to a large industry. Further efforts in research and development and competitive pressures among participants have been responsible for a significant decline in costs. If this trend continues, the cost of subsidization will also diminish, pointing to the day when it may not be necessary. Subsidization of clean energy was needed to develop renewable energy sources, but over time, with the elimination of subsidies, governments may recoup some of the subsidies by the normal process of taxing profits on companies in the solar energy business.

The marked progress that has been made in reducing solar electricity rates could be seen in late 2014 when 10 bids for a 100 mW PV solar plant were opened by the Dubai state utility. Shocking everyone, the winning bid was $0.0598/kWh and second place was $0.0613/kWh. The winning bid was far below the estimate of $0.137/kWh derived above for utility sized installation. However, the cost of financing was very low, estimated to be 5 percent, half of what is assumed in Figure 9.3. If the formula in deriving Figure 9.3 were adjusted to expand 6 hours to perhaps 8 hours considering solar conditions in the Middle East and reducing financing costs in half, Figure 9.3 values would be cut by 60 percent, clearly showing the impact of greater solar intensity and lower cost financing. As a point of reference, the highest bid submitted to the Dubai state utility was $0.147/kWh. An unsolicited bid for a 1,000 mW facility was $0.054/kWh. Previous winning bids in Brazil and India were in the $0.08–$0.09/kWh range. Solar industry observers feel that the unprecedented low winning bid, void of any subsidy, reflects the tremendous progress of technical, commercial, and financial innovation in the PV industry. The solar industry is coming of age, and these low bids will incentivize other nations to more vigorously pursue the solar option.[51] The progress of solar power to eventually making a meaningful contribution to satisfying overall energy can be seen in Figure 9.4, which shows the energy source for US power plant capacity added in 2013.[52]

Natural gas contributed 48 percent of the 14.3 gW of new electricity generating capacity. Solar is in second place at 28 percent, including residential solar that can be viewed as new generating capacity distributed among homes rather than centralized in a single facility. Coal is a distant 11 percent, as is wind at 7 percent. For 2014, of 9 gW of power plants brought into operation, 42 percent were natural gas, 27 percent wind, 13 percent "small" solar (private installations), and 18 percent "big" solar (solar electricity fed through the electricity grid).[53] These figures are net of small contributions from hydro and biomass; coal is out of the picture. Although overall solar is still a small percentage contributor to energy demand, doubling every 3 or 4 years assures that its future role will gain in importance at the expense of other sources of energy at a rapid pace.[54]

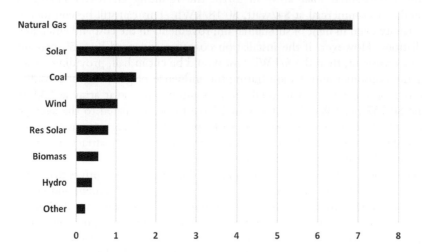

Figure 9.4 Energy Source for New US Power Plants in 2013 (gW)

Wind Power

Wind results from differences in air temperature, density, and pressure from uneven solar heating of the Earth's surface. Like ocean currents, wind currents act as giant heat exchangers, cooling the tropics and warming the poles. Successful placement of wind turbines is in areas with persistent winds, such as where geological formations force wind to flow through relatively narrow mountain passages as in California. Mountain chains channel air such as the east side of the Rockies, making the northern plain states ideal for wind turbines. Other areas of desirable wind patterns are along coastlines where, during the day, air above land heats up more quickly than air over water, causing a sea breeze of heavier, cooler air over water rushing in to take the place of rising warmer air over land. At night, a land breeze results from air cooling more rapidly over land than over water. Coastlines and offshore waters are high on the list for wind development projects to take advantage of their fairly reliable and robust wind patterns.

See the Companion Website for sections on the Historical Development of Wind Power and Government Involvement in Developing Wind Turbines: www.routledge. com/cw/nersesian.

From Tiny Acorns to Mighty Oaks

During the 1980s and 1990s wind turbine installations increased steadily in northern Europe. Denmark was the leader, drawing on its earlier role in wind energy. The higher cost of electricity and excellent wind resources in northern Europe created a small but stable market for single and cooperative-owned wind turbines. Driven by high utility power rates for wind power, the installation of 50 kW turbines rapidly gave way to

100 kW, then 200 kW, then 500 kW, and, in the mid-2000s, 1.5 mW wind turbines by cooperatives and private landowners in the Netherlands, Denmark, and Germany. The installation of over 70,000 mW (70 gW) of European wind capacity by 2009 supported a thriving private wind turbine development and manufacturing industry.

The 1990s robust wind development activity in Europe contrasted with the US penchant for low electricity rates based on cheap coal and natural gas, which when coupled with deregulation of the utility industry virtually strangled wind energy development. In the 1990s the California wind farm market was further pummeled by expiration or forced renegotiation of once attractive power purchase contracts with the major California utilities Southern California Edison and Pacific Gas and Electric. Despite this negative outlook, in 1999, "green power" initiatives in Colorado, Texas, and elsewhere spurred US wind energy development. New wind farms included a cluster of Zond Z-40 turbines operated for a southwest Texas utility, a wind farm of 46 Vestas machines at Big Spring, Texas, a 10 mW wind farm in northern Colorado with other turbines in the upper Midwest, plus "repowering" of California projects with larger and more modern units. Entrepreneur Jim Dehlsen founded the company that manufactured Zond turbines, now part of GE Energy. GE Energy is the world's largest manufacturer of wind turbines, as seen in Table 9.2.[55]

Perhaps the greatest incentive for the revival of wind energy was the fall in cost of wind electricity from $1.00 per kilowatt-hour in 1978 to under $0.05 in 1998, and as low as $0.02–$0.04 in 2012 for large wind turbines favorably located in the US.[56] However, it is difficult to accurately compare the costs of wind farms and fossil fuel plants because their respective cost drivers are so vastly different. Low installed cost per kilowatt figures for wind turbines are misleading because cost estimates are based on

Table 9.2 World's Largest Wind Turbine Manufacturers

Company	Percent Market Share	Description
GE Energy (US)	15.5	16,000 1.5 mW installed plus 2.5 mW plus 4.1 mW built for offshore
Vestas (Denmark)	14.0	43,000 turbines in 66 nations including 1.8 and 2.1 mW for onshore, 3 mW for low wind conditions plus 3 mW for offshore via MHI Vestas joint venture
Siemens (Germany)	9.5	Market leader offshore turbines 2.3 mW, 3.6 mW, and 6 mW with 150 meter diameter rotor
Enercon (Germany)	8.2	20,000 turbines worldwide including 2 mW, 2.5 mW (light winds), 3 mW, and 7.5 mW
Suzlon Group (India)	7.4	21.5 gW of installed capacity including 2.1 mW for normal and light winds. German subsidiary is REpower 1.8–6.15 mW
Gamesa (Spain)	6.1	18 gW of installed capacity including 2 mW, 4.5 mW, and 5 mW (offshore)
Goldwind (China)	6.0	World's leading manufacturer of permanent magnet direct drive turbines including 1.5 mW and 2.5 mW; other leading Chinese manufacturer is Sinovel

full capacity operation. But wind is not reliable, and actual load factors vary between 25 and 40 percent of capacity compared to average load factors for natural gas power plants of 50 to 70 percent of capacity with the ability to ramp up to 100 percent capacity at will, or coal and nuclear plants that normally operate near full capacity at all times, an attribute that wind turbines cannot replicate. Thus 200 gW of wind capacity represent at most 80 gW of conventional fossil fuel electricity generating plants. Widely dispersing wind farms and placing them in areas where acceptable wind conditions are prevalent increase their reliability. But the cost estimates of wind energy projects frequently neglect the need for backup sources of power in case the wind stops blowing and the need to construct transmission lines to the electric power grid from what could be remote areas amenable for generating wind power.

While fuel is free, wind turbines have operating costs such as insurance and maintenance. Film clips of wind farms always show a number of idle wind turbines, which gives an inkling of their reliability.[57] With the top of wind turbines a few hundred feet in the air, some method has to be devised to get repairmen up to where the electricity generating equipment is located. On land, large cranes may be necessary for lattice type wind turbines to hold ladders in place for workmen to climb to the machinery space behind the hub. Larger and more modern wind turbines have a tubular tower with an internal ladder for repairmen to climb. In offshore waters, helicopters have to be employed to lower repairmen to the dome-shaped top of wind turbines. Repair costs have to reflect the use of large cranes or helicopters and the inherent danger of climbing hundreds of feet up a ladder in gusty winds or being lowered on top of a dome shape in windy conditions compounded by the helicopter's downdraft prior to fastening oneself to a safety line. Worker safety in installing or repairing wind turbines is a critical issue.[58] Can you imagine climbing a ladder within a tubular tower to what amounts to 30–40 floors of an office building only to discover that a vital tool or part is lacking? Wind turbine manufacturers install a supervisory control and data acquisition (SCADA) system to permit the detailed monitoring of all critical aspects of wind turbine operation in order to identify potential problems early in order to initiate remedial action. Once a problem needing the attention of repairmen occurs, there is little need to do an initial investigation as to what might be the cause with information provided by SCADA.[59]

Like water flowing in a river, the amount of generated electricity is determined by energy contained in wind passing through the area swept by wind turbine blades known as wind power density. Wind power density depends on the cube of wind speed (when wind speed doubles, wind power density goes up by a factor of eight), and also on air density and temperature (lower altitudes and cooler temperatures increase wind power density). A turbine has four output phases depending on wind speed. No power is generated when wind is below a minimum speed. Above the minimum speed, electricity output rises with the cube of increasing wind speed until the wind speed attains a threshold level. Above this, electricity output is constant at the turbine's rated capacity even with increasing wind speed to avoid overstressing the wind turbine. Turbine blades are designed to rotate with a frequency that ensures optimum efficiency and maximum yield of wind power density that can be converted to electricity with minimum tower oscillation, but are also designed to become less efficient at wind speeds that exceed the rated power output and can damage the tower supporting the turbine or the blades themselves. When wind speed is too high, a wind turbine stops producing electricity and assumes a mode of operation that protects the blades and tower against physical damage.

Large commercial wind turbines operate between 10 and 20 revolutions per minute (rpm) where the rate of rotation depends on wind speed.

For wind turbines to be efficiently employed, dispatchers should have an accurate forecast of wind conditions in order to plan a short term schedule of operation for the utility's generating resources. To assist dispatchers, IBM has developed the Hybrid Renewable Energy Forecasting (HyRef) system that has weather modeling capabilities for small areas such as within a square kilometer and to vertical heights where turbine hubs and rotors are located. Sensors on turbines monitor wind speed, turbulence, temperature, and direction, and this information is integrated with satellite weather information and other data and analyzed to provide forecasts from minutes to 72 hours ahead in order to better integrate an intermittent power source into the electricity grid.[60] HyRef reduces the degree of wasted wind (and solar) power stemming from not being able to forecast short term supply.

The larger the wind turbine, the less is its impact on the environment (the greener the electricity). The cause of this is cumulative learning and experience and advancements in technology and efficiency over the course of building ever larger wind turbines. The assessed environmental progress rate of 86 percent means that for every doubling of cumulative production of wind energy, global warming potential per kilowatt-hour of wind energy is reduced by 14 percent.[61] The world's largest wind turbines in the design phase are Mitsubishi's 7 mW and Areva/Gamesa's 8 mW turbines. REpower's 6 mW is the largest turbine installed at sea. The largest installed on land is Vestas' 8 mW turbine with blades 80 meters long or a rotor diameter of 160 meters. To give perspective as to the length of a blade of 80 meters, the Airbus 380, normally carrying around 450 passengers with a maximum capacity of 840 passengers, has a tip-to-tip wingspan of 79.8 meters and a length of 73 meters.[62] The Airbus 380 can fit lengthwise and width-wise within a single blade!

Enercon's 7.5 mW turbine has been developed from its predecessor 6 mW turbine introduced in 2007 with a concrete tower and a 135 meter hub height. This is almost 450 feet to the machinery space of a wind turbine or about the same as a 40 story building. Imagine climbing up this height on an internal ladder within the tubular tower or being lowered by helicopter to the dome of the turbine! Enercon's wind turbine has segmented steel composite hybrid blades with a 127 meter rotor diameter, or a blade length of 63.5 meters.[63] Thus the distance from ground to bottom of the blade at its low point is the hub height less the blade length, or 72.5 meters or 240 feet above the ground. Samsung's 7 mW turbine is in the testing phase and 6 mW wind turbines are undergoing testing at Siemens, Alstrom Haliade, and Sinovel, which is also in the preliminary design phase for a 10 mW wind turbine. Five mW wind turbines are available from Areva, Gamesa, Bard, and XEMC.[64] These large turbines are affected by torque and thrust. Torque turns the rotors, creating power, while thrust equivalent to five F-18 engines pushes against the turbine, threatening to topple it. It requires great engineering skills to design a wind turbine that can withstand these forces and yet remain reliable.[65] In 2015, GE Energy offered 11 models of wind turbines with rated capacities between 1.6 and 3.2 mW.[66] The company however does not appear to be at the cutting edge of building larger sized wind turbines of 5–8 mW. If larger sized turbines can reduce the ratio of capital cost to electricity output, that is, provide economies of scale, this may affect GE Energy's standing as the world's largest wind turbine manufacturer. In 2012 GE Energy was the world's largest wind turbine manufacturer partially due to a last minute extension of the production tax credit (PTC) wind subsidy. However, in 2013, GE Energy sank to tenth in ranking with the expiration of the PTC, illustrating the dependence of renewables on government support. In 2013, the largest companies in terms of wind turbine installations was Vestas (4.8 gW of installed capacity and 14 percent market share), Enercon GmbH (3.7 gW and 10 percent market share), Xinjiang Goldwind (3.6 gW and 10 percent market share), Siemens (2.6 gW and 7 percent market share), and Suzlon Group (2.2 gW and 6 percent market share).[67]

Larger wind turbines are more efficient in extracting energy from the wind and their cost in terms of output falls. The dollars per megawatt-hour declined from a range between $60 and $110 in 1995 to about $55 per megawatt-hour ($0.055 per kilowatt-hour) in 2004. Thereafter the cost of a megawatt-hour of capacity increased from the rising prices of wind turbines (part higher material costs and part greater market demand) to $80 per megawatt-hour. These costs do not reflect any form of government subsidy. The future cost per megawatt-hour in 2010 dollars is expected to fall another 10 to 35 percent by 2030 from further reductions in manufacturing costs and advances in technology.[68]

The older models of wind turbines had gear boxes that would speed up the rotation of a generator several hundred fold over the rotational speed of the rotor to allow for a much smaller generator. However, gearboxes generally have a poor record of durability. The industry is moving toward direct drive permanent magnet generators, which while larger in size are actually lighter in weight because permanent magnets allow for weight savings by removing the necessity for copper coils fed by electricity to provide a magnetic field.[69] Moreover, slower rotating generators generate less heat and therefore there is less concern over cooling. The variable rate of rotation generates a variable frequency electrical current, which is converted to DC. Historically electricity was transmitted for long distances as high voltage AC, but recent technological progress now allows high voltage DC transmission. At some point before electricity enters an AC transmission system, DC is converted to a fixed frequency AC as required by the utility, such as 60 hertz or cycles per second in the US, or 50 hertz in the UK and elsewhere.

Offshore Wind Installations

A very large area for the development of European wind energy is not coastlines, but offshore waters. There are 150,000 square kilometers (58,000 square miles) of water less than 35 meters (115 feet) deep available for development with more than enough potential to fulfill the continent's electricity needs, weather permitting. Offshore installations are more costly to build, requiring specially designed jack-up rigs to install offshore wind turbines.[70] It is also more costly to connect offshore wind farms to shoreside transmission systems. Reliability is of crucial concern in the design, manufacturing, and laying of undersea cables.[71] The variable frequency output of wind turbines is converted to high voltage DC for more efficient underwater transmission before being converted to high voltage alternating current on land. Offshore wind turbines avoid problems associated with finding and acquiring suitable landside sites and, generally speaking, offshore winds are more dependable and have a higher average speed than onshore winds.[72] An acceptable offshore location is one with an annual average wind speed of at least 14 miles per hour; an ideal location is one with a persistent wind speed 25–35 miles per hour. Figure 9.5 shows the annual additions to offshore wind capacity. It is clear that

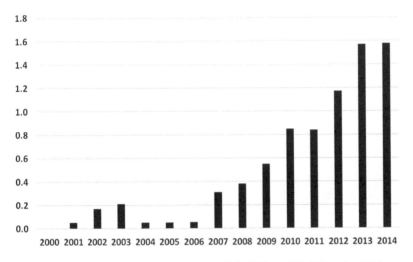

Figure 9.5 Europe: Annual Additions to Installed Offshore Wind Capacity (gW)

offshore installations are in the take-off phase of development. Annual growth from 2007 to 2014 was 26 percent.

Figure 9.6 shows the distribution of 5.4 gW of offshore wind turbines. Over half is offshore the UK, with the London Array being the largest offshore wind farm at 630 mW. Denmark was the first European nation to take a serious interest in wind technology and is now in second place with the UK (Denmark being a much smaller nation). Denmark is a major exporter of hardware (wind turbines) and software (knowledge and expertise) to other nations. China is a late-comer in offshore wind turbines but already ranks third, nearly tied with Belgium.[73]

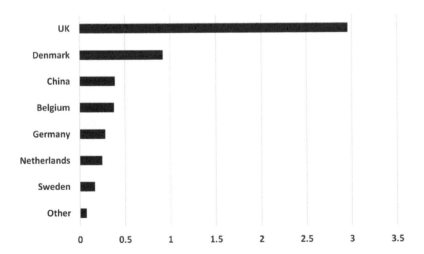

Figure 9.6 2012 Offshore Installed Wind Turbines (gW)

As of mid–2014, there were 2,300 offshore wind turbines in Europe with a combined capacity of 7.3 gW in 73 wind farms in 11 nations. During the first half of 2014, 224 off-shore wind turbines in 16 wind farms of 781 mW were fully grid connected with another 310 wind turbines awaiting grid connection, which when connected would increase capacity by 1.2 gW to 8.5 gW. Of the grid connected turbines completed during the first half of 2014, 81 percent were manufactured by Siemens and 29 percent by MHI Vestas. Total wind turbines under construction will add 4.9 gW when fully commissioned. This is nearly equal to the 5.4 gW of installed capacity as of the end of 2012 or a near doubling of capacity.[74] Plans are underway to significantly expand European offshore wind capacity. Dogger Bank Creyke Beck will initially consist of two 1.2 gW offshore installations as a prelude to further development of a total of 4.8 gW.[75] A planned expansion of the Cumbria wind farm in the Irish Sea of 0.75 gW would restore the record for this wind farm of being the largest in Europe.[76] Race Bank, east of England, is planning on expanding its capacity by 0.58 gW.[77]

The offshore waters of New Jersey and Delaware have conditions favorable for wind farms. If wind farms were built about 15 miles offshore along much of the coastline, electricity generation would make Delaware and New Jersey not only self-sufficient, but leading electricity exporting states. As with any project, a hurdle for offshore wind farms is getting the requisite permissions. Shoreside residents are reluctant to see the tips of wind turbines peeking over the horizon.[78] Nevertheless New Jersey offshore wind developmental plans have been completed, but require the Governor's approval to keep the process going. Shoreside residents in Long Island have killed offshore wind projects despite their espoused economic and energy benefits. The 468 mW offshore Cape Cod wind farm (Cape Wind project), whose blade tips will be seen just over the horizon, faced early opposition by the politically connected residents of Hyannis, Massachusetts. The project has been in continuous litigation since its inception in 2000.[79] Today the opposition is led by one of the Koch brothers, both billionaire oil men, who is strongly opposed to this project because of "visual pollution" from his several shoreside estates.[80]

Permitting offshore wind farms is extremely complex, requiring review and/or approvals under the Outer Continental Shelf Lands Act, National Environmental Policy Act, Section 10 of the Rivers and Harbors Act, Clean Water Act, Clean Air Act, Coastal Zone Management Act, various US Coast Guard laws and regulations, Marine Mammal Protection Act, Endangered Species Act, Migratory Bird Treaty Act, Magnuson-Stevens Fishery Conservation and Management Act, and National Historic Preservation Act. In addition, a project requires a number of state and local approvals. The regulatory processes involved in obtaining these approvals permit numerous opportunities for legal challenges by groups opposed to the project.[81] The outcome of this byzantine web of litigation is problematic. Or perhaps not: "extended, unprecedented and relentless litigation" delayed the project sufficiently that Cape Wind could not complete its financing by the end of 2014. Having missed this significant milestone, utilities buying the power filed to terminate their power purchase agreements, which were at substantially higher rates than conventional electricity sources.[82]

States showing interest in offshore wind power include Rhode Island, Delaware, Maryland, North Carolina, and Oregon.[83] Deepwater Wind has received financing to start construction in 2016 of five offshore wind turbines each with an output of 6 mW for a total capacity of 30 mW 3 miles southeast of Block Island in Rhode Island state waters.[84] The wind farm will generate over 125,000 mWh annually as compared to the theoretical 30 mW times 8,640 hours per year or 259,200 mWh for an efficiency of 48 percent. If true, this is significantly higher than onshore installations. Power will be exported to the mainland electricity grid via a 21 mile, bidirectional submarine HVDC cable. Deepwater Wind also proposes a wind turbine offshore Long Island, which is currently under review by the buying utility. Deepwater Wind specializes in floating wind turbines using the same technology of the oil and gas industry for deep water production from floating rigs.[85] Floating wind turbines can be located far from shoreside residents in deep waters with ideal wind conditions. Principle Power is in the approval process to build a demonstration floating wind turbine in Coos Bay, Oregon. If successful, the company is planning a 30 mW offshore wind farm, called the WindFloat Pacific Project, which would be five floating wind turbines tethered 16 nautical miles from Coos Bay in waters 1,400 feet deep.[86]

Offshore and Onshore Wind Installations

From tiny acorns planted in the 1980s in California, mighty oaks are growing. As cited in the previous edition of this book, 2008 global wind energy capacity was 120 gW, growing at a compound growth rate of 27 percent since 2000 when output was 17.4 gW. Global installed wind power in Figure 9.7 exhibits 26 percent growth since 1996, almost identical with the growth rate between 2000 and 2008.[87] Wind power has grown 330 percent between 2008 and 2014, a very impressive degree of growth.

In 2008, the leading nations with installed wind power of 120 gW were the US at 21 percent, Germany 20 percent, Spain 14 percent, and China trailing at 10 percent. A forecast made by the Global Wind Energy Council in 2008 for year 2013 was 318.1 gW, whereas actual capacity in 2013 was slightly higher at 332.1 gW, a highly accurate forecast by any measure. Figure 9.8 shows the distribution of 396.6 gW of wind power in 2014 by nation.

In 2014, the leading nation is China, followed by the US, Germany, and Spain. China and the US will continue their robust growth, but Germany and Spain will lag as a

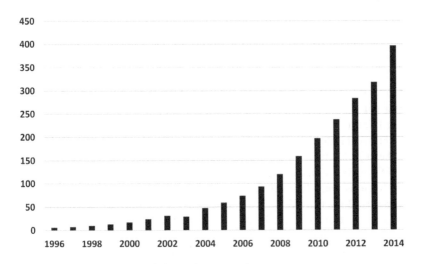

Figure 9.7 2014 Global Installed Wind Power (gW)

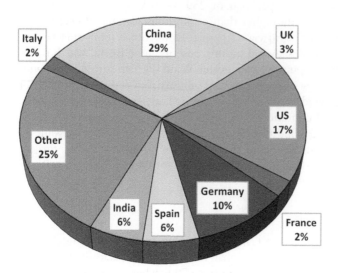

Figure 9.8 2014 Wind Power Capacity by Nation (gW)

consequence of Germany paring back renewable energy subsidies and Spain eliminating them. Europe is suffering from an economic slump and falling power demand and a growing concern to reduce the price of electricity.[88] Moreover, some of its new wind installations are repowering existing wind farms with newer and more powerful turbines in place of older and smaller turbines.[89] India is just a bit short of overtaking Spain and will be in fourth place in 2015. "Other" has doubled in just a few years, indicating the spreading globalization of wind power.

In Figure 9.7, the 2014 global wind capacity is 396.6 gW. If this operates with an efficiency of 30 percent, this is equivalent to about 120 gW of fossil fuel generating capacity. Multiplying this by 8,640 hours of operation is 1,037,000 gWh or 1,037 tWh. World electricity generation was 23,537 tWh in 2014. Thus wind, in spite of its progress, accounts for only 4.4 percent of world electricity. But if wind power continues to grow at 26 percent and if world electricity generation continues growing at 1.5 percent per year, then in 10 years wind power will provide 38 percent of electricity generation: no longer a marginal player. If wind power grows at a more realistic sustained annual growth of 20 percent, then wind power will provide 24 percent of electricity generation, still a major player on a par with natural gas. The world's largest wind farms in 2012 over 600 mW are Da'an (Gansu) at 1,000 mW; Shepherds Flat (Oregon) 845 mW; Roscoe (Texas) 782 mW; Horse Hollow (Texas) 736 mW; Alta Wind (California) 720 mW; Capricorn Ridge (Texas) 663 mW; Dabancheng (Xinjiang) 640 mW; and Anbei (Gansu) 601 mW.[90] Figure 9.9 shows the annual regional forecast for newly installed wind power.[91] Total output of the various wind farms making up Gansu Wind Farm is 5,160 mW and is anticipated to grow to 20,000 mW by 2020, near the 22,500 mW capacity of Three Gorges Dam.[92] Of course, Gansu Wind Farm can only approach the output of Three Gorges Dam when wind is within its optimal speed range.

Figure 9.10 adds the forecast to the actual figures in Figure 9.7 to obtain a projection of wind power to 2018.

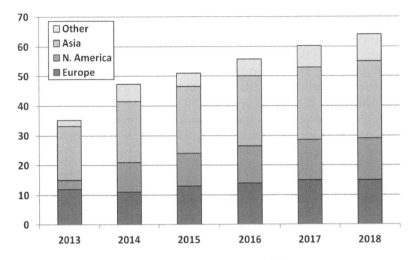

Figure 9.9 Annual Market Forecast by Region 2013–2018

Projected 2018 wind power capacity will be just under 600 gW with an overall growth rate between 2010 and 2018 of 14.8 percent, down from the previous cited 26 percent. Extremely high growth rates cannot continue because of the doubling effect of exponential growth. At 26 percent annual growth, capacity doubles every 3 years; at 14.8 percent every 5 years. Doubling at these frequencies sooner or later runs up against constraints. For instance, China's rapid development of wind power in its northern parts has breached a constraint on transmission capacity to send electricity to its southern parts where electricity is consumed. Installing new capacity in the northern parts of China will be slowed until improvements are made to the transmission infrastructure to handle higher loads, but wind development will proceed in other areas of China.

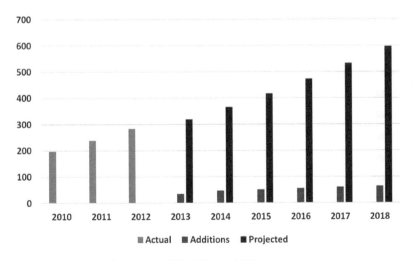

Figure 9.10 Projected Growth of Wind Power (gW)

Wind Power in the US

Figure 9.11 shows the leading states with an installed capacity of over 2 gW.[93]

Based on US total wind power of 67.8 gW in 2015, Texas has 23 percent, California 9 percent, Iowa 8 percent, and Oklahoma 6 percent.[94] In the early 2000s, the northern Great Plains states (Montana, the Dakotas, and Wyoming), self-dubbed the Saudi Arabias of wind energy, had the potential to supply the US with all its electricity needs, weather permitting, on land that would have taken up about 10 percent of the area of just one state. But these states did not become the center of wind activity from a lack of a long-distance transmission system to get the electricity to market. The so-called transmission superhighway was not authorized to be built and so today their contribution to wind power is relatively minor.

Similarly T. Boone Pickens, an oil man, had an idea of building what would have been the world's largest wind farm (4 gW) in the Texas Panhandle. The constraint was the necessity of building a long distance transmission system to connect the wind farm with the electricity grid. Without this infrastructural support by the federal government, the project was abandoned in 2009. But things change with the passage of time, when the Texas Legislature, not the federal government, authorized the spending of $7 billion for 3,600 miles of transmission lines in the belief that "if you build it, they [wind farms] will come." The cost works out to about $300 per person served by the Texas grid, which will be paid by a monthly $6 surcharge to electricity bills. As of the end of 2013, 7 gW of wind capacity is under construction in the Panhandle of Texas, which has very favorable wind conditions, with plenty of room for more expansion since the transmission lines are capable of carrying 18 gW. Special zones have been set up for wind development to ensure wind developers have access to the transmission system. The saving in electricity cost from the wind farms is estimated to be greater than the $6 per month surcharge to build the transmission system.[95]

Another proposal to link the windy plains of Kansas to electricity consumers is the Grain Belt Express Clean Line. The promoters of this project compare this transmission line to a railroad, which made it possible to transform the empty plains of Kansas into

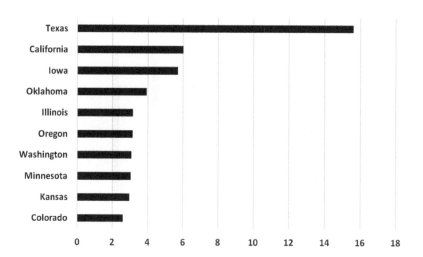

Figure 9.11 US States with More Than 2 gW Installed Wind Power (2015)

one of the nation's principal grain growing states or to a pipeline that has to be built first before oil reserves can be developed. This transmission line, once built, will make it possible to tap the wind resources of Kansas. The transmission line will be a 600,000 volt high voltage DC (HVDC) capable of transmitting 3.5 gW of electrical power. It'll run 750 miles from Kansas to Indiana where it will connect with other transmission lines, and is tentatively scheduled for completion in 2018.[96] HVDC has lower inductive losses than HVAC, no need for frequency regulation, lower voltage conversion losses, much more suitable for underground and underwater transmission, bidirectional, and fits better with connecting to independent asynchronous AC systems.[97] Unlike the transmission line in Texas connecting Panhandle to population centers in Texas, which faced no opposition from ranchers, the Grain Belt Express Clean Line is running up against opposition from farmers through whose land the transmission line must pass for both visual pollution and loss of fertile land for agricultural use.[98]

Wind Power in China

Figure 9.12 shows the phenomenal growth in wind power capacity in China.[99]

China only had minuscule wind power capacity until 2005. In 2008 China's capacity was 12 gW, 10 percent of the world's total. Then wind capacity simply exploded to 27 gW in 2009, 45 gW in 2010, and 115 gW in 2014 for an astounding 55 percent compound growth since 2001. For the last 3 years, growth has been within the range of 20–25 percent, a more sustainable growth rate. China built up its wind turbine manufacturing capacity, with its top five wind turbine manufacturers being Goldwind, Sinovel, United Power, Mingyang, and Dongfang. China has an ambitious goal for a number of regions and provinces in China to have at least 10 gW of capacity: East Inner Mongolia, West Inner Mongolia, Hebei, Jiangsu, Jilin, Gansu, Xinjiang, Shandong, and Heilongjiang. Figure 9.13 shows the provinces with the largest wind power capacity in 2012.

These regions and provinces are in the "Three Northern Area" (northwest, north, and northeast China), the center of wind power development. Northern regions are the best location for wind development both for wind conditions and vast tracts of empty land

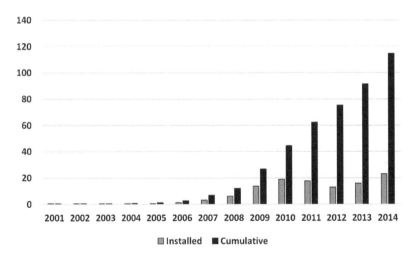

Figure 9.12 China: Annual Installed and Cumulative Wind Power (gW)

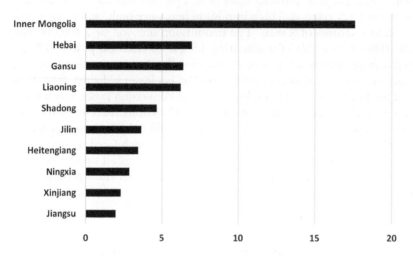

Figure 9.13 Wind Power Capacity in Provinces of China (gW)

on which to build wind farms. However, there is a mismatch between where wind farms are built in northern China and where electricity is consumed in southeast China. The transmission infrastructure had proven inadequate to handle the load, forcing producers to curtail production. In 2011, curtailment in electricity generation was necessary in East Inner Mongolia by 22 percent, Jilin by 20 percent, West Inner Mongolia by 18 percent, Gansu by 16 percent, Heilongjiang by 15 percent, and Liaoning by 10 percent.[100] The pace of building wind power units in these regions has been slowed to give time to improve the transmission infrastructure. In the meantime, wind development has moved to some extent from the northern to the central and eastern parts of China. While wind conditions are not as desirable as in northern China, there is a local market to consume electricity and a more robust transmission infrastructure to reach other population centers. China has 18,000 kilometers of shoreline and 6,000 islands where offshore installations can be built, and as seen in Figure 9.6, China is now a distant third in offshore installations from being 3 years behind its planned schedule of expansion. China considers offshore wind more risky and costly than onshore wind and is taking a more cautious stance on developing offshore wind, but who's to say where China will stand on offshore wind tomorrow?[101] As of the end of 2014, China's wind capacity was 114 gW versus the US at 67 gW. Wind power is growing fast and now exceeds nuclear power in China.

Small Can Be Beautiful

As with solar, wind farms do not have to be large to be effective. Isolated areas that are not connected to electricity grids can be served by small wind farms coupled with diesel generators as backup when the wind is calm. In addition to small wind farms, there are small wind turbines to allow individual homeowners, farmers, businesses, and public facilities to generate their own clean power to reduce electricity bills or for areas not connected to an electricity grid. Wind turbines for individual homes have a capacity of 1–10 kWh, while intermediate wind turbines of 10–100 kWh can serve villages.

Taking advantage of the 40 percent decline in wind electricity costs in the last few years, distributed wind companies are being formed to serve this market. These companies take the hassle out of wind project development including the permitting process and allow those buying wind energy to concentrate on their business interests without getting directly involved with setting up a wind farm.[102] A wind farm can be augmented by solar power when the sun is shining. Battery storage is a form of backup, but diesel power backup is still needed for those times when the battery has a low charge with the wind not blowing and the sun not shining.

While solar panel installations can be purchased by individuals for their home, it is difficult to purchase a wind turbine. But an enterprising company buys existing wind turbines and then sells shares in a wind turbine. Revenue is determined by the output of the wind turbine with rates set by a contract to a utility, and shareholders must pay an annual maintenance fee. A smartphone app allows shareholders to monitor wind speeds and electricity output in real time.[103] Remote locations far off the grid may not have small installations—mining activities are normally powered by diesel generators. Mines in Chile are using wind and solar power in excess of 100 mW to reduce the dependence on expensive diesel fuel.[104]

Another entrepreneurial company has devised "SolarMill," a combination solar panel mounted on top of vertical axis wind turbines for homes or small commercial establishments. SolarMill generates power from the sun and wind simultaneously and its largest model has a maximum solar output of 1,470 W and a wind output of 286 W with a wind speed of 11 meters per second and 1,000 W at 17 meters per second.[105] Units are scalable, meaning that a consumer can install the requisite number to meet his or her electricity demand when the sun is shining and the wind is blowing. Units are mounted on a building where both solar and wind conditions are best.

Objections to Wind Power

Usually there has been little opposition to locating wind turbines on farmland, given the long history of windmills on American farms that lasted until the mid-twentieth century. Farming operations are minimally disturbed by the presence of wind turbines, which are normally sited in pastures or along edges of fields, and are viewed favorably by farmers as a source of incremental income even though a turbine has a direct or indirect impact on about 15 acres of land. As a point of comparison, a well to frack oil or gas has an impact on about 50 acres of land, taking into consideration well pads, pipelines, water disposal ponds, and new roads to gain access to drill sites.[106] Much of the opposition to developing wind farms comes from suburbanites, real estate developers, and environmentalists for a variety of reasons.

Wind turbines are highly visible. No matter what the size, suburbanites do not want to look at them and environmentalists object to locating wind farms in scenic areas or along coastlines. Some of this opposition can be overcome by designing less obtrusive and/or more pleasing designs, such as foregoing lattice for tubular towers and blending a line of wind turbines with the contours of the land. Unsightly transmission lines can be removed by burying them. Some object to the swishing noise of the blade passing through the air, which can be heard within a few miles of a large wind farm and within several hundred feet for an individual wind turbine. Noise from a wind farm is less obtrusive than normal motor vehicle traffic, but the fact that a quiet night is no longer quiet bothers people.

To counter this, increasing the separation between a wind farm and a residential area reduces noise levels. Larger wind turbines can be quieter than smaller ones, depending on the speed of the blade tip and the design of a blade's airfoils and trailing edges. Local opposition can be mollified if the citizenry receives a monthly stipend or a reduction in property taxes for permitting a wind farm to be built. Non-local opposition cannot be bought off so easily.

Another objection was locating early wind farms in mountain passes in what turned out to be bird migratory paths. Birds were killed when they flew into the rotating blades. Siting wind farms now takes into account bird migratory paths. Even if built in a migratory path, migration is a seasonal phenomenon. Radar can be used to stop the wind turbines when a large flock of birds is about to pass through or near a wind farm. The leading cause of bird fatalities by human interference is not birds flying into wind turbines, but into buildings, windows, high-tension transmission lines, communication towers, and motor vehicles, plus fatal encounters with pet cats and pesticides. Hundreds of millions of birds are killed flying into homes and buildings and a billion by predatory cats.[107] As a point of comparison, one study concluded that about a quarter million song birds are killed annually by US and Canadian wind turbines.[108] It was thought that fewer more powerful wind turbines would reduce bird deaths, but the jury is still out on this assertion. A planned expansion of the London Array in the Thames Estuary from 630 to 1,000 mW was abandoned because of the time required to assess its impact on the winter feeding ground for 6,500 red throated divers.[109] Still wind turbines have the lowest kill rate by far among manmade encounters. The Obama administration has decided not to pursue the matter of bird and bat kills by solar and wind installations.[110]

Nevertheless wind turbines pose a hazard for birds that cannot dodge a blade whose tip speed is over 200 miles per hour. A proposed design for wind turbines with no external blade would avoid killing birds. Wind enters a vertical cylindrical structure where airfoils direct the wind against blades on a rotating vertical shaft. The vertical shaft allows the generator to be at ground level for greater ease of maintenance and reduced interference with radio, television, and communication signals. The vertical axis wind turbine is shorter in height than a traditional wind turbine, less obtrusive in appearance, creates less noise from its lower speed of rotation, and has a surrounding wire mesh to prevent birds from entering the turbine. While the vertical axis wind turbine has an optimal wind speed similar to that of traditional wind turbines of 28–33 mph, it can operate with wind speeds up to 70 mph versus 50 mph for traditional wind turbines. This higher range of wind speed increases the overall average output from 25 to 40 percent of rated capacity for traditional wind turbines to 40–45 percent.[111]

As with any utility project, there are a number of organizations a wind farm developer must successfully negotiate with before construction can begin. State governments have boards that require an environmental impact assessment for the wind farm and its transmission lines. Permits are required from land commissions before a project can move ahead. A public utility commission must grant a certificate of need. County and community planning boards ensure compliance with zoning ordinances and land use requirements. As with any real estate development, clearing land for access roads and wind turbine foundations must be done in a manner that avoids or minimizes soil erosion. These boards can also address the possibility that a wind farm might interfere with radio and television reception. If the wind project is on land, then the Bureau of Land Management or Forest Service will be involved, along with the Fish and Wildlife Service, to ensure minimal hazard to birds and other wildlife.

The views of community groups greatly influence the permit process. As described with the Cape Wind project, interest groups can challenge a site proposal through the court system if they believe that laws, regulations, and legal procedures have not been properly followed. To ensure public support, it is important for project organizers to make the public aware of the benefits of wind power, including any contribution that the wind farm is making in the form of paying local taxes in addition to steps being taken to minimize environmental objections.

Evaluating a Potential Site

While a single wind turbine can have large fluctuations in power output from abrupt changes in wind speed and direction, a wind farm covering a wide area tends to dampen the aggregate impact of shifting winds. Wind patterns can be affected for days from passing storms and weather fronts and for months from seasonal variations (winds are generally more intense in winter and spring). What counts in determining the feasibility of a potential wind farm site is not short term wind fluctuations or seasonal swings but average speed throughout the year. The economic return of a wind farm is enhanced if wind blows more during daytime when electricity is more highly valued, but in many locations the reverse is true. Night time wind electricity is often not desired or wanted because coal and nuclear plants are relatively inflexible in adjusting their loads to accommodate fluctuations in wind farm output. Wind electricity will come into its own when economical storage facilities can be built to store night time generation for dispatching during the day. In addition to average annual wind speed, wind patterns near the ground are critical in selecting the height of the hub (center of the rotor). Wind shear is the change in wind speed with height, which is influenced by solar heating, atmospheric mixing, and nature of the terrain. Forests and cities tend to increase wind shear by slowing the speed of air near the surface. A differential in air speed between the blade's lower and upper sweeps can damage the blade. Wind shear can be greatly reduced with an abrupt change in terrain height such as a sea cliff or mountain ridge. Cliffs and ridges also accelerate wind speed, as do mountain passes.

Financial Incentives

Tax shields to induce investment come in various forms such as accelerated depreciation and tax credits. A tax shield reduces a corporate or personal tax by the tax rate; for a corporation paying a tax rate on its profit of 35 percent, a $100 tax shield is worth $35 in reduced taxes. A tax credit is a far more powerful incentive than a tax shield because a tax credit is a dollar-for-dollar reduction in taxes; a $100 tax credit is worth $100 in reduced taxes as long as the corporation is paying taxes. A production tax credit is in terms of cents per kilowatt-hour produced for the first 10 years of a wind turbine's life. For a tax-paying company, this has a direct impact on lowering taxes. Tax shields and tax credits are direct subsidies that cover the higher incremental cost of wind energy, which the government absorbs in the form of decreased tax revenues. In the US, the problem with production tax credits, both at state and federal levels, is that they normally expire after a short period of time and require frequent legislative renewals, which are not always forthcoming. US production tax credits expire and are renewed on an annual or biannual basis. This on-again, off-again tax credit has predictable results. Figure 9.14 shows the annual additions to wind power capacity.[112]

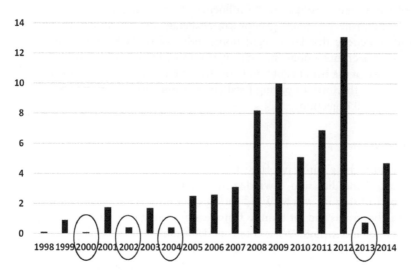

Figure 9.14 Annual Additions to US Wind Power Capacity (gW)

Following the expiration of production tax credits in 1999, 2001, 2003, and 2012, installations of new turbines fell considerably in 2000 by 92 percent, in 2002 by 76 percent, in 2004 by 76 percent, and in 2013 by 92 percent.[113] In following years when production tax credit was reinstated, wind turbine installations increased dramatically, illustrating the vital role of production tax credits in the economic decision making process for wind turbines.

One way to encourage growth in wind energy and other renewable sources is for utilities to offer customers an option to pay a premium on their electricity rates that will support the generation of electricity from renewable sources. The utilities enter into a contract to buy the output of a renewable power project at commercial rates that apply to conventional plants. Since this rate cannot economically support an investment in electricity produced from renewable energy, the utility has to find enough consumers willing to make up the difference in the form of a rate premium. Care has to be exercised to ensure that the amount of electricity that carries the premium rate covers, but does not exceed, the capacity of the renewable energy source. For utilities offering their customers a voluntary premium rate applied to electricity generated from renewable energy sources, those in the south generally favor solar power while those in the north favor wind power. Another option is to give consumers a choice of power supply such as solar, micro hydro, and wind, each with a different premium to cover their respective extra costs. This method does not assure efficiency of operation because a consumer is picking up the entire incremental cost associated with the capital and operating costs of a renewable energy electricity generating plant even if mismanaged.

Source of Employment

Solar and wind industries are important sources of employment. According to the Solar Foundation, estimated US employment in 2015 is 210,000, growing at about 20 percent per year.[114] Another estimate was that 174,000 people worked in the US solar industry in 2014 compared to 143,000 in 2013 and 93,500 in 2010. Of those employed in 2014, 97,000 were system installers, 32,000 in manufacturing, 20,000 in sales, about 15,000 in project development, and another 9,000 in other forms of work, including research.[115] As a point of reference, the number of US coal miners was 89,800 in 2012 and 80,100 in 2013, reflecting the pressure the Obama administration is placing on coal as a source of energy.[116] According to the American Wind Energy Association (AWEA), wind power created 75,000 jobs in 2013.[117] This assessment does not include indirect jobs such as accountants, computer systems analysts, and those associated with the integration of wind farms with the electricity grid and improving the electricity infrastructure to accommodate wind power. According to the European Wind Energy Association (EWEA), direct and indirect employment in 2010 was 238,000, which is expected to grow to 520,000 by 2020 and 794,000 by 2030.[118] Global employment in 2015 totaled 7.7 million, of which 2.5 million is in solar PV power, 1.8 million is in liquid biofuels, 1 million is in wind, 0.8 million is in biomass, another 0.8 million is in solar heating and concentrated solar, and the remainder is in biogas, small hydropower, and geothermal. The top ten employing nations are China, Brazil, the US, India, Germany, Indonesia, Japan, France, Bangladesh, and Colombia. Two-thirds of solar PV jobs are in China, biofuel jobs are concentrated in Brazil and the US, with more than half the jobs in wind, solar heating, and small hydro in China. Not included in these figures are construction workers for large hydro projects, of which there are 1.5 million jobs, nearly half in China.[119]

Electricity Storage

Solar and wind power have their critics. One contention is that if backup power support is near the capacity of a solar or wind farm, what then is the need for the farm? For instance, Germany experiences 10 consecutive days without wind twice a year. A total eclipse wipes out solar power when it's most needed. Having a primary source with a backup that covers a large portion of the output doubles the investment in renewables. One may as well depend on the backup energy source alone even if fossil fueled. The other is that solar and wind introduce operational risk from sudden changes in the weather that cuts supply and adversely affects grid stability. One exception is the solar thermal tower with built-in storage in the form of hot molten salt that can extend power generation into the evening and, more importantly, augment day time production in case of cloud cover to stabilize output. Other than this, intervention by dispatchers has to be quick to access an alternative or backup power supply to compensate for the inherent unreliability of solar and wind power. Backup power or spinning reserves are essentially stranded assets when the sun is shining and the wind is blowing, which add considerably to the cost of solar and wind power. But backup power cannot deal with excess generation of electricity, but grid storage capacity can. Grid storage acts as an energy buffer supplying power for current use and absorbing excess renewable power for later use. It creates value by storing wind electricity at night, which generally has little or no value, and feeding it into the electricity grid during the day when it does have value. Grid storage transforms the highly variable nature of renewable power to a reliable supply under the direct control of dispatchers. It also acts as a grid stabilizer enhancing operating efficiency while reducing the role of spinning reserves. The challenge of transforming solar and wind power into a controllable output for dispatchers is worsening with the growth of solar and wind power. In 2013, for the first time, power generation capacity additions for fossil fuel and clean energy (hydro, nuclear, solar, wind, biomass and waste, and geothermal) were equal at about 140 gW. The largest contributors to clean energy in order of importance were solar, wind, and hydro. A tie becomes a rout in the future. In 2015 it is anticipated that fossil fuel additions will be 110 gW versus 164 gW for clean energy. By 2020 it is 91 gW for fossil fuels versus 208 gW for clean energy. By 2030, the score is 64 gW for fossil fuels versus 279 gW for clean energy.[120] Since much of this is solar and wind, there has to be a major expansion of the means to store and control electricity flows to ensure system stability. The primary means today are pumped storage or gravity batteries, whereas the future may be more dependent on non-flow and flow batteries, with compressed air and hydrogen playing a minor role. Renewables are providing plenty of incentive for the development of a super battery capable of handling the challenge of adding large renewable capacity to national electricity grids.

Non-Flow or Solid State Batteries

Alessandro Volta invented the non-flow or solid state battery in the 1800s and laid the foundation of electrochemistry. A non-flow or solid state battery converts stored chemical energy into electrical energy. Each cell of a battery contains a positive terminal or cathode and a negative terminal or anode. An electrolyte allows ions to move between the electrodes and terminals, completing a path for current to flow in and out of a battery to perform work. The most common non-flow battery is the lead acid battery found in automobiles. It consists of six cells each generating 2 volts of power. Each cell has one plate made of lead and another of lead dioxide immersed in a sulfuric acid electrolyte (35 percent sulfuric acid and 65 percent water). During battery discharges, a chemical reaction deposits lead sulfate ($PbSO_4$) on the plate surfaces, depleting electrolyte of sulfuric acid. In charging a battery from an alternator, the reaction is reversed. Sulfur is reabsorbed by the electrolyte raising its sulfuric acid content while clearing plate surfaces of lead sulfate. Charging and discharging, which exchanges chemical energy with electrical energy, allows a battery to be reused time and again.[121]

Lithium Ion Battery

Nickel cadmium batteries once powered portable equipment, from wireless communications to mobile computing. Nickel metal hydride and lithium ion batteries emerged in the early 1990s, and in the race for consumer acceptance, lithium ion won. Lithium ion batteries have important advantages over competing technologies. Electrodes are made of lightweight lithium and graphite (carbon). Lithium is a highly reactive element that can store a great deal of energy in its atomic bonds for high energy density. For this reason, lithium ion batteries are much lighter than other types of rechargeable batteries of the same capacity. A lithium ion battery can store 150 Wh of electricity per kilogram of battery versus 100 Wh, and more typically 60–70 Wh per kilogram of a nickel metal hydride battery. A lead acid battery can store only 25 Wh per kilogram. Therefore it takes 6 kilograms of a lead acid battery to store the same amount of energy as a 1 kilogram lithium ion battery.

A lithium ion battery pack loses about 5 percent of its charge per month compared to a 20 percent loss per month for a nickel metal hydride battery. There is no so-called memory effect, which means that the battery does not have to be completely discharged before recharging. A lithium ion battery can handle hundreds of cycles of charging and discharging. One initial disadvantage was that a lithium ion battery started to degrade quickly and had a life of only 2 or 3 years from time of manufacture, which was subsequently improved to 7 years. However, in recent years, the longevity of a lithium ion battery has been extended to 10–15 or more years to cover the life of an electric vehicle. A lithium ion battery pack must have an onboard computer to manage battery output, increasing its cost. There is a 1 or 2 chance in a million of a lithium ion battery bursting into flame, as had occurred with a few electric vehicles, although it is said that these occurred under what one might term extreme driving conditions.[122] Researchers at Oak Ridge National Laboratory have developed a solid electrolyte to replace the liquid flammable electrolyte in lithium ion batteries. The electrolyte will enable lithium ion batteries to store 5–10 times more energy in a safer environment.[123] Researchers at the University of Southern California are trying to improve the performance of a lithium ion battery by replacing traditional graphite anodes with porous silicon nanoparticles that can hold as much as three times the energy and be recharged within 10 minutes.[124] Another potential technological breakthrough may be the lithium sulfur battery with a lithium metal anode and a sulfur based cathode. The battery has five times the power density of the lithium ion battery and would be capable of obtaining 400–500 miles for electric vehicles on a single charge. The battery will be brought to market in 2016.[125]

Manufacturers have been reluctant to disclose the cost of lithium batteries. The high/low estimates in \$/kWh for 2010 were \$1,105/\$600; for 2015 \$600/\$450; and for 2020 \$500/\$225. Between 2010 and 2020 the high end cost estimates decline 7.6 percent per year and the low end 8.5 percent per year in line with past trends.[126] Tesla Motors in partnership with Panasonic is building "Gigafactory" in Nevada. Its planned 2020 output will be 40 gWh per year, about equal to present global lithium ion battery manufacturing capacity. Gigafactory is sufficient to power 500,000 electric vehicles per year (2015 production of Tesla electric vehicles projected to be 35,000).[127] This may be the basis for the estimate by Elon Musk, founder of Tesla Motors, that battery costs will fall below \$200 per kWh in the near future.[128] There is some thought that costs could fall as low as \$100 per kWh, which would make electric cars cost competitive with gasoline powered vehicles.[129]

Batteries can form a distributive generation and storage system. Suppose that 100,000 solar array owners install a 5 kW battery backup capable of delivering 5 kW for one hour when fully charged. Even if only half of the total capacity is available, there would still be 250 mWh of capacity available for one hour to stabilize the power grid in case of a disruption or to compensate for cloud cover. About 15 gWh/year of Gigafactory 40 gWh/year capacity is intended for stationary uses, which would include storing electricity for various distributive renewable energy sources.[130] Musk has also organized SolarCity, where solar panels and lithium ion batteries are packaged into a single unit for sale to homes and businesses. Distributive batteries can be charged with electricity from any source at night when electricity rates are low for supplying electricity during the day when electricity rates are high. Even batteries installed in electric vehicles can be used for distributive storage purposes when vehicles are parked.

Tesla has set up 135 solar powered, fast-discharge, recharging stations where electric vehicles can recharge for free. NRG Energy is building a network of public charging stations in major cities for a fee per charge. These recharging stations are necessary to bolster public acceptance of electric vehicles. Musk's activities both encourage and discourage utilities: electric vehicles increase electricity demand, but batteries encourage a distributive generation of electricity where consumers can reduce their reliance or remove themselves entirely from the grid. Distributive generation with electricity storage is a disruptive force to the utility business model built on centralized power generation, transmission, and distribution.[131] System control of centralized power generation is solely in the hands of a utility with no means of interaction by consumers other than their flipping on–off switches. Distributive generation and storage of electricity put the consumer partly and even entirely in control, affecting the operation and revenue generation of a utility organized along traditional lines.

Sodium Sulfur and Sodium Chloride Batteries

Sodium based batteries are being designed for electricity grid support. They have a high energy density, long cycle life, operate in harsh environments such as temperatures as low as $-40°C$ and as high as $60°C$, and are adaptive for storing energy from intermittent solar and wind power. Sodium sulfur batteries consist of a solid ceramic electrolyte made of sodium alumina, with liquid sodium acting as the negative electrode and molten sulfur as the positive electrode. The electrolyte only allows positive charged sodium ions to pass through to create an electric current.[132] One variant is sodium–nickel chloride where the cathode is nickel chloride and the anode sodium. The electrolyte is tetrachloroaluminate and is liquid at the $270°C$ to $350°C$ operating temperature of the battery. The main advantages are no need for air conditioning, high energy density, long cycle life (2,000 cycles) and physical life of over 15 years, maintenance-free, zero emissions, and manufacturing materials are recyclable. Still another variant is the sodium sulfur battery with a solid electrolyte membrane between the anode and cathode compared to liquid metal batteries where the anode, cathode, and membrane are liquids. The cylindrical configuration is enclosed by a steel casing protected from corrosion on the inside by a chromium and molybdenum coating. The outside container serves as a positive electrode, while liquid sodium serves as a negative electrode, with an intervening membrane made of beta-alumina solid electrolyte. Once running, the heat produced by charging and discharging cycles is sufficient to maintain operating temperatures. Variants of sodium based batteries are in their early pilot project stage for developing a durable utility power storage device with 70 percent or greater efficiency and a 1,500 cycle lifetime.[133]

Advance Lead Acid and Aqueous Sodium Ion Batteries

As described in a lead acid battery, positive plate (electrode) is comprised of lead dioxide and negative of finely divided lead. Both of these active materials react with a sulfuric acid electrolyte to form a lead sulfate coating on the plates during discharge and chemical reactions are reversed on recharge. Batteries are constructed with lead grids to support the active material and individual cells are connected to produce a battery in a plastic case. The advance lead acid battery has a supercapacitor electrode composed of carbon combined with the lead acid battery negative plate to better regulate the charge and discharge of electricity, extending the power and life of the battery.[134] An aqueous sodium ion battery has a saltwater electrolyte, manganese oxide cathode, carbon composite anode, and synthetic cotton separator. Noncorrosive reactions at the anode and cathode prevent deterioration of materials and water based chemistry results in a nontoxic and noncombustible battery safe to handle and environmentally friendly.[135]

Flow Batteries

A flow battery is a rechargeable battery with three tanks holding electrolyte in different states of charge and two pumps. One tank is associated with fully charged electrolyte and the other with depleted electrolyte to be recharged. A third tank is split into two with a membrane between the cathode and anode permitting electrons to flow and supply electrical power. One side of the membrane is supplied by fully charged electrolyte from one tank, while the other side has depleted electrolyte that is pumped to the recharging tank.[136] The advantage of flow batteries is that they can be almost instantly recharged by replacing electrolyte in the electricity generating tank with fully charged electrolyte while reenergizing spent or depleted electrolyte. The fundamental difference between non-flow and flow batteries is that energy is stored in the electrode material in conventional or non-flow batteries and in the electrolyte of flow batteries. These are also known as "redox" batteries, referring to chemical reduction and oxidation reactions to charge and discharge electrical energy in the liquid electrolyte solutions which flow through a battery.[137] The energy capacity of a redox flow battery is determined by the amount of liquid electrolyte, and power is determined by the surface area of the electrodes. Various types of flow batteries are associated primarily with different electrolytes, some under development, such as vanadium redox, zinc bromine, iron chromium, hydrogen bromine, zinc chlorine, zinc ferrocyanide, and iron ferrocyanide.[138]

Research is being conducted to lower the cost of electrolytes by finding more mundane substances that can perform the same function and by improving the design. Researchers at Stanford University are looking into more simplified designed batteries such as the lithium polysulfide battery that uses only one tank and a single pump and a simple coating to avoid the need for an expensive membrane to separate the anode and cathode.[139] Researchers at Harvard University are working on a metal-free flow battery that relies on the electrochemistry of naturally abundant, inexpensive, carbon-based organic molecules called quinones similar to molecules that store energy in plants and animals.[140] Researchers at Vanderbilt University are experimenting with incorporating a battery as an integral part of a solar cell. A silicon-based capacitor added to a solar cell would store excess solar electricity generation to be drawn down as required to meet demand.[141] Researchers at Ohio State University are developing a solar cell to act as a rechargeable battery by incorporating a mesh solar panel that allows air to enter the battery to activate a process for transferring electrons between the solar panel and the battery electrode.[142]

Alevo is building a plant to manufacture a lithium cell that contains an inorganic non-flammable electrolyte of lithium ferrophosphate and graphite, which eliminates the risk of combustion and explosion. The Alevo battery also sharply reduces the debilitating effects of charging cycles and is thermodynamically stable with an electrochemical loop to minimize battery degradation during deep discharges. The battery showed no signs of increase in internal resistance after more than 30,000 cycles of overcharge followed by deep discharge. (At one cycle per day, 30,000 cycles is equivalent to an 80 year lifespan.) Alevo will be offering "Gridbank," a shipping container-sized 2 mW powered unit capable of generating 1 mWh of energy to be installed in electricity grid systems. The battery along with smart data analytics is intended to reduce a large part of the 30 percent of generated electricity currently wasted through inefficiencies in a grid delivery system. The system will act as an energy service provider, monitoring grid usage in real time and enabling the battery to handle peak shaving, frequency regulation, and the integration of renewables (solar and wind) into an electricity grid.[143] Responding to the same market, EnerVault offers a 1 mWh, 250 kW storage iron-chromium flow battery.[144] American Vanadium offers vanadium redox flow batteries of 400, 800, and 1,600 kWh with a power rating of 200 kW.[145] UniEnergy Technologies also offers a large scale advanced vanadium flow battery.[146] An example of usage of a flow battery is an onion processing plant handling 300,000 pounds of onions per day. The plant's waste is liquefied into 30,000 gallons of onion juice. Rich in sugars, the juice produces methane in an anaerobic digester, which in turn feeds two fuel cells that generate 600 kW of electricity. The remainder of the onion waste becomes cattle feed. But 600 kW is not enough, and purchases from a utility occur during periods of peak rates. The company installed an advanced design vanadium redox battery provided by Prudent Energy that is recharged at night when electricity rates are low.[147]

A potential alternative to a battery is a supercapacitor. A capacitor stores energy by means of a static charge as opposed to an electrochemical reaction. Applying a voltage differential on the positive and negative plates charges the capacitor. A capacitor charges much more quickly than a lithium ion battery, but it costs considerably more in terms of watt-hour of output and its energy density is much lower. Nevertheless there are applications or circumstances where a supercapacitor may perform better than a battery, such as fitting a supercapacitor in an electric vehicle along with a battery for more rapid acceleration.[148]

A major use of storage batteries is to smooth the output of solar and wind power. These two sources can fluctuate widely and in a short period of time responding to changing cloud patterns and wind speeds. This makes it very difficult for dispatchers who are caught in the middle of matching fluctuating supply with fluctuating demand. Often this entails having spare fossil fuel, normally natural gas, plants spinning; that is, ready to go on line in a moment's notice to compensate for the fluctuating supply. When on line, these backup plants must change power levels often, actually increasing carbon dioxide emissions, but not all agree that fluctuating power levels necessarily increase carbon emissions. One study concluded that added carbon emissions are negligible and that cycling marginally reduced sulfur and nitrous oxide emissions compared to steady power output. Moreover, even with the necessity of a backup power source, the impact of solar and wind is still a large net reduction in carbon emissions.[149] A storage battery can change this by storing solar and wind power and can be dispatched under controlled conditions in response to changing demand. Thus solar and wind can be transformed into what amounts to the reliability of a fossil fuel plant, and generation of wind electricity at night can be stored for dispatching during the day. But this requires the technological development of a super battery—low cost, high capacity, long life, reliable, and efficient in its operation. This battery is not yet here, but nevertheless, battery capacity is growing rapidly. In 2014, Europe's largest battery storage facility went into operation in Schwerin, in northeastern Germany, with a rated power of 5 mW and capacity of 5 gWh to compensate for fluctuations in the electricity grid and ensure a stable supply. A battery twice as large as the Schwerin model is being installed in Feldheim outside Berlin, and Italy is adding 70 mW of storage capacity to its transmission network. In the US, battery storage was given a boost by a California law that requires that investor owned utilities purchase 1.3 gW of storage capacity by 2020, which has greatly accelerated development of storage technologies. Southern California Edison is moving forward with the world's largest storage plant of 260 mW. The Southern California Edison Tehachapi Wind Energy Storage Project will have 8 mW of capacity that can operate for 4 hours to produce 32 mWh stored in 600,000 lithium-ion battery cells. With a cost of $50 million half-funded by the Department of Energy, the project will serve as a test bed for a larger system to provide voltage support and grid stabilization, regulate frequency, decrease transmission losses, diminish congestion, increase system reliability, defer transmission investment, optimize renewable-related transmission, integrate renewable energy (smoothing) from shifting solar and wind generation output, and replace spinning reserves. The objective is to try to meet peak load demand with stored electricity in lithium-ion batteries to minimize the need for fossil fuel backup generation.[150]

Gravity Batteries

Electricity capacity must be able to meet peak demand without consumers experiencing brownouts or blackouts. Conventional batteries cannot store sufficient quantities of electricity to smooth out the operations of an electric utility by supplementing supply when demand is high and being recharged when demand is low. Hydropower has a large capacity to "store" electricity through pumped storage plants. These plants have reversible pump-turbines that pump water during periods of low electricity demand from a body of water up to a storage reservoir located at a higher elevation. A gravity battery can be an open system where the source of water is a river or bay or a closed system of lower and upper reservoirs. An upper reservoir stores the potential energy of water before being transformed to kinetic energy by gravity to drive a turbine. During periods of high electricity demand, water flows from the storage or upper reservoir back to the body of water or lower reservoir through reversible pump-turbines to generate electricity. Motors that pump water to the storage reservoir become generators to produce electricity. Gravity batteries can absorb excess production of solar and wind power plants that can be returned to the grid when needed. For both solar and wind and tidal and wave and other forms of intermittent energy supply, gravity batteries transform an intermittent source of electricity where output cannot be controlled to a reliable source of controlled electricity. Gravity batteries being built throughout Europe are intended to stabilize the electricity grid from the Continent's ongoing commitment to expand renewable (solar and wind) power capacity.[151] Operational efficiency to handle fluctuating "charges" is enhanced by variable speed motors for pumping water to the upper reservoir.[152]

Pumped storage plants or gravity batteries reduce variability in electricity demand by increasing base load demand during times of slack demand and augmenting supplies during times of peak or high demand, reducing variability and the need for peaking plants. Pumped storage plants or gravity batteries are constrained by the availability of suitable sites that contain a sufficient volume of water to make a meaningful contribution in narrowing the gap between base load and peak demand. Required volume of water is a function of the difference in elevation between upper and lower reservoirs and power of motors/generators to both replenish the upper reservoir and generate electricity. The economic analysis of a gravity battery depends on the differential between day and night electricity rates, amount of electricity that can be generated, cost of operation, and savings from a smaller investment in peaking generators. Peaking generators are an expensive means of generating electricity as they may run only 250 hours per year. They normally are relatively low cost simple cycle gas fueled combustion turbines, similar to a jet engine, with the lowest efficiency/highest energy consumption per unit of electrical output. Gravity batteries can reduce or eliminate the need for peaking generators, which should be reflected in their economic analysis. Gravity batteries are also cheaper than flow and non-flow batteries particularly when the analysis runs for the 30 or more year life of a pumped storage plant, which represents many battery replacements. Pumped storage plants or gravity batteries are common in Europe and China, and more are being built. A 1.56 gW pumped storage plant has been announced to be built near St. Petersburg as a joint venture between Russian and Chinese companies, the first of possibly several.[153]

Gravity batteries are the largest means for storing electricity by far. In 2010, the total capacity of gravity batteries was 140,000 mW compared to 976 mW (only 0.7 percent!) for other storage alternatives. Of this, compressed air energy storage (CAES) accounted for 440 mW; sodium sulfur batteries 304 mW; lithium ion 100 mW; lead acid 70 mW; nickel cadmium 27 mW; flywheel 25 mW; and redox flow batteries 10 mW. With total battery capacity in 2010 of 536 mW, the largest pumped storage facility in the world is Bath County Pumped Storage Station (US) rated at 3,003 mW, followed by Huizhou Pumped Storage Station (China) at 2,448 mW; Guangdong Pumped Storage Station (China) at 2,400 mW; and Okutataragi Pumped Storage Station (Japan) at 1,932 mW. Of a total of 51 pumped storage facilities in the world over 1,000 mW, 14 are in China, 11 in Europe, 10 in the US, 8 in Japan, and the remaining 8 in other nations. Thirteen are under construction, of which 7 are in China, including one of 3,600 mW.[154]

Compressed Air Energy Storage

Compressed air energy storage (CAES) is similar in concept to pumped hydro storage. But instead of pumping water from a lower to an upper reservoir, ambient air is compressed and stored under pressure in an underground cavern at about 1,000 psi. The heat of compression is normally removed, which then has to be compensated during the expansion phase by heating the incoming compressed air to an expansion turbine with natural gas (called a diabatic CAES). Alternatively compressed air can retain its heat (adiabatic CAES). Two diabatic CAES plants are in existence, one in Germany and the other in Alabama. These burn natural gas in gas turbines running off compressed air, generating three times the output for the same natural gas input if the gas turbine ran off ambient air pressure. Future CAES plants are expected to follow this design. An adiabatic CAES can achieve efficiency up to 70 percent by recovering the heat of compression to reheat the compressed air during turbine operations. This removes the need to burn natural gas to warm up the decompressed air. Heat storage is in the development stage.[155]

In response to a green energy requirement in California, four energy companies are proposing an $8 billion renewable energy 2.1 gW Pathfinder project that will supply Los Angeles with more than twice the energy generated by the similarly powered 2.1 gW Hoover Dam. The Hoover Dam produced an annual average of 4.2 gWh of electricity from 1999 to 2008, whereas the Pathfinder project is expected to produce about 9.2 gWh a year via the higher utilization afforded by CAES. The Pathfinder project includes a wind farm in Wyoming and a new 525 mile (845 kilometer) transmission line to a CAES in underground salt caverns in Utah where electricity will either inject air into the CAES or be transmitted via an existing 490 mile transmission line to Los Angeles.

CAES will provide electricity to meet shortfalls in supply. If approved, the project is expected to be completed in 2023.[156]

An alternative to cavern storage is underwater compressed air energy storage (UW-CAES). Toronto Hydropower has 4–5 days per year with a shortfall of electricity. Traditional means to cover the shortfall is to expand the transmission system or install peaking generators. Both are costly in light of the degree of shortfall. To supply electricity for this short period of time, a balloon-like storage vessel made of stretched fabric is anchored in 80 meters of water 5 kilometers offshore Lake Ontario. The balloon is filled with pressurized air. When electricity is needed, air is released and pipelined ashore and converted to electricity via a turbo-expander. On a more large scale basis, a UW-CAES would be installed in water depths of 400–700 meters. Pressure within the balloon is equal to the water pressure. One difference between a UW-CAES and a land based cavern CAES is that air pressure drops as air is drawn from a land based CAES whereas air pressure is maintained by water pressure until air is exhausted for the underwater version.[157]

Flywheels

Flywheel energy storage transforms electric energy to kinetic energy, or a spinning mass called a rotor. The rotor is heavy and spins 10,000 revolutions per minute (100,000 rpm in more advanced designs) in a nearly frictionless vacuum enclosure. When electricity is needed, kinetic energy is converted to electricity through the same motor generator that converted electrical energy to kinetic energy. Flywheel farms can store megawatts of electricity for rapid response to loss of power to critical high power, low energy control systems.[158] The relative performance of storage alternatives is listed in Table 9.3.[159]

Hydrogen

Energy (heat) generates electricity for producing hydrogen by the electrolysis of water. Fuel cells reverse electrolysis by reuniting hydrogen with oxygen, producing electricity, heat, and water. Electrolysis consumes electricity when converting water to hydrogen and oxygen, and a fuel cell generates electricity by converting hydrogen and oxygen to water. A fuel cell represents a twofold generation of electricity—once to produce hydrogen by the electrolysis of water and again when a fuel cell converts hydrogen back

Table 9.3 Performance of Storage Technologies

Storage Type	Power in mW	Discharge Time	Efficiency %	Lifetime Years	Storage Cost $/mW-hour
Pumped storage	250–1,000	10 hrs	70–80	<30	$50–150
CAES	100–300	3–10 hrs	45–60	30	About $150
Flywheels	<10	<15 min	>85	20	NA
Supercapacitors	10	<30 sec	About 90	50 k cycles	NA
Vanadium RB	<10	2–8 hrs	75	5–15	$200–300
Lithium ion	5	<4 hrs	About 90	8–15	$250–500
Lead battery	3–20	<4 hrs	75	4–8	NA
Sodium sulfur	30–35	4 hrs	80	15	$50–150

to water. Hydrogen can be produced any time there is available electricity, then distributed, stored, and converted back to electricity when and as needed by fuel cells. Although one might say that hydrogen fulfills the same role as a battery, there is a major difference. A battery stores chemical energy that is converted to electricity until the chemical energy is exhausted. As such, a battery is a finite source of energy that must be recharged or discarded when the chemical energy is gone. A fuel cell converts chemical energy (hydrogen) to electricity continually up to its rated capacity as long as hydrogen supplies are available. A battery's output drops as it is exhausted of charge and has to be recharged. A hydrogen fed fuel cell runs at capacity as long as hydrogen is available. Since any quantity of hydrogen can be stored, hydrogen is far more effective in storing electricity than a battery.

Sir William Robert Grove invented the hydrogen fuel cell in the 1830s, but, without practical use, the fuel cell faded from view. It was revived in the 1960s when General Electric developed a workable fuel cell as a power supply for the Apollo and Gemini space missions. Hydrogen, the fuel for fuel cells, must be uncontaminated and can be supplied from tanks pressurized with hydrogen gas or from associated reformers that extract hydrogen from natural gas, propane, methanol, gasoline, or other types of hydrocarbons. A fuel cell consists of a proton-exchange membrane (PEM) at its center, surrounded on both sides by a catalyst. On the outside of each catalyst is an anode or a cathode electrode connected by an electrical circuit that passes through a motor or a light bulb or any electrical load. Hydrogen, passing through a flow plate at one end of the fuel cell, enters the anode catalyst, where the hydrogen is split into protons and electrons (a hydrogen molecule is two atoms of hydrogen each of one proton and one electron). The PEM only allows protons to pass through to the cathode catalyst, where they establish an electrical charge to induce the flow of the electrons from the anode electrode through the electrical load to the cathode electrode. Once through the PEM, protons pass to the cathode catalyst, where they are reunited with the returning electrons from the cathode electrode and with oxygen from air to form water and heat. The waste products, which may contain a trace of nitrous oxides from protons reacting with nitrogen rather than oxygen atoms in the air, pass through the flow plate on the other end of the fuel cell. A fuel cell stack of individual fuel cells is connected to others to form a fuel cell module that produces a desired output of electricity. Fuel cells have no moving parts and are about two to three times more efficient than an internal combustion engine in converting fuel into usable power. In addition to PEM fuel cells, there are also phosphoric acid fuel cells, molten carbonate fuel cells, and solid oxide fuel cells that have different operating temperatures and performance characteristics for specific applications.[160]

Researchers at the Georgia Institute of Technology are conducting experiments to transform a solar cell into a fuel cell with biomass as fuel by means of a solar-induced, low temperature, direct biomass to electricity hybrid fuel cell. The fuel cell relies on a polyoxometalate catalyst, which when mixed with biomass and exposed to solar energy oxidizes biomass, delivering electrons to the fuel cell's anode to generate electricity.[161] Another innovation being explored is a carbon fuel cell capable of taking a dilute air mixture of carbon dioxide, such as flue gas from a utility, and produce electricity, heat, and a pure stream of carbon dioxide, which can be sold, sequestered, or used for tertiary oil recovery. The fuel cell electrochemical reactions are supported by an electrolyte layer in which carbonate ions are a bridge completing the electrical circuit.[162]

Water waste poses a problem when operating a fuel cell exposed to freezing weather. Waste heat prevents water from freezing during operation, but when a fuel cell is shut down, residual water can turn to ice and damage a fuel cell. This, along with costs, presents a challenge for manufacturers of fuel cell powered motor vehicles. Although there has been progress in reducing costs, fuel cells are still relatively expensive to manufacture and operate given the cost of hydrogen. Further technical breakthroughs are necessary to make fuel cells competitive with gasoline engines.

There are 28 companies worldwide in fuel cell manufacturing, of which 14 are in the US, 5 in Canada, 2 each in China and Singapore, and 1 each in the UK, Italy, Taiwan, Germany, and Greece.[163] The original market for fuel cells was primarily as backup power supplies for critical communications and computer systems where a power loss can have severe operational repercussions. Hydrogen fuel cells are distributed power sources, which can be located at required sites for auxiliary power as needed. Hydrogen is usually from associated reformers that strip hydrogen from hydrocarbons. Hydrogen fuel cells supply electricity and potable water on manned space missions. Hydrogen fuel cells are used for material handling vehicles where zero emissions are important and also to power hydrogen fuel cars, trucks, and busses. They are now starting to be used to generate electricity for communities. Bridgeport, Connecticut, has installed a 14.9 mW fuel cell that can power 15,000 homes. The advantages of a fuel cell are that it is unobtrusive in appearance, quiet in operation, efficient, and reliable. Heat and water are waste products, along with carbon dioxide from stripping hydrogen from natural gas (biogas, coal gas, and propane can also be fuels). A fuel cell is 47 percent efficient in converting natural gas to electricity, which can be increased to 51 percent by capturing waste heat to generate more electricity. Two smaller electricity generating fuel cells are to be added in Bridgeport, one with an output of 1.4 mW to serve a university and the other at 2.8 mW as part of a renewable energy complex.[164] The manufacturer, FuelCell Energy, has built 300 operating fuel cell units including 21 units for the world's largest fuel cell complex of 59 mW in South Korea.[165]

Germany has taken the lead in power to gas (PtG) applications involving hydrogen. Excess electricity from solar and wind electrolyzes water to produce oxygen and hydrogen. Both are sold to commercial consumers. Some hydrogen is sold as fuel for hydrogen fuel cells either in automobiles or other applications. Some is sold to natural gas distributors who have found that hydrogen can make up 5 percent of natural gas without any adverse consequences for natural gas consumers. Hydrogen is also being combined with carbon dioxide emissions from industrial and utility plants to produce synthetic natural gas that is fed into the natural gas distribution system.[166]

Hydrogen is difficult to store in that it must be kept in high pressure tanks and, even under high pressure, has a low energy density. It is subject to leaks through fittings, as hydrogen molecules are very small compared to other compressed gases and, of course, highly flammable if it escapes into the environment. One idea is to take excess renewable electricity to electrolyze water to produce hydrogen not for storage, but to make ammonia. Ammonia is much easier to handle, can be kept liquid in conventional tanks such as those that hold LPG, and is nonflammable. Its highly distinctive odor is a *de facto* leak detector, another advantage over hydrogen. Ammonia can be shipped and stored until needed and can be converted back to energy via combustion in a modified internal combustion engine, its hydrogen can be separated to energize a fuel cell to generate electricity, or a fuel cell can be modified to consume ammonia directly with water and nitrogen as emissions.

Conventional manufacture of ammonia is from hydrogen and nitrogen separated from air. Hydrogen can be from electrolyzing water or, much more often, stripping hydrogen from methane molecules, which releases carbon dioxide as a waste product. A new technology has been devised to produce methane via a process called solid state ammonia synthesis that converts electricity, water, and nitrogen directly into ammonia at less cost and with greater energy efficiency.[167]

Problems and Projects

Problem 9.1

The almost 200-year history of mining in Kentucky has left 1.5 million acres (6.07 billion square meters) including the removal of 470 mountain tops unusable. In 2007 Kentucky produced 158 million tons of coal. Obviously producing this coal did not require 1.5 million acres of land, but the point is that 1.5 million acres were effectively desecrated by the long history of coal mining and would presumably be available for solar array installations. Using a highly efficient coal generating plant, one ton of coal can produce 3.5 mWh. How many kilowatt-hours can 158 million tons of coal produce?

Suppose that coal mining ceased and that 70 percent of this land can be covered with solar arrays. What would be the solar output power for a solar panel efficiency of 15 percent in converting solar radiation of 1,000 watts/square meter to electricity with an average cloud cover that further reduces output by 25 percent? What would be the kilowatt-hours for an effective 5 hours per day of peak output? What would then be the annual output? Compare the annual output of coal power with solar power; what is your conclusion? Can solar power actually replace coal?

Problem 9.2

Using the same basis for calculation as in Problem 9.1, what is solar power on an annual basis per square mile? Could desert land 100 miles on a side (10,000 square miles), which is equivalent to 9 percent of the area of the state of Nevada, generate enough electricity to supply the US?

Problem 9.3

Derive Figure 9.3. Let C be the capacity of the plant in watts and X be $/watt to build the plant. The capital investment for the plant is C*X and the annual charge without maintenance is 10 percent of the capital investment. The watt-hours per year is C times 6 hours per day times 365 days per year. There is no downtime for a solar array and 6 hours per day at full power takes into consideration cloud cover and times of reduced output when the sun is closer to the horizon. Convert watt-hours to kilowatt-hours and divide the annual charge by the kilowatt-hours of output per year to obtain $/kWh.

Problem 9.4

Under the heading "Sizing Home Installations," 40 panels measuring 65″ × 40″ would be sufficient to provide a home with 120,000 kWh per year. What is the roof area of this installation in square feet? Suppose that you purchased a Nissan Leaf where

34 kWh is required to drive 100 miles, or 0.34 kWh per mile. You estimate that you'll drive 13,500 miles per year charging your car in its carport. How many kWh will the car consume in a year? How large does the roof on the carport have to be to accommodate this load?

Problem 9.5

The economics of solar power depend on many variables. For example, an energy-efficient 2,000 square foot home needs about 2 kW of output from a solar array mounted on the roof. If the cost of installation is $16,000 and if there is a rebate available for $8,000, the net cost to the consumer is $8,000. The amount of electricity that the solar array can produce is 100,000 kWh over its 25-year life, assuming that the sun is shining an average of 5.5 hours per day (2 kW per hour × 5.5 hours per day × 365 days per year × 25 years). The 5.5 hours per day takes into consideration reduced output when the sun is near the horizon and during times of cloud cover for the particular location. What would be the internal rate of return on the investment of $8,000 if the average rate over the next 25 years started at $0.12 kWh and escalated at 2, 3, 4, and 5 percent a year thereafter? What if the subsidy were not available and the investment is now $16,000?

Problem 9.6

The Alamosa Solar Project (Website www.powermag.com/topplantalamosa-solar-project-san-luis-valley-colorado) can generate 76,000 mW per year on 225 acres with a rated output of 30 mW. What is the implied effective hours per day of full sunlight? How many electric vehicles (Nissan Leaf) can run off the Alamosa solar power plant? How many square feet of the project are required to fuel the Nissan Leaf for one year?

Problem 9.7

The Alamosa Solar Project has an output of 30 mW in the hours around noon when the sun's radiation is 1,000 W per square meter. What is the effective output of the Alamosa Solar Project in terms of watts per square meter?

The Ivanpah Solar Electric Generating System (Website www.nrel.gov/csp/solarpaces/project_detail.cfm/projectID=62) sits on 3,500 acres and is expected to produce 1,079,232 mWh/year. What is its effective watts per square meter? Given solar radiation of 1,000 watts per square meter, what is the effective conversion rate to electricity? How many square feet are needed to fuel a Nissan Leaf for one year?

Problem 9.8

Algenol claims in one of its videos on Website www.algenol.com that its pilot plant can make an equivalent of 9,000 gallons of ethanol per acre. Suppose that an automobile, driven 13,500 miles per year, can get 25 miles per gallon on ethanol. How many acres of ethanol-producing algae is necessary to fuel the automobile for an entire year?

Sugar cane can produce 600 gallons of ethanol per year; how many acres of sugar cane is necessary to fuel the automobile for a year? How about corn ethanol that yields 400 gallons of ethanol per year? Suppose that the automobile is powered by biodiesel and can obtain 40 miles per gallon. Palm oil produces 500 gallons per acre per year and soy diesel 57 gallons per acre per year. How many acres would be required for palm oil and soy oil to fuel the automobile for a year? How do these figures compare against the land area needed to fuel a Nissan Leaf for 1 year?

Problem 9.9

The Horse Hollow Wind Energy Center is capable of generating 735.5 mW of power covering 47,000 acres in Texas. How many 3.5 mW wind turbines would this represent? How much land on average is taken up by each wind turbine? Can you conclude anything about land use at Horse Hollow?

   Suppose that the efficiency of electricity generation is 25 percent from changing wind patterns. Suppose that 15 acres are required for a single wind turbine. How many Nissan Leafs can be powered by a single wind turbine? What is the square feet necessary to power a single vehicle?

Problem 9.10

Vestas' 8 mW turbine has blades 80 meters long or a rotor diameter of 160 meters. Suppose that it performs at 12 revolutions per minute. What is the speed in miles per hour at the tip of a blade?

Problem 9.11

In 2014, global electricity output was 23,537 tW, growing at 1.5 percent per year, and wind electricity output was estimated at 1,037 tW, growing at 26 percent a year. The portion of electricity generation satisfied by wind was 4.4 percent. What would it be in 10 years? Set the problem up in a way to make it easy to change growth rates. What would be the portion satisfied by wind if electricity demand grows at 1 percent and wind power at 20 percent?

Problem 9.12

The Hoover Dam has a power generating capacity about the same as the Pathfinder project of 2.1 gW. The Hoover Dam produced a yearly average of 4.2 million megawatt-hours of electricity from 1999 to 2008, while the 2.1 gW Pathfinder project is expected to produce about 9.2 million megawatt-hours a year. What is the utilization rate for the Hoover Dam and Pathfinder? Why do you think the difference is so large?

Project 9.1

Suppose that a solar array has an output of 2 mW. At its location, maximum output occurs for two hours a day. Other hourly segments have less power. From 6–7 am and 5–6 pm, the solar output is 0.06 mW, for 7–8 am and 4–5 pm 0.39 mW, for 8–9 am and 3–4 pm 0.88 mW, for 9–10 am and 2–3 pm 1.4 mW, for 10–11 am and 1–2 pm 1.8 mW, and for 11–12 am and 12–1 pm, 2 mW. A fossil fuel plant can operate 24 hours a day at 95 percent of its rated power. How many megawatt-hours can a fossil fuel produce in a day? How many megawatt-hours does the solar plant produce? How does a solar plant compare to a fossil fuel plant on a 24-hour day? If you conclude that solar plants are not to serve base load demand, but heightened demand during the day, how does a solar plant compare to a fossil fuel plant on a 12-hour day?

This is based on cloudless days. Suppose that there is a 60 percent chance of a clear day for the location of the solar array. On days that it's cloudy, the amount of solar radiation can vary from 100 percent for a clear day with a wisp of clouds down to 30 percent on a really cloudy day. Using random numbers to determine whether it is clear or not and then another random number to determine the degree of cloud cover, what is the effective output of the solar array?

In the cell to the right of the cloudless output of the solar cell, put in an IF statement to generate a 1 if the random number, RAND(), is less than 0.6, otherwise 0. In the next cell to the right enter the same formula derived for the project in Chapter 8 on hydropower. The intercept has a value of 0.3 when X=0 and the slope value can be easily obtained by having the line value at X=1 also being 1. Now instead of X, substitute RAND(). The next cell to the right is another IF statement that if a clear day = 1, then the output is the cloudless output for the solar array; if not, then multiply the cloudless output by the value of diminishment in the cell to the left. Hit the function key F9 to do an iteration of a simulation and record the results for at least 25 iterations (the more the better). Then using Excel Data ribbon/Data Analysis/ Regression and Histogram, a histogram of the results will show the range of output and the mean value. How does the mean value compare to the cloudless output of the solar array?

Project 9.2

In terms of percent of rated output, suppose that a wind turbine has the operating characteristics in Project Table 9.2a.

Let column A be wind speed, starting from 0 mph in cell A6, going to 80 mph in increments of 1 mph. Try to formulate Project Table 9.2a using embedded IF statements

Project Table 9.2a

Wind Speed (mph)	Power Output	Comments
0–5	None	Wind speed too low to produce power
5–20	Increases by the cube of wind speed up to 100% at 20 mph	Power output = (wind speed/20)^3 × 100%
20–40	100% rated output	Turbine operating at maximum performance
40–60	30% rated output	Power is reduced to protect the integrity of the wind turbine from high winds
Over 60	0% rated output	Objective is to preserve the wind turbine structure from damage, not generate power

in cell B6 and replicate down to see if the rated output of the wind turbine follows the specifications in the table. Chart the output as shown in Project Table 9.2b. Refer to the following formula if necessary:

$$= IF(A6 <= 5,0,IF(A6 <= 20,(A6/20)^3,IF(A6 <= 40,1,IF(A6 <= 60,0.3,0))))$$

The formula first asks whether wind speed is less than 5 mpg; if so, the output is 0. If this condition is not true, it then asks if wind speed is less than 20 mph. Since less than 5 mph has already been dealt with, this part of the formula only handles speed between 5 and 20 mph. If this condition is true, then output is the ratio of wind speed divided by 20 mph raised to the cube power. The next part deals with wind speeds between 20 and 40 mph where the output is 100 percent of capacity. Between 40 and 60 mph, output is 30 percent; if none of these conditions apply, then wind speed has to be over 60 mph and output is 0 percent.

A study has been done with the characteristics of wind speed with the discrete and cumulative probability distribution as shown in Project Table 9.2c.

Starting in cell D9, put in day 1 and replicate down to day 25. In cell E9 put in a random number generator =RAND(). Create the Excel formula that incorporates Project

Project Table 9.2b

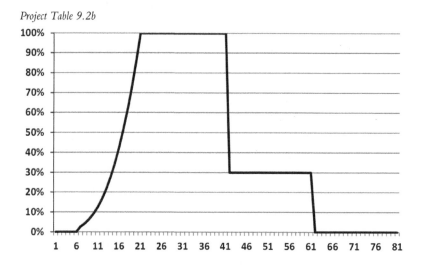

Project Table 9.2c

Probability of Wind Speed MPH	Discrete Probability	Cumulative Probability
<5	6.5%	6.5%
5-20	71.5%	78.0%
20-40	19.0%	97.0%
40-60	2.0%	99.0%
>60	1.0%	100.0%

Table 9.2c in cell F9—again embedded IF statements are necessary. Try to do this first without referring to the following:[168]

$$= IF(E9 < 0.065, 5 * RAND(), IF(E9 < 0.78, 5 + RAND()$$
$$* 15, IF(E9 < 0.97, 20 + RAND()$$
$$* 20, IF(E9 < 0.99, 40 + RAND() * 20, 60 + RAND() * 40))))$$

If the random number in cell E9 is less than 0.065, then the wind speed is between 0 and 5 mph; if this condition is not true, then see if cell E9 is less than 0.78. Note that the cumulative probability is being used. Since the probability below 0.065 has already been accounted for, the discrete probability of fulfilling this condition is 0.78 less 0.65 or 0.715, the discrete probability for wind speeds from 5 to 20 mph. If this condition is true, then the wind speed is 5 + RAND()*15 or any value from 5 to 20 mph. If this condition is not true, then the next IF statement is examined to see if the value is less than 0.97; if true, then the wind speed is between 20 and 40 mph. If none of these IF statements are true, then the is the random value less than 0.99? If so, then wind speed is between 40 and 60 mph; and again, if none so far are true, then the wind speed is between 60 and 100 mph (any speed over 60 would do). Then copy the wind speed formula from cell B6 to cell G9 and replicate F9 and G9 down for a 30-day history of performance. Notice that during the month there are occasions when there is no output from the wind turbine. Variations in daily output show the challenges facing dispatchers when managing an electricity grid. Obtain a monthly average. Press the F9 key to get iterations for a simulation. Record 25 monthly average outputs in a column and use Excel Histogram to construct a histogram of output. What is the minimum, mean, and maximum of monthly outputs? How does this compare with a fossil fuel plant?

Notes

1   Solar Energy Technologies Program, US Department of Energy Efficiency and Renewable Energy, Website http://energy.gov/eere/solarpoweringamerica/solar-powering-america-home.

2   "Trends 2014 in Photovoltaic Applications," International Energy Agency (IEA), Website www.iea-pvps.org/fileadmin/dam/public/report/statistics/IEA_PVPS_Trends_2014_in_PV_Applications_-_lr.pdf.

3   Yuhua New Material, Website www.yuhuasolar.com/Products/showproduct.php?lang=en&id=3&gclid=CKjw6NTjhMMCFbBm7Aodz2YAGw.

4   Solar 3D, Website www.solar3d.com/technology.php.

5   "Catching a Few More Rays," *The Economist* (September 1, 2012).

6   "Soitec Announces 46 Percent Efficient Solar Cell," *Renewable Energy World* (December 2, 2014), Website www.renewableenergyworld.com/rea/news/article/2014/12/soitec-announces-46-percent-efficient-solar-cell. On January 20, 2015, Soitec, the maker of concentrating photovoltaic (CPV) solar panels and the developer of CPV solar projects, announced that it plans to exit the solar industry and focus on its core semiconductor manufacturing business. Jennifer Runyon, "Soitec to Give Up on Solar CPV," *Renewable Energy World* (January 15, 2015), Website www.renewableenergyworld.com/rea/news/article/2015/01/soitec-to-give-up-on-solar-cpv?cmpid=WNL-Wednesday-January21-2015.

7   "ZSW Brings World Record Back to Stuttgart," Centre for Solar Energy and Hydrogen Research (April 12, 2014), Website www.zsw-bw.de/en/support/news/news-detail/zsw-brings-world-record-back-to-stuttgart.html. See also Chris Meehan, "Two Thin-Film Solar Efficiency Records Broken This Week," SolarReviews (February 28, 2014), Website www.solarreviews.com/news/two-thin-film-solar-records-broken-022814.

8 Cheryl Long, "Easy Solar Power," *Mother Earth News* (October/November, 2006), Website www.motherearthnews.com/renewable-energy/easy-solar-power-zmaz06onzraw. aspx#axzz3Oikd3iVg.

9 Ian Clover, "Top 10 Module Suppliers in End-of-Year Reshuffle, Says IHS," *PV Magazine* (December 3, 2014), Website www.pv-magazine.com/news/details/beitrag/top-10-module-suppliers-in-end-of-year-reshuffle--says-ihs_100017359/#axzz3P7a0jHy2.

10 Jennifer Runyon, "Global Solar Expansion: Mega Solar PV Manufacturing Plants (Reportedly) in the Works from East to West," *Renewable Energy World* (July 3, 2014), Website www. renewableenergyworld.com/rea/news/article/2014/07/global-solar-expansion-mega-solar-pv-manufacturing-plants-reportedly-in-the-works-from-east-to-west.

11 Sahara Forest Project, Website http://saharaforestproject.com.

12 "Sign of the Times: Saudis Go Solar," *UPI* (February 14, 2013).

13 Wael Mahdi, "Solar Beats Natural Gas to Unlock Middle East's Heavy Oil, Says GlassPoint Solar," *Bloomberg* (January 20, 2014). See also Jeffrey Ball, "Why the Saudis Are Going Solar," *Atlantic Monthly* (July/August, 2015), Website www.theatlantic.com/magazine/archive/2015/07/saudis-solar-energy/395315. The article also discusses how low gasoline prices and electricity rates in Saudi Arabia encourage wasteful practices and their impact on domestic consumption.

14 Natalie Pearson and Ganesh Nagarajan, "Solar Water Pumps Wean India Farmers from Grid," *Bloomberg* (February 10, 2014).

15 1366 Technologies, Website www.technologyreview.com.

16 David Chandler, "Recycling Old Batteries into Solar Cells," *MIT News* (August 18, 2014), Website http://newsoffice.mit.edu/2014/recycling-batteries-into-solar-cells-0818.

17 Zep Solar, Website www.zepsolar.com.

18 ENF, Website www.enfsolar.com.

19 "Nanotech Pushes Organic Solar Cell Efficiency Past 10 Percent," *Energy Matters* (May 16, 2013), Website www.energymatters.com.au/renewable-news/em3741.

20 Sue Holmes, "Novel Nanoparticle Production Method Could Lead to Better Lights, Lenses, and Solar Cells," Sandia National Labs (June 17, 2014), Website https://share.sandia.gov/news/resources/news_releases/nanoparticles_production/#.VM98TKMo6M8.

21 "Solar Cells: Tiny Balls of Fire," *The Economist* (June 28, 2014). The researchers discovered that their spherical light collectors resembled a moth's eyes!

22 "Lighting the Way," *The Economist* (September 1, 2012).

23 "Philippine Utility Scale Photovoltaic Case Study," and also "Juwi Enters Philippine Market with Utility Scale PV Plant," USAID, Website www.energytoolbox.org/gcre/photovoltaic_case_study. pdf.

24 Junko Movellan, "Getting Out of the Weeds: How to Control Vegetative Growth under Solar Arrays," *Renewable Energy World* (July 11, 2014), Website www.renewableenergyworld.com/rea/news/article/2014/07/weed-control-at-solar-installations-what-works-best.

25 Junko Movellan, "Running Out of Precious Land? Floating Solar PV Systems May Be a Solution," *Renewable Energy World* (November 7, 2013), Website www.renewableenergyworld.com/rea/news/article/2013/11/running-out-of-precious-land-floating-solar-pv-systems-may-be-a-solution.

26 Paula Mints (SPV Market Research/Strategies), "Off-grid Solar Applications, Where Grid Parity Is Truly Meaningless," *Renewable Energy World* (August 21, 2013), Website www.renewableenergyworld. com/rea/news/article/2013/08/off-grid-solar-applications-where-grid-parity-is-truly-meaningless.

27 "Trends 2014 in Photovoltaic Applications," International Energy Agency (IEA), Website www. iea-pvps.org/fileadmin/dam/public/report/statistics/IEA_PVPS_Trends_2014_in_PV_ Applications_-_lr.pdf. This is the source of information for Figures 9.1 and 9.2. See also Joshua Hill, "Global Solar PV Capacity Ends 2014 at 177 gW," Clean Technica, Website http://cleantechnica. com/2015/04/02/global-solar-pv-capacity-ends-2014-177-gw.

28 Travis Bradford, *Solar Revolution: The Economic Transformation of the Global Energy Industry* (New York, NY: Wiley, 2008). I originally thought the author took a rather Pollyanna outlook for solar power. In

retrospect, while the author wasn't "Pollyanna" enough, he was certainly propitious about the future role for solar!

29 Bruno Burger, "Electricity Production from Solar and Wind in Germany 2013," Fraunhofer Institute for Energy Systems (January 9, 2014), Website www.ise.fraunhofer.de/en/downloads-englisch/pdf-files-englisch/news/electricity-production-from-solar-and-wind-in-germany-in-2013.pdf.

30 Junko Movellan, "Fighting Blackouts: Japan Residential PV and Energy Storage Market Flourishing," *Renewable Energy World* (May 14, 2013), Website www.renewableenergyworld.com/rea/news/article/2013/05/fighting-blackouts-japan-residential-pv-and-energy-storage-market-flourishing.

31 In Chapter 8 under subsidies, I argued that the statistical data for solar power seemed to exclude private solar installations. The higher value contained in Figure 9.2 indicates that IEA includes private solar installations.

32 Wikipedia (The Free Encyclopedia), Website http://en.wikipedia.org/wiki/List_of_photovoltaic_power_stations.

33 A chart showing the occurrence and the magnitude of negative electricity rates is in an article by Holbert Janson, "Infrastructure Upgrades Mean Texas No Longer Wasting Wind Power," *Renewable Energy World* (August 27, 2014), Website www.renewableenergyworld.com/rea/blog/post/print/2014/08/infrastructure-upgrades-mean-texas-no-longer-wasting-wind-power.

34 Julie Johnsson and Naureen Malik, "Nuclear Industry Withers in U.S. as Wind Pummels Prices," *Bloomberg* (March 11, 2013), Website http://m.futuresmag.com/2013/03/11/nuclear-industry-withers-in-us-as-wind-pummels-pri. See also Elliott Negin (Union of Concerned Scientists), "Nuclear Giant Exelon Blasts Wind Energy," *Renewable Energy World* (June 5, 2014), Website www.renewableenergyworld.com/rea/news/article/2014/06/nuclear-giant-exelon-blasts-wind-energy.

35 Barry Cinnamon, "How Many Solar Panels Do I Need?" Solar Energy Show, Website https://soundcloud.com/cinnamonsolar.

36 "Database of State Incentives for Renewables and Efficiency," DSIRE, Website www.dsireusa.org.

37 Arizona Power Service, Website www.azenergyfuture.com.

38 "Directive 2009/28/EC," *Official Journal of the European Union of the European Parliament and Council* (April 23, 2009), Website http://eur-lex.europa.eu/legal-content/EN/TXT/PDF/?uri=CELEX:3 2009L0028&from=en.

39 "Global Renewable Energy," EIA/IRENA (International Renewable Energy Agency), Website www.iea.org/policiesandmeasures/renewableenergy.

40 Amicus, Website http://amicussolar.com.

41 Laurie Guevara-Stone, "The Rise of Solar Co-ops," Rocky Mountain Institute (April 22, 2014), Website http://blog.rmi.org/blog_2014_04_22_the_rise_of_solar_coops.

42 Mark Chediak, "NRG Energy to Sell Solar Directly to Consumers in Colorado," *Bloomberg* (January 28, 2015), Website www.bloomberg.com/news/articles/2015-01-28/nrg-energy-to-build-community-solar-projects-in-colorado.

43 Solar Energy Industries Association, Website www.seia.org/state-solar-policy/california. This Website has the solar programs for every state.

44 US Bureau of Land Management, Website www.blm.gov/wo/st/en/prog/energy/solar_energy.html.

45 Envision Solar International, Website www.envisionsolar.com.

46 Daryl Zeis, "Beat the Heat: Hotel Reduces Cooling Costs by 44 Percent with New Solar Carport," *Renewable Energy World* (July 31, 2014), Website www.renewableenergyworld.com/rea/news/article/2014/07/beating-the-heat-hampton-inn-hotel-reduces-cooling-costs-by-44-with-new-solar-carport.

47 Tom Randall, "Wal-Mart Now Draws More Solar Power Than 38 U.S. States," *Bloomberg* (October 25, 2013).

48 Alex Klein, "Corporate Giants Are Leading the Solar Charge," *The Daily Beast* (September 12, 2012), Website www.thedailybeast.com/articles/2012/09/12/corporate-giants-are-leading-the-solar-charge.html.

49 Tom Randall, "What Apple Did in Solar Is Really a Big Deal," *Bloomberg* (February 11, 2015), Website www.bloomberg.com/news/articles/2015-02-11/what-apple-just-did-in-solar-is-a-really-big-deal.

50 "Photovoltaic System Pricing Trends," US National Renewable Energy Laboratory (September 22, 2014), Website www.nrel.gov/docs/fy14osti/62558.pdf.

51 Moritz Borgmann, "Dubai Utility DEWA Procures the World's Cheapest Solar Energy Ever," Apricum (November 27, 2014), Website www.apricum-group.com/dubais-dewa-procures-worlds-cheapest-solar-energy-ever-riyadh-start-photocopiers. Apricum is a global strategy consulting and transaction advisory firm specializing in solar and wind power.

52 "Today in Energy," EIA, Website www.eia.gov/todayinenergy/detail.cfm?id=15751.

53 Google Web Image, https://www.google.com/search?q=world+power+plant+additions+2014&biw=1920&bih=918&tbm=isch&imgil=OxC72cQ0cm43kM%253A%253BvnCTgN7E1dcn4M%253Bhttp%25253A%25252F%25252Fcleantechnica.com%25252F2015%25252F03%25252F16%25252Fsmall-solar-surging-13-new-us-power-plant-capacity-2014%25252F&source=iu&pf=m&fir=OxC72cQ0cm43kM%253A%252CvnCTgN7E1dcn4M%252C_&usg=__4Q6-n-FceAPW5isZcazhL4mGxH8%3D&ved=0CDYQyjdqFQoTCIivhrC0lMcCFcRxPgod-zUAcQ&ei=f0zDVcjzEsTj-QH764CIBw#imgrc=OxC72cQ0cm43kM%3A&usg=__4Q6-n-FceAPW5isZcazhL4mGxH8%3D. Sources EIA and SEIA—such as no mention of other sources such as biomass and hydro, which would be minor in scope.

54 John Farrell, "The Three Biggest Solar Charts of 2014," Institute for Local Self-Reliance (ILSR) (January 6, 2015), Website http://ilsr.org/biggest-solar-charts-2014.

55 Navigant Consulting (March, 2013), Website www.navigant.com, for percentage market share (site no longer available); "Turbine Manufacturers," Windpower Monthly, Website www.windpowermonthly.com/turbine-manufacturers.

56 American Wind Energy Association 2012 estimates for all of the US range $0.02 to $0.10 kWh depending on the location. $0.02–$0.04 is for large turbines in favorable areas of the Midwest. Website www.awea.org/Resources/Content.aspx?ItemNumber=5547#CostofWindEnergy.

57 Passing by large wind farms in California seemed to me as a casual observer to have a fair number of idle turbines.

58 Tildy Bayar, "Keeping Safe When Working with Wind Power," *Renewable Energy World* (January 6, 2014), Website www.renewableenergyworld.com/rea/news/article/2014/01/keeping-safe-when-working-with-wind-power.

59 Justin Martino, "Using Technology to Monitor and Maintain Wind Turbines," *Power Engineering* (August 12, 2013), Website www.power-eng.com/articles/print/volume-117/issue-8/features/using-technology-to-monitor-maintain-wind-turbines.html.

60 James Montgomery, "IBM's HyRef Seeks to Solve Wind's Intermittency Problem," *Renewable Energy World* (August 13, 2013), Website www.renewableenergyworld.com/rea/news/article/2013/08/ibms-hyref-seeks-to-solve-winds-intermittency-problem. See also Jim Utsler, "Improved Weather Forecasting Could Boost the Efficiency of Renewable Energy Sources," *IBM Systems Magazine* (March, 2014), Website www.ibmsystemsmag.com/mainframe/trends/IBM-Research/hyref_treinish.

61 M. Caduff, M. Huijbreghts, H. Althaus, A. Koehler, and S. Hellweg, "Wind Power Electricity: The Bigger the Turbine, the Greener the Electricity?" *Environmental Science & Technology* (2012), Website http://pubs.acs.org/doi/pdf/10.1021/es204108n.

62 Airbus dimensions provided on Website www.google.com/search?q=airbus+dimensions&biw=1920&bih=918&source=lnms&tbm=isch&sa=X&ei=_hXFVLb7MIHasATR3YLQAQ&ved=0CAYQ_AUoAQ#imgdii=_&imgrc=JvKBN9N9Q2o20M%253A%3BHu4NUKFQD2e8iM%3Bhttp%253A%252F%252Fnewsimg.bbc.co.uk%252Fmedia%252Fimages%252F40728000%252Fgif%252F_40728825_airbus_a380416.gif%3Bhttp%253A%252F%252Fnews.bbc.co.uk%252F2%252Fhi%252Fbusiness%252F4174729.stm%3B416%3B275.

63 A photoessay on building a turbine blade has been put together by Joan Sullivan, "Making the Blade Photoessay: How and Where Wind Turbines Get Their Swoosh," *Renewable Energy World*

(October 28, 2014), Website www.renewableenergyworld.com/rea/news/article/2014/10/making-the-blade-how-and-where-wind-turbines-get-their-swoosh.

64 "The Ten Biggest Turbines in the World," Windpower Monthly, Website www.windpowermonthly.com/10-biggest-turbines.

65 Justin Martino, "Advancements in Wind Turbine Technology: Improving Efficiency and Reducing Cost," *Power Engineering* (March 14, 2014), Website www.power-eng.com/articles/print/volume-118/issue-3/features/advancements-in-wind-turbine-technology-improving-efficiency-and-reducing-cost.html.

66 "Full Wind Turbine Portfolio," GE Energy, Website https://renewables.gepower.com/wind-energy/turbines/full-portfolio.html.

67 "Vestas Back on Top as Wind Turbine Installations Leader," *Renewable Energy World* (March 12, 2014), Website www.renewableenergyworld.com/rea/news/article/2014/03/vestas-back-on-top-as-wind-turbine-installions-leader.

68 "IEA Wind Task 26: The Past and Future Cost of Wind Energy," International Energy Agency and National Renewable Energy Laboratory (May, 2012), Website www.ieawind.org/index_page_postings/WP2_task26.pdf.

69 Peter Fairley, "Wind Turbines Shed Their Gears," *MIT Technology Review* (April 27, 2010), Website www.technologyreview.com/news/418689/wind-turbines-shed-their-gears.

70 David Appleyard, "New Offshore Jack-up Vessel Commissioned by Hochtief," *Renewable Energy World* (December 13, 2013), Website www.renewableenergyworld.com/rea/news/article/2013/12/new-offshore-jack-up-vessel-commissioned-by-hochtief.

71 Tildy Bayar, "Subsea Cables Bring Offshore Wind Power to the People," *Renewable Energy World* (December 19, 2013), Website www.renewableenergyworld.com/rea/news/article/2013/12/subsea-cables-bring-offshore-wind-power-to-the-people.

72 Worldwide wind patterns along with speeds by clicking on a location can be found at Website http://earth.nullschool.net. The default screen is the Western Hemisphere, but there are YouTube presentations (search youtube earth.nullschool) on how to work the site to see the rest of the world.

73 Data sources for Figures 9.7, 9.8, and 9.10 from "Global Wind Statistics (2014)," Global Wind Energy Council, Website www.gwec.net/wp-content/uploads/2015/03/GWEC_Global_Wind_2014_Report_LR.pdf.

74 "European Offshore Statistics 1st Half 2014," European Wind Energy Association, Website www.ewea.org/fileadmin/files/library/publications/statistics/European_offshore_statistics_1st-half_2014.pdf.

75 Forewind, Website www.forewind.co.uk/projects/dogger-bank-creyke-beck.html.

76 Harley Dixon, "Plans for World's Largest Wind Farm in Cumbria," *The Telegraph* (March 12, 2013), Website www.telegraph.co.uk/news/earth/energy/windpower/9924233/Plans-for-worlds-largest-wind-farm-in-Cumbria.html.

77 "Race Bank," 4C Offshore, Website www.4coffshore.com/windfarms/race-bank-united-kingdom-uk18.html.

78 Bureau of Ocean Energy Management, Website www.boem.gov/Renewable-Energy-Program/State-Activities/NC/Offshore-North-Carolina-Visualization-Study.aspx, for visualizations of large wind turbines 10, 15, and 20 nautical miles offshore North Carolina.

79 Cape Wind project, Website www.capewind.org.

80 Katharine Seelye, "Koch Brother Wages 12-Year Fight Over Wind Farm," *New York Times* (October 22, 2013), Website www.nytimes.com/2013/10/23/us/koch-brother-wages-12-year-fight-over-wind-farm.html?pagewanted=all&_r=0.

81 David Dickman, "Wind in the Sails of Energy Projects after Cape Wind," *Law360* (May 22, 2014), Website www.law360.com/articles/539172/wind-in-the-sails-of-energy-projects-after-cape-wind.

82 "UPDATE: Cape Wind in Jeopardy as Two Utilities Seek to Terminate Power Purchase Agreements," *Renewable Energy World* (January 26, 2015), Website www.renewableenergyworld.com/rea/news/

article/2015/01/cape-wind-in-jeopardy-as-two-utilities-seek-to-terminate-power-purchase-agreements.

83 James Montgomery, "US Shifts Offshore Wind Gaze to Maryland," *Renewable Energy World* (December 17, 2013), Website www.renewableenergyworld.com/rea/news/article/2013/12/us-shifts-offshore-wind-gaze-to-maryland. New Jersey was excluded from the list of states interested in offshore wind because the first NJ offshore project was killed by the NJ Board of Public Utilities because of a seeming "lack of financial integrity" by the backers, as reported by Alexi Friedman, "State rejects $188M offshore wind farm plan," *The Star-Ledger* (March 20, 2014).

84 Justin Doom, "Deepwater Gets Financing for First US Offshore Wind Farm," *Bloomberg* (March 3, 2015), Website www.bloomberg.com/news/articles/2015-03-02/deepwater-to-begin-construction-on-first-u-s-offshore-wind-farm.

85 Deepwater Wind, Website http://dwwind.com.

86 Elizabeth Harball, "Floating Wind Turbines Coming to West Coast," *Scientific American* (February 6, 2014), Website www.scientificamerican.com/article/floating-wind-turbines-coming-to-oregon-coast.

87 Data up to 2012 from Global Wind Energy Council, Website www.gwec.net/wp-content/uploads/2013/02/GWEC-PRstats-2012_english.pdf. Data for 2012 from Website www.gwec.net/wp-content/uploads/2014/04/5_17-1_global-installed-wind-power-capacity_regional-distribution.jpg.

88 Alex Morales, "European Wind Turbine Forecasts Cut as Power Demand Falls," *Bloomberg* (July 23, 2014), Website www.bloomberg.com/news/articles/2014-07-23/european-wind-turbine-forecasts-cut-as-power-demand-falls.

89 "European Wind Repowering Continues to Gather Pace," *Renewable Energy World* (June 11, 2014), Website www.renewableenergyworld.com/rea/news/article/2014/06/european-wind-repowering-continues-to-gather-pace.

90 See the Windpower Website www.thewindpower.net/index.php for data base on wind turbines and wind farms.

91 "Annual Market Forecast by Region 2003–2018," Global Wind Energy Council, Website www.gwec.net/wp-content/uploads/2014/04/1_29–1_annual-market-forecast-by-region-2003-2018.jpg.

92 Terri Engels, "Five Landmark Renewable Energy Projects from Around the World," *Renewable Energy World* (February 5, 2015), Website www.renewableenergyworld.com/rea/blog/post/2015/02/5-landmark-renewable-energy-projects-from-around-the-world?page=all.

93 "State Wind Energy Fact," American Wind Energy Association (2014), Website www.awea.org/resources/statefactsheets.aspx?itemnumber=890.

94 "U.S. Wind Energy Market Report," American Wind Energy Association, Website www.awea.org/resources/statefactsheets.aspx?itemnumber=890.

95 Matthew Wald, "Wired for Wind: A Texas Project May Lead the Way for the Nation," *The New York Times Business Day* (July 24, 2014).

96 Grain Belt Express Clean Line, Website www.grainbeltexpresscleanline.com.

97 Jennifer Van Burkleo (Electric Light & Power), "HVDC: The Key to Revolutionizing the Renewable Energy Grid," *Renewable Energy World* (September 3, 2013), Website www.renewableenergyworld.com/rea/news/article/2014/02/solar-induced-hybrid-fuel-cell-produces-electricity-directly-from-biomass. See comments by Gerry Wootton and Carlos Loures.

98 Jim Salter (Associated Press), "Transmission Line to Carry Wind Power Across the US Midwest Sparks Controversy," *Renewable Energy World* (March 19, 2014), Website www.renewableenergyworld.com/rea/news/article/2014/03/transmission-line-to-carry-wind-power-across-the-us-midwest-sparks-controversy.

99 See Li Junfeng, "China Wind Energy Outlook 2012," Global Wind Energy Council, Website www.gwec.net/wp-content/uploads/2012/11/China-Outlook-2012-EN.pdf, for data for Figures 9.12 and 9.13.

100 Li Junfeng, "China Wind Energy Outlook 2012," Global Wind Energy Council, Website www. gwec.net/wp-content/uploads/2012/11/China-Outlook-2012-EN.pdf.

101 Feifei Shen, "China Three Years Late on Installing Offshore Wind Farms," *Bloomberg* (July 16, 2014), Website www.bloomberg.com/news/articles/2014-07-16/china-three-years-late-on-installing-offshore-wind-farms.

102 Russel Tencer (CEO, United Wind), "Distributed Wind Energy: The New Cash Crop," energycentral (July 2, 2014), Website www.energycentral.com/generationstorage/wind/articles/2966/Distributed-Wind-Energy-The-New-Cash-Crop.

103 Tildy Bayar, "Dutch Wind Turbine Purchase Sets World Crowdfunding Record," *Renewable Energy World* (September 24, 2013), Website www.renewableenergyworld.com/rea/news/article/2013/09/dutch-wind-turbine-purchase-sets-world-crowdfunding-record.

104 John Matthews, "Chile's Mines Set Hot Pace for Renewables—Australia Take Note," *Renewable Energy World* (December 24, 2014), Website www.renewableenergyworld.com/rea/news/article/2014/12/chiles-mines-set-hot-pace-on-renewables-australia-take-note.

105 Windstream Technologies, Website www.windstream-inc.com/products/solarmill/sm2-6p.

106 Kate Sheppard, "Marcellus Energy Development Could Pave Over an Area Bigger Than the State of Delaware," *Huffington Post* (February 25, 2014), Website www.huffingtonpost.com/2014/02/25/natural-gas-marcellus_n_4855927.html.

107 Andrew Curry, "Will Newer Turbines Mean Fewer Bird Deaths?" *National Geographic* (April 27, 2014), Website http://news.nationalgeographic.com/news/energy/2014/04/140427-altamont-pass-will-newer-wind-turbines-mean-fewer-bird-deaths. See also Rose Eveleth, "How Many Birds Do Wind Turbines Really Kill?" Smithsonian (December 16, 2013), Website www.smithsonianmag.com/smart-news/how-many-birds-do-wind-turbines-really-kill-180948154/?no-ist.

108 Susan Kraemer, "New Research Improves on Earlier Bird-Killing Turbine Studies," *Renewable Energy World* (September 19, 2014), Website www.renewableenergyworld.com/rea/news/article/2014/09/new-research-improves-on-earlier-bird-killing-turbine-studies.

109 "Sea Bird Halts London Array Wind Farm Expansion," BBC News (February 19, 2014), Website www.bbc.com/news/uk-england-26258271.

110 "Obama Looks the Other Way When Wind & Solar Kill Birds & Bats," Institute for Energy Research (September 2, 2014), Website http://instituteforenergyresearch.org/analysis/obama-administration-ignores-wind-solar-power-killing-birds-bats. See also Justin Doom (Bloomberg), "U.S. Eases Wind Power Bird-Death Rule," *Renewable Energy World* (December 9, 2013), Website www.renewableenergyworld.com/rea/news/article/2013/12/u-s-eases-wind-power-bird-death-rule.

111 Terra Moya Aqua (TMA), Website www.tmawind.com. See also Sauer Energy, a proponent of vertical turbines, Website www.sauerenergy.com.

112 "2013 Wind Technologies Market Report," Energy Efficiency and Renewable Energy (US DOE), Website http://emp.lbl.gov/sites/all/files/2013_Wind_Technologies_Market_Report_Final3.pdf.

113 "Federal Production Tax Credit for Wind Energy," AWEA (2014), Website http://awea.files.cms-plus.com/FileDownloads/pdfs/PTC%20Fact%20Sheet.pdf. Data for 2014 from Louise Downing, "U.S. Wind Power Installations Swelled Sixfold in 2014," *Bloomberg* (January 22, 2015), Website www.bloomberg.com/news/articles/2015-01-22/u-s-wind-power-installations-rose-sixfold-in-2014-bnef.

114 "National Solar Jobs Census," Solar Energy Industries Association (2014), Website www.seia.org/research-resources/national-solar-jobs-census.

115 Justin Doom, "US Solar Jobs Climb 22 Percent as Clean Power Aids Economic Recovery," *Bloomberg* (January 15, 2015), Website www.bloomberg.com/news/articles/2015-01-15/us-solar-jobs-climb-22-as-clean-power-aids-economic-recovery.

116 "Average Number of Employees by State and Mine Type, 2013 and 2012 (Table 18)," US Energy Information Administration Annual Coal Report (2013), Website www.eia.gov/coal/annual/pdf/table18.pdf.

117 American Wind Energy Association Press Release (January 7, 2013), Website www.awea.org/MediaCenter/pressrelease.aspx?ItemNumber=4842.

118 "Green Growth: The Impact of Wind Energy on Jobs and the Economy," European Wind Energy Association (2012), Website www.ewea.org/uploads/tx_err/Green_Growth.pdf.

119 "Renewable Energy and Jobs 2015 Annual Review," International Renewable Energy Agency (IRENA), Website www.irena.org/DocumentDownloads/Publications/IRENA_RE_Jobs_Annual_Review_2015.pdf.

120 Tom Randall, "Fossil Fuels Just Lost the Race Against Renewables," *Bloomberg* (April 15, 2015), Website www.bloomberg.com/news/articles/2015-04-14/fossil-fuels-just-lost-the-race-against-renewables.

121 Marshall Brain, "How Do Car Batteries Work?" (August 20, 2009), Website www.brainstuffshow.com/blog/how-do-car-batteries-work.

122 Marshall Brain, "How Lithium-Ion Batteries Work," Website http://electronics.howstuffworks.com/everyday-tech/lithium-ion-battery.htm.

123 Kevin Bullis, "Battery Material Prevents Fires, Stores Five Times the Energy," *MIT Technology Review* (January 25, 2013), Website www.technologyreview.com/news/510311/battery-material-prevents-fires-stores-five-times-the-energy.

124 "Cheap, Strong Lithium-Ion Battery Developed at USC," *USC (University of Southern California) News* (February 14, 2013), Website https://news.usc.edu/46778/cheap-strong-lithium-ion-battery-developed-at-usc.

125 Oxis Energy, Website www.oxisenergy.com.

126 John Voelcker, "How Much and How Fast Will Electric-Car Battery Costs Fall?" Green Car Reports (March 16, 2012), Website www.greencarreports.com/news/1074183_how-much-and-how-fast-will-electric-car-battery-costs-fall.

127 "Panasonic and Tesla Sign Agreement for the Gigafactory," Tesla Motors (July 30, 2014), Website www.teslamotors.com/blog/panasonic-and-tesla-sign-agreement-gigafactory.

128 "Battery Cost Dropping Below $200 per kWhr Soon, Says Tesla's Elon Musk," AutoBlog (February 21, 2012), Website www.autoblog.com/2012/02/21/battery-cost-dropping-below-200-per-kwh-soon-says-teslas-elon.

129 Daniel Sparks, "Tesla Motors, Inc.'s Gigafactory May Be More Revolutionary Than We Realize," *The Motley Fool* (August 20, 2014), Website www.fool.com/investing/general/2014/08/20/tesla-motors-incs-gigafactory-may-be-more-revoluti.aspx.

130 Ali Nourai, "Distributed Bulk Storage: Is This the New Shape of the Grid?" *Renewable Energy World* (January 28, 2015), Website www.renewableenergyworld.com/rea/blog/post/2015/01/distributed-bulk-storage-is-this-the-new-shape-of-the-grid.

131 Mark Chediak, "Musk's Battery Works Fill Utilities with Fear and Promise," *Bloomberg* (December 6, 2014), Website www.bloomberg.com/news/articles/2014-12-05/musk-battery-works-fill-utilities-with-fear-and-promise.

132 "Sodium Sulfur (NAS) Batteries," Energy Storage Association, Website http://energystorage.org/energy-storage/technologies/sodium-sulfur-nas-batteries.

133 "Battery Technologies," EuroBat, Website www.eurobat.org/battery-technologies#Sodium_based.

134 Advanced Lead Battery Consortium, Website www.alabc.org/publications/ultrabattery-alab-technological-breakthrough.

135 Aquion Energy, Website www.aquionenergy.com/energy-storage-technology.

136 "How Does a Battery Work?" MIT School of Engineering, Website http://engineering.mit.edu/ask/how-does-battery-work.

137 Energy Storage Association, Website http://energystorage.org.

138 See "Iron Flow Battery for Grid Storage," Arotech presentation (March, 2014), Website www.arotech.com, for comparative analysis of flow battery types.

139 "New Battery Design Could Help Solar and Wind Energy Power the Grid," US DOE SLAC National Accelerator Laboratory and Stanford University (April 24, 2014), Website www6.slac.stanford.edu/news/2013-04-24-polysulfide-flowbattery.aspx.

140 "Organic Mega Flow Battery Promises Breakthrough for Renewable Energy," *Harvard School of Engineering and Applied Sciences News* (January 8, 2014), Website www.seas.harvard.edu/news/2014/01/organic-mega-flow-battery-promises-breakthrough-for-renewable-energy.

141 Chris Meehan, "Vanderbilt Proposes Building Energy Storage into Solar Cells," SolarReviews (October 30, 2013), Website www.solarreviews.com/news/vanderbilt-supercapacitor-solar-cell-103013.

142 Pam Frost Gorder, "All-in-One Solution: Solar that Stores its Own Power," *Renewable Energy World* (October 7, 2014), Website www.renewableenergyworld.com/rea/news/article/2014/10/all-in-one-solution-solar-that-stores-its-own-power.

143 Zachary Shahan, "Talking With $1 Billion Battery Startup Alevo," CleanTechnica (November 10, 2014), Website http://cleantechnica.com/2014/11/10/alevo-1-billion-battery-startup. See also Aleva, Website http://alevo.com.

144 EnerVault, Website http://enervault.com.

145 American Vanadium, Website www.americanvanadium.com/cellcube.php. See also T. Shibato, T. Kumamoto, Y. Nagaoka, K. Kawase, and K. Yano, "Redox Flow Batteries for the Stable Supply of Renewable Energy," *SEI Technical Review*, Number 76 (April, 2013), Website http://global-sei.com/tr/pdf/feature/76-03.pdf, for a technical paper on vanadium batteries.

146 UniEnergy Technologies, Website www.uetechnologies.com.

147 "Clean Energy Storage—and Onions?" Prudent Energy, Website www.pdenergy.com/pdfs/GillsOnions-PrudentEnergy-WhitePaper-July2012.pdf.

148 "BU-209: Supercapacitor," Battery University, Website http://batteryuniversity.com/learn/article/whats_the_role_of_the_supercapacitor. See also "Supercapacitors: First One Up the Drive," *The Economist* (July 12, 2014).

149 Chris Meehan, "Do Solar and Wind Cause Power Plants to Release More Pollution?" *Renewable Energy World* (October 4, 2013), Website www.solarreviews.com/news/solar-wind-reduce-emmisions-NREL-092713.

150 Paul Hockenos, "Energy Storage Market Outlook 2015," *Renewable Energy World* (February 11, 2015), Website www.renewableenergyworld.com/rea/news/article/2015/02/energy-storage-market-outlook-2015. See also Smartgrid.gov, "Recovery Act Smart Grid Investments," Website www.smartgrid.gov/project/southern_california_edison_company_tehachapi_wind_energy_storage_project.

151 "IHA Hydropower Annual Report," International Hydropower Association, Website www.hydropower.org/2013-iha-hydropower-report.

152 Jon Are Suul, "Variable Speed Pumped Storage Hydropower Plants for Integration of Wind Power in Isolated Power System," Norwegian Institute of Science and Technology, Website http://cdn.intechopen.com/pdfs-wm/9345.pdf.

153 Michael Harris, "RusHydro, Chinese Conglomerates Sign Deals for Conventional, Pumped-Storage Development," *Hydro Review* (November 10, 2014), Website www.hydroworld.com/articles/2014/11/rushydro-chinese-conglomerates-sign-deals-for-conventional-pumped-storage-development.html.

154 "List of Pumped-Storage Hydroelectric Power Stations," Wikipedia, The Free Encyclopedia, Website http://en.wikipedia.org/wiki/List_of_pumped-storage_hydroelectric_power_stations.

155 "Compressed Air Energy Storage," Energy Storage Association, Website http://energystorage.org/compressed-air-energy-storage-caes.

156 Ehren Goossens, "Green Power for L.A. Power," *Bloomberg* (September 24, 2014), Website www.bloomberg.com/news/articles/2014-09-23/developers-plan-8-billion-green-project-for-l-a-power.

157 Karen Hampton, "Toronto Hydro to Test Cost-Competitive Underwater Energy Storage," *Energy Storage Journal* (June 3, 2013), Website www.energystoragejournal.com/toronto-hydro-to-test-cost-competitive-underwater-energy-storage.

158 "Flywheels," Energy Storage Association, Website http://energystorage.org/energy-storage/technologies/flywheels.

159 Data source Electric Power Research Institute (EPRI), International Renewable Energy Agency (IRENA), and IEA Electricity Storage Technology Brief as compiled by Bruce Dorminey, "The Wide Appeal of Batteries for the Renewable Energy Market," (*Renewable Energy World* June 5, 2014), Website www.renewableenergyworld.com/rea/news/article/2014/06/the-wide-appeal-of-batteries-for-the-renewable-energy-market.

160 See Plug Power, Website www.plugpower.com, for a description of fuel cells and their present commercial applications. See also Ballard Power Systems, Website www.ballard.com/about-ballard/fuel-cell-education-resources/how-a-fuel-cell-works.aspx.

161 John Toon (Georgia Institute of Technology), "Solar-Induced Hybrid Fuel Cell Produces Electricity Directly from Biomass," *Renewable Energy World* (February 25, 2014), Website www.renewableenergyworld.com/rea/news/article/2014/02/solar-induced-hybrid-fuel-cell-produces-electricity-directly-from-biomass.

162 "Carbon Capture," FuelCell Energy, Website www.fuelcellenergy.com/advanced-technologies/carbon-capture.

163 Source Guides, Website http://energy.sourceguides.com/businesses/byP/fcsys/byB/manufacturers/byN/byName.shtml.

164 Anthony DePalma, "A Mayor's Green-Power Moonshot," *The New York Times* (April 23, 2015).

165 FuelCell Energy, Website http://fcel.client.shareholder.com/releasedetail.cfm?ReleaseID=826618.

166 Edward Dodge, "Power-to-Gas Enables Massive Energy Storage," The Energy Collective (December 6, 2014), Website http://theenergycollective.com/ed-dodge/2166976/power-gas-enables-massive-energy-storage.

167 NHThree, Website http://nhthree.com/index.html, describes the process. See also William Leighty (Alaska Applied Sciences), "The Alaska Renewable-source Ammonia Fuel Pilot Plant: Firming Storage and Renewables Export," *Renewable Energy World* (December 23, 2013), Website www.renewableenergyworld.com/rea/news/article/2013/12/the-alaska-renewable-source-ammonia-fuel-pilot-plant-firming-storage-and-renewables-export.

168 Projects 9.1 and 9.2 adapted from Roy Nersesian, *Energy Risk Modeling* (Ithaca, NY: Palisade, 2013).

10 Hydrogen Economy, Geothermal and Ocean Power, and Climate Change

Hydrogen for storing electricity and fuel cells for converting hydrogen back to electricity were covered in the previous chapter. This chapter deals with the role of hydrogen as a motor vehicle fuel and what a hydrogen economy may be like. Geothermal energy along with enhanced geothermal systems have been grossly ignored as a source of energy. Geothermal energy has the potential of supplying much of the electricity demand in many regions of the world that possess geothermal resources that can be developed and connected to a transmission system. Tides are a major source of energy, but tidal dams are far from centers of population. While tides can be predicted with precision, their occurrence may not match demand. However, tidal dams are being built with a number of proposals on the table for potential consideration. While the initial development of wave energy is underway, only a minuscule portion of wave energy potential will ever be tapped. Climate change is the mantra of those who blame carbon dioxide buildup in the atmosphere as a sole source of problems that at times include volcanic eruptions and earthquakes. Climate change has been part of Earth's repertoire for as long as it has existed. There may be other contributors to climate change besides anthropomorphic gases. Perhaps it is time to acknowledge the ultimate unpredictability of climate rather than bet all the chips on a seemingly predictable, but often wrong, oversimplified, deterministic, single variable climate model. Ironically, this book, in looking at fossil fuels as a finite resource and what might be left in a century, concludes along with the global alarmists that reducing carbon dioxide fuels is a desirable course of action—but motivations are far different.

Hydrogen Economy

Hydrogen is the most abundant element in the universe, making up 75 percent of its mass and 90 percent of its molecules. Hydrogen, when burned as a fuel, emits only water and heat, the cleanest source of energy by far. Though plentiful in the universe, there is no free hydrogen here on Earth. While a portion is locked away in hydrocarbons and other chemicals, most is all around and in us as water, the product of hydrogen combustion.

It is interesting that human progress in energy has been marked with decarbonizing fuel sources. For most of history, humans burned wood, which has the highest ratio of carbon to hydrogen atoms, about ten carbon atoms per hydrogen atom. This means burning wood emits more carbon dioxide than burning fossil fuels for an equivalent release of energy. Coal, the fossil fuel that sparked the Industrial Revolution, has about one or two carbon atoms per hydrogen atom, which means it emits less carbon dioxide than wood. Next is oil, with one-half of a carbon atom per hydrogen atom (or one carbon atom for every two hydrogen atoms), and natural gas is last, with one-quarter of a carbon atom per hydrogen atom (or one carbon atom for every four hydrogen atoms). Thus, as people have learned to use new fuels, each one was a step down in carbon dioxide emissions for an equivalent release of energy. The ultimate step is hydrogen, which has no carbon atoms and, therefore, no carbon dioxide emissions, no emissions of carbon monoxide, sulfur, nitrous oxides, and other progenitor chemicals that create smog, and no metallic emissions (mercury, arsenic); hydrogen produces only water and heat.

See the Companion Website for sections on the Historical Background of Hydrogen Economy and Hydrogen Today: www.routledge.com/cw/nersesian.

Hydrogen as a Motor Vehicle Fuel

Hydrogen's low energy density, however, presents a serious logistics problem. Hydrogen contains only about one-third the energy content of natural gas when compressed to the same pressure. If a 20 gallon gasoline tank to power a car for 300 miles represents one unit of volume, an amount of liquid hydrogen on an energy-equivalent basis would represent two units of volume or 2×; hydrogen in chemical hydrides 2.5×; compressed 10,000 psi 3×; metal hydrides 4×; and compressed 5,000 psi 5×.[1] While liquid hydrogen has only one-third the energy content of gasoline on a volume basis, the higher efficiency of a fuel cell means less hydrogen has to be burned for a given power level and thus requires twice the volume of a gasoline tank, not three times. As a compressed gas, small molecules of hydrogen can more easily leak through cracks, porous material, and faulty fittings and gaskets than larger methane molecules. The integrity of fittings and gaskets is a technical challenge when hydrogen is compressed to 5,000 or 10,000 psi in order to store a sufficient volume for a normal 300-mile driving range. Research is being conducted on solid-state storage using metal hydrides (magnesium, lanthanum and nickel, sodium aluminum, or lithium boron) where hydrogen is stored at much less pressure within the molecular structure of metal hydrides and is released by heating the storage medium.

About 30 automobile companies are offering over 60 models of hydrogen burning automobiles.[2] Most of these models are concept cars relying on different technologies, with the most frequent being hydrogen fuel cells. Some are electric hybrids with hydrogen fuel cells. A few have a conventional engine adapted for pressurized hydrogen. One has a bi-fuel hydrogen and gasoline engine to compensate for the relative scarcity of hydrogen filling stations. Three commercial sedans—the Mercedes Benz B-Class F-Cell, Honda Clarity, and Toyota Mirai—are available to the public. The Toyota Mirai is a combination hybrid and fuel cell with 153 horsepower and can accelerate from 0–60 mph in 9 seconds. The Mirai's two 10,000 psi carbon fiber polymer fuel tanks can be refueled in 3–5 minutes and has a range of 300 miles. It has a nickel metal hydride rechargeable battery pack and a 152 horsepower electric traction motor. The Honda FCX Clarity is powered by a 100 kW V-Flow fuel cell, a lithium ion battery pack, a 95 kW electric motor, and a 5,000 psi compressed hydrogen gas storage tank for a range of 270 miles. The Mercedes-Benz F-Cell Sports Tourer is a hybrid vehicle using battery power with an assist from a hydrogen fuel cell in delivering power to the electric motors during acceleration. A battery pack is also recharged by the fuel cell and with regenerative braking common with hybrid vehicles. An electric motor generates 100 kW (136 horsepower) with a driving range of 250 miles.[3] The Ford F-250 Super Chief Tri-Flex Fuel truck has a single engine that runs gasoline and E85 carried in the same tank (flex fuel) or hydrogen in a separate tank.[4]

Fiat-Chrysler, Ford, and GM have a collaborative program to strengthen the technology base of US automobile companies called the US Council for Automotive Research (USCAR).[5] In addition to funding from private sources, there is also public funding such as the US Department of Energy's US DRIVE (Driving Research and Innovation for Vehicle Efficiency and Energy Sustainability).[6] The purpose of this research program is to develop a motor vehicle powered by a hydrogen fuel cell or other technologies such as advanced hybrid propulsion systems. To hasten development, US DRIVE has teamed up with USCAR. California, with its tough air quality laws and calls for zero-emission vehicles, has become a national testing ground for battery power and hydrogen fuel motor vehicles.

Hydrogen fuel motor vehicles represent the classic chicken-and-egg situation. No one is going to build hydrogen fueling stations without hydrogen fuel cars, and no one is going to build or buy hydrogen fuel cars without fueling stations. California is the national trendsetter with its hydrogen highway initiative program with about ten fueling stations. According to one source, the number of hydrogen fueling stations existing/planned are 40/42 in Europe; 18/15 in the US; 4/4 in Japan; 5/0 in South Korea; two existing in Taiwan and South America; and one existing in China, Malaysia, India, and Canada.[7] (Different sources quote widely differing numbers of hydrogen refilling stations.)[8]

The number of hydrogen filling stations today is less than that cited in the previous edition of this book. In other words, the hydrogen economy is taking off at a rather leisurely pace. For instance, California has some hydrogen fueling stations clustered around San Francisco and more about Los Angeles, but previous plans called for the California Hydrogen Highway stretching from Vancouver, BC, to Baja California in Mexico. The Scandinavia Hydrogen Highway links hydrogen highways in Sweden, Norway, and Denmark. The European Union Hydrogen Highway will link the Scandinavia Hydrogen Highway with Germany, the Netherlands, Belgium, France, Austria, Italy, Spain, and the UK. The Japan Hydrogen Highway connects 11 cities around Tokyo Bay (Tokyo, Kawasaki, Yokohama, and others). The South Korea Hydrogen Highway consists of a cluster of hydrogen fueling stations around Seoul with one in the center and one in the south of the nation, hardly a viable alternative for owners of hydrogen fuel vehicles.

The intent of the California, Scandinavia, European Union, Japan, and South Korea hydrogen highways is to attack the chicken-and-egg situation by ensuring an adequate number of fueling stations along highly travelled automobile corridors for the public to start buying hydrogen fuel vehicles. These vehicles will have to be owned by those whose driving patterns are more or less confined to a 100–150-mile-wide strip on either side of the highway (assuming a 200–300-mile range between fueling). Once a stretch of road can serve hydrogen fuel vehicles, then the population of hydrogen fuel vehicles can expand in communities along the hydrogen highway. As the population of hydrogen fuel vehicles grows in areas adjacent to hydrogen highways, more fueling stations can be added, increasing the area that can serve hydrogen fuel vehicles, allowing for another step-up in the population of hydrogen fuel vehicles, which encourages the opening of more hydrogen fueling stations. Once started, this process feeds on itself and could mark the start of an era of hydrogen fuel vehicles.

If this process sounds vaguely familiar, it is. The first automobiles did not have gasoline stations for fueling. Gasoline fuels (naphtha and other light-end products) were purchased in tins. The first gas stations were in city centers where the first automobiles were sold. Building gas stations and roads around city centers expanded the market for automobiles, which, in turn, expanded the market for more gas stations and roads. This process continued until the nation, and indeed much of the world, became blanketed with automobiles and gasoline stations and paved with roads and parking lots.

The probability of a massive switch to hydrogen fuel vehicles is remote at this time with a high cost of hydrogen compared to gasoline and a high cost of a hydrogen automobile compared to a conventionally fueled automobile. The most serious obstacle is the cost of a hydrogen fuel cell, even though its cost has fallen considerably in recent years. The cost was $248 per kW in 2002 and $51 per kW in 2009, with an objective to be further reduced to $30 per kW to be competitive with gasoline engines. Part of the savings has been in minimizing platinum as a coating material on a catalyst and in substituting a salt mixture of molten carbonate as an electrolyte. Fuel storage, which for a gasoline automobile is simply a metal tank, was $15–$18 per kilowatt-hour for high-pressure storage, with an objective to be reduced to $2 per kilowatt-hour to make a hydrogen vehicle more cost-competitive with a gasoline vehicle. Moreover, fuel cells are not as durable as gasoline engines and perform poorly in cold weather.[9] A European 40-passenger hydrogen fuel cell powered bus cost $2.1 million 5 years ago and $1.5 million in 2015 versus a conventional diesel powered bus costing between $300,000 and $600,000. Hydrogen fuel on an energy content basis with diesel is about twice as expensive. Hydrogen fuel busses need to be substantially subsidized to remain in service.[10] Huge developmental efforts are still necessary to improve manufacturing processes and the expected life and reliability of fuel cells, particularly those exposed to low winter temperatures. Some believe that an entirely new fuel cell technology may have to be created for another significant cost reduction. Others are convinced that necessary cost reductions and performance enhancements can be achieved with present-day technology. While the cost for hydrogen fuel is declining, it would take another oil crisis with gasoline prices at $8 per gallon for hydrogen to be cost competitive. The odds of hydrogen becoming a fuel of the future depend on what happens in the oil patch.

Hydrogen Economy Tomorrow

While hydrogen will most likely come from stripping hydrogen from hydrocarbons, black hydrogen will eventually have to give way to green hydrogen to reduce carbon dioxide emissions. The difficulty in transporting hydrogen over long distances, associated with its low density and propensity to leak through fittings and gaskets, can be overcome by generating electricity and producing hydrogen locally. Each community, or group of communities, with an aggregate population of 500,000 or more would have its local nuclear or integrated gasification combined cycle (IGCC) power plant with sequestered carbon dioxide augmented as much as possible by sustainable energy sources. Nuclear and IGCC plants would produce electricity for the electrolysis of water plus direct hydrogen production from IGCC plants. A distributed generation system would supply electricity in the local region, and excess electricity would be dedicated to generating hydrogen, which would be sold at local motor vehicle fueling stations. Electricity generators would operate close to full capacity in order to sell electricity at a low base rate for consumption by individuals, businesses, and industry or for the electrolysis of hydrogen. There would be no need to invest in generators that only operate part of the time in response to transient changes in electricity demand and also negate marginal electricity rates. This would be a return to Thomas Edison's original idea for neighborhood electricity generating plants and, if carried to its logical conclusion, would make Westinghouse's idea of large centralized power stations with long-distance transmission lines serving wide swaths of a nation obsolete.

The next step toward the hydrogen economy would be for every building and home to be fitted with a solar array and/or wind turbine, an electrolysis unit, a hydrogen storage medium, and a fuel cell module. A solar array or wind turbine would provide electricity to the building. Excess electricity would be fed to the electrolysis unit to produce hydrogen, which would be stored in a tank or storage medium. Hydrogen would be fed to the fuel cell module to generate electricity when the sun is not shining and/or the wind is not blowing. Waste heat, in the form of hot water generated when hydrogen is converted to electricity, would be recycled for personal use, running appliances, and space heating.

The ultimate dream of hydrogen aficionados is to increase the amount of electricity generated by solar energy, which would depend on improving the efficiency of converting sunlight to electricity. If solar power could be significantly stepped up, then electricity output may be large enough to produce enough hydrogen to power fuel cell motor vehicles. Motor vehicles for personal use operate only about 5 percent of the time, which means that their fuel cells are idle 95 percent of the time. This is not an efficient use of any capital investment. Once parked at its destination, a hydrogen fuel automobile would generate electricity for the electricity grid as long as there is enough hydrogen left for the return trip. If sufficient numbers of these mobile generators are available and if a sufficient volume of hydrogen can be generated from the sun and wind, this could conceivably eliminate most of the local nuclear and IGCC plants.

Utilities would still be needed for power generation to cover shortfalls and serve as backup, but their primary purpose would be providing physical connections for millions of automobiles, homes, and buildings to plug into the electric grid where every home, building, and automobile is both an electricity generating utility and a consumer. If the aggregate output of sustainable power sources were large enough, there would be no need for backup generators. Once this occurs, then distributive utilities could become as obsolete as their centralized kin for electricity generation. However, they would remain as "virtual" utilities, overseeing buying and selling of electricity among millions of users and generators and providing technology to dispatch and control millions of micro-generators. Transformation of an electricity grid with a few large generators into an interactive electricity network of millions of micro-generators would require advanced computer technologies, millions of sensors, and sophisticated software to allow electricity to flow exactly where and when needed at the lowest rate in a world where everyone is electrically and electronically connected to everyone else. Cooperatives could be set up for buying and selling electricity among their members, possibly even taking over the utility's role of providing an interactive electricity network modeled after the worldwide communications web. If cooperatives also took over responsibility of servicing and installing electrical wires and cables and connections, then the entire concept of a utility becomes obsolete.

If all this sounds esoteric, it is. It may hold true a century or two from now, but not from today's perspective. Significant technological advances have yet to be made to bring about the hydrogen economy. Other than those alarmed over its cost, few are against the concept. Hydrogen is virtually pollution-free with an unlimited supply. But for hydrogen to become a major energy source in the coming decades, sustainable sources of energy (hydro, wind, solar, geothermal) will not be enough. Nuclear power and coal burning IGCC plants with sequestered carbon dioxide will have to play a major role in generating the requisite amounts of electricity until that day when highly efficient (70 percent plus) solar installations can be the ubiquitous substitute for nearly all forms of energy. Even then hydro, nuclear, wind, and geothermal would probably be needed for backup support.

Geothermal Power

Geothermal energy, from the Greek words *geo* (Earth) and *therme* (heat), takes advantage of hot water or steam escaping from hot spots. Geothermal power is clean, renewable, sustainable, and safe, using little land area. It generates electricity for base load needs and is highly reliable, reducing the need to burn fossil fuels, and is a means to diversify energy sources. Although intended to serve base load needs, geothermal output is easily controlled by a throttle and can be used to satisfy transient demand, quite unlike nuclear and coal where operators try to avoid changing power levels to any significant degree. Geothermal plants can be built in a modular fashion to handle growing demand, boost local economies, and provide power at remote locations. The potential of geothermal power is enormous. Conceivably, geothermal power could satisfy the needs of 620 million people in 39 nations in Africa, Central and South America, and in the Pacific located within the transmission range of hot spots.

Geothermal sources are located where magma is relatively close to the surface and where rock above magma is porous and filled with subsurface water with access to the surface. Geothermal sources are found near tectonic plate boundaries that are separating (Iceland and the Great Rift Valley in East Africa) or colliding, creating subduction zones (Japan and Southeast Asia), or sliding by one another (California). Potential sites for geothermal development can be commonly found along the Pacific "Ring of Fire." Geothermal energy sources are also found near volcanoes (Mount Vesuvius in Italy, island of Hawaii, and the Yellowstone caldera), or where magma protrusions lie relatively close to the surface.

Geothermal Power for Heating

Maoris in New Zealand and Native Americans have used water from hot springs for cooking and medicinal purposes for thousands of years. The ancient Greeks and Romans had geothermal heated spas. The people of Pompeii, living too close to Mount Vesuvius, tapped hot water from the Earth to heat their buildings. The Romans used geothermal waters for treating eye and skin disease. The Japanese have enjoyed geothermal spas for centuries. American Indians have enjoyed the benefit of hot springs in California. Today geothermal sources supply 11 gW of thermal power in 40 nations for various heating purposes, plus another 35 nations that have not developed geothermal sources commercially, but enjoy the benefit of natural hot springs for bathing, such as in Japan where 4,000 hot springs attract 12 million visitors per year.[11]

The Earth's crust insulates life from the hot interior of the mantle. The normal temperature gradient is about 50°F–87°F per mile or 17°C–30°C per kilometer of depth and higher where the crust is relatively thin or near plate boundaries and volcanoes. Magma trapped beneath the crust heats up lower rock layers. If hot rock is porous and filled with continually replenished subsurface water with access to the surface, then the result is fumaroles of escaping steam and hot gases, geysers of hot water, or pools of boiling mud. As a geothermal source, the Earth becomes a boiler, and escaping hot water and steam, called hydrothermal fluids, are tapped for hot spring baths, heating greenhouses (agriculture), heating water for marine life (aquaculture), as district heating for homes, schools, commercial establishments, streets, and sidewalks to prevent ice formation, and as a source of hot water for industrial use or steam for generating electricity. Nearly all of Reykjavik, Iceland, receives hot water from geothermal sources. A well is being drilled 2 km deep in a suburb of Paris to tap heated geothermal water to expand existing district heating by 25 percent to include another 35,000 homes.[12] Boise, Idaho capital district, and Oregon Tech, both heated with geothermal water, are among 18 district heating systems in the western US. An estimated 270 western US cities are located close enough to geothermal sources to take advantage of district heating. Geothermal energy has reduced carbon emissions by 22 million tons plus 200,000 tons of nitrogen oxides and 110,000 tons of particulates annually.

Heat pumps can be used anywhere to provide clean heating and cooling. A heat pump is similar to an air conditioner, which can cool air inside a house, expelling heat to the outside. By turning an air conditioner around in a window, it can cool air on the outside environment, expelling heat into the house. The outside environment for a heat pump is a loop dug deep enough into the ground (10 or more feet) where temperature is constant year round at about 45°–55°F depending on latitude.[13] The loop is filled with water. During summer, a heat pump cools a house, transferring heat in the form of warmed water to the loop where it is cooled to 50°F. During winter, a heat pump warms a house, transferring cooled water to the loop to be warmed to 50°F. For mild climates, a heat pump can meet the entire heating and cooling needs of a house. In more severe climates, a furnace or air conditioning would be required, but their energy requirements would be less. Heat pumps reduce fossil fuel consumption by being 45 percent more efficient than the traditional means to heat and cool a house, although electricity usage will climb from near-continual pumping of water through the loop.[14] About 400,000 heat pumps are installed in the US providing 1.5 gW of heating and cooling. One idea is for homes to be fitted with rooftop solar panels for electricity coupled with heat pumps that would reduce utility costs for electricity and for natural gas or heating oil. Sainsbury, a supermarket chain in the UK and the US, is installing a system at its 100 food outlets that will store waste heat from its refrigeration systems underground and then pump heat back into the food outlets during winter months, reducing the energy requirements for heating by 30 percent.[15]

Geothermal Power for Electricity

Three types of geothermal power plants generate electricity. First is a dry steam geothermal reservoir in which emitted steam directly spins a turbine. These are relatively rare and were the first dedicated to generating electricity. One in Tuscany has been in operation since 1904, and The Geysers, 90 miles north of San Francisco, has been in operation since 1960. The Geysers represents the largest single source of tapped geothermal energy in the world and generates enough electricity to supply a city the size of San Francisco. A falloff in steam pressure in the 1990s was successfully countered by water injection to replenish the geothermal reservoir. Injected water was waste treatment water from neighboring communities, an innovative and environmentally safe method of disposal. Some thought has been given to tapping the world's largest source of geothermal energy, Yellowstone, the caldera of a supervolcano that last erupted 600,000 years ago. (Another eruption of that magnitude would wipe out half of the US and emit an ash cloud large enough to send the planet into a "volcanic" winter.) But Yellowstone, as a national park, cannot be commercially developed.

The second and most common form of geothermal power plant is a flash steam plant driven by geothermal reservoirs that emit hot, pressurized water between 300°F and 700°F. A drop in pressure inside a separator allows liquid to flash to steam, which is then directed into a turbine. Any gases in geothermal water such as carbon dioxide, hydrogen sulfide, and nitrous oxides pass to the atmosphere. Carbon dioxide emissions are about one-sixth that of an equivalent sized coal plant. But hydrogen sulfide, with its rotten egg smell, can be offensive to those living near and working at the geothermal plant. Water and steam remaining after flashing and passing through a turbine are usually reinjected to replenish water to maintain the reservoir's pressure. If reservoir pressure can be maintained, then geothermal becomes a sustainable source of nearly nonpolluting clean energy.

Shallower sources of geothermal energy in which the water temperature is between 250°F and 350°F require a binary power plant where a heat exchanger transfers the heat of geothermal water to a second or binary fluid such as isopentane or isobutane. A binary fluid boils at a lower temperature than water and its vapors pass through a turbine and are then condensed to a liquid for recycling. Binary plants are closed systems in which the hydrothermal fluid, along with any entrapped gases, is reinjected into the reservoir. A binary system may be necessary for water with a high mineral content to prevent forming a harmful scale on turbine blades. Sometimes minerals in the water can be separated and sold. Simbol Materials has perfected a method to take hot geothermal brine output from a geothermal plant to be built at Salton Sea in California and extract its high lithium and other minerals content at an economic cost with filters and absorption mediums. The technology bypasses the traditional evaporation process and can produce large volumes of lithium.[16] Hybrid plants, part flash and part binary, are also available, such as the one that supplies 25 percent of the electricity for the island of Hawaii.

Geothermal Electricity Capacity

As of 2014, there were 94 geothermal power plant sites with 10.2 gW of installed capacity, equivalent to ten large sized nuclear or coal fired plants, in 24 nations, partially or totally supplying the needs of 60 million people mainly in developing nations. Figure 10.1 shows the distribution of the principal sites and geothermal capacity by nation.[17] The sites are centers of geothermal activity and may involve several or a grouping of individual plants at each site. For instance, The Geysers consists of 23 geothermal plants, of which 19 are operational, spread over 117 square kilometers north of San Francisco. Thus the number of geothermal plants far exceeds the number of sites.

The US leads with 2.7 gW at 31 sites, mostly in California and Nevada, with The Geysers, the world's largest geothermal plant, accounting for nearly half (1.24 gW) of US capacity. Geothermal energy in the US only accounts for 0.4 percent of electricity demand, but still serves the needs of several million people, mostly in California with the

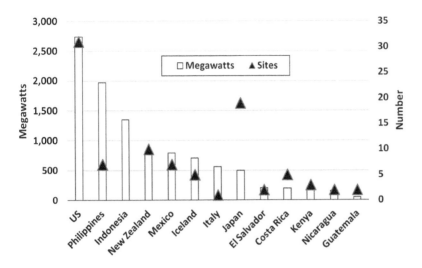

Figure 10.1 Capacity and Number of Sites of World Geothermal Plants

remainder in Nevada. Much of the growth of geothermal plants occurred in the 1980s as a consequence of PURPA legislation that compelled utilities to buy electricity from independent power producers of renewable energy sources. The second largest producer is the Philippines with 7 principal sites of nearly 2 gW of capacity, sufficient to meet 22 percent of the nation's electricity demand. Malaysia, in third place, produces 1.3 gW to satisfy 9 percent of its electricity needs.[18] New Zealand and Mexico are about tied with 0.8 gW, representing 15 and 2 percent of each nation's electricity supply respectively. Italy is 1.6 percent dependent on geothermal and Japan 0.4 percent. Italy's major geothermal site is near Mount Vesuvius on the outskirts of Naples. Another 13 mW plant in Italy is to become a hybrid biomass–geothermal plant with an associated biomass plant that will further heat geothermal steam and boost output to 18 mW. The company responsible for this, Enel, has already built a hybrid solar–geothermal plant where the electricity output of two renewable sources is combined within a single entity.[19] Japan has not taken advantage of its geothermal resources, while Iceland receives 84 percent of its energy from renewable sources (hydro and geothermal). Geothermal is responsible for 25 percent of Iceland's electricity, with a total contribution of 66 percent including thermal energy.[20] One of its geothermal plants suffered a spill and formed a pool of blue water. People began to bathe in its warm water and found that the water had therapeutic properties for treating psoriasis and other skin ailments. It is now a tourist attraction known as the Blue Lagoon.[21] Central America has a number of volcanoes with hot spots near the surface, and the intentions are to develop geothermal energy projects a safe distance away from the volcanoes. El Salvador is 22 percent reliant on geothermal power for its electricity, Costa Rica 15 percent, and Nicaragua 10 percent. Thermal uses, distinct from the generation of electricity, total another 16 thermal gW for hot springs, agriculture and aquaculture, and district heating.[22] Kenya is 19 percent dependent on geothermal power for electricity generation. There is enormous potential to vastly expand geothermal power in Central America, the Great Rift Valley in Africa, and the Pacific "Ring of Fire."

Enhanced Geothermal System (EGS)

Present-day geothermal sites were identified from escaping steam such as fumaroles and hot mud just as early oil discoveries were based on seep oil penetrating the ground. Geothermal sources are mostly limited to porous hot rock permeated with subsurface water that escaped to the surface. If water is trapped by a cover of impermeable caprock, then the geothermal reservoir must first be discovered before it can be exploited. The approach by EGS to discover hot rock formations is by employing a similar technology for discovering oil and natural gas fields without seismic instruments. It involves a search for suitable geothermal sites using satellite imagery and aerial photography aided with geologic structural mapping and geochemical and geophysical surveys, culminating in drilling to confirm the temperature gradient. The areas around volcanoes have the highest probability of being able to tap a geothermal source of energy near the surface, although many volcanoes are too remote from population areas. But not all; volcanoes in Italy, the west coast of the US, Japan, Central America, and other nations are near population centers and are more amenable for EGS development.

Hot rock underlies the entire crust. Its usefulness for geothermal extraction was a matter of depth and the presence of porous rock filled with subsurface water. But the presence of subsurface water and porous rock is no longer necessary. EGS involves drilling two separate wells deep into the Earth's crust to reach hot rock, and then fracking the rock between the two, employing methods practiced by the oil and gas industry. While similar to fracking hard shale for gas and oil, EGS fracking has significant differences. The fracking medium is water without additives or sand, but possibly with an acid additive. The purpose of fracking is to transform impermeable rock to semi-permeable to allow the passage of water by shearing rather than fracturing. Shearing creates space to ease the flow of water. The change in permeability is permanent: fracking does not have to be repeated. Water pressure for EGS is considerably less at 2,000 psi, not 9,000 psi. Once a zone has been completed, pressure is reduced to 1,000 psi and a biodegradable plastic, called diverter, is added that "gums up" cracks to keep them from propagating further. Then pressure is increased again to 2,000 psi to fracture a new zone and add another batch of diverter that can sustain a higher temperature environment. It takes about a week for the diverter to break down into water and carbon dioxide after fulfilling its function of sealing existing fractures in order to continue fracturing through a rock formation. Stimulation water does not have to be pumped back up to the surface as with gas and oil fracking; it remains part of EGS.[23] However, fracking can set off minor earthquakes usually not detectable by humans. Once EGS is completed, water is pumped down the injection well under pressure and forced through the fractured hot rock, where it is heated and rises to the surface via the production well as pressurized hydrothermal fluid. This is then flashed to produce steam and drive electricity generators or heat another liquid medium in a hybrid plant before being reinjected into the hot rock formation.[24]

Hot rock from radioactive decay in a granite formation of up to 570°F was discovered almost 3 miles below the surface in southern Australia. Geodynamics, a startup company, has drilled two wells over 14,000 feet into the hot granite formation where rock between the two wells was fractured. It takes about 9–15 days for water to make the roundtrip transit from the steam generator down the injection well, through the fractured rock where it is heated to 420 degrees, and up the production well to the steam generator. A 1 mW demonstration generator is in operation as an interim step to generating geothermal electricity on a commercial basis. Its successful operation points to the day when large electricity generators will be installed, but this became problematic with the discontinuance of clean energy initiatives and a carbon tax in Australia. Nevertheless the hot rock formation is large enough to supply a large portion, if not all, of Australia's electricity needs, though this would necessitate the building of a long distance transmission system to connect geothermal generating plants to the nation's electricity grid. In the meantime, the company is pursuing geothermal opportunities in the Pacific Islands.[25]

The US Geological Survey maintains that there are 345 gW of geothermal potential in the US.[26] If true, the US has tapped less than 1 percent of its potential. The Newberry Enhanced Geothermal Site is an EGS project in Oregon covering 15 square miles that can produce 2 gW with a potential for 5 gW of electrical power. Several production wells will be drilled around a single injection well, with fracking of the rock between the production wells and the injection well to allow for the passage of water. Another project in its formative stages is to tap a known massive hotbed (200–350°C) of geothermal resources under the Salton Sea, which is rapidly returning back to its original state as a desert. Its estimated potential is 1.5–2.9 gW of power.[27] Canada has a heated aquifer 2 miles below the Williston Basin, which extends into the northern US. This has been known for years by oil and gas drillers whose wells at times bring up more hot water than oil and gas. The aquifer is as thick as a 45 story building is tall and runs for hundreds of kilometers. It has been likened to a hot underground ocean. Deep Earth Energy Production is planning to develop this geothermal resource.[28]

China has very little geothermal energy capacity, but has announced its intention to develop geothermal resources equivalent to 50 million tons of coal by 2020 and 100 million tons by 2030. (As a point of reference, China's coal production in 2014 was 3.9 billion tons.) Some Chinese manufacturers are seriously looking into the market for geothermal equipment in response to this government announcement.[29] Geothermal projects are in the planning stage in Djibouti in Africa, British Columbia in Canada, Chile, Nicaragua, the Philippines, and Ireland.[30] Reykjavik Geothermal, an Icelandic company, has captured the nation's expertise in geothermal energy development and is spearheading projects in Ethiopia, St. Vincent and Grenadines, Rwanda, Mexico, India, Saudi Arabia, and the United Arab Emirates.[31]

A geothermal project with a negative outcome was the Swiss Deep Heat Mining Project near Basel, Switzerland. It was intended to pump water down 3 mile deep boreholes to hot rocks of 200°C. The returning superheated steam would have been sufficient to supply electrical power to 10,000 homes and hot water for another 2,700 homes. The project, partly backed with financial support by the Swiss government, was considered a safe and sustainable alternative to a nuclear power plant project opposed by the Swiss people. However, Basel is prone to earthquakes, with one in the year 1356 strong enough (6.5 on the Richter scale) to raze the city. Pumping water down the boreholes was held responsible for setting off tremors measuring 3.3 on the Richter scale up to 10 miles away from the site. The project was suspended in 2009.

A more esoteric idea is to mine heat from magma as a geothermal ore in places where it is accessible by current drilling technology. For this, a hole is drilled through the crust and a sealed pipe with a concentric inner pipe is thrust into magma. Water is pumped down the inner pipe and is transformed into high-pressure hydrothermal fluid by the magma surrounding the bottom portion of the sealed pipe. From there, hydrothermal fluid flows up the outer pipe to the surface to be flashed to steam to power electricity generators. A major obstacle to overcome is drilling all the way through the crust. The deepest bore hole ever drilled was in Russia—7.5 miles into crust 30 miles thick. Even if a bore hole were drilled into magma, precautions would have to be taken to prevent a blowout of many miles of drilling pipe, creating a mini-volcano of magma escaping to the surface. Another major obstacle is finding materials that can withstand the extreme high temperatures, pressures, and corrosive properties of being thrust into magma.[32] But if the inner heat of the planet could be tapped, geothermal energy could conceivably satisfy the world's electricity demand.

There have been two instances of accidentally drilling into magma. One occurred in Hawaii in 2007 and the hole was immediately plugged with concrete. The second was part of the Icelandic Deep Drilling Project (IDDP) to drill shafts up to 5 kilometers deep into the volcanic bedrock below Iceland. But in 2009 a bore hole near an existing geothermal plant at Krafla in northeast Iceland unexpectedly struck a pocket of magma 2,100 meters below the surface with searing temperatures of 900°C to 1000°C. Since magma did not move up the bore hole, a steel casing was cemented into the well with a perforated section near the bottom. Superheated steam emanating from the well was captured and fed into the geothermal plant for the following 2 years. The well had to be plugged after a valve failure. A second well, IDDP-2, is contemplated to be drilled in the future.[33]

Geothermal is the most untapped source of renewable energy. Its capacity utilization rate of 85 to 95 percent depending on the system compares favorably with fuel cell (95 percent), hydropower (93 percent), nuclear (90 percent), pulverized coal (85 percent), natural gas combined cycle (85 percent), natural gas combustion cycle (80 percent), bio-power (84 percent), offshore wind (43 percent), onshore wind (38 percent), concentrated or tower solar power (31 percent), and solar photovoltaic (21 percent).[34] The cost of geothermal electricity is comparable to or lower than fossil fuels for successful installations. The problem is that 40 percent of geothermal projects fail, increasing the cost of geothermal electricity.[35] Nevertheless, geothermal power has the potential of being the sole source of base load demand in areas around the Pacific Rim including the west coasts of North and South and Central America, Mediterranean nations (particularly Italy), and nations around the Great Rift Valley in East Africa. Japan can or maybe should consider geothermal energy as a potential replacement for nuclear power, but its approach to geothermal is very cautious with plans to build 15 small scale geothermal plants of about 2 mW each.[36] Malaysia, Indonesia, and the Philippines have many potential sites near volcanoes that could be developed if not too remote from population centers. As mentioned, Australia can potentially supply all of its electricity needs from one hot granite formation. It appears that a renaissance in geothermal energy, so long postponed, may be just beginning.

See the Companion Website for a section on Ocean Power: www.routledge.com/cw/nersesian.

Climate Change

First and foremost there is no such thing as a "normal" or "steady state" climate.[37] Climate change is continual with warming and cooling cycles, and within these cycles weather patterns change significantly. Treating climate change strictly as a twentieth and twenty-first-century phenomenon that started with burning fossil fuels is absurd. Although the Sahara desert is thought to be one to two million years old or possibly older, there is ample evidence of "inter-desert" periods of a few millennial with plentiful rainfall and vegetation just as there are interglacial periods of warm weather when life can thrive. These "inter-desert" periods lasted long enough to transform an unforgiving desert into lush savannahs, as attested by cave paintings in the Sahara portraying vibrant animal life on open savannahs. Satellite photographs, employing a technology that can see through sand, have revealed a world of dried riverbeds and streams. The last time savannahs reverted back to a desert from a global change in wind patterns (aka climate change) occurred about six to eight thousand years ago.[38] Tribes fleeing the rapid transition from savannah to desert are thought to have founded Egypt. Within historical times Carthage in North Africa was sustained by agricultural activities on land near the city, which is now inhospitable desert. Climate change can also occur overnight—woolly mammoths, literally freeze-dried about 20,000 years ago, were found to be "fit for eating" by Siberian natives. They're still being found today with flesh and stomach contents intact. These climate changes were not anthropomorphic, that is, due to the activities of man, and they did not evolve slowly.

Climate Dating

With modern weather record keeping barely two centuries old, a method had to be developed to track the history of climate. The first such method, counting tree rings, was devised in the early part of the twentieth century. The width of annual tree rings is a record of weather. Wide tree rings mark years of favorable growing conditions with plentiful rainfall and moderate temperatures, whereas narrow tree rings mark years of unfavorable growing conditions such as drought and extremes in temperatures. The first trees analyzed were ponderosa pine and giant sequoia in northern California, where overlapping sequences of cores taken from living and dead trees provided a history of climate going back 3,000 years. From this record, along with carbon-14 dating of wood in Anasazi cliff dwellings in the US Southwest, it was shown that this 500-year advanced Native Indian civilization collapsed in the 1200s as a consequence of a 26-year drought.

The next method for analyzing the history of climate was an examination of lake and ocean sediment. Several techniques had to be devised to make this time capsule of climate change readable. One was the discovery that certain types of plankton thrive in warm waters and others in cold, and the ratio of their calcium carbonate skeletons is a good indicator of water temperature. Another was improving the technique to bring up deep cores from lake bottoms and ocean floors with minimum distortion to sedimentary layers. Areas of ocean floors had to be found that were least disturbed by burrowing worms and other marine life whose activity blurs the distinction between layers. The discovery of radioactive carbon dating in 1947 was followed by the discovery of the ratio of two oxygen isotopes being sensitive to changes in temperature. These two measuring sticks made it possible to obtain a record of major climate changes in terms of ocean temperatures and the waxing and waning of ice sheets going back many thousands of years.

Just as tree rings showed that a severe 26-year drought brought an end to the Anasazi civilization, analysis of sediments from the bottom of a Yucatan saline lake showed that three periods of extreme drought within a 150-year dry spell brought an end to the

3,000-year Mayan civilization during the ninth century. Maya Indians, who devised a highly sophisticated calendar to keep track of time and built massive temple complexes, had an estimated population of 15 million in the centuries before the dry spell. A similar situation is thought to be have caused the demise of the Khmer Empire in present-day Cambodia. The capital of the Khmer Empire, Angkor, at its height covered an area of almost 400 square miles (the size of all five boroughs of New York City) with a population of about 750,000 inhabitants, of which 40,000 lived in the city center. Constricted growth rings in a rare type of cypress tree called "po mu" showed back-to-back mega-droughts lasting from 1363 to 1392 and again from 1415 to 1440 that spelled the end of this civilization.[39] Droughts of unusual severity can occur even when climate is reasonably stable—for example, the 1930s Dust Bowl in the US Southwest and ongoing desertification in Sub-Saharan Africa. Some feel that the unusually severe drought in 2015 in California is a harbinger of California reverting to a desert in a similar vein as the Sahara desert. Were this to occur, the US would have to find alternative sources of food as California currently produces 90 or more percent of the nation's artichokes, avocadoes, broccoli, celery, lettuce, and plums and between 80 and 90 percent of cauliflower, lemons, spinach, peaches, and strawberries. Increasing occurrences of drought in Brazil could also affect agricultural output. To blame these shifts in weather patterns on a constituent of the atmosphere measured in parts per millions is considered by some to be ludicrous.

Advances in analyzing sediment layers in lakes and oceans to discover the history of climate change were accompanied by advances in analyzing annual snowfalls that formed distinct layers in stationary ice packs in Greenland and Antarctica. The first 1,000 foot core of ice was removed from the Greenland ice pack in 1956 and cut into segments for transport to labs in Europe and the US for analysis. Technical advances in drilling allowed cores to be withdrawn from deeper depths in a more pristine state, and in 1966, a 4,500 foot core that extended down to bedrock was extracted from the Greenland ice pack. In the 1980s another core, 6,600 feet long, was extracted, followed in the 1990s by a core over 9,800 feet in length, both down to bedrock. Sediment from lake bottoms and ocean floors and cores from Greenland have provided a record of climate change for the past 100,000 years, and subsequent cores drilled in Antarctica have pushed back the record to over 400,000 years.

Before the extraction of sediment and ice cores, the theory of climate change was based on the Earth's elliptical orbit, which changes in its orientation to the sun, and its slight wobbling about its axis (precession) that induced periods of reduced solar radiation every 22,000 years in the northern hemisphere. It was thought that this would create a 22,000-year cycle of relatively short ice ages, interspersed by long periods of a stable and warm climate. This early theory on climate was in concert with a general belief that change in the natural world was gradual and resulted from existing forces operating uniformly over eons of time. This gave animals and plants ample opportunity to shift their habitat in response to the slow pace of climate change.

The record of climate gleaned from the lake and ocean sediments and Greenland and Antarctica ice packs dashed the belief in gradual and uniform change as well as the implied ability to forecast general climate conditions within reasonable bounds. The record better supports chaotic and catastrophic change measured in just a few millennium, centuries, decades, or less, to the point of leaving little time for animals and plants to adapt to shifting climate conditions. The story locked in sediment and ice cores is that there is no such thing as normal climate. Significant shifts in the ratio of oxygen isotopes testify to large changes in average temperatures over relatively short periods of time, sometimes accompanied with heavy layers of volcanic ash. Analysis of gas entrapped in the ice core showed cyclical fluctuations in methane and carbon dioxide and other greenhouse gas concentrations. The only predictable behavior regarding climate is change itself, but not its direction or magnitude.

With the exception of the past 10,000 years, variations in temperature were much more severe, transitions between cooling and warming trends were swift (about 1,000 years), and the Earth a decidedly much colder place to live for the last four hundred thousand years. The warmest part of the temperature cycle during this period would be similar to today's weather, but it did not last long before the world plunged into another frigid ice age. About 14,700 years ago, the Earth warmed and climate stabilized for about 2,000 years before there was a sudden reversion to a 1,000-year ice age, named the Younger Dryas (there are also the Older and Oldest Dryas periods). Perhaps the onslaught of this sudden cooling freeze-dried the woolly mammoths (the science fiction movie *The Day After Tomorrow* imagines a sudden freezing event).[40] Then, for inexplicable reasons, climate suddenly reversed direction and an era of unusual warmth with relatively stable temperatures began that has lasted about 12,000 years (the Holocene Epoch)—a phenomenon not experienced during the previous 400,000 years. During this 12,000-year period, there were 46 warming events where the mean rate of warming was about 1.2°C per century versus the 0.7°C per century warming experienced since 1900.[41]

How Long Has Man Been Influencing Climate?

While a few might consider the Holocene Epoch evidence of the transition from Genesis 1:2 to 1:3, some feel the cause of the sudden warming was civilization. According to this hypothesis, people have been affecting the weather for thousands of years since the advent of agriculture, much longer than the 250 years since the advent of the industrial age. Analysis of ice cores shows that the concentration of methane in the atmosphere rose and fell over the past 250,000 years, fairly closely following the 22,000-year cycles in the variation in solar radiation striking the northern hemisphere from the Earth's precession.[42] During this cycle, solar radiation on the surface of the northern hemisphere varied between 440 and 520 W per square meter, with methane, a greenhouse gas, tagging along varying between 400 and 700 parts per billion, as measured from Vostok (Antarctica) ice cores. Methane follows the 22,000-year variation in solar radiation from the Earth's precession because warm spells encourage plant life. When dead plants decay in anaerobic (without oxygen) water, copious releases of methane (swamp gas) add to natural gas seeps from underground coal, oil, and natural gas fields, increasing its concentration in the atmosphere.

This trend lasted until 5,000 years ago, when solar radiation fell as part of its normal 22,000-year cycle of the Earth's precession, but methane, rather than falling to an expected 450 parts per billion, rose to nearly 700 parts per billion. This unexpected rise in the methane concentration is hypothesized to be the result of agricultural practices, especially growing rice and breeding herds of domesticated animals. Anaerobic decay of rice stalks in flooded rice paddies and the digestive processes of grazing animals are both contributors to atmospheric methane. Thus the Earth did not cool as expected from a fall in solar radiation caused by changes in the Earth's orientation with the sun because the rise in methane, a greenhouse gas 20 times more powerful than carbon dioxide, inhibited the escape of infrared radiation from the Earth into space.

In another study that fortified this conclusion that mankind has been affecting climate for a long time, researchers tracking methane concentrations noted an unexpected rise in methane starting around 100 BCE. They attributed this to the ancient Romans increasing herds of domesticated livestock, which are natural methane emitters, the Han dynasty in China and their expansion of rice cultivation (rice harbors methane producing bacteria), and blacksmiths in both empires fashioning metal weapons. Thus assuming that mankind is responsible for adding greenhouse gas emissions primarily since the start of the industrial revolution in 1750 should be reexamined.[43] This, of course, is at variance with those who espouse that mankind's influence on climate is negligible at best.

Carbon Dioxide and Temperature over Geologic Time

There are several diagrams illustrating changes in carbon dioxide concentrations and temperature changes over vast stretches of geologic time, one of which is summarized in Table 10.1.[44]

Sometimes carbon dioxide and temperature increase and decrease in unison, sometimes they move in opposite directions, and still other times one is unchanging while the other changes. With no consistent pattern, there is no convincing evidence of a causative relationship between carbon dioxide and temperature in the geologic past covering hundreds of millions of years. Another diagram of carbon dioxide and temperature over the geological past shows that average temperature was about 22°C (72°F) over vast stretches of time with an occasional rapid dip and recovery in terms of geological time to 12°C (54°F). However, about 50 or so million years ago, perhaps concomitant with the demise of the dinosaurs, a cooling trend cut in, ending with an age of glaciers (perhaps related to the aftermath of an asteroid hit that spelled the end of the Cretaceous period).

Table 10.1 CO_2/Temperature Relationship by Geologic Age

Geologic Age	Millions Years Ago	CO_2/Temperature Relationship
Precambrian	570–600	CO_2 buildup before temperature rise
Cambrian	510–570	End of Precambrian CO_2 declined significantly, but temperature remained unchanged through Cambrian
Ordovician	439–510	CO_2 declined marginally to 2,250 ppm (much higher than today's 500 ppm!) accompanied by a significant temperature drop; CO_2 increased marginally and temperature rose significantly
Silurian	409–439	CO_2 declined while temperature remained unchanged
Devonian	363–409	CO_2 rose and fell while temperature fell
Mississippian	323–363	CO_2 fell and temperature fell
Pennsylvanian	290–323	CO_2 constant while temperature rose considerably
Permian	245–290	CO_2 constant but rose end of Permian while temperature constant
Triassic	208–245	CO_2 at 220 ppm slowly declining, but temperature constant
Jurassic	146–208	CO_2 rose while temperature fell
Cretaceous	65–146	CO_2 at 340 ppm fell while temperature rose
Subsequent ages	Post 65	Both CO_2 and temperature in general decline up to Holocene when CO_2 began to increase

Carbon dioxide concentrations started out during the Cambrian period 550 million years ago at a peak of 7,000 ppm (a bit higher than the present level of 400 ppm) and declined to present levels during the Carboniferous period 350 million years ago. Then about 250 million years ago, both carbon dioxide and temperatures rose significantly higher, together with carbon dioxide peaking at 2,000 ppm. About 170 million years ago, carbon dioxide began a long term decline to present levels. Initially temperatures fell, then subsequently rose, and the planet was in a warm phase until about 50 million years ago when the planet cooled significantly.[45] Again, as in Table 10.1, there is no consistent relationship between carbon dioxide concentrations and temperature. It is quite interesting to note the long periods of geological time when carbon dioxide was considerably higher than today's levels with an average global temperature of a balmy 72°F.

Over the last 400,000 years, carbon dioxide concentrations peaked at about 280–290 parts per million every 100,000 years within each interglacial warming cycle and bottomed out at about 200 parts per million in the depths of an ice age. This was the first evidence linking carbon dioxide with climate. Carbon dioxide peaked around 10,500 years ago, at the end of the last ice age, and began its expected retreat as it had done in the past. About 8,000 years ago, however, the retreat became an advance. By the start of the industrial era, the concentration of carbon dioxide was back to 280–290 parts per million, the "normal" peak during the previous 400,000 years.[46] Carbon dioxide was an estimated 40 parts per million higher and methane about 250 parts per billion higher than one would predict on the basis of past patterns attributable to widespread burning of biomass fuel centuries before the Industrial Revolution. This may have been compensated by a falloff in solar radiation reaching the Earth's surface from precession of the Earth's pole. Had it not been for these additional greenhouse gases pumped into the atmosphere, the Earth might have experienced a period of cooling. Conceivably humanity's activities have helped to stabilize climate for the better![47]

A more detailed history of climate change for the last 160,000 years starts with an ice age with average temperatures −6°C below today's average temperature. The data is unclear whether carbon dioxide leads or lags or occurs simultaneously with temperature increases; actually instances of all three appear to have happened. However, the fall in carbon dioxide concentrations definitely lags declines in temperatures.[48] Another analysis of Vostok data for the same period of time incorporates dust content. The initial warmings of interglacial periods starting 20,000 and 145,000 years ago are marked first by an increase in dust concentration in the atmosphere followed by a rapid increase in temperatures, perhaps signaling intense volcanic activity. Volcanic dust covering ice fields would absorb the sun's radiation, leading to melting. As ice began to retreat, exposure of darker land and water would reduce albedo or reflection of sunlight and reinforce absorption of the heat leading to a positive feedback system of ever retreating ice. A buildup of carbon dioxide, perhaps as a result of volcanic activity, appears to lead global warming in this instance. However, with the start of the next glaciation age after a warming period 145,000 years ago, a decline in carbon dioxide lagged falling temperatures. During mild warming periods between 145,000 and 20,000 years ago, the relationship between rising temperatures and carbon dioxide concentration varied between leading, lagging, no real change, or decreasing. Again, the evidence of a causal relationship between temperature and carbon dioxide is weak at best. During the significant warming taking the world out of the last ice age 20,000 years ago, again preceded by an increase in the dust concentration, carbon dioxide rose significantly about simultaneous with temperature.[49]

Carbon dioxide rising simultaneously with temperature is not a persuasive argument that carbon dioxide is a cause of global warming. To the degree that carbon dioxide lags temperature, then the inference is that carbon dioxide does not cause global warming, but is a consequence of higher temperatures. The mechanism that would cause carbon dioxide to lag a rise in temperatures would be warming oceans giving up some of their carbon dioxide content. Methane seemed to follow temperatures better than carbon dioxide throughout this 160,000-year climate history.

While oscillations of carbon dioxide and temperature appear close to concurrent during significant warming events, some interpret the data that changes in carbon dioxide concentrations generally lag temperature changes.[50] It may not be clear in viewing this data whether temperature affects carbon dioxide or vice versa, but observational evidence certainly does not present a compelling case for a single variable model (carbon dioxide) determining global temperature.[51] It is fully reasonable to assume that other variables may affect climate. One could be ocean currents having a strong impact on the length and intensity of ice ages.[52] Still another could be underwater volcanoes, in addition to onshore volcanoes, altering the climate.[53] The sun, ultimate source of all our energy, may exert a significant influence on climate. The point is that many variables may affect climate, and their relative influence on climate change may be a function depending on the state of other variables.

We believe in linear systems. Tugging a rope attached to a wagon causes the wagon to move, whose speed can be estimated by taking the force of the tug and the wagon's resistance to movement into account. But climate is a nonlinear system akin to tugging on a sleeping dragon's tail. Nothing happens tug after tug. Then that one tug, which may be weaker than the others, awakens the dragon. Now something happens. While nonlinear systems may lend themselves to statistical analysis, probabilities become quite meaningless if a set of circumstances (variations in the sun's radiation, variations in the Earth's orbit and precession, variations in greenhouse gas concentrations) all line up to induce climate to move from one equilibrium point to another. The shift between equilibrium points can be relatively swift, with dire repercussions for life on Earth, as the frozen woolly mammoths in Siberia plainly attest. Nonlinear systems are extremely complex and incapable of rational projections. A single minded assertion that for some strange reason climate has suddenly become a single variable deterministic model should sound alarms when climate is viewed in its terms of geological ages and even in its historical context.

Climate Changes during Recorded History

There have been significant changes to climate within recorded history. The period 900–1300 CE is called the Medieval Warm Period with a warming trend similar to what is happening now. Agricultural output soared, as did the human population by an estimated 40–60 million. Vineyards sprouted in England with 14 different varieties of grape, with English wine preferred over French wine in France! Greenland was not misnamed as some have thought by a real estate charlatan trying to induce prospective settlers to buy frozen land. In 985 CE Erik the Red led 25 ships with 500 settlers to found Hvalsey in southwest Greenland where there were thickets of six meter high birch trees. Hvalsey grew to 5,000 inhabitants where, as archeological evidence shows, they supported themselves for 300 years by growing food and crops for grazing herds of livestock, augmented by fishing and trading polar bear skins and walrus tusks.[54]

The start of the Little Ice Age in 1300 CE, also known as history's Big Chill, saw average temperatures fall between 4°F to 7°F. While this might not sound like much of a change, it was sufficient to bring an end to greenery in Greenland along with the hardy Viking settlements and grape vineyards in England. Agricultural output plunged, as did the population from starvation and malnutrition, which weakened resistance to disease. Between 1371 and 1791 there were 111 recorded famines in Europe, with one famine in Russia claiming a half million lives in 1601. One blame for the Black Death, which wiped out about one-third of the population of Europe, was rats seeking warmth in human habitations to escape the cold. The coldest period during the Little Ice Age, Maunder Minimum between 1645 and 1715, was a period of unusually low sunspot activity when reduced solar radiation lowered average temperatures by another 3°F. Alpine glaciers advanced rapidly, swallowing up farmland and villages. In 1658 a Swedish army marched across the Baltic Sea ice to invade Copenhagen. Hardships suffered by the people from sparse harvests contributed to social unrest, culminating in the French Revolution.[55] The Seine River in Paris froze solid every winter, as did the River Thames in London, where a tradition of annual ice festivals beginning in 1607 lasted until 1814. This was 2 years after a bitter Russian winter destroyed over 95 percent of Napoleon's army by a combination of typhus, starvation, and freezing. The Big Chill was global in nature. Sediment cores in Africa and Antarctica reflected colder weather, and glaciers in New Zealand expanded to their maximum extent.

Impact of the Sun

The Little Ice Age may have resulted from only a 0.1 percent reduction in solar radiation accompanied by changes in sunspot activity and magnetic field intensity. Changes in the sun's magnetic field and solar wind determine how far cosmic rays penetrate the atmosphere and, in turn, affect the formation of low altitude cloud formation and hence climate. When sunspot intensity is high and sun slightly warmer, more intense solar magnetic fields and solar wind cut down on cosmic rays penetrating the atmosphere, producing fewer ions. Fewer ions provide fewer cloud condensation nuclei for the formation of low altitude clouds. Less low level cloudiness allows more sunlight to reach the surface, warming the Earth. During periods of less sun spot activity, when the sun is a little less warm and its magnetic field and solar wind weaker, more cosmic rays penetrate the atmosphere, increasing the number of ions that form cloud condensing nuclei. Greater cloud cover allows less sunlight from reaching the surface, cooling the Earth. Changes in the solar magnetic field and solar wind on low altitude cloud cover amplify the small change in solar radiation of 0.1 percent on the Earth's climate by a factor of 20. Thus a small change in solar radiation has a noticeable effect on climate, not by solar temperature change, but on the sun's capacity to shield the Earth from cosmic rays. Not all agree on the influence of cosmic rays on global warming.[56] The Forbush effect, a rapid decrease in observed cosmic ray intensity following a solar coronal mass ejection (CME) that induces short term weather change, both confirms the impact of cosmic rays on weather, yet reinforces the concept of a limited cosmic ray effect on weather (or climate) change.[57]

There are several solar cycles. The most well-known solar cycle is the Schwabe solar cycle tied to maximum and minimum sunspot activity. The Schwabe cycle has an average period of 11 years, but the range between maximum and minimum sunspot activity can vary between 9 and 14 years. Other solar cycles have been identified: the Hale cycle averages 22 years, varying between 18 and 26 years; the Gleissberg cycle averages 87 years, varying between 60 and 120 years; the Suess/de Vries cycle averages 210 years, varying between 180 and 220 years; the Eddy cycle averages 1,000 years, varying between 900 and 1,100 years; and the Hallstatt cycle averages 2,300 years, varying between 2,200 and 2,400 years. These cycles, which have been detected by diverse means in different parts of the Earth, superimpose on one another, either strengthening or weakening the Schwabe solar cycle.[58] Variation in solar radiation, coupled with variations in the Earth's orbit and precession about its axis, may have induced severe cold spells during the Little Ice Age. Another explanation is slowing of the Gulf Stream conveyor belt. Normally the Gulf Stream is more saline than water in the North Atlantic. After warming the northern European atmosphere, whose latitude is the same as Newfoundland, cooled and heavier saline Gulf Stream waters sink to the bottom of the Atlantic and return to the Caribbean. The sinking of Gulf Stream waters is thought to be the driving force behind an immense conveyor belt system of carrying warm Caribbean waters to the North Atlantic. Thus the preceding Medieval Warm Period may have caused polar ice to melt, releasing vast quantities of freshwater along with a greater outpouring of freshwater from Siberian rivers. Less dense fresh water emptying into the Arctic Ocean would eventually flow into the North Atlantic, remaining near the surface and diluting the salinity of the Gulf Stream. This would decrease its density and reduce its capacity to power the conveyor belt, cooling the weather in northern Europe.

Impact of Volcanoes

Major volcanic eruptions can trigger climate change if severe enough or at least inaugurate a period of cooler weather. One that has been recently researched is the Ilopango volcanic eruption in southeastern Mesoamerica (today's El Salvador). This massive volcano eruption is thought to be responsible for the demise of the Mayan civilization in the surrounding region. The eruption is estimated to have thrown 84 cubic kilometers of volcanic debris into the atmosphere versus 3 cubic kilometers for Mount St. Helens' eruption in 1980. The Ilopango eruption set off a multi-year global volcanic winter that may have established conditions conducive to an outbreak of bubonic plague in North Africa, which spread via trading vessels to Constantinople during the time of Emperor Justinian. Agricultural failures and loss of population from the plague in the Eastern Roman Empire were so disruptive that the Emperor was forced to abandon a successful campaign of reconquering what had been the Western Roman Empire. The retreat of Byzantine armies marked the final collapse of civilization in western Europe, signaling the start of the Dark Ages.[59]

Another volcanic eruption that temporarily affected global weather was the 1815 eruption of Tambora in Indonesia, which had the force of 100 Mount St. Helens. Whereas Mount St. Helens blew off 1,300 feet of its top in 1980, 4,200 feet of Tambora's top was blasted 30 miles into the stratosphere, reducing its height from 13,500 to 9,300 feet. The eruption left behind a 5 mile wide caldera three-quarters of a mile deep, the largest on Earth within recorded history (nothing compared to the 30–50 mile wide caldera of Yellowstone). An estimated 60,000–120,000 people were killed either by instant carbonizing in 2,000°F pyroclastic flows rushing 100 miles per hour down the volcano's slopes, by tsunamis, or, more slowly, by starvation. This was just the start of the death count as Tambora, as with other large volcanic eruptions, affected global weather (climate is usually considered to be a weather phenomenon lasting more than 30 years). An enormous plume of 150 million tons of sulfate aerosols contained in 100 cubic kilometers of ash blanketed the Earth.[60] Sulfate aerosols are from ejected sulfur combining with oxygen to form sulfur oxides and then with water vapor to form an aerosol of sulfuric acid that covered the upper surfaces of clouds, reflecting incoming sunlight. With ash shading the Earth and an aerosol mist reflecting sunlight, the Earth cooled by an average of 2°F. But in the northeast US and Canada and northern Europe, cooling was more like 10°F, making 1816 the year without a summer. It snowed in northeast America, and northern Europe was drenched in cold rain, preventing crops from maturing. The eventual death toll from starvation and disease brought on by malnutrition, concentrated in Europe, is thought to be several times that of the death toll in Indonesia. In New England, the year without a summer induced a migration of farmers to begin anew in the Midwest.[61] But Asia was not left untouched—countless thousands died of starvation in Yunnan Province in China from the weather-related consequences of this volcano.

Volcanoes are "natural coal burners," releasing huge volumes of ash, sulfur, sulfur oxides, aerosols, and carbon dioxide that can affect global weather patterns for a number of years, but the amount of carbon dioxide released by volcanoes is estimated to be barely 1 percent of man's contribution.[62] Other geologists are more reticent, saying that volcanic carbon dioxide emissions are not really known because few volcanoes have actually been monitored (too small a sample size). Still others are open to the possibility that volcanic carbon dioxide may make a larger contribution.[63] Past estimates of 100 and 200 million tons of annual CO_2 emissions from volcanoes have recently been revised to 600 million tons, still a small fraction of man's 40 billion ton contribution to atmospheric CO_2.[64] Some feel that the record number of volcanic eruptions in 2013 and 2014 will induce global cooling for a few years.[65] But volcanoes eject more than carbon dioxide and sulfur oxides. The eruption of Mount Pinatubo in the Philippines in 1991 released more particulate pollution into the atmosphere in a few weeks than civilization had released since the start of the Industrial Revolution. Pinatubo also released 20 million tons of sulfur dioxide into the stratosphere, particularly large when compared to an annual average 10 million ton contribution of all volcanoes. Pinatubo brought about a couple of years of cooler weather.[66] Sulfur dioxide emitted from the Laki fissure eruption in Iceland in 1783–1784 was estimated to be over 120 million tons. This was sufficient to cool Europe for a half dozen years, sorely affecting livestock and agricultural output, including Iceland's worst episode of starvation with 23,000 deaths.[67] Nature has a way of reminding mankind of his rightful place in the general scheme of things.

In 1850 the Little Ice Age abruptly ended, inaugurating the present warming trend. There was only one major volcanic eruption, Krakatoa in 1883, which blew 45 cubic kilometers of volcanic rock into the stratosphere, killed 36,000 people, was heard 2,800 miles away in Australia, caused spectacular sunsets throughout the world, and cooled the planet by 1.2 degrees for 5 years.[68] But Krakatoa was certainly not a cause of a warming trend. Three possible explanations are an increase in solar radiation influenced by increased sunspot and magnetic field strength; the restoration of the Gulf Stream conveyor belt if it had been weakened; and adding carbon dioxide to the atmosphere by the Industrial Revolution. Each of these explanations has been advanced with no consensus as to which or what combination was responsible for a warmer climate.

Whither Thou Goest Climate?

There is no doubt that the Earth has been warming rapidly from the early 1970s to the end of the 1990s and there is no doubt that the concentration of carbon dioxide has been growing since the start of the Industrial Revolution. The current concentration of 400 ppm far exceeds levels experienced in the last 400,000 years. Despite continuing growth in carbon dioxide, the question is whether since the late 1990s the global temperature is still warming, has become stable, or is entering a cooling trend. Before that question is addressed, it is best to look at average annual temperatures from 1880 to the present alongside carbon dioxide readings, as shown in Figure 10.2.[69]

Temperatures are expressed as a differential in 0.01°C increments from the mean temperature between 1951 and 1980. Carbon dioxide is in parts per million. Superficially the two chart lines follow one another with an R-Square of a respectable 86 percent. Carbon dioxide concentration grew slowly from 1840 with a reading of 285 ppm, but then accelerated after 1950, as seen in the upward shift of the slope of the curve. In January 2015, carbon dioxide reached 400 ppm. Temperature is in terms of deviation from an average covering the entire period. The temperature in 1880 of −21 and in 2014 of +68 represents a difference of 89 increments of 0.01°C or a total rise of 0.89°C over 134 years or 0.66°C per century from the overall average temperature. The Intergovernmental Panel on Climate Change (IPCC) is projecting a gain in temperature between 0.6°C and 2.4°C from 2000 to 2050 and between 1.2°C and 5.6°C from 2000 to 2100 based on post-1970 temperature data.[70] The IPCC minimum projection is nearly twice as high as the temperature rise experienced between 1880 and 2014. Carbon dioxide concentration is projected to be between 463–623 ppm in 2050 and 478–1,099 ppm in 2100. Using a regression equation between temperature as the dependent variable and carbon dioxide as the independent variable, and if there were a causal relationship, carbon dioxide readings of this projected order of magnitude would induce unimaginably high temperatures indicating, hopefully, an essentially non-causal relationship between carbon dioxide and temperature.

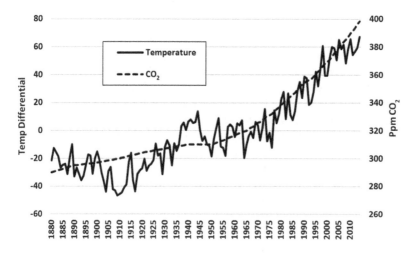

Figure 10.2 CO_2 and Temperatures 1880–2014

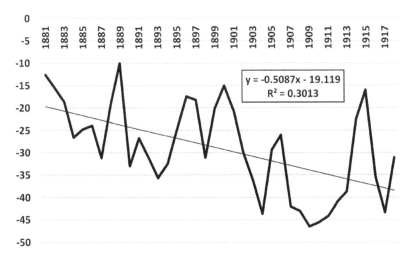

Figure 10.3 Temperature Trend 1880–1918

Unlike carbon dioxide buildup, which by any measure is a smooth curve, temperatures exhibits greater variability about an upward trend taking what amounts to, the steps seen in Figure 10.2. Figure 10.3 shows the worldwide annual temperature trend from 1880 to 1918.

Clearly there was a cooling trend for nearly 40 years. The coefficient of −0.5087 represents 1/100 of a degree Celsius change per year or 0.005087°C change per year. Hence in 100 years, the worldwide average temperature would change by −0.5087°C. This is radically different than the overall +0.66°C per century from 1880 to 2014. Figure 10.4 shows the worldwide annual temperature trend from 1919 to 1943.

A warming trend had set in where global temperature rose 1.52°C per century, over double the overall 0.66°C temperature gain per century for this period and in excess of the minimum IPCC trend of 1.2°C per century after 2000, but far lower than its maximum. Then the trend switched again in 1944 to a slight cooling trend to 1965.

The cooling trend is indeed modest, amounting to a decline of 0.033°C per century. Some have opined that, every 20–30 years, much colder water near the bottom of the ocean cycles to the top, exerting a mild cooling effect on global temperatures until the sun warms the water. Once warmed, ocean waters recycle again. The cooling trend in Figure 10.5 depends on the selected years. Figure 10.6 extends the end of the trend from 1965 to 1976.

A modest negative trend became a modest positive trend with a temperature gain of 0.0905°C per century. The point of this chart is to stress the importance of selecting start and end points in determining a trend and the ability to manage trends by careful selection of start and end points. The 1970s were marked by various forecasts of a coming ice age based on the cooling trend. Like many forecasts, it was dashed against the wall of reality. Advocates of a coming ice age were eventually silenced by a persistent warming trend starting in the 1970s and a few switched horses and became advocates for global warming. Figure 10.7 shows the warming trend from 1966 to an arbitrarily selected cut off in 1997.

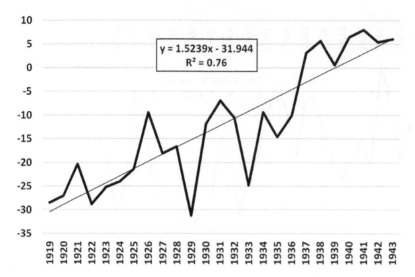

Figure 10.4 Temperature Trend 1919–1943

The trend during this period of time was 1.4°C per century, less than the warming trend of 1.52°C from 1919 to 1943, but more than the minimum IPCC trend of 1.2°C per century starting in 2000. Figure 10.8 is the temperature trend for 1998 to 2014.

The trend has been reduced by 42 percent from 1.4°C to 0.8°C, below the IPCC trend of 1.2°C starting in 2000. This is also seen in Figure 10.2 at the right end of the chart. The question is, where do we go from here? Advocates of global warming point to the continuing rise in CO_2 concentration and consider this period of apparent "stability" in temperatures just another hiatus before the unremitting staircase climb in temperatures

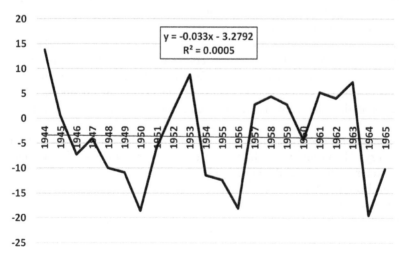

Figure 10.5 Temperature Trend 1944–1965

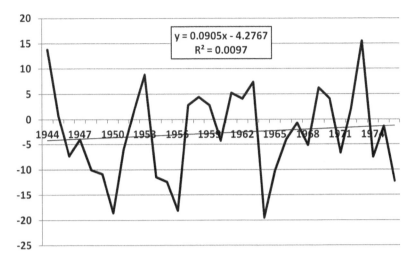

Figure 10.6 Temperature Trend 1944–1976

reassumes just as it had occurred from 1880 to 1918 and from 1976 to the late 1990s. In fact they argue that 2014 was the warmest year on record, although some back tracking was necessary as the increment of 0.02°C to beat the previous record was well within the margin of error of 0.1°C. This was also reflected in a low statistical confidence value of only 38 percent (confidence values are usually 95 or 99 percent).[71] Despite record cold during the 2014/2015 winter, there are a few warnings that the summer of 2015 may be extraordinarily hot not from CO_2 buildup, but an approaching El Niño that will be the strongest in years, possibly setting a record global temperature.[72] In fact it may be a "double

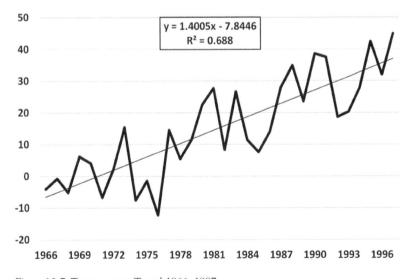

Figure 10.7 Temperature Trend 1966–1997

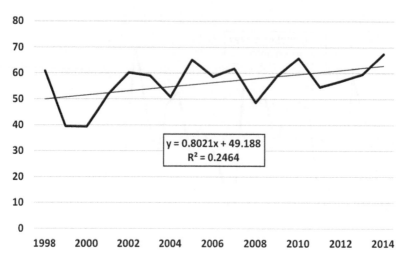

$$y = 0.8021x + 49.188$$
$$R^2 = 0.2464$$

Figure 10.8 Temperature Trend 1998–2014

El Niño" of two consecutive years of concentrated warm water in the Pacific Ocean that brings West Coast storms and Pacific cyclones, but quiet hurricane seasons in the Atlantic. A stationary "blob" of warm water in the Pacific Ocean is being blamed for bizarre weather in the US from dry spells in the West to East Coast's endless snow season. This decadal pattern is called the North Pacific Mode, a pattern of higher than normal surface temperatures that can affect North American weather. The North Pacific Mode appears to be second only to the Southern Oscillation (El Niño) in terms of affecting North American climate.[73] The two in combination, the North Pacific Mode and Southern Oscillation (El Niño), could mean the end of a landing on a climate staircase. There may be another step increase in global temperatures as warm water spreads across the Pacific, increasing evaporation and moisture content in the air and leading to more thunderstorms and tropical storms.[74] Of course, any warming can be ascribed to anthropomorphic greenhouse gases, and another potential record global temperature may be interpreted as a resumption back to the overall increasing global temperature trend *or* it may be recognized as a 1 or 2 year weather phenomenon masking an underlying climate cooling trend.[75]

The scientific community more or less conforms to a view that the warming trend will persist, but a dissenting minority maintains that a climate cooling trend has already begun, but is being temporarily masked by a counter-warming El Niño weather event. These individuals believe that the rise in carbon dioxide concentration has only a marginal impact on climate: climate is ultimately driven by the sun. As the sun has made a transition from high activity, as seen by the number of sunspots during the 1990s, to a period of quietude, its reduced radiation on the Earth's surface, measured in terms of a tenth of a percent, will lead to a cooling trend. The mechanism for this is reduced solar magnetism and solar wind blocking fewer of the incoming cosmic rays from outer space, which will interact with the lower atmosphere, increasing cloud cover and reducing solar radiation on the Earth's surface. In a way, cooling advocates have placed themselves before the people for immediate judgment. They maintain that cooling is already occurring. The most recent solar sunspot (Schwabe) cycle was weak. History records that it is not unusual for a weak cycle to be followed by one or two more weak cycles. Weak solar cycles mean cooler temperatures, and two weak cycles means 20 years of cooler weather. On top of this, the Gleissberg and Suess/de Vries cycles are also entering their weak phases, which when added to the weak Schwabe cycles can mean cooler weather from now to 2030–2050 or even longer.

Another group of cooling adherents are pointing in another direction, taking a paleo-climate view covering hundreds of thousands of years. During these long stretches of time, in rough numbers, ice ages last about 100,000 years with interglacial periods of about 12,000 years. This rhythm of climate stems from three Milankovitch cycles of variation in the shape of the Earth's orbit that has a period of 100,000 years, variation in the tilt of the Earth that has a period of 41,000 years, and the precession of the equinoxes, the Earth's wobble, that has a period of 26,000 years. These three periods, working together, are responsible for variation in the degree of solar radiation falling on the northern hemisphere, resulting in 100,000-year cycles of ice ages interspersed with 12,000-year periods of interglacial warming. Paleoclimate advocates criticize the anthropogenic global warming view of focusing on a timeline measured in decades, not tens of thousands of years. To a lesser extent, this same criticism can be applied to those who believe in solar cycles having a strong effect on climate. The real risk is that we may be at the end of the Holocene period of interglacial warming and about to plunge into the next ice age (a view, by the way, that was as popular in the 1970s as global warming is today). In fact a few of the leading alarmists of climate change/global warming had their teeth cut as ice age alarmists 40 years ago.[76] If paleoclimate or solar cycle advocates are correct and cool weather is about to descend on us, then pumping carbon dioxide into the atmosphere may turn out to be a virtue rather than a vice.

Both warming and cooling groups advocate a fairly rapid change to this period of relative stability in global temperatures. Both groups cast negative aspersions on the other. Cooling advocates maintain that it is politically correct to blame global warming/climate change almost entirely on anthropomorphic CO_2 from burning fossil fuels and the release of other anthropomorphic gases, mainly methane. The predominance of opinion in favor of global warming is partly the result of the availability of government and private grants for research in support of anthropologic global warming. Relatively little public and private funds go to those who do not support this view. Scientists and researchers go where the money is, which unfortunately can bias research activities. Moreover, some leading advocates of global warming will personally be richly rewarded if greenhouse emission programs such as cap and trade are initiated.[77]

Climate change usually reverts to global warming because it's difficult to justify global cooling with a continued rise in CO_2 concentration. Climate change is also held responsible for more occurrences of extreme weather, and in even earthquakes and volcanic eruptions. If climate change, whatever form it may take, can be predominantly associated with rising carbon dioxide concentrations from burning fossil fuels, then governments are given a self-proclaimed mandate to right a wrong. Climate change advocates want to take over the energy industry, instituting a "Marshall Plan for the Earth" to save the planet from mankind.[78] The sacrifice necessary to save the planet may entail replacing democracy and capitalism on a national scale for a global governing system led by an enlightened elite with the power to constrict carbon emissions for the good of all mankind. This would adversely affect the life styles of all; but not as drastic as a fringe group advocating depopulation as the ultimate solution to saving the planet.[79] To a growing number of opponents, climate policy is really climate politics: a massive power grab by governments ostensibly trying to protect their citizens from themselves. A proposed EPA regulation requiring carbon dioxide emissions from the utility industry be cut 32 percent below their 2005 levels by 2030 is criticized precisely on this point. Three times Congress has refused to pass legislation to reduce carbon emissions by instituting carbon emissions control programs. The utility industry is primarily under state regulation, and some states are active in setting up a system to monitor and possibly regulate carbon emissions. The proposed EPA regulation bypasses the voice of the people as expressed in Congress and usurps control over state regulation of utilities by fiat.

Global warming climatologists generally reject the idea that the sun plays a meaningful role in determining climate change. If this were true, then anthropomorphic gas emissions play a lesser role, which would enervate the impetus of righting a basic wrong through massive government intrusion in the private sector. The IPCC does not take into serious consideration other causes of climate change beyond carbon emissions. Solar radiation is dismissed perfunctorily as either marginal in effect or too difficult to model for calculating future temperatures. Difficulty in modeling should not be an excuse for ignoring something as big as the sun! The IPCC assumes that warming adds to atmospheric vapor that is itself a greenhouse gas. Thus clouds of water vapor form a positive feedback loop amplifying the impact of carbon dioxide. This is the primary reason for the high end estimates of global warming. Some scientists feel that added atmospheric vapor from a warmer Earth actually forms a negative feedback loop that counters, or dampens, the impact of carbon dioxide. If global warming from carbon dioxide emissions increases cloud cover from greater evaporation and increased cloud cover shields the Earth from the sun's rays, then this would argue in favor of a negative feedback loop. If true, this would drastically erode the high end estimates of global warming.

All agree that atmospheric vapor plays a role in determining climate—the question is, how much and what kind of a role? Water vapor increases with rising temperatures and vice versa. Continental rainfall in the form of rivers emptying into the oceans has been estimated at 37,000 cubic kilometers per year, of which about 18 percent is in the Amazon alone.[80] Taking into consideration rainfall on oceans, then evaporation of water on land and ocean to match rainfall pegs estimated annual recycling of water vapor driven by the sun's heat to about 100,000 cubic kilometers (25,000 cubic miles) per year. This recycling of water results in atmospheric water vapor making up 75 percent of greenhouse gases, accompanied by carbon dioxide at 16 percent, methane at 6 percent, and ozone at 3 percent. While there is agreement that water vapor influences global weather, there is disagreement among scientists about whether water vapor forms a positive or negative feedback system. If negative feedback, then atmospheric water vapor cannot be classed as a greenhouse gas. It is even possible that water vapor may play both roles, essentially neutralizing its contribution to climate change.[81]

In addition to atmospheric vapor content, there are huge atmospheric systems whose movements and strength can affect weather by warming or cooling for a number of years in different regions of the world. Among these are the Pacific Decadal Oscillation, Atlantic Multidecadal Oscillation, North Atlantic Oscillation, and Southern Oscillation (the warming phase of the Southern Oscillation is El Niño and the cooling phase is La Niña). These oscillations affect weather patterns by warming some regions of the Earth and cooling others. Polar vortexes are persistent cyclones around each pole that strengthen in the winter. The winter of 2014/2015 was particularly severe when the jet stream pattern shifted southward, bringing the Arctic polar vortex into the US Midwest and causing severe low temperature weather.[82] Advocates of climate change maintain that the cold winter in 2014/2015 was caused by a more energetic atmosphere from global warming being responsible for the shift in the jet stream to a more southerly track, allowing the Arctic polar vortex to penetrate further south. Support for this contention was Alaska having the least snow and one of the highest winter temperatures recorded in a century.[83] But Alaska is subject to extreme weather patterns: the 2012/2013 winter in Anchorage was one of the wettest and coldest on record since 1982; the 2011/2012 winter broke the previous record on snowfall set in 1954/1955.[84] Yet on a longer term perspective, there has been a generally rising trend in average temperatures in Alaska since 1978.[85]

IPCC models start at 1970 at the beginning of a distinct period of global warming, conveniently after 30 years of a mild cooling, which in any case would not have been projected by present models. The IPCC maintains that cooling off between 1940 and 1970 was caused by increased aerosols in the atmosphere that reflect sunlight from burning coal. The IPCC maintains that global warming began with the installation of desulfurization units on utility smokestacks. However, the major portion of desulfurization units were actually installed in the 1980s, and this argument ignores the enormous amount of aerosols added to the atmosphere since the 1990s by China's massive building of coal burning electricity generating plants without much in the way of pollution abatement. In recent years China has taken significant steps to cut pollution from coal in the form of sulfur oxides and particulate matter, which perhaps makes China partially responsible for the reduction in global warming that has been experienced![86]

Moreover there have been serious allegations over manipulating past data to support a preconceived conclusion about the future, dubbed Climate Gate, reminiscent of the Ministry of Truth's slogan in George Orwell's *1984*: "Who controls the past controls the future: who controls the present controls the past."[87] Warming advocates respond by pointing out that nearly all scientists agree with the IPCC findings and that all accusations of wrong doing are spurious and not worthy of note.[88] The contention that there is unanimity of scientific agreement on the anthropomorphic effect of carbon dioxide on climate change (aka global warming, aka extreme weather) is misleading. Over 32,000 scientists and engineers including 9,000 with PhD degrees have signed a petition presented to the US government that "there is no convincing scientific evidence that … greenhouse gases … cause catastrophic heating of the Earth's atmosphere or disruption of the Earth's climate."[89]

Perhaps the greatest criticism over the IPCC findings is the IPCC itself. It turns out that the full 2,216 page text of the 2013 IPCC report is at variance with the 20 page summary report on a number of key points. The media and politicians do not read the full report, but rely on the highly politicized summary. Within the full report are some climate scientists recanting prior claims of imminent disasters or irreversible runaway climate tipping points. There is admission that there has been a hiatus in the warming trend since 1998 and express doubt over the effectiveness of their models and their associated predictions. They acknowledge that there have been far worse floods and damaging weather prior to the twentieth century and that there is no trend of increasing hurricanes and cyclones. The principal consequence of global warming and increased carbon dioxide has been more rain and that another 2°C warming would pose no danger to mankind. In fact, it may be beneficial to humans as plants have increased growth by 6 percent between 1982 and 1999 thanks to higher levels of carbon dioxide. Moreover, the influence of carbon dioxide on global warming may be overstated by a factor of three from overly simplistic modeling.[90]

Is Chicago Experiencing a Warming or Cooling Trend?

In this light, it might be of interest to focus on a single city: Chicago. Heating degree days and cooling degree days are calculated throughout the US to help the providers of energy to assess electricity demand for air conditioning during summer and heating oil and natural gas for heating homes and buildings during winter. The temperature data bank is not "tweaked" by anyone with a hidden agenda. Heating and cooling degree days are calculated using a reference temperature of 65°F. If the average daily temperature is 75°F, this would count as 10 cooling degree days as air conditioning would be used to cool the indoor temperature; if on the other hand the average daily temperature is 55°F, then this would count as 10 heating degree days as natural gas or heating oil is burned to warm indoor temperatures. A cooling temperature trend would be seen by a larger number of heating degree days and a smaller number of cooling degree days. Figure 10.9 shows heating degree days for Chicago.[91]

The upward trend in heating degree days shows that Chicago has been suffering from colder winters on balance. Figure 10.10 shows cooling degree days for Chicago.

The downward trend means less electricity demand for air conditioning; or in other words, cooler summers. This microcosm of the Earth, a single city, clearly shows that there has been a cooling trend intact since 1998. This should not be misconstrued to apply to the entire planet, but to show that there is evidence of a start of a cooling trend at least in a single US city.

Warmer Oceans, More Hurricanes

Some espouse global climate change (aka global warming, aka more severe weather patterns) that warmer ocean waters have spurred the frequency of major hurricanes, which has been debunked by cooling advocates. In tropical ocean waters, higher average temperatures from a warming Earth spawn hurricanes and cyclones. Intense hurricanes that have struck the US in the last few years are partly caused by record water surface

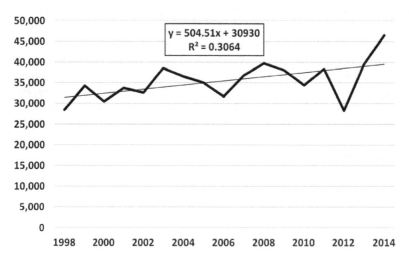

Figure 10.9 Heating Degree Days for Chicago

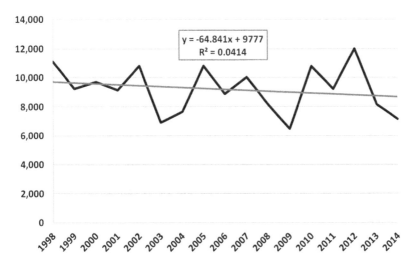

Figure 10.10 Cooling Degree Days for Chicago

temperatures in the Gulf of Mexico that can transform a low level tropical storm entering the Gulf into a Category 5 hurricane in two days' time. In 2005, Katrina struck in August killing nearly two thousand people, Rita in September, and Wilma in October in one of the worst hurricane seasons ever recorded. In 2012 hurricane Sandy killed 285 people in the Caribbean and along the US Atlantic coast, devastating buildings and shorelines wherever it struck.[92] However, global warming may not be the only cause of the increasing frequency of hurricanes because hurricane activity is itself cyclical, spanning decades. Moreover, history records devastating hurricanes and typhoons and tornadoes in the past when average temperatures were lower. For instance, a hurricane in the Caribbean in 1780 sank 1,200 ships, drowning their crews; the Galveston hurricane in 1900 killed over 6,000 people; 1955 was an extremely active year for hurricanes and tornadoes; and a 1970 typhoon drowned over one-quarter of a million people in Bangladesh.[93] Figure 10.11 shows the frequency of major Atlantic basin hurricanes since 1851.[94]

The average number of hurricanes in the Atlantic basin from 1851 to 1940 was 1.34, whereas the average from 1941 to 2014 was 2.64, nearly a double. While there is no question that major Atlantic basin hurricanes have increased in frequency in recent decades, there appears to be little statistical support for this being a global phenomenon.[95]

Polar Ice

During the 1990s, evidence of a warming trend was ample: glaciers were retreating (although there were counterexamples of some glaciers advancing) with the Arctic ice cap thinning and covering much less area, opening up the Northeast Passage for ocean shipping. Surface ice measurements of the Arctic are fairly recent, dating from the 1970s with the advent of space satellites. Retreat of the Arctic ice pack in the 1990s/2000s was thought to be unique, entirely blamable on global warming. Fear was rampant that the Arctic ice pack might disappear for an extended part of the year, bringing polar bears to

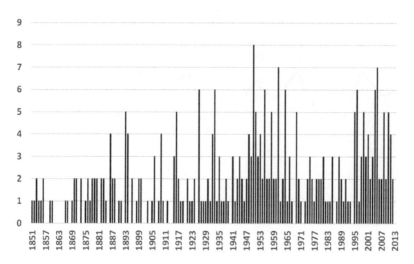

Figure 10.11 Frequency of Major Atlantic Basin Hurricanes

the edge of extinction. Shipping interests were jubilant over the prospects of opening up the Northwest Passage for ship transits for a large portion of a year. Voyage distances between the Far East and North Atlantic are much shorter transiting the Arctic Ocean than the Panama and Suez Canals. But the nuclear submarine *Skate* surfaced at the North Pole in 1958 and 1959 and found on one occasion thin ice of 2 feet, which is normally 6–8 feet thick, and on another occasion, no ice at all. Arctic ice has its own cyclic patterns of thick and thin ice based on weather, wind, and currents.[96] According to the latest European Space Agency satellite data, Arctic sea ice volume in the autumn of 2014 was above the average of low levels for the previous 5 years and up from the lows of 2011 and 2012, but still below the average first recorded by space satellites in the 1970s. That can change if Arctic winters become more severe.[97]

While Arctic ice was in retreat in the 2000s, it was thought that the thickness of the Antarctic ice pack on the continent was expanding.[98] The balance between melting in West Antarctica with ice gaining in East Antarctica, where air and water are colder, was thought to be in balance. Now two different studies have concluded that melting in West Antarctica is significantly exceeding gains in ice accumulation in East Antarctica, perhaps a red flag alert that the situation may be more alarming than earlier thought.[99] In another report primarily concerned with Arctic ice conditions, it was noted that Antarctic ice extended over 20 million square kilometers in 2014, the first time since 1980 when satellite observations of Antarctica were first available.[100] Obviously the first challenge of climate change is determining the nature of climate change! The ice cover of the Great Lakes is not a global indicator of warming or cooling and its ice coverage varies considerably, swinging between 10 and 95 percent since 1973. As a point of interest during this period, peak ice coverage occurred in 1979 at 94.5 percent; the second peak in 2014 at 91 percent; and the third in 1994 at 90.7 percent. Since 1998 when ice coverage was only 11.5 percent, the trend is increasing ice coverage subject to wide annual swings.[101]

Melting of the Arctic polar cap is sometimes cited as a cause of rising ocean levels, but floating polar ice has already displaced seawater and its melting does not affect ocean levels. This can be seen by filling a glass with ice cubes and with water to its brim where ice cubes protrude above the top of the glass. A paper towel under the glass will remain dry as the ice melts, showing that water level has not changed with the melting of floating ice. Of course this observation does not hold true for melting snow and ice on land such as Greenland and Antarctica, whose waters flow into oceans. Melting all the ice on Antarctica would raise the oceans by 73 meters and Greenland another 7 meters for a total of 80 meters or 262 feet.[102] The highest point in Florida is 312 feet, so just about all of Florida would be inundated.[103]

Reducing the surface area covered by polar ice decreases the Earth's reflectivity, or albedo. Sea ice reflects up to 80 percent of sunlight that strikes it, but reflectivity is reduced when white ice gives way to dark water. Greater absorption of solar energy by open ocean water leads to higher temperatures and more ice melting, creating larger areas of reduced albedo, an example of a positive feedback system. Another contribution to melting ice besides global warming is soot. Soot comes from burning biomass as a fuel and slash and burn farming, plus burning fossil fuels. Diesel engines emit a great deal of soot, as does burning coal without precipitators. Soot settles on ice, decreasing its albedo, allowing the sun's heat to increase melting and ice to disappear. Thus it's possible that melting Arctic ice is not caused solely by higher temperatures, but greater concentration of soot (and volcanic ash) in the air. In theory, as a positive feedback loop, once melting sets in, it should proceed without hindrance until no ice is left, but it doesn't. One reason is that the extra heat absorbed by the Arctic region during summer is given back to the environment during winter. Conversely, if cooler temperatures are experienced, glaciers expand, as do ice caps, increasing albedo—the loss of heat from a higher reflectance of the sun's rays. Thus growing ice caps induce more growth of ice caps—another example of a positive feedback system that could continue until the whole Earth is frozen in ice. It is felt that "Snowball Earths" occurred twice—once 2.2 billion years ago and again 635 million years ago. The Earth emerged after millions of years from its frozen state by volcanism that covered ice with dust and debris that absorbed sunlight along with carbon dioxide emissions, which as a greenhouse gas reduced heat lost to space.[104]

Rising Oceans

Another assertion is that the sea level is rising and will drown low lying island nations and inundate seashore properties. National Oceanic and Atmospheric Administration (NOAA) Websites that showed ocean level changes on a historic basis are no longer available.[105] When they were, sea levels in feet per century were recorded at 233 measuring spots. The conclusion was that mean sea level increase was 0.33 feet (4 inches) per century, with some measuring stations experiencing falling sea levels such as those in Arctic waters and the Pacific coast of Alaska. Most of the readings were positive between 0 and 1 feet, but there were a few examples of areas where sea levels have changed plus or minus 4 feet over the course of a century. Part of rising sea levels was from melting of Greenland and Antarctica ice packs and partly from thermal expansion of warmer ocean waters.

However, another government agency does record ocean levels available to the public. The Carbon Dioxide Information Analysis Center of the US Department of Energy estimates that since 1993 sea levels have been rising at 0.29 millimeters per year or 29 millimeters or 2.9 centimeters per century, or about a bit over an inch per century. The NOAA's assessment of 0.33 feet or 4 inches per century is higher than the US Department of Energy's assessment of 1.14 inches per century. Whichever of these assessments is more accurate does not support fears of an imminent flooding of coastal regions.[106] However, it has been noted that ocean levels along the US Northeast coast jumped by 5 inches in 2009–2010. While some were quick to let climate change take credit for this change, others noted that local sea level changes are affected by many factors including nearby ocean currents.[107]

Anthropomorphic Gas Concentration

Charles Keeling of the Scripps Institution of Oceanography began taking regular measurements of the atmospheric carbon dioxide concentration atop Mauna Loa, Hawaii, in 1958. He also began taking readings at the South Pole, but had to cease when funding was cut. Even without funding, he managed to continue taking readings in Hawaii. The Keeling curve of CO_2 concentration was backdated to the start of the Industrial Revolution by analysis of Antarctic ice cores in 1980. At that time, the concentration was 280 to 290 parts per million (ppm), already at its cyclical peak for the previous 400,000 years. For the first time in 400,000 years, carbon dioxide did not decline from its peak, but continued to rise. It reached 300 ppm in 1900; 316 ppm in 1959; 330 ppm in 1972; 370 ppm in 2000; 377 ppm in 2004; 387 ppm in 2009; and 400 ppm in 2015. Carbon dioxide concentration is increasing at a faster pace during the twentieth and twenty-first centuries than the nineteenth, correlating well with a greater consumption of fossil fuels. The observed buildup of carbon dioxide can be modeled assuming that two-thirds of carbon dioxide emissions are absorbed by oceans and land masses with the remainder accumulating in the atmosphere.

Similarly the rise of methane concentration is also accelerating. For the last 800,000 years, methane concentration varied between 450 and 550 parts per billion (ppb). From 1000 to 1800 CE, methane was about 700 ppb and rose 100 ppb during the nineteenth century to 800 ppb. In 1950 methane concentration was 1,100 ppb, reaching 1,500 ppb in 1980 and 1,750 ppb in 2015—again an accelerating trend. Nitrous oxide varied between 200 and 300 ppb for the last 800,000 years, but in recent times rose to 325 ppb in 2015. These rises are almost entirely attributable to human activities. Greater nitrous oxide emissions can be linked to nitrogen based fertilizers and burning fossil fuels.[108] Rising concentration of methane is from increased rice growing and other agricultural activities involving anaerobic decay of organic material, a far higher population of domesticated grazing animals, a higher methane-emitting termite population from deforestation, greater volumes of methane escaping from landfills, coal mining, and oil and gas activities. And, of course, vast quantities of methane entered the atmosphere from venting natural gas in oil fields in the US Southwest before construction of long distance natural gas pipelines. More methane entered the atmosphere from venting natural gas in Africa and the Middle East before the 1973 oil crisis. However, if much of this gas was flared rather than vented, then carbon dioxide replaces methane as the anthropomorphic gas. Much of the associated gas from producing fracked oil wells in North Dakota is flared. Atmospheric methane lasts only about 8 or 12 years (depending on the information source), whereas carbon dioxide lasts 20–200 years for the 65–80 percent portion eventually dissolved in oceans, and many thousands of years for the remainder.

Burning coal releases more carbon dioxide for a given quantity of energy than other fossil fuels. There is nothing that can be done about this, other than sequestering, as this is a chemical property of coal with its higher ratio of carbon to hydrogen atoms. Natural gas, with its low ratio of carbon atoms to hydrogen atoms, is the cleanest burning fossil fuel, releasing the least amount of carbon dioxide on an energy-equivalent basis plus water. Table 10.2 calculates the global release of carbon from burning of fossil fuels for 2014.[109]

Table 10.2 excludes human consumption of biomass, which has a higher carbon release factor than coal. However, plants and trees absorb carbon dioxide before being harvested for biomass. Rounding to take into account some net carbon release from deforestation, the approximate amount of annual carbon release into the atmosphere from human activities is a little over 10 billion tons, which works out to be about 40 billion tons of carbon dioxide.[110] Forty billion tons of CO_2 added to the atmosphere are impressive until one realizes that the atmosphere weighs 6 quadrillion tons.[111] Thus the annual contribution to the atmosphere by human activity of an additional 40 billion tons is divided by 6 quadrillion tons for a staggering 0.00067 percent, yet is sufficient to contribute to the buildup of carbon dioxide in the atmosphere.

As seen in Table 10.2, coal adds a proportionally greater amount of carbon dioxide to the atmosphere than other fossil fuels. It contributes 43 percent to carbon dioxide emissions, but represents only 35 percent of fossil fuels consumed in terms of energy release. Moreover, old coal burning electricity generating plants, particularly in India and China, are energy inefficient compared to those in developed nations. Replacing these coal fired plants (plus old plants in OECD nations) with new natural gas energy efficient plants would reduce carbon dioxide emissions two ways—natural gas releases less carbon dioxide than coal for an equivalent output of energy and less fuel would be burned for an equivalent output of electricity. Furthermore, natural gas does not emit sulfur and nitrogen oxides or heavy metals, nor does it desecrate the landscape or affect water supplies. One can see why nations prefer to abandon coal in favor of natural gas. But reality is that the supply of natural gas is not sufficient to replace coal and its higher price in Europe and Asia compared to coal would add to energy costs.

Lest we become too enthralled with our capacity to influence the weather, 40 billion tons of anthropomorphic carbon dioxide, which is equivalent to 10 billion tons of carbon added to the atmosphere per year, are dwarfed by nature's global carbon recycling program. Ninety billion tons of carbon are recycled between ocean and atmosphere and living plants absorb 120 billion tons, about equal to that released to the atmosphere by decaying plants. A higher concentration of carbon dioxide, in itself, should spur plant growth, which would absorb greater quantities of carbon dioxide from the atmosphere. However, plants eventually die, and the incremental carbon dioxide absorbed is given back through plant decay. Agriculture and land use by humans releases and absorbs

Table 10.2 Calculating Anthropomorphic Global Release of Carbon Dioxide

	World Consumptions Billions TOE	*Percent of Total*	*CO_2 Release Factor*	*CO_2 Release Billion Tons*	*Percent Carbon Emissions*
Coal	3.882	34.8%	3.96	15.372	43.3%
Oil	4.211	37.7%	3.07	12.927	36.4%
Natural Gas	3.066	27.5%	2.35	7.205	20.3%
Total	11.159	100%		35.504	100%
Carbon Equivalent (Billion Tons)				9.683	

about 1 billion tons of carbon, a rounding error in what nature recycles. In terms of carbon inventory, plants contain 560 billion tons of carbon, atmosphere 750 billion tons, soil 1,500 billion tons, fossil fuel resources 4,000 billion tons, deep ocean 38,000 billion tons, and the Earth's crust 100,000,000 billion tons.[112] With an annual exchange of 200 billion tons of carbon between vegetation and oceans with the atmosphere, and considering the size of the carbon inventory, scientists ponder why a paltry 5 percent addition to nature's recycling program is making such a big difference to the atmospheric concentration of carbon dioxide.[113] The increase in anthropomorphic carbon dioxide in the atmosphere can be explained by about one-third remaining in the atmosphere and the remaining two-thirds being absorbed by land and ocean. Yet why is this relatively small increment of anthropomorphic gas not being recycled along with the much larger natural volumes of carbon dioxide exchanged between the atmosphere and Earth?

Ocean Acidification

An acid donates hydrogen ions, and when dissolved in water, the balance between hydrogen ions and hydroxide ions shifts toward more hydrogen ions, which makes the solution more acidic. A base is a substance that accepts hydrogen ions. When dissolved in water, the balance between hydrogen ions and hydroxide ions shifts in favor of hydroxide ions, making the solution basic or alkaline. The range of pH values is between 0 and 14, with the pH of distilled water at 7.0, a neutral point. Basic or alkaline solutions have pH values above 7 to as high as 14, whereas acidic solutions have pH values below 7 to as low as 0. A kitchen drain cleaner has high pH values, whereas battery acid has low pH values, both depending on their strength.[114] Each unit of a pH scale represents a factor of 10 in a substance being more basic or acidic.[115] A change of 0.1 in pH value represents about a 25 percent change in strength of an acid or base. The addition of carbon dioxide in seawater forms a mixture of bicarbonate and carbonate and hydrogen ions, the latter associated with carbonic acid, whose strength is dependent on sea water temperature and alkalinity. One-third of anthropomorphic carbon dioxide is absorbed by land and oceans, and oceans alone absorb about one-quarter of anthropomorphic carbon dioxide. About one-half of absorbed carbon dioxide is retained in the upper 400 meters of the ocean depth and the remaining half penetrates deeper waters from an internal ocean circulation driven by differences in density and by winds. Changes in pH in deep ocean depths are expected to lag changes in surface pH by a few centuries.

An extreme form of ocean acidification occurred about 56 million years ago at the Paleocene–Eocene Thermal Maximum (PETM) when, for unknown reasons, massive amounts of carbon dioxide entered the atmosphere. Volcanism is one possible cause, another is a warming sufficient to release methane from methane hydrate. Whatever the cause, the Earth warmed about 5°C to 7°C. Increased ocean acidification from adding 1.5 to 7 gigatons of carbon to the atmosphere was sufficient to dissolve carbonate sediments in ocean basins. PETM is recorded as a layer of red clay sandwiched between white layers of calcium carbonate in ocean bottom sediment. A large number of species of marine life with calcium carbonate shells became extinct. Animal and plant life was sorely affected by this extinction event that followed the demise of the dinosaurs by ten million years.[116] The effects of increased ocean acidification (so-called carbon dioxide's evil twin) can be seen today at a small island, Castello Aragonese, 17 miles offshore Naples. The island is surrounded by vents emitting large volumes of volcanic carbon dioxide that has acidified local waters. The impact on shell covered marine life around this island is evident. Most barnacles and mussels cannot survive in the more acidic waters, and those that do have shells so thin that they're almost transparent. About one-third of species of marine life found not far from Castello Aragonese, where waters are normal, are absent around the island.[117] Under the auspices of Prince Albert II of Monaco, the Monaco Declaration, a strongly worded statement made by 150 scientists, asserted that ocean acidification would destroy the world's coral reefs as a habitat for marine life with severe ramifications on ocean life and the ocean economy. The Monaco Declaration was presented to the United Nations Climate Change Conference in Copenhagen in 2009.[118]

It is felt that the ocean has always been slightly basic, averaging a pH of 8.1–8.2 for millions of years. Actual measurements since 1910 show that most readings oscillate in range from 7.9 to 8.2. In the early 1980s, pH readings were clustered around 8.15. Since then pH readings started a steady decline, reaching 7.95, with a trend projecting further declines. While these readings are still within their historical range, the consistency of the current trend suggests that pH readings will continue to fall. The reading of 7.8 at Castello Aragonese is not that far away, but bear in mind that a lowering of pH by a value of 0.1 means 25 percent greater acidity. On the other hand, if pH remains above its historical lower limit of 7.9, then the worst of the impact on marine life envisioned in the Monaco Declaration will not occur.[119]

A more acid environment does not mean that all shell life suffers equally. Some suffer more than others and there are species that do not seem affected by increased acidity. Perhaps nature will fight ocean acidification for us. Twelve thousand species of diatoms in oceans and lakes are a sink, or source of natural removal, of carbon dioxide. Diatoms are single-celled algae that convert carbon dioxide, water, and sunlight into food and release oxygen. Unlike other phytoplankton, diatoms also absorb carbon dioxide to create microscopic shells that sink to the bottom of the lake or ocean when they die. It is estimated that diatoms remove about half as much carbon dioxide as photosynthesis, a huge volume of carbon dioxide. One potential way of reducing carbon dioxide would be expanding the population of diatoms, but it cannot be expected that diatoms can do the whole job.[120]

Which climate change model do you select? This is an important decision because carbon dioxide control measures such as cap and trade or a carbon tax will cost taxpayers billions of dollars and have a significant impact on the level and direction of future economic activity. Truth unfortunately appears to be a manageable entity to serve either economic interests or political goals. Nevertheless, whichever path future temperatures follow, winners will gloat and losers will shirk off the media stage and hope that people will forget what they had prophesized to be the future just as what happened to the ice age advocates in the mid-1970s. If a cooling trend does set in, just as in the 1970s when ice agers transmogrified into leading spokespeople for global warming, perhaps some of today's global warming enthusiasts will be leading massive demonstrations demanding that more coal be burned to help raise the Earth's temperature!

Problems and Projects

Problem 10.1

A wind turbine and a turbine powered by river or tidal flow work off the same equation. Maximum power (Pmax) is ½ * efficiency of turbine * density of water * volume of water flowing through the turbine per second * velocity squared. But volume of water flowing is the area of the turbine blades * velocity.

Thus: Pmax = Efficiency * Water density * Area of blade * Velocity cubed.

Water density is 1,000 kilograms per cubic meter. Suppose that the radius of the blade is two meters and velocity of water is two meters per second and turbine efficiency is 90 percent. What is the power output in terms of kilogram * meters squared/seconds cubed? A joule is defined as 1 kilogram * meter/seconds squared and a watt is defined as a joule/second. What is the power output in kilowatts?

Problem 10.2

What is the weight of the atmosphere? The Earth has a radius of 4,000 miles—calculate the number of square miles, square feet, and square inches in the Earth's area. Atmospheric pressure is 14.7 pounds per square inch—calculate the pounds and then tons (2,000 pounds per ton) to obtain the weight.

Problem 10.3

The addition of carbon dioxide is 40 billion tons annually. If all the anthropomorphic carbon dioxide remains in the atmosphere, what will be the impact in terms of parts per million per year? This can be obtained by getting the fraction of carbon dioxide added to the atmosphere with the result in the previous problem. By multiplying this fraction by one million, you'll get the fraction in terms of parts per million (ppm). In 2011, the ppm of CO_2 was 391 and 400 in 2015. Assuming that we've been dumping 40 billion tons each year, what percentage of 40 billion tons is being absorbed by land and ocean and what percentage is remaining in the atmosphere?

Problem 10.4

Carbon dioxide makes up 400 ppm in the atmosphere; what is the equivalent billion tons of carbon dioxide and carbon?

Problem 10.5

The low estimate of the PETM extinction event is an emission of 1,500 gigatons of carbon with other estimates of a range between 2,000 and 7,000 gigatons. Assuming no absorption by the Earth, what is the incremental ppm of carbon dioxide added to the atmosphere for these different estimates?

Project 10.1

The EPA regulation announced in August 2015 calls for electric utilities to lower carbon emissions by 32 percent from 2005 levels by 2030. The purpose of this project is to look at both feasibility and repercussions of compliance.[121] From *BP Energy Statistics*, what was the terawatt-hours of US electricity output in 2005 and 2014? What is the rate of growth over these 9 years? With an expanding population, how do you explain

Project Table 10.1

	2005	2014
Coal	49%	39%
Natural Gas	19%	27%
Nuclear	19%	20%
Hydro	7%	6%
Renewables	2%	7%
Others	4%	1%

such a low rate of growth? Using this rate of growth, what is the projected electricity consumption in 2030?

Energy sources by percentage for generating electricity in 2005 and 2014 are shown in Project Table 10.1 above.

Using the relationship that coal produces 2.13 pounds of carbon dioxide per kilowatt-hour and natural gas 1.21 pounds of carbon dioxide per kilowatt-hour, and using the terawatt-hour output from BP, how much carbon dioxide was emitted in 2005 and 2014? What is the percentage decline without EPA regulations? Why did this happen?

Set up a similar Excel table for the 2030 projection of electricity, but with the proportion of coal and natural gas with an initial value of zero. Enter what you think should be the percentage contribution for nuclear, hydro, renewables, and other. Renewables could reflect a weighted average of growth for solar and wind. Using Solver, the objective is total carbon dioxide for 2030 to be 68 percent of 2005 carbon dioxide emissions; the variables are percentages of coal and natural gas, with a constraint that all energy sources must total 100 percent. Look at the result—is it feasible, and what are the repercussions?

Electricity makes up 38 percent of total energy consumption. With no carbon dioxide emission cuts for residential, commercial, industrial, and transportation energy sectors, what would be the overall reduction in US carbon dioxide emissions in 2030 if these sectors exhibited no growth? If they grew by 1.2 percent per year, obtain the new percentage share of electricity to calculate the net overall reduction. Without any cooperation from India and China, will the EPA regulation have any effect on global carbon emissions? If not, what have we gained by spending billions to reduce carbon emissions? Will the rise in electricity costs affect the US, competitive position? Why do you think this regulation was implemented?

Project 10.2

Visit Website http://data.giss.nasa.gov/gistemp/tabledata_v3/GLB.Ts+dSST.txt to obtain the temperature data used to construct the trend lines in Figures 10.3 to 10.8. Use the Text to Columns icon on Data tab to convert to columns of data from which average annual values can be calculated. Create your own set of trend lines accompanied with a story line as to how you interpret the data.

Project 10.3

Visit Website www.weatherdatadepot.com and select a city or a small group of cities or regions and chart warming and cooling degree days and see whether these localities have warming or cooling trends in place similar to Chicago.

Notes

1 Alternative Fuels Data Center, Energy Efficiency & Renewable Energy, Website www.afdc.energy. gov/fuels/hydrogen_basics.html.

2 Hydrogen Cars Now, Website www.hydrogencarsnow.com, lists every model, their technical specifications, and stage of development including a listing of hydrogen filling stations.

3 Alternative Fuels Data Center, Energy Efficiency & Renewable Energy, Website www.afdc.energy. gov/vehicles/search/results/?vehicle_type=light&category_id=27&fuel_id=9.

4 "Ford F-250 SuperChief Tri-Flex Fuel Truck," Hydrogen Cars Now, Website www.hydrogencars now.com/ford-superchief-f250-pickup.htm.

5 "Sharing Technology for a Stronger America," USCAR, Website www.uscar.org.

6 US Drive, Website www1.eere.energy.gov/vehiclesandfuels/pdfs/program/us_drive_partnership_ plan_mar2013.pdf.

7 "Hydrogen Filling Stations Worldwide," netinform, Website www.netinform.net/H2/H2Stations/ H2Stations.aspx?Continent=NA&StationID=-1. Different sources provide wide variance on the number of hydrogen filling stations. See next footnote.

8 Simon Wright, "Foot on the Gas: Hydrogen-Powered Cars Hit the Road," *The Economist* (The World in 2015), reports that California has 10 filling stations and is building another 28, Japan should have 100 hydrogen filling stations by 2015, South Korea should reach 43, and Germany 100 by 2017.

9 Energy Efficiency and Renewable Energy (EERE), Website www.fueleconomy.gov/feg/fcv_chal lenges.shtml.

10 "Hydrogen Buses Struggle with Expense," *Scientific American* (December 16, 2013), Website www. scientificamerican.com/article/hydrogen-buses-struggle-with-expense. See also Christopher Mac Kechnie, "How Much Does a Bus Cost to Purchase and Operate?" About Money, Website http:// publictransport.about.com/od/Transit_Vehicles/a/How-Much-Does-A-Bus-Cost-To-Purchase- And-Operate.htm, for the cost of a bus.

11 Geothermal Education Office, Website http://geothermal.marin.org/GEOpresentation/sld001. htm, is a principal source of information.

12 Tara Patel, "A Mile Below Paris Drillers Hit Hot Pools to Warm Houses," *Bloomberg* (September 2, 2014), Website www.bloomberg.com/news/articles/2014-09-01/a-mile-below-paris-drillers-hit- hot-pools-to-warm-houses.

13 Barry Cinnamon, "Listen Up: Geothermal Heat Pumps and Rooftop Solar are a Perfect Match," *Renewable Energy World* (November 7, 2014), Website www.renewableenergyworld.com/rea/news/ article/2014/11/listen-up-heat-pumps-and-rooftop-solar-are-a-perfect-match.

14 Ted Clutter, "Why Geothermal Heat Pumps Should be a Carbon Reduction Tool for Coal Plants," Global Energy Products (November 19, 2014), Website http://gep-solar.com/why-geothermal- heat-pumps-should-be-a-carbon-reduction-tool-for-coal-plants.

15 "UK Supermarket to be Powered Exclusively by Waste-to-Energy Plant," *Renewable Energy World* (August 20, 2014), Website www.renewableenergyworld.com/rea/news/article/2014/08/uk- supermarket-to-be-powered-exclusively-by-waste-to-energy-plant.

16 Meg Cichon, "Energy Storage and Geothermal Markets Look to Team Up in the Hunt for Lithium," *Renewable Energy World* (July 27, 2015), Website www.renewableenergyworld.com/articles/print/ volume-18/issue-4/features/geothermal/energy-storage-and-geothermal-markets-look-to-team- up-in-the-hunt-for-lithium.html. See also Simbol Materials, Website www.simbolmaterials.com.

17 "Current List of Geothermal Power Plants," Global Energy Observatory, Website http://global energyobservatory.org/list.php?db=PowerPlants&type=Geothermal.

18 Malaysia was omitted from the previous footnote, and its output, but not the number of sites, was obtained from "Hot Rocks," *The Economist* (August 16, 2014).

19 Charles Thurston, "Enel Moves Hybrid Renewables Forward Again with World's First Biomass and Geothermal Project," *Renewable Energy World* (December 24, 2014), Website www.renewable energyworld.com/rea/news/article/2014/12/enel-moves-hybrid-renewables-forward-again.

20 National Energy Authority (Iceland), Website www.nea.is/geothermal.

21 Alexander Richter, "Excess Water from Iceland Geothermal Plant Source of Thriving Spa Business," GEP Products, Website http://gep-solar.com/excess-water-from-iceland-geothermal-plant-source-of-thriving-spa-business.

22 Geothermal Resources Council, Website www.geothermal.org.

23 Philippe Dumas and Luca Angelino, "Geothermal Energy: Why It Is Different from Shale Gas," *Renewable Energy World* (September 23, 2013), Website www.renewableenergyworld.com/rea/news/article/2013/09/geothermal-why-it-is-different-to-shale-gas. See also Meg Cichon, "Is Fracking for Enhanced Geothermal Systems the Same as Fracking for Natural Gas?" *Renewable Energy World* (July 16, 2013), Website www.renewableenergyworld.com/rea/news/article/2013/07/is-fracking-for-enhanced-geothermal-systems-the-same-as-fracking-for-natural-gas.

24 "What is an Enhanced Geothermal System (EGS)?" EERE Geothermal Technologies Office, Website www.geothermal.energy.gov. See also "The Future of Geothermal Energy," MIT (2006), Website http://geothermal.inel.gov/publications/future_of_geothermal_energy.pdf.

25 Geodynamics, Website www.geodynamics.com.au.

26 Meg Cichon, "The Dream Becomes Real: Touring the Newberry Enhanced Geothermal Site," *Renewable Energy World* (December 15, 2014), Website www.renewableenergyworld.com/rea/news/article/2014/12/the-dream-becomes-real-touring-the-newberry-enhanced-geothermal-site. See also the video on the Alta Rock project, Website http://altarockenergy.com/#&panel1-1.

27 Meg Cichon, "Can Geothermal Energy Save California's Salton Sea?" *Renewable Energy World* (June 4, 2015), Website www.renewableenergyworld.com/rea/news/print/article/2014/06/can-geothermal-energy-save-californias-salton-sea.

28 Andrew Herndon, "Deep Earth Plans Geothermal Plant Amid Canadian Oil Wells," *Bloomberg* (May 24, 2013), Website www.bloomberg.com/news/articles/2013-05-24/deep-Earth-plans-canada-s-first-geothermal-power-amid-oil-wells. See also Deep Earth Energy Production, Website www.deepcorp.ca.

29 Liu Yuanyuan, "China's Geothermal Energy Sector Demonstrates Great Growth Potential," *Renewable Energy World* (January 8, 2015), Website www.renewableenergyworld.com/rea/news/article/2015/01/chinas-geothermal-energy-sector-demonstrates-great-growth-potential. See also Liu Yuanyuan, "Geothermal Energy to Become Next New Source of Chinese Renewable Growth," *Renewable Energy World* (July 24, 2014), Website www.renewableenergyworld.com/rea/news/article/2014/07/geothermal-energy-to-become-next-new-source-of-china-renewable-growth.

30 Leslie Blodgett, "Global Geothermal News Roundup: US Plants Near Completion, South America Closer to Tapping Resource," Global Energy Products (May 21, 2014), Website http://gep-solar.com/global-geothermal-news-roundup-us-plants-near-completion-south-america-closer-to-tapping-resource.

31 Reykjavik Geothermal, Website www.rg.is/en/home.

32 Wendell A. Duffield and John H. Sass, *Geothermal Energy—Clean Power from the Earth's Heat*, Circular 1249 (Washington, DC: US Geological Survey, US Department of the Interior, 2003).

33 Michael Parker (The Conversation), "Icelandic Drilling Project Opens Door to Volcano-Powered Electricity," *Scientific American* (July 29, 2014), Website www.scientificamerican.com/article/icelandic-drilling-project-opens-door-to-volcano-powered-electricity.

34 Leslie Blodgett, "Geothermal Visual: Capacity Factors for Assorted Energy Systems," *Renewable Energy World*, including data from DOE and NREL's Transparent Costs Database (February 20, 2015), Website www.renewableenergyworld.com/rea/blog/post/2015/02/geothermal-visual-capacity-factors-for-assorted-energy-systems.html.

35 Leslie Blodgett, "IFC Study Says Over 60% of Geothermal Wells Drilled Globally are Successful," *Renewable Energy World* (June 17, 2013), Website www.renewableenergyworld.com/rea/news/article/2013/06/ifc-study-says-over-60-of-geothermal-wells-drilled-globally-are-successful?cmpid=rss.

36 Chisaki Watanabe, "Orix Plans to Build as Many as 15 Geothermal Plants in Japan," *Bloomberg* (July 22, 2014), Website www.bloomberg.com/news/articles/2014-07-23/orix-plans-to-build-as-many-as-15-geothermal-plants-in-japan.

37 John D. Cox, *Climate Crash* (Washington, DC: Joseph Henry Press, 2005).

38 Bjorn Carey, "Sahara Desert Was Once Lush and Populated," livescience (July 20, 2006), Website www.livescience.com/4180-sahara-desert-lush-populated.html.

39 "Answers From Angkor" by Richard Stone, *National Geographic* (July, 2009).

40 ClimateSight, Website http://climatesight.org/2012/04/26/the-day-after-tomorrow-a-scientific-critique critiques the scientific misrepresentations in the movie, yet the sudden cooling event during the Younger Dryas is a scientific fact; the question is one of cause.

41 Fritz Vahrenholt and Sebastian Luning, *The Neglected Sun* (London, UK: Stacy International, 2013).

42 Climate Data Information, Website www.climatedata.info/forcing/milankovitch-cycles. Milankovitch cycles were developed in the 1930s by Serbian mathematician Milutin Milankovitch and account for three variations in the orbit of the Earth around the sun: Earth's orbit varying from being nearly circular to slightly elliptical (eccentricity); variations in the angle of tilt of the Earth's axis from 22.1° to 24.5° (obliquity); and variation in the direction of tilt (precession).

43 "Classical Gas," *Smithsonian Magazine* (February, 2013).

44 Image "Geological Timescale: Concentration of CO2 and Temperature Fluctuations," Website www.google.com/search?q=temperature+and+carbon+dioxide+prehistoric+levels&biw=1920&bih=916&tbm=isch&imgil=CPZxHjDBVR0dNM%253A%253BXEzBa6goh_Kz_M%253Bhttp%25253A%25252F%25252Fbiocab.org%25252FClimate_Geologic_Timescale.html&source=iu&pf=m&fir=CPZxHjDBVR0dNM%253A%252CXEzBa6goh_Kz_M%252C_&usg=__3C9W89peQykCxOQWTQye4BZ2VXM%3D&ved=0CCcQyjc&ei=N4zoVNidBMmgNt-lgugF#imgdii=_&imgrc=s8ssDP_5dFQVaM%253A%3Beptuj_H4Y2CHjM%3Bhttp%253A%252F%252Fwww.biocab.org%252FCarbon_Dioxide_Geological.jpg%3Bhttp%253A%252F%252Fwww.answerbag.com%252Fq_view%252F2944387%3B713%3B534.

45 Image "Atmospheric CO2 versus Average Global Temperature," Website www.google.com/search?q=image+temperature+carbon+dioxide+geological+past&biw=1920&bih=918&tbm=isch&imgil=nqMMwMKAfosvaM%253A%253ByCyJqB-rRBgbNM%253Bhttp%25253A%25252F%25252.

46 In 1942 a squadron of Lockheed Lightnings was abandoned in Greenland. In 1993 a search was made for these planes and they were eventually discovered buried surprisingly in 250 feet of ice. There were many more layers than years and it is thought that each layer actually represents a passage of a storm, not a passage of a year. To say the least, this would significantly affect the time line of ice core dating.

47 William F. Ruddiman, "Did Humans Stop an Ice Age?" *Scientific American* (March, 2005).

48 J. Barnola et al., "Vostok Ice Core Provides 160,000-Year Record of Atmospheric CO2," *Nature*, Vol. 329 (October 1, 1987), Website http://shadow.eas.gatech.edu/~kcobb/warming_papers/barnola87.pdf.

49 Image of Vostok Climate Records (note references at bottom of image), Website http://shum.cc.huji.ac.il/~cariel/climate5763/160.html.

50 J. Petit et al., "Climate and Atmospheric History of the Past 420,000 Years from the Vostok Ice Core, Antarctica," *Nature*, Vol. 399 (June 3, 1999), Website www.jerome-chappellaz.com/files/publications/climate-and-atmospheric-history-of-the-past-420-000-years-from-the-vostok-ice-core-antarctica-38.pdf. The article confirms the strong correlation between atmospheric greenhouse gas concentrations and Antarctic temperatures. The article notes that carbon dioxide lags temperature declines. On the important note of whether carbon dioxide leads or lags temperature declines, the article notes that Fischer and others have concluded that carbon dioxide also lags temperature rises, but Petit feels that the uncertainty in timing might not support such a conclusion. Leading or lagging is absolutely critical in assessing the causal relationship between carbon dioxide and temperature. See also H. Fischer et al., "Ice Core Records of Atmospheric CO2 around the Last Three Glacial Terminations," *Science*, Vol. 283, No. 5408 (March 12, 1999), Website www.sciencemag.org/

content/283/5408/1712.abstract, and "Ice Core Studies Prove that CO2 is Not the Powerful Climate Driver Climate Alarmists Make it Out to Be," *CO2 Science*, Vol. 6, No. 26 (June 25, 2003), Website www.co2science.org/articles/V6/N26/EDIT.php.

51 B. Geerts and E. Linacre, "Ice Cores, CO2 Concentration, and Climate," Atmospheric Science, University of Wyoming (2002), Website www-das.uwyo.edu/~geerts/cwx/notes/chap01/icecore.html.

52 L. Pena, "Ancient Ocean Currents May Have Changed Pacing and Intensity of Ice Ages," National Science Foundation (June 26, 2014), Website www.nsf.gov/news/news_summ.jsp?cntn_id=131830&org=NSF&from=news.

53 "Seafloor Pulses May Alter Climate," The Earth Institute, Columbia University (February 5, 2015), Website www.Earth.columbia.edu/articles/view/3231.

54 Steve Goreham, *The Mad, Mad, Mad World of Climatism* (New Lenox, IL: New Lenox Press, 2012).

55 Brian M. Fagan, *The Little Ice Age: How Climate Made History (1300–1850)* (New York, NY: Basic Books, 2001).

56 "Solar Variability and Terrestrial Climate," National Aeronautics and Space Administration (NASA), Science News (January 8, 2013), Website http://science.nasa.gov/science-news/science-at-nasa/2013/08jan_sunclimate. See also *National Academy of Sciences of the United States of America* (Vol. 112, No. 11), Website www.pnas.org/content/112/11/3253.full. The article concludes that cosmic rays affect short term global temperatures, but there is a lack of statistical evidence that cosmic rays affect long term global temperatures.

57 A. Dragic et al., "Forbush Decreases—Clouds Relation to the Neutron Monitor Era," Astrophysics and Space Science Transactions (ASTRA), No. 7, Pages 315–318 (2011), Website www.astrophys-space-sci-trans.net/7/315/2011/astra-7-315-2011.pdf.

58 Fritz Vahrenholt and Sebastian Luning, *The Neglected Sun* (London, UK: Stacy International, 2013). The book describes the methodology of detecting these solar cycles and how solar radiative power and its associated magnetic field in attenuating incoming cosmic radiation affects cloud cover and ultraviolet radiation and their impact on climate.

59 Robert Dull, University of Texas, Website www.utexas.edu/experts/robert_dull. An investigative documentary of Dull's work in San Salvador is well worth watching. See also John Black, "Why Is the Global Climatic Cataclysm of the Sixth Century Virtually Unheard Of?" Ancient Origins (February 19, 2014), Website www.ancient-origins.net/unexplained-phenomena/why-global-climatic-cataclysm-sixth-century-virtually-unheard-001360.

60 "After Tambora," *The Economist* (April 11, 2015).

61 Volcano Discovery, Website www.volcanodiscovery.com/tambora.html. See also Robert Evans, "Blast from the Past," *Smithsonian Magazine* (July, 2002), Website www.smithsonianmag.com/history/blast-from-the-past-65102374/?no-ist.

62 "Do Volcanoes Emit More CO2 than Humans?" Skeptical Science, Website www.skepticalscience.com/volcanoes-and-global-warming.htm.

63 Timothy Casey, "Volcanic Carbon Dioxide," Consulting Engineer, Website http://carbon-budget.geologist-1011.net.

64 Robin Wylie, "Long Invisible, Research Shows Volcanic CO2 Levels Are Staggering," livescience (October 15, 2013), Website www.livescience.com/40451-volcanic-co2-levels-are-staggering.html.

65 Michael Snyder, "Record Number of Volcano Eruptions in 2013—Is Catastrophic Global Cooling Dead Ahead?" mensnewsdaily MND (December 5, 2013), Website http://michaelsnyder.mensnewsdaily.com/2014/09/the-number-of-volcanic-eruptions-is-increasing-and-that-could-lead-to-an-extremely-cold-winter.

66 S. Self et al., "The Atmospheric Impact of the 1991 Mount Pinatubo Eruption," US Geological Survey (June, 1999), Website http://pubs.usgs.gov/pinatubo/self. Total bulk volume of volcanic ejecta was 8.4–10.4 cubic kilometers.

67 "Volcanic Eruption: An Incitement for Lowering Earth's Temperature," academic.edu, Website www.academia.edu/8784934/Volcanic_eruption_An_incitement_for_lowering_Earths_temperature.

See also T. Thordarson and S. Self, "Atmospheric and Environmental Effects of the 1783–1784 Laki Eruption: A Review and Reassessment," *Journal of Geophysical Research*, Vol. 108, No. D1 (January, 2003), Website http://seismo.berkeley.edu/~manga/LIPS/thordarson03.pdf.

68 Mary Bagley, "Krakatoa Volcano: Facts About 1883 Eruption," *livescience*, Website www.livescience.com/28186-krakatoa.html.

69 Earth System Research Laboratory of National Oceanic and Atmospheric Administration (NOAA), Website ftp://aftp.cmdl.noaa.gov/products/trends/co2/co2_annmean_mlo.txt, Mauna Loa CO_2 readings 1959 to present. For CO_2 readings prior to 1960, Climate Data Information, Website www.climatedata.info/forcing/gases/carbon-dioxide. See also "GLOBAL Land-Ocean Temperature Index in 0.01 Degrees Celsius Base Period: 1951–1980," National Aeronautics and Space Administration (NASA), Website http://data.giss.nasa.gov/gistemp/tabledata_v3/GLB.Ts+dSST.txt, for source of global average annual temperatures.

70 Intergovernmental Panel on Climate Change, Website www.ipcc.ch/ipccreports/tar/wg2/index.php?idp=29.

71 David Rose, "Nasa Climate Scientists: We Said 2014 was the Warmest Year on Record…But We're Only 38% Sure We Were Right," *The Daily Mail* (January 17, 2015), Website www.dailymail.co.uk/news/article-2915061/Nasa-climate-scientists-said-2014-warmest-year-record-38-sure-right.html.

72 Rolf Schuttenhelm, "Two Hottest Years Ever: 2014 Will Set New World Temperature Record—and 2015 Will Break It," bits of science (April 7, 2014), Website www.bitsofscience.org/hottest-years-ever-2014-world-temperature-record-2015-6545.

73 Tia Ghose, "Warm 'Blob' in Pacific Ocean to Blame for Wonky US Weather, livescience (April 10, 2015), Website www.livescience.com/50445-warm-blob-causes-weird-weather.html.

74 Jared Goyette, "Welcome to the 'Double El Niño'—and More Extreme Weather," Public Radio International (March 22, 2015), Website www.pri.org/stories/2015-03-22/welcome-double-el-nio-and-more-extreme-weather.

75 "NASA Scientists Puzzled by Global Cooling on Land and Sea," Newsmax (October 6, 2014), Website www.newsmax.com/Newsfront/Science-US-climate-oceans/2014/10/06/id/598864. See also Space and Science Research Corporation, Website www.spaceandscience.net/id1.html, and the bio on John Casey at Website www.spaceandscience.net/sitebuildercontent/sitebuilderfiles/casey-johnbioandphotocurrent.pdf.

76 Scientists can be as fickle in their beliefs as teenage crushes and depend on their past pronouncements being lost in time as much as politicians.

77 One major oil company, long a critic of global warming with a clear articulation of its position, is now a global warming fan. Makes one wonder about their motivation—a search for truth or government favors?

78 Naomi Klein, "If Enough of Us Decide that Climate Change is a Crisis Worthy of Marshall Plan Levels of Response, Then It Will Become One," *The Guardian* (March 6, 2015), Website www.theguardian.com/environment/2015/mar/06/dont-look-away-now-the-climate-crisis-needs-you?CMP=ema_565.

79 Speeches advocating a 90 percent reduction in world population have at times been received with acclamation—makes one wonder how the audience knows that it would escape whatever means are used to achieve depopulation.

80 A. Dai and K. Trenberth, "New Estimates of Continental Discharge and Oceanic Freshwater Transport," National Center for Atmospheric Research (2003), Website www.cgd.ucar.edu/cas/adai/papers/Dai_discharge_AMS03.pdf.

81 "It's Water Vapor, Not the CO2," American Chemical Society, Website www.acs.org/content/acs/en/climatescience/climatesciencenarratives/its-water-vapor-not-the-co2.html.

82 Pallab Ghosh, "Wavier Jet Stream 'May Drive Weather Shift,'" BBC News (February 15, 2014), Website www.bbc.com/news/science-environment-26023166.

83 "Record High Temperatures Recorded in Alaska," newsminer.com (February 19, 2015), Website www.newsminer.com/arctic_cam/record-high-temperatures-recorded-in-alaska/article_bff09598-b87d-11e4-a09a-a74bf2e704a7.html.

84 Ben Anderson, "Brrrrrrr! Last Year Coldest in Three Decades for Anchorage," *Alaska Dispatch News* (January 3, 2013), Website www.adn.com/article/brrrrrrr-last-year-coldest-three-decades-anchorage.

85 "Temperature Changes in Alaska," The Alaska Climate Research Center, Website http://climate.gi.alaska.edu/ClimTrends/Change/TempChange.html.

86 Steve Goreham, *The Mad, Mad, Mad World of Climatism* (New Lenox, IL: New Lenox Books, 2012). This book is a thorough critique of global warming.

87 Christopher Booker, "Climate Change: This is the Worst Scientific Scandal of Our Generation," *The Telegraph* (November 28, 2009), Website www.telegraph.co.uk/comment/columnists/christopherbooker/6679082/Climate-change-this-is-the-worst-scientific-scandal-of-our-generation.html. See also Christopher Booker, "The Scandal of Fiddled Global Warming Data," *The Telegraph* (June 21, 2014), Website www.telegraph.co.uk/news/Earth/environment/10916086/The-scandal-of-fiddled-global-warming-data.html; Christopher Booker, "Climategate, the Sequel: How We are STILL Being Tricked with Flawed Data on Global Warming," *The Telegraph* (January 27, 2015), Website www.telegraph.co.uk/comment/11367272/Climategate-the-sequel-How-we-are-STILL-being-tricked-with-flawed-data-on-global-warming.html; Christopher Booker, "The Fiddling with Temperature Data is the Biggest Science Scandal Ever," *The Telegraph* (February 7, 2015), Website www.telegraph.co.uk/news/earth/environment/globalwarming/11395516/The-fiddling-with-temperature-data-is-the-biggest-science-scandal-ever.html; Peter Ferrara, "To the Horror of Global Alarmists, Global Cooling Is Here," *Forbes* (May 26, 2013), Website www.forbes.com/sites/peterferrara/2013/05/26/to-the-horror-of-global-warming-alarmists-global-cooling-is-here; "Ice Age Now: Major Danish Daily Warns—'Globe May Be on Path to Little Ice Age…'" (August 16, 2013), Website http://notrickszone.com/2013/08/09/major-danish-daily-warns-globe-may-be-on-path-to-little-ice-age-much-colder-winters-dramatic-consequences/#sthash.1Iii5R3m.dpbs; David Rose, "And Now it's Global COOLING! Record Return of Arctic Ice Cap as it Grows by 60% in a Year," *The Daily Mail* (September 7, 2013), Website www.dailymail.co.uk/news/article-2415191/And-global-COOLING-Return-Arctic-ice-cap-grows-29-year.html; "Climate Science: Stubborn Things," *The Economist* (October 5, 2013); "Global Warming: Who Pressed the Pause Button?" *The Economist* (March 8, 2014); "No Global Warming for 17 Years 3 Months—A Monckton Analysis," Climate Depot (December 18, 2013), Website www.climatedepot.com/2013/12/18/no-global-warming-for-17-years-3-months-a-monckton-analysis; and Thomas Karl, Antony Arguez, et al., "Possible Artifacts of Data Biases in the Recent Global Surface Warming Hiatus," American Association for the Advancement of Science (AAAS) (June 4, 2015), Website www.sciencemag.org/content/early/2015/06/03/science.aaa5632.full—a paper on overestimating temperatures prior to 2000, which if substituted into the historical temperature record would show that the "hiatus" in temperature rises since 2000 is a statistical aberration; that is, global warming has not slowed. This begs the question as to the reliability of temperature data to support global warming.

88 "Why Scientists are (Almost) Certain that Climate Change is Man-Made," *The Economist* (November 2, 2014).

89 Global Warming Petition Project, Website www.petitionproject.org.

90 See the Cliff Claven comments contained in article "Major European Utility Set for Dramatic Renewable Energy Transformation," *Renewable Energy World* (October 31, 2013), Website www.renewableenergyworld.com/rea/news/article/2013/10/major-european-utility-set-for-dramatic-transformation. The Cliff Claven comments also include a Website to upload the 2013 IPCC report and a study on exaggerating the impact of CO_2. See Websites www.climatechange2013.org/images/report/WG1AR5_ALL_FINAL.pdf and http://marshall.org/climate-change/why-has-there-been-no-global-warming-for-the-last-decade. Note the pedigree of the authors in the latter report.

91 Weather Data Depot, Website www.weatherdatadepot.com.

92 "The Frankenstorm," livescience, Website www.livescience.com/24380-hurricane-sandy-status-data.html.

93 "Looking Back" and "Making Records," *Weatherwise* (January/February, 2006).

94 Hurricane Research Division of National Oceanic and Atmospheric Administration (NOAA), Website www.aoml.noaa.gov/hrd/tcfaq/E11.html.

95 "Hurricanes and Climate Change," Union of Concerned Scientists, Website www.ucsusa.org/global_warming/science_and_impacts/impacts/hurricanes-and-climate-change.html#.Vcn31PkZl_A. This Website shows that the proportion of category 4 and 5 hurricanes on a global basis is increasing; that is, storms are becoming more severe. However, that does not mean that their number is increasing.

    The following Website concludes that "the collective global frequency of all global hurricane landfalls and the minor and major subsets shows considerable interannual variability but no significant linear trend," which is reflected in Figure 2 on the Website. This means little statistical support for a rise, or fall, in the number of global hurricanes/cyclones. J. Weinkle, R. Maue, and R. Pielke, "Historical Tropical Cyclone Landfalls," American Meteorological Society (July 1, 2012), Website http://sciencepolicy.colorado.edu/admin/publication_files/2012.04.pdf.

96 Anthony Watts, "Ice at the North Pole in 1958 and 1959—Not So Thick," Watts Up With That? (April 26, 2009), Website http://wattsupwiththat.com/2009/04/26/ice-at-the-north-pole-in-1958-not-so-thick.

97 "Arctic Sea Ice 'More Resilient' Than Thought," Reporting Climate Science (December 15, 2014), Website www.reportingclimatescience.com/news-stories/article/arctic-sea-ice-more-resilient-than-thought.html. See also Danish Meteorological Institute, Website http://ocean.dmi.dk/arctic/ice-cover.uk.php.

98 "Why is Antarctic Sea Ice Increasing as Arctic Ice Declines?" EarthSky (September 27, 2014), Website http://Earthsky.org/Earth/while-arctic-sea-ice-declines-in-2014-antarctic-sea-ice-increases.

99 Luis Henao and Seth Borenstein, "Glacial Melting in Antarctica Makes Continent the 'Ground Zero of Global Climate Change,'" *Huffington Post* (February 27, 2015), Website www.huffingtonpost.com/2015/02/27/the-big-melt-antarctica_n_6766290.html.

100 "December Ends, 2014 in Review," National Snow and Ice Data Center (January, 2015), Website www.nsidc.org/arcticseaicenews/2015/01/december-ends.

101 "National Overview—Great Lakes Ice," National Oceanic and Atmospheric Administration (NOAA) National Climatic Data Center (February, 2015), Website www.ncdc.noaa.gov/sotc/national/2014/2/supplemental/page-6.

102 R. Poore, R. Williams, and C. Tracey, "Sea Level and Climate," Fact Sheet 002-00, US Coast Guard, Website http://pubs.usgs.gov/fs/fs2-00.

103 "Treading Water," *National Geographic* (February, 2015), describes what Florida will be like if the climatologists' assessments of a five foot rise in the ocean level and a 3°F+ rise in temperatures by 2100 occurred. In the Southeast, an average of 95°F or more days would increase from an annual 8 days to an additional 48–130 days.

104 Snowball Earth, Website www.snowballEarth.org.

105 It is disconcerting that NOAA Websites showing statistical data on ocean levels that were previously available when preparing this book are gone ("No server is available to handle this request"), such as "Tides and Currents," Website http://tidesandcurrents.noaa.gov/sltrends/mslGlobalTrendsTable.htm, and "Sea Level Trends," Website http://tidesandcurrents.noaa.gov/sltrends/sltrends.html. A search of the NOAA Website provided no data on ocean levels other than bland statements that ocean levels are rising. Withdrawing vital data from a public arena makes it difficult to have an informed public making rational decisions.

106 "Global Mean Sea Level," Carbon Dioxide Information Analysis Center, US Department of Energy, Website http://cdiac.ornl.gov/trends/sea_level.html.

107 Helen Briggs, "US Sea Level North of New York City 'Jumped by 128mm,'" BBC News Science & Environment (February 24, 2015), Website www.bbc.com/news/science-environment-31604953.

108 "Atmospheric Concentrations of Greenhouse Gases," Environmental Protection Agency (EPA), Website www.epa.gov/climatechange/science/indicators/ghg/ghg-concentrations.html.

109 *BP Energy Statistics* (London, UK: British Petroleum, 2015).

110 The atomic weight of carbon is 12, and is 16 for oxygen. The atomic weight of carbon dioxide of one carbon atom and two oxygen atoms is 44. Thus a ton of carbon, when burned, produces 44/12 tons of carbon dioxide; or alternatively tons of carbon dioxide can be converted to tons of carbon equivalent by the ratio 12/44.

111 PhysLink.com, Website www.physlink.com/Education/AskExperts/ae328.cfm. The calculation is actually straightforward, starting with atmospheric pressure of 14.7 pounds per square inch and multiplying by the area of the Earth with a radius of 4,000 miles expressed in square inches.

112 "Global Carbon Cycle," University of New Hampshire, Website http://globecarboncycle.unh.edu/CarbonCycleBackground.pdf. (A petagram is 1 billion metric tons.)

113 "The Case of the Missing Carbon," *National Geographic* (February, 2004).

114 "Acids, Bases, & the pH Scale," Science Buddies, Website www.sciencebuddies.org/science-fair-projects/project_ideas/Chem_AcidsBasespHScale.shtml.

115 "A Primer on pH," National Oceanic and Atmospheric Administration (NOAA), Website www.pmel.noaa.gov/co2/story/A+primer+on+pH.

116 Phil Jardine, "Patterns in Palaeontology: The Paleocene–Eocene Thermal Maximum," Palaeontology, Website www.palaeontologyonline.com/articles/2011/the-paleocene-eocene-thermal-maximum.

117 "Ocean Acidification: Carbon Dioxide Is Putting Shelled Animals at Risk," National Geographic Critical Issues, Website http://ocean.nationalgeographic.com/ocean/critical-issues-ocean-acidification. See also "Ocean Acidification," Wikipedia: The Free Encyclopedia, Website http://en.wikipedia.org/wiki/Ocean_acidification.

118 David Braun, "Ocean Acidification Threatens Food Webs, 150 Scientists Warn," National Geographic Ocean Views (February 2, 2009), Website http://voices.nationalgeographic.com/2009/02/02/ocean_acidification.

119 James Delingpole, "NOAAgate: How 'Ocean Acidification' Could Turn Out to be the Biggest Con Since Michael Mann's Hockey Stick," Breitbart (December 23, 2014), Website www.breitbart.com/london/2014/12/23/noaagate-how-ocean-acidification-could-turn-out-to-be-the-biggest-con-since-michael-manns-hockey-stick.

120 "Gas Guzzlers" by Deborah Franklin, *Smithsonian* (February, 2004).

121 Euan Mearns, "What is the Real Price of Obama's CO2 Plans?" Oilprice.com (August 6, 2015), Website http://oilprice.com/Latest-Energy-News/World-News/What-Is-The-Real-Price-Of-Obamas-CO2-Plans.html, is the primary source of data.

11 Environment and Energy Sustainability

No one argues that anthropomorphic carbon dioxide has raised levels to 400 ppm, far beyond that experienced in the last 400,000 years. During this time, carbon dioxide cycled from 200 ppm during long periods of glaciation to 280–290 ppm during short interglacial periods of warm climate, the same level at the start of the Industrial Revolution. Now at 400 ppm, the central question is how anthropomorphic carbon dioxide affects climate. No one really knows the outcome of heightened carbon dioxide emissions and addition of pollutants (SOx and NOx, hydrocarbons of which methane figures predominantly) to the atmosphere, and that is the crux of the matter. Climate is a nonlinear, discontinuous, chaotic system chock full of feedback systems beyond our comprehension. We find ourselves unarmed in an arena that no one has been in before and we do not know what is behind the closed gate and we do not want to know. Yet the gate will be opened.

This concluding chapter begins with actions that have been taken to protect the atmospheric environment with a focus on US regulations. They were pathfinders and have inspired other national governments to develop environmental regulations concerning the atmosphere on their own and then morphed into international regulations under UN auspices. US environmental policies have contributed to a significant decline in water and airborne pollution. They internalized what had been an external cost of environmental degradation not borne by private industry. By internalizing these costs, a favorable cost–benefit relationship could be constructed to act as an incentive for industry to clean up its act. A series of climate change conferences have been held on anthropomorphic carbon dioxide influences on climate.

Energy efficiency and conservation are means to sustain an acceptable life style with less energy consumption. Efficiency is driving the same distance in an automobile that gets better mileage saving both on cost and energy. Conservation is living a life with less energy intensity such as substituting a healthier lifestyle of some bicycling and walking for driving. Efficiency and conservation can reduce per capita energy consumption without affecting living standards. Efficiency and conservation play vital roles in addressing energy needs, but they can be outdone by population growth, by raising the living standards of billions of those who live somewhere between severe and abject poverty, and by a return to cheap energy, which removes the incentive to be efficient and conserve energy.

The chapter ends with guidelines for an energy sustainable society that applies to today's world, but contains principles that will last for centuries, not decades. Massive population growth in the last century and a societal and economic structure built on a foundation of fossil fuel energy makes us vulnerable to another Easter Island tragedy. Doing nothing and exhausting fossil fuels will not be the destruction of a civilization on one small remote island in the Pacific Ocean; this time we are talking about an entire planet. Thus on a time horizon spanning centuries, human society has to take actions that will lead to a slow but inexorable elimination of fossil fuels before these resources are entirely consumed. This is not a hypothetical exercise because one day, even if a century away, fossil fuels as a finite resource will be exhausted; if not one century, then two. What difference does it make when human history is 6,000 years old and a single lifetime in today's world can easily span nearly a century? We should be thinking about the next 600, not the next 60, years. The sustainability of society that we have constructed is not threatened but extinguished if we run out of fossil fuels before alternative sources of energy have been substituted. But we do have time, and actions are already underway to reduce our dependence on fossil fuels; it is just a matter to ensure that we stay the course and not be diverted away from this ultimate goal.

Environment

Speculation concerning climate change over the next 100 years tends to mask what is happening to the environment now, best epitomized by the Asian brown cloud, which on its own is an agent of climate change.[1] The Asian brown cloud covers thousands of square miles and can be seen from space. It has been estimated that 4,000 people die daily from the effects of the Asian brown cloud in China alone. The principal culprit is PM2.5s, a fine particulate matter with a diameter smaller than 2.5 microns, while human hair has a diameter between 40 and 120 microns. These particles, lodged in the lungs, are capable of triggering heart attacks, strokes, lung cancer, and asthma, affecting 1.6 million a year and responsible for 17 percent of China's mortalities.[2] The World Health Organization (WHO) maintains that those immersed in a cloud of pollution suffer from an increased incidence of acute respiratory infections, pulmonary disease, lung cancer, tuberculosis, and asthma. WHO estimates that outdoor air pollution kills an estimated 2.6 million people per year in Asia (not just China), and indoor pollution from burning biomass and coal for cooking and heating kills another 3.3 million, which when adjusted for those who die from a combination of outdoor and indoor air pollution raises the total to seven million deaths per year.[3]

The Asian brown cloud originates mostly in China and India from burning biomass and coal without environmental safeguards as required in developed nations. In the developed world, electrostatic precipitators capture over 99 percent of the fly ash, solid particles in combustion emissions, which is trucked to a disposal site or consumed in making cinder blocks. Desulfurization units (sulfur scrubbers) remove about 98 percent of sulfur before it can enter the atmosphere. In India and China, much of the particulate residues and sulfur emissions from burning a generally low-quality, low-energy coal enter the atmosphere as ash, soot, sulfur dioxide, and other pollutants. However, it must be said that China has taken action to install precipitators and desulfurization units on its utility plants in recent years and to build more environmentally sound and energy efficient coal burning utilities to replace old smokers. But China still has a long way to go, as any photo taken in Beijing "clearly" shows.

Burning coal is not entirely to blame; other major contributors are burning biomass and exhaust fumes from a rapidly growing population of motor vehicles throughout Asia. Some motor vehicles made in Asia (not in Japan) have substandard environmental safeguards compared to those produced in the West and cannot be exported because they would fail pollution emission standards. These vehicles contribute to airborne pollution more than

Western-made motor vehicles. Two-cycle gasoline engines found on small motorcycles throughout Asia are horrific polluters. However, China is embarking on a program to enhance the emission standards of its domestically manufactured motor vehicles, not only to try to clean up its environment but also to open export markets in the West.

The Asian brown cloud hovers over mainland Asia and island nations of Southeast Asia, affecting the health of billions of people. At times the overhanging haze is so thick that one can look directly at the diffused light of the sun. The 2-mile-thick Asian brown cloud reduces the amount of sunlight reaching the ground by 10–15 percent, causing global dimming, just the opposite of global warming. Sunlight warming the lower atmosphere, or troposphere, rather than the Earth's surface, is a form of global cooling, but it increases the frequency and strength of thermal inversions, which trap large amounts of pollution near the Earth's surface. With less sunlight reaching the Earth's surface, the Asian brown cloud reduces evaporation and photosynthesis, affecting the amount and pattern of precipitation and agricultural productivity.

Seasonal prevailing winds over India spread pollution to Nepal in the Himalayas or over much of the Indian Ocean. Seasonal prevailing winds over China spread pollution to otherwise isolated, idyllic, and pristine tourist meccas in the Pacific Islands where it is noticed, or at times as far away as Los Angeles where it goes unnoticed. The Los Angeles basin frequently suffers from a temperature inversion that traps pollution near the surface, unable to escape over the surrounding mountains. Early explorers noted overhanging smoke from native Indian fires, but now it is caused by the hydrocarbon emissions of motor vehicles. As late as the 1930s, the probability of having a very clear summer afternoon, with a visual range in excess of 35 miles, was 21 percent, but by the 1940s, increased population of automobiles had dropped the probability by a factor of 100 to 0.2 percent. However, California's strict emission regulations in recent decades have noticeably ameliorated air pollution.

Since global dimming prevents the full force of the sun's radiation from reaching the surface of the Earth, it counteracts global warming. Mankind may be trapped in a web of pollutants that to some degree counterbalance the worst effects of the other. Both global dimming and warming have to be dealt with together to avoid one or the other from unduly influencing the climate to the detriment of humanity. Another example of one type of pollution counteracting another is carbon dioxide, methane, and sulfur oxides. Carbon dioxide and methane hinder the escape of infrared radiation from the Earth to space, heating up the atmosphere. An aerosol mist of sulfuric acid from SOx emissions collects on cloud tops, increasing their albedo, or reflectivity, thereby reducing the amount of sunlight that enters the atmosphere. SOx eventually falls to the Earth as acid rain, inhibiting wetland bacteria from producing methane (swamp gas) from decaying plant matter. Combustion particles (soot) can hang in the atmosphere, shielding the sun from the Earth's surface (global dimming), but, when deposited on glaciers, reduces albedo and accelerates melting (global warming).

Records over the past 35 years of a declining rate of water evaporation on the Earth's surface, despite higher average air temperatures, confirm that less sunlight is reaching the surface. Solar radiation reaching the surface of the Earth, measured in watts per square meter, has declined on average from 191 in 1958 to 190 in 1965 to 182 in 1975 to 176 in 1985 to 171 in 1992, an accelerating trend.[4] Overall, between 1950 and the 1990s, global dimming has reduced solar radiation by 9 percent in Antarctica, 10 percent in the US, 30 percent in Russia, and 16 percent in the UK for an overall reduction of 22 percent.[5] Evidence suggests that global dimming is continuing into the twenty-first century.[6]

Global dimming may be an antidote for global warming by reducing the amount of solar radiation reaching the Earth's surface, but it also affects agricultural output by reducing evaporation, resulting in less rainfall and photosynthesis. Global dimming may be partly responsible for severe droughts afflicting parts of the Earth.

See the Companion Website for a section on US Clean Air Acts: www.routledge. com/cw/nersesian.

Cap-and-Trade Emissions Trading

The innovative part of the 1990 Clean Air Act took advantage of internalizing an externality by instituting an economic benefit to encourage pollution abatement through emissions trading. Installing scrubbers based on a coal price differential between high- and low-sulfur coal was an example of an economic incentive to reduce pollution, but emissions trading takes a more direct approach. Although the beginning of emissions trading can be traced back to the 1977 Act, the 1990 Act brought it to the forefront. The Act introduced a market-based system for the buying and selling of rights or allowances to release pollution emissions. A pollution emitting plant could invest in environmental equipment to decrease its emissions. If the equipment installation lowered sulfur emissions below the cited allowance or right of a company to emit a pollutant, the company had the right to sell emission allowances (or rights to pollute), up to its maximum allowance, to companies that exceeded their mandatory emission allowances. The value of these emission allowances was to be determined by the market forces of supply and demand, just like the value of corporate shares and commodities.

Buying and selling pollution emission allowances do not in any way abrogate the reduction in total emissions required by the Act. It simply redistributes the amount of allowed pollution among emitting plants. This gives companies flexibility to reduce emissions either by taking direct action to do so by investing in pollution reduction equipment or by buying excess allowances from other emitters. At the end of a compliance period, every emitter must have Environmental Protection Agency (EPA) issued and purchased allowances equal to its pollution emissions to avoid having to pay stiff fines. This ability to buy allowances is called allowance trading, or cap and trade. Cap and trade means that there is an aggregate emissions cap, or a maximum limit, on total allowable emissions. The overall cap on emissions is initially set lower than the historical level of emissions, which gives value to allowances. As the overall cap is progressively lowered with time, so is each individual pollution emitter's allowance limit. If a company's emissions are less than its allowance limit as determined by the EPA, then the company has the right to sell the difference to those whose emissions are above their allowance limit. If a company's emissions are above its allowance limit, then it must buy the difference or reduce operations to cut pollution or install pollution abatement equipment. Cap and trade allows companies to act in the most economical way to reduce pollution by investing in pollution abatement equipment, by buying allowances from a company that has available allowances, by reducing operating levels, or any combination thereof that best serves their financial interests.

Rights to pollute have a positive impact in that plants that go the full mile to reduce pollution are rewarded for beating their individual allowance limit by making money selling their excess emission allowances. Plants that have not fully complied with their individual allowance limits now have a financial incentive to do so because of the cost of buying emission allowances above their allotted allowances. A plant can use the revenue from selling excess emission allowances to justify its investment in reducing pollution emissions below the legal requirement. A plant buying sulfur emission allowances can use the cost to justify investing in emission abatement equipment. As the aggregate cap on emissions shrinks with time, these allowances, or rights to pollute, are apt to gain value to the greater benefit of those who are below their allowance limit and to the detriment of those who are above. Bonus allowances are rewarded to power plants that install clean coal technology to further reduce pollution emissions, use nonpolluting renewable energy sources such as wind and solar, or encourage energy conservation to reduce the amount of power that has to be generated. Allowances earned by not having to generate megawatts of electricity via energy efficiency or conservation can be considered nega-watts, which under these circumstances have monetary value, meaning that money can be earned by not producing electricity. Bonus allowances can be saved for future use or sold to justify taking more costly actions to reduce pollution. Negawatts embody the concept of fewer resources and less energy to achieve the same results.

Since 1997, between 15 and 25 million tons of sulfur allowances have been traded annually at a generally increasing price of $100 per ton in 1997 to a little over $200 per ton in early 2004. The price escalated sharply in the second half of 2004, reaching $485 in the fall of 2004, $700 in early 2005, and broke through $1,000 in October 2005, peaking at $1,600 at the beginning of 2006, before sharply falling thereafter to $500 in mid-2006 and to a little below $400 in the first half of 2008. Prices continued to fall to $150 per ton in July 2008 and to less than $100 per ton in March 2009 as demand for sulfur allowances waned in the wake of reduced electricity output caused by the economic recession. In 2010, most sulfur allowances sold around $39 per ton, $2–$5 per ton in 2011, $0.50–$1 per ton in 2012, and less in 2013 and 2014 with a significant shrinkage in volume.[7] The reason for sulfur allowances becoming essentially worthless was the success of Obama's "war on coal" that led to the closure of many coal burning generating plants where coal was replaced by non-sulfur emitting natural gas and renewable energy. Sulfur allowances have little value when aggregate sulfur emissions are below the maximum allowed, and most companies are below their allowable limits.

The benefit of cap and trade is lowering overall investment in pollution control equipment by making it possible for companies to avoid high pollution abatement costs by buying excess allowances from companies with low pollution abatement costs. However, at $1,600 per ton, companies must have taken a second look at investing in pollution control equipment rather than buying excess allowances, whereas their thinking changed with a falloff in the value of allowances. Nevertheless, cap and trade emissions trading is estimated to have reduced the overall cost of pollution abatement by about one-third over a cost indifferent command requirement. This resulted in smaller electricity rate hikes for consumers, who, ultimately, foot the bill for pollution abatement.

See the Companion Website for a section on the Cross-State Air Pollution Rule: www.routledge.com/cw/nersesian.

Classifying Carbon Dioxide as a Pollutant

The public was largely unaware of global warming when the Clean Air Acts were originally legislated and for that reason did not include carbon dioxide and other greenhouse gas emissions as air pollutants. In April 2009 EPA declared that the effects of carbon dioxide and five other greenhouse gases endangered public welfare and human health as a consequence of global warming. Considering carbon dioxide a pollutant was contentious, as this "pollutant" is absolutely vital to plant growth and the existence of plant eating animals. It is also vital to retaining global heat, otherwise the planet could cool anywhere from 2°C to 30°C, which would be intolerably cold for life and may lead to another episode of snowball Earth.[8] Moreover, defining carbon dioxide as a pollutant makes humans and animals polluters simply by exhaling. SOx and NOx are pollution emissions, and a Supreme Court decision that carbon dioxide is a pollutant is a political decision, not scientific fact. The purpose of declaring carbon dioxide along with other greenhouse gases (some of which are pollutants) was a prelude to establishing a national cap and trade program in GHG (greenhouse gas) emissions. One might argue that a national GHG emission program was in reaction to regional consortia of Canadian provinces and US states taking the initiative to set up GHG emission reduction programs. These included the Western Climate Initiative (7 states, 4 provinces), Midwest Greenhouse Gas Reduction Accord (6 states, 1 province), and Regional Greenhouse Gas Initiative (10 states).[9] A single standard for the entire nation would be preferable to states or regions having differing standards.

Clean Air Acts have proven to be contentious, complicated, and difficult to administrate. The succession of acts and amendments to the acts manifest the challenges faced by the federal government in trying to improve the quality of the air in 50 states. While one can argue that the environment is far from pollution-free and we still have a way to go for a clean air environment, nevertheless, Clean Air Acts have been effective in reducing pollution. Between 1980 and 2012, sulfur dioxide emissions were down by 78 percent, nitrogen dioxide 55 percent, ozone 25 percent, fine particles 37 percent, and course particles 27 percent, plus marked reductions in carbon monoxide, VOCs, and lead emissions by a whopping 98 percent, the single greatest achievement of Clean Air Acts.[10]

Montreal Protocol

Ozone is a molecule of three oxygen atoms, not the normal two, and is constantly being created and destroyed in the stratosphere, 9 to 30 miles above the Earth. In an unpolluted stratosphere, the natural cycle of production and decomposition is at the right equilibrium to maintain a protective layer of ozone to filter out harmful ultraviolet B-rays that cause skin cancer. But manmade chemicals such as chlorofluorocarbons (CFCs) affect the ozone layer. CFCs are a refrigerant in refrigerators and air conditioning units, a propellant in aerosol sprays, and are used in solvents and foam-blowing agents. CFCs escape into the atmosphere through leaks in refrigerators and air conditioning units in buildings, rooms, and motor vehicles, and from the failure to remove CFCs from disposed units. As an aerosol propellant, CFCs ultimately end up in the atmosphere where they rise to the stratosphere and decompose, releasing chlorine, which acts as a catalyst speeding up the decomposition of ozone. This thins the ozone layer to the point of creating an ozone hole, first noticed over Antarctica, where it grew in size to include the southern tip of

South America. Those caught in the ozone hole were exposed to ultraviolet B-rays and began to suffer from a higher incidence of malignant melanoma, a dangerous form of skin cancer. While the ozone hole was mostly restricted to Antarctica, there was also evidence of thinning of the ozone layer over the Arctic that could potentially affect those living in northern Europe.

The Montreal Protocol on Substances That Deplete the Ozone Layer is a landmark international agreement for controlling air pollution on a global scale. Originally signed in 1987 and substantially amended in 1990 and 1992, the Montreal Protocol made it obligatory on the part of signatory nations to phase out production of CFCs and substitute other chemicals that fulfill the same function without affecting ozone. The Protocol's timetable calls for an 85 percent phase-out of CFCs by 2007, a 100 percent phase-out of CFCs and halons (used in fire extinguishers) by 2010, and a 100 percent phase-out of methyl bromide (a fumigant) by 2015.[11] The Montreal Protocol was very successful in reducing CFCs and its success encouraged world leaders to proceed with the Kyoto Protocol to reduce greenhouse gas emissions for countering global warming. With regard to the ozone hole, the peak 2014 hole was 23 million square kilometers, about the same as in 2013, but less than peak values in 2006–2009.[12]

Kyoto Protocol

The Kyoto Protocol is an international agreement signed in 1997 to reduce carbon dioxide and other greenhouse gas emissions.[13] The Protocol calls for a reduction in greenhouse gas emissions to an average of 5 percent below 1990 levels to be achieved between 2008 and 2012. Greenhouse gases are defined as carbon dioxide, methane, nitrous oxides, hydrofluorocarbons (HFCs), perfluorocarbons (PFCs), and sulfur hexafluoride. Table 11.1 shows the relative strength of the greenhouse effect of these gases compared to carbon dioxide and their average lifetime once in the atmosphere.[14]

HFCs and PFCs represent two families of similar chemicals reflected by the wide spread in their global warming factors and lifetimes. Table 11.1 is a bit unsettling in that carbon dioxide has the lowest impact on global warming of all greenhouse gases. Methane has 28 times the impact as the same volume of carbon dioxide. One unit of volume of sulfur hexafluoride has the warming potential of 23,900 units of volume of carbon dioxide. Of course, there is far less methane and other greenhouse gases in the atmosphere than carbon dioxide. The lifetime of carbon dioxide varies considerably depending on whether it is absorbed relatively quickly by the ocean or more slowly by photosynthesis or by marine

Table 11.1 Global Warming Potential and Atmospheric Lifetime of Greenhouse Gases

Greenhouse Gas	Average Lifetime in Atmosphere (Years)	100-Year Global Warming Potential
Carbon dioxide	Varies: 20–many thousands	1
Methane	8–12	28
Nitrous oxide	121	265
Hydrofluorocarbons	1.5–264	140–11,700
Perfluorocarbons	3,200–50,000	6,500–9,200
Sulfur hexafluoride	3,200	23,900

shells, or if it simply remains part of the atmosphere for thousands of years. Methane has a much shorter lifetime of about 8–12 years (depending on information source) before being removed by oxidation, and through a complex set of reactions transitions to carbon dioxide. But HFCs and PFCs and sulfur hexafluoride, once in the atmosphere, remain forever from a human perspective. Figure 11.1 shows the largest greenhouse gas emitting nations in terms of carbon dioxide.[15]

Historically the largest emitter of carbon dioxide was the US. In 2008 China overtook the US with a 22 percent share of global emissions versus 20 percent for the US. With China's reliance on coal burning electricity generating plants to meet much of its incremental demand for electricity and with the US decreasing its reliance on coal, China is now far ahead of the US as a greenhouse gas emitter. The two nations are responsible for 38 percent of global carbon dioxide emissions, while every other nation pales in comparison. Any leadership in reducing carbon dioxide emissions must come first and foremost from China followed by the US. The EU, in the aggregate, would also have to be an important participant in reducing greenhouse gas emissions. However, the EU has already focused on reducing greenhouse gas emissions for years by the aggressive pursuit of renewable energy sources.

Voting for ratifying the Kyoto Protocol was both a straight vote by nation and a weighted vote, depending on a country's volume of greenhouse emissions. The US, the world's greatest contributor to greenhouse gas emissions at that time, had a single vote as a nation and the largest weighted vote based on emissions. The ratification of the Kyoto Protocol required the approval by a minimum of 55 nations, representing an aggregate contribution of 55 percent of greenhouse gas emissions.[16] In 2002, over 90 individual nations had ratified the Protocol, but their aggregate contribution to greenhouse gas emissions was only 37 percent. Ratification of the Protocol was in doubt. The principal objection to the Kyoto Protocol was that, if ratified, only 38 developed nations were obliged to take action to reduce their greenhouse gas emissions. The obligor nations were mainly in Europe, including those in transition to a market economy in central and eastern Europe, plus Ukraine and Russia. Nations outside Europe obliged to reduce

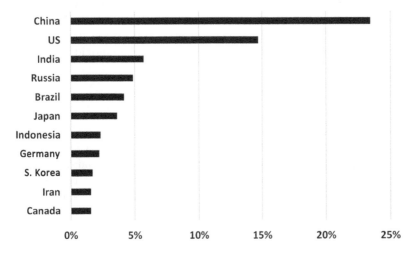

Figure 11.1 Share of Global Carbon Dioxide Emissions (2014)

their greenhouse emissions were the US, Canada, Japan, Australia, and New Zealand. Although developing nations could vote in favor to ratify the Protocol, they were exempt from taking any action to reduce greenhouse gas emissions.

The rationale for limiting the obligation to reduce greenhouse gases to 38 nations (actually 37, since one signatory was the European Community, whose members were separate signatories) was that these nations were most responsible for the presence of greenhouse gases already in the atmosphere. Since developing nations were not responsible for creating the greenhouse gas problem, they should not be held responsible for decreasing their emissions. The counterargument to the obligation being limited to developed nations was that China, India, Mexico, and Brazil, representing 40 percent of the world's population, had become major greenhouse gas emitters in their own right and were expected to be the largest contributors to projected gains.

In 2003, the US and Russia announced that they would not sign the Kyoto Protocol. Both nations feared the adverse economic impact of complying with the Kyoto Protocol on their respective economies and accompanying economic advantage that would accrue to nations that did not have to comply. The combined voting power in terms of greenhouse gas emissions of Russia and the US was sufficient to prevent the Kyoto Protocol from coming into force, but either one switching would swing the vote the other way. In 2004, with 123 nations having ratified the Protocol, representing 44 percent of total emissions, Russia signed the Kyoto Protocol under pressure from European nations, bringing the Protocol into force in February 2005. Australia, a long-time holdout by virtue of being a coal dominated economy, signed in 2008. Excluding the US, the remaining 36 nations became responsible for putting into place policies and procedures to reduce their greenhouse gas emissions to 95 percent of their 1990 levels between 2008 and 2012. Australia eventually agreed to reduce its 2000 emissions by 60 percent by 2050.

The UK and Germany were already close to compliance because of their switch from coal to natural gas for electricity generation after 1990. Other nations had a tougher row to hoe. Compliance could be accomplished by reducing methane, nitrous oxides, HFCs, PFCs, and sulfur hexafluoride rather than focusing on carbon dioxide since these greenhouse gases have a much greater impact on global warming than carbon dioxide on a unit volume basis. Thus a relatively small reduction in these gases counts the same as a relatively large reduction in carbon dioxide emissions at potentially less cost. Greenhouse gas emissions can be reduced by building nuclear and sustainable power plants (hydro, wind, solar, tidal), switching from coal to natural gas, and by creating carbon dioxide sinks such as reforestation projects.

Doha Amendment

The Kyoto Protocol operated under the Marrakesh Rules from 2008 to 2010. The Doha Amendment to the Kyoto Protocol was adopted in late 2012 to cover the period 2013 to 2020. As of August 2015, 40 nations have ratified the Doha Amendment where 144 instruments of acceptance are required for the amendment to enter into force.[17] Most of the mandated reduction on greenhouse gas emissions falls on European nations where they're obligated to reduce greenhouse gas emissions 8 percent from 1980 base levels if the Protocol enters into force. Australia, New Zealand, Canada, and Japan are also included but with different goals. No nation among the developing world including China, India, and Brazil have any obligation under the Doha Amendment, although, as in the Kyoto Protocol, they are eligible to vote for its ratification.[18] The central weakness of the Kyoto Protocol remains unaddressed: the largest emitters and those with the greatest growth in greenhouse gas emissions have no obligation to cut their emissions. And those nations that do have such obligations, namely Europe, have already taken massive steps to cut greenhouse gas emissions. Thus the Protocol as amended has no real substance in reducing greenhouse gas emissions.

Emissions Trading System (ETS)

A cap and trade program for greenhouse gases in terms of tons of carbon was set up by the signatory nations to the Kyoto Protocol. Its structure is similar to the cap and trade program established by the US Clean Air Act of 1990 for sulfur oxide emissions. The emissions trading system (ETS) for the EU is built around a National Allocation Plan, whereby each member nation is assigned an annual allotment of greenhouse gas emissions. These are broken down and reassigned to an estimated 12,000 greenhouse gas emitters targeted for emission reduction. These include power and heat generation facilities, oil refineries, coking ovens, and production facilities for ferrous metals, cement, glass, brick, porcelain, pulp, and paper, which, in the aggregate, are responsible for nearly half of European carbon emissions. Targeted companies can participate in an offset program, which compensates for additional emissions from a new plant or an expansion of an existing plant. Targeted companies can select a downstream emissions program, which focuses on reducing greenhouse gas emissions at the point of release to the atmosphere such as during combustion, or an upstream program, which focuses on the characteristics of a fuel such as substituting natural gas for coal.

ETS was set up by first establishing an aggregate limit or cap on emissions that is stepped down over time. For trading to be successful, individual participants must have divergent compliance costs in order to create different cost saving benefits. Companies that can reduce their emissions at a lower cost than others should do so to the maximum practicable extent. This allows the companies to profit from selling emission allowances that are below their stipulated maximum allowances to those facing a high cost for lowering emissions. By purchasing these allowances, companies can avoid making a costly investment in pollution abatement equipment. The accurate monitoring of actual emissions and effective enforcement are also part of an emissions trading program to ensure that every greenhouse gas emitter holds enough emission entitlements and trading allowances to cover its actual emissions or face stiff fines.[19]

Exchange markets have been established, with others in the process of being set up, in Europe, the US, China, Korea, Japan, and New Zealand for trading greenhouse gas emissions plus trading pollution allowances for SOx and NOx. The largest ETS market accounting for 75 percent of greenhouse gas emissions trading is the EU followed by the US. In 2005, 2.15 billion tons of carbon dioxide equivalent were traded globally, in 2010 2.3 billion tons, in 2013 3.15 billion tons, in 2015 4.6 billion tons, and the estimated volume traded in 2016 is expected to be 6.78 billion tons of carbon dioxide equivalent.[20]

Emissions trading requires a properly organized exchange market to provide ease of trading, transparency of market information to ensure that all participants know the price and volume of every transaction, and standardization of contracts between buyers and sellers to simplify ownership and transfer plus settlement of disputes. A well-organized market provides access to speculators and traders, whose participation lends depth (volume) to the market. This gives hedgers an opportunity to take a position against an adverse change in the price of greenhouse gas emission rights. Hedging is important if the future value of greenhouse gas emission rights is financially supporting the purchase of pollution abatement equipment.

An alternative to cap and trade is baseline and credit, a method in which an emissions baseline is defined. A participant takes actions to reduce emissions below the baseline. If successful, an emitter is granted credits for the difference between actual emissions and the baseline at the end of the compliance period. These credits can then be sold to those emitters requiring credits to meet their emission baselines or banked for future use or sale. Borrowing involves the use of allowances or credits on the basis that they will be credited in the future when, for instance, emission control devices have been installed. Banking and borrowing can be similar to the workings of a commercial bank where banked credits (deposits) are borrowed at some "interest" charge.[21]

Clean Development Mechanism (CDM)

In addition to emissions trading, the Kyoto Protocol established the Clean Development Mechanism (CDM) as another means of reducing greenhouse gas emissions. This allows nonparticipants, that is, nongreenhouse gas emitters, to earn carbon credits by implementing a program that reduces emissions or creates a greenhouse gas sink. Carbon credits can then be sold to emitters in need of emission allowances.[22] The economic basis for CDM is that reduction of carbon dioxide at its source may cost $15 to $100 per ton of carbon, whereas developing a carbon dioxide sink may cost as little as $1 to $4 per ton. The World Bank is a proactive investment banker for carbon finance, and manages a large portfolio of "carbon" loans. The World Bank has set up the Prototype Carbon Fund to demonstrate how to reduce greenhouse gas emissions through the use of CDM in a cost-effective fashion. The Community Development Carbon Fund and Bio Carbon Fund are designed so that small rural communities can benefit from carbon finance by selling credits in sustainable energy projects.

An example of carbon financing is a project to substitute charcoal for coal in pig iron production in Brazil. A plantation of eucalyptus trees was established on degraded pastureland where growing trees are treated as a carbon dioxide sink. After 7 years, trees are harvested and transformed into charcoal as a substitute for coal. Financing was based partly on the economics of the project in the form of revenue generated by selling eucalyptus trees for charcoal production and partly on the sale of carbon credits generated by the plantation as a carbon sink. Another example was an electricity generating plant fueled by methane emissions from a landfill. The project could not be financed solely on the sale of electricity. By selling the project's carbon credits through a World Bank facility to a company obliged to cut greenhouse emissions in accordance with the Kyoto Protocol, enough incremental revenue would be earned for the project to obtain the necessary financing. The financing draws on both the economic benefit of the project to generate electricity and on its environmental benefit of lowering methane emissions to the atmosphere. Nearly 500 projects are in the pipeline in 2015.[23] As of 2015 there are nearly 2,600 registered projects that have already issued certified emission reduction (CER) credits, which by the end of their crediting periods will contribute emissions reductions totaling 4 billion tons of carbon dioxide equivalent. Moreover there are 7,600 projects in the process of being registered plus another 200 projects requesting registration that will contribute another 8.6 billion tons of carbon dioxide by the end of their crediting periods.[24] Projects in the pipeline must run the gamut of conceptualization, approval, validation, registration, and implementation and, in order of importance, are associated with wind, hydro, biomass energy, solar, methane, HDCs, and NOX. Historically, reforestation projects were quite popular. The leading sponsoring nations (beneficiaries) of registered projects are the UK with 33 percent of all projects, Switzerland (28 percent), the Netherlands (9 percent), Japan (8 percent), Sweden (7 percent), and Germany (5 percent). The leading host nations for registered projects are China (49 percent), India (20 percent), and Brazil (4 percent), with Vietnam, Mexico, Indonesia, Thailand, and Malaysia each at 2 percent.

China and India have added a new wrinkle to the story. The Kyoto Protocol sets up the CDM, which permits a company of a signatory nation (primarily European) to either reduce its carbon emissions or buy credits via CDMs where carbon emissions can be reduced at less cost than direct investment in carbon emission controls at the company's facilities. Carbon reduction of planting trees in a reforestation project was a low cost alternative that could be purchased by a carbon emitting utility or industrial plant rather than investing in much more expensive means to reduce carbon emissions at their source. A better example today of CDMs is wind or solar energy projects in developing nations. The irony is that China and India, along with other developing nations, do not participate in the Kyoto Protocol. They do not want to be placed under a mandatory program of reducing carbon emissions because, in their minds, the industrial West is entirely responsible for the buildup of carbon dioxide in the atmosphere. The fact that they now number among the world's heaviest carbon and other pollutant emitters is irrelevant. Yet China, India, and other developing nations enter into CDM projects and freely sell carbon emission credits to participating Kyoto Protocol signatory nations based on wind, solar, and other carbon reducing projects. Then these nations utilize the revenue from selling carbon emission credits to help finance wind, solar, and other carbon reducing projects generating the carbon credits. Selling carbon credits by developing and nonparticipating nations to the Kyoto Protocol participating nations has been criticized as nothing more than a wealth transfer program from developed to developing nations.

The number of projects entering validation peaked at a little over 300 at the start of 2012 and has subsequently collapsed to about 25 since the start of 2013.[25] Fewer projects are a direct consequence of a significant decline in the price of EU ETS and UN CDM allowances because of economic doldrums in Europe and growth in non–carbon emitting solar and wind power installations. Actual carbon dioxide emissions being below maximum allowable amounts for many companies limits the market for allowances.[26] The price of a carbon allowance was 30 euros per ton carbon dioxide in 2008 and fell to an average of 15 euros per ton in 2009 and 2010. In 2011 the price fell further to 8 euros and remained there in 2012, and then fell to an average price of 6 euros in 2013 and 2014.[27] Moreover the number of projects being initiated has also collapsed as low carbon allowance values no longer economically support carbon reduction projects. Since the loss of value is associated with a surplus of allowances, the EU agreed to cut greenhouse gas emissions 40 percent from 1990 levels by 2030, which eventually will restore value to greenhouse gas allowances.[28] But in the meantime, the EU Emission Trading Scheme is languishing, and the lower the price of carbon, the greater the cost differential between renewables and fossil fuels. In addition, more carbon emissions can be added to the atmosphere without a punitive charge, such as burning lignite in Germany and importing coal in the UK for electricity generation.[29]

Non-Kyoto Initiatives to Reduce Greenhouse Gas Emissions

Nonparticipating nations to the Kyoto Protocol are at least concerned about cutting their emissions, which of course include carbon dioxide. China, with much of its population immersed in a heavy haze of pollution, is paying more than lip service to cleaning up its air. China is trying to reduce its reliance on coal and is taking action to cut the exhaust emissions of its domestically produced automobiles, a necessity if China wants to become a major world exporter of automobiles. China's largest automaker has teamed up with Toyota to assemble fuel efficient hybrid automobiles in China. Toyota is also having conversations with two other potential partners to expand production.[30] Beijing was able to significantly reduce air pollution for the 2008 Summer Olympics by curtailing the use of coal by substituting more expensive diesel fuel to generate electricity. Shanghai has taken action along a same vein. Beijing reverted back to coal once the Summer Olympics were over.

Several US states are requiring companies to report on their carbon dioxide emissions, a possible precursor to setting up a program to place a limit on or decrease emissions. A few states require either a carbon cap or an offset requirement for new plants, a few others have set up committees to explore the possibility of carbon sequestration, and a fair number are developing climate action plans. Many states have instituted some means of keeping track of greenhouse gas inventories and/or have issued mandates for renewable energy to play a specified role in meeting electricity demand. The Regional Greenhouse Gas Initiative (RGGI) is the first market-based regulatory program to reduce greenhouse gas emissions from the power sector. Its membership includes Connecticut, Delaware, Maine, Maryland, Massachusetts, New Hampshire, New York, Rhode Island, and Vermont. As a cooperative effort, RGGI implemented a new 2014 cap of 91 million short tons of carbon emissions for the power sector, which then declines 2.5 percent each year from 2015 to 2020. Member states sell emission allowances through auctions and invest the proceeds in energy efficiency, renewable energy, and other consumer benefit programs, spurring innovation in the clean energy economy and creating green jobs.[31] How the August 2015 proposed EPA regulation on reducing carbon emissions by electricity utilities will affect these state and regional initiatives is not known.

The mayors of 850 US cities representing 80 million people have responded to an idea put forth by the mayor of Seattle to have cities contact greenhouse gas emitters to take an inventory of gas emissions. Once the amount of greenhouse gases is known, then it would be possible to establish a goal for cutting emissions. This led to the formation of the US Conference of Mayors Climate Protection Agreement that called for a 7 percent reduction in greenhouse gas emissions from 1990 levels by 2012. While this objective has not been generally met, the organization is active in taking steps and spreading ideas on reducing greenhouse gas emissions.[32] Some utilities are initiating actions to cut greenhouse gases. One utility gave land to the US Fish and Wildlife Service for incorporation into the national refuge system to grow trees as a carbon sink to counter its carbon emissions. Others are looking into carbon sequestration as a means to reduce their carbon emissions. Companies emitting greenhouse gases may one day face potential public and/or shareholder approbation for failing to take some sort of action.

In 2005 the California Air Resources Board adopted the first rules in the US to reduce greenhouse gas emissions from automobiles sold within its jurisdiction. The new rules require automakers to cut greenhouse gas emissions by as much as 25 percent, beginning in the 2009 model year and increasing to 34 percent for 2016 models. Although this unilateral action appears to be in defiance of a provision in the Clean Air Act that requires one set of automobile pollution emission standards for the nation, the Clean Air Act did not originally deal with greenhouse gases until 2009 when they were declared to be air pollutants, therefore subject to EPA regulation. In California, purchasers are required to buy any one of an assortment of environmentally desirable cars. The lowest level is LEV (low emission vehicles) whose emissions of NOX and hydrocarbons are less than those imposed by EPA. To aid in compliance, California imposed gasoline specifications that allowed LEV vehicles to meet state standards. ULEV (ultra low emission vehicles) have emissions 50 percent less than the average new car; SULEV (super ultra low emission vehicles) have emissions less than 90 percent of an average new car; PZEV (partial zero emission vehicles) are the same as SULEV except that there are zero evaporative emissions when the vehicle is idling; and ZEV (zero emission vehicles) are typically electric plug-in or hydrogen fuel vehicles.[33] Hybrid automobiles can meet the more stringent pollution emission standards. In addition, all California residents are required to inspect their vehicles for smog emissions every 2 years.[34] New York State requires that registered vehicles comply with California emission requirements.[35] EPA under the Obama Administration will be promulgating new standards and regulations on motor vehicle greenhouse gas emissions from the smallest motor vehicles to the largest trucks. In recognition of California's initiatives, EPA has provided a waiver to let California set its own standards for greenhouse gas emissions.[36]

Automobile manufacturers have warned that reducing greenhouse gas emissions increases the cost of automobiles from having to redesign the engine, transmission, and air-conditioning systems. But this same warning was given to reduce pollution emissions stemming from earlier Clean Air Acts. Like all corporate costs, the incremental costs of pollution abatement are passed on to consumers in the form of higher prices. When carbon emission legislation is established in the US, then automobiles imported into the world's largest market will also have to abide by these rules. Once a company's automobiles marked for export have reduced their greenhouse gas emissions for sale in the US, it may be cumbersome to have differently designed, higher polluting automobiles marked for domestic consumption. Thus, what California initiated for reducing greenhouse gas emissions from automobiles sold within its jurisdiction may end up not only with the federal government setting uniform standards for the nation, but also affect the entire global automobile manufacturing industry.

Governor Arnold Schwarzenegger signed an executive order in 2005 establishing greenhouse gas emission targets for California to reduce GHG emissions to 1990 levels by 2020 and 80 percent below 1990 levels by 2050. The 2020 GHG reduction target was subsequently codified in California's Global Warming Solutions Act of 2006. In 2013 a bill was introduced that requires the state to plan for carbon reductions through 2050. A "Road to 2050 Board" was set up consisting of the California Energy Commission (CEC), California Air Resources Board (CARB), California Public Utilities Commission (CPUC), California Alternative Energy and Advanced Transportation Financing Authority, California Environmental Protection Agency, California Independent System Operator, and the Governor's Office. The board is to study the best way for meeting a goal of reducing greenhouse gas emissions by 80 percent of 1990 emission levels by 2050 plus the integration of renewable electricity generation into the electric grid to ensure cost-effectiveness and reliability. While some opined that an 80 percent reduction is probably technologically impossible, it might be possible to achieve a 60 percent decline.

The work of the committee will result in new GHG legislation.[37] Passage of such a bill will open the door for emissions trading in greenhouse gases in California. Emissions trading in California and elsewhere would be a boon for solar and wind power providers because their sale of carbon credits would aid in financing new sustainable energy projects. Emissions trading would be a financial burden to coal burning electricity generators and to agriculture, a heavy user of fossil fuels.

See the Companion Website for a section on Climate Change Conferences: www. routledge.com/cw/nersesian.

Efficiency and Conservation

Efficiency is giving up an SUV that gets 10 miles to the gallon for a hybrid that gets 50 miles to the gallon. Thus driving an automobile the same distance consumes less gasoline. Conservation is driving the automobile fewer miles by combining trips, carpooling, and eliminating unnecessary travel. Efficiency is adding insulation to a house to keep it at the same temperature, thereby consuming less heating oil or natural gas. Conservation is lowering the temperature and wearing a warm woolen sweater. Efficiency implies that the same function can be accomplished with less energy. Conservation implies less need for a function.

Energy conservation is a particular way of thinking, or having a mindset, about energy for individuals to undertake a whole range of energy saving actions. These can take the form of wearing heavier clothing rather than tropical short sleeved shirts and shorts inside a house during winter in order to lower room temperatures, cleaning furnace filters, sealing air leaks around windows and doors, and installing insulation. During the summer the largest source of energy savings is relying less on air conditioning and more on natural air circulation, perhaps enduring higher, though not uncomfortable, temperatures. Regardless of the season, turning off unnecessary lights and electronic equipment (televisions, computers), buying "smart" appliances that turn themselves off automatically when not needed, and adopting common sense practices such as running dishwashers and washing machines with full loads can save energy. Though each act saves only a smidgen of energy, the aggregate impact of many individual acts by tens or hundreds of millions of individuals can have a significant impact on energy demand, energy prices, and pollution emissions.[38] Both energy efficiency and conservation have an economic benefit of lower energy costs by reducing demand and an environmental side benefit of reducing pollution emissions.

However, the very success of energy efficiency and conservation programs in lowering energy demand has a perverse effect of increasing energy consumption when prices fall such as driving an energy efficient car on longer trips because of low gasoline prices, or offering vacations in remote locations or importing fresh fruit from New Zealand and Chile because of low jet fuel prices. People who trade in inefficient refrigerators and air conditioning units take advantage of the greater efficiencies by buying larger capacity refrigerators and air conditioning units, negating much of the anticipated savings in energy. The "Rebound Dilemma" is that inefficient refrigerators and air conditioners don't disappear—they appear in second hand markets at greatly discounted prices, purchased by those who cannot afford new models. Thus the impact of introducing greater efficiency appliances is not a saving in energy, but perversely an increase in energy consumption.[39] While there has been a pronounced reduction in power requirements to run refrigerators, this has been somewhat matched by increased power requirements for larger sized and higher definition televisions. China has boosted its sales of fuel efficient vehicles and now requires that all new coal plants over 600 mW be of a supercritical design that reduces fuel consumption by about a third.[40] While this is commendable, larger numbers of vehicles and power plants regardless of their energy efficiency increase energy consumption. Moreover there are circumstances such as larger sized and higher definition televisions where consumers eschew efficiency and energy cost savings for satisfaction.

Energy efficiency is sometimes called the "first fuel" in that it reduces the need for energy. It is also known as "avoided energy"—energy that would have been expanded had the means of enhancing efficiency not been put in place. "First fuel" avoids purchasing larger amounts of energy, but it is not free because of investments needed to enhance efficiency. Worldwide investments in efficiency enhancements in 2012 are estimated to be between $310 and $360 billion. In 2011, 11 IEA member nations in Europe, the US, Japan, and Australia reported avoided energy or energy savings of a cumulative total since 2001 of 1,337 million tons of oil equivalent. As an order of magnitude, this is about twice the annual energy consumption of all Central and South America, about twice that of the Russian Federation, and half of the total energy consumption of China. For 18 IEA nations, the cumulative saving is about 1,740 million tons of oil equivalent since 2001. Avoided energy is decomposed to activities, structure, and efficiency and covers residential, commercial, transportation, and electricity generation.[41]

See the Companion Website for sections on the Energy Star Program, Light Emitting Diodes and Compact Fluorescent Light Bulbs, and the US Green Building Council/LEED: www.routledge.com/cw/nersesian.

Sustainable Energy

The 1987 *Report of the United Nations World Commission on Environment and Development* had a succinct definition of sustainability:

Meeting the needs of the present without compromising the ability of future generations to meet their own needs.

Native American View of Sustainability

Mohawk Indian Chief:

Not until the last tree has fallen, the last river has been poisoned, the last fish has been caught, will man realize that money isn't edible!

Native Indian Proverb:

> We do not inherit the earth from our ancestors; we borrow it from our children.

Extracted from the Great Law of the Iroquois Confederacy:

> In our deliberations, we must consider the impact of our decisions on the next seven generations.

Founding Fathers View on Financial Sustainability

We do well to ponder the thoughts of Thomas Jefferson and George Washington.

Thomas Jefferson:

> Then I say the earth belongs to each...generation during its course, fully and in its own right. The second generation receives it clear of the debts and encumbrances, the third of the second, and so on. For if the first could charge it with a debt, then the earth would belong to the dead and not to the living generation. Then, no generation can contract debts greater than may be paid during the course of its own existence.

George Washington:

> No generation has a right to contract debts greater than what can be paid off during the course of its existence.

Quite obviously we haven't followed the advice of our Founding Fathers, as we have already sunk into a morass of debt that no number of future generations will ever be able to pay off. And we surely don't follow the advice of Native Americans, as our society is anything but sustainable. But the central thought of Native Americans about preserving the future for their posterity can be found in Theodore Roosevelt's concern with preserving the natural heritage of the nation for future generations:

> The greatest good for the greatest number applies to the [number of] people within the womb of time, compared to which those now alive form but an insignificant fraction. Our duty to the whole, including the unborn generations, bids us to restrain an unprincipled present-day minority from wasting the heritage of these unborn generations.

The first national park was Yellowstone, founded in 1872 by President Ulysses Grant. Theodore Roosevelt, remembered as the "conservation" President, founded five national parks, which, with others, became the responsibility of the National Park Service established in 1916 by President Woodrow Wilson.[42]

Easter Island

Easter Island is over 2,000 miles from Tahiti and Chile. To the original inhabitants, Easter Island was an isolated island of plentiful, but finite, resources surrounded by a seemingly infinite ocean. What happened on Easter Island when it ultimately exhausted its resources is pertinent because Earth is an isolated planet of plentiful, but finite, resources surrounded by seemingly infinite space. Whether we admit it or not, we are in danger of exhausting our natural resources. Rough, and some deem optimistic, estimates of 60 years for oil, 80 years for natural gas, and 100 years for coal are not particularly comforting when viewed from the perspective of civilization with at least a 6,000 year history. Like Easter Islanders who had nowhere to go, this is our home planet now and for the foreseeable future. Space travel is a long way off, and a few flying off to Mars to escape a manmade calamity on Earth leaving billions stranded to their fate is not a particularly inviting prospect.

Examination of soil layers on Easter Island, or Rapa Nui to the present inhabitants, revealed an island with abundant plant and animal life for tens of thousands of years. Then around 400 CE the island was discovered and settled by Polynesians, who originally named the island Te Pito O Te Henua (Navel of the World). Natives survived on the bounty of natural animal and plant life on the island and fish in the surrounding waters. Critical for survival were 80-foot-tall Easter Island palms that provided sap and nuts for human consumption and wood to make canoes for fishing. Palms also provided the means to move the massive stone Moai, stone figures for which the island is famous, which now stand in mute testimony to an ecological catastrophe that unfolded around 1500 CE. By then the estimated population had grown to somewhere between 10,000 and 15,000 inhabitants.[43]

This sounds like an awful lot of people descended from a few settlers, but this is the nature of exponential growth. If a party of ten people originally settled on Easter Island and grew at a modest 1 percent per year (which, by the way, is mathematically impossible for the first few generations, but less than the current growth in world population), the number of Easter Islanders would double about every 70 years. That would make nearly 16 doublings of the population in the 1,100 years from 400 to 1500 CE. Double ten 16 times and see what you get. In theory the population would have grown to 567,000, a mathematical consequence of compound exponential growth at 1 percent per year for 1,100 years. It would never have reached this level because, as proven in 1500, a population in excess of 10,000 was sufficient to exhaust the island's natural resources.

A growing population with an increased demand for meat eventually led to the natives feasting on the last animal. More people and no animals promoted more intensive tilling of the land, which first had to be cleared of palms. With fewer palms, erosion increased and, coupled with the pressure to grow more crops, soil fertility declined. Of course, the palms did not go to waste as they were needed to support the leading industry on Easter Island: construction and moving of the Moai plus, of course, making canoes. Fish became more important in the diet as the population grew, animals disappeared, and crop yields fell. Around 1500 the last palm tree was cut down. Social disintegration marked by bloody intertribal warfare, cannibalism, and starvation marked the demise of a civilization.

On Easter of 1722, Dutch explorer Jacob Roggeveen rediscovered the island. It presented a great mystery as the few surviving and impoverished natives had no memory of the tragedy nor did they understand the meaning of the Moai. The gift of Western civilization—infectious disease—ultimately reduced the native population to a remnant of 111 by 1800. In 1888, when the island was annexed by Chile and renamed Rapa Nui, the population had risen to 2,000 (a growth rate considerably in excess of 1 percent!).

Mathematics of Resource Extinction

Suppose that we depend on a forest for supplying wood for fuel and building material. If the forest grows at 3 percent per year and we remove 2 percent of the forest per year, the resource will last forever (a sustainable resource). The forest also lasts forever if 3 percent is removed per year, but care has to be exercised to ensure that removal does not exceed 3 percent. (This is the secret for Native Indians' sustainable society; if a wild herd of deer numbering 1,000 and growing at a rate of 5 percent a year was the sole source of meat, then the annual hunt was not allowed to exceed 50 deer, preferably bucks.) If consumption exceeds the natural rate of production of a forest as a consequence of a growing population that needs more wood for fuel and shelter, or if a new technology is introduced that consumes a great deal of wood such as glass and metal making, then the forest will eventually be consumed (a nonsustainable society).

Referring to Figure 11.2, suppose that a forest consists of 1,000 units of usable wood that increases naturally by 3 percent per year. While the forest is a sustainable resource if consumption is limited to 3 percent or less, at 3.5 and 4 percent the forest as a resource will be reduced by 40 percent and 62 percent in a century. One hundred years in the recorded 6,000 year history of humanity is not very long—for a growing portion of a population, a single lifetime. But this does not accurately describe the situation. What is wrong with this projection is that demand declines in absolute terms over time. For example, in the first year the forest gains 30 units and consumption at 4 percent is 40 units, leaving 990 units for the next year. When the forest is down to 800 units, consumption at 4 percent falls from 40 to 32 units. This is not realistic; there is no reason for demand to decline simply because supply is dwindling. Suppose that consumption remains constant at 40 units with 3 percent growth in forest reserves. Then the forest is transformed to barren land in 52 years. What is more realistic is consumption climbing at 1 unit per year: 40 units in the first year, 41 units the second, and so on, which is reflective of a growing population. Now the forest is gone in 35 years, a single generation. An even more realistic assessment would be consumption starting at 40, but increasing at 2.5 percent per year. Exhaustion occurs even quicker at 27 years.

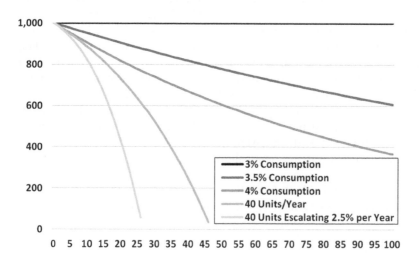

Figure 11.2 Mathematics of Resource Exhaustion

Before the resource is exhausted, other mitigating factors come into play. One is price, a factor not at play on Easter Island. As the forest diminishes in size and consumers and suppliers realize that wood supplies are becoming increasingly scarce, price would increase. The more serious the situation becomes, the higher the price. Higher prices dampen demand and act as an incentive to search for other forests or alternative sources for wood such as coal for energy and plastic for wood products (neither option available to the Easter Islanders). The salubrious impact of price can be seen in world fishing. Fish in the open oceans are being depleted by what can be best described as strip mining the world's oceans. Fishing nets stretch tens of miles, fishing fleets replete with sonar detect schools of fish, and floating fish factories process hundreds of tons of fish operating 24/7. The collapse of cod fishing off Newfoundland's Grand Banks is a case in point of reckless disregard for sustainability.[44] As wild or natural fish stocks were depleted, fish prices increased to a level to spawn a new industry: aquaculture or domestic farming of fish. Figure 11.3 shows growth in aquaculture, which in 2011 supplied 41 percent of the world's fish supply and is growing.[45]

Annual wild fish take has stabilized, indeed may be at the early stages of declining, but increasing demand is now handled by aquaculture. Price would certainly have caused a change of some sort to deal with the oncoming crisis in Easter Island, but would not have affected the eventual outcome. A very high price for the last Easter Island palm would not have saved a civilization from extinction. The individual who became rich selling the last palm would have spent his last dime buying the last fish. Easter Island is not the only civilization that collapsed from a shortage or loss of natural resources. It is believed that a fall in agricultural output from a prolonged drought led to the demise of the Mayan civilization in Central America among others. Ruins of dead civilizations litter the Earth, a humbling reminder of their impermanence, or shall we say lack of sustainability?

Interestingly, we have a history of responding to finite natural resources in danger of exhaustion. We exhausted forests in Europe at the start of the Industrial Age in our quest for making glass and metals and we nearly drove whales to the point of extinction during the nineteenth century in our quest for whale oil for lighting. Fortunately we found ways

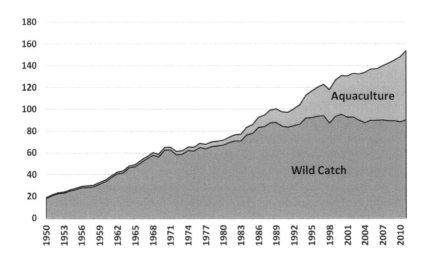

Figure 11.3 Wild Fish and Aquaculture Production (mm tons)

to avert what could have been a terminal crisis. Forests in Europe were saved from the axe by discovery of coal as an alternative to wood in glass and metal making and heating homes. Whales were saved from extinction by finding an alternative source for lighting in the form of kerosene. While we discovered the technology to strip mine the open oceans of fish life, we also developed another technology in aquaculture to save a resource from exhaustion. We have the power, if accompanied by sufficient will, to prevent exhaustion of a natural resource such as taking effective action to rejuvenate a threatened species of marine animal (whales).

In the case of energy, it is true that immense energy reserves have been found that have kept up with our horrific appetite for energy, making mincemeat of Theodore Roosevelt's prediction that we will soon, from the vantage point of the early twentieth century, exhaust our natural resources. A key question facing us is whether the future pace of discovery can keep ahead of our growing appetite for energy; that is, will Roosevelt ultimately be proven right? Just because we run short of a natural resource does not necessarily mean that we can find an alternative. The tragedy of Easter Island was a lack of alternatives.

See the Companion Website for a section on Energy Returned on Energy Invested (EROEI): www.routledge.com/cw/nersesian.

We Need to Identify the Relevant Goal

I'm convinced that we're on Easter Island. I do not believe that climate change is even relevant. The relevant issue is that we are exhausting fossil fuel resources at an alarming rate, which, by the way, would ultimately solve the problem of climate change! Exhaustion of resources can occur; as a case in point, we long ago exhausted our reserves of anthracite coal. This was not fatal, as vast quantities of a second-rate substitute, bituminous coal, were available. Reserve to production ratios of fossil fuels are meaningless if we start looking out centuries into the future. Civilization, as we know it, is about 6,000 years old. However, as an energy-intensive civilization, it is only 200 years old. Fossil fuel reserves are less than 100 years. Suppose from new discoveries they can last 200 years. What is 200 years in human history? The percentage of people living to 80 or 90 or more years is increasing, thanks to advances in medical technology. So 200 years can fit into two to three lifetimes. Babies born today may still be alive when oil and natural gas are down to residual flows and coal down to its last seams; if not them, then certainly their children or, being truly optimistic, their grandchildren. What then?

Take a close look at our civilization. We are utterly dependent on coal and natural gas for most of our electricity generation and oil for just about all our transportation needs. Oil and natural gas are indispensable for petrochemical feedstock to produce a wide variety of consumer products. They are also vital in agriculture for pesticides and fertilizers and fuel for operating farm machinery and for processing and distributing food. Life in suburbia depends on automobiles. The world's highways are congested with a billion automobiles, trucks, and busses and are becoming more so. What happens if oil were to run out? Civilization simply collapses.

My wife and I lived through Hurricane Sandy in 2012. For about nine days, we could have sat in a cold house eating food from the refrigerator before it spoiled, then switch over to canned food (lucky for us, one of our daughters did not lose electricity). I stood outside a four-floor old age home located directly across the street from a supermarket. Elderly residents could not leave their rooms because elevators were not working and they could not manage going up and down stairwells. A store within easy walking distance chock full of food could not be opened to sell nonperishable foods because checkout counters required electricity and apparently store personnel could not handle cash sales. The elderly, confined to cold rooms with no electricity for lighting and powering medical devices, lived on sandwiches provided by the staff for as long as food was in the pantry. Gas stations could not operate without electricity to run pumps. People with gasoline fueled electricity generators were driving to Pennsylvania to fill up their cars and cans with gasoline for their generators. Had the power outage continued for a few more weeks and encompassed a wider area, civil strife would have broken out as hunger drove people out into the streets. This experience brought home the vulnerability of modern society when energy is no longer available. Actually energy was still available—the problem was failure of delivery systems. Nevertheless the crisis had all the earmarks of energy exhaustion. Thus we have identified the relevant goal: find substitutable and alternative energy sources for fossil fuels before we transform planet Earth into planet Easter Island.

Population

The greatest impediment to achieving this goal is population growth. It's simply working against us. Even as late as the 1930s the world's population was a manageable 2 billion. A recent study on population growth concluded that the 2010 population of 6.9 billion (2015 population 7.3 billion) will supposedly stabilize around 9.3 billion by 2050. But it will not be evenly distributed around the world. Several European nations, Russia, and Japan have birthrates far below the sustainable 2.11 children per family for developed nations. This locks in population declines for native Europeans (not counting immigrants), Russia, and Japan. With immigration, European population has stabilized, but the mix of native Europeans and immigrants will change significantly in the coming decades.[46] Japan will be a far advanced geriatric state with an aged population, with only one working person supporting an elderly person by 2050; the number is now 1.7.[47] Clearly this is an untenable position, but there is a solution of retirees returning to the work force, which is already occurring.[48] China is about 20 years behind Japan and will eventually face the same problem of too many retirees in relation to those employed. Moreover the consequences of one child (meaning one boy) per family on China's population profile will come back to haunt them.

There is some thought that population will not level off at 9.5 billion, but peak at about 9 billion, and then begin a long decline, reaching 8 billion in 2100 and continue declining thereafter. The basis for this projection is that birth rates are dropping in nearly every nation. With the exception of the US because of immigration, OECD nations plus Brazil, Russia, and China are below the replacement rate, meaning that maintenance of populations is primarily due to people living longer, not reproduction. As the expanding population bulge of elderly begin dying in significant numbers, then deaths will exceed births and population will decline after 2050. The birth rate of developing nations requires 2.3 children per family for a sustainable population. These are also falling, with India approaching a point of just being able to replenish its population. It is felt that this trend will spread to populations with the highest current reproduction rates and become a global phenomenon despite political and social pressure in some societies to continue having large families to achieve hegemonic power.[49] Of course, population declines can also emanate from conflicts- and diseases-without-borders, which have amply demonstrated their effectiveness in reducing populations on a number of occasions.

Figure 11.4 is the global population in billions and per capita energy consumption in terms of barrels of oil equivalent per year since 1965.[50]

The relevant goal, or challenge, of finding alternative sources of energy to substitute for fossil fuels is daunting. Not only is population increasing, but so is per capita energy consumption. Between 1965 and 2013, population grew by 0.978 percent annually, whereas per capita energy consumption grew more rapidly at 1.67 percent. Overall energy consumption, which couples both population and per capita growth, has been increasing at a rather brisk pace of 2.58 percent. Using 2000 as a base year, annual population growth is 1.21 percent, per capital energy growth is 1.52 percent, and aggregate energy growth is 2.41 percent. Population growth is speeding up, but there has been some taming of growth rates for per capita energy consumption and overall energy growth.

While it's true that Europe has stabilized and Japan has reduced energy consumption, China's appetite for energy is voracious. Even if surfeited in coming years, India is about to take on the mantle of energy consumer extraordinaire followed in close sequence by Southeast Asia, the Middle East, Sub-Saharan Africa, and Latin America. Many of the world's indigent poor of two to three billion are not going to make the ultimate energy sacrifice for the good of mankind or the benefit of those living high off the energy hog if that choice were given to them. One of the arguments against renewable energy is that it is expensive relative to coal and natural gas. Higher electricity rates hurt the world's poor by depriving them of the benefits of electricity. But keeping electricity rates low by intentional dependence on fossil fuels at the expense of higher cost

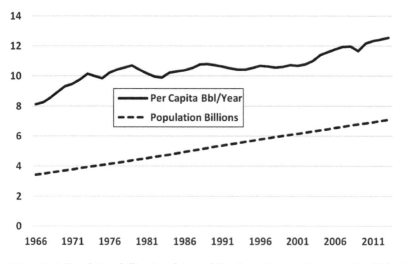

Figure 11.4 Population (billions) and Annual Per Capita Energy Consumption (bbl of oil equivalent)

renewable energy will ultimately not be in the best interests of the world's poor when the cupboard for fossil fuels is bare.

If by 2050 the world's population levels out at 9.3 billion, and if aggregate energy growth slows to 2 percent per year, then aggregate energy demand will be 26,500 million tons oil equivalent versus the 2013 value of 12,730 million tons, the power of exponential growth. The consumption of fossil fuels in 2013 was 11,030 million tons of oil equivalent, and the oil equivalent of nuclear, hydro, and renewables was 1,700 million tons. Suppose that 2050 fossil fuel consumption were 11,000 million tons, essentially unchanged from 2013; renewables including nuclear and hydro would then have to increase from the present 1,700 million tons to 15,500 million tons, a nine-fold increase in 37 years. This would represent an annual growth rate of 6.2 percent per year. While this might sound doable, nuclear power is in a slow decline as the first generation of commercial plants are retired after 50–60 years of service, or possibly longer. Much of the rebirth of interest in nuclear power taking place in Asia will, from a global viewpoint, largely replace retired units in the US and Europe. Hydro has been expanding a little over 3 percent annually since 2005 and will probably continue at this pace, compensating for any fall-off in nuclear power. If hydro and nuclear are holding their own, the onus for non-fossil energy supplies filling the energy gap falls primarily on the smallest segment: solar and wind, and other forms of renewables. Renewables, accounting for only 279 million tons of oil equivalent, would have to expand by 14 percent per year to fill the gap. While current growth rates are around 20 percent per year, a sustained 14 percent over many years might tax the credulity of the most ebullient renewable supporters when one takes into account the rapidly enlarging infrastructure necessary to support such a high level of growth. And this calculation does not remove one barrel of oil or one cubic meter of natural gas or one ton of coal from present consumption. Indeed, an energy forecast by the *World Energy Outlook* calls for increasing consumption of natural gas and oil and a more subdued growth or near-leveling out for coal over the coming decades. Clearly there has to be a renaissance in nuclear power for any hope of replacing fossil fuels; depending entirely on sun and wind may be dicey. We can safely conclude that elimination of fossil fuels is impossible by 2050 and probably rank as a not-so-minor miracle if we can keep fossil fuels from expanding much beyond present levels. It appears that the goal of finding alternative energy sources for fossil fuels may be concomitant with their exhaustion, not a pretty picture.

It's Not Just Energy

It is clear that this planet is not sustainable in energy or water at its present population, never mind adding a couple of billion more.[51] Water is critical to support human life and agriculture. It is also critical to energy generation. As energy demand increases, so does demand for water. Much of the water is not consumed as such, but is required for cooling purposes. Most conventional and nuclear plants use either a "once-through" system or a cooling tower. A once-through system takes water from a river or lake and cycles the water through the power plant once to capture waste heat, which is then discharged back to the environment as warmed water. Cooling towers end up using 30–70 percent more water than once-through systems since cooling is through evaporation. One can argue that no water is being consumed as all water returns to the environment either in a vapor or a warmed liquid state. That misses the point.

Water is absolutely critical for the operation of a power plant; without cooling water, no output. A nuclear plant requires 0.5 to 2.8 liters of water per kilowatt-hour generated for once-through and 2.2–4.5 liters of water for a cooling tower. A plant cannot operate unless this volume of water is available. Corresponding values for coal plants are 0.2–1.2 liters for once-through and 1.8–2.8 liters for cooling tower per kilowatt-hour; natural gas combined cycle 0.2–1.8 liters for once-through and 0.3–2.0 liters for cooling tower per kilowatt-hour; biomass 1.9–3.5 liters (mostly in growing crops) per kilowatt-hour; hydro 3.6 liters per kilowatt-hour; and virtually no water required for solar and wind.[52] Water availability and siting problems associated with water supply are incentives for air cooled condensers where heated air from condensing turbine exhaust steam to water rises in a cooling tower, allowing cool air to enter the bottom.[53] A number of natural gas plants are air cooled despite being less efficient than water cooled, but coal and nuclear plants depend almost entirely on water for cooling.

Towards an Energy Sustainable Society

Biofuels

Fuel for food has run its course. Corn ethanol does little to reduce oil consumption. Whatever is saved in displacing gasoline by corn ethanol is essentially consumed as fossil fuels in running tractors and machinery to grow and harvest corn, in manufacturing and distributing fertilizers and pesticides, and in producing and distributing ethanol. Because there is almost as much fossil fuels consumed in making ethanol as there are fossil fuel savings in burning ethanol, greenhouse gas emissions are down marginally at most. Not all agree; some feel that corn ethanol has a carbon footprint 20 percent greater than burning standard gasoline and 13 percent greater than gasoline made from Canadian oil sands. In addition corn ethanol emits more benzene, a carcinogen, plus loss of carbon absorbing plant mass by converting 23 million acres of wetland and grassland to cropland.[54] Corn ethanol should be recognized for what it really is: a government support program for corn growers and ethanol producers. On the other hand, as discussed in Chapter 3, sugar ethanol in Brazil has been effective in reducing fossil fuel consumption, and hence greenhouse gas emissions. Replacement of biodiesel for petrodiesel in running sugar plantations will further reduce fossil fuel demand and its associated greenhouse gas emissions. Brazil has plenty of pasture and grazing land available for conversion to sugar plantations to expand sugar ethanol production without resorting to deforesting the Amazon.

Biobutanol, a hydrocarbon with a chemical structure similar to gasoline, has the advantage of being compatible within the existing gasoline distribution system, eliminating special logistics requirements associated with ethanol and its limits as a fuel other than flex-fuel vehicles. The cost of converting ethanol to biobutanol exceeds the savings in logistics at this time. But a cost-effective way of converting ethanol to biobutanol would expand the marketability of ethanol. Brazil's adoption of biobutanol would enhance sugar ethanol for export by being a straight substitute for gasoline. Just as corn ethanol is a price support system for corn growers, sugar ethanol plays the same role for sugar growers. Sugar grown in excess of what's needed as food can be converted into ethanol or biobutanol to fuel motor vehicles. An economical means to convert ethanol to biobutanol would open the market for a major expansion of sugar production in the Caribbean, Africa, and Southeast Asia that would reduce gasoline imports, be a source of local employment, and an earner of foreign exchange. Angola is developing a 104,000 acre (162 square miles) sugar plantation with an output of 254,000 tons per year of sugar to be completed by 2025. The project is to provide local jobs and displace current sugar imports, with the remainder sold as either sugar or ethanol into the international market, whichever provides the better return. This could be further enhanced by a cost effective way of converting ethanol to biobutanol.[55]

Cellulosic and algal sources of motor vehicle fuels are not price competitive at this time. But there is enough wood waste and marginal and nonagricultural land fit for fast growing plants and trees to produce enough cellulosic ethanol production to supply most of US automobile fuel—another massive market for biobutanol. Continued support of cellulosic and algal ethanol is warranted to achieve a technological breakthrough that would make these sources economically attractive vis-à-vis crude oil. Of course, a severe run up in the price of oil would make cellulosic and algal ethanol price competitive, but no infrastructure exists to support a massive increase in cellulosic and algal ethanol at this time. Private and public funding to enhance the technology of cellulosic and algal ethanol can be viewed as a means of risk mitigation against a major disruption in oil supplies.

Research efforts to foster biofuels are underway with new areas opening up such as fungi-based biofuels.[56] An alga (Latin word for seaweed) in coastal waters of the Mediterranean introduced accidentally from a local aquarium (*Caulerpa taxifolia alga*) is strangling native marine plants and emitting a toxin that affects young fish. It grows profusely to ten feet in length and is rapidly spreading to new areas. If the proper technology could be developed, this seaweed could be harvested and processed on specially fitted floating factories to transform this menace to marine life to biofuels and animal feed. Perhaps a genetically modified seaweed not harmful to the native environment could be developed that grows fast, can be easily harvested, and produces a great deal of oil. A flat area of the ocean free of protrusions would allow growing and harvesting seaweed similar to growing and harvesting wheat in the plains states.

Jatropha, a weed, bears a nonedible oil seed that can be converted to biodiesel along with other oil bearing nonedible seed plants grown on land unfit for agriculture. This would be a boon to farmers who can obtain another cash crop from unusable or marginal land. Mali, Bangladesh, and a host of other impoverished nations can transform themselves from petroleum importing to biofuel exporting nations, bettering the lives of their people in terms of cash and in greater availability of animal feed from the residue of biodiesel production. Using biodiesel to operate farm equipment to plant and harvest and distribute biodiesel reduces demand for petrodiesel even further.

Bonaire, an island off the coast of Venezuela, has a plan to eliminate fossil fuels for electricity generation partially from biomass. Bonaire has installed 11 mW of wind power capacity that can meet 90 percent of the island's electricity demand at times of optimal wind speeds and 40–45 percent on average. The rest is supplied by diesel generation. To replace petrodiesel, Bonaire is growing algae in large salt flats for eventual production of biodiesel. When this conversion is complete, electricity would be generated solely by renewable power.[57] A more populous nation, Denmark, has an objective to be coal-free by 2025 and generate 70 percent of its total energy from renewable sources including biomass. Its plan is to depend on wind power to the maximum possible extent supported financially by Danes participating in ownership cooperatives. Additional electricity is obtained by substituting biomass for coal and by importing electricity from hydro plants in Sweden. Denmark has also established a successful and economically sound method of district heating supplied by natural gas and a growing portion by biomass including burning waste. Entire neighborhoods and towns are served via a network of underground pipes from a centralized location with highly efficient boilers producing steam and hot water. District heating networks also capture and redistribute surplus heat from factories, power stations, public transport systems, and geothermal sources, resulting in lower cost and lower carbon content hot water. To achieve a completely fossil-free environment by 2050, electricity would have to replace gasoline and biodiesel replace petrodiesel for motor vehicles.[58]

Fats and offal from slaughterhouses, used tires, and municipal waste can be converted to biofuels using current technology with beneficial results for the environment. Trucks require relatively little in modification to switch from petro to biodiesel. Biodiesel is a promising replacement for petrodiesel given the developed state of its technology and the amount of nonagricultural land in Africa, South America, and Asia that could be dedicated to jatropha and other nonedible oil seed plants. Another advantage of biodiesel is that it can be handled by the current infrastructure for petrodiesel with little modifications, the same as biobutanol in the current infrastructure for gasoline. Biogas production from municipal and human waste would not only be beneficial as a new energy source, but would help reduce the negative environmental impact of current disposal practices. Household waste after separation of paper, metals, glass, and other recyclables should be burned in environmentally sound electricity generating plants rather than dumped into oceans and landfills. Continued growth of wood pellets for home heating and as a utility fuel reduces demand for fossil fuels and cuts emissions of greenhouse gases.

Coal

The problem with coal is the size of the problem. Coal is the principal fuel in many nations for generating electricity. Projections out to 2030 call for increased consumption, or at best a near-leveling of consumption, resulting in coal losing market share to natural gas and renewables, but not in being displaced. The only nation that has cut coal consumption significantly is the US and this trend will continue. The 2015 proposed EPA regulation on reducing carbon emissions by utilities can be satisfied by increasing the efficiency of current fossil fuel plants, favoring natural gas over coal plants by converting coal burning plants to natural gas or by building natural gas plants and retiring coal plants, continuing the use of existing nuclear power plants, continued expansion of renewable energy, and greater reliance on energy efficiency and conservation to reduce electricity demand.[59]

Despite efforts to reduce greenhouse gas emissions, Germany resumed burning coal as a consequence of shutting down its nuclear plants. The UK imported coal from the US to counter high natural gas prices, but has recently stopped importing. China ramped up coal consumption, as has India to a lesser extent, to satisfy their insatiable appetites for electricity. Global coal consumption, which had previously been growing about 4 percent per year, has been reduced to 1 percent since 2012 primarily through reduced economic growth, environmental opposition in OECD nations, and increases in renewables on a global scale. The irony is that, though coal production to reserves ratios for certain nations are measured in hundreds of years with an aggregate global ratio of a bit over 100 years, China has only 30 years of reserves left at the current rate of production. Higher prices can change coal resources to reserves and more coal discoveries can be made, as in

Mongolia. But even so, China's low reserves may help explain its aggressive stance for developing all types of energy sources such as natural gas imports from Russia, building of LNG import terminals, and massive additions to nuclear, hydro, wind, and solar power. Although China can import vast quantities of coal from Australia and elsewhere including the US and prolong its days as a coal dependent nation, China may actually have to lead the world in cutting the umbilical cord to coal.

There seems to be little progress in sequestering carbon dioxide from burning coal. First, sequestering would not work for existing coal plants because carbon dioxide makes up about 17 percent of flue gas. IGCC plants produce a solid stream of carbon dioxide that can be sequestered in deep underground geologic permeable or water filled formations. The problem is one of economics—IGCC plants are major capital investments and burn about one-third more coal than an equivalent sized conventional coal fired electricity generating plant to provide the necessary energy for sequestering carbon dioxide deep within the earth. The cost of electricity for IGCCs with sequestration is high enough to support building nuclear plants with no greenhouse gas emissions. Building IGCC plants with sequestration that burn one-third more coal for the same energy output only hastens the day when coal reserves are exhausted.

Oil

Oil is the most critical of the fossil fuels by far, but rumors that we are at the end of the line with oil have all proven wrong, beginning with Theodore Roosevelt. Rather than running out of oil, discoveries made after his death created an enormous surplus that oil companies have had to contend with for decades. Oil company executives today say that there is plenty of oil under the ground, but that the problem is above ground. Drilling restrictions, xenophobia among producers, difficulties in negotiating contracts, and rescinding contracts without restitution are some of the above ground challenges faced by oil companies. Below ground, oil companies have improved technology for finding oil and developing oil fields in difficult locations such as 2 miles below the ocean surface and then another 5 miles into the ocean bottom. For offshore Brazilian sub-salt oil formations, the drill pipe had to be super-controlled to make it through the seismic distorting salt layers to penetrate underlying relatively small sized, highly productive reservoirs. The oil industry has mastered techniques necessary to develop oil and gas in tight sands and shale and bitumen deposits that heretofore were out of reach for commercial development. Tertiary means of recovery have reached a point where as much as half of the oil can be drained from an oil reservoir versus a third without advanced recovery methods.

The fact that no giant oil field has been discovered in half a century is disconcerting. In the sense of legacy oil, or massive discoveries of low cost crude whose internal pressure propels oil up a well bore, we've passed Hubbert's peak. Existing giant oil fields are showing distinct signs of aging, which is another way of saying we're exhausting our oil reserves in terms of legacy oil—a wasting asset in terms of financial accounting. Many old legacy fields are in a terminal decline that cannot be stopped by drilling more wells. Some high cost fields are in a death spiral; most notably, North Sea. Exploration keeps reducing the probability for finding a giant oil field as each well drilled eliminates another potential site.

Legacy oil is cheap oil. A giant oil field of low cost oil may yet be discovered in largely unexplored Iraq (if Humpty Dumpty Iraq can be put back together again from its warring sectarian factions) or in the South China Sea (if conflicting jurisdictional claims between China and other littoral nations can be resolved). A growing possibility to resolving conflicting littoral claims in the South China Sea is China asserting and enforcing hegemonic claims via naval power, thus ending any further discussion on conflicting claims. Relying on a yet-to-be-made discovery of a giant oil field to maintain legacy oil reserves is like a single large bet at a roulette wheel. With slim chances of winning, what if you lose? Actually a timed sequence of giant oil fields equivalent to a number of Saudi Arabias need to be discovered to delay Hubbert's peak in terms of legacy oil. While there is a certain degree of comfort that the ratio of oil reserves to production is growing, much of this has been from adding oil sands and bitumen to traditional oil reserves and by writing up existing reserves. Writing up existing reserves may be valid since reserves can be better estimated as oil is pumped out of a field. Nevertheless it is still disheartening to see additions of light and medium grade oil from discoveries of traditional oil fields significantly lagging consumption. While at this time oil in tight shale and tight sand geologic formations are not included in oil reserves in *BP Energy Statistics*, fracked oil along with oil sands and bitumen requires high oil prices to be economically feasible and eligible to be counted as reserves.

The oil share of the energy pie has declined from 44 percent in 1980 to 39 percent in 1990 through 2000, and then down to 35 percent in 2008 before falling further to 33 percent in 2014. Coal and natural gas shares have risen to fill the gap. Part of the eroding share of oil is a long term decline in per capita oil consumption in Europe and, in the last few years, joined by North America and Japan primarily from smaller and more efficient automobiles driven fewer miles per year. This partially compensates for the growth in oil consumption in China, India, Southeast Asia, the Middle East, and South America. Several billion humans making up the economically deprived portion of the world population consume little oil. It is going to remain nil for these people because many third world oil importing nations have little in the way of hard currency reserves to pay for oil imports.

Although the share of oil may be declining, its volume is rising, just not quite as fast as coal and natural gas. Oil has the lowest ratio of production to reserves of traditional reserves, but has expanded in recent years by counting bitumen deposits in Venezuela and oil sands in Canada. Including these, the production to reserves ratio is 51 years compared to 40 years in the previous edition of this book. But bitumen deposits in Venezuela are not developed and probably won't be as long as the present government remains in power. New projects in Canadian oil sands cannot be economically supported at mid-2015 oil prices. North America may face significant production declines if oil remains below $80 per barrel from cessation of fracking new oil wells.

OPEC controls 72 percent of reserves, but OPEC does not mean infinite oil—Indonesia, a founding member of OPEC, is now a non-OPEC oil importing nation producing only half of its needs. Domestic oil consumption in OPEC nations is growing at a fast pace partially from prices for oil products being heavily subsidized by the government. This cuts into available oil for export. A worrisome aspect of OPEC oil is that half of OPEC reserves is located in the politically volatile Middle East, which accounts for one-third of global production. In retrospect, President George H.W. Bush made the right decision to defeat Iraq in Kuwait, but not invading Iraq, leaving Saddam Hussein in power in the first Gulf War. In hindsight, President George W. Bush made the wrong decision to invade Iraq and uproot Saddam in the second Gulf War. From the perspective of 2015, no matter what a butcher of his people Saddam may have been, Iraqi people would have been better off under his misrule. The same can be said for President Obama's uprooting of Gaddafi. No matter how bad Gaddafi may have been, the people of Libya would also have been better off under his misrule. More people live in greater misery and fear and more have died than when these political miscreants (Hussein and Gaddafi) were in power. Iraq and Libya are now failed states, joining Syria and Yemen and others being torn apart by sectarian violence.

US intrusion into the Middle East has not benefited global oil security. Nearly every Middle Eastern state is now at war. The geopolitical risk of the Middle East collapsing leading to a cessation of oil exports is rising with each passing day. Cessation of Middle East exports would simply shut down the Asian economies. The US imports little Middle East oil, which can easily be replaced by diverting, by force if necessary, a relatively small portion of West Africa and/or Venezuela exports to Asia. But the US will suffer along with the rest of the world with extremely expensive oil that will crush global economic activity.

While we may have passed Hubbert's Peak with regard to low cost or legacy oil, there are huge reserves of high cost oil left to exploit. If incremental oil production is needed, then oil prices have to rise to clear the cost of marginal oil. "Cheap" oil at $50–$60 per barrel in 2015 has brought to a halt further development of fracking hard shale, Canadian oil sands, and deep ocean drilling other than completing well-advanced projects. Oil prices will have to rise to a minimum of $70–$80 per barrel to resuscitate these sources and to $100 per barrel for OPEC nations to satisfy the social expectations of their populations. Canadian oil sands and Venezuelan bitumen deposits require huge volumes of natural gas to both desulfurize and hydrogenate heavy oil/bitumen to make them acceptable as a refinery crude feedstock. For Canadian oil sands, natural gas is also needed to heat a mixture of oil sands and water to separate oil from sand. Thus gasoline made from heavy oil/bitumen has higher greenhouse gas content from upgrading operations that more rapidly depletes natural gas resources and lowers its EROEI ratio. Natural gas availability may be a future constraint facing Canadian oil sands that would not be faced in developing Venezuelan bitumen with its huge untapped reserves of natural gas.

Although reserves for fracked oil are enormous, the need for well replacement on a 3 year schedule may impose physical constraints that form a real barrier to development in terms of the number of qualified crews and drilling rigs, and possibly the availability of water for fracking. But the industry is also changing. Although fracking new wells is not financially justified with oil prices at $50–$60 per barrel in 2015, new well output is nearly double that of older wells as operators take advantage of what they've learned from experience. This includes improved grades of sand and mixes of water and chemicals and better placement of drill holes within tight shale and sand formations. Shortening drilling time from 21–35 days to 17 days and falling day rates from idle drilling equipment have reduced average investment per well from $4.5 million to $3.5 million. Improved output and reduced investment lower breakeven oil prices for new wells by tens of dollars per barrel.[60] There is a growing sense that the new global swing producer will be the US as higher than breakeven oil prices turn fracking "on" and lower than breakeven prices turn fracking "off." Given the short life of fracked wells, supply declines fairly rapidly. As supply nears demand, increasing oil prices will again turn fracking "on." Saudi Arabia will no longer be the swing producer making decisions based on both political and economic considerations, but by the US where "on" and "off" fracking decisions are purely economic in nature.[61] If this occurs, then supply will oscillate around demand, more or less keeping both in balance. Technological development to substitute propane or another petroleum liquid as a fracking medium would eliminate the need for huge volumes of fresh water for fracking and the problem of disposing of huge volumes of contaminated water after fracking. Moreover a petroleum fracking medium could be separated either at the well or at a refinery and recycled.

High cost crude oil is a necessity to dampen demand, promote efficiency and conservation, provide an incentive for alternative fueled vehicles, and to divert US drivers' love affair with heavy duty gas guzzling SUVs. The sales ratio of economical hybrid automobiles with gas guzzling SUVs closely follows gasoline prices. When gasoline prices decline significantly, SUV sales explode at the expense of hybrids. In 2015 with relatively low gasoline prices, automobile manufacturers were having a tough time keeping up with demand for trucks for personal use and SUVs while hybrid and electric vehicle sales languished.[62] Thus high oil prices are necessary to enforce a decision to buy better mileage motor vehicles and encourage the commercial development of cellulosic and algal ethanol and greater reliance on electric cars.

Electric cars are expensive, and further technological progress is necessary in battery development to reduce costs. Apple, Google, Tesla, BMW, and GM are all involved with developmental work on electric automobiles that can get 300 or more miles on a single charge and cost around $35,000. Development of a low cost, high capacity, long life, reliable super battery of five times the capacity at one-fifth of the cost of existing lithium batteries is at the core of the electric automobile revolution. It is true that electric cars save on gasoline, but if electricity is predominantly from burning coal and natural gas, little progress will be made in reducing the role of fossil fuels.

Further savings in oil consumption can be made by shifting long distance truck traffic to the fuel economy of railroads such as building an intermodal rail line augmented by the short sea ferry service from Halifax to Miami. Europe has developed a fast ferry service connecting ports on the North and Baltic and Mediterranean Seas that reduce truck traffic. High speed trains and express bus transportation reduces automobile congestion, itself a great waste of energy. Gains in engine efficiency and smaller sized vehicles improve mileage. To meet EPA demand of 54.5 mpg by 2025, automobile manufacturers hope to save 5 percent fuel consumption for every 10 percent reduction in weight that can be achieved by greater use of polymer composites, carbon fiber composites, aluminum, and advanced (thinner) steels. Smooth, streamlined shapes save another 5 percent, and 2 percent can be saved from automatically opening and closing shutters on the grill to minimize turbulent wind flow and provide air for cooling. Engine enhancements can reduce fuel consumption 5 percent by variable valve timing, 7.5 percent by cylinder deactivation, 12 percent by direct fuel injection, 7.5 percent by turbocharging, 3.6 percent by waste heat harvesting for electricity generation for cooling systems and accessories, and 6 percent by automated and continuously variable transmissions.[63]

Companies have adopted programs whose objective is to increase fuel efficiency. FedEx has a goal of a 30 percent gain in fleet fuel efficiency by 2020 after achieving a previous goal of a 20 percent increase in 2012. The program involves adoption of nearly 600 light weight hybrid electric and electric delivery vehicles along with taking the initiative to test new technologies and adopt energy boosting features such as smoothing air flow around vehicles.[64] All of these are beneficial, but fuel efficiency and a switch of some small percentage of the fleet to hybrids and electric vehicles do not address the crux of the matter of how to significantly reduce the role of oil in transportation for a billion automobiles and hundreds of millions of trucks (large and small), plus innumerable off-road bulldozers, construction machinery, cranes, pumps, and diesel generated electricity, as well as trains, planes, and ships.

Let's take another tack to describe the problem of oil. The world population in 2013 was 7.1 billion and world oil production was 91.3 million barrels per day (mmBpd). In 2050, the earth's population is projected to be 9.3 billion people. Assuming no change in per capita oil consumption, the projected world oil production would have to be 119.6 mmBpd, or incremental growth of 28.3 mmBpd. Saudi Arabia produced 11.5 mmBpd in 2014, or about 2.4 Saudi Arabias would have to be added to maintain per capita oil production. If the current production of oil declines by 1.5 percent per year, an admittedly low estimate, then another 41 mmBpd of oil would have to be replaced by 2050, or 3.6 Saudi Arabias, bringing the grand total of additional oil production to satisfy incremental demand and replace production declines to six Saudi Arabias. Expressed in these terms, it is clear that it is going to be a challenge just to stand still. As presently constituted, electricity and cellulosic and algal ethanol, along with growing oilseeds on marginal agricultural lands for biodiesel, don't even begin to address the magnitude of the problem with oil. The technological development of motor vehicle storage batteries and biofuels has to be hastened along with the adoption of natural gas as a motor vehicle fuel to avert an oil crisis in the future.

Natural Gas

The ratio of production to reserves is higher for natural gas than oil, and natural gas is a more secure source of energy, having less geopolitical risk other than those receiving pipeline imports from Russia and LNG imports from the Middle East. It is by far the cleanest burning fossil fuel both in terms of greenhouse gas and pollution emissions. Natural gas could be a temporary stop gap alternative to reducing dependence on oil in the transition to a fossil fuel free world. For advocates of climate change, shifting to natural gas decarbonizes motor vehicle fuels. In the case of the US, one starting point, perhaps unlikely to occur, could be conversion of railroads to LNG. Diesel engines can be converted to burn either LNG or diesel fuel as done on modern LNG carriers. LNG would be transported in LNG tank cars similar to LNG carriage in trucks to customers not connected by pipeline to LNG receiving terminals. LNG storage depots would be located at critical points along the nation's railway system. From there LNG would be transferred to LNG fueling tank cars on freight trains that would also have diesel tank cars for dual fuel capacity. As the system becomes more fully developed, railroads could end up relying entirely on LNG. Having LNG depots spanning the nation's rail lines opens the way for dual LNG/diesel fueled trucks on the nation's interstate highway system, particularly those interstate highways relatively near rail lines. Truck stops would have LNG refueling dispensers that could be served from the railroad LNG storage tanks. Trucks normally have to leave the interstate system for delivery and pickup of trailers and would have to be dual fueled to cover areas not served by LNG. Getting railroads and trucks on natural gas would markedly lessen oil dependence. Since railroad locomotives are diesel electric, incorporating regenerative braking, whose generated electricity would have to be stored in a battery, would be a significant saving in fuel consumption.[65] However, a more likely alternative to diesel fuel is electrification of the rail system that would inhibit transformation of interstate trucks to natural gas.[66]

As an alternative to LNG, compressed natural gas should be instituted at central locations that serve local transport in trucks, busses, and motor vehicles such as taxis. The US

Post Office would be a good place to start as local postal trucks operate out of a central location, but private industry has seized the initiative. FeDex and UPS are in the process of developing centralized natural gas refueling stations for their local delivery trucks, as are Waste Management and other waste disposal companies. Any fleet of trucks, busses, and cars (e.g., taxis) housed in a centralized place with access to natural gas can be converted from petrofuels to natural gas. Automobiles can be converted to run on natural gas for homes supplied by natural gas. Garage pressurizers are available for an overnight charge. Some automobiles built in Brazil are dual fuel for pressurized natural gas or any mix of gasoline and ethanol (flex fuel). Automobiles in a number of oil exporting and importing nations with stranded natural gas reserves are being converted to run on natural gas to enhance a nation's oil exports or reduce its oil imports. Natural gas would be a vital stop-gap plan to reduce dependence on oil during the transition to electric or cellulosic and algal ethanol or biobutanol fueled vehicles.

Nuclear Power

A fresh look is needed for nuclear power. China is building two pebble bed reactors. These reactors are fail-safe, where a total loss of coolant such as suffered at Chernobyl and Fukushima would have no impact on plant integrity. Of all reactor types, the pebble bed reactor has the greatest simplicity of design, the lowest cost of construction, operation, and maintenance, and, most of all, the greatest inherent safety. A core meltdown, the worst type of reactor accident, cannot occur in a reactor that has no core. The highest achievable temperature from a loss of coolant is less than the melting temperature of the ceramic cladding surrounding each of the 10,000–15,000 fuel microspheres within each pebble. Pebble bed reactors are smaller in capacity (100–250 mW) as an inherent safety feature to allow dissipation of residual heat to avoid ceramic melting if coolant is lost. A collection of six or so pebble bed reactors would be necessary to equate to a single large 1,500 mW (1.5 gW) coal or nuclear plant. Though this is perfectly feasible, it is also possible to build these plants to serve the needs of local communities in a distributive form of electricity generation without relying on long distance transmission lines as originally envisioned by Thomas Edison. If pebble bed reactors perform as expected, there should be a massive expansion of nuclear power as a means to substitute for coal and natural gas in electricity generation. The fail-safe thorium reactor should also be developed to take advantage of thorium reserves that can provide power, along with reprocessing of uranium fuel modules and fast breeder reactors, for thousands of years.

With regard to conventional pressurized and boiling water reactors, reprocessing of spent fuel should be adopted by the US as a means to reduce the volume of radioactive waste by about 97 percent, greatly easing permanent storage requirements, and capturing unused U235 and plutonium for fuel recycling. Although some would object, the safest means of storage for residual and highly radioactive reprocessing waste is to encapsulate it in neutron absorbing glass and drop the glass encased waste in deep ocean trenches. Radioactivity will be long gone when reactor waste once again surfaces many millions of years from now by geologic recycling of the earth's crust. Another approach to handling nearly 70,000 tons of nuclear waste is a proposed waste-annihilating molten salt reactor where a mixture of molten fluoride salt and spent fuel pellets flow through a reactor core that utilizes fissionable materials in the fuel pellets to create heat energy. Heat from the molten salt and spent fuel mixture is transferred to a second loop of nonradioactive pure molten salt and from there to a third loop of water, which is flashed to steam to generate electricity. This process can capture 98 percent of the energy in spent fuel pellets and drastically reduce spent fuel waste to only a small percentage of its former weight, which in a couple of hundred years becomes inert, not millions for present spent fuel waste.[67] This method, if proven feasible, would be preferable to deep ocean burying in that further energy can be extracted from nuclear waste before eventual disposal with much less radioactivity. Various proposals have been made to expose spent fuel to fast neutrons to transform long-lived radionuclides to shorter lived radionuclides via fissioning. Capturing heat given off by fissioning long-lived radionuclides for commercial purposes would reduce processing costs.

Nuclear power is the logical choice as a substitute for coal and natural gas for electricity generation. A nuclear plant program should adopt the French model where one central authority controls the industry with a single basic reactor design and a limited number of output capacities. A "cookie cutter" approach to nuclear design, construction, licensing, and operation is the only way to control construction costs and schedules and to ensure nuclear safety integrity. A carefully crafted program of pebble bed reactors, conventional reactors with reprocessing of spent fuel, thorium reactors, factory produced small modular reactors, and fast breeder reactors, which produce more fuel than consumed, can make nuclear power sustainable by extending fuel reserves for millennia.

The essential problem with nuclear power is Chernobyl and Fukushima. Although pebble bed and thorium reactors are immune from the circumstances that cause core meltdowns, they are still nuclear reactors. Moreover the economics of the pebble bed reactors are not known with precision, but the building of pebble bed reactors in China will demonstrate the effectiveness of this type of reactor to generate electricity in an economical, safe, and reliable manner. The thorium reactor does not exist, but development efforts should be made to have another type of fail-safe reactor available and to place relatively plentiful thorium on the list of fissionable materials.

Those opposed to nuclear power state that alternatives should be preferred, particularly renewable power sources. In the last 10 years, the US has added 100 gW of renewable power (55 gW of utility wind power, 17 gW of rooftop PV solar, 10 gW of utility PV solar, 15 gW of biomass and biogas, and 3 gW of geothermal) for an effective output of 42 gW. This is equivalent to 40 nuclear reactors' worth of electricity. In the next 10 years, it is anticipated that there would be an additional 305 gW of renewable power (130 gW of utility wind power, 75 gW of rooftop PV solar, 35 gW of utility PV solar, 60 gW of biomass and biogas, and 5 gW of geothermal) for an effective output of 131 gW, or another 130 nuclear plants. These future assessments include no advances in wind and solar efficiency and no grid storage. If improvements can be made in these areas, then the contribution of renewables will be greater.[68] While renewables may be sufficient to substitute for replacement nuclear power plants for those approaching 60 years of continuous service, nuclear plants will still have to be built, preferably fail-safe plants, to expand nuclear capacity sufficiently to reduce the role of coal and natural gas as principal utility fuels.

Hydro Power

Unlike pebble reactors, hydropower is not fail-safe. Dams are vulnerable to earthquakes and construction faults. The drive to use hydropower as a substitute for fossil fuels will continue with new dams, despite siting challenges, providing a continuation of 3 percent annual growth in capacity. While there are major expansions in Churchill Falls in Labrador and in Africa, much of this growth will be in China and nations around China who will sell a large portion of their hydropower to China. The incentive to build large dams to capture water flowing from the Tibetan plateau often in remote locations necessitating long distance transmission lines may be weakened if pebble reactors can provide comparable cost electricity from locations within the market. A safe alternative to conventional dams are river dams that generate electricity from the momentum of water flow. The dam is low, the "reservoir" small, and power is generated by water flow through turbines mounted in the dam. Another is tunneling alongside fast moving streams between two elevations where water flow through turbines mounted at the end of the tunnel provides the power to run electricity generators.

Some of these tunnels are located in Nepal, devastated by an earthquake in May 2015. This earthquake was so mammoth that a region of Nepal rose by about 2 meters while another region of the Himalayas north of Nepal subsided an equal distance.[69] Fourteen hydropower dams were affected, but there were no dam failures, although one suffered cracks. Hydropower output fell by 30 percent from landslides and rock falls.[70] Perhaps the major impact of the Nepal earthquake is on China's plans to harness water flow from the Tibetan plateau in a number of mega-sized dams whose output, after satisfying demand in electricity-short Tibet, Nepal, and other nearby areas, is slated to be transmitted to eastern China. An alternative to a large scale hydropower project is several medium and mini sized hydropower projects to serve local areas in an economical fashion. In addition to the risk of potentially damaging earthquakes, hydropower is at the mercy of rain. Without rain in the hinterlands to replenish reservoirs, hydropower can be severely curtailed, as around Sao Paulo in Brazil and in California and Arizona in 2015 when reservoir levels dropped to historical lows.

Solar Power

Solar power is coming into its own, but like wind power, it can't be relied upon like a fossil fuel plant. Fossil fuel plants respond to the whims of a dispatcher, whereas solar and wind power respond to the whims of clouds and wind. Two technical developments are needed for solar power to assume its rightful place. One is the development of storage battery capacity at a cost that will provide adequate backup to transform an unreliable source into a reliable source under the direct control of a dispatcher. The so-called super battery at five times the storage capacity at one-fifth the cost of what's available at this time would be charged with solar and/or wind power and a dispatcher could draw on battery power whenever needed in a steady and reliable manner similar to a conventional power plant for as long as the battery remains charged.[71] Sizing the battery is similar in concept to determining the size of a hydropower reservoir. A reservoir is large enough to hold enough water that falls as rainfall in the hinterlands to generate the requisite power needed by a dispatcher. Reservoir level is a function of the relationship between output (water to turn the turbine generators) and input (water flowing into the reservoir). This is a classic example of a stock and flow diagram from system analysis where stock is the inventory of water measured in, say, cubic meters, whereas flow is the input and output of water measured in, say, cubic meters per minute. Reservoir level is determined by flow of water in and out of a reservoir and level change a function of the area of a reservoir. The same is true for a battery; it should be large enough to absorb all the excess electricity generated by solar and wind farms for dispatching to the grid when needed without "wasting" any solar and wind generated electricity from either a lack of storage capacity or an inadequate load to fully utilize their output. The battery should also be able to deliver enough current at the requisite voltage when transient demand exceeds transient supply.

Unreliability is now addressed by spinning reserves to compensate for changing cloud cover and wind conditions. Having what amounts to nearly full power backup is a cost often hidden from the economic analysis of solar and wind power plants. This cost is not only considerable, but when added to the cost of unsubsidized solar and wind power, along with the possibility of having to build new transmission lines to remote locations, makes for rather expensive electricity.[72] One way to deal with this situation would be to end all subsidies to fossil fuel plants to narrow the cost differential between renewables and fossil fuels. Another way to narrow the cost differential is to incorporate externalities associated with burning fossil fuels into electricity rates such as a tax on pollution and carbon emissions. The tax should be sufficient not only to narrow the cost differential, but also end all subsidies for renewable energy.

Backup plants for solar and wind experience major swings in output over short periods, adding to carbon emissions.[73] However, there is also an opposing view that rapid changes in backup power supplies are not major contributors to incremental carbon dioxide and pollution emissions.[74] Backup suppliers were up and running when a predicted eclipse of the sun occurred on March 20, 2015, significantly reducing solar power in Europe.[75] The European power grid handled the eclipse without difficulty. But a more difficult test would be a major weather front that adversely affects solar and wind power over a wide area for a period of time to effectively demonstrate that the electricity grid can cope with the challenges of clean power.[76]

Germany meets its reliability goals by having nuclear (those units still operating) and large gas and coal fired turbines for base load demand and let wind and solar generate whatever they can as dictated by wind conditions and clouds. The remaining ups and downs are handled by highly dispatchable, load-following resources such as hydro and gas fired peaking generators.[77] The need for backup plants can be reduced by further integration of the European electricity grid connecting solar and wind farms over a wide geographic area to take advantage of varying solar and wind conditions to smooth output. An 8-year effort to fully integrate the German and French electricity grid with the rest of central and western Europe was completed in 2015. This means that some of the extreme fluctuations in solar and wind output which had plagued German utility operations will be compensated with access to a much broader market. Leveling of electricity rates across the region is occurring, along with reducing volatility in both supply and demand.[78] German utilities, suffering from a series of financial losses, are taking corrective actions to remain vital players in the German electricity market by divesting fossil fuel plants, reorganizing themselves to better respond to a new market environment, and changing their focus from traditional energy sources to renewables.[79]

On the surface, net metering is fair in that excess electricity from solar power installed on a residence or building is sold back to the utility at the same rate for electricity consumed by a residence or building when solar power is not sufficient to meet needs. The problem with this arrangement is that the utility loses revenue when a home or building is fitted with solar power, yet is expected to maintain the transmission and distribution system to guarantee a consumer's access to electricity if and when needed. Utilities want a charge placed on electricity they must purchase from consumers to reflect the cost of maintaining transmission and distribution systems for the consumers' benefit.[80] Individuals selling excess electricity back to the utility are not in a strong bargaining position. But they can be by forming a yet-to-be-developed virtual power plant (VPP), an aggregation of many individuals acting collectively as a single entity by coordinating the individual solar installations as a unified and flexible resource. VPPs, as concentrated power suppliers, would be able to offer utilities greater flexibility to manage their grids for supplying dependable power at the lowest cost. VPPs would rely on computer software systems to remotely and automatically dispatch and optimize generation in a single, secure web-connected system.[81]

The other needed technical development is enhancing the efficiency of transforming incoming solar radiation to electricity. The present rate of 15–17 percent is too low; a doubling or tripling would make an enormous difference in the area and presumably the investment needed to provide solar power. There are a number of technological developments underway that point to improving solar efficiency. One is a hybrid device that combines silicon solar photovoltaics and glass voltaics to boost efficiencies to over 30 percent and another is incorporating Fresnel lenses with solar panels.[82] The economics of solar power would be improved if incremental capital costs do not exceed the degree of improvement in solar efficiency.

Solar panels ought to be installed in sunny climates; Germany does not sound like an optimal choice for solar installations. This would, however, necessitate a major investment in long distance transmission systems.[83] Europe could be supplied with huge solar electricity installations in North Africa and the US from similar sized solar electricity installations in southwestern states like Arizona. DESERTEC is an organization that promotes renewable sources with an emphasis on deserts and their potential to power nations. Tapping only a small percentage of solar energy in deserts could supply the world with electricity.[84] Thermal solar electricity generating plants are being built and will remain a choice along with solar photovoltaic electricity for investors in solar power. But the future of solar power plainly lies with photovoltaic cells.

Yet solar power, despite these caveats, may spread faster than anticipated. Bangladesh aims to be the first "solar nation" by installing 250 W solar panels on rooftops of all homes not connected to an electricity grid. Six million households are planned to have solar panels installed in 2017 with the objective of all homes not connected to an electricity grid be fitted with solar panels by 2021. With attached batteries, a modicum of lighting plus power for a small television or computer would be provided to all. People already connected to solar power prefer solar power over being connected to a grid that suffers frequent blackouts. Homes already connected with solar panels are saving the nation 200,000 tons of kerosene a year for an estimated $180 million. This saving can be diverted as financial aid in the form of loans to pay for the $640 solar installation.[85]

Wind Power

Wind power is gaining in popularity as a concentrated power source for utilities, but not for residences. It, too, suffers from unreliability. Fluctuating wind speeds and periods of prolonged calm reduce the effectiveness of wind power. Wind power in many places has greater output at night when power is not needed than during the day. Battery storage, as already described, could transform an unreliable source into a reliable source and convert night time electricity generation to day time usage when it's needed. Wind turbines work best where there are steady winds such as along coastal areas with regular day and night breezes or mountain passages, or in areas of dependable prevailing winds such as northern China. Offshore wind turbines, though more costly, normally have a higher output than many onshore wind turbines. Offshore wind turbines can be built far enough out in the water to not disturb the quiet of the night and blight the landscape of the day. However, in the US, the mere sight of blade tips turning just over the horizon marring the ocean vistas of beachfront vacation homes and weekend pleasure craft has been sufficient to end the development of offshore turbines. Were it not for these objections, Delaware and New Jersey could be transformed into electricity exporting states by a line of offshore wind turbines 10 or more miles out at sea stretching along their entire coastline. Europe has taken a more aggressive stance toward building offshore wind turbine farms. Europeans are more keenly aware of the environmental benefits of wind power versus burning fossil fuels, whereas Americans want the benefits of renewables as long as they're not in their backyard. Americans cannot seem able to comprehend the consequences of being simultaneously against fossil fuels and renewables. Wind turbines may be reaching their upper limits with regard to economies of scale and output unlike solar cells that need further technological development. Larger sized turbines with slower blade speeds create less noise and give birds a better chance of surviving an encounter. Research efforts are underway to improve radars serving wind farms to better identify incoming birds. Once this information is available, then operational procedures can be adopted to minimize bird kills.

Resistance to Renewable Energy

Both solar and wind are the principal mainstays of renewable energy, but are still more expensive than fossil fuels. While their economics are improving with time, they still require financial assistance either by government subsidies or by higher rates via feed-in tariffs. Europeans have been quite aggressive in introducing renewables into their energy mix. In Germany, renewables (biomass, sun, wind) make up about 23 percent of the energy required for electricity generation, with a goal of 80 percent by 2050 for electricity generation and 60 percent of total energy consumption. If these goals can be met, then emissions of greenhouse gases are expected to fall by 70 percent in 2040 and 80–95 percent in 2050 relative to 1990 emissions. But public resistance is growing against higher cost electricity, and industry is complaining about a loss of competitive position and have moved some of their heavy industry enterprises offshore to obtain lower cost electricity. German natural gas consumption is declining to mitigate against the geopolitical risk of relying too heavily on Russian sources, and nuclear plant output has been slashed by forced phasing out of older units. This leaves Germany burning more lignite coal than it did in 1990. Lignite, the least energy efficient and dirtiest of coals, has caused overall greenhouse gas emissions in Germany to increase despite the significant advancement in renewable energy.[86]

A proposal to cut German feed-in tariffs was not received with open arms by renewable energy supporters.[87] One way to contain electricity rates is to recommission nuclear power plants that have been shut down in reaction to the Fukushima accident, the cause of which could not occur in Germany. Germany along with Spain, the UK, and Italy have trimmed renewable energy subsidies after a boom in biomass, solar, and wind installations resulted in more costly power for consumers. One can appreciate the negative reaction coming from lower to middle income people when one realizes how expensive electricity is in Europe. The average cost of residential electricity in the US in 2013 was 12 cents per kilowatt-hour versus Denmark at 39.5 cents, Germany at 39 cents, Ireland at 31 cents, Italy at 30.5 cents, Spain at 30 cents, and the UK at 23 cents. France, relying heavily on nuclear power, has a cost of 20 cents per kilowatt-hour, half that of Germany. The overall weighted average for the EU-28 is 27 cents per kilowatt-hour.[88] With such high priced electricity, one can understand why Europe is attempting to clarify an energy policy balancing cost of renewables with reducing greenhouse gas emissions.[89] This same problem has occurred in Japan which offered, like Germany, overly attractive feed-in tariff rates that made it quite profitable for individuals to install solar panels. The cost of expensive electricity paid by the utilities is ultimately incorporated into electricity rates. In response to complaints over costly electricity, Japanese utilities are making it difficult for homeowners with solar installations to feed excess electricity into the grid.[90] Australia had an ambitious clean energy program that would have involved $20 billion in clean energy investments to be paid by higher electricity rates and a carbon tax. In 2014, reeling from lower prices and volume for export commodities to China and the depressing effect of higher electricity rates on its domestic economy, Australia dismantled its carbon tax program and cut government spending from A$1.3 billion on clean energy projects for the first six months of 2013 to A$58 million for the first six months of 2014.[91] Similar economic considerations caused Ohio to roll back 2008 legislation requiring the state to acquire 12.5 percent of its energy from renewables and to reduce energy consumption by 22 percent by 2025.[92] Its renewable portfolio standard and energy consumption reduction will be reevaluated at some future time. Other nations, regions, and states are thinking of reconsidering their clean energy mandate programs in light of their costs.

Public receptivity towards renewables displacing fossil fuels is measured by the Renewable Energy Country Attractiveness Index (RECAI), published by Ernst & Young. The index on renewable energy outcomes is based on economic and political stability, ease of doing business, prioritization of renewables and bankability, project attractiveness, and magnitude of renewable energy investments. The top ten leading nations in 2015 for receptivity are China, the US, Germany, Japan, India, Canada, France, the UK, Brazil, and Australia. The RECAI report has commentary for select nations on current activities, plans for the future, relevant happenings such as inauguration or reduction of renewable energy subsidies, and degree of popular and political support for mandated programs.[93]

Renewable Energy in China and the US

China will be burning more coal at least to 2030. But China intends to add enough renewable power capacity to contribute over half of new capacity growth in electricity generation. Natural gas and renewables (nuclear, hydro, solar, wind) are expected to reach the same capacity of coal by 2030 in generating electricity. The share of coal fired power generation is expected to decline from 67 percent in 2012 to 44 percent in 2030. Natural gas and renewables are expected to rise from 27 percent in 2012 to 44 percent in 2030, growing at 47 gW per year. Moreover, massive investments will continue to be made in infrastructure such as long distance transmission lines, smart grid, energy storage, and demand response systems. This process will be aided when China fully implements an emissions trading scheme along with a relatively low carbon tax of $16 per ton carbon dioxide equivalent.[94]

US renewables accounted for 75 percent of new generating capacity during the first quarter of 2015. Of the total of 1,229 mW of electricity generating capacity placed into service, 647 mW was wind, 214 mW solar, 45 mW geothermal, 21 mW hydropower, and the remainder natural gas. At this time renewables made up 17 percent of installed operating generating capacity, of which 8.5 percent is hydro, 5.7 percent wind, 1.4 per-cent biomass, 1 percent solar, and 0.3 percent geothermal. These figures reflect capacity additions, not actual output, which for wind and solar is far below capacity. While solar has just topped 1 percent of electricity generating capacity, this figure may not include solar installations on homes and buildings unassociated with utilities; if so, then the role of solar is understated.[95]

Renewables Displacing Fossil Fuels

Figure 11.5 shows the rapidity of the transition from fossil to renewable energy electric-ity generating units from a starting position of 1,000 units, of which 900 are fossil fueled. Fossil fueled units are phased out 25 units per year and replaced by 40 percent fossil fueled and 60 percent renewables to maintain total output at 1,000 units. As seen, it would take nearly 30 years for renewables to satisfy half of electricity generating capacity and 60 years to fully displace fossil fueled units.

Figure 11.6 has the same starting point but with total energy growing by 1 percent per year and fossil fuel plants being phased out by 2.5 percent per year. This means that retiring of capacity slows over time as the inventory of fossil fuel plants declines. For renewables having 60, 70, and 80 percent of new capacity additions, Figure 11.6 shows that the share of renewables reaches 50 percent in 25–40 years depending on the percent-age of renewables in new capacity additions and asymptotically reaches market saturation at the percentage of renewable capacity additions after 70 or so years.

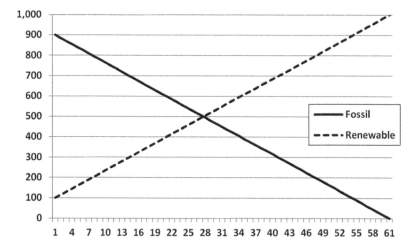

Figure 11.5 Displacement of Fossil Fueled Units by Renewables

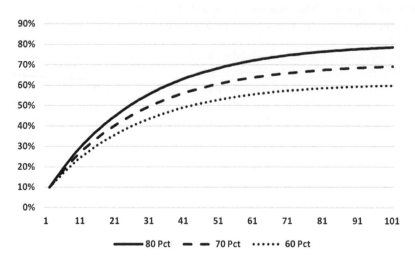

Figure 11.6 Penetration of Renewables for Various Percentages of New Capacity Additions

Thus by having renewables making up over half of new capacity additions, fossil fuel plants can be phased out over 50 years or so with an endpoint being the fraction of renewables to new capacity additions. For fossil fuels to eventually make up 10 percent of plant capacity, then renewables will have to make up 90 percent of new capacity additions.

Can the World Run on Renewable Energy?

Denmark is producing 43 percent of its energy from renewables and is aiming at 70 percent by 2020. Germany is presently 25 percent now and will be achieving 30 percent renewables shortly and aims at 40–50 percent renewable power by 2025, 55–60 percent by 2035, and 80 percent by 2050. Whether Germany achieves these levels depends on how its population reacts to ever higher electricity bills unless this new capacity eventually can be added at the same cost as traditional sources of electric power. Moreover the financial implications for German utilities heavily invested in fossil fuel plants are dire to say the least unless they continue to take drastic action to revamp their business plans.[96] The US lags at 13 percent renewable, but some regions, notably California, point the way forward where some developers are incorporating solar panels into every newly constructed house. Perhaps solar panels should be installed in all newly constructed homes in states where the sun shines much of the time. Perhaps there should be a program to cover every large parking lot and every large flat roof for a commercial building with solar panels.

Despite China's enormous commitment to renewables, it still remains highly reliant on coal. From 2005 to 2011, China added the equivalent of two 600 mW coal burning plants every week and from 2011 to 2013 increased coal burning plant capacity by about half of US capacity. Yet at the same time, China has achieved 20 percent dependence on renewables including hydro power and has become the world's largest solar panel manufacturer. One source has estimated that a renewable energy takeover will require 3.8

million wind turbines, 90,000 utility scale solar plants, 490,000 tidal turbines, 5,350 geo-thermal sites, and 900 hydroelectric plants. The cost for this is not expected to be higher than if this electricity capacity were built for fossil fuel consumption or nuclear power.[97] The problem, of course, is that it's physically impossible to build that much capacity, and if it were built, many conventional plants are going to be retired before the end of their physical lives and funding stranded costs will ultimately raise the price of electricity.

Funding of renewables could follow the German model. Nearly half of Germany's wind and solar power is owned locally by millions of Germans building their retirement nest eggs around wind and solar power plants supplying power to their local communities. These individuals are not only rate payers, but dividend recipients; not only consumers, but producers.[98] Another example of the democratizing of energy is the Province of Ontario, which has experienced difficulties in eliminating coal from its energy structure and substituting renewables. Its one crowning achievement has been the MicroFIT pro-gram that has added over 100 mW of renewables by having 15,000 individuals and small businesses generate their own solar power.[99] Yet despite this progress, there are many who believe that while renewables will certainly make a dent in fossil fuel consumption, the word "eliminate" is entirely inappropriate. The world will be strongly dependent on fossil fuels for decades to come, although there will be regions where renewables may have an upper hand over fossil fuels.

Battery Storage

Prime locations for both wind and solar energy are remote from population areas. Large scale investments in transmission systems are necessary before wind and solar can achieve their full potential. Even so, there appears to be an upper limit for solar and wind power to total electricity demand, given the poor reliability associated with supply being dependent on cloud cover and wind conditions. Higher levels depend on having adequate backup support generally in the form of natural gas and hydro plants that can be rapidly ramped up and down in response to the volatile output of solar and wind. This operational restriction could be relaxed were there sufficiently large capacity super batteries available to store the output of wind turbines and solar arrays until a dispatcher decides to feed stored electricity into the electric grid as though they were quasi-fossil fuel plants. The near term objective is for storage batteries to have four hours of capac-ity, but that isn't nearly enough to operate solar and wind without backup support.[100] Technological advances have to be made in battery design in terms of cost and capacity before such large scale storage of electricity is possible. If such a development took place, storage batteries would face exponential growth. Even so, today's battery technology is being put to good use to smooth the output of solar and wind and to shift power to more desirable times that enhances utilization of generating capacity without having to add peaking generators. By focusing on distributive electricity, storage batteries would increase utilization of existing transmission and distribution systems, obviating some of the need for new investment.

Gravity batteries (pumped hydroelectric storage between two reservoirs at different elevations) are by far the most common source of stored electricity. Using spare electricity to compress air stored in caves and then using compressed air as a power source to gener-ate electricity when needed has been proposed, but only a few units exist. Another form of storage is electrolyzing water with excess electricity to produce hydrogen. Hydrogen, a stored form of electricity, can be consumed as needed by fuel cells to generate electricity. But fuel cells are nowhere near the point of being large generators of electricity. Existing batteries are too small in capacity and too expensive. The best solution would be a low cost dependable storage of immense amounts of electrical charge—a super battery. This technological development is becoming more pressing as renewables exceed fossil fuel in new electricity generating capacity.

Geothermal Power

Geothermal has the potential to power much of the world, but not nearly enough effort is being dedicated to transform geothermal into something other than a marginal contributor to energy supply. More effort in developing geothermal energy is warranted. For instance, Japan could replace a significant portion of its nuclear capacity with much safer geothermal energy. Japan has 100 volcanoes and a potential for 23 gW of geothermal power, the third largest in the world. With a gigawatt being about the average output of a nuclear plant and a bit over 40 reactors currently offline, the development of geothermal energy could replace about half of them. Japan's actual geothermal output is 0.5 gW, with expected growth to 1–1.3 gW by 2030, a proverbial drop in a bucket. The problem is that nearly 80 percent of Japan's geothermal resources are located within national parks or protected hot springs that place severe restrictions on development of any kind.[101] This same problem affects Yellowstone National Park, which has enough geothermal power potential to supply a large portion, if not all, of US electricity demand were it legal and desirable to do so. Another form of geothermal power is combined heating and cooling systems that uses Earth as a heat source or sink. These systems can be reasonably installed in homes under construction in temperate climates. Perhaps geothermal heating and cooling systems, along with solar panels, should be required in new home construction in areas that can benefit from these renewable sources. A massive expansion of geothermal would have to be accomplished on a global scale to make a dent in fossil fuel consumption for electricity generation.

Tidal and Wave Power

River and tidal currents and ocean waves will be marginal contributors under any foreseeable scenario; nevertheless, any contribution these sources can make should not be overlooked. Tides and waves are particularly useful for communities located on isolated islands or in lightly populated shore locations. But tidal power should not be dismissed out of hand. Tidal Lagoon's first project in the UK will produce electricity at $248 per megawatt-hour (24.8 cents per kilowatt-hour), while the second plant will double output at half the cost, which by European standards is low cost electricity.[102]

Efficiency and Conservation

Efficiency and conservation have and will continue to make serious inroads into energy consumption by either accomplishing the same task or enjoying the same functionality with less energy or by adopting a less energy intensive life style. One major area where energy can be captured is waste. In some places, waste material along with sewer sludge is burned for electricity or converted into soil enhancers or into fuels. Europe has led the way of transforming waste into electricity as an alternative to transforming the landscape into a landfill. China is dealing with its mountains of waste by inaugurating waste-to-energy investments for generating electricity, steam, and hot water for industrial use.[103] Ideally human and animal sewage should be placed in a biodigester first to remove methane that can be burned as a biofuel and the remaining sludge either burned to generate electricity or transformed into soil additives. Some oil wells emit large quantities of hot water that is pumped back down the well to maintain reservoir pressure. Thought has been given to operating small geothermal plants to capture the heat before the water is pumped back into the reservoir.[104] Research is being conducted to capture relatively low temperature differences of less than 100°C using the thermogalvanic effect of charging and discharging batteries to capture this source of waste energy.[105]

A source of wasted energy that could be captured is flaring natural gas. This is very common in fracking oil where gas is mixed with oil, but the volume of gas is not sufficient to be gathered and moved to a major natural gas pipeline. CNG-in-a-Box is a mobile technology that captures natural gas intended to be flared and produces compressed natural gas (CNG) that can serve as a motor vehicle fuel and power drilling equipment, reducing demand for gasoline and diesel fuel.[106] Waste-to-energy projects can go a long way to defossilizing energy sources.

Utility Adaptation

The utility industry is under attack, but not like the attack faced by canals with the advent of railroads. This attack can be managed and perhaps corralled for the ultimate benefit of utilities, which is occurring in Europe and elsewhere. What is under attack is not utilities as a concept, but how they had previously modeled their investments. Utilities have historically built base load plants, typically nuclear and coal, which operate 24/7 at full power. Day time demand was typically natural gas. With time-of-day auctions run by utility pools and access provided to independent power producers (IPPs), IPPs would build power stations intended for peak demand. Part of their output was fixed by contract to the utility to assure a credit rating for their underlying bonds that would be satisfactory for investors. Some of the remaining output could be placed in short term contracts for a few years or months at a time and the rest of their output was free to be sold to the utility during the course of the day at higher than base rates to cover spot shortfalls. These short term and spot contracts would determine the return on the equity investment.

Renewables are threatening this cozy arrangement and there is little a utility or an IPP, which is more vulnerable than a utility, can do to prevent renewables from entering the picture. Laws, regulations, renewable portfolio standards, subsidies, feed-in tariffs, and a now well-established renewables industry, particularly solar and wind, with their spokespeople and political influence, have put renewables on the map. The problem with renewables is that supply cannot be controlled and utilities for the most part are obligated to purchase the entire solar and wind output regardless of circumstances. Thus if renewables are available, they must be consumed even at the cost of cutting back or shutting down fossil fuel plants. Advocates of renewables state that this is exactly what should happen to cut greenhouse gas emissions. But look at the implications to the traditional utility model. In Germany, on perfectly sunny days with just the right wind speed, the output of renewables is capable of converting peak demand to a peak trough where the output of solar and wind can cover as much as 78 percent of day time demand. The implications on the classical utility model of base load plants operating 24/7 and natural gas plants satisfying peak demand are disastrous. Investments in IPP plants built to serve peak demand, with the return on investment hinging on electricity rates during peak demand, are in danger of liquidation unless there is enough long term contract coverage to cover their debt obligations. Even base load plants are vulnerable to cut backs that affect their investment return. Utility or IPP owned natural gas plants would have no revenue stream except for those times when solar and wind energy are not available. Under these circumstances, this makes for rather expensive backup electricity and, more to the point, rather poor financial returns for investors. Development of a super battery to smooth solar and wind output and store excess generation such as wind energy at night for dispatching during the day would reduce the need for fossil fuel backup in the form of spinning reserves, further weakening the financial return of fossil fuel generating units.

Another challenge facing the utility industry is a lack of growth in electricity demand in Europe and North America. The year 2000 marked a watershed in electricity consumption when annual gains of 100 kWh per year per person ceased. In 2010 US per capita electricity consumption curve turned negative, reflecting efficiency gains, offshoring of US manufacturing, and a declining standard of living.[107] While global electricity demand is growing modestly, a number of nations are experiencing shrinking electricity demand partly as a result of an economy in the doldrums, partly the impact of efficiency in reducing demand, and partly the rising cost of electricity. In 2014, UK electricity consumption was below 1995 levels, Italy below 2001 levels, France 2002, Germany 2004, and North America 2008. Australia and Japan have declining electricity consumption. These are incredible when the old economic model predicted that economic progress and electricity consumption would go hand in hand. This is a major reversal for the utility industry. The benefit of growth in demand is that it eventually covers the all-too-human error of adding too much capacity before it's actually needed. Without growth in demand, excess capacity weighs on the profitability of utilities by generating stranded costs that eventually are covered by rate increases.

Another challenge is pressure to close coal plants that provide low cost electricity from cheap coal coupled with low capital charges of more or less fully amortized plants. Closing coal plants for replacement by renewable energy adds to the cost of electricity. The 2014 levelized cost of electricity is ranked in Table 11.2. Levelized costs for solar and wind have been in an ongoing downward trend, which is expected to continue at least for another decade. By this time solar and wind without government incentives may be comparable to conventional power plants.

The principal risks facing utilities making investments in new plant capacity are choice of plant, initial cost, fuel costs, regulatory changes, carbon policies, water constraints, stock price shock, and planning errors. Investments in efficiency have the lowest cost and risk profile by far, with its only risk being initial cost.[108]

Utilities have to be aware of the repercussions of government regulation of carbon emissions, which will place high carbon emitters (coal) at greatest risk; need for greater grid resilience towards natural catastrophes; security against both physical and cyberattacks on electricity facilities; and disruptive challenges that are shifting utility business models from simple cost of service to one of carbon reduction and customer engagement. Moreover the continual lowering of cost of natural gas and renewables accentuates the need for greater flexibility in selecting energy sources. In particular, as discussed, solar and wind may replace afternoon demand peak with an afternoon

Table 11.2 Ranking of Costs and Risks for Types of Electricity Generating Plants

Type	Ranking in Costs	Ranking in Risks
Unsubsidized solar thermal	1	Low
Unsubsidized solar PV distributed (primarily home installations)	2	Low
IGCC coal plants with carbon sequestration	3	High
Distributed solar PV with government incentives	4	Low
Nuclear	5	High
Biomass	6	Medium
Conventional pulverized coal plants	7	Medium
Geothermal	8	Medium
Biomass with government incentives	9	Medium
Utility scale solar PV	10	Low
Onshore wind	11	Low
Natural gas combined cycle plants	12	Medium
Utility scale solar PV with incentives	13	Low
Onshore wind with government incentives	14	Low
Efficiency gains (by far lowest cost and lowest risk)	15	Lowest

demand trough for conventional sources of electricity. The trough is caused by solar power peaking at the same time as peak demand. If solar power is significant enough, then peak demand less solar and wind power yields a demand curve for conventional plants where night time or base load demand is higher than what had been day time peak demand. So instead of adding conventional units of power generation into the grid as the day progresses, fossil fuel units have to be taken off line and, in the case of an extreme trough, base load generators such as nuclear and coal would have to be cut back. This is not a hypothetical happenstance—electricity rates have turned negative in order to force cutbacks on nonrenewable power sources.[109] This has turned the demand model for electricity upside down!

Several states have taken the initiative to pursue market and regulatory structures to emphasize cleaner, smarter, and a more decentralized electric grid. Utilities will have to deal in a world with an imperative to increase clean energy even at higher costs than traditional sources. This is not a problem for utilities if rates are allowed to increase compensating for the higher costs, but it might be a problem for electricity consumers. Utilities will have to deal with a greater emphasis on distributed energy resources rather than traditional centralized energy resources. New analytical methods and modeling tools are needed for planning investments. Regulation must continue to evolve to deal with an evolving utility industry. Lastly, collaboration and transparency between utilities and regulators will become more essential than in the past.[110]

The final challenge facing utilities is contending with what amounts to defecting customers. Net zero living is generating enough power to equal the power provided by the grid. Typically a net zero house is powered by photovoltaic solar and is orientated to take full advantage of the sun's rays both for photovoltaic cells for electricity and passive thermal solar heat for hot water and warming a house. It is usually advantageous from an economic standpoint not to invest in a battery. Excess electricity can be sold to the utility and electricity can be drawn from the grid to meet needs when solar power is not available. However, without a battery, a homeowner is vulnerable to a disruption in the grid, whereas a homeowner with an adequately sized battery is now independent of the grid even to the point of dispensing with a hookup altogether.

Net zero homes located in colder climates are highly insulated with triple-pane windows and doors, virtually airtight, and all electric, including baseboard heaters, stoves, hot water heaters, and space heaters. With no connections to natural gas, propane, or heating oil, a modestly sized 1,500 square foot home requires a 4 kW solar system or, in some cases, less. Since the house is air tight, a ventilation system is needed to exchange fresh incoming air with outgoing stale air where incoming air is warmed through a heat recovery exchanger by outgoing air. LED bulbs provide lighting, and a low-flow shower head reduces hot water usage.[111] Net zero homes (sometimes referred to as zero net energy) represent lost business for utilities, yet utilities are responsible for maintaining a distribution system to accept electricity whether desired or not and provide electricity under all circumstances. With buying and selling electricity netting out to zero, net zero homes are effectively a cost to utilities. With batteries, these homes are no longer on the grid, which is probably preferred by utilities as they are no longer responsible for maintaining a hookup. This trend is growing from net zero homes to net zero energy communities. In 2015 a net zero community of 20 residences was completed in Scottsdale, Arizona. The homes are connected to the grid from which they can draw needed electricity or sell excess electricity. Each home is fitted with high-efficiency solar PV panels, an electricity powered and energy efficient heating, ventilation, and air conditioning system, spray foam insulation for walls and roof, highly insulated windows, energy efficient lighting, smart chargers for timing battery charging, and smart appliances, which automatically turn off when not in use or automatically reduce their output when certain conditions apply. Whereas a net zero home of equivalent size requires 7–10 kW of solar electricity, these homes need only 3.5–4.5 kW. Their energy usage is only 60 percent of homes, in compliance with the latest California Energy Code.[112]

Georgetown, Texas, will be receiving 100 percent of its electricity from renewable energy by 2017. Georgetown is supplied by electricity from its municipal utility, which owns no power plant. All its electricity is contractual, which gives Georgetown flexibility to change power sources with maturing of contracts. Georgetown will receive its electricity half from solar and half from wind, with contracts that will ensure sufficient supply even with fluctuations in cloud cover and wind speed. The town still remains connected to the Texas grid just in case there is no sun and wind and to sell its excess electricity. From the perspective of traditional utilities and IPPs in the Texas grid, Georgetown is equivalent to a net zero house.[113]

Higashimatsushima, a town of 40,000 people, devastated by the 2011 tsunami that caused the Fukushima nuclear tragedy, is being rebuilt as a net zero energy town by 2022. The system will be half photovoltaic solar power and half biodiesel generators with a large capacity battery. The town government will serve as a municipal utility and be responsible for setting up a microgrid system including smart grid infrastructure, distribution substations, and smart meters. The town will remain hooked up to the regional utility for the purchase and sale of electricity on a net zero energy basis, and its battery storage capacity will be sufficient to supply power for a number of days in case of a grid blackout.[114]

The flexibility of a municipal utility to take unilateral action to determine power suppliers for a community or city has been adopted in Europe. Municipal utilities, while majority state-owned, have been successful in providing combined heat and power, and in some cases water and steam, to clients, something that traditional utilities don't do.

Municipal utilities represent the decentralization of the older, monolithic utility organization prevalent in the past. Decentralization is ongoing in Germany and is growing in Scandinavia and eastern Europe by establishing municipal utilities. Yet the monolithic utility organization still exists to tie municipalities together to distribute electricity among themselves and to ensure system reliability, resilience, and stability.[115] One could look at this as just another step toward total decentralization where everyone's solar installation becomes a potential power source to feed a microgrid connected to consumers where consumers have a choice of not just power supplier, but a host of power suppliers competing for the consumers' business. Again, some overarching monolithic information technology utility would be necessary to ensure reliability, security, and stability.

One enterprising individual purchased a wrecked Tesla electric vehicle and salvaged the mattress-sized battery and hooked it up to his solar installation, which when expanded by more solar panels will become his own electric company selling electricity to his neighbors.[116] This concept could be expanded to include other homeowners with solar installations, who become members of a microgrid where electricity can be exchanged, or bought and sold, among themselves as necessary to meet their power demands or dispose of excess electricity generation. One company, experiencing outages from the grid, organized a microgrid consisting of solar panels, battery storage, and fossil fuel generators that can provide full electricity backup indefinitely in case of a blackout or a voluntary desire to disconnect from the grid. The microgrid controls the output of the energy sources in terms of minimizing cost.[117]

The utility industry was originally based on a single supplier powering a home or business. Deregulation/liberalization reorganized the utility industry by introducing competition that lowered electricity rates, but did not reduce the utility's mission as a supplier of electricity to consumers. However, microgrids are a direct threat to the *raison d'être* of the whole industry. It is a way for a community or area to remain linked to a utility, but at its volition to divorce itself and supply its own power. It is also a way to completely divorce itself from a utility if a microgrid's cost of electricity is competitive or lower and its reliability is equal or superior to that of the utility. The future may be communities setting up microgrids built around solar power, with utilities distributing power among microgrids to enhance their economic performance. It is not unlike the situation when passenger traffic was dependent on railroads for long distance and trolleys for local transport. Microgrids represent automobiles when passenger traffic became an individual affair totally divorced from train and trolley schedules. Utilities may become something like railroads serving freight and airlines serving passengers over long distances on high volume routes, but where people take care of their local needs via pickup trucks and automobiles. The mission of utilities would be to tie grids together for better efficiency and reliability, but the bulk of electricity would be supplied by millions of microgrids built around solar arrays. For this to occur, microgrids would have to demonstrate their affordability and equitable access to electricity, sustainability, reliability, and resiliency of supply from storms or cyberattacks. If successful, microgrids could be a new business model for utilities where building large scale coal, natural gas, and nuclear plants will no longer assure a utility a place in the sun.[118] And the future certainly seems headed in that direction. In 2015, there are only about 30 commercial microgrid systems installed such as eBay and the US Food and Drug Administration. But this number is anticipated to climb to 300 over the next 2 years in the US, with another 400 in different nations. The potential commercial market for microgrids is estimated to be 24,000 in the US alone.

One company sets up microgrid systems for groups of homeowners powered by rooftop solar panels, which are leased to homeowners at a saving of 10–30 percent off grid prices.[119]

Some believe that the utility industry is facing its eventual demise. The threat is solar power, where solar power coupled with a sufficiently sized storage battery has a declining cost curve, whereas utility rates are experiencing an escalating cost curve from aging transmission and distribution systems in need of upgrading plus new investments in smart grids, generating capacity system in need of replacement, more demanding environmental regulations increasing operating costs, and success in energy efficiency that reduces demand. Reducing demand pushes rates up to reimburse utilities for stranded costs stemming from declining utilization rates of existing plants. When the two cost lines of solar power and conventional utilities cross, the incentive would be for residential users, particularly in states with plenty of sunshine and high electricity rates such as Hawaii and California, to defect from the grid, worsening the problems faced by utilities. Defecting customers will see benefits in greater reliability and resilience to system damage with no exposure to grid blackouts, lower cost electricity, and personal satisfaction in switching to clean energy. Defecting customers will, for the most part, not participate in blackouts except to the degree that they are still dependent on the grid. Blackouts affect millions of utility customers. Over 8 million people were without power in the wake of Superstorm Sandy in October 2012, 4 million customers in 11 Midwest and MidAtlantic states from the Derecho Summer storm in June 2012, 3 million customers from a Nor'easter in October 2011, nearly 3 million customers from a Southeastern blackout in September 2011, 5 million customers from Hurricane Irene in August 2011, and on it goes (2011 was a particularly bad year for blackouts). With utilities making investments on a 30 year time horizon and with consumers taking energy matters into their own hands, it's possible that utilities will face financial losses by not being able to sell the originally intended output of its conventionally fueled generating plants over their useful lives.[120]

One proposal that is just the opposite of a microgrid built around decentralization is the building of a worldwide high voltage direct current (HVDC) transmission system connecting all the continents. HVDC can carry electricity underwater with minimal losses compared to high voltage alternating current (HVAC) transmission. Underwater cables would be minimized in length by using land masses and islands to the maximum practical extent such as in connecting Australia with Asia. Laying a trans-Atlantic cable just south of Greenland can minimize the underwater distance between Europe and the nearest landfall in Canada. The benefit of the Global Renewable Energy Grid (GREG) would be to interconnect solar and wind installations from the Pacific coast of North America to the Pacific coast of Asia. On this basis, solar power would be available around 18 hours a day and wind would be much more reliable by connecting wind farms in far-flung locations. Regional shortages can be matched with regional surpluses by a global HVDC transmission network. Night time production from one part of the globe can be shunted to day time demand in another. Centralized electricity storage can be integrated into the system to further enhance reliability and economic performance. Of course, how this system will be regulated and operated and financed are major hurdles at this time, but the idea is intriguing.[121]

It is clear that the electricity industry in OECD nations needs more demand to keep their investment in electricity generating facilities operating at profitable levels. Just as a century ago when the kerosene market was waning from the intrusion of electricity into lighting, the automobile proved the salvation of the oil industry. Once again the automobile may be called upon to save the electricity generating industry. The only real alternative to reducing fossil fuels for transportation is to switch to electric vehicles. Coupling recharging of electric vehicles with a smart grid would increase and flatten the electricity demand curve. The smart grid would control the timing of recharging automobile batteries or, possibly, for producing hydrogen in a manner that essentially eliminates variable demand. With electricity generating units running close to full capacity, electricity rates would fall to base rates, perhaps low enough for electricity to substitute for heating oil and natural gas in heating and cooling homes and buildings, further reducing reliance on fossil fuels. However, some excess capacity has to be built into the system to cover down times for planned maintenance and unexpected repairs. Such a system would require plenty of renewable sources augmented with a healthy stake in fail-safe nuclear power plants. Smart meters, which ostensibly let consumers select when to run appliances to take advantage of lower electricity rates, would actually become a means to control loads during times when demand is taxing electricity generating capacity. Smart meters coupled with smart grids will be necessary to accommodate the recharging of electric cars and/or electrolysis of water for hydrogen in a world of distributive systems of renewable energy sources (wind farms and solar arrays) coupled with a host of fail-safe nuclear reactors serving local communities.

Summary of Disruptive Challenges Facing the Utility Industry

Disruptive challenges, which have been previously mentioned, can be summarized as:

- Falling costs of distributed energy resources, particularly solar;
- Enhanced focus on development of distributed energy resources;
- Increased consumer, regulatory, and political interest in demand side management technologies;
- Government programs incentivizing the promotion of selected technologies;
- Declining price of natural gas and its impact on other forms of energy to generate electricity;
- Slowing economic growth and its impact on electricity consumption; and
- Rising electricity rates to compensate for falling demand.

Utility investments are normally made over a 30 year period on the presumption that the basic business model will not change appreciably. This is now in question and it's possible that a disruptive challenge can lead to underemployed assets and an inability to recoup the original investment with an intended rate of return. This is already occurring in Europe where recently built natural gas plants have been mothballed or operate at a fraction of their intended output. Part of this is to accommodate rising renewable sources of energy, which has legal priority over fossil fuels, and partly switching to lower cost coal to save money and reduce reliance on Russian gas.[122] This pressure on the utility sector by renewables cutting away at their core business can be seen in the decline of credit ratings for US utilities. In 1970, a few utilities had triple A ratings and 95 percent had A ratings or above. In 1980 B ratings made up 25 percent, which by 2011 had grown to nearly 70 percent of all utilities. Triple A and double A ratings are gone and about 30 percent are single A ratings. Lower ratings mean higher interest rates on long term utility debt, which of course in the present era of zero interest rates for short term paper does not mean that interest rates have climbed as they would have in the past when interest rates were not actively managed by governments. But presumably, in the future, interest rates could climb. Meanwhile electricity consumption is declining in OECD nations for previously cited reasons plus utility customers defecting from the grid and supplying their own power, mainly by solar. Potentially rising interest rates and declining consumption point in only one direction: higher electricity rates. This, perversely, makes installation of solar power for home use and forming microgrids more attractive, compounding the problem. The problem is worsened by the significant subsidizing of solar panels and public policies that encourage renewable energy development such as renewable portfolio standards. There is strong public support for net metering that allows customers to sell excess electricity back to a utility at retail prices. This price has no allowance for the utility to maintain the requisite distribution systems in the face of falling revenue from defecting customers who are both avoiding buying electricity from a utility and selling excess electricity back to a utility at what amounts to a premium rate. (Some utilities already buy electricity from residential users at a wholesale price, about half that of retail.) The utility must adjust its generating units to make room for those who are transmitting electricity into the system, as a utility is obliged to purchase excess electricity from those defecting from the grid. Time-of-use rates encourage utility customers to switch their loads (clothes washers and dryers and hot water heaters) to night time use to take advantage of lower rates. This shifting of load from day time peak to base load was meant to save money for consumers and also to lessen peak demand, and therefore rates, for day time operations of businesses and industries. But higher day time rates were necessary to attract investments in natural gas plants built specifically to address day time peak loads. Lowering day time peak rates by load shifting to night time and emphasizing solar power, a day time peak load satisfier, threatens the financial viability of natural gas electricity generating plants. Wind energy affects base load plants built on a basis of 24 hour a day operation along with affecting peak load conditions. With solar power supplying peak load and wind supplying peak and base load, coupled with public policies that give electricity from renewable energy sources priority over fossil fuels, the net result is consumers paying high rates for electricity to support renewable energy incentives. Meanwhile the wholesale market for traditionally fueled electricity producers is suffering from lack of demand. In this upside down world where retail prices are high and wholesale costs are low, traditional utilities are losing money by owning fossil fuel plants!

Taken to the extreme, the entire utility model described in Chapter 2 may go the way of the dodo bird. This has occurred before. In the 1970s, the US airline industry was regulated and airlines were facing bankruptcy because rising internal costs passed on to passengers in the form of higher fares reduced airline traffic to below self-sustaining. The industry was deregulated, some airlines failed, and others merged, but with the end of subsidies airlines were forced to operate efficiently, fares fell, traffic grew, and the industry prospered. The US telecommunication business in 1978 is unrecognizable today. AT&T essentially had a monopoly on long distance phone lines and telephone charges were high. The monopoly status of AT&T was successfully challenged in court by MCI Communications and today telecommunication companies, using far different technologies, compete, and telephone rates on a per call basis have virtually disappeared with monthly connect fees being the primary means of revenue. The US Post Office is hopelessly in debt, but a government agency is not allowed to fail. Better delivery of packages offered by FedEx and UPS and the switch from mail to email for paying bills and general communications should have been the death-knell for the postal service as presently structured. But maybe not. While FedEx and UPS have taken a great deal of "long distance" packages away from the post office, these companies have recently joined forces with post offices to complete the last stage of delivery for small packages. One long standing suggestion has been to put junk mail on a self-sustaining basis, as junk mail is a major operating loss for the post office, a source of irritation for its customers, and a horrible waste of resources and energy. Congress refuses to consider such a suggestion, pressured by small businesses who consider junk mail part of their marketing strategy. Perhaps the answer is privatization of the post office and let it do whatever needs to be done to ensure its survival.

Companies facing extinction must change; if not, they're another Kodak, a world premier company in film photography that ignored the advent of digital photography. In like manner, the utility industry must adapt its way of doing business, change its models for making investment decisions, and usurp leadership in the transition to renewables that is going to occur independent of the desires of entrenched utility managers. There are just too many companies and individuals seeking ways to bypass utilities for them to succeed by hunkering down in the trenches hoping that the enemy will somehow disappear.[123]

Technology Developments

A great deal of technological progress has been made in lowering the levelized cost of electricity generated from solar and wind. A breakthrough in technological progress in enhancing the efficiency of the conversion of solar power to electricity would make solar power more attractive as an investment by individuals, businesses, and utilities. Wind and solar power need a breakthrough in the development of a super battery. This would enhance the reliability and attractiveness of solar and wind power by smoothing their output and by storing wind electricity generated when it's not needed for dispatching when it is. It would also give a much needed boost to the electric car to get 300 or more miles per charge. Further technological enhancements to the fuel cell are necessary before hydrogen, which is stored electricity, can be considered a viable alternative to the gasoline internal combustion engine. Cellulosic and algal biofuels also need technological breakthroughs to ramp up their volume and become price competitive with gasoline. A more economic means of producing biobutanol from ethanol would incorporate ethanol into the existing gasoline distribution infrastructure. The technology of smart meters is developed—it's a matter of cost and public acceptance. The smart grid, absolutely necessary for managing distributive power sources and recharging electric motor vehicles, has a long way to go in terms of technological development, investment funding, and planning horizons.

Breakthroughs can also come from unexpected directions. Automobile manufacturer Audi in association with the German startup firm Sunfire in Dresden has produced its first batches of e-diesel made from carbon dioxide and water. The process requires low cost electricity from renewable sources to produce hydrogen from water via electrolysis. Carbon dioxide from the air or from utility exhaust (at Audi, carbon dioxide is from a biogas plant) is first converted to carbon monoxide and then, via two chemical processes replete with a number of reactions, into either synthetic methane (e-gas) or a liquid called "blue crude" of long-chain hydrocarbons. Waste heat generated by making e-gas or blue crude is captured and consumed in other industrial processes. Blue crude is then refined to produce synthetic diesel (e-diesel) which can be mixed with petrodiesel to improve its performance similar to biodiesel. The price of e-diesel can be close to petrodiesel, but this depends on low cost electricity.[124] This is an example of turning carbon emissions into a revenue stream rather than a cost to sequester. Other ideas are to turn captured carbon dioxide emissions into useful products such as baking soda, hydrochloric acid, and limestone used in making paper, glass, cement, and other products.[125]

A more futuristic idea is developing a mutant yeast strain to enhance biofuel and biochemical production.[126] Another is an electrolytic cation exchange module capable of removing carbon dioxide from sea water both as a gas and in its carbonate and bicarbonate forms, which would be converted to carbon monoxide and hydrogen, then to liquid hydrocarbons in a catalytic reactor, and finally to jet fuel.[127] More esoteric technologies are fusion-triggered fission where lasers coax electricity from spent nuclear fuel; solar gasoline where concentrated sunlight and carbon dioxide produce hydrogen and carbon monoxide that can then be converted to synthetic motor vehicle fuels; quantum photovoltaics where hot electrons double solar cell efficiency; heat engines where shape-memory alloys produce extra power for cars, appliances, and machinery; the shockwave auto engine where gas turbine cars have five times the mileage of piston powered hybrids; magnetic air conditioners where unusual alloys keep rooms cool and food cold; and clean(er) coal where salt sucks carbon from smokestacks.[128] Other esoteric ideas are Dutch windwheels, electrostatic wind energy converters, solar wind energy towers, and wind trees.[129] The future is anyone's guess!

Taxing Carbon

Two proposals for taxing carbon emissions to create an incentive to switch to renewables are the carbon cap and trade program and a straight carbon tax. A carbon cap and trade program would be suboptimal for a system intended to divorce mankind from fossil fuels. A cap and trade program allows an electric utility to continue operating a coal burning plant as long as it can purchase carbon credits, such as planting trees in Sub-Saharan Africa. This does not deal with the goal of eliminating coal. Cap and trade is great for Wall Street intermediaries as money paid by utilities and companies for carbon credits is funneled to tree farms in developing nations (to be fair, wind and solar farms are being partially financed in China and India by European utilities and manufacturing companies having to buy carbon credits). A carbon tax provides direct revenue to the government, which can then be spent to fund, for example, a transmission highway to connect regions with optimal solar and wind power generation capabilities to the existing electricity grid. A carefully crafted carbon tax creates a world where utilities look at renewables as an economically viable means of replacing fossil fuel generating units. A carbon tax deals directly with the phase out of fossil fuels, whereas a carbon cap and trade program finds alternatives to phasing out fossil fuels, which may not always be effective.[130] A carbon tax, which would increase the price of gasoline and electricity, provides an incentive not just to utilize alternative fuels, but to be more efficient in using less energy to accomplish the same purpose or be more conservative in energy consumption. The latter years of the 1980s and the 1990s provided ample evidence that energy efficiency and conservation fall by the wayside when energy is cheap.

Of course, the presence of a carbon tax would swing the economics in favor of biofuels versus petrofuels and electricity generated by nuclear and renewable energy. A $30 carbon tax would be equivalent to a gasoline tax of 24.4 cents per gallon.[131] Such a tax could be tax-neutral by reducing some combination of personal and corporate tax rates and possibly capital gains taxes to stimulate investments in renewable energy, yet remain a strong incentive to redirect energy consumption from fossil to renewable fuels. A carbon tax, properly constructed, could end all subsidies to solar, wind, and nuclear, along with all subsidies to fossil fuels, a great saving for government expenditures.[132] If cancelling subsidies for fossil fuels in developed nations leads to higher electricity prices, then this just makes alternative fuels more attractive while at the same time saving the government money. If the differential in subsidies paid to fossil fuel companies is large compared to subsidies paid to renewable energy, then it may be possible to eliminate all energy subsidies and still reduce cost differentials between electricity from fossil fuels and renewable energy.

The fossil fuel industry started with coal in the eighteenth century, natural gas in the early nineteenth century, and oil in the late nineteenth century. Obviously surviving companies have been successful. Why do they still have to be coddled by the government? IEA nations paid $550 billion a year to fossil fuel energy suppliers and only $121 billion to renewables in 2013, which is expected to rise to $230 billion in 2030.[133] The fossil fuel industry response is that some of the so-called subsidies are essentially deductions that any company is allowed to take and should not be treated otherwise.[134] In addition to IEA subsidies are non-IEA nation coal subsidies in coal producing developing nations to keep coal prices low for domestic consumption and oil subsidies by oil exporters to keep motor vehicle fuel prices low for domestic consumption. While one thinks that these subsidies benefit the poor, which they do, they also benefit the rich who have established energy consuming businesses that depend on cheap energy supplies for their profitability.

But reduction in carbon emissions by a carbon tax isn't entirely necessary. One can reduce carbon emissions and save money by means of a negative abatement cost (saving energy and money) by switching to LED lighting, insulating buildings, pursuing energy efficiency, capturing waste heat for electricity generation or as a source of hot water, generating electricity from landfill methane, and producing biofuels. Low but positive abatement costs to cut greenhouse gas emissions are restoring degraded land, enabling afforestation, building energy efficient buildings or renovating them with better insulation, providing more efficient heating and cooling systems, installing geothermal energy systems, and enabling better grass land management. More expensive means to reduce greenhouse gases are solar and wind power. The highest abatement cost to reduce greenhouse gas emissions is carbon sequestration of coal burning utilities.[135] Reducing greenhouse gases is just another facet of reducing fossil fuel consumption, which is what sustainable energy is all about.

The major argument opposing a carbon tax, and cap and trade, is that they add to energy costs. If a carbon tax or cap and trade were universally applied via some type of Kyoto Treaty, then all societies would be footing the same bill for an equivalent usage of energy. When only one region of the world, or a select number of nations, make a carbon tax or cap and trade obligatory, then these nations are operating at an economic disadvantage as heavy energy consumers migrate to nations without an obligatory carbon tax or cap and trade. This observation holds for obligatory renewable energy projects that have, at least in the past, been more expensive than traditional fossil fuel plants. As with a carbon tax or cap and trade, the resulting higher energy cost of renewable energy has a baneful effect on local industries. Spain reacted to ever higher electricity rates from renewable energy by reneging on previously arranged subsidy packages that left investors high and dry.[136] Germany is putting a brake on new renewable energy projects by cutting subsidies in its attempt to stabilize the cost of electricity. Either way, investments in renewables suffer. One idea that has been put forward to make investments in renewables more attractive and reduce their financing cost is pooling various projects into one package. For investors, pooling mitigates risk of loss in a single project by being invested in many different types of projects, which is reflected in lower interest costs for participating projects. Lower financing costs reduce required electricity rates for renewables, marginally calming the waters of public criticism over paying high rates.[137]

The Essential Problem Is the Magnitude of the Problem

There are two different approaches to consider. One is to accept the call for "keeping fossil fuels in the ground" to stop climate change.[138] Astonishingly there's no mention of the consequences of suddenly turning off three-quarters of electricity generation and abandoning the world's oil refineries. Just follow the simple minded approach of keeping fossil fuels in the ground and all will be well! The other approach is to accept the reality that Big Oil, Big Natural Gas, and Big Coal are going to be around for decades to come and there is nothing that can be done about it because the magnitude of the problem overwhelms human and capital resources to expand manufacturing and construction capacity to the degree necessary for a rapid transformation of a basic industry. Some blame climate change solely on carbon dioxide emissions and for that reason want to wipe the planet clean of fossil fuels with alternative energy sources. My point is that the fossil fuel industry will be wiped out as their resources are exhausted, and for that reason, alternative energy sources have to be developed at a pace to avoid the ultimate energy crisis.[139] These differences of opinion are like two individuals walking in opposite directions on what appears to be an infinite plane—they never intend to meet. But they do meet face to face because they didn't realize that they were on a large sphere. Energy sustainability means that in a century, possibly two, a lifespan of two or three rather long lived individuals, recoverable fossil fuels will be exhausted. If nuclear, hydro, solar, wind, geothermal, and other renewables have not taken up the slack to essentially power everything, then planet Earth may well end as planet Easter Island.

Getting rid of fossil fuels should make everyone happy . . . but, of course, it won't. Environmental objections over wind farms, perhaps solar installations, and certainly nuclear power plants, even of a fail-safe design, will remain persistent. If these groups are effective in blocking the conversion process, as they've been in the past, particularly in the US, then turning away from fossil fuels cannot occur. By thwarting progress in finding a solution to the fossil fuel problem, perhaps the more extreme environmentalists' solution of eliminating 90 percent of the world population in order to save planet Earth may become more than just a talking point.

There Is Always an Alternative

The alternative is very simple. Do nothing—which is what we did for the first 30–35 years after the 1973 oil crisis. It is remarkable that this book contains nothing new had it been written in the 1970s, other than technological progress in manufacturing wind turbines, solar panels, and hybrid cars, and by extending fossil fuel reserves in developing deep water oil fields, bitumen resources, and fracking hard shale and tight sand. Only in recent years have wind and solar taken off as significant new energy sources. Europe, the US, and Japan adopted energy policies fairly early on, with China and India tagging along. Many nations have no coherent national energy policies or, if a nation has one, there is no effectual action plan to accomplish it. Since the 1973 energy crisis, much of the world has been to various degrees adrift with regard to energy policies that reduce fossil fuels. Even with progress made to date with renewable energy, we are consuming more fossil fuels than ever before. Since 1973, world oil consumption has climbed nearly 50 percent and is continuing to grow, although at a slower pace than other fossil fuels. Natural gas is up 190 percent and coal 145 percent, with both still growing and expected to continue growing. The primary reason for this is unrelenting growth in population and per capita energy consumption. By any measure the scope of the problem is getting worse. We can drift for the next 50 years consuming more and more fossil fuels, but I don't think this luxury will be available forever. I don't think we have the capability of adding multiple Saudi Arabias to oil production, which would be necessary just to keep up with modest growth in demand and declining production of existing fields. Fracking is not a long term solution with its 3 year life span for a producing well. It is a short term breather to give us more time to deal with the long term problem of fossil fuels. Fracking will, by the mathematics of the situation, eventually transform the countryside into an industrial waste land of abandoned well sites. Reliance on carbon rich oil sands and bitumen also gives us a breather, but not a solution.

The solution is electricity from renewables including fail-safe nuclear power plants and biofuels from nonfood sources. We have to be blind not to see the danger of relying on the Middle East for a third of the world's oil production when geopolitical risk is growing daily. We are close to a major conflict in the Middle East that is only tangentially related to oil. It is actually a hegemonic conflict among competing cultures in an area of the world which, incidentally, houses a large portion of global oil reserves and production. Moreover, petroleum has the lowest reserves to production ratio of fossil fuels. This makes petroleum much more important on the fossil fuel priority list than natural gas and coal. We've accomplished nothing for being involved in the Middle East for a generation despite a body count of thousands, maimed bodies and minds of tens of thousands, and two trillion wasted dollars. If oil carried a Security Premium to cover the cost of these Middle East conflicts, certainly an externality that should have been internalized in the aftermath of the first Gulf War, we would have a different perspective and a stronger incentive on trying to reduce petroleum usage in favor of natural gas, electricity, and biofuels.

Asia has yet to react with the apparent US abandonment of its decades' old policy of having a strong military presence in the Middle East. Asia, more vulnerable to an oil shock than the US, appears to have no contingency plans in place other than China's expanding its strategic oil reserves. Perhaps China's and Japan's building up its naval forces ostensibly for hegemonic control over the South China Sea may have another mission. The industrial world becoming a collection of third world nations of endless depression and poverty and social unrest is the risk we are taking when we continue drifting without an effective action plan to reduce dependence on fossil fuels, particularly oil. When the infrastructure of refineries, pipelines, storage tanks, and filling stations of the most vulnerable of the fossil fuels runs dry, then what do we do?

Problems

Problem 11.1

Complete Problem Table 11.1 to obtain the total cost of lighting for 50,000 hours of illumination.

Problem Table 11.1

	LED	CFL	Incandescent
Lifespan in hours	50,000	10,000	1,200
Watts per bulb equivalent to lumens of 60 W bulb	10	14	60
Cost per bulb	$36	$4	$1.25
kWh over 50,000 hours			
Electricity cost at $0.12/kWh			
# bulbs for 50,000 hours' usage			
Cost of bulbs in 50,000 hours' usage			
Total cost of 50,000 hours' usage			

Problem 11.2

A CFL bulb contains 5 milligrams of mercury, which is released if broken. How much mercury is released to the environment by burning coal to generate electricity to power an incandescent bulb and a CFL for 50,000 hours of illumination? Start with the fact that coal fired power plants produced 1,971 billion kilowatt-hours of electricity while emitting 50.7 tons of mercury into the air in 2006. Assuming tons of mercury is in short tons of 2,000 pounds, first convert 50.7 short tons to metric tons and from that calculate the milligrams of mercury released producing 1 kWh of electricity. Adjust this value for 10 percent loss in transmission and distribution to obtain milligrams of mercury per kilowatt-hour consumed in a home. Then multiply this by the kilowatt-hours consumed for 50,000 hours of operation for the CFL and incandescent bulb calculated in the previous problem. While it is true that 5 milligrams of mercury in a CFL bulb would only be released to the environment if broken, considering the disposal methods of household waste, the bulb would most probably be broken. Multiplying 5 milligrams of mercury content per bulb for the number of CFL bulbs for 50,000 hours from the previous problem, which type of bulb releases more mercury to the environment?

Problem 11.3

This problem derives the mathematics of exhaustion shown in Figure 11.2. Let Column A be years from 0 to 100 starting in row 5. Supply for year 0 is 1,000 for all columns. Column B is 3 percent growth for the resource with 3.5 percent growth in consumption for a formula in cell B6 of =B5*(1.03–0.035). Column C is 3 percent growth in the resource coupled with 4 percent growth in consumption. Column D is consumption of 40 units per year and column E is consumption of 40 units per year escalating at 2.5 percent. The results should be the same as cited in the text.

Problem 11.4

This problem derives that the current EROEI is about 40; or one unit of energy input is necessary to generate 40 units of energy output. Using the EROEI values in

Figure CW11.1 and global energy consumption from *BP Energy Statistics*, derive the weighted average value of EROEI. The percentage assigned to renewables may require some intelligent estimations, but this will not materially affect EROEI as the overall percentage of renewables is quite small compared to conventional sources of energy.

Problem 11.5

This problem derives the values for Figure CW11.2 on what would be the energy input and output curves if energy consumption is growing by 1 percent per year and the initial weighted average EROEI of 40 is declining by 2.5 percent per year indefinitely (say 300 years). Let column B be 100 escalating at 1 percent per year, column C be 40 deescalating at 2.5 percent per year, and column D being column B divided by column C to obtain energy input taking both growing energy output and declining EROEI into consideration.

Problem 11.6

Suppose that a base load coal plant of 1,000 mW operating at 95 percent utilization requires 2 liters per kilowatt-hour. How many cubic meters of water are required primarily for cooling purposes on an annual basis? How about global electricity generation net of renewables (solar, wind) of 23,000 tWh in water demand in cubic meters and cubic kilometers?

Problem 11.7

This problem derives the values for Figure 11.5. Suppose that current energy supply consists of 1,000 units of which 900 represent fossil fuel plants and 100 renewables. Twenty-five units of fossil fuel capacity are being phased out each year from fossil fuel alone. Replacement capacity is 60 percent renewables and 40 percent fossil fuel. How many years until renewables are about 50 percent of total capacity and how many years before there are no fossil fuel plants left? The percentage replacement fossil fuel should be (1 − replacement renewables)—why? This problem is relatively simple to formulate with replacement in absolute terms. What are the weak points of this approach?

Problem 11.8

This problem derives the values for Figure 11.6. Similar to Problem 11.7, this problem is set up in relative terms. Total demand for 1,000 units of capacity is growing by 1 percent a year and phase out of old fossil fuel plants are 2.5 percent per year. Replacement capacity is 60 percent renewables and 40 percent fossil fuel. First calculate annual demand for new plants which is incremental growth in demand plus annual phase out of older fossil plants. Notice how phase out in terms of capacity declines with time as the number of fossil fuel plant units drop. Net incremental demand is then divided into new renewables and fossil fuel capacity. The cumulative total of new additions has to be used to get the projected capacity. How many years until renewables are 50 percent of total capacity? Repeat this for replacement capacity of 70 percent renewables/30 percent fossil fuels and 80 percent renewables/20 percent fossil fuels. Examine the nature of the projected percentage of renewable capacity—can you explain why the curve approaches the percentage of new renewable capacity asymptotically? What would be your critical analysis of this approach?

Problem 11.9

This problem is to set up a spreadsheet to project the number of Saudi Arabias that have to be added to oil production given per capita oil consumption, global population, and decline rate in existing oil production. Obtain the annual rate for 7.1 billion people to grow to 9.3 billion people by 2050 and apply this growth to the 7.1 billion for each year between now and 2050. For year zero (2013), the per capita Bpd is the current population divided by 91.3 million Bpd. Construct a column where this can be escalated or deescalated by any desired percentage which is applied to the 2013 per capita Bpd. Then multiply these two columns to obtain a projection of oil consumption. In a similar fashion construct a column for production starting at 91.3 million Bpd deescalating by an arbitrarily selected percentage such as −1.5 percent. Then take the difference between production and consumption divided by 11.5 million Bpd to obtain the number of Saudi Arabias. For 0% growth for per capita consumption and 1.5% decline for existing production, the projection should be 5.9 Saudi Arabias of additional production in 2050. Then experiment with other value assessments for per capita consumption growth and natural decline of existing production. Note how minor changes in assumptions can have a major impact on projected results.

Notes

1 "Asian Brown Cloud: Climate and Other Environmental Impacts," United Nations Environment Programme (UNEP) (2002). See also Bob Hershon, "Asian Brown Cloud," AAAS Science Update, Website http://sciencenetlinks.com/science-news/science-updates/asian-brown-cloud; Indian Ocean Experiment, Website http://idn.ceos.org/KeywordSearch/Metadata.do?Portal=idn_ceos&Keywo rdPath=[Keyword%3D%27INODEX%27]&OrigMetadataNode=GCMD&EntryId=INDOEX_ UCAR_JOSS_NOAA_CODIAC&MetadataView=Full&MetadataType=0&lbnode=mdlb3; and Syd Perkins, "Asian Brown Cloud Threatens U.S.," *AAAS Science News* (May 25, 2012), Website http://news.sciencemag.org/asia/2012/05/asian-brown-cloud-threatens-u.s.
2 Alex Morales, "China's Air Pollution Kills 4,000 People a Day," *Bloomberg Business* (August 13, 2015), Website www.bloomberg.com/news/articles/2015-08-13/china-air-pollution-kills-4-000-people-a-day-researchers.
3 "7 Million Premature Deaths Annually Linked to Air Pollution," World Health Organization (March 25, 2014), Website www.who.int/mediacentre/news/releases/2014/air-pollution/en.
4 G. Stanhill and S. Cohen, "Global Dimming: A Review of the Evidence," *Agricultural and Forest Meteorology*, Vol. 107 (2001).
5 "What is Global Dimming?" Conserve Energy Future, Website www.conserve-energy-future.com/causes-and-effects-of-global-dimming.php.
6 Rob Painting, "Global Dimming in the Hottest Decade," *Skeptical Science* (October 25, 2012), Website www.skepticalscience.com/Global-Dimming-in-the-Hottest-Decade.html.
7 "SO2 Allowance Auctions," EPA, Website www2.epa.gov/airmarkets/so2-allowance-auctions.
8 Chris Colose, "What Would a CO2-Free Atmosphere Look Like?" *Skeptical Science* (March 11, 2011), Website www.skepticalscience.com/What-would-a-CO2-free-atmosphere-look-like.html.
9 "Electric Market National Overview (Slide 13), Federal Energy Regulatory Commission, Website www.ferc.gov/market-oversight/mkt-electric/overview/2009/08-2009-elec-ovr-archive.pdf.
10 "Progress Cleaning the Air and Improving People's Health," EPA, Website www.epa.gov/air/caa/progress.html.

11 "The Montreal Protocol on Substances That Deplete the Ozone Layer," United Nations Environment Programme: Ozone Secretariat, Website http://ozone.unep.org/en/handbook-montreal-protocol-substances-deplete-ozone-layer/5.

12 The Ozone Hole, Website www.theozonehole.com/2014ozonehole.htm.

13 "Kyoto Protocol," United Nations Framework Convention on Climate Change, Website http://unfccc.int/kyoto_protocol/items/2830.php.

14 "Climate Change Indicators in US," EPA, Website www3.epa.gov/climatechange/ghgemissions/gases.html. See also "Greenhouse Gas," Wikipedia: The Free Encyclopedia, Website http://en.wikipedia.org/wiki/Greenhouse_gas.

15 "The Largest Producers of CO2 Emissions Worldwide in 2014, Based on Their Share of Global CO2 Emissions," statista, Website www.statista.com/statistics/271748/the-largest-emitters-of-co2-in-the-world.

16 "The Convention and Kyoto Protocol," UN, Website www.unfccc.int/resource/convkp.html.

17 "Status of the Doha Amendment," United Nations Framework Convention on Climate Change, Website http://unfccc.int/kyoto_protocol/doha_amendment/items/7362.php.

18 "Doha Amendment to the Kyoto Protocol," United Nations Framework Convention on Climate Change, Website http://unfccc.int/files/kyoto_protocol/application/pdf/kp_doha_amendment_english.pdf.

19 *Emissions Trading and Utilities: What's the Impact?* (Albuquerque, NM: UtiliPoint International, 2005). See also "Climate Change," European Commission, Website http://ec.europa.eu/clima/policies/ets/index_en.htm.

20 "International Carbon Action Partnership (ICAP): Status Report 2015" (Page 24), Website https://icapcarbonaction.com/images/StatusReport2015/ICAP_Report_2015_02_10_online_version.pdf.

21 *A Guide to Emissions Trading* (New York, NY: United Nations Environmental Programme, 2002). See also "International Emissions Trading," United Nations Framework Convention on Climate Change, Website http://unfccc.int/kyoto_protocol/mechanisms/emissions_trading/items/2731.php.

22 "Clean Development Mechanism (CDM)," United Nations Framework Convention on Climate Change, Website http://unfccc.int/kyoto_protocol/mechanisms/clean_development_mechanism/items/2718.php.

23 "Climate Finance," World Bank, Website https://wbcarbonfinance.org/Router.cfm?Page=ProjPort&ItemID=24702.

24 "CDM Project Activities," United Nations Framework Convention on Climate Change, Website http://cdm.unfccc.int/Statistics/Public/CDMinsights/index.html.

25 "Trend of Types of Projects Registered and Registering," United Nations Framework Convention on Climate Change, Website http://cdm.unfccc.int/Statistics/Public/files/201502/regtypenum.pdf.

26 "European Carbon Price 'Inching Ever Closer to Zero,'" *The Economist* (February 7, 2013).

27 "Carbon Markets: Complete Disaster in the Making," *The Economist* (September 15, 2012).

28 Christian Oliver and Pilata Clark, "EU Plans to Revive Lifeless Carbon Market," *Carbon Markets: Financial Times* (October 13, 2014), Website www.ft.com/cms/s/0/23d2b622-4fce-11e4-a0a4-00144feab7de.html#axzz3Ux5WUDmn.

29 Paul Hockenos, "Europe Sinks Its Flagship Carbon Trading Scheme," *Renewable Energy World* (May 10, 2013), Website www.renewableenergyworld.com/rea/news/article/2013/05/europe-sinks-its-flagship-carbon-trading-scheme. See also "Europe's Dirty Secret: The Unwelcome Renaissance," *The Economist* (January 5, 2013).

30 "Green Car Congress: Toyota to Develop Hybrid Vehicles with Two Chinese Partners" (November 21, 2013), Green Car Congress, Website www.greencarcongress.com/2013/11/20131120-tmc.html. See also "Guangzhou Toyota Begins Production," 75 Years of Toyota, Website www.toyota-global.com/company/history_of_toyota/75years/text/leaping_forward_as_a_global_corporation/chapter4/section4/item1_b.html.

31 Regional Greenhouse Gas Initiative, Website www.rggi.org.

32 US Conference of Mayors Climate Protection Agreement, Website www.usmayors.org/climate protection/agreement.htm. For current activities see Website www.usmayors.org/climateprotection/revised.

33 Patrick George, "How the California Air Resources Board Works," howstuffworks, Website http://auto.howstuffworks.com/fuel-efficiency/fuel-economy/carb2.htm.

34 "Smog Check in California," DMV.ORG (privately owned), Website www.dmv.org/ca-california/smog-check.php.

35 New York State Department of Motor Vehicles, Website http://dmv.ny.gov/registration/california-emissions-standards.

36 EPA Regulation and Standards, Website www.epa.gov/otaq/climate/regulations.htm. See also EPA Emission Standards Reference Guide, Website www.epa.gov/otaq/standards/index.htm.

37 Justin Gerds, "How Will California Slash Greenhouse Gas Emissions by 80% by 2050?" *Forbes* (February 27, 2013), Website www.forbes.com/sites/justingerdes/2013/02/27/how-will-california-slash-greenhouse-gas-emissions-80-by-2050.

38 "Energy Conservation & Efficiency Tips," just energy, Website www.justenergy.com/green-energy/energy-conservation-efficiency-tips.

39 Robert Michaels, "The Hidden Flaw of Energy Efficiency," *The Wall Street Journal* (August 20, 2012), Website www.wsj.com/articles/SB10001424052702303933704577532610425105168.

40 "Negawatt Hour: The Energy Conservation Business is Booming," *The Economist* (March 1, 2014).

41 "Energy Efficiency Market Report," OECD/IEA (2014).

42 National Park Services, Website www.nps.gov/thrb/learn/historyculture/trandthenpsystem.htm.

43 Jarad Diamond, *Collapse: How Societies Choose to Fail or Succeed* (New York, NY: Penguin Publishing Group, 2011).

44 This ecological disaster has been well documented, such as "The Collapse of the Cod Fishery of the Grand Banks," Website www.sjsu.edu/faculty/watkins/grandbanks.htm.

45 "The State of World Fisheries and Aquaculture," Food and Agricultural Organization of the United Nations (2012), Website www.fao.org/docrep/016/i2727e/i2727e01.pdf. Earlier data obtained from other FAO sites.

46 "The Future of World Religions: Population Growth Projections, 2010–2050," Pew Research Center (April 2, 2015), Website www.pewforum.org/2015/04/02/religious-projections-2010-2050.

47 "Ratio of Workers to Retirees in Japan (2000–2050)," The Japan Institute for Labor Policy and Training, Website www.jil.go.jp/english/index.html.

48 Kanoko Matsuyama, "In Japan, Retirees Go on Working," *Bloomberg Business* (August 30, 2012), Website www.bloomberg.com/bw/articles/2012-08-30/in-japan-retirees-go-on-working.

49 Max Roser, "Future World Population Data—Our World in Data," Our World in Data (2014), Website http://ourworldindata.org/data/population-growth-vital-statistics/future-world-population-growth.

50 Data sources *BP Energy Statistics* and US Census Bureau.

51 The Website https://populationspeakout.org/the-book/view-book shows stunning photographs of what's afflicting this world.

52 Nick Cunningham, "How Much Water Does the Energy Sector Use?" Oil Price (April 13, 2015), Website http://oilprice.com/Energy/Energy-General/How-Much-Water_Does-The-Energy-Sector-Use.html.

53 William Wurtz (SPX Cooling Technologies) and Robert Peltier, "Air-Cooled Condensers Eliminate Plant Water Use," *Power* (September 15, 2008), Website www.powermag.com/air-cooled-condensers-eliminate-plant-water-use.

54 Robert Bryce, "Corn Ethanol is Worse than Keystone," *Bloomberg View* (June 2, 2015), Website www.bloombergview.com/articles/2015-06-02/corn-ethanol-is-worse-than-keystone.

55 Manuel Soque and Colin McClelland, "Angola's $750 Million Sugar-to-Fuel Project to Start in June," *Bloomberg* (May 26, 2015), Website www.bloomberg.com/news/articles/2015-05-26/angola-sugar-to-fuel-farm-delayed-for-tests-as-costs-rise-50-.

56 Roy Hales, "Why Fungi-Based Biofuels Could Eventually Replace Conventional Jet Fuel," *Renewable Energy World* (May 8, 2015), Website www.renewableenergyworld.com/rea/news/article/2015/05/why-fungi-based-biofuels-could-eventually-replace-conventional-jet-fuel.

57 Kaitlyn Bunker (RMI),"A Caribbean Island Says Goodbye Diesel and Hello 100 Percent Renewable Electricity," *Renewable Energy World* (January 9, 2015), Website www.renewableenergyworld.com/rea/news/article/2015/01/a-caribbean-island-says-goodbye-diesel-and-hello-100-percent-renewable-electricity.

58 Paul Hockenos, "Brave Little Denmark Leads War Against Coal," Aljazeera (November 17, 2014), Website http://america.aljazeera.com/opinions/2014/11/denmark-war-againstcoalgermanyrenewableenergy.html.

59 Elisa Wood,"Obama's New Carbon Plan Makes History for Clean Energy," *Renewable Energy World* (June 2, 2014), Website www.renewableenergyworld.com/articles/2014/06/obamas-new-carbon-plan-makes-history-for-clean-energy.html.

60 Andy Tully (Oil Price),"The Oil Price War has Just Begun," *Business Insider* (May 18, 2015), Website www.businessinsider.com/the-oil-price-war-has-just-begun-2015-5.

61 "The Oil Industry: After OPEC," *The Economist* (May 16, 2015).

62 Brent Snavely and Alisa Priddle, "Ford to Lay Off 700 Workers at Michigan Assembly Due to Slow Car Sales," *Detroit Free Press* (April 23, 2015), Website www.freep.com/story/money/cars/ford/2015/04/23/ford-cuts-shift-michigan-assembly-plant-focus-cmax/26251933.

63 "Infographic of the Day: Automobile Fuel Efficiency Technology," Global Economic Intersection (April 4, 2013), Website http://econintersect.com/b2evolution/blog1.php/2013/04/04/automobile-fuel-efficiency-technology.

64 Wayne Risher, "FedEx Races Past Fuel Economy Goal," knoxnews.com (March 6, 2013), Website www.knoxnews.com/news/2013/mar/06/fedex-races-past-fuel-economy-goal.

65 Charles Cook (Maxwell Technologies), "Transforming the Transportation Industry with Renewable Energy," *Renewable Energy World* (September 18, 2014), Website www.renewableenergyworld.com/rea/news/article/2014/09/transforming-the-transportation-industry-with-renewable-energy.

66 Philip Longman, "Back on Tracks," *Washington Monthly* (January–February, 2009), Website www.washingtonmonthly.com/features/2009/0901.longman.html.

67 David Ferris,"The Future of Energy: Next-Next-Gen Nuclear Power," *Popular Science* (June, 2013).

68 Tom DeRosa, "Renewables vs. Nuclear: Do We Need More Nuclear Power?" *Renewable Energy World* (April 28, 2015), Website www.renewableenergyworld.com/rea/blog/post/2015/04/renewables-vs-nuclear-do-we-need-more-nuclear-power.

69 "European Space Agency's Sentinel-1A Satellite Observes Major Displacement of Land Following the Mega-Quake in Nepal," European Space Agency (April 17–29, 2015), Website http://earthobservatory.nasa.gov/IOTD/view.php.

70 "Nepal Earthquake Damages at Least 14 Hydropower Dams," circle of blue (May 5, 2015), Website www.circleofblue.org/waternews/2015/world/nepal-earthquake-damages-at-least-14-hydropower-dams.

71 "Grid-Scale Energy Storage: Smooth Operators," *The Economist* (December 6, 2014).

72 "Wind and Solar Power are Even More Expensive than is Commonly Thought," *The Economist* (July 26, 2014).

73 Rachel Morison, "Europe Divided on Supply Security as Green Power Gains: Energy," *Bloomberg* (February 4, 2014), Website www.bloomberg.com/news/articles/2014-02-04/europe-divided-on-supply-security-as-green-power-gains-energy.

74 Chris Meehan, "Do Solar and Wind Cause Power Plants to Release More Pollution?" Solar Reviews, (September 27, 2013), Website www.solarreviews.com/news/solar-wind-reduce-emmisions-NREL-092713.

75 S. Nicola, W. Zha, L. Totaro, and D. Bennett, "German Solar Age's First Eclipse Passes with Brief Surge in Power Price," *Bloomberg New Energy Finance* as reported by *Renewable Energy World* (March 20, 2015), Website www.renewableenergyworld.com/rea/news/article/2015/03/german-solar-ages-first-eclipse-passes-with-brief-surge-in-power-price.

76 John Moore, "Experts Agree: Electric Grid Will Stay Ahead of the Curve on the Clean Power Plan," Natural Resources Defense Council (May 12, 2015), Website http://switchboard.nrdc.org/blogs/jmoore/experts_agree_electric_grid_wi.html.

77 Arno Harris, "Chicken Little and the 'Crisis' of Grid Reliability," Recurrent Energy (March 1, 2013), Website http://recurrentenergy.com/dev/blogchicken-little-and-crisis-grid-reliability.

78 Rachel Morison and Weizin Zha, "Renewable Power Can Now Flow All Over Europe," *Renewable Energy World* (May 20, 2015), Website www.renewableenergyworld.com/articles/2015/05/renew able-power-can-now-flow-all-over-europe.html?eid=291117084&bid=1077409.

79 Tino Andresen, "Germany's Powerhouse Feels Pinch of Shift to Renewables," *Bloomberg* (May 12, 2015), Website www.bloomberg.com/news/articles/2015-05-12/germany-s-powerhouse-feels-pinch-of-shift-to-renewables. See also Philippe Paelinck (Alstom), "Moving Towards the European Super Grid," *Renewable Energy World* (April 30, 2014), Website www.renewableenergyworld.com/articles/2014/04/moving-towards-the-european-super-grid.html.

80 Christopher Martin, "NRDC and U.S. Utilities Urge Grid Payments for Solar," *Bloomberg* (February 13, 2014), Website www.bloomberg.com/news/articles/2014-02-12/nrdc-and-u-s-utilities-seek-compensation-for-rooftop-solar-cost.

81 Tildy Bayar, "Virtual Power Plants: A New Model for Renewables Integration," *Renewable Energy World* (September 30, 2013), Website www.renewableenergyworld.com/rea/news/article/2013/09/virtual-power-plants-a-new-model-for-renewables-integration.

82 "Flat-Pack Lens Boosts Solar Power: Fresnel Lens Concentrates Solar without Bulk," ScienceDaily (February 10, 2014), Website www.sciencedaily.com/releases/2014/02/140210101945.htm.

83 "5 Energy Innovators Driving Personal Energy Independence," *Renewable Energy World* (July 7, 2014), Website www.renewableenergyworld.com/rea/news/article/2014/07/5-energy-innovators-driving-personal-energy-independence?page=all.

84 DESERTEC, Website www.desertec.org/global-mission.

85 Pantho Rahaman, "Bangladesh Plans to be World's 'First Solar Nation,'" Reuters (January 25, 2015), Website http://in.reuters.com/article/2015/01/25/bangladesh-solar-idINKBN0KY0O2 20150125.

86 "Germany's Energy Transition: Sunny, Windy, Costly and Dirty," *The Economist* (January 18, 2014).

87 "Germany Energy Minister Proposes Cuts to Renewable Subsidies, Industry Reacts," *Bloomberg News* as reported by *Renewable Energy World* (January 20, 2014), Website www.renewableenergyworld.com/rea/news/article/2014/01/german-energy-minister-proposes-cuts-to-renewable-subsidies-industry-reacts.

88 "European Residential Electricity Prices Increasing Faster than Prices in United States," US Energy Information Administration (EIA) (November 18, 2014), Website www.eia.gov/todayin energy/detail.cfm?id=18851.

89 Alex Morales and Sally Bakewell, "Renewable Energy Loses Out in Europe's 'Lame-Duck' Climate Plan," *Bloomberg* (January 24, 2014), Website www.bloomberg.com/news/articles/2014-01-23/eu-renewable-energy-loses-out-on-bloc-s-lame-duck-plan.

90 "Electricity Firms in Japan: Solar Shambles," *The Economist* (November 29, 2014).

91 Mike Anderson, James Paton, and Jason Scott, "Australia Chills Hopes for $20 Billion Clean Energy Industry," *Bloomberg* (August 20, 2014), Website www.bloomberg.com/news/articles/2014-08-20/australia-review-chills-20-billion-clean-energy-industry.

92 Steven Mufson and Tom Hamburger, "Ohio Governor Signs Bill Freezing Renewable-Energy Standards," *The Washington Post* (June 13, 2014), Website www.washingtonpost.com/business/economy/ohio-governor-signs-bill-freezing-renewable-energy-standards/2014/06/13/730d8b44-f33b-11e3-9ebc-2ee6f81ed217_story.html.

93 "Renewable Energy Country Attractiveness Index (RECAI)," Website www.ey.com/Publication/vwLUAssets/Renewable_Energy_Country_Attractiveness_Index_43/$FILE/RECAI%2043_March%202015.pdf. The current report can be obtained from Website www.ey.com/GL/en/Industries/Power---Utilities/Renewable-Energy-Country-Attractiveness-Index.

94 "China's Power Sector Heads toward a Cleaner Future," *Bloomberg New Energy Finance* (August 27, 2013), Website http://about.bnef.com/press-releases/chinas-power-sector-heads-towards-a-cleaner-future.

95 Kenneth Bossong (SUN DAY Campaign), "Renewables Account for 75 Percent of New US Generating Capacity in First Quarter of 2015," *Renewable Energy World* (April 23, 2015), Website www.renewableenergyworld.com/rea/news/article/2015/04/renewables-account-for-75-percent-of-new-us-generating-capacity-in-first-quarter-of-2015.

96 Tino Andresen, "German Utilities Hammered in Market Favoring Renewable Energy," *Bloomberg* (August 12, 2013) as reported by *Renewable Energy World*, Website www.renewableenergyworld. com/rea/news/article/2013/08/german-utilities-hammered-in-market-favoring-renewable-energy?cmpid=rss.

97 "Can the World Run on Renewable Energy?" Wharton (University of Pennsylvania) (April 23, 2015), Website http://knowledge.wharton.upenn.edu/article/can-the-world-run-on-renewable-energy.

98 John Farrell, "3 Reasons Germans are Going Renewable 'At All Costs,'" Clean Technica (October 23, 2013), Website http://cleantechnica.com/2013/10/23/3-reasons-germans-going-renewable-costs.

99 John Farrell, "Ontario Kills Coal, But Local Renewables Program Falters," grist (October 15, 2013), Website http://grist.org/article/ontario-kills-coal-but-local-renewables-program-falters.

100 Michael Kanellos, "Will Lithium Ion Work for Grid-Scale Storage?" *Renewable Energy World* (October 2, 2014), Website www.renewableenergyworld.com/rea/blog/post/2014/10/will-lithium-ion-work-for-grid-scale-storage.

101 Meg Cichon, "Is Japan the Next Boom Market for the Geothermal Energy Industry?" *Renewable Energy World* (May 30, 2015), Website www.renewableenergyworld.com/articles/print/volume-18/issue-3/features/geothermal/is-japan-the-next-boom-market-for-the-geothermal-energy-industry.html.

102 Louise Downing (Bloomberg), "Tidal Lagoon's Next Plant May Produce Power on Par with Nuclear," *Renewable Energy World* (March 20, 2015), Website www.renewableenergyworld.com/rea/news/article/2015/03/tidal-lagoons-next-plant-may-produce-power-on-par-with-nuclear.

103 Liu Yuanyuan, "Chinese Waste-to-Energy Market Experiences Rapid Growth During Last Five Years," *Renewable Energy World* (April 28, 2015), Website www.renewableenergyworld.com/rea/news/article/2015/04/chinese-waste-to-energy-market-experiences-rapid-growth-during-last-five-years.

104 Jeremy van Loon, "Turning Bakken Oil Well Waste Water into Clean Geothermal Power," *Bloomberg* (April 22, 2015), Website www.bloomberg.com/news/articles/2015-04-22/turning-bakken-oil-well-waste-water-into-clean-geothermal-power.

105 David Chandler, "A New Way to Harness Waste Heat," MIT (May 21, 2014), Website http://newsoffice.mit.edu/2014/new-way-harness-waste-heat-0521.

106 General Electric ecomagination, Website www.ecomagination.com/portfolio/cng-in-a-box.

107 John Farrell, "Is Energy Efficiency the More Persistent Threat to Utilities?" Clean Technica (March 9, 2015), Website http://cleantechnica.com/2015/03/09/energy-efficiency-persistent-threat-utilities.

108 "Levelized Cost of Electricity Renewable Energy Technologies," Fraunhofer Institute (November, 2013), Website www.ise.fraunhofer.de/en/publications/veroeffentlichungen-pdf-dateien-en/studien-und-konzeptpapiere/study-levelized-cost-of-electricity-renewable-energies.pdf.

109 "How to Lose Half a Trillion Euros: Europe's Electricity Providers Face an Existential Threat," *The Economist* (October 12, 2013).

110 "Practicing Risk-Aware Electricity Regulation," Ceres (2014), Website www.ceres.org/resources/reports/practicing-risk-aware-electricity-regulation/view. See also "Updated Cost & Risk Rankings of New Generation Resources," Ceres (2014), Website www.ceres.org/resources/reports/practicing-risk-aware-electricity-regulation-2014-update.

111 Sarah Lozanova, "Net Zero Living in an Ultra Energy Efficient Home," *Renewable Energy World* (January 15, 2015), Website www.renewableenergyworld.com/rea/blog/post/2015/01/net-zero-living-in-a-ultra-energy-efficient-home-1.

112 Junko Movellan, "California's First Zero Net Energy Community Opens on Earth Day to Support Bold State Goals," *Renewable Energy World* (April 22, 2015), Website www.renewableenergyworld. com/rea/news/article/2015/04/californias-first-zero-net-energy-community-opens-on-earth-day-to-support-bold-state-goals.

113 John Farrell, "Can Other Cities Match Georgetown's Low-Cost Switch to 100 Percent Wind and Sun?" Institute for Local Self-Reliance (April 14, 2015), Website http://ilsr.org/can-other-cities-match-georgetowns-low-cost-switch-to-100-wind-and-sun.

114 Junko Movellan, "Born from Disaster: Japan Establishes First Microgrid Community," *Renewable Energy World* (May 18, 2015), Website www.renewableenergyworld.com/articles/2015/05/born-from-disaster-japans-first-microgrid-community-represents-future-of-energy.html?eid= 291117084&bid=1075329.

115 Nigel Blackaby (Power Engineering International), "Can Europe Achieve a Clean, Affordable Power Balance?" *Renewable Energy World* (March 27, 2014), Website www.renewableenergyworld. com/rea/news/article/2014/03/maintaining-the-power-balance-in-europe.

116 Matthew Campbell, Tim Loh, and Mark Chediak, "Battery Hackers Are Building the Future in the Garage," *Bloomberg* (March 11, 2015), Website www.bloomberg.com/news/features/2015-03-11/battery-hackers-are-building-the-future-in-the-garage.

117 "Oncor Launches Paradigm-Breaking Microgrid in Texas," *Renewable Energy World* (April 13, 2015), Website www.renewableenergyworld.com/rea/news/article/2015/04/oncor-launches-paradigm-breaking-microgrid-in-texas. Associated video at Website https://edelmanftp.app.box.com/s/sxab1h210w4bawlwdoqzm5kj8r0n7tru.

118 Mahesh Bhave (Indian Institute of Management), "A Requiem for Today's Grid," *Renewable Energy World* (August 6, 2014), Website www.renewableenergyworld.com/rea/news/article/2014/08/a-requiem-for-todays-grid.

119 Ken Wells and Mark Chediak (Bloomberg), "Big Corporations Embracing Microgrids: A Threat for Utilities?" *Renewable Energy World* (October 22, 2013), Website www.renewableenergyworld.com/rea/news/article/2013/10/big-corporations-embracing-microgrids-a-threat-for-utilities.

120 "The Economics of Grid Defection," Rocky Mountain Institute and Cohn & Reznick (February, 2014), Website www.rmi.org/electricity_load_defection.

121 Mohammed Safiuddin and Robert Finton, "Global Renewable Energy Grid Project: Integrating Renewables via HVDC and Centralized Storage," *Renewable Energy World* (February 19, 2014), Website www.renewableenergyworld.com/rea/news/article/2014/02/global-renewable-energy-grid-project-integrating-renewables-via-hvdc-and-centralized-storage.

122 Tino Andresen and Tara Patel (Bloomberg), "What Do Struggling Gas-Fired Plants Mean for Renewables?" *Renewable Energy World* (March 13, 2013), Website www.renewableenergyworld. com/rea/news/article/2013/03/what-do-struggling-gas-fired-plants-mean-for-renewables.

123 Peter Kind (Energy Infrastructure Advocates), "Disruptive Challenges: Financial Implications and Strategic Responses to a Changing Retail Electric Business," *Edison Electric Institute* (January, 2013).

124 Eric Mack, "Audi Just Created Diesel Fuel from Air and Water," Gizmag (April, 2015), Website www.gizmag.com/audi-creates-e-diesel-from-co2/37130.

125 Ron Pernick, "Turning Carbon Emissions into a Revenue Stream," Clean Edge (June 4, 2014), Website http://cleanedge.com/views/Turning-Carbon-Emissions-into-a-Revenue-Stream.

126 "Engineers Develop New Yeast Strain to Enhance Biofuel and Biochemical Production," Cockrell School of Engineering, University of Texas at Austin (March 24, 2015), Website www.engr.utexas. edu/news/7931-alper-new-yeast-strain.

127 Daniel Parry, "Scale Model WWII Craft Takes Flight with the Sea Concept," US Naval Research Laboratory (May 7, 2014), Website www.nrl.navy.mil/media/news-releases/2014/scale-model-wwii-craft-takes-flight-with-fuel-from-the-sea-concept.

128 "Radical Energy Solutions," *Scientific American* (May, 2011).

129 Andrew Williams, "Wheels, Towers and Trees: Unconventional Renewable Energy Technologies in the Pipeline," *Renewable Energy World* (May 15, 2015), Website www.renewableenergyworld.com/

articles/2015/05/wheels-towers-and-trees-unconventional-renewable-energy-technologies-in-the-pipeline.html?eid=291117084&bid=1075329.

130 Wilson Dizard, "Carbon Trading Harms Climate, Says Europe Study," Al Jazeera America (August 25, 2015), Website http://america.aljazeera.com/articles/2015/8/25/european-climate-credits-fail. html.

131 Dale Jorgenson, "Time to Tax Carbon," *Harvard Magazine* (September–October, 2014).

132 "Seize the Day: The Fall in the Price of Oil and Gas Provides a Once-in-a-Generation Opportunity to Fix Bad Energy Policies," *The Economist* (January 17, 2015).

133 *World Energy Outlook*, IEA (2014).

134 "Cashing in on All of the Above: U.S. Fossil Fuel Production Subsidies under Obama," Oil Change International (July, 2014), Website http://priceofoil.org/2014/07/09/cashing-in-on-all-of-the-above-u-s-fossil-fuel-production-subsidies-under-obama.

135 "Greenhouse Gas Cost Abatement Curves," McKinsey (2015), Website www.mckinsey.com/client_service/sustainability/latest_thinking/greenhouse_gas_abatement_cost_curves.

136 Toby Couture (IFOK GmbH), "The Lesson in Renewable Energy Development from Spain," *Renewable Energy World* (July 30, 2013), Website www.renewableenergyworld.com/rea/u/toby-couture-261896. See also "Renewable Energy in Spain: The Cost Del Sol," *The Economist* (July 20, 2013).

137 Toby Couture (IFOK GmbH) and Sean Flannery (Meister Consultants Group), "Can Climate Bonds Advance Renewable Energy Finance?" *Renewable Energy World* (July 11, 2013), Website www.renewableenergyworld.com/rea/news/article/2013/07/can-climate-bonds-advance-renewable-energy-finance.

138 George Monbiot, "Keep Fossil Fuels in the Ground to Stop Climate Change," *The Guardian* (2015), Website www.theguardian.com/environment/2015/mar/10/keep-fossil-fuels-in-the-ground-to-stop-climate-change.

139 "Deep Decarbonization Pathway Project," Institute for Sustainable Development and International Relations (IDDRI) (2014), Website www.iddri.org/Projets/The-Deep-Decarbonization-Pathway-Project.

Index

For Product Safety Concerns and Information please contact our
EU representative GPSR@taylorandfrancis.com Taylor & Francis
Verlag GmbH, Kaufingerstraße 24, 80331 München, Germany